The MIDDLE LENGTH DISCOURSES of the BUDDHA

THE TEACHINGS OF THE BUDDHA

The Middle Length Discourses of the Buddha

A Translation of the Majjhima Nikāya

Translated from the Pali

ORIGINAL TRANSLATION
by
Bhikkhu Ñāṇamoli

TRANSLATION EDITED AND REVISED
by
Bhikkhu Bodhi

Second Edition

WISDOM PUBLICATIONS • BOSTON
in association with the
Barre Center for Buddhist Studies

First Published in 1995
Second Edition 2001

WISDOM PUBLICATIONS
199 ELM STREET
SOMERVILLE, MASSACHUSETTS 02144 USA

ISBN 0-86171-072-X

Library of Congress Cataloging-in-Publication Data
(cataloging data from first edition)
Tipiṭaka. Suttapiṭaka. Majjhimaṇikāya. English
The middle length discourses of the Buddha : a new translation of the Majjhima Nikāya / original translation by Bhikkhu Ñāṇamoli ; translation edited and revised by Bhikkhu Bodhi.
p. cm. — (Teachings of the Buddha)
Includes bibliographical references and index.
ISBN 0-86171-072-X
I. Ñāṇamoli, Bhikkhu, d. 1960. II. Bodhi, Bhikkhu.
III. Series.
BQ1312.E5N36 1995
294.3'823—dc20 94-37636

06 05 04 03
9 8 7 6

Cover Design by: L·J·Sawlit

Set in DPalatino 10 on 12.4 point by John Bullitt and L J.Sawlit

Wisdom Publications' books are printed on acid-free paper and meet the guidelines for permanence and durability of the Committee on Production Guidelines for Book Longevity of the Council on Library Resources.

Printed in Canada

Contents

5 THE DIVISION ON BRAHMINS (*Brāhmaṇavagga*)

PART THREE: THE FINAL FIFTY DISCOURSES (*Uparipaṇṇāsapāḷi*)

1 THE DIVISION AT DEVADAHA (*Devadahavagga*)

2 THE DIVISION OF ONE BY ONE (*Anupadavagga*)

5 THE DIVISION OF THE SIXFOLD BASE (*Saḷāyatanavagga*)

Preface

THE PRESENT WORK OFFERS a complete translation of the *Majjhima Nikāya, The Middle Length Discourses of the Buddha,* one of the major collections in the *Sutta Piṭaka* or "Basket of Discourses" belonging to the Pali Canon. This vast body of scriptures, recorded in the ancient Indian language now known as Pali, is regarded by the Theravāda school of Buddhism as the definitive recension of the Buddha-word, and among scholars too it is generally considered our most reliable source for the original teachings of the historical Buddha Gotama.

This translation is an extensively revised version of an original draft translation made by the distinguished English scholar-monk Bhikkhu Ñāṇamoli (1905–1960). During his eleven years' life in the Buddhist Order, passed entirely at the Island Hermitage in south Sri Lanka, Ven. Ñāṇamoli had rendered into English some of the most difficult and intricate texts of Pali Buddhism, among them the encyclopaedic *Visuddhimagga.* Following his premature death at the age of fifty-five, three thick, hand-bound notebooks containing a handwritten translation of the entire Majjhima Nikāya were found among his effects. However, although all 152 *suttas* of the Majjhima had been translated, the work was obviously still in an ongoing process of revision, with numerous crossouts and overwritings and a fair number of unresolved inconsistencies. The translation also employed an experimental scheme of highly original renderings for Pali doctrinal terms that Ven. Ñāṇamoli had come to prefer to his earlier scheme and had overwritten into the notebooks. He had used this new set of renderings in several of his final publications, offering an explanation for his choices in an appendix to *The Minor Readings and The Illustrator of*

Ultimate Meaning, his translation of the *Khuddakapāṭha* and its commentary.

In 1976 Bhikkhu Khantipālo made a selection of ninety suttas from the notebooks, which he edited into a fairly consistent and readable version rearranged according to a topical sequence he himself devised. This was published in Thailand in three volumes under the title *A Treasury of the Buddha's Words*. In this edition Ven. Khantipālo had endeavoured to make as few changes as possible in the original translation by Ven. Ñāṇamoli, though he inevitably found it desirable to replace some of the latter's innovative renderings with better-known equivalents, generally choosing the terminology that Ven. Ñāṇamoli had used in *The Path of Purification*, his excellent translation of the *Visuddhimagga*.

The present work contains finished translations of all 152 suttas. In editing the ninety suttas selected by Ven. Khantipālo, I have worked from the version found in *A Treasury of the Buddha's Words*, referring to Ven. Ñāṇamoli's notebooks whenever questions arose or problematic passages were encountered. The other sixty-two suttas had to be freshly edited from the notebooks. The translations of all 152 suttas have been checked against the original Pali texts and I hope that all errors and omissions have been rectified.

My aim in editing and revising this material, I must frankly state, has not been to reconstruct the suttas in a way that would conform as closely as possible to the intentions of the original translator. My aim has been, rather, to turn out a translation of the Majjhima Nikāya that simultaneously approaches two ideals: first, fidelity to the intended meaning of the texts themselves; and second, the expression of that meaning in an idiom that would be intelligible to a modern reader seeking in the Pali suttas personal guidance in the proper understanding and conduct of life. Terminological exactitude and internal consistency have been important guidelines underlying the endeavour to achieve those ideals, but care has been taken that their pursuit should leave the translation transparent as to the meaning.

To produce a translation of the Majjhima Nikāya that is both technically precise and lucid in expression required numerous revisions in the manuscript version. Most were quite minor but a few were substantial. Numerous alterations were made in the rendering of Pali doctrinal terms, most of Ven. Khantipālo's changes having been incorporated. In place of Ven. Ñāṇamoli's novel renderings I have in most cases returned to the clearer and better established terminology he employed in *The Path of Purification*. When doubts arose I always turned for help to Ven. Nyanaponika Mahāthera, whose wise advice helped to steer this translation closer towards its two guiding ideals. The handling of several important technical terms is discussed at the end of the Introduction, to which is attached a list showing the terminological changes that were made for this edition. By consulting the list the reader can obtain some idea of how the manuscript translation read. A glossary in the back gives the English renderings used for the major Pali doctrinal terms found in the Majjhima Nikāya as well as Pali words and meanings not included in the Pali Text Society's *Pali-English Dictionary*. The subject index also includes, for most entries, the Pali term after its chosen English rendering. Botanical names that could not be easily rendered by familiar English equivalents have been left untranslated.

Ven. Ñāṇamoli's translation was based primarily on the Pali Text Society's roman-script edition of the Majjhima Nikāya, published in three volumes, the first edited by V. Trenckner (1888), the second two by Robert Chalmers (1898, 1899). This edition was also used to check the translation, but on problematic passages I consulted as well two other editions: the Burmese Buddhasāsana Samiti's Sixth Buddhist Council edition in Burmese script and the Sinhala-script Buddha Jayanti edition published in Sri Lanka. Instances are not unusual where the reading in one or the other of these editions was preferred to that of the PTS edition, though only occasionally are these mentioned in the notes. Seldom too do the notes refer to I. B. Horner's long-standing English translation of the Majjhima Nikāya, *The Collection of the Middle Length Sayings*, with which I sometimes compared Ven. Ñāṇamoli's translation. Since the first volume of that translation was published in 1954, and the next two in 1957 and 1959, while Ven. Ñāṇamoli's manuscript indicates that he did his revised translation between 1953 and 1956, it seems unlikely that he had consulted Horner's version in preparing his own; at most, he might have had access to the first volume after he had completed his first volume.

The text of the translation is divided into numerical sections. These divisions were introduced by Ven. Ñāṇamoli into his manuscript version of the suttas and are not found in the PTS edition of the Majjhima Nikāya. Sometimes, when logic seemed to dictate it, I have made minor alterations in the divisions. The section numbers are included in the sutta references in the Introduction, Notes, and Indexes. Thus, for example, a reference to MN 26.18 means Majjhima Sutta No. 26, section 18.

The numbers at the top of the pages refer to the volume and page number of the PTS edition of the Majjhima Nikāya, as do the bracketed numbers embedded in the text (except for MN 92 and MN 98, wherein the numbers refer to the PTS edition of the Sutta Nipāta).

The Introduction aims to provide the reader with a thorough study guide to the Majjhima Nikāya by systematically surveying the principal teachings of the Buddha contained in this collection along with references to the suttas where fuller expositions of those teachings can be found. More elementary information on the Pali Canon and on Pali Buddhism in general will be found in Maurice Walshe's introduction to his recent translation of the complete Dīgha Nikāya, *Thus Have I Heard,* which the present publication is intended to parallel. As a way of easing the reader's entrance into the canonical texts themselves, a summary of the Majjhima's 152 suttas follows the Introduction.

To clarify difficult passages in the suttas and to shed additional light on passages whose meaning is richer than appears at first sight, a copious set of back notes has been provided. Many of these notes are drawn from the commentaries on the Majjhima, of which there are two. One is the commentary proper, the *Majjhima Nikāya Aṭṭhakathā,* also known as the *Papañcasūdanī.* This was composed in the fifth century by the great Buddhist commentator, Ācariya Buddhaghosa, who based it on the ancient commentaries (no longer extant) that had been preserved for centuries by the Sangha of the Mahāvihāra at Anuradhapura in Sri Lanka. The commentary is of value not only for elucidating the meaning of the texts but also for filling in the background of events that led to the promulgation of the discourses. The other commentarial work is the subcommentary, the *Majjhima Nikāya Ṭīkā,* ascribed to Ācariya Dhammapāla, who probably lived and worked in South India a century or more later than Ācariya Buddhaghosa. The main purpose of the Ṭīkā is to clear up obscure or difficult points in the Aṭṭhakathā, but in doing so the author often sheds additional light on the meaning of the canonical text. In order to keep the notes as concise as possible, almost always the commentaries have been paraphrased rather than quoted directly.

I am aware that the Notes sometimes repeat things already explained in the Introduction, but in a work of this nature such repetitions can be of use, particularly as novel ideas briefly treated in the Introduction may slip the reader's memory at the time of reading a sutta to which they pertain.

In conclusion I want to mention the contributions that others have made to the completion of this project.

First, I wish to thank Ven. Nyanaponika Mahāthera for first encouraging me to take up this task, which seemed so daunting at the outset, and then for providing valuable advice at every crucial turn along the way. Not only was he always ready to discuss difficult points, but despite deteriorating vision, which drastically reduced the time he had available for reading, he still read through the Introduction, the Notes, and the knottier suttas, offering helpful suggestions.

Second, I thank Ven. Khantipālo (now Laurence Mills) for permission to use his versions of the ninety suttas in *A Treasury of the Buddha's Words* as the working basis for this edition. The work he did on those suttas almost two decades ago greatly facilitated the preparation of this volume.

Third, I must mention the tremendous help received from Ayyā Nyanasirī, who subedited the initial draft, made numerous suggestions for minor improvements, and typed out the entire manuscript. Even though, as my conception of the editorial task changed, several suttas had to be typed a second time, and a few a third time, this was always done with patience and understanding.

Fourth, I thank two fellow bhikkhus, Ven. Ṭhānissaro (U.S.A.) and Ven. Dhammavihārī (Sri Lanka), for reading portions of the manuscript and suggesting minor improvements.

Finally, I wish to express my appreciation to Dr. Nicholas Ribush for his encouragement and helpfulness and to Wisdom Publications for doing such a fine job of production.

I am particularly grateful to John Bullitt for his careful and precise management of this project.

For any errors or defects that remain, I myself am fully responsible.

BHIKKHU BODHI
Forest Hermitage
Kandy, Sri Lanka

Note to the Second Edition

This second edition of *The Middle Length Discourses of the Buddha* (2001) incorporates a number of corrections and minor changes in the terminology that I have been making over the years to the text of the original edition. It also includes some additions and alterations to the Notes.

B.B.

Introduction

THE MAJJHIMA NIKĀYA AS A COLLECTION

THE MAJJHIMA NIKĀYA is the second collection of the Buddha's discourses found in the Sutta Piṭaka of the Pali Canon. Its title means literally the Middle Collection, and it is so called because the suttas it contains are generally of middle length, compared with the longer suttas of the Dīgha Nikāya, which precedes it, and the shorter suttas making up the two major collections that follow it, the Saṁyutta Nikāya and the Anguttara Nikāya.

The Majjhima Nikāya consists of 152 suttas. These are divided into three parts called Sets of Fifty (*paṇṇāsa*), though the last set actually contains fifty-two suttas. Within each part the suttas are further grouped into chapters or divisions (*vagga*) of ten suttas each, the next to the last division containing twelve suttas. The names assigned to these divisions are often derived solely from the titles of their opening sutta (or, in some cases, pair of suttas) and thus are scarcely indicative of the material found within the divisions themselves. A partial exception is the Middle Fifty, where the division titles usually refer to the principal type of interlocutor or key figure in each of the suttas they contain. Even then the connection between the title and the contents is sometimes tenuous. The entire system of classification appears to have been devised more for the purpose of convenience than because of any essential homogeneity of subject matter in the suttas comprised under a single division.

There is also no particular pedagogical sequence in the suttas, no unfolding development of thought. Thus while different suttas illuminate each other and one will fill in ideas merely suggested by another, virtually any sutta may be taken up for individual study and will be found comprehensible on its own. Of course, the study of the entire compilation will naturally yield the richest harvest of understanding.

If the Majjhima Nikāya were to be characterised by a single phrase to distinguish it from among the other books of the Pali Canon, this might be done by describing it as the collection that combines the richest variety of contextual settings with the deepest and most comprehensive assortment of teachings. Like the Dīgha Nikāya, the Majjhima is replete with drama and narrative, while lacking much of its predecessor's tendency towards imaginative embellishment and profusion of legend. Like the Saṁyutta, it contains some of the profoundest discourses in the Canon, disclosing the Buddha's radical insights into the nature of existence; and like the Anguttara, it covers a wide range of topics of practical applicability. In contrast to those two Nikāyas, however, the Majjhima sets forth this material not in the form of short, self-contained utterances, but in the context of a fascinating procession of scenarios that exhibit the Buddha's resplendence of wisdom, his skill in adapting his teachings to the needs and proclivities of his interlocutors, his wit and gentle humour, his majestic sublimity, and his compassionate humanity.

Naturally the greatest number of discourses in the Majjhima are addressed to the bhikkhus—the monks—since they lived in closest proximity to the Master and had followed him into homelessness to take upon themselves his complete course of training. But in the Majjhima we do not meet the Buddha only in his role as head of the Order. Repeatedly we see him engaged in living dialogue with people from the many different strata of ancient Indian society—with kings and princes, with brahmins and ascetics, with simple villagers and erudite philosophers, with earnest seekers and vain disputants. It is perhaps in this scripture above all others that the Buddha emerges in the role ascribed to him in the canonical verse of homage to the Blessed One as "the incomparable leader of persons to be tamed, the teacher of gods and humans."

It is not the Buddha alone who appears in the Majjhima in the role of teacher. The work also introduces us to the accomplished disciples he produced who carried on the transmission of his teaching. Of the 152 suttas in the collection, nine are spoken by the venerable Sāriputta, the General of the Dhamma; three of these (MN 9, MN 28, MN 141) have become basic texts for the study of Buddhist doctrine in monastic schools throughout the Theravāda Buddhist world. The venerable Ānanda, the Buddha's personal attendant during the last twenty-five years of his life, delivers seven suttas and participates in many more. Four suttas are spoken by the venerable Mahā Kaccāna, who excelled in elaborating upon the brief but enigmatic sayings of the Master, and two by the second chief disciple, the venerable Mahā Moggallāna, one of which (MN 15) has been recommended for a monk's daily reflections. A dialogue between the venerable Sāriputta and the venerable Puṇṇa Mantāṇiputta (MN 24) explores a scheme of seven stages of purification that was to form the outline for Ācariya Buddhaghosa's great treatise on the Buddhist path, the *Visuddhimagga*. Another dialogue (MN 44) introduces the bhikkhunī Dhammadinnā, whose replies to a series of probing questions were so adroit that the Buddha sealed them for posterity with the words "I would have explained it to you in the same way."

The formats of the suttas are also highly variegated. The majority take the form of discourses proper, expositions of the teaching that pour forth uninterrupted from the mouth of the Enlightened One. A few among these are delivered in a series of unadorned instructional propositions or guidelines to practice, but most are interlaced with striking similes and parables, which flash through and light up the dense mass of doctrine in ways that impress it deeply upon the mind. Other suttas unfold in dialogue and discussion, and in some the dramatic or narrative element predominates. Perhaps the best known and most widely appreciated among these is the *Angulimāla Sutta* (MN 86), which relates how the Buddha subdued the notorious bandit Angulimāla and transformed him into an enlightened saint. Equally moving, though in a different way, is the story of Raṭṭhapāla (MN 82), the youth of wealthy family whose precocious insight into the universality of suffering was so compelling that he was prepared to die rather than accept his parents' refusal to permit him to go forth into homelessness. Several suttas centre upon debate, and these highlight the Buddha's wit and delicate sense of irony as well as his dialectical skills. Particular mention might be made of MN 35 and MN 56, with their subtle humour leavening the seriousness of their contents. In a class of its own is the *Brahmanimantanika Sutta* (MN 49), in which the Buddha visits the Brahma-world to detach a deluded deity from his illusions of grandeur and soon finds himself locked in a gripping contest with Māra the Evil One—an inconceivable alliance of Divinity and Devil defending the sanctity of being against the Buddha's call for deliverance into Nibbāna, the cessation of being.

THE BUDDHA IN THE MAJJHIMA NIKĀYA

Biographical information for its own sake was never an overriding concern of the redactors of the Pali Canon, and thus the data the Majjhima provides on the life of the Buddha is scanty and uncoordinated, included principally because of the light it sheds on the Buddha as the ideal exemplar of the spiritual quest and the fully qualified teacher. Nevertheless, though it subordinates biography to other concerns, the Majjhima does give us the fullest canonical account of the Master's early life as a Bodhisatta, a seeker of enlightenment. With the Dīgha it shares the miraculous story of his conception and birth (MN 123), but its version of his great renunciation has been stripped to bare essentials and related in the stark terms of existential realism. In his youth, having seen through the sensual delights to which his princely status entitled him (MN 75.10), the Bodhisatta decided that it was futile to pursue things subject like himself to ageing and death and thus, with his parents weeping, he left the home life and went in search of the ageless and deathless, Nibbāna (MN 26.13). MN 26 tells of his discipleship under two accomplished meditation teachers of the day, his mastery of their systems, and his consequent disillusionment. MN 12 and MN 36 describe his ascetic practices during his six hard years of striving, a path he pursued almost to the point of death. MN 26 and MN 36 both relate in lean and unembellished terms his attainment of enlightenment, which they view from different angles, while MN 26 takes us past the enlightenment to the decision to teach and the instruction of his first disciples. From that point on connected biography breaks off in the Majjhima and can only be reconstructed partially and hypothetically.

Again, despite the absence of any systematic account, the Majjhima offers a sufficient number of cameo portraits of the

Buddha for us to obtain, with the aid of information provided by other sources, a fairly satisfactory picture of his daily activities and annual routine during the forty-five years of his ministry. A commentarial text shows the Buddha's daily schedule as having been divided between periods of instructing the bhikkhus, giving discourses to the laity, and secluded meditation, during which he usually dwelt either in the "abode of voidness" (MN 121.3, MN 122.6) or in the attainment of great compassion. The day's single meal was always taken in the forenoon, either received by invitation or collected on almsround, and his sleep was restricted to a few hours per night, except in the summer, when he rested briefly during the middle of the day (MN 36.46). The annual routine was determined by the Indian climate, which divided the year into three seasons—a cold season from November through February, a hot season from March through June, and a rainy season from July through October. As was customary among the ascetics of ancient India, the Buddha and his monastic community would remain at a fixed residence during the rainy season, when torrential rains and swollen rivers made travel almost impossible. During the rest of the year he would wander through the Ganges Valley expounding his teachings to all who were prepared to listen.

The Buddha's main seats of residence for the rains retreat (*vassa*) were located at Sāvatthī in the state of Kosala and Rājagaha in the state of Magadha. At Sāvatthī he would usually stay at Jeta's Grove, a park offered to him by the wealthy merchant Anāthapiṇḍika, and accordingly a great number of Majjhima discourses are recorded as having been given there. Occasionally at Sāvatthī he would reside instead at the Eastern Park, offered by the devout lay-woman Visākhā, also known as "Migāra's mother." In Rājagaha he often stayed at the Bamboo Grove, offered by the king of Magadha, Seniya Bimbisāra, or for greater seclusion, on Vulture Peak outside the city. His wanderings, during which he was usually accompanied by a large retinue of bhikkhus, ranged from the Angan country (close to modern West Bengal) to the Himalayan foothills and the Kuru country (modern Delhi). Occasionally, when he saw that a special case required his individual attention, he would leave the Sangha and travel alone (see MN 75, MN 86, MN 140).

Although the Canon is precise and reliable in affording such details, for the early Buddhist community interest focuses upon the Buddha not so much in his concrete historical particularity as in his archetypal significance. Whereas outsiders might view him as merely one among the many spiritual teachers of the day—as "the recluse Gotama"—to his disciples "he is vision, he is knowledge, he is the Dhamma, he is the holy one,...the giver of the Deathless, the lord of the Dhamma, the Tathāgata" (MN 18.12). The last term in this series is the epithet the Buddha uses most often when referring to himself and it underscores his significance as the Great Arrival who brings to fulfilment a cosmic, repetitive pattern of events. The Pali commentators explain the word as meaning "thus come" (*tathā āgata*) and "thus gone" (*tathā gata*), that is, the one who *comes* into our midst bearing the message of deathlessness to which he has *gone* by his own practice of the path. As the Tathāgata he possesses the ten powers of knowledge and the four intrepidities, which enable him to roar his "lion's roar" in the assemblies (MN 12.9–20). He is not merely a wise sage or a benevolent moralist but the latest in the line of Fully Enlightened Ones, each of whom arises singly in an age of spiritual darkness, discovers the deepest truths about the nature of existence, and establishes a Dispensation (*sāsana*) through which the path to deliverance again becomes accessible to the world. Even those of his disciples who have attained unsurpassable vision, practice, and deliverance still honour and venerate the Tathāgata as one who, enlightened himself, teaches others for the sake of their enlightenment (MN 35.26). Looking back at him following his demise, the first generation of monks could say: "The Blessed One was the arouser of the unarisen path, the producer of the unproduced path, the declarer of the undeclared path; he was the knower of the path, the finder of the path, the one skilled in the path," which is followed by and attained to afterwards by his disciples (MN 108.5).

THE FOUR NOBLE TRUTHS

The Buddha's teaching is called the Dhamma, a word that can signify both the truth transmitted by the teaching and the conceptual-verbal medium by which that truth is expressed in order that it can be communicated and made comprehensible. The

Dhamma is not a body of immutable dogmas or a system of speculative thought. It is essentially a means, a raft for crossing over from the "near shore" of ignorance, craving, and suffering to the "far shore" of transcendental peace and freedom (MN 22.13). Because his aim in setting forth his teaching is a pragmatic one—deliverance from suffering—the Buddha can dismiss the whole gamut of metaphysical speculation as a futile endeavour. Those committed to it he compares to a man struck by a poisoned arrow who refuses the surgeon's help until he knows the details about his assailant and his weaponry (MN 63.5). Being struck by the arrow of craving, afflicted by ageing and death, humanity is in urgent need of help. The remedy the Buddha brings as the surgeon for the world (MN 105.27) is the Dhamma, which discloses both the truth of our existential plight and the means by which we can heal our wounds.

The Dhamma that the Buddha discovered and taught consists at its core in Four Noble Truths:

- the noble truth of suffering (*dukkha*)
- the noble truth of the origin of suffering (*dukkhasamudaya*)
- the noble truth of the cessation of suffering (*dukkhanirodha*)
- the noble truth of the way leading to the cessation of suffering (*dukkhanirodhagāminī paṭipadā*)

It is these four truths that the Buddha awakened to on the night of his enlightenment (MN 4.31, MN 36.42), made known to the world when he set rolling the matchless Wheel of the Dhamma at Benares (MN 141.2), and held aloft through the forty-five years of his ministry as "the teaching special to the Buddhas" (MN 56.18). In the Majjhima Nikāya the Four Noble Truths are expounded concisely at MN 9.14–18 and in detail in MN 141, while in MN 28 the venerable Sāriputta develops an original exposition of the truths unique to that sutta. Yet, though they may be brought forth explicitly only on occasion, the Four Noble Truths structure the entire teaching of the Buddha, containing its many other principles just as the elephant's footprint contains the footprints of all other animals (MN 28.2).

The pivotal notion around which the truths revolve is that of *dukkha*, translated here as "suffering." The Pali word originally meant simply pain and suffering, a meaning it retains in the texts when it is used as a quality of feeling: in these cases it has been rendered as "pain" or "painful." As the first noble truth, however, dukkha has a far wider significance, reflective of a comprehensive philosophical vision. While it draws its affective colouring from its connection with pain and suffering, and certainly includes these, it points beyond such restrictive meanings to the inherent unsatisfactoriness of everything conditioned. This unsatisfactoriness of the conditioned is due to its impermanence, its vulnerability to pain, and its inability to provide complete and lasting satisfaction.

The notion of impermanence (*aniccatā*) forms the bedrock for the Buddha's teaching, having been the initial insight that impelled the Bodhisatta to leave the palace in search of a path to enlightenment. Impermanence, in the Buddhist view, comprises the totality of conditioned existence, ranging in scale from the cosmic to the microscopic. At the far end of the spectrum the Buddha's vision reveals a universe of immense dimensions evolving and disintegrating in repetitive cycles throughout beginningless time—"many aeons of world-contraction, many aeons of world-expansion, many aeons of world-contraction and expansion" (MN 4.27). In the middle range the mark of impermanence comes to manifestation in our inescapable mortality, our condition of being bound to ageing, sickness, and death (MN 26.5), of possessing a body that is subject "to being worn and rubbed away, to dissolution and disintegration" (MN 74.9). And at the close end of the spectrum, the Buddha's teaching discloses the radical impermanence uncovered only by sustained attention to experience in its living immediacy: the fact that all the constituents of our being, bodily and mental, are in constant process, arising and passing away in rapid succession from moment to moment without any persistent underlying substance. In the very act of observation they are undergoing "destruction, vanishing, fading away, and ceasing" (MN 74.11).

This characteristic of impermanence that marks everything conditioned leads directly to the recognition of the universality of dukkha or suffering. The Buddha underscores this all-pervasive aspect of dukkha when, in his explanation of the first noble truth, he says, "In short, the five aggregates affected by clinging are suffering." The five aggregates affected by clinging (*pañc'upādānakkhandhā*) are a classificatory scheme that the Buddha had devised for demonstrating the composite nature of personality. The scheme comprises every possible type of conditioned state, which it distributes into five categories—material form, feeling, perception, mental formations, and consciousness. The aggregate of material form (*rūpa*) includes the physical body with its sense faculties as well as external material objects. The aggregate of feeling (*vedanā*) is the affective element in experience, either pleasant, painful, or neutral. Perception (*saññā*), the third aggregate, is the factor responsible for noting the qualities of things and also accounts for recognition and memory. The formations aggregate (*sankhārā*) is an umbrella term that includes all volitional, emotive, and intellective aspects of mental life. And consciousness (*viññāṇa*), the fifth aggregate, is the basic awareness of an object indispensable to all cognition. As the venerable Sāriputta shows in his masterly analysis of the first noble truth, representatives of all five aggregates are present on every occasion of experience, arising in connection with each of the six sense faculties and their objects (MN 28.28).

The Buddha's statement that the five aggregates are dukkha thus reveals that the very things we identify with and hold to as the basis for happiness, rightly seen, are the basis for the suffering that we dread. Even when we feel ourselves comfortable and secure, the instability of the aggregates is itself a source of oppression and keeps us perpetually exposed to suffering in its more blatant forms. The whole situation becomes multiplied further to dimensions beyond calculation when we take into account the Buddha's disclosure of the fact of rebirth. All beings in whom ignorance and craving remain present wander on in the cycle of repeated existence, *saṁsāra*, in which each turn brings them the suffering of new birth, ageing, illness, and death. All states of existence within saṁsāra, being necessarily transitory and subject to change, are incapable of providing lasting security. Life in any world is unstable, it is swept away, it has no shelter and protector, nothing of its own (MN 82.36).

THE TEACHING OF NON-SELF

Inextricably tied up with impermanence and suffering is a third principle intrinsic to all phenomena of existence. This is the characteristic of non-self (*anattā*), and the three together are called the three marks or characteristics (*tilakkhaṇa*). The Buddha teaches, contrary to our most cherished beliefs, that our individual being—the five aggregates—cannot be identified as self, as an enduring and substantial ground of personal identity. The notion of self has only a conventional validity, as a convenient shorthand device for denoting a composite insubstantial situation. It does not signify any ultimate immutable entity subsisting at the core of our being. The bodily and mental factors are transitory phenomena, constantly arising and passing away, processes creating the appearance of selfhood through their causal continuity and interdependent functioning. Nor does the Buddha posit a self outside and beyond the five aggregates. The notion of selfhood, treated as an ultimate, he regards as a product of ignorance, and all the diverse attempts to substantiate this notion by identifying it with some aspect of the personality he describes as "clinging to a doctrine of self."

In several suttas in the Majjhima Nikāya, the Buddha gives forceful expression to his repudiation of views of self. In MN 102 he undertakes a far-reaching survey of the various propositions put forth about the self, declaring them all to be "conditioned and gross." In MN 2.8 six views of self are branded as "the thicket of views, the wilderness of views, the contortion of views, the vacillation of views, the fetter of views." In MN 11 he compares his teaching point by point with those of other recluses and brahmins and shows that beneath their apparent similarities, they finally diverge on just this one crucial point—the rejection of views of self—which undermines the agreements. MN 22 offers a series of arguments against the view of self, culminating in the Buddha's declaration that he does not see any doctrine of self that would not lead to sorrow, lamentation, pain, grief, and despair. In his map of the steps to liberation, identity view (*sakkāyadiṭṭhi*), the positing of a self in relation to the five aggregates, is held to be the first fetter to be broken with the arising of the "vision of the Dhamma."

The principle of non-self is shown in the suttas to follow logically from the two marks of impermanence and suffering. The standard formula states that what is impermanent is pain or suffering, and what is impermanent, suffering, and subject to change cannot be regarded as mine, I, or self (MN 22.26, MN 35.20, etc.). Other passages highlight the relationship among the three characteristics from different angles. MN 28 points out that when the external physical elements—earth, water, fire, and air—vast as they are, are periodically destroyed in cosmic cataclysms, there can be no considering this transitory body as self. MN 148 demonstrates by a *reductio ad absurdum* argument that impermanence implies non-self: when all the factors of being are clearly subject to rise and fall, to identify anything among them with self is to be left with the untenable thesis that self is subject to rise and fall. MN 35.19 connects the mark of non-self with that of dukkha by arguing that because we cannot bend the five aggregates to our will, they cannot be taken as mine, I, or self.

THE ORIGIN AND CESSATION OF SUFFERING

The second of the Four Noble Truths makes known the origin or cause of suffering, which the Buddha identifies as craving (*taṇhā*) in its three aspects: craving for sensual pleasures; craving for being, that is, for continued existence; and craving for non-being, that is, for personal annihilation. The third truth states the converse of the second truth, that with the elimination of craving the suffering that originates from it will cease without remainder.

The Buddha's discovery of the causal link between craving and suffering accounts for the apparent "pessimistic" streak that emerges in several suttas of the Majjhima Nikāya: in MN 13 with its disquisition on the dangers in sensual pleasures, form, and feeling; in MN 10 and MN 119 with their cemetery meditations; in MN 22, MN 54, and MN 75 with their shocking similes for sensual pleasures. Such teachings are part of the Buddha's tactical approach to guiding his disciples to liberation. By its own inherent nature craving springs up and thrives wherever it finds something that appears pleasant and delightful. It proliferates through mistaken perception—the perception of sense objects as enjoyable—and thus to break the grip of craving on the mind, exhortation is often not enough. The Buddha must make people see that the things they yearn for and frantically pursue are really suffering, and he does this by exposing the dangers concealed beneath their sweet and charming exteriors.

Although the second and third noble truths have an immediate psychological validity, they also have a deeper aspect brought to light in the suttas. The middle two truths as stated in the general formulation of the Four Noble Truths are actually telescoped versions of a longer formulation that discloses the origin and cessation of bondage in saṁsāra. The doctrine in which this expanded version of the two truths is set forth is called *paṭicca samuppāda,* dependent origination. In its fullest statement the doctrine spells out the origination and cessation of suffering in terms of twelve factors connected together in eleven propositions. This formulation, laid down schematically, will be found at MN 38.17 in its order of arising and at MN 38.20 in its order of ceasing. MN 115.11 includes both sequences together preceded by a statement of the general principle of conditionality that underlies the applied doctrine. A more elaborate version giving a factorial analysis of each term in the series is presented at MN 9.21–66, and a version exemplified in the course of an individual life at MN 38.26–40. Condensed versions are also found, notably at MN 1.171, MN 11.16, and MN 75.24–25. The venerable Sāriputta quotes the Buddha as saying that one who sees dependent origination sees the Dhamma and one who sees the Dhamma sees dependent origination (MN 28.28).

According to the usual interpretation, the series of twelve factors extends over three lives and divides into causal and resultant phases. The gist of it can be briefly explained as follows. Because of ignorance (*avijjā*)—defined as non-knowledge of the Four Noble Truths—a person engages in volitional actions or *kamma,* which may be bodily, verbal, or mental, wholesome or unwholesome. These kammic actions are the formations (*saṅkhārā*), and they ripen in states of consciousness (*viññāṇa*)—first as the rebirth-consciousness at the moment of conception and thereafter as the passive states of consciousness resulting from kamma that matures in the course of a lifetime. Along with consciousness there arises mentality-materiality (*nāmarūpa*), the psychophysical organism, which is equipped with the sixfold base (*saḷāyatana*), the five physical sense faculties and mind as the faculty of the higher cognitive functions. Via the sense faculties contact (*phassa*) takes place between consciousness and its objects, and contact conditions feeling (*vedanā*). The links from consciousness through feeling are the products of past kamma, of the causal phase represented by ignorance and formations. With the next link the kammically active phase of the present life begins, productive of a new existence in the future. Conditioned by feeling, craving (*taṇhā*) arises, this being the second noble truth. When craving intensifies it gives rise to clinging (*upādāna*), through which one again engages in volitional actions pregnant with a renewal of existence (*bhava*). The new existence begins with birth (*jāti*), which inevitably leads to ageing and death (*jarāmaraṇa*).

The teaching of dependent origination also shows how the round of existence can be broken. With the arising of true knowledge, full penetration of the Four Noble Truths, ignorance is eradicated. Consequently the mind no longer indulges in craving and clinging, action loses its potential to generate rebirth, and deprived thus of its fuel, the round comes to an end. This marks the goal of the teaching signalled by the third noble truth, the cessation of suffering.

NIBBĀNA

The state that supervenes when ignorance and craving have been uprooted is called Nibbāna (Sanskrit, *Nirvāṇa*), and no conception in the Buddha's teaching has proved so refractory to conceptual pinning down as this one. In a way such elusiveness is only to be expected, since Nibbāna is described precisely as "profound, hard to see and hard to understand,...unattainable by mere reasoning" (MN 26.19). Yet in this same passage the Buddha also says that Nibbāna is to be experienced by the wise and in the suttas he gives enough indications of its nature to convey some idea of its desirability.

The Pali Canon offers sufficient evidence to dispense with the opinion of some interpreters that Nibbāna is sheer annihilation; even the more sophisticated view that Nibbāna is merely the destruction of defilements and the extinction of existence cannot stand up under scrutiny. Probably the most compelling testimony against that view is the well-known passage from the *Udāna* that declares with reference to Nibbāna that "there is an unborn, unbecome, unmade, unconditioned," the existence of which makes possible "escape from the born, become, made, and conditioned" (Ud 8:3/80). The Majjhima Nikāya characterises Nibbāna in similar ways. It is "the unborn, unageing, unailing, deathless, sorrowless, undefiled supreme security from bondage," which the Buddha attained to on the night of his enlightenment (MN 26.18). Its pre-eminent reality is affirmed by the Buddha when he calls Nibbāna the supreme foundation of truth, whose nature is undeceptive and which ranks as the supreme noble truth (MN 140.26). Nibbāna cannot be perceived by those who live in lust and hate, but it can be seen with the arising of spiritual vision, and by fixing the mind upon it in the depths of meditation, the disciple can attain the destruction of the taints (MN 26.19, MN 75.24, MN 64.9).

The Buddha does not devote many words to a philosophical definition of Nibbāna. One reason is that Nibbāna, being unconditioned, transcendent, and supramundane, does not easily lend itself to definition in terms of concepts that are inescapably tied to the conditioned, manifest, and mundane. Another is that the Buddha's objective is the practical one of leading beings to release from suffering, and thus his principal approach to the characterisation of Nibbāna is to inspire the incentive to attain it and to show what must be done to accomplish this. To show Nibbāna as desirable, as the aim of striving, he describes it as the highest bliss, as the supreme state of sublime peace, as the ageless, deathless, and sorrowless, as the supreme security from bondage. To show what must be done to attain Nibbāna, to indicate that the goal implies a definite task, he describes it as the stilling of all formations, the relinquishing of all acquisitions, the destruction of craving, dispassion (MN 26.19). Above all, Nibbāna is the cessation of suffering, and for those who seek an end to suffering such a designation is enough to beckon them towards the path.

THE WAY TO THE CESSATION OF SUFFERING

The fourth noble truth completes the pattern established by the first three truths by revealing the means to eliminate craving and thereby bring an end to suffering. This truth teaches the "Middle Way" discovered by the Buddha, the Noble Eightfold Path:

1. right view (*sammā diṭṭhi*)
2. right intention (*sammā sankappa*)
3. right speech (*sammā vācā*)

4. right action (*sammā kammanta*)
5. right livelihood (*sammā ājīva*)
6. right effort (*sammā vāyāma*)
7. right mindfulness (*sammā sati*)
8. right concentration (*sammā samādhi*)

Mentioned countless times throughout the Majjhima Nikāya, the Noble Eightfold Path is explained in detail in two full suttas. MN 141 gives a factorial analysis of the eight components of the path using the definitions that are standard in the Pali Canon; MN 117 expounds the path from a different angle under the rubric of "noble right concentration with its supports and its requisites." The Buddha there makes the important distinction between the mundane and supramundane stages of the path, defines the first five factors for both stages, and shows how the path factors function in unison in the common task of providing an outlet from suffering. Other suttas explore in greater detail individual components of the path. Thus MN 9 provides an in-depth exposition of right view, MN 10 of right mindfulness, MN 19 of right intention. MN 44.11 explains that the eight factors can be incorporated into three "aggregates" of training. Right speech, right action, and right livelihood make up the aggregate of virtue or moral discipline (*sīla*); right effort, right mindfulness, and right concentration make up the aggregate of concentration (*samādhi*); and right view and right intention make up the aggregate of understanding or wisdom (*paññā*). This threefold sequence in turn serves as the basic outline for the gradual training, to be discussed later.

In the Pali Canon the practices conducing to Nibbāna are often elaborated into a more complex set comprising seven groups of intersecting factors. The later tradition designates them the thirty-seven aids to enlightenment (*bodhipakkhiyā dhammā*), but the Buddha himself simply speaks of them without a collective name as "the things that I have taught you after directly knowing them" (MN 103.3, MN 104.5). Towards the end of his life he stressed to the Sangha that the long duration of his teaching in the world depends upon the accurate preservation of these factors and their being practised by his followers in harmony, free from contention.

The constituents of this set are as follows:

- the four foundations of mindfulness (*satipaṭṭhāna*)
- the four right kinds of striving (*sammappadhāna*)
- the four bases for spiritual power (*iddhipāda*)
- the five faculties (*indriya*)
- the five powers (*bala*)
- the seven enlightenment factors (*bojjhanga*)
- the Noble Eightfold Path (*ariya aṭṭhangika magga*)

Each group is defined in full at MN 77.15–21. As examination will show, most of these groups are simply subdivisions or rearrangements of factors of the eightfold path made to highlight different aspects of the practice. Thus, for example, the four foundations of mindfulness are an elaboration of right mindfulness; the four right kinds of striving, an elaboration of right effort. The development of the groups is therefore integral and not sequential. MN 118, for example, shows how the practice of the four foundations of mindfulness fulfils the development of the seven enlightenment factors, and MN 149.10 states that one engaged in insight meditation on the senses brings to maturity all thirty-seven aids to enlightenment.

Factorial analysis of the thirty-seven aids to enlightenment brings to light the central importance of four factors among them—energy, mindfulness, concentration, and wisdom. From this a clear picture of the essential practice can be sketched. One begins with a conceptual understanding of the Dhamma and an intention to achieve the goal, the first two path factors. Then, out of faith, one accepts the moral discipline regulating speech, action, and livelihood. With virtue as a basis one energetically applies the mind to cultivating the four foundations of mindfulness. As mindfulness matures it issues in deepened concentration, and the concentrated mind, by investigation, arrives at wisdom, a penetrative understanding of the principles originally grasped only conceptually.

THE GRADUAL TRAINING

In the Majjhima Nikāya the Buddha often expounds the practice of the path as a gradual training (*anupubbasikkhā*), which unfolds in stages from the first step to the final goal. This gradual training is a finer subdivision of the threefold division of the path into virtue, concentration, and wisdom. Invariably in the suttas the sequence on the gradual training is shown to start with the going forth into homelessness and the adoption of the lifestyle of a bhikkhu, a Buddhist monk. This immediately calls attention to the importance of the monastic life in the Buddha's Dispensation. In principle the entire practice of the Noble Eightfold Path is open to people from any mode of life, monastic or lay, and the Buddha confirms that many among his lay followers were accomplished in the Dhamma and had attained the first three of the four supramundane stages (MN 68.18–23; MN 73.9–22; the Theravādin position is that lay followers can also attain the fourth stage, arahantship, but having done so they immediately seek the going forth or pass away). However, the fact remains that the household life inevitably tends to impede the single-hearted quest for deliverance by fostering a multitude of worldly concerns and personal attachments. Hence the Buddha himself went forth into homelessness as the preliminary step in his own noble quest, and after his enlightenment he established the Sangha, the order of bhikkhus and bhikkhunīs, as the resort for those who wish to devote themselves fully to the practice of his teaching undeflected by the cares of household life.

The main paradigm for the gradual training found in the Majjhima Nikāya is that laid out in MN 27 and MN 51; alternative versions are found at MN 38, MN 39, MN 53, MN 107, and MN 125, and some of the more important variations will be briefly noted. The sequence opens with the appearance of a Tathāgata in the world and his exposition of the Dhamma, hearing which the disciple acquires faith and follows the Teacher into homelessness. Having gone forth, he undertakes and observes the rules of discipline that promote the purification of conduct and livelihood. The next three steps—contentment, restraint of the sense faculties, and mindfulness and full awareness—are intended to internalise the process of purification and thereby bridge the transition from virtue to concentration. Alternative versions (MN 39, MN 53, MN 107, MN 125) insert two additional steps here, moderation in eating and devotion to wakefulness.

The direct training in concentration comes to prominence in the section on the abandonment of the five hindrances. The five hindrances—sensual desire, ill will, sloth and torpor, restlessness and remorse, and doubt—are the primary obstacles to meditative development and their removal is therefore essential for the mind to be brought to a state of calm and unification. In the sequence on the gradual training the overcoming of the hindrances is treated only schematically; other parts of the Canon provide more practical instruction, amplified still more in the commentaries. The passage on the hindrances is graced in MN 39 by a series of similes illustrating the contrast between the bondage imposed by the hindrances and the joyful sense of freedom that is won when they are abandoned.

The next stage in the sequence describes the attainment of the *jhānas,* profound states of concentration in which the mind becomes fully absorbed in its object. The Buddha enumerates four jhānas, named simply after their numerical position in the series, each more refined and elevated than its predecessor. The jhānas are always described by the same formulas, which in several suttas (MN 39, MN 77, MN 119) are augmented by similes of great beauty. Although in the Theravāda tradition the jhānas are not regarded as indispensable to the attainment of enlightenment, the Buddha invariably includes them in the full gradual training because of the contribution they make to the intrinsic perfection of the path and because the deep concentration they induce provides a solid base for the cultivation of insight. While still mundane the jhānas are the "footsteps of the Tathāgata" (MN 27.19–22) and foretokens of the bliss of Nibbāna that lies at the training's end.

From the fourth jhāna three alternative lines of further development become possible. In a number of passages outside the sequence on the gradual training (MN 8, MN 25, MN 26, MN 66, etc.) the Buddha mentions four meditative states that continue the mental unification established by the jhānas. These states, described as "the liberations that are peaceful and immaterial," are, like the jhānas, also mundane. Distinguished from the jhānas by their transcendence of the subtle mental image that forms the object in the jhānas, they are named after their own exalted objects: the base of infinite space, the base of infinite consciousness, the base of nothingness, and the base of neither-perception-nor-non-perception. In the Pali commentaries these states came to be called the immaterial or formless jhānas (*arūpajjhāna*).

A second line of development disclosed by the suttas is the acquisition of supernormal knowledge. The Buddha frequently mentions six types as a group, which come to be called the six kinds of direct knowledge (*chaḷabhiññā*; the expression does not occur in the Majjhima). The last of these, the knowledge of the destruction of the taints, is supramundane and thus properly belongs to the third line of development. But the other five are all mundane, products of the extraordinarily powerful degree of mental concentration achieved in the fourth jhāna: the supernormal powers, the divine ear, the ability to read the minds of others, the recollection of past lives, and the divine eye (MN 6, MN 73, MN 77, MN 108).

The jhānas and the mundane types of direct knowledge by themselves do not issue in enlightenment and liberation. As lofty and peaceful as these attainments are, they can only suppress the defilements that sustain the round of rebirths but cannot eradicate them. To uproot the defilements at the most fundamental level, and thereby yield the fruits of enlightenment and deliverance, the meditative process must be redirected along a third line of development, one which does not necessarily presuppose the former two. This is the contemplation of "things as they actually are," which results in increasingly deeper insights into the nature of existence and culminates in the final goal, the attainment of arahantship.

This line of development is the one the Buddha pursues in the sequence on the gradual training, though he precedes it by descriptions of two of the direct knowledges, the recollection of past lives and the divine eye. The three together, which figured prominently in the Buddha's own enlightenment (MN 4.27–30), are collectively called the three true knowledges (*tevijjā*). Although the first two among these are not essential to the realisation of arahantship, we may assume that the Buddha includes them here because they reveal the truly vast and profound dimensions of suffering in saṁsāra and thereby prepare the mind for the penetration of the Four Noble Truths, in which that suffering is diagnosed and surmounted.

The process of contemplation by which the meditator develops insight is not explicitly shown as such in the sequence on the gradual training. It is only implied by the exhibiting of its final fruit, here called the knowledge of the destruction of the taints. The *āsavas* or taints are a classification of defilements considered in their role of sustaining the saṁsāric round. The commentaries derive the word from a root *su* meaning "to flow." Scholars differ as to whether the flow implied by the prefix *ā* is inward or outward; hence some have rendered it as "influxes" or "influences," others as "outflows" or "effluents." A stock passage in the suttas indicates the term's real significance independently of etymology when it describes the *āsavas* as states "that defile, bring renewal of being, give trouble, ripen in suffering, and lead to future birth, ageing, and death" (MN 36.47, etc.). Thus other translators, bypassing the literal meaning, have rendered it "cankers," "corruptions," or "taints," the latter being the choice of Ven. Ñāṇamoli. The three taints mentioned in the suttas are virtual synonyms for craving for sensual pleasures, craving for being, and the ignorance that appears at the head of the formula for dependent origination. When the disciple's mind has been liberated from the taints by the completion of the path of arahantship, he reviews his newly won freedom and roars his lion's roar: "Birth is destroyed, the holy life has been lived, what had to be done has been done, there is no more coming to any state of being."

APPROACHES TO MEDITATION

The methods of meditation taught by the Buddha in the Pali Canon fall into two broad systems. One is the development of serenity (*samatha*), which aims at concentration (*samādhi*); the other is the development of insight (*vipassanā*), which aims at understanding or wisdom (*paññā*). In the Buddha's system of mental training the role of serenity is subordinated to that of insight because the latter is the crucial instrument needed to uproot the ignorance at the bottom of saṁsāric bondage. The attainments possible through serenity meditation were known to Indian contemplatives long before the advent of the Buddha. The Buddha himself mastered the two highest stages under his early teachers but found that, on their own, they only led to higher planes of rebirth, not to genuine enlightenment (MN 26.15–16). However, because the unification of mind induced by the practice of concentration contributes to clear understanding, the Buddha incorporated the techniques of serenity meditation and the resulting levels of absorption into his own system, treating them as a foundation and preparation for insight and as a "pleasant abiding here and now."

The attainments reached by the practice of serenity meditation are, as mentioned in the preceding section, the eight absorptions—the four jhānas and the four immaterial states—each of which serves as the basis for the next. Strangely, the suttas do not explicitly prescribe specific meditation subjects as the means for attaining the jhānas, but the commentarial literature such as the *Visuddhimagga* enables us to make the connections. Among the meditation topics enumerated in the suttas, eight of the ten *kasiṇas* (MN 77.24) are recognised as suitable for attaining all four jhānas, the last two being the respective supports for the first two immaterial attainments. The eight bases for transcendence seem to be a more finely differentiated treatment of meditation on the colour kasiṇas, as are the first three of the eight liberations (MN 77.22–23). Mindfulness of breathing, to which the Buddha devotes an entire sutta (MN 118), provides an ever accessible meditation subject that can be pursued through all four jhānas and also used to develop insight. Another method for attaining the jhānas mentioned in the suttas is the four divine abodes (*brahmavihāra*)—boundless loving-kindness, compassion, altruistic joy (i.e., gladness at others' success), and equanimity (MN 7, MN 40, etc.). Tradition holds the first three to be capable of leading to the three lower jhānas, the last of inducing the fourth jhāna. The immaterial attainments are to be reached by fixing the mind on the specific object of each attainment—infinite space, infinite consciousness, nothingness, and the state that can only be described as neither percipient nor as non-percipient.

Whereas in serenity meditation the meditator attempts to focus upon a single uniform object abstracted from actual experience, in insight meditation the endeavour is made to contemplate, from a position of detached observation, the ever-shifting flux of experience itself in order to penetrate through to the essential nature of bodily and mental phenomena. The Buddha teaches that the craving and clinging that hold us in bondage are sustained by a network of "conceivings" (*maññita*)—deluded views, conceits, and suppositions that the mind fabricates by an internal process of mental commentary or "proliferation" (*papañca*) and then projects out upon the world, taking them to possess objective validity. The task of insight meditation is to sever our attachments by enabling us to pierce through this net of conceptual projections in order to see things as they really are.

To see things as they really are means to see them in terms of the three characteristics—as impermanent, as painful or suffering, and as not self. Since the three characteristics are closely interlinked, any one of them can be made the main portal for entering the domain of insight, but the Buddha's usual approach is to show all three together—impermanence implying suffering and the two in conjunction implying the absence of self. When the noble disciple sees all the factors of being as stamped with these three marks, he no longer identifies with them, no longer appropriates them by taking them to be mine, I, or self. Seeing thus, he becomes disenchanted with all formations. When he becomes disenchanted, his lust and attachment fade away and his mind is liberated from the taints.

Instructions for the development of insight in the Majjhima Nikāya, though concise, are many and diverse. The single most important lesson on the practice conducing to insight is the *Satipaṭṭhāna Sutta*, the Discourse on the Foundations of Mindfulness (MN 10; also found in the Dīgha Nikāya with an amplified section on the Four Noble Truths). The sutta sets forth a comprehensive system called *satipaṭṭhāna* designed to train the mind to see with microscopic precision the true nature of the body, feelings, states of mind, and mental objects. The system is sometimes taken to be the paradigm for the practice of "bare insight"—the direct contemplation of mental and bodily phenomena without a prior foundation of jhāna—and, while several exercises described in the sutta can also lead to the jhānas, the arousing of insight is clearly the intent of the method.

Other suttas in the Majjhima Nikāya describe approaches to developing insight that either elaborate upon the *satipaṭṭhāna* contemplations or reach them from a different starting point. Thus MN 118 shows how the practice of mindfulness of breathing fulfils all four foundations of mindfulness, not the first alone as shown in MN 10. Several suttas—MN 28, MN 62, MN 140—present more detailed instructions on the contemplation of the elements. MN 37, MN 74, and MN 140 contain illuminating passages on the contemplation of feeling. In some suttas the Buddha uses the five aggregates as the groundwork for insight contemplation (e.g., MN 22, MN 109); in some, the six sense bases (e.g., MN 137, MN 148, MN 149); in some, the two combined (MN 147). MN 112 has sections dealing with insight based on the five aggregates, the six elements, and the six sense bases, and as resulting from the gradual training. MN 52 and MN 64 show that insight can also be aroused with the jhānas, the immaterial attainments, and the divine abodes as its objects: the disciple enters any of these states and contemplates its constituent factors as subject to the three characteristics.

Several sequences of meditative states mentioned in the Majjhima culminate in an attainment called the cessation of perception and feeling (*saññāvedayitanirodha*). Although this state always follows the last immaterial attainment, it is not, as may be supposed, merely one higher step in the scale of concentration. Strictly speaking, the attainment of cessation pertains neither to serenity nor to insight. It is a state reached by the combined powers of serenity and insight in which all mental processes are temporarily suspended. The attainment is said to be accessible only to non-returners and arahants who have also mastered the jhānas and immaterial states. Detailed canonical discussions of it are found in MN 43 and MN 44.

THE FOUR PLANES OF LIBERATION

The practice of the Buddhist path evolves in two distinct stages, a mundane (*lokiya*) or preparatory stage and a supramundane (*lokuttara*) or consummate stage. The mundane path is developed when the disciple undertakes the gradual training in virtue, concentration, and wisdom. This reaches its peak in the practice of insight meditation, which deepens direct experience of the three characteristics of existence. When the practitioner's faculties have arrived at an adequate degree of maturity, the mundane path gives birth to the supramundane path, so called because it leads directly and infallibly out of (*uttara*) the world (*loka*) comprising the three realms of existence to the attainment of "the deathless element," Nibbāna.

Progress along the supramundane path is marked by four major breakthroughs, each of which ushers the disciple through two subordinate phases called the path (*magga*) and its fruit (*phala*). The phase of path has the special function of eliminating a determinate number of defilements to which it is directly opposed, the mental impediments that hold us in bondage to the round of rebirths. When the work of the path has been completed, the disciple realises its corresponding fruit, the degree of liberation made accessible by that particular path. The canonical formula of homage to the Sangha refers obliquely to these four planes of liberation—each with its phase of path and fruit—when it extols the Blessed One's community of noble disciples as comprising "the four pairs of persons, the eight types of individuals" (MN 7.7). These four pairs are obtained by taking, for each stage, the one who has entered upon the way to realisation of the fruit and the one who has attained the fruit.

In the suttas the Buddha highlights the specific characteristics of each supramundane stage in two ways: by mentioning the defilements that are abandoned on each plane and the consequences its attainment bears on the process of rebirth (see, e.g., MN 6.11–13, 19; MN 22.42–45, etc.). He handles the elimination of the defilements by classifying these into a tenfold group called the ten fetters (*saṁyojana*). The disciple enters upon the first supramundane path either as a Dhamma-follower (*dhammānusārin*) or as a faith-follower (*saddhānusārin*); the former is one in whom wisdom is the dominant faculty, the latter one who progresses by the impetus of faith. This path, the path of stream-entry, has the task of eradicating the grossest three fetters: identity view, i.e., the view of a self among the five aggregates; doubt in the Buddha and his teaching; and adherence to external rules and observances, either ritualistic or ascetic, in the belief that they can bring purification. When the disciple realises the fruit of this path he becomes a stream-enterer (*sotāpanna*), who has entered the "stream" of the Noble Eightfold Path that will carry him irreversibly to Nibbāna. The stream-enterer is bound to reach final liberation in a maximum of seven more births, which all occur either in the human world or in the heavenly realms.

The second supramundane path attenuates to a still greater degree the root defilements of lust, hatred, and delusion, though without yet eradicating them. On realising the fruit of this path the disciple becomes a once-returner (*sakadāgāmin*), who is due to return to this world (i.e., the sense-sphere realm) only one more time and then make an end of suffering. The third path eradicates the next two fetters, sensual desire and ill will; it issues in the fruit of the non-returner (*anāgāmin*), who is due to reappear by spontaneous birth in one of the special celestial realms called the Pure Abodes, and there attain final Nibbāna without ever returning from that world.

The fourth and last supramundane path is the path of arahantship. This path eradicates the five higher fetters: desire for rebirth in the fine-material realm and in the immaterial realm, conceit, restlessness, and ignorance. By realisation of the fruit of this path the practitioner becomes an arahant, a fully liberated one, who "here and now enters upon and abides in the deliverance of mind and deliverance by wisdom that are taintless with the destruction of the taints." The arahant will be discussed further in the next section.

The commentaries (often referred to in the notes to this translation) develop an interpretation of the paths and fruits based upon the systemisation of the Buddha's teachings known as the Abhidhamma. Drawing upon the Abhidhamma depiction of the mind as a sequence of discrete momentary acts of consciousness, called *cittas*, the commentaries understand each supramundane path to be a single occasion of consciousness arising at the climax of a series of insights into the Dhamma. Each of the four momentary path cittas eliminates its own fixed set of defilements, to be followed immediately by its fruition, which consists of a string of momentary cittas that enjoy the bliss of Nibbāna made accessible by the breakthrough of the path. Though this conception of the paths and fruits is regularly employed by the commentators as an hermeneutical tool for interpreting the suttas, it is not explicitly formulated as such in the old Nikāyas and at times there even appears to be a tension between the two (for example, in the passage at MN 142.5 describing the four persons on the path as distinct recipients of offerings).

THE ARAHANT

The ideal figure of the Majjhima Nikāya, as of the Pali Canon as a whole, is the arahant. The word "arahant" itself derives from a root meaning "to be worthy." Ven. Ñāṇamoli renders it "accomplished" and "Accomplished One" when it is used as an epithet of the Buddha, probably to be consistent with his practice of translating all the Buddha's epithets. In its other occurrences he leaves it untranslated. The word seems to have been of pre-Buddhist coinage but was taken over by the Buddha to designate the individual who has reached the final fruit of the path.

The suttas employ a stock description of the arahant that summarises his accomplishments: he is "one with taints destroyed, who has lived the holy life, done what had to be done, laid down the burden, reached his own goal, destroyed the fetters of being, and is completely liberated through final knowledge" (MN 1.51, etc.). Variant descriptions emphasise different aspects of the arahant's attainment. Thus one sutta offers a series of metaphorical epithets that the Buddha himself interprets as representing the arahant's abandoning of ignorance, craving, and conceit, his eradication of fetters, and his freedom from the round of births (MN 22.30–35). Elsewhere the Buddha ascribes a different set of epithets to the arahant—several of brahmanical currency—deriving these terms by imaginative etymology from the arahant's elimination of all evil unwholesome states (MN 39.22–29).

The Majjhima records differences of type among the arahants, which are ascribed to the diversity in their faculties. In MN 70 the Buddha introduces a basic distinction between those arahants who are "liberated-in-both-ways" and those who are "liberated-by-wisdom": whereas the former are capable of abiding in the immaterial attainments, the latter lack that capacity. Arahants are further distinguished as those who possess, besides the knowledge of the destruction of the taints necessary to all arahants, all three of the true knowledges and all six of the direct knowledges. In MN 108 the venerable Ānanda indicates that those arahants who possessed the six direct knowledges were accorded special veneration and authority in the Sangha following the Buddha's passing away.

Beneath these incidental differences, however, all arahants alike share the same essential accomplishments—the destruction of all defilements and the freedom from future rebirths. They possess three unsurpassable qualities—unsurpassable vision, unsurpassable practice of the way, and unsurpassable deliverance (MN 35.26). They are endowed with the ten factors of one beyond training—the eight factors of the Noble Eightfold Path augmented by right knowledge and right deliverance (MN 65.34, MN 78.14). They possess the four foundations—the foundations of wisdom, of truth, of relinquishment, and of peace (MN 140.11). And by the eradication of lust, hate, and delusion all arahants have access to a unique meditative attainment called the fruition attainment of arahantship, described as the unshakeable deliverance of mind, the immeasurable deliverance of mind, the void deliverance of mind, the deliverance of mind through nothingness, and the signless deliverance of mind (MN 43.35–37).

KAMMA AND REBIRTH

According to the Buddha's teaching, all beings except the arahants are subject to "renewal of being in the future" (*punabbhava*), that is, to rebirth. Rebirth, in the Buddhist conception, is not the transmigration of a self or soul but the continuation of a process, a flux of becoming in which successive lives are linked together by causal transmission of influence rather than by substantial identity. The basic causal pattern underlying the process is that defined by the teaching of dependent origination (see above, pp. 30–31), which also demonstrates how rebirth is possible without a reincarnating self.

The process of rebirth, the Buddha teaches, exhibits a definite lawfulness essentially ethical in character. This ethical character is established by the fundamental dynamism that determines the states into which beings are reborn and the circumstances they encounter in the course of their lives. That dynamism is *kamma*, volitional action of body, speech, and mind. Those beings who engage in bad actions—actions motivated by the three unwholesome roots of greed, hate, and delusion—generate unwholesome kamma that leads them to rebirth into lower states of existence and, if it ripens in the human world, brings them pain and misfortune. Those beings who engage in good actions—actions motivated by the three wholesome roots of non-greed, non-hate, and non-delusion—generate wholesome kamma that leads them to higher states of existence and ripens in the human world as happiness and good fortune. Because the deeds a person performs in the course of a single life can be extremely varied, the type of rebirth that lies ahead of him can be very unpredictable, as the Buddha shows in MN 136. But despite this empirical variability, an invariable law governs the direct relationship between types of actions and the types of results they yield, the basic correlations being sketched by the Buddha in MN 57 and laid out in greater detail in MN 135.

In several suttas of the Majjhima Nikāya the Buddha refers to various planes of existence into which rebirth can occur and he also gives some indication of the types of kamma that lead to those planes. This cosmological typography is not, from the Buddhist standpoint, the product of conjecture or fantasy but a matter directly known to the Buddha through his "Tathāgata's powers of knowledge" (MN 12.36); to some extent the process is also verifiable by those who gain the divine eye (e.g., MN 39.20). A brief overview may be given here of the planes of rebirth recognised in Buddhist cosmology and of their kammic antecedents, as systematised in the developed Theravāda tradition.

The Buddhist cosmos is divided into three broad realms—the sense-sphere realm, the fine-material realm, and the immaterial realm. Each of these comprises a range of subsidiary planes, amounting to a total of thirty-one planes of existence.

The sense-sphere realm, so called because sensual desire predominates there, consists of eleven planes divided into two groups, the bad destinations and the good destinations. The bad destinations or "states of deprivation" (*apāya*) are four in number: the hells, which are states of intense torment as described in MN 129 and MN 130; the animal kingdom; the sphere of ghosts (*peta*), beings afflicted with incessant hunger and thirst; and the sphere of titans (*asura*), beings involved in constant combat (not mentioned as a separate plane in the Majjhima). The courses of kamma leading to rebirth into these planes are classified into a set of ten—three of body, four of speech, and three of mind. These are enumerated briefly at MN 9.4 and explicated in MN 41. Gradations in the gravity of the evil intentions responsible for these deeds account for specific differences in the mode of rebirth resulting from such actions.

The good destinations in the sense-sphere realm are the human world and the heavenly planes. The latter are sixfold: the gods under the Four Great Kings; the gods of the Thirty-three (*tāvatiṁsa*), who are presided over by Sakka, a Buddhist metamorphosis of Indra, depicted as a devotee of the Buddha, faithful, but prone to negligence (MN 37); the Yāma gods; the gods of the Tusita heaven, the abode of the Bodhisatta before his final birth (MN 123); the gods who delight in creating; and the gods who wield power over others' creations. The last is said to be the abode of Māra, the Tempter in Buddhism, who besides being a symbol for Desire and Death, is also regarded as a powerful deity with evil designs, keen to prevent beings from escaping the net of saṁsāra. The kammic cause for rebirth into the good destinations of the sense-sphere realm is the practice of the ten courses of wholesome action, defined at MN 9.8 and in MN 41.

In the fine-material realm the grosser types of matter are absent and the bliss, power, luminosity, and vitality of its denizens are far superior to those in the sense-sphere realm. The fine-material realm consists of sixteen planes, which are the objective counterparts of the four jhānas. Attainment of the first jhāna leads to rebirth among Brahmā's Assembly, the Ministers of Brahmā and the Mahā Brahmās, according to whether it is developed to an inferior, middling, or superior degree. Baka the Brahmā (MN 49) and Brahmā Sahampati (MN 26, MN 67) seem to be residents of the last-named plane. The suttas mention especially the divine abodes as the path to the company of Brahmā (MN 99.24–27). Attainment of the second jhāna in the same three degrees leads respectively to rebirth among the gods of Limited Radiance, of Immeasurable Radiance, and of Streaming Radiance; the third jhāna to rebirth among the gods of Limited Glory, of Immeasurable Glory, and of Refulgent Glory. The fourth jhāna ordinarily leads to rebirth among the gods of Great Fruit, but if it is developed with a desire to attain an insentient mode of existence, it will conduce to rebirth among the non-percipient beings, for whom consciousness is temporarily suspended. The fine-material realm also contains five special planes that are exclusively for the rebirth of non-returners. These are the Pure Abodes—the Aviha, the Atappa, the Sudassa, the Sudassī, and the Akaniṭṭha. In each of these planes in the fine-material realm the lifespan is said to be of enormous duration and to increase significantly in each higher plane.

The third realm of being is the immaterial realm, where matter has become non-existent and only mental processes exist. This realm consists of four planes, which are the objective counterparts of the four immaterial meditative attainments, from which they result and whose names they share: the bases of infinite space, infinite consciousness, nothingness, and neither-perception-nor-non-perception. The lifespans ascribed to them are respectively 20,000; 40,000; 60,000; and 84,000 great aeons.

In Buddhist cosmology existence in every realm, being the product of a kamma with a finite potency, is necessarily impermanent. Beings take rebirth in accordance with their deeds, experience the good or bad results, and then, when the generative kamma has spent its force, they pass away to take rebirth elsewhere as determined by still another kamma that has found the opportunity to ripen. Hence the torments of hell as well as the bliss of heaven, no matter how long they may last, are bound to pass. For this reason the Buddha does not locate the final goal of his teaching anywhere within the conditioned world. He guides those whose spiritual faculties are still tender to aspire for a heavenly rebirth and teaches them the lines of conduct that conduce to the fulfilment of their aspirations (MN 41, MN 120). But for those whose faculties are mature and who can grasp the unsatisfactory nature of everything conditioned, he urges determined effort to put an end to wandering in saṁsāra and to reach Nibbāna, which transcends all planes of being.

THE BUDDHA AND HIS CONTEMPORARIES

The Middle Country of India in which the Buddha lived and taught in the fifth century B.C. teemed with a luxuriant variety of religious and philosophical beliefs propagated by teachers equally varied in their ways of life. The main division was into the brahmins and the non-brahmanic ascetics, the *samaṇas* or "strivers." The brahmins were the hereditary priesthood of India, the custodians of the ancient orthodoxy. They accepted the authority of the Vedas, which they studied, chanted at countless rituals, sacrifices, and ceremonies, and turned to as the source of their philosophical speculations. Thus they are characterised in the suttas as traditionalists (*anussavika*), who teach their doctrines on the basis of oral tradition (MN 100.7). The Pali Canon generally depicts them as living a comfortably settled life, as marrying and begetting progeny, and in some cases as enjoying royal patronage. The more learned among them gathered a company of students—all necessarily of brahmin birth—to whom they taught the Vedic hymns.

The samaṇas, on the other hand, did not accept the authority of the Vedas, for which reason from the perspective of the brahmins they stood in the ranks of heterodoxy. They were usually celibate, lived a life of mendicancy, and acquired their status by voluntary renunciation rather than by birth. The samaṇas roamed the Indian countryside sometimes in company, sometimes as solitaries, preaching their doctrines to the populace, debating with other ascetics, engaging in their spiritual practices, which often involved severe austerities (see MN 51.8). Some teachers in the samaṇa camp taught entirely on the basis of reasoning and speculation, while others taught on the basis of their experiences in meditation. The Buddha placed himself among the latter, as one who teaches a Dhamma that he has directly known for himself (MN 100.7).

The Buddha's encounters with brahmins were usually friendly, their conversations marked by courtesy and mutual regard. Several suttas in the Majjhima Nikāya concern the brahmins' claim to superiority over those in other social classes. In the Buddha's age the caste system was only beginning to take shape in northeast India and had not yet spawned the countless subdivisions and rigid regulations that were to manacle Indian society through the centuries. Society was divided into four broad social classes: the *brahmins,* who performed the priestly functions; the *khattiyas,* the nobles, warriors, and administrators; the *vessas,* the merchants and agriculturalists; and the *suddas,* the menials and serfs. From the Pali suttas it appears that the brahmins, while vested with authority in religious matters, had not yet risen to the position of unchallengeable hegemony they were to gain after the promulgation of the *Laws of Manu.* They had, however, already embarked on their drive for domination and did so by propagating the thesis that brahmins are the highest caste, the fairest caste, the divinely blessed offspring of Brahmā who are alone capable of purification. Anxiety that this claim of the brahmins might actually be true seems to have spread among the royalty, who must have been fearful of the threat it posed to their own power (see MN 84.4, MN 90.9–10).

Contrary to certain popular notions, the Buddha did not explicitly repudiate the class divisions of Indian society or appeal for the abolition of this social system. Within the Sangha, however, all caste distinctions were abrogated from the moment of ordination.

Thus people from any of the four castes who went forth under the Buddha renounced their class titles and prerogatives and instead became known simply as disciples of the Sakyan son (see Ud 5:5/55). Whenever the Buddha or his disciples were confronted with the brahmins' claim to superiority, they argued vigorously against them, maintaining that all such claims were groundless. Purification, they contended, was the result of conduct, not of birth, and was thus accessible to those of all four castes (MN 40.13–14, MN 84, MN 90.12, MN 93). The Buddha even stripped the term "brahmin" of its hereditary accretions, and hearkening back to its original connotation of holy man, he defined the true brahmin as the arahant (MN 98). Those among the brahmins who were not yet hampered by class prejudice responded appreciatively to the Buddha's teaching. Some of the most eminent brahmins of the time, in whom there still burned the ancient Vedic yearning for light, knowledge, and truth, recognised in the Buddha the All-Enlightened One for whom they longed and declared themselves his disciples (see especially MN 91.34). Several even renounced their class privileges and with their retinues entered the Sangha (MN 7.22, MN 92.15–24).

The samaṇas were a much more diversified group which, lacking a common scriptural authority, promulgated a plethora of philosophical doctrines ranging from the diabolical to the superdivine. The Pali Canon frequently mentions six teachers in particular as contemporaries of the Buddha, and as they are each described as "the head of an order...regarded by many as a saint" (MN 77.5), they must have been quite influential at the time. The Majjhima Nikāya mentions both the set of six and, separately, states their individual doctrines; it does not, however, correlate the names with the doctrines. The connections between names and doctrines are made in the *Sāmaññaphala Sutta* of the Dīgha Nikāya.

Pūraṇa Kassapa, who is always mentioned first in the list, taught a doctrine of inaction (*akiriyavāda*) that denied the validity of moral distinctions (MN 60.13, MN 76.10). Makkhali Gosāla was the leader of the sect known as the Ājīvakas (or Ājivikas), which survived in India down into the medieval period. He taught a doctrine of fatalism that denied causality (*ahetukavāda*) and claimed that the entire cosmic process is rigidly controlled by a principle called fate or destiny (*niyati*); beings have no volitional control over their actions but move helplessly caught in the grip of fate (MN 60.21, MN 76.13). Ajita Kesakambalin was a moral nihilist (*natthikavāda*) who propounded a materialist philosophy that rejected the existence of an afterlife and kammic retribution (MN 60.5, MN 76.7); his doctrine is always cited by the Buddha as the paradigmatic instance of wrong view among the unwholesome courses of action. Pakudha Kaccāyana advocated an atomism on the basis of which he repudiated the basic tenets of morality (MN 76.16). Sañjaya Belaṭṭhiputta, a sceptic, refused to take a stand on the crucial moral and philosophical issues of the day, probably claiming that such knowledge was beyond our capacity for verification (MN 76.30). The sixth teacher, the Nigaṇṭha Nātaputta, is identified with Mahāvīra, the historical progenitor of Jainism. He taught that there exists a plurality of monadic souls entrapped in matter by the bonds of past kamma and that the soul is to be liberated by exhausting its kammic bonds through the practice of severe self-mortification.

Whereas the Pali suttas are generally cordial but critical towards the brahmins, they are trenchant in their rejection of the rival doctrines of the samaṇas. In one sutta (MN 60) the Buddha contends that the firm adoption of any of the first three doctrines (and by implication the fourth) entails a chain of unwholesome states generating evil kamma strong enough to bring a descent into the lower realms. Similarly the venerable Ānanda describes these views as four "negations of the holy life" (MN 76). The scepticism of Sañjaya, while not regarded as so pernicious, is taken as an indication of its proponent's dullness and confusion; it is described as "eel-wriggling" (*amarāvikkhepa*) because of its evasiveness and classified among the types of holy life that are without consolation (MN 76.30–31). The Jain doctrine, though sharing certain similarities with the Buddha's teaching, was held to be sufficiently mistaken in basic assumptions as to call for refutation, which the Buddha undertook on several occasions (MN 14, MN 56, MN 101). The repudiation of these erroneous views was seen, from the Buddhist perspective, to be a necessary measure not only to sound a clear warning against tenets that were spiritually detrimental, but also to cut away the obstacles against the acceptance of right view, which as the forerunner of the Buddha's path (MN 117.4) was a prerequisite to progress along the road to final deliverance.

TECHNICAL NOTES

There remain to be discussed only a few technical points concerning this translation: first a general problem inevitably facing any translator from the Pali Canon, then certain changes that have been made in Ven. Ñāṇamoli's renderings of important doctrinal terms.

THE REPETITIONS

Readers of Pali suttas, particularly in the original language, will immediately be struck by the frequency and length of the repetitive passages. The repetitions, if examined, will be found to be of different kinds and thus probably stem from different sources. We may consider three main types.

First are the narrative repetitions within a single sutta as well as the repetition of statements in ordinary conversation. These doubtlessly originate from the method of oral transmission by which the suttas were preserved for the first four centuries of their existence, such repetition serving as a useful mnemonic device to ensure that details would not be lost. In this translation these repetitions have usually been bridged over with ellipsis points and occasionally the liberty was taken of contracting them.

A second type of repetition stems from the use of stock formulas to describe fixed sets of doctrinal categories or aspects of the training. A common example of this is the formulas for the four jhānas and the three true knowledges. These formulas were almost certainly part of the Buddha's repertory of instructions, employed by him in the countless discourses he gave during his forty-five years' ministry in order to preserve the unity and consistency of his teaching. Here the shorter stereotyped formulas have generally been allowed to stand except when they play a subordinate role to a larger theme, in which case only the main clauses have been retained; an example is the treatment of the jhāna formula at MN 53.18. The longer formulas that appear very often have been abridged, with references usually given to the passages where they appear in full; examples are the treatment of the first two true knowledges at MN 27.23–24 and of the gradual training at MN 38.31–38.

A third type of repetition stems from the Buddha's application of an identical method of exposition to a series of doctrinal terms belonging to a fixed set. Examples are the formula for insight that is attached to each of the exercises in the *Satipaṭṭhāna Sutta* (MN 10.5), and the exposition on the three characteristics applied to each of the five aggregates (MN 22.26). These repetitions, contrary to modernistic suppositions, were very likely integral to the Buddha's own pedagogical method and served to drive home the points he wanted to convey. We can well imagine that such repetitions, delivered by a fully enlightened teacher to those earnestly striving for awakening, must have sunk down deep into the minds of those who heard them and in many cases triggered off a glimpse of the truth. In the translation this type of repetition has usually been handled by repeating the method of exposition only for the first and last terms in the set—as is often done in the Pali editions of the texts—except when the method of exposition is especially long (as at MN 118.37–39), in which case it is shown in full only for the first term and in much abbreviated form for the rest. Those who read the suttas as an exercise in contemplation, and not merely for information, may try mentally filling in the entire sequence and exploring its range of implications.

DHAMMA

In his later translations Ven. Ñāṇamoli appears to have set himself two goals: to render virtually every Pali word into English (*arahant* and *bodhisatta* are rare exceptions); and to do so in obedience to a very rigorous standard of consistency. In effect the principle that guided his work was: one Pali word, one corresponding English word. This principle he also applied to his treatment of the multiplex word *dhamma*, of which he wrote elsewhere that "the need for unity in the rendering is so great as to be almost desperate" (*Minor Readings and Illustrator*, p. 331). He chose as his root rendering the word "idea," which he attempted to deploy for the Pali word in all its diverse occurrences. Even when *dhamma* is used in the suttas to signify the Buddha's teaching, he still remained faithful to his choice by translating it "the True Idea."

Needless to say, this experiment was not successful. Recognising this, Ven. Khantipālo, in his edition of the ninety suttas, opted instead to retain the Pali word in most of its occurrences. This decision, however, seems to have been unnecessary when the relinquishment of the demand for strict consistency allows for smooth and reliable translation without loss of meaning. While the many different uses of the Pali word *dhamma* may originally have had some underlying connection of meaning, by the time of the Pali Canon such connection had already receded so far into the background as to be virtually irrelevant to the understanding of the texts. The commentaries ascribe at least ten different contextual meanings to the word as it occurs in the Canon and they do not try to read any philosophical significance into this variability of application. The goal of lucid translation therefore seems to require that the word be rendered differently according to its context, which generally makes the intended meaning clear.

In revising Ven. Ñāṇamoli's translation I have retained the Pali word *Dhamma* only when it refers to the Buddha's teaching, or in several cases to a rival teaching with which the Buddha's is contrasted (as at MN 11.13 and MN 104.2). In its other uses the context has been allowed to decide the rendering. Thus when *dhamma* occurs in the plural as a general ontological reference term it has been rendered "things" (as at MN 1.2 and MN 2.5). When it acquires a more technical nuance, in the sense either of the phenomena of existence or of mental constituents, it has been rendered "states" (as at MN 64.9 and MN 111.4). This term, however, must be divested of its overtone of staticity, *dhammas* being events within a dynamic process, and it must also not be taken to refer to some persisting entity that undergoes the states, entities themselves being nothing but connected series of *dhammas*. The last two meanings of *dhamma* are not always separable in the texts and sometimes naturalness of English diction had to be used as the factor for deciding which should be selected.

As the fourth foundation of mindfulness and as the sixth external sense base (*āyatana*), *dhamma* has been rendered "mind-objects" (even here "ideas" is too narrow). In still other contexts it has been rendered as qualities (MN 15.3, MN 48.6) and teachings (MN 46.2, MN 47.3). When used as a suffix it acquires the idiomatic sense of "to be subject to" and so it has been translated, e.g., *vipariṇāmadhamma* as "subject to change."

SANKHĀRA

Although this word as used in the suttas has different specific references in different contexts, unlike *dhamma* it retains enough unity of meaning to permit, with rare exceptions, a uniform rendering. The problem, however, is to decide which of the many proposed renderings is the most adequate, or, if none are found fitting, to coin a new one that is.

The root idea suggested by the word *sankhāra* is "making together." The Pali commentators explain that the word allows for both an active and a passive sense. Thus the *sankhāras* are either factors (or forces) that function together in producing an effect, or they are the things that are produced by a combination of co-operating factors. In his translation of the *Visuddhimagga* Ven. Ñāṇamoli had rendered *sankhāras* as "formations," a rendering favoured by many other translators. In his later translation scheme he had experimented with rendering it as "determinations" and had attempted to incorporate that new choice into his manuscript of the Majjhima. In editing the manuscript Ven. Khantipālo chose to return to the translator's earlier and better known "formations," and in this edition I have followed suit. Though this word has the disadvantage of accentuating the passive aspect of *sankhāras*, it avoids the problems into which "determinations" runs and seems colourless enough to take on the meaning determined by the context.

The word *sankhāra* occurs in four major contexts in the Pali suttas: (1) As the second factor in the formula of dependent origination it is used to mean volitional actions, suggesting their active role of generating results in the process of rebirth. (2) As the fourth of the five aggregates the *sankhāras* comprise all the mental factors not included in the other three mental aggregates; this group is probably assigned the name *sankhārakkhandha* after its chief member, volition (*cetanā*), which is responsible for forming all the other aggregates. (3) *Sankhāra* is also used in a very comprehensive sense to signify everything produced by conditions. In this sense it comprises all five aggregates (as at MN 35.4 and MN 115.12). Here the word bears the passive sense, being explained by the commentators as *sankhatasankhārā*, "formations consisting in the conditioned." This usage comes close in meaning to the ontological use of *dhamma*, except that the latter is wider in range since it includes the unconditioned element Nibbāna and concepts (*paññatti*), both of which are excluded from *sankhāra*. (4) In still another context the word *sankhāra* is used in relation to *kāya*, *vacī*, and *citta*—body, speech, and mind—to mean the bodily formation, which is in-and-out breathing; the verbal formation, which is applied thought and sustained thought; and the mental formation, which is perception and feeling. The first and third are things that are dependent respectively upon the body and the mind, the second the things that activate speech. This triad is discussed at MN 44.13–15.

Sankhāra is also employed outside these major contexts, and in one such case Ven. Ñāṇamoli's sense of "determination" has been retained. This is where it occurs in the compound *padhānasankhāra*, which has been rendered "determined striving" (as at MN 16.26). The rare and involved idiom, *sankhāraṁ padahati*, has similarly been rendered "he strives with determination" (MN 101.23). In another case (MN 120), following the commentarial gloss, *sankhāra* is rendered "aspiration."

NĀMARŪPA

Ven. Ñāṇamoli had translated this compound literally as "name-and-form." In this edition the compound has been changed back to the rendering used in his translation of the *Visuddhimagga*, "mentality-materiality," though with regret that this cumbersome Latinate expression lacks the concision and punch of "name-and-form." The word *nāma* originally meant "name," but in the Pali suttas it is used in this compound as a collective term for the mental factors associated with consciousness, as will be seen in the definition at MN 9.54. The commentaries explain *nāma* here as deriving from the word *namati*, to bend, and as being applied to the mental factors because they "bend" towards the object in the act of cognizing it. *Rūpa* is used in two major contexts in the suttas: as the first of the five aggregates and as the specific object of eye-consciousness. The former is a broader category that includes the latter as one among many other species of *rūpa*. Ven. Ñāṇamoli, aiming at consistency in his manuscript translation, had used "form" for *rūpa* as visible object (in preference to the "visible-datum" used in his earlier translation scheme). But when *rūpa* is used to signify the first of the five aggregates, it has been changed to "material form." This rendering should indicate more precisely the meaning of *rūpa* in that context while preserving the connection with *rūpa* as visible object. Occasionally in the texts the word seems to straddle both meaning without allowing an exclusive delimitation, as in the context of certain meditative attainments such as the first two liberations (MN 77.22).

BRAHMA

The word *brahma* provided Ven. Ñāṇamoli with another challenge to his endeavour to achieve complete consistency. The word itself, going back to the Vedic period, originally meant holy power, the sacred power that sustains the cosmos and that was contacted through the prayers and rituals of the Vedas. Though the word retained its significance of "holy" or "sacred," by the Buddha's time it had undergone two distinct lines of development. One culminated in the conception of Brahman (neuter) as an impersonal absolute reality hidden behind and manifesting itself through the changing phenomena of the world. This conception is the keynote of the Upanishads, but the word *brahma* never appears in this sense in the Pali Canon. The other line of development culminated in the conception of Brahmā (masculine singular) as an eternal personal God who creates and regulates the world. This conception was held by the brahmins as depicted in the Pali suttas. The Buddhists themselves asserted that Brahmā was not a single creator God but a collective name for several classes of high deities whose chiefs, forgetting that they are still transient beings in the grip of kamma, were prone to imagine themselves to be the omnipotent everlasting creator (see MN 49).

Ven. Ñāṇamoli attempted to fulfil his guideline of consistency by rendering the word *brahma* in its various occurrences by "divine" or its cognates. Thus Brahmā the deity was rendered "the Divinity," *brāhmaṇa* (= brahmin) was rendered "divine" (as a noun meaning a priestly theologian), and the expression *brahmacariya*, in which *brahma* functions as an adjective, was rendered "the Life Divine." The result of this experiment was again the sacrifice of clarity for the sake of consistency, even at the risk of generating misunderstanding, and therefore in the revisionary process I decided to treat these expressions in line with more conventional practices. Thus Brahmā and brahmin have been left untranslated (the latter word is probably already more familiar to modern readers than the archaic noun "divine"). The word *brahma,* as it appears in compounds, has usually been rendered "holy"—e.g., *brahmacariya* as "the holy life" except when it is used to signify total sexual abstinence, in which case it has been rendered in accordance with its intended meaning as "celibacy." The word "divine" has, however, been retained in the expression *brahmavihāra,* rendered "divine abode" (MN 83.6) with reference to the "immeasurable" meditations on loving-kindness, compassion, altruistic joy, and equanimity, which are the dwellings of the divinity Brahmā (MN 55.7) and the path to rebirth in the Brahma-world (MN 99.22).

A NOTE ON PRONUNCIATION

The pronunciation of Pali words and names is quite easy providing the following simple rules are heeded. Among the vowels:

a	i	u	as in "but," "pin," "duke";
ā	ī	ū	as in "father," "keen," "pool";
e	and	o	as in "way" and "home."

Among the consonants, *g* is pronounced as in "girl," *c* as in "church," *ñ* as in "canyon." The cerebrals—*ṭ, ḍ, ṇ, ḷ*—are spoken with the tongue on the roof of the mouth; the dentals—*t, d, n, l*—with the tongue on the upper teeth. *ṁ* is a nasal as in "sing." The aspirates—*kh, gh, ch, jh, ṭh, ḍh, th, dh, ph, and bh*—are single consonants pronounced with a slight outward puff of breath, e.g., *th* as in "Thomas" (not as in "that"), *ph* as in "top hat" (not as in "phone"). Double consonants are always enunciated separately, e.g., *dd* as in "mad dog," *gg* as in "big gun."

An *o* and an *e* always carry a stress, otherwise the stress falls on a long vowel—*ā, ī, or ū*—or on a double consonant, or on *ṁ*.

MAJOR CHANGES IN TERMINOLOGY

This list shows the most important of the changes in Ven. Ñāṇamoli's manuscript terminology that were made for this edition. Changes marked with an asterisk were already introduced by Ven. Khantipālo in *A Treasury of the Buddha's Words.*

PALI TERM	MS RENDERING	REVISED RENDERING
akusala	unprofitable	unwholesome
ajjhosāna	cleaving	holding
abhinivesa	insistence	adherence
arūpa	formless	immaterial
**asekha*	the Adept	one beyond training
iddhi	success	(1) supernormal power; (2) spiritual power; (3) success
uddhacca-kukkucca	agitation and worry	restlessness and remorse
upadhi	essentials of existence	acquisition(s)
ottappa	shame	fear of wrongdoing
kāmā	sensual desires	sensual pleasures
kusala	profitable	wholesome
khaya	exhaustion	destruction
**citta*	cognizance	mind
chanda	zeal	(1) desire; (2) zeal
**jhāna*	illumination	jhāna
**tathāgata*	the Perfect One	the Tathāgata
thīna-middha	lethargy and drowsiness	sloth and torpor
**dhamma*	the True Idea	the Dhamma
dhammā	ideas	(1) things, states, factors; (2) mind-objects; (3) qualities; (4) teachings
nandī	relishing	delight
nāma	name	mentality

PALI TERM	MS RENDERING	REVISED RENDERING
nāmarūpa	name-and-form	mentality-materiality
**nibbāna*	extinction	Nibbāna
nibbidā	dispassion	disenchantment
paññā	understanding	wisdom
paṭigha	resistance	(1) sensory impact; (2) aversion
padhāna	endeavour	striving
papañca	diversification	proliferation
paritassanā	anguish	agitation
pīti	happiness	rapture
**buddha*	the Enlightened One	the Buddha
brahma	divine	holy, divine
brahmā	the Divinity	Brahmā
brāhmaṇa	divine (caste)	brahmin
bhāvanā	maintaining in being	development
muditā	gladness	altruistic joy
rūpa	form	(1) form; (2) material form, materiality; (3) fine-material (being)
vicāra	pondering	sustained thought
vicikicchā	uncertainty	doubt
vitakka	thought, thinking	thought, applied thought
virāga	fading away of lust	dispassion
sakkāya	embodiment	identity
**sankhārā*	determinations	formations
**sangha*	the Community	the Sangha
**sattā*	creatures	beings
samaṇa	monk	recluse
**sekha*	the Initiate	the disciple in higher training
hiri	conscience	shame

A Summary of the 152 Suttas

PART ONE: THE ROOT FIFTY DISCOURSES

1 *Mūlapariyāya Sutta*: The Root of All Things. The Buddha analyses the cognitive processes of four types of individuals—the untaught ordinary person, the disciple in higher training, the arahant, and the Tathāgata. This is one of the deepest and most difficult suttas in the Pali Canon, and it is therefore suggested that the earnest student read it only in a cursory manner on a first reading of the Majjhima Nikāya, returning to it for an in-depth study after completing the entire collection.

2 *Sabbāsava Sutta*: All the Taints. The Buddha teaches the bhikkhus seven methods for restraining and abandoning the taints, the fundamental defilements that maintain bondage to the round of birth and death.

3 *Dhammadāyāda Sutta*: Heirs in Dhamma. The Buddha enjoins the bhikkhus to be heirs in Dhamma, not heirs in material things. The venerable Sāriputta then continues on the same theme by explaining how disciples should train themselves to become the Buddha's heirs in Dhamma.

4 *Bhayabherava Sutta*: Fear and Dread. The Buddha describes to a brahmin the qualities required of a monk who wishes to live alone in the forest. He then relates an account of his own attempts to conquer fear when striving for enlightenment.

5 *Anangaṇa Sutta*: Without Blemishes. The venerable Sāriputta gives a discourse to the bhikkhus on the meaning of blemishes, explaining that a bhikkhu becomes blemished when he falls under the sway of evil wishes.

6 *Ākankheyya Sutta*: If a Bhikkhu Should Wish. The Buddha begins by stressing the importance of virtue as the foundation for a bhikkhu's training; he then goes on to enumerate

the benefits that a bhikkhu can reap by properly fulfilling the training.

7 *Vatthūpama Sutta*: The Simile of the Cloth. With a simple simile the Buddha illustrates the difference between a defiled mind and a pure mind.

8 *Sallekha Sutta*: Effacement. The Buddha rejects the view that the mere attainment of the meditative absorptions is effacement and explains how effacement is properly practised in his teaching.

9 *Sammādiṭṭhi Sutta*: Right View. A long and important discourse by the venerable Sāriputta, with separate sections on the wholesome and the unwholesome, nutriment, the Four Noble Truths, the twelve factors of dependent origination, and the taints.

10 *Satipaṭṭhāna Sutta*: The Foundations of Mindfulness. This is one of the fullest and most important suttas by the Buddha dealing with meditation, with particular emphasis on the development of insight. The Buddha begins by declaring the four foundations of mindfulness to be the direct path for the realisation of Nibbāna, then gives detailed instructions on the four foundations: the contemplation of the body, feelings, mind, and mind-objects.

11 *Cūḷasīhanāda Sutta*: The Shorter Discourse on the Lion's Roar. The Buddha declares that only in his Dispensation can the four grades of noble individuals be found, explaining how his teaching can be distinguished from other creeds through its unique rejection of all doctrines of self.

12 *Mahāsīhanāda Sutta*: The Greater Discourse on the Lion's Roar. The Buddha expounds the ten powers of a Tathāgata, his four kinds of intrepidity, and other superior qualities, which entitle him to "roar his lion's roar in the assemblies."

13 *Mahādukkhakkhandha Sutta*: The Greater Discourse on the Mass of Suffering. The Buddha explains the full understanding of sensual pleasures, material form, and feelings; there is a long section on the dangers in sensual pleasures.

14 *Cūḷadukkhakkhandha Sutta*: The Shorter Discourse on the Mass of Suffering. A variation on the preceding, ending in a discussion with Jain ascetics on the nature of pleasure and pain.

15 *Anumāna Sutta*: Inference. The venerable Mahā Moggallāna enumerates the qualities that make a bhikkhu difficult to admonish and teaches how one should examine oneself to remove the defects in one's character.

16 *Cetokhila Sutta*: The Wilderness in the Heart. The Buddha explains to the bhikkhus the five "wildernesses in the heart" and the five "shackles in the heart."

17 *Vanapattha Sutta*: Jungle Thickets. A discourse on the conditions under which a meditative monk should remain living in a jungle thicket and the conditions under which he should go elsewhere.

18 *Madhupiṇḍika Sutta*: The Honeyball. The Buddha utters a deep but enigmatic statement about "the source through which perceptions and notions tinged by mental proliferation beset a man." This statement is elucidated by the venerable Mahā Kaccāna, whose explanation is praised by the Buddha.

19 *Dvedhāvitakka Sutta*: Two Kinds of Thought. With reference to his own struggle for enlightenment, the Buddha explains the way to overcome unwholesome thoughts and replace them by wholesome thoughts.

20 *Vitakkasaṇṭhāna Sutta*: The Removal of Distracting Thoughts. The Buddha teaches five methods for dealing with the unwholesome thoughts that may arise in the course of meditation.

21 *Kakacūpama Sutta*: The Simile of the Saw. A discourse on the need to maintain patience when addressed with disagreeable words.

22 *Alagaddūpama Sutta*: The Simile of the Snake. A bhikkhu named Ariṭṭha gives rise to a pernicious view that conduct prohibited by the Buddha is not really an obstruction. The Buddha reprimands him and, with a series of memorable similes, stresses the dangers in misapplying and misrepresenting the Dhamma. The sutta culminates in one of the most impressive disquisitions on non-self found in the Canon.

23 *Vammika Sutta*: The Ant-hill. A deity presents a monk with an obscure riddle, which is unravelled for him by the Buddha.

24 *Rathavinīta Sutta*: The Relay Chariots. The venerable Puṇṇa

Mantāṇiputta explains to Sāriputta that the goal of the holy life, final Nibbāna, is to be reached by way of the seven stages of purification.

25 *Nivāpa Sutta*: The Bait. The Buddha uses the analogy of deer-trappers to make known to the bhikkhus the obstacles that confront them in their effort to escape from Māra's control.

26 *Ariyapariyesanā Sutta*: The Noble Search. The Buddha gives the bhikkhus a long account of his own quest for enlightenment from the time of his life in the palace up to his transmission of the Dhamma to his first five disciples.

27 *Cūḷahatthipadopama Sutta*: The Shorter Discourse on the Simile of the Elephant's Footprint. Using the analogy of a woodsman tracking down a big bull elephant, the Buddha explains how a disciple arrives at complete certainty of the truth of his teaching. The sutta presents a full account of the step-by-step training of the Buddhist monk.

28 *Mahāhatthipadopama Sutta*: The Greater Discourse on the Simile of the Elephant's Footprint. The venerable Sāriputta begins with a statement of the Four Noble Truths, which he then expounds by way of the contemplation of the four elements and the dependent origination of the five aggregates.

29 *Mahāsāropama Sutta*: The Greater Discourse on the Simile of the Heartwood.

30 *Cūḷasāropama Sutta*: The Shorter Discourse on the Simile of the Heartwood.

These two discourses emphasise that the proper goal of the holy life is the unshakeable deliverance of the mind, to which all other benefits are subsidiary.

31 *Cūḷagosinga Sutta*: The Shorter Discourse in Gosinga. The Buddha meets three bhikkhus who are living in concord, "blending like milk and water," and inquires how they succeed in living together so harmoniously.

32 *Mahāgosinga Sutta*: The Greater Discourse in Gosinga. On a beautiful moonlit night a number of senior disciples meet together in a sāla-tree wood and discuss what kind of bhikkhu could illuminate the wood. After each has answered according to his personal ideal, they go to the Buddha, who provides his own answer.

33 *Mahāgopālaka Sutta*: The Greater Discourse on the

Cowherd. The Buddha teaches eleven qualities that prevent a bhikkhu's growth in the Dhamma and eleven qualities that contribute to his growth.

34 *Cūḷagopālaka Sutta*: The Shorter Discourse on the Cowherd. The Buddha explains the types of bhikkhus who "breast Māra's stream" and get safely across to the further shore.

35 *Cūḷasaccaka Sutta*: The Shorter Discourse to Saccaka. The debater Saccaka boasts that in debate he can shake the Buddha up and down and thump him about, but when he finally meets the Buddha their discussion takes some unexpected turns.

36 *Mahāsaccaka Sutta*: The Greater Discourse to Saccaka. The Buddha meets again with Saccaka and in the course of a discussion on "development of body" and "development of mind" he relates a detailed narrative on his own spiritual quest.

37 *Cūḷataṇhāsankhaya Sutta*: The Shorter Discourse on the Destruction of Craving. The venerable Mahā Moggallāna overhears the Buddha give a brief explanation to Sakka, ruler of gods, as to how a bhikkhu is liberated through the destruction of craving. Wishing to know if Sakka understood the meaning, he makes a trip to the heaven of the Thirty-three to find out.

38 *Mahātaṇhāsankhaya Sutta*: The Greater Discourse on the Destruction of Craving. A bhikkhu named Sāti promulgates the pernicious view that the same consciousness transmigrates from life to life. The Buddha reprimands him with a lengthy discourse on dependent origination, showing how all phenomena of existence arise and cease through conditions.

39 *Mahā-Assapura Sutta*: The Greater Discourse at Assapura. The Buddha elucidates "the things that make one a recluse" with a discourse covering many aspects of the bhikkhu's training.

40 *Cūḷa-Assapura Sutta*: The Shorter Discourse at Assapura. The Buddha explains "the way proper to the recluse" to be not the mere outward practice of austerities but the inward purification from defilements.

41 *Sāleyyaka Sutta*: The Brahmins of Sālā.

42 *Verañjaka Sutta*: The Brahmins of Verañja.

In these two nearly identical suttas the Buddha explains to groups of brahmin householders the courses of conduct leading to rebirth in lower realms and the courses leading to higher rebirth and deliverance.

43 *Mahāvedalla Sutta*: The Greater Series of Questions and Answers.

44 *Cūḷavedalla Sutta*: The Shorter Series of Questions and Answers.

These two discourses take the form of discussions on various subtle points of Dhamma, the former between the venerable Mahā Koṭṭhita and the venerable Sāriputta, the latter between the bhikkhunī Dhammadinnā and the lay follower Visākha.

45 *Cūḷadhammasamādāna Sutta*: The Shorter Discourse on Ways of Undertaking Things.

46 *Mahādhammasamādāna Sutta*: The Greater Discourse on Ways of Undertaking Things.

The Buddha explains, differently in each of the two suttas, four ways of undertaking things, distinguished according to whether they are painful or pleasant now and whether they ripen in pain or pleasure in the future.

47 *Vīmaṁsaka Sutta*: The Inquirer. The Buddha invites the bhikkhus to make a thorough investigation of himself in order to find out whether or not he can be accepted as fully enlightened.

48 *Kosambiya Sutta*: The Kosambians. During the period when the bhikkhus at Kosambi are divided by a dispute, the Buddha teaches them the six qualities that create love and respect and conduce to unity. He then explains seven extraordinary knowledges possessed by a noble disciple who has realised the fruit of stream-entry.

49 *Brahmanimantanika Sutta*: The Invitation of a Brahmā. Baka the Brahmā, a high divinity, adopts the pernicious view that the heavenly world over which he presides is eternal and that there is no higher state beyond. The Buddha visits him to dissuade him from that wrong view and engages him in a contest of Olympian dimensions.

50 *Māratajjanīya Sutta*: The Rebuke to Māra. Māra attempts to harass the venerable Mahā Moggallāna, but the latter relates

a story of the distant past to warn Māra of the dangers in creating trouble for a disciple of the Buddha.

PART TWO: THE MIDDLE FIFTY DISCOURSES

51 *Kandaraka Sutta*: To Kandaraka. The Buddha discusses four kinds of persons found in the world—the one who torments himself, the one who torments others, the one who torments both himself and others, and the one who torments neither but lives a truly holy life.

52 *Aṭṭhakanāgara Sutta*: The Man from Aṭṭhakanagara. The venerable Ānanda teaches eleven "doors to the Deathless" by which a bhikkhu can attain the supreme security from bondage.

53 *Sekha Sutta*: The Disciple in Higher Training. At the Buddha's request the venerable Ānanda gives a discourse on the practices undertaken by a disciple in higher training.

54 *Potaliya Sutta*: To Potaliya. The Buddha teaches a presumptuous interlocutor the meaning of "the cutting off of affairs" in his discipline. The sutta offers a striking series of similes on the dangers in sensual pleasures.

55 *Jīvaka Sutta*: To Jīvaka. The Buddha explains the regulations he has laid down concerning meat-eating and defends his disciples against unjust accusations.

56 *Upāli Sutta*: To Upāli. The wealthy and influential householder Upāli, a prominent supporter of the Jains, proposes to go to the Buddha and refute his doctrine. Instead, he finds himself converted by the Buddha's "converting magic."

57 *Kukkuravatika Sutta*: The Dog-Duty Ascetic. The Buddha meets two ascetics, one who imitates the behaviour of a dog, the other who imitates the behaviour of an ox. He reveals to them the futility of their practices and gives them a discourse on kamma and its fruit.

58 *Abhayarājakumāra Sutta*: To Prince Abhaya. The Jain leader, Nigaṇṭha Nātaputta, teaches Prince Abhaya a "two-horned question" with which he can refute the Buddha's doctrine. The Buddha escapes the dilemma and explains what kind of speech he would and would not utter.

59 *Bahuvedanīya Sutta*: The Many Kinds of Feeling. After

resolving a disagreement about the classification of feelings, the Buddha enumerates the different kinds of pleasure and joy that beings can experience.

60 *Apaṇṇaka Sutta*: The Incontrovertible Teaching. The Buddha gives a group of brahmin householders an "incontrovertible teaching" that will help them steer clear of the tangle in contentious views.

61 *Ambalaṭṭhikārāhulovāda Sutta*: Advice to Rāhula at Ambalaṭṭhikā. The Buddha admonishes his son, the novice Rāhula, on the dangers in lying and stresses the importance of constant reflection on one's motives.

62 *Mahārāhulovāda Sutta*: The Greater Discourse of Advice to Rāhula. The Buddha teaches Rāhula the meditation on the elements, on mindfulness of breathing, and other topics.

63 *Cūḷamālunkya Sutta*: The Shorter Discourse to Mālunkyāputta. A bhikkhu threatens to leave the Order unless the Buddha answers his metaphysical questions. With the simile of the man struck by a poisoned arrow, the Buddha makes plain exactly what he does and does not teach.

64 *Mahāmālunkya Sutta*: The Greater Discourse to Mālunkyāputta. The Buddha teaches the path to the abandoning of the five lower fetters.

65 *Bhaddāli Sutta*: To Bhaddāli. The Buddha admonishes a recalcitrant monk and explains the disadvantages of refusing to submit to the training.

66 *Laṭukikopama Sutta*: The Simile of the Quail. The Buddha drives home the importance of abandoning all fetters, no matter how harmless and trifling they may seem.

67 *Cātumā Sutta*: At Cātumā. The Buddha teaches a group of newly ordained monks four dangers to be overcome by those who have gone forth into homelessness.

68 *Naḷakapāna Sutta*: At Naḷakapāna. The Buddha explains why, when his disciples die, he declares their level of attainment and plane of rebirth.

69 *Gulissāni Sutta*: Gulissāni. The venerable Sāriputta gives a discourse on the proper training of a forest-dwelling bhikkhu.

70 *Kīṭāgiri Sutta*: At Kīṭāgiri. The Buddha admonishes a group of disobedient monks, in the course of which he presents an important sevenfold classification of noble disciples.

71 *Tevijjavacchagotta Sutta*: To Vacchagotta on the Threefold

True Knowledge. The Buddha denies possessing complete knowledge of everything at all times and defines the threefold knowledge he does possess.

72 *Aggivacchagotta Sutta*: To Vacchagotta on Fire. The Buddha explains to a wanderer why he does not hold any speculative views. With the simile of an extinguished fire he tries to indicate the destiny of the liberated being.

73 *Mahāvacchagotta Sutta*: The Greater Discourse to Vacchagotta. The story of the wanderer Vacchagotta's full conversion to the Dhamma, his going forth, and his attainment of arahantship.

74 *Dīghanakha Sutta*: To Dīghanakha. The Buddha counters the disclaimers of a sceptic and teaches him the way to liberation through the contemplation of feelings.

75 *Māgandiya Sutta*: To Māgandiya. The Buddha meets the hedonist philosopher Māgandiya and points out to him the dangers in sensual pleasures, the benefits of renunciation, and the meaning of Nibbāna.

76 *Sandaka Sutta*: To Sandaka. The venerable Ānanda teaches a group of wanderers four ways that negate the living of the holy life and four kinds of holy life without consolation. Then he explains the holy life that is truly fruitful.

77 *Mahāsakuludāyi Sutta*: The Greater Discourse to Sakuludāyin. The Buddha teaches a group of wanderers the reasons why his disciples venerate him and look to him for guidance.

78 *Samaṇamaṇḍikā Sutta*: Samaṇamaṇḍikāputta. The Buddha explains how a man is "one who has attained to the supreme attainment."

79 *Cūḷasakuludāyi Sutta*: The Shorter Discourse to Sakuludāyin. The Buddha examines the doctrine of a wandering ascetic, using the simile of "the most beautiful girl in the country" to expose the folly of his claims.

80 *Vekhanassa Sutta*: To Vekhanassa. A discourse partly similar to the preceding one, with an additional section on sensual pleasure.

81 *Ghaṭīkāra Sutta*: Ghaṭīkāra the Potter. The Buddha recounts the story of the chief lay supporter of the past Buddha Kassapa.

82 *Raṭṭhapāla Sutta*: On Raṭṭhapāla. The story of a young man

who goes forth into homelessness against the wishes of his parents and later returns to visit them.

83 *Makhādeva Sutta*: King Makhādeva. The story of an ancient lineage of kings and how their virtuous tradition was broken due to negligence.

84 *Madhurā Sutta*: At Madhurā. The venerable Mahā Kaccāna examines the brahmin claim that brahmins are the highest caste.

85 *Bodhirājakumāra Sutta*: To Prince Bodhi. The Buddha counters the claim that pleasure is to be gained through pain with an account of his own quest for enlightenment.

86 *Angulimāla Sutta*: On Angulimāla. The story of how the Buddha subdued the notorious criminal Angulimāla and led him to the attainment of arahantship.

87 *Piyajātika Sutta*: Born from Those Who Are Dear. Why the Buddha teaches that sorrow and grief arise from those who are dear.

88 *Bāhitika Sutta*: The Cloak. The venerable Ānanda answers King Pasenadi's questions on the Buddha's behaviour.

89 *Dhammacetiya Sutta*: Monuments to the Dhamma. King Pasenadi offers ten reasons why he shows such deep veneration to the Buddha.

90 *Kaṇṇakatthala Sutta*: At Kaṇṇakatthala. King Pasenadi questions the Buddha on omniscience, on caste distinctions, and on the gods.

91 *Brahmāyu Sutta*: Brahmāyu. An old and erudite brahmin learns about the Buddha, goes to meet him, and becomes his disciple.

92 *Sela Sutta*: To Sela. The brahmin Sela questions the Buddha, gains faith in him, and becomes a monk along with his company of pupils.

93 *Assalāyana Sutta*: To Assalāyana. A young brahmin approaches the Buddha to argue the thesis that the brahmins are the highest caste.

94 *Ghoṭamukha Sutta*: To Ghoṭamukha. A discussion between a brahmin and a bhikkhu on whether the renunciate life accords with the Dhamma.

95 *Cankī Sutta*: With Cankī. The Buddha instructs a young brahmin on the preservation of truth, the discovery of truth, and the final arrival at truth.

96 *Esukārī Sutta*: To Esukārī. The Buddha and a brahmin discuss the brahmins' claim to superiority over the other castes.

97 *Dhānañjāni Sutta*: To Dhānañjāni. The venerable Sāriputta admonishes a brahmin who tries to excuse his negligence by appeal to his many duties. Later, when he is close to death, Sāriputta guides him to rebirth in the Brahma-world but is reprimanded by the Buddha for having done so.

98 *Vāseṭṭha Sutta*: To Vāseṭṭha. The Buddha resolves a dispute between two young brahmins on the qualities of a true brahmin.

99 *Subha Sutta*: To Subha. The Buddha answers a young brahmin's questions and teaches him the way to rebirth in the Brahma-world.

100 *Sangārava Sutta*: To Sangārava. A brahmin student questions the Buddha about the basis on which he teaches the fundamentals of the holy life.

PART THREE: THE FINAL FIFTY DISCOURSES

101 *Devadaha Sutta*: At Devadaha. The Buddha examines the Jain thesis that liberation is to be attained by self-mortification, proposing a different account of how striving becomes fruitful.

102 *Pañcattaya Sutta*: The Five and Three. A survey of various speculative views about the future and the past and of misconceptions about Nibbāna.

103 *Kinti Sutta*: What Do You Think About Me? The Buddha explains how the monks can resolve disagreements about the Dhamma.

104 *Sāmagāma Sutta*: At Sāmagāma. The Buddha lays down disciplinary procedures for the guidance of the Sangha to ensure its harmonious functioning after his demise.

105 *Sunakkhatta Sutta*: To Sunakkhatta. The Buddha discusses the problem of an individual's overestimation of his progress in meditation.

106 *Āneñjasappāya Sutta*: The Way to the Imperturbable. The Buddha explains the approaches to various levels of higher meditative states culminating in Nibbāna.

107 *Gaṇakamoggallāna Sutta*: To Gaṇaka Moggallāna. The

Buddha sets forth the gradual training of the Buddhist monk and describes himself as the "shower of the way."

108 *Gopakamoggallāna Sutta*: With Gopaka Moggallāna. The venerable Ānanda explains how the Sangha maintains its unity and internal discipline after the passing away of the Buddha.

109 *Mahāpuṇṇama Sutta*: The Greater Discourse on the Full-moon Night. A bhikkhu questions the Buddha on the five aggregates, clinging, personality view, and the realisation of non-self.

110 *Cūḷapuṇṇama Sutta*: The Shorter Discourse on the Full-Moon Night. The Buddha explains the differences between an "untrue man" and a "true man."

111 *Anupada Sutta*: One by One As They Occurred. The Buddha describes the venerable Sāriputta's development of insight when he was training for the attainment of arahantship.

112 *Chabbisodhana Sutta*: The Sixfold Purity. The Buddha explains how a bhikkhu should be interrogated when he claims final knowledge and how he would answer if his claim is genuine.

113 *Sappurisa Sutta*: The True Man. The Buddha distinguishes the character of a true man from that of an untrue man.

114 *Sevitabbāsevitabba Sutta*: To Be Cultivated and Not To Be Cultivated. The Buddha sets up three brief outlines of things to be cultivated and not to be cultivated, and the venerable Sāriputta fills in the details.

115 *Bahudhātuka Sutta*: The Many Kinds of Elements. The Buddha expounds in detail the elements, the sense bases, dependent origination, and the kinds of situations that are possible and impossible in the world.

116 *Isigili Sutta*: Isigili: The Gullet of the Seers. An enumeration of the names and epithets of paccekabuddhas who formerly dwelt on the mountain Isigili.

117 *Mahācattārīsaka Sutta*: The Great Forty. The Buddha defines the factors of the Noble Eightfold Path and explains their inter-relationships.

118 *Ānāpānasati Sutta*: Mindfulness of Breathing. An exposition of sixteen steps in mindfulness of breathing and of the relation of this meditation to the four foundations of mindfulness and the seven enlightenment factors.

119 *Kāyagatāsati Sutta*: Mindfulness of the Body. The Buddha

explains how mindfulness of the body should be developed and cultivated and the benefits to which it leads.

120 *Sankhārupapatti Sutta*: Reappearance by Aspiration. The Buddha teaches how one can be reborn in accordance with one's wish.

121 *Cūḷasuññata Sutta*: The Shorter Discourse on Voidness. The Buddha instructs Ānanda on the "genuine, undistorted, pure descent into voidness."

122 *Mahāsuññata Sutta*: The Greater Discourse on Voidness. Upon finding that the bhikkhus have grown fond of socialising, the Buddha stresses the need for seclusion in order to abide in voidness.

123 *Acchariya-abbhūta Sutta*: Wonderful and Marvellous. At a gathering of bhikkhus the venerable Ānanda recounts the wonderful and marvellous events that preceded and attended the birth of the Buddha.

124 *Bakkula Sutta*: Bakkula. The elder disciple Bakkula enumerates his austere practices during his eighty years in the Sangha and exhibits a remarkable death.

125 *Dantabhūmi Sutta:* The Grade of the Tamed. By analogy with the taming of an elephant, the Buddha explains how he tames his disciples.

126 *Bhūmija Sutta*: Bhūmija. The Buddha brings forward a series of similes to illustrate the natural fruitfulness of the Noble Eightfold Path.

127 *Anuruddha Sutta*: Anuruddha. The venerable Anuruddha clarifies the difference between the immeasurable deliverance of mind and the exalted deliverance of mind.

128 *Upakkilesa Sutta*: Imperfections. The Buddha discusses the various impediments to meditative progress he encountered during his quest for enlightenment, with particular reference to the divine eye.

129 *Bālapaṇḍita Sutta*: Fools and Wise Men. The sufferings of hell and animal life into which a fool is reborn through his evil deeds, and the pleasures of heaven that a wise man reaps through his good deeds.

130 *Devadūta Sutta*: The Divine Messengers. The Buddha describes the sufferings of hell that await the evil-doer after death.

131 *Bhaddekaratta Sutta*: A Single Excellent Night.

132 *Ānandabhaddekaratta Sutta*: Ānanda and A Single Excellent Night.

133 *Mahākaccānabhaddekaratta Sutta*: Mahā Kaccāna and A Single Excellent Night.

134 *Lomasakangiyabhaddekaratta Sutta*: Lomasakangiya and A Single Excellent Night.

The above four suttas all revolve around a stanza spoken by the Buddha emphasising the need for present effort in developing insight into things as they are.

135 *Cūḷakammavibhanga Sutta*: The Shorter Exposition of Action. The Buddha explains how kamma accounts for the fortune and misfortune of beings.

136 *Mahākammavibhanga Sutta*: The Greater Exposition of Action. The Buddha reveals subtle complexities in the workings of kamma that overturn simplistic dogmas and sweeping generalizations.

137 *Saḷāyatanavibhanga Sutta*: The Exposition of the Sixfold Base. The Buddha expounds the six internal and external sense bases and other related topics.

138 *Uddesavibhanga Sutta*: The Exposition of a Summary. The venerable Mahā Kaccāna elaborates upon a brief saying of the Buddha on the training of consciousness and the overcoming of agitation.

139 *Araṇavibhanga Sutta*: The Exposition of Non-conflict. The Buddha gives a detailed discourse on things that lead to conflict and things that lead away from conflict.

140 *Dhātuvibhanga Sutta*: The Exposition of Elements. Stopping at a potter's workshop for the night, the Buddha meets a monk named Pukkusāti and gives him a profound discourse on the elements culminating in the four foundations of arahantship.

141 *Saccavibhanga Sutta*: The Exposition of the Truths. The venerable Sāriputta gives a detailed analysis of the Four Noble Truths.

142 *Dakkhiṇāvibhanga Sutta*: The Exposition of Offerings. The Buddha enumerates fourteen kinds of personal offerings and seven kinds of offerings made to the Sangha.

143 *Anāthapiṇḍikovāda Sutta*: Advice to Anāthapiṇḍika. The venerable Sāriputta is called to Anāthapiṇḍika's deathbed and gives him a stirring sermon on non-attachment.

144 *Channovāda Sutta*: Advice to Channa. The venerable Channa, gravely ill, takes his own life despite the attempts of two brother-monks to dissuade him.

145 *Puṇṇovāda Sutta*: Advice to Puṇṇa. The bhikkhu Puṇṇa receives a short exhortation from the Buddha and decides to go live among the fierce people of a remote territory.

146 *Nandakovāda Sutta*: Advice from Nandaka. The venerable Nandaka gives the nuns a discourse on impermanence.

147 *Cūḷarāhulovāda Sutta*: The Shorter Discourse of Advice to Rāhula. The Buddha gives Rāhula a discourse that leads him to the attainment of arahantship.

148 *Chachakka Sutta*: The Six Sets of Six. An especially profound and penetrating discourse on the contemplation of all the factors of sense experience as not-self.

149 *Mahāsaḷāyatanika Sutta*: The Great Sixfold Base. How wrong view about the six kinds of sense experience leads to future bondage, while right view about them leads to liberation.

150 *Nagaravindeyya Sutta*: To the Nagaravindans. The Buddha explains to a group of brahmin householders what kind of recluses and brahmins should be venerated.

151 *Piṇḍapātapārisuddhi Sutta*: The Purification of Almsfood. The Buddha teaches Sāriputta how a bhikkhu should review himself to make himself worthy of almsfood.

152 *Indriyabhāvanā Sutta*: The Development of the Faculties. The Buddha explains the supreme development of control over the sense faculties and the arahant's mastery over his perceptions.

Plan of central and eastern India showing some of the principal place names mentioned in the Pali Tipiṭaka with modern names in brackets (sources: *Cambridge History of India*, vol. 1 map 5; T. W. Rhys Davids, *Buddhist India*).

The MAJJHIMA NIKĀYA

The MIDDLE LENGTH DISCOURSES *of the* BUDDHA

NAMO TASSA BHAGAVATO
ARAHATO SAMMĀSAMBUDDHASSA

HOMAGE TO THE BLESSED ONE,
ACCOMPLISHED AND FULLY ENLIGHTENED

Part One

The Root Fifty Discourses

(*Mūlapaṇṇāsapāḷi*)

1
The Division of the Discourse on the Root
(Mūlapariyāyavagga)

1 *Mūlapariyāya Sutta*
The Root of All Things

[1] 1. THUS HAVE I HEARD.[1] On one occasion the Blessed One was living in Ukkaṭṭhā in the Subhaga Grove at the root of a royal sāla tree. There he addressed the bhikkhus thus: "Bhikkhus."[2]—"Venerable sir," they replied. The Blessed One said this:

2. "Bhikkhus, I shall teach you a discourse on the root of all things.[3] Listen and attend closely to what I shall say."—"Yes, venerable sir," the bhikkhus replied. The Blessed One said this:

(THE ORDINARY PERSON)

3. "Here, bhikkhus, an untaught ordinary person,[4] who has no regard for noble ones and is unskilled and undisciplined in their Dhamma, who has no regard for true men and is unskilled and undisciplined in their Dhamma, perceives earth as earth.[5] Having perceived earth as earth, he conceives [himself as] earth, he conceives [himself] in earth, he conceives [himself apart] from earth, he conceives earth to be 'mine,' he delights in earth.[6] Why is that? Because he has not fully understood it, I say.[7]

4. "He perceives water as water. Having perceived water as water, he conceives [himself as] water, he conceives [himself] in water, he conceives [himself apart] from water, he conceives water to be 'mine,' he delights in water. Why is that? Because he has not fully understood it, I say.

5. "He perceives fire as fire. Having perceived fire as fire, he conceives [himself as] fire, he conceives [himself] in fire, he conceives [himself apart] from fire, he conceives fire to be 'mine,' he delights in fire. Why is that? Because he has not fully understood it, I say.

6. "He perceives air as air. Having perceived air as air, he conceives [himself as] air, he conceives [himself] in air, he conceives

[himself apart] from air, he conceives air to be 'mine,' he delights in air. Why is that? Because he has not fully understood it, I say. [2]

7. "He perceives beings as beings.[8] Having perceived beings as beings, he conceives beings, he conceives [himself] in beings, he conceives [himself apart] from beings, he conceives beings to be 'mine,' he delights in beings. Why is that? Because he has not fully understood it, I say.

8. "He perceives gods as gods.[9] Having perceived gods as gods, he conceives gods, he conceives [himself] in gods, he conceives [himself apart] from gods, he conceives gods to be 'mine,' he delights in gods. Why is that? Because he has not fully understood it, I say.

9. "He perceives Pajāpati as Pajāpati.[10] Having perceived Pajāpati as Pajāpati, he conceives Pajāpati, he conceives [himself] in Pajāpati, he conceives [himself apart] from Pajāpati, he conceives Pajāpati to be 'mine,' he delights in Pajāpati. Why is that? Because he has not fully understood it, I say.

10. "He perceives Brahmā as Brahmā.[11] Having perceived Brahmā as Brahmā, he conceives Brahmā, he conceives [himself] in Brahmā, he conceives [himself apart] from Brahmā, he conceives Brahmā to be 'mine,' he delights in Brahmā. Why is that? Because he has not fully understood it, I say.

11. "He perceives the gods of Streaming Radiance as the gods of Streaming Radiance.[12] Having perceived the gods of Streaming Radiance as the gods of Streaming Radiance, he conceives the gods of Streaming Radiance, he conceives [himself] in the gods of Streaming Radiance, he conceives [himself apart] from the gods of Streaming Radiance, he conceives the gods of Streaming Radiance to be 'mine,' he delights in the gods of Streaming Radiance. Why is that? Because he has not fully understood it, I say.

12. "He perceives the gods of Refulgent Glory as the gods of Refulgent Glory.[13] Having perceived the gods of Refulgent Glory as the gods of Refulgent Glory, he conceives the gods of Refulgent Glory, he conceives [himself] in the gods of Refulgent Glory, he conceives [himself apart] from the gods of Refulgent Glory, he conceives the gods of Refulgent Glory to be 'mine,' he delights in the gods of Refulgent Glory. Why is that? Because he has not fully understood it, I say.

13. "He perceives the gods of Great Fruit as the gods of Great Fruit.[14] Having perceived the gods of Great Fruit as the gods of Great Fruit, he conceives the gods of Great Fruit, he conceives [himself] in the gods of Great Fruit, he conceives [himself apart] from the gods of Great Fruit, he conceives the gods of Great Fruit to be 'mine,' he delights in the gods of Great Fruit. Why is that? Because he has not fully understood it, I say.

14. "He perceives the Overlord as the Overlord.[15] Having perceived the Overlord as the Overlord, he conceives the Overlord, he conceives [himself] in the Overlord, he conceives [himself apart] from the Overlord, he conceives the Overlord to be 'mine,' he delights in the Overlord. Why is that? Because he has not fully understood it, I say.

15. "He perceives the base of infinite space as the base of infinite space.[16] Having perceived the base of infinite space as the base of infinite space, he conceives [himself as] the base of infinite space, he conceives [himself] in the base of infinite space, he conceives [himself apart] from the base of infinite space, he conceives the base of infinite space to be 'mine,' he delights in the base of infinite space. Why is that? Because he has not fully understood it, I say.

16. "He perceives the base of infinite consciousness as the base of infinite consciousness. Having perceived the base of infinite consciousness as the base of infinite consciousness, [3] he conceives [himself as] the base of infinite consciousness, he conceives [himself] in the base of infinite consciousness, he conceives [himself apart] from the base of infinite consciousness, he conceives the base of infinite consciousness to be 'mine,' he delights in the base of infinite consciousness. Why is that? Because he has not fully understood it, I say.

17. "He perceives the base of nothingness as the base of nothingness. Having perceived the base of nothingness as the base of nothingness, he conceives [himself as] the base of nothingness, he conceives [himself] in the base of nothingness, he conceives [himself apart] from the base of nothingness, he conceives the base of nothingness to be 'mine,' he delights in the base of nothingness. Why is that? Because he has not fully understood it, I say.

18. "He perceives the base of neither-perception-nor-non-perception as the base of neither-perception-nor-non-perception. Having perceived the base of neither-perception-nor-non-perception

as the base of neither-perception-nor-non-perception, he conceives [himself as] the base of neither-perception-nor-non-perception, he conceives [himself] in the base of neither-perception-nor-non-perception, he conceives [himself apart] from the base of neither-perception-nor-non-perception, he conceives the base of neither-perception-nor-non-perception to be 'mine,' he delights in the base of neither-perception-nor-non-perception. Why is that? Because he has not fully understood it, I say.

19. "He perceives the seen as the seen.[17] Having perceived the seen as the seen, he conceives [himself as] the seen, he conceives [himself] in the seen, he conceives [himself apart] from the seen, he conceives the seen to be 'mine,' he delights in the seen. Why is that? Because he has not fully understood it, I say.

20. "He perceives the heard as the heard. Having perceived the heard as the heard, he conceives [himself as] the heard, he conceives [himself] in the heard, he conceives [himself apart] from the heard, he conceives the heard to be 'mine,' he delights in the heard. Why is that? Because he has not fully understood it, I say.

21. "He perceives the sensed as the sensed. Having perceived the sensed as the sensed, he conceives [himself as] the sensed, he conceives [himself] in the sensed, he conceives [himself apart] from the sensed, he conceives the sensed to be 'mine,' he delights in the sensed. Why is that? Because he has not fully understood it, I say.

22. "He perceives the cognized as the cognized. Having perceived the cognized as the cognized, he conceives [himself as] the cognized, he conceives [himself] in the cognized, he conceives [himself apart] from the cognized, he conceives the cognized to be 'mine,' he delights in the cognized. Why is that? Because he has not fully understood it, I say.

23. "He perceives unity as unity.[18] Having perceived unity as unity, he conceives [himself as] unity, he conceives [himself] in unity, he conceives [himself apart] from unity, he conceives unity to be 'mine,' he delights in unity. Why is that? Because he has not fully understood it, I say.

24. "He perceives diversity as diversity. Having perceived diversity as diversity, he conceives [himself as] diversity, he conceives [himself] in diversity, he conceives [himself apart] from diversity, he conceives diversity to be 'mine,' he delights

in diversity. Why is that? Because he has not fully understood it, I say.

25. "He perceives all as all.[19] Having perceived all as all, he conceives [himself as] all, [4] he conceives [himself] in all, he conceives [himself apart] from all, he conceives all to be 'mine,' he delights in all. Why is that? Because he has not fully understood it, I say.

26. "He perceives Nibbāna as Nibbāna.[20] Having perceived Nibbāna as Nibbāna, he conceives [himself as] Nibbāna, he conceives [himself] in Nibbāna, he conceives [himself apart] from Nibbāna, he conceives Nibbāna to be 'mine,' he delights in Nibbāna. Why is that? Because he has not fully understood it, I say.

(THE DISCIPLE IN HIGHER TRAINING)

27. "Bhikkhus, a bhikkhu who is in higher training,[21] whose mind has not yet reached the goal, and who is still aspiring to the supreme security from bondage, directly knows earth as earth.[22] Having directly known earth as earth, he should not conceive [himself as] earth, he should not conceive [himself] in earth, he should not conceive [himself apart] from earth, he should not conceive earth to be 'mine,' he should not delight in earth. Why is that? So that he may fully understand it, I say.[23]

28–49. "He directly knows water as water...He directly knows all as all...

50. "He directly knows Nibbāna as Nibbāna. Having directly known Nibbāna as Nibbāna, he should not conceive [himself as] Nibbāna, he should not conceive [himself] in Nibbāna, he should not conceive [himself apart] from Nibbāna, he should not conceive Nibbāna to be 'mine,' he should not delight in Nibbāna. Why is that? So that he may fully understand it, I say.

(THE ARAHANT—I)

51. "Bhikkhus, a bhikkhu who is an arahant with taints destroyed, who has lived the holy life, done what had to be done, laid down the burden, reached his own goal, destroyed the fetters of being, and is completely liberated through final knowledge,[24] directly knows earth as earth. Having directly

known earth as earth, he does not conceive [himself as] earth, he does not conceive [himself] in earth, he does not conceive [himself apart] from earth, he does not conceive earth to be 'mine,' he does not delight in earth. Why is that? Because he has fully understood it, I say.[25]

52–74. "He directly knows water as water...Nibbāna as Nibbāna...Why is that? Because he has fully understood it, I say.

(THE ARAHANT—II)

75. "Bhikkhus, a bhikkhu who is an arahant...completely liberated through final knowledge, [5] directly knows earth as earth. Having directly known earth as earth, he does not conceive [himself as] earth, he does not conceive [himself] in earth, he does not conceive [himself apart] from earth, he does not conceive earth to be 'mine,' he does not delight in earth. Why is that? Because he is free from lust through the destruction of lust.[26]

76–98. "He directly knows water as water...Nibbāna as Nibbāna...Why is that? Because he is free from lust through the destruction of lust.

(THE ARAHANT—III)

99. "Bhikkhus, a bhikkhu who is an arahant...completely liberated through final knowledge, directly knows earth as earth. Having directly known earth as earth, he does not conceive [himself as] earth, he does not conceive [himself] in earth, he does not conceive [himself apart] from earth, he does not conceive earth to be 'mine,' he does not delight in earth. Why is that? Because he is free from hate through the destruction of hate.

100–122. "He directly knows water as water...Nibbāna as Nibbāna...Why is that? Because he is free from hate through the destruction of hate.

(THE ARAHANT—IV)

123. "Bhikkhus, a bhikkhu who is an arahant...completely liberated through final knowledge, directly knows earth as earth. Having directly known earth as earth, he does not conceive [himself as] earth, he does not conceive [himself] in earth, he

does not conceive [himself apart] from earth, he does not conceive earth to be 'mine,' he does not delight in earth. Why is that? Because he is free from delusion through the destruction of delusion.

124–146. "He directly knows water as water...Nibbāna as Nibbāna...Why is that? Because he is free from delusion through the destruction of delusion.

(THE TATHĀGATA—I)

147. "Bhikkhus, the Tathāgata,[27] accomplished and fully enlightened, directly knows earth as earth. Having directly known earth as earth, he does not conceive [himself as] earth, he does not conceive [himself] in earth, he does not conceive [himself apart] from earth, he does not conceive earth to be 'mine,' he does not delight in earth. [6] Why is that? Because the Tathāgata has fully understood it to the end, I say.[28]

148–170. "He directly knows water as water...Nibbāna as Nibbāna...Why is that? Because the Tathāgata has fully understood it to the end, I say.

(THE TATHĀGATA—II)

171. "Bhikkhus, the Tathāgata, accomplished and fully enlightened, directly knows earth as earth. Having directly known earth as earth, he does not conceive [himself as] earth, he does not conceive [himself] in earth, he does not conceive [himself apart] from earth, he does not conceive earth to be 'mine,' he does not delight in earth. Why is that? Because he has understood that delight is the root of suffering, and that with being [as condition] there is birth, and that for whatever has come to be there is ageing and death.[29] Therefore, bhikkhus, through the complete destruction, fading away, cessation, giving up, and relinquishing of cravings, the Tathāgata has awakened to supreme full enlightenment, I say.[30]

172–194. "He directly knows water as water...Nibbāna as Nibbāna...Why is that? Because he has understood that delight is the root of suffering, and that with being [as condition] there is birth, and that for whatever has come to be there is ageing and death. Therefore, bhikkhus, through the complete destruction, fading away, cessation, giving up, and relinquishing of cravings, the Tathāgata has awakened to supreme full enlightenment, I say."

That is what the Blessed One said. But those bhikkhus did *not* delight in the Blessed One's words.[31]

2 *Sabbāsava Sutta*
All the Taints

1. THUS HAVE I HEARD. On one occasion the Blessed One was living at Sāvatthī in Jeta's Grove, Anāthapiṇḍika's Park. There he addressed the bhikkhus thus: "Bhikkhus."—"Venerable sir," they replied. The Blessed One said this:

2. "Bhikkhus, I shall teach you a discourse on the restraint of all the taints.[32] [7] Listen and attend closely to what I shall say."—"Yes, venerable sir," the bhikkhus replied. The Blessed One said this:

(SUMMARY)

3. "Bhikkhus, I say that the destruction of the taints is for one who knows and sees, not for one who does not know and see. Who knows and sees what? Wise attention and unwise attention.[33] When one attends unwisely, unarisen taints arise and arisen taints increase. When one attends wisely, unarisen taints do not arise and arisen taints are abandoned.

4. "Bhikkhus, there are taints that should be abandoned by seeing. There are taints that should be abandoned by restraining. There are taints that should be abandoned by using. There are taints that should be abandoned by enduring. There are taints that should be abandoned by avoiding. There are taints that should be abandoned by removing. There are taints that should be abandoned by developing.[34]

(TAINTS TO BE ABANDONED BY SEEING)

5. "What taints, bhikkhus, should be abandoned by seeing?[35] Here, bhikkhus, an untaught ordinary person, who has no regard for noble ones and is unskilled and undisciplined in their

Dhamma, who has no regard for true men and is unskilled and undisciplined in their Dhamma, does not understand what things are fit for attention and what things are unfit for attention. Since that is so, he attends to those things unfit for attention and he does not attend to those things fit for attention.[36]

6. "What are the things unfit for attention that he attends to? They are things such that when he attends to them, the unarisen taint of sensual desire arises in him and the arisen taint of sensual desire increases, the unarisen taint of being arises in him and the arisen taint of being increases, the unarisen taint of ignorance arises in him and the arisen taint of ignorance increases. These are the things unfit for attention that he attends to.[37] And what are the things fit for attention that he does not attend to? They are things such that when he attends to them, the unarisen taint of sensual desire does not arise in him and the arisen taint of sensual desire is abandoned, the unarisen taint of being does not arise in him and the arisen taint of being is abandoned, the unarisen taint of ignorance does not arise in him and the arisen taint of ignorance is abandoned. These are the things fit for attention that he does not attend to. [8] By attending to things unfit for attention and by not attending to things fit for attention, both unarisen taints arise in him and arisen taints increase.

7. "This is how he attends unwisely: 'Was I in the past? Was I not in the past? What was I in the past? How was I in the past? Having been what, what did I become in the past? Shall I be in the future? Shall I not be in the future? What shall I be in the future? How shall I be in the future? Having been what, what shall I become in the future?' Or else he is inwardly perplexed about the present thus: 'Am I? Am I not? What am I? How am I? Where has this being come from? Where will it go?'[38]

8. "When he attends unwisely in this way, one of six views arises in him.[39] The view 'self exists for me' arises in him as true and established; or the view 'no self exists for me' arises in him as true and established; or the view 'I perceive self with self' arises in him as true and established; or the view 'I perceive not-self with self' arises in him as true and established; or the view 'I perceive self with not-self' arises in him as true and established; or else he has some such view as this: 'It is this self of mine that speaks and feels and experiences here and there the result of good and bad actions; but this self of mine is permanent,

everlasting, eternal, not subject to change, and it will endure as long as eternity.'[40] This speculative view, bhikkhus, is called the thicket of views, the wilderness of views, the contortion of views, the vacillation of views, the fetter of views. Fettered by the fetter of views, the untaught ordinary person is not freed from birth, ageing, and death, from sorrow, lamentation, pain, grief, and despair; he is not freed from suffering, I say.

9. "Bhikkhus, a well-taught noble disciple, who has regard for noble ones and is skilled and disciplined in their Dhamma, who has regard for true men and is skilled and disciplined in their Dhamma, understands what things are fit for attention and what things are unfit for attention. Since that is so, [9] he does not attend to those things unfit for attention and he attends to those things fit for attention.

10. "What are the things unfit for attention that he does not attend to? They are things such that when he attends to them, the unarisen taint of sensual desire arises in him...(*as §6*)...and the arisen taint of ignorance increases. These are the things unfit for attention that he does not attend to. And what are the things fit for attention that he attends to? They are things such that when he attends to them, the unarisen taint of sensual desire does not arise in him...(*as §6*)...and the arisen taint of ignorance is abandoned. These are the things fit for attention that he attends to. By not attending to things unfit for attention and by attending to things fit for attention, unarisen taints do not arise in him and arisen taints are abandoned.

11. "He attends wisely: 'This is suffering'; he attends wisely: 'This is the origin of suffering'; he attends wisely: 'This is the cessation of suffering'; he attends wisely: 'This is the way leading to the cessation of suffering.'[41] When he attends wisely in this way, three fetters are abandoned in him: personality view, doubt, and adherence to rules and observances. These are called the taints that should be abandoned by seeing.[42]

(TAINTS TO BE ABANDONED BY RESTRAINING)

12. "What taints, bhikkhus, should be abandoned by restraining?[43] Here a bhikkhu, reflecting wisely, abides with the eye faculty restrained. While taints, vexation, and fever might arise in one who abides with the eye faculty unrestrained, there are no

taints, vexation, or fever in one who abides with the eye faculty restrained.[44] Reflecting wisely, he abides with the ear faculty restrained...with the nose faculty restrained...with the tongue faculty restrained...with the body faculty restrained...with the mind faculty restrained...While taints, vexation, and fever might arise in one who abides with the faculties unrestrained, [10] there are no taints, vexation, or fever in one who abides with the faculties restrained. These are called the taints that should be abandoned by restraining.

(TAINTS TO BE ABANDONED BY USING)

13. "What taints, bhikkhus, should be abandoned by using?[45] Here a bhikkhu, reflecting wisely, uses the robe only for protection from cold, for protection from heat, for protection from contact with gadflies, mosquitoes, wind, the sun, and creeping things, and only for the purpose of concealing the private parts.

14. "Reflecting wisely, he uses almsfood neither for amusement nor for intoxication nor for the sake of physical beauty and attractiveness, but only for the endurance and continuance of this body, for ending discomfort, and for assisting the holy life, considering: 'Thus I shall terminate old feelings without arousing new feelings and I shall be healthy and blameless and shall live in comfort.'

15. "Reflecting wisely, he uses the resting place only for protection from cold, for protection from heat, for protection from contact with gadflies, mosquitoes, wind, the sun, and creeping things, and only for the purpose of warding off the perils of climate and for enjoying retreat.

16. "Reflecting wisely, he uses the medicinal requisites only for protection from arisen afflicting feelings and for the benefit of good health.

17. "While taints, vexation, and fever might arise in one who does not use the requisites thus, there are no taints, vexation, or fever in one who uses them thus. These are called the taints that should be abandoned by using.

(TAINTS TO BE ABANDONED BY ENDURING)

18. "What taints, bhikkhus, should be abandoned by enduring? Here a bhikkhu, reflecting wisely, bears cold and heat, hunger and

thirst, and contact with gadflies, mosquitoes, wind, the sun, and creeping things; he endures ill-spoken, unwelcome words and arisen bodily feelings that are painful, racking, sharp, piercing, disagreeable, distressing, and menacing to life. While taints, vexation, and fever might arise in one who does not endure such things, there are no taints, vexation, or fever in one who endures them. These are called the taints that should be abandoned by enduring.

(TAINTS TO BE ABANDONED BY AVOIDING)

19. "What taints, bhikkhus, should be abandoned by avoiding? Here a bhikkhu, reflecting wisely, avoids a wild elephant, a wild horse, a wild bull, a wild dog, a snake, a stump, [11] a bramble patch, a chasm, a cliff, a cesspit, a sewer. Reflecting wisely, he avoids sitting on unsuitable seats, wandering to unsuitable resorts,[46] and associating with bad friends, since if he were to do so wise companions in the holy life might suspect him of evil conduct. While taints, vexation, and fever might arise in one who does not avoid these things, there are no taints, vexation, and fever in one who avoids them. These are called the taints that should be abandoned by avoiding.

(TAINTS TO BE ABANDONED BY REMOVING)

20. "What taints, bhikkhus, should be abandoned by removing? Here a bhikkhu, reflecting wisely, does not tolerate an arisen thought of sensual desire; he abandons it, removes it, does away with it, and annihilates it. He does not tolerate an arisen thought of ill will...He does not tolerate an arisen thought of cruelty...He does not tolerate arisen evil unwholesome states; he abandons them, removes them, does away with them, and annihilates them.[47] While taints, vexation, and fever might arise in one who does not remove these thoughts, there are no taints, vexation, or fever in one who removes them. These are called the taints that should be abandoned by removing.

(TAINTS TO BE ABANDONED BY DEVELOPING)

21. "What taints, bhikkhus, should be abandoned by developing? Here a bhikkhu, reflecting wisely, develops the mindfulness

enlightenment factor, which is supported by seclusion, dispassion, and cessation, and ripens in relinquishment. He develops the investigation-of-states enlightenment factor...the energy enlightenment factor...the rapture enlightenment factor...the tranquillity enlightenment factor...the concentration enlightenment factor...the equanimity enlightenment factor, which is supported by seclusion, dispassion, and cessation, and ripens in relinquishment.[48] While taints, vexation, and fever might arise in one who does not develop these enlightenment factors, there are no taints, vexation, or fever in one who develops them. These are called the taints that should be abandoned by developing.[49]

(CONCLUSION)

22. "Bhikkhus, when for a bhikkhu the taints that should be abandoned by seeing have been abandoned by seeing, when the taints that should be abandoned by restraining have been abandoned by restraining, when the taints that should be abandoned by using have been abandoned by using, when the taints that should be abandoned by enduring have been abandoned by enduring, when the taints that should be abandoned by avoiding [12] have been abandoned by avoiding, when the taints that should be abandoned by removing have been abandoned by removing, when the taints that should be abandoned by developing have been abandoned by developing—then he is called a bhikkhu who dwells restrained with the restraint of all the taints. He has severed craving, flung off the fetters, and with the complete penetration of conceit he has made an end of suffering."[50]

That is what the Blessed One said. The bhikkhus were satisfied and delighted in the Blessed One's words.

3 *Dhammadāyāda Sutta*
Heirs in Dhamma

1. THUS HAVE I HEARD. On one occasion the Blessed One was living in Sāvatthī in Jeta's Grove, Anāthapiṇḍika's Park. There he addressed the bhikkhus thus: "Bhikkhus."[51]—"Venerable sir," they replied. The Blessed One said this:

2. "Bhikkhus, be my heirs in Dhamma, not my heirs in material things. Out of compassion for you I have thought: 'How shall my disciples be my heirs in Dhamma, not my heirs in material things?' If you are my heirs in material things, not my heirs in Dhamma, you will be reproached thus: 'The Teacher's disciples live as his heirs in material things, not as heirs in Dhamma'; and I will be reproached thus: 'The Teacher's disciples live as his heirs in material things, not as his heirs in Dhamma.'

"If you are my heirs in Dhamma, not my heirs in material things, you will not be reproached [as it will be said]: 'The Teacher's disciples live as his heirs in Dhamma, not as his heirs in material things'; and I will not be reproached [as it will be said]: 'The Teacher's disciples live as his heirs in Dhamma, not as his heirs in material things.' Therefore, bhikkhus, be my heirs in Dhamma, not my heirs in material things. Out of compassion for you I have thought: 'How shall my disciples be my heirs in Dhamma, not my heirs in material things?'

3. "Now, bhikkhus, suppose that I had eaten, refused more food, had my fill, finished, had enough, had what I needed, and some almsfood was left over to be thrown away. Then two bhikkhus arrived [13] hungry and weak, and I told them: 'Bhikkhus, I have eaten...had what I needed, but there is this almsfood of mine left over to be thrown away. Eat if you like; if you do not eat then I shall throw it away where there is no greenery or drop it into water where there is no life.' Then one bhikkhu thought: 'The Blessed One has eaten...had what he

needed, but there is this almsfood of the Blessed One left over to be thrown away; if we do not eat it the Blessed One will throw it away...But this has been said by the Blessed One: "Bhikkhus, be my heirs in Dhamma, not my heirs in material things." Now this almsfood is one of the material things. Suppose that instead of eating this almsfood I pass the night and day hungry and weak.' And instead of eating that almsfood he passed that night and day hungry and weak. Then the second bhikkhu thought: 'The Blessed One has eaten...had what he needed, but there is this almsfood of the Blessed One left over to be thrown away...Suppose that I eat this almsfood and pass the night and day neither hungry nor weak.' And after eating that almsfood he passed the night and day neither hungry nor weak. Now although that bhikkhu by eating that almsfood passed the night and day neither hungry nor weak, yet the first bhikkhu is more to be respected and commended by me. Why is that? Because that will for long conduce to his fewness of wishes, contentment, effacement, easy support, and arousal of energy.[52] Therefore, bhikkhus, be my heirs in Dhamma, not my heirs in material things. Out of compassion for you I have thought: 'How shall my disciples be my heirs in Dhamma, not my heirs in material things?'"

4. That is what the Blessed One said. Having said this, the Sublime One rose from his seat and went into his dwelling. Soon after he had left, the venerable Sāriputta addressed the bhikkhus thus: "Friends, bhikkhus."—"Friend," they replied. [14] The venerable Sāriputta said this:

5. "Friends, in what way do disciples of the Teacher who lives secluded not train in seclusion? And in what way do disciples of the Teacher who lives secluded train in seclusion?"

"Indeed, friend, we would come from far away to learn from the venerable Sāriputta the meaning of this statement. It would be good if the venerable Sāriputta would explain the meaning of this statement. Having heard it from him the bhikkhus will remember it."

"Then, friends, listen and attend closely to what I shall say."

"Yes, friend," the bhikkhus replied. The venerable Sāriputta said this:

6. "Friends, in what way do disciples of the Teacher who lives secluded not train in seclusion? Here disciples of the Teacher who lives secluded do not train in seclusion; they do not abandon

what the Teacher tells them to abandon; they are luxurious and careless, leaders in backsliding, neglectful of seclusion.

"In this the elder bhikkhus are to be blamed for three reasons.[53] As disciples of the Teacher who lives secluded they do not train in seclusion: they are to be blamed for this first reason. They do not abandon what the Teacher tells them to abandon: they are to be blamed for this second reason. They are luxurious and careless, leaders in backsliding, neglectful of seclusion: they are to be blamed for this third reason. The elder bhikkhus are to be blamed for these three reasons.

"In this the middle bhikkhus are to be blamed for three reasons. As disciples of the Teacher who lives secluded they do not train in seclusion: they are to be blamed for this first reason. They do not abandon what the Teacher tells them to abandon: they are to be blamed for this second reason. They are luxurious and careless, leaders in backsliding, neglectful of seclusion: they are to be blamed for this third reason. The middle bhikkhus are to be blamed for these three reasons.

"In this the new bhikkhus are to be blamed for three reasons. As disciples of the Teacher who lives secluded they do not train in seclusion: they are to be blamed for this first reason. They do not abandon what the Teacher tells them to abandon: they are to be blamed for this second reason. They are luxurious and careless, leaders in backsliding, neglectful of seclusion: they are to be blamed for this third reason. The new bhikkhus are to be blamed for these three reasons.

"It is in this way that disciples of the Teacher who lives secluded do not train in seclusion.

7. "In what way, friends, do disciples of the Teacher who lives secluded [15] train in seclusion? Here disciples of the Teacher who lives secluded train in seclusion; they abandon what the Teacher tells them to abandon; they are not luxurious and careless, they are keen to avoid backsliding, and are leaders in seclusion.

"In this the elder bhikkhus are to be commended for three reasons. As disciples of the Teacher who lives secluded they train in seclusion: they are to be commended for this first reason. They abandon what the Teacher tells them to abandon: they are to be commended for this second reason. They are not luxurious and careless; they are keen to avoid backsliding and are leaders in seclusion: they are to be commended for this third reason. The elder bhikkhus are to be commended for these three reasons.

"In this the middle bhikkhus are to be commended for three reasons. As disciples of the Teacher who lives secluded they train in seclusion: they are to be commended for this first reason. They abandon what the Teacher tells them to abandon: they are to be commended for this second reason. They are not luxurious and careless; they are keen to avoid backsliding and are leaders in seclusion: they are to be commended for this third reason. The middle bhikkhus are to be commended for these three reasons.

"In this the new bhikkhus are to be commended for three reasons. As disciples of the Teacher who lives secluded they train in seclusion: they are to be commended for this first reason. They abandon what the Teacher tells them to abandon: they are to be commended for this second reason. They are not luxurious and careless; they are keen to avoid backsliding and are leaders in seclusion: they are to be commended for this third reason. The new bhikkhus are to be commended for these three reasons.

"It is in this way that disciples of the Teacher who lives secluded train in seclusion.

8. "Friends, the evil herein is greed and hate.[54] There is a Middle Way for the abandoning of greed and hate, giving vision, giving knowledge, which leads to peace, to direct knowledge, to enlightenment, to Nibbāna. And what is that Middle Way? It is just this Noble Eightfold Path; that is, right view, right intention, right speech, right action, right livelihood, right effort, right mindfulness, and right concentration. This is the Middle Way giving vision, giving knowledge, which leads to peace, to direct knowledge, to enlightenment, to Nibbāna.[55]

9–15. "The evil herein is anger and resentment...contempt and insolence...envy and avarice...deceit and fraud...obstinacy [16] and rivalry...conceit and arrogance...vanity and negligence. There is a Middle Way for the abandoning of vanity and negligence, giving vision, giving knowledge, which leads to peace, to direct knowledge, to enlightenment, to Nibbāna. And what is that Middle Way? It is just this Noble Eightfold Path; that is, right view, right intention, right speech, right action, right livelihood, right effort, right mindfulness, and right concentration.

This is the Middle Way giving vision, giving knowledge, which leads to peace, to direct knowledge, to enlightenment, to Nibbāna."

That is what the venerable Sāriputta said. The bhikkhus were satisfied and delighted in the venerable Sāriputta's words.

4 *Bhayabherava Sutta*
Fear and Dread

1. THUS HAVE I HEARD. On one occasion the Blessed One was living at Sāvatthī in Jeta's Grove, Anāthapiṇḍika's Park.

2. Then the brahmin Jāṇussoṇi[56] went to the Blessed One and exchanged greetings with him. When this courteous and amiable talk was finished, he sat down at one side and said: "Master Gotama, when clansmen have gone forth from the home life into homelessness out of faith in Master Gotama, do they have Master Gotama for their leader, their helper, and their guide? And do these people follow the example of Master Gotama?"[57]

"That is so, brahmin, that is so. When clansmen have gone forth from the home life into homelessness out of faith in me, they have me for their leader, their helper, and their guide. And these people follow my example."

"But, Master Gotama, remote jungle-thicket resting places in the forest are hard to endure, seclusion is hard to practise, and it is hard to enjoy solitude. One would think the jungles must rob a bhikkhu of his mind, if he has no concentration." [17]

"That is so, brahmin, that is so. Remote jungle-thicket resting places in the forest are hard to endure, seclusion is hard to practise, and it is hard to enjoy solitude. One would think the jungles must rob a bhikkhu of his mind, if he has no concentration.

3. "Before my enlightenment, while I was still only an unenlightened Bodhisatta, I too considered thus: 'Remote jungle-thicket resting places in the forest are hard to endure...the jungles must rob a bhikkhu of his mind, if he has no concentration.'

4. "I considered thus: 'Whenever recluses or brahmins unpurified in bodily conduct resort to remote jungle-thicket resting places in the forest, then owing to the defect of their unpurified bodily conduct these good recluses and brahmins evoke unwholesome fear and dread. But I do not resort to remote jungle-thicket

resting places in the forest unpurified in bodily conduct. I am purified in bodily conduct. I resort to remote jungle-thicket resting places in the forest as one of the noble ones with bodily conduct purified.' Seeing in myself this purity of bodily conduct, I found great solace in dwelling in the forest.

5–7. "I considered thus: 'Whenever recluses or brahmins unpurified in verbal conduct...unpurified in mental conduct...unpurified in livelihood resort to remote jungle-thicket resting places in the forest...they evoke unwholesome fear and dread. But...I am purified in livelihood. I resort to remote jungle-thicket resting places in the forest as one of the noble ones with livelihood purified.' Seeing in myself this purity of livelihood, I found great solace in dwelling in the forest.

8. "I considered thus: 'Whenever recluses or brahmins who are covetous and full of lust...I am uncovetous...' [18]

9. "'...with a mind of ill will and intentions of hate...I have a mind of loving-kindness...'

10. "'...overcome by sloth and torpor...I am without sloth and torpor...'

11. "'...overcome with restless and unpeaceful in mind...I have a peaceful mind...'

12. "'...uncertain and doubting...I have gone beyond doubt...'

13. "'[19]...given to self-praise and disparagement of others...I am not given to self-praise and disparagement of others...'

14. "'...subject to alarm and terror...I am free from trepidation...'

15. "'...desirous of gain, honour, and renown...I have few wishes...'

16. "'...lazy and wanting in energy...I am energetic...'

17. "'...[20] unmindful and not fully aware...I am established in mindfulness...'

18. "'...unconcentrated and with straying minds...I am possessed of concentration...'

19. "I considered thus: 'Whenever recluses or brahmins devoid of wisdom, drivellers, resort to remote jungle-thicket resting places in the forest, then owing to the defect of their being devoid of wisdom and drivellers these good recluses and brahmins evoke unwholesome fear and dread. But I do not resort to remote jungle-thicket resting places in the forest devoid of wisdom, a driveller. I am possessed of wisdom.[58] I resort to

remote jungle-thicket resting places in the forest as one of the noble ones possessed of wisdom.' Seeing in myself this possession of wisdom, I found great solace in dwelling in the forest.

20. "I considered thus: 'There are the specially auspicious nights of the fourteenth, the fifteenth, and the eighth of the fortnight.[59] Now what if, on such nights as these, I were to dwell in such awe-inspiring, horrifying abodes as orchard shrines, woodland shrines, and tree shrines? Perhaps I might encounter that fear and dread.' And later, on such specially auspicious nights as the fourteenth, the fifteenth, and the eighth of the fortnight, I dwelt in such awe-inspiring, horrifying abodes as orchard shrines, woodland shrines, and tree shrines. And while I dwelt there, a wild animal would come up to me, or a peacock [21] would knock off a branch, or the wind would rustle the leaves. I thought: 'What now if this is the fear and dread coming?' I thought: 'Why do I dwell always expecting fear and dread? What if I subdue that fear and dread while keeping the same posture that I am in when it comes upon me?'[60]

"While I walked, the fear and dread came upon me; I neither stood nor sat nor lay down till I had subdued that fear and dread. While I stood, the fear and dread came upon me; I neither walked nor sat nor lay down till I had subdued that fear and dread. While I sat, the fear and dread came upon me; I neither walked nor stood nor lay down till I had subdued that fear and dread. While I lay down, the fear and dread came upon me; I neither walked nor stood nor sat down till I had subdued that fear and dread.

21. "There are, brahmin, some recluses and brahmins who perceive day when it is night and night when it is day. I say that on their part this is an abiding in delusion. But I perceive night when it is night and day when it is day. Rightly speaking, were it to be said of anyone: 'A being not subject to delusion has appeared in the world for the welfare and happiness of many, out of compassion for the world, for the good, welfare, and happiness of gods and humans,' it is of me indeed that rightly speaking this should be said.

22. "Tireless energy was aroused in me and unremitting mindfulness was established, my body was tranquil and untroubled, my mind concentrated and unified.[61]

23. "Quite secluded from sensual pleasures, secluded from

unwholesome states, I entered upon and abided in the first jhāna, which is accompanied by applied and sustained thought, with rapture and pleasure born of seclusion.[62]

24. "With the stilling of applied and sustained thought, I entered upon and abided in the second jhāna, which has self-confidence and singleness of mind [22] without applied and sustained thought, with rapture and pleasure born of concentration.

25. "With the fading away as well of rapture, I abided in equanimity, and mindful and fully aware, still feeling pleasure with the body, I entered upon and abided in the third jhāna, on account of which noble ones announce: 'He has a pleasant abiding who has equanimity and is mindful.'

26. "With the abandoning of pleasure and pain, and with the previous disappearance of joy and grief, I entered upon and abided in the fourth jhāna, which has neither-pain-nor-pleasure and purity of mindfulness due to equanimity.

27. "When my concentrated mind was thus purified, bright, unblemished, rid of imperfection, malleable, wieldy, steady, and attained to imperturbability, I directed it to knowledge of the recollection of past lives.[63] I recollected my manifold past lives, that is, one birth, two births, three births, four births, five births, ten births, twenty births, thirty births, forty births, fifty births, a hundred births, a thousand births, a hundred thousand births, many aeons of world-contraction, many aeons of world-expansion, many aeons of world-contraction and expansion: 'There I was so named, of such a clan, with such an appearance, such was my nutriment, such my experience of pleasure and pain, such my life-term; and passing away from there, I reappeared elsewhere; and there too I was so named, of such a clan, with such an appearance, such was my nutriment, such my experience of pleasure and pain, such my life-term; and passing away from there, I reappeared here.' Thus with their aspects and particulars I recollected my manifold past lives.

28. "This was the first true knowledge attained by me in the first watch of the night. Ignorance was banished and true knowledge arose, darkness was banished and light arose, as happens in one who abides diligent, ardent, and resolute.

29. "When my concentrated mind was thus purified, bright, unblemished, rid of imperfection, malleable, wieldy, steady, and attained to imperturbability, I directed it to knowledge of the

passing away and reappearance of beings.[64] With the divine eye, which is purified and surpasses the human, I saw beings passing away and reappearing, inferior and superior, fair and ugly, fortunate and unfortunate. I understood how beings pass on according to their actions thus: 'These worthy beings who were ill conducted in body, speech, and mind, revilers of noble ones, wrong in their views, giving effect to wrong view in their actions, on the dissolution of the body, after death, have reappeared in a state of deprivation, in a bad destination, in perdition, even in hell; but these worthy beings who were well conducted in body, [23] speech, and mind, not revilers of noble ones, right in their views, giving effect to right view in their actions, on the dissolution of the body, after death, have reappeared in a good destination, even in the heavenly world.' Thus with the divine eye, which is purified and surpasses the human, I saw beings passing away and reappearing, inferior and superior, fair and ugly, fortunate and unfortunate, and I understood how beings pass on according to their actions.

30. "This was the second true knowledge attained by me in the middle watch of the night. Ignorance was banished and true knowledge arose, darkness was banished and light arose, as happens in one who abides diligent, ardent, and resolute.

31. "When my concentrated mind was thus purified, bright, unblemished, rid of imperfection, malleable, wieldy, steady, and attained to imperturbability, I directed it to knowledge of the destruction of the taints. I directly knew as it actually is: 'This is suffering'; I directly knew as it actually is: 'This is the origin of suffering'; I directly knew as it actually is: 'This is the cessation of suffering'; I directly knew as it actually is: 'This is the way leading to the cessation of suffering.' I directly knew as it actually is: 'These are the taints'; I directly knew as it actually is: 'This is the origin of the taints'; I directly knew as it actually is: 'This is the cessation of the taints'; I directly knew as it actually is: 'This is the way leading to the cessation of the taints.'[65]

32. "When I knew and saw thus, my mind was liberated from the taint of sensual desire, from the taint of being, and from the taint of ignorance. When it was liberated, there came the knowledge: 'It is liberated.'[66] I directly knew: 'Birth is destroyed, the holy life has been lived, what had to be done has been done, there is no more coming to any state of being.'[67]

33. "This was the third true knowledge attained by me in the last watch of the night. Ignorance was banished and true knowledge arose, darkness was banished and light arose, as happens in one who abides diligent, ardent, and resolute.

34. "Now, brahmin, it might be that you think: 'Perhaps the recluse Gotama is not free from lust, hate, and delusion even today, which is why he still resorts to remote jungle-thicket resting places in the forest.' But you should not think thus. It is because I see two benefits that I still resort to remote jungle-thicket resting places in the forest: I see a pleasant abiding for myself here and now, and I have compassion for future generations."[68]

35. "Indeed, it is because Master Gotama is an Accomplished One, a Fully Enlightened One, that he has compassion for future generations. [24] Magnificent, Master Gotama! Magnificent, Master Gotama! Master Gotama has made the Dhamma clear in many ways, as though he were turning upright what had been overthrown, revealing what was hidden, showing the way to one who was lost, or holding up a lamp in the dark for those with eyesight to see forms. I go to Master Gotama for refuge and to the Dhamma and to the Sangha of bhikkhus. From today let Master Gotama remember me as a lay follower who has gone to him for refuge for life."

5 *Anangaṇa Sutta*
Without Blemishes

1. THUS HAVE I HEARD. On one occasion the Blessed One was living at Sāvatthī in Jeta's Grove, Anāthapiṇḍika's Park. There the venerable Sāriputta addressed the bhikkhus thus. "Friends, bhikkhus."—"Friend," they replied. The venerable Sāriputta said this:

2. "Friends, there are these four kinds of persons found existing in the world.[69] What four? Here some person with a blemish does not understand it as it actually is thus: 'I have a blemish in myself.' Here some person with a blemish understands it as it actually is thus: 'I have a blemish in myself.' Here some person with no blemish does not understand it as it actually is thus: 'I have no blemish in myself.' Here some person with no blemish understands it as it actually is thus: 'I have no blemish in myself.'

"Herein, the person with a blemish who does not understand it as it actually is thus: 'I have a blemish in myself' is called the inferior of these two persons with a blemish. Herein, the person with a blemish who understands it as it actually is thus: 'I have a blemish in myself' is called the superior of these two persons with a blemish.

"Herein, the person with no blemish [25] who does not understand it as it actually is thus: 'I have no blemish' is called the inferior of these two persons with no blemish. Herein, the person with no blemish who understands it as it actually is thus: 'I have no blemish' is called the superior of these two persons with no blemish."

3. When this was said, the venerable Mahā Moggallāna asked the venerable Sāriputta: "Friend Sāriputta, what is the cause and reason why, of these two persons with a blemish, one is called the inferior man and one is called the superior man? What is the

cause and reason why, of these two persons with no blemish, one is called the inferior man and one is called the superior man?"

4. "Herein, friend, when a person with a blemish does not understand it as it actually is thus: 'I have a blemish in myself,' it can be expected that he will not arouse zeal, make effort, or instigate energy to abandon that blemish, and that he will die with lust, hate, and delusion, with a blemish, with mind defiled. Suppose a bronze dish were brought from a shop or a smithy covered with dirt and stains, and the owners neither used it nor had it cleaned but put it away in a dusty corner. Would the bronze dish thus get more defiled and stained later on?"—"Yes, friend."—"So too, friend, when a person with a blemish does not understand it as it actually is thus: 'I have a blemish in myself,' it can be expected...that he will die...with mind defiled.

5. "Herein, when a person with a blemish understands it as it actually is thus: 'I have a blemish in myself,' it can be expected that he will arouse zeal, make effort, and instigate energy to abandon that blemish, and that he will die without lust, hate, and delusion, without blemish, with mind undefiled. Suppose a bronze dish were brought from a shop or a smithy covered with dirt and stains, and the owners used it and had it cleaned and did not put it in a dusty corner. [26] Would the bronze dish thus get cleaner and brighter later on?"—"Yes, friend."—"So too, friend, when a person with a blemish understands it as it actually is thus: 'I have a blemish in myself,' it can be expected...that he will die...with mind undefiled.

6. "Herein, when a person with no blemish does not understand it as it actually is thus: 'I have no blemish in myself,' it can be expected that he will give attention to the sign of the beautiful,[70] that by his doing so lust will infect his mind, and that he will die with lust, hate, and delusion, with a blemish, with mind defiled. Suppose a bronze dish were brought from a shop or smithy clean and bright, and the owners neither used it nor had it cleaned but put it in a dusty corner. Would the bronze dish thus get more defiled and more stained later on?"—"Yes, friend."—"So too, friend, when a person with no blemish does not understand it as it actually is thus: 'I have no blemish in myself,' it can be expected that he will die...with mind defiled.

7. "Herein, when a person with no blemish understands it as it actually is thus: 'I have no blemish in myself, ' it can be expected

that he will not give attention to the sign of the beautiful, that by his not doing so lust will not infect his mind, and that he will die without lust, hate, and delusion, without blemish, with mind undefiled. Suppose a bronze dish were brought from a shop or smithy clean and bright, and the owners used it and had it cleaned and did not put it in a dusty corner. Would the bronze dish thus get cleaner and brighter later on?"—"Yes, friend."—"So too, friend, when a person with no blemish understands it as it actually is thus: 'I have no blemish in myself,' it can be expected...that he will die...with mind undefiled. [27]

8. "This is the cause and reason why, of these two persons with a blemish, one is called the inferior man and one is called the superior man. This is the cause and reason why, of these two persons with no blemish, one is called the inferior man and one is called the superior man.

9. "'Blemish, blemish,' is said, friend, but what is this word 'blemish' a term for? 'Blemish,' friend, is a term for the spheres of evil unwholesome wishes.

10. "It is possible that a bhikkhu here might wish: 'If I commit an offence, let the bhikkhus not know that I have committed an offence.' And it is possible that the bhikkhus come to know that that bhikkhu has committed an offence. So he is angry and bitter thus: 'The bhikkhus know I have committed an offence.' The anger and bitterness are both a blemish.

11. "It is possible that a bhikkhu here might wish: 'I have committed an offence. The bhikkhus should admonish me in private, not in the midst of the Sangha.' And it is possible that the bhikkhus admonish that bhikkhu in the midst of the Sangha, not in private. So he is angry and bitter thus: 'The bhikkhus admonish me in the midst of the Sangha, not in private.' The anger and bitterness are both a blemish.

12. "It is possible that a bhikkhu here might wish: 'I have committed an offence. A person who is my equal should admonish me, not a person who is not my equal.' And it is possible that a person not his equal admonishes him, not a person his equal. So he is angry and bitter thus: 'A person not my equal admonishes me, not a person my equal.' The anger and bitterness are both a blemish.

13. "It is possible that a bhikkhu here might wish: 'Oh that the Teacher might teach the Dhamma to the bhikkhus by asking a

series of questions of me, not of some other bhikkhu!' And it is possible that the Teacher teaches the Dhamma to the bhikkhus by asking a series of questions of some other bhikkhu, [28] not of that bhikkhu. So he is angry and bitter thus: 'The Teacher teaches the Dhamma to the bhikkhus by asking a series of questions of some other bhikkhu, not of me.' The anger and bitterness are both a blemish.

14. "It is possible that a bhikkhu here might wish: 'Oh that the bhikkhus might enter the village for alms putting me in the forefront, not some other bhikkhu!' And it is possible that the bhikkhus enter the village for alms putting some other bhikkhu in the forefront, not that bhikkhu. So he is angry and bitter thus: 'The bhikkhus enter the village for alms putting some other bhikkhu in the forefront, not me.' The anger and bitterness are both a blemish.

15. "It is possible that a bhikkhu here might wish: 'Oh that I might get the best seat, the best water, the best almsfood in the refectory, not some other bhikkhu!' And it is possible that some other bhikkhu gets the best seat...

16. "It is possible that a bhikkhu here might wish: 'Oh that I might give the blessing in the refectory after the meal, not some other bhikkhu!' And it is possible that some other bhikkhu gives the blessing...

17–20. "It is possible that a bhikkhu here might wish: 'Oh that I might teach the Dhamma to the bhikkhus...that I might teach the Dhamma to the bhikkhunīs...men lay followers...women lay followers visiting the monastery, not some other bhikkhu!' And it is possible that some other bhikkhu teaches the Dhamma [29]...

21–24. "It is possible that a bhikkhu here might wish: 'Oh that the bhikkhus...bhikkhunīs...men lay followers...women lay followers might honour, respect, revere, and venerate me, not some other bhikkhu!' And it is possible that they honour...some other bhikkhu...

25–28. "It is possible that a bhikkhu here might wish: 'Oh that I might be the one to get a superior robe, [30]...superior almsfood...a superior resting place...superior medicinal requisites, not some other bhikkhu!' And it is possible that some other bhikkhu is the one to get superior medicinal requisites, not that bhikkhu. So he is angry and bitter thus: 'Another bhikkhu is the one to get superior medicinal requisites, not me.' The anger and the bitterness are both a blemish.

"'Blemish,' friend, is a term for the spheres of these evil unwholesome wishes.

29. "If the spheres of these evil unwholesome wishes are seen and heard to be unabandoned in any bhikkhu, then for all he may be a forest dweller, a frequenter of remote abodes, an almsfood eater, a house-to-house seeker, a refuse-rag wearer, a wearer of rough robes,[71] still his fellows in the holy life do not honour, respect, revere, and venerate him. Why is that? Because the spheres of these evil unwholesome wishes are seen and heard to be unabandoned in that venerable one.

"Suppose a bronze dish were brought from a shop or a smithy clean and bright; and the owners put the carcass of a snake or a dog or a human being in it and, covering it with another dish, went back to the market; then people seeing it said: 'What is that you are carrying about like a treasure?' Then, raising the lid and uncovering it, they looked in, and as soon as they saw they were inspired with such loathing, repugnance, and disgust that even those who were hungry would not want to eat, not to speak of those who were full.

"So too, if the spheres of these evil unwholesome wishes are seen and heard to be unabandoned in any bhikkhu, then for all he may be a forest dweller...[31]...unabandoned in that venerable one.

30. "If the spheres of these evil unwholesome wishes are seen and heard to be abandoned in any bhikkhu, then for all he may be a village dweller, an acceptor of invitations, a wearer of robes given him by householders,[72] yet his fellows in the holy life honour, respect, revere, and venerate him. Why is that? Because the spheres of these evil unwholesome wishes are seen and heard to be abandoned in that venerable one.

"Suppose a bronze dish were brought from a shop or a smithy clean and bright; and the owners put clean boiled rice and various soups and sauces into it, and, covering it with another dish, went back to the market; then people seeing it said: 'What is that you are carrying about like a treasure?' Then raising the lid and uncovering it, they looked in, and as soon as they saw they were inspired with such liking, appetite, and relish that even those who were full would want to eat, not to speak of those who were hungry.

"So too, friend, if the spheres of these evil unwholesome wishes are seen and heard to be abandoned in any bhikkhu, then for all he may be a village dweller...abandoned in that venerable one."

31. When this was said, the venerable Mahā Moggallāna said to the venerable Sāriputta: "A simile occurs to me, friend Sāriputta."—"State it, friend Moggallāna."—"On one occasion, friend, I was living at the Hill Fort at Rājagaha. Then, when it was morning, I dressed, and taking my bowl and outer robe, I went into Rājagaha for alms. Now on that occasion Samīti the cartwright's son was planing a felloe and the Ājīvaka Paṇḍuputta, son of a former cartwright, was standing by.[73] Then this thought arose in the Ājīvaka Paṇḍuputta's mind: 'Oh that this Samīti the cartwright's son might plane this bend, this twist, this fault, out of the felloe so that it would be without bends, twists, or faults, and come to consist purely of heartwood.' [32] And just as this thought came to pass in his mind, so did Samīti the cartwright's son plane that bend, that twist, that fault, out of the felloe. Then the Ājīvaka Paṇḍuputta, son of a former cartwright, was glad and he voiced his gladness thus: 'He planes just as if he knew my heart with his heart!'

32. "So too, friend, there are persons who are faithless and have gone forth from the home life into homelessness not out of faith but seeking a livelihood, who are fraudulent, deceitful, treacherous, haughty, hollow, personally vain, rough-tongued, loose-spoken, unguarded in their sense faculties, immoderate in eating, undevoted to wakefulness, unconcerned with recluseship, not greatly respectful of training, luxurious, careless, leaders in backsliding, neglectful of seclusion, lazy, wanting in energy, unmindful, not fully aware, unconcentrated, with straying minds, devoid of wisdom, drivellers. The venerable Sāriputta with his discourse on the Dhamma planes out their faults just as if he knew my heart with his heart![74]

"But there are clansmen who have gone forth out of faith from the home life into homelessness, who are not fraudulent, deceitful, treacherous, haughty, hollow, personally vain, rough-tongued, or loose-spoken; who are guarded in their sense faculties, moderate in eating, devoted to wakefulness, concerned with recluseship, greatly respectful of training, not luxurious or careless, who are keen to avoid backsliding, leaders in seclusion, energetic, resolute, established in mindfulness, fully aware, concentrated, with unified minds, possessing wisdom, not drivellers.

These, on hearing the venerable Sāriputta's discourse on the Dhamma, drink it in and eat it, as it were, by word and thought. Good indeed it is that he makes his fellows in the holy life emerge from the unwholesome and establish themselves in the wholesome.

33. "Just as a woman—or a man—young, youthful, fond of adornments, with head bathed, having received a garland of lotuses, jasmine, or roses, would take it with both hands and place it on the head, so too there are clansmen who have gone forth out of faith...not drivellers. These, on hearing the venerable Sāriputta's discourse on the Dhamma, drink it in and eat it, as it were, by word and thought. Good indeed it is that he makes his fellows in the holy life emerge from the unwholesome and establish themselves in the wholesome."

Thus it was that these two great beings rejoiced in each other's good words.[75]

6 *Ākankheyya Sutta*
If a Bhikkhu Should Wish

[33] 1. THUS HAVE I HEARD. On one occasion the Blessed One was living at Sāvatthī in Jeta's Grove, Anāthapiṇḍika's Park. There he addressed the bhikkhus thus: "Bhikkhus."—"Venerable sir," they replied. The Blessed One said this:

2. "Bhikkhus, dwell possessed of virtue, possessed of the Pātimokkha, restrained with the restraint of the Pātimokkha, perfect in conduct and resort, and seeing fear in the slightest fault, train by undertaking the training precepts.[76]

3. "If a bhikkhu should wish: 'May I be dear and agreeable to my companions in the holy life, respected and esteemed by them,' let him fulfil the precepts, be devoted to internal serenity of mind, not neglect meditation, be possessed of insight, and dwell in empty huts.[77]

4. "If a bhikkhu should wish: 'May I be one to obtain robes, almsfood, resting place, and medicinal requisites,' let him fulfil the precepts...

5. "If a bhikkhu should wish: 'May the services of those whose robes, almsfood, resting place, and medicinal requisites I use bring them great fruit and benefit,' let him fulfil the precepts...

6. "If a bhikkhu should wish: 'When my kinsmen and relatives who have passed away and died remember me with confidence in their minds, may that bring them great fruit and great benefit,' let him fulfil the precepts...[78]

7. "If a bhikkhu should wish: 'May I become a conqueror of discontent and delight, and may discontent not conquer me; may I abide transcending discontent whenever it arises,' let him fulfil the precepts...

8. "If a bhikkhu should wish: 'May I become a conqueror of fear and dread, and may fear and dread not conquer me; may I

abide transcending fear and dread whenever they arise,' let him fulfil the precepts...

9. "If a bhikkhu should wish: 'May I become one to obtain at will, without trouble or difficulty, the four jhānas that constitute the higher mind and provide a pleasant abiding here and now,' let him fulfil the precepts...

10. "If a bhikkhu should wish: 'May I contact with the body and abide in those liberations that are peaceful and immaterial, transcending forms,' let him fulfil the precepts...[34][79]

11. "If a bhikkhu should wish: 'May I, with the destruction of three fetters, become a stream-enterer, no longer subject to perdition, bound [for deliverance], headed for enlightenment,' let him fulfil the precepts...[80]

12. "If a bhikkhu should wish: 'May I, with the destruction of three fetters and with the attenuation of lust, hate, and delusion, become a once-returner, returning once to this world to make an end of suffering,' let him fulfil the precepts...

13. "If a bhikkhu should wish: 'May I, with the destruction of the five lower fetters, become due to reappear spontaneously [in the Pure Abodes] and there attain final Nibbāna, without ever returning from that world,' let him fulfil the precepts...[81]

14. "If a bhikkhu should wish:[82] 'May I wield the various kinds of supernormal power: having been one, may I become many; having been many, may I become one; may I appear and vanish; may I go unhindered through a wall, through an enclosure, through a mountain as though through space; may I dive in and out of the earth as though it were water; may I walk on water without sinking as though it were earth; seated cross-legged, may I travel in space like a bird; with my hand may I touch and stroke the moon and sun so powerful and mighty; may I wield bodily mastery, even as far as the Brahma-world,' let him fulfil the precepts...

15. "If a bhikkhu should wish: 'May I, with the divine ear element, which is purified and surpasses the human, hear both kinds of sounds, the divine and the human, those that are far as well as near,' let him fulfil the precepts...

16. "If a bhikkhu should wish: 'May I understand the minds of other beings, of other persons, having encompassed them with my own mind. May I understand a mind affected by lust as affected by lust and a mind unaffected by lust as unaffected by

lust; may I understand a mind affected by hate as affected by hate and a mind unaffected by hate as unaffected by hate; may I understand a mind affected by delusion as affected by delusion and a mind unaffected by delusion as unaffected by delusion; may I understand a contracted mind as contracted and a distracted mind as distracted; may I understand an exalted mind as exalted and an unexalted mind as unexalted; may I understand a surpassed mind as surpassed and an unsurpassed mind as unsurpassed; may I understand a concentrated mind as concentrated [35] and an unconcentrated mind as unconcentrated; may I understand a liberated mind as liberated and an unliberated mind as unliberated,' let him fulfil the precepts…

17. "If a bhikkhu should wish: 'May I recollect my manifold past lives, that is, one birth, two births…(*as Sutta 4, §27*)…Thus with their aspects and their particulars may I recollect my manifold past lives,' let him fulfil the precepts…

18. "If a bhikkhu should wish: 'May I, with the divine eye, which is purified and surpasses the human, see beings passing away and reappearing, inferior and superior, fair and ugly, fortunate and unfortunate; may I understand how beings pass on according to their actions thus:'…(*as Sutta 4, §29*)…let him fulfil the precepts…

19. "If a bhikkhu should wish: 'May I, by realising for myself with direct knowledge, here and now enter upon and abide in the deliverance of mind and deliverance by wisdom that are taintless with the destruction of the taints,'[83] [36] let him fulfil the precepts, be devoted to internal serenity of mind, not neglect meditation, be possessed of insight, and dwell in empty huts.

20. "So it was with reference to this that it was said: 'Bhikkhus, dwell possessed of virtue, possessed of the Pātimokkha, restrained with the restraint of the Pātimokkha, perfect in conduct and resort, and seeing fear in the slightest fault, train by undertaking the training precepts.'"

That is what the Blessed One said. The bhikkhus were satisfied and delighted in the Blessed One's words.

7 *Vatthūpama Sutta*
The Simile of the Cloth

1. THUS HAVE I HEARD.[84] On one occasion the Blessed One was living at Sāvatthī in Jeta's Grove, Anāthapiṇḍika's Park. There he addressed the bhikkhus thus: "Bhikkhus."—"Venerable sir," they replied. The Blessed One said this:

2. "Bhikkhus, suppose a cloth were defiled and stained, and a dyer dipped it in some dye or other, whether blue or yellow or red or pink; it would look poorly dyed and impure in colour. Why is that? Because of the impurity of the cloth. So too, when the mind is defiled, an unhappy destination may be expected.[85] Bhikkhus, suppose a cloth were pure and bright, and a dyer dipped it in some dye or other, whether blue or yellow or red or pink; it would look well dyed and pure in colour. Why is that? Because of the purity of the cloth. So too, when the mind is undefiled, a happy destination may be expected.

3. "What, bhikkhus, are the imperfections that defile the mind?[86] Covetousness and unrighteous greed is an imperfection that defiles the mind. Ill will...anger...resentment...contempt... insolence...envy...avarice...deceit...fraud...obstinacy...rivalry...conceit...arrogance...vanity...[37]...negligence is an imperfection that defiles the mind.[87]

4. "Knowing that covetousness and unrighteous greed is an imperfection that defiles the mind, a bhikkhu abandons it.[88] Knowing that ill will...negligence is an imperfection that defiles the mind, a bhikkhu abandons it.

5. "When a bhikkhu has known that covetousness and unrighteous greed is an imperfection that defiles the mind and has abandoned it; when a bhikkhu has known that ill will...negligence is an imperfection that defiles the mind and has abandoned it, he acquires perfect confidence in the Buddha thus:[89] 'The Blessed One is accomplished, fully enlightened, perfect in

true knowledge and conduct, sublime, knower of worlds, incomparable leader of persons to be tamed, teacher of gods and humans, enlightened, blessed.'

6. "He acquires perfect confidence in the Dhamma thus: 'The Dhamma is well proclaimed by the Blessed One, visible here and now, immediately effective, inviting inspection, onward leading, to be experienced by the wise for themselves.'

7. "He acquires perfect confidence in the Sangha thus: 'The Sangha of the Blessed One's disciples is practising the good way, practising the straight way, practising the true way, practising the proper way, that is, the four pairs of persons, the eight types of individuals; this Sangha of the Blessed One's disciples is worthy of gifts, worthy of hospitality, worthy of offerings, worthy of reverential salutation, the unsurpassed field of merit for the world.'

8. "When he has given up, expelled, released, abandoned, and relinquished [the imperfections of the mind] in part,[90] he considers thus: 'I am possessed of perfect confidence in the Buddha,' and he gains inspiration in the meaning, gains inspiration in the Dhamma,[91] gains gladness connected with the Dhamma. When he is glad, rapture is born in him; in one who is rapturous, the body becomes tranquil; one whose body is tranquil feels pleasure; in one who feels pleasure, the mind becomes concentrated.[92]

9. "He considers thus: 'I am possessed of perfect confidence in the Dhamma,' and he gains inspiration in the meaning, gains inspiration in the Dhamma, gains gladness connected with the Dhamma. When he is glad...the mind becomes concentrated. [38]

10. "He considers thus: 'I am possessed of perfect confidence in the Sangha,' and he gains inspiration in the meaning, gains inspiration in the Dhamma, gains gladness connected with the Dhamma. When he is glad...the mind becomes concentrated.

11. "He considers thus: '[The imperfections of the mind] have in part been given up, expelled, released, abandoned, and relinquished by me,' and he gains inspiration in the meaning, gains inspiration in the Dhamma, gains gladness connected with the Dhamma. When he is glad, rapture is born in him; in one who is rapturous, the body becomes tranquil; one whose body is tranquil feels pleasure; in one who feels pleasure, the mind becomes concentrated.

12. "Bhikkhus, if a bhikkhu of such virtue, such a state [of concentration], and such wisdom[93] eats almsfood consisting of choice hill rice along with various sauces and curries, even that will be no obstacle for him.[94] Just as a cloth that is defiled and stained becomes pure and bright with the help of clear water, or just as gold becomes pure and bright with the help of a furnace, so too, if a bhikkhu of such virtue...eats almsfood...that will be no obstacle for him.

13. "He abides pervading one quarter with a mind imbued with loving-kindness,[95] likewise the second, likewise the third, likewise the fourth; so above, below, around, and everywhere, and to all as to himself, he abides pervading the all-encompassing world with a mind imbued with loving-kindness, abundant, exalted, immeasurable, without hostility and without ill will.

14–16. "He abides pervading one quarter with a mind imbued with compassion...with a mind imbued with altruistic joy...with a mind imbued with equanimity, likewise the second, likewise the third, likewise the fourth; so above, below, around, and everywhere, and to all as to himself, he abides pervading the all-encompassing world with a mind imbued with equanimity, abundant, exalted, immeasurable, without hostility and without ill will.

17. "He understands thus: 'There is this, there is the inferior, there is the superior, and beyond there is an escape from this whole field of perception.'[96]

18. "When he knows and sees thus, his mind is liberated from the taint of sensual desire, from the taint of being, and from the taint of ignorance. When it is liberated there comes the knowledge: 'It is liberated.' He understands: 'Birth is destroyed, the holy life has been lived, what had to be done has been done, there is no more coming to any state of being.' [39] Bhikkhus, this bhikkhu is called one bathed with the inner bathing."[97]

19. Now on that occasion the brahmin Sundarika Bhāradvāja was sitting not far from the Blessed One. Then he said to the Blessed One: "But does Master Gotama go to the Bāhukā River to bathe?"

"Why, brahmin, go to the Bāhukā River? What can the Bāhukā River do?"

"Master Gotama, the Bāhukā River is held by many to give liberation, it is held by many to give merit, and many wash away their evil actions in the Bāhukā River."

20. Then the Blessed One addressed the brahmin Sundarika Bhāradvāja in stanzas:

"Bāhukā and Adhikakkā,
Gayā and Sundarikā too,
Payāga and Sarassatī,
And the stream Bahumatī—[98]
A fool may there forever bathe
Yet will not purify dark deeds.

What can the Sundarikā bring to pass?
What the Payāga? What the Bāhukā?
They cannot purify an evil-doer,
A man who has done cruel and brutal deeds.

One pure in heart has evermore
The Feast of Spring, the Holy Day;[99]
One fair in act, one pure in heart
Brings his virtue to perfection.

It is here, brahmin, that you should bathe,
To make yourself a refuge for all beings.
And if you speak no falsehood
Nor work harm for living beings,
Nor take what is offered not,
With faith and free from avarice,
What need for you to go to Gayā?
For any well will be your Gayā."

21. When this was said, the brahmin Sundarika Bhāradvāja said: "Magnificent, Master Gotama! Magnificent, Master Gotama! Master Gotama has made the Dhamma clear in many ways, as though he were turning upright what had been overthrown, revealing what was hidden, showing the way to one who was lost, or holding up a lamp in the dark for those with eyesight to see forms. I go to Master Gotama for refuge and to the Dhamma and to the Sangha of bhikkhus. I would receive the

going forth under Master Gotama, I would receive the full admission."[100]

22. And the brahmin Sundarika Bhāradvāja received the going forth under the Blessed One, and he received the full admission. [40] And soon, not long after his full admission, dwelling alone, withdrawn, diligent, ardent, and resolute, the venerable Bhāradvāja, by realising for himself with direct knowledge, here and now entered upon and abided in that supreme goal of the holy life for the sake of which clansmen rightly go forth from the home life into homelessness. He directly knew: "Birth is destroyed, the holy life has been lived, what had to be done has been done, there is no more coming to any state of being." And the venerable Bhāradvāja became one of the arahants.

8 *Sallekha Sutta*
Effacement

1. THUS HAVE I HEARD.[101] On one occasion the Blessed One was living at Sāvatthī in Jeta's Grove, Anāthapiṇḍika's Park.

2. Then, when it was evening, the venerable Mahā Cunda rose from meditation and went to the Blessed One. After paying homage to the Blessed One he sat down at one side and said to him:

3. "Venerable sir, various views arise in the world associated either with doctrines of a self or with doctrines about the world.[102] Now does the abandoning and relinquishing of those views come about in a bhikkhu who is attending only to the beginning [of his meditative training]?"[103]

"Cunda, as to those various views that arise in the world associated either with doctrines of a self or with doctrines about the world: if [the object] in relation to which those views arise, which they underlie, and which they are exercised upon[104] is seen as it actually is with proper wisdom thus: 'This is not mine, this I am not, this is not my self,' then the abandoning and relinquishing of those views comes about.[105]

(THE EIGHT ATTAINMENTS)

4. "It is possible here, Cunda, that quite secluded from sensual pleasures, secluded from unwholesome states, some bhikkhu enters upon and abides in the first jhāna, which is accompanied by applied and sustained thought, with rapture and pleasure born of seclusion. He might think thus: 'I am abiding in effacement.' But it is not these attainments that are called 'effacement' in the Noble One's Discipline: these are called 'pleasant abidings here and now' [41] in the Noble One's Discipline.[106]

5. "It is possible here that with the stilling of applied and sustained thought, some bhikkhu enters upon and abides in the second jhāna, which has self-confidence and singleness of mind without applied and sustained thought, with rapture and pleasure born of concentration. He might think thus: 'I am abiding in effacement.' But...these are called 'pleasant abidings here and now' in the Noble One's Discipline.

6. "It is possible here that with the fading away as well of rapture, some bhikkhu abides in equanimity, and mindful and fully aware, still feeling pleasure with the body, he enters upon and abides in the third jhāna, on account of which noble ones announce: 'He has a pleasant abiding who has equanimity and is mindful.' He might think thus: 'I am abiding in effacement.' But...these are called 'pleasant abidings here and now' in the Noble One's Discipline.

7. "It is possible here that with the abandoning of pleasure and pain, and with the previous disappearance of joy and grief, some bhikkhu enters upon and abides in the fourth jhāna, which has neither-pain-nor-pleasure and purity of mindfulness due to equanimity. He might think thus: 'I am abiding in effacement.' But it is not these attainments that are called 'effacement' in the Noble One's Discipline: these are called 'pleasant abidings here and now' in the Noble One's Discipline.

8. "It is possible here that with the complete surmounting of perceptions of form, with the disappearance of perceptions of sensory impact, with non-attention to perceptions of diversity, aware that 'space is infinite,' some bhikkhu enters upon and abides in the base of infinite space. He might think thus: 'I am abiding in effacement.' But it is not these attainments that are called 'effacement' in the Noble One's Discipline: these are called 'peaceful abidings' in the Noble One's Discipline.

9. "It is possible here that by completely surmounting the base of infinite space, aware that 'consciousness is infinite,' some bhikkhu enters upon and abides in the base of infinite consciousness. He might think thus: 'I am abiding in effacement.' But...these are called 'peaceful abidings' in the Noble One's Discipline.

10. "It is possible here that by completely surmounting the base of infinite consciousness, aware that 'there is nothing,' some bhikkhu enters upon and abides in the base of nothingness. He

might think thus: 'I am abiding in effacement.' But...these are called 'peaceful abidings' in the Noble One's Discipline.

11. "It is possible here that by completely surmounting the base of nothingness, some bhikkhu enters upon and abides in the base of neither-perception-nor-non-perception. He might think thus: 'I am abiding in effacement.' [42] But these attainments are not called 'effacement' in the Noble One's Discipline: these are called 'peaceful abidings' in the Noble One's Discipline.

(EFFACEMENT)

12. "Now, Cunda, here effacement should be practised by you:[107]

(1) 'Others will be cruel; we shall not be cruel here': effacement should be practised thus.[108]

(2) 'Others will kill living beings; we shall abstain from killing living beings here': effacement should be practised thus.

(3) 'Others will take what is not given; we shall abstain from taking what is not given here': effacement should be practised thus.

(4) 'Others will be uncelibate; we shall be celibate here': effacement should be practised thus.

(5) 'Others will speak falsehood; we shall abstain from false speech here': effacement should be practised thus.

(6) 'Others will speak maliciously; we shall abstain from malicious speech here': effacement should be practised thus.

(7) 'Others will speak harshly; we shall abstain from harsh speech here': effacement should be practised thus.

(8) 'Others will gossip; we shall abstain from gossip here': effacement should be practised thus.

(9) 'Others will be covetous; we shall be uncovetous here': effacement should be practised thus.

(10) 'Others will have ill will; we shall be without ill will here': effacement should be practised thus.

(11) 'Others will be of wrong view; we shall be of right view here': effacement should be practised thus.

(12) 'Others will be of wrong intention; we shall be of right intention here': effacement should be practised thus.

(13) 'Others will be of wrong speech; we shall be of right speech here': effacement should be practised thus.

(14) 'Others will be of wrong action; we shall be of right action here': effacement should be practised thus.

(15) 'Others will be of wrong livelihood; we shall be of right livelihood here': effacement should be practised thus.

(16) 'Others will be of wrong effort; we shall be of right effort here': effacement should be practised thus.

(17) 'Others will be of wrong mindfulness; we shall be of right mindfulness here': effacement should be practised thus.

(18) 'Others will be of wrong concentration; we shall be of right concentration here': effacement should be practised thus.

(19) 'Others will be of wrong knowledge; we shall be of right knowledge here': effacement should be practised thus.

(20) 'Others will be of wrong deliverance; we shall be of right deliverance here': effacement should be practised thus.

(21) 'Others will be overcome by sloth and torpor; we shall be free from sloth and torpor here': effacement should be practised thus.

(22) 'Others will be restless; we shall not be restless here': effacement should be practised thus.

(23) 'Others will be doubters; we shall go beyond doubt here': effacement should be practised thus.

(24) 'Others will be angry; we shall not be angry here': effacement should be practised thus.

(25) 'Others will be resentful; we shall not be resentful here': effacement should be practised thus. [43]

(26) 'Others will be contemptuous; we shall not be contemptuous here': effacement should be practised thus.

(27) 'Others will be insolent; we shall not be insolent here': effacement should be practised thus.

(28) 'Others will be envious; we shall not be envious here': effacement should be practised thus.

(29) 'Others will be avaricious; we shall not be avaricious here': effacement should be practised thus.

(30) 'Others will be fraudulent; we shall not be fraudulent here': effacement should be practised thus.

(31) 'Others will be deceitful; we shall not be deceitful here': effacement should be practised thus.

(32) 'Others will be obstinate; we shall not be obstinate here': effacement should be practised thus.

(33) 'Others will be arrogant; we shall not be arrogant here': effacement should be practised thus.

(34) 'Others will be difficult to admonish; we shall be easy to admonish here': effacement should be practised thus.

(35) 'Others will have bad friends; we shall have good friends here': effacement should be practised thus.

(36) 'Others will be negligent; we shall be diligent here': effacement should be practised thus.

(37) 'Others will be faithless; we shall be faithful here': effacement should be practised thus.

(38) 'Others will be shameless; we shall be shameful here': effacement should be practised thus.

(39) 'Others will have no fear of wrongdoing; we shall be afraid of wrongdoing here': effacement should be practised thus.

(40) 'Others will be of little learning; we shall be of great learning here': effacement should be practised thus.

(41) 'Others will be lazy; we shall be energetic here': effacement should be practised thus.

(42) 'Others will be unmindful; we shall be established in mindfulness here': effacement should be practised thus.

(43) 'Others will lack wisdom; we shall possess wisdom here': effacement should be practised thus.

(44) 'Others will adhere to their own views, hold on to them tenaciously, and relinquish them with difficulty;[109] we shall not adhere to our own views or hold on to them tenaciously, but shall relinquish them easily': effacement should be practised thus.

(INCLINATION OF MIND)

13. "Cunda, I say that even the inclination of mind towards wholesome states is of great benefit, so what should be said of bodily and verbal acts conforming [to such a state of mind]?[110] Therefore, Cunda:

(1) Mind should be inclined thus: 'Others will be cruel; we shall not be cruel here.'

(2) Mind should be inclined thus: 'Others will kill living beings; we shall abstain from killing living beings here.'

(3–43) Mind should be inclined thus:...

(44) Mind should be inclined thus: 'Others will adhere to their own views, hold on to them tenaciously, and relinquish them with difficulty; we shall not adhere to our own views or hold on to them tenaciously, but shall relinquish them easily.'

(AVOIDANCE)

14. "Cunda, suppose there were an uneven path and another even path by which to avoid it; and suppose there were an uneven ford and another even ford by which to avoid it. [44] So too:

(1) A person given to cruelty has non-cruelty by which to avoid it.

(2) One given to killing living beings has abstention from killing living beings by which to avoid it.

(3) One given to taking what is not given has abstention from taking what is not given by which to avoid it.

(4) One given to be uncelibate has celibacy by which to avoid it.

(5) One given to false speech has abstention from false speech by which to avoid it.

(6) One given to malicious speech has abstention from malicious speech by which to avoid it.

(7) One given to harsh speech has abstention from harsh speech by which to avoid it.

(8) One given to gossip has abstention from gossip by which to avoid it.

(9) One given to covetousness has uncovetousness by which to avoid it.

(10) One given to ill will has non-ill will by which to avoid it.

(11) One given to wrong view has right view by which to avoid it.

(12) One given to wrong intention has right intention by which to avoid it.

(13) One given to wrong speech has right speech by which to avoid it.

(14) One given to wrong action has right action by which to avoid it.

(15) One given to wrong livelihood has right livelihood by which to avoid it.

(16) One given to wrong effort has right effort by which to avoid it.

(17) One given to wrong mindfulness has right mindfulness by which to avoid it.

(18) One given to wrong concentration has right concentration by which to avoid it.

(19) One given to wrong knowledge has right knowledge by which to avoid it.

(20) One given to wrong deliverance has right deliverance by which to avoid it.

(21) One given to sloth and torpor has freedom from sloth and torpor by which to avoid it.

(22) One given to restlessness has non-restlessness by which to avoid it.

(23) One given to doubt has the state beyond doubt by which to avoid it.

(24) One given to anger has non-anger by which to avoid it.

(25) One given to resentment has non-resentment by which to avoid it.

(26) One given to contempt has non-contempt by which to avoid it.

(27) One given to insolence has non-insolence by which to avoid it.

(28) One given to envy has non-envy by which to avoid it.

(29) One given to avarice has non-avarice by which to avoid it.

(30) One given to fraud has non-fraud by which to avoid it.

(31) One given to deceit has non-deceit by which to avoid it.

(32) One given to obstinacy has non-obstinacy by which to avoid it.

(33) One given to arrogance has non-arrogance by which to avoid it.

(34) One given to being difficult to admonish has being easy to admonish by which to avoid it.

(35) One given to making bad friends has making good friends by which to avoid it.

(36) One given to negligence has diligence by which to avoid it.

(37) One given to faithlessness has faith by which to avoid it.

(38) One given to shamelessness has shame by which to avoid it.

(39) One given to fearlessness of wrongdoing has fear of wrongdoing by which to avoid it.

(40) One given to little learning has great learning by which to avoid it.

(41) One given to laziness has the arousal of energy by which to avoid it.

(42) One given to unmindfulness has the establishment of mindfulness by which to avoid it.

(43) One given to lack of wisdom has the acquisition of wisdom by which to avoid it.

(44) One given to adhere to his own views, who holds on to them tenaciously and relinquishes them with difficulty, has non-adherence to his own views, not holding on to them tenaciously and relinquishing them easily, by which to avoid it.

(THE WAY LEADING UPWARDS)

15. "Cunda, just as all unwholesome states lead downwards and all wholesome states lead upwards, so too:

(1) A person given to cruelty has non-cruelty to lead him upwards.

(2) One given to killing living beings has abstention from killing living beings to lead him upwards.

(3–43) One given to...to lead him upwards.

(44) One given to adhere to his own views, who holds on to them tenaciously [45] and relinquishes them with difficulty, has non-adherence to his own views, not holding on to them tenaciously and relinquishing them easily, to lead him upwards.

(THE WAY OF EXTINGUISHING)

16. "Cunda, that one who is himself sinking in the mud should pull out another who is sinking in the mud is impossible; that one who is not himself sinking in the mud should pull out another who is sinking in the mud is possible. That one who is himself untamed, undisciplined, [with defilements] unextinguished, should tame another, discipline him, and help extinguish [his defilements] is impossible; that one who is himself tamed, disciplined, [with defilements] extinguished, should tame another, discipline him, and help extinguish [his defilements] is possible.[111] So too:

(1) A person given to cruelty has non-cruelty by which to extinguish it.[112]

(2) One given to killing living beings has abstention from killing living beings by which to extinguish it.

(3–43) One given to...[46]...by which to extinguish it.

(44) One given to adhere to his own views, who holds on to them tenaciously and relinquishes them with difficulty, has

non-adherence to his own views, not holding on to them tenaciously and relinquishing them easily, by which to extinguish it.

(CONCLUSION)

17. "So, Cunda, the way of effacement has been taught by me, the way of inclining the mind has been taught by me, the way of avoidance has been taught by me, the way leading upwards has been taught by me, and the way of extinguishing has been taught by me.

18. "What should be done for his disciples out of compassion by a teacher who seeks their welfare and has compassion for them, that I have done for you, Cunda.[113] There are these roots of trees, these empty huts. Meditate, Cunda, do not delay or else you will regret it later. This is our instruction to you."

That is what the Blessed One said. The venerable Mahā Cunda was satisfied and delighted in the Blessed One's words.

9 *Sammādiṭṭhi Sutta*
Right View

1. THUS HAVE I HEARD. On one occasion the Blessed One was living at Sāvatthī in Jeta's Grove, Anāthapiṇḍika's Park. There the venerable Sāriputta addressed the bhikkhus thus: "Friends, bhikkhus."—"Friend," they replied. The venerable Sāriputta said this:

2. "'One of right view, one of right view,' is said, friends. In what way is a noble disciple one of right view, whose view is straight, who has perfect confidence in the Dhamma, and has arrived at this true Dhamma?"[114]

"Indeed, friend, we would come from far away to learn from the venerable Sāriputta the meaning of this statement. It would be good if the venerable Sāriputta would explain the meaning of this statement. Having heard it from him, the bhikkhus will remember it."

"Then, friends, listen and attend closely to what I shall say."

"Yes, friend," the bhikkhus replied. The venerable Sāriputta said this:

(THE WHOLESOME AND THE UNWHOLESOME)

3. "When, friends, a noble disciple understands the unwholesome and the root of the unwholesome, the wholesome and the root of the wholesome, [47] in that way he is one of right view, whose view is straight, who has perfect confidence in the Dhamma and has arrived at this true Dhamma.

4. "And what, friends, is the unwholesome, what is the root of the unwholesome, what is the wholesome, what is the root of the wholesome? Killing living beings is unwholesome; taking what is not given is unwholesome; misconduct in sensual pleasures is unwholesome; false speech is unwholesome; malicious

speech is unwholesome; harsh speech is unwholesome; gossip is unwholesome; covetousness is unwholesome; ill will is unwholesome; wrong view is unwholesome. This is called the unwholesome.[115]

5. "And what is the root of the unwholesome? Greed is a root of the unwholesome; hate is a root of the unwholesome; delusion is a root of the unwholesome. This is called the root of the unwholesome.[116]

6. "And what is the wholesome? Abstention from killing living beings is wholesome; abstention from taking what is not given is wholesome; abstention from misconduct in sensual pleasures is wholesome; abstention from false speech is wholesome; abstention from malicious speech is wholesome; abstention from harsh speech is wholesome; abstention from gossip is wholesome; uncovetousness is wholesome; non-ill will is wholesome; right view is wholesome. This is called the wholesome.[117]

7. "And what is the root of the wholesome? Non-greed is a root of the wholesome; non-hate is a root of the wholesome; non-delusion is a root of the wholesome. This is called the root of the wholesome.

8. "When a noble disciple has thus understood the unwholesome and the root of the unwholesome, the wholesome and the root of the wholesome,[118] he entirely abandons the underlying tendency to lust, he abolishes the underlying tendency to aversion, he extirpates the underlying tendency to the view and conceit 'I am,' and by abandoning ignorance and arousing true knowledge he here and now makes an end of suffering.[119] In that way too a noble disciple is one of right view, whose view is straight, who has perfect confidence in the Dhamma, and has arrived at this true Dhamma."

(NUTRIMENT)

9. Saying, "Good, friend," the bhikkhus delighted and rejoiced in the venerable Sāriputta's words. Then they asked him a further question: "But, friend, might there be another way in which a noble disciple is one of right view...and has arrived at this true Dhamma?"—"There might be, friends.

10. "When, friends, a noble disciple understands nutriment, the origin of nutriment, the cessation of nutriment, and the way

leading to the cessation of nutriment, in that way he is one of right view...and has arrived [48] at this true Dhamma.

11. "And what is nutriment, what is the origin of nutriment, what is the cessation of nutriment, what is the way leading to the cessation of nutriment? There are four kinds of nutriment for the maintenance of beings that already have come to be and for the support of those seeking a new existence. What four? They are: physical food as nutriment, gross or subtle; contact as the second; mental volition as the third; and consciousness as the fourth.[120] With the arising of craving there is the arising of nutriment. With the cessation of craving there is the cessation of nutriment. The way leading to the cessation of nutriment is just this Noble Eightfold Path; that is, right view, right intention, right speech, right action, right livelihood, right effort, right mindfulness, and right concentration.

12. "When a noble disciple has thus understood nutriment, the origin of nutriment, the cessation of nutriment, and the way leading to the cessation of nutriment, he entirely abandons the underlying tendency to greed, he abolishes the underlying tendency to aversion, he extirpates the underlying tendency to the view and conceit 'I am,' and by abandoning ignorance and arousing true knowledge he here and now makes an end of suffering. In that way too a noble disciple is one of right view, whose view is straight, who has perfect confidence in the Dhamma, and has arrived at this true Dhamma."

(THE FOUR NOBLE TRUTHS)

13. Saying, "Good, friend," the bhikkhus delighted and rejoiced in the venerable Sāriputta's words. Then they asked him a further question: "But, friend, might there be another way in which a noble disciple is one of right view...and has arrived at this true Dhamma?"—"There might be, friends.

14. "When, friends, a noble disciple understands suffering, the origin of suffering, the cessation of suffering, and the way leading to the cessation of suffering, in that way he is one of right view...and has arrived at this true Dhamma.

15. "And what is suffering, what is the origin of suffering, what is the cessation of suffering, what is the way leading to the cessation of suffering? Birth is suffering; ageing is suffering;

sickness is suffering; death is suffering; sorrow, lamentation, pain, grief, and despair are suffering; not to obtain what one wants is suffering; in short, the five aggregates affected by clinging are suffering. This is called suffering.

16. "And what is the origin of suffering? It is craving, which brings renewal of being, is accompanied by delight and lust, and delights in this and that; that is, craving for sensual pleasures [49], craving for being, and craving for non-being. This is called the origin of suffering.

17. "And what is the cessation of suffering? It is the remainderless fading away and ceasing, the giving up, relinquishing, letting go, and rejecting of that same craving. This is called the cessation of suffering.

18. "And what is the way leading to the cessation of suffering? It is just this Noble Eightfold Path; that is, right view...right concentration. This is called the way leading to the cessation of suffering.

19. "When a noble disciple has thus understood suffering, the origin of suffering, the cessation of suffering, and the way leading to the cessation of suffering...he here and now makes an end of suffering. In that way too a noble disciple is one of right view...and has arrived at this true Dhamma."

(AGEING AND DEATH)

20. Saying, "Good, friend," the bhikkhus delighted and rejoiced in the venerable Sāriputta's words. Then they asked him a further question: "But, friend, might there be another way in which a noble disciple is one of right view...and has arrived at this true Dhamma?"—"There might be, friends.

21. "When, friends, a noble disciple understands ageing and death, the origin of ageing and death, the cessation of ageing and death, and the way leading to the cessation of ageing and death, in that way he is one of right view...and has arrived at this true Dhamma.[121]

22. "And what is ageing and death, what is the origin of ageing and death, what is the cessation of ageing and death, what is the way leading to the cessation of ageing and death? The ageing of beings in the various orders of beings, their old age, brokenness of teeth, greyness of hair, wrinkling of skin, decline of life, weakness of faculties—this is called ageing. The passing of beings out

of the various orders of beings, their passing away, dissolution, disappearance, dying, completion of time, dissolution of the aggregates,[122] laying down of the body—this is called death. So this ageing and this death are what is called ageing and death. With the arising of birth there is the arising of ageing and death. With the cessation of birth there is the cessation of ageing and death. The way leading to the cessation of ageing and death is just this Noble Eightfold Path; that is, right view...right concentration.

23. "When a noble disciple has thus understood ageing and death, the origin of ageing and death, the cessation of ageing and death, and the way leading to the cessation of ageing and death...he here and now makes an end of suffering. In that way too a noble disciple is one of right view...and has arrived at this true Dhamma."

(BIRTH)

24. Saying, "Good, friend," the bhikkhus delighted and rejoiced in the venerable Sāriputta's words. Then they asked him a further question: "But, friend, might there be another way in which a noble disciple is one of right view...and has arrived at this true Dhamma?"—[50] "There might be, friends.

25. "When, friends, a noble disciple understands birth, the origin of birth, the cessation of birth, and the way leading to the cessation of birth, in that way he is one of right view...and has arrived at this true Dhamma.

26. "And what is birth, what is the origin of birth, what is the cessation of birth, what is the way leading to the cessation of birth? The birth of beings in the various orders of beings, their coming to birth, precipitation [in a womb], generation, manifestation of the aggregates, obtaining the bases for contact[123]—this is called birth. With the arising of being there is the arising of birth. With the cessation of being there is the cessation of birth. The way leading to the cessation of birth is just this Noble Eightfold Path; that is, right view...right concentration.

27. "When a noble disciple has thus understood birth, the origin of birth, the cessation of birth, and the way leading to the cessation of birth...he here and now makes an end of suffering. In that way too a noble disciple is one of right view...and has arrived at this true Dhamma."

(BEING)

28. Saying, "Good, friend," the bhikkhus delighted and rejoiced in the venerable Sāriputta's words. Then they asked him a further question: "But, friend, might there be another way in which a noble disciple is one of right view...and has arrived at this true Dhamma?"—"There might be, friends.

29. "When, friends, a noble disciple understands being, the origin of being, the cessation of being, and the way leading to the cessation of being, in that way he is one of right view...and has arrived at this true Dhamma.

30. "And what is being, what is the origin of being, what is the cessation of being, what is the way leading to the cessation of being? There are these three kinds of being: sense-sphere being, fine-material being, and immaterial being.[124] With the arising of clinging there is the arising of being. With the cessation of clinging there is the cessation of being. The way leading to the cessation of being is just this Noble Eightfold Path; that is, right view...right concentration.

31. "When a noble disciple has thus understood being, the origin of being, the cessation of being, and the way leading to the cessation of being...he here and now makes an end of suffering. In that way too a noble disciple is one of right view...and has arrived at this true Dhamma."

(CLINGING)

32. Saying, "Good, friend," the bhikkhus delighted and rejoiced in the venerable Sāriputta's words. Then they asked him a further question: "But, friend, might there be another way in which a noble disciple is one of right view...and has arrived at this true Dhamma?"—"There might be, friends.

33. "When, friends, a noble disciple understands clinging, the origin of clinging, the cessation of clinging, and the way leading to the cessation of clinging, in that way he is one of right view... and has arrived at this true Dhamma.

34. "And what is clinging, what is the origin of clinging, what is the cessation of clinging, what is the way leading to the cessation of clinging? There are these four [51] kinds of clinging: clinging to sensual pleasures, clinging to views, clinging to rules

and observances, and clinging to a doctrine of self.[125] With the arising of craving there is the arising of clinging. With the cessation of craving there is the cessation of clinging. The way leading to the cessation of clinging is just this Noble Eightfold Path; that is, right view...right concentration.

35. "When a noble disciple has thus understood clinging, the origin of clinging, the cessation of clinging, and the way leading to the cessation of clinging...he here and now makes an end of suffering. In that way too a noble disciple is one of right view... and has arrived at this true Dhamma."

(CRAVING)

36. Saying, "Good, friend," the bhikkhus delighted and rejoiced in the venerable Sāriputta's words. Then they asked him a further question: "But, friend, might there be another way in which a noble disciple is one of right view...and has arrived at this true Dhamma?"—"There might be, friends.

37. "When, friends, a noble disciple understands craving, the origin of craving, the cessation of craving, and the way leading to the cessation of craving, in that way he is one of right view... and has arrived at this true Dhamma.

38. "And what is craving, what is the origin of craving, what is the cessation of craving, what is the way leading to the cessation of craving? There are these six classes of craving: craving for forms, craving for sounds, craving for odours, craving for flavours, craving for tangibles, craving for mind-objects.[126] With the arising of feeling there is the arising of craving. With the cessation of feeling there is the cessation of craving. The way leading to the cessation of craving is just this Noble Eightfold Path; that is, right view...right concentration.

39. "When a noble disciple has thus understood craving, the origin of craving, the cessation of craving, and the way leading to the cessation of craving...he here and now makes an end of suffering. In that way too a noble disciple is one of right view... and has arrived at this true Dhamma."

(FEELING)

40. Saying, "Good, friend," the bhikkhus delighted and rejoiced in the venerable Sāriputta's words. Then they asked him a further question: "But, friend, might there be another way in which a noble disciple is one of right view…and has arrived at this true Dhamma?"—"There might be, friends.

41. "When, friends, a noble disciple understands feeling, the origin of feeling, the cessation of feeling, and the way leading to the cessation of feeling, in that way he is one of right view…and has arrived at this true Dhamma.

42. "And what is feeling, what is the origin of feeling, what is the cessation of feeling, what is the way leading to the cessation of feeling? There are these six classes of feeling: feeling born of eye-contact, feeling born of ear-contact, feeling born of nose-contact, feeling born of tongue-contact, feeling born of body-contact, feeling born of mind-contact. With the arising of contact there is the arising of feeling. With the cessation of contact there is the cessation of feeling. The way leading to the cessation of feeling is just this Noble Eightfold Path; that is, right view… right concentration. [52]

43. "When a noble disciple has thus understood feeling, the origin of feeling, the cessation of feeling, and the way leading to the cessation of feeling…he here and now makes an end of suffering. In that way too a noble disciple is one of right view…and has arrived at this true Dhamma."

(CONTACT)

44. Saying, "Good, friend," the bhikkhus delighted and rejoiced in the venerable Sāriputta's words. Then they asked him a further question: "But, friend, might there be another way in which a noble disciple is one of right view…and has arrived at this true Dhamma?"—"There might be, friends.

45. "When, friends, a noble disciple understands contact, the origin of contact, the cessation of contact, and the way leading to the cessation of contact, in that way he is one of right view…and has arrived at this true Dhamma.

46. "And what is contact, what is the origin of contact, what is the cessation of contact, what is the way leading to the cessation

of contact? There are these six classes of contact: eye-contact, ear-contact, nose-contact, tongue-contact, body-contact, mind-contact.[127] With the arising of the sixfold base there is the arising of contact. With the cessation of the sixfold base there is the cessation of contact. The way leading to the cessation of contact is just this Noble Eightfold Path; that is, right view...right concentration.

47. "When a noble disciple has thus understood contact, the origin of contact, the cessation of contact, and the way leading to the cessation of contact...he here and now makes an end of suffering. In that way too a noble disciple is one of right view...and has arrived at this true Dhamma."

(THE SIXFOLD BASE)

48. Saying, "Good, friend," the bhikkhus delighted and rejoiced in the venerable Sāriputta's words. Then they asked him a further question: "But, friend, might there be another way in which a noble disciple is one of right view...and has arrived at this true Dhamma?"—"There might be, friends.

49. "When, friends, a noble disciple understands the sixfold base, the origin of the sixfold base, the cessation of the sixfold base, and the way leading to the cessation of the sixfold base, in that way he is one of right view...and has arrived at this true Dhamma.

50. "And what is the sixfold base, what is the origin of the sixfold base, what is the cessation of the sixfold base, what is the way leading to the cessation of the sixfold base? There are these six bases: the eye-base, the ear-base, the nose-base, the tongue-base, the body-base, the mind-base.[128] With the arising of mentality-materiality there is the arising of the sixfold base. With the cessation of mentality-materiality there is the cessation of the sixfold base. The way leading to the cessation of the sixfold base is just this Noble Eightfold Path; that is, right view...right concentration.

51. "When a noble disciple has thus understood the sixfold base, the origin of the sixfold base, the cessation of the sixfold base, and [53] the way leading to the cessation of the sixfold base...he here and now makes an end of suffering. In that way too a noble disciple is one of right view...and has arrived at this true Dhamma."

(MENTALITY-MATERIALITY)

52. Saying, "Good, friend," the bhikkhus delighted and rejoiced in the venerable Sāriputta's words. Then they asked him a further question: "But, friend, might there be another way in which a noble disciple is one of right view...and has arrived at this true Dhamma?"—"There might be, friends.

53. "When, friends, a noble disciple understands mentality-materiality, the origin of mentality-materiality, the cessation of mentality-materiality, and the way leading to the cessation of mentality-materiality, in that way he is one of right view...and has arrived at this true Dhamma.[129]

54. "And what is mentality-materiality, what is the origin of mentality-materiality, what is the cessation of mentality-materiality, what is the way leading to the cessation of mentality-materiality? Feeling, perception, volition, contact, and attention—these are called mentality. The four great elements and the material form derived from the four great elements—these are called materiality. So this mentality and this materiality are what is called mentality-materiality. With the arising of consciousness there is the arising of mentality-materiality. With the cessation of consciousness there is the cessation of mentality-materiality. The way leading to the cessation of mentality-materiality is just this Noble Eightfold Path; that is, right view...right concentration.

55. "When a noble disciple has thus understood mentality-materiality, the origin of mentality-materiality, the cessation of mentality-materiality, and the way leading to the cessation of mentality-materiality...he here and now makes an end of suffering. In that way too a noble disciple is one of right view...and has arrived at this true Dhamma."

(CONSCIOUSNESS)

56. Saying, "Good, friend," the bhikkhus delighted and rejoiced in the venerable Sāriputta's words. Then they asked him a further question: "But, friend, might there be another way in which a noble disciple is one of right view...and has arrived at this true Dhamma?"—"There might be, friends.

57. "When, friends, a noble disciple understands consciousness, the origin of consciousness, the cessation of consciousness, and

the way leading to the cessation of consciousness, in that way he is one of right view...and has arrived at this true Dhamma.

58. "And what is consciousness, what is the origin of consciousness, what is the cessation of consciousness, what is the way leading to the cessation of consciousness? There are these six classes of consciousness: eye-consciousness, ear-consciousness, nose-consciousness, tongue-consciousness, body-consciousness, mind-consciousness.[130] With the arising of formations there is the arising of consciousness. With the cessation of formations there is the cessation of consciousness. The way leading to the cessation of consciousness is just this Noble Eightfold Path; that is, right view...right concentration.

59. "When a noble disciple has thus understood consciousness, the origin of consciousness, the cessation of consciousness, and the way leading to the cessation of consciousness [54]...he here and now makes an end of suffering. In that way too a noble disciple is one of right view...and has arrived at this true Dhamma."

(FORMATIONS)

60. Saying, "Good, friend," the bhikkhus delighted and rejoiced in the venerable Sāriputta's words. Then they asked him a further question: "But, friend, might there be another way in which a noble disciple is one of right view...and has arrived at this true Dhamma?"—"There might be, friends.

61. "When, friends, a noble disciple understands formations, the origin of formations, the cessation of formations, and the way leading to the cessation of formations, in that way he is one of right view...and has arrived at this true Dhamma.

62. "And what are formations, what is the origin of formations, what is the cessation of formations, what is the way leading to the cessation of formations? There are these three kinds of formations: the bodily formation, the verbal formation, the mental formation.[131] With the arising of ignorance there is the arising of formations. With the cessation of ignorance there is the cessation of formations. The way leading to the cessation of formations is just this Noble Eightfold Path; that is, right view...right concentration.

63. "When a noble disciple has thus understood formations, the origin of formations, the cessation of formations, and the way leading to the cessation of formations...he here and now

makes an end of suffering. In that way too a noble disciple is one of right view...and has arrived at this true Dhamma."

(IGNORANCE)

64. Saying, "Good, friend," the bhikkhus delighted and rejoiced in the venerable Sāriputta's words. Then they asked him a further question: "But, friend, might there be another way in which a noble disciple is one of right view...and has arrived at this true Dhamma?"—"There might be, friends.

65. "When, friends, a noble disciple understands ignorance, the origin of ignorance, the cessation of ignorance, and the way leading to the cessation of ignorance, in that way he is one of right view...and has arrived at this true Dhamma.

66. "And what is ignorance, what is the origin of ignorance, what is the cessation of ignorance, what is the way leading to the cessation of ignorance? Not knowing about suffering, not knowing about the origin of suffering, not knowing about the cessation of suffering, not knowing about the way leading to the cessation of suffering—this is called ignorance. With the arising of the taints there is the arising of ignorance. With the cessation of the taints there is the cessation of ignorance. The way leading to the cessation of ignorance is just this Noble Eightfold Path; that is, right view...right concentration.

67. "When a noble disciple has thus understood ignorance, the origin of ignorance, the cessation of ignorance, and the way leading to the cessation of ignorance...he here and now makes an end of suffering. In that way too a noble disciple is one of right view...and has arrived at this true Dhamma."

(TAINTS)

68. Saying, "Good, friend," the bhikkhus delighted and rejoiced in the venerable Sāriputta's words. Then they asked him a further question: "But, friend, might there be another [55] way in which a noble disciple is one of right view, whose view is straight, who has perfect confidence in the Dhamma, and has arrived at this true Dhamma?"—"There might be, friends.

69. "When, friends, a noble disciple understands the taints, the origin of the taints, the cessation of the taints, and the way

leading to the cessation of the taints, in that way he is one of right view, whose view is straight, who has perfect confidence in the Dhamma, and has arrived at this true Dhamma.

70. "And what are the taints, what is the origin of the taints, what is the cessation of the taints, what is the way leading to the cessation of the taints? There are these three taints: the taint of sensual desire, the taint of being, and the taint of ignorance. With the arising of ignorance there is the arising of the taints.[132] With the cessation of ignorance there is the cessation of the taints. The way leading to the cessation of the taints is just this Noble Eightfold Path; that is, right view, right intention, right speech, right action, right livelihood, right effort, right mindfulness, and right concentration.

71. "When a noble disciple has thus understood the taints, the origin of the taints, the cessation of the taints, and the way leading to the cessation of the taints, he entirely abandons the underlying tendency to lust, he abolishes the underlying tendency to aversion, he extirpates the underlying tendency to the view and conceit 'I am,' and by abandoning ignorance and arousing true knowledge he here and now makes an end of suffering. In that way too a noble disciple is one of right view, whose view is straight, who has perfect confidence in the Dhamma, and has arrived at this true Dhamma."

That is what the venerable Sāriputta said. The bhikkhus were satisfied and delighted in the venerable Sāriputta's words.

10 *Satipaṭṭhāna Sutta*
The Foundations of Mindfulness

1. THUS HAVE I HEARD.[133] On one occasion the Blessed One was living in the Kuru country where there was a town of the Kurus named Kammāsadhamma.[134] There he addressed the bhikkhus thus: "Bhikkhus."—"Venerable sir," they replied. The Blessed One said this:

2. "Bhikkhus, this is the direct path[135] for the purification of beings [56], for the surmounting of sorrow and lamentation, for the disappearance of pain and grief, for the attainment of the true way, for the realisation of Nibbāna—namely, the four foundations of mindfulness.[136]

3. "What are the four? Here, bhikkhus, a bhikkhu[137] abides contemplating the body as a body, ardent, fully aware, and mindful, having put away covetousness and grief for the world.[138] He abides contemplating feelings as feelings, ardent, fully aware, and mindful, having put away covetousness and grief for the world. He abides contemplating mind as mind, ardent, fully aware, and mindful, having put away covetousness and grief for the world. He abides contemplating mind-objects as mind-objects, ardent, fully aware, and mindful, having put away covetousness and grief for the world.[139]

(CONTEMPLATION OF THE BODY)

(*1. Mindfulness of Breathing*)

4. "And how, bhikkhus, does a bhikkhu abide contemplating the body as a body? Here a bhikkhu, gone to the forest or to the root of a tree or to an empty hut, sits down; having folded his legs crosswise, set his body erect, and established mindfulness in front of him, ever mindful he breathes in, mindful he breathes

out. Breathing in long, he understands: 'I breathe in long'; or breathing out long, he understands: 'I breathe out long.' Breathing in short, he understands: 'I breathe in short'; or breathing out short, he understands: 'I breathe out short.'[140] He trains thus: 'I shall breathe in experiencing the whole body'; he trains thus: 'I shall breathe out experiencing the whole body.'[141] He trains thus: 'I shall breathe in tranquillising the bodily formation'; he trains thus: 'I shall breathe out tranquillising the bodily formation.'[142] Just as a skilled turner or his apprentice, when making a long turn, understands: 'I make a long turn'; or, when making a short turn, understands: 'I make a short turn'; so too, breathing in long, a bhikkhu understands: 'I breathe in long'...he trains thus: 'I shall breathe out tranquillising the bodily formation.'

(INSIGHT)

5. "In this way he abides contemplating the body as a body internally, or he abides contemplating the body as a body externally, or he abides contemplating the body as a body both internally and externally.[143] Or else he abides contemplating in the body its nature of arising, or he abides contemplating in the body its nature of vanishing, or he abides contemplating in the body its nature of both arising and vanishing.[144] Or else mindfulness that 'there is a body' is simply established in him to the extent necessary for bare knowledge and mindfulness.[145] And he abides independent, not clinging to anything in the world. That is how a bhikkhu abides contemplating the body as a body.

(2. *The Four Postures*)

6. "Again, bhikkhus, when walking, a bhikkhu understands: 'I am walking'; when standing, he understands: 'I am standing'; when sitting, [57] he understands: 'I am sitting'; when lying down, he understands: 'I am lying down'; or he understands accordingly however his body is disposed.[146]

7. "In this way he abides contemplating the body as a body internally, externally, and both internally and externally...And he abides independent, not clinging to anything in the world. That too is how a bhikkhu abides contemplating the body as a body.

(*3. Full Awareness*)

8. "Again, bhikkhus, a bhikkhu is one who acts in full awareness when going forward and returning;[147] who acts in full awareness when looking ahead and looking away; who acts in full awareness when flexing and extending his limbs; who acts in full awareness when wearing his robes and carrying his outer robe and bowl; who acts in full awareness when eating, drinking, consuming food, and tasting; who acts in full awareness when defecating and urinating; who acts in full awareness when walking, standing, sitting, falling asleep, waking up, talking, and keeping silent.

9. "In this way he abides contemplating the body as a body internally, externally, and both internally and externally... And he abides independent, not clinging to anything in the world. That too is how a bhikkhu abides contemplating the body as a body.

(*4. Foulness—The Bodily Parts*)

10. "Again, bhikkhus, a bhikkhu reviews this same body up from the soles of the feet and down from the top of the hair, bounded by skin, as full of many kinds of impurity thus: 'In this body there are head-hairs, body-hairs, nails, teeth, skin, flesh, sinews, bones, bone-marrow, kidneys, heart, liver, diaphragm, spleen, lungs, intestines, mesentery, contents of the stomach, feces, bile, phlegm, pus, blood, sweat, fat, tears, grease, spittle, snot, oil of the joints, and urine.'[148] Just as though there were a bag with an opening at both ends full of many sorts of grain, such as hill rice, red rice, beans, peas, millet, and white rice, and a man with good eyes were to open it and review it thus: 'This is hill rice, this is red rice, these are beans, these are peas, this is millet, this is white rice'; so too, a bhikkhu reviews this same body...as full of many kinds of impurity thus: 'In this body there are head-hairs...and urine.'

11. "In this way he abides contemplating the body as a body internally, externally, and both internally and externally... And he abides independent, not clinging to anything in the world. That too is how a bhikkhu abides contemplating the body as a body.

(5. Elements)

12. "Again, bhikkhus, a bhikkhu reviews this same body, however it is placed, however disposed, as consisting of elements thus: 'In this body there are the earth element, the water element, the fire element, and the air element.'[149] [58] Just as though a skilled butcher or his apprentice had killed a cow and was seated at the crossroads with it cut up into pieces; so too, a bhikkhu reviews this same body...as consisting of elements thus: 'In this body there are the earth element, the water element, the fire element, and the air element.'

13. "In this way he abides contemplating the body as a body internally, externally, and both internally and externally...And he abides independent, not clinging to anything in the world. That too is how a bhikkhu abides contemplating the body as a body.

(6–14. The Nine Charnel Ground Contemplations)

14. "Again, bhikkhus, as though he were to see a corpse thrown aside in a charnel ground, one, two, or three days dead, bloated, livid, and oozing matter, a bhikkhu compares this same body with it thus: 'This body too is of the same nature, it will be like that, it is not exempt from that fate.'[150]

15. "In this way he abides contemplating the body as a body internally, externally, and both internally and externally...And he abides independent, not clinging to anything in the world. That too is how a bhikkhu abides contemplating the body as a body.

16. "Again, as though he were to see a corpse thrown aside in a charnel ground, being devoured by crows, hawks, vultures, dogs, jackals, or various kinds of worms, a bhikkhu compares this same body with it thus: 'This body too is of the same nature, it will be like that, it is not exempt from that fate.'

17. "...That too is how a bhikkhu abides contemplating the body as a body.

18–24. "Again, as though he were to see a corpse thrown aside in a charnel ground, a skeleton with flesh and blood, held together with sinews...a fleshless skeleton smeared with blood, held together with sinews...a skeleton without flesh and blood, held together with sinews...disconnected bones scattered in all directions—here a hand-bone, there a foot-bone, here a shin-bone, there a thigh-bone, here a hip-bone, there a back-bone, here a rib-bone, there a breast-bone, here an arm-bone, there a shoulder-bone, here a neck-bone, there a jaw-bone, here a tooth, there the skull—a bhikkhu compares this same body with it thus: 'This body too is of the same nature, it will be like that, it is not exempt from that fate.'[151]

25. "...That too is how a bhikkhu abides contemplating the body as a body.

26–30. "Again, as though he were to see a corpse thrown aside in a charnel ground, bones bleached white, the colour of shells... bones heaped up, more than a year old...bones rotted and crumbled to dust [59], a bhikkhu compares this same body with it thus: 'This body too is of the same nature, it will be like that, it is not exempt from that fate.'

(INSIGHT)

31. "In this way he abides contemplating the body as a body internally, or he abides contemplating the body as a body externally, or he abides contemplating the body as a body both internally and externally. Or else he abides contemplating in the body its nature of arising, or he abides contemplating in the body its nature of vanishing, or he abides contemplating in the body its nature of both arising and vanishing. Or else mindfulness that 'there is a body' is simply established in him to the extent necessary for bare knowledge and mindfulness. And he abides independent, not clinging to anything in the world. That too is how a bhikkhu abides contemplating the body as a body.

(CONTEMPLATION OF FEELING)

32. "And how, bhikkhus, does a bhikkhu abide contemplating feelings as feelings?[152] Here, when feeling a pleasant feeling, a bhikkhu understands: 'I feel a pleasant feeling'; when feeling a painful feeling, he understands: 'I feel a painful feeling'; when feeling a neither-painful-nor-pleasant feeling, he understands: 'I feel a neither-painful-nor-pleasant feeling.' When feeling a worldly pleasant feeling, he understands: 'I feel a worldly pleasant feeling'; when feeling an unworldly pleasant feeling, he understands: 'I feel an unworldly pleasant feeling'; when feeling

a worldly painful feeling, he understands: 'I feel a worldly painful feeling'; when feeling an unworldly painful feeling, he understands: 'I feel an unworldly painful feeling'; when feeling a worldly neither-painful-nor-pleasant feeling, he understands: 'I feel a worldly neither-painful-nor-pleasant feeling'; when feeling an unworldly neither-painful-nor-pleasant feeling, he understands: 'I feel an unworldly neither-painful-nor-pleasant feeling.'

(INSIGHT)

33. "In this way he abides contemplating feelings as feelings internally, or he abides contemplating feelings as feelings externally, or he abides contemplating feelings as feelings both internally and externally. Or else he abides contemplating in feelings their nature of arising, or he abides contemplating in feelings their nature of vanishing, or he abides contemplating in feelings their nature of both arising and vanishing.[153] Or else mindfulness that 'there is feeling' is simply established in him to the extent necessary for bare knowledge and mindfulness. And he abides independent, not clinging to anything in the world. That is how a bhikkhu abides contemplating feelings as feelings.

(CONTEMPLATION OF MIND)

34. "And how, bhikkhus, does a bhikkhu abide contemplating mind as mind?[154] Here a bhikkhu understands mind affected by lust as mind affected by lust, and mind unaffected by lust as mind unaffected by lust. He understands mind affected by hate as mind affected by hate, and mind unaffected by hate as mind unaffected by hate. He understands mind affected by delusion as mind affected by delusion, and mind unaffected by delusion as mind unaffected by delusion. He understands contracted mind as contracted mind, and distracted mind as distracted mind. He understands exalted mind as exalted mind, and unexalted mind as unexalted mind. He understands surpassed mind as surpassed mind, and unsurpassed mind as unsurpassed mind. He understands concentrated mind as concentrated mind, and unconcentrated mind as unconcentrated mind. He understands liberated mind as liberated mind, and unliberated mind as unliberated mind.[155]

(INSIGHT)

35. "In this way he abides contemplating mind as mind internally, or he abides contemplating mind as mind externally, or he abides contemplating mind as mind both internally and externally. Or else he abides contemplating in mind its nature of arising, [60] or he abides contemplating in mind its nature of vanishing, or he abides contemplating in mind its nature of both arising and vanishing.[156] Or else mindfulness that 'there is mind' is simply established in him to the extent necessary for bare knowledge and mindfulness. And he abides independent, not clinging to anything in the world. That is how a bhikkhu abides contemplating mind as mind.

(CONTEMPLATION OF MIND-OBJECTS)

(*1. The Five Hindrances*)

36. "And how, bhikkhus, does a bhikkhu abide contemplating mind-objects as mind-objects?[157] Here a bhikkhu abides contemplating mind-objects as mind-objects in terms of the five hindrances.[158] And how does a bhikkhu abide contemplating mind-objects as mind-objects in terms of the five hindrances? Here, there being sensual desire in him, a bhikkhu understands: 'There is sensual desire in me'; or there being no sensual desire in him, he understands: 'There is no sensual desire in me'; and he also understands how there comes to be the arising of unarisen sensual desire, and how there comes to be the abandoning of arisen sensual desire, and how there comes to be the future non-arising of abandoned sensual desire.'

"There being ill will in him...There being sloth and torpor in him...There being restlessness and remorse in him...There being doubt in him, a bhikkhu understands: 'There is doubt in me'; or there being no doubt in him, he understands: 'There is no doubt in me'; and he understands how there comes to be the arising of unarisen doubt, and how there comes to be the abandoning of arisen doubt, and how there comes to be the future non-arising of abandoned doubt.

(INSIGHT)

37. "In this way he abides contemplating mind-objects as mind-objects internally, or he abides contemplating mind-objects as mind-objects externally, or he abides contemplating mind-objects as mind-objects both internally and externally. Or else he abides contemplating in mind-objects their nature of arising, or he abides contemplating in mind-objects their nature of vanishing, or he abides contemplating in mind-objects their nature of both arising and vanishing. Or else mindfulness that 'there are mind-objects' is simply established in him to the extent necessary for bare knowledge and mindfulness. And he abides independent, not clinging to anything in the world. That is how a bhikkhu abides contemplating mind-objects as mind-objects in terms of the five hindrances.

(2. *The Five Aggregates*)

38. "Again, bhikkhus, a bhikkhu abides contemplating mind-objects as mind-objects [61] in terms of the five aggregates affected by clinging.[159] And how does a bhikkhu abide contemplating mind-objects as mind-objects in terms of the five aggregates affected by clinging? Here a bhikkhu understands: 'Such is material form, such its origin, such its disappearance; such is feeling, such its origin, such its disappearance; such is perception, such its origin, such its disappearance; such are the formations, such their origin, such their disappearance; such is consciousness, such its origin, such its disappearance.'

39. "In this way he abides contemplating mind-objects as mind-objects internally, externally, and both internally and externally...And he abides independent, not clinging to anything in the world. That is how a bhikkhu abides contemplating mind-objects as mind-objects in terms of the five aggregates affected by clinging.

(3. *The Six Bases*)

40. "Again, bhikkhus, a bhikkhu abides contemplating mind-objects as mind-objects in terms of the six internal and external bases.[160] And how does a bhikkhu abide contemplating mind-

objects as mind-objects in terms of the six internal and external bases? Here a bhikkhu understands the eye, he understands forms, and he understands the fetter that arises dependent on both; and he also understands how there comes to be the arising of the unarisen fetter, and how there comes to be the abandoning of the arisen fetter, and how there comes to be the future non-arising of the abandoned fetter.

"He understands the ear, he understands sounds...He understands the nose, he understands odours...He understands the tongue, he understands flavours...He understands the body, he understands tangibles...He understands the mind, he understands mind-objects, and he understands the fetter that arises dependent on both; and he also understands how there comes to be the arising of the unarisen fetter, and how there comes to be the abandoning of the arisen fetter, and how there comes to be the future non-arising of the abandoned fetter.

41. "In this way he abides contemplating mind-objects as mind-objects internally, externally, and both internally and externally...And he abides independent, not clinging to anything in the world. That is how a bhikkhu abides contemplating mind-objects as mind-objects in terms of the six internal and external bases.

(*4. The Seven Enlightenment Factors*)

42. "Again, bhikkhus, a bhikkhu abides contemplating mind-objects as mind-objects in terms of the seven enlightenment factors.[161] And how does a bhikkhu abide contemplating mind-objects as mind-objects in terms of the seven enlightenment factors? Here, there being the mindfulness enlightenment factor in him, a bhikkhu understands: 'There is the mindfulness enlightenment factor in me'; or there being no mindfulness enlightenment factor in him, he understands: [62] 'There is no mindfulness enlightenment factor in me'; and he also understands how there comes to be the arising of the unarisen mindfulness enlightenment factor, and how the arisen mindfulness enlightenment factor comes to fulfilment by development.

"There being the investigation-of-states enlightenment factor in him[162]...There being the energy enlightenment factor in him...There being the rapture enlightenment factor in him...There being the tranquillity enlightenment factor in him...There being the concentration enlightenment factor in him...There being the equanimity enlightenment factor in him, a bhikkhu understands: 'There is the equanimity enlightenment factor in me'; or there being no equanimity enlightenment factor in him, he understands: 'There is no equanimity enlightenment factor in me'; and he also understands how there comes to be the arising of the unarisen equanimity enlightenment factor, and how the arisen equanimity enlightenment factor comes to fulfilment by development.[163]

43. "In this way he abides contemplating mind-objects as mind-objects internally, externally, and both internally and externally...And he abides independent, not clinging to anything in the world. That is how a bhikkhu abides contemplating mind-objects as mind-objects in terms of the seven enlightenment factors.

(*5. The Four Noble Truths*)

44. "Again, bhikkhus, a bhikkhu abides contemplating mind-objects as mind-objects in terms of the Four Noble Truths.[164] And how does a bhikkhu abide contemplating mind-objects as mind-objects in terms of the Four Noble Truths? Here a bhikkhu understands as it actually is: 'This is suffering'; he understands as it actually is: 'This is the origin of suffering'; he understands as it actually is: 'This is the cessation of suffering'; he understands as it actually is: 'This is the way leading to the cessation of suffering.'

(INSIGHT)

45. "In this way he abides contemplating mind-objects as mind-objects internally, or he abides contemplating mind-objects as mind-objects externally, or he abides contemplating mind-objects as mind-objects both internally and externally. Or else he abides contemplating in mind-objects their nature of arising, or he abides contemplating in mind-objects their nature of vanishing, or he abides contemplating in mind-objects their nature of both arising and vanishing. Or else mindfulness that 'there are mind-

objects' is simply established in him to the extent necessary for bare knowledge and mindfulness. And he abides independent, not clinging to anything in the world. That is how a bhikkhu abides contemplating mind-objects as mind-objects in terms of the Four Noble Truths.

(CONCLUSION)

46. "Bhikkhus, if anyone should develop these four foundations of mindfulness in such a way for seven years, one of two fruits could be expected for him: either final knowledge here and now, or if there is a trace of clinging left, non-return.[165]

"Let alone seven years, bhikkhus. [63] If anyone should develop these four foundations of mindfulness in such a way for six years...for five years...for four years...for three years...for two years...for one year, one of two fruits could be expected for him: either final knowledge here and now, or if there is a trace of clinging left, non-return.

"Let alone one year, bhikkhus. If anyone should develop these four foundations of mindfulness in such a way for seven months...for six months...for five months...for four months...for three months...for two months...for one month...for half a month, one of two fruits could be expected for him: either final knowledge here and now, or if there is a trace of clinging left, non-return.

"Let alone half a month, bhikkhus. If anyone should develop these four foundations of mindfulness in such a way for seven days, one of two fruits could be expected for him: either final knowledge here and now, or if there is a trace of clinging left, non-return.

47. "So it was with reference to this that it was said: 'Bhikkhus, this is the direct path for the purification of beings, for the surmounting of sorrow and lamentation, for the disappearance of pain and grief, for the attainment of the true way, for the realisation of Nibbāna—namely, the four foundations of mindfulness.'"

That is what the Blessed One said. The bhikkhus were satisfied and delighted in the Blessed One's words.

2

The Division of the Lion's Roar

(*Sīhanādavagga*)

11 *Cūḷasīhanāda Sutta*
The Shorter Discourse on the Lion's Roar

1. THUS HAVE I HEARD. On one occasion the Blessed One was living at Sāvatthī in Jeta's Grove, Anāthapiṇḍika's Park. There he addressed the bhikkhus thus: "Bhikkhus."—"Venerable sir," they replied. The Blessed One said this:

2. "Bhikkhus, only here is there a recluse, only here a second recluse, only here a third recluse, only here a fourth recluse. The doctrines of others are devoid [64] of recluses: that is how you should rightly roar your lion's roar.[166]

3. "It is possible, bhikkhus, that wanderers of other sects might ask: 'But on the strength of what [argument] or with the support of what [authority] do the venerable ones say thus?' Wanderers of other sects who ask thus may be answered in this way: 'Friends, four things have been declared to us by the Blessed One who knows and sees, accomplished and fully enlightened; on seeing these in ourselves we say thus: "Only here is there a recluse, only here a second recluse, only here a third recluse, only here a fourth recluse. The doctrines of others are devoid of recluses." What are the four? We have confidence in the Teacher, we have confidence in the Dhamma, we have fulfilled the precepts, and our companions in the Dhamma are dear and agreeable to us whether they are laymen or those gone forth. These are the four things declared to us by the Blessed One who knows and sees, accomplished and fully enlightened, on seeing which in ourselves we say as we do.'

4. "It is possible, bhikkhus, that wanderers of other sects might say thus: 'Friends, we too have confidence in the Teacher, that is, in our Teacher; we too have confidence in the Dhamma, that is, in our Dhamma; we too have fulfilled the precepts, that is, our precepts; and our companions in the Dhamma are dear and agreeable to us too whether they are laymen or those gone

forth. What is the distinction here, friends, what is the variance, what is the difference between you and us?'

5. "Wanderers of other sects who ask thus may be answered in this way: 'How then, friends, is the goal one or many?' Answering rightly, the wanderers of other sects would answer thus: 'Friends, the goal is one, not many.'[167]—'But, friends, is that goal for one affected by lust or free from lust?' Answering rightly, the wanderers of other sects would answer thus: 'Friends, that goal is for one free from lust, not for one affected by lust.'—'But, friends, is that goal for one affected by hate or free from hate?' Answering rightly, they would answer: 'Friends, that goal is for one free from hate, not for one affected by hate.'—'But, friends, is that goal for one affected by delusion or free from delusion?' Answering rightly, they would answer: 'Friends, that goal is for one free from delusion, not for one affected by delusion.'—'But, friends, is that goal for one affected by craving or free from craving?' [65] Answering rightly, they would answer: 'Friends, that goal is for one free from craving, not for one affected by craving.'—'But, friends, is that goal for one affected by clinging or free from clinging?' Answering rightly, they would answer: 'Friends, that goal is for one free from clinging, not for one affected by clinging.'—'But, friends, is that goal for one who has vision or for one without vision?' Answering rightly, they would answer: 'Friends, that goal is for one with vision, not for one without vision.'—'But, friends, is that goal for one who favours and opposes, or for one who does not favour and oppose?' Answering rightly, they would answer: 'Friends, that goal is for one who does not favour and oppose, not for one who favours and opposes.'[168]—'But, friends, is that goal for one who delights in and enjoys proliferation, or for one who does not delight in and enjoy proliferation?' Answering rightly, they would answer: 'Friends, that goal is for one who does not delight in and enjoy proliferation, not for one who delights in and enjoys proliferation.'[169]

6. "Bhikkhus, there are these two views: the view of being and the view of non-being. Any recluses or brahmins who rely on the view of being, adopt the view of being, accept the view of being, are opposed to the view of non-being. Any recluses or brahmins who rely on the view of non-being, adopt the view of non-being, accept the view of non-being, are opposed to the view of being.[170]

7. "Any recluses or brahmins who do not understand as they actually are the origin, the disappearance, the gratification, the danger, and the escape[171] in the case of these two views are affected by lust, affected by hate, affected by delusion, affected by craving, affected by clinging, without vision, given to favouring and opposing, and they delight in and enjoy proliferation. They are not freed from birth, ageing, and death; from sorrow, lamentation, pain, grief, and despair; they are not freed from suffering, I say.

8. "Any recluses or brahmins who understand as they actually are the origin, the disappearance, the gratification, the danger, and the escape in the case of these two views are without lust, without hate, without delusion, without craving, without clinging, with vision, not given to favouring and opposing, and they do not delight in and enjoy proliferation. They are freed from birth, ageing, and death; from sorrow, lamentation, pain, grief, and despair; they are freed from suffering, I say. [66]

9. "Bhikkhus, there are these four kinds of clinging. What four? Clinging to sensual pleasures, clinging to views, clinging to rules and observances, and clinging to a doctrine of self.

10. "Though certain recluses and brahmins claim to propound the full understanding of all kinds of clinging, they do not completely describe the full understanding of all kinds of clinging.[172] They describe the full understanding of clinging to sensual pleasures without describing the full understanding of clinging to views, clinging to rules and observances, and clinging to a doctrine of self. Why is that? Those good recluses and brahmins do not understand these three instances of clinging as they actually are. Therefore, though they claim to propound the full understanding of all kinds of clinging, they describe only the full understanding of clinging to sensual pleasures without describing the full understanding of clinging to views, clinging to rules and observances, and clinging to a doctrine of self.

11. "Though certain recluses and brahmins claim to propound the full understanding of all kinds of clinging...they describe the full understanding of clinging to sensual pleasures and clinging to views without describing the full understanding of clinging to rules and observances and clinging to a doctrine of self. Why is that? They do not understand two instances...therefore they describe only the full understanding of clinging to sensual

pleasures and clinging to views without describing the full understanding of clinging to rules and observances and clinging to a doctrine of self.

12. "Though certain recluses and brahmins claim to propound the full understanding of all kinds of clinging...they describe the full understanding of clinging to sensual pleasures, clinging to views, and clinging to rules and observances without describing the full understanding of clinging to a doctrine of self. They do not understand one instance...therefore they describe only the full understanding of clinging to sensual pleasures, clinging to views, and clinging to rules and observances without describing the full understanding of clinging to a doctrine of self.[173]

13. "Bhikkhus, in such a Dhamma and Discipline as that, it is plain that confidence in the Teacher is not rightly directed, that confidence in the Dhamma is not rightly directed, that fulfilment of the precepts is not rightly directed, and that the affection among companions in the Dhamma is not rightly directed. Why is that? Because that is how it is when the Dhamma and Discipline is [67] badly proclaimed and badly expounded, unemancipating, unconducive to peace, expounded by one who is not fully enlightened.

14. "Bhikkhus, when a Tathāgata, accomplished and fully enlightened, claims to propound the full understanding of all kinds of clinging, he completely describes the full understanding of all kinds of clinging: he describes the full understanding of clinging to sensual pleasures, clinging to views, clinging to rules and observances, and clinging to a doctrine of self.[174]

15. "Bhikkhus, in such a Dhamma and Discipline as that, it is plain that confidence in the Teacher is rightly directed, that confidence in the Dhamma is rightly directed, that fulfilment of the precepts is rightly directed, and that the affection among companions in the Dhamma is rightly directed. Why is that? Because that is how it is when the Dhamma and Discipline is well proclaimed and well expounded, emancipating, conducive to peace, expounded by one who is fully enlightened.

16. "Now these four kinds of clinging have what as their source, what as their origin, from what are they born and produced? These four kinds of clinging have craving as their source, craving as their origin, they are born and produced from craving.[175] Craving has what as its source...? Craving has feeling as its

source...Feeling has what as its source...? Feeling has contact as its source...Contact has what as its source...? Contact has the sixfold base as its source...The sixfold base has what as its source...? The sixfold base has mentality-materiality as its source...Mentality-materiality has what as its source...? Mentality-materiality has consciousness as its source...Consciousness has what as its source...? Consciousness has formations as its source...Formations have what as their source...? Formations have ignorance as their source, ignorance as their origin, they are born and produced from ignorance.

17. "Bhikkhus, when ignorance is abandoned and true knowledge has arisen in a bhikkhu, then with the fading away of ignorance and the arising of true knowledge he no longer clings to sensual pleasures, no longer clings to views, no longer clings to rules and observances, no longer clings to a doctrine of self.[176] When he does not cling, he is not agitated. When he is not agitated, he personally attains Nibbāna. He understands: 'Birth is destroyed, the holy life has been lived, what had to be done has been done, there is no more coming to any state of being.'" [68]

That is what the Blessed One said. The bhikkhus were satisfied and delighted in the Blessed One's words.

12 *Mahāsīhanāda Sutta* The Greater Discourse on the Lion's Roar

1. THUS HAVE I HEARD. On one occasion the Blessed One was living at Vesālī in the grove outside the city to the west.

2. Now on that occasion Sunakkhatta, son of the Licchavis, had recently left this Dhamma and Discipline.[177] He was making this statement before the Vesālī assembly: "The recluse Gotama does not have any superhuman states, any distinction in knowledge and vision worthy of the noble ones.[178] The recluse Gotama teaches a Dhamma [merely] hammered out by reasoning, following his own line of inquiry as it occurs to him, and when he teaches the Dhamma to anyone, it leads him when he practises it to the complete destruction of suffering."[179]

3. Then, when it was morning, the venerable Sāriputta dressed, and taking his bowl and outer robe, went into Vesālī for alms. Then he heard Sunakkhatta, son of the Licchavis, making this statement before the Vesālī assembly. When he had wandered for alms in Vesālī and had returned from his almsround, after his meal he went to the Blessed One, and after paying homage to him, he sat down at one side and told the Blessed One what Sunakkhatta was saying.

4. [The Blessed One said:] "Sāriputta, the misguided man Sunakkhatta is angry and his words are spoken out of anger. Thinking to discredit the Tathāgata, he actually praises him; [69] for it is praise of the Tathāgata to say of him: 'When he teaches the Dhamma to anyone, it leads him when he practises it to the complete destruction of suffering.'

5. "Sāriputta, this misguided man Sunakkhatta will never infer of me according to Dhamma: 'That Blessed One is accomplished, fully enlightened, perfect in true knowledge and conduct, sublime, knower of worlds, incomparable leader of persons to be tamed, teacher of gods and humans, enlightened, blessed.'[180]

6. "And he will never infer of me according to Dhamma: 'That Blessed One enjoys the various kinds of supernormal power: having been one, he becomes many; having been many, he becomes one; he appears and vanishes; he goes unhindered through a wall, through an enclosure, through a mountain, as though through space; he dives in and out of the earth as though it were water; he walks on water without sinking as though it were earth; seated cross-legged, he travels in space like a bird; with his hand he touches and strokes the moon and sun so powerful and mighty; he wields bodily mastery even as far as the Brahma-world.'

7. "And he will never infer of me according to Dhamma: 'With the divine ear element, which is purified and surpasses the human, that Blessed One hears both kinds of sounds, the heavenly and the human, those that are far as well as near.'

8. "And he will never infer of me according to Dhamma: 'That Blessed One encompasses with his own mind the minds of other beings, other persons. He understands a mind affected by lust as affected by lust and a mind unaffected by lust as unaffected by lust; he understands a mind affected by hate as affected by hate and a mind unaffected by hate as unaffected by hate; he understands a mind affected by delusion as affected by delusion and a mind unaffected by delusion as unaffected by delusion; he understands a contracted mind as contracted and a distracted mind as distracted; he understands an exalted mind as exalted and an unexalted mind as unexalted; he understands a surpassed mind as surpassed and an unsurpassed mind as unsurpassed; he understands a concentrated mind as concentrated and an unconcentrated mind as unconcentrated; he understands a liberated mind as liberated and an unliberated mind as unliberated.'

(TEN POWERS OF A TATHĀGATA)

9. "Sāriputta, the Tathāgata has these ten Tathāgata's powers, possessing which he claims the herd-leader's place, roars his lion's roar in the assemblies, and sets rolling the Wheel of Brahmā.[181] What are the ten?

10. (1) "Here, the Tathāgata understands as it actually is the possible as possible and the impossible as impossible.[182] And that [70] is a Tathāgata's power that the Tathāgata has, by virtue

of which he claims the herd-leader's place, roars his lion's roar in the assemblies, and sets rolling the Wheel of Brahmā.

11. (2) "Again, the Tathāgata understands as it actually is the results of actions undertaken, past, future, and present, with possibilities and with causes. That too is a Tathāgata's power...[183]

12. (3) "Again, the Tathāgata understands as it actually is the ways leading to all destinations. That too is a Tathāgata's power...[184]

13. (4) "Again, the Tathāgata understands as it actually is the world with its many and different elements. That too is a Tathāgata's power...[185]

14. (5) "Again, the Tathāgata understands as it actually is how beings have different inclinations. That too is a Tathāgata's power...[186]

15. (6) "Again, the Tathāgata understands as it actually is the disposition of the faculties of other beings, other persons. That too is a Tathāgata's power...[187]

16. (7) "Again, the Tathāgata understands as it actually is the defilement, the cleansing, and the emergence in regard to the jhānas, liberations, concentrations, and attainments. That too is a Tathāgata's power...[188]

17. (8) "Again, the Tathāgata recollects his manifold past lives, that is, one birth, two births...(*as Sutta 4, §27*)...Thus with their aspects and particulars he recollects his manifold past lives. That too is a Tathāgata's power...

18. (9) "Again, with the divine eye, which is purified and surpasses the human, the Tathāgata sees beings passing away and reappearing, inferior and superior, fair and ugly, fortunate and unfortunate...(*as Sutta 4, §29*) [71]...and he understands how beings pass on according to their actions. That too is a Tathāgata's power...

19. (10) "Again, by realising for himself with direct knowledge, the Tathāgata here and now enters upon and abides in the deliverance of mind and deliverance by wisdom that are taintless with the destruction of the taints. That too is a Tathāgata's power that the Tathāgata has, by virtue of which he claims the herd-leader's place, roars his lion's roar in the assemblies, and sets rolling the Wheel of Brahmā.

20. "The Tathāgata has these ten Tathāgata's powers, possessing

which he claims the herd-leader's place, roars his lion's roar in the assemblies, and sets rolling the Wheel of Brahmā.

21. "Sāriputta, when I know and see thus, should anyone say of me: 'The recluse Gotama does not have any superhuman states, any distinction in knowledge and vision worthy of the noble ones. The recluse Gotama teaches a Dhamma [merely] hammered out by reasoning, following his own line of inquiry as it occurs to him'—unless he abandons that assertion and that state of mind and relinquishes that view, then as [surely as if he had been] carried off and put there he will wind up in hell.[189] Just as a bhikkhu possessed of virtue, concentration, and wisdom would here and now enjoy final knowledge, so it will happen in this case, I say, that unless he abandons that assertion and that state of mind and relinquishes that view, then as [surely as if he had been] carried off and put there he will wind up in hell.

(FOUR KINDS OF INTREPIDITY)

22. "Sāriputta, the Tathāgata has these four kinds of intrepidity, possessing which he claims the herd-leader's place, roars his lion's roar in the assemblies, and sets rolling the Wheel of Brahmā. What are the four?

23. "Here, I see no ground on which any recluse or brahmin or god or Māra or Brahmā or anyone else at all in the world could, in accordance with the Dhamma, accuse me thus: 'While you claim full enlightenment, you are not fully enlightened in regard to certain things.' [72] And seeing no ground for that, I abide in safety, fearlessness, and intrepidity.

24. "I see no ground on which any recluse...or anyone at all could accuse me thus: 'While you claim to have destroyed the taints, these taints are undestroyed by you.' And seeing no ground for that, I abide in safety, fearlessness, and intrepidity.

25. "I see no ground on which any recluse...or anyone at all could accuse me thus: 'Those things called obstructions by you are not able to obstruct one who engages in them.' And seeing no ground for that, I abide in safety, fearlessness, and intrepidity.

26. "I see no ground on which any recluse...or anyone at all could accuse me thus: 'When you teach the Dhamma to someone, it does not lead him when he practises it to the complete

destruction of suffering.' And seeing no ground for that, I abide in safety, fearlessness, and intrepidity.

27. "A Tathāgata has these four kinds of intrepidity, possessing which he claims the herd-leader's place, roars his lion's roar in the assemblies, and sets rolling the Wheel of Brahmā.

28. "Sāriputta, when I know and see thus, should anyone say of me...he will wind up in hell.

(THE EIGHT ASSEMBLIES)

29. "Sāriputta, there are these eight assemblies. What are the eight? An assembly of nobles, an assembly of brahmins, an assembly of householders, an assembly of recluses, an assembly of gods of the heaven of the Four Great Kings, an assembly of gods of the heaven of the Thirty-three, an assembly of Māra's retinue, an assembly of Brahmās. Possessing these four kinds of intrepidity, the Tathāgata approaches and enters these eight assemblies.

30. "I recall having approached many hundred assemblies of nobles...many hundred assemblies of brahmins...many hundred assemblies of householders...many hundred assemblies of recluses...many hundred assemblies of gods of the heaven of the Four Great Kings...many hundred assemblies of gods of the heaven of the Thirty-three...many hundred assemblies of Māra's retinue...many hundred assemblies of Brahmās. And formerly I had sat with them there and talked with them and held conversations with them, yet I see no ground for thinking that fear or timidity might come upon me there. And seeing no ground for that, I abide in safety, fearlessness, and intrepidity. [73]

31. "Sāriputta, when I know and see thus, should anyone say of me...he will wind up in hell.

(FOUR KINDS OF GENERATION)

32. "Sāriputta, there are these four kinds of generation. What are the four? Egg-born generation, womb-born generation, moisture-born generation, and spontaneous generation.

33. "What is egg-born generation? There are these beings born by breaking out of the shell of an egg; this is called egg-born generation. What is womb-born generation? There are these beings born by breaking out from the caul; this is called womb-

born generation. What is moisture-born generation? There are these beings born in a rotten fish, in a rotten corpse, in rotten porridge, in a cesspit, or in a sewer; this is called moisture-born generation. What is spontaneous generation? There are gods and denizens of hell and certain human beings and some beings in the lower worlds; this is called spontaneous generation. These are the four kinds of generation.

34. "Sāriputta, when I know and see thus, should anyone say of me...he will wind up in hell.

(THE FIVE DESTINATIONS AND NIBBĀNA)

35. "Sāriputta, there are these five destinations. What are the five? Hell, the animal realm, the realm of ghosts, human beings, and gods.[190]

36. (1) "I understand hell, and the path and way leading to hell. And I also understand how one who has entered this path will, on the dissolution of the body, after death, reappear in a state of deprivation, in an unhappy destination, in perdition, in hell.

(2) "I understand the animal realm, and the path and way leading to the animal realm. And I also understand how one who has entered this path will, on the dissolution of the body, after death, reappear in the animal realm.

(3) "I understand the realm of ghosts, and the path and way leading to the realm of ghosts. And I also understand how one who has entered this path will, on the dissolution of the body, after death, reappear in the realm of ghosts.

(4) "I understand human beings, and the path and way leading to the human world. And I also understand how one who has entered this path will, on the dissolution of the body, after death, reappear among human beings.

(5) "I understand the gods, and the path and way leading to the world of the gods. And I also understand how one who has entered this path will, on the dissolution of the body, after death, reappear in a happy destination, in the heavenly world.

(6) "I understand Nibbāna, and the path and way leading to Nibbāna. [74] And I also understand how one who has entered this path will, by realising for himself with direct knowledge, here and now enter upon and abide in the deliverance of mind

and deliverance by wisdom that are taintless with the destruction of the taints.

37. (1) "By encompassing mind with mind I understand a certain person thus: 'This person so behaves, so conducts himself, has taken such a path that on the dissolution of the body, after death, he will reappear in a state of deprivation, in an unhappy destination, in perdition, in hell.' And then later on, with the divine eye, which is purified and surpasses the human, I see that on the dissolution of the body, after death, he has reappeared in a state of deprivation, in an unhappy destination, in perdition, in hell, and is experiencing exclusively painful, racking, piercing feelings. Suppose there were a charcoal pit deeper than a man's height full of glowing coals without flame or smoke; and then a man scorched and exhausted by hot weather, weary, parched, and thirsty, came by a path going in one way only and directed to that same charcoal pit. Then a man with good sight on seeing him would say: 'This person so behaves, so conducts himself, has taken such a path, that he will come to this same charcoal pit'; and then later on he sees that he has fallen into that charcoal pit and is experiencing exclusively painful, racking, piercing feelings. So too, by encompassing mind with mind...piercing feelings.

38. (2) "By encompassing mind with mind I understand a certain person thus: 'This person so behaves, so conducts himself, has taken such a path that on the dissolution of the body, after death, he will reappear in the animal realm.' And then later on, with the divine eye, which is purified and surpasses the human, I see that on the dissolution of the body, after death, he has reappeared in the animal realm and is experiencing painful, racking, piercing feelings. Suppose there were a cesspit deeper than a man's height full of filth; and then a man [75] scorched and exhausted by hot weather, weary, parched, and thirsty, came by a path going in one way only and directed to that same cesspit. Then a man with good sight on seeing him would say: 'This person so behaves...that he will come to this same cesspit'; and then later on he sees that he has fallen into that cesspit and is experiencing painful, racking, piercing feelings. So too, by encompassing mind with mind...piercing feelings.

39. (3) "By encompassing mind with mind I understand a certain person thus: 'This person so behaves, so conducts himself,

has taken such a path that on the dissolution of the body, after death, he will reappear in the realm of ghosts.' And then later on...I see that...he has reappeared in the realm of ghosts and is experiencing much painful feeling. Suppose there were a tree growing on uneven ground with scanty foliage casting a dappled shadow; and then a man scorched and exhausted by hot weather, weary, parched, and thirsty, came by a path going in one way only and directed to that same tree. Then a man with good sight on seeing him would say: 'This person so behaves... that he will come to this same tree'; and then later on he sees that he is sitting or lying in the shade of that tree experiencing much painful feeling. So too, by encompassing mind with mind ...much painful feeling.

40. (4) "By encompassing mind with mind I understand a certain person thus: 'This person so behaves, so conducts himself, has taken such a path that on the dissolution of the body, after death, he will reappear among human beings.' And then later on...I see that...he has reappeared among human beings and is experiencing much pleasant feeling. Suppose there were a tree growing on even ground with thick foliage casting a deep shade; and then a man scorched and exhausted by hot weather, weary, parched, and thirsty, came by a path going in one way only and directed to that same tree. Then a man with good sight on seeing him would say: 'This person so behaves...that he will come to this same tree'; and then later on he sees that he is sitting or lying in the shade of that tree experiencing much pleasant feeling. So too, by encompassing mind with mind...much pleasant feeling. [76]

41. (5) "By encompassing mind with mind I understand a certain person thus: 'This person so behaves, so conducts himself, has taken such a path that on the dissolution of the body, after death, he will reappear in a happy destination, in the heavenly world.' And then later on...I see that...he has reappeared in a happy destination, in the heavenly world, and is experiencing exclusively pleasant feelings. Suppose there were a mansion, and it had an upper chamber plastered within and without, shut off, secured by bars, with shuttered windows, and in it there was a couch spread with rugs, blankets, and sheets, with a deerskin coverlet, with a canopy as well as crimson pillows for both [head and feet]; and then a man scorched and exhausted by hot

weather, weary, parched, and thirsty, came by a path going in one way only and directed to that same mansion. Then a man with good sight on seeing him would say: 'This person so behaves...that he will come to this same mansion'; and then later on he sees that he is sitting or lying in that upper chamber in that mansion experiencing exclusively pleasant feelings. So too, by encompassing mind with mind...exclusively pleasant feelings.

42. (6) "By encompassing mind with mind I understand a certain person thus: 'This person so behaves, so conducts himself, has taken such a path that by realising for himself with direct knowledge, he here and now will enter upon and abide in the deliverance of mind and deliverance by wisdom that are taintless with the destruction of the taints.' And then later on I see that by realising for himself with direct knowledge, he here and now enters upon and abides in the deliverance of mind and deliverance by wisdom that are taintless with the destruction of the taints, and is experiencing exclusively pleasant feelings.[191] Suppose there were a pond with clean, agreeable, cool water, transparent, with smooth banks, delightful, and nearby a dense wood; and then a man scorched and exhausted by hot weather, weary, parched, and thirsty, came by a path going in one way only towards that same pond. Then a man with good sight on seeing him would say: 'This person so behaves...that he will come to this same pond'; and then later on he sees that he has plunged into the pond, bathed, drunk, and relieved all his distress, fatigue, and fever and has come out again and is sitting or lying in the wood [77] experiencing exclusively pleasant feelings. So too, by encompassing mind with mind...exclusively pleasant feelings. These are the five destinations.

43. "Sāriputta, when I know and see thus, should anyone say of me: 'The recluse Gotama does not have any superhuman states, any distinction in knowledge and vision worthy of the noble ones. The recluse Gotama teaches a Dhamma [merely] hammered out by reasoning, following his own line of inquiry as it occurs to him'—unless he abandons that assertion and that state of mind and relinquishes that view, then as [surely as if he had been] carried off and put there he will wind up in hell. Just as a bhikkhu possessed of virtue, concentration, and wisdom would here and now enjoy final knowledge, so it will happen in this case, I say, that unless he abandons that assertion and that

state of mind and relinquishes that view, then as [surely as if he had been] carried off and put there he will wind up in hell.

(THE BODHISATTA'S AUSTERITIES)

44. "Sāriputta, I recall having lived a holy life possessing four factors. I have been an ascetic—a supreme ascetic; I have been coarse—supremely coarse; I have been scrupulous—supremely scrupulous; I have been secluded—supremely secluded.[192]

45. "Such was my asceticism, Sāriputta, that I went naked, rejecting conventions, licking my hands, not coming when asked, not stopping when asked; I did not accept food brought or food specially made or an invitation to a meal; I received nothing from a pot, from a bowl, across a threshold, across a stick, across a pestle, from two eating together, from a pregnant woman, from a woman giving suck, from a woman lying in the midst of men, from where food was advertised to be distributed, from where a dog was waiting, from where flies were buzzing; I accepted no fish or meat, I drank no liquor, wine, or fermented brew. I kept to one house, to one morsel; I kept to two [78] houses, to two morsels;...I kept to seven houses, to seven morsels. I lived on one saucerful a day, on two saucerfuls a day...on seven saucerfuls a day; I took food once a day, once every two days...once every seven days; thus even up to once every fortnight, I dwelt pursuing the practice of taking food at stated intervals. I was an eater of greens or millet or wild rice or hide-parings or moss or ricebran or rice-scum or sesamum flour or grass or cowdung. I lived on forest roots and fruits; I fed on fallen fruits. I clothed myself in hemp, in hemp-mixed cloth, in shrouds, in refuse rags, in tree bark, in antelope hide, in strips of antelope hide, in kusa-grass fabric, in bark fabric, in wood-shavings fabric, in head-hair wool, in animal wool, in owls' wings. I was one who pulled out hair and beard, pursuing the practice of pulling out hair and beard. I was one who stood continuously, rejecting seats. I was one who squatted continuously, devoted to maintaining the squatting position. I was one who used a mattress of spikes; I made a mattress of spikes my bed. I dwelt pursuing the practice of bathing in water three times daily including the evening. Thus in such a variety of ways I dwelt pursuing the practice of tormenting and mortifying the body. Such was my asceticism.

46. "Such was my coarseness, Sāriputta, that just as the bole of a tindukā tree, accumulating over the years, cakes and flakes off, so too, dust and dirt, accumulating over the years, caked off my body and flaked off. It never occurred to me: 'Oh, let me rub this dust and dirt off with my hand, or let another rub this dust and dirt off with his hand'—it never occurred to me thus. Such was my coarseness.

47. "Such was my scrupulousness, Sāriputta, that I was always mindful in stepping forwards and stepping backwards. I was full of pity even in regard to a drop of water thus: 'Let me not hurt the tiny creatures in the crevices of the ground.'[193] Such was my scrupulousness.

48. "Such was my seclusion, Sāriputta, that [79] I would plunge into some forest and dwell there. And when I saw a cowherd or a shepherd or someone gathering grass or sticks, or a woodsman, I would flee from grove to grove, from thicket to thicket, from hollow to hollow, from hillock to hillock. Why was that? So that they should not see me or I see them. Just as a forest-bred deer, on seeing human beings, flees from grove to grove, from thicket to thicket, from hollow to hollow, from hillock to hillock, so too, when I saw a cowherd or a shepherd...Such was my seclusion.

49. "I would go on all fours to the cow-pens when the cattle had gone out and the cowherd had left them, and I would feed on the dung of the young suckling calves. As long as my own excrement and urine lasted, I fed on my own excrement and urine. Such was my great distortion in feeding.

50. "I would plunge into some awe-inspiring grove and dwell there—a grove so awe-inspiring that normally it would make a man's hair stand up if he were not free from lust. When those cold wintry nights came during the 'eight-days interval of frost,' I would dwell by night in the open and by day in the grove.[194] In the last month of the hot season I would dwell by day in the open and by night in the grove. And there came to me spontaneously this stanza never heard before:

'Chilled by night and scorched by day,
Alone in awe-inspiring groves,
Naked, no fire to sit beside,
The sage yet pursues his quest.'

51. "I would make my bed in a charnel ground with the bones of the dead for a pillow. And cowherd boys came up and spat on me, urinated on me, threw dirt at me, and poked sticks into my ears. Yet I do not recall that I ever aroused an evil mind [of hate] against them. Such was my abiding in equanimity. [80]

52. "Sāriputta, there are certain recluses and brahmins whose doctrine and view is this: 'Purification comes about through food.'[195] They say: 'Let us live on kola-fruits,' and they eat kola-fruits, they eat kola-fruit powder, they drink kola-fruit water, and they make many kinds of kola-fruit concoctions. Now I recall having eaten a single kola-fruit a day. Sāriputta, you may think that the kola-fruit was bigger at that time, yet you should not regard it so: the kola-fruit was then at most the same size as now. Through feeding on a single kola-fruit a day, my body reached a state of extreme emaciation. Because of eating so little my limbs became like the jointed segments of vine stems or bamboo stems. Because of eating so little my backside became like a camel's hoof. Because of eating so little the projections on my spine stood forth like corded beads. Because of eating so little my ribs jutted out as gaunt as the crazy rafters of an old roofless barn. Because of eating so little the gleam of my eyes sank far down in their sockets, looking like a gleam of water that has sunk far down in a deep well. Because of eating so little my scalp shrivelled and withered as a green bitter gourd shrivels and withers in the wind and sun. Because of eating so little my belly skin adhered to my backbone; thus if I wanted to touch my belly skin I encountered my backbone, and if I wanted to touch my backbone I encountered my belly skin. Because of eating so little, if I wanted to defecate or urinate, I fell over on my face right there. Because of eating so little, if I tried to ease my body by rubbing my limbs with my hands, the hair, rotted at its roots, fell from my body as I rubbed.

53–55. "Sāriputta, there are certain recluses and brahmins whose doctrine and view is this: 'Purification comes about through food.' They say: 'Let us live on beans,'...'Let us live on sesamum,'...'Let us live on rice,' and they eat rice, they eat rice powder, [81] they drink rice water, and they make many kinds of rice concoctions. Now I recall having eaten a single rice grain a day. Sāriputta, you may think that the rice grain was bigger at that time, yet you should not regard it so: the rice grain was then at most the same size as now. Through feeding on a single rice grain a day, my body reached a state of extreme emaciation. Because of eating so little...the hair, rotted at its roots, fell from my body as I rubbed.

56. "Yet, Sāriputta, by such conduct, by such practice, by such performance of austerities, I did not attain any superhuman states, any distinction in knowledge and vision worthy of the noble ones. Why was that? Because I did not attain that noble wisdom which when attained is noble and emancipating and leads the one who practises in accordance with it to the complete destruction of suffering.

57. "Sāriputta, there are certain recluses and brahmins whose doctrine and view is this: 'Purification comes about through the round of rebirths.' But it is not easy to find a realm in the round that I have not already [82] passed through in this long journey, except for the gods of the Pure Abodes; and had I passed through the round as a god in the Pure Abodes, I would never have returned to this world.[196]

58. "There are certain recluses and brahmins whose doctrine and view is this: 'Purification comes about through [some particular kind of] rebirth.' But it is not easy to find a kind of rebirth that I have not been reborn in already in this long journey, except for the gods of the Pure Abodes...

59. "There are certain recluses and brahmins whose doctrine and view is this: 'Purification comes about through [some particular] abode.' But it is not easy to find a kind of abode that I have not already dwelt in...except for the gods of the Pure Abodes...

60. "There are certain recluses and brahmins whose doctrine and view is this: 'Purification comes about through sacrifice.' But it is not easy to find a kind of sacrifice that has not already been offered up by me in this long journey, when I was either a head-anointed noble king or a well-to-do brahmin.

61. "There are certain recluses and brahmins whose doctrine and view is this: 'Purification comes through fire-worship.' But it is not easy to find a kind of fire that has not already been worshipped by me in this long journey, when I was either a head-anointed noble king or a well-to-do brahmin.

62. "Sāriputta, there are certain recluses and brahmins whose doctrine and view is this: 'As long as this good man is still

young, a black-haired young man endowed with the blessing of youth, in the prime of life, so long is he perfect in his lucid wisdom. But when this good man is old, aged, burdened with years, advanced in life, and come to the last stage, being eighty, ninety, or a hundred years old, then the lucidity of his wisdom is lost.' But it should not be regarded so. I am now old, aged, burdened with years, advanced in life, and come to the last stage: my years have turned eighty. Now suppose that I had four disciples with a hundred years' lifespan, perfect in mindfulness, retentiveness, memory, and lucidity of wisdom.[197] Just as a skilled archer, trained, practised, and tested, could easily shoot a light arrow across the shadow of a palm tree, suppose that they were even to that extent perfect in mindfulness, retentiveness, [83] memory, and lucidity of wisdom. Suppose that they continuously asked me about the four foundations of mindfulness and that I answered them when asked and that they remembered each answer of mine and never asked a subsidiary question or paused except to eat, drink, consume food, taste, urinate, defecate, and rest in order to remove sleepiness and tiredness. Still the Tathāgata's exposition of the Dhamma, his explanations of factors of the Dhamma, and his replies to questions would not yet come to an end, but meanwhile those four disciples of mine with their hundred years' lifespan would have died at the end of those hundred years. Sāriputta, even if you have to carry me about on a bed, still there will be no change in the lucidity of the Tathāgata's wisdom.

63. "Rightly speaking, were it to be said of anyone: 'A being not subject to delusion has appeared in the world for the welfare and happiness of many, out of compassion for the world, for the good, welfare, and happiness of gods and humans,' it is of me indeed that rightly speaking this should be said."

64. Now on that occasion the venerable Nāgasamāla was standing behind the Blessed One fanning him.[198] Then he said to the Blessed One: "It is wonderful, venerable sir, it is marvellous! As I listened to this discourse on the Dhamma, the hairs of my body stood up. Venerable sir, what is the name of this discourse on the Dhamma?"

"As to that, Nāgasamāla, you may remember this discourse on the Dhamma as 'The Hair-Raising Discourse.'"[199]

That is what the Blessed One said. The venerable Nāgasamāla was satisfied and delighted in the Blessed One's words.

13 *Mahādukkhakkhandha Sutta* The Greater Discourse on the Mass of Suffering

1. THUS HAVE I HEARD. On one occasion the Blessed One was living at Sāvatthī in Jeta's Grove, Anāthapiṇḍika's Park.

2. Then, when it was morning, a number of bhikkhus dressed, and taking their bowls and outer robes, [84] went into Sāvatthī for alms. Then they thought: "It is still too early to wander for alms in Sāvatthī. Suppose we went to the park of the wanderers of other sects." So they went to the park of the wanderers of other sects and exchanged greetings with the wanderers. When this courteous and amiable talk was finished, they sat down at one side. The wanderers said to them:

3. "Friends, the recluse Gotama describes the full understanding of sensual pleasures, and we do so too; the recluse Gotama describes the full understanding of material form, and we do so too; the recluse Gotama describes the full understanding of feelings, and we do so too. What then is the distinction here, friends, what is the variance, what is the difference between the recluse Gotama's teaching of the Dhamma and ours, between his instructions and ours?"[200]

4. Then those bhikkhus neither approved nor disapproved of the wanderers' words. Without doing either they rose from their seats and went away, thinking: "We shall come to understand the meaning of these words in the Blessed One's presence."

5. When they had wandered for alms in Sāvatthī and had returned from their almsround, after the meal they went to the Blessed One, and after paying homage to him, they sat down at one side and told him what had taken place. [The Blessed One said:] [85]

6. "Bhikkhus, wanderers of other sects who speak thus should be questioned thus: 'But, friends, what is the gratification, what is the danger, and what is the escape in the case of sensual

pleasures? What is the gratification, what is the danger, and what is the escape in the case of material form? What is the gratification, what is the danger, and what is the escape in the case of feelings?' Being questioned thus, wanderers of other sects will fail to account for the matter, and what is more, they will get into difficulties. Why is that? Because it is not their province. Bhikkhus, I see no one in the world with its gods, its Māras, and its Brahmās, in this generation with its recluses and brahmins, with its princes and its people, who could satisfy the mind with a reply to these questions, except for the Tathāgata or his disciple or one who has learned it from them.

(SENSUAL PLEASURES)

7. (i) "And what, bhikkhus, is the gratification in the case of sensual pleasures? Bhikkhus, there are these five cords of sensual pleasure. What are the five? Forms cognizable by the eye that are wished for, desired, agreeable and likeable, connected with sensual desire, and provocative of lust. Sounds cognizable by the ear...Odours cognizable by the nose...Flavours cognizable by the tongue...Tangibles cognizable by the body that are wished for, desired, agreeable and likeable, connected with sensual desire, and provocative of lust. These are the five cords of sensual pleasure. Now the pleasure and joy that arise dependent on these five cords of sensual pleasure are the gratification in the case of sensual pleasures.

8. (ii) "And what, bhikkhus, is the danger in the case of sensual pleasures? Here, bhikkhus, on account of the craft by which a clansman makes a living—whether checking or accounting or calculating or farming or trading or husbandry or archery or the royal service, or whatever craft it may be—he has to face cold, he has to face heat, he is injured by contact with gadflies, mosquitoes, wind, sun, and creeping things; he risks death by hunger and thirst. Now this is a danger in the case of sensual pleasures, a mass of suffering visible here and now, having sensual pleasures as its cause, sensual pleasures as its source, sensual pleasures as its basis, [86] the cause being simply sensual pleasures.

9. "If no property comes to the clansman while he works and strives and makes an effort thus, he sorrows, grieves, and laments, he weeps beating his breast and becomes distraught,

crying: 'My work is in vain, my effort is fruitless!' Now this too is a danger in the case of sensual pleasures, a mass of suffering visible here and now...the cause being simply sensual pleasures.

10. "If property comes to the clansman while he works and strives and makes an effort thus, he experiences pain and grief in protecting it: 'How shall neither kings nor thieves make off with my property, nor fire burn it, nor water sweep it away, nor hateful heirs make off with it?' And as he guards and protects his property, kings or thieves make off with it, or fire burns it, or water sweeps it away, or hateful heirs make off with it. And he sorrows, grieves, and laments, he weeps beating his breast and becomes distraught, crying: 'What I had I have no longer!' Now this too is a danger in the case of sensual pleasures, a mass of suffering visible here and now...the cause being simply sensual pleasures.

11. "Again, with sensual pleasures as the cause, sensual pleasures as the source, sensual pleasures as the basis, the cause being simply sensual pleasures, kings quarrel with kings, nobles with nobles, brahmins with brahmins, householders with householders; mother quarrels with son, son with mother, father with son, son with father; brother quarrels with brother, brother with sister, sister with brother, friend with friend. And here in their quarrels, brawls, and disputes they attack each other with fists, clods, sticks, or knives, whereby they incur death or deadly suffering. Now this too is a danger in the case of sensual pleasures, a mass of suffering here and now...the cause being simply sensual pleasures.

12. "Again, with sensual pleasures as the cause...men take swords and shields and buckle on bows and quivers, and they charge into battle massed in double array with arrows and spears flying and swords flashing; and there they are wounded by arrows and spears, and their heads are cut off by swords, whereby they incur death or deadly suffering. Now this too is a danger in the case of sensual pleasures, a mass of suffering here and now...the cause being simply sensual pleasures.

13. "Again, with sensual pleasures as the cause...men take swords and shields and buckle on bows and quivers, and they charge slippery bastions, with arrows and spears flying [87] and swords flashing; and there they are wounded by arrows and spears and splashed with boiling liquids and crushed

under heavy weights, and their heads are cut off by swords, whereby they incur death or deadly suffering. Now this too is a danger in the case of sensual pleasures, a mass of suffering here and now…the cause being simply sensual pleasures.

14. "Again, with sensual pleasures as the cause…men break into houses, plunder wealth, commit burglary, ambush highways, seduce others' wives, and when they are caught, kings have many kinds of torture inflicted on them. The kings have them flogged with whips, beaten with canes, beaten with clubs; they have their hands cut off, their feet cut off, their hands and feet cut off; their ears cut off, their noses cut off, their ears and noses cut off; they have them subjected to the 'porridge pot,' to the 'polished-shell shave,' to the 'Rāhu's mouth,' to the 'fiery wreath,' to the 'flaming hand,' to the 'blades of grass,' to the 'bark dress,' to the 'antelope,' to the 'meat hooks,' to the 'coins,' to the 'lye pickling,' to the 'pivoting pin,' to the 'rolled-up palliasse';[201] and they have them splashed with boiling oil, and they have them thrown to be devoured by dogs, and they have them impaled alive on stakes, and they have their heads cut off with swords—whereby they incur death or deadly suffering. Now this too is a danger in the case of sensual pleasures, a mass of suffering here and now…the cause being simply sensual pleasures.

15. "Again, with sensual pleasures as the cause, sensual pleasures as the source, sensual pleasures as the basis, the cause being simply sensual pleasures, people indulge in misconduct of body, speech, and mind. Having done so, on the dissolution of the body, after death, they reappear in states of deprivation, in an unhappy destination, in perdition, even in hell. Now this is a danger in the case of sensual pleasures, a mass of suffering in the life to come,[202] having sensual pleasures as its cause, sensual pleasures as its source, sensual pleasures as its basis, the cause being simply sensual pleasures.

16. (iii) "And what, bhikkhus, is the escape in the case of sensual pleasures? It is the removal of desire and lust, the abandonment of desire and lust for sensual pleasures.[203] This is the escape in the case of sensual pleasures.

17. "That those recluses and brahmins who do not understand as it actually is the gratification as gratification, the danger as danger, and the escape as escape in the case of sensual

pleasures, can either themselves fully understand sensual pleasures or instruct another so that he can fully understand sensual pleasures—that is impossible. That those recluses and brahmins who understand as it actually is [88] the gratification as gratification, the danger as danger, and the escape as escape in the case of sensual pleasures, can either themselves fully understand sensual pleasures or instruct another so that he can fully understand sensual pleasures—that is possible.

(MATERIAL FORM)

18. (i) "And what, bhikkhus, is the gratification in the case of material form? Suppose there were a girl of the noble class or the brahmin class or of householder stock, in her fifteenth or sixteenth year, neither too tall nor too short, neither too thin nor too fat, neither too dark nor too fair. Is her beauty and loveliness then at its height?"—"Yes, venerable sir."—"Now the pleasure and joy that arise in dependence on that beauty and loveliness are the gratification in the case of material form.

19. (ii) "And what, bhikkhus, is the danger in the case of material form? Later on one might see that same woman here at eighty, ninety, or a hundred years, aged, as crooked as a roof bracket, doubled up, supported by a walking stick, tottering, frail, her youth gone, her teeth broken, grey-haired, scanty-haired, bald, wrinkled, with limbs all blotchy. What do you think, bhikkhus? Has her former beauty and loveliness vanished and the danger become evident?"—"Yes, venerable sir."—"Bhikkhus, this is a danger in the case of material form.

20. "Again, one might see that same woman afflicted, suffering, and gravely ill, lying fouled in her own urine and excrement, lifted up by some and set down by others. What do you think, bhikkhus? Has her former beauty and loveliness vanished and the danger become evident?"—"Yes, venerable sir."—"Bhikkhus, this too is a danger in the case of material form.

21. "Again, one might see that same woman as a corpse thrown aside in a charnel ground, one, two, or three days dead, bloated, livid, and oozing matter. What do you think, bhikkhus? Has her former beauty and loveliness vanished and the danger become evident?"—"Yes, venerable sir."—"Bhikkhus, this too is a danger in the case of material form.

22–29. "Again, one might see that same woman as a corpse thrown aside in a charnel ground, being devoured by crows, hawks, vultures, dogs, jackals, or various kinds of worms... [89]...a skeleton with flesh and blood, held together with sinews...a fleshless skeleton smeared with blood, held together with sinews...a skeleton without flesh and blood, held together with sinews...disconnected bones scattered in all directions—here a hand-bone, there a foot-bone, here a thigh-bone, there a rib-bone, here a hip-bone, there a back-bone, here the skull...bones bleached white, the colour of shells...bones heaped up, more than a year old...bones rotted and crumbled to dust. What do you think, bhikkhus? Has her former beauty and loveliness vanished and the danger become evident?"—"Yes, venerable sir."—"Bhikkhus, this too is a danger in the case of material form.

30. (iii) "And what, bhikkhus, is the escape in the case of material form? It is the removal of desire and lust, the abandonment of desire and lust for material form. This is the escape in the case of material form.

31. "That those recluses and brahmins who do not understand as it actually is the gratification as gratification, the danger as danger, and the escape as escape in the case of material form, can either themselves fully understand material form or instruct another so that he can fully understand material form—that is impossible. That those recluses and brahmins who understand as it actually is the gratification as gratification, the danger as danger, and the escape as escape in the case of material form, can either themselves fully understand material form or instruct another so that he can fully understand material form—that is possible.

(FEELINGS)

32. (i) "And what, bhikkhus, is the gratification in the case of feelings? Here, bhikkhus, quite secluded from sensual pleasures, secluded from unwholesome states, a bhikkhu enters upon and abides in the first jhāna, which is accompanied by applied and sustained thought, with rapture and pleasure born of seclusion.[204] On such an occasion he does not choose for his own affliction, or for another's affliction, or for the affliction of both.

[90] On that occasion he feels only feeling that is free from affliction. The highest gratification in the case of feelings is freedom from affliction, I say.

33–35. "Again, with the stilling of applied and sustained thought, a bhikkhu enters upon and abides in the second jhāna...With the fading away as well of rapture...he enters upon and abides in the third jhāna...With the abandoning of pleasure and pain he enters upon and abides in the fourth jhāna...On such an occasion he does not choose for his own affliction, or for another's affliction, or for the affliction of both. On that occasion he feels only feeling that is free from affliction. The highest gratification in the case of feelings is freedom from affliction, I say.

36. (ii) "And what, bhikkhus, is the danger in the case of feelings? Feelings are impermanent, suffering, and subject to change. This is the danger in the case of feelings.

37. (iii) "And what, bhikkhus, is the escape in the case of feelings? It is the removal of desire and lust, the abandonment of desire and lust for feelings. This is the escape in the case of feelings.

38. "That those recluses and brahmins who do not understand as it actually is the gratification as gratification, the danger as danger, and the escape as escape in the case of feelings, can either themselves fully understand feelings or instruct another so that he can fully understand feelings—that is impossible. That those recluses and brahmins who understand as it actually is the gratification as gratification, the danger as danger, and the escape as escape in the case of feelings, can either themselves fully understand feelings or instruct another so that he can fully understand feelings—that is possible."

That is what the Blessed One said. The bhikkhus were satisfied and delighted in the Blessed One's words.

14 *Cūḷadukkhakkhandha Sutta*
The Shorter Discourse on the Mass of Suffering

[91] 1. THUS HAVE I HEARD. On one occasion the Blessed One was living in the Sakyan country at Kapilavatthu in Nigrodha's Park.

2. Then Mahānāma the Sakyan[205] went to the Blessed One, and after paying homage to him, he sat down at one side and said: "Venerable sir, I have long understood the Dhamma taught by the Blessed One thus: 'Greed is an imperfection that defiles the mind, hate is an imperfection that defiles the mind, delusion is an imperfection that defiles the mind.' Yet while I understand the Dhamma taught by the Blessed One thus, at times states of greed, hate, and delusion invade my mind and remain. I have wondered, venerable sir, what state is still unabandoned by me internally, owing to which at times these states of greed, hate, and delusion invade my mind and remain."[206]

3. "Mahānāma, there is still a state unabandoned by you internally, owing to which at times states of greed, hate, and delusion invade your mind and remain; for were that state already abandoned by you internally you would not be living the home life, you would not be enjoying sensual pleasures.[207] It is because that state is unabandoned by you internally that you are living the home life and enjoying sensual pleasures.

4. "Even though a noble disciple has seen clearly as it actually is with proper wisdom how sensual pleasures provide little gratification, much suffering, and much despair, and how great is the danger in them, as long as he still does not attain to the rapture and pleasure that are apart from sensual pleasures, apart from unwholesome states, or to something more peaceful than that, he may still be attracted to sensual pleasures.[208] But when a noble disciple has seen clearly as it actually is with proper wisdom how sensual pleasures provide little gratification, much suffering, and much despair, and how great is the danger in

them, and he attains to the rapture and pleasure that are apart from sensual pleasures, apart from unwholesome states, or to something more peaceful than that, then he is no longer attracted to sensual pleasures. [92]

5. "Before my enlightenment, while I was still only an unenlightened Bodhisatta, I too clearly saw as it actually is with proper wisdom how sensual pleasures provide little gratification, much suffering, and much despair, and how great is the danger in them, but as long as I still did not attain to the rapture and pleasure that are apart from sensual pleasures, apart from unwholesome states, or to something more peaceful than that, I recognised that I still could be attracted to sensual pleasures. But when I clearly saw as it actually is with proper wisdom how sensual pleasures provide little gratification, much suffering, and much despair, and how great is the danger in them, and I attained to the rapture and pleasure that are apart from sensual pleasures, apart from unwholesome states, or to something more peaceful than that, I recognised that I was no longer attracted to sensual pleasures.

6–14. "And what is the gratification in the case of sensual pleasures? Mahānāma, there are these five cords of sensual pleasure...(*as Sutta 13, §§7–15*)...Now this is a danger in the case of sensual pleasures, a mass of suffering in the life to come, having sensual pleasures as its cause, sensual pleasures as its source, sensual pleasures as its basis, the cause being simply sensual pleasures.

15. "Now, Mahānāma, on one occasion I was living at Rājagaha on the mountain Vulture Peak. On that occasion a number of Niganṭhas living on the Black Rock on the slopes of Isigili were practising continuous standing, rejecting seats, and were experiencing painful, racking, piercing feelings due to exertion.[209]

16. "Then, when it was evening, I rose from meditation and went to the Niganṭhas there. I asked them: 'Friends, why do you practise continuous standing, rejecting seats, and experience painful, racking, piercing feelings due to exertion?'

17. "When this was said, they replied: 'Friend, the Niganṭha Nātaputta is omniscient and all-seeing and claims to have complete knowledge and vision thus: "Whether I am walking or standing or asleep or awake, [93] knowledge and vision are continuously and uninterruptedly present to me." He says thus:

"Nigaṇṭhas, you have done evil actions in the past; exhaust them with the performance of piercing austerities. And when you are here and now restrained in body, speech, and mind, that is doing no evil actions for the future. So by annihilating with asceticism past actions and by doing no fresh actions, there will be no consequence in the future. With no consequence in the future, there is the destruction of action. With the destruction of action, there is the destruction of suffering. With the destruction of suffering, there is the destruction of feeling. With the destruction of feeling, all suffering will be exhausted." This is [the doctrine] we approve of and accept, and we are satisfied with it.'

18. "When this was said, I told them: 'But, friends, do you know that you existed in the past, and that it is not the case that you did not exist?'—'No, friend.'—'But, friends, do you know that you did evil actions in the past and did not abstain from them?'—'No, friend.'—'But, friends, do you know that you did such and such evil actions?'—'No, friend.'—'But, friends, do you know that so much suffering has already been exhausted, or that so much suffering has still to be exhausted, or that when so much suffering has been exhausted all suffering will have been exhausted?'—'No, friend.'—'But, friends, do you know what the abandoning of unwholesome states is and what the cultivation of wholesome states is here and now?'—'No, friend.'

19. "'So, friends, it seems that you do not know that you existed in the past and that it is not the case that you did not exist; or that you did evil actions in the past and did not abstain from them; or that you did such and such evil actions; or that so much suffering has already been exhausted, or that so much suffering has still to be exhausted, or that when so much suffering has been exhausted all suffering will have been exhausted; or what the abandoning of unwholesome states is and what the cultivation of wholesome states is here and now. That being so, those who are murderers, bloody-handed evil-doers in the world, when they are reborn among human beings, go forth into homelessness as Nigaṇṭhas.'[210]

20. "'Friend Gotama, pleasure is not to be gained through pleasure; pleasure is to be gained through pain. [94] For were pleasure to be gained through pleasure, then King Seniya Bimbisāra of Magadha would gain pleasure, since he abides in greater pleasure than the venerable Gotama.'

"'Surely the venerable Nigaṇṭhas have uttered those words rashly and without reflection. Rather it is I who ought to be asked: "Who abides in greater pleasure, King Seniya Bimbisāra of Magadha or the venerable Gotama?"'

"'Surely, friend Gotama, we uttered those words rashly and without reflection. But let that be. Now we ask the venerable Gotama: Who abides in greater pleasure, King Seniya Bimbisāra of Magadha or the venerable Gotama?'

21. "'Then, friends, I shall ask you a question in return. Answer it as you like. What do you think, friends? Can King Seniya Bimbisāra of Magadha abide without moving his body or uttering a word, experiencing exclusively pleasure for seven days and nights?'—'No, friend.'—'Can King Seniya Bimbisāra of Magadha abide without moving his body or uttering a word, experiencing exclusively pleasure for six, five, four, three, or two days and nights?...for one day and night?'—'No, friend.'

22. "'But, friends, I can abide without moving my body or uttering a word, experiencing exclusively pleasure for one day and night...for two, three, four, five, and six days and nights...for seven days and nights.[211] What do you think, friends? That being so, who dwells in greater pleasure, King Seniya Bimbisāra of Magadha or I?'

"'That being so, [95] the venerable Gotama abides in greater pleasure than King Seniya Bimbisāra of Magadha.'"

That is what the Blessed One said. Mahānāma the Sakyan was satisfied and delighted in the Blessed One's words.

15 *Anumāna Sutta*
Inference

1. THUS HAVE I HEARD. On one occasion the venerable Mahā Moggallāna was living in the Bhagga country at Suṁsumāragira in the Bhesakalā Grove, the Deer Park. There he addressed the bhikkhus thus: "Friends, bhikkhus."—"Friend," they replied. The venerable Mahā Moggallāna said this:

2. "Friends, though a bhikkhu asks thus: 'Let the venerable ones admonish me,[212] I need to be admonished by the venerable ones,' yet if he is difficult to admonish and possesses qualities that make him difficult to admonish, if he is impatient and does not take instruction rightly, then his companions in the holy life think that he should not be admonished or instructed, they think of him as a person not to be trusted.

3. "What qualities make him difficult to admonish?

(1) Here a bhikkhu has evil wishes and is dominated by evil wishes;[213] this is a quality that makes him difficult to admonish.

(2) Again, a bhikkhu lauds himself and disparages others; this is a quality that makes him difficult to admonish.

(3) Again, a bhikkhu is angry and is overcome by anger; this is a quality…

(4) Again, a bhikkhu is angry, and resentful because of anger…

(5) Again, a bhikkhu is angry, and stubborn because of anger…

(6) Again, a bhikkhu is angry, and he utters words bordering on anger…

(7) Again, a bhikkhu is reproved, and he resists the reprover…

(8) Again, a bhikkhu is reproved, and he denigrates the reprover…

(9) Again, [96] a bhikkhu is reproved, and he counter-reproves the reprover…

(10) Again, a bhikkhu is reproved, and he prevaricates, leads the talk aside, and shows anger, hate, and bitterness...

(11) Again, a bhikkhu is reproved, and he fails to account for his conduct...

(12) Again, a bhikkhu is contemptuous and insolent...

(13) Again, a bhikkhu is envious and avaricious...

(14) Again, a bhikkhu is fraudulent and deceitful...

(15) Again, a bhikkhu is obstinate and arrogant...

(16) Again, a bhikkhu adheres to his own views, holds on to them tenaciously, and relinquishes them with difficulty; this is a quality that makes him difficult to admonish.[214]

"Friends, these are called the qualities that make him difficult to admonish.

4. "Friends, though a bhikkhu does not ask thus: 'Let the venerable ones admonish me; I need to be admonished by the venerable ones,' yet if he is easy to admonish and possesses qualities that make him easy to admonish, if he is patient and takes instruction rightly, then his companions in the holy life think that he should be admonished and instructed, and they think of him as a person to be trusted.

5. "What qualities make him easy to admonish?

(1) Here a bhikkhu has no evil wishes and is not dominated by evil wishes; this is a quality that makes him easy to admonish.

(2) Again, a bhikkhu does not laud himself nor disparage others; this is a quality...

(3) He is not angry nor allows anger to overcome him...

(4) He is not angry or resentful because of anger...

(5) He is not angry or stubborn because of anger...

(6) He is not angry, and he does not utter words bordering on anger...

(7) He is reproved, and he does not resist the reprover...

(8) He is reproved, and he does not denigrate the reprover...[97]

(9) He is reproved, and he does not counter-reprove the reprover...

(10) He is reproved, and he does not prevaricate, lead the talk aside, and show anger, hate, and bitterness...

(11) He is reproved, and he does not fail to account for his conduct...

(12) He is not contemptuous or insolent...

(13) He is not envious or avaricious...

(14) He is not fraudulent or deceitful...

(15) He is not obstinate or arrogant...

(16) Again, a bhikkhu does not adhere to his own views or hold on to them tenaciously, and he relinquishes them easily; this is a quality that makes him easy to admonish.

"Friends, these are called the qualities that make him easy to admonish.

6. "Now, friends, a bhikkhu ought to infer about himself in the following way: [215]

(1) 'A person with evil wishes and dominated by evil wishes is displeasing and disagreeable to me. If I were to have evil wishes and be dominated by evil wishes, I would be displeasing and disagreeable to others.' A bhikkhu who knows this should arouse his mind thus: 'I shall not have evil wishes and be dominated by evil wishes.'

(2–16) 'A person who lauds himself and disparages others... [98]...A person who adheres to his own views, holds on to them tenaciously, and relinquishes them with difficulty is displeasing and disagreeable to me. If I were to adhere to my own views, hold on to them tenaciously, and relinquish them with difficulty, I would be displeasing and disagreeable to others.' A bhikkhu who knows this should arouse his mind thus: 'I shall not adhere to my own views, hold on to them tenaciously, and I shall relinquish them easily.'

7. "Now, friends, a bhikkhu should review himself thus:

(1) 'Do I have evil wishes and am I dominated by evil wishes?' If, when he reviews himself, he knows: 'I have evil wishes, I am dominated by evil wishes,' then he should make an effort to abandon those evil unwholesome states. But if, when he reviews himself, he knows: 'I have no evil wishes, I am not dominated by evil wishes,' then he can abide happy and glad, training day and night in wholesome states.

(2–16) Again, a bhikkhu should review himself thus: 'Do I praise myself and disparage others?'...[99]...'Do I adhere to my own views, hold on to them tenaciously, and relinquish them with difficulty?' If, when he reviews himself, he knows: 'I adhere to my own views...,' then [100] he should make an effort to abandon those evil unwholesome states. But if, when he reviews himself, he knows: 'I do not adhere to my own views...,' then he can abide happy and glad, training day and night in wholesome states.

8. "Friends, when a bhikkhu reviews himself thus, if he sees that these evil unwholesome states are not all abandoned in himself, then he should make an effort to abandon them all. But if, when he reviews himself thus, he sees that they are all abandoned in himself, then he can abide happy and glad, training day and night in wholesome states.[216]

"Just as when a woman—or a man—young, youthful, fond of ornaments, on viewing the image of her own face in a clear bright mirror or in a basin of clear water, sees a smudge or a blemish on it, she makes an effort to remove it, but if she sees no smudge or blemish on it, she becomes glad thus: 'It is a gain for me that it is clean'; so too when a bhikkhu reviews himself thus...then he can abide happy and glad, training day and night in wholesome states."

That is what the venerable Mahā Moggallāna said. The bhikkhus were satisfied and delighted in the venerable Mahā Moggallāna's words.

16 *Cetokhila Sutta*
The Wilderness in the Heart

[101] 1. THUS HAVE I HEARD. On one occasion the Blessed One was living at Sāvatthī in Jeta's Grove, Anāthapiṇḍika's Park. There he addressed the bhikkhus thus: "Bhikkhus."—"Venerable sir," they replied. The Blessed One said this:

2. "Bhikkhus, that any bhikkhu who has not abandoned five wildernesses in the heart and not severed five shackles in the heart should come to growth, increase, and fulfilment in this Dhamma and Discipline—that is impossible.[217]

3. "What, bhikkhus, are the five wildernesses in the heart that he has not abandoned? Here a bhikkhu is doubtful, uncertain, undecided, and unconfident about the Teacher, and thus his mind does not incline to ardour, devotion, perseverance, and striving. As his mind does not incline to ardour, devotion, perseverance, and striving, that is the first wilderness in the heart that he has not abandoned.

4. "Again, a bhikkhu is doubtful, uncertain, undecided, and unconfident about the Dhamma[218]...As his mind does not incline to ardour...that is the second wilderness in the heart that he has not abandoned.

5. "Again, a bhikkhu is doubtful, uncertain, undecided, and unconfident about the Sangha...As his mind does not incline to ardour...that is the third wilderness in the heart that he has not abandoned.

6. "Again, a bhikkhu is doubtful, uncertain, undecided, and unconfident about the training...As his mind does not incline to ardour...that is the fourth wilderness in the heart that he has not abandoned.

7. "Again, a bhikkhu is angry and displeased with his companions in the holy life, resentful and callous towards them, and thus his mind does not incline to ardour, devotion, perseverance,

and striving. As his mind does not incline to ardour, devotion, perseverance, and striving, that is the fifth wilderness in the heart that he has not abandoned.

"These are the five wildernesses in the heart that he has not abandoned.

8. "What, bhikkhus, are the five shackles in the heart that he has not severed? Here a bhikkhu is not free from lust, desire, affection, thirst, fever, and craving for sensual pleasures, and thus his mind does not incline to ardour, devotion, perseverance, and striving. As his mind does not incline to ardour, devotion, perseverance, and striving, that is the first shackle in the heart that he has not severed.

9. "Again, a bhikkhu is not free from lust, desire, affection, thirst, fever, and craving for the body[219]...As his mind does not incline to ardour...that is the second shackle in the heart that he has not severed. [102]

10. "Again, a bhikkhu is not free from lust, desire, affection, thirst, fever, and craving for form...As his mind does not incline to ardour...that is the third shackle in the heart that he has not severed.

11. "Again, a bhikkhu eats as much as he likes until his belly is full and indulges in the pleasures of sleeping, lolling, and drowsing...As his mind does not incline to ardour...that is the fourth shackle in the heart that he has not severed.

12. "Again, a bhikkhu lives the holy life aspiring to some order of gods thus: 'By this virtue or observance or asceticism or holy life, I shall become a [great] god or some [lesser] god,' and thus his mind does not incline to ardour, devotion, perseverance, and striving. As his mind does not incline to ardour, devotion, perseverance, and striving, this is the fifth shackle in the heart that he has not severed.

"These are the five shackles in the heart that he has not severed.

13. "Bhikkhus, that any bhikkhu who has not abandoned these five wildernesses in the heart and severed these five shackles in the heart should come to growth, increase, and fulfilment in this Dhamma and Discipline—that is impossible.

14. "Bhikkhus, that any bhikkhu who has abandoned five wildernesses in the heart and severed five shackles in the heart should come to growth, increase, and fulfilment in this Dhamma and Discipline—that is possible.

15. "What, bhikkhus, are the five wildernesses in the heart that he has abandoned? Here a bhikkhu is not doubtful, uncertain, undecided, or unconfident about the Teacher, and thus his mind inclines to ardour, devotion, perseverance, and striving. As his mind inclines to ardour, devotion, perseverance, and striving, this first wilderness in the heart has been abandoned by him.

16. "Again, a bhikkhu is not doubtful, uncertain, undecided, or unconfident about the Dhamma...As his mind inclines to ardour...this second wilderness in the heart has been abandoned by him.

17. "Again, a bhikkhu is not doubtful, uncertain, undecided, or unconfident about the Sangha...As his mind inclines to ardour...this third wilderness in the heart has been abandoned by him.

18. "Again, a bhikkhu is not doubtful, uncertain, undecided, or unconfident about the training...As his mind inclines to ardour...this fourth wilderness in the heart has been abandoned by him.

19. "Again, a bhikkhu is not angry and displeased with his companions in the holy life, nor resentful and callous towards them, and thus his mind inclines to ardour, devotion, perseverance, and striving. [103] As his mind inclines to ardour, devotion, perseverance, and striving, this fifth wilderness in the heart has been abandoned by him.

"These are the five wildernesses in the heart that he has abandoned.

20. "What, bhikkhus, are the five shackles in the heart that he has severed? Here a bhikkhu is free from lust, desire, affection, thirst, fever, and craving for sensual pleasures, and thus his mind inclines to ardour, devotion, perseverance, and striving. As his mind inclines to ardour, devotion, perseverance, and striving, this first shackle in the heart has been severed by him.

21. "Again, a bhikkhu is free from lust, desire, affection, thirst, fever, and craving for the body...As his mind inclines to ardour...this second shackle in the heart has been severed by him.

22. "Again, a bhikkhu is free from lust, desire, affection, thirst, fever, and craving for form...As his mind inclines to ardour...this third shackle in the heart has been severed by him.

23. "Again, a bhikkhu does not eat as much as he likes until his belly is full and does not indulge in the pleasures of sleeping,

lolling, and drowsing...As his mind inclines to ardour...this fourth shackle in the heart has been severed by him.

24. "Again, a bhikkhu does not live the holy life aspiring to some order of gods thus: 'By this virtue or observance or asceticism or holy life, I shall become a [great] god or some [lesser] god,' and thus his mind inclines to ardour, devotion, perseverance, and striving. As his mind inclines to ardour, devotion, perseverance, and striving, this fifth shackle in the heart has been severed by him.

"These are the five shackles in the heart that he has severed.

25. "Bhikkhus, that any bhikkhu who has abandoned these five wildernesses in the heart and severed these five shackles in the heart should come to growth, increase, and fulfilment in this Dhamma and Discipline—that is possible.

26. "He develops the basis for spiritual power consisting in concentration due to zeal and determined striving; he develops the basis for spiritual power consisting in concentration due to energy and determined striving; he develops the basis for spiritual power consisting in concentration due to [purity of] mind and determined striving; he develops the basis for spiritual power consisting in concentration due to investigation and determined striving. And enthusiasm is the fifth.[220]

27. "A bhikkhu who thus possesses the fifteen factors including enthusiasm is [104] capable of breaking out, capable of enlightenment, capable of attaining the supreme security from bondage.[221]

"Suppose there were a hen with eight, ten, or twelve eggs, which she had covered, incubated, and nurtured properly. Even though she did not wish: 'Oh, that my chicks might pierce their shells with the points of their claws and beaks and hatch out safely!' yet the chicks are capable of piercing their shells with the points of their claws and beaks and hatching out safely.[222] So too, a bhikkhu who thus possesses the fifteen factors including enthusiasm is capable of breaking out, capable of enlightenment, capable of attaining the supreme security from bondage."

That is what the Blessed One said. The bhikkhus were satisfied and delighted in the Blessed One's words.

17 *Vanapattha Sutta*
Jungle Thickets

1. THUS HAVE I HEARD. On one occasion the Blessed One was living at Sāvatthī in Jeta's Grove, Anāthapiṇḍika's Park. There he addressed the bhikkhus thus: "Bhikkhus."—"Venerable sir," they replied. The Blessed One said this:

2. "Bhikkhus, I shall teach you a discourse on jungle thickets. Listen and attend closely to what I shall say."—"Yes, venerable sir," the bhikkhus replied. The Blessed One said this:

3. "Here, bhikkhus, a bhikkhu lives in some jungle thicket.[223] While he is living there his unestablished mindfulness does not become established, his unconcentrated mind does not become concentrated, his undestroyed taints do not come to destruction, he does not attain the unattained supreme security from bondage; and also the requisites of life that should be obtained by one gone forth—robes, almsfood, resting place, and medicinal requisites—are hard to come by. The bhikkhu [105] should consider thus: 'I am living in this jungle thicket. While I am living here my unestablished mindfulness does not become established...I do not attain the unattained supreme security from bondage; and also the requisites of life...are hard to come by.' That bhikkhu should depart from that jungle thicket that very night or that very day; he should not continue living there.

4. "Here, bhikkhus, a bhikkhu lives in some jungle thicket. While he is living there his unestablished mindfulness does not become established, his unconcentrated mind does not become concentrated, his undestroyed taints do not come to destruction, he does not attain the unattained supreme security from bondage; yet the requisites of life that should be obtained by one gone forth...are easy to come by. The bhikkhu should consider thus: 'I am living in this jungle thicket. While I am living here my unestablished mindfulness does not become established...I do

not attain the unattained supreme security from bondage; yet the requisites of life that should be obtained by one gone forth...are easy to come by. However, I did not go forth from the home life into homelessness for the sake of robes, almsfood, resting place, and medicinal requisites. Moreover, while I am living here my unestablished mindfulness does not become established...I do not attain the unattained supreme security from bondage.' Having reflected thus, that bhikkhu should depart from that jungle thicket; he should not continue living there.

5. "Here, bhikkhus, a bhikkhu lives in some jungle thicket. While he is living there his unestablished mindfulness becomes established, his unconcentrated mind becomes concentrated, his undestroyed taints come to destruction, he attains the unattained supreme security from bondage; yet the requisites of life that should be obtained by one gone forth...are hard to come by. The bhikkhu should consider thus: [106] 'I am living in this jungle thicket. While I am living here my unestablished mindfulness has become established...I have attained the unattained supreme security from bondage; yet the requisites of life...are hard to come by. However, I did not go forth from the home life into homelessness for the sake of robes, almsfood, resting place, and medicinal requisites. Moreover, while I am living here my unestablished mindfulness has become established...I have attained the unattained supreme security from bondage.' Having reflected thus, that bhikkhu should continue living in that jungle thicket; he should not depart.

6. "Here, bhikkhus, a bhikkhu lives in some jungle thicket. While he is living there his unestablished mindfulness becomes established, his unconcentrated mind becomes concentrated, his undestroyed taints come to destruction, he attains the unattained supreme security from bondage; and also the requisites of life that should be obtained by one gone forth—robes, almsfood, resting place, and medicinal requisites—are easy to come by. The bhikkhu should consider thus: 'I am living in this jungle thicket. While I am living here my unestablished mindfulness has become established...I have attained the unattained supreme security from bondage; and also the requisites of life...are easy to come by.' That bhikkhu should continue living in that jungle thicket as long as life lasts; he should not depart.

7–10. "Here, bhikkhus, a bhikkhu lives in dependence upon a certain village...[224]

11–14. "Here, bhikkhus, a bhikkhu lives in dependence upon a certain town...

15–18. "Here, bhikkhus, a bhikkhu lives in dependence upon a certain city...

19–22. "Here, bhikkhus, a bhikkhu lives in dependence upon a certain country...

23. "Here, bhikkhus, a bhikkhu lives in dependence upon a certain person...(*as in* §3) [107]...That very night or that very day, that bhikkhu should depart from that person without taking leave; he should not continue following him.

24. "Here, bhikkhus, a bhikkhu lives in dependence upon a certain person...(*as in* §4)...Having reflected thus, that bhikkhu should depart from that person after taking leave;[225] he should not continue following him.

25. "Here, bhikkhus, a bhikkhu lives in dependence upon a certain person...(*as in* §5)...Having reflected thus, that bhikkhu should continue following that person; he should not depart from him.

26. "Here, bhikkhus, a bhikkhu lives in dependence upon a certain person...(*as in* §6) [108]...That bhikkhu should continue following that person as long as life lasts; he should not depart from him even if told to go away."

That is what the Blessed One said. The bhikkhus were satisfied and delighted in the Blessed One's words.

18 *Madhupiṇḍika Sutta*
The Honeyball

1. THUS HAVE I HEARD. On one occasion the Blessed One was living in the Sakyan country at Kapilavatthu in Nigrodha's Park.

2. Then, when it was morning, the Blessed One dressed, and taking his bowl and outer robe, went into Kapilavatthu for alms. When he had wandered for alms in Kapilavatthu and had returned from his almsround, after his meal he went to the Great Wood for the day's abiding, and entering the Great Wood, sat down at the root of a bilva sapling for the day's abiding.

3. Daṇḍapāni the Sakyan, while walking and wandering for exercise, also went to the Great Wood, and when he had entered the Great Wood, he went to the bilva sapling where the Blessed One was and exchanged greetings with him. When this courteous and amiable talk was finished, he stood at one side leaning on his stick and asked the Blessed One: "What does the recluse assert, what does he proclaim?"[226]

4. "Friend, I assert and proclaim [my teaching] in such a way that one does not quarrel with anyone in the world with its gods, its Māras, and its Brahmās, in this generation with its recluses and brahmins, its princes and its people; in such a way that perceptions no more underlie that brahmin who abides detached from sensual pleasures, without perplexity, shorn of worry, free from craving for any kind of being."[227]

5. When this was said, Daṇḍapāni the Sakyan shook his head, [109] wagged his tongue, and raised his eyebrows until his forehead was puckered in three lines.[228] Then he departed, leaning on his stick.

6. Then, when it was evening, the Blessed One rose from meditation and went to Nigrodha's Park, where he sat down on a seat made ready for him and told the bhikkhus what had taken place. Then a certain bhikkhu asked the Blessed One:

7. "But, venerable sir, how does the Blessed One assert and proclaim [his teaching] in such a way that he does not quarrel with anyone in the world with its gods, its Māras, and its Brahmās, in this generation with its recluses and brahmins, its princes and its people? And, venerable sir, how is it that perceptions no more underlie the Blessed One, that brahmin who abides detached from sensual pleasures, without perplexity, shorn of worry, free from craving for any kind of being?"

8. "Bhikkhu, as to the source through which perceptions and notions [born of] mental proliferation beset a man: if nothing is found there to delight in, welcome and hold to, this is the end of the underlying tendency to lust, of the underlying tendency to aversion, [110] of the underlying tendency to views, of the underlying tendency to doubt, of the underlying tendency to conceit, of the underlying tendency to desire for being, of the underlying tendency to ignorance; this is the end of resorting to rods and weapons, of quarrels, brawls, disputes, recrimination, malicious words, and false speech; here these evil unwholesome states cease without remainder."[229]

9. That is what the Blessed One said. Having said this, the Sublime One rose from his seat and went into his dwelling.

10. Then, soon after the Blessed One had gone, the bhikkhus considered: "Now, friends, the Blessed One has risen from his seat and gone into his dwelling after giving a summary in brief without expounding the detailed meaning. Now who will expound this in detail?" Then they considered: "The venerable Mahā Kaccāna is praised by the Teacher and esteemed by his wise companions in the holy life.[230] He is capable of expounding the detailed meaning. Suppose we went to him and asked him the meaning of this."

11. Then the bhikkhus went to the venerable Mahā Kaccāna and exchanged greetings with him. When this courteous and amiable talk was finished, they sat down to one side and told him what had taken place, [111] adding: "Let the venerable Mahā Kaccāna expound it to us."

12. [The venerable Mahā Kaccāna replied:] "Friends, it is as though a man needing heartwood, seeking heartwood, wandering in search of heartwood, thought that heartwood should be sought for among the branches and leaves of a great tree standing possessed of heartwood, after he had passed over the root

and the trunk. And so it is with you, venerable sirs, that you think that I should be asked about the meaning of this, after you passed the Blessed One by when you were face to face with the Teacher. For knowing, the Blessed One knows; seeing, he sees; he is vision, he is knowledge, he is the Dhamma, he is the holy one;[231] he is the sayer, the proclaimer, the elucidator of meaning, the giver of the Deathless, the lord of the Dhamma, the Tathāgata. That was the time when you should have asked the Blessed One the meaning. As he told you, so you should have remembered it."

13. "Surely, friend Kaccāna, knowing, the Blessed One knows; seeing, he sees; he is vision...the Tathāgata. That was the time when we should have asked the Blessed One the meaning. As he told us, so we should have remembered it. Yet the venerable Mahā Kaccāna is praised by the Teacher and esteemed by his wise companions in the holy life. The venerable Mahā Kaccāna is capable of expounding the detailed meaning of this summary given in brief by the Blessed One without expounding the detailed meaning. Let the venerable Mahā Kaccāna expound it without finding it troublesome."

14. "Then listen, friends, and attend closely to what I shall say."—"Yes, friend," the bhikkhus replied. The venerable Mahā Kaccāna said this:

15. "Friends, when the Blessed One rose from his seat and went into his dwelling after giving a summary in brief without expounding the detailed meaning, that is: 'Bhikkhu, as to the source through which perceptions and notions [born of] mental proliferation beset a man: if nothing is found there to delight in, welcome, and hold to, this is the end of the underlying tendency to lust...this is the end of resorting to rods and weapons...here these evil unwholesome states cease without remainder,' I understand the detailed meaning of it to be as follows:

16. "Dependent on the eye and forms, eye-consciousness arises. The meeting of the three is contact. With contact as condition there is feeling. What one feels, that one perceives. [112] What one perceives, that one thinks about. What one thinks about, that one mentally proliferates. With what one has mentally proliferated as the source, perceptions and notions [born of] mental proliferation beset a man with respect to past, future, and present forms cognizable through the eye.[232]

"Dependent on the ear and sounds...Dependent on the nose and odours...Dependent on the tongue and flavours...Dependent on the body and tangibles...Dependent on the mind and mind-objects, mind-consciousness arises. The meeting of the three is contact. With contact as condition there is feeling. What one feels, that one perceives. What one perceives, that one thinks about. What one thinks about, that one mentally proliferates. With what one has mentally proliferated as the source, perceptions and notions [born of] mental proliferation beset a man with respect to past, future, and present mind-objects cognizable through the mind.

17. "When there is the eye, a form, and eye-consciousness, it is possible to point out the manifestation of contact.[233] When there is the manifestation of contact, it is possible to point out the manifestation of feeling. When there is the manifestation of feeling, it is possible to point out the manifestation of perception. When there is the manifestation of perception, it is possible to point out the manifestation of thinking. When there is the manifestation of thinking, it is possible to point out the manifestation of besetment by perceptions and notions [born of] mental proliferation.

"When there is the ear, a sound, and ear-consciousness...When there is the nose, an odour, and nose-consciousness...When there is the tongue, a flavour, and tongue-consciousness...When there is the body, a tangible, and body-consciousness...When there is the mind, a mind-object, and mind-consciousness...it is possible to point out the manifestation of besetment by perceptions and notions [born of] mental proliferation.

18. "When there is no eye, no form, and no eye-consciousness, it is impossible to point out the manifestation of contact. When there is no manifestation of contact, it is impossible to point out the manifestation of feeling. When there is no manifestation of feeling, it is impossible to point out the manifestation of perception. When there is no manifestation of perception, it is impossible to point out the manifestation of thinking. When there is no manifestation of thinking, it is impossible to point out the manifestation of besetment by perceptions and notions [born of] mental proliferation.

"When there is no ear, no sound, and no ear-consciousness... When there is no nose, no odour, and no nose-consciousness... When there is no tongue, no flavour, and no tongue-consciousness... When there is no body, no tangible, and no body-consciousness...When there is no mind, no mind-object, and no mind-consciousness...it is impossible to point out the manifestation of besetment by perceptions and notions [born of] mental proliferation.

19. "Friends, when the Blessed One [113] rose from his seat and went into his dwelling after giving a summary in brief without expounding the detailed meaning, that is: 'Bhikkhu, as to the source through which perceptions and notions [born of] mental proliferation beset a man: if nothing is found there to delight in, welcome, and hold to, this is the end of the underlying tendency to lust, of the underlying tendency to aversion, of the underlying tendency to views, of the underlying tendency to doubt, of the underlying tendency to conceit, of the underlying tendency to desire for being, of the underlying tendency to ignorance; this is the end of resorting to rods and weapons, of quarrels, brawls, disputes, recrimination, malicious words, and false speech; here these evil unwholesome states cease without remainder,' I understand the detailed meaning of this summary to be thus. Now, friends, if you wish, go to the Blessed One and ask him about the meaning of this. As the Blessed One explains it to you, so you should remember it."

20. Then the bhikkhus, having delighted and rejoiced in the venerable Mahā Kaccāna's words, rose from their seats and went to the Blessed One. After paying homage to him, they sat down at one side and told the Blessed One all that had taken place after he had left, adding: "Then, venerable sir, we went to the venerable Mahā Kaccāna and asked him about the meaning. [114] The venerable Mahā Kaccāna expounded the meaning to us with these terms, statements, and phrases."

21. "Mahā Kaccāna is wise, bhikkhus, Mahā Kaccāna has great wisdom. If you had asked me the meaning of this, I would have explained it to you in the same way that Mahā Kaccāna has explained it. Such is the meaning of this, and so you should remember it."

22. When this was said, the venerable Ānanda said to the Blessed One: "Venerable sir, just as if a man exhausted by hunger and weakness came upon a honeyball,[234] wherever he would taste it he would find a sweet delectable flavour; so too, venerable sir, any able-minded bhikkhu, wherever he might

scrutinize with wisdom the meaning of this discourse on the Dhamma, would find satisfaction and confidence of mind. Venerable sir, what is the name of this discourse on the Dhamma?"

"As to that, Ānanda, you may remember this discourse on the Dhamma as 'The Honeyball Discourse.'"

That is what the Blessed One said. The venerable Ānanda was satisfied and delighted in the Blessed One's words.

19 *Dvedhāvitakka Sutta*
Two Kinds of Thought

1. THUS HAVE I HEARD. On one occasion the Blessed One was living at Sāvatthī in Jeta's Grove, Anāthapiṇḍika's Park. There he addressed the bhikkhus thus: "Bhikkhus."—"Venerable sir," they replied. The Blessed One said this:

2. "Bhikkhus, before my enlightenment, while I was still only an unenlightened Bodhisatta, it occurred to me: 'Suppose that I divide my thoughts into two classes.'[235] Then I set on one side thoughts of sensual desire, thoughts of ill will, and thoughts of cruelty, and I set on the other side thoughts of renunciation, thoughts of non-ill will, and thoughts of non-cruelty.[236]

3. "As I abided thus, diligent, ardent, and resolute, [115] a thought of sensual desire arose in me. I understood thus: 'This thought of sensual desire has arisen in me. This leads to my own affliction, to others' affliction, and to the affliction of both; it obstructs wisdom, causes difficulties, and leads away from Nibbāna.' When I considered: 'This leads to my own affliction,' it subsided in me; when I considered: 'This leads to others' affliction,' it subsided in me; when I considered: 'This leads to the affliction of both,' it subsided in me; when I considered: 'This obstructs wisdom, causes difficulties, and leads away from Nibbāna,' it subsided in me. Whenever a thought of sensual desire arose in me, I abandoned it, removed it, did away with it.

4–5. "As I abided thus, diligent, ardent, and resolute, a thought of ill will arose in me...a thought of cruelty arose in me. I understood thus: 'This thought of cruelty has arisen in me. This leads to my own affliction, to others' affliction, and to the affliction of both; it obstructs wisdom, causes difficulties, and leads away from Nibbāna.' When I considered thus...it subsided in me. Whenever a thought of cruelty arose in me, I abandoned it, removed it, did away with it.

6. "Bhikkhus, whatever a bhikkhu frequently thinks and ponders upon, that will become the inclination of his mind. If he frequently thinks and ponders upon thoughts of sensual desire, he has abandoned the thought of renunciation to cultivate the thought of sensual desire, and then his mind inclines to thoughts of sensual desire. If he frequently thinks and ponders upon thoughts of ill will...upon thoughts of cruelty, he has abandoned the thought of non-cruelty to cultivate the thought of cruelty, and then his mind inclines to thoughts of cruelty.

7. "Just as in the last month of the rainy season, in the autumn, when the crops thicken, a cowherd would guard his cows by constantly tapping and poking them on this side and that with a stick to check and curb them. Why is that? Because he sees that he could be flogged, imprisoned, fined, or blamed [if he let them stray into the crops]. So too I saw in unwholesome states danger, degradation, and defilement, and in wholesome states the blessing of renunciation, the aspect of cleansing. [116]

8. "As I abided thus, diligent, ardent, and resolute, a thought of renunciation arose in me. I understood thus: 'This thought of renunciation has arisen in me. This does not lead to my own affliction, or to others' affliction, or to the affliction of both; it aids wisdom, does not cause difficulties, and leads to Nibbāna. If I think and ponder upon this thought even for a night, even for a day, even for a night and day, I see nothing to fear from it. But with excessive thinking and pondering I might tire my body, and when the body is tired, the mind becomes disturbed, and when the mind is disturbed, it is far from concentration.' So I steadied my mind internally, quieted it, brought it to singleness, and concentrated it. Why is that? So that my mind should not be disturbed.[237]

9–10. "As I abided thus, diligent, ardent, and resolute, a thought of non-ill will arose in me...a thought of non-cruelty arose in me. I understood thus: 'This thought of non-cruelty has arisen in me. This does not lead to my own affliction, or to others' affliction, or to the affliction of both; it aids wisdom, does not cause difficulties, and leads to Nibbāna. If I think and ponder upon this thought even for a night, even for a day, even for a night and day, I see nothing to fear from it. But with excessive thinking and pondering I might tire my body, and when the body is tired, the mind becomes disturbed, and when the mind is disturbed, it is far from concentration.' So I steadied my mind internally, quieted it, brought it to singleness, and concentrated it. Why is that? So that my mind should not be disturbed.

11. "Bhikkhus, whatever a bhikkhu frequently thinks and ponders upon, that will become the inclination of his mind. If he frequently thinks and ponders upon thoughts of renunciation, he has abandoned the thought of sensual desire to cultivate the thought of renunciation, and then his mind inclines to thoughts of renunciation. If he frequently thinks and ponders upon thoughts of non-ill will...upon thoughts of non-cruelty, he has abandoned the thought of cruelty to cultivate the thought of non-cruelty, and then his mind inclines to thoughts of non-cruelty.

12. "Just as in the last month of the hot season, when all the crops have been brought inside the villages, [117] a cowherd would guard his cows while staying at the root of a tree or out in the open, since he needs only to be mindful that the cows are there; so too, there was need for me only to be mindful that those states were there.

13. "Tireless energy was aroused in me and unremitting mindfulness was established, my body was tranquil and untroubled, my mind concentrated and unified.

14–23. "Quite secluded from sensual pleasures, secluded from unwholesome states, I entered upon and abided in the first jhāna...*(as Sutta 4, §§23–32)*...I directly knew: 'Birth is destroyed, the holy life has been lived, what had to be done has been done, there is no more coming to any state of being.'

24. "This was the third true knowledge attained by me in the last watch of the night. Ignorance was banished and true knowledge arose, darkness was banished and light arose, as happens in one who abides diligent, ardent, and resolute.

25. "Suppose, bhikkhus, that in a wooded range there was a great low-lying marsh near which a large herd of deer lived. Then a man appeared desiring their ruin, harm, and bondage, and he closed off the safe and good path that led to their happiness, and he opened up a false path, and he put out a decoy and set up a dummy so that the large herd of deer might later come upon calamity, disaster, and loss. But another man came desiring their good, welfare, and protection, and he reopened the safe and good path that led to their happiness, and he closed off the false path, and he removed the decoy and destroyed the

dummy, so that the large herd of deer might later come to growth, increase, and fulfilment.

26. "Bhikkhus, I have given this simile in order to convey a meaning. [118] This is the meaning: 'The great low-lying marsh' is a term for sensual pleasures. 'The large herd of deer' is a term for beings. 'The man desiring their ruin, harm, and bondage' is a term for Māra the Evil One. 'The false path' is a term for the wrong eightfold path, that is: wrong view, wrong intention, wrong speech, wrong action, wrong livelihood, wrong effort, wrong mindfulness, and wrong concentration. 'The decoy' is a term for delight and lust. 'The dummy' is a term for ignorance. 'The man desiring their good, welfare, and protection' is a term for the Tathāgata, accomplished and fully enlightened. 'The safe and good path that led to their happiness' is a term for the Noble Eightfold Path, that is: right view, right intention, right speech, right action, right livelihood, right effort, right mindfulness, and right concentration.

"So, bhikkhus, the safe and good path that leads to happiness has been reopened by me, the wrong path has been closed off, the decoy removed, the dummy destroyed.

27. "What should be done for his disciples out of compassion by a teacher who seeks their welfare and has compassion for them, that I have done for you, bhikkhus. There are these roots of trees, these empty huts. Meditate, bhikkhus, do not delay or else you will regret it later. This is our instruction to you."

That is what the Blessed One said. The bhikkhus were satisfied and delighted in the Blessed One's words.

20 *Vitakkasaṇṭhāna Sutta*
The Removal of Distracting Thoughts

1. THUS HAVE I HEARD.[238] On one occasion the Blessed One was living at Sāvatthī in Jeta's Grove, Anāthapiṇḍika's Park. There he addressed the bhikkhus thus: "Bhikkhus."—"Venerable sir," [119] they replied. The Blessed One said this:

2. "Bhikkhus, when a bhikkhu is pursuing the higher mind, from time to time he should give attention to five signs.[239] What are the five?

3. (i) "Here, bhikkhus, when a bhikkhu is giving attention to some sign, and owing to that sign there arise in him evil unwholesome thoughts connected with desire, with hate, and with delusion, then he should give attention to some other sign connected with what is wholesome.[240] When he gives attention to some other sign connected with what is wholesome, then any evil unwholesome thoughts connected with desire, with hate, and with delusion are abandoned in him and subside. With the abandoning of them his mind becomes steadied internally, quieted, brought to singleness, and concentrated. Just as a skilled carpenter or his apprentice might knock out, remove, and extract a coarse peg by means of a fine one, so too...when a bhikkhu gives attention to some other sign connected with what is wholesome...his mind becomes steadied internally, quieted, brought to singleness, and concentrated.

4. (ii) "If, while he is giving attention to some other sign connected with what is wholesome, there still arise in him evil unwholesome thoughts connected with desire, with hate, and with delusion, then he should examine the danger in those thoughts thus: 'These thoughts are unwholesome, they are reprehensible, they result in suffering.'[241] When he examines the danger in those thoughts, then any evil unwholesome thoughts connected with desire, with hate, and with delusion are abandoned

in him and subside. With the abandoning of them his mind becomes steadied internally, quieted, brought to singleness, and concentrated. Just as a man or a woman, young, youthful, and fond of ornaments, would be horrified, humiliated, and disgusted if the carcass of a snake or a dog or a human being [120] were hung around his or her neck, so too...when a bhikkhu examines the danger in those thoughts...his mind becomes steadied internally, quieted, brought to singleness, and concentrated.

5. (iii) "If, while he is examining the danger in those thoughts, there still arise in him evil unwholesome thoughts connected with desire, with hate, and with delusion, then he should try to forget those thoughts and should not give attention to them. When he tries to forget those thoughts and does not give attention to them, then any evil unwholesome thoughts connected with desire, with hate, and with delusion are abandoned in him and subside. With the abandoning of them his mind becomes steadied internally, quieted, brought to singleness, and concentrated. Just as a man with good eyes who did not want to see forms that had come within range of sight would either shut his eyes or look away, so too...when a bhikkhu tries to forget those thoughts and does not give attention to them...his mind becomes steadied internally, quieted, brought to singleness, and concentrated.

6. (iv) "If, while he is trying to forget those thoughts and is not giving attention to them, there still arise in him evil unwholesome thoughts connected with desire, with hate, and with delusion, then he should give attention to stilling the thought-formation of those thoughts.[242] When he gives attention to stilling the thought-formation of those thoughts, then any evil unwholesome thoughts connected with desire, with hate, and with delusion are abandoned in him and subside. With the abandoning of them his mind becomes steadied internally, quieted, brought to singleness, and concentrated. Just as a man walking fast might consider: 'Why am I walking fast? What if I walk slowly?' and he would walk slowly; then he might consider: 'Why am I walking slowly? What if I stand?' and he would stand; then he might consider: 'Why am I standing? What if I sit?' and he would sit; then he might consider: 'Why am I sitting? What if I lie down?' and he would lie down. By doing so he would substitute for each grosser posture one that was subtler. So too...when a

bhikkhu gives attention to stilling the thought-formation of those thoughts...his mind becomes steadied internally, quieted, brought to singleness, and concentrated.

7. (v) "If, while he is giving attention to stilling the thought-formation of those thoughts, there still arise in him evil unwholesome thoughts connected with desire, with hate, and with delusion, then, with his teeth clenched and his tongue pressed against the roof of his mouth, he should beat down, constrain, and crush mind with mind.[243] [121] When, with his teeth clenched and his tongue pressed against the roof of his mouth, he beats down, constrains, and crushes mind with mind, then any evil unwholesome thoughts connected with desire, with hate, and with delusion are abandoned in him and subside. With the abandoning of them his mind becomes steadied internally, quieted, brought to singleness, and concentrated. Just as a strong man might seize a weaker man by the head or shoulders and beat him down, constrain him, and crush him, so too...when, with his teeth clenched and his tongue pressed against the roof of his mouth, a bhikkhu beats down, constrains, and crushes mind with mind...his mind becomes steadied internally, quieted, brought to singleness, and concentrated.

8. "Bhikkhus, when a bhikkhu is giving attention to some sign, and owing to that sign there arise in him evil unwholesome thoughts connected with desire, with hate, and with delusion, then when he gives attention to some other sign connected with what is wholesome, any such evil unwholesome thoughts are abandoned in him and subside, and with the abandoning of them his mind becomes steadied internally, quieted, brought to singleness, and concentrated. When he examines the danger in those thoughts...When he tries to forget those thoughts and does not give attention to them...When he gives attention to stilling the thought-formation of those thoughts...When, with his teeth clenched and his tongue pressed against the roof of his mouth, he beats down, constrains, and crushes mind with mind, any such evil unwholesome thoughts are abandoned in him...and his mind becomes steadied internally, quieted, [122] brought to singleness, and concentrated. This bhikkhu is then called a master of the courses of thought. He will think whatever thought he wishes to think and he will not think any thought that he does not wish to think. He has severed craving,

flung off the fetters, and with the complete penetration of conceit he has made an end of suffering."[244]

That is what the Blessed One said. The bhikkhus were satisfied and delighted in the Blessed One's words.

3

The Third Division

(*Tatiyavagga*)

21 *Kakacūpama Sutta*
The Simile of the Saw

1. THUS HAVE I HEARD. On one occasion the Blessed One was living at Sāvatthī in Jeta's Grove, Anāthapiṇḍika's Park.

2. Now on that occasion the venerable Moliya Phagguna was associating overmuch with bhikkhunīs.[245] He was associating so much with bhikkhunīs that if any bhikkhu spoke dispraise of those bhikkhunīs in his presence, he would become angry and displeased and would make a case of it; and if any bhikkhu spoke dispraise of the venerable Moliya Phagguna in those bhikkhunīs' presence, they would become angry and displeased and would make a case of it. So much was the venerable Moliya Phagguna associating with bhikkhunīs.

3. Then a certain bhikkhu went to the Blessed One, and after paying homage to him, he sat down at one side and told the Blessed One what was taking place.

4. Then the Blessed One addressed a certain bhikkhu thus: "Come, [123] bhikkhu, tell the bhikkhu Moliya Phagguna in my name that the Teacher calls him."—"Yes, venerable sir," he replied, and he went to the venerable Moliya Phagguna and told him: "The Teacher calls you, friend Phagguna."—"Yes, friend," he replied, and he went to the Blessed One, and after paying homage to him, sat down at one side. The Blessed One asked him:

5. "Phagguna, is it true that you are associating overmuch with bhikkhunīs, that you are associating so much with bhikkhunīs that if any bhikkhu speaks dispraise of those bhikkhunīs in your presence, you become angry and displeased and make a case of it; and if any bhikkhu speaks dispraise of you in those bhikkhunīs' presence, they become angry and displeased and make a case of it? Are you associating so much with bhikkhunīs, as it seems?"—"Yes, venerable sir."—"Phagguna,

are you not a clansman who has gone forth out of faith from the home life into homelessness?"—"Yes, venerable sir."

6. "Phagguna, it is not proper for you, a clansman gone forth out of faith from the home life into homelessness, to associate overmuch with bhikkhunīs. Therefore, if anyone speaks dispraise of those bhikkhunīs in your presence, you should abandon any desires and any thoughts based on the household life. And herein you should train thus: 'My mind will be unaffected, and I shall utter no evil words; I shall abide compassionate for his welfare, with a mind of loving-kindness, without inner hate.' That is how you should train, Phagguna.

"If anyone gives those bhikkhunīs a blow with his hand, with a clod, with a stick, or with a knife in your presence, you should abandon any desires and any thoughts based on the household life. And herein you should train thus: 'My mind will be unaffected...' If anyone speaks dispraise in your presence, you should abandon any desires and any thoughts based on the household life. And herein you should train thus: 'My mind will be unaffected...' If anyone should give you a blow with his hand, with a clod, with a stick, or with a knife, [124] you should abandon any desires and any thoughts based on the household life. And herein you should train thus: 'My mind will be unaffected, and I shall utter no evil words; I shall abide compassionate for his welfare, with a mind of loving-kindness, without inner hate.' That is how you should train, Phagguna.

7. Then the Blessed One addressed the bhikkhus thus: "Bhikkhus, there was an occasion when the bhikkhus satisfied my mind. Here I addressed the bhikkhus thus: 'Bhikkhus, I eat at a single session. By so doing, I am free from illness and affliction, and I enjoy health, strength, and a comfortable abiding. Come, bhikkhus, eat at a single session. By so doing, you will be free from illness and affliction, and you will enjoy health, strength, and a comfortable abiding.' And I had no need to keep on instructing those bhikkhus; I had only to arouse mindfulness in them.[246] Suppose there were a chariot on even ground at the crossroads, harnessed to thoroughbreds, waiting with goad lying ready, so that a skilled trainer, a charioteer of horses to be tamed, might mount it, and taking the reins in his left hand and the goad in his right hand, might drive out and back by any road whenever he likes. So too, I had no need to

keep on instructing those bhikkhus; I had only to arouse mindfulness in them.

8. "Therefore, bhikkhus, abandon what is unwholesome and devote yourselves to wholesome states, for that is how you will come to growth, increase, and fulfilment in this Dhamma and Discipline. Suppose there were a big sāla-tree grove near a village or town, and it was choked with castor-oil weeds, and some man would appear desiring its good, welfare, and protection. He would cut down and throw out the crooked saplings that robbed the sap, and he would clean up the interior of the grove and tend the straight well-formed saplings, so that the sāla-tree grove later on would come to growth, increase, and fulfilment. So too, bhikkhus, abandon what is unwholesome and devote yourselves to wholesome states, [125] for that is how you will come to growth, increase, and fulfilment in this Dhamma and Discipline.

9. "Formerly, bhikkhus, in this same Sāvatthī there was a housewife named Vedehikā. And a good report about Mistress Vedehikā had spread thus: 'Mistress Vedehikā is gentle, Mistress Vedehikā is meek, Mistress Vedehikā is peaceful.' Now Mistress Vedehikā had a maid named Kālī, who was clever, nimble, and neat in her work. The maid Kālī thought: 'A good report about my lady has spread thus: "Mistress Vedehikā is gentle, Mistress Vedehikā is meek, Mistress Vedehikā is peaceful." How is it now, while she does not show anger, is it nevertheless actually present in her or is it absent? Or else is it just because my work is neat that my lady shows no anger though it is actually present in her? Suppose I test my lady.'

"So the maid Kālī got up late. The Mistress Vedehikā said: 'Hey, Kālī!'—'What is it, madam?'—'What is the matter that you get up so late?'—'Nothing is the matter, madam.'—'Nothing is the matter, you wicked girl, yet you get up so late!' and she was angry and displeased, and she scowled. Then the maid Kālī thought: 'The fact is that while my lady does not show anger, it is actually present in her, not absent; and it is just because my work is neat that my lady shows no anger though it is actually present in her, not absent. Suppose I test my lady a little more.'

"So the maid Kālī got up later in the day. Then Mistress Vedehikā said: 'Hey, Kālī!'—'What is it, madam?'—'What is the matter that you get up later in the day?'—'Nothing is the matter, madam.'—'Nothing is the matter, you wicked girl, yet you get up later in the day!' and she was angry and displeased, and she spoke words of displeasure. Then the maid Kālī thought: 'The fact is that while my lady does not show anger, it is actually present in her, not absent; and it is just because my work is neat that my lady shows no anger though it is actually present in her, not absent. Suppose I test my lady a little more.'

"So the maid Kālī got up still later in the day. Then Mistress Vedehikā [126] said: 'Hey, Kālī!'—'What is it, madam?'—'What is the matter that you get up still later in the day?'—'Nothing is the matter, madam.'—'Nothing is the matter, you wicked girl, yet you get up still later in the day!' and she was angry and displeased, and she took a rolling-pin, gave her a blow on the head, and cut her head.

"Then the maid Kālī, with blood running from her cut head, denounced her mistress to the neighbours: 'See, ladies, the gentle lady's work! See, ladies, the meek lady's work! See, ladies, the peaceful lady's work! How can she become angry and displeased with her only maid for getting up late? How can she take a rolling-pin, give her a blow on the head, and cut her head?' Then later on a bad report about Mistress Vedehikā spread thus: 'Mistress Vedehikā is rough, Mistress Vedehikā is violent, Mistress Vedehikā is merciless.'

10. "So too, bhikkhus, some bhikkhu is extremely gentle, extremely meek, extremely peaceful, so long as disagreeable courses of speech do not touch him. But it is when disagreeable courses of speech touch him that it can be understood whether that bhikkhu is really kind, gentle, and peaceful. I do not call a bhikkhu easy to admonish who is easy to admonish and makes himself easy to admonish only for the sake of getting robes, almsfood, a resting place, and medicinal requisites. Why is that? Because that bhikkhu is not easy to admonish nor makes himself easy to admonish when he gets no robes, almsfood, resting place, and medicinal requisites. But when a bhikkhu is easy to admonish and makes himself easy to admonish because he honours, respects, and reveres the Dhamma, him I call easy to admonish. Therefore, bhikkhus, you should train thus: 'We shall be easy to admonish and make ourselves easy to admonish because we honour, respect, and revere the Dhamma.' That is how you should train, bhikkhus.

11. "Bhikkhus, there are these five courses of speech that others may use when they address you: their speech may be timely or untimely, true or untrue, gentle or harsh, connected with good or with harm, spoken with a mind of loving-kindness or with inner hate. When others address you, their speech may be timely or untimely; when others address you, their speech may be true or untrue; when others address you, their speech may be gentle or harsh; when others address you, their speech may be connected with good [127] or with harm; when others address you, their speech may be spoken with a mind of loving-kindness or with inner hate. Herein, bhikkhus, you should train thus: 'Our minds will remain unaffected, and we shall utter no evil words; we shall abide compassionate for their welfare, with a mind of loving-kindness, without inner hate. We shall abide pervading that person with a mind imbued with loving-kindness, and starting with him,[247] we shall abide pervading the all-encompassing world with a mind imbued with loving-kindness, abundant, exalted, immeasurable, without hostility and without ill will.' That is how you should train, bhikkhus.

12. "Bhikkhus, suppose a man came with a hoe and a basket and said: 'I shall make this great earth to be without earth.' He would dig here and there, strew the soil here and there, spit here and there, and urinate here and there, saying: 'Be without earth, be without earth!' What do you think, bhikkhus? Could that man make this great earth to be without earth?"—"No, venerable sir. Why is that? Because this great earth is deep and immense; it is not easy to make it be without earth. Eventually the man would reap only weariness and disappointment."

13. "So too, bhikkhus, there are these five courses of speech... (*as in §11*)...Herein, bhikkhus, you should train thus: 'Our minds will remain unaffected...and starting with him, we shall abide pervading the all-encompassing world with a mind similar to the earth, abundant, exalted, immeasurable, without hostility and without ill will.' That is how you should train, bhikkhus.

14. "Bhikkhus, suppose a man came with crimson, turmeric, indigo, or carmine and said: 'I shall draw pictures and make pictures appear on empty space.' What do you think, bhikkhus? Could that man draw pictures and make pictures appear on empty space?"—"No, venerable sir. Why is that? Because empty space is formless and non-manifestive; it is not easy to draw

pictures there or make pictures appear there. [128] Eventually the man would reap only weariness and disappointment."

15. "So too, bhikkhus, there are these five courses of speech...Herein, bhikkhus, you should train thus: 'Our minds will remain unaffected...and starting with him, we shall abide pervading the all-encompassing world with a mind similar to empty space, abundant, exalted, immeasurable, without hostility and without ill will.' That is how you should train, bhikkhus.

16. "Bhikkhus, suppose a man came with a blazing grass-torch and said: 'I shall heat up and burn away the river Ganges with this blazing grass-torch.' What do you think, bhikkhus? Could that man heat up and burn away the river Ganges with that blazing grass-torch?"—"No, venerable sir. Why is that? Because the river Ganges is deep and immense; it is not easy to heat it up or burn it away with a blazing grass-torch. Eventually the man would reap only weariness and disappointment."

17. "So too, bhikkhus, there are these five courses of speech...Herein, bhikkhus, you should train thus: 'Our minds will remain unaffected...and starting with him, we shall abide pervading the all-encompassing world with a mind similar to the river Ganges, abundant, exalted, immeasurable, without hostility and without ill will.' That is how you should train, bhikkhus.

18. "Bhikkhus, suppose there were a catskin bag that was rubbed, well rubbed, thoroughly well rubbed, soft, silky, rid of rustling, rid of crackling, and a man came with a stick or a potsherd and said: 'There is this catskin bag that is rubbed...rid of rustling, rid of crackling. I shall make it rustle and crackle.' What do you think, bhikkhus? Could that man make it rustle or crackle with the stick or the potsherd?"—"No, venerable sir. Why is that? Because that catskin bag being rubbed...rid of rustling, rid of crackling, it is not easy to make it rustle or crackle with the stick or the potsherd. Eventually the man would reap only weariness and disappointment."

19. "So too, bhikkhus, there are these five courses of speech that others may use when they address you: their speech may be timely [129] or untimely, true or untrue, gentle or harsh, connected with good or with harm, spoken with a mind of loving-kindness or with inner hate. When others address you, their speech may be timely or untimely; when others address you, their speech may be true or untrue; when others address you,

their speech may be gentle or harsh; when others address you, their speech may be connected with good or with harm; when others address you, their speech may be spoken with a mind of loving-kindness or with inner hate. Herein, bhikkhus, you should train thus: 'Our minds will remain unaffected, and we shall utter no evil words; we shall abide compassionate for their welfare, with a mind of loving-kindness, without inner hate. We shall abide pervading that person with a mind imbued with loving-kindness; and starting with him, we shall abide pervading the all-encompassing world with a mind similar to a catskin bag, abundant, exalted, immeasurable, without hostility and without ill will.' That is how you should train, bhikkhus.

20. "Bhikkhus, even if bandits were to sever you savagely limb by limb with a two-handled saw, he who gave rise to a mind of hate towards them would not be carrying out my teaching. Herein, bhikkhus, you should train thus: 'Our minds will remain unaffected, and we shall utter no evil words; we shall abide compassionate for their welfare, with a mind of loving-kindness, without inner hate. We shall abide pervading them with a mind imbued with loving-kindness; and starting with them, we shall abide pervading the all-encompassing world with a mind imbued with loving-kindness, abundant, exalted, immeasurable, without hostility and without ill will.' That is how you should train, bhikkhus.

21. "Bhikkhus, if you keep this advice on the simile of the saw constantly in mind, do you see any course of speech, trivial or gross, that you could not endure?"—"No, venerable sir."—"Therefore, bhikkhus, you should keep this advice on the simile of the saw constantly in mind. That will lead to your welfare and happiness for a long time."

That is what the Blessed One said. The bhikkhus were satisfied and delighted in the Blessed One's words.

22 *Alagaddūpama Sutta*
The Simile of the Snake

(SETTING)

[130] 1. THUS HAVE I HEARD.[248] On one occasion the Blessed One was living at Sāvatthī in Jeta's Grove, Anāthapiṇḍika's Park.

2. Now on that occasion a pernicious view had arisen in a bhikkhu named Ariṭṭha, formerly of the vulture killers, thus: "As I understand the Dhamma taught by the Blessed One, those things called obstructions by the Blessed One are not able to obstruct one who engages in them."[249]

3. Several bhikkhus, having heard about this, went to the bhikkhu Ariṭṭha and asked him: "Friend Ariṭṭha, is it true that such a pernicious view has arisen in you?"

"Exactly so, friends. As I understand the Dhamma taught by the Blessed One, those things called obstructions by the Blessed One are not able to obstruct one who engages in them."

Then these bhikkhus, desiring to detach him from that pernicious view, pressed and questioned and cross-questioned him thus: "Friend Ariṭṭha, do not say so. Do not misrepresent the Blessed One; it is not good to misrepresent the Blessed One. The Blessed One would not speak thus. For in many ways the Blessed One has stated how obstructive things are obstructions, and how they are able to obstruct one who engages in them. The Blessed One has stated how sensual pleasures provide little gratification, much suffering, and much despair, and how great is the danger in them. With the simile of the skeleton...with the simile of the piece of meat...with the simile of the grass torch...with the simile of the pit of coals...with the simile of the dream...with the simile of the borrowed goods...with the simile of fruits on a tree...with the simile of the butcher's knife and block...with the simile of the sword stake...with the simile of the snake's head, the Blessed One has stated how sensual pleasures provide little gratification, much suffering, and much despair, and how great is the danger in them."[250]

Yet although pressed and questioned and cross-questioned by those bhikkhus in this way, the bhikkhu Ariṭṭha, formerly of the vulture killers, still obstinately adhered to that pernicious view and continued to insist upon it.

4. Since the bhikkhus were unable to detach him [131] from that pernicious view, they went to the Blessed One, and after paying homage to him, they sat down at one side and told him all that had occurred, adding: "Venerable sir, since we could not detach the bhikkhu Ariṭṭha, formerly of the vulture killers, from this pernicious view, we have reported this matter to the Blessed One."

5. Then the Blessed One addressed a certain bhikkhu thus: "Come, bhikkhu, tell the bhikkhu Ariṭṭha, formerly of the vulture killers, in my name that the Teacher calls him."—[132] "Yes, venerable sir," he replied, and he went to the bhikkhu Ariṭṭha and told him: "The Teacher calls you, friend Ariṭṭha."

"Yes, friend," he replied, and he went to the Blessed One, and after paying homage to him, sat down at one side. The Blessed One then asked him: "Ariṭṭha, is it true that the following pernicious view has arisen in you: 'As I understand the Dhamma taught by the Blessed One, those things called obstructions by the Blessed One are not able to obstruct one who engages in them'?"

"Exactly so, venerable sir. As I understand the Dhamma taught by the Blessed One, those things called obstructions by the Blessed One are not able to obstruct one who engages in them."

6. "Misguided man, to whom have you ever known me to teach the Dhamma in that way? Misguided man, have I not stated in many ways how obstructive things are obstructions, and how they are able to obstruct one who engages in them? I have stated how sensual pleasures provide little gratification, much suffering, and much despair, and how great is the danger in them. With the simile of the skeleton...with the simile of the piece of meat...with the simile of the grass torch...with the simile of the pit of coals...with the simile of the dream...with the simile of the borrowed goods...with the simile of fruits on a tree...with the simile of the butcher's knife and block...with the simile of the sword stake...with the simile of the snake's head, I have stated how sensual pleasures provide little gratification,

much suffering, and much despair, and how great is the danger in them. But you, misguided man, have misrepresented us by your wrong grasp and injured yourself and stored up much demerit; for this will lead to your harm and suffering for a long time."[251]

7. Then the Blessed One addressed the bhikkhus thus: "Bhikkhus, what do you think? Has this bhikkhu Ariṭṭha, formerly of the vulture killers, kindled even a spark of wisdom in this Dhamma and Discipline?"

"How could he, venerable sir? No, venerable sir."

When this was said, the bhikkhu Ariṭṭha, formerly of the vulture killers, sat silent, dismayed, with shoulders drooping and head down, glum, and without response. Then, knowing this, the Blessed One told him: "Misguided man, you will be recognised by your own pernicious view. I shall question the bhikkhus on this matter."

8. Then the Blessed One addressed the bhikkhus thus: "Bhikkhus, [133] do you understand the Dhamma taught by me as this bhikkhu Ariṭṭha, formerly of the vulture killers, does when he misrepresents us by his wrong grasp and injures himself and stores up much demerit?"

"No, venerable sir. For in many ways the Blessed One has stated how obstructive things are obstructions, and how they are able to obstruct one who engages in them. The Blessed One has stated how sensual pleasures provide little gratification, much suffering, and much despair, and how great is the danger in them. With the simile of the skeleton...with the simile of the snake's head, the Blessed One has stated...how great is the danger in them."

"Good, bhikkhus. It is good that you understand the Dhamma taught by me thus. For in many ways I have stated how obstructive things are obstructions, and how they are able to obstruct one who engages in them. I have stated how sensual pleasures provide little gratification, much suffering, and much despair, and how great is the danger in them. With the simile of the skeleton...with the simile of the snake's head, I have stated...how great is the danger in them. But this bhikkhu Ariṭṭha, formerly of the vulture killers, misrepresents us by his wrong grasp and injures himself and stores up much demerit; for this will lead to this misguided man's harm and suffering for a long time.

9. "Bhikkhus, that one can engage in sensual pleasures without sensual desires, without perceptions of sensual desire, without thoughts of sensual desire—that is impossible.[252]

(THE SIMILE OF THE SNAKE)

10. "Here, bhikkhus, some misguided men learn the Dhamma—discourses, stanzas, expositions, verses, exclamations, sayings, birth stories, marvels, and answers to questions—but having learned the Dhamma, they do not examine the meaning of those teachings with wisdom. Not examining the meaning of those teachings with wisdom, they do not gain a reflective acceptance of them. Instead they learn the Dhamma only for the sake of criticising others and for winning in debates, and they do not experience the good for the sake of which they learned the Dhamma. Those teachings, being wrongly grasped by them, conduce to their harm and suffering for a long time.[253] Why is that? Because of the wrong grasp of those teachings.

"Suppose a man needing a snake, seeking a snake, wandering in search of a snake, saw a large snake and grasped its coils or its tail. It would turn back on him and bite his hand or his arm or one of his limbs, [134] and because of that he would come to death or deadly suffering. Why is that? Because of his wrong grasp of the snake. So too, here some misguided men learn the Dhamma...Why is that? Because of the wrong grasp of those teachings.

11. "Here, bhikkhus, some clansmen learn the Dhamma—discourses...answers to questions—and having learned the Dhamma, they examine the meaning of those teachings with wisdom. Examining the meaning of those teachings with wisdom, they gain a reflective acceptance of them. They do not learn the Dhamma for the sake of criticising others and for winning in debates, and they experience the good for the sake of which they learned the Dhamma. Those teachings, being rightly grasped by them, conduce to their welfare and happiness for a long time. Why is that? Because of the right grasp of those teachings.

"Suppose a man needing a snake, seeking a snake, wandering in search of a snake, saw a large snake and caught it rightly with a cleft stick, and having done so, grasped it rightly by the neck. Then although the snake might wrap its coils round his hand or his arm or his limbs, still he would not come to death or deadly suffering because of that. Why is that? Because of his right grasp of the snake. So too, here some clansmen learn the Dhamma... Why is that? Because of the right grasp of those teachings.

12. "Therefore, bhikkhus, when you understand the meaning of my statements, remember it accordingly; and when you do not understand the meaning of my statements, then ask either me about it or those bhikkhus who are wise.

(THE SIMILE OF THE RAFT)

13. "Bhikkhus, I shall show you how the Dhamma is similar to a raft, being for the purpose of crossing over, not for the purpose of grasping.[254] Listen and attend closely to what I shall say."—"Yes, venerable sir," the bhikkhus replied. The Blessed One said this:

"Bhikkhus, suppose a man in the course of a journey saw a great expanse of water, whose near shore was dangerous and fearful and whose further shore was safe and free from fear, but there was no ferryboat or bridge for going to the far shore. [135] Then he thought: 'There is this great expanse of water, whose near shore is dangerous and fearful and whose further shore is safe and free from fear, but there is no ferryboat or bridge for going to the far shore. Suppose I collect grass, twigs, branches, and leaves and bind them together into a raft, and supported by the raft and making an effort with my hands and feet, I got safely across to the far shore.' And then the man collected grass, twigs, branches, and leaves and bound them together into a raft, and supported by the raft and making an effort with his hands and feet, he got safely across to the far shore. Then, when he had got across and had arrived at the far shore, he might think thus: 'This raft has been very helpful to me, since supported by it and making an effort with my hands and feet, I got safely across to the far shore. Suppose I were to hoist it on my head or load it on my shoulder, and then go wherever I want.' Now, bhikkhus, what do you think? By doing so, would that man be doing what should be done with that raft?"

"No, venerable sir."

"By doing what would that man be doing what should be done with that raft? Here, bhikkhus, when that man got across and had arrived at the far shore, he might think thus: 'This raft has been very helpful to me, since supported by it and making an effort with my hands and feet, I got safely across to the far shore. Suppose I were to haul it onto the dry land or set it adrift in the water, and then go wherever I want.' Now, bhikkhus, it is by so doing that that man would be doing what should be done with that raft. So I have shown you how the Dhamma is similar to a raft, being for the purpose of crossing over, not for the purpose of grasping.

14. "Bhikkhus, when you know the Dhamma to be similar to a raft, you should abandon even the teachings, how much more so things contrary to the teachings.[255]

(STANDPOINTS FOR VIEWS)

15. "Bhikkhus, there are these six standpoints for views.[256] What are the six? Here, bhikkhus, an untaught ordinary person, who has no regard for noble ones and is unskilled and undisciplined in their Dhamma, who has no regard for true men and is unskilled and undisciplined in their Dhamma, regards material form thus: 'This is mine, this I am, this is my self.'[257] He regards feeling thus: 'This is mine, this I am, this is my self.' He regards perception thus: 'This is mine, this I am, this is my self.' He regards formations thus: 'This is mine, this I am, this is my self.' He regards what is seen, heard, sensed, cognized, encountered, sought, mentally pondered thus: 'This is mine, this I am, this is my self.'[258] And this standpoint for views, namely, 'That which is the self is the world; after death I shall be permanent, everlasting, eternal, not subject to change; [136] I shall endure as long as eternity'—this too he regards thus: 'This is mine, this I am, this is my self.'[259]

16. "Bhikkhus, a well-taught noble disciple who has regard for noble ones and is skilled and disciplined in their Dhamma, who has regard for true men and is skilled and disciplined in their Dhamma, regards material form thus: 'This is not mine, this I am not, this is not my self.' He regards feeling thus: 'This is not mine, this I am not, this is not my self.' He regards perception thus: 'This is not mine, this I am not, this is not my self.' He regards formations thus: 'This is not mine, this I am not, this is not my self.' He regards what is seen, heard, sensed, cognized, encountered, sought, mentally pondered thus: 'This is not mine,

this I am not, this is not my self.' And this standpoint for views, namely, 'That which is the self is the world; after death I shall be permanent, everlasting, eternal, not subject to change; I shall endure as long as eternity'—this too he regards thus: 'This is not mine, this I am not, this is not my self.'

17. "Since he regards them thus, he is not agitated about what is non-existent."[260]

(AGITATION)

18. When this was said, a certain bhikkhu asked the Blessed One: "Venerable sir, can there be agitation about what is non-existent externally?"

"There can be, bhikkhu," the Blessed One said. "Here, bhikkhu, someone thinks thus: 'Alas, I had it! Alas, I have it no longer! Alas, may I have it! Alas, I do not get it!' Then he sorrows, grieves, and laments, he weeps beating his breast and becomes distraught. That is how there is agitation about what is non-existent externally."

19. "Venerable sir, can there be no agitation about what is non-existent externally?"

"There can be, bhikkhu," the Blessed One said. "Here, bhikkhu, someone does not think thus: 'Alas I had it! Alas, I have it no longer! Alas, may I have it! Alas, I do not get it!' Then he does not sorrow, grieve, and lament, he does not weep beating his breast and become distraught. That is how there is no agitation about what is non-existent externally."

20. "Venerable sir, can there be agitation about what is non-existent internally?"

"There can be, bhikkhu," the Blessed One said. "Here, bhikkhu, someone has the view: 'That which is the self is the world; after death I shall be permanent, everlasting, eternal, not subject to change; I shall endure as long as eternity.' He hears the Tathāgata or a disciple of the Tathāgata teaching the Dhamma for the elimination of all standpoints, decisions, obsessions, adherences, and underlying tendencies, for the stilling of all formations, for the relinquishing of all attachments, for the destruction of craving, for dispassion, for cessation, for Nibbāna. He [137] thinks thus: 'So I shall be annihilated! So I shall perish! So I shall be no more!' Then he sorrows, grieves, and laments, he weeps beating his breast and becomes distraught. That is how there is agitation about what is non-existent internally."

21. "Venerable sir, can there be no agitation about what is non-existent internally?"

"There can be, bhikkhu," the Blessed One said. "Here, bhikkhu, someone does not have the view: 'That which is the self is the world...I shall endure as long as eternity.' He hears the Tathāgata or a disciple of the Tathāgata teaching the Dhamma for the elimination of all standpoints, decisions, obsessions, adherences, and underlying tendencies, for the stilling of all formations, for the relinquishing of all attachments, for the destruction of craving, for dispassion, for cessation, for Nibbāna. He does not think thus: 'So I shall be annihilated! So I shall perish! So I shall be no more!' Then he does not sorrow, grieve, and lament, he does not weep beating his breast and become distraught. That is how there is no agitation about what is non-existent internally.

(IMPERMANENCE AND NOT SELF)

22. "Bhikkhus, you may well acquire that possession that is permanent, everlasting, eternal, not subject to change, and that might endure as long as eternity.[261] But do you see any such possession, bhikkhus?"—"No, venerable sir."—"Good, bhikkhus. I too do not see any possession that is permanent, everlasting, eternal, not subject to change, and that might endure as long as eternity.

23. "Bhikkhus, you may well cling to that doctrine of self that would not arouse sorrow, lamentation, pain, grief, and despair in one who clings to it.[262] But do you see any such doctrine of self, bhikkhus?"—"No, venerable sir."—"Good, bhikkhus. I too do not see any doctrine of self that would not arouse sorrow, lamentation, pain, grief, and despair in one who clings to it.

24. "Bhikkhus, you may well take as a support that view that would not arouse sorrow, lamentation, pain, grief, and despair in one who takes it as a support.[263] But do you see any such support of views, bhikkhus?"—"No, venerable sir."—"Good, bhikkhus. I too do not see any support of views [138] that would not arouse sorrow, lamentation, pain, grief, and despair in one who takes it as a support.

25. "Bhikkhus, there being a self, would there be for me what belongs to a self?"[264]—"Yes, venerable sir."—"Or, there being what belongs to a self, would there be for me a self?"—"Yes, venerable sir."—"Bhikkhus, since a self and what belongs to a self are not apprehended as true and established, then this standpoint for views, namely, 'That which is the self is the world; after death I shall be permanent, everlasting, eternal, not subject to change; I shall endure as long as eternity'—would it not be an utterly and completely foolish teaching?"

"What else could it be, venerable sir, but an utterly and completely foolish teaching?"

26. "Bhikkhus, what do you think? Is material form permanent or impermanent?"—"Impermanent, venerable sir."—"Is what is impermanent suffering or happiness?"—"Suffering, venerable sir."—"Is what is impermanent, suffering, and subject to change, fit to be regarded thus: 'This is mine, this I am, this is my self'?"—"No, venerable sir."

"Bhikkhus, what do you think? Is feeling...Is perception... Are formations...Is consciousness permanent or impermanent?"—"Impermanent, venerable sir."—"Is what is impermanent suffering or happiness?"—"Suffering, venerable sir."—"Is what is impermanent, suffering, and subject to change, fit to be regarded thus: 'This is mine, this I am, this is my self'?"—"No, venerable sir."

27. "Therefore, bhikkhus, any kind of material form whatever, whether past, future, or present, internal or external, [139] gross or subtle, inferior or superior, far or near, all material form should be seen as it actually is with proper wisdom thus: 'This is not mine, this I am not, this is not my self.' Any kind of feeling whatever...Any kind of perception whatever...Any kind of formations whatever...Any kind of consciousness whatever, whether past, future, or present, internal or external, gross or subtle, inferior or superior, far or near, all consciousness should be seen as it actually is with proper wisdom thus: 'This is not mine, this I am not, this is not my self.'

28. "Seeing thus, bhikkhus, a well-taught noble disciple becomes disenchanted with material form, disenchanted with feeling, disenchanted with perception, disenchanted with formations, disenchanted with consciousness.

29. "Being disenchanted, he becomes dispassionate. Through

dispassion [his mind] is liberated.[265] When it is liberated there comes the knowledge: 'It is liberated.' He understands: 'Birth is destroyed, the holy life has been lived, what had to be done has been done, there is no more coming to any state of being.'

(THE ARAHANT)

30. "Bhikkhus, this bhikkhu is called one whose shaft has been lifted, whose trench has been filled in, whose pillar has been uprooted, one who has no bar, a noble one whose banner is lowered, whose burden is lowered, who is unfettered.

31. "And how is the bhikkhu one whose shaft has been lifted? Here the bhikkhu has abandoned ignorance, has cut it off at the root, made it like a palm stump, done away with it, so that it is no longer subject to future arising. That is how the bhikkhu is one whose shaft has been lifted.

32. "And how is the bhikkhu one whose trench has been filled in? Here the bhikkhu has abandoned the round of births that brings renewed being, has cut it off at the root...so that it is no longer subject to future arising. That is how the bhikkhu is one whose trench has been filled in.

33. "And how is the bhikkhu one whose pillar has been uprooted? Here the bhikkhu has abandoned craving, has cut it off at the root...so that it is no longer subject to future arising. That is how the bhikkhu is one whose pillar has been uprooted.

34. "And how is the bhikkhu one who has no bar? Here the bhikkhu has abandoned the five lower fetters, has cut them off at the root...so that they are no longer subject to future arising. That is how the bhikkhu is one who has no bar.

35. "And how is the bhikkhu a noble one whose banner is lowered, whose burden is lowered, who is unfettered? Here a bhikkhu has abandoned the conceit 'I am,' has cut it off at the root [140]...so that it is no longer subject to future arising. That is how the bhikkhu is a noble one whose banner is lowered, whose burden is lowered, who is unfettered.

36. "Bhikkhus, when the gods with Indra, with Brahmā and with Pajāpati seek a bhikkhu who is thus liberated in mind, they do not find [anything of which they could say]: 'The consciousness of one thus gone is supported by this.' Why is that? One thus gone, I say, is untraceable here and now.[266]

(MISREPRESENTATION OF THE TATHĀGATA)

37. "So saying, bhikkhus, so proclaiming, I have been baselessly, vainly, falsely, and wrongly misrepresented by some recluses and brahmins thus: 'The recluse Gotama is one who leads astray; he teaches the annihilation, the destruction, the extermination of an existing being.'[267] As I am not, as I do not proclaim, so have I been baselessly, vainly, falsely, and wrongly misrepresented by some recluses and brahmins thus: 'The recluse Gotama is one who leads astray; he teaches the annihilation, the destruction, the extermination of an existing being.'

38. "Bhikkhus, both formerly and now what I teach is suffering and the cessation of suffering.[268] If others abuse, revile, scold, and harass the Tathāgata for that, the Tathāgata on that account feels no annoyance, bitterness, or dejection of the heart. And if others honour, respect, revere, and venerate the Tathāgata for that, the Tathāgata on that account feels no delight, joy, or elation of the heart. If others honour, respect, revere, and venerate the Tathāgata for that, the Tathāgata on that account thinks thus: 'They perform such services as these towards that which earlier was fully understood.'[269]

39. "Therefore, bhikkhus, if others abuse, revile, scold, and harass you, on that account you should not entertain any annoyance, bitterness, or dejection of the heart. And if others honour, respect, revere, and venerate you, on that account you should not entertain any delight, joy, or elation of the heart. If others honour, respect, revere, and venerate you, on that account you should think thus: 'They perform such services as these towards that which earlier was fully understood.'

(NOT YOURS)

40. "Therefore, bhikkhus, whatever is not yours, abandon it; when you have abandoned it, that will lead to your welfare and happiness for a long time. What is it that is not yours? Material form is not yours. Abandon it. When you have abandoned it, that will lead to your welfare and happiness for a long time. Feeling is not yours. [141] Abandon it. When you have abandoned it, that will lead to your welfare and happiness for a long time. Perception is not yours. Abandon it. When you have

abandoned it, that will lead to your welfare and happiness for a long time. Formations are not yours. Abandon them. When you have abandoned them, that will lead to your welfare and happiness for a long time. Consciousness is not yours. Abandon it. When you have abandoned it, that will lead to your welfare and happiness for a long time.[270]

41. "Bhikkhus, what do you think? If people carried off the grass, sticks, branches, and leaves in this Jeta Grove, or burned them, or did what they liked with them, would you think: 'People are carrying us off or burning us or doing what they like with us'?"—"No, venerable sir. Why not? Because that is neither our self nor what belongs to our self."—"So too, bhikkhus, whatever is not yours, abandon it; when you have abandoned it, that will lead to your welfare and happiness for a long time. What is it that is not yours? Material form is not yours...Feeling is not yours...Perception is not yours...Formations are not yours...Consciousness is not yours. Abandon it. When you have abandoned it, that will lead to your welfare and happiness for a long time.

(IN THIS DHAMMA)

42. "Bhikkhus, the Dhamma well proclaimed by me thus is clear, open, evident, and free of patchwork.[271] In the Dhamma well proclaimed by me thus, which is clear, open, evident, and free of patchwork, there is no [future] round for manifestation in the case of those bhikkhus who are arahants with taints destroyed, who have lived the holy life, done what had to be done, laid down the burden, reached their own goal, destroyed the fetters of being, and are completely liberated through final knowledge.[272]

43. "Bhikkhus, the Dhamma well proclaimed by me thus is clear...free of patchwork. In the Dhamma well proclaimed by me thus, which is clear...free of patchwork, those bhikkhus who have abandoned the five lower fetters are all due to reappear spontaneously [in the Pure Abodes] and there attain final Nibbāna, without ever returning from that world.

44. "Bhikkhus, the Dhamma well proclaimed by me thus is clear...free of patchwork. In the Dhamma well proclaimed by me thus, which is clear...free of patchwork, those bhikkhus who

have abandoned three fetters and attenuated lust, hate, and delusion are all once-returners, returning once to this world to make an end of suffering.

45. "Bhikkhus, the Dhamma well proclaimed by me thus is clear...free of patchwork. In the Dhamma well proclaimed by me thus, which is clear...free of patchwork, those bhikkhus who have abandoned three fetters are all stream-enterers, no longer subject to perdition, [142] bound [for deliverance] and headed for enlightenment.

46. "Bhikkhus, the Dhamma well proclaimed by me thus is clear...free of patchwork. In the Dhamma well proclaimed by me thus, which is clear...free of patchwork, those bhikkhus who are Dhamma-followers or faith-followers are all headed for enlightenment.[273]

47. "Bhikkhus, the Dhamma well proclaimed by me thus is clear, open, evident, and free of patchwork. In the Dhamma well proclaimed by me thus, which is clear, open, evident, and free of patchwork, those who have sufficient faith in me, sufficient love for me, are all headed for heaven."[274]

That is what the Blessed One said. The bhikkhus were satisfied and delighted in the Blessed One's words.

23 *Vammika Sutta*
The Ant-hill

1. THUS HAVE I HEARD. On one occasion the Blessed One was living at Sāvatthī in Jeta's Grove, Anāthapiṇḍika's Park. Now on that occasion the venerable Kumāra Kassapa was living in the Blind Men's Grove.[275]

Then, when the night was well advanced, a certain deity of beautiful appearance who illuminated the whole of the Blind Men's Grove approached the venerable Kumāra Kassapa and stood at one side.[276] So standing, the deity said to him:

2. "Bhikkhu, bhikkhu, this ant-hill fumes by night and flames by day.[277]

"Thus spoke the brahmin: 'Delve with the knife, thou wise one.' Delving with the knife, the wise one saw a bar: 'A bar, O venerable sir.'

"Thus spoke the brahmin: 'Throw out the bar; delve with the knife, thou wise one.' Delving with the knife, the wise one saw a toad: 'A toad, O venerable sir.'

"Thus spoke the brahmin: 'Throw out the toad; delve with the knife, thou wise one.' Delving with the knife, the wise one saw a fork: 'A fork, O venerable sir.'

"Thus spoke the brahmin: 'Throw out the fork; delve with the knife, thou wise one.' Delving with the knife, the wise one saw a sieve: 'A sieve, O venerable sir.'

"Thus spoke the brahmin: [143] 'Throw out the sieve; delve with the knife, thou wise one.' Delving with the knife, the wise one saw a tortoise: 'A tortoise, O venerable sir.'

"Thus spoke the brahmin: 'Throw out the tortoise; delve with the knife, thou wise one.' Delving with the knife, the wise one saw a butcher's knife and block: 'A butcher's knife and block, O venerable sir.'

"Thus spoke the brahmin: 'Throw out the butcher's knife and

block; delve with the knife, thou wise one.' Delving with the knife, the wise one saw a piece of meat: 'A piece of meat, O venerable sir.'

"Thus spoke the brahmin: 'Throw out the piece of meat; delve with the knife, thou wise one.' Delving with the knife, the wise one saw a Nāga serpent: 'A Nāga serpent, O venerable sir.'

"Thus spoke the brahmin: 'Leave the Nāga serpent; do not harm the Nāga serpent; honour the Nāga serpent.'

"Bhikkhu, you should go to the Blessed One and ask him about this riddle. As the Blessed One tells you, so should you remember it. Bhikkhu, other than the Tathāgata or a disciple of the Tathāgata or one who has learned it from them, I see no one in this world with its gods, its Māras, and its Brahmās, in this generation with its recluses and brahmins, its princes and its people, whose explanation of this riddle might satisfy the mind."

That is what was said by the deity, who thereupon vanished at once.

3. Then, when the night was over, the venerable Kumāra Kassapa went to the Blessed One. After paying homage to him, he sat down at one side and told the Blessed One what had occurred. Then he asked: "Venerable sir, what is the ant-hill, what the fuming by night, what the flaming by day? Who is the brahmin, who the wise one? What is the knife, what the delving, what the bar, what the toad, what the fork, what the sieve, what the tortoise, what the butcher's knife and block, what the piece of meat, what the Nāga serpent?" [144]

4. "Bhikkhu, the ant-hill is a symbol for this body, made of material form, consisting of the four great elements, procreated by a mother and father, built up out of boiled rice and porridge,[278] and subject to impermanence, to being worn and rubbed away, to dissolution and disintegration.

"What one thinks and ponders by night based upon one's actions during the day is the 'fuming by night.'

"The actions one undertakes during the day by body, speech, and mind after thinking and pondering by night is the 'flaming by day.'

"The brahmin is a symbol for the Tathāgata, accomplished and fully enlightened. The wise one is a symbol for a bhikkhu in higher training. The knife is a symbol for noble wisdom. The delving is a symbol for the arousing of energy.

"The bar is a symbol for ignorance.[279] 'Throw out the bar:

abandon ignorance. Delve with the knife, thou wise one.' This is the meaning.

"The toad is a symbol for the despair due to anger. 'Throw out the toad: abandon despair due to anger. Delve with the knife, thou wise one.' This is the meaning.

"The fork is a symbol for doubt.[280] 'Throw out the fork: abandon doubt. Delve with the knife, thou wise one.' This is the meaning.

"The sieve is a symbol for the five hindrances, namely, the hindrance of sensual desire, the hindrance of ill will, the hindrance of sloth and torpor, the hindrance of restlessness and remorse, and the hindrance of doubt. 'Throw out the sieve: abandon the five hindrances. Delve with the knife, thou wise one.' This is the meaning.

"The tortoise is a symbol for the five aggregates affected by clinging,[281] namely, the material form aggregate affected by clinging, the feeling aggregate affected by clinging, the perception aggregate affected by clinging, the formations aggregate affected by clinging, and the consciousness aggregate affected by clinging. 'Throw out the tortoise: abandon the five aggregates affected by clinging. Delve with the knife, thou wise one.' This is the meaning.

"The butcher's knife and block is a symbol for the five cords of sensual pleasure[282]—forms cognizable by the eye that are wished for, desired, agreeable, and likeable, connected with sensual desire, and provocative of lust; sounds cognizable by the ear...odours cognizable by the nose...flavours cognizable by the tongue...tangibles cognizable by the body that are wished for, desired, agreeable, and likeable, connected with sensual desire, [145] and provocative of lust. 'Throw out the butcher's knife and block: abandon the five cords of sensual pleasure. Delve with the knife, thou wise one.' This is the meaning.

"The piece of meat is a symbol for delight and lust.[283] 'Throw out the piece of meat: abandon delight and lust. Delve with the knife, thou wise one.' This is the meaning.

"The Nāga serpent is a symbol for a bhikkhu who has destroyed the taints.[284] 'Leave the Nāga serpent; do not harm the Nāga serpent; honour the Nāga serpent.' This is the meaning."

That is what the Blessed One said. The venerable Kumāra Kassapa was satisfied and delighted in the Blessed One's words.

24 *Rathavinīta Sutta*
The Relay Chariots

1. THUS HAVE I HEARD. On one occasion the Blessed One was living at Rājagaha in the Bamboo Grove, the Squirrels' Sanctuary.

2. Then a number of bhikkhus from [the Blessed One's] native land,[285] who had spent the Rains there, went to the Blessed One, and after paying homage to him, sat down at one side. The Blessed One asked them: "Bhikkhus, who in [my] native land is esteemed by the bhikkhus there, by his companions in the holy life, in this way: 'Having few wishes himself, he talks to the bhikkhus on fewness of wishes; content himself, he talks to the bhikkhus on contentment; secluded himself, he talks to the bhikkhus on seclusion; aloof from society himself, he talks to the bhikkhus on aloofness from society; energetic himself, he talks to the bhikkhus on arousing energy; attained to virtue himself, he talks to the bhikkhus on the attainment of virtue; attained to concentration himself, he talks to the bhikkhus on the attainment of concentration; attained to wisdom himself, he talks to the bhikkhus on the attainment of wisdom; attained to deliverance himself, he talks to the bhikkhus on the attainment of deliverance; attained to the knowledge and vision of deliverance himself, he talks to the bhikkhus on the attainment of the knowledge and vision of deliverance;[286] he is one who advises, informs, instructs, urges, [146] rouses, and gladdens his companions in the holy life'?"

"Venerable sir, the venerable Puṇṇa Mantāṇiputta is so esteemed in the [Blessed One's] native land by the bhikkhus there, by his companions in the holy life."[287]

3. Now on that occasion the venerable Sāriputta was seated near the Blessed One. Then it occurred to the venerable Sāriputta: "It is a gain for the venerable Puṇṇa Mantāṇiputta, it is a great gain for him that his wise companions in the holy life

praise him point by point in the Teacher's presence. Perhaps sometime or other we might meet the venerable Puṇṇa Mantāṇiputta and have some conversation with him."

4. Then, when the Blessed One had stayed at Rājagaha as long as he chose, he set out to wander by stages to Sāvatthī. Wandering by stages, he eventually arrived at Sāvatthī, and there he lived in Jeta's Grove, Anāthapiṇḍika's Park.

5. The venerable Puṇṇa Mantāṇiputta heard: "The Blessed One has arrived at Sāvatthī and is living in Jeta's Grove, Anāthapiṇḍika's Park." Then the venerable Puṇṇa Mantāṇiputta set his resting place in order, and taking his outer robe and bowl, set out to wander by stages to Sāvatthī. Wandering by stages, he eventually arrived at Sāvatthī and went to Jeta's Grove, Anāthapiṇḍika's Park, to see the Blessed One. After paying homage to the Blessed One, he sat down at one side and the Blessed One instructed, urged, roused, and gladdened him with talk on the Dhamma. Then the venerable Puṇṇa Mantāṇiputta, instructed, urged, roused, and gladdened by the Blessed One's talk on the Dhamma, delighting and rejoicing in the Blessed One's words, rose from his seat, and after paying homage to the Blessed One, keeping him on his right, he went to the Blind Men's Grove for the day's abiding.

6. Then a certain bhikkhu went to the venerable Sāriputta and said to him: "Friend Sāriputta, the bhikkhu Puṇṇa Mantāṇiputta of whom you have always spoken highly [147] has just been instructed, urged, roused, and gladdened by the Blessed One with talk on the Dhamma; after delighting and rejoicing in the Blessed One's words, he rose from his seat, and after paying homage to the Blessed One, keeping him on his right, he has gone to the Blind Men's Grove for the day's abiding."

7. Then the venerable Sāriputta quickly picked up a mat and followed close behind the venerable Puṇṇa Mantāṇiputta, keeping his head in sight. Then the venerable Puṇṇa Mantāṇiputta entered the Blind Men's Grove and sat down for the day's abiding at the root of a tree. The venerable Sāriputta also entered the Blind Men's Grove and sat down for the day's abiding at the root of a tree.

8. Then, when it was evening, the venerable Sāriputta rose from meditation, went to the venerable Puṇṇa Mantāṇiputta, and exchanged greetings with him. When this courteous and

amiable talk was finished, he sat down at one side and said to the venerable Puṇṇa Mantāṇiputta:

9. "Is the holy life lived under our Blessed One, friend?"—"Yes, friend."—"But, friend, is it for the sake of purification of virtue that the holy life is lived under the Blessed One?"—"No, friend."—"Then is it for the sake of purification of mind that the holy life is lived under the Blessed One?"—"No, friend."—"Then is it for the sake of purification of view that the holy life is lived under the Blessed One?"—"No, friend."—"Then is it for the sake of purification by overcoming doubt that the holy life is lived under the Blessed One?"—"No, friend."—"Then is it for the sake of purification by knowledge and vision of what is the path and what is not the path that the holy life is lived under the Blessed One?"—"No, friend."—"Then is it for the sake of purification by knowledge and vision of the way that the holy life is lived under the Blessed One?"—"No, friend."—"Then is it for the sake of purification by knowledge and vision that the holy life is lived under the Blessed One?"—"No, friend."[288]

10. "Friend, when asked: 'But, friend, is it for the sake of purification of virtue that the holy life is lived under the Blessed One?' you replied: 'No, friend.' When asked: 'Then is it for the sake of purification of mind...purification of view...purification by overcoming doubt...purification by knowledge and vision of what is the path and what is not the path...purification by knowledge and vision of the way...purification by knowledge and vision that the holy life is lived under the Blessed One?' you replied: 'No, friend.' For the sake of what then, friend, [148] is the holy life lived under the Blessed One?"

"Friend, it is for the sake of final Nibbāna without clinging that the holy life is lived under the Blessed One."[289]

11. "But, friend, is purification of virtue final Nibbāna without clinging?"—"No, friend."—"Then is purification of mind final Nibbāna without clinging?"—"No, friend."—"Then is purification of view final Nibbāna without clinging?"—"No, friend."—"Then is purification by overcoming doubt final Nibbāna without clinging?"—"No, friend."—"Then is purification by knowledge and vision of what is the path and what is not the path final Nibbāna without clinging?"—"No, friend."—"Then is purification by knowledge and vision of the way final Nibbāna without clinging?"—"No, friend."—"Then is purification by knowledge and

vision final Nibbāna without clinging?"—"No, friend."—"But, friend, is final Nibbāna without clinging to be attained without these states?"—"No, friend."

12. "When asked: 'But, friend, is purification of virtue final Nibbāna without clinging?' you replied: 'No, friend.' When asked: 'Then is purification of mind...purification of view...purification by overcoming doubt...purification by knowledge and vision of what is the path and what is not the path...purification by knowledge and vision of the way...purification by knowledge and vision final Nibbāna without clinging?' you replied: 'No, friend.' And when asked: 'But, friend, is final Nibbāna without clinging to be attained without these states?' you replied: 'No, friend.' But how, friend, should the meaning of these statements be regarded?"

13. "Friend, if the Blessed One had described purification of virtue as final Nibbāna without clinging, he would have described what is still accompanied by clinging as final Nibbāna without clinging. If the Blessed One had described purification of mind...purification of view...purification by overcoming doubt...purification by knowledge and vision of what is the path and what is not the path...purification by knowledge and vision of the way...purification by knowledge and vision as final Nibbāna without clinging, he would have described what is still accompanied by clinging as final Nibbāna without clinging.[290] And if final Nibbāna without clinging were to be attained without these states, then an ordinary person would have attained final Nibbāna, for an ordinary person is without these states.

14. "As to that, friend, I shall give you a simile, for some wise men understand the meaning of a statement by means of a simile. Suppose that King Pasenadi of Kosala while living at Sāvatthī [149] had some urgent business to settle at Sāketa, and that between Sāvatthī and Sāketa seven relay chariots were kept ready for him. Then King Pasenadi of Kosala, leaving Sāvatthī through the inner palace door, would mount the first relay chariot, and by means of the first relay chariot he would arrive at the second relay chariot; then he would dismount from the first chariot and mount the second chariot, and by means of the second chariot, he would arrive at the third chariot...by means of the third chariot, he would arrive at the fourth chariot...by means of the fourth chariot, he would arrive at the fifth chariot...by

means of the fifth chariot, he would arrive at the sixth chariot...by means of the sixth chariot, he would arrive at the seventh chariot, and by means of the seventh chariot he would arrive at the inner palace door in Sāketa. Then, when he had come to the inner palace door, his friends and acquaintances, his kinsmen and relatives, would ask him: 'Sire, did you come from Sāvatthī to the inner palace door in Sāketa by means of this relay chariot?' How then should King Pasenadi of Kosala answer in order to answer correctly?"

"In order to answer correctly, friend, he should answer thus: 'Here, while living at Sāvatthī I had some urgent business to settle at Sāketa, and between Sāvatthī and Sāketa seven relay chariots were kept ready for me. Then, leaving Sāvatthī through the inner palace door, I mounted the first relay chariot, and by means of the first relay chariot I arrived at the second relay chariot; then I dismounted from the first chariot and mounted the second chariot, and by means of the second chariot I arrived at the third...fourth...fifth...sixth...seventh chariot, and by means of the seventh chariot I arrived at the inner palace door in Sāketa.' In order to answer correctly he should answer thus."

15. "So too, friend, purification of virtue is for the sake of reaching purification of mind; purification of mind is for the sake of reaching purification of view; purification of view is for the sake of reaching purification by overcoming doubt; purification by overcoming doubt [150] is for the sake of reaching purification by knowledge and vision of what is the path and what is not the path; purification by knowledge and vision of what is the path and what is not the path is for the sake of reaching purification by knowledge and vision of the way; purification by knowledge and vision of the way is for the sake of reaching purification by knowledge and vision; purification by knowledge and vision is for the sake of reaching final Nibbāna without clinging. It is for the sake of final Nibbāna without clinging that the holy life is lived under the Blessed One."

16. When this was said, the venerable Sāriputta asked the venerable Puṇṇa Mantāṇiputta: "What is the venerable one's name, and how do his companions in the holy life know the venerable one?"[291]

"My name is Puṇṇa, friend, and my companions in the holy life know me as Mantāṇiputta."

"It is wonderful, friend, it is marvellous! Each profound question has been answered, point by point, by the venerable Puṇṇa Mantāṇiputta as a learned disciple who understands the Teacher's Dispensation correctly. It is a gain for his companions in the holy life, it is a great gain for them that they have the opportunity to see and honour the venerable Puṇṇa Mantāṇiputta. Even if it were by carrying the venerable Puṇṇa Mantāṇiputta about on a cushion on their heads that his companions in the holy life would get the opportunity to see and honour him, it would be a gain for them, a great gain for them. And it is a gain for us, a great gain for us that we have the opportunity to see and honour the venerable Puṇṇa Mantāṇiputta."

17. When this was said, the venerable Puṇṇa Mantāṇiputta asked the venerable Sāriputta: "What is the venerable one's name, and how do his companions in the holy life know the venerable one?"

"My name is Upatissa, friend, and my companions in the holy life know me as Sāriputta."

"Indeed, friend, we did not know that we were talking with the venerable Sāriputta, the disciple who is like the Teacher himself.[292] If we had known that this was the venerable Sāriputta, we should not have said so much. It is wonderful, friend, it is marvellous! Each profound question has been posed, point by point, by the venerable Sāriputta as a learned disciple who understands the Teacher's Dispensation correctly. It is a gain for his companions in the holy life, it is a great gain for them that they have the opportunity to see and honour the venerable Sāriputta. Even if it were by carrying the venerable Sāriputta about on a cushion on their heads that his companions in the holy life would get the opportunity to see and honour him, [151] it would be a gain for them, a great gain for them. And it is a gain for us, a great gain for us that we have the opportunity to see and honour the venerable Sāriputta."

Thus it was that these two great beings rejoiced in each other's good words.

25 *Nivāpa Sutta*
The Bait

1. THUS HAVE I HEARD. On one occasion the Blessed One was living at Sāvatthī in Jeta's Grove, Anāthapiṇḍika's Park. There he addressed the bhikkhus thus: "Bhikkhus."—"Venerable sir," they replied. The Blessed One said this:

2. "Bhikkhus, a deer-trapper does not lay down bait for a deer herd intending thus: 'May the deer herd enjoy this bait that I have laid down and so be long-lived and handsome and endure for a long time.' A deer-trapper lays down bait for a deer herd intending thus: 'The deer herd will eat food unwarily by going right in amongst the bait that I have laid down; by so doing they will become intoxicated; when they are intoxicated, they will fall into negligence; when they are negligent, I can do with them as I like on account of this bait.'

3. "Now the deer of the first herd ate food unwarily by going right in amongst the bait that the deer-trapper had laid down; by so doing they became intoxicated; when they were intoxicated, they fell into negligence; when they were negligent, the deer-trapper did with them as he liked on account of that bait. That is how the deer of the first herd failed to get free from the deer-trapper's power and control.

4. "Now the deer of a second herd reckoned thus: 'The deer of that first herd, by acting as they did without precaution, [152] failed to get free from the deer-trapper's power and control. Suppose we altogether shun that bait food; shunning that fearful enjoyment, let us go out into the forest wilds and live there.' And they did so. But in the last month of the hot season when the grass and the water were used up, their bodies were reduced to extreme emaciation; with that they lost their strength and energy; when they had lost their strength and energy, they returned to that same bait that the deer-trapper had laid down.

They ate food unwarily by going right in amongst it. By so doing they became intoxicated; when they were intoxicated they fell into negligence; when they were negligent, the deer-trapper did with them as he liked on account of that bait. And that is how the deer of the second herd also failed to get free from the deer-trapper's power and control.

5. "Now the deer of a third herd reckoned thus: 'The deer of that first herd, by acting as they did without precaution, failed to get free from the deer-trapper's power and control. The deer of that second herd, by reckoning how the deer of the first herd had failed and by planning and acting as they did with the precaution of going to live in the forest wilds, also failed to get free from the deer-trapper's power and control. Suppose we make our dwelling place within range of the deer-trapper's bait. [153] Then, having done so, we shall eat food not unwarily and without going right in amongst the bait that the deer-trapper has laid down; by doing so we shall not become intoxicated; when we are not intoxicated, we shall not fall into negligence; when we are not negligent, the deer-trapper shall not do with us as he likes on account of that bait.' And they did so.

"But then the deer-trapper and his following considered thus: 'These deer of this third herd are as cunning and crafty as wizards and sorcerers. They eat the bait laid down without our knowing how they come and go. Suppose we have the bait that is laid down completely surrounded all round over a wide area with wicker hurdles; then perhaps we might see the third deer herd's dwelling place, where they go to hide.' They did so, and they saw the third herd's dwelling place, where they went to hide. And that is how the deer of the third herd also failed to get free from the deer-trapper's power and control.

6. "Now the deer of a fourth herd reckoned thus: 'The deer of that first herd, by acting as they did without precaution, failed to get free from the deer-trapper's power and control. The deer of that second herd, by reckoning how the deer of the first herd had failed and by planning and acting as they did with the precaution of going to live in the forest wilds, also failed to get free from the deer-trapper's power and control. And the deer of that third herd, by reckoning how the deer of the first herd [154] and also the deer of the second herd had failed, and by planning and acting as they did with the precaution of making their dwelling

place within range of the deer-trapper's bait, also failed to get free from the deer-trapper's power and control. Suppose we make our dwelling place where the deer-trapper and his following cannot go. Then, having done so, we shall eat food not unwarily and without going right in amongst the bait that the deer-trapper has laid down; by doing so we shall not become intoxicated; when we are not intoxicated, we shall not fall into negligence; when we are not negligent, [155] the deer-trapper shall not do with us as he likes on account of that bait.' And they did so.

"But then the deer-trapper and his following considered thus: 'These deer of this fourth herd are as cunning and crafty as wizards and sorcerers. They eat the bait laid down without our knowing how they come and go. Suppose we have the bait that is laid down completely surrounded all round over a wide area with wicker hurdles; then perhaps we might see the fourth deer herd's dwelling place, where they go to hide.' They did so, but they did not see the fourth deer herd's dwelling place, where they went to hide. Then the deer-hunter and his following considered thus: 'If we scare the fourth deer herd, being scared they will alert others, and so the deer herds will all desert this bait that we have laid down. Suppose we treat the fourth deer herd with indifference.' They did so. And that was how the deer of the fourth deer herd got free from the deer-trapper's power and control.

7. "Bhikkhus, I have given this simile in order to convey a meaning. This is the meaning: 'Bait' is a term for the five cords of sensual pleasure. 'Deer-trapper' is a term for Māra the Evil One. 'The deer-trapper's following' is a term for Māra's following. 'Deer herd' is a term for recluses and brahmins.

8. "Now recluses and brahmins of the first kind ate food unwarily by going right in amongst the bait and the material things of the world that Māra had laid down; [156] by so doing they became intoxicated; when they were intoxicated, they fell into negligence; when they were negligent, Māra did with them as he liked on account of that bait and those material things of the world. That is how the recluses and brahmins of the first kind failed to get free from Māra's power and control. Those recluses and brahmins, I say, are just like the deer of the first herd.

9. "Now recluses and brahmins of the second kind reckoned thus: 'Those recluses and brahmins of the first kind, by acting as they did without precaution, failed to get free from Māra's

power and control. Suppose we altogether shun that bait food and those material things of the world; shunning that fearful enjoyment, let us go out into the forest wilds and live there.' And they did so. There they were eaters of greens or millet or wild rice or hide-parings or moss or rice-bran or the discarded scum of boiled rice or sesamum flour or grass or cowdung; they lived on forest roots and fruits, they fed on fallen fruits.

"But in the last month of the hot season when the grass and the water were used up, their bodies were reduced to extreme emaciation; with that they lost their strength and energy; when they had lost their strength and energy, they lost their deliverance of mind;[293] with the loss of their deliverance of mind, they returned to that same bait that Māra had laid down and those material things of the world; they ate food unwarily by going right in amongst it; by so doing they became intoxicated; when they were intoxicated, they fell into negligence; when they were negligent, Māra did with them as he liked on account of that bait and those material things of the world. That is how those recluses and brahmins of the second kind failed to get free from Māra's power and control. [157] Those recluses and brahmins, I say, are just like the deer of the second herd.

10. "Now recluses and brahmins of the third kind reckoned thus: 'Those recluses and brahmins of the first kind, by acting as they did without precaution, failed to get free from Māra's power and control. Those recluses and brahmins of the second kind, by reckoning how the recluses and brahmins of the first kind had failed, and then planning and acting as they did with the precaution of going to live in the forest wilds, also failed to get free from Māra's power and control. Suppose we make our dwelling place within range of that bait that Māra has laid down and those material things of the world. Then, having done so, we shall eat food not unwarily and without going right in amongst the bait that Māra has laid down and the material things of the world. By doing so we shall not become intoxicated; when we are not intoxicated, we shall not fall into negligence; when we are not negligent, Māra shall not do with us as he likes on account of that bait and those material things of the world.' And they did so.

"But then they came to hold views such as 'the world is eternal' and 'the world is not eternal' and 'the world is finite' and 'the world is infinite' and 'the soul and the body are the same' and 'the soul is one thing and the body another' and 'after death a Tathāgata exists' and 'after death a Tathāgata does not exist' and 'after death a Tathāgata both exists and does not exist' and 'after death a Tathāgata neither exists nor does not exist.'[294] [158] That is how those recluses and brahmins of the third kind failed to get free from Māra's power and control. Those recluses and brahmins, I say, are just like the deer of the third herd.

11. "Now recluses and brahmins of the fourth kind reckoned thus: 'Those recluses and brahmins of the first kind, by acting as they did without precaution, failed to get free from Māra's power and control. Those recluses and brahmins of the second kind, by reckoning how the recluses and brahmins of the first kind had failed, and by planning and acting as they did with the precaution of going to live in the forest wilds, also failed to get free from Māra's power and control. And the recluses and brahmins of the third kind, by reckoning how the recluses and brahmins of the first kind and also the recluses and brahmins of the second kind had failed, and by planning and acting as they did with the precaution of making their dwelling place within range of the bait that Māra had laid down and the material things of the world, also failed to get free from Māra's power and control. Suppose we make our dwelling place where Māra and his following cannot go. Then, having done so, we shall eat food not unwarily and without going right in amongst the bait that Māra has laid down and the material things of the world. By doing so we shall not become intoxicated; when we are not intoxicated, we shall not fall into negligence; when we are not negligent, Māra shall not do with us as he likes on account of that bait and those material things of the world.' And they did so. [159] And that is how those recluses and brahmins of the fourth kind got free from Māra's power and control. Those recluses and brahmins, I say, are just like the deer of the fourth herd.

12. "And where is it that Māra and his following cannot go? Here, quite secluded from sensual pleasures, secluded from unwholesome states, a bhikkhu enters upon and abides in the first jhāna, which is accompanied by applied and sustained thought, with rapture and pleasure born of seclusion. This bhikkhu

is said to have blindfolded Māra, to have become invisible to the Evil One by depriving Māra's eye of its opportunity.[295]

13. "Again, with the stilling of applied and sustained thought, a bhikkhu enters upon and abides in the second jhāna, which has self-confidence and singleness of mind without applied and sustained thought, with rapture and pleasure born of concentration. This bhikkhu is said to have blindfolded Māra…

14. "Again, with the fading away as well of rapture, a bhikkhu abides in equanimity, and mindful and fully aware, still feeling pleasure with the body, he enters upon and abides in the third jhāna, on account of which the noble ones announce: 'He has a pleasant abiding who has equanimity and is mindful.' This bhikkhu is said to have blindfolded Māra…

15. "Again, with the abandoning of pleasure and pain, and with the previous disappearance of joy and grief, a bhikkhu enters upon and abides in the fourth jhāna, which has neither-pain-nor-pleasure and purity of mindfulness due to equanimity. This bhikkhu is said to have blindfolded Māra…

16. "Again, with the complete surmounting of perceptions of form, with the disappearance of perceptions of sensory impact, with non-attention to perceptions of diversity, aware that 'space is infinite,' a bhikkhu enters upon and abides in the base of infinite space. This bhikkhu is said to have blindfolded Māra…

17. "Again, by completely surmounting the base of infinite space, aware that 'consciousness is infinite,' a bhikkhu enters upon and abides in the base of infinite consciousness. This bhikkhu is said to have blindfolded Māra…

18. "Again, by completely surmounting the base of infinite consciousness, [160] aware that 'there is nothing,' a bhikkhu enters upon and abides in the base of nothingness. This bhikkhu is said to have blindfolded Māra…

19. "Again, by completely surmounting the base of nothingness, a bhikkhu enters upon and abides in the base of neither-perception-nor-non-perception. This bhikkhu is said to have blindfolded Māra, to have become invisible to the Evil One by depriving Māra's eye of its opportunity.

20. "Again, by completely surmounting the base of neither-perception-nor-non-perception, a bhikkhu enters upon and abides in the cessation of perception and feeling. And his taints are destroyed by his seeing with wisdom. This bhikkhu is said

to have blindfolded Māra, to have become invisible to the Evil One by depriving Māra's eye of its opportunity, and to have crossed beyond attachment to the world."[296]

That is what the Blessed One said. The bhikkhus were satisfied and delighted in the Blessed One's words.

26 *Ariyapariyesanā Sutta*
The Noble Search

1. THUS HAVE I HEARD.[297] On one occasion the Blessed One was living at Sāvatthī in Jeta's Grove, Anāthapiṇḍika's Park.

2. Then, when it was morning, the Blessed One dressed, and taking his bowl and outer robe, went into Sāvatthī for alms. Then a number of bhikkhus went to the venerable Ānanda and said to him: "Friend Ānanda, it is long since we heard a talk on the Dhamma from the Blessed One's own lips. It would be good if we could get to hear such a talk, friend Ānanda."—"Then let the venerable ones go to the brahmin Rammaka's hermitage. Perhaps you will get to hear a talk on the Dhamma from the Blessed One's own lips."—"Yes, friend," they replied.

3. Then, when the Blessed One had wandered for alms in Sāvatthī and had returned from his almsround, after his meal he addressed the venerable Ānanda: "Ānanda, let us go to the Eastern Park, to the Palace of Migāra's Mother, for the day's abiding."—"Yes, venerable sir," the venerable Ānanda replied. [161] Then the Blessed One went with the venerable Ānanda to the Eastern Park, the Palace of Migāra's Mother, for the day's abiding.

Then, when it was evening, the Blessed One rose from meditation and addressed the venerable Ānanda: "Ānanda, let us go to the Eastern Bathing Place to bathe."—"Yes, venerable sir," the venerable Ānanda replied. Then the Blessed One went with the venerable Ānanda to the Eastern Bathing Place to bathe. When he was finished, he came up out of the water and stood in one robe drying his limbs. Then the venerable Ānanda said to the Blessed One: "Venerable sir, the brahmin Rammaka's hermitage is nearby. That hermitage is agreeable and delightful. Venerable sir, it would be good if the Blessed One went there out of compassion." The Blessed One consented in silence.

4. Then the Blessed One went to the brahmin Rammaka's hermitage. Now on that occasion a number of bhikkhus were sitting together in the hermitage discussing the Dhamma. The Blessed One stood outside the door waiting for their discussion to end. When he knew that it was over, he coughed and knocked, and the bhikkhus opened the door for him. The Blessed One entered, sat down on a seat made ready, and addressed the bhikkhus thus: "Bhikkhus, for what discussion are you sitting together here now? And what was your discussion that was interrupted?"

"Venerable sir, our discussion on the Dhamma that was interrupted was about the Blessed One himself. Then the Blessed One arrived."

"Good, bhikkhus. It is fitting for you clansmen who have gone forth out of faith from the home life into homelessness to sit together to discuss the Dhamma. When you gather together, bhikkhus, you should do either of two things: hold discussion on the Dhamma or maintain noble silence.[298]

(TWO KINDS OF SEARCH)

5. "Bhikkhus, there are these two kinds of search: the noble search and the ignoble search. And what is the ignoble search? Here someone being himself subject to birth seeks what is also subject to birth; being himself subject to ageing, [162] he seeks what is also subject to ageing; being himself subject to sickness, he seeks what is also subject to sickness; being himself subject to death, he seeks what is also subject to death; being himself subject to sorrow, he seeks what is also subject to sorrow; being himself subject to defilement, he seeks what is also subject to defilement.

6. "And what may be said to be subject to birth? Wife and children are subject to birth, men and women slaves, goats and sheep, fowl and pigs, elephants, cattle, horses, and mares, gold and silver are subject to birth. These acquisitions[299] are subject to birth; and one who is tied to these things, infatuated with them, and utterly committed to them, being himself subject to birth, seeks what it also subject to birth.

7. "And what may be said to be subject to ageing? Wife and children are subject to ageing, men and women slaves, goats

and sheep, fowl and pigs, elephants, cattle, horses, and mares, gold and silver are subject to ageing. These acquistions are subject to ageing; and one who is tied to these things, infatuated with them, and utterly committed to them, being himself subject to ageing, seeks what is also subject to ageing.

8. "And what may be said to be subject to sickness? Wife and children are subject to sickness, men and women slaves, goats and sheep, fowl and pigs, elephants, cattle, horses, and mares are subject to sickness. These acquisitions are subject to sickness; and one who is tied to these things, infatuated with them, and utterly committed to them, being himself subject to sickness, seeks what is also subject to sickness.[300]

9. "And what may be said to be subject to death? Wife and children are subject to death, men and women slaves, goats and sheep, fowl and pigs, elephants, cattle, horses, and mares are subject to death. These acquisitions are subject to death; and one who is tied to these things, infatuated with them, and utterly committed to them, being himself subject to death, seeks what is also subject to death.

10. "And what may be said to be subject to sorrow? Wife and children are subject to sorrow, men and women slaves, goats and sheep, fowl and pigs, elephants, cattle, horses, and mares are subject to sorrow. These acquisitions are subject to sorrow; and one who is tied to these things, infatuated with them, and utterly committed to them, being himself subject to sorrow, seeks what is also subject to sorrow.

11. "And what may be said to be subject to defilement? Wife and children are subject to defilement, men and women slaves, goats and sheep, fowl and pigs, elephants, cattle, horses, and mares, gold and silver are subject to defilement. These acquisitions are subject to defilement; and one who is tied to these things, infatuated with them, and utterly committed to them, being himself subject to defilement, seeks what is also subject to defilement. This is the ignoble search.

12. "And what is the noble search? Here someone being himself subject to birth, having understood the danger in what is subject to birth, [163] seeks the unborn supreme security from bondage, Nibbāna; being himself subject to ageing, having understood the danger in what is subject to ageing, he seeks the unageing supreme security from bondage, Nibbāna; being

himself subject to sickness, having understood the danger in what is subject to sickness, he seeks the unailing supreme security from bondage, Nibbāna; being himself subject to death, having understood the danger in what is subject to death, he seeks the deathless supreme security from bondage, Nibbāna; being himself subject to sorrow, having understood the danger in what is subject to sorrow, he seeks the sorrowless supreme security from bondage, Nibbāna; being himself subject to defilement, having understood the danger in what is subject to defilement, he seeks the undefiled supreme security from bondage, Nibbāna. This is the noble search.

(THE SEARCH FOR ENLIGHTENMENT)

13. "Bhikkhus, before my enlightenment, while I was still only an unenlightened Bodhisatta, I too, being myself subject to birth, sought what was also subject to birth; being myself subject to ageing, sickness, death, sorrow, and defilement, I sought what was also subject to ageing, sickness, death, sorrow, and defilement. Then I considered thus: 'Why, being myself subject to birth, do I seek what is also subject to birth? Why, being myself subject to ageing, sickness, death, sorrow, and defilement, do I seek what is also subject to ageing, sickness, death, sorrow, and defilement? Suppose that, being myself subject to birth, having understood the danger in what is subject to birth, I seek the unborn supreme security from bondage, Nibbāna. Suppose that, being myself subject to ageing, sickness, death, sorrow, and defilement, having understood the danger in what is subject to ageing, sickness, death, sorrow, and defilement, I seek the unageing, unailing, deathless, sorrowless, and undefiled supreme security from bondage, Nibbāna.'

14. "Later, while still young, a black-haired young man endowed with the blessing of youth, in the prime of life, though my mother and father wished otherwise and wept with tearful faces, I shaved off my hair and beard, put on the yellow robe, and went forth from the home life into homelessness.

15. "Having gone forth, bhikkhus, in search of what is wholesome, seeking the supreme state of sublime peace, I went to Āḷāra Kālāma and said to him: 'Friend Kālāma, I want to lead the holy life in this Dhamma and Discipline.' Āḷāra Kālāma

replied: 'The venerable one may stay here. This Dhamma is such that a wise man [164] can soon enter upon and abide in it, realising for himself through direct knowledge his own teacher's doctrine.' I soon quickly learned that Dhamma. As far as mere lip-reciting and rehearsal of his teaching went, I could speak with knowledge and assurance, and I claimed, 'I know and see'—and there were others who did likewise.

"I considered: 'It is not through mere faith alone that Āḷāra Kālāma declares: "By realising for myself with direct knowledge, I enter upon and abide in this Dhamma." Certainly Āḷāra Kālāma abides knowing and seeing this Dhamma.' Then I went to Āḷāra Kālāma and asked him: 'Friend Kālāma, in what way do you declare that by realising for yourself with direct knowledge you enter upon and abide in this Dhamma?' In reply he declared the base of nothingness.[301]

"I considered: 'Not only Āḷāra Kālāma has faith, energy, mindfulness, concentration, and wisdom. I too have faith, energy, mindfulness, concentration, and wisdom. Suppose I endeavour to realise the Dhamma that Āḷāra Kālāma declares he enters upon and abides in by realising for himself with direct knowledge?'

"I soon quickly entered upon and abided in that Dhamma by realising for myself with direct knowledge. Then I went to Āḷāra Kālāma and asked him: 'Friend Kālāma, is it in this way that you declare that you enter upon and abide in this Dhamma by realising for yourself with direct knowledge?'—'That is the way, friend.'—'It is in this way, friend, that I also enter upon and abide in this Dhamma by realising for myself with direct knowledge.'—'It is a gain for us, friend, it is a great gain for us that we have such a venerable one for our companion in the holy life. So the Dhamma that I declare I enter upon and abide in by realising for myself with direct knowledge is the Dhamma that you enter upon and abide in by realising for yourself with direct knowledge. [165] And the Dhamma that you enter upon and abide in by realising for yourself with direct knowledge is the Dhamma that I declare I enter upon and abide in by realising for myself with direct knowledge. So you know the Dhamma that I know and I know the Dhamma that you know. As I am, so are you; as you are, so am I. Come, friend, let us now lead this community together.'

"Thus Āḷāra Kālāma, my teacher, placed me, his pupil, on an equal footing with himself and awarded me the highest honour. But it occurred to me: 'This Dhamma does not lead to disenchantment, to dispassion, to cessation, to peace, to direct knowledge, to enlightenment, to Nibbāna, but only to reappearance in the base of nothingness.'[302] Not being satisfied with that Dhamma, disappointed with it, I left.

16. "Still in search, bhikkhus, of what is wholesome, seeking the supreme state of sublime peace, I went to Uddaka Rāmaputta and said to him: 'Friend, I want to lead the holy life in this Dhamma and Discipline.'[303] Uddaka Rāmaputta replied: 'The venerable one may stay here. This Dhamma is such that a wise man can soon enter upon and abide in it, himself realising through direct knowledge his own teacher's doctrine.' I soon quickly learned that Dhamma. As far as mere lip-reciting and rehearsal of his teaching went, I could speak with knowledge and assurance, and I claimed, 'I know and see'—and there were others who did likewise.

"I considered: 'It was not through mere faith alone that Rāma declared: "By realising for myself with direct knowledge, I enter upon and abide in this Dhamma." Certainly Rāma abided knowing and seeing this Dhamma.' Then I went to Uddaka Rāmaputta and asked him: 'Friend, in what way did Rāma declare that by realising for himself with direct knowledge he entered upon and abided in this Dhamma?' In reply Uddaka Rāmaputta declared the base of neither-perception-nor-non-perception.

"I considered: 'Not only Rāma had faith, [166] energy, mindfulness, concentration, and wisdom. I too have faith, energy, mindfulness, concentration, and wisdom. Suppose I endeavour to realise the Dhamma that Rāma declared he entered upon and abided in by realising for himself with direct knowledge.'

"I soon quickly entered upon and abided in that Dhamma by realising for myself with direct knowledge. Then I went to Uddaka Rāmaputta and asked him: 'Friend, was it in this way that Rāma declared that he entered upon and abided in this Dhamma by realising for himself with direct knowledge?'—'That is the way, friend.'—'It is in this way, friend, that I also enter upon and abide in this Dhamma by realising for myself with direct knowledge.'—'It is a gain for us, friend, it is a great gain for us that we have such a venerable one for our companion in the holy life. So the Dhamma that Rāma declared he entered upon and abided in by realising for himself with direct knowledge is the Dhamma that you enter upon and abide in by realising for yourself with direct knowledge. And the Dhamma that you enter upon and abide in by realising for yourself with direct knowledge is the Dhamma that Rāma declared he entered upon and abided in by realising for himself with direct knowledge. So you know the Dhamma that Rāma knew and Rāma knew the Dhamma that you know. As Rāma was, so are you; as you are, so was Rāma. Come, friend, now lead this community.'

"Thus Uddaka Rāmaputta, my companion in the holy life, placed me in the position of a teacher and accorded me the highest honour. But it occurred to me: 'This Dhamma does not lead to disenchantment, to dispassion, to cessation, to peace, to direct knowledge, to enlightenment, to Nibbāna, but only to reappearance in the base of neither-perception-nor-non-perception.' Not being satisfied with that Dhamma, disappointed with it, I left.

17. "Still in search, bhikkhus, of what is wholesome, seeking the supreme state of sublime peace, I wandered by stages through the Magadhan country until eventually I arrived at Senānigama near Uruvelā. [167] There I saw an agreeable piece of ground, a delightful grove with a clear-flowing river with pleasant, smooth banks and nearby a village for alms resort. I considered: 'This is an agreeable piece of ground, this is a delightful grove with a clear-flowing river with pleasant, smooth banks and nearby a village for alms resort. This will serve for the striving of a clansman intent on striving.' And I sat down there thinking: 'This will serve for striving.'[304]

(ENLIGHTENMENT)

18. "Then, bhikkhus, being myself subject to birth, having understood the danger in what is subject to birth, seeking the unborn supreme security from bondage, Nibbāna, I attained the unborn supreme security from bondage, Nibbāna; being myself subject to ageing, having understood the danger in what is subject to ageing, seeking the unageing supreme security from bondage, Nibbāna, I attained the unageing supreme security from bondage, Nibbāna; being myself subject to sickness, having understood the danger in what is subject to sickness, seeking the

unailing supreme security from bondage, Nibbāna, I attained the unailing supreme security from bondage, Nibbāna; being myself subject to death, having understood the danger in what is subject to death, seeking the deathless supreme security from bondage, Nibbāna, I attained the deathless supreme security from bondage, Nibbāna; being myself subject to sorrow, having understood the danger in what is subject to sorrow, seeking the sorrowless supreme security from bondage, Nibbāna, I attained the sorrowless supreme security from bondage, Nibbāna; being myself subject to defilement, having understood the danger in what is subject to defilement, seeking the undefiled supreme security from bondage, Nibbāna, I attained the undefiled supreme security from bondage, Nibbāna. The knowledge and vision arose in me: 'My deliverance is unshakeable; this is my last birth; now there is no renewal of being.'

19. "I considered: 'This Dhamma that I have attained is profound, hard to see and hard to understand, peaceful and sublime, unattainable by mere reasoning, subtle, to be experienced by the wise.[305] But this generation delights in worldliness, takes delight in worldliness, rejoices in worldliness.[306] It is hard for such a generation to see this truth, namely, specific conditionality, dependent origination. And it is hard to see this truth, namely, the stilling of all formations, the relinquishing of all acquisitions, the destruction of craving, dispassion, cessation, Nibbāna. [168] If I were to teach the Dhamma, others would not understand me, and that would be wearying and troublesome for me.' Thereupon there came to me spontaneously these stanzas never heard before:

'Enough with teaching the Dhamma
That even I found hard to reach;
For it will never be perceived
By those who live in lust and hate.

Those dyed in lust, wrapped in darkness
Will never discern this abstruse Dhamma
Which goes against the worldly stream,
Subtle, deep, and difficult to see.'

Considering thus, my mind inclined to inaction rather than to teaching the Dhamma.[307]

20. "Then, bhikkhus, the Brahmā Sahampati knew with his mind the thought in my mind and he considered: 'The world will be lost, the world will perish, since the mind of the Tathāgata, accomplished and fully enlightened, inclines to inaction rather than to teaching the Dhamma.' Then, just as quickly as a strong man might extend his flexed arm or flex his extended arm, the Brahmā Sahampati vanished in the Brahma-world and appeared before me. He arranged his upper robe on one shoulder, and extending his hands in reverential salutation towards me, said: 'Venerable sir, let the Blessed One teach the Dhamma, let the Sublime One teach the Dhamma. There are beings with little dust in their eyes who are wasting through not hearing the Dhamma. There will be those who will understand the Dhamma.' The Brahmā Sahampati spoke thus, and then he said further:

'In Magadha there have appeared till now
Impure teachings devised by those still stained.
Open the doors to the Deathless! Let them hear
The Dhamma that the Stainless One has found.

Just as one who stands on a mountain peak
Can see below the people all around,
So, O Wise One, All-seeing Sage,
Ascend the palace of the Dhamma.
Let the Sorrowless One survey this human breed,
Engulfed in sorrow, overcome by birth and old age. [169]

Arise, victorious hero, caravan leader,
Debtless one, and wander in the world.
Let the Blessed One teach the Dhamma,
There will be those who will understand.'

21. "Then I listened to the Brahmā's pleading, and out of compassion for beings I surveyed the world with the eye of a Buddha. Surveying the world with the eye of a Buddha, I saw beings with little dust in their eyes and with much dust in their eyes, with keen faculties and with dull faculties, with good qualities and with bad qualities, easy to teach and hard to teach, and some who dwelt seeing fear in blame and in the other world. Just as in a pond of blue or red or white lotuses, some lotuses that are born

and grow in the water thrive immersed in the water without rising out of it, and some other lotuses that are born and grow in the water rest on the water's surface, and some other lotuses that are born and grow in the water rise out of the water and stand clear, unwetted by it; so too, surveying the world with the eye of a Buddha, I saw beings with little dust in their eyes and with much dust in their eyes, with keen faculties and with dull faculties, with good qualities and with bad qualities, easy to teach and hard to teach, and some who dwelt seeing fear in blame and in the other world. Then I replied to the Brahmā Sahampati in stanzas:

> 'Open for them are the doors to the Deathless,
> Let those with ears now show their faith.
> Thinking it would be troublesome, O Brahmā,
> I did not speak the Dhamma subtle and sublime.'

Then the Brahmā Sahampati thought: 'I have created the opportunity for the Blessed One to teach the Dhamma.' And after paying homage to me, keeping me on the right, he thereupon departed at once.

22. "I considered thus: 'To whom should I first teach the Dhamma? Who will understand this Dhamma quickly?' It then occurred to me: 'Āḷāra Kālāma is wise, intelligent, and discerning; he has long had little dust in his eyes. Suppose I [170] taught the Dhamma first to Āḷāra Kālāma. He will understand it quickly.' Then deities approached me and said: 'Venerable sir, Āḷāra Kālāma died seven days ago.' And the knowledge and vision arose in me: 'Āḷāra Kālāma died seven days ago.' I thought: 'Āḷāra Kālāma's loss is a great one. If he had heard this Dhamma, he would have understood it quickly.'

23. "I considered thus: 'To whom should I first teach the Dhamma? Who will understand this Dhamma quickly?' It then occurred to me: 'Uddaka Rāmaputta is wise, intelligent, and discerning; he has long had little dust in his eyes. Suppose I taught the Dhamma first to Uddaka Rāmaputta. He will understand it quickly.' Then deities approached me and said: 'Venerable sir, Uddaka Rāmaputta died last night.' And the knowledge and vision arose in me: 'Uddaka Rāmaputta died last night.' I thought: 'Uddaka Rāmaputta's loss is a great one. If he had heard this Dhamma, he would have understood it quickly.'

24. "I considered thus: 'To whom should I first teach the Dhamma? Who will understand this Dhamma quickly?' It then occurred to me: 'The bhikkhus of the group of five who attended upon me while I was engaged in my striving were very helpful.[308] Suppose I taught the Dhamma first to them.' Then I thought: 'Where are the bhikkhus of the group of five now living?' And with the divine eye, which is purified and surpasses the human, I saw that they were living at Benares in the Deer Park at Isipatana.

(THE TEACHING OF THE DHAMMA)

25. "Then, bhikkhus, when I had stayed at Uruvelā as long as I chose, I set out to wander by stages to Benares. Between Gayā and the Place of Enlightenment the Ājīvaka Upaka saw me on the road and said: 'Friend, your faculties are clear, the colour of your skin is pure and bright. Under whom have you gone forth, friend? Who is your teacher? Whose Dhamma do you [171] profess?' I replied to the Ājīvaka Upaka in stanzas:

'I am one who has transcended all, a knower of all,
Unsullied among all things, renouncing all,
By craving's ceasing freed. Having known this all
For myself, to whom should I point as teacher?

I have no teacher, and one like me
Exists nowhere in all the world
With all its gods, because I have
No person for my counterpart.

I am the Accomplished One in the world,
I am the Teacher Supreme.
I alone am a Fully Enlightened One
Whose fires are quenched and extinguished.

I go now to the city of Kāsi
To set in motion the Wheel of Dhamma.
In a world that has become blind
I go to beat the drum of the Deathless.'

'By your claims, friend, you ought to be the Universal Victor.'[309]

'The victors are those like me
Who have won to destruction of taints.
I have vanquished all evil states,
Therefore, Upaka, I am a victor.'

"When this was said, the Ājīvaka Upaka said: 'May it be so, friend.' Shaking his head, he took a bypath and departed.[310]

26. "Then, bhikkhus, wandering by stages, I eventually came to Benares, to the Deer Park at Isipatana, and I approached the bhikkhus of the group of five. The bhikkhus saw me coming in the distance, and they agreed among themselves thus: 'Friends, here comes the recluse Gotama who lives luxuriously, who gave up his striving, and reverted to luxury. We should not pay homage to him or rise up for him or receive his bowl and outer robe. But a seat may be prepared for him. If he likes, he may sit down.' However, as I approached, those bhikkhus found themselves unable to keep their pact. One came to meet me and took my bowl and outer robe, another prepared a seat, and another set out water for my feet; however, they addressed me by name and as 'friend.'[311]

27. "Thereupon I told them: 'Bhikkhus, do not address the Tathāgata by name and as "friend." The Tathāgata is an Accomplished One, [172] a Fully Enlightened One. Listen, bhikkhus, the Deathless has been attained. I shall instruct you, I shall teach you the Dhamma. Practising as you are instructed, by realising for yourselves here and now through direct knowledge you will soon enter upon and abide in that supreme goal of the holy life for the sake of which clansmen rightly go forth from the home life into homelessness.'

"When this was said, the bhikkhus of the group of five answered me thus: 'Friend Gotama, by the conduct, the practice, and the performance of austerities that you undertook, you did not achieve any superhuman states, any distinction in knowledge and vision worthy of the noble ones.[312] Since you now live luxuriously, having given up your striving and reverted to luxury, how will you have achieved any superhuman states, any distinction in knowledge and vision worthy of the noble ones?' When this was said, I told them: 'The Tathāgata does not live luxuriously, nor has he given up his striving and reverted to luxury. The Tathāgata is an Accomplished One, a Fully Enlightened One.

Listen, bhikkhus, the Deathless has been attained...from the home life into homelessness.'

"A second time the bhikkhus of the group of five said to me: 'Friend Gotama...how will you have achieved any superhuman states, any distinction in knowledge and vision worthy of the noble ones?' A second time I told them: 'The Tathāgata does not live luxuriously...from the home life into homelessness.' A third time the bhikkhus of the group of five said to me: 'Friend Gotama...how will you have achieved any superhuman states, any distinction in knowledge and vision worthy of the noble ones?'

28. "When this was said I asked them: 'Bhikkhus, have you ever known me to speak like this before?'—'No, venerable sir.'[313]—'Bhikkhus, the Tathāgata is an Accomplished One, a Fully Enlightened One. Listen, bhikkhus, the Deathless has been attained. I shall instruct you, I shall teach you the Dhamma. Practising as you are instructed, by realising for yourselves here and now through direct knowledge you will soon enter upon and abide in that supreme goal of the holy life for the sake of which clansmen rightly go forth from the home life into homelessness.' [173]

29. "I was able to convince the bhikkhus of the group of five.[314] Then I sometimes instructed two bhikkhus while the other three went for alms, and the six of us lived on what those three bhikkhus brought back from their almsround. Sometimes I instructed three bhikkhus while the other two went for alms, and the six of us lived on what those two bhikkhus brought back from their almsround.

30. "Then the bhikkhus of the group of five, thus taught and instructed by me, being themselves subject to birth, having understood the danger in what is subject to birth, seeking the unborn supreme security from bondage, Nibbāna, attained the unborn supreme security from bondage, Nibbāna; being themselves subject to ageing, sickness, death, sorrow, and defilement, having understood the danger in what is subject to ageing, sickness, death, sorrow, and defilement, seeking the unageing, unailing, deathless, sorrowless, and undefiled supreme security from bondage, Nibbāna, they attained the unageing, unailing, deathless, sorrowless, and undefiled supreme security from bondage, Nibbāna. The knowledge and vision arose in them:

'Our deliverance is unshakeable; this is our last birth; there is no renewal of being.'

(SENSUAL PLEASURE)

31. "Bhikkhus, there are these five cords of sensual pleasure.[315] What are the five? Forms cognizable by the eye that are wished for, desired, agreeable and likeable, connected with sensual desire, and provocative of lust. Sounds cognizable by the ear...Odours cognizable by the nose...Flavours cognizable by the tongue...Tangibles cognizable by the body that are wished for, desired, agreeable and likeable, connected with sensual desire, and provocative of lust. These are the five cords of sensual pleasure.

32. "As to those recluses and brahmins who are tied to these five cords of sensual pleasure, infatuated with them and utterly committed to them, and who use them without seeing the danger in them or understanding the escape from them, it may be understood of them: 'They have met with calamity, met with disaster, the Evil One may do with them as he likes.' Suppose a forest deer who was bound lay down on a heap of snares; it might be understood of him: 'He has met with calamity, met with disaster, the hunter can do with him as he likes, and when the hunter comes he cannot go where he wants.' So too, as to those recluses and brahmins who are tied to these five cords of sensual pleasure...it may be understood of them: 'They have met with calamity, met with disaster, the Evil One may do with them as he likes.'

33. "As to those recluses and brahmins who are not tied to these five cords of sensual pleasure, who are not infatuated with them or utterly committed to them, and who use them seeing the danger in them and understanding the escape from them, [174] it may be understood of them: 'They have not met with calamity, not met with disaster, the Evil One cannot do with them as he likes.'[316] Suppose a forest deer who was unbound lay down on a heap of snares; it might be understood of him: 'He has not met with calamity, not met with disaster, the hunter cannot do with him as he likes, and when the hunter comes he can go where he wants.' So too, as to those recluses and brahmins who are not tied to these five cords of sensual pleasure...it may

be understood of them: 'They have not met with calamity, not met with disaster, the Evil One cannot do with them as he likes.'

34. "Suppose a forest deer is wandering in the forest wilds: he walks confidently, stands confidently, sits confidently, lies down confidently. Why is that? Because he is out of the hunter's range. So too, quite secluded from sensual pleasures, secluded from unwholesome states, a bhikkhu enters upon and abides in the first jhāna, which is accompanied by applied and sustained thought, with rapture and pleasure born of seclusion. This bhikkhu is said to have blindfolded Māra, to have become invisible to the Evil One by depriving Māra's eye of its opportunity.[317]

35. "Again, with the stilling of applied and sustained thought, a bhikkhu enters upon and abides in the second jhāna, which has self-confidence and singleness of mind without applied and sustained thought, with rapture and pleasure born of concentration. This bhikkhu is said to have blindfolded Māra...

36. "Again, with the fading away as well of rapture, a bhikkhu abides in equanimity, and mindful and fully aware, still feeling pleasure with the body, he enters upon and abides in the third jhāna, on account of which noble ones announce: 'He has a pleasant abiding who has equanimity and is mindful.' This bhikkhu is said to have blindfolded Māra...

37. "Again, with the abandoning of pleasure and pain, and with the previous disappearance of joy and grief, a bhikkhu enters upon and abides in the fourth jhāna, which has neither-pain-nor-pleasure and purity of mindfulness due to equanimity. This bhikkhu is said to have blindfolded Māra...

38. "Again, with the complete surmounting of perceptions of form, with the disappearance of perceptions of sensory impact, with non-attention to perceptions of diversity, aware that 'space is infinite,' a bhikkhu enters upon and abides in the base of infinite space. This bhikkhu is said to have blindfolded Māra...

39. "Again, by completely surmounting the base of infinite space, aware that 'consciousness is infinite,' a bhikkhu enters upon and abides in the base of infinite consciousness. This bhikkhu is said to have blindfolded Māra...

40. "Again, by completely surmounting the base of infinite consciousness, aware that 'there is nothing,' a bhikkhu enters upon and abides in the base of nothingness. This bhikkhu is said to have blindfolded Māra...

41. "Again, by completely surrounding the base of nothingness, [175] a bhikkhu enters upon and abides in the base of neither-perception-nor-non-perception. This bhikkhu is said to have blindfolded Māra, to have become invisible to the Evil One by depriving Māra's eye of its opportunity.

42. "Again, by completely surmounting the base of neither-perception-nor-non-perception, a bhikkhu enters upon and abides in the cessation of perception and feeling. And his taints are destroyed by his seeing with wisdom. This bhikkhu is said to have blindfolded Māra, to have become invisible to the Evil One by depriving Māra's eye of its opportunity, and to have crossed beyond attachment to the world.[318] He walks confidently, stands confidently, sits confidently, lies down confidently. Why is that? Because he is out of the Evil One's range."

That is what the Blessed One said. The bhikkhus were satisfied and delighted in the Blessed One's words.

27 *Cūḷahatthipadopama Sutta*
The Shorter Discourse on the Simile of the Elephant's Footprint

1. THUS HAVE I HEARD.[319] On one occasion the Blessed One was living at Sāvatthī in Jeta's Grove, Anāthapiṇḍika's Park.

2. Now on that occasion the brahmin Jāṇussoṇi was driving out of Sāvatthī in the middle of the day in an all-white chariot drawn by white mares. He saw the wanderer Pilotika coming in the distance and asked him: "Now where is Master Vacchāyana coming from in the middle of the day?"[320]

"Sir, I am coming from the presence of the recluse Gotama."

"What does Master Vacchāyana think of the recluse Gotama's lucidity of wisdom? He is wise, is he not?"

"Sir, who am I to know the recluse Gotama's lucidity of wisdom? One would surely have to be his equal to know the recluse Gotama's lucidity of wisdom."

"Master Vacchāyana praises the recluse Gotama with high praise indeed."

"Sir, who am I to praise the recluse Gotama? The recluse Gotama is praised by the praised as best among gods and humans."

"What reasons does Master Vacchāyana see that he has such firm confidence in the recluse Gotama?"

3. "Sir, suppose a wise elephant woodsman were to enter an elephant wood and were to see in the elephant wood [176] a big elephant's footprint, long in extent and broad across. He would come to the conclusion: 'Indeed, this is a big bull elephant.' So too, when I saw four footprints of the recluse Gotama, I came to the conclusion: 'The Blessed One is fully enlightened, the Dhamma is well proclaimed by the Blessed One, the Sangha is practising the good way.' What are the four?

4. "Sir, I have seen here certain learned nobles who were clever, knowledgeable about the doctrines of others, as sharp as

hairsplitting marksmen; they wander about, as it were, demolishing the views of others with their sharp wits. When they hear: 'The recluse Gotama will visit such and such a village or town,' they formulate a question thus: 'We will go to the recluse Gotama and ask him this question. If he is asked like this, he will answer like this, and so we will refute his doctrine in this way; and if he is asked like that, he will answer like that, and so we will refute his doctrine in that way.'

"They hear: 'The recluse Gotama has come to visit such and such a village or town.' They go to the recluse Gotama, and the recluse Gotama instructs, urges, rouses, and gladdens them with a talk on the Dhamma. After they have been instructed, urged, roused, and gladdened by the recluse Gotama with a talk on the Dhamma, they do not so much as ask him the question, so how should they refute his doctrine? In actual fact, they become his disciples. When I saw this first footprint of the recluse Gotama, I came to the conclusion: 'The Blessed One is fully enlightened, the Dhamma is well proclaimed by the Blessed One, the Sangha is practising the good way.'

5. "Again, I have seen certain learned brahmins who were clever...In actual fact, they too become his disciples. When I saw this second footprint of the recluse Gotama, I came to the conclusion: 'The Blessed One is fully enlightened...'

6. "Again, I have seen certain learned householders who were clever...[177]...In actual fact, they too become his disciples. When I saw this third footprint of the recluse Gotama, I came to the conclusion: 'The Blessed One is fully enlightened...'

7. "Again, I have seen certain learned recluses who were clever...They do not so much as ask him the question, so how should they refute his doctrine? In actual fact, they ask the recluse Gotama to allow them to go forth from the home life into homelessness, and he gives them the going forth. Not long after they have gone forth, dwelling alone, withdrawn, diligent, ardent, and resolute, by realising for themselves with direct knowledge they here and now enter upon and abide in that supreme goal of the holy life for the sake of which clansmen rightly go forth from the home life into homelessness. They say thus: 'We were very nearly lost, we very nearly perished, for formerly we claimed that we were recluses though we were not really recluses; we claimed that we were brahmins though we

were not really brahmins; we claimed that we were arahants though we were not really arahants. But now we are recluses, now we are brahmins, now we are arahants.' When I saw this fourth footprint of the recluse Gotama, I came to the conclusion: 'The Blessed One is fully enlightened…'

"When I saw these four footprints of the recluse Gotama, I came to the conclusion: 'The Blessed One is fully enlightened, the Dhamma is well proclaimed by the Blessed One, the Sangha is practising the good way.'"

8. When this was said, the brahmin Jāṇussoṇi got down from his all-white chariot drawn by white mares, and arranging his upper robe on one shoulder, he extended his hands in reverential salutation towards the Blessed One and uttered this exclamation three times: "Honour to the Blessed One, accomplished and fully enlightened! Honour to the Blessed One, accomplished and fully enlightened! Honour to the Blessed One, accomplished and fully enlightened! Perhaps some time or other [178] we might meet Master Gotama and have some conversation with him."

9. Then the brahmin Jāṇussoṇi went to the Blessed One and exchanged greetings with him. When this courteous and amiable talk was finished, he sat down at one side and related to the Blessed One his entire conversation with the wanderer Pilotika. Thereupon the Blessed One told him: "At this point, brahmin, the simile of the elephant's footprint has not yet been completed in detail. As to how it is completed in detail, listen and attend carefully to what I shall say."—"Yes, sir," the brahmin Jāṇussoṇi replied. The Blessed One said this:

10. "Brahmin, suppose an elephant woodsman were to enter an elephant wood and were to see in the elephant wood a big elephant's footprint, long in extent and broad across. A wise elephant woodsman would not yet come to the conclusion: 'Indeed, this is a big bull elephant.' Why is that? In an elephant wood there are small she-elephants that leave a big footprint, and this might be one of their footprints. He follows it and sees in the elephant wood a big elephant's footprint, long in extent and broad across, and some scrapings high up. A wise elephant woodsman would not yet come to the conclusion: 'Indeed, this is a big bull elephant.' Why is that? In an elephant wood there are tall she-elephants that have prominent teeth and leave a big footprint, and this might be one of their footprints. He follows it

further and sees in the elephant wood a big elephant's footprint, long in extent and broad across, and some scrapings high up, and marks made by tusks. A wise elephant woodsman would not yet come to the conclusion: 'Indeed, this is a big bull elephant.' Why is that? In an elephant wood there are tall she-elephants that have tusks and leave a big footprint, and this might be one of their footprints. He follows it further and sees in the elephant wood a big elephant's footprint, long in extent and broad across, and some scrapings high up, and marks made by tusks, and broken-off branches. And he sees that bull elephant at the root of a tree or in the open, walking about, sitting, or lying down. He comes to the conclusion: 'This is that big bull elephant.'

11. "So too, [179] brahmin, here a Tathāgata appears in the world, accomplished, fully enlightened, perfect in true knowledge and conduct, sublime, knower of worlds, incomparable leader of persons to be tamed, teacher of gods and humans, enlightened, blessed. He declares this world with its gods, its Māras, and its Brahmās, this generation with its recluses and brahmins, its princes and its people, which he has himself realised with direct knowledge. He teaches the Dhamma good in the beginning, good in the middle, and good in the end, with the right meaning and phrasing, and he reveals a holy life that is utterly perfect and pure.

12. "A householder or householder's son or one born in some other clan hears that Dhamma. On hearing the Dhamma he acquires faith in the Tathāgata. Possessing that faith, he considers thus: 'Household life is crowded and dusty; life gone forth is wide open. It is not easy, while living in a home, to lead the holy life utterly perfect and pure as a polished shell. Suppose I shave off my hair and beard, put on the yellow robe, and go forth from the home life into homelessness.' On a later occasion, abandoning a small or a large fortune, abandoning a small or a large circle of relatives, he shaves off his hair and beard, puts on the yellow robe, and goes forth from the home life into homelessness.

13. "Having thus gone forth and possessing the bhikkhu's training and way of life, abandoning the killing of living beings, he abstains from killing living beings; with rod and weapon laid aside, gentle and kindly, he abides compassionate to all living beings. Abandoning the taking of what is not given, he abstains

from taking what is not given; taking only what is given, expecting only what is given, by not stealing he abides in purity. Abandoning incelibacy, he observes celibacy, living apart, abstaining from the vulgar practice of sexual intercourse.

"Abandoning false speech, he abstains from false speech; he speaks truth, adheres to truth, is trustworthy and reliable, one who is no deceiver of the world. Abandoning malicious speech, he abstains from malicious speech; he does not repeat elsewhere what he has heard here in order to divide [those people] from these, nor does he repeat to these people what he has heard elsewhere in order to divide [these people] from those; thus he is one who reunites those who are divided, a promoter of friendships, who enjoys concord, rejoices in concord, delights in concord, a speaker of words that promote concord. Abandoning harsh speech, he abstains from harsh speech; he speaks such words as are gentle, pleasing to the ear, and loveable, as go to the heart, are courteous, desired by many [180] and agreeable to many. Abandoning gossip, he abstains from gossip; he speaks at the right time, speaks what is fact, speaks on what is good, speaks on the Dhamma and the Discipline; at the right time he speaks such words as are worth recording, reasonable, moderate, and beneficial.

"He abstains from injuring seeds and plants. He practises eating only one meal a day, abstaining from eating at night and outside the proper time.[321] He abstains from dancing, singing, music, and theatrical shows. He abstains from wearing garlands, smartening himself with scent, and embellishing himself with unguents. He abstains from high and large couches. He abstains from accepting gold and silver. He abstains from accepting raw grain. He abstains from accepting raw meat. He abstains from accepting women and girls. He abstains from accepting men and women slaves. He abstains from accepting goats and sheep. He abstains from accepting fowl and pigs. He abstains from accepting elephants, cattle, horses, and mares. He abstains from accepting fields and land. He abstains from going on errands and running messages. He abstains from buying and selling. He abstains from false weights, false metals, and false measures. He abstains from cheating, deceiving, defrauding, and trickery. He abstains from wounding, murdering, binding, brigandage, plunder, and violence.

14. "He becomes content with robes to protect his body and with almsfood to maintain his stomach, and wherever he goes, he sets out taking only these with him. Just as a bird, wherever it goes, flies with its wings as its only burden, so too the bhikkhu becomes content with robes to protect his body and with almsfood to maintain his stomach, and wherever he goes, he sets out taking only these with him. Possessing this aggregate of noble virtue, he experiences within himself a bliss that is blameless.

15. "On seeing a form with the eye, he does not grasp at its signs and features. Since, if he left the eye faculty unguarded, evil unwholesome states of covetousness and grief might invade him, he practises the way of its restraint, he guards the eye faculty, he undertakes the restraint of the eye faculty.[322] On hearing a sound with the ear…On smelling an odour with the nose…On tasting a flavour with the tongue…On touching a tangible with the body…On cognizing a mind-object with the mind, he does not grasp at its signs and features. Since, if he left the mind faculty unguarded, evil unwholesome states of covetousness and grief might invade him, he practises the way of its restraint, [181] he guards the mind faculty, he undertakes the restraint of the mind faculty. Possessing this noble restraint of the faculties, he experiences within himself a bliss that is unsullied.

16. "He becomes one who acts in full awareness when going forward and returning; who acts in full awareness when looking ahead and looking away; who acts in full awareness when flexing and extending his limbs; who acts in full awareness when wearing his robes and carrying his outer robe and bowl; who acts in full awareness when eating, drinking, consuming food, and tasting; who acts in full awareness when defecating and urinating; who acts in full awareness when walking, standing, sitting, falling asleep, waking up, talking, and keeping silent.

17. "Possessing this aggregate of noble virtue, and this noble restraint of the faculties, and possessing this noble mindfulness and full awareness, he resorts to a secluded resting place: the forest, the root of a tree, a mountain, a ravine, a hillside cave, a charnel ground, a jungle thicket, an open space, a heap of straw.

18. "On returning from his almsround, after his meal he sits down, folding his legs crosswise, setting his body erect, and establishing mindfulness before him. Abandoning covetousness for the world, he abides with a mind free from covetousness; he

purifies his mind from covetousness.[323] Abandoning ill will and hatred, he abides with a mind free from ill will, compassionate for the welfare of all living beings; he purifies his mind from ill will and hatred. Abandoning sloth and torpor, he abides free from sloth and torpor, percipient of light, mindful and fully aware; he purifies his mind from sloth and torpor. Abandoning restlessness and remorse, he abides unagitated with a mind inwardly peaceful; he purifies his mind from restlessness and remorse. Abandoning doubt, he abides having gone beyond doubt, unperplexed about wholesome states; he purifies his mind from doubt.

19. "Having thus abandoned these five hindrances, imperfections of the mind that weaken wisdom, quite secluded from sensual pleasures, secluded from unwholesome states, he enters upon and abides in the first jhāna, which is accompanied by applied and sustained thought, with rapture and pleasure born of seclusion. This, brahmin, is called a footprint of the Tathāgata, something scraped by the Tathāgata, something marked by the Tathāgata, but a noble disciple does not yet come to the conclusion: 'The Blessed One is fully enlightened, the Dhamma is well proclaimed by the Blessed One, the Sangha is practising the good way.'[324]

20. "Again, with the stilling of applied and sustained thought, a bhikkhu enters upon and abides in the second jhāna, which has self-confidence and singleness of mind without applied and sustained thought, with rapture and pleasure born of concentration. This too, brahmin, is called a footprint of the Tathāgata... but a noble [182] disciple does not yet come to the conclusion: 'The Blessed One is fully enlightened...'

21. "Again, with the fading away as well of rapture, a bhikkhu abides in equanimity, and mindful and fully aware, still feeling pleasure with the body, he enters upon and abides in the third jhāna, on account of which noble ones announce: 'He has a pleasant abiding who has equanimity and is mindful.' This too, brahmin, is called a footprint of the Tathāgata...but a noble disciple does not yet come to the conclusion: 'The Blessed One is fully enlightened...'

22. "Again, with the abandoning of pleasure and pain, and with the previous disappearance of joy and grief, a bhikkhu enters upon and abides in the fourth jhāna, which has neither-

pain-nor-pleasure and purity of mindfulness due to equanimity. This too, brahmin, is called a footprint of the Tathāgata...but a noble disciple does not yet come to the conclusion: 'The Blessed One is fully enlightened...'

23. "When his concentrated mind is thus purified, bright, unblemished, rid of imperfection, malleable, wieldy, steady, and attained to imperturbability, he directs it to knowledge of the recollection of past lives. He recollects his manifold past lives, that is, one birth, two births, three births, four births, five births, ten births, twenty births, thirty births, forty births, fifty births, a hundred births, a thousand births, a hundred thousand births, many aeons of world-contraction, many aeons of world-expansion, many aeons of world-contraction and expansion: ...(*as Sutta 4, §27*)...Thus with their aspects and particulars he recollects his manifold past lives. This too, brahmin, is called a footprint of the Tathāgata...but a noble disciple does not yet come to the conclusion: 'The Blessed One is fully enlightened...' [183]

24. "When his concentrated mind is thus purified, bright, unblemished, rid of imperfection, malleable, wieldy, steady, and attained to imperturbability, he directs it to knowledge of the passing away and reappearance of beings. With the divine eye, which is purified and surpasses the human, he sees beings passing away and reappearing, inferior and superior, fair and ugly, fortunate and unfortunate. He understands how beings pass on according to their actions thus:...(*as Sutta 4, §29*)...Thus with the divine eye, which is purified and surpasses the human, he sees beings passing away and reappearing, inferior and superior, fair and ugly, fortunate and unfortunate, and he understands how beings pass on according to their actions. This too, brahmin, is called a footprint of the Tathāgata...but a noble disciple does not yet come to the conclusion: 'The Blessed One is fully enlightened...'

25. "When his concentrated mind is thus purified, bright, unblemished, rid of imperfection, malleable, wieldy, steady, and attained to imperturbability, he directs it to knowledge of the destruction of the taints. He understands as it actually is: 'This is suffering';...'This is the origin of suffering';...'This is the cessation of suffering';...'This is the way leading to the cessation of suffering';...'These are the taints';...'This is the origin of the taints';...'This is the cessation of the taints';...'This is the way leading to the cessation of the taints.'

"This too, brahmin, is called a footprint of the Tathāgata, something scraped by the Tathāgata, something marked by the Tathāgata, but a noble disciple still has not yet come to the conclusion: 'The Blessed One is fully enlightened, the Dhamma is well proclaimed by the Blessed One, the Sangha is practising the good way.' Rather, he is in the process of coming to this conclusion.[325]

26. "When he knows and sees thus, his mind is liberated from the taint of sensual desire, [184] from the taint of being, and from the taint of ignorance. When it is liberated there comes the knowledge: 'It is liberated.' He understands: 'Birth is destroyed, the holy life has been lived, what had to be done has been done, there is no more coming to any state of being.'

"This too, brahmin, is called a footprint of the Tathāgata, something scraped by the Tathāgata, something marked by the Tathāgata. It is at this point that a noble disciple has come to the conclusion: 'The Blessed One is fully enlightened, the Dhamma is well proclaimed by the Blessed One, the Sangha is practising the good way.'[326] And it is at this point, brahmin, that the simile of the elephant's footprint has been completed in detail."

27. When this was said, the brahmin Jāṇussoṇi said to the Blessed One: "Magnificent, Master Gotama! Magnificent, Master Gotama! Master Gotama has made the Dhamma clear in many ways, as though he were turning upright what had been overthrown, revealing what was hidden, showing the way to one who was lost, or holding up a lamp in the dark for those with eyesight to see forms. I go to Master Gotama for refuge and to the Dhamma and to the Sangha of bhikkhus. From today let Master Gotama remember me as a lay follower who has gone to him for refuge for life."

28 *Mahāhatthipadopama Sutta* The Greater Discourse on the Simile of the Elephant's Footprint

1. THUS HAVE I HEARD.[327] On one occasion the Blessed One was living at Sāvatthī in Jeta's Grove, Anāthapiṇḍika's Park. There the venerable Sāriputta addressed the bhikkhus thus: "Friends, bhikkhus."—"Friend," they replied. The venerable Sāriputta said this:

2. "Friends, just as the footprint of any living being that walks can be placed within an elephant's footprint, and so the elephant's footprint is declared the chief of them because of its great size; so too, all wholesome states can be included in the Four Noble Truths.[328] In what four? In the noble truth of suffering, [185] in the noble truth of the origin of suffering, in the noble truth of the cessation of suffering, and in the noble truth of the way leading to the cessation of suffering.

3. "And what is the noble truth of suffering? Birth is suffering, ageing is suffering, death is suffering; sorrow, lamentation, pain, grief, and despair are suffering; not to obtain what one wants is suffering; in short, the five aggregates affected by clinging are suffering.

4. "And what are the five aggregates affected by clinging? They are: the material form aggregate affected by clinging, the feeling aggregate affected by clinging, the perception aggregate affected by clinging, the formations aggregate affected by clinging, and the consciousness aggregate affected by clinging.

5. "And what is the material form aggregate affected by clinging? It is the four great elements and the material form derived from the four great elements. And what are the four great elements? They are the earth element, the water element, the fire element, and the air element.

(THE EARTH ELEMENT)

6. "What, friends, is the earth element? The earth element may be either internal or external. What is the internal earth element? Whatever internally, belonging to oneself, is solid, solidified, and clung-to; that is, head-hairs, body-hairs, nails, teeth, skin, flesh, sinews, bones, bone-marrow, kidneys, heart, liver, diaphragm, spleen, lungs, intestines, mesentery, contents of the stomach, feces, or whatever else internally, belonging to oneself, is solid, solidified, and clung-to: this is called the internal earth element.[329] Now both the internal earth element and the external earth element are simply earth element.[330] And that should be seen as it actually is with proper wisdom thus: 'This is not mine, this I am not, this is not my self.' When one sees it thus as it actually is with proper wisdom, one becomes disenchanted with the earth element and makes the mind dispassionate toward the earth element.

7. "Now there comes a time when the water element is disturbed and then the external earth element vanishes.[331] When even this external earth element, great as it is, is seen to be impermanent, subject to destruction, disappearance, and change, what of this body, which is clung to by craving and lasts but a while? There can be no considering that as 'I' or 'mine' or 'I am.'[332]

8. "So then, if others abuse, revile, scold, and harass a bhikkhu [who has seen this element as it actually is], he understands thus: 'This painful feeling born of ear-contact has arisen in me. That is dependent, not independent. Dependent on what? [186] Dependent on contact.'[333] Then he sees that contact is impermanent, that feeling is impermanent, that perception is impermanent, that formations are impermanent, and that consciousness is impermanent. And his mind, having made an element its objective support, enters into [that new objective support] and acquires confidence, steadiness, and resolution.[334]

9. "Now, if others attack that bhikkhu in ways that are unwished for, undesired, and disagreeable, by contact with fists, clods, sticks, or knives, he understands thus: 'This body is of such a nature that contact with fists, clods, sticks, and knives assail it.[335] But this has been said by the Blessed One in his "advice on the simile of the saw": "Bhikkhus, even if bandits

were to sever you savagely limb by limb with a two-handled saw, he who gave rise to a mind of hate towards them would not be carrying out my teaching."[336] So tireless energy shall be aroused in me and unremitting mindfulness established, my body shall be tranquil and untroubled, my mind concentrated and unified. And now let contact with fists, clods, sticks, and knives assail this body; for this is just how the Buddha's teaching is practised.'

10. "When that bhikkhu thus recollects the Buddha, the Dhamma, and the Sangha, if equanimity supported by the wholesome does not become established in him, then he arouses a sense of urgency thus: 'It is a loss for me, it is no gain for me, it is bad for me, it is no good for me, that when I thus recollect the Buddha, the Dhamma, and the Sangha, equanimity supported by the wholesome does not become established in me.'[337] Just as when a daughter-in-law sees her father-in-law, she arouses a sense of urgency [to please him], so too, when that bhikkhu thus recollects the Buddha, the Dhamma, and the Sangha, if equanimity supported by the wholesome does not become established in him, then he arouses a sense of urgency. But if, when he recollects the Buddha, the Dhamma, and the Sangha, equanimity supported by the wholesome becomes established in him, [187] then he is satisfied with it. At that point, friends, much has been done by that bhikkhu.

(THE WATER ELEMENT)

11. "What, friends, is the water element? The water element may be either internal or external. What is the internal water element? Whatever internally, belonging to oneself, is water, watery, and clung-to; that is, bile, phlegm, pus, blood, sweat, fat, tears, grease, spittle, snot, oil-of-the-joints, urine, or whatever else internally, belonging to oneself, is water, watery, and clung-to: this is called the internal water element. Now both the internal water element and the external water element are simply water element. And that should be seen as it actually is with proper wisdom thus: 'This is not mine, this I am not, this is not my self.' When one sees it thus as it actually is with proper wisdom, one becomes disenchanted with the water element and makes the mind dispassionate toward the water element.

12. "Now there comes a time when the external water element is disturbed. It carries away villages, towns, cities, districts, and countries. There comes a time when the waters in the great ocean sink down a hundred leagues, two hundred leagues, three hundred leagues, four hundred leagues, five hundred leagues, six hundred leagues, seven hundred leagues. There comes a time when the waters in the great ocean stand seven palms deep, six palms deep...two palms deep, only a palm deep. There comes a time when the waters in the great ocean stand seven fathoms deep, six fathoms deep...two fathoms deep, only a fathom deep. There comes a time when the waters in the great ocean stand half a fathom deep, only waist deep, only knee deep, only ankle deep. There comes a time when the waters in the great ocean are not enough to wet even the joint of a finger. When even this external water element, great as it is, [188] is seen to be impermanent, subject to destruction, disappearance, and change, what of this body, which is clung to by craving and lasts but a while? There can be no considering that as 'I' or 'mine' or 'I am.'

13–15. "So then, if others abuse, revile, scold, and harass a bhikkhu [who has seen this element as it actually is], he understands thus:...(*repeat §§8–10*)...At that point too, friends, much has been done by that bhikkhu.

(THE FIRE ELEMENT)

16. "What, friends, is the fire element? The fire element may be either internal or external. What is the internal fire element? Whatever internally, belonging to oneself, is fire, fiery, and clung-to; that is, that by which one is warmed, ages, and is consumed, and that by which what is eaten, drunk, consumed, and tasted gets completely digested, or whatever else internally, belonging to oneself, is fire, fiery, and clung-to: this is called the internal fire element. Now both the internal fire element and the external fire element are simply fire element. And that should be seen as it actually is with proper wisdom thus: 'This is not mine, this I am not, this is not my self.' When one sees it thus as it actually is with proper wisdom, one becomes disenchanted with the fire element and makes the mind dispassionate toward the fire element.

17. "Now there comes a time when the external fire element is disturbed. It burns up villages, towns, cities, districts, and countries. It goes out due to lack of fuel only when it comes to green grass, or to a road, or to a rock, or to water, or to a fair open space. There comes a time when they seek to make a fire even with a cock's feather or a hide-paring. When even this external fire element, great as it is, is seen to be impermanent, subject to destruction, disappearance, and change, what of this body, which is clung to by craving and lasts but a while? There can be no considering that as 'I' or 'mine' or 'I am.'

18–20. "So then, if others abuse, revile, scold, and harass a bhikkhu [who has seen this element as it actually is], he understands thus:...(*repeat §§8–10*)...At that point too, friends, much has been done by that bhikkhu.

(THE AIR ELEMENT)

21. "What, friends, is the air element? The air element may be either internal or external. What is the internal air element? Whatever internally, belonging to oneself, is air, airy, and clung-to; that is, up-going winds, down-going winds, winds in the belly, winds in the bowels, winds that course through the limbs, in-breath and out-breath, or whatever else internally, belonging to oneself, is air, airy, and clung-to: this is called the internal air element. Now both the internal air element and the external air element are simply air element. And that should be seen as it actually is with proper wisdom thus: 'This is not mine, this I am not, this is not my self.' When one sees it thus as it actually is with proper wisdom, one becomes disenchanted with the air element and makes the mind dispassionate toward the air element. [189]

22. "Now there comes a time when the external air element is disturbed. It sweeps away villages, towns, cities, districts, and countries. There comes a time in the last month of the hot season when they seek wind by means of a fan or bellows and even the strands of straw in the drip-fringe of the thatch do not stir. When even this external air element, great as it is, is seen to be impermanent, subject to destruction, disappearance, and change, what of this body, which is clung to by craving and lasts but a while? There can be no considering that as 'I' or 'mine' or 'I am.'

23–25. "So then, if others abuse, revile, scold, and harass a bhikkhu [who has seen this element as it actually is], he understands thus:...[190] (*repeat §§8–10*)...At that point too, friends, much has been done by that bhikkhu.

26. "Friends, just as when a space is enclosed by timber and creepers, grass, and clay, it comes to be termed 'house,' so too, when a space is enclosed by bones and sinews, flesh and skin, it comes to be termed 'material form.'[338]

27. "If, friends, internally the eye is intact but no external forms come into its range, and there is no corresponding [conscious] engagement, then there is no manifestation of the corresponding class of consciousness.[339] If internally the eye is intact and external forms come into its range, but there is no corresponding [conscious] engagement, then there is no manifestation of the corresponding class of consciousness. But when internally the eye is intact and external forms come into its range and there is the corresponding [conscious] engagement, then there is the manifestation of the corresponding class of consciousness.

28. "The material form in what has thus come to be is included in the material form aggregate affected by clinging.[340] The feeling in what has thus come to be is included in the feeling aggregate affected by clinging. The perception in what has thus come to be is included in the perception aggregate affected by clinging. The formations in what has thus come to be are included in the formations aggregate affected by clinging. The consciousness in what has thus come to be is included in the consciousness aggregate affected by clinging. He understands thus: 'This, indeed, is how there comes to be the inclusion, gathering, and amassing of things into these five aggregates affected by clinging. Now this has been said by the Blessed One: "One who sees [191] dependent origination sees the Dhamma; one who sees the Dhamma sees dependent origination."[341] And these five aggregates affected by clinging are dependently arisen. The desire, indulgence, inclination, and holding based on these five aggregates affected by clinging is the origin of suffering.[342] The removal of desire and lust, the abandonment of desire and lust for these five aggregates affected by clinging is the cessation of suffering.' At that point too, friends, much has been done by that bhikkhu.[343]

29–30. "If, friends, internally the ear is intact but no external sounds come into its range...(*as in §§27–28*)...At that point too, friends, much has been done by that bhikkhu.

31–32. "If, friends, internally the nose is intact but no external smells come into its range...At that point too, friends, much has been done by that bhikkhu.

33–34. "If, friends, internally the tongue is intact but no external flavours come into its range...At that point too, friends, much has been done by that bhikkhu.

35–36. "If, friends, internally the body is intact but no external tangibles come into its range...At that point too, friends, much has been done by that bhikkhu.

37. "If, friends, internally the mind is intact but no external mind-objects come into its range, and there is no corresponding [conscious] engagement, then there is no manifestation of the corresponding class of consciousness.[344] If internally the mind is intact and external mind-objects come into its range, but there is no corresponding [conscious] engagement, then there is no manifestation of the corresponding class of consciousness.[345] But when internally the mind is intact and external mind-objects come into its range and there is the corresponding [conscious] engagement, then there is the manifestation of the corresponding class of consciousness.

38. "The material form in what has thus come to be is included in the material form aggregate affected by clinging. The feeling in what has thus come to be is included in the feeling aggregate affected by clinging. The perception in what has thus come to be is included in the perception aggregate affected by clinging. The formations in what has thus come to be are included in the formations aggregate affected by clinging. The consciousness in what has thus come to be is included in the consciousness aggregate affected by clinging. He understands thus: 'This, indeed, is how there comes to be the inclusion, gathering, and amassing of things into these five aggregates affected by clinging. Now this has been said by the Blessed One: "One who sees dependent origination sees the Dhamma; one who sees the Dhamma sees dependent origination." And these five aggregates affected by clinging are dependently arisen. The desire, indulgence, inclination, and holding based on these five aggregates affected by clinging is the origin of suffering. The removal of desire and

lust, the abandonment of desire and lust for these five aggregates affected by clinging is the cessation of suffering.' At that point too, friends, much has been done by that bhikkhu."

That is what the venerable Sāriputta said. The bhikkhus were satisfied and delighted in the venerable Sāriputta's words.

29 *Mahāsāropama Sutta*
The Greater Discourse on the Simile of the Heartwood

[192] 1. THUS HAVE I HEARD. On one occasion the Blessed One was living at Rājagaha on the mountain Vulture Peak; it was soon after Devadatta had left.[346] There, referring to Devadatta, the Blessed One addressed the bhikkhus thus:

2. "Bhikkhus, here some clansman goes forth out of faith from the home life into homelessness, considering: 'I am a victim of birth, ageing, and death, of sorrow, lamentation, pain, grief, and despair; I am a victim of suffering, a prey to suffering. Surely an ending of this whole mass of suffering can be known.' When he has gone forth thus, he acquires gain, honour, and renown. He is pleased with that gain, honour, and renown, and his intention is fulfilled. On account of it he lauds himself and disparages others thus: 'I have gain, honour, and renown, but these other bhikkhus are unknown, of no account.' He becomes intoxicated with that gain, honour, and renown, grows negligent, falls into negligence, and being negligent, he lives in suffering.

"Suppose a man needing heartwood, seeking heartwood, wandering in search of heartwood, came to a great tree standing possessed of heartwood. Passing over its heartwood, its sapwood, its inner bark, and its outer bark, he would cut off its twigs and leaves and take them away thinking they were heartwood. Then a man with good sight, seeing him, might say: 'This good man did not know the heartwood, the sapwood, the inner bark, the outer bark, or the twigs and leaves. Thus, while needing heartwood, seeking heartwood, wandering in search of heartwood, he came to a great tree standing possessed of heartwood, and passing over its heartwood, its sapwood, its inner bark, and its outer bark, he cut off its twigs and leaves and took them away thinking they were heartwood. Whatever it was this good man had to make with heartwood, his purpose will not be served.' So too, bhikkhus, here some clansman goes forth out of faith...[193]...he lives in suffering. This bhikkhu is called one who has taken the twigs and leaves of the holy life and stopped short with that.

3. "Here, bhikkhus, some clansman goes forth out of faith from the home life into homelessness, considering: 'I am a victim of birth, ageing, and death, of sorrow, lamentation, pain, grief, and despair; I am a victim of suffering, a prey to suffering. Surely an ending of this whole mass of suffering can be known.' When he has gone forth thus, he acquires gain, honour, and renown. He is not pleased with that gain, honour, and renown, and his intention is not fulfilled. He does not, on account of it, laud himself and disparage others. He does not become intoxicated with that gain, honour, and renown; he does not grow negligent and fall into negligence. Being diligent, he achieves the attainment of virtue. He is pleased with that attainment of virtue and his intention is fulfilled. On account of it he lauds himself and disparages others thus: 'I am virtuous, of good character, but these other bhikkhus are immoral, of evil character.' He becomes intoxicated with that attainment of virtue, grows negligent, falls into negligence, and being negligent, he lives in suffering.

"Suppose a man needing heartwood, seeking heartwood, wandering in search of heartwood, came to a great tree standing possessed of heartwood. Passing over its heartwood, its sapwood, and its inner bark, he would cut off its outer bark and take it away thinking it was heartwood. Then a man with good sight, seeing him, might say: 'This good man did not know the heartwood...or the twigs and leaves. Thus, while needing heartwood...he cut off its outer bark and took it away thinking it was heartwood. Whatever it was this good man had to make with heartwood, his purpose will not be served.' So too, bhikkhus, here some clansman goes forth out of faith...he lives in suffering. [194] This bhikkhu is called one who has taken the outer bark of the holy life and stopped short with that.

4. "Here, bhikkhus, some clansman goes forth out of faith from the home life into homelessness, considering: 'I am a victim of birth, ageing, and death, of sorrow, lamentation, pain, grief, and despair; I am a victim of suffering, a prey to suffering. Surely an ending of this whole mass of suffering can be known.'

When he has gone forth thus, he acquires gain, honour, and renown. He is not pleased with that gain, honour, and renown, and his intention is not fulfilled...Being diligent, he achieves the attainment of virtue. He is pleased with that attainment of virtue, but his intention is not fulfilled. He does not, on account of it, laud himself and disparage others. He does not become intoxicated with that attainment of virtue; he does not grow negligent and fall into negligence. Being diligent, he achieves the attainment of concentration. He is pleased with that attainment of concentration and his intention is fulfilled. On account of it he lauds himself and disparages others thus: 'I am concentrated, my mind is unified, but these other bhikkhus are unconcentrated, with their minds astray.' He becomes intoxicated with that attainment of concentration, grows negligent, falls into negligence, and being negligent, he lives in suffering.

"Suppose a man needing heartwood, seeking heartwood, wandering in search of heartwood, came to a great tree standing possessed of heartwood. Passing over its heartwood and its sapwood, he would cut off its inner bark and take it away thinking it was heartwood. Then a man with good sight, seeing him, might say: 'This good man did not know the heartwood...or the twigs and leaves. Thus, while needing heartwood...he cut off its inner bark and took it away thinking it was heartwood. Whatever it was this good man had to make with heartwood, his purpose will not be served.' So too, bhikkhus, here some clansman goes forth out of faith...he lives in suffering. [195] This bhikkhu is called one who has taken the inner bark of the holy life and stopped short with that.

5. "Here, bhikkhus, some clansman goes forth out of faith from the home life into homelessness, considering: 'I am a victim of birth, ageing, and death, of sorrow, lamentation, pain, grief, and despair; I am a victim of suffering, a prey to suffering. Surely an ending of this whole mass of suffering can be known.' When he has gone forth thus, he acquires gain, honour, and renown. He is not pleased with that gain, honour, and renown, and his intention is not fulfilled...Being diligent, he achieves the attainment of virtue. He is pleased with that attainment of virtue, but his intention is not fulfilled...Being diligent, he achieves the attainment of concentration. He is pleased with that attainment of concentration, but his intention is not fulfilled. He

does not, on account of it, laud himself and disparage others. He does not become intoxicated with that attainment of concentration; he does not grow negligent and fall into negligence. Being diligent, he achieves knowledge and vision.[347] He is pleased with that knowledge and vision and his intention is fulfilled. On account of it he lauds himself and disparages others thus: 'I live knowing and seeing, but these other bhikkhus live unknowing and unseeing.' He becomes intoxicated with that knowledge and vision, grows negligent, falls into negligence, and being negligent, he lives in suffering.

"Suppose a man needing heartwood, seeking heartwood, wandering in search of heartwood, came to a great tree standing possessed of heartwood. Passing over its heartwood, he would cut off its sapwood and take it away thinking it was heartwood. Then a man with good sight, seeing him, might say: 'This good man did not know the heartwood...or the twigs and leaves. Thus, while needing heartwood...he cut off its sapwood and took it away thinking it was heartwood. Whatever it was this good man had to make with heartwood, his purpose will not be served.' [196] So too, bhikkhus, here some clansman goes forth out of faith...he lives in suffering. This bhikkhu is called one who has taken the sapwood of the holy life and stopped short with that.

6. "Here, bhikkhus, some clansman goes forth out of faith from the home life into homelessness, considering: 'I am a victim of birth, ageing, and death, of sorrow, lamentation, pain, grief, and despair; I am a victim of suffering, a prey to suffering. Surely an ending of this whole mass of suffering can be known.' When he has gone forth thus, he acquires gain, honour, and renown. He is not pleased with that gain, honour, and renown, and his intention is not fulfilled...When he is diligent, he achieves the attainment of virtue. He is pleased with that attainment of virtue, but his intention is not fulfilled...When he is diligent, he achieves the attainment of concentration. He is pleased with that attainment of concentration, but his intention is not fulfilled...When he is diligent, he achieves knowledge and vision. He is pleased with that knowledge and vision, but his intention is not fulfilled. He does not, on account of it, laud himself and disparage others. He does not become intoxicated with that knowledge and vision; he does not grow negligent and

fall into negligence. Being diligent, he attains perpetual liberation. And it is impossible for that bhikkhu to fall away from that perpetual deliverance.[348]

"Suppose a man needing heartwood, seeking heartwood, wandering in search of heartwood, came to a great tree standing possessed of heartwood, and cutting off only its heartwood, he would take it away knowing it was heartwood. Then a man with good sight, seeing him, might say: 'This good man knew the heartwood, the sapwood, the inner bark, the outer bark, and the twigs and leaves. Thus, while needing heartwood, seeking heartwood, wandering in search of heartwood, [197] he came to a great tree standing possessed of heartwood, and cutting off only its heartwood, he took it away knowing it was heartwood. Whatever it was this good man had to make with heartwood, his purpose will be served.' So too, bhikkhus, here some clansman goes forth out of faith...When he is diligent, he attains perpetual liberation. And it is impossible for that bhikkhu to fall away from that perpetual deliverance.

7. "So this holy life, bhikkhus, does not have gain, honour, and renown for its benefit, or the attainment of virtue for its benefit, or the attainment of concentration for its benefit, or knowledge and vision for its benefit. But it is this unshakeable deliverance of mind that is the goal of this holy life, its heartwood, and its end."[349]

That is what the Blessed One said. The bhikkhus were satisfied and delighted in the Blessed One's words.

30 *Cūḷasāropama Sutta*
The Shorter Discourse on the Simile of the Heartwood

[198] 1. THUS HAVE I HEARD. On one occasion the Blessed One was living at Sāvatthī in Jeta's Grove, Anāthapiṇḍika's Park.

2. Then the brahmin Pingalakoccha went to the Blessed One and exchanged greetings with him. When this courteous and amiable talk was finished, he sat down at one side and said to the Blessed One:

"Master Gotama, there are these recluses and brahmins, each the head of an order, the head of a group, the teacher of a group, a well-known and famous founder of a sect regarded by many as a saint—that is, Pūraṇa Kassapa, Makkhali Gosāla, Ajita Kesakambalin, Pakudha Kaccāyana, Sañjaya Belaṭṭhiputta, and the Nigaṇṭha Nātaputta.[350] Have they all had direct knowledge as they claim, or have none of them had direct knowledge, or have some of them had direct knowledge and some not?"

"Enough, brahmin! Let this be!—'Have they all had direct knowledge as they claim, or have none of them had direct knowledge, or have some of them had direct knowledge and some not?' I shall teach you the Dhamma, brahmin. Listen and attend closely to what I shall say."[351]

"Yes, sir," the brahmin Pingalakoccha replied. The Blessed One said this:

3. "Suppose, brahmin, a man needing heartwood, seeking heartwood, wandering in search of heartwood, came to a great tree standing possessed of heartwood. Passing over its heartwood, its sapwood, its inner bark, and its outer bark, he would cut off its twigs and leaves and take them away thinking they were heartwood. Then a man with good sight, seeing him, might say: 'This good man did not know the heartwood, the sapwood, the inner bark, the outer bark, or the twigs and leaves. Thus, while needing heartwood, seeking heartwood, wandering

in search of heartwood, he came to a great tree standing possessed of heartwood, and passing over its heartwood, its sapwood, its inner bark, and its outer bark, he cut off its twigs and leaves and took them away thinking they were heartwood. Whatever it was this good man had to make with heartwood, his purpose will not be served.'

4. "Suppose a man needing heartwood, seeking heartwood, wandering in search of heartwood, came to a great tree standing possessed of heartwood. Passing over its heartwood, its sapwood [199] and its inner bark, he would cut off its outer bark and take it away thinking it was heartwood. Then a man with good sight, seeing him, might say: 'This good man did not know the heartwood...or the twigs and leaves. Thus, while needing heartwood...he cut off its outer bark and took it away thinking it was heartwood. Whatever it was this good man had to make with heartwood, his purpose will not be served.'

5. "Suppose a man needing heartwood, seeking heartwood, wandering in search of heartwood, came to a great tree standing possessed of heartwood. Passing over its heartwood and its sapwood, he would cut off its inner bark and take it away thinking it was heartwood. Then a man with good sight, seeing him, might say: 'This good man did not know the heartwood...or the twigs and leaves. Thus, while needing heartwood...he cut off its inner bark and took it away thinking it was heartwood. Whatever it was this good man had to make with heartwood, his purpose will not be served.'

6. "Suppose a man needing heartwood, seeking heartwood, wandering in search of heartwood, came to a great tree standing possessed of heartwood. Passing over its heartwood, he would cut off its sapwood and take it away thinking it was heartwood. Then a man with good sight, seeing him, might say: 'This good man did not know the heartwood...or the twigs and leaves. Thus, while needing heartwood...he cut off its sapwood and took it away thinking it was heartwood. Whatever it was this good man had to make with heartwood, his purpose will not be served.'

7. "Suppose a man needing heartwood, seeking heartwood, wandering in search of heartwood, came to a great tree standing possessed of heartwood, and cutting off only its heartwood, he would take it away knowing it was heartwood. Then a man

with good sight, seeing him, might say: 'This good man knew the heartwood, the sapwood, the inner bark, the outer bark, and the twigs and leaves. Thus, while needing heartwood, seeking heartwood, wandering in search of heartwood, he came to a great tree standing possessed of heartwood, and cutting off only its heartwood, [200] he took it away knowing it was heartwood. Whatever it was this good man had to make with heartwood, his purpose will be served.'

8. "So too, brahmin, here some clansman goes forth out of faith from the home life into homelessness, considering: 'I am a victim of birth, ageing, and death, of sorrow, lamentation, pain, grief, and despair; I am a victim of suffering, a prey to suffering. Surely an ending of this whole mass of suffering can be known.' When he has gone forth thus, he acquires gain, honour, and renown. He is pleased with that gain, honour, and renown, and his intention is fulfilled. On account of it he lauds himself and disparages others thus: 'I have gain, honour, and renown, but these other bhikkhus are unknown, of no account.' So he arouses no desire to act, he makes no effort for the realisation of those other states that are higher and more sublime than gain, honour, and renown; he hangs back and slackens.[352] I say that this person is like the man needing heartwood, who came to a great tree standing possessed of heartwood, and passing over its heartwood, its sapwood, its inner bark, and its outer bark, cut off its twigs and leaves and took them away thinking they were heartwood; and so whatever it was he had to make with heartwood, his purpose will not have been served.

9. "Here, brahmin, some clansman goes forth out of faith from the home life into homelessness, considering: 'I am a victim of birth, ageing, and death, of sorrow, lamentation, pain, grief, and despair; I am a victim of suffering, a prey to suffering. Surely an ending of this whole mass of suffering can be known.' When he has gone forth thus, he acquires gain, honour, and renown. He is not pleased with that gain, honour, and renown, and his intention is not fulfilled. He does not, on account of it, laud himself and disparage others. He arouses desire to act and he makes an effort for the realisation of those other states that are higher and more sublime than gain, honour, and renown; he does not hang back and slacken. He achieves the attainment of virtue. He is pleased with that attainment of virtue and his

intention is fulfilled. On account of it he lauds himself and disparages others thus: 'I am virtuous, of good character, but these other bhikkhus are immoral, of evil character.' So he arouses no desire to act, he makes no effort for the realisation of those other states that are higher and more sublime than the attainment of virtue; [201] he hangs back and slackens. I say that this person is like the man needing heartwood...who passing over its heartwood, its sapwood, and its inner bark, cut off its outer bark and took it away thinking it was heartwood; and so whatever it was he had to make with heartwood, his purpose will not have been served.

10. "Here, brahmin, some clansman goes forth out of faith from the home life into homelessness, considering: 'I am a victim of birth, ageing, and death, of sorrow, lamentation, pain, grief, and despair; I am a victim of suffering, a prey to suffering. Surely an ending of this whole mass of suffering can be known.' When he has gone forth thus, he acquires gain, honour, and renown. He is not pleased with that gain, honour, and renown, and his intention is not fulfilled. He achieves the attainment of virtue. He is pleased with that attainment of virtue, but his intention is not fulfilled. He does not, on account of it, laud himself and disparage others. He arouses desire to act and he makes an effort for the realisation of those other states that are higher and more sublime than the attainment of virtue; he does not hang back and slacken. He achieves the attainment of concentration. He is pleased with that attainment of concentration and his intention is fulfilled. On account of it he lauds himself and disparages others thus: 'I am concentrated, my mind is unified, but these other bhikkhus are unconcentrated, with their minds astray.' So he arouses no desire to act, he makes no effort for the realisation of those other states that are higher and more sublime than the attainment of concentration; he hangs back and slackens. I say that this person is like the man needing heartwood...who passing over its heartwood and its sapwood, cut off its inner bark and took it away thinking it was heartwood; and so whatever it was he had to make with heartwood, his purpose will not have been served.

11. "Here, brahmin, some clansman goes forth out of faith from the home life into homelessness, considering: 'I am a victim of birth, ageing, and death, [202] of sorrow, lamentation, pain,

grief, and despair; I am a victim of suffering, a prey to suffering. Surely an ending of this whole mass of suffering can be known.' When he has gone forth thus, he acquires gain, honour, and renown. He is not pleased with that gain, honour, and renown, and his intention is not fulfilled...He achieves the attainment of virtue. He is pleased with that attainment of virtue, but his intention is not fulfilled...He achieves the attainment of concentration. He is pleased with that attainment of concentration, but his intention is not fulfilled. He does not, on account of it, laud himself and disparage others. He arouses desire to act and he makes an effort for the realisation of those other states that are higher and more sublime than the attainment of concentration; he does not hang back and slacken. He achieves knowledge and vision. He is pleased with that knowledge and vision and his intention is fulfilled. On account of it he lauds himself and disparages others thus: 'I live knowing and seeing, but these other bhikkhus live unknowing and unseeing.' So he arouses no desire to act, he makes no effort for the realisation of those other states that are higher and more sublime than knowledge and vision; he hangs back and slackens. I say that this person is like the man needing heartwood...who passing over its heartwood, cut off its sapwood and took it away thinking it was heartwood; and so whatever it was he had to make with heartwood, his purpose will not have been served.

12. "Here, brahmin, some clansman goes forth out of faith from the home life into homelessness, considering: 'I am a victim of birth, ageing, and death, of sorrow, lamentation, pain, grief, and despair; I am a victim of suffering, a prey to suffering. Surely an ending of this whole mass of suffering can be known.' When he has gone forth thus, [203] he acquires gain, honour, and renown. He is not pleased with that gain, honour, and renown, and his intention is not fulfilled...He achieves the attainment of virtue. He is pleased with that attainment of virtue, but his intention is not fulfilled...He achieves the attainment of concentration. He is pleased with that attainment of concentration, but his intention is not fulfilled...He achieves knowledge and vision. He is pleased with that knowledge and vision, but his intention is not fulfilled. He does not, on account of it, laud himself and disparage others. He arouses desire to act and he makes an effort for the realisation of those other states

that are higher and more sublime than knowledge and vision; he does not hang back and slacken.

"But what, brahmin, are the states that are higher and more sublime than knowledge and vision?

13. "Here, brahmin, quite secluded from sensual pleasures, secluded from unwholesome states, a bhikkhu enters upon and abides in the first jhāna, which is accompanied by applied and sustained thought, with rapture and pleasure born of seclusion. This is a state higher and more sublime than knowledge and vision.[353]

14. "Again, with the stilling of applied and sustained thought, a bhikkhu enters upon and abides in the second jhāna, which has self-confidence and singleness of mind without applied and sustained thought, with rapture and pleasure born of concentration. This too is a state higher and more sublime than knowledge and vision.

15. "Again, with the fading away as well of rapture, a bhikkhu abides in equanimity, and mindful and fully aware, still feeling pleasure with the body, he enters upon and abides in the third jhāna, on account of which noble ones announce: 'He has a pleasant abiding who has equanimity and is mindful.' This too [204] is a state higher and more sublime than knowledge and vision.

16. "Again, with the abandoning of pleasure and pain, and with the previous disappearance of joy and grief, a bhikkhu enters upon and abides in the fourth jhāna, which has neither-pain-nor-pleasure and purity of mindfulness due to equanimity. This too is a state higher and more sublime than knowledge and vision.

17. "Again, with the complete surmounting of perceptions of form, with the disappearance of perceptions of sensory impact, with non-attention to perceptions of diversity, aware that 'space is infinite', a bhikkhu enters upon and abides in the base of infinite space. This too is a state higher and more sublime than knowledge and vision.

18. "Again, by completely surmounting the base of infinite space, aware that 'consciousness is infinite,' a bhikkhu enters upon and abides in the base of infinite consciousness. This too is a state higher and more sublime than knowledge and vision.

19. "Again, by completely surmounting the base of infinite consciousness, aware that 'there is nothing,' a bhikkhu enters

upon and abides in the base of nothingness. This too is a state higher and more sublime than knowledge and vision.

20. "Again, by completely surmounting the base of nothingness, a bhikkhu enters upon and abides in the base of neither-perception-nor-non-perception. This too is a state higher and more sublime than knowledge and vision.

21. "Again, by completely surmounting the base of neither-perception-nor-non-perception, a bhikkhu enters upon and abides in the cessation of perception and feeling. And his taints are destroyed by seeing with wisdom. This too is a state higher and more sublime than knowledge and vision. These are the states that are higher and more sublime than knowledge and vision.

22. "I say that this person, brahmin, is like a man needing heartwood, seeking heartwood, wandering in search of heartwood, who came to a great tree standing possessed of heartwood, and cutting off its heartwood, took it away knowing it was heartwood; and so whatever it was he had to make with heartwood, his purpose will have been served.

23. "So this holy life, brahmin, does not have gain, honour, and renown for its benefit, or the attainment of virtue for its benefit, or the attainment of concentration for its benefit, or knowledge and vision for its benefit. But it is [205] this unshakeable deliverance of mind that is the goal of this holy life, its heartwood, and its end."

24. When this was said, the brahmin Pingalakoccha said to the Blessed One: "Magnificent, Master Gotama! Magnificent, Master Gotama! Master Gotama has made the Dhamma clear in many ways, as though he were turning upright what had been overthrown, revealing what was hidden, showing the way to one who was lost, or holding up a lamp in the dark for those with eyesight to see forms. I go to Master Gotama for refuge and to the Dhamma and to the Sangha of bhikkhus. From today let Master Gotama remember me as a lay follower who has gone to him for refuge for life."

4

The Great Division of Pairs

(*Mahāyamakavagga*)

31 *Cūḷagosinga Sutta*
The Shorter Discourse in Gosinga

1. THUS HAVE I HEARD. On one occasion the Blessed One was living at Nādikā in the Brick House.

2. Now on that occasion the venerable Anuruddha, the venerable Nandiya, and the venerable Kimbila were living at the Park of the Gosinga Sāla-tree Wood.[354]

3. Then, when it was evening, the Blessed One rose from meditation and went to the Park of the Gosinga Sāla-tree Wood. The park keeper saw the Blessed One coming in the distance and told him: "Do not enter this park, recluse. There are three clansmen here seeking their own good. Do not disturb them."

4. The venerable Anuruddha heard the park keeper speaking to the Blessed One and told him: "Friend park keeper, do not keep the Blessed One out. It is our Teacher, the Blessed One, who has come." Then the venerable Anuruddha went to the venerable Nandiya and the venerable Kimbila and said: "Come out, venerable sirs, come out! Our Teacher, [206] the Blessed One, has come."

5. Then all three went to meet the Blessed One. One took his bowl and outer robe, one prepared a seat, and one set out water for washing the feet. The Blessed One sat down on the seat made ready and washed his feet. Then those three venerable ones paid homage to the Blessed One and sat down at one side. When they were seated, the Blessed One said to them: "I hope you are all keeping well, Anuruddha, I hope you are all comfortable, I hope you are not having any trouble getting almsfood."

"We are keeping well, Blessed One, we are comfortable, and we are not having any trouble getting almsfood."

6. "I hope, Anuruddha, that you are all living in concord, with mutual appreciation, without disputing, blending like milk and water, viewing each other with kindly eyes."

"Surely, venerable sir, we are living in concord, with mutual appreciation, without disputing, blending like milk and water, viewing each other with kindly eyes."

"But, Anuruddha, how do you live thus?"

7. "Venerable sir, as to that, I think thus: 'It is a gain for me, it is a great gain for me, that I am living with such companions in the holy life.' I maintain bodily acts of loving-kindness towards those venerable ones both openly and privately; I maintain verbal acts of loving-kindness towards them both openly and privately; I maintain mental acts of loving-kindness towards them both openly and privately.[355] I consider: 'Why should I not [207] set aside what I wish to do and do what these venerable ones wish to do?' Then I set aside what I wish to do and do what these venerable ones wish to do. We are different in body, venerable sir, but one in mind."

The venerable Nandiya and the venerable Kimbila each spoke likewise, adding: "That is how, venerable sir, we are living in concord, with mutual appreciation, without disputing, blending like milk and water, viewing each other with kindly eyes."

8. "Good, good, Anuruddha. I hope that you all abide diligent, ardent, and resolute."

"Surely, venerable sir, we abide diligent, ardent, and resolute."

"But, Anuruddha, how do you abide thus?"

9. "Venerable sir, as to that, whichever of us returns first from the village with almsfood prepares the seats, sets out the water for drinking and for washing, and puts the refuse bucket in its place. Whichever of us returns last eats any food left over, if he wishes; otherwise he throws it away where there is no greenery or drops it into water where there is no life. He puts away the seats and the water for drinking and for washing. He puts away the refuse bucket after washing it and he sweeps out the refectory. Whoever notices that the pots of water for drinking, washing, or the latrine are low or empty takes care of them. If they are too heavy for him, he calls someone else by a signal of the hand and they move it by joining hands, but because of this we do not break out into speech. But every five days we sit together all night discussing the Dhamma. That is how we abide diligent, ardent, and resolute."

10. "Good, good, Anuruddha. But while you abide thus diligent, ardent, and resolute, have you attained any superhuman

state, a distinction in knowledge and vision worthy of the noble ones, a comfortable abiding?"

"Why not, venerable sir? Here, venerable sir, whenever we want, quite secluded from sensual pleasures, secluded from unwholesome states, we enter upon and abide in the first jhāna, which is accompanied by applied and sustained thought, with rapture and pleasure born of seclusion. Venerable sir, this is a superhuman state, a distinction in knowledge and vision worthy of the noble ones, a comfortable abiding, which we have attained while abiding diligent, ardent, and resolute."

11–13. "Good, good, Anuruddha. But is there any other superhuman state, a distinction in knowledge and vision worthy of the noble ones, a comfortable abiding, which you have attained by surmounting that abiding, [208] by making that abiding subside?"

"Why not, venerable sir? Here, venerable sir, whenever we want, with the stilling of applied and sustained thought, we enter upon and abide in the second jhāna...With the fading away as well of rapture...we enter upon and abide in the third jhāna...With the abandoning of pleasure and pain...we enter upon and abide in the fourth jhāna...Venerable sir, this is another superhuman state, a distinction in knowledge and vision worthy of the noble ones, a comfortable abiding, which we have attained by surmounting the preceding abiding, by making that abiding subside."

14. "Good, good, Anuruddha. But is there any other superhuman state...which you have attained by surmounting that abiding, by making that abiding subside?"

"Why not, venerable sir? Here, venerable sir, whenever we want, with the complete surmounting of perceptions of form, with the disappearance of perceptions of sensory impact, with non-attention to perceptions of diversity, aware that 'space is infinite,' [209] we enter upon and abide in the base of infinite space. Venerable sir, this is another superhuman state...which we have attained by surmounting the preceding abiding, by making that abiding subside."

15–17. "Good, good, Anuruddha. But is there any other superhuman state...which you have attained by surmounting that abiding, by making that abiding subside?"

"Why not, venerable sir? Here, venerable sir, whenever we want, by completely surmounting the base of infinite space, aware that 'consciousness is infinite,' we enter upon and abide in the base of infinite consciousness...By completely surmounting the base of infinite consciousness, aware that 'there is nothing,' we enter upon and abide in the base of nothingness...By completely surmounting the base of nothingness, we enter upon and abide in the base of neither-perception-nor-non-perception. Venerable sir, this is another superhuman state...which we have attained by surmounting the preceding abiding, by making that abiding subside."

18. "Good, good Anuruddha. But is there any other superhuman state, a distinction in knowledge and vision worthy of the noble ones, a comfortable abiding, which you have attained by surmounting that abiding, by making that abiding subside?"

"Why not, venerable sir? Here, venerable sir, whenever we want, by completely surmounting the base of neither-perception-nor-non-perception, we enter upon and abide in the cessation of perception and feeling. And our taints are destroyed by our seeing with wisdom. Venerable sir, this is another superhuman state, a distinction in knowledge and vision worthy of the noble ones, a comfortable abiding, which we have attained by surmounting the preceding abiding, by making that abiding subside. And, venerable sir, we do not see any other comfortable abiding higher or more sublime than this one."

"Good, good Anuruddha. There is no other comfortable abiding higher or more sublime than that one."

19. Then, when the Blessed One had instructed, urged, roused, and gladdened the venerable Anuruddha, the venerable Nandiya, and the venerable Kimbila with a talk on the Dhamma, he rose from his seat and departed.

20. After they had accompanied the Blessed One a little way and turned back again, the venerable [210] Nandiya and the venerable Kimbila asked the venerable Anuruddha: "Have we ever reported to the venerable Anuruddha that we have obtained those abidings and attainments that the venerable Anuruddha, in the Blessed One's presence, ascribed to us up to the destruction of the taints?"

"The venerable ones have never reported to me that they have obtained those abidings and attainments. Yet by encompassing the venerable ones' minds with my own mind, I know that they have obtained those abidings and attainments. And deities have also reported to me: 'These venerable ones have obtained those abidings and attainments.' Then I declared it when directly questioned by the Blessed One."

21. Then the spirit Dīgha Parajana[356] went to the Blessed One. After paying homage to the Blessed One, he stood at one side and said: "It is a gain for the Vajjians, venerable sir, a great gain for the Vajjian people that the Tathāgata, accomplished and fully enlightened, dwells among them and these three clansmen, the venerable Anuruddha, the venerable Nandiya, and the venerable Kimbila!" On hearing the exclamation of the spirit Dīgha Parajana, the earth gods exclaimed: "It is a gain for the Vajjians, a great gain for the Vajjian people that the Tathāgata, accomplished and fully enlightened, dwells among them and these three clansmen, the venerable Anuruddha, the venerable Nandiya, and the venerable Kimbila!" On hearing the exclamation of the earth gods, the gods of the heaven of the Four Great Kings...the gods of the heaven of the Thirty-three...the Yāma gods...the gods of the Tusita heaven...the gods who delight in creating...the gods who wield power over others' creations...the gods of Brahmā's retinue exclaimed: "It is a gain for the Vajjians, a great gain for the Vajjian people that the Tathāgata, accomplished and fully enlightened, dwells among them and these three clansmen, the venerable Anuruddha, the venerable Nandiya, and the venerable Kimbila!" Thus at that instant, at that moment, those venerable ones were known as far as the Brahma-world.

22. [The Blessed One said:] "So it is, Dīgha, so it is! And if the clan from which those three clansmen went forth from the home life into homelessness should remember them with confident heart, that would lead to the welfare and happiness of that clan for a long time. And if the retinue of the clan from which those three clansmen went forth [211]...the village from which they went forth...the town from which they went forth...the city from which they went forth...the country from which those three clansmen went forth from the home life into homelessness should remember them with confident heart, that would lead to the welfare and happiness of that country for a long time. If all nobles should remember those three clansmen with confident heart, that would lead to the welfare and happiness of the nobles for a long time. If all brahmins...all merchants...all workers

should remember those three clansmen with confident heart, that would lead to the welfare and happiness of the workers for a long time. If the world with its gods, its Māras, and its Brahmās, this generation with its recluses and brahmins, its princes and its people, should remember those three clansmen with confident heart, that would lead to the welfare and happiness of the world for a long time. See, Dīgha, how those three clansmen are practising for the welfare and happiness of the many, out of compassion for the world, for the good, welfare and happiness of gods and humans."

That is what the Blessed One said. The spirit Dīgha Parajana was satisfied and delighted in the Blessed One's words.

32 *Mahāgosinga Sutta*
The Greater Discourse in Gosinga

[212] 1. THUS HAVE I HEARD. On one occasion the Blessed One was living in the Park of the Gosinga Sāla-tree Wood together with a number of very well-known elder disciples—the venerable Sāriputta, the venerable Mahā Moggallāna, the venerable Mahā Kassapa, the venerable Anuruddha, the venerable Revata, the venerable Ānanda, and other very well known elder disciples.

2. Then, when it was evening, the venerable Mahā Moggallāna rose from meditation, went to the venerable Mahā Kassapa, and said to him: "Friend Kassapa, let us go to the venerable Sāriputta to listen to the Dhamma."—"Yes, friend," the venerable Mahā Kassapa replied. Then the venerable Mahā Moggallāna, the venerable Mahā Kassapa, and the venerable Anuruddha went to the venerable Sāriputta to listen to the Dhamma.

3. The venerable Ānanda saw them going to the venerable Sāriputta to listen to the Dhamma. Thereupon he went to the venerable Revata and said to him: "Friend Revata, those true men are going to the venerable Sāriputta to listen to the Dhamma. Let us also go to the venerable Sāriputta to listen to the Dhamma."—"Yes, friend," the venerable Revata replied. Then the venerable Revata and the venerable Ānanda went to the venerable Sāriputta to listen to the Dhamma.

4. The venerable Sāriputta saw the venerable Revata and the venerable Ānanda coming in the distance and said to the venerable Ānanda: "Let the venerable Ānanda come, welcome to the venerable Ānanda, the Blessed One's attendant, who is always in the Blessed One's presence. Friend Ānanda, the Gosinga Sāla-tree Wood is delightful, the night is moonlit, the sāla trees are all in blossom, and heavenly scents seem to be floating in the air. What kind of bhikkhu, friend Ānanda, could illuminate the Gosinga Sāla-tree Wood?"

"Here, friend [213] Sāriputta, a bhikkhu has learned much, remembers what he has learned, and consolidates what he has learned. Such teachings as are good in the beginning, good in the middle, and good in the end, with the right meaning and phrasing, and which affirm a holy life that is utterly perfect and pure—such teachings as these he has learned much of, remembered, mastered verbally, investigated with the mind, and penetrated well by view. And he teaches the Dhamma to the four assemblies with well-rounded and coherent statements and phrases for the eradication of the underlying tendencies.[357] That kind of bhikkhu could illuminate this Gosinga Sāla-tree Wood."

5. When this was said, the venerable Sāriputta addressed the venerable Revata thus: "Friend Revata, the venerable Ānanda has spoken according to his own inspiration.[358] Now we ask the venerable Revata: Friend Revata, the Gosinga Sāla-tree Wood is delightful, the night is moonlit, the sāla trees are all in blossom, and heavenly scents seem to be floating in the air. What kind of bhikkhu, friend Revata, could illuminate this Gosinga Sāla-tree Wood?"

"Here, friend Sāriputta, a bhikkhu delights in solitary meditation and takes delight in solitary meditation; he is devoted to internal serenity of mind, does not neglect meditation, possesses insight, and dwells in empty huts.[359] That kind of bhikkhu could illuminate this Gosinga Sāla-tree Wood."

6. When this was said, the venerable Sāriputta addressed the venerable Anuruddha thus: "Friend Anuruddha, the venerable Revata has spoken according to his own inspiration. Now we ask the venerable Anuruddha: Friend Anuruddha, the Gosinga Sāla-tree Wood is delightful...What kind of bhikkhu, friend Anuruddha, could illuminate this Gosinga Sāla-tree Wood?"

"Here, friend Sāriputta, with the divine eye, which is purified and surpasses the human, a bhikkhu surveys a thousand worlds. Just as a man with good sight, when he has ascended to the upper palace chamber, might survey a thousand wheel-rims, so too, with the divine eye, which is purified and surpasses the human, a bhikkhu surveys a thousand worlds.[360] That kind of bhikkhu could illuminate this Gosinga Sāla-tree Wood."

7. When this was said, the venerable Sāriputta addressed the venerable Mahā Kassapa thus: "Friend Kassapa, the venerable Anuruddha has spoken according to his own inspiration. Now

we ask the venerable Mahā Kassapa: Friend Kassapa, the Gosinga Sāla-tree Wood is delightful...What kind of bhikkhu, friend Kassapa, [214] could illuminate this Gosinga Sāla-tree Wood?"

"Here, friend Sāriputta, a bhikkhu is a forest dweller himself and speaks in praise of forest dwelling; he is an almsfood eater himself and speaks in praise of eating almsfood; he is a refuse-rag wearer himself and speaks in praise of wearing refuse-rag robes; he is a triple-robe wearer himself and speaks in praise of wearing the triple robe;[361] he has few wishes himself and speaks in praise of fewness of wishes; he is content himself and speaks in praise of contentment; he is secluded himself and speaks in praise of seclusion; he is aloof from society himself and speaks in praise of aloofness from society; he is energetic himself and speaks in praise of arousing energy; he has attained to virtue himself and speaks in praise of the attainment of virtue; he has attained to concentration himself and speaks in praise of the attainment of concentration; he has attained to wisdom himself and speaks in praise of the attainment of wisdom; he has attained to deliverance himself and speaks in praise of the attainment of deliverance; he has attained to the knowledge and vision of deliverance himself and speaks in praise of the attainment of the knowledge and vision of deliverance. That kind of bhikkhu could illuminate this Gosinga Sāla-tree Wood."

8. When this was said, the venerable Sāriputta addressed the venerable Mahā Moggallāna thus: "Friend Moggallāna, the venerable Mahā Kassapa has spoken according to his own inspiration. Now we ask the venerable Mahā Moggallāna: Friend Moggallāna, the Gosinga Sāla-tree Wood is delightful...What kind of bhikkhu, friend Moggallāna, could illuminate this Gosinga Sāla-tree Wood?"

"Here, friend Sāriputta, two bhikkhus engage in a talk on the higher Dhamma[362] and they question each other, and each being questioned by the other answers without foundering, and their talk rolls on in accordance with the Dhamma. That kind of bhikkhu could illuminate this Gosinga Sāla-tree Wood."

9. When this was said, the venerable Mahā Moggallāna addressed the venerable Sāriputta thus: "Friend Sāriputta, we have all spoken according to our own inspiration. Now we ask the venerable Sāriputta: Friend Sāriputta, the Gosinga Sāla-tree Wood is delightful, the night is moonlit, the sāla trees are all in

blossom, and heavenly scents seem to be floating in the air. What kind of bhikkhu, friend Sāriputta, could illuminate this Gosinga Sāla-tree Wood?"

"Here, friend Moggallāna, a bhikkhu wields mastery over his mind, he does not let the mind wield mastery over him. In the morning he abides in whatever abiding or attainment he wants [215] to abide in during the morning; at midday he abides in whatever abiding or attainment he wants to abide in at midday; in the evening he abides in whatever abiding or attainment he wants to abide in during the evening. Suppose a king or a king's minister had a chest full of variously coloured garments. In the morning he could put on whatever pair of garments he wanted to put on in the morning; at midday he could put on whatever pair of garments he wanted to put on at midday; in the evening he could put on whatever pair of garments he wanted to put on in the evening. So too, a bhikkhu wields mastery over his mind, he does not let the mind wield mastery over him. In the morning...at midday...in the evening he abides in whatever abiding or attainment he wants to abide in during the evening. That kind of bhikkhu could illuminate this Gosinga Sāla-tree Wood."

10. Then the venerable Sāriputta addressed those venerable ones thus: "Friends, we have all spoken according to our own inspiration. Let us go to the Blessed One and report this matter to him. As the Blessed One answers, so let us remember it."—"Yes, friend," they replied. Then those venerable ones went to the Blessed One, and after paying homage to him, they sat down at one side. The venerable Sāriputta said to the Blessed One:

11. "Venerable sir, the venerable Revata and the venerable Ānanda came to me to listen to the Dhamma. I saw them coming in the distance and [216] said to the venerable Ānanda: 'Let the venerable Ānanda come, welcome to the venerable Ānanda...Friend Ānanda, the Gosinga Sāla-tree Wood is delightful...What kind of bhikkhu, friend Ānanda, could illuminate this Gosinga Sāla-tree Wood?' When asked, venerable sir, the venerable Ānanda replied: 'Here, friend Sāriputta, a bhikkhu has learned much...(*as in §4*)...That kind of bhikkhu could illuminate this Gosinga Sāla-tree Wood.'"

"Good, good, Sāriputta. Ānanda, speaking rightly, should speak just as he did. For Ānanda has learned much, remembers what he has learned, and consolidates what he has learned. Such teachings as are good in the beginning, good in the middle, and good in the end, with the right meaning and phrasing, and which affirm a holy life that is utterly perfect and pure—such teachings as these he has learned much of, remembered, mastered verbally, investigated with the mind, and penetrated well by view. And he teaches the Dhamma to the four assemblies with well-rounded and coherent statements and phrases for the eradication of the underlying tendencies."

12. "When this was said, venerable sir, I addressed the venerable Revata thus: 'Friend Revata...What kind of bhikkhu could illuminate this Gosinga Sāla-tree Wood?' And the venerable Revata replied: 'Here, friend Sāriputta, a bhikkhu delights in solitary meditation...(*as in* §5)...That kind of bhikkhu could illuminate this Gosinga Sāla-tree Wood.'"

"Good, good, Sāriputta. Revata, speaking rightly, should speak just as he did. For Revata delights in solitary meditation, takes delight in solitary meditation, is devoted to internal serenity of mind, does not neglect meditation, possesses insight, and dwells in empty huts." [217]

13. "When that was said, venerable sir, I addressed the venerable Anuruddha thus: 'Friend Anuruddha...What kind of bhikkhu could illuminate this Gosinga Sāla-tree Wood?' And the venerable Anuruddha replied: 'Here, friend Sāriputta, with the divine eye...(*as in* §6)...That kind of bhikkhu could illuminate this Gosinga Sāla-tree Wood.'"

"Good, good, Sāriputta. Anuruddha, speaking rightly, should speak just as he did. For with the divine eye, which is purified and surpasses the human, Anuruddha surveys a thousand worlds."

14. "When this was said, venerable sir, I addressed the venerable Mahā Kassapa thus: 'Friend Kassapa...What kind of bhikkhu could illuminate this Gosinga Sāla-tree Wood?' And the venerable Mahā Kassapa replied: 'Here, friend Sāriputta, a bhikkhu is a forest-dweller himself...(*as in* §7)...That kind of bhikkhu could illuminate this Gosinga Sāla-tree Wood.'" [218]

"Good, good, Sāriputta. Kassapa, speaking rightly, should speak just as he did. For Kassapa is a forest-dweller himself and speaks in praise of forest dwelling...he has attained to the knowledge and vision of deliverance himself and speaks in praise of the attainment of the knowledge and vision of deliverance."

15. "When this was said, venerable sir, I addressed the venerable Mahā Moggallāna thus: 'Friend Moggallāna...What kind of bhikkhu could illuminate this Gosinga Sāla-tree Wood?' And the venerable Mahā Moggallāna replied: 'Here, friend Sāriputta, two bhikkhus engage in a talk on the higher Dhamma...(*as in §8*)...That kind of bhikkhu could illuminate this Gosinga Sāla-tree Wood.'"

"Good, good, Sāriputta. Moggallāna, speaking rightly, should speak just as he did. For Moggallāna is one who talks on the Dhamma."

16. When that was said, the venerable Mahā Moggallāna told the Blessed One: "Then, venerable sir, I addressed the venerable Sāriputta thus: 'Friend Sāriputta...What kind of bhikkhu could illuminate this Gosinga Sāla-tree Wood?' And the venerable Sāriputta replied: 'Here, friend Moggallāna, a bhikkhu wields mastery over his mind...[219] (*as in §9*)...That kind of bhikkhu could illuminate this Gosinga Sāla-tree Wood.'"

"Good, good, Moggallāna. Sāriputta, speaking rightly, should speak just as he did. For Sāriputta wields mastery over his mind, he does not let the mind wield mastery over him. In the morning he abides in whatever abiding or attainment he wants to abide in during the morning; at midday he abides in whatever abiding or attainment he wants to abide in at midday; in the evening he abides in whatever abiding or attainment he wants to abide in during the evening."

17. When this was said, the venerable Sāriputta asked the Blessed One: "Venerable sir, which of us has spoken well?"

"You have all spoken well, Sāriputta, each in his own way. Hear also from me what kind of bhikkhu could illuminate this Gosinga Sāla-tree Wood. Here, Sāriputta, when a bhikkhu has returned from his almsround, after his meal, he sits down, folds his legs crosswise, sets his body erect, and establishing mindfulness in front of him, resolves: 'I shall not break this sitting position until through not clinging my mind is liberated from the taints.' That kind of bhikkhu could illuminate this Gosinga Sāla-tree Wood."[363]

That is what the Blessed One said. Those venerable ones were satisfied and delighted in the Blessed One's words.

33 *Mahāgopālaka Sutta*
The Greater Discourse on the Cowherd

[220] 1. THUS HAVE I HEARD. On one occasion the Blessed One was living at Sāvatthī in Jeta's Grove, Anāthapiṇḍika's Park. There he addressed the bhikkhus thus: "Bhikkhus."—"Venerable sir," they replied. The Blessed One said this:

2. "Bhikkhus, when a cowherd possesses eleven factors, he is incapable of keeping and rearing a herd of cattle. What eleven? Here a cowherd has no knowledge of form, he is unskilled in characteristics, he fails to pick out flies' eggs, he fails to dress wounds, he fails to smoke out the sheds, he does not know the watering place, he does not know what it is to have drunk, he does not know the road, he is unskilled in pastures, he milks dry, and he shows no extra veneration to those bulls who are fathers and leaders of the herd. When a cowherd possesses these eleven factors, he is incapable of keeping and rearing a herd of cattle.

3. "So too, bhikkhus, when a bhikkhu possesses eleven qualities, he is incapable of growth, increase, and fulfilment in this Dhamma and Discipline. What eleven? Here a bhikkhu has no knowledge of form, he is unskilled in characteristics, he fails to pick out flies' eggs, he fails to dress wounds, he fails to smoke out the sheds, he does not know the watering place, he does not know what it is to have drunk, he does not know the road, he is unskilled in pastures, he milks dry, and he shows no extra veneration to those elder bhikkhus of long-standing who have long gone forth, the fathers and leaders of the Sangha.

4. "How has a bhikkhu no knowledge of form? Here a bhikkhu does not understand as it actually is thus: 'All material form of whatever kind consists of the four great elements and the material form derived from the four great elements.' That is how a bhikkhu has no knowledge of form.

5. "How is a bhikkhu unskilled in characteristics? Here a

bhikkhu does not understand as it actually is thus: 'A fool is characterised by his actions; a wise man is characterised by his actions.' That is how a bhikkhu is unskilled in characteristics.[364]

6. "How does a bhikkhu fail to pick out flies' eggs? Here, when a thought of sensual desire has arisen, a bhikkhu tolerates it; he does not abandon it, remove it, do away with it, and annihilate it. When a thought of ill will has arisen...When a thought of cruelty has arisen...When evil unwholesome states have arisen, a bhikkhu tolerates them; [221] he does not abandon them, remove them, do away with them, and annihilate them. That is how a bhikkhu fails to pick out flies' eggs.

7. "How does a bhikkhu fail to dress wounds? Here, on seeing a form with the eye, a bhikkhu grasps at its signs and features. Even though, when he leaves the eye faculty unguarded, evil unwholesome states of covetousness and grief might invade him, he does not practise the way of its restraint, he does not guard the eye faculty, he does not undertake the restraint of the eye faculty. On hearing a sound with the ear...On smelling an odour with the nose...On tasting a flavour with the tongue...On touching a tangible with the body...On cognizing a mind-object with the mind, he grasps at its signs and features. Even though, when he leaves the mind faculty unguarded, evil unwholesome states of covetousness and grief might invade him, he does not practise the way of its restraint, he does not guard the mind faculty, he does not undertake the restraint of the mind faculty. That is how a bhikkhu fails to dress wounds.

8. "How does a bhikkhu fail to smoke out the sheds? Here a bhikkhu does not teach others in detail the Dhamma as he has learned it and mastered it. That is how a bhikkhu fails to smoke out the sheds.

9. "How does a bhikkhu not know the watering place? Here a bhikkhu does not go from time to time to those bhikkhus who have learned much, who are well versed in the tradition, who maintain the Dhamma, the Discipline, and the Codes,[365] and he does not enquire and ask questions of them thus: 'How is this, venerable sir? What is the meaning of this?' These venerable ones do not reveal to him what has not been revealed, do not clarify what is not clear, or remove his doubts about the numerous things that give rise to doubt. That is how a bhikkhu does not know the watering place.

10. "How does a bhikkhu not know what it is to have drunk? Here, when the Dhamma and Discipline proclaimed by the Tathāgata is being taught, a bhikkhu does not gain inspiration in the meaning, does not gain inspiration in the Dhamma, does not gain gladness connected with the Dhamma.[366] That is how a bhikkhu does not know what it is to have drunk.

11. "How does a bhikkhu not know the road? Here a bhikkhu does not understand the Noble Eightfold Path as it actually is. That is how a bhikkhu does not know the road.

12. "How is a bhikkhu unskilled in pastures? Here a bhikkhu does not understand the four foundations of mindfulness as they actually are. That is how [222] a bhikkhu is unskilled in pastures.[367]

13. "How does a bhikkhu milk dry? Here, when faithful householders invite a bhikkhu to take as much as he likes of robes, almsfood, resting places, and medicinal requisites, the bhikkhu does not know moderation in accepting. That is how a bhikkhu milks dry.

14. "How does a bhikkhu show no extra veneration to those elder bhikkhus of long-standing who have long gone forth, the fathers and leaders of the Sangha? Here a bhikkhu does not maintain bodily acts of loving-kindness both openly and privately towards those elder bhikkhus; he does not maintain verbal acts of loving-kindness towards them both openly and privately; he does not maintain mental acts of loving-kindness towards them both openly and privately. That is how a bhikkhu shows no extra veneration to those elder bhikkhus of long-standing who have long gone forth, the fathers and leaders of the Sangha.

"When a bhikkhu possesses these eleven qualities, he is incapable of growth, increase, and fulfilment in this Dhamma and Discipline.

15. "Bhikkhus, when a cowherd possesses eleven factors, he is capable of keeping and rearing a herd of cattle. What eleven? Here a cowherd has knowledge of form, he is skilled in characteristics, he picks out flies' eggs, he dresses wounds, he smokes out the sheds, he knows the watering place, he knows what it is to have drunk, he knows the road, he is skilled in pastures, he does not milk dry, and he shows extra veneration to those bulls who are fathers and leaders of the herd. When a cowherd

possesses these eleven factors, he is capable of keeping and rearing a herd of cattle.

16. "So too, bhikkhus, when a bhikkhu possesses these eleven qualities, he is capable of growth, increase, and fulfilment in this Dhamma and Discipline. What eleven? Here a bhikkhu has knowledge of form, he is skilled in characteristics, he picks out flies' eggs, he dresses wounds, he smokes out the sheds, he knows the watering place, he knows what it is to have drunk, he knows the road, he is skilled in pastures, he does not milk dry, and he shows extra veneration to those elder bhikkhus of long-standing who have long since gone forth, the fathers and leaders of the Sangha.

17. "How does a bhikkhu have knowledge of form? Here a bhikkhu understands as it actually is thus: 'All material form of whatever kind consists of the four [223] great elements and the material form derived from the four great elements.' That is how a bhikkhu has knowledge of form.

18. "How is a bhikkhu skilled in characteristics? Here a bhikkhu understands as it actually is thus: 'A fool is characterised by his actions; a wise man is characterised by his actions.' That is how a bhikkhu is skilled in characteristics.

19. "How does a bhikkhu pick out flies' eggs? Here, when a thought of sensual desire has arisen, a bhikkhu does not tolerate it; he abandons it, removes it, does away with it, and annihilates it. When a thought of ill will has arisen...When a thought of cruelty has arisen...When evil unwholesome states have arisen, a bhikkhu does not tolerate them; he abandons them, removes them, does away with them, and annihilates them. That is how a bhikkhu picks out flies' eggs.

20. "How does a bhikkhu dress wounds? Here, on seeing a form with the eye, a bhikkhu does not grasp at its signs and features. Since if he left the eye faculty unguarded, evil unwholesome states of covetousness and grief might invade him, he practises the way of its restraint, he guards the eye faculty, he undertakes the restraint of the eye faculty. On hearing a sound with the ear...On smelling an odour with the nose...On tasting a flavour with the tongue...On touching a tangible with the body...On cognizing a mind-object with the mind, a bhikkhu does not grasp at its signs and features. Since, if he left the mind faculty unguarded, evil unwholesome states of covetousness

and grief might invade him, he practises the way of its restraint, he guards the mind faculty, he undertakes the restraint of the mind faculty. That is how a bhikkhu dresses wounds.

21. "How does a bhikkhu smoke out the sheds? Here a bhikkhu teaches others in detail the Dhamma as he has learned it and mastered it. That is how a bhikkhu smokes out the sheds.

22. "How does a bhikkhu know the watering place? Here a bhikkhu goes from time to time to such bhikkhus who have learned much, who are well versed in the tradition, who maintain the Dhamma, the Discipline, and the Codes, and he enquires and asks questions of them thus: 'How is this, venerable sir? What is the meaning of this?' These venerable ones reveal to him what has not been revealed, clarify what is not clear, and remove his doubts about the numerous things that give rise to doubt. That is how a bhikkhu knows the watering place.

23. "How does [224] a bhikkhu know what it is to have drunk? Here, when the Dhamma and Discipline proclaimed by the Tathāgata is being taught, a bhikkhu gains inspiration in the meaning, gains inspiration in the Dhamma, gains gladness connected with the Dhamma. That is how a bhikkhu knows what it is to have drunk.

24. "How does a bhikkhu know the road? Here a bhikkhu understands the Noble Eightfold Path as it actually is. That is how a bhikkhu understands the road.

25. "How is a bhikkhu skilled in pastures? Here a bhikkhu understands the four foundations of mindfulness as they actually are. That is how a bhikkhu is skilled in pastures.

26. "How does a bhikkhu not milk dry? Here, when faithful householders invite a bhikkhu to take as much as he likes of robes, almsfood, resting places, and medicinal requisites, the bhikkhu knows moderation in accepting. That is how a bhikkhu does not milk dry.

27. "How does a bhikkhu show extra veneration to those elder bhikkhus of long-standing who have long gone forth, the fathers and leaders of the Sangha? Here a bhikkhu maintains bodily acts of loving-kindness both openly and privately towards those elder bhikkhus; he maintains verbal acts of loving-kindness towards them both openly and privately; he maintains mental acts of loving-kindness towards them both openly and privately. That is how a bhikkhu shows extra veneration to those elder

bhikkhus of long-standing who have long gone forth, the fathers and leaders of the Sangha.

"When a bhikkhu possesses these eleven qualities, he is capable of growth, increase, and fulfilment in this Dhamma and Discipline."

That is what the Blessed One said. The bhikkhus were satisfied and delighted in the Blessed One's words.

34 *Cūḷagopālaka Sutta*
The Shorter Discourse on the Cowherd

[225] 1. THUS HAVE I HEARD. On one occasion the Blessed One was living in the Vajjian country at Ukkācelā on the banks of the river Ganges. There he addressed the bhikkhus thus: "Bhikkhus."—"Venerable sir," they replied. The Blessed One said this:

2. "Bhikkhus, there was once a foolish Magadhan cowherd who, in the last month of the rainy season, in the autumn, without examining the near shore or the further shore of the river Ganges, drove his cattle across to the other shore in the Videhan country at a place that had no ford. Then the cattle bunched together in mid-stream in the river Ganges, and they met with calamity and disaster. Why was that? Because that foolish Magadhan cowherd, in the last month of the rainy season, in the autumn, without examining the near shore or the further shore of the river Ganges, drove his cattle across to the other shore in the Videhan country at a place that had no ford.

3. "So too, bhikkhus, as to those recluses and brahmins who are unskilled in this world and the other world, unskilled in Māra's realm and what is outside Māra's realm, unskilled in the realm of Death and what is outside the realm of Death—it will lead to the harm and suffering for a long time of those who think they should listen to them and place faith in them.

4. "Bhikkhus, there was once a wise Magadhan cowherd who, in the last month of the rainy season, in the autumn, after examining the near shore and the further shore of the river Ganges, drove his cattle across to the other shore in the Videhan country at a place that had a ford. He made the bulls, the fathers and leaders of the herd, enter first, and they breasted the stream of the Ganges and got safely across to the further shore. He made the strong cattle and the cattle to be tamed enter next,

and they too breasted the stream of the Ganges and got safely across to the further shore. He made the heifers and young oxen enter next, and they too breasted the stream of the Ganges and got safely across to the further shore. He made the calves and the feeble cattle enter next, and they too breasted the stream of the Ganges and got safely across to the further shore. At the time there was a tender calf just born, and being urged on by its mother's lowing, it too breasted the stream of the Ganges and got safely across to the further shore. Why was that? Because that wise Magadhan cowherd, [226] in the last month of the rainy season, in the autumn, after examining the near shore and the further shore of the river Ganges, drove his cattle across to the other shore in the Videhan country at a place that had a ford.

5. "So too, bhikkhus, as to those recluses and brahmins who are skilled in this world and the other world, skilled in Māra's realm and what is outside Māra's realm, skilled in the realm of Death and what is outside the realm of Death—it will lead to the welfare and happiness for a long time of those who think they should listen to them and place faith in them.

6. "Bhikkhus, just as the bulls, the fathers and leaders of the herd, breasted the stream of the Ganges and got safely across to the further shore, so too, those bhikkhus who are arahants with taints destroyed, who have lived the holy life, done what had to be done, laid down the burden, reached their own goal, destroyed the fetters of being, and are completely liberated through final knowledge—by breasting Māra's stream they have gotten safely across to the further shore.

7. "Just as the strong cattle and the cattle to be tamed breasted the stream of the Ganges and got safely across to the further shore, so too, those bhikkhus who, with the destruction of the five lower fetters, will reappear spontaneously [in the Pure Abodes] and there attain final Nibbāna without ever returning from that world—by breasting Māra's stream they will get safely across to the further shore.

8. "Just as the heifers and young oxen breasted the stream of the Ganges and got safely across to the further shore, so too, those bhikkhus who, with the destruction of three fetters and with the attenuation of lust, hate, and delusion, are once-returners, returning once to this world to make an end of suffering—by

breasting Māra's stream they too will get safely across to the further shore.

9. "Just as the calves and the feeble cattle breasted the stream of the Ganges and got safely across to the further shore, so too, those bhikkhus who, with the destruction of three fetters, are stream-enterers, no longer subject to perdition, bound [for deliverance], headed for enlightenment—by breasting Māra's stream they too will get safely across to the further shore.

10. "Just as that tender calf just born, being urged on by its mother's lowing, also breasted the stream of the Ganges and got safely across to the further shore, so too, those bhikkhus who are Dhamma-followers and faith-followers—by breasting Māra's stream they too will get safely across to the further shore.[368]

11. "Bhikkhus, I am [227] skilled in this world and in the other world, skilled in Māra's realm and in what is outside Māra's realm, skilled in the realm of Death and in what is outside the realm of Death. It will lead to the welfare and happiness for a long time of those who think they should listen to me and place faith in me."

12. That is what the Blessed One said. When the Sublime One had said that, the Teacher said further:

"Both this world and the world beyond
Are well described by the one who knows,
And what is still in Māra's reach
And what is out of reach of Death.

Knowing directly all the world,
The Enlightened One who understands
Opened the door to the deathless state
By which Nibbāna may be safely reached;

For Māra's stream is breasted now,
Its current blocked, its reeds removed;
Rejoice then, bhikkhus, mightily
And set your hearts where safety lies."

35 *Cūḷasaccaka Sutta*
The Shorter Discourse to Saccaka

1. THUS HAVE I HEARD. On one occasion the Blessed One was living at Vesālī in the Great Wood in the Hall with the Peaked Roof.

2. Now on that occasion Saccaka the Nigaṇṭha's son was staying at Vesālī, a debater and a clever speaker regarded by many as a saint.[369] He was making this statement before the Vesālī assembly: "I see no recluse or brahmin, the head of an order, the head of a group, the teacher of a group, even one claiming to be accomplished and fully enlightened, who would not shake, shiver, and tremble, and sweat under the armpits if he were to engage in debate with me. Even if I were to engage a senseless post in debate, it would shake, shiver, and tremble if it were to engage in debate with me, so what shall I say of a human being?"

3. Then, when it was morning, the venerable Assaji dressed, and taking his bowl and outer robe, went into Vesālī for alms.[370] As Saccaka the Nigaṇṭha's son was walking and wandering for exercise in Vesālī, [228] he saw the venerable Assaji coming in the distance and went up to him and exchanged greetings with him. When this courteous and amiable talk was finished, Saccaka the Nigaṇṭha's son stood at one side and said to him:

4. "Master Assaji, how does the recluse Gotama discipline his disciples? And how is the recluse Gotama's instruction usually presented to his disciples?"

"This is how the Blessed One disciplines his disciples, Aggivessana, and this is how the Blessed One's instruction is usually presented to his disciples: 'Bhikkhus, material form is impermanent, feeling is impermanent, perception is impermanent, formations are impermanent, consciousness is impermanent. Bhikkhus, material form is not self, feeling is not self, perception is not self, formations are not self, consciousness is not self. All formations are impermanent; all things are not self.'[371] That is how the

Blessed One disciplines his disciples, and that is how the Blessed One's instruction is usually presented to his disciples."

"If we have heard what the recluse Gotama asserts, we have indeed heard what is disagreeable. Perhaps sometime or other we might meet Master Gotama and have some conversation with him. Perhaps we might detach him from that evil view."

5. Now at that time five hundred Licchavis had met together in an assembly hall for some business or other. Then Saccaka the Nigaṇṭha's son went to them and said: "Come forth, good Licchavis, come forth! Today there will be some conversation between me and the recluse Gotama. If the recluse Gotama maintains before me what was maintained before me by one of his famous disciples, the bhikkhu named Assaji, then just as a strong man might seize a long-haired ram by the hair and drag him to and drag him fro and drag him round about, so in debate I will drag the recluse Gotama to and drag him fro and drag him round about. Just as a strong brewer's workman might throw a big brewer's sieve into a deep water tank, and taking it by the corners, drag it to and drag it fro and drag it round about, so in debate I will drag the recluse Gotama to and drag him fro and drag him round about. Just as a strong brewer's mixer [229] might take a strainer by the corners and shake it down and shake it up and thump it about, so in debate I will shake the recluse Gotama down and shake him up and thump him about. And just as a sixty-year-old elephant might plunge into a deep pond and enjoy playing the game of hemp-washing, so I shall enjoy playing the game of hemp-washing with the recluse Gotama.[372] Come forth, good Licchavis, come forth! Today there will be some conversation between me and the recluse Gotama."

6. Thereupon some Licchavis said: "Who is the recluse Gotama that he could refute Saccaka the Nigaṇṭha's son's assertions? On the contrary, Saccaka the Nigaṇṭha's son will refute the recluse Gotama's assertions." And some Licchavis said: "Who is Saccaka the Nigaṇṭha's son that he could refute the Blessed One's assertions? On the contrary, the Blessed One will refute Saccaka the Nigaṇṭha's son's assertions." Then Saccaka the Nigaṇṭha's son went with five hundred Licchavis to the Hall with the Peaked Roof in the Great Wood.

7. Now on that occasion a number of bhikkhus were walking up and down in the open. Then Saccaka the Nigaṇṭha's son

went up to them and asked: "Where is Master Gotama staying now, sirs? We want to see Master Gotama."

"The Blessed One has entered the Great Wood, Aggivessana, and is sitting at the root of a tree for the day's abiding."

8. Then Saccaka the Nigaṇṭha's son, together with a large following of Licchavis, entered the Great Wood and went to the Blessed One. He exchanged greetings with the Blessed One, and after this courteous and amiable talk was finished, sat down at one side. Some of the Licchavis paid homage to the Blessed One and sat down at one side; some exchanged greetings with him, and when this courteous and amiable talk was finished, sat down at one side; some extended their hands in reverential salutation towards the Blessed One and sat down at one side; some pronounced their name and clan in the Blessed One's presence and sat down at one side; some kept silent and sat down at one side.

9. When Saccaka the Nigaṇṭha's son had sat down, he said to the Blessed One: "I would like to question Master Gotama on a certain point, if Master Gotama would grant me the favour of an answer to the question."

"Ask what you like, Aggivessana." [230]

"How does Master Gotama discipline his disciples? And how is Master Gotama's instruction usually presented to his disciples?"

"This is how I discipline my disciples, Aggivessana, and this is how my instruction is usually presented to my disciples: 'Bhikkhus, material form is impermanent, feeling is impermanent, perception is impermanent, formations are impermanent, consciousness is impermanent. Bhikkhus, material form is not self, feeling is not self, perception is not self, formations are not self, consciousness is not self. All formations are impermanent; all things are not self.' That is the way I discipline my disciples, and that is how my instruction is usually presented to my disciples."

10. "A simile occurs to me, Master Gotama."

"Explain how it occurs to you, Aggivessana," the Blessed One said.

"Just as when seeds and plants, whatever their kind, reach growth, increase, and maturation, all do so in dependence upon the earth, based upon the earth; and just as when strenuous works, whatever their kind, are done, all are done in dependence upon the earth, based upon the earth—so too, Master

Gotama, a person has material form as self, and based upon material form he produces merit or demerit. A person has feeling as self, and based upon feeling he produces merit or demerit. A person has perception as self, and based upon perception he produces merit or demerit. A person has formations as self, and based upon formations he produces merit or demerit. A person has consciousness as self, and based upon consciousness he produces merit or demerit."

11. "Aggivessana, are you not asserting thus: 'Material form is my self, feeling is my self, perception is my self, formations are my self, consciousness is my self'?"

"I assert thus, Master Gotama: 'Material form is my self, feeling is my self, perception is my self, formations are my self, consciousness is my self.' And so does this great multitude."[373]

"What has this great multitude to do with you, Aggivessana? Please confine yourself to your own assertion alone."

"Then, Master Gotama, I assert thus: 'Material form is my self, feeling is my self, perception is my self, formations are my self, consciousness is my self.'"

12. "In that case, Aggivessana, I shall ask you a question in return. Answer it as you choose. [231] What do you think, Aggivessana? Would a head-anointed noble king—for example, King Pasenadi of Kosala or King Ajātasattu Vedehiputta of Magadha—exercise the power in his own realm to execute those who should be executed, to fine those who should be fined, and to banish those who should be banished?"

"Master Gotama, a head-anointed noble king—for example, King Pasenadi of Kosala or King Ajātasattu Vedehiputta of Magadha—would exercise the power in his own realm to execute those who should be executed, to fine those who should be fined, and to banish those who should be banished. For even these [oligarchic] communities and societies such as the Vajjians and the Mallians exercise the power in their own realm to execute those who should be executed, to fine those who should be fined, and to banish those who should be banished; so all the more so should a head-anointed noble king such as King Pasenadi of Kosala or King Ajātasattu Vedehiputta of Magadha. He would exercise it, Master Gotama, and he would be worthy to exercise it."

13. "What do you think, Aggivessana? When you say thus: 'Material form is my self,' do you exercise any such power over

that material form as to say: 'Let my form be thus; let my form not be thus'?"[374] When this was said, Saccaka the Nigaṇṭha's son was silent.

A second time the Blessed One asked the same question, and a second time Saccaka the Nigaṇṭha's son was silent. Then the Blessed One said to him: "Aggivessana, answer now. Now is not the time to be silent. If anyone, when asked a reasonable question up to the third time by the Tathāgata, still does not answer, his head splits into seven pieces there and then."

14. Now on that occasion a thunderbolt-wielding spirit holding an iron thunderbolt that burned, blazed, and glowed, appeared in the air above Saccaka the Nigaṇṭha's son, thinking: "If this Saccaka the Nigaṇṭha's son, when asked a reasonable question up to the third time by the Blessed One, still does not answer, I shall split his head into seven pieces here and now."[375] The Blessed One saw the thunderbolt-wielding spirit and so did Saccaka the Nigaṇṭha's son. Then Saccaka the Nigaṇṭha's son was frightened, alarmed, and terrified. [232] Seeking his shelter, asylum, and refuge in the Blessed One himself, he said: "Ask me, Master Gotama, I will answer."

15. "What do you think, Aggivessana? When you say thus: 'Material form is my self,' do you exercise any such power over that material form as to say: 'Let my form be thus; let my form not be thus'?"—"No, Master Gotama."

16. "Pay attention, Aggivessana, pay attention how you reply! What you said afterwards does not agree with what you said before, nor does what you said before agree with what you said afterwards. What do you think, Aggivessana? When you say thus: 'Feeling is my self,' do you exercise any power over that feeling as to say: 'Let my feeling be thus; let my feeling not be thus'?"—"No, Master Gotama."

17. "Pay attention, Aggivessana, pay attention how you reply! What you said afterwards does not agree with what you said before, nor does what you said before agree with what you said afterwards. What do you think, Aggivessana? When you say thus: 'Perception is my self,' do you exercise any power over that perception as to say: 'Let my perception be thus; let my perception not be thus'?"—"No, Master Gotama."

18. "Pay attention, Aggivessana, pay attention how you reply! What you said afterwards does not agree with what you

said before, nor does what you said before agree with what you said afterwards. What do you think, Aggivessana? When you say thus: 'Formations are my self,' do you exercise any such power over those formations as to say: 'Let my formations be thus; let my formations not be thus'?"—"No, Master Gotama."

19. "Pay attention, Aggivessana, pay attention how you reply! What you said afterwards does not agree with what you said before, nor does what you said before agree with what you said afterwards. What do you think, Aggivessana? When you say thus: 'Consciousness is my self,' do you exercise any such power over that consciousness as to say: 'Let my consciousness be thus; let my consciousness not be thus'?"—"No, Master Gotama."

20. "Pay attention, Aggivessana, pay attention how you reply! What you said afterwards does not agree with what you said before, nor does what you said before agree with what you said afterwards. What do you think, Aggivessana, is material form permanent or impermanent?"—"Impermanent, Master Gotama."—"Is what is impermanent suffering or happiness?"—"Suffering, Master Gotama."—"Is what is impermanent, suffering, and subject to change fit to be regarded thus: 'This is mine, this I am, [233] this is my self'?"—"No, Master Gotama."

"What do you think, Aggivessana? Is feeling permanent or impermanent?...Is perception permanent or impermanent?...Are formations permanent or impermanent?...Is consciousness permanent or impermanent?"—"Impermanent, Master Gotama."—"Is what is impermanent suffering or happiness?"—"Suffering, Master Gotama."—"Is what is impermanent, suffering, and subject to change fit to be regarded thus: 'This is mine, this I am, this is my self'?"—"No, Master Gotama."

21. "What do you think, Aggivessana? When one adheres to suffering, resorts to suffering, holds to suffering, and regards what is suffering thus: 'This is mine, this I am, this is my self,' could one ever fully understand suffering oneself or abide with suffering utterly destroyed?"

"How could one, Master Gotama? No, Master Gotama."

*"What do you think, Aggivessana? That being so, do you not adhere to suffering, resort to suffering, hold to suffering, and regard what is suffering thus: 'This is mine, this I am, this is my self'?"

"How could I not, Master Gotama? Yes, Master Gotama."*[376]

22. "It is as though a man needing heartwood, seeking heartwood, wandering in search of heartwood, were to take a sharp axe and enter the wood, and there he would see a large plantain trunk, straight, young, with no fruit-bud core. Then he would cut it down at the root, cut off the crown, and unroll the leaf-sheaths; but as he went on unrolling the leaf sheaths, he would never come even to any sapwood, let alone heartwood. So too, Aggivessana, when you are pressed, questioned, and cross-questioned by me about your own assertion, you turn out to be empty, vacant, and mistaken. But it was you who made this statement before the Vesālī assembly: 'I see no recluse or brahmin, the head of an order, the head of a group, the teacher of a group, even one claiming to be accomplished and fully enlightened, who would not shake, shiver, and tremble and sweat under the armpits if he were to engage in debate with me. Even if I were to engage a senseless post in debate, it would shake, shiver, and tremble if it were to engage in debate with me, so what shall I say of a human being?' Now there are drops of sweat on your forehead and they have soaked through your upper robe and fallen to the ground. But there is no sweat on my body now." And the Blessed One uncovered his golden-coloured body before the assembly. [234] When this was said, Saccaka the Nigaṇṭha's son sat silent, dismayed, with shoulders drooping and head down, glum, and without response.

23. Then Dummukha, the son of the Licchavis, seeing Saccaka the Nigaṇṭha's son in such a condition, said to the Blessed One: "A simile occurs to me, Master Gotama."

"Explain how it occurs to you, Dummukha."

"Suppose, venerable sir, not far from a village or town there was a pond with a crab in it. And then a party of boys or girls went out from the town or village to the pond, went into the water, and pulled the crab out of the water and put it on dry land. And whenever the crab extended a leg, they cut it off, broke it, and smashed it with sticks and stones, so that the crab with all its legs cut off, broken, and smashed, would be unable to get back to the pond as before. So too, all Saccaka the Nigaṇṭha's son's contortions, writhings, and vacillations have been cut off, broken, and smashed by the Blessed One, and now he cannot get near the Blessed One again for the purpose of debate."

24. When this was said, Saccaka the Nigaṇṭha's son told him: "Wait, Dummukha, wait! We are not speaking with you, here we are speaking with Master Gotama."

[Then he said]: "Let be, Master Gotama, that talk of ours and of other ordinary recluses and brahmins. It was mere prattle, I think. But in what way is a disciple of the Master Gotama one who carries out his instruction, who responds to his advice, who has crossed beyond doubt, become free from perplexity, gained intrepidity, and become independent of others in the Teacher's Dispensation?"[377]

"Here, Aggivessana, any kind of material form whatever, whether past, future, or present, internal or external, gross or subtle, inferior or superior, far or near—a disciple of mine sees all material form as it actually is with proper wisdom thus: 'This is not mine, this I am not, this is not my self.' [235] Any kind of feeling whatever...Any kind of perception whatever...Any kind of formations whatever...Any kind of consciousness whatever, whether past, future, or present, internal or external, gross or subtle, inferior or superior, far or near—a disciple of mine sees all consciousness as it actually is with proper wisdom thus: 'This is not mine, this I am not, this is not my self.' It is in this way that a disciple of mine is one who carries out my instruction, who responds to my advice, who has crossed beyond doubt, become free from perplexity, gained intrepidity, and become independent of others in the Teacher's Dispensation."

25. "Master Gotama, in what way is a bhikkhu an arahant with taints destroyed, one who has lived the holy life, done what had to be done, laid down the burden, reached his own goal, destroyed the fetters of being, and is completely liberated through final knowledge?"

"Here, Aggivessana, any kind of material form whatever, whether past, future, or present, internal or external, gross or subtle, inferior or superior, far or near—a bhikkhu has seen all material form as it actually is with proper wisdom thus: 'This is not mine, this I am not, this is not my self,' and through not clinging he is liberated. Any kind of feeling whatever...Any kind of perception whatever...Any kind of formations whatever ...Any kind of consciousness whatever, whether past, future, or present, internal or external, gross or subtle, inferior or superior, far or near—a bhikkhu has seen all consciousness as it actually is with proper wisdom thus: 'This is not mine, this I am not, this is not my self,' and through not clinging he is liberated. It is in this way that a bhikkhu is an arahant with taints destroyed, one who has lived the holy life, done what had to be done, laid down the burden, reached his own goal, destroyed the fetters of being, and is completely liberated through final knowledge.

26. "When a bhikkhu's mind is thus liberated, he possesses three unsurpassable qualities: unsurpassable vision, unsurpassable practice, and unsurpassable deliverance.[378] When a bhikkhu is thus liberated, he still honours, respects, reveres, and venerates the Tathāgata thus: 'The Blessed One is enlightened and he teaches the Dhamma for the sake of enlightenment. The Blessed One is tamed and he teaches the Dhamma for taming oneself. The Blessed One is at peace and he teaches the Dhamma for the sake of peace. The Blessed One has crossed over and he teaches the Dhamma for crossing over. The Blessed One has attained Nibbāna and he teaches the Dhamma for attaining Nibbāna.'"

27. When this was said, Saccaka the Nigaṇṭha's son [236] replied: "Master Gotama, we were bold and impudent in thinking we could attack Master Gotama in debate. A man might attack a mad elephant and find safety, yet he could not attack Master Gotama and find safety. A man might attack a blazing mass of fire and find safety, yet he could not attack Master Gotama and find safety. A man might attack a terrible poisonous snake and find safety, yet he could not attack Master Gotama and find safety. We were bold and impudent in thinking we could attack Master Gotama in debate.

"Let the Blessed One together with the Sangha of bhikkhus consent to accept tomorrow's meal from me." The Blessed One consented in silence.

28. Then, knowing that the Blessed One had consented, Saccaka the Nigaṇṭha's son addressed the Licchavis: "Hear me, Licchavis. The recluse Gotama together with the Sangha of good bhikkhus has been invited by me for tomorrow's meal. You may bring to me whatever you think would be suitable for him."

29. Then, when the night had ended, the Licchavis brought five hundred ceremonial dishes of milk rice as gifts of food. Then Saccaka the Nigaṇṭha's son had good food of various kinds prepared in his own park and had the time announced to the Blessed One: "It is time, Master Gotama, the meal is ready."

30. Then, it being morning, the Blessed One dressed, and taking his bowl and outer robe, he went with the Sangha of bhikkhus to the park of Saccaka the Nigaṇṭha's son and sat down on the seat made ready. Then, with his own hands, Saccaka the Nigaṇṭha's son served and satisfied the Sangha of bhikkhus headed by the Buddha with the various kinds of good food. When the Blessed One had eaten and had put his bowl aside, Saccaka the Nigaṇṭha's son took a low seat, sat down at one side, and said to the Blessed One: "Master Gotama, may the merit and the great meritorious fruits of this act of giving be for the happiness of the givers."

"Aggivessana, whatever comes about from giving to a recipient such as yourself—one who is not free from lust, not free from hate, not free from delusion—[237] that will be for the givers. And whatever comes about from giving to a recipient such as myself—one who is free from lust, free from hate, free from delusion—that will be for you."[379]

36 *Mahāsaccaka Sutta*
The Greater Discourse to Saccaka

1. THUS HAVE I HEARD. On one occasion the Blessed One was living at Vesālī in the Great Wood in the Hall with the Peaked Roof.

2. Now on that occasion, when it was morning, the Blessed One had finished dressing and had taken his bowl and outer robe, desiring to go into Vesālī for alms.

3. Then, as Saccaka the Nigaṇṭha's son was walking and wandering for exercise, he came to the Hall with the Peaked Roof in the Great Wood.[380] The venerable Ānanda saw him coming in the distance and said to the Blessed One: "Venerable sir, here comes Saccaka the Nigaṇṭha's son, a debater and a clever speaker regarded by many as a saint. He wants to discredit the Buddha, the Dhamma, and the Sangha. It would be good if the Blessed One would sit down for a while out of compassion."[381] The Blessed One sat down on the seat made ready. Then Saccaka the Nigaṇṭha's son went up to the Blessed One and exchanged greetings with him. When this courteous and amiable talk was finished, he sat down at one side and said to the Blessed One:

4. "Master Gotama, there are some recluses and brahmins who abide pursuing development of body, but not development of mind.[382] They are touched by bodily painful feeling. In the past, when one was touched by bodily painful feeling, one's thighs would become rigid, one's heart would burst, hot blood would gush from one's mouth, and one would go mad, go out of one's mind. So then the mind was subservient to the body, the body wielded mastery over it. Why is that? [238] Because the mind was not developed. But there are some recluses and brahmins who abide pursuing development of mind, but not development of body. They are touched by mental painful feeling. In the past, when one was touched by mental painful feeling, one's

thighs would become rigid, one's heart would burst, hot blood would gush from one's mouth, and one would go mad, go out of one's mind. So then the body was subservient to the mind, the mind wielded mastery over it. Why is that? Because the body was not developed. Master Gotama, it has occurred to me: 'Surely Master Gotama's disciples abide pursuing development of mind, but not development of body.'"

5. "But, Aggivessana, what have you learned about development of body?"

"Well, there are, for example, Nanda Vaccha, Kisa Sankicca, Makkhali Gosāla.[383] They go naked, rejecting conventions, licking their hands, not coming when asked, not stopping when asked; they do not accept food brought or food specially made or an invitation to a meal; they receive nothing from a pot, from a bowl, across a threshold, across a stick, across a pestle, from two eating together, from a pregnant woman, from a woman giving suck, from a woman in the midst of men, from where food is advertised to be distributed, from where a dog is waiting, from where flies are buzzing; they accept no fish or meat, they drink no liquor, wine, or fermented brew. They keep to one house, to one morsel; they keep to two houses, to two morsels...they keep to seven houses, to seven morsels. They live on one saucerful a day, on two saucerfuls a day...on seven saucerfuls a day. They take food once a day, once every two days...once every seven days; thus even up to once every fortnight, they dwell pursuing the practice of taking food at stated intervals."

6. "But do they subsist on so little, Aggivessana?"

"No, Master Gotama, sometimes they consume excellent hard food, eat excellent soft food, taste excellent delicacies, drink excellent drinks. Thereby they again regain their strength, fortify themselves, and become fat."

"What they earlier abandoned, Aggivessana, they later gather together again. That is how there is increase and decrease of this body. But what have you learned about development of mind?" [239]

When Saccaka the Nigaṇṭha's son was asked by the Blessed One about development of mind, he was unable to answer.

7. Then the Blessed One told him: "What you have just spoken of as development of body, Aggivessana, is not development of

body according to the Dhamma in the Noble One's Discipline. Since you do not know what development of body is, how could you know what development of mind is? Nevertheless, Aggivessana, as to how one is undeveloped in body and undeveloped in mind, and developed in body and developed in mind, listen and attend closely to what I shall say."—"Yes, sir," Saccaka the Nigaṇṭha's son replied. The Blessed One said this:

8. "How, Aggivessana, is one undeveloped in body and undeveloped in mind? Here, Aggivessana, pleasant feeling arises in an untaught ordinary person. Touched by that pleasant feeling, he lusts after pleasure and continues to lust after pleasure. That pleasant feeling of his ceases. With the cessation of the pleasant feeling, painful feeling arises. Touched by that painful feeling, he sorrows, grieves, and laments, he weeps beating his breast and becomes distraught. When that pleasant feeling has arisen in him, it invades his mind and remains because body is not developed. And when that painful feeling has arisen in him, it invades his mind and remains because mind is not developed. Anyone in whom, in this double manner, arisen pleasant feeling invades his mind and remains because body is not developed, and arisen painful feeling invades his mind and remains because mind is not developed, is thus undeveloped in body and undeveloped in mind.

9. "And how, Aggivessana, is one developed in body and developed in mind? Here, Aggivessana, pleasant feeling arises in a well-taught noble disciple. Touched by that pleasant feeling, he does not lust after pleasure or continue to lust after pleasure. That pleasant feeling of his ceases. With the cessation of the pleasant feeling, painful feeling arises. Touched by that painful feeling, he does not sorrow, grieve, and lament, he does not weep beating his breast and become distraught. When that pleasant feeling has arisen in him, it does not invade his mind and remain because body is developed. And when that painful feeling has arisen in him, it does not invade his mind and remain because mind is developed. Anyone in whom, in this double manner, arisen pleasant feeling [240] does not invade his mind and remain because body is developed, and arisen painful feeling does not invade his mind and remain because mind is developed, is thus developed in body and developed in mind."[384]

10. "I have confidence in Master Gotama thus: 'Master Gotama is developed in body and developed in mind.'"

"Surely, Aggivessana, your words are offensive and discourteous, but still I will answer you. Since I shaved off my hair and beard, put on the yellow robe, and went forth from the home life into homelessness, it has not been possible for arisen pleasant feeling to invade my mind and remain or for arisen painful feeling to invade my mind and remain."

11. "Has there never arisen in Master Gotama a feeling so pleasant that it could invade his mind and remain? Has there never arisen in Master Gotama a feeling so painful that it could invade his mind and remain?"

12. "Why not, Aggivessana?[385] Here, Aggivessana, before my enlightenment, while I was still only an unenlightened Bodhisatta, I thought: 'Household life is crowded and dusty; life gone forth is wide open. It is not easy, while living in a home, to lead the holy life utterly perfect and pure as a polished shell. Suppose I shave off my hair and beard, put on the yellow robe, and go forth from the home life into homelessness.'

13–16. "Later, while still young, a black-haired young man endowed with the blessing of youth, in the prime of life...(*as Sutta 26, §§14–17*)...And I sat down there thinking: 'This will serve for striving.'

17. "Now these three similes occurred to me spontaneously, never heard before. Suppose there were a wet sappy piece of wood lying in water, and a man came with an upper fire-stick, thinking: 'I shall light a fire, I shall produce heat.' What do you think, Aggivessana? Could the man light a fire and produce heat by taking the upper fire-stick and rubbing it against the wet sappy piece of wood lying in the water?"

"No, Master Gotama. Why not? Because it is a wet sappy piece of wood, [241] and it is lying in water. Eventually the man would reap only weariness and disappointment."

"So too, Aggivessana, as to those recluses and brahmins who still do not live bodily withdrawn from sensual pleasures, and whose sensual desire, affection, infatuation, thirst, and fever for sensual pleasures has not been fully abandoned and suppressed internally, even if those good recluses and brahmins feel painful, racking, piercing feelings due to exertion, they are incapable of knowledge and vision and supreme enlightenment;

and even if those good recluses and brahmins do not feel painful, racking, piercing feelings due to exertion, they are incapable of knowledge and vision and supreme enlightenment. This was the first simile that occurred to me spontaneously, never heard before.

18. "Again, Aggivessana, a second simile occurred to me spontaneously, never heard before. Suppose there were a wet sappy piece of wood lying on dry land far from water, and a man came with an upper fire-stick, thinking: 'I shall light a fire, I shall produce heat.' What do you think, Aggivessana? Could the man light a fire and produce heat by taking the upper fire-stick and rubbing it against the wet sappy piece of wood lying on dry land far from water?"

"No, Master Gotama. Why not? Because it is a wet sappy piece of wood, even though it is lying on dry land far from water. Eventually the man would reap only weariness and disappointment."

"So too, Aggivessana, as to those recluses and brahmins who live bodily withdrawn from sensual pleasures,[386] but whose sensual desire, affection, infatuation, thirst, and fever for sensual pleasures has not been fully abandoned and suppressed internally, even if those good recluses and brahmins feel painful, racking, piercing feelings due to exertion, they are incapable of knowledge and vision and supreme enlightenment; and even if those good recluses and brahmins do not feel painful, racking, piercing feelings due to exertion, they are incapable of knowledge and vision and supreme enlightenment. This was the second simile that occurred to me spontaneously, never heard before.

19. "Again, Aggivessana, a third simile occurred to me [242] spontaneously, never heard before. Suppose there were a dry sapless piece of wood lying on dry land far from water, and a man came with an upper fire-stick, thinking: 'I shall light a fire, I shall produce heat.' What do you think, Aggivessana? Could the man light a fire and produce heat by rubbing it against the dry sapless piece of wood lying on dry land far from water?"

"Yes, Master Gotama. Why so? Because it is a dry sapless piece of wood, and it is lying on dry land far from water."

"So too, Aggivessana, as to those recluses and brahmins who live bodily withdrawn from sensual pleasures, and whose sensual desire, affection, infatuation, thirst, and fever for sensual pleasures has been fully abandoned and suppressed internally, even if those good recluses and brahmins feel painful, racking, piercing feelings due to exertion, they are capable of knowledge and vision and supreme enlightenment; and even if those good recluses and brahmins do not feel painful, racking, piercing feelings due to exertion, they are capable of knowledge and vision and supreme enlightenment.[387] This was the third simile that occurred to me spontaneously, never heard before. These are the three similes that occurred to me spontaneously, never heard before.

20. "I thought: 'Suppose, with my teeth clenched and my tongue pressed against the roof of my mouth, I beat down, constrain, and crush mind with mind.' So, with my teeth clenched and my tongue pressed against the roof of my mouth, I beat down, constrained, and crushed mind with mind. While I did so, sweat ran from my armpits. Just as a strong man might seize a weaker man by the head or shoulders and beat him down, constrain him, and crush him, so too, with my teeth clenched and my tongue pressed against the roof of my mouth, I beat down, constrained, and crushed mind with mind, and sweat ran from my armpits. But although tireless energy was aroused in me and unremitting mindfulness was established, my body was overwrought [243] and uncalm because I was exhausted by the painful striving. But such painful feeling that arose in me did not invade my mind and remain.[388]

21. "I thought: 'Suppose I practise the breathingless meditation.' So I stopped the in-breaths and out-breaths through my mouth and nose. While I did so, there was a loud sound of winds coming out from my earholes. Just as there is a loud sound when a smith's bellows are blown, so too, while I stopped the in-breaths and out-breaths through my nose and ears, there was a loud sound of winds coming out from my earholes. But although tireless energy was aroused in me and unremitting mindfulness was established, my body was overwrought and uncalm because I was exhausted by the painful striving. But such painful feeling that arose in me did not invade my mind and remain.

22. "I thought: 'Suppose I practise further the breathingless meditation.' So I stopped the in-breaths and out-breaths through

my mouth, nose, and ears. While I did so, violent winds cut through my head. Just as if a strong man were splitting my head open with a sharp sword, so too, while I stopped the in-breaths and out-breaths through my mouth, nose, and ears, violent winds cut through my head. But although tireless energy was aroused in me and unremitting mindfulness was established, my body was overwrought and uncalm because I was exhausted by the painful striving. But such painful feeling that arose in me did not invade my mind and remain.

23. "I thought: 'Suppose I practise further the breathingless meditation.' So I stopped the in-breaths and out-breaths through my mouth, nose, and ears. While I did so, there were violent pains in my head. Just as if a strong man [244] were tightening a tough leather strap around my head as a headband, so too, while I stopped the in-breaths and out-breaths through my mouth, nose, and ears, there were violent pains in my head. But although tireless energy was aroused in me and unremitting mindfulness was established, my body was overwrought and uncalm because I was exhausted by the painful striving. But such painful feeling that arose in me did not invade my mind and remain.

24. "I thought: 'Suppose I practise further the breathingless meditation.' So I stopped the in-breaths and out-breaths through my mouth, nose, and ears. While I did so, violent winds carved up my belly. Just as if a skilled butcher or his apprentice were to carve up an ox's belly with a sharp butcher's knife, so too, while I stopped the in-breaths and out-breaths through my mouth, nose, and ears, violent winds carved up my belly. But although tireless energy was aroused in me and unremitting mindfulness was established, my body was overwrought and uncalm because I was exhausted by the painful striving. But such painful feeling that arose in me did not invade my mind and remain.

25. "I thought: 'Suppose I practise further the breathingless meditation.' So I stopped the in-breaths and out-breaths through my mouth, nose, and ears. While I did so, there was a violent burning in my body. Just as if two strong men were to seize a weaker man by both arms and roast him over a pit of hot coals, so too, while I stopped the in-breaths and out-breaths through my mouth, nose, and ears, there was a violent burning in my body. But although tireless energy was aroused in me and

unremitting mindfulness was established, my body was overwrought and uncalm because I was exhausted by the painful striving. But such painful feeling that arose in me did not invade my mind and remain.

26. "Now when [245] deities saw me, some said: 'The recluse Gotama is dead.' Other deities said: 'The recluse Gotama is not dead, he is dying.' And other deities said: 'The recluse Gotama is not dead nor dying; he is an arahant, for such is the way arahants abide.'

27. "I thought: 'Suppose I practise entirely cutting off food.' Then deities came to me and said: 'Good sir, do not practise entirely cutting off food. If you do so, we shall infuse heavenly food into the pores of your skin and you will live on that.' I considered: 'If I claim to be completely fasting while these deities infuse heavenly food into the pores of my skin and I live on that, then I shall be lying.' So I dismissed those deities, saying: 'There is no need.'

28. "I thought: 'Suppose I take very little food, a handful each time, whether of bean soup or lentil soup or vetch soup or pea soup.' So I took very little food, a handful each time, whether of bean soup or lentil soup or vetch soup or pea soup. While I did so, my body reached a state of extreme emaciation. Because of eating so little my limbs became like the jointed segments of vine stems or bamboo stems. Because of eating so little my backside became like a camel's hoof. Because of eating so little the projections on my spine stood forth like corded beads. Because of eating so little my ribs jutted out as gaunt as the crazy rafters of an old roofless barn. Because of eating so little the gleam of my eyes sank far down in their sockets, looking like the gleam of water that has sunk far down in a deep well. Because of eating so little my scalp shrivelled and withered as [246] a green bitter gourd shrivels and withers in the wind and sun. Because of eating so little my belly skin adhered to my backbone; thus if I touched my belly skin I encountered my backbone and if I touched my backbone I encountered my belly skin. Because of eating so little, if I defecated or urinated, I fell over on my face there. Because of eating so little, if I tried to ease my body by rubbing my limbs with my hands, the hair, rotted at its roots, fell from my body as I rubbed.

29. "Now when people saw me, some said: 'The recluse Gotama

is black.' Other people said: 'The recluse Gotama is not black, he is brown.' Other people said: 'The recluse Gotama is neither black nor brown, he is golden-skinned.' So much had the clear, bright colour of my skin deteriorated through eating so little.

30. "I thought: 'Whatever recluses or brahmins in the past have experienced painful, racking, piercing feelings due to exertion, this is the utmost, there is none beyond this. And whatever recluses and brahmins in the future will experience painful, racking, piercing feelings due to exertion, this is the utmost, there is none beyond this. And whatever recluses and brahmins at present experience painful, racking, piercing feelings due to exertion, this is the utmost, there is none beyond this. But by this racking practice of austerities I have not attained any superhuman states, any distinction in knowledge and vision worthy of the noble ones. Could there be another path to enlightenment?'

31. "I considered: 'I recall that when my father the Sakyan was occupied, while I was sitting in the cool shade of a rose-apple tree, quite secluded from sensual pleasures, secluded from unwholesome states, I entered upon and abided in the first jhāna, which is accompanied by applied and sustained thought, with rapture and pleasure born of seclusion.[389] Could that be the path to enlightenment?' Then, following on that memory, came the realisation: 'That is the path to enlightenment.'

32. "I thought: 'Why [247] am I afraid of that pleasure that has nothing to do with sensual pleasures and unwholesome states?' I thought: 'I am not afraid of that pleasure since it has nothing to do with sensual pleasures and unwholesome states.'[390]

33. "I considered: 'It is not easy to attain that pleasure with a body so excessively emaciated. Suppose I ate some solid food—some boiled rice and bread.' And I ate some solid food—some boiled rice and bread. Now at that time five bhikkhus were waiting upon me, thinking: 'If our recluse Gotama achieves some higher state, he will inform us.' But when I ate the boiled rice and bread, the five bhikkhus were disgusted and left me, thinking: 'The recluse Gotama now lives luxuriously; he has given up his striving and reverted to luxury.'

34. "Now when I had eaten solid food and regained my strength, then quite secluded from sensual pleasures, secluded from unwholesome states, I entered upon and abided in the first jhāna, which is accompanied by applied and sustained thought,

with rapture and pleasure born of seclusion. But such pleasant feeling that arose in me did not invade my mind and remain.[391]

35–37. "With the stilling of applied and sustained thought, I entered upon and abided in the second jhāna...With the fading away as well of rapture...I entered upon and abided in the third jhāna...With the abandoning of pleasure and pain...I entered upon and abided in the fourth jhāna...But such pleasant feeling that arose in me did not invade my mind and remain.

38. "When my concentrated mind was thus purified, bright, unblemished, rid of imperfection, malleable, wieldy, steady, and attained to imperturbability, [248] I directed it to knowledge of the recollection of past lives. I recollected my manifold past lives, that is, one birth, two births...(*as Sutta 4, §27*)...Thus with their aspects and particulars I recollected my manifold past lives.

39. "This was the first true knowledge attained by me in the first watch of the night. Ignorance was banished and true knowledge arose, darkness was banished and light arose, as happens in one who abides diligent, ardent, and resolute. But such pleasant feeling that arose in me did not invade my mind and remain.

40. "When my concentrated mind was thus purified, bright, unblemished, rid of imperfection, malleable, wieldy, steady, and attained to imperturbability, I directed it to knowledge of the passing away and reappearance of beings...(*as Sutta 4, §29*)... Thus with the divine eye, which is purified and surpasses the human, I saw beings passing away and reappearing, inferior and superior, fair and ugly, fortunate and unfortunate, and I understood how beings pass on according to their actions.

41. "This was the second true knowledge attained by me in the middle watch of the night. Ignorance was banished and true knowledge arose, [249] darkness was banished and light arose, as happens in one who abides diligent, ardent, and resolute. But such pleasant feeling that arose in me did not invade my mind and remain.

42. "When my concentrated mind was thus purified, bright, unblemished, rid of imperfection, malleable, wieldy, steady, and attained to imperturbability, I directed it to knowledge of the destruction of the taints. I directly knew as it actually is: 'This is suffering';...'This is the origin of suffering';...'This is the cessa-

tion of suffering';...'This is the way leading to the cessation of suffering';...'These are the taints';...'This is the origin of the taints';...'This is the cessation of the taints';...'This is the way leading to the cessation of the taints.'

43. "When I knew and saw thus, my mind was liberated from the taint of sensual desire, from the taint of being, and from the taint of ignorance. When it was liberated there came the knowledge: 'It is liberated.' I directly knew: 'Birth is destroyed, the holy life has been lived, what had to be done has been done, there is no more coming to any state of being.'

44. "This was the third true knowledge attained by me in the last watch of the night. Ignorance was banished and true knowledge arose, darkness was banished and light arose, as happens in one who abides diligent, ardent, and resolute. But such pleasant feeling that arose in me did not invade my mind and remain.

45. "Aggivessana, I recall teaching the Dhamma to an assembly of many hundreds. Perhaps each person thinks: 'The recluse Gotama is teaching the Dhamma especially for me.' But it should not be so regarded; the Tathāgata teaches the Dhamma to others only to give them knowledge. When the talk is finished, Aggivessana, then I steady my mind internally, quieten it, bring it to singleness, and concentrate it on that same sign of concentration as before, in which I constantly abide."[392]

"This can be believed of Master Gotama, since he is accomplished and fully enlightened. But does Master Gotama recall sleeping during the day?"[393]

46. "I recall, Aggivessana, in the last month of the hot season, on returning from my almsround, after my meal I lay out my outer robe folded in four, and lying down on my right side, I fall asleep mindful and fully aware."

"Some recluses and brahmins call that abiding in delusion, Master Gotama." [250]

"It is not in such a way that one is deluded or undeluded, Aggivessana. As to how one is deluded or undeluded, listen and attend closely to what I shall say."—"Yes, sir," Saccaka the Nigaṇṭha's son replied. The Blessed One said this:

47. "Him I call deluded, Aggivessana, who has not abandoned the taints that defile, bring renewal of being, give trouble, ripen in suffering, and lead to future birth, ageing, and death; for it is with the non-abandoning of the taints that one is deluded. Him I

call undeluded who has abandoned the taints that defile, bring renewal of being, give trouble, ripen in suffering, and lead to future birth, ageing, and death; for it is with the abandoning of the taints that one is undeluded. The Tathāgata, Aggivessana, has abandoned the taints that defile, bring renewal of being, give trouble, ripen in suffering, and lead to future birth, ageing, and death; he has cut them off at the root, made them like a palm stump, done away with them so that they are no longer subject to future arising. Just as a palm tree whose crown is cut off is incapable of further growth, so too, the Tathāgata has abandoned the taints that defile...done away with them so that they are no longer subject to future arising."

48. When this was said, Saccaka the Nigaṇṭha's son said: "It is wonderful, Master Gotama, it is marvellous how when Master Gotama is spoken to offensively again and again, assailed by discourteous courses of speech, the colour of his skin brightens and the colour of his face clears, as is to be expected of one who is accomplished and fully enlightened. I recall, Master Gotama, engaging Pūraṇa Kassapa in debate, and then he prevaricated, led the talk aside, and showed anger, hate, and bitterness. But when Master Gotama is spoken to offensively again and again, assaulted by discourteous courses of speech, the colour of his skin brightens and the colour of his face clears, as is to be expected of one who is accomplished and fully enlightened. I recall, Master Gotama, engaging Makkhali Gosāla...Ajita Kesakambalin...Pakudha Kaccāyana...Sañjaya Belaṭṭhiputta...the Nigaṇṭha Nātaputta in debate, [251] and then he prevaricated, led the talk aside, and showed anger, hate, and bitterness. But when Master Gotama is spoken to offensively again and again, assailed by discourteous courses of speech, the colour of his skin brightens and the colour of his face clears, as is to be expected of one who is accomplished and fully enlightened. And now, Master Gotama, we depart. We are busy and have much to do."

"Now is the time, Aggivessana, to do as you think fit."

Then Saccaka the Nigaṇṭha's son, having delighted and rejoiced in the Blessed One's words, got up from his seat and departed.[394]

37 *Cūḷataṇhāsankhaya Sutta*
The Shorter Discourse on the Destruction of Craving

1. THUS HAVE I HEARD. On one occasion the Blessed One was living at Sāvatthī in the Eastern Park, in the Palace of Migāra's Mother.

2. Then Sakka, ruler of gods, went to the Blessed One, and after paying homage to him, he stood at one side and asked: "Venerable sir, how in brief is a bhikkhu liberated in the destruction of craving, one who has reached the ultimate end, the ultimate security from bondage, the ultimate holy life, the ultimate goal, one who is foremost among gods and humans?"[395]

3. "Here, ruler of gods, a bhikkhu has heard that nothing is worth adhering to. When a bhikkhu has heard that nothing is worth adhering to, he directly knows everything; having directly known everything, he fully understands everything; having fully understood everything, whatever feeling he feels, whether pleasant or painful or neither-painful-nor-pleasant, he abides contemplating impermanence in those feelings, contemplating fading away, contemplating cessation, contemplating relinquishment. Contemplating thus, he does not cling to anything in the world. When he does not cling, he is not agitated. When he is not agitated, he personally attains Nibbāna.[396] [252] He understands: 'Birth is destroyed, the holy life has been lived, what had to be done has been done, there is no more coming to any state of being.' Briefly, it is in this way, ruler of gods, that a bhikkhu is liberated in the destruction of craving, one who has reached the ultimate end, the ultimate security from bondage, the ultimate holy life, the ultimate goal, one who is foremost among gods and humans."

4. Then Sakka, ruler of gods, delighting and rejoicing in the Blessed One's words, paid homage to the Blessed One, and keeping him on his right, he vanished at once.

5. Now on that occasion the venerable Mahā Moggallāna was sitting not far from the Blessed One. Then he considered: "Did that spirit penetrate to the meaning of the Blessed One's words when he rejoiced, or did he not? Suppose I found out whether he did or not."

6. Then, just as quickly as a strong man might extend his flexed arm or flex his extended arm, the venerable Mahā Moggallāna vanished from the Palace of Migāra's Mother in the Eastern Park and appeared among the gods of the Thirty-three.

7. Now on that occasion Sakka, ruler of gods, was furnished and endowed a hundredfold with the five kinds of heavenly music, and he was enjoying it in the Pleasure Park of the Single Lotus. When he saw the venerable Mahā Moggallāna coming in the distance, he dismissed the music, went to the venerable Mahā Moggallāna, and said to him: "Come, good sir Moggallāna! Welcome, good sir Moggallāna! It is long, good sir Moggallāna, since you found an opportunity to come here. Sit down, good sir Moggallāna; this seat is ready."

The venerable Mahā Moggallāna sat down on the seat made ready, and Sakka took a low seat and sat down at one side. The venerable Mahā Moggallāna then asked him:

8. "Kosiya,[397] how did the Blessed One state to you in brief deliverance in the destruction of craving? It would be good if we might also get to hear that statement."

"Good sir Moggallāna, we are so busy, we have so much to do, not only with our own business, but also with the business of the gods of the Thirty-three. Besides, good sir Moggallāna, what was well heard, well learned, [253] well attended to, well remembered, suddenly vanished from us. Good sir Moggallāna, it once happened that war broke out between the gods and the titans.[398] In that war the gods won and the titans were defeated. When I had won that war and returned from it as a conqueror, I had the Vejayanta Palace built. Good sir Moggallāna, the Vejayanta Palace has a hundred towers, and each tower has seven hundred upper chambers, and each upper chamber has seven nymphs, and each nymph has seven maids. Would you like to see the loveliness of the Vejayanta Palace, good sir Moggallāna?" The venerable Mahā Moggallāna consented in silence.

9. Then Sakka, ruler of gods, and the divine King Vessavaṇa[399]

went to the Vejayanta Palace, giving precedence to the venerable Mahā Moggallāna. When the maids of Sakka saw the venerable Mahā Moggallāna coming in the distance, they were embarrassed and ashamed and they went each into their own rooms. Just as a daughter-in-law is embarrassed and ashamed on seeing her father-in-law, so too, when the maids of Sakka saw the venerable Mahā Moggallāna coming, they were embarrassed and ashamed and they went each into their own rooms.

10. Then Sakka, ruler of gods, and the divine King Vessavaṇa had the venerable Mahā Moggallāna walk all over and explore the Vejayanta Palace: "See, good sir Moggallāna, this loveliness of the Vejayanta Palace! See, good sir Moggallāna, this loveliness of the Vejayanta Palace!"

"It does the venerable Kosiya credit as one who has formerly made merit; and whenever human beings see anything lovely, they say: 'Sirs, it does credit to the gods of the Thirty-three!' It does the venerable Kosiya credit as one who has formerly made merit."

11. Then the venerable Mahā Moggallāna considered thus: "This spirit is living much too negligently. What if I stirred up a sense of urgency in him?" Then the venerable Mahā Moggallāna performed such a feat of supernormal power that with the point of his toe he made the Vejayanta Palace shake and quake and tremble.[400] [254] Sakka and the divine King Vessavaṇa and the gods of the Thirty-three were filled with wonder and amazement, and they said: "Sirs, it is wonderful, it is marvellous, what power and might the recluse has, that with the point of his toe he makes the heavenly region shake and quake and tremble!"

12. When the venerable Mahā Moggallāna knew that Sakka, ruler of the gods, was stirred to a sense of urgency with his hair standing on end, he asked him: "Kosiya, how did the Blessed One state to you in brief deliverance in the destruction of craving? It would be good if we might also get to hear that statement."

"Good sir Moggallāna, I went to the Blessed One, and after paying homage to him, I stood at one side and said: 'Venerable sir,...[*as in §2*]...of gods and humans?' When this was said, good sir Moggallāna, the Blessed One told me: 'Here, ruler of gods,... [*as in §3*]...of gods and humans.' That is how the Blessed One stated to me in brief deliverance in the destruction of craving, good sir Moggallāna."

13. Then the venerable Mahā Moggallāna delighted and rejoiced in the words of Sakka, ruler of gods. [255] Then, just as quickly as a strong man might extend his flexed arm or flex his extended arm, he vanished from among the gods of the Thirty-three and appeared in the Eastern Park in the Palace of Migāra's Mother.

14. Then, soon after the venerable Mahā Moggallāna had gone, the attendants of Sakka, ruler of gods, asked him: "Good sir, was that your teacher, the Blessed One?"—"No, good sirs, that was not my teacher, the Blessed One. That was one of my companions in the holy life, the venerable Mahā Moggallāna."[401]—"Good sir, it is a gain for you that your companion in the holy life is so powerful and mighty. Oh, how much more so must be the Blessed One, your teacher!"

15. Then the venerable Mahā Moggallāna went to the Blessed One, and after paying homage to him, he sat down at one side and asked him: "Venerable sir, does the Blessed One recall stating in brief—to a certain one of the renowned spirits with a great following—deliverance in the destruction of craving?"

"I do recall doing so, Moggallāna. Here Sakka, ruler of gods, came to me, and after paying homage to me, he stood at one side and asked: 'Venerable sir, how in brief is a bhikkhu liberated in the destruction of craving, one who has reached the ultimate end, the ultimate security from bondage, the ultimate holy life, the ultimate goal, one who is foremost among gods and humans?' When this was said, I told him: 'Here, ruler of gods, a bhikkhu has heard that nothing is worth adhering to. When a bhikkhu has heard that nothing is worth adhering to, he directly knows everything; having directly known everything, he fully understands everything; having fully understood everything, whatever feeling he feels, whether pleasant or painful or neither-painful-nor-pleasant, he abides contemplating impermanence in those feelings, contemplating fading away, contemplating cessation, contemplating relinquishment. Contemplating thus, he does not cling to anything in the world. When he does not cling, he is not agitated. When he is not agitated, he personally attains Nibbāna. He understands: "Birth is destroyed, the holy life has been lived, [256] what had to be done has been done, there is no more coming to any state of being." Briefly, it is in this way, ruler of gods, that a bhikkhu is liberated in the destruction of craving...one who is foremost among gods and humans.' That is how I recall stating in brief to Sakka, ruler of gods, deliverance in the destruction of craving."

That is what the Blessed One said. The venerable Mahā Moggallāna was satisfied and delighted in the Blessed One's words.

38 *Mahātaṇhāsankhaya Sutta*
The Greater Discourse on the Destruction of Craving

(SETTING)

1. THUS HAVE I HEARD. On one occasion the Blessed One was living at Sāvatthī in Jeta's Grove, Anāthapiṇḍika's Park.

2. Now on that occasion a pernicious view had arisen in a bhikkhu named Sāti, son of a fisherman, thus: "As I understand the Dhamma taught by the Blessed One, it is this same consciousness that runs and wanders through the round of rebirths, not another."[402]

3. Several bhikkhus, having heard about this, went to the bhikkhu Sāti and asked him: "Friend Sāti, is it true that such a pernicious view has arisen in you?"

"Exactly so, friends. As I understand the Dhamma taught by the Blessed One, it is this same consciousness that runs and wanders through the round of rebirths, not another."

Then those bhikkhus, desiring to detach him from that pernicious view, pressed and questioned and cross-questioned him thus: "Friend Sāti, do not say so. Do not misrepresent the Blessed One; it is not good to misrepresent the Blessed One. The Blessed One would not speak thus. For in many ways the Blessed One has stated consciousness to be dependently arisen, [257] since without a condition there is no origination of consciousness."

Yet although pressed and questioned and cross-questioned by those bhikkhus in this way, the bhikkhu Sāti, son of a fisherman, still obstinately adhered to that pernicious view and continued to insist upon it.

4. Since the bhikkhus were unable to detach him from that pernicious view, they went to the Blessed One, and after paying homage to him, they sat down at one side and told him all that

had occurred, adding: "Venerable sir, since we could not detach the bhikkhu Sāti, son of a fisherman, from this pernicious view, we have reported this matter to the Blessed One."

5. Then the Blessed One addressed a certain bhikkhu thus: "Come, [258] bhikkhu, tell the bhikkhu Sāti, son of a fisherman, in my name that the Teacher calls him."—"Yes, venerable sir," he replied, and he went to the bhikkhu Sāti and told him: "The Teacher calls you, friend Sāti."

"Yes, friend," he replied, and he went to the Blessed One, and after paying homage to him, sat down at one side. The Blessed One then asked him: "Sāti, is it true that the following pernicious view has arisen in you: 'As I understand the Dhamma taught by the Blessed One, it is this same consciousness that runs and wanders through the round of rebirths, not another'?"

"Exactly so, venerable sir. As I understand the Dhamma taught by the Blessed One, it is this same consciousness that runs and wanders through the round of rebirths, not another."

"What is that consciousness, Sāti?"

"Venerable sir, it is that which speaks and feels and experiences here and there the result of good and bad actions."[403]

"Misguided man, to whom have you ever known me to teach the Dhamma in that way? Misguided man, have I not stated in many ways consciousness to be dependently arisen, since without a condition there is no origination of consciousness? But you, misguided man, have misrepresented us by your wrong grasp and injured yourself and stored up much demerit; for this will lead to your harm and suffering for a long time."

6. Then the Blessed One addressed the bhikkhus thus: "Bhikkhus, what do you think? Has this bhikkhu Sāti, son of a fisherman, kindled even a spark of wisdom in this Dhamma and Discipline?"

"How could he, venerable sir? No, venerable sir."

When this was said, the bhikkhu Sāti, son of a fisherman, sat silent, dismayed, with shoulders drooping and head down, glum, and without response. Then, knowing this, the Blessed One told him: "Misguided man, you will be recognised by your own pernicious view. I shall question the bhikkhus on this matter."

7. Then the Blessed One addressed the bhikkhus thus: "Bhikkhus, do you understand the Dhamma taught by me as this bhikkhu Sāti, [259] son of a fisherman, does when he mis-

represents us by his wrong grasp and injures himself and stores up much demerit?"

"No, venerable sir. For in many discourses the Blessed One has stated consciousness to be dependently arisen, since without a condition there is no origination of consciousness."

"Good, bhikkhus. It is good that you understand the Dhamma taught by me thus. For in many ways I have stated consciousness to be dependently arisen, since without a condition there is no origination of consciousness. But this bhikkhu Sāti, son of a fisherman, misrepresents us by his wrong grasp and injures himself and stores up much demerit; for this will lead to the harm and suffering of this misguided man for a long time.

(CONDITIONALITY OF CONSCIOUSNESS)

8. "Bhikkhus, consciousness is reckoned by the particular condition dependent upon which it arises. When consciousness arises dependent on the eye and forms, it is reckoned as eye-consciousness; when consciousness arises dependent on the ear and sounds, it is reckoned as ear-consciousness; when consciousness arises dependent on the nose and odours, [260] it is reckoned as nose-consciousness; when consciousness arises dependent on the tongue and flavours, it is reckoned as tongue-consciousness; when consciousness arises dependent on the body and tangibles, it is reckoned as body-consciousness; when consciousness arises dependent on the mind and mind-objects, it is reckoned as mind-consciousness. Just as fire is reckoned by the particular condition dependent on which it burns—when fire burns dependent on logs, it is reckoned as a log fire; when fire burns dependent on faggots, it is reckoned as a faggot fire; when fire burns dependent on grass, it is reckoned as a grass fire; when fire burns dependent on cowdung, it is reckoned as a cowdung fire; when fire burns dependent on chaff, it is reckoned as a chaff fire; when fire burns dependent on rubbish, it is reckoned as a rubbish fire—so too, consciousness is reckoned by the particular condition dependent on which it arises.[404] When consciousness arises dependent on the eye and forms, it is reckoned as eye-consciousness...when consciousness arises dependent on the mind and mind-objects, it is reckoned as mind-consciousness.

(GENERAL QUESTIONNAIRE ON BEING)

9. "Bhikkhus, do you see: 'This has come to be'?"[405]—"Yes, venerable sir."—"Bhikkhus, do you see: 'Its origination occurs with that as nutriment'?"—"Yes, venerable sir."—"Bhikkhus, do you see: 'With the cessation of that nutriment, what has come to be is subject to cessation'?"—"Yes, venerable sir."

10. "Bhikkhus, does doubt arise when one is uncertain thus: 'Has this come to be'?"—"Yes, venerable sir."—"Bhikkhus, does doubt arise when one is uncertain thus: 'Does its origination occur with that as nutriment'?"—"Yes, venerable sir."—"Bhikkhus, does doubt arise when one is uncertain thus: 'With the cessation of that nutriment, is what has come to be subject to cessation'?"—"Yes, venerable sir."

11. "Bhikkhus, is doubt abandoned in one who sees as it actually is with proper wisdom thus: 'This has come to be'?"—"Yes, venerable sir."—"Bhikkhus, is doubt abandoned in one who sees as it actually is with proper wisdom thus: 'Its origination occurs with that as nutriment'?"—"Yes, venerable sir."—"Bhikkhus, is doubt abandoned in one who sees as it actually is with proper wisdom thus: 'With the cessation of that nutriment, what has come to be is subject to cessation'?"—"Yes, venerable sir."

12. "Bhikkhus, are you thus free from doubt here: 'This has come to be'?"—"Yes, venerable sir."—"Bhikkhus, are you thus free from doubt here: 'Its origination occurs with that as nutriment'?"—"Yes, venerable sir."—"Bhikkhus, are you thus free from doubt here: 'With the cessation of that nutriment, what has come to be is subject to cessation'?"—"Yes, venerable sir."

13. "Bhikkhus, has it been seen well by you as it actually is with proper wisdom thus: 'This has come to be'?"—"Yes, venerable sir."—"Bhikkhus, has it been seen well by you as it actually is with proper wisdom thus: 'Its origination occurs with that as nutriment'?"—"Yes, venerable sir."—"Bhikkhus, has it been seen well by you as it actually is with proper wisdom thus: 'With the cessation of that nutriment, what has come to be is subject to cessation'?"—"Yes, venerable sir."

14. "Bhikkhus, purified and bright as this view is, if you adhere to it, cherish it, treasure it, and treat it as a possession, would you then understand that the Dhamma has been taught as similar to a raft, being for the purpose of crossing over, not

for the purpose of grasping?"[406]—"No, venerable sir."—"Bhikkhus, purified and bright as this view is, [261] if you do not adhere to it, cherish it, treasure it, and treat it as a possession, would you then understand that the Dhamma has been taught as similar to a raft, being for the purpose of crossing over, not for the purpose of grasping?"—"Yes, venerable sir."

(NUTRIMENT AND DEPENDENT ORIGINATION)

15. "Bhikkhus, there are these four kinds of nutriment for the maintenance of beings that already have come to be and for the support of those seeking a new existence. What four? They are: physical food as nutriment, gross or subtle; contact as the second; mental volition as the third; and consciousness as the fourth.[407]

16. "Now, bhikkhus, these four kinds of nutriment have what as their source, what as their origin, from what are they born and produced? These four kinds of nutriment have craving as their source, craving as their origin; they are born and produced from craving. And this craving has what as its source...? Craving has feeling as its source...And this feeling has what as its source...? Feeling has contact as its source...And this contact has what as its source...? Contact has the sixfold base as its source...And this sixfold base has what as its source...? The sixfold base has mentality-materiality as its source...And this mentality-materiality has what as its source...? Mentality-materiality has consciousness as its source...And this consciousness has what as its source...? Consciousness has formations as its source...And these formations have what as their source, what as their origin, from what are they born and produced? Formations have ignorance as their source, ignorance as their origin; they are born and produced from ignorance.

(FORWARD EXPOSITION ON ARISING)

17. "So, bhikkhus, with ignorance as condition, formations [come to be]; with formations as condition, consciousness; with consciousness as condition, mentality-materiality; with mentality-materiality as condition, the sixfold base; with the sixfold base as condition, contact; with contact as condition, feeling; with feeling as condition, craving; with craving as condition, clinging;

with clinging as condition, being; with being as condition, birth; with birth as condition, ageing and death, sorrow, lamentation, pain, grief, and despair come to be. Such is the origin of this whole mass of suffering.

(REVERSE ORDER QUESTIONNAIRE ON ARISING)

18. "'With birth as condition, ageing and death': so it was said. Now, bhikkhus, do ageing and death have birth as condition or not, or how do you take it in this case?"

"Ageing and death have birth as condition, venerable sir. Thus we take it in this case: 'With birth as condition, ageing and death.'"

"'With being as condition, birth': so it was said. Now, bhikkhus, does birth have being as condition or not, or how do you take it in this case?"

"Birth has being as condition, [262] venerable sir. Thus we take it in this case: 'With being as condition, birth.'"

"'With clinging as condition, being': so it was said. Now, bhikkhus, does being have clinging as condition or not, or how do you take it in this case?"

"Being has clinging as condition, venerable sir. Thus we take it in this case: 'With clinging as condition, being.'"

"'With craving as condition, clinging': so it was said. Now, bhikkhus, does clinging have craving as condition or not, or how do you take it in this case?"

"Clinging has craving as condition, venerable sir. Thus we take it in this case: 'With craving as condition, clinging.'"

"'With feeling as condition, craving': so it was said. Now, bhikkhus, does craving have feeling as condition or not, or how do you take it in this case?"

"Craving has feeling as condition, venerable sir. Thus we take it in this case: 'With feeling as condition, craving.'"

"'With contact as condition, feeling': so it was said. Now, bhikkhus, does feeling have contact as condition or not, or how do you take it in this case?"

"Feeling has contact as condition, venerable sir. Thus we take it in this case: 'With contact as condition, feeling.'"

"'With the sixfold base as condition, contact': so it was said. Now, bhikkhus, does contact have the sixfold base as condition or not, or how do you take it in this case?"

"Contact has the sixfold base as condition, venerable sir. Thus we take it in this case: 'With the sixfold base as condition, contact.'"

"'With mentality-materiality as condition, the sixfold base': so it was said. Now, bhikkhus, does the sixfold base have mentality-materiality as condition or not, or how do you take it in this case?"

"The sixfold base has mentality-materiality as condition, venerable sir. Thus we take it in this case: 'With mentality-materiality as condition, the sixfold base.'"

"'With consciousness as condition, mentality-materiality': so it was said. Now, bhikkhus, does mentality-materiality have consciousness as condition or not, or how do you take it in this case?"

"Mentality-materiality has consciousness as condition, venerable sir. Thus we take it in this case: 'With consciousness as condition, mentality-materiality.'"

"'With formations as condition, consciousness': so it was said. Now, bhikkhus, does consciousness have formations as condition or not, or how do you take it in this case?"

"Consciousness has formations as condition, venerable sir. Thus we take it in this case: 'With formations as condition, consciousness.'"

"'With ignorance as condition, formations': so it was said. Now, bhikkhus, do formations have ignorance as condition or not, or how do you take it in this case?"

"Formations have ignorance as condition, venerable sir. Thus we take it in this case: 'With formations as condition, ignorance.'"

(RECAPITULATION ON ARISING)

19. "Good, bhikkhus. So you say thus, and I also say thus: 'When this exists, that comes to be; [263] with the arising of this, that arises.'[408] That is, with ignorance as condition, formations [come to be]; with formations as condition, consciousness; with consciousness as condition, mentality-materiality; with mentality-materiality as condition, the sixfold base; with the sixfold base as condition, contact; with contact as condition, feeling; with feeling as condition, craving; with craving as condition, clinging;

with clinging as condition, being; with being as condition, birth; with birth as condition, ageing and death, sorrow, lamentation, pain, grief, and despair come to be. Such is the origin of this whole mass of suffering.

(FORWARD EXPOSITION ON CESSATION)

20. "But with the remainderless fading away and cessation of ignorance comes cessation of formations; with the cessation of formations, cessation of consciousness; with the cessation of consciousness, cessation of mentality-materiality; with the cessation of mentality-materiality, cessation of the sixfold base; with the cessation of the sixfold base, cessation of contact; with the cessation of contact, cessation of feeling; with the cessation of feeling, cessation of craving; with the cessation of craving, cessation of clinging; with the cessation of clinging, cessation of being; with the cessation of being, cessation of birth; with the cessation of birth, ageing and death, sorrow, lamentation, pain, grief, and despair cease. Such is the cessation of this whole mass of suffering.

(REVERSE ORDER QUESTIONNAIRE ON CESSATION)

21. "'With the cessation of birth, cessation of ageing and death': so it was said. Now, bhikkhus, do ageing and death cease with the cessation of birth or not, or how do you take it in this case?"

"Ageing and death cease with the cessation of birth, venerable sir. Thus we take it in this case: 'With the cessation of birth, cessation of ageing and death.'"

"'With the cessation of being, cessation of birth'...'With the cessation of clinging, cessation of being'...'With the cessation of craving, cessation of clinging'...'With the cessation of feeling, cessation of craving'...'With the cessation of contact, cessation of feeling' [264]...'With the cessation of the sixfold base, cessation of contact'...'With the cessation of mentality-materiality, cessation of the sixfold base'...'With the cessation of consciousness, cessation of mentality-materiality'...'With the cessation of formations, cessation of consciousness'...'With the cessation of ignorance, cessation of formations': so it was said. Now, bhikkhus, do formations cease with the cessation of ignorance or not, or how do you take it in this case?"

"Formations cease with the cessation of ignorance, venerable sir. Thus we take it in this case: 'With the cessation of ignorance, cessation of formations.'"

(RECAPITULATION ON CESSATION)

22. "Good, bhikkhus. So you say thus, and I also say thus: 'When this does not exist, that does not come to be; with the cessation of this, that ceases.' That is, with the cessation of ignorance comes cessation of formations; with the cessation of formations, cessation of consciousness; with the cessation of consciousness, cessation of mentality-materiality; with the cessation of mentality-materiality, cessation of the sixfold base; with the cessation of the sixfold base, cessation of contact; with the cessation of contact, cessation of feeling; with the cessation of feeling, cessation of craving; with the cessation of craving, cessation of clinging; with the cessation of clinging, cessation of being; with the cessation of being, cessation of birth; with the cessation of birth, ageing and death, sorrow, lamentation, pain, grief, and despair cease. Such is the cessation of this whole mass of suffering.

(PERSONAL KNOWLEDGE)

23. "Bhikkhus, knowing and seeing in this way, [265] would you run back to the past thus: 'Were we in the past? Were we not in the past? What were we in the past? How were we in the past? Having been what, what did we become in the past?'?"—"No, venerable sir."—"Knowing and seeing in this way, would you run forward to the future thus: 'Shall we be in the future? Shall we not be in the future? What shall we be in the future? How shall we be in the future? Having been what, what shall we become in the future?'?"—"No, venerable sir."—"Knowing and seeing in this way, would you now be inwardly perplexed about the present thus: 'Am I? Am I not? What am I? How am I? Where has this being come from? Where will it go?'?"—"No, venerable sir."

24. "Bhikkhus, knowing and seeing in this way, would you speak thus: 'The Teacher is respected by us. We speak as we do out of respect for the Teacher'?"—"No, venerable sir."—"Knowing and seeing in this way, would you speak thus: 'The

Recluse says this, and we speak thus at the bidding of the Recluse'?"[409]—"No, venerable sir."—"Knowing and seeing in this way, would you acknowledge another teacher?"—"No, venerable sir."—"Knowing and seeing in this way, would you return to the observances, tumultuous debates, and auspicious signs of ordinary recluses and brahmins, taking them as the core [of the holy life]?"—"No, venerable sir."—"Do you speak only of what you have known, seen, and understood for yourselves?"—"Yes, venerable sir."

25. "Good, bhikkhus. So you have been guided by me with this Dhamma, which is visible here and now, immediately effective, inviting inspection, onward leading, to be experienced by the wise for themselves. For it was with reference to this that it has been said: 'Bhikkhus, this Dhamma is visible here and now, immediately effective, inviting inspection, onward leading, to be experienced by the wise for themselves.'

(THE ROUND OF EXISTENCE: CONCEPTION TO MATURITY)

26. "Bhikkhus, the descent of the embryo takes place through the union of three things.[410] Here, there is the union of the mother and father, but the mother is not in season, and the *gandhabba*[411] is not present—in this case no [266] descent of an embryo takes place. Here, there is the union of the mother and father, and the mother is in season, but the *gandhabba* is not present—in this case too no descent of the embryo takes place. But when there is the union of the mother and father, and the mother is in season, and the *gandhabba* is present, through the union of these three things the descent of the embryo takes place.

27. "The mother then carries the embryo in her womb for nine or ten months with much anxiety, as a heavy burden. Then, at the end of nine or ten months, the mother gives birth with much anxiety, as a heavy burden. Then, when the child is born, she nourishes it with her own blood; for the mother's breast-milk is called blood in the Noble One's Discipline.

28. "When he grows up and his faculties mature, the child plays at such games as toy ploughs, tipcat, somersaults, toy windmills, toy measures, toy cars, and a toy bow and arrow.

29. "When he grows up and his faculties mature [still further], the youth enjoys himself provided and endowed with the five

cords of sensual pleasure, with forms cognizable by the eye... sounds cognizable by the ear...odours cognizable by the nose... flavours cognizable by the tongue...tangibles cognizable by the body that are wished for, desired, agreeable and likeable, connected with sensual desire, and provocative of lust.

(THE CONTINUATION OF THE ROUND)

30. "On seeing a form with the eye, he lusts after it if it is pleasing; he dislikes it if it is unpleasing. He abides with mindfulness of the body unestablished, with a limited mind, and he does not understand as it actually is the deliverance of mind and deliverance by wisdom wherein those evil unwholesome states cease without remainder. Engaged as he is in favouring and opposing, whatever feeling he feels—whether pleasant or painful or neither-painful-nor-pleasant—he delights in that feeling, welcomes it, and remains holding to it.[412] As he does so, delight arises in him. Now delight in feelings is clinging. With his clinging as condition, being [comes to be]; with being as condition, birth; with birth as condition, ageing and death, sorrow, lamentation, pain, grief, and despair come to be. Such is the origin of this whole mass of suffering.

"On hearing a sound with the ear...On smelling an odour with the nose...On tasting a flavour with the tongue...On touching a tangible with the body...On cognizing a mind-object with the mind, [267] he lusts after it if it is pleasing; he dislikes it if it is unpleasing...Now delight in feelings is clinging. With his clinging as condition, being [comes to be]; with being as condition, birth; with birth as condition, ageing and death, sorrow, lamentation, pain, grief, and despair come to be. Such is the origin of this whole mass of suffering.

(THE ENDING OF THE ROUND: THE GRADUAL TRAINING)

31–38. "Here, bhikkhus, a Tathāgata appears in the world, accomplished, fully enlightened...(*as Sutta 27, §§11–18*) [268–69]...he purifies his mind from doubt. [270]

39. "Having thus abandoned these five hindrances, imperfections of the mind that weaken wisdom, quite secluded from sensual pleasures, secluded from unwholesome states, he

enters upon and abides in the first jhāna...With the stilling of applied and sustained thought, he enters upon and abides in the second jhāna...With the fading away as well of rapture...he enters upon and abides in the third jhāna...With the abandoning of pleasure and pain...he enters upon and abides in the fourth jhāna...which has neither-pain-nor-pleasure and purity of mindfulness due to equanimity.

(THE ENDING OF THE ROUND: FULL CESSATION)

40. "On seeing a form with the eye, he does not lust after it if it is pleasing; he does not dislike it if it is unpleasing. He abides with mindfulness of the body established, with an immeasurable mind, and he understands as it actually is the deliverance of mind and deliverance by wisdom wherein those evil unwholesome states cease without remainder.[413] Having thus abandoned favouring and opposing, whatever feeling he feels, whether pleasant or painful or neither-painful-nor-pleasant, he does not delight in that feeling, welcome it, or remain holding to it.[414] As he does not do so, delight in feelings ceases in him. With the cessation of his delight comes cessation of clinging; with the cessation of clinging, cessation of being; with the cessation of being, cessation of birth; with the cessation of birth, ageing and death, sorrow, lamentation, pain, grief, and despair cease. Such is the cessation of this whole mass of suffering.

"On hearing a sound with the ear...On smelling an odour with the nose...On tasting a flavour with the tongue...On touching a tangible with the body...On cognizing a mind-object with the mind, he does not lust after it if it is pleasing; he does not dislike it if it is unpleasing...With the cessation of his delight comes cessation of clinging; with the cessation of clinging, cessation of being; with the cessation of being, cessation of birth; with the cessation of birth, ageing and death, sorrow, lamentation, pain, grief, and despair cease. Such is the cessation of this whole mass of suffering.

(CONCLUSION)

41. "Bhikkhus, remember this deliverance in the destruction of craving as taught in brief by me; but [remember] the bhikkhu Sāti,

[271] son of a fisherman, as caught up in a vast net of craving, in the trammel of craving."

That is what the Blessed One said. The bhikkhus were satisfied and delighted in the Blessed One's words.

39 *Mahā-Assapura Sutta*
The Greater Discourse at Assapura

1. THUS HAVE I HEARD. On one occasion the Blessed One was living in the Angan country at a town of the Angans named Assapura. There the Blessed One addressed the bhikkhus thus: "Bhikkhus."—"Venerable sir," they replied. The Blessed One said this:

2. "'Recluses, recluses,' bhikkhus, that is how people perceive you. And when you are asked, 'What are you?', you claim that you are recluses. Since that is what you are designated and what you claim to be, you should train thus: 'We will undertake and practise those things that make one a recluse, that make one a brahmin,[415] so that our designations may be true and our claims genuine, and so that the services of those whose robes, almsfood, resting place, and medicinal requisites we use shall bring them great fruit and benefit, and so that our going forth shall not be in vain but fruitful and fertile.'

(CONDUCT AND LIVELIHOOD)

3. "And what, bhikkhus, are the things that make one a recluse, that make one a brahmin? Bhikkhus, you should train thus: 'We will be possessed of shame and fear of wrongdoing.'[416] Now, bhikkhus, you may think thus: 'We are possessed of shame and fear of wrongdoing. That much is enough, that much has been done, the goal of recluseship has been reached, there is nothing more for us to do'; and you may rest content with that much. Bhikkhus, I inform you, I declare to you: You who seek the recluse's status, do not fall short of the goal of recluseship while there is more to be done.[417]

4. "What more is to be done? [272] Bhikkhus, you should train thus: 'Our bodily conduct shall be purified, clear and open,

flawless and restrained, and we will not laud ourselves and disparage others on account of that purified bodily conduct.' Now, bhikkhus, you may think thus: 'We are possessed of shame and fear of wrongdoing and our bodily conduct has been purified. That much is enough, that much has been done, the goal of recluseship has been reached, there is nothing more for us to do'; and you may rest content with that much. Bhikkhus, I inform you, I declare to you: You who seek the recluse's status, do not fall short of the goal of recluseship while there is more to be done.

5. "What more is to be done? Bhikkhus, you should train thus: 'Our verbal conduct shall be purified, clear and open, flawless and restrained, and we will not laud ourselves and disparage others on account of that purified verbal conduct.' Now, bhikkhus, you may think thus: 'We are possessed of shame and fear of wrongdoing, our bodily conduct has been purified, and our verbal conduct has been purified. That much is enough...'; and you may rest content with that much. Bhikkhus, I inform you, I declare to you: You who seek the recluse's status, do not fall short of the goal of recluseship while there is more to be done.

6. "What more is to be done? Bhikkhus, you should train thus: 'Our mental conduct shall be purified, clear and open, flawless and restrained, and we will not laud ourselves and disparage others on account of that purified mental conduct.' Now, bhikkhus, you may think thus: 'We are possessed of shame and fear of wrongdoing, our bodily conduct and verbal conduct have been purified, and our mental conduct has been purified. That much is enough...'; and you may rest content with that much. Bhikkhus, I inform you, I declare to you: You who seek the recluse's status, do not fall short of the goal of recluseship while there is more to be done.

7. "What more is to be done? Bhikkhus, you should train thus: 'Our livelihood shall be purified, clear and open, flawless and restrained, and we will not laud ourselves and disparage others on account of that purified livelihood.' Now, bhikkhus, you may think thus: 'We are possessed of shame and fear of wrongdoing, our bodily conduct, verbal conduct, and mental conduct have been purified, and our livelihood has been purified. [273] That much is enough...'; and you may rest content with that much.

Bhikkhus, I inform you, I declare to you: You who seek the recluse's status, do not fall short of the goal of recluseship while there is more to be done.

(RESTRAINT OF THE SENSES)

8. "What more is to be done? Bhikkhus, you should train thus: 'We will guard the doors of our sense faculties. On seeing a form with the eye, we will not grasp at its signs and features. Since, if we left the eye faculty unguarded, evil unwholesome states of covetousness and grief might invade us, we will practise the way of its restraint, we will guard the eye faculty, we will undertake the restraint of the eye faculty. On hearing a sound with the ear...On smelling an odour with the nose...On tasting a flavour with the tongue...On touching a tangible with the body...On cognizing a mind-object with the mind, we will not grasp at its signs and features. Since, if we left the mind faculty unguarded, evil unwholesome states of covetousness and grief might invade us, we will practise the way of its restraint, we will guard the mind faculty, we will undertake the restraint of the mind faculty.' Now, bhikkhus, you may think thus: 'We are possessed of shame and fear of wrongdoing, our bodily conduct, verbal conduct, mental conduct, and livelihood have been purified, and we guard the doors of our sense faculties. That much is enough...'; and you may rest content with that much. Bhikkhus, I inform you, I declare to you: You who seek the recluse's status, do not fall short of the goal of recluseship while there is more to be done.

(MODERATION IN EATING)

9. "What more is to be done? Bhikkhus, you should train thus: 'We will be moderate in eating. Reflecting wisely, we will take food neither for amusement nor for intoxication nor for the sake of physical beauty and attractiveness, but only for the endurance and continuance of this body, for ending discomfort, and for assisting the holy life, considering: "Thus I shall terminate old feelings without arousing new feelings and I shall be healthy and blameless and shall live in comfort."' Now, bhikkhus, you may think thus: 'We are possessed of shame and

fear of wrongdoing, our bodily conduct, verbal conduct, mental conduct, and livelihood have been purified, we guard the doors of our sense faculties, and we are moderate in eating. That much is enough...'; and you may rest content with that much. Bhikkhus, I inform you, I declare to you: You who seek the recluse's status, do not fall short of the goal of recluseship while there is more to be done.

(WAKEFULNESS)

10. "What more is to be done? Bhikkhus, you should train thus: 'We will be devoted to wakefulness. During the day, while walking back and forth and sitting, we will purify our minds of obstructive states. In the first watch of the night, [274] while walking back and forth and sitting, we will purify our minds of obstructive states. In the middle watch of the night we will lie down on the right side in the lion's pose with one foot overlapping the other, mindful and fully aware, after noting in our minds the time for rising. After rising, in the third watch of the night, while walking back and forth and sitting, we will purify our minds of obstructive states.' Now, bhikkhus, you may think thus: 'We are possessed of shame and fear of wrongdoing, our bodily conduct, verbal conduct, mental conduct, and livelihood have been purified, we guard the doors of our sense faculties, we are moderate in eating, and we are devoted to wakefulness. That much is enough...'; and you may rest content with that much. Bhikkhus, I inform you, I declare to you: You who seek the recluse's status, do not fall short of the goal of recluseship while there is more to be done.

(MINDFULNESS AND FULL AWARENESS)

11. "What more is to be done? Bhikkhus, you should train thus: 'We will be possessed of mindfulness and full awareness. We will act in full awareness when going forward and returning; we will act in full awareness when looking ahead and looking away; we will act in full awareness when flexing and extending our limbs; we will act in full awareness when wearing our robes and carrying our outer robe and bowl; we will act in full awareness when eating, drinking, consuming food, and tasting; we

will act in full awareness when defecating and urinating; we will act in full awareness when walking, standing, sitting, falling asleep, waking up, talking, and keeping silent.' Now, bhikkhus, you may think thus: 'We are possessed of shame and fear of wrongdoing, our bodily conduct, verbal conduct, mental conduct, and livelihood have been purified, we guard the doors of our sense faculties, we are moderate in eating, we are devoted to wakefulness, and we are possessed of mindfulness and full awareness. That much is enough, that much has been done, the goal of recluseship has been reached, there is nothing more for us to do'; and you may rest content with that much. Bhikkhus, I inform you, I declare to you: You who seek the recluse's status, do not fall short of the goal of recluseship while there is more to be done.

(ABANDONING OF THE HINDRANCES)

12. "What more is to be done? Here, bhikkhus, a bhikkhu resorts to a secluded resting place: the forest, the root of a tree, a mountain, a ravine, a hillside cave, a charnel ground, a jungle thicket, an open space, a heap of straw.

13. "On returning from his almsround, after his meal he sits down, folding his legs crosswise, setting his body erect and establishing mindfulness before him. Abandoning covetousness for the world, he abides with a mind free from covetousness; he purifies his mind from covetousness. Abandoning ill will and hatred, he abides with a mind free from ill will, compassionate for the welfare of all living beings; [275] he purifies his mind from ill will and hatred. Abandoning sloth and torpor, he abides free from sloth and torpor, percipient of light, mindful and fully aware; he purifies his mind from sloth and torpor. Abandoning restlessness and remorse, he abides unagitated with a mind inwardly peaceful; he purifies his mind from restlessness and remorse. Abandoning doubt, he abides having gone beyond doubt, unperplexed about wholesome states; he purifies his mind from doubt.

14. "Bhikkhus, suppose a man were to take a loan and undertake business and his business were to succeed so that he could repay all the money of the old loan and there would remain enough extra to maintain a wife; then on considering this, he

would be glad and full of joy. Or suppose a man were afflicted, suffering and gravely ill, and his food would not agree with him and his body had no strength, but later he would recover from the affliction and his food would agree with him and his body would regain strength; then on considering this, he would be glad and full of joy. Or suppose a man were imprisoned in a prisonhouse, but later he would be released from prison, safe and secure, with no loss to his property; then on considering this, he would be glad and full of joy. Or suppose a man were a slave, not self-dependent but dependent on others, unable to go where he wants, but later on he would be released from slavery, self-dependent, independent of others, a freed man able to go where he wants; then on considering this, [276] he would be glad and full of joy. Or suppose a man with wealth and property were to enter a road across a desert, but later on he would cross over the desert, safe and secure, with no loss to his property; then on considering this, he would be glad and full of joy. So too, bhikkhus, when these five hindrances are unabandoned in himself, a bhikkhu sees them respectively as a debt, a disease, a prisonhouse, slavery, and a road across a desert. But when these five hindrances have been abandoned in himself, he sees that as freedom from debt, healthiness, release from prison, freedom from slavery, and a land of safety.[418]

(THE FOUR JHĀNAS)

15. "Having abandoned these five hindrances, imperfections of the mind that weaken wisdom, quite secluded from sensual pleasures, secluded from unwholesome states, he enters upon and abides in the first jhāna, which is accompanied by applied and sustained thought, with rapture and pleasure born of seclusion. He makes the rapture and pleasure born of seclusion drench, steep, fill, and pervade this body, so that there is no part of his whole body unpervaded by the rapture and pleasure born of seclusion. Just as a skilled bath man or a bath man's apprentice heaps bath powder in a metal basin and, sprinkling it gradually with water, kneads it until the moisture wets his ball of bath powder, soaks it, and pervades it inside and out, yet the ball itself does not ooze; so too, a bhikkhu makes the rapture and pleasure born of seclusion drench, steep, fill, and pervade

this body, so that there is no part of his whole body unpervaded by the rapture and pleasure born of seclusion.

16. "Again, bhikkhus, with the stilling of applied and sustained thought, a bhikkhu enters upon and abides in the second jhāna, which has self-confidence and singleness of mind without applied and sustained thought, with rapture and pleasure born of concentration. He makes the rapture and pleasure born of concentration drench, steep, fill, and pervade this body, so that there is no part of his whole body unpervaded by the rapture and pleasure born of concentration. Just as though there were a lake whose waters welled up from below [277] and it had no inflow from east, west, north, or south, and would not be replenished from time to time by showers of rain, then the cool fount of water welling up in the lake would make the cool water drench, steep, fill, and pervade the lake, so that there would be no part of the whole lake unpervaded by cool water; so too, a bhikkhu makes the rapture and pleasure born of concentration drench, steep, fill, and pervade this body, so that there is no part of his whole body unpervaded by the rapture and pleasure born of concentration.

17. "Again, bhikkhus, with the fading away as well of rapture, a bhikkhu abides in equanimity, and mindful and fully aware, still feeling pleasure with the body, he enters upon and abides in the third jhāna, on account of which noble ones announce: 'He has a pleasant abiding who has equanimity and is mindful.' He makes the pleasure divested of rapture drench, steep, fill, and pervade this body, so that there is no part of his whole body unpervaded by the pleasure divested of rapture. Just as, in a pond of blue or red or white lotuses, some lotuses that are born and grow in the water thrive immersed in the water without rising out of it, and cool water drenches, steeps, fills, and pervades them to their tips and their roots, so that there is no part of all those lotuses unpervaded by cool water; so too, a bhikkhu makes the pleasure divested of rapture drench, steep, fill, and pervade this body, so that there is no part of his whole body unpervaded by the pleasure divested of rapture.

18. "Again, bhikkhus, with the abandoning of pleasure and pain, and with the previous disappearance of joy and grief, a bhikkhu enters upon and abides in the fourth jhāna, which has neither-pain-nor-pleasure and purity of mindfulness due to equanimity. He sits pervading this body with a pure bright

mind, so that there is no part of his whole body unpervaded by the pure bright mind. Just as though a man were sitting covered from the head down with a white cloth, so that there would be no part of his whole [278] body unpervaded by the white cloth; so too, a bhikkhu sits pervading this body with a pure bright mind, so that there is no part of his whole body unpervaded by the pure bright mind.

(THE THREE TRUE KNOWLEDGES)

19. "When his concentrated mind is thus purified, bright, unblemished, rid of imperfection, malleable, wieldy, steady, and attained to imperturbability, he directs it to knowledge of the recollection of past lives. He recollects his manifold past lives, that is, one birth, two births...(*as Sutta 4, §27*)...Thus with their aspects and particulars he recollects his manifold past lives. Just as a man might go from his own village to another village and then back again to his own village, he might think: 'I went from my own village to that village, and there I stood in such a way, sat in such a way, spoke in such a way, kept silent in such a way; and from that village I went to that other village, and there I stood in such a way, sat in such a way, spoke in such a way, kept silent in such a way; and from that village I came back again to my own village.' So too, a bhikkhu recollects his manifold past lives...Thus with their aspects and particulars he recollects his manifold past lives.

20. "When his concentrated mind is thus purified, bright, unblemished, rid of imperfection, malleable, wieldy, steady, and attained to imperturbability, he directs it to knowledge of the passing away and reappearance of beings...(*as Sutta 4, §29*) [279]...Thus with the divine eye, which is purified and surpasses the human, he sees beings passing away and reappearing, inferior and superior, fair and ugly, fortunate and unfortunate, and he understands how beings pass on according to their actions. Just as though there were two houses with doors and a man with good sight standing there between them saw people entering the houses and coming out and passing to and fro, so too, with the divine eye, which is purified and surpasses the human, a bhikkhu sees beings passing away and reappearing...and he understands how beings pass on according to their actions.

21. "When his concentrated mind is thus purified, bright, unblemished, rid of imperfection, malleable, wieldy, steady, and attained to imperturbability, he directs it to knowledge of the destruction of the taints. He understands as it actually is: 'This is suffering';...'This is the origin of suffering';...'This is the cessation of suffering';...'This is the way leading to the cessation of suffering';...'These are the taints';...'This is the origin of the taints';...'This is the cessation of the taints';...'This is the way leading to the cessation of the taints.'

"When he knows and sees thus, his mind is liberated from the taint of sensual desire, from the taint of being, and from the taint of ignorance. When it is liberated there comes the knowledge: 'It is liberated.' He understands: 'Birth is destroyed, the holy life has been lived, what had to be done has been done, there is no more coming to any state of being.'

"Just as if there were a lake in a mountain recess, clear, limpid, and undisturbed, so that a man with good sight standing on the bank could see shells, gravel, and pebbles, and also shoals of fish swimming about and resting, he might think: 'There is this lake, clear, limpid, and undisturbed, and there are these [280] shells, gravel, and pebbles, and also these shoals of fish swimming about and resting.' So too, a bhikkhu understands as it actually is: 'This is suffering.'...He understands: 'Birth is destroyed, the holy life has been lived, what had to be done has been done, there is no more coming to any state of being.'

(THE ARAHANT)

22. "Bhikkhus, a bhikkhu such as this is called a recluse, a brahmin, one who has been washed, one who has attained to knowledge, a holy scholar, a noble one, an arahant.[419]

23. "And how is a bhikkhu a recluse? He has quieted down evil unwholesome states that defile, bring renewal of being, give trouble, ripen in suffering, and lead to future birth, ageing, and death. That is how a bhikkhu is a recluse.

24. "And how is a bhikkhu a brahmin? He has expelled evil unwholesome states that defile...and lead to future birth, ageing, and death. That is how a bhikkhu is a brahmin.

25. "And how is a bhikkhu one who has been washed?[420] He has washed off evil unwholesome states that defile...and lead to

future birth, ageing, and death. That is how a bhikkhu is one who has been washed.

26. "And how is a bhikkhu one who has attained to knowledge? He has known evil unwholesome states that defile...and lead to future birth, ageing, and death. That is how a bhikkhu is one who has attained to knowledge.

27. "And how is a bhikkhu a holy scholar?[421] The evil unwholesome states that defile...and lead to future birth, ageing, and death, have streamed away from him. That is how a bhikkhu is a holy scholar.

28. "And how is a bhikkhu a noble one? Evil unwholesome states that defile...and lead to future birth, ageing, and death, are far away from him. That is how a bhikkhu is a noble one.

29. "And how is a bhikkhu an arahant? Evil unwholesome states that defile, bring renewal of being, give trouble, ripen in suffering, and lead to future birth, ageing, and death, are far away from him. That is how a bhikkhu is an arahant."

That is what the Blessed One said. The bhikkhus were satisfied and delighted in the Blessed One's words.

40 *Cūḷa-Assapura Sutta*
The Shorter Discourse at Assapura

[281] 1. THUS HAVE I HEARD. On one occasion the Blessed One was living in the Angan country at a town of the Angans named Assapura. There the Blessed One addressed the bhikkhus thus: "Bhikkhus."—"Venerable sir," they replied. The Blessed One said this:

2. "'Recluses, recluses,' bhikkhus, that is how people perceive you. And when you are asked, 'What are you?' you claim that you are recluses. Since that is what you are designated and what you claim to be, you should train thus: 'We will practise the way proper to the recluse[422] so that our designations may be true and our claims genuine, and so that the services of those whose robes, almsfood, resting place, and medicinal requisites we use shall bring them great fruit and benefit, and so that our going forth shall not be in vain but fruitful and fertile.'

3. "How, bhikkhus, does a bhikkhu not practise the way proper to the recluse? For so long as a bhikkhu who is covetous has not abandoned covetousness, who has a mind of ill will has not abandoned ill will, who is angry has not abandoned anger, who is resentful has not abandoned resentment, who is contemptuous has not abandoned contempt, who is insolent has not abandoned insolence, who is envious has not abandoned envy, who is avaricious has not abandoned avarice, who is fraudulent has not abandoned fraud, who is deceitful has not abandoned deceit, who has evil wishes has not abandoned evil wishes, who has wrong view has not abandoned wrong view,[423] for so long he does not practise the way proper to the recluse, I say, because of his failure to abandon these stains for the recluse, these faults for the recluse, these dregs for the recluse, which are grounds for rebirth in a state of deprivation and whose results are to be experienced in an unhappy destination.

4. "Suppose the weapon called a *mataja*, well whetted on both edges, were enclosed and encased in a patchwork sheath. I say that such a bhikkhu's going forth is comparable to that.

5. "I do not say that the recluse's status comes about in a patchwork-cloak wearer through the mere wearing of the patchwork cloak, nor in a naked ascetic through mere nakedness, nor in a dweller in dust and dirt through mere dust and dirt, nor in a washer in water through mere washing in water, nor in a tree-root dweller through mere [282] dwelling at the root of a tree, nor in an open-air dweller through mere dwelling in the open air, nor in a practitioner of continuous standing through mere continuous standing, nor in a taker of food at stated intervals through mere taking of food at stated intervals, nor in a reciter of incantations through mere recitation of incantations; nor do I say that the recluse's status comes about in a matted-hair ascetic through mere wearing of the hair matted.

6. "Bhikkhus, if through the mere wearing of the patchwork cloak a patchwork-cloak wearer who was covetous abandoned covetousness, who had a mind of ill will abandoned ill will... who had wrong view abandoned wrong view, then his friends and companions, his kinsmen and relatives, would make him a patchwork-cloak wearer as soon as he was born and have him undertake the patchwork-cloak wearing thus: 'Come, my dear, be a patchwork-cloak wearer so that, by the mere wearing of the patchwork-cloak, when you are covetous you will abandon covetousness, when you have a mind of ill will you will abandon ill will...when you have wrong view you will abandon wrong view.' But I see here a patchwork-cloak wearer who is covetous, who has a mind of ill will...who has wrong view; and that is why I do not say that the recluse's status comes about in a patchwork-cloak wearer through the mere wearing of the patchwork cloak.

"If through mere nakedness a naked ascetic who was covetous abandoned covetousness...If through mere dust and dirt...If through mere washing in water...If through mere dwelling at the root of a tree...If through mere dwelling in the open air...If through mere continuous standing...If through mere taking of food at stated intervals...If through mere recitation of incantations...If through mere wearing of the hair matted...[283]...and that is why I do not say that the recluse's status comes about in a matted-hair ascetic through the mere wearing of the hair matted.

7. "How, bhikkhus, does a bhikkhu practise the way proper to the recluse? When any bhikkhu who was covetous has abandoned covetousness, who had a mind of ill will has abandoned ill will, who was angry has abandoned anger, who was resentful has abandoned resentment, who was contemptuous has abandoned contempt, who was insolent has abandoned insolence, who was envious has abandoned envy, who was avaricious has abandoned avarice, who was fraudulent has abandoned fraud, who was deceitful has abandoned deceit, who had evil wishes has abandoned evil wishes, who had wrong view has abandoned wrong view, then he practises the way proper to the recluse, I say, because of his abandoning these stains for the recluse, these faults for the recluse, these dregs for the recluse, which are grounds for rebirth in a state of deprivation and whose results are to be experienced in an unhappy destination.

8. "He sees himself purified of all these evil unwholesome states, he sees himself liberated from them. When he sees this, gladness is born in him. When he is glad, rapture is born in him; in one who is rapturous, the body becomes tranquil; one whose body is tranquil feels pleasure; in one who feels pleasure, the mind becomes concentrated.

9. "He abides pervading one quarter with a mind imbued with loving-kindness, likewise the second, likewise the third, likewise the fourth; so above, below, around, and everywhere, and to all as to himself, he abides pervading the all-encompassing world with a mind imbued with loving-kindness, abundant, exalted, immeasurable, without hostility and without ill will.

10–12. "He abides pervading one quarter with a mind imbued with compassion...with a mind imbued with altruistic joy...with a mind imbued with equanimity...abundant, exalted, immeasurable, without hostility and without ill will.

13. "Suppose there were a pond with clear, agreeable cool water, transparent, with smooth banks, delightful. [284] If a man, scorched and exhausted by hot weather, weary, parched, and thirsty, came from the east or from the west or from the north or from the south or from where you will, having come upon the pond he would quench his thirst and his hot-weather fever. So too, bhikkhus, if anyone from a clan of nobles goes forth from the home life into homelessness, and after encountering the Dhamma and Discipline proclaimed by the Tathāgata, develops

loving-kindness, compassion, appreciative joy, and equanimity, and thereby gains internal peace, then because of that internal peace he practises the way proper to the recluse, I say. And if anyone from a clan of brahmins goes forth...If anyone from a clan of merchants goes forth...If anyone from a clan of workers goes forth from the home life into homelessness, and after encountering the Dhamma and Discipline proclaimed by the Tathāgata, develops loving-kindness, compassion, appreciative joy, and equanimity, and thereby gains internal peace, then because of that internal peace he practises the way proper to the recluse, I say.

14. "Bhikkhus, if anyone from a clan of nobles goes forth from the home life into homelessness, and by realising for himself with direct knowledge here and now enters upon and abides in the deliverance of mind and deliverance by wisdom that are taintless with the destruction of the taints, then he is already a recluse because of the destruction of the taints.[424] And if anyone from a clan of brahmins goes forth...If anyone from a clan of merchants goes forth...If anyone from a clan of workers goes forth from the home life into homelessness, and by realising for himself with direct knowledge here and now enters upon and abides in the deliverance of mind and deliverance by wisdom that are taintless with the destruction of the taints, then he is already a recluse because of the destruction of the taints."

That is what the Blessed One said. The bhikkhus were satisfied and delighted in the Blessed One's words.

5

The Shorter Division of Pairs

(*Cūḷayamakavagga*)

41 *Sāleyyaka Sutta*
The Brahmins of Sālā

See also #135 pg. 1053

[285] 1. THUS HAVE I HEARD. On one occasion the Blessed One was wandering by stages in the Kosalan Country with a large Sangha of bhikkhus, and eventually he arrived at a Kosalan brahmin village named Sālā.

2. The brahmin householders of Sālā heard: "The recluse Gotama, the son of the Sakyans who went forth from a Sakyan clan, has been wandering in the Kosalan country with a large Sangha of bhikkhus and has come to Sālā. Now a good report of Master Gotama has been spread to this effect: 'That Blessed One is accomplished, fully enlightened, perfect in true knowledge and conduct, sublime, knower of worlds, incomparable leader of persons to be tamed, teacher of gods and humans, enlightened, blessed. He declares this world with its gods, its Māras, and its Brahmās, this generation with its recluses and brahmins, its princes and its people, which he has himself realised with direct knowledge. He teaches the Dhamma good in the beginning, good in the middle, and good in the end, with the right meaning and phrasing, and he reveals a holy life that is utterly perfect and pure.' Now it is good to see such arahants."

3. Then the brahmin householders of Sālā went to the Blessed One. Some paid homage to the Blessed One and sat down at one side; some exchanged greetings with him, and when this courteous and amiable talk was finished, sat down at one side; some extended their hands in reverential salutation towards the Blessed One and sat down at one side; some pronounced their name and clan in the Blessed One's presence and sat down at one side; some kept silent and sat down at one side.

4. When they were seated, they said to the Blessed One: "Master Gotama, what is the cause and condition why some beings here, on the dissolution of the body, after death, reappear

in states of deprivation, in an unhappy destination, in perdition, even in hell? And what is the cause and condition why some beings here, on the dissolution of the body, after death, reappear in a happy destination, even in the heavenly world?"

5. "Householders, it is by reason of conduct not in accordance with the Dhamma, by reason of unrighteous conduct that some beings here, on the dissolution of the body, after death, reappear in states of deprivation, in an unhappy destination, in perdition, even in hell. It is by reason of conduct in accordance with the Dhamma, by reason of righteous conduct that some beings here, on the dissolution of the body, after death, reappear in a happy destination, even in the heavenly world." [286]

6. "We do not understand the detailed meaning of Master Gotama's utterance, which he has spoken in brief without expounding the detailed meaning. It would be good if Master Gotama would teach us the Dhamma so that we might understand the detailed meaning of his utterance."

"Then, householders, listen and attend closely to what I shall say."

"Yes, venerable sir," they replied. The Blessed One said this:

7. "Householders, there are three kinds of bodily conduct not in accordance with the Dhamma, unrighteous conduct. There are four kinds of verbal conduct not in accordance with the Dhamma, unrighteous conduct. There are three kinds of mental conduct not in accordance with the Dhamma, unrighteous conduct.

8. "And how, householders, are there three kinds of bodily conduct not in accordance with the Dhamma, unrighteous conduct? Here someone kills living beings; he is murderous, bloody-handed, given to blows and violence, merciless to living beings. He takes what is not given; he takes by way of theft the wealth and property of others in the village or forest. He misconducts himself in sensual pleasures; he has intercourse with women who are protected by their mother, father, mother and father, brother, sister, or relatives, who have a husband, who are protected by law, and even with those who are garlanded in token of betrothal. That is how there are three kinds of bodily conduct not in accordance with the Dhamma, unrighteous conduct.

9. "And how, householders, are there four kinds of verbal conduct not in accordance with the Dhamma, unrighteous conduct? Here someone speaks falsehood; when summoned to a court, or

to a meeting, or to his relatives' presence, or to his guild, or to the royal family's presence, and questioned as a witness thus: 'So, good man, tell what you know,' not knowing, he says, 'I know,' or knowing, he says, 'I do not know'; not seeing, he says, 'I see,' or seeing, he says, 'I do not see'; in full awareness he speaks falsehood for his own ends, or for another's ends, or for some trifling worldly end. He speaks maliciously; he repeats elsewhere what he has heard here in order to divide [those people] from these, or he repeats to these people what he has heard elsewhere in order to divide [these people] from those; thus he is one who divides those who are united, a creator of divisions, who enjoys discord, rejoices in discord, delights in discord, a speaker of words that create discord. He speaks harshly; he utters such words as are rough, hard, hurtful to others, offensive to others, bordering on anger, unconducive to concentration. [287] He is a gossip; he speaks at the wrong time, speaks what is not fact, speaks what is useless, speaks contrary to the Dhamma and the Discipline; at the wrong time he speaks such words as are worthless, unreasonable, immoderate, and unbeneficial. That is how there are four kinds of verbal conduct not in accordance with the Dhamma, unrighteous conduct.

10. "And how, householders, are there three kinds of mental conduct not in accordance with the Dhamma, unrighteous conduct? Here someone is covetous; he covets the wealth and property of others thus: 'Oh, may what belongs to another be mine!' Or he has a mind of ill will and intentions of hate thus: 'May these beings be slain and slaughtered, may they be cut off, perish, or be annihilated!' Or he has wrong view, distorted vision, thus: 'There is nothing given, nothing offered, nothing sacrificed; no fruit or result of good and bad actions; no this world, no other world; no mother, no father; no beings who are reborn spontaneously; no good and virtuous recluses and brahmins in the world who have themselves realised by direct knowledge and declare this world and the other world.'[425] That is how there are three kinds of mental conduct not in accordance with the Dhamma, unrighteous conduct. So, householders, it is by reason of such conduct not in accordance with the Dhamma, by reason of such unrighteous conduct that some beings here on the dissolution of the body, after death, reappear in states of deprivation, in an unhappy destination, in perdition, even in hell.

11. "Householders, there are three kinds of bodily conduct in accordance with the Dhamma, righteous conduct. There are four kinds of verbal conduct in accordance with the Dhamma, righteous conduct. There are three kinds of mental conduct in accordance with the Dhamma, righteous conduct.

12. "And how, householders, are there three kinds of bodily conduct in accordance with the Dhamma, righteous conduct? Here someone, abandoning the killing of living beings, abstains from killing living beings; with rod and weapon laid aside, gentle and kindly, he abides compassionate to all living beings. Abandoning the taking of what is not given, he abstains from taking what is not given; he does not take by way of theft the wealth and property of others in the village or in the forest. Abandoning misconduct in sensual pleasures, he abstains from misconduct in sensual pleasures; he does not have intercourse with women who are protected by their mother, father, mother and father, brother, sister, or relatives, who have a husband, who are protected by law, or with those who are garlanded in token of betrothal. That is how there are three kinds of bodily conduct in accordance with the Dhamma, righteous conduct. [288]

13. "And how, householders, are there four kinds of verbal conduct in accordance with the Dhamma, righteous conduct? Here someone, abandoning false speech, abstains from false speech; when summoned to a court, or to a meeting, or to his relatives' presence, or to his guild, or to the royal family's presence, and questioned as a witness thus: 'So, good man, tell what you know,' not knowing, he says, 'I do not know,' or knowing, he says, 'I know'; not seeing, he says, 'I do not see,' or seeing, he says, 'I see'; he does not in full awareness speak falsehood for his own ends, or for another's ends, or for some trifling worldly end. Abandoning malicious speech, he abstains from malicious speech; he does not repeat elsewhere what he has heard here in order to divide [those people] from these, nor does he repeat to these people what he has heard elsewhere in order to divide [these people] from those; thus he is one who reunites those who are divided, a promoter of friendships, who enjoys concord, rejoices in concord, delights in concord, a speaker of words that promote concord. Abandoning harsh speech, he abstains from harsh speech; he speaks such words as are gentle, pleasing to the ear, and loveable, as go to the heart, are courteous,

desired by many, and agreeable to many. Abandoning gossip, he abstains from gossip; he speaks at the right time, speaks what is fact, speaks on what is good, speaks on the Dhamma and the Discipline; at the right time he speaks such words as are worth recording, reasonable, moderate, and beneficial. That is how there are four kinds of verbal conduct in accordance with the Dhamma, righteous conduct.

14. "And how, householders, are there three kinds of mental conduct in accordance with the Dhamma, righteous conduct? Here someone is not covetous; he does not covet the wealth and property of others thus: 'Oh, may what belongs to another be mine!' His mind is without ill will and he has intentions free from hate thus: 'May these beings be free from enmity, affliction and anxiety! May they live happily!' He has right view, undistorted vision, thus: 'There is what is given and what is offered and what is sacrificed; there is fruit and result of good and bad actions; there is this world and the other world; there is mother and father; there are beings who are reborn spontaneously; there are good and virtuous recluses and brahmins in the world who have themselves realised by direct knowledge and declare this world and the other world.' That is how there are three kinds of mental conduct in accordance with the Dhamma, righteous conduct. So, householders, it is by reason of such conduct in accordance with the Dhamma, by reason of such righteous conduct that some beings here, on the dissolution of the body, after death, reappear in a happy destination, even in the heavenly world. [289]

15. "If, householders, one who observes conduct in accordance with the Dhamma, righteous conduct, should wish: 'Oh, that on the dissolution of the body, after death, I might reappear in the company of well-to-do nobles!' it is possible that, on the dissolution of the body, after death, he will reappear in the company of well-to-do nobles. Why is that? Because he observes conduct that is in accordance with the Dhamma, righteous conduct.

16–17. "If, householders, one who observes conduct in accordance with the Dhamma, righteous conduct, should wish: 'Oh, that on the dissolution of the body, after death, I might reappear in the company of well-to-do brahmins!...in the company of well-to-do householders!' it is possible that, on the dissolution of the body, after death, he will reappear in the company of well-to-do householders. Why is that? Because he observes conduct that is in accordance with the Dhamma, righteous conduct.

18–42. "If, householders, one who observes conduct in accordance with the Dhamma, righteous conduct, should wish: 'Oh, that on the dissolution of the body, after death, I might reappear in the company of the gods of the heaven of the Four Great Kings!...in the company of the gods of the heaven of the Thirty-three...the Yāma gods...the gods of the Tusita heaven...the gods who delight in creating...the gods who wield power over others' creations...the gods of Brahmā's retinue...the gods of Radiance[426]...the gods of Limited Radiance...the gods of Immeasurable Radiance...the gods of Streaming Radiance...the gods of Glory...the gods of Limited Glory...the gods of Immeasurable Glory...the gods of Refulgent Glory...the gods of Great Fruit...the Aviha gods...the Atappa gods...the Sudassa gods...the Sudassī gods...the Akaniṭṭha gods...the gods of the base of infinite space...the gods of the base of infinite consciousness...the gods of the base of nothingness...the gods of the base of neither-perception-nor-non-perception!' it is possible that on the dissolution of the body, after death, he will reappear in the company of the gods of neither-perception-nor-non-perception. Why is that? Because he observes conduct in accordance with the Dhamma, righteous conduct.

43. "If, householders, one who observes conduct in accordance with the Dhamma, righteous conduct, should wish: 'Oh, that by realising for myself with direct knowledge I might here and now enter upon and abide in the deliverance of mind and deliverance by wisdom that are taintless with the destruction of the taints!' it is possible that, by realising for himself with direct knowledge, he will here and now enter upon and abide in the deliverance of mind and deliverance by wisdom that are taintless with the destruction of the taints. Why is that? Because he observes conduct in accordance with the Dhamma, righteous conduct."[427] [290]

44. When this was said, the brahmin householders of Sālā said to the Blessed One: "Magnificent, Master Gotama! Magnificent, Master Gotama! Master Gotama has made the Dhamma clear in many ways, as though he were turning upright what had been overthrown, revealing what was hidden, showing the way to one who was lost, or holding up a lamp in the darkness for

those with eyesight to see forms. We go to Master Gotama for refuge and to the Dhamma and to the Sangha of bhikkhus. From today let Master Gotama accept us as lay followers who have gone to him for refuge for life."

42 *Verañjaka Sutta*
The Brahmins of Verañja

1. THUS HAVE I HEARD. On one occasion the Blessed One was living at Sāvatthī in Jeta's Grove, Anāthapiṇḍika's Park.

2. Now on that occasion some brahmin householders of Verañja were on a visit to Sāvatthī for some business or other. [291]

3–44. [*The text of this sutta is the same as that of Sutta 41, except that where the preceding sutta is phrased in terms of* "conduct not in accordance with the Dhamma, unrighteous conduct" (§§7–10) *and* "conduct in accordance with the Dhamma, righteous conduct" (§§11–14), *this sutta is phrased in terms of* "one who does not observe conduct in accordance with the Dhamma, one of unrighteous conduct" *and* "one who observes conduct in accordance with the Dhamma, one of righteous conduct"; *substitute* "Verañja" *for* "Sālā" *throughout.*]

43 *Mahāvedalla Sutta*
The Greater Series of Questions and Answers

[292] 1. THUS HAVE I HEARD. On one occasion the Blessed One was living at Sāvatthī in Jeta's Grove, Anāthapiṇḍika's Park.

Then, when it was evening, the venerable Mahā Koṭṭhita rose from meditation, went to the venerable Sāriputta, and exchanged greetings with him.[428] When this courteous and amiable talk was finished, he sat down at one side and said to the venerable Sāriputta:

(WISDOM)

2. "'One who is unwise, one who is unwise' is said, friend. With reference to what is this said, 'one who is unwise'?"

"'One does not wisely understand, one does not wisely understand,' friend; that is why it is said, 'one who is unwise.' And what doesn't one wisely understand? One does not wisely understand: 'This is suffering'; one does not wisely understand: 'This is the origin of suffering'; one does not wisely understand: 'This is the cessation of suffering'; one does not wisely understand: 'This is the way leading to the cessation of suffering.' 'One does not wisely understand, one does not wisely understand,' friend; that is why it is said, 'one who is unwise.'"

Saying, "Good, friend," the venerable Mahā Koṭṭhita delighted and rejoiced in the venerable Sāriputta's words. Then he asked him a further question:

3. "'One who is wise, one who is wise,' is said, friend. With reference to what is this said, 'one who is wise'?"

"'One wisely understands, one wisely understands,' friend; that is why it is said, 'one who is wise.' What does one wisely understand? One wisely understands: 'This is suffering'; one wisely understands: 'This is the origin of suffering'; one wisely understands: 'This is the cessation of suffering'; one wisely understands: 'This is the way leading to the cessation of suffering.' 'One wisely understands, one wisely understands,' friend; that is why it is said, 'one who is wise.'"[429]

(CONSCIOUSNESS)

4. "'Consciousness, consciousness' is said, friend. With reference to what is 'consciousness' said?"

"'It cognizes, it cognizes,' friend; that is why 'consciousness' is said.[430] What does it cognize? It cognizes: '[This is] pleasant'; it cognizes: '[This is] painful'; it cognizes: '[This is] neither-painful-nor-pleasant.' 'It cognizes, it cognizes,' friend; that is why 'consciousness' is said."[431]

5. "Wisdom and consciousness, friend—are these states conjoined or disjoined? And is it possible to separate each of these states from the other in order to describe the difference between them?"

"Wisdom and consciousness, friend—these states are conjoined, not disjoined, and it is impossible to separate each of these states from the other in order to describe the difference between them. For what one wisely understands, that one cognizes, and what one cognizes, that one wisely understands. [293] That is why these states are conjoined, not disjoined, and it is impossible to separate each of these states from the other in order to describe the difference between them."[432]

6. "What is the difference, friend, between wisdom and consciousness, these states that are conjoined, not disjoined?"

"The difference, friend, between wisdom and consciousness, these states that are conjoined, not disjoined, is this: wisdom is to be developed, consciousness is to be fully understood."[433]

(FEELING)

7. "'Feeling, feeling' is said, friend. With reference to what is 'feeling' said?"

"'It feels, it feels,' friend; that is why 'feeling' is said. What does it feel? It feels pleasure, it feels pain, it feels neither-pain-nor-pleasure. 'It feels, it feels,' friend, that is why 'feeling' is said."[434]

(PERCEPTION)

8. "'Perception, perception,' is said, friend. With reference to what is 'perception' said?"

"'It perceives, it perceives,' friend; that is why 'perception' is said. What does it perceive? It perceives blue, it perceives yellow, it perceives red, and it perceives white. 'It perceives, it perceives,' friend; that is why 'perception' is said."[435]

9. "Feeling, perception, and consciousness, friend—are these states conjoined or disjoined? And is it possible to separate each of these states from the others in order to describe the difference between them?"

"Feeling, perception, and consciousness, friend—these states are conjoined, not disjoined, and it is impossible to separate each of these states from the others in order to describe the difference between them. For what one feels, that one perceives; and what one perceives, that one cognizes. That is why these states are conjoined, not disjoined, and it is impossible to separate each of these states from the others in order to describe the difference between them."[436]

(KNOWABLE BY MIND ALONE)

10. "Friend, what can be known by purified mind-consciousness released from the five faculties?"

"Friend, by purified mind-consciousness released from the five faculties the base of infinite space can be known thus: 'Space is infinite'; the base of infinite consciousness can be known thus: 'Consciousness is infinite'; and the base of nothingness can be known thus: 'There is nothing.'"[437]

11. "Friend, with what does one understand a state that can be known?"

"Friend, one understands a state that can be known with the eye of wisdom."[438]

12. "Friend, what is the purpose of wisdom?"

"The purpose of wisdom, friend, is direct knowledge, its purpose is full understanding, its purpose is abandoning."[439]

(RIGHT VIEW)

[294] 13. "Friend, how many conditions are there for the arising of right view?"

"Friend, there are two conditions for the arising of right view: the voice of another and wise attention. These are the two conditions for the arising of right view."[440]

14. "Friend, by how many factors is right view assisted when it has deliverance of mind for its fruit, deliverance of mind for its fruit and benefit, when it has deliverance by wisdom for its fruit, deliverance by wisdom for its fruit and benefit?"

"Friend, right view is assisted by five factors when it has deliverance of mind for its fruit, deliverance of mind for its fruit and benefit, when it has deliverance by wisdom for its fruit, deliverance by wisdom for its fruit and benefit. Here, friend, right view is assisted by virtue, learning, discussion, serenity, and insight. Right view assisted by these five factors has deliverance of mind for its fruit, deliverance of mind for its fruit and benefit; it has deliverance by wisdom for its fruit, deliverance by wisdom for its fruit and benefit."[441]

(BEING)

15. "Friend, how many kinds of being are there?"

"There are these three kinds of being, friend: sense-sphere being, fine-material being, and immaterial being."

16. "Friend, how is renewal of being in the future generated?"

"Friend, renewal of being in the future is generated through the delighting in this and that on the part of beings who are hindered by ignorance and fettered by craving."[442]

17. "Friend, how is renewal of being in the future not generated?"

"Friend, with the fading away of ignorance, with the arising of true knowledge, and with the cessation of craving, renewal of being in the future is not generated."

(THE FIRST JHĀNA)

18. "Friend, what is the first jhāna?"

"Here, friend, quite secluded from sensual pleasures, secluded from unwholesome states, a bhikkhu enters upon and abides in the first jhāna, which is accompanied by applied and sustained thought, with rapture and pleasure born of seclusion. This is called the first jhāna."

19. "Friend, how many factors does the first jhāna have?"

"Friend, the first jhāna has five factors. Here, when a bhikkhu has entered upon the first jhāna, there occur applied thought, sustained thought, rapture, pleasure, and unification of mind. That is how the first jhāna has five factors."

20. "Friend, how many factors are abandoned in the first jhāna and how many factors are possessed?"

"Friend, in the first jhāna five factors are abandoned and five factors are possessed. Here, when a bhikkhu has entered upon the first jhāna, sensual desire is abandoned, ill will is abandoned, sloth and torpor are abandoned, restlessness and remorse [295] are abandoned, and doubt is abandoned; and there occur applied thought, sustained thought, rapture, pleasure, and unification of mind. That is how in the first jhāna five factors are abandoned and five factors are possessed."

(THE FIVE FACULTIES)

21. "Friend, these five faculties each have a separate field, a separate domain, and do not experience each other's field and domain, that is, the eye faculty, the ear faculty, the nose faculty, the tongue faculty, and the body faculty. Now of these five faculties, each having a separate field, a separate domain, not experiencing each other's field and domain, what is their resort, what experiences their fields and domains?"[443]

"Friend, these five faculties each have a separate field, a separate domain, and do not experience each other's field and domain, that is, the eye faculty, the ear faculty, the nose faculty, the tongue faculty, and the body faculty. Now these five faculties, each having a separate field, a separate domain, not experiencing each other's field and domain, have mind as their resort, and mind experiences their fields and domains."

22. "Friend, as to these five faculties—that is, the eye faculty, the ear faculty, the nose faculty, the tongue faculty, and the body faculty—what do these five faculties stand in dependence on?"

"Friend, as to these five faculties—that is, the eye faculty, the ear faculty, the nose faculty, the tongue faculty, and the body faculty—these five faculties stand in dependence on vitality."[444]

"Friend, what does vitality stand in dependence on?"

"Vitality stands in dependence on heat."[445]

"Friend, what does heat stand in dependence on?"

"Heat stands in dependence on vitality."

"Just now, friend, we understood the venerable Sāriputta to have said: 'Vitality stands in dependence on heat'; and now we understand him to say: 'Heat stands in dependence on vitality.' How should the meaning of these statements be regarded?"

"In that case, friend, I shall give you a simile, for some wise men here understand the meaning of a statement by means of a simile. Just as when an oil-lamp is burning, its radiance is seen in dependence on its flame and its flame is seen in dependence on its radiance; so too, vitality stands in dependence on heat and heat stands in dependence on vitality."

(VITAL FORMATIONS)

23. "Friend, are vital formations things that can be felt or are vital formations one thing and things that can be felt another?" [296]

"Vital formations, friend, are not things that can be felt.[446] If vital formations were things that can be felt, then a bhikkhu who has entered upon the cessation of perception and feeling would not be seen to emerge from it. Because vital formations are one thing and things that can be felt another, a bhikkhu who has entered upon the cessation of perception and feeling can be seen to emerge from it."

24. "Friend, when this body is bereft of how many states is it then discarded and forsaken, left lying senseless like a log?"[447]

"Friend, when this body is bereft of three states—vitality, heat, and consciousness—it is then discarded and forsaken, left lying senseless like a log."

25. "Friend, what is the difference between one who is dead, who has completed his time, and a bhikkhu who has entered upon the cessation of perception and feeling?"

"Friend, in the case of one who is dead, who has completed his time, his bodily formations have ceased and subsided, his verbal formations have ceased and subsided, his mental formations have ceased and subsided, his vitality is exhausted, his heat has been dissipated, and his faculties are fully broken up. In the case of a bhikkhu who has entered upon the cessation of perception and feeling, his bodily formations have ceased and subsided, his verbal formations have ceased and subsided, his mental formations have ceased and subsided, but his vitality is not exhausted, his heat has not been dissipated, and his faculties become exceptionally clear.[448] This is the difference between one who is dead, who has completed his time, and a bhikkhu who has entered upon the cessation of perception and feeling."

(DELIVERANCE OF MIND)

26. "Friend, how many conditions are there for the attainment of the neither-painful-nor-pleasant deliverance of mind?"

"Friend, there are four conditions for the attainment of the neither-painful-nor-pleasant deliverance of mind: here, with the abandoning of pleasure and pain, and with the previous disappearance of joy and grief, a bhikkhu enters upon and abides in the fourth jhāna, which has neither-pain-nor-pleasure and purity of mindfulness due to equanimity. These are the four conditions for the attainment of the neither-painful-nor-pleasant deliverance of mind."

27. "Friend, how many conditions are there for the attainment of the signless deliverance of mind?"

"Friend, there are two conditions for the attainment of the signless deliverance of mind: non-attention to all signs and attention to the signless element. These are the two conditions for the attainment of the signless deliverance of mind."[449]

28. "Friend, how many conditions are there for the persistence of the signless deliverance of mind?"

"Friend, there are three conditions for the persistence of the signless deliverance of mind: [297] non-attention to all signs, attention to the signless element, and the prior determination [of its duration]. These are the three conditions for the persistence of the signless deliverance of mind."

29. "Friend, how many conditions are there for emergence from the signless deliverance of mind?"

"Friend, there are two conditions for emergence from the signless deliverance of mind: attention to all signs and non-attention to the signless element. These are the two conditions for emergence from the signless deliverance of mind."

30. "Friend, the immeasurable deliverance of mind, the deliverance of mind through nothingness, the deliverance of mind through voidness, and the signless deliverance of mind: are these states different in meaning and different in name, or are they one in meaning and different only in name?"

"Friend, the immeasurable deliverance of mind, the deliverance of mind through nothingness, the deliverance of mind through voidness, and the signless deliverance of mind: there is a way in which these states are different in meaning and different in name, and there is a way in which they are one in meaning and different only in name.

31. "What, friend, is the way in which these states are different in meaning and different in name? Here a bhikkhu abides pervading one quarter with a mind imbued with loving-kindness, likewise the second, likewise the third, likewise the fourth; so above, below, around, and everywhere, and to all as to himself, he abides pervading the all-encompassing world with a mind imbued with loving-kindness, abundant, exalted, immeasurable, without hostility and without ill will. He abides pervading one quarter with a mind imbued with compassion...He abides pervading one quarter with a mind imbued with altruistic joy...He abides pervading one quarter with a mind imbued with equanimity, likewise the second, likewise the third, likewise the fourth; so above, below, around, and everywhere, and to all as to himself, he abides pervading the all-encompassing world with a mind imbued with equanimity, abundant, exalted, immeasurable, without hostility and without ill will. This is called the immeasurable deliverance of mind.

32. "And what, friend, is the deliverance of mind through nothingness? Here, with the complete surmounting of the base of infinite consciousness, aware that 'there is nothing,' a bhikkhu enters upon and abides in the base of nothingness. This is called the deliverance of mind through nothingness.

33. "And what, friend, is the deliverance of mind through voidness? Here a bhikkhu, gone to the forest or to the root of a tree or to an empty hut, reflects thus: 'This is void of a self or of what belongs to a self.' [298] This is called the deliverance of mind through voidness.[450]

34. "And what, friend, is the signless deliverance of mind? Here, with non-attention to all signs, a bhikkhu enters upon and abides in the signless concentration of mind. This is called the signless deliverance of mind.[451] This is the way in which these states are different in meaning and different in name.

35. "And what, friend, is the way in which these states are one in meaning and different only in name? Lust is a maker of measurement, hate is a maker of measurement, delusion is a maker of measurement.[452] In a bhikkhu whose taints are destroyed, these are abandoned, cut off at the root, made like a palm stump, done away with so that they are no longer subject to future arising. Of all the kinds of immeasurable deliverance of mind, the unshakeable deliverance of mind is pronounced the best. Now that unshakeable deliverance of mind is void of lust, void of hate, void of delusion.[453]

36. "Lust is a something, hate is a something, delusion is a something.[454] In a bhikkhu whose taints are destroyed, these are abandoned, cut off at the root, made like a palm stump, done away with so that they are no longer subject to future arising. Of all the kinds of deliverance of mind through nothingness, the unshakeable deliverance of mind is pronounced the best.[455] Now that unshakeable deliverance of mind is void of lust, void of hate, void of delusion.

37. "Lust is a maker of signs, hate is a maker of signs, delusion is a maker of signs.[456] In a bhikkhu whose taints are destroyed, these are abandoned, cut off at the root, made like a palm stump, done away with so that they are no longer subject to future arising. Of all the kinds of signless deliverance of mind, the unshakeable deliverance of mind is pronounced the best.[457] Now that unshakeable deliverance of mind is void of lust, void of hate, void of delusion. This is the way in which these states are one in meaning and different only in name."[458]

That is what the venerable Sāriputta said. The venerable Mahā Koṭṭhita was satisfied and delighted in the venerable Sāriputta's words.

44 *Cūḷavedalla Sutta*
The Shorter Series of Questions and Answers

[299] 1. THUS HAVE I HEARD. On one occasion the Blessed One was living at Rājagaha in the Bamboo Grove, the Squirrels' Sanctuary. Then the lay follower Visākha went to the bhikkhunī Dhammadinnā,[459] and after paying homage to her, he sat down at one side and asked her:

(IDENTITY)

2. "Lady, 'identity, identity' is said. What is called identity by the Blessed One?"

"Friend Visākha, these five aggregates affected by clinging are called identity by the Blessed One; that is, the material form aggregate affected by clinging, the feeling aggregate affected by clinging, the perception aggregate affected by clinging, the formations aggregate affected by clinging, and the consciousness aggregate affected by clinging. These five aggregates affected by clinging are called identity by the Blessed One."[460]

Saying, "Good, lady," the lay follower Visākha delighted and rejoiced in the bhikkhunī Dhammadinnā's words. Then he asked her a further question:

3. "Lady, 'origin of identity, origin of identity' is said. What is called the origin of identity by the Blessed One?"

"Friend Visākha, it is craving, which brings renewal of being, is accompanied by delight and lust, and delights in this and that; that is, craving for sensual pleasures, craving for being, and craving for non-being. This is called the origin of identity by the Blessed One."

4. "Lady, 'cessation of identity, cessation of identity' is said. What is called the cessation of identity by the Blessed One?"

"Friend Visākha, it is the remainderless fading away and ceasing, the giving up, relinquishing, letting go, and rejecting of that same craving. This is called the cessation of identity by the Blessed One."

5. "Lady, 'the way leading to the cessation of identity, the way leading to the cessation of identity' is said. What is called the way leading to the cessation of identity by the Blessed One?"

"Friend Visākha, it is just this Noble Eightfold Path; that is, right view, right intention, right speech, right action, right livelihood, right effort, right mindfulness, and right concentration."

6. "Lady, is that clinging the same as these five aggregates affected by clinging, or is the clinging something apart from the five aggregates affected by clinging?"

"Friend Visākha, that clinging is neither the same as these five aggregates affected by clinging [300] nor is clinging something apart from the five aggregates affected by clinging. It is the desire and lust in regard to the five aggregates affected by clinging that is the clinging there."[461]

(IDENTITY VIEW)

7. "Lady, how does identity view come to be?"

"Here, friend Visākha, an untaught ordinary person, who has no regard for noble ones and is unskilled and undisciplined in their Dhamma, who has no regard for true men and is unskilled and undisciplined in their Dhamma, regards material form as self, or self as possessed of material form, or material form as in self, or self as in material form. He regards feeling as self, or self as possessed of feeling, or feeling as in self, or self as in feeling. He regards perception as self, or self as possessed of perception, or perception as in self, or self as in perception. He regards formations as self, or self as possessed of formations, or formations as in self, or self as in formations. He regards consciousness as self, or self as possessed of consciousness, or consciousness as in self, or self as in consciousness. That is how identity view comes to be."[462]

8. "Lady, how does identity view not come to be?"

"Here, friend Visākha, a well-taught noble disciple, who has regard for noble ones and is skilled and disciplined in their Dhamma, who has regard for true men and is skilled and disciplined in their Dhamma, does not regard material form as self, or self as possessed of material form, or material form as in self, or self as in material form. He does not regard feeling as self, or self as possessed of feeling, or feeling as in self, or self as in feeling. He does not regard perception as self, or self as possessed of perception, or perception as in self, or self as in perception. He does not regard formations as self, or self as possessed of formations, or formations as in self, or self as in formations. He does not regard consciousness as self, or self as possessed of consciousness, or consciousness as in self, or self as in consciousness. That is how identity view does not come to be."

(THE NOBLE EIGHTFOLD PATH)

9. "Lady, what is the Noble Eightfold Path?"

"Friend Visākha, it is just this Noble Eightfold Path; that is, right view, right intention, right speech, right action, right livelihood, right effort, right mindfulness, and right concentration."

10. "Lady, is the Noble Eightfold Path conditioned or unconditioned?"

"Friend Visākha, the Noble Eightfold Path is [301] conditioned."

11. "Lady, are the three aggregates included by the Noble Eightfold Path, or is the Noble Eightfold Path included by the three aggregates?"[463]

"The three aggregates are not included by the Noble Eightfold Path, friend Visākha, but the Noble Eightfold Path is included by the three aggregates. Right speech, right action, and right livelihood—these states are included in the aggregate of virtue. Right effort, right mindfulness, and right concentration—these states are included in the aggregate of concentration. Right view and right intention—these states are included in the aggregate of wisdom."

(CONCENTRATION)

12. "Lady, what is concentration? What is the basis of concentration? What is the equipment of concentration? What is the development of concentration?"

"Unification of mind, friend Visākha, is concentration; the four foundations of mindfulness are the basis of concentration; the four right kinds of striving are the equipment of concentration;

the repetition, development, and cultivation of these same states is the development of concentration therein."[464]

(FORMATIONS)

13. "Lady, how many formations are there?"

"There are these three formations, friend Visākha: the bodily formation, the verbal formation, and the mental formation."

14. "But, lady, what is the bodily formation? What is the verbal formation? What is the mental formation?"

"In-breathing and out-breathing, friend Visākha, are the bodily formation; applied thought and sustained thought are the verbal formation; perception and feeling are the mental formation."[465]

15. "But, lady, why are in-breathing and out-breathing the bodily formation? Why are applied thought and sustained thought the verbal formation? Why are perception and feeling the mental formation?"

"Friend Visākha, in-breathing and out-breathing are bodily, these are states bound up with the body; that is why in-breathing and out-breathing are the bodily formation. First one applies thought and sustains thought, and subsequently one breaks out into speech; that is why applied thought and sustained thought are the verbal formation. Perception and feeling are mental, these are states bound up with the mind; that is why perception and feeling are the mental formation."[466]

(THE ATTAINMENT OF CESSATION)

16. "Lady, how does the attainment of the cessation of perception and feeling come to be?"

"Friend Visākha, when a bhikkhu is attaining the cessation of perception and feeling, it does not occur to him: 'I shall attain the cessation of perception and feeling,' or 'I am attaining the cessation of perception and feeling,' or 'I have attained the cessation of perception and feeling'; but rather his mind has previously been developed in such a way that it leads him to that state."[467] [302]

17. "Lady, when a bhikkhu is attaining the cessation of perception and feeling, which states cease first in him: the bodily formation, the verbal formation, or the mental formation?"

"Friend Visākha, when a bhikkhu is attaining the cessation of perception and feeling, first the verbal formation ceases, then the bodily formation, then the mental formation."[468]

18. "Lady, how does emergence from the attainment of the cessation of perception and feeling come to be?"

"Friend Visākha, when a bhikkhu is emerging from the attainment of the cessation of perception and feeling, it does not occur to him: 'I shall emerge from the attainment of the cessation of perception and feeling,' or 'I am emerging from the attainment of the cessation of perception and feeling,' or 'I have emerged from the attainment of the cessation of perception and feeling'; but rather his mind has previously been developed in such a way that it leads him to that state."[469]

19. "Lady, when a bhikkhu is emerging from the attainment of the cessation of perception and feeling, which states arise first in him: the bodily formation, the verbal formation, or the mental formation?"

"Friend Visākha, when a bhikkhu is emerging from the attainment of the cessation of perception and feeling, first the mental formation arises, then the bodily formation, then the verbal formation."[470]

20. "Lady, when a bhikkhu has emerged from the attainment of the cessation of perception and feeling, how many kinds of contact touch him?"

"Friend Visākha, when a bhikkhu has emerged from the attainment of the cessation of perception and feeling, three kinds of contact touch him: voidness contact, signless contact, desireless contact."[471]

21. "Lady, when a bhikkhu has emerged from the attainment of the cessation of perception and feeling, to what does his mind incline, to what does it lean, to what does it tend?"

"Friend Visākha, when a bhikkhu has emerged from the attainment of the cessation of perception and feeling, his mind inclines to seclusion, leans to seclusion, tends to seclusion."[472]

(FEELING)

22. "Lady, how many kinds of feeling are there?"

"Friend Visākha, there are three kinds of feeling: pleasant feeling, painful feeling, and neither-painful-nor-pleasant feeling."

23. "But, lady, what is pleasant feeling? What is painful feeling? What is neither painful-nor-pleasant feeling?"

"Friend Visākha, whatever is felt bodily or mentally as pleasant and soothing is pleasant feeling. Whatever is felt bodily or mentally as painful and hurting is painful feeling. Whatever is felt bodily or mentally as neither soothing nor hurting [303] is neither-painful-nor-pleasant feeling."

24. "Lady, what is pleasant and what is painful in regard to pleasant feeling? What is painful and what is pleasant in regard to painful feeling? What is pleasant and what is painful in regard to neither-painful-nor-pleasant feeling?"

"Friend Visākha, pleasant feeling is pleasant when it persists and painful when it changes. Painful feeling is painful when it persists and pleasant when it changes. Neither-painful-nor-pleasant feeling is pleasant when there is knowledge [of it] and painful when there is no knowledge [of it]."

(UNDERLYING TENDENCIES)

25. "Lady, what underlying tendency underlies pleasant feeling? What underlying tendency underlies painful feeling? What underlying tendency underlies neither-painful-nor-pleasant feeling?"

"Friend Visākha, the underlying tendency to lust underlies pleasant feeling. The underlying tendency to aversion underlies painful feeling. The underlying tendency to ignorance underlies neither-painful-nor-pleasant feeling."[473]

26. "Lady, does the underlying tendency to lust underlie all pleasant feeling? Does the underlying tendency to aversion underlie all painful feeling? Does the underlying tendency to ignorance underlie all neither-painful-nor-pleasant feeling?"

"Friend Visākha, the underlying tendency to lust does not underlie all pleasant feeling. The underlying tendency to aversion does not underlie all painful feeling. The underlying tendency to ignorance does not underlie all neither-painful-nor-pleasant feeling."

27. "Lady, what should be abandoned in regard to pleasant feeling? What should be abandoned in regard to painful feeling? What should be abandoned in regard to neither-painful-nor-pleasant feeling?"

"Friend Visākha, the underlying tendency to lust should be

abandoned in regard to pleasant feeling. The underlying tendency to aversion should be abandoned in regard to painful feeling. The underlying tendency to ignorance should be abandoned in regard to neither-painful-nor-pleasant feeling."

28. "Lady, does the underlying tendency to lust have to be abandoned in regard to all pleasant feeling? Does the underlying tendency to aversion have to be abandoned in regard to all painful feeling? Does the underlying tendency to ignorance have to be abandoned in regard to all neither-painful-nor-pleasant feeling?"

"Friend Visākha, the underlying tendency to lust does not have to be abandoned in regard to all pleasant feeling. The underlying tendency to aversion does not have to be abandoned in regard to all painful feeling. The underlying tendency to ignorance does not have to be abandoned in regard to all neither-painful-nor-pleasant feeling.

"Here, friend Visākha, quite secluded from sensual pleasures, secluded from unwholesome states, a bhikkhu enters upon and abides in the first jhāna, which is accompanied by applied and sustained thought, with rapture and pleasure born of seclusion. With that he abandons lust, and the underlying tendency to lust does not underlie that.[474]

"Here a bhikkhu considers thus: 'When shall I enter upon and abide in that base that the noble ones now enter upon and abide in?' In one who thus generates a longing for the supreme liberations, [304] grief arises with that longing as condition. With that he abandons aversion, and the underlying tendency to aversion does not underlie that.[475]

"Here, with the abandoning of pleasure and pain, and with the previous disappearance of joy and grief, a bhikkhu enters upon and abides in the fourth jhāna, which has neither-pain-nor-pleasure and purity of mindfulness due to equanimity. With that he abandons ignorance, and the underlying tendency to ignorance does not underlie that."[476]

(COUNTERPARTS)

29. "Lady, what is the counterpart of pleasant feeling?"[477]

"Friend Visākha, painful feeling is the counterpart of pleasant feeling."

"What is the counterpart of painful feeling?"

"Pleasant feeling is the counterpart of painful feeling."

"What is the counterpart of neither-painful-nor-pleasant feeling?"

"Ignorance is the counterpart of neither-painful-nor pleasant feeling."[478]

"What is the counterpart of ignorance?"

"True knowledge is the counterpart of ignorance."

"What is the counterpart of true knowledge?"

"Deliverance is the counterpart of true knowledge."

"What is the counterpart of deliverance?"

"Nibbāna is the counterpart of deliverance."

"Lady, what is the counterpart of Nibbāna?"

"Friend Visākha, you have pushed this line of questioning too far; you were not able to grasp the limit to questions.[479] For the holy life, friend Visākha, is grounded upon Nibbāna, culminates in Nibbāna, ends in Nibbāna. If you wish, friend Visākha, go to the Blessed One and ask him about the meaning of this. As the Blessed One explains it to you, so you should remember it."

(CONCLUSION)

30. Then the lay follower Visākha, having delighted and rejoiced in the bhikkhunī Dhammadinnā's words, rose from his seat, and after paying homage to her, keeping her on his right, he went to the Blessed One. After paying homage to him, he sat down at one side and told the Blessed One his entire conversation with the bhikkhunī Dhammadinnā. When he finished speaking, the Blessed One told him:

31. "The bhikkhunī Dhammadinnā is wise, Visākha, the bhikkhunī Dhammadinnā has great wisdom. If you had asked me the meaning of this, I would have explained it to you [305] in the same way that the bhikkhunī Dhammadinnā has explained it. Such is its meaning, and so you should remember it."[480]

That is what the Blessed One said. The lay follower Visākha was satisfied and delighted in the Blessed One's words.

45 *Cūḷadhammasamādāna Sutta*
The Shorter Discourse on Ways of Undertaking Things

1. THUS HAVE I HEARD. On one occasion the Blessed One was living at Sāvatthī in Jeta's Grove, Anāthapiṇḍika's Park. There he addressed the bhikkhus thus: "Bhikkhus."—"Venerable sir," they replied. The Blessed One said this:

2. "Bhikkhus, there are four ways of undertaking things. What are the four? There is a way of undertaking things that is pleasant now and ripens in the future as pain. There is a way of undertaking things that is painful now and ripens in the future as pain. There is a way of undertaking things that is painful now and ripens in the future as pleasure. There is a way of undertaking things that is pleasant now and ripens in the future as pleasure.

3. "What, bhikkhus, is the way of undertaking things that is pleasant now and ripens in the future as pain? Bhikkhus, there are certain recluses and brahmins whose doctrine and view is this: 'There is no harm in sensual pleasures.' They take to gulping down sensual pleasures and divert themselves with women wanderers who wear their hair bound in a topknot. They say thus: 'What future fear do these good recluses and brahmins see in sensual pleasures when they speak of abandoning sensual pleasures and describe the full understanding of sensual pleasures? Pleasant is the touch of this woman wanderer's tender soft downy arm!' Thus they take to gulping down sensual pleasures, and having done so, on the dissolution of the body, after death, they reappear in a state of deprivation, in an unhappy destination, in perdition, even in hell. There they feel painful, racking, piercing feelings. They say thus: 'This is the future fear those good recluses and brahmins saw in sensual pleasures when they spoke of abandoning sensual pleasures and described the full understanding of sensual pleasures. For it is

by reason of sensual pleasures, [306] owing to sensual pleasures, that we are now feeling painful, racking, piercing feelings.'

4. "Bhikkhus, suppose that in the last month of the hot season a māluva-creeper pod burst open and a māluva-creeper seed fell at the foot of a sāla tree. Then a deity living in that tree became fearful, perturbed, and frightened; but the deity's friends and companions, kinsmen and relatives—garden deities, park deities, tree deities, and deities inhabiting medicinal herbs, grass, and forest-monarch trees—gathered together and reassured that deity thus: 'Have no fear, sir, have no fear. Perhaps a peacock will swallow the māluva-creeper seed or a wild animal will eat it or a forest fire will burn it or woodsmen will carry it off or white ants will devour it or it may not even be fertile.' But no peacock swallowed that seed, no wild animal ate it, no forest fire burned it, no woodsmen carried it off, no white ants devoured it, and it was in fact fertile. Then, being moistened by rain from a rain-bearing cloud, the seed in due course sprouted and the māluva creeper's tender soft downy tendril wound itself around that sāla tree. Then the deity living in the sāla tree thought: 'What future fear did my friends and companions, kinsmen and relatives...see in that māluva-creeper seed when they gathered together and reassured me as they did? Pleasant is the touch of this māluva creeper's tender soft downy tendril!' Then the creeper enfolded the sāla tree, made a canopy over it, draped a curtain all around it, and split the main branches of the tree. The deity who lived in the tree then realised: 'This is the future fear they saw in that māluva-creeper seed. [307] Because of that māluva-creeper seed I am now feeling painful, racking, piercing feelings.'

"So too, bhikkhus, there are certain recluses and brahmins whose doctrine and view is this: 'There is no harm in sensual pleasures.'...They say thus: 'This is the future fear those good recluses and brahmins saw in sensual pleasures...that we are now feeling painful, racking, piercing feelings.' This is called the way of undertaking things that is pleasant now and ripens in the future as pain.

5. "And what, bhikkhus, is the way of undertaking things that is painful now and ripens in the future as pain? Here, bhikkhus, someone goes naked, rejecting conventions, licking his hands, not coming when asked, not stopping when asked...(*as Sutta 12, §45*) [308]...He dwells pursuing the practice of bathing in water three times daily including the evening. Thus in such a variety

of ways he dwells pursuing the practice of tormenting and mortifying the body. On the dissolution of the body, after death, he reappears in a state of deprivation, in an unhappy destination, in perdition, even in hell. This is called the way of undertaking things that is painful now and ripens in the future as pain.

6. "And what, bhikkhus, is the way of undertaking things that is painful now and ripens in the future as pleasure? Here, bhikkhus, someone by nature has strong lust, and he constantly experiences pain and grief born of lust; by nature he has strong hate, and he constantly experiences pain and grief born of hate; by nature he has strong delusion, and he constantly experiences pain and grief born of delusion. Yet in pain and grief, weeping with tearful face, he leads the perfect and pure holy life. On the dissolution of the body, after death, he reappears in a happy destination, even in the heavenly world. This is called the way of undertaking things that is painful now and ripens in the future as pleasure.

7. "And what, bhikkhus, is the way of undertaking things that is pleasant now and ripens in the future as pleasure? Here, bhikkhus, someone by nature does not have strong lust, and he does not constantly experience pain and grief born of lust; by nature he does not have strong hate, and he does not constantly experience pain and grief born of hate; by nature he does not have strong delusion, [309] and he does not constantly experience pain and grief born of delusion. Quite secluded from sensual pleasures, secluded from unwholesome states, he enters upon and abides in the first jhāna...With the stilling of applied and sustained thought, he enters upon and abides in the second jhāna...With the fading away as well of rapture...he enters upon and abides in the third jhāna...With the abandoning of pleasure and pain...he enters upon and abides in the fourth jhāna...On the dissolution of the body, after death, he reappears in a happy destination, even in the heavenly world. This is called the way of undertaking things that is pleasant now and ripens in the future as pleasure. These, bhikkhus, are the four ways of undertaking things."

That is what the Blessed One said. The bhikkhus were satisfied and delighted in the Blessed One's words.

46 *Mahādhammasamādāna Sutta*
The Greater Discourse on Ways of Undertaking Things

1. THUS HAVE I HEARD. On one occasion the Blessed One was living at Sāvatthī in Jeta's Grove, Anāthapiṇḍika's Park. There he addressed the bhikkhus thus: "Bhikkhus."—"Venerable sir," they replied. The Blessed One said this:

2. "Bhikkhus, for the most part beings have this wish, desire, and longing: 'If only unwished for, undesired, disagreeable things would diminish and wished for, desired, agreeable things would increase!' Yet although beings have this wish, desire, and longing, unwished for, undesired, disagreeable things increase for them and wished for, desired, agreeable things diminish. Now, bhikkhus, what do you think is the reason for that?"

"Venerable sir, our teachings are rooted in the Blessed One, [310] guided by the Blessed One, have the Blessed One as their resort. It would be good if the Blessed One would explain the meaning of these words. Having heard it from the Blessed One, the bhikkhus will remember it."

"Then listen, bhikkhus, and attend closely to what I shall say."

"Yes, venerable sir," they replied. The Blessed One said this:

3. "Here, bhikkhus, an untaught ordinary person who has no regard for noble ones and is unskilled and undisciplined in their Dhamma, who has no regard for true men and is unskilled and undisciplined in their Dhamma, does not know what things should be cultivated and what things should not be cultivated, he does not know what things should be followed and what things should not be followed. Not knowing this, he cultivates things that should not be cultivated and does not cultivate things that should be cultivated, he follows things that should not be followed and does not follow things that should be followed.[481] It is because he does this that unwished for, undesired, disagreeable things increase for him and wished for, desired, agreeable

things diminish. Why is that? That is what happens to one who does not see.

4. "The well-taught noble disciple who has regard for noble ones and is skilled and disciplined in their Dhamma, who has regard for true men and is skilled and disciplined in their Dhamma, knows what things should be cultivated and what things should not be cultivated, he knows what things should be followed and what things should not be followed. Knowing this, he cultivates things that should be cultivated and does not cultivate things that should not be cultivated, he follows things that should be followed and does not follow things that should not be followed. It is because he does this that unwished for, undesired, disagreeable things diminish for him and wished for, desired, agreeable things increase. Why is that? That is what happens to one who sees.

5. "Bhikkhus, there are four ways of undertaking things. What are the four? There is a way of undertaking things that is painful now and ripens in the future as pain. There is [311] a way of undertaking things that is pleasant now and ripens in the future as pain. There is a way of undertaking things that is painful now and ripens in the future as pleasure. There is a way of undertaking things that is pleasant now and ripens in the future as pleasure.

(THE IGNORANT PERSON)

6. (1) "Now, bhikkhus, one who is ignorant, not knowing this way of undertaking things that is painful now and ripens in the future as pain, does not understand it as it actually is thus: 'This way of undertaking things is painful now and ripens in the future as pain.' Not knowing it, not understanding it as it actually is, the ignorant one cultivates it and does not avoid it; because he does so, unwished for, undesired, disagreeable things increase for him and wished for, desired, agreeable things diminish. Why is that? That is what happens to one who does not see.

7. (2) "Now, bhikkhus, one who is ignorant, not knowing this way of undertaking things that is pleasant now and ripens in the future as pain, does not understand it as it actually is thus: 'This way of undertaking things is pleasant now and ripens in the future as pain.' Not knowing it, not understanding it as it actually

is, the ignorant one cultivates it and does not avoid it; because he does so, unwished for...things increase for him and wished for...things diminish. Why is that? That is what happens to one who does not see.

8. (3) "Now, bhikkhus, one who is ignorant, not knowing this way of undertaking things that is painful now and ripens in the future as pleasure, does not understand it as it actually is thus: 'This way of undertaking things is painful now and ripens in the future as pleasure.' Not knowing it, not understanding it as it actually is, the ignorant one does not cultivate it but avoids it; because he does so, unwished for...things increase for him and wished for...things diminish. Why is that? That is what happens to one who does not see.

9. (4) "Now, bhikkhus, one who is ignorant, not knowing the way of undertaking things that is pleasant now and ripens in the future as pleasure, does not understand it as it actually is thus: 'This way of undertaking things is pleasant now and ripens in the future as pleasure.' Not knowing it, not understanding it as it actually is, the ignorant one does not cultivate it but avoids it; because he does so, [312] unwished for...things increase for him and wished for...things diminish. Why is that? That is what happens to one who does not see.

(THE WISE PERSON)

10. (1) "Now, bhikkhus, one who is wise, knowing this way of undertaking things that is painful now and ripens in the future as pain, understands it as it actually is thus: 'This way of undertaking things is painful now and ripens in the future as pain.' Knowing it, understanding it as it actually is, the wise one does not cultivate it but avoids it; because he does so, unwished for, undesired, disagreeable things diminish for him and wished for, desired, agreeable things increase. Why is that? That is what happens to one who sees.

11. (2) "Now, bhikkhus, one who is wise, knowing this way of undertaking things that is pleasant now and ripens in the future as pain, understands it as it actually is thus: 'This way of undertaking things is pleasant now and ripens in the future as pain.' Knowing it, understanding it as it actually is, the wise one does not cultivate it but avoids it; because he does so, unwished

for...things diminish for him and wished for...things increase. Why is that? That is what happens to one who sees.

12. (3) "Now, bhikkhus, one who is wise, knowing this way of undertaking things that is painful now and ripens in the future as pleasure, understands it as it actually is thus: 'This way of undertaking things is painful now and ripens in the future as pleasure.' Knowing it, understanding it as it actually is, the wise one does not avoid it but cultivates it; because he does so, unwished for things...diminish for him and wished for...things increase. Why is that? That is what happens to one who sees.

13. (4) "Now, bhikkhus, one who is wise, knowing this way of undertaking things that is pleasant now and ripens in the future as pleasure, understands it as it actually is thus: 'This way of undertaking things is pleasant now and ripens in the future as pleasure.' Knowing it, understanding it as it actually is, the wise one does not avoid it but cultivates it; because he does so, unwished for...things diminish for him and wished for...things increase. Why is that? That is what happens to one who sees. [313]

(THE FOUR WAYS)

14. (1) "What, bhikkhus, is the way of undertaking things that is painful now and ripens in the future as pain? Here, bhikkhus, someone in pain and grief kills living beings, and he experiences pain and grief that have killing of living beings as condition. In pain and grief he takes what is not given...misconducts himself in sensual pleasures...speaks falsehood...speaks maliciously... speaks harshly...gossips...is covetous...has a mind of ill will...holds wrong view, and he experiences pain and grief that have wrong view as condition. On the dissolution of the body, after death, he reappears in a state of deprivation, in an unhappy destination, in perdition, even in hell. This is called the way of undertaking things that is painful now and ripens in the future as pain.

15. (2) "What, bhikkhus, is the way of undertaking things that is pleasant now and ripens in the future as pain? Here, bhikkhus, someone in pleasure and joy kills living beings, and he experiences pleasure and joy that have killing of living beings as condition. In pleasure and joy he takes what is not given...

[314]...holds wrong view, and he experiences pleasure and joy that have wrong view as condition. On the dissolution of the body, after death, he reappears in a state of deprivation, in an unhappy destination, in perdition, even in hell. This is called the way of undertaking things that is pleasant now and ripens in the future as pain.

16. (3) "What, bhikkhus, is the way of undertaking things that is painful now and ripens in the future as pleasure? Here, bhikkhus, someone in pain and grief abstains from killing living beings, and he experiences pain and grief that have abstention from killing living beings as condition. In pain and grief he abstains from taking what is not given...from misconduct in sensual pleasures...from speaking falsehood...from speaking maliciously...from speaking harshly...from gossiping...he is not covetous...he does not have a mind of ill will...[315]...he holds right view, and he experiences pain and grief that have right view as condition. On the dissolution of the body, after death, he reappears in a happy destination, even in the heavenly world. This is called the way of undertaking things that is painful now and ripens in the future as pleasure.

17. (4) "What, bhikkhus, is the way of undertaking things that is pleasant now and ripens in the future as pleasure? Here, bhikkhus, someone in pleasure and joy abstains from killing living beings, and he experiences pleasure and joy that have abstention from killing living beings as condition. In pleasure and joy he abstains from taking what is not given...he holds right view, and he experiences pleasure and joy that have right view as condition. On the dissolution of the body, after death, he reappears in a happy destination, even in the heavenly world. This is called the way of undertaking things that is pleasant now and ripens in the future as pleasure.

(THE SIMILES)

18. (1) "Bhikkhus, suppose there were a bitter gourd mixed with poison, and a man came who wanted to live, not to die, who wanted pleasure and recoiled from pain, and they told him: 'Good man, this bitter gourd is mixed with poison. Drink from it if you want; [316] as you drink from it, its colour, smell, and taste will not agree with you, and after drinking from it, you

will come to death or deadly suffering.' Then he drank from it without reflecting and did not relinquish it. As he drank from it, its colour, smell, and taste did not agree with him, and after drinking from it, he came to death or deadly suffering. Similar to that, I say, is the way of undertaking things that is painful now and ripens in the future as pain.

19. (2) "Suppose there were a bronze cup of beverage possessing a good colour, smell, and taste, but it was mixed with poison, and a man came who wanted to live, not to die, who wanted pleasure and recoiled from pain, and they told him: 'Good man, this bronze cup of beverage possesses a good colour, smell, and taste, but it is mixed with poison. Drink from it if you want; as you drink from it, its colour, smell, and taste will agree with you, but after drinking from it, you will come to death or deadly suffering.' Then he drank from it without reflecting and did not relinquish it. As he drank from it, its colour, smell, and taste agreed with him, but after drinking from it, he came to death or deadly suffering. Similar to that, I say, is the way of undertaking things that is pleasant now and ripens in the future as pain.

20. (3) "Suppose there were fermented urine mixed with various medicines, and a man came sick with jaundice, and they told him: 'Good man, this fermented urine is mixed with various medicines. Drink from it if you want; as you drink from it, its colour, smell, and taste will not agree with you, but after drinking from it, you will be well.' Then he drank from it after reflecting, and did not relinquish it. As he drank from it, its colour, taste, and smell did not agree with him, but after drinking from it, he became well. Similar to that, I say, is the way of undertaking things that is painful now and ripens in the future as pleasure.

21. (4) "Suppose there were curd, honey, ghee, and molasses mixed together, and a man with dysentery came, and they told him: 'Good man, [317] this is curd, honey, ghee, and molasses mixed together. Drink from it if you want; as you drink from it, its colour, smell, and taste will agree with you, and after drinking from it you will be well.' Then he drank from it after reflecting, and did not relinquish it. As he drank from it, its colour, smell, and taste agreed with him, and after drinking from it, he became well. Similar to that, I say, is the way of undertaking things that is pleasant now and ripens in the future as pleasure.

22. "Just as, in autumn, in the last month of the rainy season, when the sky is clear and cloudless, the sun rises above the earth dispelling all darkness from space with its shining and beaming and radiance, so too, the way of undertaking things that is pleasant now and ripens in the future as pleasure dispels with its shining and beaming and radiance any other doctrines whatsoever of ordinary recluses and brahmins."

That is what the Blessed One said. The bhikkhus were satisfied and delighted in the Blessed One's words.

47 *Vīmaṁsaka Sutta*
The Inquirer

1. THUS HAVE I HEARD. On one occasion the Blessed One was living at Sāvatthī in Jeta's Grove, Anāthapiṇḍika's Park. There he addressed the bhikkhus thus: "Bhikkhus."—"Venerable sir," they replied. The Blessed One said this:

2. "Bhikkhus, a bhikkhu who is an inquirer, not knowing how to gauge another's mind,[482] should make an investigation of the Tathāgata in order to find out whether or not he is fully enlightened."

3. "Venerable sir, our teachings are rooted in the Blessed One, guided by the Blessed One, have the Blessed One as their resort. It would be good if the Blessed One would explain the meaning of these words. Having heard it from the Blessed One, the bhikkhus will remember it."

"Then listen, bhikkhus, and attend closely to [318] what I shall say."

"Yes, venerable sir," the bhikkhus replied. The Blessed One said this:

4. "Bhikkhus, a bhikkhu who is an inquirer, not knowing how to gauge another's mind, should investigate the Tathāgata with respect to two kinds of states, states cognizable through the eye and through the ear thus: 'Are there found in the Tathāgata or not any defiled states cognizable through the eye or through the ear?'[483] When he investigates him, he comes to know: 'No defiled states cognizable through the eye or through the ear are found in the Tathāgata.'

5. "When he comes to know this, he investigates him further thus: 'Are there found in the Tathāgata or not any mixed states cognizable through the eye or through the ear?'[484] When he investigates him, he comes to know: 'No mixed states cognizable through the eye or through the ear are found in the Tathāgata.'

6. "When he comes to know this, he investigates him further thus: 'Are there found in the Tathāgata or not cleansed states cognizable through the eye or through the ear?' When he investigates him, he comes to know: 'Cleansed states cognizable through the eye or through the ear are found in the Tathāgata.'

7. "When he comes to know this, he investigates him further thus: 'Has this venerable one attained this wholesome state over a long time or did he attain it recently?' When he investigates him, he comes to know: 'This venerable one has attained this wholesome state over a long time; he did not attain it only recently.'

8. "When he comes to know this, he investigates him further thus: 'Has this venerable one acquired renown and attained fame, so that the dangers [connected with renown and fame] are found in him?' For, bhikkhus, as long as a bhikkhu has not acquired renown and attained fame, the dangers [connected with renown and fame] are not found in him; but when he has acquired renown and attained fame, those dangers are found in him.[485] When he investigates him, he comes to know: 'This venerable one has acquired renown and attained fame, but the dangers [connected with renown and fame] are not found in him.'

9. "When he comes to know this, [319] he investigates him further thus: 'Is this venerable one restrained without fear, not restrained by fear, and does he avoid indulging in sensual pleasures because he is without lust through the destruction of lust?' When he investigates him, he comes to know: 'This venerable one is restrained without fear, not restrained by fear, and he avoids indulging in sensual pleasure because he is without lust through the destruction of lust.'

10. "Now, bhikkhus, if others should ask that bhikkhu thus: 'What are the venerable one's reasons and what is his evidence whereby he says: "That venerable one is restrained without fear, not restrained by fear, and he avoids indulging in sensual pleasures because he is without lust through the destruction of lust"?'—answering rightly, that bhikkhu would answer thus: 'Whether that venerable one dwells in the Sangha or alone, while some there are well behaved and some are ill behaved and some there teach a group,[486] while some here are seen concerned about material things and some are unsullied by material things, still that venerable one does not despise anyone because of

that.[487] And I have heard and learned this from the Blessed One's own lips: "I am restrained without fear, not restrained by fear, and I avoid indulging in sensual pleasures because I am without lust through the destruction of lust."'

11. "The Tathāgata, bhikkhus, should be questioned further about that thus: 'Are there found in the Tathāgata or not any defiled states cognizable through the eye or through the ear?' The Tathāgata would answer thus: 'No defiled states cognizable through the eye or through the ear are found in the Tathāgata.'

12. "If asked, 'Are there found in the Tathāgata or not any mixed states cognizable through the eye or through the ear?' the Tathāgata would answer thus: 'No mixed states cognizable through the eye or through the ear are found in the Tathāgata.'

13. "If asked, 'Are there found in the Tathāgata or not cleansed states cognizable through the eye or through the ear?' the Tathāgata would answer thus: 'Cleansed states cognizable through the eye or through the ear are found in the Tathāgata. They are my pathway and my domain, yet I do not identify with them.'[488]

14. "Bhikkhus, a disciple should approach the Teacher who speaks thus in order to hear the Dhamma. The Teacher teaches him the Dhamma with its higher and higher levels, with its more and more sublime levels, with its dark and bright counterparts. As the Teacher teaches the Dhamma to a bhikkhu in this way, through direct knowledge of a certain teaching here in that Dhamma, [320] the bhikkhu comes to a conclusion about the teachings.[489] He places confidence in the Teacher thus: 'The Blessed One is fully enlightened, the Dhamma is well proclaimed by the Blessed One, the Sangha is practising the good way.'

15. "Now if others should ask that bhikkhu thus: 'What are the venerable one's reasons and what is his evidence whereby he says, "The Blessed One is fully enlightened, the Dhamma is well proclaimed by the Blessed One, the Sangha is practising the good way"?'—answering rightly, that bhikkhu would answer thus: 'Here, friends, I approached the Blessed One in order to hear the Dhamma. The Blessed One taught me the Dhamma with its higher and higher levels, with its more and more sublime levels, with its dark and bright counterparts. As the Blessed One taught the Dhamma to me in this way, through direct knowledge of a certain teaching here in that Dhamma, I came to

a conclusion about the teachings. I placed confidence in the Teacher thus: "The Blessed One is fully enlightened, the Dhamma is well proclaimed by the Blessed One, the Sangha is practising the good way."'

16. "Bhikkhus, when anyone's faith has been planted, rooted, and established in the Tathāgata through these reasons, terms, and phrases, his faith is said to be supported by reasons, rooted in vision, firm;[490] it is invincible by any recluse or brahmin or god or Māra or Brahmā or by anyone in the world. That is how, bhikkhus, there is an investigation of the Tathāgata in accordance with the Dhamma, and that is how the Tathāgata is well investigated in accordance with the Dhamma."

That is what the Blessed One said. The bhikkhus were satisfied and delighted in the Blessed One's words.

48 *Kosambiya Sutta*
The Kosambians

1. THUS HAVE I HEARD. On one occasion the Blessed One was living at Kosambī in Ghosita's Park.

2. Now on that occasion the bhikkhus at Kosambī had taken to quarrelling and brawling and were deep in disputes, stabbing each other with verbal daggers. They could neither convince each other nor be convinced by others; they could neither persuade each other nor be persuaded by others.[491]

3. Then [321] a certain bhikkhu went to the Blessed One, and after paying homage to him, he sat down at one side and informed him of what was happening.

4. Then the Blessed One addressed a certain bhikkhu thus: "Come, bhikkhu, tell those bhikkhus in my name that the Teacher calls them."—"Yes, venerable sir," he replied, and he went to those bhikkhus and told them: "The Teacher calls the venerable ones."

"Yes, friend," they replied, and they went to the Blessed One, and after paying homage to him, they sat down at one side. The Blessed One then asked them: "Bhikkhus, is it true that you have taken to quarrelling and brawling and are deep in disputes, stabbing each other with verbal daggers; that you can neither convince each other nor be convinced by others, that you can neither persuade each other nor be persuaded by others?"

"Yes, venerable sir."

5. "Bhikkhus, what do you think? When you take to quarrelling and brawling and are deep in disputes, stabbing each other with verbal daggers, do you on that occasion maintain acts of loving-kindness by body, speech, and mind in public and in private towards your companions in the holy life?"

"No, venerable sir."

"So, bhikkhus, when you take to quarrelling and brawling and are deep in disputes, stabbing each other with verbal dangers, on that occasion you do not maintain acts of loving-kindness by body, speech, and mind in public and in private towards your companions in the holy life. Misguided men, what can you possibly know, what can you see, that you take to quarrelling and brawling and are deep in disputes, [322] stabbing each other with verbal daggers? That you can neither convince each other nor be convinced by others, that you can neither persuade each other nor be persuaded by others? Misguided men, that will lead to your harm and suffering for a long time."

6. Then the Blessed One addressed the bhikkhus thus: "Bhikkhus, there are these six principles of cordiality[492] that create love and respect and conduce to cohesion, to non-dispute, to concord, and to unity. What are the six?

"Here a bhikkhu maintains bodily acts of loving-kindness both in public and in private towards his companions in the holy life. This is a principle of cordiality that creates love and respect, and conduces to cohesion, to non-dispute, to concord, and to unity.

"Again, a bhikkhu maintains verbal acts of loving-kindness both in public and in private towards his companions in the holy life. This too is a principle of cordiality that creates love and respect, and conduces to...unity.

"Again, a bhikkhu maintains mental acts of loving-kindness both in public and in private towards his companions in the holy life. This too is a principle of cordiality that creates love and respect, and conduces to...unity.

"Again, a bhikkhu uses things in common with his virtuous companions in the holy life; without making reservations, he shares with them any gain of a kind that accords with the Dhamma and has been obtained in a way that accords with the Dhamma, including even the contents of his bowl. This too is a principle of cordiality that creates love and respect, and conduces to...unity.

"Again, a bhikkhu dwells both in public and in private possessing in common with his companions in the holy life those virtues that are unbroken, untorn, unblotched, unmottled, liberating, commended by the wise, not misapprehended, and conducive to concentration. This too is a principle of cordiality that creates love and respect, and conduces to...unity.

"Again, a bhikkhu dwells both in public and in private possessing in common with his companions in the holy life that view that is noble and emancipating, and leads one who practises in accordance with it to the complete destruction of suffering.[493] This too is a principle of cordiality that creates love and respect, and conduces to cohesion, to non-dispute, to concord, and to unity.

"These are the six principles of cordiality that create love and respect, and conduce to cohesion, to non-dispute, to concord, and to unity.

7. "Of these six principles of cordiality, the chief, the most cohesive, the most unifying is this view that is noble and emancipating, and which leads the one who practises in accordance with it to the complete destruction of suffering. Just as the chief, the most cohesive, the most unifying part of a pinnacled house is the pinnacle itself, so too, [323] of these six principles of cordiality, the chief...is this view that is noble and emancipating...

8. "And how does this view that is noble and emancipating lead the one who practises in accordance with it to the complete destruction of suffering?

"Here a bhikkhu, gone to the forest or to the root of a tree or to an empty hut, considers thus: 'Is there any obsession unabandoned in myself that might so obsess my mind that I cannot know or see things as they actually are?' If a bhikkhu is obsessed by sensual lust, then his mind is obsessed. If he is obsessed by ill will, then his mind is obsessed. If he is obsessed by sloth and torpor, then his mind is obsessed. If he is obsessed by restlessness and remorse, then his mind is obsessed. If he is obsessed by doubt, then his mind is obsessed. If a bhikkhu is absorbed in speculation about this world, then his mind is obsessed. If a bhikkhu is absorbed in speculation about the other world, then his mind is obsessed. If a bhikkhu takes to quarrelling and brawling and is deep in disputes, stabbing others with verbal daggers, then his mind is obsessed.

"He understands thus: 'There is no obsession unabandoned in myself that might so obsess my mind that I cannot know and see things as they actually are. My mind is well disposed for awakening to the truths.'[494] This is the first knowledge attained by him that is noble, supramundane, not shared by ordinary people.

9. "Again, a noble disciple considers thus: 'When I pursue, develop, and cultivate this view, do I obtain internal serenity, do I personally obtain stillness?'

"He understands thus: 'When I pursue, develop, and cultivate this view, I obtain internal serenity, I personally obtain stillness.' This is the second knowledge attained by him that is noble, supramundane, not shared by ordinary people.

10. "Again, a noble disciple considers thus: 'Is there any other recluse or brahmin outside [the Buddha's Dispensation] possessed of a view such as I possess?'

"He understands thus: 'There is no other recluse or brahmin outside [the Buddha's Dispensation] possessed of a view [324] such as I possess.' This is the third knowledge attained by him that is noble, supramundane, not shared by ordinary people.

11. "Again, a noble disciple considers thus: 'Do I possess the character[495] of a person who possesses right view?' What is the character of a person who possesses right view? This is the character of a person who possesses right view: although he may commit some kind of offence for which a means of rehabilitation has been laid down,[496] still he at once confesses, reveals, and discloses it to the Teacher or to wise companions in the holy life, and having done that, he enters upon restraint for the future. Just as a young, tender infant lying prone at once draws back when he puts his hand or his foot on a live coal, so too, that is the character of a person who possesses right view.

"He understands thus: 'I possess the character of a person who possesses right view.' This is the fourth knowledge attained by him that is noble, supramundane, not shared by ordinary people.

12. "Again, a noble disciple considers thus: 'Do I possess the character of a person who possesses right view?' What is the character of a person who possesses right view? This is the character of a person who possesses right view: although he may be active in various matters for his companions in the holy life, yet he has a keen regard for training in the higher virtue, training in the higher mind, and training in the higher wisdom. Just as a cow with a new calf, while she grazes watches her calf, so too, that is the character of a person who possesses right view.

"He understands thus: 'I possess the character of a person who possesses right view.' This is the fifth knowledge attained by him that is noble, supramundane, not shared by ordinary people. [325]

13. "Again, a noble disciple considers thus: 'Do I possess the strength of a person who possesses right view?' What is the strength of a person who possesses right view? This is the strength of a person who possesses right view: when the Dhamma and Discipline proclaimed by the Tathāgata is being taught, he heeds it, gives it attention, engages it with all his mind, hears the Dhamma as with eager ears.

"He understands thus: 'I possess the strength of a person who possesses right view.' This is the sixth knowledge attained by him that is noble, supramundane, not shared by ordinary people.

14. "Again, a noble disciple considers thus: 'Do I possess the strength of a person who possesses right view?' What is the strength of a person who possesses right view? This is the strength of a person who possesses right view: when the Dhamma and Discipline proclaimed by the Tathāgata is being taught, he gains inspiration in the meaning, gains inspiration in the Dhamma, gains gladness connected with the Dhamma.[497]

"He understands thus: 'I possess the strength of a person who possesses right view.' This is the seventh knowledge attained by him that is noble, supramundane, not shared by ordinary people.

15. "When a noble disciple is thus possessed of seven factors, he has well sought the character for realisation of the fruit of stream-entry. When a noble disciple is thus possessed of seven factors, he possesses the fruit of stream-entry."[498]

That is what the Blessed One said. The bhikkhus were satisfied and delighted in the Blessed One's words.

49 *Brahmanimantanika Sutta*
The Invitation of a Brahmā

[326] 1. THUS HAVE I HEARD. On one occasion the Blessed One was living at Sāvatthī in Jeta's Grove, Anāthapiṇḍika's Park. There he addressed the bhikkhus thus: "Bhikkhus."—"Venerable sir," they replied. The Blessed One said this:

2. "Bhikkhus, on one occasion I was living at Ukkaṭṭhā in the Subhaga Grove at the root of a royal sāla tree.[499] Now on that occasion a pernicious view had arisen in Baka the Brahmā thus: 'This is permanent, this is everlasting, this is eternal, this is total, this is not subject to pass away; for this is where one is neither born nor ages nor dies nor passes away nor reappears, and beyond this there is no escape.'[500]

3. "I knew with my mind the thought in the mind of Baka the Brahmā, so just as quickly as a strong man might extend his flexed arm or flex his extended arm, I vanished from the root of the royal sāla tree in the Subhaga Grove at Ukkaṭṭhā and appeared in that Brahma-world. Baka the Brahmā saw me coming in the distance and said: 'Come, good sir! Welcome, good sir! It is long, good sir, since you found an opportunity to come here. Now, good sir, this is permanent, this is everlasting, this is eternal, this is total, this is not subject to pass away; for this is where one is neither born nor ages nor dies nor passes away nor reappears, and beyond this there is no escape.'

4. "When this was said, I told Baka the Brahmā: 'The worthy Baka the Brahmā has lapsed into ignorance; he has lapsed into ignorance in that he says of the impermanent that it is permanent, of the transient that it is everlasting, of the non-eternal that it is eternal, of the incomplete that it is total, of what is subject to pass away that it is not subject to pass away, of where one is born, ages, dies, passes away, and reappears, that here one is neither born nor ages nor dies nor passes away nor reappears;

and when there is an escape beyond this, he says that there is no escape beyond this.'

5. "Then Māra the Evil One took possession of a member of the Brahmā's Assembly,[501] and he told me: 'Bhikkhu, bhikkhu, do not disparage him, do not disparage him; for this Brahmā is the Great Brahmā, [327] the Overlord, the Untranscended, of Infallible Vision, Wielder of Mastery, Lord Maker and Creator, Most High Providence, Master and Father of those that are and ever can be. Before your time, bhikkhu, there were recluses and brahmins in the world who condemned earth through disgust with earth,[502] who condemned water through disgust with water, who condemned fire through disgust with fire, who condemned air through disgust with air, who condemned beings through disgust with beings, who condemned gods through disgust with gods, who condemned Pajāpati through disgust with Pajāpati, who condemned Brahmā through disgust with Brahmā; and on the dissolution of the body, when their life was cut off, they became established in an inferior body.[503] Before your time, bhikkhu, there were also recluses and brahmins in the world who lauded earth through delight in earth,[504] who lauded water through delight in water, who lauded fire through delight in fire, who lauded air through delight in air, who lauded beings through delight in beings, who lauded gods through delight in gods, who lauded Pajāpati through delight in Pajāpati, who lauded Brahmā through delight in Brahmā; and on the dissolution of the body, when their life was cut off, they became established in a superior body.[505] So, bhikkhu, I tell you this: Be sure, good sir, to do only as the Brahmā says; never overstep the word of the Brahmā. If you overstep the word of the Brahmā, bhikkhu, then, like a man trying to deflect an approaching beam of light with a stick, or like a man losing his hold on the earth with his hands and feet as he slips into a deep chasm, so it will befall you, bhikkhu. Be sure, good sir, to do only as the Brahmā says; never overstep the word of the Brahmā. Do you not see the Brahmā's Assembly seated here, bhikkhu?' And Māra the Evil One thus called to witness the Brahmā's Assembly.[506]

6. "When this was said, I told Māra the Evil One: 'I know you, Evil One. Do not think: "He does not know me." You are Māra, Evil One, and the Brahmā and the Brahmā's Assembly and the

members of the Brahmā's Assembly have all fallen into your hands, they have all fallen into your power. You, Evil One, think: "This one too has fallen into my hands, he too has fallen into my power"; but I have not fallen into your hands, Evil One, I have not fallen into your power.'

7. "When this was said, Baka the Brahmā told me: 'Good sir, I say of the permanent that it is permanent, [328] of the everlasting that it is everlasting, of the eternal that it is eternal, of the total that it is total, of what is not subject to pass away that it is not subject to pass away, of where one is neither born nor ages nor dies nor passes away nor reappears that here one is neither born nor ages nor dies nor passes away nor reappears; and when there is no escape beyond this, I say that there is no escape beyond this. Before your time, bhikkhu, there were recluses and brahmins in the world whose asceticism lasted as long as your whole life. They knew, when there is an escape beyond, that there is an escape beyond, and when there is no escape beyond, that there is no escape beyond. So, bhikkhu, I tell you this: You will find no escape beyond, and eventually you will reap only weariness and disappointment. If you will hold to earth, you will be close to me, within my domain, for me to work my will upon and punish.[507] If you hold to water...to fire...to air...to beings...to gods...to Pajāpati...to Brahmā, you will be close to me, within my domain, for me to work my will upon and punish.'

8. "'I know that too, Brahmā. If I will hold to earth, I shall be close to you, within your domain, for you to work your will upon and punish. If I will hold to water...to fire...to air...to beings...to gods...to Pajāpati...to Brahmā, I shall be close to you, within your domain, for you to work your will upon and punish. Further, I understand your reach and your sway to extend thus: Baka the Brahmā has this much power, this much might, this much influence.'

"'Now, good sir, how far do you understand my reach and my sway to extend?'

9. "'As far as moon and sun revolve
Shining and lighting up the quarters,
Over a thousandfold such world
Does your sovereignty extend.

And there you know the high and low,
And those with lust and free from lust,
The state that is thus and otherwise,
The coming and going of beings.

Brahmā, I understand your reach and your sway to extend thus: Baka the Brahmā has this much power, this much might, [329] this much influence.[508]

10. "'But, Brahmā, there are three other bodies, which you neither know nor see, and which I know and see. There is the body called [the gods of] Streaming Radiance, from which you passed away and reappeared here.[509] Because you have dwelt here long, your memory of that has lapsed, and hence you do not know or see it, but I know and see it. Thus, Brahmā, in regard to direct knowledge I do not stand merely at the same level as you, how then could I know less? Rather, I know more than you.[510]

"'There is the body called [the gods of] Refulgent Glory... There is the body called [the gods of] Great Fruit. You do not know or see that, but I know and see it. Thus, Brahmā, in regard to direct knowledge I do not stand merely at the same level as you, how then could I know less? Rather, I know more than you.

11. "'Brahmā, having directly known earth as earth, and having directly known that which is not commensurate with the earthness of earth, I did not claim to be earth, I did not claim to be in earth, I did not claim to be apart from earth, I did not claim earth to be "mine," I did not affirm earth.[511] Thus, Brahmā, in regard to direct knowledge I do not stand merely at the same level as you, how then could I know less? Rather, I know more than you.

12–23. "'Brahmā, having directly known water as water...fire as fire...air as air...beings as beings...gods as gods...Pajāpati as Pajāpati...Brahmā as Brahmā...the gods of Streaming Radiance as the gods of Streaming Radiance...the gods of Refulgent Glory as the gods of Refulgent Glory...the gods of Great Fruit as the gods of Great Fruit...the Overlord as the Overlord...all as all, and having directly known that which is not commensurate with the allness of all, I did not claim to be all, I did not claim to be in all, I did not claim to be apart from all, I did not claim all to be "mine," I did not affirm all. Thus, Brahmā, in regard to direct knowledge, I do not stand merely at the same level as you, how then could I know less? Rather, I know more than you.'

24. "'Good sir, if that is not partaken of by the allness of all, may it not turn out to be vacuous and empty for you!'[512]

25. "'Consciousness non-manifesting,
Boundless, luminous all-round:[513]

that is not commensurate with the earthness of earth, that is not commensurate with the waterness of water...[330]...that is not commensurate with the allness of all.'

26. "'Good sir, I shall vanish from you.'

"'Vanish from me if you can, Brahmā.'

"Then Baka the Brahmā, saying: 'I shall vanish from the recluse Gotama, I shall vanish from the recluse Gotama,' was unable to vanish. Thereupon I said: 'Brahmā, I shall vanish from you.'

"'Vanish from me if you can, good sir.'

"Then I performed such a feat of supernormal power that the Brahmā and the Brahmā's Assembly and the members of the Brahmā's Assembly could hear my voice but could not see me. After I had vanished, I uttered this stanza:

27. "'Having seen fear in every mode of being
And in being bound to cease to be,
I did not affirm any mode of being,
Nor did I cling to any delight [in being].'[514]

28. "At that the Brahmā and the Brahmā's Assembly and the members of the Brahmā's Assembly were struck with wonder and amazement, saying: 'It is wonderful, sirs, it is marvellous, the great power and great might of the recluse Gotama! We have never before seen or heard of any other recluse or brahmin who had such great power and such great might as has this recluse Gotama, who went forth from a Sakyan clan. Sirs, though living in a generation that delights in being, that takes delight in being, that rejoices in being, he has extirpated being together with its root.'

29. "Then Māra the Evil One took possession of a member of the Brahmā's Assembly, and he said to me: 'Good sir, if that is what you know, if that is what you have discovered, do not guide your [lay] disciples or those gone forth, do not teach the Dhamma to your [lay] disciples or to those gone forth, create no

yearning in your [lay] disciples or in those gone forth. Before your time, bhikkhu, there were recluses and brahmins in the world claiming to be accomplished and fully enlightened, and they guided their [lay] disciples and those gone forth; they taught the Dhamma to their [lay] disciples and to those gone forth; they created yearning in their [lay] disciples and in those gone forth; and on the dissolution of the body, when their life was cut off, they became established in an inferior body. Before your time, bhikkhu, there were also recluses and brahmins in the world claiming to be accomplished and fully enlightened, [331] and they did not guide their [lay] disciples or those gone forth; they did not teach the Dhamma to their [lay] disciples or to those gone forth; they created no yearning in their [lay] disciples or in those gone forth; and on the dissolution of the body, when their life was cut off, they became established in a superior body. So, bhikkhu, I tell you this: Be sure, good sir, to abide inactive, devoted to a pleasant abiding here and now; this is better left undeclared, and so, good sir, do not advise anyone else.'[515]

30. "When this was said, I told Māra the Evil One: 'I know you, Evil One. Do not think: "He does not know me." You are Māra, Evil One. It is not out of compassion for their welfare that you speak thus, it is without compassion for their welfare that you speak thus. You think thus, Evil One: "Those to whom the recluse Gotama teaches the Dhamma will escape from my sphere." Those recluses and brahmins of yours, Evil One, who claimed to be fully enlightened, were not fully enlightened. But I, who claim to be fully enlightened, am fully enlightened. If the Tathāgata teaches the Dhamma to disciples he is such, Evil One, and if the Tathāgata does not teach the Dhamma to disciples he is such.[516] If the Tathāgata guides disciples he is such, Evil One, and if the Tathāgata does not guide disciples he is such. Why is that? Because the Tathāgata has abandoned the taints that defile, bring renewal of being, give trouble, ripen in suffering, and lead to future birth, ageing, and death; he has cut them off at the root, made them like a palm stump, done away with them so that they are no longer subject to future arising. Just as a palm tree whose crown is cut off is incapable of further growth, so too, the Tathāgata has abandoned the taints that defilethem off at the root, made them like a palm stump, done away with them so that they are no longer subject to future arising.'"

31. Thus, because Māra was unable to reply, and because [it began] with the Brahmā's invitation, this discourse is entitled "On the Invitation of a Brahmā."

50 *Māratajjanīya Sutta*
The Rebuke to Māra

[332] 1. THUS HAVE I HEARD. On one occasion the venerable Mahā Moggallāna was living in the Bhagga country at Suṁsumāragira in the Bhesakaḷā Grove, the Deer Park.

2. Now on that occasion the venerable Mahā Moggallāna was walking up and down in the open. And on that occasion Māra the Evil One went into the venerable Mahā Moggallāna's belly and entered his bowels. Then the venerable Mahā Moggallāna considered thus: "Why is my belly so heavy? One would think it full of beans." Thus he left the walk and went into his dwelling, where he sat down on a seat made ready.

3. When he had sat down, he gave thorough attention to himself, and he saw that Māra the Evil One had gone into his belly and had entered his bowels. When he saw this, he said: "Come out, Evil One! Come out, Evil One! Do not harass the Tathāgata, do not harass the Tathāgata's disciple, or it will lead to your harm and suffering for a long time."

4. Then Māra the Evil One thought: "This recluse does not know me, he does not see me when he says that. Even his teacher would not know me so soon, so how can this disciple know me?"

5. Then the venerable Mahā Moggallāna said: "Even thus I know you, Evil One. Do not think: 'He does not know me.' You are Māra, Evil One. You were thinking thus, Evil One: 'This recluse does not know me, he does not see me when he says that. Even his teacher would not know me so soon, so how can this disciple know me?'"

6. Then Māra the Evil One thought: "The recluse knew me, he saw me when he said that," whereupon he [333] came up from the venerable Mahā Moggallāna's mouth and stood against the door bar.

7. The venerable Mahā Moggallāna saw him standing there and said: "I see you there too, Evil One. Do not think: 'He does not see me.' You are standing against the door bar, Evil One.

8. "It happened once, Evil One, that I was a Māra named Dūsī,[517] and I had a sister named Kālī. You were her son, so you were my nephew.

9. "Now on that occasion the Blessed One Kakusandha, accomplished and fully enlightened, had appeared in the world.[518] The Blessed One Kakusandha, accomplished and fully enlightened, had an auspicious pair of chief disciples named Vidhura and Sañjīva. Among all the disciples of the Blessed One Kakusandha, accomplished and fully enlightened, there was none equal to the venerable Vidhura in teaching the Dhamma. That was how the venerable Vidhura came to have the designation 'Vidhura.'[519] But the venerable Sañjīva, gone to the forest or to the root of a tree or to an empty hut, entered without difficulty upon the cessation of perception and feeling.

10. "It happened once, Evil One, that the venerable Sañjīva had seated himself at the root of a certain tree and entered upon the cessation of perception and feeling. Some cowherds, shepherds, ploughmen, and travellers saw the venerable Sañjīva sitting at the root of the tree having entered upon the cessation of perception and feeling, and they thought: 'It is wonderful, sirs, it is marvellous! There is this recluse sitting here dead. Let us cremate him.' Then the cowherds, shepherds, ploughmen, and travellers collected grass, wood, and cowdung, and having piled it up against the venerable Sañjīva's body, they set fire to it and went on their way.

11. "Now, Evil One, when the night had ended, the venerable Sañjīva emerged from the attainment.[520] He shook his robe, and then, it being morning, he dressed, and taking his bowl and outer robe, he went into the village for alms. The cowherds, shepherds, ploughmen, and travellers saw the venerable Sañjīva wandering for alms, and they thought: 'It is wonderful, sirs, it is marvellous! This recluse who was sitting there dead has come back to life!' [334] That was how the venerable Sañjīva came to have the designation 'Sañjīva.'[521]

12. "Then, Evil One, the Māra Dūsī considered thus: 'There are these virtuous bhikkhus of good character, but I do not know their coming or their going. Let me now take possession of the

brahmin householders, telling them: "Come now, abuse, revile, scold, and harass the virtuous bhikkhus of good character; then perhaps, when they are abused, reviled, scolded, and harassed by you, some change will come about in their minds whereby the Māra Dūsī may find an opportunity."'[522]

13. "Then, Evil One, the Māra Dūsī took possession of those brahmin householders, telling them: 'Come now, abuse, revile, scold, and harass the virtuous bhikkhus of good character; then perhaps, when they are abused, reviled, scolded, and harassed by you, some change will come about in their minds whereby the Māra Dūsī may find an opportunity.' Then, when the Māra Dūsī had taken possession of the brahmin householders, they abused, reviled, scolded, and harassed the virtuous bhikkhus of good character thus:[523] 'These bald-pated recluses, these swarthy menial offspring of the Kinsman's feet,[524] claim: "We are meditators, we are meditators!" and with shoulders drooping, heads down and all limp, they meditate, premeditate, out-meditate, and mismeditate.[525] Just as an owl on a branch waiting for a mouse meditates, premeditates, out-meditates, and mismeditates, or just as a jackal on a river-bank waiting for fish meditates, premeditates, out-meditates, and mismeditates, or just as a cat, waiting for a mouse by an alley or drain or rubbish bin, meditates, premeditates, out-meditates, and mismeditates, or just as a donkey unladen, standing by a door-post or a dust-bin or a drain, meditates, premeditates, out-meditates, and mismeditates, so too, these bald-pated recluses, these swarthy menial offspring of the Kinsman's feet, claim: "We are meditators, we are meditators!" and with shoulders drooping, heads down and all limp, they meditate, premeditate, out-meditate, and mismeditate.' Now, Evil One, on that occasion most of those human beings, when they died, reappeared on the dissolution of the body, after death, in a state of deprivation, in an unhappy destination, in perdition, even in hell. [335]

14. "Then the Blessed One Kakusandha, accomplished and fully enlightened, addressed the bhikkhus thus: 'Bhikkhus, the Māra Dūsī has taken possession of the brahmin householders, telling them: "Come now, abuse, revile, scold, and harass the virtuous bhikkhus of good character; then perhaps, when they are abused, reviled, scolded, and harassed by you, some change will come about in their mind whereby the Māra Dūsī may find

an opportunity." Come, bhikkhus, abide pervading one quarter with a mind imbued with loving-kindness, likewise the second, likewise the third, likewise the fourth; so above, below, around, and everywhere, and to all as to yourselves, abide pervading the all-encompassing world with a mind imbued with loving-kindness, abundant, exalted, immeasurable, without hostility and without ill will. Abide pervading one quarter with a mind imbued with compassion...with a mind imbued with altruistic joy...with a mind imbued with equanimity... abundant, exalted, immeasurable, without hostility and without ill will.'[526]

15. "So, Evil One, when those bhikkhus had been thus advised and instructed by the Blessed One Kakusandha, accomplished and fully enlightened, then, gone to the forest or to the root of a tree or to an empty hut, they abided pervading one quarter with a mind imbued with loving-kindness...with a mind imbued with compassion...with a mind imbued with appreciative joy...with a mind imbued with equanimity...without hostility and without ill will.

16. "Then, Evil One, the Māra Dūsī considered thus: 'Though I do as I am doing, still I do not know the coming or the going of these virtuous bhikkhus of good character. Let me now take possession of the brahmin householders, telling them: "Come now, honour, respect, revere, and venerate the virtuous bhikkhus of good character; [336] then perhaps, when they are honoured, respected, revered, and venerated by you, some change will come about in their minds whereby the Māra Dūsī may find an opportunity."'[527]

17. "Then, Evil One, the Māra Dūsī took possession of those brahmin householders, telling them: 'Come now, honour, respect, revere, and venerate the virtuous bhikkhus of good character; then perhaps, when they are honoured, respected, revered, and venerated by you, some change will come about in their minds whereby the Māra Dūsī may find an opportunity.' Then, when the Māra Dūsī had taken possession of the brahmin householders, they honoured, respected, revered, and venerated the virtuous bhikkhus of good character. Now, Evil One, on that occasion most of those human beings, when they died, reappeared on the dissolution of the body, after death, in a happy destination, even the heavenly world.

18. "Then, Evil One, the Blessed One Kakusandha, accomplished and fully enlightened, addressed the bhikkhus thus: 'Bhikkhus, the Māra Dūsī has taken possession of those brahmin householders, telling them: "Come now, honour, respect, revere, and venerate the virtuous bhikkhus of good character; then perhaps, when they are honoured, respected, revered, and venerated by you, some change will come about in their minds whereby the Māra Dūsī may find an opportunity." Come, bhikkhus, abide contemplating foulness in the body, perceiving repulsiveness in nutriment, perceiving disenchantment with all the world, contemplating impermanence in all formations.'[528]

19. "So, Evil One, when those bhikkhus had been thus advised and instructed by the Blessed One Kakusandha, accomplished and fully enlightened, then, gone to the forest or to the root of a tree or to an empty hut, they abided contemplating foulness in the body, perceiving repulsiveness in nutriment, perceiving disenchantment with all the world, contemplating impermanence in all formations.

20. "Then, when it was morning, the Blessed One Kakusandha, accomplished and fully enlightened, dressed, and taking his bowl and outer robe, he went into the village for alms with the venerable Vidhura as his attendant.

21. "Then the Māra Dūsī took possession of a certain boy, and picking up a stone, he struck the venerable Vidhura on the head with it and cut his head. With blood running from his cut head, [337] the venerable Vidhura followed close behind the Blessed One Kakusandha, accomplished and fully enlightened. Then the Blessed One Kakusandha, accomplished and fully enlightened, turned around and looked at him with the elephant look: 'This Māra Dūsī knows no bounds.' And with that look, Evil One, the Māra Dūsī fell from that place and reappeared in the Great Hell.[529]

22. "Now, Evil One, there are three names for the Great Hell: the hell of the six bases for contact, the hell of the impalement with stakes, and the hell to be felt for oneself.[530] Then, Evil One, the wardens of hell came up to me and said: 'Good sir, when stake meets stake in your heart, then you will know: "I have been roasting in hell for a thousand years."'

23. "For many a year, Evil One, for many a century, for many a millennium, I roasted in that Great Hell. For ten millennia I roasted in the auxiliary of that Great Hell, experiencing the

feeling called that of emergence from ripening.[531] My body had the same form as a human body, Evil One, but my head had the form of a fish's head.

24. "What can hell be well compared to
Wherein Dūsī roasted, assailant
Of Vidhura the disciple
And the brahmin Kakusandha?[532]
Stakes of steel, even a hundred,
Each one suffered separately;
These can hell be well compared to
Wherein Dūsī roasted, assailant
Of Vidhura the disciple
And the brahmin Kakusandha.

Dark One, you have much to suffer
By assaulting such a bhikkhu,
An Enlightened One's disciple
Who directly knows this fact.

25. "In the middle of the ocean
There are mansions aeon-lasting,
Sapphire-shining, fiery-gleaming
With a clear translucent lustre,
Where iridescent sea-nymphs dance
In complex, intricate rhythms.

Dark One, you have much to suffer...
Who directly knows this fact.

26. "I am one who, when exhorted
By the Enlightened One in person,
Shook Migāra's Mother's Palace
With his toe, the Order watching.[533]

Dark One, you have much to suffer...
Who directly knows this fact.

27. "I am one who, wielding firmly
Strength of supernormal powers,

Shook all Vejayanta Palace
With his toe to incite the gods:[534] [338]

Dark One, you have much to suffer…
Who directly knows this fact.

28. "I am one who, in that palace,
Posed to Sakka this question:
'Do you know then, friend, deliverance
In craving's utter destruction?'
Whereupon Sakka then answered
Truly to the question asked him:[535]

Dark One, you have much to suffer…
Who directly knows this fact.

29. "I am one who thought of posing
Brahmā this question
In Sudhamma Hall in heaven:
'Is there still found in you, friend,
The wrong view you once accepted?
Is the radiance of heaven
Clearly seen by you as passing?'
Brahmā then answered my question
Truthfully and in due sequence:
'There is found in me no longer,
Sir, the wrong view that once I held;
All the radiance of heaven
I now clearly see as passing;
I disclaim my prior claim
That it is permanent, eternal':[536]

Dark One, you have much to suffer…
Who directly knows this fact.

30. "I am one who, by liberation,
Has touched the peak of Mount Sineru,
Visited India and Pubbavideha
And all the regions of the earth.[537]

Dark One, you have much to suffer
By assaulting such a bhikkhu,
An Enlightened One's disciple
Who directly knows this fact.

31. "There has never been found a fire
Which intends, 'Let me burn the fool,'
But a fool who assaults a fire
Burns himself by his own doing.
So it is with you, O Māra:
By assaulting the Tathāgata,
Like a fool who plays with fire
You only burn yourself alone.
By assaulting the Tathāgata,
You generate much demerit.
Evil One, do you imagine
That your evil will not ripen?
Doing thus, you store up evil
Which will last long, O End-maker!
Māra, shun the Enlightened One,
Play no more your tricks on bhikkhus."

So the bhikkhu chastened Māra
In the Bhesakaḷā thicket
Whereupon the sombre spirit
Disappeared right then and there.

Part Two
The Middle Fifty Discourses
(*Majjhimapaṇṇāsapāḷi*)

1

The Division on Householders

(*Gahapativagga*)

51 *Kandaraka Sutta*
To Kandaraka

[339] 1. THUS HAVE I HEARD. On one occasion the Blessed One was living at Campā on the banks of the Gaggarā Lake with a large Sangha of bhikkhus. Then Pessa, the elephant driver's son, and Kandaraka the wanderer went to the Blessed One. Pessa, after paying homage to the Blessed One, sat down at one side, while Kandaraka exchanged greetings with the Blessed One, and when this courteous and amiable talk was finished, he stood at one side.[538] Standing there, he surveyed the Sangha of bhikkhus sitting in complete silence,[539] and then he said to the Blessed One:

2. "It is wonderful, Master Gotama, it is marvellous how the Sangha of bhikkhus has been led to practise the right way by Master Gotama. Those who were Blessed Ones, accomplished and fully enlightened in the past, at most only led the Sangha of bhikkhus to practise the right way as is done by Master Gotama now. And those who will be Blessed Ones, accomplished and fully enlightened in the future, at most will only lead the Sangha of bhikkhus to practise the right way as is done by Master Gotama now."[540]

3. "So it is, Kandaraka, so it is! Those who were Blessed Ones, accomplished and fully enlightened in the past, at most only led the Sangha of bhikkhus to practise the right way as is done by me now. And those who will be Blessed Ones, accomplished and fully enlightened in the future, at most will only lead the Sangha of bhikkhus to practise the right way as is done by me now.

"Kandaraka, in this Sangha of bhikkhus there are bhikkhus who are arahants with taints destroyed, who have lived the holy life, done what had to be done, laid down the burden, reached the true goal, destroyed the fetters of being, and who are completely liberated through final knowledge. In this Sangha of bhikkhus there are bhikkhus in higher training, of constant virtue, living a life of constant virtue, sagacious, living a life of constant sagacity. They abide with their minds well established in the four foundations of mindfulness.[541] What four? Here, Kandaraka, [340] a bhikkhu abides contemplating the body as a body, ardent, fully aware, and mindful, having put away covetousness and grief for the world. He abides contemplating feelings as feelings, ardent, fully aware, and mindful, having put away covetousness and grief for the world. He abides contemplating mind as mind, ardent, fully aware, and mindful, having put away covetousness and grief for the world. He abides contemplating mind-objects as mind-objects, ardent, fully aware, and mindful, having put away covetousness and grief for the world."

4. When this was said, Pessa, the elephant driver's son, said: "It is wonderful, venerable sir, it is marvellous how well the four foundations of mindfulness have been made known by the Blessed One: for the purification of beings, for the surmounting of sorrow and lamentation, for the disappearance of pain and grief, for the attainment of the true way, for the realisation of Nibbāna. From time to time, venerable sir, we white-clothed lay people also abide with our minds well established in these four foundations of mindfulness.[542] Here, venerable sir, we abide contemplating the body as a body...feelings as feelings...mind as mind...mind-objects as mind-objects, ardent, fully aware, and mindful, having put away covetousness and grief for the world. It is wonderful, venerable sir, it is marvellous how amid man's tangle, corruption, and deceptions, the Blessed One knows the welfare and harm of beings. For humankind is a tangle but the animal is open enough. Venerable sir, I can drive an elephant to be tamed, and in the time it takes to make a trip back and forth in Campā, that elephant will show every kind of deception, duplicity, crookedness, and fraud [he is capable of].[543] But those who are called our slaves, messengers, and servants behave in one way with the body, in another way by speech, while their minds work in still another way. It is wonderful, venerable sir, it is marvellous how amid man's tangle, corruption, and deceptions, the Blessed One knows the welfare and harm of beings. For humankind is a tangle but the animal is open enough."

5. "So it is, Pessa, so it is! [341] Humankind is a tangle but the animal is open enough. Pessa, there are four kinds of persons to be found existing in the world.[544] What four? Here a certain kind of person torments himself and pursues the practice of torturing himself. Here a certain kind of person torments others and pursues the practice of torturing others. Here a certain kind of person torments himself and pursues the practice of torturing himself, and he also torments others and pursues the practice of torturing others. Here a certain kind of person does not torment himself or pursue the practice of torturing himself, and he does not torment others or pursue the practice of torturing others. Since he torments neither himself nor others, he is here and now hungerless, extinguished, and cooled, and he abides experiencing bliss, having himself become holy.[545] Which of these four kinds of persons satisfies your mind, Pessa?"

"The first three do not satisfy my mind, venerable sir, but the last one satisfies my mind."

6. "But, Pessa, why don't the first three kinds of persons satisfy your mind?"

"Venerable sir, the kind of person who torments himself and pursues the practice of torturing himself, torments and tortures himself though he desires pleasure and recoils from pain; that is why this kind of person does not satisfy my mind. And the kind of person who torments others and pursues the practice of torturing others, torments and tortures others who desire pleasure and recoil from pain; that is why this kind of person does not satisfy my mind. And the kind of person who torments himself and pursues the practice of torturing himself, and who also torments others and pursues the practice of torturing others, torments and tortures himself and others, both of whom desire pleasure and recoil from pain; that is why this kind of person does not satisfy my mind. [342] But the kind of person who does not torment himself or pursue the practice of torturing himself and who does not torment others or pursue the practice of torturing others; who, since he torments neither himself nor others, is here and now hungerless, extinguished, and cooled, and abides experiencing bliss, having himself become holy—he does not torment and torture either himself or others, both of whom desire pleasure and recoil from pain. That is why this kind of person satisfies my mind. And now, venerable sir, we depart. We are busy and have much to do."

"You may go, Pessa, at your own convenience."

Then Pessa, the elephant driver's son, having delighted and rejoiced in the Blessed One's words, rose from his seat, and after paying homage to the Blessed One, keeping him on his right, he departed.

7. Soon after he had left, the Blessed One addressed the bhikkhus thus: "Bhikkhus, Pessa, the elephant driver's son, is wise, he has great wisdom. If he had sat a while longer until I had expounded for him in detail these four kinds of persons, he would have greatly benefited. Still he has already greatly benefited even as it is."[546]

"This is the time, Blessed One, this is the time, Sublime One, for the Blessed One to expound in detail these four kinds of persons. Having heard it from the Blessed One, the bhikkhus will remember it."

"Then, bhikkhus, listen and attend closely to what I shall say."

"Yes, venerable sir," the bhikkhus replied. The Blessed One said this:

8. "Bhikkhus, what kind of person torments himself and pursues the practice of torturing himself?[547] Here a certain person goes naked, rejecting conventions, licking his hands, not coming when asked, not stopping when asked; he does not accept food brought or food specially made or an invitation to a meal; he receives nothing from a pot, from a bowl, across a threshold, across a stick, across a pestle, from two eating together, from a pregnant woman, from a woman giving suck, from a woman in the midst of men, from where food is advertised to be distributed, from where a dog is waiting, from where flies are buzzing; he accepts no fish or meat, he drinks no liquor, wine, or fermented brew. He keeps to one house, to one morsel; he keeps to two houses to two morsels;...he keeps to seven houses, to seven morsels. He lives on one saucerful a day, on two saucerfuls a day...on seven saucerfuls a day. He takes food once a day, [343] once every two days...once every seven days; thus even up to once every fortnight, he dwells pursuing the practice of taking food at stated intervals. He is an eater of greens or millet or wild rice or hide-parings or moss or ricebran or rice-scum or sesamum flour or grass or cowdung. He lives on forest roots and fruits, he

feeds on fallen fruits. He clothes himself in hemp, in hemp-mixed cloth, in shrouds, in refuse rags, in tree bark, in antelope hide, in strips of antelope hide, in kusa-grass fabric, in bark fabric, in wood-shavings fabric, in head-hair wool, in animal wool, in owls' wings. He is one who pulls out hair and beard, pursuing the practice of pulling out hair and beard. He is one who stands continuously, rejecting seats. He is one who squats continuously, devoted to maintaining the squatting position. He is one who uses a mattress of spikes; he makes a mattress of spikes his bed. He dwells pursuing the practice of bathing in water three times daily including the evening. Thus in such a variety of ways he dwells pursuing the practice of tormenting and mortifying the body. This is called the kind of person who torments himself and pursues the practice of torturing himself.

9. "What kind of person, bhikkhus, torments others and pursues the practice of torturing others? Here a certain person is a butcher of sheep, a butcher of pigs, a fowler, a trapper of wild beasts, a hunter, a fisherman, a thief, an executioner, a prison warden, or one who follows any other such bloody occupation. This is called the kind of person who torments others and pursues the practice of torturing others.

10. "What kind of person, bhikkhus, torments himself and pursues the practice of torturing himself and also torments others and pursues the practice of torturing others? Here some person is a head-anointed noble king or a well-to-do brahmin.[548] Having had a new sacrificial temple built to the east of the city, and having shaved off his hair and beard, dressed himself in rough hide, and greased his body with ghee and oil, scratching his back with a deer's horn, he enters the sacrificial temple together with his chief queen and his brahmin high priest. There he lies down on the bare ground with the grass on it. The king lives on the milk in the first teat of a cow with a calf of the same colour [344] while the chief queen lives on the milk in the second teat and the brahmin high priest lives on the milk in the third teat; the milk in the fourth teat they pour onto the fire, and the calf lives on what is left. He says thus: 'Let so many bulls be slaughtered for sacrifice, let so many bullocks be slaughtered for sacrifice, let so many heifers be slaughtered for sacrifice, let so many goats be slaughtered for sacrifice, let so many sheep be slaughtered for sacrifice, let so many trees be

felled for the sacrificial posts, let so much grass be cut for the sacrificial grass.' And then his slaves, messengers, and servants make preparations, weeping with tearful faces, being spurred on by threats of punishment and by fear. This is called the kind of person who torments himself and pursues the practice of torturing himself and who torments others and pursues the practice of torturing others.

11. "What kind of person, bhikkhus, does not torment himself or pursue the practice of torturing himself and does not torment others or pursue the practice of tormenting others—the one who, since he torments neither himself nor others, is here and now hungerless, extinguished, and cooled, and abides experiencing bliss, having himself become holy?[549]

12. "Here, bhikkhus, a Tathāgata appears in the world, accomplished, fully enlightened, perfect in true knowledge and conduct, sublime, knower of worlds, incomparable leader of persons to be tamed, teacher of gods and humans, enlightened, blessed. He declares this world with its gods, its Māras, and its Brahmās, this generation with its recluses and brahmins, its princes and its people, which he has himself realised by direct knowledge. He teaches the Dhamma good in the beginning, good in the middle, and good in the end, with the right meaning and phrasing, and he reveals a holy life that is utterly perfect and pure.

13. "A householder or householder's son or one born in some other clan hears that Dhamma. On hearing the Dhamma he acquires faith in the Tathāgata. Possessing that faith, he considers thus: 'Household life is crowded and dusty; life gone forth is wide open. It is not easy, while living in a home, to lead the holy life utterly perfect and pure as a polished shell. Suppose I shave off my hair and beard, put on the yellow robe, and go forth from the home life into homelessness.' On a later occasion, abandoning a small or a large fortune, [345] abandoning a small or a large circle of relatives, he shaves off his hair and beard, puts on the yellow robe, and goes forth from the home life into homelessness.

14. "Having thus gone forth and possessing the bhikkhus' training and way of life, abandoning the killing of living beings, he abstains from killing living beings; with rod and weapon laid aside, gentle and kindly, he abides compassionate to all living beings. Abandoning the taking of what is not given, he abstains

from taking what is not given; taking only what is given, expecting only what is given, by not stealing he abides in purity. Abandoning incelibacy, he observes celibacy, living apart, abstaining from the vulgar practice of sexual intercourse.

"Abandoning false speech, he abstains from false speech; he speaks truth, adheres to truth, is trustworthy and reliable, one who is no deceiver of the world. Abandoning malicious speech, he abstains from malicious speech; he does not repeat elsewhere what he has heard here in order to divide [those people] from these, nor does he repeat to these people what he has heard elsewhere in order to divide [these people] from those; thus he is one who reunites those who are divided, a promoter of friendships, who enjoys concord, rejoices in concord, delights in concord, a speaker of words that promote concord. Abandoning harsh speech, he abstains from harsh speech; he speaks such words as are gentle, pleasing to the ear, and loveable, as go to the heart, are courteous, desired by many and agreeable to many. Abandoning gossip, he abstains from gossip; he speaks at the right time, speaks what is fact, speaks on what is good, speaks on the Dhamma and the Discipline; at the right time he speaks such words as are worth recording, reasonable, moderate, and beneficial.

"He abstains from injuring seeds and plants. He practises eating only meal a day, abstaining from eating at night and outside the proper time. He abstains from dancing, singing, music, and theatrical shows. He abstains from wearing garlands, smartening himself with scent, and embellishing himself with unguents. He abstains from high and large couches. He abstains from accepting gold and silver. He abstains from accepting raw grain. He abstains from accepting raw meat. He abstains from accepting women and girls. He abstains from accepting men and women slaves. He abstains from accepting goats and sheep. He abstains from accepting fowl and pigs. He abstains from accepting elephants, cattle, horses, and mares. He abstains from accepting fields and land. He abstains from going on errands and running messages. He abstains from buying and selling. He abstains from false weights, false metals, and false measures. [346] He abstains from cheating, deceiving, defrauding, and trickery. He abstains from wounding, murdering, binding, brigandage, plunder, and violence.

15. "He becomes content with robes to protect his body and with almsfood to maintain his stomach, and wherever he goes he sets out taking only these with him. Just as a bird, wherever it goes, flies with its wings as its only burden, so too, the bhikkhu becomes content with robes to protect his body and with almsfood to maintain his stomach, and wherever he goes he sets out taking only these with him. Possessing this aggregate of noble virtue, he experiences within himself a bliss that is blameless.

16. "On seeing a form with the eye, he does not grasp at its signs and features. Since, if he left the eye faculty unguarded, evil unwholesome states of covetousness and grief might invade him, he practises the way of its restraint, he guards the eye faculty, he undertakes the restraint of the eye faculty. On hearing a sound with the ear...On smelling an odour with the nose...On tasting a flavour with the tongue...On touching a tangible with the body...On cognizing a mind-object with the mind, he does not grasp at its signs and features. Since, if he left the mind faculty unguarded, evil unwholesome states of covetousness and grief might invade him, he practises the way of its restraint, he guards the mind faculty, he undertakes the restraint of the mind faculty. Possessing this noble restraint of the faculties, he experiences within himself a bliss that is unsullied.

17. "He becomes one who acts in full awareness when going forward and returning; who acts in full awareness when looking ahead and looking away; who acts in full awareness when flexing and extending his limbs; who acts in full awareness when wearing his robes and carrying his outer robe and bowl; who acts in full awareness when eating, drinking, consuming food, and tasting; who acts in full awareness when defecating and urinating; who acts in full awareness when walking, standing, sitting, falling asleep, waking up, talking, and keeping silent.

18. "Possessing this aggregate of noble virtue, and this noble restraint of the faculties, and possessing this noble mindfulness and full awareness, he resorts to a secluded resting place: the forest, the root of a tree, a mountain, a ravine, a hillside cave, a charnel ground, a jungle thicket, an open space, a heap of straw.

19. "On returning from his almsround, after his meal he sits down, folding his legs crosswise, setting his body erect, and establishing mindfulness before him. [347] Abandoning covetousness for the world, he abides with a mind free from covetousness;

he purifies his mind from covetousness. Abandoning ill will and hatred, he abides with a mind free from ill will, compassionate for the welfare of all living beings; he purifies his mind from ill will and hatred. Abandoning sloth and torpor, he abides free from sloth and torpor, percipient of light, mindful and fully aware; he purifies his mind from sloth and torpor. Abandoning restlessness and remorse, he abides unagitated with a mind inwardly peaceful; he purifies his mind from restlessness and remorse. Abandoning doubt, he abides having gone beyond doubt, unperplexed about wholesome states; he purifies his mind from doubt.

20. "Having thus abandoned these five hindrances, imperfections of the mind that weaken wisdom, quite secluded from sensual pleasures, secluded from unwholesome states, he enters upon and abides in the first jhāna, which is accompanied by applied and sustained thought, with rapture and pleasure born of seclusion.

21. "Again, with the stilling of applied and sustained thought, he enters upon and abides in the second jhāna, which has self-confidence and singleness of mind without applied and sustained thought, with rapture and pleasure born of concentration.

22. "Again, with the fading away as well of rapture, he abides in equanimity, and mindful and fully aware, still feeling pleasure with the body, he enters upon and abides in the third jhāna, on account of which noble ones announce: 'He has a pleasant abiding who has equanimity and is mindful.'

23. "Again, with the abandoning of pleasure and pain, and with the previous disappearance of joy and grief, he enters upon and abides in the fourth jhāna, which has neither-pain-nor-pleasure and purity of mindfulness due to equanimity.

24. "When his concentrated mind is thus purified, bright, unblemished, rid of imperfection, malleable, wieldy, steady, and attained to imperturbability, he directs it to knowledge of the recollection of past lives. He recollects his manifold past lives, that is, one birth, two births, three births, four births, five births, ten births, twenty births, thirty births, forty births, fifty births, a hundred births, a thousand births, a hundred thousand births, many aeons of world-contraction, many aeons of world-expansion, many aeons of world-contraction and expansion: 'There I was so named, of such a clan, with such an appearance, such

was my nutriment, such my experience of pleasure and pain, such my life-term; and passing away from there, I reappeared elsewhere; and there too I was so named, of such a clan, with such an appearance, such was my nutriment, such my experience of pleasure and pain, [348] such my life-term; and passing away from there, I reappeared here.' Thus with their aspects and particulars he recollects his manifold past lives.

25. "When his concentrated mind is thus purified, bright, unblemished, rid of imperfection, malleable, wieldy, steady, and attained to imperturbability, he directs it to knowledge of the passing away and reappearance of beings. With the divine eye, which is purified and surpasses the human, he sees beings passing away and reappearing, inferior and superior, fair and ugly, fortunate and unfortunate. He understands how beings pass on according to their actions thus: 'These worthy beings who were ill conducted in body, speech, and mind, revilers of noble ones, wrong in their views, giving effect to wrong view in their actions, on the dissolution of the body, after death, have reappeared in a state of deprivation, in a bad destination, in perdition, even in hell; but these worthy beings who were well conducted in body, speech, and mind, not revilers of noble ones, right in their views, giving effect to right view in their actions, on the dissolution of the body, after death, have reappeared in a good destination, even in the heavenly world.' Thus with the divine eye, which is purified and surpasses the human, he sees beings passing away and reappearing, inferior and superior, fair and ugly, fortunate and unfortunate, and he understands how beings pass on according to their actions.

26. "When his concentrated mind is thus purified, bright, unblemished, rid of imperfection, malleable, wieldy, steady, and attained to imperturbability, he directs it to knowledge of the destruction of the taints. He understands as it actually is: 'This is suffering'; he understands as it actually is: 'This is the origin of suffering'; he understands as it actually is: 'This is the cessation of suffering'; he understands as it actually is: 'This is the way leading to the cessation of suffering.' He understands as it actually is: 'These are the taints'; he understands as it actually is: 'This is the origin of the taints'; he understands as it actually is: 'This is the cessation of the taints'; he understands as it actually is: 'This is the way leading to the cessation of the taints.'

27. "When he knows and sees thus, his mind is liberated from the taint of sensual desire, from the taint of being, and from the taint of ignorance. When it is liberated there comes the knowledge: 'It is liberated.' He understands: 'Birth is destroyed, the holy life has been lived, what had to be done has been done, there is no more coming to any state of being.'

28. "This, bhikkhus, is called the kind of person who does not torment himself or pursue the practice of torturing himself and who does not torment others or pursue the practice of torturing others [349]—the one who, since he torments neither himself nor others, is here and now hungerless, extinguished, and cooled, and abides experiencing bliss, having himself become holy."

That is what the Blessed One said. The bhikkhus were satisfied and delighted in the Blessed One's words.

52 *Aṭṭhakanāgara Sutta*
The Man from Aṭṭhakanāgara

1. THUS HAVE I HEARD. On one occasion the Venerable Ānanda was living at Beluvagāmaka near Vesālī.

2. Now on that occasion the householder Dasama of Aṭṭhakanāgara had arrived at Pāṭaliputta for some business or other. Then he went to a certain bhikkhu in Kukkuṭa's Park, and after paying homage to him, he sat down at one side and asked him: "Where does the venerable Ānanda live now, venerable sir? I wish to see the venerable Ānanda."

"The venerable Ānanda is living at Beluvagāmaka near Vesālī, householder."

3. When the householder Dasama had completed his business at Pāṭaliputta, he went to the venerable Ānanda at Beluvagāmaka near Vesālī. After paying homage to him, he sat down at one side and asked him:

"Venerable Ānanda, has any one thing been proclaimed by the Blessed One who knows and sees, accomplished and fully enlightened, wherein if a bhikkhu abides diligent, ardent, and resolute, his unliberated mind comes to be liberated, his undestroyed taints come to be destroyed, and he attains the supreme security from bondage that he had not attained before?"[550]

"Yes, householder, one such thing has been proclaimed by the Blessed One." [350]

"What is that one thing, venerable Ānanda?"

4. "Here, householder, quite secluded from sensual pleasures, secluded from unwholesome states, a bhikkhu enters upon and abides in the first jhāna, which is accompanied by applied and sustained thought, with rapture and pleasure born of seclusion. He considers this and understands it thus: 'This first jhāna is conditioned and volitionally produced.[551] But whatever is conditioned and volitionally produced is impermanent, subject to

cessation.' If he is steady in that, he attains the destruction of the taints.[552] But if he does not attain the destruction of the taints because of that desire for the Dhamma, that delight in the Dhamma,[553] then with the destruction of the five lower fetters he becomes one due to reappear spontaneously [in the Pure Abodes] and there attain final Nibbāna without ever returning from that world.

"This is one thing proclaimed by the Blessed One who knows and sees, accomplished and fully enlightened, wherein if a bhikkhu abides diligent, ardent, and resolute, his unliberated mind comes to be liberated, his undestroyed taints come to be destroyed, and he attains the supreme security from bondage that he had not attained before.

5. "Again, with the stilling of applied and sustained thought, a bhikkhu enters and abides in the second jhāna...He considers this and understands it thus: 'This second jhāna is conditioned and volitionally produced. But whatever is conditioned and volitionally produced is impermanent, subject to cessation.' If he is steady in that, he attains the destruction of the taints. But if he does not attain the destruction of the taints...without ever returning from that world.

"This too is one thing proclaimed by the Blessed One [351]... wherein if a bhikkhu abides diligent, ardent, and resolute...he attains the supreme security from bondage that he had not attained before.

6. "Again, with the fading away as well of rapture, a bhikkhu...enters upon and abides in the third jhāna...He considers this and understands it thus: 'This third jhāna is conditioned and volitionally produced. But whatever is conditioned and volitionally produced is impermanent, subject to cessation.' If he is steady in that, he attains the destruction of the taints. But if he does not attain the destruction of the taints...without ever returning from that world.

"This too is one thing proclaimed by the Blessed One... wherein if a bhikkhu abides diligent, ardent, and resolute...he attains the supreme security from bondage that he had not attained before.

7. "Again, with the abandoning of pleasure and pain...a bhikkhu enters upon and abides in the fourth jhāna...He considers this and understands it thus: 'This fourth jhāna is conditioned

and volitionally produced. But whatever is conditioned and volitionally produced is impermanent, subject to cessation.' If he is steady in that, he attains the destruction of the taints. But if he does not attain the destruction of the taints...without ever returning from that world.

"This too is one thing proclaimed by the Blessed One... wherein if a bhikkhu abides diligent, ardent, and resolute...he attains the supreme security from bondage that he had not attained before.

8. "Again, a bhikkhu abides pervading one quarter with a mind imbued with loving-kindness, likewise the second, likewise the third, likewise the fourth; so above, below, around, and everywhere, and to all as to himself, he abides pervading the all-encompassing world with a mind imbued with loving-kindness, abundant, exalted, immeasurable, without hostility and without ill will. He considers this and understands it thus: 'This deliverance of mind through loving-kindness is conditioned and volitionally produced. But whatever is conditioned and volitionally produced is impermanent, subject to cessation.' If he is steady in that, he attains the destruction of the taints. But if he does not attain the destruction of the taints...without ever returning from that world.

"This too is one thing proclaimed by the Blessed One... wherein if a bhikkhu abides diligent, ardent, and resolute...he attains the supreme security from bondage that he had not attained before.

9. "Again, a bhikkhu abides pervading one quarter with a mind imbued with compassion...without ill will. He considers this and understands it thus: 'This deliverance of mind through compassion is conditioned and volitionally produced. But whatever is conditioned and volitionally produced is impermanent, subject to cessation.' If he is steady in that, he attains the destruction of the taints. But if he does not attain the destruction of the taints...without ever returning from that world.

"This too is one thing proclaimed by the Blessed One... wherein if a bhikkhu abides diligent, ardent, and resolute...he attains the supreme security from bondage that he had not attained before.

10. "Again, a bhikkhu abides pervading one quarter with a mind imbued with altruistic joy...without ill will. He considers

this and understands it thus: 'This deliverance of mind through altruistic joy is conditioned and volitionally produced. But whatever is conditioned and volitionally produced is impermanent, subject to cessation.' If he is steady in that, he attains the destruction of the taints. But if he does not attain the destruction of the taints...without ever returning from that world.

"This too is one thing proclaimed by the Blessed One... wherein if a bhikkhu abides diligent, ardent, and resolute...he attains the supreme security from bondage that he had not attained before.

11. "Again, a bhikkhu abides pervading one quarter with a mind imbued with equanimity...without ill will. He considers this and understands it thus: 'This deliverance of mind through equanimity is conditioned and volitionally produced. But whatever is conditioned and volitionally produced is impermanent, [352] subject to cessation.' If he is steady in that, he attains the destruction of the taints. But if he does not attain the destruction of the taints...without ever returning from that world.

"This too is one thing proclaimed by the Blessed One... wherein if a bhikkhu abides diligent, ardent, and resolute...he attains the supreme security from bondage that he had not attained before.

12. "Again, with the complete surmounting of perceptions of form, with the disappearance of perceptions of sensory impact, with non-attention to perceptions of diversity, aware that 'space is infinite,' a bhikkhu enters upon and abides in the base of infinite space. He considers this and understands it thus: 'This attainment of the base of infinite space is conditioned and volitionally produced. But whatever is conditioned and volitionally produced is impermanent, subject to cessation.' If he is steady in that, he attains the destruction of the taints. But if he does not attain the destruction of the taints...without ever returning from that world.

"This too is one thing proclaimed by the Blessed One... wherein if a bhikkhu abides diligent, ardent, and resolute...he attains the supreme security from bondage that he had not attained before.

13. "Again, by completely surmounting the base of infinite space, aware that 'consciousness is infinite,' a bhikkhu enters upon and abides in the base of infinite consciousness. He considers this and understands it thus: 'This attainment of the base of

infinite consciousness is conditioned and volitionally produced. But whatever is conditioned and volitionally produced is impermanent, subject to cessation.' If he is steady in that, he attains the destruction of the taints. But if he does not attain the destruction of the taints...without ever returning from that world.

"This too is one thing proclaimed by the Blessed One... wherein if a bhikkhu abides diligent, ardent, and resolute...he attains the supreme security from bondage that he had not attained before.

14. "Again, by completely surmounting the base of infinite consciousness, aware that 'there is nothing,' a bhikkhu enters upon and abides in the base of nothingness. He considers this and understands it thus: 'This attainment of the base of nothingness is conditioned and volitionally produced. But whatever is conditioned and volitionally produced is impermanent, subject to cessation.' If he is steady in that, he attains the destruction of the taints. But if he does not attain the destruction of the taints because of that desire for the Dhamma, that delight in the Dhamma, then with the destruction of the five lower fetters he becomes one due to reappear spontaneously [in the Pure Abodes] and there attain final Nibbāna without ever returning from that world.

"This too is one thing proclaimed by the Blessed One who knows and sees, accomplished and fully enlightened, wherein if a bhikkhu abides diligent, ardent, and resolute, his unliberated mind comes to be liberated, his undestroyed taints come to be destroyed, and he attains the supreme security from bondage that he had not attained before."[554]

15. When venerable Ānanda had spoken, the householder Dasama of Aṭṭhakanāgara said to him: "Venerable Ānanda, just as if a man seeking one entrance to a hidden treasure came all at once upon eleven [353] entrances to a hidden treasure, so too, while I was seeking one door to the Deathless, I have come all at once to hear of eleven doors to the Deathless.[555] Just as if a man had a house with eleven doors and when that house caught on fire, he could flee to safety by any one of these eleven doors, so I can flee to safety by any one of these eleven doors to the Deathless. Venerable sir, these sectarians will even seek a teacher's fee for their teachers; why shouldn't I make an offering to the venerable Ānanda?"

16. Then the householder Dasama of Aṭṭhakanāgara assembled the Sangha of bhikkhus from Pāṭaliputta and Vesālī, and with his own hands he served and satisfied them with various kinds of good food. He presented a pair of cloths to each bhikkhu, and he presented a triple robe to the venerable Ānanda, and he had a dwelling worth five hundred[556] built for the venerable Ānanda.

53 *Sekha Sutta*
The Disciple in Higher Training

1. THUS HAVE I HEARD. On one occasion the Blessed One was living in the Sakyan country at Kapilavatthu in Nigrodha's Park.

2. Now on that occasion a new assembly hall had recently been built for the Sakyans of Kapilavatthu and it had not yet been inhabited by any recluse or brahmin or human being at all. Then the Sakyans of Kapilavatthu went to the Blessed One. After paying homage to him, they sat down at one side and said to him:

"Venerable sir, a new assembly hall has recently been built here for the Sakyans of Kapilavatthu and it has not yet been inhabited by any recluse or brahmin or human being at all. Venerable sir, let the Blessed One be the first to use it. When the Blessed One has used it first, then the Sakyans of Kapilavatthu will use it afterwards. That will lead to their welfare and happiness for a long time."[557] [354]

3. The Blessed One consented in silence. Then, when they saw that he had consented, they got up from their seats, and after paying homage to him, keeping him on their right, they went to the assembly hall. They covered it completely with coverings and prepared seats, and they put out a large water jug and hung up an oil-lamp. Then they went to the Blessed One, and after paying homage to him, they stood at one side and said:

"Venerable sir, the assembly hall has been covered completely with coverings and seats have been prepared, a large water jug has been put out and an oil-lamp hung up. Let the Blessed One come at his own convenience."

4. Then the Blessed One dressed, and taking his bowl and outer robe, he went with the Sangha of bhikkhus to the assembly hall. When he arrived, he washed his feet and then entered the hall and sat down by the central pillar facing the east. And the bhikkhus washed their feet and then entered the hall and sat

down by the western wall facing the east, with the Blessed One before them. And the Sakyans of Kapilavatthu washed their feet and entered the hall and sat down by the eastern wall facing the west, with the Blessed One before them.

5. Then, when the Blessed One had instructed, urged, roused, and gladdened the Sakyans of Kapilavatthu with talk on the Dhamma for much of the night, he said to the venerable Ānanda:

"Ānanda, speak to the Sakyans of Kapilavatthu about the disciple in higher training who has entered upon the way.[558] My back is uncomfortable. I will rest it."

"Yes, venerable sir," the venerable Ānanda replied.

Then the Blessed One prepared his patchwork cloak folded in four and lay down on his right side in the lion's pose, with one foot overlapping the other, mindful and fully aware, after noting in his mind the time for rising.

6. Then the venerable Ānanda addressed Mahānāma the Sakyan thus:

"Mahānāma, here a noble disciple is possessed of virtue, guards the doors of his sense faculties, is moderate in eating, and devoted to wakefulness; he possesses seven good qualities; and he is one who obtains at will, without trouble or difficulty, the four jhānas that constitute the higher mind and provide a pleasant abiding here and now. [355]

7. "And how is a noble disciple possessed of virtue? Here a noble disciple is virtuous, he dwells restrained with the restraint of the Pātimokkha, he is perfect in conduct and resort, and seeing fear in the slightest fault, he trains by undertaking the training precepts. This is how a noble disciple is possessed of virtue.

8. "And how does a noble disciple guard the doors of his sense faculties? On seeing a form with the eye, a noble disciple does not grasp at its signs and features. Since, if he left the eye faculty unguarded, evil unwholesome states of covetousness and grief might invade him, he practises the way of its restraint, he guards the eye faculty, he undertakes the restraint of the eye faculty. On hearing a sound with the ear...On smelling an odour with the nose...On tasting a flavour with the tongue...On touching a tangible with the body...on cognizing a mind-object with the mind, a noble disciple does not grasp at its signs and features. Since, if he left the mind faculty unguarded, evil unwholesome states of covetousness and grief

might invade him, he practises the way of its restraint, he guards the mind faculty, he undertakes the restraint of the mind faculty. That is how a noble disciple guards the doors of his sense faculties.

9. "And how is a noble disciple moderate in eating? Here, reflecting wisely, a noble disciple takes food neither for amusement nor for intoxication nor for the sake of physical beauty and attractiveness, but only for the endurance and continuance of this body, for ending discomfort, and for assisting the holy life, considering: 'Thus I shall terminate old feelings without arousing new feelings and I shall be healthy and blameless and shall live in comfort.' That is how a noble disciple is moderate in eating.

10. "And how is a noble disciple devoted to wakefulness? Here, during the day, while walking back and forth and sitting, a noble disciple purifies his mind of obstructive states. In the first watch of the night, while walking back and forth and sitting, he purifies his mind of obstructive states. In the middle watch of the night he lies down on the right side in the lion's pose with one foot overlapping the other, mindful and fully aware, after noting in his mind the time for rising. After rising, in the third watch of the night, while walking back and forth and sitting, he purifies his mind of obstructive states. That is how a noble disciple is devoted to wakefulness. [356]

11. "And how does a noble disciple possess seven good qualities? Here a noble disciple has faith; he places his faith in the Tathāgata's enlightenment thus: 'The Blessed One is accomplished, fully enlightened, perfect in true knowledge and conduct, sublime, knower of worlds, incomparable leader of persons to be tamed, teacher of gods and humans, enlightened, blessed.'

12. "He has shame; he is ashamed of misconduct in body, speech, and mind, ashamed of engaging in evil unwholesome deeds.

13. "He has fear of wrongdoing; he is afraid of misconduct in body, speech, and mind, afraid of engaging in evil unwholesome deeds.[559]

14. "He has learned much, remembers what he has learned, and consolidates what he has learned. Such teachings as are good in the beginning, good in the middle, and good in the end,

with the right meaning and phrasing, and affirm a holy life that is utterly perfect and pure—such teachings as these he has learned much of, remembered, recited verbally, investigated with the mind and penetrated well by view.

15. "He is energetic in abandoning unwholesome states and in undertaking wholesome states; he is steadfast, firm in striving, not remiss in developing wholesome states.

16. "He has mindfulness; he possesses the highest mindfulness and skill; he recalls and recollects what was done long ago and spoken long ago.[560]

17. "He is wise; he possesses wisdom regarding rise and disappearance that is noble and penetrative and leads to the complete destruction of suffering.[561] That is how a noble disciple possesses seven good qualities.

18. "And how is a noble disciple one who obtains at will, without trouble or difficulty, the four jhānas that constitute the higher mind and provide a pleasant abiding here and now? Here, quite secluded from sensual pleasures, secluded from unwholesome states, a noble disciple enters upon and abides in the first jhāna...With the stilling of applied and sustained thought, he enters upon and abides in the second jhāna...With the fading away as well of rapture...he enters upon and abides in the third jhāna...With the abandoning of pleasure and pain...he enters upon and abides in the fourth jhāna, which has neither-pain-nor-pleasure and purity of mindfulness due to equanimity. That is how a noble disciple is one who obtains at will, without trouble or difficulty, the four jhānas that constitute the higher mind and provide a pleasant abiding here and now.

19. "When a noble disciple has thus become one who is possessed of virtue, who guards the doors of his sense faculties, who is moderate in eating, who is devoted to wakefulness, who possesses seven good qualities, [357] who obtains at will, without trouble or difficulty, the four jhānas that constitute the higher mind and provide a pleasant abiding here and now, he is called one in higher training who has entered upon the way. His eggs are unspoiled; he is capable of breaking out, capable of enlightenment, capable of attaining the supreme security from bondage.

"Suppose there were a hen with eight or ten or twelve eggs, which she had covered, incubated, and nurtured properly.[562]

Even though she did not wish: 'Oh, that my chicks might pierce their shells with the points of their claws and beaks and hatch out safely!' yet the chicks are capable of piercing their shells with the points of their claws and beaks and hatching out safely. So too, when a noble disciple has thus become one who is possessed of virtue...he is called one in higher training who has entered upon the way. His eggs are unspoiled; he is capable of breaking out, capable of enlightenment, capable of attaining the supreme security from bondage.

20. "Based upon that same supreme mindfulness whose purity is due to equanimity,[563] this noble disciple recollects his manifold past lives...(*as Sutta 51, §24*)...Thus with their aspects and particulars he recollects his manifold past lives. This is his first breaking out like that of the hen's chicks from their shells.

21. "Based upon that same supreme mindfulness whose purity is due to equanimity, with the divine eye, which is purified and surpasses the human, this noble disciple sees beings passing away and reappearing...(*as Sutta 51, §25*)...he understands how beings pass on according to their actions. This is his second breaking out like that of the hen's chicks from their shells.

22. "Based upon that same supreme mindfulness whose purity is due to equanimity, by realising for himself with direct knowledge, this noble disciple here and now enters upon and abides in the deliverance of mind and deliverance by wisdom that are taintless with the destruction of the taints. [358] This is his third breaking out like that of the hen's chicks from their shells.[564]

23. "When a noble disciple is possessed of virtue, that pertains to his conduct. When he guards the doors of his sense faculties, that pertains to his conduct. When he is moderate in eating, that pertains to his conduct. When he is devoted to wakefulness, that pertains to his conduct. When he possesses seven good qualities, that pertains to his conduct. When he is one who obtains at will, without trouble or difficulty, the four jhānas that constitute the higher mind and provide a pleasant abiding here and now, that pertains to his conduct.[565]

24. "When he recollects his manifold past lives...with their aspects and particulars, that pertains to his true knowledge. When, with the divine eye...he sees beings passing away and reappearing and understands how beings pass on according to

their actions, that pertains to his true knowledge. When, by realising for himself with direct knowledge, he here and now enters upon and abides in the deliverance of mind and deliverance by wisdom that are taintless with the destruction of the taints, that pertains to his true knowledge.

25. "This noble disciple is thus said to be perfect in true knowledge, perfect in conduct, perfect in true knowledge and conduct. And this stanza was uttered by the Brahmā Sanankumāra:

> 'The noble clan is held to be
> The best of people as to lineage;
> But best of gods and humans is one
> Perfect in true knowledge and conduct.'

"Now that stanza was well sung by the Brahmā Sanankumāra, not ill sung; it was well spoken, not ill spoken; it has a meaning, and is not meaningless; and it was approved by the Blessed One."[566]

26. Then the Blessed One rose and addressed the venerable Ānanda thus: "Good, good, Ānanda! It is good that you have spoken to the Sakyans of Kapilavatthu about the disciple in higher training who has entered upon the way." [359]

That is what the venerable Ānanda said. The Teacher approved. The Sakyans of Kapilavatthu were satisfied and delighted in the venerable Ānanda's words.

54 *Potaliya Sutta*
To Potaliya

1. THUS HAVE I HEARD. On one occasion the Blessed One was living in the country of the Anguttarāpans where there was a town of theirs named Āpaṇa.

2. Then, when it was morning, the Blessed One dressed, and taking his bowl and outer robe, went into Āpaṇa for alms. When he had wandered for alms in Āpaṇa and had returned from his almsround, after his meal he went to a certain grove for the day's abiding. Having entered the grove, he sat down at the root of a tree.

3. Potaliya the householder, while walking and wandering for exercise, wearing full dress with parasol and sandals, also went to the grove, and having entered the grove, he went to the Blessed One and exchanged greetings with him. When this courteous and amiable talk was finished, he stood at one side. The Blessed One said to him: "There are seats, householder, sit down if you like."

When this was said, the householder Potaliya thought: "The recluse Gotama addresses me as 'householder,'" and angry and displeased, he remained silent.

A second time the Blessed One said to him: "There are seats, householder, sit down if you like." And a second time the householder Potaliya thought: "The recluse Gotama addresses me as 'householder,'" and angry and displeased, he remained silent.

A third time the Blessed One said to him: "There are seats, householder, sit down if you like." When this was said, the householder Potaliya thought: "The recluse Gotama addresses me as 'householder,'" and angry and displeased, he said to the Blessed One: [360] "Master Gotama, it is neither fitting nor proper that you address me as 'householder.'"

"Householder, you have the aspects, marks, and signs of a householder."

"Nevertheless, Master Gotama, I have given up all my works and cut off all my affairs."

"In what way, householder, have you given up all your works and cut off all your affairs?"

"Master Gotama, I have given all my wealth, grain, silver, and gold to my children as their inheritance. Without advising or admonishing them, I live merely on food and clothing. That is how I have given up all my works and cut off all my affairs."

"Householder, the cutting off of affairs as you describe it is one thing, but in the Noble One's Discipline the cutting off of affairs is different."

"What is the cutting off of affairs like in the Noble One's Discipline, venerable sir? It would be good, venerable sir, if the Blessed One would teach me the Dhamma, showing what the cutting off of affairs is like in the Noble One's Discipline."

"Then listen, householder, and attend closely to what I shall say."

"Yes, venerable sir," Potaliya the householder replied. The Blessed One said this:

4. "Householder, there are these eight things in the Noble One's Discipline that lead to the cutting off of affairs. What are the eight? With the support of the non-killing of living beings, the killing of living beings is to be abandoned. With the support of taking only what is given, the taking of what is not given is to be abandoned. With the support of truthful speech, false speech is to be abandoned. With the support of unmalicious speech, malicious speech is to be abandoned. With the support of refraining from rapacious greed,[567] rapacious greed is to be abandoned. With the support of refraining from spiteful scolding, spiteful scolding is to be abandoned. With the support of refraining from angry despair, angry despair is to be abandoned. With the support of non-arrogance, arrogance is to be abandoned. These are the eight things, stated in brief without being expounded in detail, that lead to the cutting off of affairs in the Noble One's Discipline."

5. "Venerable sir, it would be good if, out of compassion, the Blessed One would expound to me in detail these eight things that lead to the cutting off of affairs in the Noble One's

Discipline, which have been stated in brief by the Blessed One without being expounded in detail."

"Then listen, householder, and attend closely to what I shall say."

"Yes, venerable sir," Potaliya the householder replied. The Blessed One said this: [361]

6. "'With the support of the non-killing of living beings, the killing of living beings is to be abandoned.' So it was said. And with reference to what was this said? Here a noble disciple considers thus: 'I am practising the way to the abandoning and cutting off of those fetters because of which I might kill living beings. If I were to kill living beings, I would blame myself for doing so; the wise, having investigated, would censure me for doing so; and on the dissolution of the body, after death, because of killing living beings an unhappy destination would be expected. But this killing of living beings is itself a fetter and a hindrance.[568] And while taints, vexation, and fever might arise through the killing of living beings, there are no taints, vexation, and fever for one who abstains from killing living beings.' So it is with reference to this that it was said: 'With the support of the non-killing of living beings, the killing of living beings is to be abandoned.'

7. "'With the support of taking only what is given, the taking of what is not given is to be abandoned.' So it was said...

8. "'With the support of truthful speech, false speech is to be abandoned.' So it was said...[362]

9. "'With the support of unmalicious speech, malicious speech is to be abandoned.' So it was said...

10. "'With the support of refraining from rapacious greed, rapacious greed is to be abandoned.' So it was said...

11. "'With the support of refraining from spiteful scolding, spiteful scolding is to be abandoned.' So it was said...[363]

12. "'With the support of refraining from angry despair, angry despair is to be abandoned.' So it was said...

13. "'With the support of non-arrogance, arrogance is to be abandoned.' So it was said. And with reference to what was this said? Here a noble disciple considers thus: 'I am practising the way to the abandoning and cutting off of those fetters because of which I might be arrogant. If I were to be arrogant, I would blame myself for this; the wise, having investigated, would censure me

for this; and on the dissolution of the body, after death, because of being arrogant an unhappy destination would be expected. But this arrogance is itself a fetter and a hindrance. And while taints, vexation, and fever might arise through arrogance, there are no taints, vexation, and fever for one who is not arrogant.' So it is with reference to this that it was said: 'With the support of non-arrogance, arrogance is to be abandoned.'[569] [364]

14. "These eight things that lead to the cutting off of affairs in the Noble One's Discipline have now been expounded in detail. But the cutting off of affairs in the Noble One's Discipline has not yet been achieved entirely and in all ways."

"Venerable sir, how is the cutting off of affairs in the Noble One's Discipline achieved entirely and in all ways? It would be good, venerable sir, if the Blessed One would teach me the Dhamma, showing me how the cutting off of affairs in the Noble One's Discipline is achieved entirely and in all ways."

"Then listen, householder, and attend closely to what I shall say."

"Yes, venerable sir," Potaliya the householder replied. The Blessed One said this:

15. "Householder, suppose a dog, overcome by hunger and weakness, was waiting by a butcher's shop.[570] Then a skilled butcher or his apprentice would toss the dog a well hacked, clean hacked skeleton of meatless bones smeared with blood. What do you think, householder? Would that dog get rid of his hunger and weakness by gnawing such a well hacked, clean hacked skeleton of meatless bones smeared with blood?"

"No, venerable sir. Why is that? Because that was a skeleton of well hacked, clean hacked meatless bones smeared with blood. Eventually that dog would reap weariness and disappointment."

"So too, householder, a noble disciple considers thus: 'Sensual pleasures have been compared to a skeleton by the Blessed One; they provide much suffering and much despair, while the danger in them is great.' Having seen this thus as it actually is with proper wisdom, he avoids the equanimity that is diversified, based on diversity, and develops the equanimity that is unified, based on unity,[571] where clinging to the material things of the world utterly ceases without remainder.

16. "Householder, suppose a vulture, a heron, or a hawk seized a piece of meat and flew away, and then vultures, herons,

and hawks pursued it and pecked and clawed it. What do you think, householder? If that vulture, heron, or hawk does not quickly let go of that piece of meat, wouldn't it incur death or deadly suffering because of that?"

"Yes, venerable sir."

"So too, householder, a noble disciple considers thus: 'Sensual pleasures have been compared to a piece of meat by the Blessed One; they provide much suffering and much despair, while the danger in them is great.' [365] Having seen this thus as it actually is with proper wisdom...clinging to the material things of the world utterly ceases without remainder.

17. "Householder, suppose a man took a blazing grass torch and went against the wind. What do you think, householder? If that man does not quickly let go of that blazing grass torch, wouldn't that blazing grass torch burn his hand or his arm or some other part of his body, so that he might incur death or deadly suffering because of that?"

"Yes, venerable sir."

"So too, householder, a noble disciple considers thus: 'Sensual pleasures have been compared to a grass torch by the Blessed One; they provide much suffering and much despair, while the danger in them is great.' Having seen this thus as it actually is with proper wisdom...clinging to the material things of the world utterly ceases without remainder.

18. "Householder, suppose there were a charcoal pit deeper than a man's height full of glowing coals without flame or smoke. Then a man came who wanted to live and not to die, who wanted pleasure and recoiled from pain, and two strong men seized him by both arms and dragged him towards that charcoal pit. What do you think, householder? Would that man twist his body this way and that?"

"Yes, venerable sir. Why is that? Because that man knows that if he falls into that charcoal pit, he will incur death or deadly suffering because of that."

"So too, householder, a noble disciple considers thus: 'Sensual pleasures have been compared to a charcoal pit by the Blessed One; they provide much suffering and much despair, while the danger in them is great.' Having seen this thus as it actually is with proper wisdom...clinging to the material things of the world utterly ceases without remainder.

19. "Householder, suppose a man dreamt about lovely parks, lovely groves, lovely meadows, and lovely lakes, and on waking he saw nothing of it. So too, householder, a noble disciple considers thus: 'Sensual pleasures have been compared to a dream by the Blessed One; they provide much suffering and much despair, while the danger in them is great.' Having seen this thus as it actually is with proper wisdom...clinging to the material things of the world utterly ceases without remainder.

20. "Householder, suppose a man borrowed goods on loan [366]—a fancy carriage and fine-jewelled earrings—and preceded and surrounded by those borrowed goods he went to the marketplace. Then people, seeing him, would say: 'Sirs, that is a rich man! That is how the rich enjoy their wealth!' Then the owners, whenever they saw him, would take back their things. What do you think, householder? Would that be enough for that man to become dejected?"

"Yes, venerable sir. Why is that? Because the owners took back their things."

"So too, householder, a noble disciple considers thus: 'Sensual pleasures have been compared to borrowed goods by the Blessed One; they provide much suffering and much despair, while the danger in them is great.' Having seen this thus as it actually is with proper wisdom...clinging to material things of the world utterly ceases without remainder.

21. "Householder, suppose there were a dense grove not far from some village or town, within which there was a tree laden with fruit but none of its fruit had fallen to the ground. Then a man came needing fruit, seeking fruit, wandering in search of fruit, and he entered the grove and saw the tree laden with fruit. Thereupon he thought: 'This tree is laden with fruit but none of its fruit has fallen to the ground. I know how to climb a tree, so let me climb this tree, eat as much fruit as I want, and fill my bag.' And he did so. Then a second man came needing fruit, seeking fruit, wandering in search of fruit, and taking a sharp axe, he too entered the grove and saw that tree laden with fruit. Thereupon he thought: 'This tree is laden with fruit but none of its fruit has fallen to the ground. I do not know how to climb a tree, so let me cut this tree down at its root, eat as much fruit as I want, and fill my bag.' And he did so. What do you think, householder? If that first man who had climbed the tree doesn't

come down quickly, when the tree falls, wouldn't he break his hand or his foot or some other part of his body, [367] so that he might incur death or deadly suffering because of that?"

"Yes, venerable sir."

"So too, householder, a noble disciple considers thus: 'Sensual pleasures have been compared to fruits on a tree by the Blessed One; they provide much suffering and much despair, while the danger in them is great.' Having seen this thus as it actually is with proper wisdom, he avoids the equanimity that is diversified, based on diversity, and develops the equanimity that is unified, based on unity, where clinging to the material things of the world utterly ceases without remainder.

22. "Based upon that same supreme mindfulness whose purity is due to equanimity, this noble disciple recollects his manifold past lives, that is, one birth, two births...(*as Sutta 51, §24*)...Thus with their aspects and particulars he recollects his manifold past lives.

23. "Based upon that same supreme mindfulness whose purity is due to equanimity, with the divine eye, which is purified and surpasses the human, this noble disciple sees beings passing away and reappearing, inferior and superior, fair and ugly, fortunate and unfortunate...(*as Sutta 51, §25*)...and he understands how beings pass on according to their actions.

24. "Based upon that same supreme mindfulness whose purity is due to equanimity, by realising for himself with direct knowledge, this noble disciple here and now enters upon and abides in the deliverance of mind and deliverance by wisdom that are taintless with the destruction of the taints.

25. "At this point, householder, the cutting off of affairs in the Noble One's Discipline has been achieved entirely and in all ways. What do you think, householder? Do you see in yourself any cutting off of affairs like this cutting off of affairs in the Noble One's Discipline when it is achieved entirely and in all ways?"

"Venerable sir, who am I that I should possess any cutting off of affairs entirely and in all ways like that in the Noble One's Discipline? I am far indeed, venerable sir, from that cutting off of affairs in the Noble One's Discipline when it has been achieved entirely and in all ways. For, venerable sir, though the wanderers of other sects are not thoroughbreds, we imagined that they are thoroughbreds;[572] though they are not thoroughbreds, we fed them the food of thoroughbreds; though they are not thoroughbreds, we set them in the place of thoroughbreds. But though the bhikkhus are thoroughbreds, we imagined that they are not thoroughbreds; though they are thoroughbreds, we fed them the food of those who are not thoroughbreds; though they are thoroughbreds, we set them in the place of those who are not thoroughbreds. But now, venerable sir, [368] as the wanderers of other sects are not thoroughbreds, we shall understand that they are not thoroughbreds; as they are not thoroughbreds, we shall feed them the food of those who are not thoroughbreds; as they are not thoroughbreds, we shall set them in the place of those who are not thoroughbreds. But as the bhikkhus are thoroughbreds, we shall understand that they are thoroughbreds; as they are thoroughbreds, we shall feed them the food of thoroughbreds; as they are thoroughbreds, we shall set them in the place of those who are thoroughbreds. Venerable sir, the Blessed One has inspired in me love for recluses, confidence in recluses, reverence for recluses.

26. "Magnificent, Master Gotama! Magnificent, Master Gotama! Master Gotama has made the Dhamma clear in many ways, as though he were turning upright what had been overthrown, revealing what was hidden, showing the way to one who was lost, or holding up a lamp in the dark for those with eyesight to see forms. I go to Master Gotama for refuge and to the Dhamma and to the Sangha of bhikkhus. From today let Master Gotama remember me as a lay follower who has gone to him for refuge for life."

55 *Jīvaka Sutta*
To Jīvaka

1. THUS HAVE I HEARD. On one occasion the Blessed One was living at Rājagaha in the Mango Grove of Jīvaka Komārabhacca.[573]

2. Then Jīvaka Komārabhacca went to the Blessed One, and after paying homage to him, he sat down at one side and said to the Blessed One:

3. "Venerable sir, I have heard this: 'They slaughter living beings for the recluse Gotama; the recluse Gotama knowingly eats meat prepared for him from animals killed for his sake.' Venerable sir, do those who speak thus say what has been said by the Blessed One, and not misrepresent him with what is contrary to fact? Do they explain in accordance with the Dhamma in such a way that nothing which provides a ground for censure can be legitimately deduced from their assertions?" [369]

4. "Jīvaka, those who speak thus do not say what has been said by me, but misrepresent me with what is untrue and contrary to fact.

5. "Jīvaka, I say that there are three instances in which meat should not be eaten: when it is seen, heard, or suspected [that the living being has been slaughtered for oneself]. I say that meat should not be eaten in these three instances. I say that there are three instances in which meat may be eaten: when it is not seen, not heard, and not suspected [that the living being has been slaughtered for oneself]. I say that meat may be eaten in these three instances.[574]

6. "Here, Jīvaka, some bhikkhu lives in dependence upon a certain village or town. He abides pervading one quarter with a mind imbued with loving-kindness, likewise the second, likewise the third, likewise the fourth; so above, below, around, and everywhere, and to all as to himself, he abides pervading the all-encompassing world with a mind imbued with loving-kindness,

abundant, exalted, immeasurable, without hostility and without ill will. Then a householder or a householder's son comes to him and invites him for the next day's meal. The bhikkhu accepts, if he likes. When the night is ended, in the morning he dresses, and taking his bowl and outer robe, goes to the house of that householder or householder's son and sits down on a seat made ready. Then the householder or householder's son serves him with good almsfood. He does not think: 'How good that the householder or householder's son serves me with good almsfood! If only a householder or householder's son might serve me with such good almsfood in the future!' He does not think thus. He eats that almsfood without being tied to it, infatuated with it, and utterly committed to it, seeing the danger in it and understanding the escape from it. What do you think, Jīvaka? Would that bhikkhu on such an occasion choose for his own affliction, or for another's affliction, or for the affliction of both?"—"No, venerable sir."—"Does not that bhikkhu sustain himself with blameless food on that occasion?"

7. "Yes, venerable sir. I have heard this, venerable sir: 'Brahmā abides in loving-kindness.' Venerable sir, the Blessed One is my visible witness to that; for the Blessed One abides in loving-kindness."

"Jīvaka, any lust, [370] any hate, any delusion whereby ill will might arise have been abandoned by the Tathāgata, cut off at the root, made like a palm stump, done away with so that they are no longer subject to future arising.[575] If what you said referred to that, then I allow it to you."

"Venerable sir, what I said referred to precisely that."

8–10. "Here, Jīvaka, a bhikkhu lives in dependence upon a certain village or town. He abides pervading one quarter with a mind imbued with compassion...with a mind imbued with altruistic joy...with a mind imbued with equanimity, likewise the second, likewise the third, likewise the fourth; so above, below, around, and everywhere, and to all as to himself, he abides pervading the all-encompassing world with a mind imbued with equanimity, abundant, exalted, immeasurable, without hostility and without ill will. Then a householder or a householder's son comes to him and invites him for the next day's meal. The bhikkhu accepts, if he likes...What do you think, Jīvaka? Would that bhikkhu on such an occasion choose for his own affliction, or for another's affliction, or for the affliction of both?"—"No, venerable sir."—"Does not that bhikkhu sustain himself with blameless food on that occasion?"

11. "Yes, venerable sir. I have heard this, venerable sir: 'Brahmā abides in equanimity.' Venerable sir, the Blessed One is my visible witness to that; for the Blessed One abides in equanimity."

"Jīvaka, any lust, any hate, any delusion whereby cruelty or discontent or aversion might arise have been abandoned by the Tathāgata, cut off at the root, made like a palm stump, done away with so that they are no longer subject to future arising.[576] If what you said referred to that, then I allow it to you." [371]

"Venerable sir, what I said referred to precisely that."

12. "If anyone slaughters a living being for the Tathāgata or his disciple, he lays up much demerit in five instances. When he says: 'Go and fetch that living being,' this is the first instance in which he lays up much demerit. When that living being experiences pain and grief on being led along with a neck-halter, this is the second instance in which he lays up much demerit. When he says: 'Go and slaughter that living being,' this is the third instance in which he lays up much demerit. When that living being experiences pain and grief on being slaughtered, this is the fourth instance in which he lays up much demerit. When he provides the Tathāgata or his disciple with food that is not permissible, this is the fifth instance in which he lays up much demerit. Anyone who slaughters a living being for the Tathāgata or his disciple lays up much demerit in these five instances."

13. When this was said, Jīvaka Komārabhacca said to the Blessed One: "It is wonderful, venerable sir, it is marvellous! The bhikkhus sustain themselves with permissible food. The bhikkhus sustain themselves with blameless food. Magnificent, venerable sir! Magnificent, venerable sir!...From today let the Blessed One remember me as a lay follower who has gone to him for refuge for life."[577]

56 *Upāli Sutta*
To Upāli

1. THUS HAVE I HEARD. On one occasion the Blessed One was living at Nāḷandā in Pāvārika's Mango Grove.

2. Now on that occasion the Nigaṇṭha Nātaputta was staying at Nāḷandā with a large assembly of Nigaṇṭhas. Then, when the Nigaṇṭha [named] Dīgha Tapassī[578] had wandered for alms in Nāḷandā and had returned from his almsround, after his meal he went to Pāvārika's Mango Grove to see the Blessed One. [372] He exchanged greetings with the Blessed One, and when this courteous and amiable talk was finished, he stood at one side. As he stood there, the Blessed One said to him: "There are seats, Tapassī, sit down if you like."

3. When this was said, Dīgha Tapassī took a low seat and sat down at one side. Then the Blessed One asked him: "Tapassī, how many kinds of action does the Nigaṇṭha Nātaputta describe for the performance of evil action, for the perpetration of evil action?"

"Friend Gotama, the Nigaṇṭha Nātaputta is not accustomed to use the description 'action, action'; the Nigaṇṭha Nātaputta is accustomed to use the description 'rod, rod.'"[579]

"Then, Tapassī, how many kinds of rod does the Nigaṇṭha Nātaputta describe for the performance of evil action, for the perpetration of evil action?"

"Friend Gotama, the Nigaṇṭha Nātaputta describes three kinds of rod for the performance of evil action, for the perpetration of evil action; that is, the bodily rod, the verbal rod, and the mental rod."[580]

"How then, Tapassī, is the bodily rod one, the verbal rod another, and the mental rod still another?"

"The bodily rod is one, friend Gotama, the verbal rod is another, and the mental rod is still another."

"Of these three kinds of rod, Tapassī, thus analysed and distinguished, which kind of rod does the Nigaṇṭha Nātaputta describe as the most reprehensible for the performance of evil action, for the perpetration of evil action: the bodily rod or the verbal rod or the mental rod?"

"Of these three kinds of rod, friend Gotama, thus analysed and distinguished, the Nigaṇṭha Nātaputta describes the bodily rod as the most reprehensible for the performance of evil action, for the perpetration of evil action, and not so much the verbal rod and the mental rod."

"Do you say the bodily rod, Tapassī?"

"I say the bodily rod, friend Gotama."

"Do you say the bodily rod, Tapassī?"

"I say the bodily rod, friend Gotama."

"Do you say the bodily rod, Tapassī?"

"I say the bodily rod, friend Gotama."

Thus the Blessed One made the Nigaṇṭha Dīgha Tapassī maintain his statement up to the third time. [373]

4. Then the Nigaṇṭha Dīgha Tapassī asked the Blessed One: "And you, friend Gotama, how many kinds of rod do you describe for the performance of evil action, for the perpetration of evil action?"

"Tapassī, the Tathāgata is not accustomed to use the description 'rod, rod'; the Tathāgata is accustomed to use the description 'action, action.'"

"But, friend Gotama, how many kinds of action do you describe for the performance of evil action, for the perpetration of evil action?"

"Tapassī, I describe three kinds of action for the performance of evil action, for the perpetration of evil action: that is, bodily action, verbal action, and mental action."

"How then, friend Gotama, is bodily action one, verbal action another, and mental action still another?"

"Bodily action is one, Tapassī, verbal action is another, and mental action is still another."

"Of these three kinds of action, friend Gotama, thus analysed and distinguished, which kind of action do you describe as the most reprehensible for the performance of evil action, for the perpetration of evil action: bodily action or verbal action or mental action?"

"Of these three kinds of action, Tapassī, thus analysed and distinguished, I describe mental action as the most reprehensible for the performance of evil action, for the perpetration of evil action, and not so much bodily action and verbal action."[581]

"Do you say mental action, friend Gotama?"

"I say mental action, Tapassī."

"Do you say mental action, friend Gotama?"

"I say mental action, Tapassī."

"Do you say mental action, friend Gotama?"

"I say mental action, Tapassī."

Thus the Nigaṇṭha Dīgha Tapassī made the Blessed One maintain his statement up to the third time, after which he rose from his seat and went to the Nigaṇṭha Nātaputta.

5. Now on that occasion the Nigaṇṭha Nātaputta was seated together with a very large assembly of laymen from Bālaka, most prominent among them being Upāli. The Nigaṇṭha Nātaputta saw the Nigaṇṭha Dīgha Tapassī coming in the distance and asked him: "Now where are you coming from in the middle of the day, Tapassī?"

"I am coming from the presence of the recluse Gotama, venerable sir."

"Did you have some conversation with the recluse Gotama, Tapassī?" [374]

"I had some conversation with the recluse Gotama, venerable sir."

"What was your conversation with him like, Tapassī?"

Then the Nigaṇṭha Dīgha Tapassī related to the Nigaṇṭha Nātaputta his entire conversation with the Blessed One.

6. When this was said, the Nigaṇṭha Nātaputta told him: "Good, good, Tapassī! The Nigaṇṭha Dīgha Tapassī has answered the recluse Gotama like a well-taught disciple who understands his teacher's dispensation rightly. What does the trivial mental rod count for in comparison with the gross bodily rod? On the contrary, the bodily rod is the most reprehensible for the performance of evil action, for the perpetration of evil action, and not so much the verbal rod and the mental rod."

7. When this was said, the householder Upāli said to the Nigaṇṭha Nātaputta: "Good, good, venerable sir, [on the part of] Dīgha Tapassī! The venerable Tapassī has answered the recluse Gotama like a well-taught disciple who understands his

teacher's dispensation rightly. What does the trivial mental rod count for in comparison with the gross bodily rod? On the contrary, the bodily rod is the most reprehensible for the performance of evil action, for the perpetration of evil action, and not so much the verbal rod and the mental rod. Now, venerable sir, I shall go and refute the recluse Gotama's doctrine on the basis of this statement. If the recluse Gotama maintains before me what the venerable Dīgha Tapassī made him maintain, then just as a strong man[582] might seize a long-haired ram by the hair and drag him to and drag him fro and drag him round about, so in debate I will drag the recluse Gotama to and drag him fro and drag him round about. Just as a strong brewer's workman might throw a big brewer's sieve into a deep water tank, and taking it by the corners, might drag it to and drag it fro and drag it round about, so in debate I will drag the recluse Gotama to and drag him fro and drag him round about. Just as a strong brewer's mixer might take a strainer by the corners and shake it down and shake it up and thump it about, so in debate I will shake the recluse Gotama down [375] and shake him up and thump him about. And just as a sixty-year-old elephant might plunge into a deep pond and enjoy playing the game of hemp-washing, so I shall enjoy playing the game of hemp-washing with the recluse Gotama. Venerable sir, I shall go and refute the recluse Gotama's doctrine on the basis of this statement."

"Go, householder, and refute the recluse Gotama's doctrine on the basis of this statement. For either I should refute the recluse Gotama's doctrine or else the Nigaṇṭha Dīgha Tapassī or you yourself."

8. When this was said, the Nigaṇṭha Dīgha Tapassī said to the Nigaṇṭha Nātaputta: "Venerable sir, I do not agree that the householder Upāli should [try to] refute the recluse Gotama's doctrine. For the recluse Gotama is a magician and knows a converting magic by which he converts disciples of other sectarians."

"It is impossible, Tapassī, it cannot happen that the householder Upāli should go over to discipleship under the recluse Gotama; but it is possible, it can happen that the recluse Gotama might come over to discipleship under the householder Upāli. Go, householder, and refute the recluse Gotama's doctrine. For either I should refute the recluse Gotama's doctrine or else the Nigaṇṭha Dīgha Tapassī or you yourself."

For the second time…For the third time, the Nigaṇṭha Dīgha Tapassī said to the Nigaṇṭha Nātaputta: "Venerable sir, I do not agree that the householder Upāli should [try to] refute the recluse Gotama's doctrine. For the recluse Gotama is a magician and knows a converting magic by which he converts disciples of other sectarians."

"It is impossible, Tapassī, it cannot happen that the householder Upāli should go over to discipleship under the recluse Gotama; but it is possible, it can happen that the recluse Gotama might come over to discipleship under the householder Upāli. Go, householder, and refute the recluse Gotama's doctrine. For either I should refute the recluse Gotama's doctrine or else the Nigaṇṭha Dīgha Tapassī or you yourself."

9. "Yes, venerable sir," the householder Upāli replied, and he rose from his seat, and after paying homage to the Nigaṇṭha Nātaputta, keeping him on his right, he left to go to the Blessed One in Pāvārika's Mango Grove. [376] There, after paying homage to the Blessed One, he sat down at one side and asked the Blessed One: "Venerable sir, did the Nigaṇṭha Dīgha Tapassī come here?"

"The Nigaṇṭha Dīgha Tapassī came here, householder."

"Venerable sir, did you have some conversation with him?"

"I had some conversation with him, householder."

"What was your conversation with him like, venerable sir?"

Then the Blessed One related to the householder Upāli his entire conversation with the Nigaṇṭha Dīgha Tapassī.

10. When this was said, the householder Upāli said to the Blessed One: "Good, good, venerable sir, on the part of Tapassī! The Nigaṇṭha Dīgha Tapassī has answered the Blessed One like a well-taught disciple who understands his teacher's dispensation rightly. What does the trivial mental rod count for in comparison with the gross bodily rod? On the contrary, the bodily rod is the most reprehensible for the performance of evil action, for the perpetration of evil action, and not so much the verbal rod and the mental rod."

"Householder, if you will debate on the basis of truth, we might have some conversation about this."

"I will debate on the basis of truth, venerable sir, so let us have some conversation about this."

11. "What do you think, householder? Here some Nigaṇṭha might be afflicted, suffering, and gravely ill [with an illness

needing treatment by cold water, which his vows prohibit] and he might refuse cold water [though mentally longing for it] and use only [the permissible] hot water [thus keeping his vows bodily and verbally]. Because he does not get cold water he might die. Now, householder, where would the Nigaṇṭha Nātaputta describe his rebirth [as taking place]?"

"Venerable sir, there are gods called 'mind-bound'; he would be reborn there. Why is that? Because when he died he was still bound [by attachment] in the mind."[583]

"Householder, householder, pay attention how you reply! What you said afterwards does not agree with what you said before, nor does what you said before agree with what you said afterwards. Yet you made this statement: 'I will debate on the basis of truth, venerable sir, so let us have some conversation about this.'"

"Venerable sir, although the Blessed One has spoken thus, yet the bodily rod is the most reprehensible for the performance of evil action, for the perpetration of evil action, and not so much the verbal rod and the mental rod."[584]

12. "What do you think, [377] householder? Here some Nigaṇṭha might be restrained with four checks—curbed by all curbs, clamped by all curbs, cleansed by all curbs, and claimed by all curbs[585]—and yet when going forward and returning he brings about the destruction of many small living beings. What result does the Nigaṇṭha Nātaputta describe for him?"

"Venerable sir, the Nigaṇṭha Nātaputta does not describe what is unintended as greatly reprehensible."

"But if one intends it, householder?"

"Then it is greatly reprehensible, venerable sir."

"But under which [of the three rods] does the Nigaṇṭha Nātaputta describe volition, householder?"

"Under the mental rod, venerable sir."[586]

"Householder, householder, pay attention how you reply! What you said afterwards does not agree with what you said before, nor does what you said before agree with what you said afterwards. Yet you made this statement: 'I will debate on the basis of truth, venerable sir, so let us have some conversation about this.'"

"Venerable sir, although the Blessed One has spoken thus, yet the bodily rod is the most reprehensible for the performance of evil action, for the perpetration of evil action, and not so much the verbal rod and the mental rod."

13. "What do you think, householder? Is this town of Nāḷandā successful and prosperous, is it populous and crowded with people?"

"Yes, venerable sir, it is."

"What do you think, householder? Suppose a man came here brandishing a sword and spoke thus: 'In one moment, in one instant, I will make all the living beings in this town of Nāḷandā into one mass of flesh, into one heap of flesh.' What do you think, householder, would that man be able to do that?"

"Venerable sir, ten, twenty, thirty, forty, or even fifty men would not be able to make all the living beings in this town of Nāḷandā into one mass of flesh, into one heap of flesh in one moment or instant, so what does a single trivial man count for?"

"What do you think, householder? Suppose some recluse or brahmin came here possessed of supernormal power and attained to mastery of mind, and he spoke thus: 'I will reduce this town of Nāḷandā to ashes with one mental act of hate.' What do you think, householder, would such a recluse or brahmin be able to do that?" [378]

"Venerable sir, such a recluse or brahmin possessed of supernormal power and attained to mastery of mind would be able to reduce ten, twenty, thirty, forty, or even fifty Nāḷandās to ashes with one mental act of hate, so what does a single trivial Nāḷandā count for?"

"Householder, householder, pay attention how you reply! What you said afterwards does not agree with what you said before, nor does what you said before agree with what you said afterwards. Yet you made this statement: 'I will debate on the basis of truth, venerable sir, so let us have some conversation about this.'"

"Venerable sir, although the Blessed One has spoken thus, yet the bodily rod is the most reprehensible for the performance of evil action, for the perpetration of evil action, and not so much the verbal rod and the mental rod."

14. "What do you think, householder? Have you heard how the Daṇḍaka, Kālinga, Mejjha, and Mātanga forests became forests?"[587]—"Yes, venerable sir."—"As you heard it, how did they become forests?"—"Venerable sir, I heard that they became forests by means of a mental act of hate on the part of the seers."

"Householder, householder, pay attention how you reply! What you said before does not agree with what you said afterwards, nor does what you said afterwards agree with what you said before. Yet you made this statement: 'I will debate on the basis of truth, venerable sir, so let us have some conversation about this.'"

15. "Venerable sir, I was satisfied and pleased by the Blessed One's very first simile. Nevertheless, I thought I would oppose the Blessed One thus since I desired to hear the Blessed One's varied solutions to the problem. Magnificent, venerable sir! Magnificent, venerable sir! The Blessed One has made the Dhamma clear in many ways, as though he were turning upright what had been overthrown, revealing what was hidden, showing the way to one who was lost, or holding up a lamp in the dark for those with eyesight to see forms. Venerable sir, I go to the Blessed One for refuge [379] and to the Dhamma and to the Sangha of bhikkhus. Let the Blessed One remember me as a lay follower who has gone to him for refuge for life."

16. "Investigate thoroughly, householder. It is good for such well-known people like you to investigate thoroughly."

"Venerable sir, I am even more satisfied and pleased with the Blessed One for telling me that. For the other sectarians, on acquiring me as their disciple, would carry a banner all over Nāḷandā announcing: 'The householder Upāli has come to discipleship under us.' But, on the contrary, the Blessed One tells me: 'Investigate thoroughly, householder. It is good for such well-known people like you to investigate thoroughly.' So for the second time, venerable sir, I go to the Blessed One for refuge and to the Dhamma and to the Sangha of bhikkhus. Let the Blessed One remember me as a lay follower who has gone to him for refuge for life."

17. "Householder, your family has long supported the Nigaṇṭhas and you should consider that alms should be given to them when they come."

"Venerable sir, I am even more satisfied and pleased with the Blessed One for telling me that. Venerable sir, I have heard that the recluse Gotama says thus: 'Gifts should be given only to me; gifts should not be given to others. Gifts should be given only to my disciples; gifts should not be given to others' disciples. Only what is given to me is very fruitful, not what is given to others.

Only what is given to my disciples is very fruitful, not what is given to others' disciples.' But, on the contrary, the Blessed One encourages me to give gifts to the Nigaṇṭhas. Anyway we shall know the time for that, venerable sir. So for the third time, venerable sir, I go to the Blessed One for refuge and to the Dhamma and to the Sangha of bhikkhus. Let the Blessed One remember me as a lay follower who has gone to him for refuge for life."

18. Then the Blessed One gave the householder Upāli progressive instruction, that is, talk on giving, talk on virtue, talk on the heavens; he explained the danger, degradation, and defilement in sensual pleasures and the blessing of renunciation. When he knew that the householder Upāli's mind [380] was ready, receptive, free from hindrances, elated, and confident, he expounded to him the teaching special to the Buddhas: suffering, its origin, its cessation, and the path. Just as a clean cloth with all marks removed would take dye evenly, so too, while the householder Upāli sat there, the spotless immaculate vision of the Dhamma arose in him: "All that is subject to arising is subject to cessation."[588] Then the householder Upāli saw the Dhamma, attained the Dhamma, understood the Dhamma, fathomed the Dhamma; he crossed beyond doubt, did away with perplexity, gained intrepidity, and became independent of others in the Teacher's Dispensation.[589] Then he said to the Blessed One: "Now, venerable sir, we must go. We are busy and have much to do."

"You may go, householder, at your own convenience."

19. Then the householder Upāli, having delighted and rejoiced in the Blessed One's words, rose from his seat, and after paying homage to the Blessed One, keeping him on his right, he left to return to his own house. There he addressed the doorkeeper thus: "Good doorkeeper, from today on I close my door to the Nigaṇṭhas and the Nigaṇṭhīs, and I open my door to the Blessed One's bhikkhus, bhikkhunīs, men lay followers, and women lay followers. If any Nigaṇṭha comes, then tell him thus: 'Wait, venerable sir, do not enter. From today on the householder Upāli has gone over to discipleship under the recluse Gotama. He has closed his door to the Nigaṇṭhas and Nigaṇṭhīs, and he has opened it to the Blessed One's bhikkhus, bhikkhunīs, men lay followers, and women lay followers. Venerable sir, if you need alms, wait here; they will bring it to you here.'"—"Yes, venerable sir," the doorkeeper replied.

20. The Nigaṇṭha Dīgha Tapassī heard: "The householder Upāli has gone over to discipleship under the recluse Gotama." Then he went to the Nigaṇṭha Nātaputta and told him: "Venerable sir, I have heard thus: 'The householder Upāli has gone over to discipleship under the recluse Gotama.'"

"It is impossible, Tapassī, it cannot happen that the householder Upāli should go over to discipleship under the recluse Gotama; but it is possible, it can happen that the recluse Gotama might come over to discipleship under the householder Upāli." [381]

A second time...And a third time the Nigaṇṭha Dīgha Tapassī told the Nigaṇṭha Nātaputta: "Venerable sir, I have heard thus: 'The householder Upāli has gone over to discipleship under the recluse Gotama.'"

"It is impossible, Tapassī, it cannot happen..."

"Venerable sir, shall I go and find out whether or not the householder Upāli has gone over to discipleship under the recluse Gotama?"

"Go, Tapassī, and find out whether or not he has gone over to discipleship under the recluse Gotama."

21. Then the Nigaṇṭha Dīgha Tapassī went to the householder Upāli's house. The doorkeeper saw him coming in the distance and told him: "Wait, venerable sir, do not enter. From today on the householder Upāli has gone over to discipleship under the recluse Gotama. He has closed his door to the Nigaṇṭhas and Nigaṇṭhīs, and he has opened it to the Blessed One's bhikkhus, bhikkhunīs, men lay followers, and women lay followers. Venerable sir, if you need alms, wait here; they will bring it to you here."

"I do not need alms, friend," he said, and he turned back and went to the Nigaṇṭha Nātaputta and told him: "Venerable sir, it is only too true that the householder Upāli has gone over to discipleship under the recluse Gotama. Venerable sir, I did not get your consent when I told you: 'Venerable sir, I do not agree that the householder Upāli should [try to] refute the recluse Gotama's doctrine. For the recluse Gotama is a magician and knows a converting magic by which he converts disciples of other sectarians.' And now, venerable sir, your householder Upāli has been converted by the recluse Gotama with his converting magic!"

"It is impossible, Tapassī, it cannot happen that the householder Upāli should go over to discipleship under the recluse Gotama; but it is possible, it can happen that the recluse Gotama might come over to discipleship under the householder Upāli."

A second time...And a third time the Nigaṇṭha Dīgha Tapassī told the Nigaṇṭha Nātaputta: "Venerable sir, it is only too true that the householder Upāli has gone over to discipleship under the recluse Gotama [382]...with his converting magic!"

"It is impossible, Tapassī, it cannot happen...it can happen that the recluse Gotama might come over to discipleship under the householder Upāli. Now I shall go myself and find out whether or not he has gone over to discipleship under the recluse Gotama."

22. Then the Nigaṇṭha Nātaputta went with a large assembly of Nigaṇṭhas to the householder Upāli's house. The doorkeeper saw him coming in the distance and told him: "Wait, venerable sir, do not enter. From today on the householder Upāli has gone over to discipleship under the recluse Gotama. He has closed his door to the Nigaṇṭhas and Nigaṇṭhīs, and he has opened his door to the Blessed One's bhikkhus, bhikkhunīs, men lay followers, and women lay followers. Venerable sir, if you need alms, wait here; they will bring it to you here."

"Good doorkeeper, go to the householder Upāli and tell him: 'Venerable sir, the Nigaṇṭha Nātaputta is standing at the outer gate with a large assembly of Nigaṇṭhas; he wishes to see you.'"

"Yes, venerable sir," he replied, and he went to the householder Upāli and told him: "Venerable sir, the Nigaṇṭha Nātaputta is standing at the outer gate with a large assembly of Nigaṇṭhas; he wishes to see you."

"In that case, good doorkeeper, make seats ready in the hall of the central door."

"Yes, venerable sir," he replied, and after he had made seats ready in the hall of the central door, he returned to the householder Upāli and told him: "Venerable sir, the seats are made ready in the hall of the central door. You may come at your own convenience."

23. Then the householder Upāli [383] went to the hall of the central door and sat down on the highest, best, chief, most excellent seat there. Then he told the doorkeeper: "Now, good doorkeeper, go to the Nigaṇṭha Nātaputta and tell him:

'Venerable sir, the householder Upāli says: "Enter, venerable sir, if you wish."'"

"Yes, venerable sir," he replied, and he went to the Nigaṇṭha Nātaputta and told him: "Venerable sir, the householder Upāli says: 'Enter, venerable sir, if you wish.'"

Then the Nigaṇṭha Nātaputta went with the large assembly of Nigaṇṭhas to the hall of the central door.

24. Previously, when the householder Upāli saw the Nigaṇṭha Nātaputta coming in the distance, he used to go out to meet him, dust off the highest, best, chief, most excellent seat there with an upper robe, and having arranged it all around, have him seated on it. But now, while seated himself on the highest, best, chief, most excellent seat, he told Nigaṇṭha Nātaputta: "Venerable sir, there are seats; sit down if you wish."

25. When this was said, the Nigaṇṭha Nātaputta said: "Householder, you are mad, you are an imbecile. You went saying: 'Venerable sir, I shall refute the recluse Gotama's doctrine,' and you have come back caught by the vast net of his doctrine. Just as if a man went to castrate someone and came back castrated on both sides, just as if a man went to put out someone's eyes and came back with both his eyes put out; so you too, householder, went saying: 'Venerable sir, I shall refute the recluse Gotama's doctrine,' and you have come back caught by the vast net of his doctrine. Householder, you have been converted by the recluse Gotama with his converting magic!"

26. "Auspicious is that converting magic, venerable sir, good is that converting magic![590] Venerable sir, if my beloved kinsmen and relatives were to be converted by this conversion, it would lead to the welfare and happiness of my beloved kinsmen and relatives for a long time. If all nobles were to be converted by this conversion, it would lead to the welfare and happiness of the nobles for a long time. [384] If all brahmins...all merchants... all workers were to be converted by this conversion, it would lead to the welfare and happiness of the workers for a long time. If the world with its gods, its Māras, and its Brahmās, this generation with its recluses and brahmins, its princes and its people, were to be converted by this conversion, it would lead to the welfare and happiness of the world for a long time. As to this, venerable sir, I shall give you a simile; for some wise men here understand the meaning of a statement by a simile.

27. "Venerable sir, there was once a brahmin who was old, aged, and burdened with years, and he had as a wife a young brahmin girl who was pregnant and near her confinement. Then she told him: 'Go, brahmin, buy a young monkey in the market and bring it back to me as a playmate for my child.' He replied: 'Wait, madam, till you have borne the child. If you bear a boy, then I will go to the market and buy a young male monkey and bring it back to you as a playmate for your little boy; but if you bear a girl, then I will go to the market and buy a young female monkey and bring it back to you as a playmate for your little girl.' For the second time she made the same request and received the same answer. For the third time she made the same request. Then, since his mind was bound to her with love, he went to the market, bought a young male monkey, brought it back, and told her: 'I have bought this young male monkey in the market [385] and brought it back to you as a playmate for your child.' Then she told him: 'Go, brahmin, take this young male monkey to Rattapāṇi the dyer's son and tell him: "Good Rattapāṇi, I want this young male monkey dyed the colour called yellow-unguent, pounded and re-pounded, and smoothened out on both sides."' Then, since his mind was bound to her with love, he took the young male monkey to Rattapāṇi the dyer's son and told him: 'Good Rattapāṇi, I want this young male monkey dyed the colour called yellow-unguent, pounded and re-pounded, and smoothened out on both sides.' Rattapāṇi the dyer's son told him: 'Venerable sir, this young male monkey will take a dyeing but not a pounding or a smoothening out.' So too, venerable sir, the doctrine of the foolish Nigaṇṭhas will give delight to fools but not to the wise, and it will not withstand testing or being smoothened out.

"Then, venerable sir, on another occasion that brahmin took a pair of new garments to Rattapāṇi the dyer's son and told him: 'Good Rattapāṇi, I want this pair of new garments dyed the colour called yellow-unguent, pounded and re-pounded, and smoothened out on both sides.' Rattapāṇi the dyer's son told him: 'Venerable sir, this pair of new garments will take a dyeing and a pounding and a smoothening out.' So too, venerable sir, the doctrine of that Blessed One, accomplished and fully enlightened, will give delight to the wise but not to fools, and it will withstand testing and being smoothened out."

28. "Householder, the assembly and the king know you thus: 'The householder Upāli is a disciple of the Nigaṇṭha Nātaputta.' Whose disciple should we consider you to be?"

When this was said, the householder Upāli rose from his seat, and arranging his upper robe on one shoulder, [386] he extended his hands in reverential salutation in the direction of the Blessed One and told the Nigaṇṭha Nātaputta:

29. "In that case, venerable sir, hear whose disciple I am:

He is the Wise One who has cast off delusion,
abandoned the heart's wilderness,[591] victor in battle;
He knows no anguish, is perfectly even-minded,
mature in virtue, of excellent wisdom;
Beyond all temptations,[592] he is without stain:
The Blessed One is he, and I am his disciple.

Free from perplexity, he abides contented,
spurning worldly gains, a vessel of gladness;
A human being who has done the recluse's duty,
a man who bears his final body;
He is utterly peerless and utterly spotless:
The Blessed One is he, and I am his disciple.

He is free from doubt and skilful,
the discipliner and excellent leader.
None can surpass his resplendent qualities;
without hesitation, he is the illuminator;
Having severed conceit, he is the hero:
The Blessed One is he, and I am his disciple.

The leader of the herd, he cannot be measured,
his depths are unfathomed, he attained to the silence;[593]
Provider of safety, possessor of knowledge,
he stands in the Dhamma, inwardly restrained;
Having overcome all bondage, he is liberated:
The Blessed One is he, and I am his disciple.

The immaculate tusker, living in remoteness,
with fetters all shattered, fully freed;
Skilled in discussion, imbued with wisdom,

his banner lowered,[594] he no longer lusts;
Having tamed himself, he no more proliferates:[595]
The Blessed One is he, and I am his disciple.

The best of seers,[596] with no deceptive schemes,
gained the triple knowledge, attained to holiness;
His heart cleansed, a master of discourse,
he lives ever tranquil, the finder of knowledge;
The first of all givers, he is ever capable:
The Blessed One is he, and I am his disciple.

He is the Noble One, developed in mind,
who has gained the goal and expounds the truth;
Endowed with mindfulness and penetrative insight,
he leans neither forwards nor back;[597]
Free from perturbation, attained to mastery:
The Blessed One is he, and I am his disciple.

He has fared rightly and abides in meditation,
inwardly undefiled, in purity perfect;
He is independent and altogether fearless,[598]
living secluded, attained to the summit;
Having crossed over himself, he leads us across:
The Blessed One is he, and I am his disciple.

Of supreme serenity, with extensive wisdom,
a man of great wisdom, devoid of all greed;
He is the Tathāgata, he is the Sublime One,
the person unrivalled, the one without equal;
He is intrepid, proficient in all:
The Blessed One is he, and I am his disciple.

He has severed craving and become the Enlightened One,
cleared of all clouds, completely untainted;
Most worthy of gifts, most mighty of spirits,
most perfect of persons, beyond estimation;
The greatest in grandeur, attained the peak of glory:
The Blessed One is he, and I am his disciple."

30. "When did you concoct that hymn of praise to the recluse Gotama, householder?"

"Venerable sir, suppose there were a great heap of many kinds of flowers, [387] and then a clever garland-maker or garland-maker's apprentice were to knot them into a multicoloured garland; so too, venerable sir, the Blessed One has many praiseworthy qualities, many hundred praiseworthy qualities. Who, venerable sir, would not praise the praiseworthy?"

31. Then, since the Nigaṇṭha Nātaputta was unable to bear this honour done to the Blessed One, hot blood then and there gushed from his mouth.[599]

57 *Kukkuravatika Sutta*
The Dog-Duty Ascetic

1. THUS HAVE I HEARD. On one occasion the Blessed One was living in the Koliyan country where there was a town of the Koliyans named Haliddavasana.

2. Then Puṇṇa, son of the Koliyans, an ox-duty ascetic, and also Seniya, a naked dog-duty ascetic, went to the Blessed One.[600] Puṇṇa, the ox-duty ascetic, paid homage to the Blessed One and sat down at one side, while Seniya, the naked dog-duty ascetic, exchanged greetings with the Blessed One, and when this courteous and amiable talk was finished, he too sat down at one side curled up like a dog. Puṇṇa, the ox-duty ascetic, said to the Blessed One: "Venerable sir, this Seniya is a naked dog-duty ascetic who does what is hard to do: he eats his food when it is thrown to the ground. He has long taken up and practised that dog-duty. What will be his destination? What will be his future course?"

"Enough, Puṇṇa, let that be. Do not ask me that."

A second time...And a third time Puṇṇa, the ox-duty ascetic, said to the Blessed One: "Venerable sir, this Seniya is a naked dog-duty ascetic who does what is hard to do: he eats his food when it is thrown to the ground. He has long taken up and practised that dog-duty. What will be his destination? What will be his future course?"

"Well, Puṇṇa, since I certainly cannot persuade you when I say: 'Enough, Puṇṇa, let that be. Do not ask me that,' I shall therefore answer you.

3. "Here, Puṇṇa, someone develops the dog-duty fully and uninterruptedly; he develops the dog-habit fully and uninterruptedly; he develops the dog-mind fully [388] and uninterruptedly; he develops dog-behaviour fully and uninterruptedly. Having done so, on the dissolution of the body, after death, he

reappears in the company of dogs. But if he has such a view as this: 'By this virtue or observance or asceticism or holy life I shall become a [great] god or some [lesser] god,' that is wrong view in his case. Now there are two destinations for one with wrong view, I say: hell or the animal realm.[601] So, Puṇṇa, if his dog-duty succeeds, it will lead him to the company of dogs; if it fails, it will lead him to hell."

4. When this was said, Seniya the naked dog-duty ascetic cried out and burst into tears. Then the Blessed One told Puṇṇa, son of the Koliyans, the ox-duty ascetic: "Puṇṇa, I could not persuade you when I said: 'Enough, Puṇṇa, let that be. Do not ask me that.'"

[Then Seniya the naked dog-duty ascetic said:] "Venerable sir, I am not crying because the Blessed One has said this about me, but because I have long taken up and practised this dog-duty. Venerable sir, this Puṇṇa, son of the Koliyans, is an ox-duty ascetic. He has long taken up and practised that ox-duty. What will be his destination? What will be his future course?"

"Enough, Seniya, let that be. Do not ask me that."

A second time...And a third time Seniya the naked dog-duty ascetic asked the Blessed One: "Venerable sir, this Puṇṇa, son of the Koliyans, is an ox-duty ascetic. He has long taken up and practised that ox-duty. What will be his destination? What will be his future course?"

"Well, Seniya, since I certainly cannot persuade you when I say: 'Enough, Seniya, let that be. Do not ask me that,' I shall therefore answer you.

5. "Here, Seniya, someone develops the ox-duty fully and uninterruptedly; he develops the ox-habit fully and uninterruptedly; he develops the ox-mind fully and uninterruptedly; he develops ox-behaviour fully and uninterruptedly. Having done so, on the dissolution of the body, after death, he reappears in the company of oxen. [389] But if he has such a view as this: 'By this virtue or observance or asceticism or holy life I shall become a [great] god or some [lesser] god,' that is wrong view in his case. Now there are two destinations for one with wrong view, I say: hell or the animal realm. So, Seniya, if his ox-duty succeeds, it will lead him to the company of oxen; if it fails, it will lead him to hell."

6. When this was said, Puṇṇa, son of the Koliyans, the ox-duty ascetic cried out and burst into tears. Then the Blessed One told

Seniya the naked dog-duty ascetic: "Seniya, I could not persuade you when I said: 'Enough, Seniya, let that be. Do not ask me that.'"

[Then Puṇṇa the ox-duty ascetic said:] "Venerable sir, I am not crying because the Blessed One has said this about me, but because I have long taken up and practised this ox-duty. Venerable sir, I have confidence in the Blessed One thus: 'The Blessed One is capable of teaching me the Dhamma in such a way that I can abandon this ox-duty and that this Seniya the naked dog-duty ascetic can abandon that dog-duty.'"

"Then, Puṇṇa, listen and attend closely to what I shall say."—"Yes, venerable sir," he replied. The Blessed One said this:

7. "Puṇṇa, there are four kinds of action proclaimed by me after realising them for myself with direct knowledge. What are the four? There is dark action with dark result; there is bright action with bright result; there is dark-and-bright action with dark-and-bright result; and there is action that is neither dark nor bright with neither-dark-nor-bright result, action that leads to the destruction of action.

8. "And what, Puṇṇa, is dark action with dark result? Here someone generates an afflictive bodily formation, an afflictive verbal formation, an afflictive mental formation.[602] Having generated an afflictive bodily formation, an afflictive verbal formation, an afflictive mental formation, he reappears in an afflictive world.[603] When he has reappeared in an afflictive world, afflictive contacts touch him. Being touched by afflictive contacts, he feels afflictive feelings, exclusively painful, as in the case of the beings in [390] hell. Thus a being's reappearance is due to a being:[604] one reappears through the actions one has performed. When one has reappeared, contacts touch one. Thus I say beings are the heirs of their actions. This is called dark action with dark result.

9. "And what, Puṇṇa, is bright action with bright result? Here someone generates an unafflictive bodily formation, an unafflictive verbal formation, an unafflictive mental formation.[605] Having generated an unafflictive bodily formation, an unafflictive verbal formation, an unafflictive mental formation, he reappears in an unafflictive world.[606] When he has reappeared in an unafflictive world, unafflictive contacts touch him. Being touched by unafflictive contacts, he feels unafflictive feelings, exclusively pleasant, as in the case of the gods of Refulgent Glory. Thus a being's reappearance is due to a being; one reappears through

the actions one has performed. When one has reappeared, contacts touch one. Thus I say beings are the heirs of their actions. This is called bright action with bright result.

10. "And what, Puṇṇa, is dark-and-bright action with dark-and-bright result? Here someone generates a bodily formation that is both afflictive and unafflictive, a verbal formation that is both afflictive and unafflictive, a mental formation that is both afflictive and unafflictive.[607] Having generated a bodily formation, a verbal formation, a mental formation that is both afflictive and unafflictive, he reappears in a world that is both afflictive and unafflictive. When he has reappeared in a world that is both afflictive and unafflictive, both afflictive and unafflictive contacts touch him. Being touched by both afflictive and unafflictive contacts, he feels both afflictive and unafflictive feelings, mingled pleasure and pain, as in the case of human beings and some gods and some beings in the lower worlds. Thus a being's reappearance is due to a being: one reappears through the actions one has performed. When one has reappeared, contacts touch one. Thus I say beings are the heirs to their actions. This is called dark-and-bright action with dark-and-bright result. [391]

11. "And what, Puṇṇa, is action that is neither dark nor bright with neither-dark-nor-bright result, action that leads to the destruction of action? Therein, the volition for abandoning the kind of action that is dark with dark result, and the volition for abandoning the kind of action that is bright with bright result, and the volition for abandoning the kind of action that is dark and bright with dark-and-bright result: this is called action that is neither dark nor bright with neither-dark-nor-bright result, action that leads to the destruction of action.[608] These are the four kinds of action proclaimed by me after realising them for myself with direct knowledge."

12. When this was said, Puṇṇa, son of the Koliyans, the ox-duty ascetic said to the Blessed One: "Magnificent, venerable sir! Magnificent, venerable sir! The Blessed One has made the Dhamma clear in many ways...From today let the Blessed One remember me as a lay follower who has gone to him for refuge for life."

13. But Seniya the naked dog-duty ascetic said to the Blessed One: "Magnificent, venerable sir! Magnificent, venerable sir! The Blessed One has made the Dhamma clear in many ways, as

though he were turning upright what had been overthrown, revealing what was hidden, showing the way to one who was lost, or holding up a lamp in the dark for those with eyesight to see forms. I go to the Blessed One for refuge and to the Dhamma and to the Sangha of bhikkhus. I would receive the going forth under the Blessed One, I would receive the full admission."

14. "Seniya, one who formerly belonged to another sect and desires the going forth and the full admission in this Dhamma and Discipline lives on probation for four months.[609] At the end of four months, if the bhikkhus are satisfied with him, they give him the going forth and the full admission to the bhikkhus' state. But I recognise individual differences in this matter."[610]

"Venerable sir, if those who formerly belonged to another sect and desire the going forth and the full admission in this Dhamma and Discipline live on probation for four months, and if at the end of the four months the bhikkhus being satisfied with them give them the going forth and the full admission to the bhikkhus' state, then I will live on probation for four years. At the end of the four years if the bhikkhus are satisfied with me, let them give me the going forth and the full admission to the bhikkhus' state."

15. Then Seniya the naked dog-duty ascetic received the going forth under the Blessed One, and he received the full admission. And soon, not long after his full admission, dwelling alone, withdrawn, [392] diligent, ardent, and resolute, the venerable Seniya, by realising for himself with direct knowledge, here and now entered upon and abided in that supreme goal of the holy life for the sake of which clansmen rightly go forth from the home life into homelessness. He directly knew: "Birth is destroyed, the holy life has been lived, what had to be done has been done, there is no more coming to any state of being." And the venerable Seniya became one of the arahants.

58 *Abhayarājakumāra Sutta*
To Prince Abhaya

1. THUS HAVE I HEARD. On one occasion the Blessed One was living at Rājagaha in the Bamboo Grove, the Squirrels' Sanctuary.

2. Then Prince Abhaya[611] went to the Nigaṇṭha Nātaputta, and after paying homage to him, sat down at one side. Thereupon the Nigaṇṭha Nātaputta said to him:

3. "Come, prince, refute the recluse Gotama's doctrine, and a good report of you will be spread to this effect: 'Prince Abhaya has refuted the doctrine of the recluse Gotama, who is so powerful and mighty.'"

"But how, venerable sir, shall I refute his doctrine?"

"Come, prince, go to the recluse Gotama and say: 'Venerable sir, would the Tathāgata utter speech that would be unwelcome and disagreeable to others?' If the recluse Gotama, on being asked thus, answers: 'The Tathāgata, prince, would utter speech that would be unwelcome and disagreeable to others,' then say to him: 'Then, venerable sir, what is the difference between you and an ordinary person? For an ordinary person also would utter speech that would be unwelcome and disagreeable to others.' But if the recluse Gotama, on being asked thus, answers: 'The Tathāgata, prince, would not utter speech [393] that would be unwelcome and disagreeable to others,' then say to him: 'Then, venerable sir, why have you declared of Devadatta: "Devadatta is destined for the states of deprivation, Devadatta is destined for hell, Devadatta will remain [in hell] for the aeon, Devadatta is incorrigible"? Devadatta was angry and displeased with that speech of yours.' When the recluse Gotama is posed this two-horned question by you, he will not be able either to throw it up or to gulp it down. If an iron spike were stuck in a man's throat, he would not be able either to throw it up or to gulp it down; so too, prince, when the recluse Gotama is posed this two-horned question by you, he will not be able either to throw it up or to gulp it down."

4. "Yes, venerable sir," Prince Abhaya replied. Then he rose from his seat, and after paying homage to the Nigaṇṭha Nātaputta, keeping him on his right, he left and went to the Blessed One. After paying homage to the Blessed One, he sat down at one side, looked at the sun, and thought: "It is too late today to refute the Blessed One's doctrine. I shall refute the Blessed One's doctrine in my own house tomorrow." Then he said to the Blessed One: "Venerable sir, let the Blessed One with three others consent to accept tomorrow's meal from me." The Blessed One consented in silence.

5. Then, knowing that the Blessed One had consented, Prince Abhaya rose from his seat, and after paying homage to him, keeping him on his right, he departed. Then, when the night had ended, it being morning, the Blessed One dressed, and taking his bowl and outer robe, he went to Prince Abhaya's house and sat down on the seat made ready. Then, with his own hands, Prince Abhaya served and satisfied the Blessed One with various kinds of good food. When the Blessed One had eaten and had withdrawn his hand from the bowl, Prince Abhaya took a low seat, sat down at one side, and said to the Blessed One:

6. "Venerable sir, would a Tathāgata utter such speech as would be unwelcome and disagreeable to others?"

"There is no one-sided answer to that, prince."

"Then, venerable sir, the Nigaṇṭhas have lost in this."

"Why do you say this, prince: [394] 'Then, venerable sir, the Nigaṇṭhas have lost in this'?"[612]

Prince Abhaya then reported to the Blessed One his entire conversation with the Nigaṇṭha Nātaputta.

7. Now on that occasion a young tender infant was lying prone on Prince Abhaya's lap. Then the Blessed One said to Prince Abhaya: [395] "What do you think, prince? If, while you or your nurse were not attending to him, this child were to put a stick or a pebble in his mouth, what would you do to him?"

"Venerable sir, I would take it out. If I could not take it out at once, I would take his head in my left hand, and crooking a finger of my right hand, I would take it out even if it meant drawing blood. Why is that? Because I have compassion for the child."

8. "So too, prince, such speech as the Tathāgata knows to be untrue, incorrect, and unbeneficial, and which is also unwelcome and disagreeable to others: such speech the Tathāgata does not utter. Such speech as the Tathāgata knows to be true and correct but unbeneficial, and which is also unwelcome and disagreeable to others: such speech the Tathāgata does not utter. Such speech as the Tathāgata knows to be true, correct, and beneficial, but which is unwelcome and disagreeable to others: the Tathāgata knows the time to use such speech.[613] Such speech as the Tathāgata knows to be untrue, incorrect, and unbeneficial, but which is welcome and agreeable to others: such speech the Tathāgata does not utter. Such speech as the Tathāgata knows to be true and correct but unbeneficial, and which is welcome and agreeable to others: such speech the Tathāgata does not utter. Such speech as the Tathāgata knows to be true, correct, and beneficial, and which is welcome and agreeable to others: the Tathāgata knows the time to use such speech. Why is that? Because the Tathāgata has compassion for beings."

9. "Venerable sir, when learned nobles, learned brahmins, learned householders, and learned recluses, after formulating a question, then go to the Blessed One and pose it, has there already been in the Blessed One's mind the thought: 'If they come to me and ask me thus, I shall answer thus'? Or does that answer occur to the Tathāgata on the spot?"

10. "As to that, prince, I shall ask you a question in return. Answer it as you choose. What do you think, prince? Are you skilled in the parts of a chariot?"

"Yes, venerable sir, I am."

"What do you think, prince? When people come to you and ask: 'What is the name of this part of the chariot?' has there already been in your mind the thought: [396] 'If they come to me and ask me thus, I shall answer them thus'? Or does that answer occur to you on the spot?"

"Venerable sir, I am well known as a charioteer skilled in the parts of a chariot. All the parts of a chariot are well known to me. That answer would occur to me on the spot."

11. "So too, prince, when learned nobles, learned brahmins, learned householders, and learned recluses, after formulating a question, then come to the Tathāgata and pose it, the answer occurs to the Tathāgata on the spot. Why is that? That element

of things has been fully penetrated by the Tathāgata, through the full penetration of which the answer occurs to the Tathāgata on the spot."[614]

12. When this was said, Prince Abhaya said: "Magnificent, venerable sir! Magnificent, venerable sir! The Blessed One has made the Dhamma clear in many ways...From today let the Blessed One remember me as a lay follower who has gone to him for refuge for life."

59 *Bahuvedanīya Sutta*
The Many Kinds of Feeling

1. THUS HAVE I HEARD. On one occasion the Blessed One was living at Sāvatthī in Jeta's Grove, Anāthapiṇḍika's Park.

2. Then the carpenter Pañcakanga[615] went to the venerable Udāyin, and after paying homage to him, he sat down at one side and asked him:

3. "Venerable sir, how many kinds of feeling have been stated by the Blessed One?"

"Three kinds of feeling have been stated by the Blessed One, householder: pleasant feeling, painful feeling, and neither-painful-nor-pleasant feeling. [397] These three kinds of feeling have been stated by the Blessed One."

"Not three kinds of feeling have been stated by the Blessed One, venerable Udāyin; two kinds of feeling have been stated by the Blessed One: pleasant feeling and painful feeling. This neither-painful-nor-pleasant feeling has been stated by the Blessed One as a peaceful and sublime kind of pleasure."

A second time and a third time the venerable Udāyin stated his position, and a second time and a third time the carpenter Pañcakanga stated his. But the venerable Udāyin could not convince the carpenter Pañcakanga nor could the carpenter Pañcakanga convince the venerable Udāyin.

4. The venerable Ānanda heard their conversation. Then he went to the Blessed One, and after paying homage to him, he sat down at one side and reported to the Blessed One the entire conversation between the venerable Udāyin and the carpenter Pañcakanga. When he had finished, the Blessed One told the venerable Ānanda:

5. "Ānanda, it was actually a true presentation that the carpenter Pañcakanga would not accept from Udāyin, and it was actually a true presentation that Udāyin would not accept from

the carpenter Pañcakanga. I have stated two kinds of feeling in one presentation; [398] I have stated three kinds of feeling in another presentation; I have stated five kinds of feeling in another presentation; I have stated six kinds of feeling in another presentation; I have stated eighteen kinds of feeling in another presentation; I have stated thirty-six kinds of feeling in another presentation; I have stated one hundred and eight kinds of feeling in another presentation.[616] That is how the Dhamma has been shown by me in [different] presentations.

"When the Dhamma has thus been shown by me in [different] presentations, it may be expected of those who will not concede, allow, and accept what is well stated and well spoken by others that they will take to quarreling, brawling, and disputing, stabbing each other with verbal daggers. But it may be expected of those who concede, allow, and accept what is well stated and well spoken by others that they will live in concord, with mutual appreciation, without disputing, blending like milk and water, viewing each other with kindly eyes.

6. "Ānanda, there are these five cords of sensual pleasure. What are the five? Forms cognizable by the eye that are wished for, desired, agreeable, and likeable, connected with sensual desire and provocative of lust. Sounds cognizable by the ear... Odours cognizable by the nose...Flavours cognizable by the tongue...Tangibles cognizable by the body that are wished for, desired, agreeable, and likeable, connected with sensual desire and provocative of lust. These are the five cords of sensual pleasure. Now the pleasure and joy that arise dependent on these five cords of sensual pleasure are called sensual pleasure.

7. "Should anyone say: 'That is the utmost pleasure and joy that beings experience,' I would not concede that to him. Why is that? Because there is another kind of pleasure loftier and more sublime than that pleasure. And what is that other kind of pleasure? Here, Ānanda, quite secluded from sensual pleasures, secluded from unwholesome states, a bhikkhu enters upon and abides in the first jhāna, which is accompanied by applied and sustained thought, with rapture and pleasure born of seclusion. This is that other kind of pleasure loftier and more sublime than the previous pleasure.

8. "Should anyone say: 'That is the utmost pleasure and joy that beings experience,' I would not concede that to him. [399]

Why is that? Because there is another kind of pleasure loftier and more sublime than that pleasure. And what is that other kind of pleasure? Here, Ānanda, with the stilling of applied and sustained thought, a bhikkhu enters upon and abides in the second jhāna, which has self-confidence and singleness of mind without applied and sustained thought, with rapture and pleasure born of concentration. This is that other kind of pleasure loftier and more sublime than the previous pleasure.

9. "Should anyone say...And what is that other kind of pleasure? Here, Ānanda, with the fading away as well of rapture, a bhikkhu abides in equanimity, mindful and fully aware, and still feeling pleasure with the body, he enters upon and abides in the third jhāna, on account of which noble ones announce: 'He has a pleasant abiding who has equanimity and is mindful.' This is that other kind of pleasure loftier and more sublime than the previous pleasure.

10. "Should anyone say...And what is that other kind of pleasure? Here, Ānanda, with the abandoning of pleasure and pain, and with the previous disappearance of joy and grief, a bhikkhu enters upon and abides in the fourth jhāna, which has neither-pain-nor-pleasure and purity of mindfulness due to equanimity. This is that other kind of pleasure loftier and more sublime than the previous pleasure.[617]

11. "Should anyone say...And what is that other kind of pleasure? Here, Ānanda, with the complete surmounting of perceptions of form, with the disappearance of perceptions of sensory impact, with non-attention to perceptions of diversity, aware that 'space is infinite,' a bhikkhu enters upon and abides in the base of infinite space. This is that other kind of pleasure loftier and more sublime than the previous pleasure.

12. "Should anyone say...And what is that other kind of pleasure? Here, Ānanda, by completely surmounting the base of infinite space, aware that 'consciousness is infinite,' a bhikkhu enters upon and abides in the base of infinite consciousness. This is that other kind of pleasure loftier and more sublime than the previous pleasure.

13. "Should anyone say...And what is that other kind of pleasure? Here, Ānanda, by completely surmounting the base of infinite consciousness, aware that 'there is nothing,' a bhikkhu enters upon and abides in the base of nothingness. This is that

other kind of pleasure loftier and more sublime than the previous pleasure. [400]

14. "Should anyone say...And what is that other kind of pleasure? Here, Ānanda, by completely surmounting the base of nothingness, a bhikkhu enters upon and abides in the base of neither-perception-nor-non-perception. This is that other kind of pleasure loftier and more sublime than the previous pleasure.

15. "Should anyone say: 'That is the utmost pleasure and joy that beings experience,' I would not concede that to him. Why is that? Because there is another kind of pleasure loftier and more sublime than that pleasure. And what is that other kind of pleasure? Here, Ānanda, by completely surmounting the base of neither-perception-nor-non-perception, a bhikkhu enters upon and abides in the cessation of perception and feeling. This is that other kind of pleasure loftier and more sublime than the previous pleasure.

16. "It is possible, Ānanda, that wanderers of other sects might speak thus: 'The recluse Gotama speaks of the cessation of perception and feeling and he describes that as pleasure. What is this, and how is this?' Wanderers of other sects who speak thus should be told: 'Friends, the Blessed One describes pleasure not only with reference to pleasant feeling; rather, friends, the Tathāgata describes as pleasure any kind of pleasure wherever and in whatever way it is found.'"[618]

That is what the Blessed One said. The venerable Ānanda was satisfied and delighted in the Blessed One's words.

60 *Apaṇṇaka Sutta*
The Incontrovertible Teaching

1. THUS HAVE I HEARD. On one occasion the Blessed One was wandering in the Kosalan country with a large Sangha of bhikkhus, and eventually he arrived at a Kosalan brahmin village named Sālā.

2. The brahmin householders of Sālā heard: "The recluse Gotama, the son of the Sakyans who went forth from a Sakyan clan, has been wandering in the Kosalan country [401] with a large Sangha of bhikkhus and has come to Sālā. Now a good report of Master Gotama has been spread to this effect: 'That Blessed One is accomplished, fully enlightened, perfect in true knowledge and conduct, sublime, knower of worlds, incomparable leader of persons to be tamed, teacher of gods and humans, enlightened, blessed. He declares this world with its gods, its Māras, and its Brahmās, this generation with its recluses and brahmins, its princes and its people, which he has himself realised with direct knowledge. He teaches the Dhamma good in the beginning, good in the middle, and good in the end, with the right meaning and phrasing, and he reveals a holy life that is utterly perfect and pure.' Now it is good to see such arahants."

3. Then the brahmin householders of Sālā went to the Blessed One. Some paid homage to the Blessed One and sat down at one side; some exchanged greetings with him, and when this courteous and amiable talk was finished, sat down at one side; some extended their hands in reverential salutation towards the Blessed One and sat down at one side; some pronounced their name and clan in the Blessed One's presence and sat down at one side; some kept silent and sat down at one side.

4. When they were seated, the Blessed One asked them: "Householders, is there any teacher agreeable to you in whom you have acquired faith supported by reasons?"[619]

"No, venerable sir, there is no teacher agreeable to us in whom we have acquired faith supported by reasons."

"Since, householders, you have not found an agreeable teacher, you may undertake and practise this incontrovertible teaching;[620] for when the incontrovertible teaching is accepted and undertaken, it will lead to your welfare and happiness for a long time. And what is the incontrovertible teaching?[621]

(I. THE DOCTRINE OF NIHILISM)

5. (A) "Householders, there are some recluses and brahmins whose doctrine and view is this: 'There is nothing given, nothing offered, nothing sacrificed; no fruit or result of good and bad actions; no this world, no other world; no mother, no father; no beings who are reborn spontaneously; no good and virtuous recluses and brahmins in the world who have themselves realised by direct knowledge and declare this world and the other world.'[622] [402]

6. (B) "Now there are some recluses and brahmins whose doctrine is directly opposed to that of those recluses and brahmins, and they say thus: 'There is what is given and what is offered and what is sacrificed; there is fruit and result of good and bad actions; there is this world and the other world; there is mother and father; there are beings who are reborn spontaneously; there are good and virtuous recluses and brahmins in the world who have themselves realised by direct knowledge and declare this world and the other world.' What do you think, householders? Don't these recluses and brahmins hold doctrines directly opposed to each other?"—"Yes, venerable sir."

7. (A.i) "Now, householders, of those recluses and brahmins whose doctrine and view is this: 'There is nothing given...no good and virtuous recluses and brahmins in the world who have themselves realised by direct knowledge and declare this world and the other world,' it is to be expected that they will avoid these three wholesome states, namely, good bodily conduct, good verbal conduct, and good mental conduct, and that they will undertake and practise these three unwholesome states, namely, bodily misconduct, verbal misconduct, and mental misconduct. Why is that? Because those good recluses and brahmins do not see in unwholesome states the danger,

degradation, and defilement, nor do they see in wholesome states the blessing of renunciation, the aspect of cleansing.

8. (A.ii) "Since there actually is another world, one who holds the view 'there is no other world' has wrong view. Since there actually is another world, one who intends 'there is no other world' has wrong intention. Since there actually is another world, one who makes the statement 'there is no other world' has wrong speech. Since there actually is another world, one who says 'there is no other world' is opposed to those arahants who know the other world. Since there actually is another world, one who convinces another 'there is no other world' convinces him to accept an untrue Dhamma; and because he convinces another to accept an untrue Dhamma, he praises himself and disparages others. Thus any pure virtue that he formerly had is abandoned and corrupt conduct is substituted.[623] And this wrong view, wrong intention, wrong speech, opposition to noble ones, convincing another to accept an untrue Dhamma, and self-praise and disparagement of others—these several evil unwholesome states thus come into being with wrong view as their condition. [403]

9. (A.iii) "About this a wise man considers thus: 'If there is no other world, then on the dissolution of the body this good person will have made himself safe enough.[624] But if there is another world, then on the dissolution of the body, after death, he will reappear in a state of deprivation, in an unhappy destination, in perdition, even in hell. Now whether or not the word of those good recluses and brahmins is true, let me assume that there is no other world: still this good person is here and now censured by the wise as an immoral person, one of wrong view who holds the doctrine of nihilism.[625] But on the other hand, if there is another world, then this good person has made an unlucky throw on both counts: since he is censured by the wise here and now, and since on the dissolution of the body, after death, he will reappear in a state of deprivation, in an unhappy destination, in perdition, even in hell. He has wrongly accepted and undertaken this incontrovertible teaching in such a way that it extends only to one side and excludes the wholesome alternative.'[626]

10. (B.i) "Now, householders, of those recluses and brahmins whose doctrine and view is this: 'There is what is given...there are good and virtuous recluses and brahmins in the world who

have themselves realised by direct knowledge and declare this world and the other world,' it is to be expected that they will avoid these three unwholesome states, namely, bodily misconduct, verbal misconduct, and mental misconduct, and that they will undertake and practise these three wholesome states, namely, good bodily conduct, good verbal conduct, and good mental conduct. Why is that? Because those good recluses and brahmins see in unwholesome states the danger, degradation, and defilement, and they see in wholesome states the blessing of renunciation, the aspect of cleansing.

11. (B.ii) "Since there actually is another world, one who holds the view 'there is another world' has right view. Since there actually is another world, one who intends 'there is another world' has right intention. Since there actually is another world, one who makes the statement 'there is another world' has right speech. Since there actually is another world, one who says 'there is another world' is not opposed to those arahants who know the other world. Since there actually is another world, one who convinces another 'there is another world' [404] convinces him to accept true Dhamma; and because he convinces another to accept true Dhamma, he does not praise himself and disparage others. Thus any corrupt conduct that he formerly had is abandoned and pure virtue is substituted. And this right view, right intention, right speech, non-opposition to noble ones, convincing another to accept true Dhamma, and avoidance of self-praise and disparagement of others—these several wholesome states thus come into being with right view as their condition.

12. (B.iii) "About this a wise man considers thus: 'If there is another world, then on the dissolution of the body, after death, this good person will reappear in a happy destination, even in the heavenly world. Now whether or not the word of those good recluses and brahmins is true, let me assume that there is no other world: still this good person is here and now praised by the wise as a virtuous person, one with right view who holds the doctrine of affirmation.[627] And on the other hand, if there is another world, then this good person has made a lucky throw on both counts: since he is praised by the wise here and now, and since on the dissolution of the body, after death, he will reappear in a happy destination, even in the heavenly world. He has rightly accepted and undertaken this incontrovertible

teaching in such a way that it extends to both sides and excludes the unwholesome alternative.'[628]

(II. THE DOCTRINE OF NON-DOING)

13. (A) "Householders, there are some recluses and brahmins whose doctrine and view is this:[629] 'When one acts or makes others act, when one mutilates or makes others mutilate, when one tortures or makes others inflict torture, when one inflicts sorrow or makes others inflict sorrow, when one oppresses or makes others inflict oppression, when one intimidates or makes others inflict intimidation, when one kills living beings, takes what is not given, breaks into houses, plunders wealth, commits burglary, ambushes highways, seduces another's wife, utters falsehood—no evil is done by the doer. If, with a razor-rimmed wheel, one were to make the living beings on this earth into one mass of flesh, into one heap of flesh, because of this there would be no evil and no outcome of evil. If one were to go along the south bank of the Ganges killing and slaughtering, mutilating and making others mutilate, torturing and making others inflict torture, because of this there would be no evil and no outcome of evil. If one were to go along the north bank of the Ganges giving gifts and making others give gifts, making offerings and making others make offerings, because of this there would be no merit and no outcome of merit. By giving, by taming oneself, by restraint, by speaking truth, there is no merit and no outcome of merit.'

14. (B) "Now there are some recluses and brahmins [405] whose doctrine is directly opposed to that of those recluses and brahmins, and they say thus: 'When one acts or makes others act, when one mutilates or makes others mutilate...utters falsehood—evil is done by the doer. If, with a razor-rimmed wheel, one were to make the living beings on this earth into one mass of flesh, into one heap of flesh, because of this there would be evil and the outcome of evil. If one were to go along the south bank of the Ganges killing and slaughtering, mutilating and making others mutilate, torturing and making others inflict torture, because of this there would be evil and the outcome of evil. If one were to go along the north bank of the Ganges giving gifts and making others give gifts, making offerings and

making others make offerings, because of this there would be merit and the outcome of merit. By giving, by taming oneself, by restraint, by speaking truth, there is merit and the outcome of merit.' What do you think, householders? Don't these recluses and brahmins hold doctrines directly opposed to each other?"—"Yes, venerable sir."

15. (A.i) "Now, householders, of those recluses and brahmins whose doctrine and view is this: 'When one acts or makes others act...there is no merit and no outcome of merit,' it is to be expected that they will avoid these three wholesome states, namely, good bodily conduct, good verbal conduct and good mental conduct, and that they will undertake and practise these three unwholesome states, namely, bodily misconduct, verbal misconduct, and mental misconduct. Why is that? Because those good recluses and brahmins do not see in unwholesome states the danger, degradation, and defilement, nor do they see in wholesome states the blessing of renunciation, the aspect of cleansing.

16. (A.ii) "Since there actually is doing, one who holds the view 'there is no doing' has wrong view. Since there actually is doing, one who intends 'there is no doing' has wrong intention. Since there actually is doing, one who makes the statement 'there is no doing' has wrong speech. Since there actually is doing, one who says 'there is no doing' is opposed to those arahants who hold the doctrine that there is doing. Since there actually is doing, one who convinces another 'there is no doing' convinces him to accept an untrue Dhamma; and because he convinces another to accept an untrue Dhamma, he praises himself and disparages others. Thus any pure virtue that he formerly had is abandoned and corrupt conduct is substituted. [406] And this wrong view, wrong intention, wrong speech, opposition to noble ones, convincing another to accept an untrue Dhamma, and self-praise and disparagement of others—these several evil unwholesome states thus come into being with wrong view as their condition.

17. (A.iii) "About this a wise man considers thus: 'If there is no doing, then on the dissolution of the body this good person will have made himself safe enough. But if there is doing, then on the dissolution of the body, after death, he will reappear in a state of deprivation, in an unhappy destination, in perdition, even in hell. Now whether or not the word of those good recluses and

brahmins is true, let me assume that there is no doing: still this good person is here and now censured by the wise as an immoral person, one of wrong view who holds the doctrine of non-doing. But on the other hand, if there is doing, then this good person has made an unlucky throw on both counts: since he is censured by the wise here and now, and since on the dissolution of the body, after death, he will reappear in a state of deprivation, in an unhappy destination, in perdition, even in hell. He has wrongly accepted and undertaken this incontrovertible teaching in such a way that it extends only to one side and excludes the wholesome alternative.'

18. (B.i) "Now, householders, of those recluses and brahmins whose doctrine and view is this: 'When one acts or makes others act...there is merit and outcome of merit,' it is to be expected that they will avoid these three unwholesome states, namely, bodily misconduct, verbal misconduct, and mental misconduct, and that they will undertake and practise these three wholesome states, namely, good bodily conduct, good verbal conduct, and good mental conduct. Why is that? Because those good recluses and brahmins see in unwholesome states the danger, degradation, and defilement, and they see in wholesome states the blessing of renunciation, the aspect of cleansing.

19. (B.ii) "Since there actually is doing, one who holds the view 'there is doing' has right view. Since there actually is doing, one who intends 'there is doing' has right intention. Since there actually is doing, one who makes the statement 'there is doing' has right speech. Since there actually is doing, one who says 'there is doing' is not opposed to those arahants who hold the doctrine that there is doing. Since there actually is doing, one who convinces another 'there is doing' convinces him to accept true Dhamma; [407] and because he convinces another to accept true Dhamma, he does not praise himself and disparage others. Thus any corrupt conduct that he formerly had is abandoned and pure virtue is substituted. And this right view, right intention, right speech, non-opposition to noble ones, convincing another to accept true Dhamma, and avoidance of self-praise and disparagement of others—these several wholesome states thus come into being with right view as their condition.

20. (B.iii) "About this a wise man considers thus: 'If there is doing, then on the dissolution of the body, after death, this good

person will reappear in a happy destination, even in the heavenly world. Now whether or not the word of those good recluses and brahmins is true, let me assume that there is no doing: still this good person is here and now praised by the wise as a virtuous person, one with right view who holds the doctrine of doing. And on the other hand, if there is doing, then this good person has made a lucky throw on both counts: since he is praised by the wise here and now, and since on the dissolution of the body, after death, he will reappear in a happy destination, even in the heavenly world. He has rightly accepted and undertaken this incontrovertible teaching in such a way that it extends to both sides and excludes the unwholesome alternative.'

(III. THE DOCTRINE OF NON-CAUSALITY)

21. (A) "Householders, there are some recluses and brahmins whose doctrine and view is this:[630] 'There is no cause or condition for the defilement of beings; beings are defiled without cause or condition. There is no cause or condition for the purification of beings; beings are purified without cause or condition. There is no power, no energy, no manly strength, no manly endurance. All beings, all living things, all creatures, all souls are without mastery, power, and energy; moulded by destiny, circumstance, and nature, they experience pleasure and pain in the six classes.'[631]

22. (B) "Now there are some recluses and brahmins whose doctrine is directly opposed to that of those recluses and brahmins, and they say thus: 'There is a cause and condition for the defilement of beings; beings are defiled owing to a cause and condition. There is a cause and condition for the purification of beings; beings are purified owing to a cause and condition. There is power, energy, manly strength, manly endurance. It is not the case that all beings, all living things, all creatures, all souls are without mastery, power, and energy, or that moulded by destiny, circumstance, and nature, they experience pleasure and pain in the six classes.' What do you think, householders? [408] Don't these recluses and brahmins hold doctrines directly opposed to each other?"—"Yes, venerable sir."

23. (A.i) "Now, householders, of those recluses and brahmins whose doctrine and view is this: 'There is no cause or condition

for the defilement of beings...they experience pleasure and pain in the six classes,' it is to be expected that they will avoid these three wholesome states, namely, good bodily conduct, good verbal conduct, and good mental conduct, and that they will undertake and practise these three unwholesome states, namely, bodily misconduct, verbal misconduct, and mental misconduct. Why is that? Because those good recluses and brahmins do not see in unwholesome states the danger, degradation, and defilement, nor do they see in wholesome states the blessing of renunciation, the aspect of cleansing.

24. (A.ii) "Since there actually is causality, one who holds the view 'there is no causality' has wrong view. Since there actually is causality, one who intends 'there is no causality' has wrong intention. Since there actually is causality, one who makes the statement 'there is no causality' has wrong speech. Since there actually is causality, one who says 'there is no causality' is opposed to those arahants who hold the doctrine of causality. Since there actually is causality, one who convinces another 'there is no causality' convinces him to accept an untrue Dhamma; and because he convinces another to accept an untrue Dhamma, he praises himself and disparages others. Thus any pure virtue that he formerly had is abandoned and corrupt conduct is substituted. And this wrong view, wrong intention, wrong speech, opposition to noble ones, convincing another to accept an untrue Dhamma, and self-praise and disparagement of others—these several evil unwholesome states thus come into being with wrong view as their condition.

25. (A.iii) "About this a wise man considers thus: 'If there is no causality, then on the dissolution of the body this good person will have made himself safe enough. But if there is causality, then on the dissolution of the body, after death, he will reappear in a state of deprivation, in an unhappy destination, in perdition, even in hell. Now whether or not the word of those good recluses and brahmins is true, let me assume that there is no causality: still this good person is here and now censured by the wise as an immoral person, one of wrong view who holds the doctrine of non-causality. But on the other hand, if there is causality, then this good person has made an unlucky throw on both counts: [409] since he is censured by the wise here and now, and since on the dissolution of the body, after death, he

will reappear in a state of deprivation, in an unhappy destination, in perdition, even in hell. He has wrongly accepted and undertaken this incontrovertible teaching in such a way that it extends only to one side and excludes the wholesome alternative.'

26. (B.i) "Now, householders, of those recluses and brahmins whose doctrine and view is this: 'There is a cause and condition for the defilement of beings…they experience pleasure and pain in the six classes,' it is to be expected that they will avoid these three unwholesome states, namely, bodily misconduct, verbal misconduct, and mental misconduct, and that they will undertake and practise these three wholesome states, namely, good bodily conduct, good verbal conduct, and good mental conduct. Why is that? Because those good recluses and brahmins see in unwholesome states the danger, degradation, and defilement, and they see in wholesome states the blessing of renunciation, the aspect of cleansing.

27. (B.ii) "Since there actually is causality, one who holds the view 'there is causality' has right view. Since there actually is causality, one who intends 'there is causality' has right intention. Since there actually is causality, one who makes the statement 'there is causality' has right speech. Since there actually is causality, one who says 'there is causality' is not opposed to those arahants who hold the doctrine of causality. Since there actually is causality, one who convinces another 'there is causality' convinces him to accept true Dhamma; and because he convinces another to accept true Dhamma, he does not praise himself and disparage others. Thus any corrupt conduct that he formerly had is abandoned and pure virtue is substituted. And this right view, right intention, right speech, non-opposition to noble ones, convincing another to accept true Dhamma, and avoidance of self-praise and disparagement of others—these several wholesome states thus come into being with right view as their condition.

28. (B.iii) "About this a wise man considers thus: 'If there is causality, then on the dissolution of the body, after death, this good person will reappear in a happy destination, even in the heavenly world. Now whether or not the word of those good recluses and brahmins is true, let me assume that there is no causality: still this good person is here and now praised by the wise as a virtuous person, one with right view who holds the

doctrine of causality. And on the other hand, if there is [410] causality, then this good person has made a lucky throw on both counts: since he is praised by the wise here and now, and since on the dissolution of the body, after death, he will reappear in a happy destination, even in the heavenly world. He has rightly accepted and undertaken this incontrovertible teaching in such a way that it extends to both sides and excludes the unwholesome alternative.'

(IV. THERE ARE NO IMMATERIAL REALMS)

29. "Householders, there are some recluses and brahmins whose doctrine and view is this: 'There are definitely no immaterial realms.'[632]

30. "Now there are some recluses and brahmins whose doctrine is directly opposed to that of those recluses and brahmins, and they say thus: 'There definitely are immaterial realms.' What do you think, householders? Don't these recluses and brahmins hold doctrines directly opposed to each other?"—"Yes, venerable sir."

31. "About this a wise man considers thus: 'These good recluses and brahmins hold the doctrine and view "there are definitely no immaterial realms," but that has not been seen by me. And these other good recluses and brahmins hold the doctrine and view "there definitely are immaterial realms," but that has not been known by me. If, without knowing and seeing, I were to take one side and declare: "Only this is true, anything else is wrong," that would not be fitting for me. Now as to the recluses and brahmins who hold the doctrine and view "there definitely are no immaterial realms," if their word is true then it is certainly still possible that I might reappear [after death] among the gods of the fine-material realms who consist of mind.[633] But as to the recluses and brahmins who hold the doctrine and view "there definitely are immaterial realms," if their word is true then it is certainly possible that I might reappear [after death] among the gods of the immaterial realms who consist of perception. The taking up of rods and weapons, quarrels, brawls, disputes, recrimination, malice, and false speech are seen to occur based on material form, but this does not exist at all in the immaterial realms.' After reflecting thus, he practises the way

to disenchantment with material forms, to the fading away and cessation of material forms.[634]

(V. THERE IS NO CESSATION OF BEING)

32. "Householders, there are some recluses and brahmins whose doctrine and view is this: 'There is definitely no cessation of being.'[635]

33. "Now there are some recluses and brahmins whose doctrine is directly opposed to that of those recluses and brahmins, and they say thus: 'There definitely [411] is a cessation of being.' What do you think, householders? Don't these recluses and brahmins hold doctrines directly opposed to each other?"—"Yes, venerable sir."

34. "About this a wise man considers thus: 'These good recluses and brahmins hold the doctrine and view "there is definitely no cessation of being," but that has not been seen by me. And these other good recluses and brahmins hold the doctrine and view "there definitely is a cessation of being," but that has not been known by me. If, without knowing and seeing, I were to take one side and declare: "Only this is true, anything else is wrong," that would not be fitting for me. Now as to the recluses and brahmins who hold the doctrine and view "there definitely is no cessation of being," if their word is true then it is certainly still possible that I might reappear [after death] among the gods of the immaterial realms who consist of perception. But as to the recluses and brahmins who hold the doctrine and view "there definitely is a cessation of being," if their word is true then it is possible that I might here and now attain final Nibbāna. The view of those good recluses and brahmins who hold the doctrine and view "there definitely is no cessation of being" is close to lust, close to bondage, close to delighting, close to holding, close to clinging; but the view of those good recluses and brahmins who hold the doctrine and view "there definitely is cessation of being" is close to non-lust, close to non-bondage, close to non-delighting, close to non-holding, close to non-clinging.' After reflecting thus, he practises the way to disenchantment with being, to the fading away and cessation of being.[636]

(FOUR KINDS OF PERSONS)

35. "Householders, there are four kinds of persons to be found existing in the world. What four? Here a certain kind of person torments himself and pursues the practice of torturing himself. Here a certain kind of person torments others and pursues the practice of torturing others. Here a certain kind of person torments himself and pursues the practice of torturing himself, and he also torments others and pursues the practice of torturing others. Here a certain kind of person does not torment himself or pursue the practice of torturing himself, and he does not torment others or pursue the practice of torturing others. [412] Since he torments neither himself nor others, he is here and now hungerless, extinguished, and cooled, and he abides experiencing bliss, having himself become holy.

36. "What kind of person, householders, torments himself and pursues the practice of torturing himself? Here a certain person goes naked, rejecting conventions...(*as Sutta 51, §8*)...Thus in such a variety of ways he dwells pursuing the practice of tormenting and mortifying the body. This is called the kind of person who torments himself and pursues the practice of torturing himself.

37. "What kind of person, householders, torments others and pursues the practice of torturing others? Here a certain person is a butcher of sheep...(*as Sutta 51, §9*)...or one who follows any other such bloody occupation. This is called the kind of person who torments others and pursues the practice of torturing others.

38. "What kind of a person, householders, torments himself and pursues the practice of torturing himself and also torments others and pursues the practice of torturing others? Here some person is a head-anointed noble king or a well-to-do brahmin... (*as Sutta 51, §10*)...And then his slaves, messengers, and servants make preparations, weeping with tearful faces, being spurred on by threats of punishment and by fear. This is called the kind of person who torments himself and pursues the practice of torturing himself and who torments others and pursues the practice of torturing others.

39. "What kind of person, householders, does not torment himself or pursue the practice of torturing himself and does not torment others or pursue the practice of torturing others—the

one who, since he torments neither himself nor others, is here and now hungerless, extinguished, and cooled, and abides experiencing bliss, having himself become holy?

40–55. "Here, householders, a Tathāgata appears in the world...(*as Sutta 51, §§12–27*) [413]...He understands: 'Birth is destroyed, the holy life has been lived, what had to be done has been done, there is no more coming to any state of being.'

56. "This, householders, is called the kind of person who does not torment himself or pursue the practice of torturing himself and who does not torment others or pursue the practice of torturing others—the one who, since he torments neither himself nor others, is here and now hungerless, extinguished, and cooled, and abides experiencing bliss, having himself become holy."

57. When this was said, the brahmin householders of Sālā said to the Blessed One: "Magnificent, Master Gotama! Magnificent, Master Gotama! Master Gotama has made the Dhamma clear in many ways, as though he were turning upright what had been overthrown, revealing what was hidden, showing the way to one who was lost, or holding up a lamp in the darkness for those with eyesight to see forms. We go to Master Gotama for refuge and to the Dhamma and to the Sangha of bhikkhus. From today let Master Gotama accept us as lay followers who have gone to him for refuge for life."

2
The Division on Bhikkhus
(*Bhikkhuvagga*)

61 *Ambalaṭṭhikārāhulovāda Sutta*
Advice to Rāhula at Ambalaṭṭhikā

[414] 1. THUS HAVE I HEARD. On one occasion the Blessed One was living at Rājagaha in the Bamboo Grove, the Squirrels' Sanctuary.

2. Now on that occasion the venerable Rāhula was living at Ambalaṭṭhikā.[637] Then, when it was evening, the Blessed One rose from meditation and went to the venerable Rāhula at Ambalaṭṭhikā. The venerable Rāhula saw the Blessed One coming in the distance and made a seat ready and set out water for washing the feet. The Blessed One sat down on the seat made ready and washed his feet. The venerable Rāhula paid homage to him and sat down at one side.

3. Then the Blessed One left a little water in the water vessel and asked the venerable Rāhula: "Rāhula, do you see this little water left in the water vessel?"—"Yes, venerable sir."—"Even so little, Rāhula, is the recluseship of those who are not ashamed to tell a deliberate lie."

4. Then the Blessed One threw away the little water that was left and asked the venerable Rāhula: "Rāhula, do you see that little water that was thrown away?"—"Yes, venerable sir."—"Even so, Rāhula, those who are not ashamed to tell a deliberate lie have thrown away their recluseship."

5. Then the Blessed One turned the water vessel upside down and asked the venerable Rāhula: "Rāhula, do you see this water vessel turned upside down?"—"Yes, venerable sir."—"Even so, Rāhula, those who are not ashamed to tell a deliberate lie have turned their recluseship upside down."

6. Then the Blessed One turned the water vessel right way up again and asked the venerable Rāhula: "Rāhula, do you see this hollow, empty water vessel?"—"Yes, venerable sir."—"Even so

hollow and empty, Rāhula, is the recluseship of those who are not ashamed to tell a deliberate lie."

7. "Suppose, Rāhula, there were a royal tusker elephant with tusks as long as chariot poles, full-grown in stature, high-bred, and accustomed to battle. In battle he would perform his task with his forefeet and his hindfeet, with his forequarters and his hindquarters, with his head and his ears, with his tusks and his tail, [415] yet he would keep back his trunk. Then his rider would think: 'This royal tusker elephant with tusks as long as chariot poles...performs his task in battle with his forefeet and his hindfeet...yet he keeps back his trunk. He has not yet given up his life.' But when the royal tusker elephant...performs his task in battle with his forefeet and his hindfeet, with his forequarters and his hindquarters, with his head and his ears, with his tusks and his tail, and also with his trunk, then his rider would think: 'This royal tusker elephant with tusks as long as chariot poles...performs his task in battle with his forefeet and his hindfeet...and also with his trunk. He has given up his life. Now there is nothing this royal tusker elephant would not do.' So too, Rāhula, when one is not ashamed to tell a deliberate lie, there is no evil, I say, that one would not do. Therefore, Rāhula, you should train thus: 'I will not utter a falsehood even as a joke.'

8. "What do you think, Rāhula? What is the purpose of a mirror?"

"For the purpose of reflection, venerable sir."

"So too, Rāhula, an action with the body should be done after repeated reflection; an action by speech should be done after repeated reflection; an action by mind should be done after repeated reflection.

9. "Rāhula, when you wish to do an action with the body, you should reflect upon that same bodily action thus: 'Would this action that I wish to do with the body lead to my own affliction, or to the affliction of others, or to the affliction of both? Is it an unwholesome bodily action with painful consequences, with painful results?' When you reflect, if you know: 'This action that I wish to do with the body would lead to my own affliction, or to the affliction of others, or to the affliction of both; it is an unwholesome bodily action with painful consequences, with painful results,' then you definitely should not

do such an action with the body. [416] But when you reflect, if you know: 'This action that I wish to do with the body would not lead to my own affliction, or to the affliction of others, or to the affliction of both; it is a wholesome bodily action with pleasant consequences, with pleasant results,' then you may do such an action with the body.

10. "Also, Rāhula, while you are doing an action with the body, you should reflect upon that same bodily action thus: 'Does this action that I am doing with the body lead to my own affliction, or to the affliction of others, or to the affliction of both? Is it an unwholesome bodily action with painful consequences, with painful results?' When you reflect, if you know: 'This action that I am doing with the body leads to my own affliction, or to the affliction of others, or to the affliction of both; it is an unwholesome bodily action with painful consequences, with painful results,' then you should suspend such a bodily action. But when you reflect, if you know: 'This action that I am doing with the body does not lead to my own affliction, or to the affliction of others, or to the affliction of both; it is a wholesome bodily action with pleasant consequences, with pleasant results,' then you may continue in such a bodily action.

11. "Also, Rāhula, after you have done an action with the body, you should reflect upon that same bodily action thus: 'Did this action that I did with the body lead to my own affliction, or to the affliction of others, or to the affliction of both? Was it an unwholesome bodily action with painful consequences, with painful results?' When you reflect, if you know: 'This action that I did with the body led to my own affliction, or to the affliction of others, or to the affliction of both; it was an unwholesome bodily action with painful consequences, with painful results,' then you should confess such a bodily action, reveal it, and lay it open to the Teacher or to your wise companions in the holy life. Having confessed it, revealed it, and laid it open, [417] you should undertake restraint for the future.[638] But when you reflect, if you know: 'This action that I did with the body did not lead to my own affliction, or to the affliction of others, or to the affliction of both; it was a wholesome bodily action with pleasant consequences, pleasant results,' you can abide happy and glad, training day and night in wholesome states.

12. "Rāhula, when you wish to do an action by speech...(*complete*

as in §9, substituting "speech" *for* "body")...you may do such an action by speech.

13. "Also, Rāhula, while you are doing an action by speech... (*complete as in §10, substituting* "speech" *for* "body") [418]...you may continue in such an action by speech.

14. "Also, Rāhula, after you have done an action by speech... (*complete as in §11, substituting* "speech" *for* "body")...you can abide happy and glad, training day and night in wholesome states.

15. "Rāhula, when you wish to do an action by mind...(*complete as in §9, substituting* "mind" *for* "body") [419]...you may do such an action by mind.

16. "Also, Rāhula, while you are doing an action by mind... (*complete as in §10, substituting* "mind" *for* "body")...you may continue in such a mental action.

17. "Also, Rāhula, after you have done an action by mind... (*complete as in §11, substituting* "mind" *for* "body"[639])...you can abide happy and glad, training day and night in wholesome states. [420]

18. "Rāhula, whatever recluses and brahmins in the past purified their bodily action, their verbal action, and their mental action, all did so by repeatedly reflecting thus. Whatever recluses and brahmins in the future will purify their bodily action, their verbal action, and their mental action, all will do so by repeatedly reflecting thus. Whatever recluses and brahmins in the present are purifying their bodily action, their verbal action, and their mental action, all are doing so by repeatedly reflecting thus. Therefore, Rāhula, you should train thus: 'We will purify our bodily action, our verbal action, and our mental action by repeatedly reflecting upon them.'"

That is what the Blessed One said. The venerable Rāhula was satisfied and delighted in the Blessed One's words.

62 *Mahārāhulovāda Sutta*
The Greater Discourse of Advice to Rāhula

1. THUS HAVE I HEARD.[640] On one occasion the Blessed One was living at Sāvatthī in Jeta's Grove, Anāthapiṇḍika's Park.

2. Then, when it was morning, the Blessed One dressed, and taking his bowl and outer robe, went into Sāvatthī for alms. The venerable Rāhula also [421] dressed, and taking his bowl and outer robe, followed close behind the Blessed One.

3. Then the Blessed One looked back and addressed the venerable Rāhula thus:[641] "Rāhula, any kind of material form whatever, whether past, future, or present, internal or external, gross or subtle, inferior or superior, far or near, all material form should be seen as it actually is with proper wisdom thus: 'This is not mine, this I am not, this is not my self.'"

"Only material form, Blessed One? Only material form, Sublime One?"

"Material form, Rāhula, and feeling, perception, formations, and consciousness."

4. Then the venerable Rāhula considered thus: "Who would go into the town for alms today when personally admonished by the Blessed One?" Thus he turned back and sat down at the root of a tree, folding his legs crosswise, setting his body erect, and establishing mindfulness in front of him.

5. The venerable Sāriputta saw him sitting there and addressed him thus: "Rāhula, develop mindfulness of breathing. When mindfulness of breathing is developed and cultivated, it is of great fruit and great benefit."[642]

6. Then, when it was evening, the venerable Rāhula rose from meditation and went to the Blessed One. After paying homage to him, he sat down at one side and asked the Blessed One:

7. "Venerable sir, how is mindfulness of breathing developed and cultivated, so that it is of great fruit and great benefit?"

(THE FOUR GREAT ELEMENTS)

8. "Rāhula,[643] whatever internally, belonging to oneself, is solid, solidified, and clung-to, that is, head-hairs, body-hairs, nails, teeth, skin, flesh, sinews, bones, bone-marrow, kidneys, heart, liver, diaphragm, spleen, lungs, large intestines, small intestines, contents of the stomach, feces, or whatever else internally, belonging to oneself, is solid, solidified, and clung-to: this is called the internal earth element. Now both the internal earth element and the external earth element are simply earth element. And that should be seen as it actually is with proper wisdom thus: 'This is not mine, this I am not, this is not my self.' [422] When one sees it thus as it actually is with proper wisdom, one becomes disenchanted with the earth element and makes the mind dispassionate towards the earth element.

9. "What, Rāhula, is the water element? The water element may be either internal or external. What is the internal water element? Whatever internally, belonging to oneself, is water, watery, and clung-to, that is, bile, phlegm, pus, blood, sweat, fat, tears, grease, spittle, snot, oil-of-the-joints, urine, or whatever else internally, belonging to oneself, is water, watery, and clung-to: this is called the internal water element. Now both the internal water element and the external water element are simply water element. And that should be seen as it actually is with proper wisdom thus: 'This is not mine, this I am not, this is not my self.' When one sees it thus as it actually is with proper wisdom, one becomes disenchanted with the water element and makes the mind dispassionate towards the water element.

10. "What, Rāhula, is the fire element? The fire element may be either internal or external. What is the internal fire element? Whatever internally, belonging to oneself, is fire, fiery, and clung-to, that is, that by which one is warmed, ages, and is consumed, and that by which what is eaten, drunk, consumed, and tasted gets completely digested, or whatever else internally, belonging to oneself, is fire, fiery, and clung-to: this is called the internal fire element. Now both the internal fire element and the external fire element are simply fire element. And that should be seen as it actually is with proper wisdom thus: 'This is not mine, this I am not, this is not my self.' When one sees it thus as it actually is with proper wisdom, one becomes disenchanted with

the fire element and makes the mind dispassionate towards the fire element.

11. "What, Rāhula, is the air element? The air element may be either internal or external. What is the internal air element? Whatever internally, belonging to oneself, is air, airy, and clung-to, that is, up-going winds, down-going winds, winds in the belly, winds in the bowels, winds that course through the limbs, in-breath and out-breath, or whatever else internally, belonging to oneself, is air, airy, and clung-to: this is called the internal air element. Now both the internal air element and the external air element are simply air element. And that should be seen as it actually is with proper wisdom thus: 'This is not mine, this I am not, this is not my self.' [423] When one sees it thus as it actually is with proper wisdom, one becomes disenchanted with the air element and makes the mind dispassionate towards the air element.

12. "What, Rāhula, is the space element?[644] The space element may be either internal or external. What is the internal space element? Whatever internally, belonging to oneself, is space, spatial, and clung-to, that is, the holes of the ears, the nostrils, the door of the mouth, and that [aperture] whereby what is eaten, drunk, consumed, and tasted gets swallowed, and where it collects, and whereby it is excreted from below, or whatever else internally, belonging to oneself, is space, spatial, and clung-to: this is called the internal space element. Now both the internal space element and the external space element are simply space element. And that should be seen as it actually is with proper wisdom thus: 'This is not mine, this I am not, this is not my self.' When one sees it thus as it actually is with proper wisdom, one becomes disenchanted with the space element and makes the mind dispassionate towards the space element.

13. "Rāhula, develop meditation that is like the earth; for when you develop meditation that is like the earth, arisen agreeable and disagreeable contacts will not invade your mind and remain.[645] Just as people throw clean things and dirty things, excrement, urine, spittle, pus, and blood on the earth, and the earth is not repelled, humiliated, and disgusted because of that, so too, Rāhula, develop meditation that is like the earth; for when you develop meditation that is like the earth, arisen agreeable and disagreeable contacts will not invade your mind and remain.

14. "Rāhula, develop meditation that is like water; for when you develop meditation that is like water, arisen agreeable and disagreeable contacts will not invade your mind and remain. Just as people wash clean things and dirty things, excrement, urine, spittle, pus, and blood in water, and the water is not repelled, humiliated, and disgusted because of that, so too, [424] Rāhula, develop meditation that is like water; for when you develop meditation that is like water, arisen agreeable and disagreeable contacts will not invade your mind and remain.

15. "Rāhula, develop meditation that is like fire; for when you develop meditation that is like fire, arisen agreeable and disagreeable contacts will not invade your mind and remain. Just as people burn clean things and dirty things, excrement, urine, spittle, pus, and blood in fire, and the fire is not repelled, humiliated, and disgusted because of that, so too, Rāhula, develop meditation that is like fire; for when you develop meditation that is like fire, arisen agreeable and disagreeable contacts will not invade your mind and remain.

16. "Rāhula, develop meditation that is like air; for when you develop meditation that is like air, arisen agreeable and disagreeable contacts will not invade your mind and remain. Just as the air blows on clean things and dirty things, on excrement, urine, spittle, pus, and blood, and the air is not repelled, humiliated, and disgusted because of that, so too, Rāhula, develop meditation that is like air; for when you develop meditation that is like air, arisen agreeable and disagreeable contacts will not invade your mind and remain.

17. "Rāhula, develop meditation that is like space; for when you develop meditation that is like space, arisen agreeable and disagreeable contacts will not invade your mind and remain. Just as space is not established anywhere, so too, Rāhula, develop meditation that is like space; for when you develop meditation that is like space, arisen agreeable and disagreeable contacts will not invade your mind and remain.

18. "Rāhula, develop meditation on loving-kindness; for when you develop meditation on loving-kindness, any ill will will be abandoned.

19. "Rāhula, develop meditation on compassion; for when you develop meditation on compassion, any cruelty will be abandoned.

20. "Rāhula, develop meditation on altruistic joy; for when you develop meditation on altruistic joy, any discontent will be abandoned.

21. "Rāhula, develop meditation on equanimity; for when you develop meditation on equanimity, any aversion will be abandoned.

22. "Rāhula, develop meditation on foulness; for when you develop meditation on foulness, any lust will be abandoned.

23. "Rāhula, develop meditation on the perception of impermanence; [425] for when you develop meditation on the perception of impermanence, the conceit 'I am' will be abandoned.

24. "Rāhula, develop meditation on mindfulness of breathing. When mindfulness of breathing is developed and cultivated, it is of great fruit and great benefit. And how is mindfulness of breathing developed and cultivated, so that it is of great fruit and great benefit?

25. "Here, Rāhula, a bhikkhu, gone to the forest or to the root of a tree or to an empty hut, sits down; having folded his legs crosswise, set his body erect, and established mindfulness in front of him, ever mindful he breathes in, mindful he breathes out.[646]

26. "Breathing in long, he understands: 'I breathe in long'; or breathing out long, he understands: 'I breathe out long.' Breathing in short, he understands: 'I breathe in short'; or breathing out short, he understands: 'I breathe out short.' He trains thus: 'I shall breathe in experiencing the whole body'; he trains thus: 'I shall breathe out experiencing the whole body.' He trains thus: 'I shall breathe in tranquillising the bodily formation'; he trains thus: 'I shall breathe out tranquillising the bodily formation.'

27. "He trains thus: 'I shall breathe in experiencing rapture'; he trains thus: 'I shall breathe out experiencing rapture.' He trains thus: 'I shall breathe in experiencing pleasure'; he trains thus: 'I shall breathe out experiencing pleasure.' He trains thus: 'I shall breathe in experiencing the mental formation'; he trains thus: 'I shall breathe out experiencing the mental formation.' He trains thus: 'I shall breathe in tranquillising the mental formation'; he trains thus: 'I shall breathe out tranquillising the mental formation.'

28. "He trains thus: 'I shall breathe in experiencing the mind'; he trains thus: 'I shall breathe out experiencing the mind.' He

trains thus: 'I shall breathe in gladdening the mind'; he trains thus: 'I shall breathe out gladdening the mind.' He trains thus: 'I shall breathe in concentrating the mind'; he trains thus: 'I shall breathe out concentrating the mind.' He trains thus: 'I shall breathe in liberating the mind'; he trains thus: 'I shall breathe out liberating the mind.'

29. "He trains thus: 'I shall breathe in contemplating impermanence'; he trains thus: 'I shall breathe out contemplating impermanence.' He trains thus: 'I shall breathe in contemplating fading away'; he trains thus: 'I shall breathe out contemplating fading away.' He trains thus: 'I shall breathe in contemplating cessation'; he trains thus: 'I shall breathe out contemplating cessation.' He trains thus: 'I shall breathe in contemplating relinquishment'; he trains thus: 'I shall breathe out contemplating relinquishment.'

30. "Rāhula, that is how mindfulness of breathing is developed and cultivated, so that it is of great fruit and great benefit. When mindfulness of breathing is developed and cultivated in this way, [426] even the final in-breaths and out-breaths are known as they cease, not unknown."[647]

That is what the Blessed One said. The venerable Rāhula was satisfied and delighted in the Blessed One's words.

63 *Cūḷamālunkya Sutta*
The Shorter Discourse to Mālunkyāputta

1. THUS HAVE I HEARD. On one occasion the Blessed One was living at Sāvatthī in Jeta's Grove, Anāthapiṇḍika's Park.

2. Then, while the venerable Mālunkyāputta was alone in meditation, the following thought arose in his mind:

"These speculative views have been left undeclared by the Blessed One, set aside and rejected by him, namely: 'the world is eternal' and 'the world is not eternal'; 'the world is finite' and 'the world is infinite'; 'the soul is the same as the body' and 'the soul is one thing and the body another'; and 'after death a Tathāgata exists' and 'after death a Tathāgata does not exist' and 'after death a Tathāgata both exists and does not exist' and 'after death a Tathāgata neither exists nor does not exist.' The Blessed One does not declare these to me, and I do not approve of and accept the fact that he does not declare these to me, so I shall go to the Blessed One and ask him the meaning of this. If he declares to me either 'the world is eternal' or 'the world is not eternal'...or 'after death a Tathāgata neither exists nor does not exist,' then I will lead the holy life under him; if he does not declare these to me, then I will abandon the training and return to the low life." [427]

3. Then, when it was evening, the venerable Mālunkyāputta rose from meditation and went to the Blessed One. After paying homage to him, he sat down at one side and told him:

"Here, venerable sir, while I was alone in meditation, the following thought arose in my mind: 'These speculative views have been left undeclared by the Blessed One...If he does not declare these to me, then I will abandon the training and return to the low life.' If the Blessed One knows 'the world is eternal,' let the Blessed One declare to me 'the world is eternal'; if the Blessed One knows 'the world is not eternal,' let the Blessed One declare to me 'the world is not eternal.' If the Blessed One does not know either 'the world is eternal' or 'the world is not eternal,' then it is straightforward for one who does not know and does not see to say: 'I do not know, I do not see.'

"If the Blessed One knows 'the world is finite,'...'the world is infinite,'...'the soul is the same as the body,'...'the soul is one thing and the body another,'...'after death a Tathāgata exists,' [428]...'after death a Tathāgata does not exist,'...If the Blessed One knows 'after death a Tathāgata both exists and does not exist,' let the Blessed One declare that to me; if the Blessed One knows 'after death a Tathāgata neither exists nor does not exist,' let the Blessed One declare that to me. If the Blessed One does not know either 'after death a Tathāgata both exists and does not exist' or 'after death a Tathāgata neither exists nor does not exist,' then it is straightforward for one who does not know and does not see to say: 'I do not know, I do not see.'"

4. "How then, Mālunkyāputta, did I ever say to you: 'Come, Mālunkyāputta, lead the holy life under me and I will declare to you "the world is eternal"...or "after death a Tathāgata neither exists nor does not exist"'?"—"No, venerable sir."—"Did you ever tell me: 'I will lead the holy life under the Blessed One, and the Blessed One will declare to me "the world is eternal"...or "after death a Tathāgata neither exists nor does not exist"'?"—"No, venerable sir."—"That being so, misguided man, who are you and what are you abandoning?

5. "If anyone should say thus: 'I will not lead the holy life under the Blessed One until the Blessed One declares to me "the world is eternal"...or "after death a Tathāgata neither exists nor does not exist,"' [429] that would still remain undeclared by the Tathāgata and meanwhile that person would die. Suppose, Mālunkyāputta, a man were wounded by an arrow thickly smeared with poison, and his friends and companions, his kinsmen and relatives, brought a surgeon to treat him. The man would say: 'I will not let the surgeon pull out this arrow until I know whether the man who wounded me was a noble or a brahmin or a merchant or a worker.' And he would say: 'I will not let the surgeon pull out this arrow until I know the name and clan of the man who wounded me;...until I know whether the man who wounded me was tall or short or of middle height;... until I know whether the man who wounded me was dark or

brown or golden-skinned;...until I know whether the man who wounded me lives in such a village or town or city;...until I know whether the bow that wounded me was a long bow or a crossbow;...until I know whether the bowstring that wounded me was fibre or reed or sinew or hemp or bark;...until I know whether the shaft that wounded me was wild or cultivated;... until I know with what kind of feathers the shaft that wounded me was fitted—whether those of a vulture or a heron or a hawk or a peacock or a stork;...until I know with what kind of sinew the shaft that wounded me was bound—whether that of an ox or a buffalo or a deer or a monkey;...until I know what kind of arrow it was that wounded me—whether it was hoof-tipped or curved or barbed or calf-toothed or oleander.' [430]

"All this would still not be known to that man and meanwhile he would die. So too, Mālunkyāputta, if anyone should say thus: 'I will not lead the holy life under the Blessed One until the Blessed One declares to me: "the world is eternal"...or "after death a Tathāgata neither exists nor does not exist,"' that would still remain undeclared by the Tathāgata and meanwhile that person would die.

6. "Mālunkyāputta, if there is the view 'the world is eternal,' the holy life cannot be lived; and if there is the view 'the world is not eternal,' the holy life cannot be lived. Whether there is the view 'the world is eternal' or the view 'the world is not eternal,' there is birth, there is ageing, there is death, there are sorrow, lamentation, pain, grief, and despair, the destruction of which I prescribe here and now.

"If there is the view 'the world is finite,'...'the world is infinite,'...'the soul is the same as the body,'...'the soul is one thing and the body another,'...'after death a Tathāgata exists,'...'after death a Tathāgata does not exist,' the holy life cannot be lived... [431] If there is the view 'after death a Tathāgata both exists and does not exist,' the holy life cannot be lived; and if there is the view 'after death a Tathāgata neither exists nor does not exist,' the holy life cannot be lived. Whether there is the view 'after death a Tathāgata both exists and does not exist' or the view 'after death a Tathāgata neither exists nor does not exist,' there is birth, there is ageing, there is death, there are sorrow, lamentation, pain, grief, and despair, the destruction of which I prescribe here and now.

7. "Therefore, Mālunkyāputta, remember what I have left undeclared as undeclared, and remember what I have declared as declared. And what have I left undeclared? 'The world is eternal'—I have left undeclared. 'The world is not eternal'—I have left undeclared. 'The world is finite'—I have left undeclared. 'The world is infinite'—I have left undeclared. 'The soul is the same as the body'—I have left undeclared. 'The soul is one thing and the body another'—I have left undeclared. 'After death a Tathāgata exists'—I have left undeclared. 'After death a Tathāgata does not exist'—I have left undeclared. 'After death a Tathāgata both exists and does not exist'—I have left undeclared. 'After death a Tathāgata neither exists nor does not exist'—I have left undeclared.

8. "Why have I left that undeclared? Because it is unbeneficial, it does not belong to the fundamentals of the holy life, it does not lead to disenchantment, to dispassion, to cessation, to peace, to direct knowledge, to enlightenment, to Nibbāna. That is why I have left it undeclared.

9. "And what have I declared? 'This is suffering'—I have declared. 'This is the origin of suffering'—I have declared. 'This is the cessation of suffering'—I have declared. 'This is the way leading to the cessation of suffering'—I have declared.

10. "Why have I declared that? Because it is beneficial, it belongs to the fundamentals of the holy life, it leads to disenchantment, to dispassion, to cessation, to peace, to direct knowledge, to enlightenment, to Nibbāna. That is why I have declared it.

"Therefore, Mālunkyāputta, [432] remember what I have left undeclared as undeclared, and remember what I have declared as declared."

That is what the Blessed One said. The venerable Mālunkyāputta was satisfied and delighted in the Blessed One's words.[648]

64 *Mahāmālunkya Sutta*
The Greater Discourse to Mālunkyāputta

5 lower fetters

1. THUS HAVE I HEARD. On one occasion the Blessed One was living at Sāvatthī in Jeta's Grove, Anāthapiṇḍika's Park. There he addressed the bhikkhus thus: "Bhikkhus."—"Venerable sir," they replied. The Blessed One said this:

2. "Bhikkhus, do you remember the five lower fetters as taught by me?"

When this was said, the venerable Mālunkyāputta replied: "Venerable sir, I remember the five lower fetters as taught by the Blessed One."[649]

"But, Mālunkyāputta, in what way do you remember the five lower fetters as taught by me?"

"Venerable sir, I remember identity view as a lower fetter taught by the Blessed One. I remember doubt as a lower fetter taught by the Blessed One. I remember adherence to rules and observances as a lower fetter taught by the Blessed One. I remember sensual desire as a lower fetter taught by the Blessed One. I remember ill will as a lower fetter taught by the Blessed One. It is in this way, venerable sir, that I remember the five lower fetters as taught by the Blessed One."

3. "Mālunkyāputta, to whom do you remember my having taught these five lower fetters in that way?[650] Would not the wanderers of other sects confute you with the simile of the infant? For a young tender infant lying prone does not even have the notion 'identity,' [433] so how could identity view arise in him? Yet the underlying tendency to identity view lies within him.[651] A young tender infant lying prone does not even have the notion 'teachings,'[652] so how could doubt about the teachings arise in him? Yet the underlying tendency to doubt lies within him. A young tender infant lying prone does not even have the notion 'rules,' so how could adherence to rules and

observances arise in him? Yet the underlying tendency to adhere to rules and observances lies within him. A young tender infant lying prone does not even have the notion 'sensual pleasures,' so how could sensual desire arise in him? Yet the underlying tendency to sensual lust lies within him. A young tender infant lying prone does not even have the notion 'beings,' so how could ill will towards beings arise in him? Yet the underlying tendency to ill will lies within him. Would not the wanderers of other sects confute you with this simile of the infant?"

4. Thereupon, the venerable Ānanda said: "It is the time, Blessed One, it is the time, Sublime One, for the Blessed One to teach the five lower fetters. Having heard it from the Blessed One, the bhikkhus will remember it."

"Then listen, Ānanda, and attend closely to what I shall say."

"Yes, venerable sir," the venerable Ānanda replied.

The Blessed One said this:

5. "Here, Ānanda, an untaught ordinary person who has no regard for noble ones and is unskilled and undisciplined in their Dhamma, who has no regard for true men and is unskilled and undisciplined in their Dhamma, abides with a mind obsessed and enslaved by identity view, and he does not understand as it actually is the escape from the arisen identity view; and when that identity view has become habitual and is uneradicated in him, it is a lower fetter. He abides with a mind obsessed and enslaved by doubt...by adherence to rules and observances ...by sensual lust [434]...by ill will, and he does not understand as it actually is the escape from arisen ill will; and when that ill will has become habitual and is uneradicated in him, it is a lower fetter.

6. "A well-taught noble disciple who has regard for noble ones and is skilled and disciplined in their Dhamma, who has regard for true men and is skilled and disciplined in their Dhamma, does not abide with a mind obsessed and enslaved by identity view; he understands as it actually is the escape from the arisen identity view, and identity view together with the underlying tendency to it is abandoned in him.[653] He does not abide with a mind obsessed and enslaved by doubt...by adherence to rules and observances...by sensual lust...by ill will; he understands as it actually is the escape from the arisen ill will, and ill will together with the underlying tendency to it is abandoned in him.

7. "There is a path, Ānanda, a way to the abandoning of the five lower fetters; that anyone, without relying on that path, on that way, shall know or see or abandon the five lower fetters—this is not possible. Just as when there is a great tree standing possessed of heartwood, it is not possible that anyone shall cut out its heartwood without cutting through its bark and sapwood, so too, there is a path...this is not possible.

"There is a path, Ānanda, a way to the abandoning of the five lower fetters; [435] that someone, by relying on that path, on that way, shall know and see and abandon the five lower fetters—this is possible. Just as, when there is a great tree standing possessed of heartwood, it is possible that someone shall cut out its heartwood by cutting through its bark and sapwood, so too, there is a path...this is possible.

8. "Suppose, Ānanda, the river Ganges were full of water right up to the brim so that crows could drink from it, and then a feeble man came thinking: 'By swimming across the stream with my arms, I shall get safely across to the further shore of this river Ganges'; yet he would not be able to get safely across. So too, when the Dhamma is being taught to someone for the cessation of personality, if his mind does not enter into it and acquire confidence, steadiness, and resolution, then he can be regarded as like the feeble man.

"Suppose, Ānanda, the river Ganges were full of water right up to the brim so that crows could drink from it, and then a strong man came thinking: 'By swimming across the stream with my arms, I shall get safely across to the further shore of this river Ganges'; and he would be able to get safely across. So too, when the Dhamma is being taught to someone for the cessation of personality, if his mind enters into it and acquires confidence, steadiness, and resolution, then he can be regarded as like the strong man.

9. "And what, Ānanda, is the path, the way to the abandoning of the five lower fetters? Here, with seclusion from the acquisitions,[654] with the abandoning of unwholesome states, with the complete tranquillization of bodily inertia, quite secluded from sensual pleasures, secluded from unwholesome states, a bhikkhu enters upon and abides in the first jhāna, which is accompanied by applied and sustained thought, with rapture and pleasure born of seclusion.

"Whatever exists therein of material form, feeling, perception, formations, and consciousness, he sees those states as impermanent, as suffering, as a disease, as a tumour, as a barb, as a calamity, as an affliction, as alien, as disintegrating, as void, as not self.[655] He turns his mind away from those states [436] and directs it towards the deathless element thus: 'This is the peaceful, this is the sublime, that is, the stilling of all formations, the relinquishing of all attachments, the destruction of craving, dispassion, cessation, Nibbāna.'[656] If he is steady in that, he attains the destruction of the taints. But if he does not attain the destruction of the taints because of that desire for the Dhamma, that delight in the Dhamma,[657] then with the destruction of the five lower fetters he becomes one due to reappear spontaneously [in the Pure Abodes] and there attain final Nibbāna without ever returning from that world. This is the path, the way to the abandoning of the five lower fetters.

10–12. "Again, with the stilling of applied and sustained thought, a bhikkhu enters upon and abides in the second jhāna...Again, with the fading away as well of rapture, a bhikkhu...enters upon and abides in the third jhāna...Again, with the abandoning of pleasure and pain...a bhikkhu enters upon and abides in the fourth jhāna, which has neither-pain-nor-pleasure and purity of mindfulness due to equanimity.

"Whatever exists therein of material form, feeling, perception, formations, and consciousness, he sees those states as impermanent...as not self. He turns his mind away from those states and directs it towards the deathless element...This is the path, the way to the abandoning of the five lower fetters.

13. "Again, with the complete surmounting of perceptions of form, with the disappearance of perceptions of sensory impact, with non-attention to perceptions of diversity, aware that 'space is infinite,' a bhikkhu enters upon and abides in the base of infinite space.

"Whatever exists therein of feeling, perception, formations, and consciousness,[658] he sees those states as impermanent...as not self. He turns his mind away from those states and directs it towards the deathless element...This is the path, the way to the abandoning of the five lower fetters.

14. "Again, by completely surmounting the base of infinite space, aware that 'consciousness is infinite,' a bhikkhu enters upon and abides in the base of infinite consciousness.

"Whatever exists therein of feeling, perception, formations, and consciousness, he sees those states as impermanent...as not self. He turns his mind away from those states and directs it towards the deathless element...This is the path, the way to the abandoning of the five lower fetters.

15. "Again, by completely surmounting the base of infinite consciousness, aware that 'there is nothing,' a bhikkhu enters upon and abides in the base of nothingness.

"Whatever exists therein of feeling, perception, formations, and consciousness, he sees those states as impermanent, as suffering, as a disease, as a tumour, as a barb, as a calamity, as an affliction, as alien, as disintegrating, as void, as not self. He turns his mind away from those states and directs it towards the deathless element thus: 'This is the peaceful, this is the sublime, that is, the stilling of all formations, the relinquishing of all attachments, the destruction of craving, dispassion, cessation, Nibbāna.' If he is steady in that, [437] he attains the destruction of the taints. But if he does not attain the destruction of the taints because of that desire for the Dhamma, that delight in the Dhamma, then with the destruction of the five lower fetters he becomes one due to reappear spontaneously [in the Pure Abodes] and there attain final Nibbāna without ever returning from that world. This is the path, the way to the abandoning of the five lower fetters."

16. "Venerable sir, if this is the path, the way to the abandoning of the five lower fetters, then how is it that some bhikkhus here [are said to] gain deliverance of mind and some [are said to] gain deliverance by wisdom?"

"The difference here, Ānanda, is in their faculties, I say."[659]

That is what the Blessed One said. The venerable Ānanda was satisfied and delighted in the Blessed One's words.

65 *Bhaddāli Sutta*
To Bhaddāli

1. THUS HAVE I HEARD. On one occasion the Blessed One was living at Sāvatthi in Jeta's Grove, Anāthapiṇḍika's Park. There he addressed the bhikkhus thus: "Bhikkhus."—"Venerable sir," they replied. The Blessed One said this:

2. "Bhikkhus, I eat at a single session. By so doing, I am free from illness and affliction, and I enjoy health, strength, and a comfortable abiding.[660] Come, bhikkhus, eat at a single session. By so doing, you too will be free from illness and affliction, and you will enjoy health, strength, and a comfortable abiding."

3. When this was said, the venerable Bhaddāli told the Blessed One: "Venerable sir, I am not willing to eat at a single session; for if I were to do so, I might have worry and anxiety about it."[661]

"Then, Bhaddāli, eat one part there where you are invited and bring away one part to eat. By eating in that way, [438] you will maintain yourself."

"Venerable sir, I am not willing to eat in that way either; for if I were to do so, I might also have worry and anxiety about it."[662]

4. Then, when this training precept was being made known by the Blessed One,[663] the venerable Bhaddāli publicly declared in the Sangha of bhikkhus his unwillingness to undertake the training. Then the venerable Bhaddāli did not present himself to the Blessed One for the whole of that three-month period [of the Rains], as he did not fulfil the training in the Teacher's Dispensation.

5. Now on that occasion a number of bhikkhus were engaged in making up a robe for the Blessed One, thinking: "With his robe completed, at the end of the three months [of the Rains], the Blessed One will set out wandering."

6. Then the venerable Bhaddāli went to those bhikkhus and exchanged greetings with them, and when this courteous and

amiable talk was finished, he sat down at one side. When he had done so, they said to him: "Friend Bhaddāli, this robe is being made up for the Blessed One. With his robe completed, at the end of the three months [of the Rains], the Blessed One will set out wandering. Please, friend Bhaddāli, give proper attention to your declaration. Do not let it become more difficult for you later on."

7. "Yes, friends," he replied, and he went to the Blessed One, and after paying homage to him, he sat down at one side and said: "Venerable sir, a transgression overcame me, in that like a fool, confused and blundering, when a training precept was being made known by the Blessed One, I publicly declared in the Sangha of bhikkhus my unwillingness to undertake the training. Venerable sir, may the Blessed One forgive my transgression seen as such for the sake of restraint in the future."

8. "Surely, Bhaddāli, a transgression overcame you, in that like a fool, confused and blundering, when a training precept was being made known by me, you publicly declared in the Sangha of bhikkhus your unwillingness to undertake the training.

9. "Bhaddāli, this circumstance was not recognised by you: 'The Blessed One is living at Sāvatthī, and the Blessed One will know me thus: "The bhikkhu named Bhaddāli is one who does not fulfil the training in the Teacher's Dispensation."' This circumstance was not recognised by you.

"Also, this circumstance was not recognised by you: 'Many [439] bhikkhus have taken up residence at Sāvatthī for the Rains, and they too will know me thus: "The bhikkhu named Bhaddāli is one who does not fulfil the training in the Teacher's Dispensation."' This circumstance too was not recognised by you.

"Also, this circumstance was not recognised by you: 'Many bhikkhunīs have taken up residence at Sāvatthī for the Rains, and they too will know me thus: "The bhikkhu named Bhaddāli is one who does not fulfil the training in the Teacher's Dispensation."' This circumstance too was not recognised by you.

"Also, this circumstance was not recognised by you: 'Many men lay followers...Many women lay followers are staying at Sāvatthī, and they too will know me thus: "The bhikkhu named Bhaddāli is one who does not fulfil the training in the Teacher's Dispensation."' This circumstance too was not recognised by you.

"Also, this circumstance was not recognised by you: 'Many

recluses and brahmins of other sects have taken up residence at Sāvatthī for the Rains, and they too will know me thus: "The bhikkhu named Bhaddāli, an elder disciple of the recluse Gotama, is one who does not fulfil the training in the Teacher's Dispensation."' This circumstance too was not recognised by you."

10. "Venerable sir, a transgression overcame me, in that like a fool, confused and blundering, when a training precept was being made known by the Blessed One, I publicly declared in the Sangha of bhikkhus my unwillingness to undertake the training. Venerable sir, may the Blessed One forgive my transgression seen as such for the sake of restraint in the future."

"Surely, Bhaddāli, a transgression overcame you, in that like a fool, confused and blundering, when a training precept was being made known by me, you publicly declared in the Sangha of bhikkhus your unwillingness to undertake the training.

11. "What do you think, Bhaddāli? Suppose a bhikkhu here were one liberated-in-both-ways,[664] and I told him: 'Come, bhikkhu, be a plank for me across the mud.' Would he walk across himself,[665] or would he dispose his body otherwise, or would he say 'No'?"

"No, venerable sir."

"What do you think, Bhaddāli? Suppose a bhikkhu here were one liberated-by-wisdom...a body-witness...one attained-to-view...one liberated-by-faith...a Dhamma-follower...a faith-follower, and I told him: 'Come, bhikkhu, be a plank for me across the mud.' Would he walk across himself, or would he dispose his body otherwise, or would he say 'No'?"

"No, venerable sir."

12. "What do you think, Bhaddāli? Were you on that occasion one liberated-in-both-ways or [440] one liberated-by-wisdom or a body-witness or one attained-to-view or one liberated-by-faith or a Dhamma-follower or a faith-follower?"

"No, venerable sir."

"Bhaddāli, on that occasion were you not an empty, hollow wrong-doer?"

13. "Yes, venerable sir. Venerable sir, a transgression overcame me, in that like a fool, confused and blundering, when a training precept was being made known by the Blessed One, I publicly declared in the Sangha of bhikkhus my unwillingness to undertake the training. Venerable sir, may the Blessed One

forgive my transgression seen as such for the sake of restraint in the future."

"Surely, Bhaddāli, a transgression overcame you, in that like a fool, confused and blundering, when a training precept was being made known by me, you publicly declared in the Sangha of bhikkhus your unwillingness to undertake the training. But since you see your transgression as such and make amends in accordance with the Dhamma, we forgive you; for it is growth in the Noble One's Discipline when one sees one's transgression as such and makes amends in accordance with the Dhamma by undertaking restraint for the future.

14. "Here, Bhaddāli, some bhikkhu does not fulfil the training in the Teacher's Dispensation. He considers thus: 'Suppose I were to resort to a secluded resting place: the forest, the root of a tree, a mountain, a ravine, a hillside cave, a charnel ground, a jungle thicket, an open space, a heap of straw—perhaps I might realise a superhuman state, a distinction in knowledge and vision worthy of the noble ones.' He resorts to some such secluded resting place. While he lives thus withdrawn, the Teacher censures him, wise companions in the holy life who have made investigation censure him, gods censure him, and he censures himself. Being censured in this way by the Teacher, by wise companions in the holy life, by gods, and by himself, he realises no superhuman state, no distinction in knowledge and vision worthy of the noble ones. Why is that? That is how it is with one who does not fulfil the training in the Teacher's Dispensation.

15. "Here, Bhaddāli, some bhikkhu does fulfil the training in the Teacher's Dispensation. He considers thus: 'Suppose I were to resort to a secluded resting place: the forest, the root of a tree, a mountain, a ravine, a hillside cave, a charnel ground, a jungle thicket, [441] an open space, a heap of straw—perhaps I might realise a superhuman state, a distinction in knowledge and vision worthy of the noble ones.' He resorts to some such secluded resting place. While he lives thus withdrawn, the Teacher does not censure him, wise companions in the holy life who have made investigation do not censure him, gods do not censure him, and he does not censure himself. Being uncensured in this way by the Teacher, by wise companions in the holy life, by gods, and by himself, he realises a superhuman

state, a distinction in knowledge and vision worthy of the noble ones.

16. "Quite secluded from sensual pleasures, secluded from unwholesome states, he enters upon and abides in the first jhāna, which is accompanied by applied and sustained thought, with rapture and pleasure born of seclusion. Why is that? That is how it is with one who fulfils the training in the Teacher's Dispensation.

17. "With the stilling of applied and sustained thought, he enters upon and abides in the second jhāna...With the fading away as well of rapture...he enters upon and abides in the third jhāna...With the abandoning of pleasure and pain...he enters upon and abides in the fourth jhāna...Why is that? That is how it is with one who fulfils the training in the Teacher's Dispensation.

18. "When his concentrated mind is thus purified and bright, unblemished, rid of imperfection, malleable, wieldy, steady, and attained to imperturbability, he directs it to knowledge of the recollection of past lives...(*as Sutta 51, §24*)...Thus with their aspects and particulars he recollects his manifold past lives. Why is that? That is how [442] it is with one who fulfils the training in the Teacher's Dispensation.

19. "When his concentrated mind is thus purified and bright...attained to imperturbability, he directs it to knowledge of the passing away and reappearance of beings...(*as Sutta 51, §25*)...Thus with the divine eye, which is purified and surpasses the human, he understands how beings pass on according to their actions. Why is that? That is how it is with one who fulfils the training in the Teacher's Dispensation.

20. "When his concentrated mind is thus purified and bright...attained to imperturbability, he directs it to knowledge of the destruction of the taints. He understands as it actually is: 'This is suffering'...(*as Sutta 51, §26*)...He understands as it actually is: 'This is the way leading to the cessation of the taints.'

21. "When he knows and sees thus, his mind is liberated from the taint of sensual desire, from the taint of being, and from the taint of ignorance. When it is liberated there comes the knowledge: 'It is liberated.' He understands: 'Birth is destroyed, the holy life has been lived, what had to be done has been done, there is no more coming to any state of being.' Why is that? That

is how it is with one who fulfils the training in the Teacher's Dispensation."

22. Thereupon the venerable Bhaddāli asked: "Venerable sir, what is the cause, what is the reason, why they take action against some bhikkhu here by repeatedly admonishing him? What is the cause, what is the reason, why they do not take such action against some bhikkhu here by repeatedly admonishing him?"

23. "Here, Bhaddāli, some bhikkhu is a constant offender with many offences. When he is corrected by the bhikkhus, he prevaricates, leads the talk aside, shows disturbance, hate, and bitterness; he does not proceed rightly, he does not comply, he does not clear himself, he does not say: 'Let me so act that the Sangha will be satisfied.' [443] Bhikkhus, taking account of this matter, think: 'It would be good if the venerable ones examine this bhikkhu in such a way that this litigation against him is not settled too quickly.' And the bhikkhus examine that bhikkhu in such a way that the litigation against him is not settled too quickly.

24. "But here some bhikkhu is a constant offender with many offences. When he is corrected by the bhikkhus, he does not prevaricate, lead the talk aside, or show disturbance, hate, and bitterness; he proceeds rightly, he complies, he clears himself, he says: 'Let me so act that the Sangha will be satisfied.' Bhikkhus, taking account of this matter, think: 'It would be good if the venerable ones examine this bhikkhu in such a way that this litigation against him is settled quickly.' And the bhikkhus examine that bhikkhu in such a way that the litigation against him is settled quickly.

25. "Here some bhikkhu is a chance offender without many offences. When he is corrected by the bhikkhus, he prevaricates...(*repeat rest of §23*)...And the bhikkhus examine that bhikkhu in such a way that [444] the litigation against him is not settled too quickly.

26. "But here some bhikkhu is a chance offender without many offences. When he is corrected by the bhikkhus, he does not prevaricate...(*repeat rest of §24*)...And the bhikkhus examine that bhikkhu in such a way that the litigation against him is settled quickly.

27. "Here some bhikkhu progresses by a measure of faith and love.[666] In this case bhikkhus consider thus: 'Friends, this

bhikkhu progresses by a measure of faith and love. Let him not lose that measure of faith and love, as he may if we take action against him by repeatedly admonishing him.' Suppose a man had only one eye; then his friends and companions, his kinsmen and relatives, would guard his eye, thinking: 'Let him not lose his one eye.' So too, some bhikkhu progresses by a measure of faith and love...'Let him not lose that measure of faith and love, as he may if we take action against him by repeatedly admonishing him.'

28. "This is the cause, this is the reason, why they take action against some bhikkhu here by repeatedly admonishing him; this is the cause, this is the reason, why they do not take such action against some bhikkhu here by repeatedly admonishing him."

29. "Venerable sir, what is the cause, what is the reason, why there were previously [445] fewer training rules and more bhikkhus became established in final knowledge? What is the cause, what is the reason, why there are now more training rules and fewer bhikkhus become established in final knowledge?"

30. "That is how it is, Bhaddāli. When beings are deteriorating and the true Dhamma is disappearing, then there are more training rules and fewer bhikkhus become established in final knowledge. The Teacher does not make known the training rule for disciples until certain things that are the basis for taints become manifest here in the Sangha;[667] but when certain things that are the basis for taints become manifest here in the Sangha, then the Teacher makes known the training rule for disciples in order to ward off those things that are the basis for taints.

31. "Those things that are the basis for taints do not become manifest here in the Sangha until the Sangha has reached greatness; but when the Sangha has reached greatness, then those things that are the basis for taints become manifest here in the Sangha, and then the Teacher makes known the training rule for disciples in order to ward off those things that are the basis for taints. Those things that are the basis for taints do not become manifest here in the Sangha until the Sangha has reached the acme of worldly gain...the acme of fame...the acme of great learning...the acme of long-standing renown; but when the Sangha has reached the acme of long-standing renown, then those things that are the basis for taints become manifest here in the Sangha, and then the Teacher makes known the training rule

for disciples in order to ward off those things that are the basis for taints.

32. "There were few of you, Bhaddāli, when I taught an exposition of the Dhamma through the simile of the young thoroughbred colt. Do you remember that, Bhaddāli?"

"No, venerable sir."

"To what reason do you attribute that?"

"Venerable sir, I have long been one who did not fulfil the training in the Teacher's Dispensation."

"That is not the only cause or the only reason. But rather, by encompassing your mind with my mind, I have long known you thus: 'When I am teaching the Dhamma, this misguided man does not heed it, does not give it attention, does not engage it with all his mind, does not hear the Dhamma with eager ears.' Still, Bhaddāli, I will teach you an exposition of the Dhamma through the simile of the young thoroughbred colt. Listen and attend closely [446] to what I shall say."

"Yes, venerable sir," the venerable Bhaddāli replied.

The Blessed One said this:

33. "Bhaddāli, suppose a clever horse-trainer obtains a fine thoroughbred colt. He first makes him get used to wearing the bit. While the colt is being made to get used to wearing the bit, because he is doing something that he has never done before, he displays some contortion, writhing, and vacillation, but through constant repetition and gradual practice, he becomes peaceful in that action.[668]

"When the colt has become peaceful in that action, the horse-trainer further makes him get used to wearing the harness. While the colt is being made to get used to wearing the harness, because he is doing something that he has never done before, he displays some contortion, writhing, and vacillation, but through constant repetition and gradual practice, he becomes peaceful in that action.

"When the colt has become peaceful in that action, the horse-trainer further makes him act in keeping in step, in running in a circle, in prancing, in galloping, in charging, in the kingly qualities, in the kingly heritage, in the highest speed, in the highest fleetness, in the highest gentleness. While the colt is being made to get used to doing these things, because he is doing something that he has never done before, he displays some contortion, writhing, and vacillation, but through constant repetition and gradual practice, he becomes peaceful in those actions.

"When the colt has become peaceful in these actions, the horse-trainer further rewards him with a rubbing down and a grooming. When a fine thoroughbred colt possesses these ten factors, he is worthy of the king, in the king's service, and considered one of the factors of a king.

34. "So too, Bhaddāli, when a bhikkhu possesses ten qualities, he is worthy of gifts, worthy of hospitality, worthy of offerings, worthy of reverential salutation, an unsurpassed field of merit for the world. What are the ten? Here, Bhaddāli, a bhikkhu possesses the right view of one beyond training,[669] the right intention of one beyond training, the right speech of one beyond training, the right action of one beyond training, the right livelihood of one beyond training, the right effort of one beyond training, [447] the right mindfulness of one beyond training, the right concentration of one beyond training, the right knowledge of one beyond training, and the right deliverance of one beyond training.[670] When a bhikkhu possesses these ten qualities, he is worthy of gifts, worthy of hospitality, worthy of offerings, worthy of reverential salutation, an unsurpassed field of merit for the world."

That is what the Blessed One said. The venerable Bhaddāli was satisfied and delighted in the Blessed One's words.

66 *Laṭukikopama Sutta*
The Simile of the Quail

1. THUS HAVE I HEARD. On one occasion the Blessed One was living in the country of the Anguttarāpans where there was a town of theirs named Āpaṇa.

2. Then, when it was morning, the Blessed One dressed, and taking his bowl and outer robe, went into Āpaṇa for alms. When he had wandered for alms in Āpaṇa and had returned from his almsround, after his meal he went to a certain grove for the day's abiding. Having entered the grove, he sat down at the root of a tree for the day's abiding.

3. When it was morning, the venerable Udāyin dressed, and taking his bowl and outer robe, he too went into Āpaṇa for alms. When he had wandered for alms in Āpaṇa and had returned from his almsround, after his meal he went to that same grove for the day's abiding. Having entered the grove, he sat down at the root of a tree for the day's abiding.

4. Then, while the venerable Udāyin was alone in meditation, the following thought arose in his mind: "How many painful states has the Blessed One rid us of! How many pleasant states has the Blessed One brought us! How many unwholesome states has the Blessed One rid us of! How many wholesome states has the Blessed One brought us!"

5. Then, when it was evening, the venerable Udāyin rose from meditation, went to the Blessed One, and after paying homage to him, he sat down at one side [448] and told him:

6. "Here, venerable sir, while I was alone in meditation, the following thought arose in my mind: 'How many painful states has the Blessed One rid us of!...How many wholesome states has the Blessed One brought us!' Venerable sir, formerly we used to eat in the evening, in the morning, and during the day outside the proper time. Then there was an occasion when the

Blessed One addressed the bhikkhus thus: 'Bhikkhus, please abandon that daytime meal, which is outside the proper time.'[671] Venerable sir, I was upset and sad, thinking: 'Faithful householders give us good food of various kinds during the day outside the proper time, yet the Blessed One tells us to abandon it, the Sublime One tells us to relinquish it.' Out of our love and respect for the Blessed One, and out of shame and fear of wrongdoing, we abandoned that daytime meal, which was outside the proper time.

"Then we ate only in the evening and in the morning. Then there was an occasion when the Blessed One addressed the bhikkhus thus: 'Bhikkhus, please abandon that night meal, which is outside the proper time.' Venerable sir, I was upset and sad, thinking: 'The Blessed One tells us to abandon the more sumptuous of our two meals, the Sublime One tells us to relinquish it.' Once, venerable sir, a certain man had obtained some soup during the day and he said: 'Put that aside and we will all eat it together in the evening.' [Nearly] all dishes are prepared at night, few by day. Out of our love and respect for the Blessed One, and out of shame and fear of wrongdoing, we abandoned that night meal, which was outside the proper time.

"It has happened, venerable sir, that bhikkhus wandering for alms in the thick darkness of the night have walked into a cesspit, fallen into a sewer, walked into a thornbush, and walked into a sleeping cow; they have met hoodlums who had already committed a crime and those planning one, and they have been sexually enticed by women. Once, venerable sir, I went wandering for alms in the thick darkness of the night. A woman washing a pot saw me by a flash of lightning and screamed out in terror: 'Mercy me, a devil has come for me!' I told her: 'Sister, I am no devil, I am a bhikkhu [449] waiting for alms.'—'Then it's a bhikkhu whose ma's died and whose pa's died![672] Better, bhikkhu, that you get your belly cut open with a sharp butcher's knife than this prowling for alms for your belly's sake in the thick darkness of the night!' Venerable sir, when I recollected that I thought: 'How many painful states has the Blessed One rid us of! How many pleasant states has the Blessed One brought us! How many unwholesome states has the Blessed One rid us of! How many wholesome states has the Blessed One brought us!'"

7. "So too, Udāyin, there are certain misguided men here who, when told by me 'Abandon this,' say: 'What, such a mere trifle, such a little thing as this? This recluse is much too exacting!' And they do not abandon that and they show discourtesy towards me as well as towards those bhikkhus desirous of training. For them that thing becomes a strong, stout, tough, unrotting tether and a thick yoke.

8. "Suppose, Udāyin, a quail were tethered by a rotting creeper and would thereby expect injury, captivity, or death. Now suppose someone said: 'The rotting creeper by which that quail is tethered and thereby expects injury, captivity, or death, is for her a feeble, weak, rotting, coreless tether.' Would he be speaking rightly?"

"No, venerable sir. For that quail the rotting creeper by which she is tethered and thereby expects injury, captivity, or death, is a strong, stout, tough, unrotting tether and a thick yoke."

"So too, Udāyin there are certain misguided men here who, when told by me 'Abandon this'...do not abandon that and they show discourtesy towards me as well as towards those bhikkhus desirous of training. For them that thing becomes a strong, stout, tough, unrotting tether and a thick yoke.

9. "Udāyin, there are certain clansmen here who, [450] when told by me 'Abandon this,' say: 'What, such a mere trifle, such a little thing to be abandoned as this, the Blessed One tells us to abandon, the Sublime One tells us to relinquish.' Yet they abandon that and do not show discourtesy towards me or towards those bhikkhus desirous of training. Having abandoned it, they live at ease, unruffled, subsisting on others' gifts, with mind [as aloof] as a wild deer's. For them that thing becomes a feeble, weak, rotting, coreless tether.

10. "Suppose, Udāyin, a royal tusker elephant with tusks as long as chariot-poles, full-grown in stature, high-bred and accustomed to battle, were tethered by stout leather thongs, but by simply twisting his body a little he could break and burst the thongs and then go where he likes. Now suppose someone said: 'The stout leather thongs by which this royal tusker elephant is tethered...are for him a strong, stout, tough, unrotting tether and a thick yoke.' Would he be speaking rightly?"

"No, venerable sir. The stout leather thongs by which that royal tusker elephant is tethered, which by simply twisting his body a little he could break and burst and then go where he likes, are for him a feeble, weak, rotting, coreless tether."

"So too, Udāyin, there are certain clansmen here who, when told by me 'Abandon this'...abandon that and do not show discourtesy towards me or towards those bhikkhus desirous of training. Having abandoned it, they live at ease, unruffled, subsisting on others' gifts, with mind [as aloof] as a wild deer's. For them that thing becomes a feeble, weak, rotting, coreless tether.

11. "Suppose, Udāyin, there were a poor, penniless, destitute man, and he had one dilapidated hovel open to the crows, not the best kind, and one dilapidated wicker bedstead, not the best kind, [451] and some grain and pumpkin seeds in a pot, not the best kind, and one hag of a wife, not the best kind. He might see a bhikkhu in a monastery park sitting in the shade of a tree, his hands and feet well washed after he had eaten a delicious meal, devoting himself to the higher mind. He might think: 'How pleasant the recluse's state is! How healthy the recluse's state is! If only I could shave off my hair and beard, put on the yellow robe, and go forth from the home life into homelessness!' But being unable to abandon his one dilapidated hovel open to the crows, not the best kind, and his one dilapidated wicker bedstead, not the best kind, and his grain and pumpkin seeds in a pot, not the best kind, and his hag of a wife, not the best kind, he is unable to shave off his hair and beard, put on the yellow robe, and go forth from the home life into homelessness. Now suppose someone said: 'The tethers by which that man is tethered so that he cannot abandon his one dilapidated hovel...and his hag of a wife, not the best kind, and shave off his hair and beard, put on the yellow robe, and go forth from the home life into homelessness—for him those are a feeble, weak, rotting, coreless tether.' Would he be speaking rightly?"

"No, venerable sir. The tethers by which that man is tethered so that he cannot abandon his one dilapidated hovel...and his hag of a wife, not the best kind, and shave off his hair and beard, put on the yellow robe, and go forth from the home life into homelessness—for him those are a strong, stout, tough, unrotting tether and a thick yoke."

"So too, Udāyin, there are certain misguided men here who, when told by me 'Abandon this'...do not abandon that and they show discourtesy towards me as well as towards those bhikkhus desirous of training. For them that thing becomes a strong, stout, tough, unrotting tether and a thick yoke.

12. "Suppose, Udāyin, there were a rich householder or a householder's son, [452] with great wealth and property, with a vast number of gold ingots, a vast number of granaries, a vast number of fields, a vast amount of land, a vast number of wives, and a vast number of men and women slaves. He might see a bhikkhu in a monastery park sitting in the shade of a tree, his hands and feet well washed after he had eaten a delicious meal, devoting himself to the higher mind. He might think: 'How pleasant the recluse's state is! How healthy the recluse's state is! If only I could shave off my hair and beard, put on the yellow robe, and go forth from the home life into homelessness!' And being able to abandon his vast number of gold ingots, his vast number of granaries, his vast number of fields, his vast amount of land, his vast number of wives, and his vast number of men and women slaves, he is able to shave off his hair and beard, put on the yellow robe, and go forth from the home life into homelessness. Now suppose someone said: 'The tethers by which that householder or householder's son is tethered so that he can abandon his vast number of gold ingots...his vast number of men and women slaves, and shave off his hair and beard, put on the yellow robe, and go forth from the home life into homelessness—for him those are a strong, stout, tough, unrotting tether and a thick yoke.' Would he be speaking rightly?"

"No, venerable sir. The tethers by which that householder or householder's son is tethered so that he can abandon his vast number of gold ingots...his vast number of men and women slaves, and shave off his hair and beard, put on the yellow robe, and go forth from the home life into homelessness—for him those are a feeble, weak, rotting, coreless tether."

"So too, Udāyin, there are certain clansmen here who, when told by me 'Abandon this'...abandon that and do not show discourtesy towards me or towards those bhikkhus desirous of training. [453] Having abandoned it, they live at ease, unruffled, subsisting on others' gifts, with mind [as aloof] as a wild deer's. For them that thing becomes a feeble, weak, rotting, coreless tether.

13. "Udāyin, there are four kinds of persons to be found existing in the world. What are the four?[673]

14. "Here, Udāyin, some person practises the way to the abandoning of the acquisitions, to the relinquishing of the acquisitions.[674] When he is practising the way, memories and intentions associated with the acquisitions beset him. He tolerates them; he does not abandon them, remove them, do away with them, and annihilate them. Such a person I call fettered, not unfettered. Why is that? Because I have known the particular diversity of faculties in this person.

15. "Here, Udāyin, some person practises the way to the abandoning of the acquisitions, to the relinquishing of the acquisitions. When he is practising the way, memories and intentions associated with the acquisitions beset him. He does not tolerate them; he abandons them, removes them, does away with them, and annihilates them. Such a person too I call fettered, not unfettered. Why is that? Because I have known the particular diversity of faculties in this person.[675]

16. "Here, Udāyin, some person practises the way to the abandoning of the acquisitions, to the relinquishing of the acquisitions. When he is practising the way, memories and intentions associated with the acquisitions beset him now and then through lapses of mindfulness. His mindfulness may be slow in arising, but he quickly abandons them, removes them, does away with them, and annihilates them.[676] Just as if a man were to let two or three drops of water fall onto an iron plate heated for a whole day, the falling of the water drops might be slow but they would quickly vaporise and vanish. So too, here some person practises the way...His mindfulness may be slow in arising, but he quickly abandons them, removes them, does away with them, and annihilates them. Such a person too I call fettered, not unfettered. [454] Why is that? Because I have known the particular diversity of faculties in this person.

17. "Here, Udāyin, some person, having understood that acquisition is the root of suffering, divests himself of the acquisitions and is liberated in the destruction of the acquisitions. Such a person I call unfettered, not fettered.[677] Why is that? Because I have known the particular diversity of faculties in this person.

18. "There are, Udāyin, five cords of sensual pleasure. What are the five? Forms cognizable by the eye that are wished for, desired, agreeable, and likeable, connected with sensual desire and provocative of lust. Sounds cognizable by the ear...Odours

cognizable by the nose...Flavours cognizable by the tongue... Tangibles cognizable by the body that are wished for, desired, agreeable, and likeable, connected with sensual desire and provocative of lust. These are the five cords of sensual pleasure.

19. "Now, Udāyin, the pleasure and joy that arise dependent on these five cords of sensual pleasure are called sensual pleasure—a filthy pleasure, a coarse pleasure, an ignoble pleasure. I say of this kind of pleasure that it should not be pursued, that it should not be developed, that it should not be cultivated, that it should be feared.

20. "Here, Udāyin, quite secluded from sensual pleasures, secluded from unwholesome states, a bhikkhu enters upon and abides in the first jhāna...With the stilling of applied and sustained thought, he enters upon and abides in the second jhāna...With the fading away as well of rapture...he enters upon and abides in the third jhāna...With the abandoning of pleasure and pain...he enters upon and abides in the fourth jhāna...

21. "This is called the bliss of renunciation, the bliss of seclusion, the bliss of peace, the bliss of enlightenment.[678] I say of this kind of pleasure that it should be pursued, that it should be developed, that it should be cultivated, that it should not be feared.

22. "Here, Udāyin, quite secluded from sensual pleasures, secluded from unwholesome states, a bhikkhu enters upon and abides in the first jhāna...Now this, I say, belongs to the perturbable.[679] And what therein belongs to the perturbable? The applied thought and sustained thought that have not ceased therein, that is what belongs to the perturbable.

23. "Here, Udāyin, with the stilling of applied and sustained thought, a bhikkhu enters upon and abides in the second jhāna...Now this, I say, also belongs to the perturbable. And what therein belongs to the perturbable? The rapture and pleasure that have not ceased therein, that is what belongs to the perturbable.

24. "Here, Udāyin, with the fading away as well of rapture...a bhikkhu enters upon and abides in the third jhāna...Now this, I say, also belongs to the perturbable. And what therein belongs to the perturbable? The equanimity [455] and pleasure that have not ceased therein, that is what belongs to the perturbable.

25. "Here, Udāyin, with the abandoning of pleasure and pain...a bhikkhu enters upon and abides in the fourth jhāna... Now this, I say, belongs to the imperturbable.

26. "Here, Udāyin, quite secluded from sensual pleasures, secluded from unwholesome states, a bhikkhu enters upon and abides in the first jhāna...That, I say, is not enough.[680] Abandon it, I say; surmount it, I say. And what surmounts it?

27. "Here, Udāyin, with the stilling of applied and sustained thought, a bhikkhu enters upon and abides in the second jhāna...That surmounts it. But that too, I say, is not enough. Abandon it, I say; surmount it, I say. And what surmounts it?

28. "Here, Udāyin, with the fading away as well of rapture...a bhikkhu enters upon and abides in the third jhāna...That surmounts it. But that too, I say, is not enough. Abandon it, I say; surmount it, I say. And what surmounts it?

29. "Here, Udāyin, with the abandoning of pleasure and pain...a bhikkhu enters upon and abides in the fourth jhāna... That surmounts it. But that too, I say, is not enough. Abandon it, I say; surmount it, I say. And what surmounts it?

30. "Here, Udāyin, with the complete surmounting of perceptions of form, with the disappearance of perceptions of sensory impact, with non-attention to perceptions of diversity, aware that 'space is infinite,' a bhikkhu enters upon and abides in the base of infinite space. That surmounts it. But that too, I say, is not enough. Abandon it, I say; surmount it, I say. And what surmounts it?

31. "Here, Udāyin, by completely surmounting the base of infinite space, aware that 'consciousness is infinite,' a bhikkhu enters upon and abides in the base of infinite consciousness. That surmounts it. But that too, I say, is not enough. Abandon it, I say; surmount it, I say. And what surmounts it?

32. "Here, Udāyin, by completely surmounting the base of infinite consciousness, aware that 'there is nothing,' a bhikkhu enters upon and abides in the base of nothingness. That surmounts it. But that too, I say, is not enough. Abandon it, I say; surmount it, I say. And what surmounts it?

33. "Here, Udāyin, by completely surmounting the base of nothingness, a bhikkhu enters upon and abides in the base of neither-perception-nor-non-perception. [456] That surmounts it. But that too, I say, is not enough. Abandon it, I say; surmount it, I say. And what surmounts it?

34. "Here, Udāyin, by completely surmounting the base of neither-perception-nor-non-perception, a bhikkhu enters upon

and abides in the cessation of perception and feeling.[681] That surmounts it. Thus I speak of the abandoning even of the base of neither-perception-nor-non-perception. Do you see, Udāyin, any fetter, small or great, of whose abandoning I do not speak?"

"No, venerable sir."

That is what the Blessed One said. The venerable Udāyin was satisfied and delighted in the Blessed One's words.

67 *Cātumā Sutta*
At Cātumā

1. THUS HAVE I HEARD. On one occasion the Blessed One was living at Cātumā in a myrobalan grove.

2. Now on that occasion five hundred bhikkhus headed by the venerable Sāriputta and the venerable Mahā Moggallāna had come to Cātumā to see the Blessed One. While the visiting bhikkhus were exchanging greetings with the resident bhikkhus, and were preparing resting places and putting away their bowls and outer robes, they were very loud and noisy.

3. Then the Blessed One addressed the venerable Ānanda thus: "Ānanda, who are these loud and noisy people? One would think they were fishermen hawking fish."[682]

"Venerable sir, they are five hundred bhikkhus headed by Sāriputta and Moggallāna who have come to Cātumā to see the Blessed One. And while the visiting bhikkhus were exchanging greetings with the resident bhikkhus, and were preparing resting places and putting away their bowls and outer robes, they have been very loud and noisy."

4. "Then, Ānanda, tell those bhikkhus in my name that the Teacher calls the venerable ones."

"Yes, venerable sir," he replied, and he went to those bhikkhus and told them: "The Teacher calls the venerable ones."

"Yes, friend," they [457] replied, and they went to the Blessed One, and after paying homage to him, sat down at one side. When they had done so, the Blessed One asked them: "Bhikkhus, why are you so loud and noisy? One would think you were fishermen hawking fish."

"Venerable sir, we are five hundred bhikkhus headed by Sāriputta and Moggallāna who have come to Cātumā to see the Blessed One. And it was while we visiting bhikkhus were exchanging greetings with the resident bhikkhus, and were preparing resting places and putting away our bowls and outer robes, that we were very loud and noisy."

5. "Go, bhikkhus, I dismiss you. You should not live near me."

"Yes, venerable sir," they replied, and they rose from their seats, and after paying homage to the Blessed One, keeping him on their right, they put away the things in their resting places, and taking their bowls and outer robes, they departed.

6. Now on that occasion the Sakyans of Cātumā had met together in their assembly hall for some business or other. Seeing the bhikkhus coming in the distance, they went to them and asked: "Where are you going, venerable sirs?"

"Friends, the Sangha of bhikkhus has been dismissed by the Blessed One."

"Then let the venerable ones be seated awhile. Perhaps we shall be able to restore his confidence."

"Yes, friends," they replied.

7. Then the Sakyans of Cātumā went to the Blessed One, and after paying homage to him, they sat down at one side and said:

"Venerable sir, let the Blessed One delight in the Sangha of bhikkhus; venerable sir, let the Blessed One welcome the Sangha of bhikkhus; venerable sir, let the Blessed One help the Sangha of bhikkhus now as he used to help it in the past. Venerable sir, there are new bhikkhus here, just gone forth, recently come to this Dhamma and Discipline. If they get no opportunity to see the Blessed One, there may take place in them some change or alteration. Venerable sir, just as when young seedlings get no water there may take place in them some change or alteration, so too, venerable sir, there are [458] new bhikkhus here, just gone forth, recently come to this Dhamma and Discipline. If they get no opportunity to see the Blessed One, there may take place in them some change or alteration. Venerable sir, just as when a young calf does not see its mother there may take place in it some change or alteration, so too, venerable sir, there are new bhikkhus here, just gone forth, recently come to this Dhamma and Discipline. If they get no opportunity to see the Blessed One, there may take place in them some change or alteration. Venerable sir, let the Blessed One delight in the Sangha of the bhikkhus; venerable sir, let the Blessed One welcome the Sangha of bhikkhus; venerable sir, let the Blessed One help the Sangha of bhikkhus now as he used to help it in the past."

8. Then the Brahmā Sahampati[683] knew with his mind the thought in the Blessed One's mind, so just as quickly as a strong man might extend his flexed arm or flex his extended arm, he vanished in the Brahma-world and appeared before the Blessed One. Then he arranged his upper robe on one shoulder, and extending his hands in reverential salutation towards the Blessed One, he said:

9. "Venerable sir, let the Blessed One delight in the Sangha of bhikkhus; venerable sir, let the Blessed One welcome the Sangha of bhikkhus;...(*as in §7*)...[459] now as he used to help it in the past."

10. The Sakyans of Cātumā and the Brahmā Sahampati were able to restore the Blessed One's confidence with the similes of the seedlings and the young calf.

11. Then the venerable Mahā Moggallāna addressed the bhikkhus thus: "Get up, friends, take your bowls and outer robes. The Blessed One's confidence has been restored by the Sakyans of Cātumā and the Brahmā Sahampati with the similes of the seedlings and the young calf."

12. "Yes, friend," they replied and, getting up from their seats, taking their bowls and outer robes, went to the Blessed One, and after paying homage to him, sat down at one side. The Blessed One then asked the venerable Sāriputta: "What did you think, Sāriputta, when the Sangha of bhikkhus was dismissed by me?"

"Venerable sir, I thought thus: 'The Sangha of bhikkhus has been dismissed by the Blessed One. The Blessed One will now abide inactive, devoted to pleasant abiding here and now; and we too shall now abide inactive, devoted to pleasant abiding here and now.'"

"Stop, Sāriputta, stop! Such a thought should not be entertained by you again."[684]

13. Then the Blessed One addressed the venerable Mahā Moggallāna: "What did you think, Moggallāna, when the Sangha of bhikkhus was dismissed by me?"

"Venerable sir, I thought thus: 'The Sangha of bhikkhus has been dismissed by the Blessed One. The Blessed One will now abide inactive, devoted to pleasant abiding here and now. Now the venerable Sāriputta and I shall lead the Sangha of bhikkhus.'"

"Good, good, Moggallāna! Either I shall lead the Sangha of bhikkhus or else Sāriputta and Moggallāna shall lead it."

14. Then the Blessed One addressed the bhikkhus thus:

"Bhikkhus, there are these four kinds of fears to be expected by those who go down to the water.[685] What are the four? They are: fear of waves, fear of crocodiles, fear of whirlpools, and fear of sharks. These are the four kinds of fears to be expected by those who go down to the water.

15. "So too, bhikkhus, there are four kinds of fears to be expected by certain persons who have gone forth from the home life into homelessness in this Dhamma and Discipline. What are [460] the four? They are: fear of waves, fear of crocodiles, fear of whirlpools, and fear of sharks.

16. "What, bhikkhus, is fear of waves? Here some clansman goes forth out of faith from the home life into homelessness, considering: 'I am a victim of birth, ageing, and death, of sorrow, lamentation, pain, grief, and despair; I am a victim of suffering, a prey to suffering. Surely an ending of this whole mass of suffering can be known.' Then, after he has gone forth thus, his companions in the holy life advise and instruct him thus: 'You should move to and fro thus; you should look ahead and look away thus; you should flex and extend the limbs thus; you should wear the patched cloak, bowl, and robes thus.' Then he thinks: 'Formerly, when we were in the home life, we advised and instructed others, and now these [bhikkhus], who seem like they might be our sons or our grandsons, think that they can advise and instruct us.' And so he forsakes the training and reverts to the low life. He is called one who has forsaken the training and reverted to the low life because he was frightened by the fear of waves. Now 'waves' is a term for angry despair.

17. "What, bhikkhus, is fear of crocodiles? Here some clansman goes forth out of faith from the home life into homelessness, considering: 'I am a victim of birth, ageing, and death, of sorrow, lamentation, pain, grief, and despair; I am a victim of suffering, a prey to suffering. Surely an ending of this whole mass of suffering can be known.' Then, after he has gone forth thus, his companions in the holy life advise and instruct him thus: 'This can be consumed by you, this cannot be consumed by you; this can be eaten by you, this cannot be eaten by you; this can be tasted by you, this cannot be tasted by you; this can be drunk by you, this cannot be drunk by you.[686] You can consume what is allowable, you cannot consume what is not allowable; you can eat what is

allowable, you cannot eat what is not allowable; you can taste what is allowable, you cannot taste what is not allowable; you can drink what is allowable, you cannot drink what is not allowable. You can consume food within the proper time, you cannot consume food outside the proper time; you can eat within the proper time, you cannot eat outside the proper time; you can taste food within the proper time, you cannot taste food outside the proper time; you can drink within the proper time, you cannot drink outside the proper time.'[687] [461]

"Then he thinks: 'Formerly, when we were in the home life, we consumed what we liked and did not consume what we did not like; we ate what we liked and did not eat what we did not like; we tasted what we liked and did not taste what we did not like; we drank what we liked and did not drink what we did not like. We consumed what was allowable and what was not allowable; we ate what was allowable and what was not allowable; we tasted what was allowable and what was not allowable; we drank what was allowable and what was not allowable. We consumed food within the proper time and outside the proper time; we ate within the proper time and outside the proper time; we tasted food within the proper time and outside the proper time; we drank within the proper time and outside the proper time. Now, when faithful householders give us good food of various kinds during the day outside the proper time, it seems these [bhikkhus] put a muzzle on our mouths.' And so he forsakes the training and reverts to the low life. He is called one who has forsaken the training and reverted to the low life because he was frightened by the fear of crocodiles. Now 'crocodiles' is a term for gluttony.

18. "What, bhikkhus, is fear of whirlpools? Here some clansman goes forth out of faith from the home life into homelessness, considering: 'I am a victim of birth, ageing, and death, of sorrow, lamentation, pain, grief, and despair; I am a victim of suffering, a prey to suffering. Surely an ending of this whole mass of suffering can be known.' Then, after he has gone forth thus, when it is morning he dresses, and taking his bowl and outer robe, he goes into a village or town for alms with his body unguarded, with his speech unguarded, with mindfulness unestablished, and with sense faculties unrestrained. He sees some householder there or householder's son furnished and

endowed with the five cords of sensual pleasure enjoying himself with them. He considers thus: 'Formerly, when we were in the home life, we were furnished and endowed with the five cords of sensual pleasure and we enjoyed ourselves with them. My family has wealth; I can both enjoy wealth and make merit.' And so he forsakes the training and reverts to the low life. He is called one who has forsaken the training and reverted to the low life because he was frightened by the fear of whirlpools. Now 'whirlpools' is a term for the five cords of sensual pleasure.

19. "What, bhikkhus, is fear of sharks? Here [462] some clansman goes forth out of faith from the home life into homelessness, considering: 'I am a victim of birth, ageing, and death, of sorrow, lamentation, pain, grief, and despair; I am a victim of suffering, a prey to suffering. Surely an ending of this whole mass of suffering can be known.' Then, after he has gone forth thus, when it is morning he dresses, and taking his bowl and outer robe, he goes into a village or town for alms with his body unguarded, with his speech unguarded, with mindfulness unestablished, and with sense faculties unrestrained. He sees a woman there lightly clothed, lightly dressed. When he sees such a woman, lust infects his mind. Because his mind has been infected by lust, he forsakes the training and reverts to the low life. He is called one who has forsaken the training and reverted to the low life because he was frightened by the fear of sharks. Now 'sharks' is a term for women.

20. "Bhikkhus, these are the four kinds of fears to be expected by certain persons who have gone forth from the home life into homelessness in this Dhamma and Discipline."

That is what the Blessed One said. The bhikkhus were satisfied and delighted in the Blessed One's words.

68 *Naḷakapāna Sutta*
At Naḷakapāna

1. THUS HAVE I HEARD. On one occasion the Blessed One was living in the Kosalan country at Naḷakapāna in the Palāsa Grove.

2. Now on that occasion many very well known clansmen had gone forth out of faith from the home life into homelessness under the Blessed One—the venerable Anuruddha, the venerable Nandiya, the venerable Kimbila, the venerable Bhagu, the venerable Kuṇḍadhāna, the venerable Revata, the venerable Ānanda, and other very well-known clansmen.

3. And on that occasion the Blessed One was [463] seated in the open surrounded by the Sangha of bhikkhus. Then, referring to those clansmen, he addressed the bhikkhus thus: "Bhikkhus, those clansmen who have gone forth out of faith from the home life into homelessness under me—do they delight in the holy life?"

When this was said, those bhikkhus were silent.

A second and a third time, referring to those clansmen, he addressed the bhikkhus thus: "Bhikkhus, those clansmen who have gone forth out of faith from the home life into homelessness under me—do they delight in the holy life?"

For a second and a third time, those bhikkhus were silent.

4. Then the Blessed One considered thus: "Suppose I question those clansmen?"

Then he addressed the venerable Anuruddha thus: "Anuruddha, do you all delight in the holy life?"

"Surely, venerable sir, we delight in the holy life."

5. "Good, good, Anuruddha! It is proper for all you clansmen who have gone forth out of faith from the home life into homelessness to delight in the holy life. As you are still endowed with the blessing of youth, black-haired young men in the prime of life, you could have indulged in sensual pleasures, yet you have gone forth from the home life into homelessness. It is not because

you have been driven by kings that you have gone forth from the home life into homelessness, or because you have been driven by thieves, or owing to debt, fear, or want of a livelihood. Rather, did you not go forth out of faith from the home life into homelessness after considering thus: 'I am a victim of birth, ageing, and death, of sorrow, lamentation, pain, grief, and despair; I am a victim of suffering, a prey to suffering. Surely an ending of this whole mass of suffering can be known'?"—"Yes, venerable sir."

6. "What should be done, Anuruddha, by a clansman who has gone forth thus? While he still does not attain to the rapture and pleasure that are secluded from sensual pleasures and secluded from unwholesome states, or to something more peaceful than that,[688] covetousness invades his mind and remains, ill will invades his mind and remains, sloth and torpor invade his mind and remain, restlessness and remorse invade his mind and remain, doubt invades [464] his mind and remains, discontent invades his mind and remains, weariness invades his mind and remains. That is so while he still does not attain to the rapture and pleasure that are secluded from sensual pleasures and secluded from unwholesome states, or to something more peaceful than that. When he attains to the rapture and pleasure that are secluded from sensual pleasures and secluded from unwholesome states, or to something more peaceful than that, covetousness does not invade his mind and remain, ill will... sloth and torpor...restlessness and remorse...doubt...discontent...weariness does not invade his mind and remain. That is so when he attains to the rapture and pleasure that are secluded from sensual pleasures and secluded from unwholesome states, or to something more peaceful than that.

7. "How then, Anuruddha, do you all think of me in this way: 'The Tathāgata has not abandoned the taints that defile, bring renewal of being, give trouble, ripen in suffering, and lead to future birth, ageing, and death. That is why the Tathāgata uses one thing after reflecting, endures another thing after reflecting, avoids another thing after reflecting, and removes another thing after reflecting'?"[689]

"No, venerable sir, we do not think of the Blessed One in that way. We think of the Blessed One in this way: 'The Tathāgata has abandoned the taints that defile, bring renewal of being, give trouble, ripen in suffering, and lead to future birth, ageing, and death. That is why the Tathāgata uses one thing after reflecting, endures another thing after reflecting, avoids another thing after reflecting, and removes another thing after reflecting."

"Good, good, Anuruddha! The Tathāgata has abandoned the taints that defile, bring renewal of being, give trouble, ripen in suffering, and lead to future birth, ageing, and death; he has cut them off at the root, made them like a palm stump, done away with them so that they are no longer subject to future arising. Just as a palm tree whose crown is cut off is incapable of further growth, so too, the Tathāgata has abandoned the taints that defile...cut them off at the root, made them like a palm stump, done away with them so that they are no longer subject to future arising.

8. "What do you think, Anuruddha? What purpose does the Tathāgata see that when a disciple has died, he declares his reappearance thus: 'So-and-so has reappeared in such-and-such a place; so-and-so has reappeared in such-and-such a place'?"[690] [465]

"Venerable sir, our teachings are rooted in the Blessed One, guided by the Blessed One, have the Blessed One as their resort. It would be good if the Blessed One would explain the meaning of these words. Having heard it from the Blessed One, the bhikkhus will remember it."

9. "Anuruddha, it is not for the purpose of scheming to deceive people or for the purpose of flattering people or for the purpose of gain, honour, or renown, or with the thought, 'Let people know me to be thus,' that when a disciple has died, the Tathāgata declares his reappearance thus: 'So-and-so has reappeared in such-and-such a place; so-and-so has reappeared in such-and-such a place.' Rather, it is because there are faithful clansmen inspired and gladdened by what is lofty, who when they hear that, direct their minds to such a state, and that leads to their welfare and happiness for a long time.

10. "Here a bhikkhu hears thus: 'The bhikkhu named so-and-so has died; the Blessed One has declared of him: "He was established in final knowledge."'[691] And he has either seen that venerable one for himself or heard it said of him: 'That venerable one's virtue was thus, his state [of concentration] was thus, his wisdom was thus, his abiding [in attainments] was thus, his deliverance was thus.' Recollecting his faith, virtue, learning,

generosity, and wisdom, he directs his mind to such a state. In this way a bhikkhu has a comfortable abiding.

11. "Here a bhikkhu hears thus: 'The bhikkhu named so-and-so has died; the Blessed One has declared of him: "With the destruction of the five lower fetters he has reappeared spontaneously [in the Pure Abodes] and there will attain final Nibbāna without ever returning from that world."' And he has either seen that venerable one for himself...he directs his mind to such a state. In this way too a bhikkhu has a comfortable abiding.

12. "Here a bhikkhu hears thus: 'The bhikkhu named so-and-so has died; the Blessed One has declared of him: "With the destruction of three fetters and with the attenuation of lust, hate, and delusion, he has become a once-returner, returning once to this world to make an end of suffering."' And he has either seen that venerable one for himself...[466] he directs his mind to such a state. In this way too a bhikkhu has a comfortable abiding.

13. "Here a bhikkhu hears thus: 'The bhikkhu named so-and-so has died; the Blessed One has declared of him: "With the destruction of three fetters he has become a stream-enterer, no longer subject to perdition, bound [for deliverance], headed for enlightenment."' And he has either seen that venerable one for himself...he directs his mind to such a state. In this way too a bhikkhu has a comfortable abiding.

14. "Here a bhikkhunī hears thus: 'The bhikkhunī named so-and-so has died; the Blessed One has declared of her: "She was established in final knowledge."' And she has either seen that sister for herself or heard it said of her: 'That sister's virtue was thus, her state [of concentration] was thus, her wisdom was thus, her abiding [in attainments] was thus, her deliverance was thus.' Recollecting her faith, virtue, learning, generosity, and wisdom, she directs her mind to such a state. In this way a bhikkhunī has a comfortable abiding.

15. "Here a bhikkhunī hears thus: 'The bhikkhunī named so-and-so has died; the Blessed One has declared of her: "With the destruction of the five lower fetters she has reappeared spontaneously [in the Pure Abodes] and will there attain final Nibbāna without ever returning from that world."...

16. "'He has declared of her: "With the destruction of three fetters and with the attenuation of lust, hate, and delusion, she

has become a once-returner, returning once to this world to make an end of suffering."...

17. "'He has declared of her: "With the destruction of three fetters she has become a stream-enterer, no longer subject to perdition, bound [for deliverance], headed for enlightenment."' [467] And she has either seen that sister for herself...she directs her mind to such a state. In this way too a bhikkhunī has a comfortable abiding.

18. "Here a man lay follower hears thus: 'The man lay follower named so-and-so has died; the Blessed One has declared of him: "With the destruction of the five lower fetters he has reappeared spontaneously [in the Pure Abodes] and will there attain final Nibbāna without ever returning from that world."...

19. "'He has declared of him: "With the destruction of three fetters and with the attenuation of lust, hate, and delusion, he has become a once-returner, returning once to this world to make an end of suffering."...

20. "'He has declared of him: "With the destruction of three fetters he has become a stream-enterer, no longer subject to perdition, bound [for deliverance], headed for enlightenment."' And he has either seen that venerable one for himself or heard it said of him: 'That venerable one's virtue was thus, his state [of concentration] was thus, his wisdom was thus, his abiding [in attainments] was thus, his deliverance was thus.' Recollecting his faith, virtue, learning, generosity, and wisdom, he directs his mind to such a state. In this way too a man lay follower has a comfortable abiding.

21. "Here a woman lay follower hears thus: 'The woman lay follower named so-and-so has died; the Blessed One has declared of her: "With the destruction of the five lower fetters she has reappeared spontaneously [in the Pure Abodes] and will there attain final Nibbāna without ever returning from that world." [468]...

22. "'He has declared of her: "With the destruction of three fetters and with the attenuation of lust, hate, and delusion, she has become a once-returner, returning once to this world to make an end of suffering."...

23. "'He has declared of her: "With the destruction of three fetters she has become a stream-enterer, no longer subject to perdition, bound [for deliverance], headed for enlightenment."'

And she has either seen that sister for herself or heard it said of her: 'That sister's virtue was thus, her state [of concentration] was thus, her wisdom was thus, her abiding [in attainments] was thus, her deliverance was thus.' Recollecting her faith, virtue, learning, generosity, and wisdom, she directs her mind to such a state. In this way too a woman lay follower has a comfortable abiding.

24. "So, Anuruddha, it is not for the purpose of scheming to deceive people or for the purpose of flattering people or for the purpose of gain, honour, and renown, or with the thought, 'Let people know me to be thus,' that when a disciple has died, the Tathāgata declares his reappearance thus: 'So-and-so has reappeared in such-and-such a place; so-and-so has reappeared in such-and-such a place.' Rather, it is because there are faithful clansmen inspired and gladdened by what is lofty, who when they hear that, direct their minds to such a state, and that leads to their welfare and happiness for a long time."

That is what the Blessed One said. The venerable Anuruddha was satisfied and delighted in the Blessed One's words.

69 *Gulissāni Sutta*
Gulissāni

[469] 1. THUS HAVE I HEARD. On one occasion the Blessed One was living at Rājagaha in the Bamboo Grove, the Squirrels' Sanctuary.

2. Now on that occasion a bhikkhu named Gulissāni, a forest-dweller of lax behaviour, had come on a visit to stay in the midst of the Sangha for some business or other. The venerable Sāriputta addressed the bhikkhus with reference to the bhikkhu Gulissāni thus:

3. "Friends, when a forest-dwelling bhikkhu comes to the Sangha and is living in the Sangha, he should be respectful and deferential towards his companions in the holy life. If he is disrespectful and undeferential towards his companions in the holy life, there will be those who would say of him: 'What has this venerable forest-dweller gained by his dwelling alone in the forest, doing as he likes, since he is disrespectful and undeferential towards his companions in the holy life?' Since there would be those who would say this of him, a forest-dwelling bhikkhu who has come to the Sangha and is living in the Sangha should be respectful and deferential towards his companions in the holy life.

4. "When a forest-dwelling bhikkhu comes to the Sangha and is living in the Sangha, he should be skilled in good behaviour regarding seats thus: 'I shall sit down in such a way that I do not encroach upon elder bhikkhus and do not deny new bhikkhus a seat.' If he is not skilled in good behaviour regarding seats, there will be those who would say of him: 'What has this venerable forest-dweller gained by his dwelling alone in the forest, doing as he likes, since he does not even know what pertains to good behaviour?' Since there would be those who would say this of him, a forest-dwelling bhikkhu who has come to the Sangha and

is living in the Sangha should be skilled in good behaviour regarding seats.

5. "When a forest-dwelling bhikkhu comes to the Sangha and is living in the Sangha, he should not enter the village too early or return late in the day. If he enters the village too early and returns late in the day, there will be those who would say of him: 'What has this venerable forest-dweller gained by his dwelling alone in the forest, doing as he likes, since he enters the village too early and returns late in the day?' Since there would be those who would say this of him, a forest-dwelling bhikkhu who has come to the Sangha and is living in the Sangha should not enter the village too early or return late in the day.

6. "When a forest-dwelling bhikkhu comes to the Sangha and is living in the Sangha, [470] he should not go before the meal or after the meal to visit families.[692] If he goes before the meal or after the meal to visit families, there will be those who would say of him: 'Surely this venerable forest-dweller, while dwelling alone in the forest, doing as he likes, must be used to making untimely visits, since he behaves thus when he has come to the Sangha.' Since there would be those who would say this of him, a forest-dwelling bhikkhu who has come to the Sangha and is living in the Sangha should not go before the meal or after the meal to visit families.

7. "When a forest-dwelling bhikkhu comes to the Sangha and is living in the Sangha, he should not be haughty and personally vain. If he is haughty and personally vain, there will be those who would say of him: 'Surely this venerable forest-dweller, while dwelling alone in the forest, doing as he likes, must generally be haughty and personally vain, since he behaves thus when he has come to the Sangha.' Since there would be those who would say this of him, a forest-dwelling bhikkhu who has come to the Sangha and is living in the Sangha should not be haughty and personally vain.

8. "When a forest-dwelling bhikkhu comes to the Sangha and is living in the Sangha, he should not be rough-tongued and loose-spoken. If he is rough-tongued and loose-spoken, there will be those who would say of him: 'What has this venerable forest-dweller gained by his dwelling alone in the forest, doing as he likes, since he is rough-tongued and loose-spoken?' Since there would be those who would say this of him, a forest-dwelling

bhikkhu who has come to the Sangha and is living in the Sangha should not be rough-tongued and loose-spoken.

9. "When a forest-dwelling bhikkhu comes to the Sangha and is living in the Sangha, he should be easy to correct and should associate with good friends. If he is difficult to correct and associates with bad friends, there will be those who would say of him: 'What has this venerable forest-dweller gained by his dwelling alone in the forest, doing as he likes, since he is difficult to correct and associates with bad friends?' Since there would be those who would say this of him, a forest-dwelling bhikkhu who has come to the Sangha and is living in the Sangha should be easy to correct and should associate with good friends.

10. "A forest-dwelling bhikkhu should guard the doors of his sense faculties. If he does not guard the doors of his sense faculties, there will be those who would say of him: 'What has this venerable forest-dweller gained by his dwelling alone in the forest, doing as he likes, since [471] he does not guard the doors of his sense faculties?' Since there would be those who would say this of him, a forest-dwelling bhikkhu should guard the doors of his sense faculties.

11. "A forest-dwelling bhikkhu should be moderate in eating. If he is not moderate in eating, there will be those who would say of him: 'What has this venerable forest-dweller gained by his dwelling alone in the forest, doing as he likes, since he is not moderate in eating?' Since there would be those who would say this of him, a forest-dwelling bhikkhu should be moderate in eating.

12. "A forest-dwelling bhikkhu should be devoted to wakefulness. If he is not devoted to wakefulness, there will be those would say of him: 'What has this venerable forest-dweller gained by his dwelling alone in the forest, doing as he likes, since he is not devoted to wakefulness?' Since there would be those who would say this of him, a forest-dwelling bhikkhu should be devoted to wakefulness.

13. "A forest-dwelling bhikkhu should be energetic. If he is not energetic, there will be those who would say of him: 'What has this venerable forest-dweller gained by his dwelling alone in the forest, doing as he likes, since he is lazy?' Since there would be those who would say this of him, a forest-dwelling bhikkhu should be energetic.

14. "A forest-dwelling bhikkhu should be established in mindfulness. If he is unmindful, there will be those who would say of him: 'What has this venerable forest-dweller gained by his dwelling alone in the forest, doing as he likes, since he is unmindful?' Since there would be those who would say this of him, a forest-dwelling bhikkhu should be established in mindfulness.

15. "A forest-dwelling bhikkhu should be concentrated. If he is not concentrated, there will be those who would say of him: 'What has this venerable forest-dweller gained by his dwelling alone in the forest, doing as he likes, since he is not concentrated?' Since there would be those who would say this of him, a forest-dwelling bhikkhu should be concentrated.

16. "A forest-dwelling bhikkhu should be wise. If he is not wise, there will be [472] those who would say of him: 'What has this venerable forest-dweller gained by his dwelling alone in the forest, doing as he likes, since he is not wise?' Since there would be those who would say this of him, a forest-dwelling bhikkhu should be wise.

17. "A forest-dwelling bhikkhu should apply himself to the higher Dhamma and the higher Discipline.[693] There are those who ask a forest-dwelling bhikkhu a question about the higher Dhamma and the higher Discipline. If, when so asked, he fails to reply, there will be those who would say of him: 'What has this venerable forest-dweller gained by his dwelling alone in the forest, doing as he likes, since when he is asked a question about the higher Dhamma and the higher Discipline he fails to reply?' Since there will be those who would say this of him, a forest-dwelling bhikkhu should apply himself to the higher Dhamma and the higher Discipline.

18. "A forest-dwelling bhikkhu should apply himself to those liberations that are peaceful and immaterial, transcending forms.[694] There are those who ask a forest-dwelling bhikkhu a question on the liberations that are peaceful and immaterial, transcending forms. If, when so asked, he fails to reply, there will be those who would say of him: 'What has this venerable forest-dweller gained by his dwelling alone in the forest, doing as he likes, since when he is asked a question about those liberations that are peaceful and immaterial, transcending forms, he fails to reply?' Since there will be those who would say this of him, a forest-dwelling bhikkhu should

apply himself to those liberations that are peaceful and immaterial, transcending forms.

19. "A forest-dwelling bhikkhu should apply himself to the superhuman state. There are those who ask a forest-dwelling bhikkhu a question on the superhuman state.[695] If, when so asked, he fails to reply, there will be those who would say of him: 'What has this venerable forest-dweller gained by his dwelling alone in the forest, doing as he likes, since he does not even know the purpose for the sake of which he went forth?' Since there will be those who would say this of him, a forest-dwelling bhikkhu should apply himself to the superhuman state."

20. When this was said, the venerable Mahā Moggallāna asked the venerable Sāriputta: "Friend Sāriputta, should these things be undertaken and practised only by a forest-dwelling bhikkhu or [473] by one who dwells near a village as well?"

"Friend Moggallāna, these things should be undertaken and practised not only by a forest-dwelling bhikkhu, but by a town-dwelling bhikkhu as well."

70 *Kīṭāgiri Sutta*
At Kīṭāgiri

1. THUS HAVE I HEARD. On one occasion the Blessed One was wandering in the Kāsi country together with a large Sangha of bhikkhus. There he addressed the bhikkhus thus:

2. "Bhikkhus, I abstain from eating at night. By so doing, I am free from illness and affliction, and I enjoy health, strength, and a comfortable abiding. Come, bhikkhus, abstain from eating at night. By so doing, you too will be free from illness and affliction, and you will enjoy health, strength, and a comfortable abiding."[696]

"Yes, venerable sir," they replied.

3. Then, as the Blessed One was wandering by stages in the Kāsi country, he eventually arrived at a Kāsi town called Kīṭāgiri. There he lived in this Kāsi town, Kīṭāgiri.

4. Now on that occasion the bhikkhus named Assaji and Punabbasuka were residing at Kīṭāgiri.[697] Then a number of bhikkhus went and told them: "Friends, the Blessed One and the Sangha of bhikkhus now abstain from eating at night. By so doing, they are free from illness and affliction, and they enjoy health, strength, and a comfortable abiding. Come, friends, abstain from eating at night. By so doing, you too will be free from illness and affliction, and you will enjoy health, strength, and a comfortable abiding." [474] When this was said, the bhikkhus Assaji and Punabbasuka told those bhikkhus: "Friends, we eat in the evening, in the morning, and in the day outside the proper time. By so doing, we are free from illness and affliction, and we enjoy health, strength, and a comfortable abiding. Why should we abandon [a benefit] visible here and now to pursue [a benefit to be achieved] at a future time? We shall eat in the evening, in the morning, and in the day outside the proper time."

5. Since the bhikkhus were unable to convince the bhikkhus Assaji and Punabbasuka, they went to the Blessed One. After paying homage to him, they sat down at one side and told him all that had occurred, adding: "Venerable sir, since we were unable to convince the bhikkhus Assaji and Punabbasuka, we have reported this matter to the Blessed One."

6. Then the Blessed One addressed a certain bhikkhu thus: "Come, bhikkhu, tell the bhikkhus Assaji and Punabbasuka in my name that the Teacher calls them."

"Yes, venerable sir," he replied, and he went to the bhikkhus Assaji and Punabbasuka and told them: "The Teacher calls you, friends."

"Yes, friend," they replied, and they went to the Blessed One, and after paying homage to him, sat down at one side. The Blessed One then said: "Bhikkhus, is it true that when a number of bhikkhus went and told you: 'Friends, the Blessed One and the Sangha now abstain from eating at night...Come, friends, abstain from eating at night [475]...,' you told those bhikkhus: 'Friends, we eat in the evening...Why should we abandon [a benefit] visible here and now to pursue [a benefit to be achieved] at a future time? We shall eat in the evening, in the morning, and in the day outside the proper time'?"—"Yes, venerable sir."

"Bhikkhus, have you known me to teach the Dhamma in such a way as this: 'Whatever this person experiences, whether pleasant or painful or neither-painful-nor-pleasant, unwholesome states diminish in him and wholesome states increase'?"[698]—"No, venerable sir."

7. "Bhikkhus, have you not known me to teach the Dhamma in such a way as this: 'Here, when someone feels a certain kind of pleasant feeling, unwholesome states increase in him and wholesome states diminish; but when someone feels another kind of pleasant feeling, unwholesome states diminish in him and wholesome states increase.[699] Here, when someone feels a certain kind of painful feeling, unwholesome states increase in him and wholesome states diminish; but when someone feels another kind of painful feeling, unwholesome states diminish in him and wholesome states increase. Here, when someone feels a certain kind of neither-painful-nor-pleasant feeling, unwholesome states increase in him and wholesome states diminish; but when someone feels another kind of neither-painful-nor-pleasant

feeling, unwholesome states diminish in him and wholesome states increase'?"—"Yes, venerable sir."

8. "Good, bhikkhus.[700] And if it were unknown by me, unseen, unfound, unrealised, uncontacted by wisdom thus: 'Here, when someone feels a certain kind of pleasant feeling, unwholesome states increase in him and wholesome states diminish,' would it be fitting for me, not knowing that, to say: 'Abandon such a kind of pleasant feeling'?"—"No, venerable sir."

"But because it is known by me, seen, found, realised, contacted by wisdom thus: 'Here, when someone feels a certain kind of pleasant feeling [476], unwholesome states increase in him and wholesome states diminish,' that I therefore say: 'Abandon such a kind of pleasant feeling.'

"If it were unknown by me, unseen, unfound, unrealised, uncontacted by wisdom thus: 'Here, when someone feels another kind of pleasant feeling, unwholesome states diminish in him and wholesome states increase,' would it be fitting for me, not knowing that, to say: 'Enter upon and abide in such a kind of pleasant feeling'?"—"No, venerable sir."

"But because it is known by me, seen, found, realised, contacted by wisdom thus: 'Here, when someone feels another kind of pleasant feeling, unwholesome states diminish in him and wholesome states increase,' that I therefore say: 'Enter upon and abide in such a kind of pleasant feeling.'

9. "If it were unknown by me...But because it is known by me...contacted by wisdom thus: 'Here, when someone feels a certain kind of painful feeling, unwholesome states increase in him and wholesome states diminish,' that I therefore say: 'Abandon such a kind of painful feeling.'

"If it were unknown by me...But because it is known by me...contacted by wisdom thus: 'Here, when someone feels another kind of painful feeling, unwholesome states diminish in him and wholesome states increase,' that I therefore say: 'Enter upon and abide in such a kind of painful feeling.'

10. "If it were unknown by me...But because it is known by me...contacted by wisdom thus: 'Here, when someone feels a certain kind of neither-painful-nor-pleasant feeling, unwholesome states increase in him and wholesome states diminish,' that I therefore say: 'Abandon such a kind of neither-painful-nor-pleasant feeling.'

"If it were unknown by me...But because it is known by me...contacted by wisdom thus: 'Here, when someone feels another kind of neither-painful-nor-pleasant feeling, unwholesome states diminish in him and wholesome states increase,' that I therefore say: [477] 'Enter upon and abide in such a kind of neither-painful-nor-pleasant feeling.'

11. "Bhikkhus, I do not say of all bhikkhus that they still have work to do with diligence; nor do I say of all bhikkhus that they have no more work to do with diligence.

12. "I do not say of those bhikkhus who are arahants with taints destroyed, who have lived the holy life, done what had to be done, laid down the burden, reached the true goal, destroyed the fetters of being, and are completely liberated through final knowledge, that they still have work to do with diligence. Why is that? They have done their work with diligence; they are no more capable of being negligent.

13. "I say of such bhikkhus who are in higher training, whose minds have not yet reached the goal, and who are still aspiring to the supreme security from bondage, that they still have work to do with diligence. Why is that? Because when those venerable ones make use of suitable resting places and associate with good friends and balance their spiritual faculties, they may by realising for themselves with direct knowledge here and now enter upon and abide in that supreme goal of the holy life for the sake of which clansmen rightly go forth from the home life into homelessness. Seeing this fruit of diligence for these bhikkhus, I say that they still have work to do with diligence.

14. "Bhikkhus, there are seven kinds of persons to be found existing in the world.[701] What seven? They are: one liberated-in-both ways, one liberated-by-wisdom, a body-witness, one attained-to-view, one liberated-by-faith, a Dhamma-follower, and a faith-follower.

15. "What kind of person is one liberated-in-both-ways? Here some person contacts with the body and abides in those liberations that are peaceful and immaterial, transcending forms, and his taints are destroyed by his seeing with wisdom. This kind of person is called one liberated-in-both-ways.[702] I do not say of such a bhikkhu that he still has work to do with diligence. Why is that? He has done his work with diligence; he is no more capable of being negligent.

16. "What kind of person is one liberated-by-wisdom? Here some person does not contact with the body and abide in those liberations that are peaceful and immaterial, transcending forms, but his taints are destroyed by his seeing with wisdom. This kind of person is called one liberated-by-wisdom.[703] [478] I do not say of such a bhikkhu that he still has work to do with diligence. Why is that? He has done his work with diligence; he is no more capable of being negligent.

17. "What kind of person is a body-witness? Here some person contacts with the body and abides in those liberations that are peaceful and immaterial, transcending forms, and some of his taints are destroyed by his seeing with wisdom. This kind of person is called a body-witness.[704] I say of such a bhikkhu that he still has work to do with diligence. Why is that? Because when that venerable one makes use of suitable resting places and associates with good friends and balances his spiritual faculties, he may by realising for himself with direct knowledge here and now enter upon and abide in that supreme goal of the holy life for the sake of which clansmen rightly go forth from the home life into homelessness. Seeing this fruit of diligence for such a bhikkhu, I say that he still has work to do with diligence.

18. "What kind of person is one attained-to-view? Here some person does not contact with the body and abide in those liberations that are peaceful and immaterial, transcending forms, but some of his taints are destroyed by his seeing with wisdom, and he has reviewed and examined with wisdom the teachings proclaimed by the Tathāgata. This kind of person is called one attained-to-view.[705] I say of such a bhikkhu that he still has work to do with diligence. Why is that? Because when that venerable one...into homelessness. Seeing this fruit of diligence for such a bhikkhu, I say that he still has work to do with diligence.

19. "What kind of person is one liberated-by-faith? Here some person does not contact with the body and abide in those liberations that are peaceful and immaterial, transcending forms, but some of his taints are destroyed by his seeing with wisdom, and his faith is planted, rooted, and established in the Tathāgata.[706] This kind of person is called one liberated-by-faith. I say of such a bhikkhu that he still has work to do with diligence. Why is that? Because when that venerable one [479]...into homelessness.

Seeing this fruit of diligence for such a bhikkhu, I say that he still has work to do with diligence.

20. "What kind of person is a Dhamma-follower? Here some person does not contact with the body and abide in those liberations that are peaceful and immaterial, transcending forms, and his taints are not yet destroyed by his seeing with wisdom, but those teachings proclaimed by the Tathāgata are accepted by him after reflecting on them sufficiently with wisdom. Furthermore, he has these qualities: the faith faculty, the energy faculty, the mindfulness faculty, the concentration faculty, and the wisdom faculty. This kind of person is called a Dhamma-follower.[707] I say of such a bhikkhu that he still has work to do with diligence. Why is that? Because when that venerable one...into homelessness. Seeing this fruit of diligence for such a bhikkhu, I say that he still has work to do with diligence.

21. "What kind of person is a faith-follower? Here some person does not contact with the body and abide in those liberations that are peaceful and immaterial, transcending forms, and his taints are not yet destroyed by his seeing with wisdom, yet he has sufficient faith in and love for the Tathāgata. Furthermore, he has these qualities: the faith faculty, the energy faculty, the mindfulness faculty, the concentration faculty, and the wisdom faculty. This kind of person is called a faith-follower. I say of such a bhikkhu that he still has work to do with diligence. Why is that? Because when that venerable one makes use of suitable resting places and associates with good friends and balances his spiritual faculties, he may by realising for himself with direct knowledge here and now enter upon and abide in that supreme goal of the holy life for the sake of which clansmen rightly go forth from the home life into homelessness. Seeing this fruit of diligence for such a bhikkhu, I say that he still has work to do with diligence.

22. "Bhikkhus, I do not say that final knowledge is achieved all at once. On the contrary, final knowledge is achieved by gradual training, by gradual practice, by gradual progress. [480]

23. "And how is final knowledge achieved by gradual training, gradual practice, gradual progress? Here one who has faith [in a teacher] visits him; when he visits him, he pays respect to him; when he pays respect to him, he gives ear; one who gives ear hears the Dhamma; having heard the Dhamma, he memorises

it; he examines the meaning of the teachings he has memorised; when he examines their meaning, he gains a reflective acceptance of those teachings; when he has gained a reflective acceptance of those teachings, zeal springs up in him; when zeal has sprung up, he applies his will; having applied his will, he scrutinises; having scrutinised, he strives; resolutely striving, he realises with the body the supreme truth and sees it by penetrating it with wisdom.[708]

24. "There has not been that faith,[709] bhikkhus, and there has not been that visiting, and there has not been that paying of respect, and there has not been that giving ear, and there has not been that hearing of the Dhamma, and there has not been that memorising of the Dhamma, and there has not been that examination of the meaning, and there has not been that reflective acceptance of the teachings, and there has not been that zeal, and there has not been that application of will, and there has not been that scrutiny, and there has not been that striving. Bhikkhus, you have lost your way; bhikkhus, you have been practising the wrong way. How far you have strayed, misguided men, from this Dhamma and Discipline!

25. "Bhikkhus, there is a four-phrased statement, and when it is recited a wise man would quickly understand it.[710] I shall recite it to you, bhikkhus. Try to understand it."

"Venerable sir, who are we that we should understand the Dhamma?"

26. "Bhikkhus, even with a teacher who is concerned with material things, an heir to material things, attached to material things, such haggling [by his disciples] would not be proper: 'If we get this, we will do it; if we don't get this, we won't do it'; so what [should be said when the teacher is] the Tathāgata, who is utterly detached from material things?

27. "Bhikkhus, for a faithful disciple who is intent on fathoming the Teacher's Dispensation, it is proper that he conduct himself thus: 'The Blessed One is the Teacher, I am a disciple; the Blessed One knows, I do not know.' For a faithful disciple who is intent on fathoming the Teacher's Dispensation, the Teacher's Dispensation is nourishing and refreshing. For a faithful disciple who is intent on fathoming the Teacher's Dispensation, [481] it is proper that he conduct himself thus: 'Willingly, let only my skin, sinews, and bones remain, and let the flesh and blood dry

up on my body, but my energy shall not be relaxed so long as I have not attained what can be attained by manly strength, manly energy, and manly persistence.'[711] For a faithful disciple who is intent on fathoming the Teacher's Dispensation, one of two fruits may be expected: either final knowledge here and now or, if there is a trace of clinging left, non-return."

That is what the Blessed One said. The bhikkhus were satisfied and delighted in the Blessed One's words.

3
The Division on Wanderers

(*Paribbājakavagga*)

71 *Tevijjavacchagotta Sutta*
To Vacchagotta on the Threefold True Knowledge

1. THUS HAVE I HEARD. On one occasion the Blessed One was living at Vesālī in the Great Wood in the Hall with the Peaked Roof.

2. Now on that occasion the wanderer Vacchagotta was staying in the Wanderers' Park of the Single White-lotus Mango Tree.[712]

3. Then, when it was morning, the Blessed One dressed, and taking his bowl and outer robe, went into Vesālī for alms. Then the Blessed One thought: "It is still too early to wander for alms in Vesālī. Suppose I went to the wanderer Vacchagotta in the Wanderers' Park of the Single White-lotus Mango Tree."

4. Then the Blessed One went to the wanderer Vacchagotta in the Wanderers' Park of the Single White-lotus Mango Tree. The wanderer Vacchagotta saw the Blessed One coming in the distance and said to him: "Let the Blessed One come, venerable sir! Welcome to the Blessed One! It is long since the Blessed One found an opportunity to come here. Let the Blessed One be seated; this seat is ready." The Blessed One sat down on the seat made ready, and the wanderer Vacchagotta [482] took a low seat, sat down at one side, and said to the Blessed One:

5. "Venerable sir, I have heard this: 'The recluse Gotama claims to be omniscient and all-seeing, to have complete knowledge and vision thus: "Whether I am walking or standing or sleeping or awake, knowledge and vision are continuously and uninterruptedly present to me."'[713] Venerable sir, do those who speak thus say what has been said by the Blessed One, and not misrepresent him with what is contrary to fact? Do they explain in accordance with the Dhamma in such a way that nothing which provides a ground for censure can be legitimately deduced from their assertion?"

"Vaccha, those who say thus do not say what has been said

by me, but misrepresent me with what is untrue and contrary to fact."[714]

6. "Venerable sir, how should I answer that I may say what has been said by the Blessed One and not misrepresent him with what is contrary to fact? How may I explain in accordance with the Dhamma in such a way that nothing which provides a ground for censure can be legitimately deduced from my assertion?"

"Vaccha, if you answer thus: 'The recluse Gotama has the threefold true knowledge,' you will be saying what has been said by me and will not misrepresent me with what is contrary to fact. You will explain in accordance with the Dhamma in such a way that nothing which provides a ground for censure can be legitimately deduced from your assertion.

7. "For in so far as I wish, I recollect my manifold past lives, that is, one birth, two births...(*as Sutta 51, §24*)...Thus with their aspects and particulars I recollect my manifold past lives.

8. "And in so far as I wish, with the divine eye, which is purified and surpasses the human, I see beings passing away and reappearing, inferior and superior, fair and ugly, fortunate and unfortunate, and I understand how beings pass on according to their actions...(*as Sutta 51, §25*)...

9. "And by realising for myself with direct knowledge, I here and now enter upon and abide in the deliverance of mind and deliverance by wisdom that are taintless with the destruction of the taints.

10. "If you answer thus: 'The recluse Gotama has the threefold true knowledge,' [483] you will be saying what has been said by me and will not misrepresent me with what is contrary to fact. You will explain in accordance with the Dhamma in such a way that nothing which provides a ground for censure can be legitimately deduced from your assertion."

11. When this was said, the wanderer Vacchagotta asked the Blessed One: "Master Gotama, is there any householder who, without abandoning the fetter of householdership, on the dissolution of the body has made an end of suffering?"[715]

"Vaccha, there is no householder who, without abandoning the fetter of householdership, on the dissolution of the body has made an end of suffering."

12. "Master Gotama, is there any householder who, without

abandoning the fetter of householdership, on the dissolution of the body has gone to heaven?"

"Vaccha, there are not only one hundred or two or three or four or five hundred, but far more householders who, without abandoning the fetter of householdership, on the dissolution of the body have gone to heaven."

13. "Master Gotama, is there any Ājīvaka who, on the dissolution of the body, has made an end of suffering?"[716]

"Vaccha, there is no Ājīvaka who, on the dissolution of the body, has made an end of suffering."

14. "Master Gotama, is there any Ājīvaka who, on the dissolution of the body, has gone to heaven?"

"When I recollect the past ninety-one aeons, Vaccha, I do not recall any Ājīvaka who, on the dissolution of the body, went to heaven, with one exception, and he held the doctrine of the moral efficacy of action, the doctrine of the moral efficacy of deeds."[717]

15. "That being so, Master Gotama, that sectarian fold is empty even of one who goes to heaven."

"That being so, Vaccha, that sectarian fold is empty even of one who goes to heaven."

That is what the Blessed One said. The wanderer Vacchagotta was satisfied and delighted in the Blessed One's words.

72 *Aggivacchagotta Sutta*
To Vacchagotta on Fire

1. THUS HAVE I HEARD. On one occasion the Blessed One was living at Sāvatthī in Jeta's Grove, Anāthapiṇḍika's Park.

2. Then the wanderer Vacchagotta went to the Blessed One [484] and exchanged greetings with him. When this courteous and amiable talk was finished, he sat down at one side and asked the Blessed One:

3. "How is it, Master Gotama, does Master Gotama hold the view: 'The world is eternal: only this is true, anything else is wrong'?"

"Vaccha, I do not hold the view: 'The world is eternal: only this is true, anything else is wrong.'"

4. "How then, does Master Gotama hold the view: 'The world is not eternal: only this is true, anything else is wrong'?"

"Vaccha, I do not hold the view: 'The world is not eternal: only this is true, anything else is wrong.'"

5. "How is it, Master Gotama, does Master Gotama hold the view: 'The world is finite: only this is true, anything else is wrong'?"

"Vaccha, I do not hold the view: 'The world is finite: only this is true, anything else is wrong.'"

6. "How then, does Master Gotama hold the view: 'The world is infinite: only this is true, anything else is wrong'?"

"Vaccha, I do not hold the view: 'The world is infinite: only this is true, anything else is wrong.'"

7. "How is it, Master Gotama, does Master Gotama hold the view: 'The soul and the body are the same: only this is true, anything else is wrong'?"[718]

"Vaccha, I do not hold the view: 'The soul and the body are the same: only this is true, anything else is wrong.'"

8. "How then, does Master Gotama hold the view: 'The soul

is one thing and the body another: only this is true, anything else is wrong'?"

"Vaccha, I do not hold the view: 'The soul is one thing and the body another: only this is true, anything else is wrong.'"

9. "How is it, Master Gotama, does Master Gotama hold the view: 'After death a Tathāgata exists: only this is true, anything else is wrong'?"[719]

"Vaccha, I do not hold the view: 'After death a Tathāgata exists: only this is true, anything else is wrong.'"

10. "How then, does Master Gotama hold the view: 'After death a Tathāgata does not exist: only this is true, anything else is wrong'?"

"Vaccha, I do not hold the view: 'After death a Tathāgata does not exist: only this is true, anything else is wrong.'"

11. "How is it, Master Gotama, does Master Gotama hold the view: 'After death a Tathāgata both exists and does not exist: only this is true, anything else is wrong.'?" [485]

"Vaccha, I do not hold the view: 'After death a Tathāgata both exists and does not exist: only this is true, anything else is wrong.'"

12. "How then, does Master Gotama hold the view: 'After death a Tathāgata neither exists nor does not exist: only this is true, anything else is wrong'?"

"Vaccha, I do not hold the view: 'After death a Tathāgata neither exists nor does not exist: only this is true, anything else is wrong.'"

13. "How is it then, Master Gotama? When Master Gotama is asked each of these ten questions, he replies: 'I do not hold that view.' What danger does Master Gotama see that he does not take up any of these speculative views?"

14. "Vaccha, the speculative view that the world is eternal is a thicket of views, a wilderness of views, a contortion of views, a vacillation of views, a fetter of views. It is beset by suffering, by vexation, by despair, and by fever, and it does not lead to disenchantment, to dispassion, to cessation, to peace, to direct knowledge, to enlightenment, to Nibbāna.

"The speculative view that the world is not eternal...that the world is finite...that the world is infinite...that the soul and the body are the same...that the soul is one thing and the body another...that after death a Tathāgata exists [486]...that after death a Tathāgata does not exist...that after death a Tathāgata both exists and does not exist...that after death a Tathāgata neither exists nor does not exist is a thicket of views, a wilderness of views, a contortion of views, a vacillation of views, a fetter of views. It is beset by suffering, by vexation, by despair, and by fever, and it does not lead to disenchantment, to dispassion, to cessation, to peace, to direct knowledge, to enlightenment, to Nibbāna. Seeing this danger, I do not take up any of these speculative views."

15. "Then does Master Gotama hold any speculative view at all?"

"Vaccha, 'speculative view' is something that the Tathāgata has put away. For the Tathāgata, Vaccha, has seen[720] this: 'Such is material form, such its origin, such its disappearance; such is feeling, such its origin, such its disappearance; such is perception, such its origin, such its disappearance; such are formations, such their origin, such their disappearance; such is consciousness, such its origin, such its disappearance.' Therefore, I say, with the destruction, fading away, cessation, giving up, and relinquishing of all conceivings, all excogitations, all I-making, mine-making, and the underlying tendency to conceit, the Tathāgata is liberated through not clinging."

16. "When a bhikkhu's mind is liberated thus, Master Gotama, where does he reappear [after death]?"

"The term 'reappears' does not apply, Vaccha."[721]

"Then he does not reappear, Master Gotama?"

"The term 'does not reappear' does not apply, Vaccha."

"Then he both reappears and does not reappear, Master Gotama?"

"The term 'both reappears and does not reappear' does not apply, Vaccha."

"Then he neither reappears nor does not reappear, Master Gotama?"

"The term 'neither reappears nor does not reappear' does not apply, Vaccha."

17. "When Master Gotama is asked these four questions, he replies: 'The term "reappears" does not apply, Vaccha; the term "does not reappear" does not apply, Vaccha; the term "both reappears and does not reappear" does not apply, Vaccha; the term "neither reappears nor [487] does not reappear" does not apply, Vaccha.' Here I have fallen into bewilderment, Master Gotama, here I have fallen into confusion, and the measure of

confidence I had gained through previous conversation with Master Gotama has now disappeared."

18. "It is enough to cause you bewilderment, Vaccha, enough to cause you confusion. For this Dhamma, Vaccha, is profound, hard to see and hard to understand, peaceful and sublime, unattainable by mere reasoning, subtle, to be experienced by the wise. It is hard for you to understand it when you hold another view, accept another teaching, approve of another teaching, pursue a different training, and follow a different teacher. So I shall question you about this in return, Vaccha. Answer as you choose.

19. "What do you think, Vaccha? Suppose a fire were burning before you. Would you know: 'This fire is burning before me'?"

"I would, Master Gotama."

"If someone were to ask you, Vaccha: 'What does this fire burning before you burn in dependence on?'—being asked thus, what would you answer?"

"Being asked thus, Master Gotama, I would answer: 'This fire burning before me burns in dependence on grass and sticks.'"

"If that fire before you were to be extinguished, would you know: 'This fire before me has been extinguished'?"

"I would, Master Gotama."

"If someone were to ask you, Vaccha: 'When that fire before you was extinguished, to which direction did it go: to the east, the west, the north, or the south?'—being asked thus, what would you answer?"

"That does not apply, Master Gotama. The fire burned in dependence on its fuel of grass and sticks. When that is used up, if it does not get any more fuel, being without fuel, it is reckoned as extinguished."

20. "So too, Vaccha, the Tathāgata has abandoned that material form by which one describing the Tathāgata might describe him;[722] he has cut it off at the root, made it like a palm stump, done away with it so that it is no longer subject to future arising. The Tathāgata is liberated from reckoning in terms of material form, Vaccha, he is profound, immeasurable, unfathomable like the ocean. The term 'reappears' does not apply, the term 'does not reappear' does not apply, [488] the term 'both reappears and does not reappear' does not apply, the term 'neither reappears nor does not reappear' does not apply.[723] The Tathāgata has

abandoned that feeling by which one describing the Tathāgata might describe him...has abandoned that perception by which one describing the Tathāgata might describe him...has abandoned those formations by which one describing the Tathāgata might describe him...has abandoned that consciousness by which one describing the Tathāgata might describe him; he has cut it off at the root, made it like a palm stump, done away with it so that it is no longer subject to future arising. The Tathāgata is liberated from reckoning in terms of consciousness, Vaccha; he is profound, immeasurable, unfathomable like the ocean. The term 'reappears' does not apply, the term 'does not reappear' does not apply, the term 'both reappears and does not reappear' does not apply, the term 'neither appears nor does not appear' does not apply."

21. When this was said, the wanderer Vacchagotta said to the Blessed One: "Master Gotama, suppose there were a great sāla tree not far from a village or town, and impermanence wore away its branches and foliage, its bark and sapwood, so that on a later occasion, being divested of branches and foliage, divested of bark and sapwood, it became pure, consisting entirely of heartwood; so too, this discourse of Master Gotama's is divested of branches and foliage, divested of bark and sapwood, and is pure, consisting entirely of heartwood.

22. "Magnificent, Master Gotama! Magnificent, Master Gotama! Master Gotama has made the Dhamma clear in many ways, as though he were turning upright what had been overthrown, revealing what was hidden, showing the way to one who was lost, or holding up a lamp in the dark [489] for those with eyesight to see forms. I go to Master Gotama for refuge and to the Dhamma and to the Sangha of bhikkhus. From today let Master Gotama remember me as a lay follower who has gone to him for refuge for life."

73 *Mahāvacchagotta Sutta*
The Greater Discourse to Vacchagotta

1. THUS HAVE I HEARD. On one occasion the Blessed One was living at Rājagaha in the Bamboo Grove, the Squirrels' Sanctuary.

2. Then the wanderer Vacchagotta went to the Blessed One and exchanged greetings with him. When this courteous and amiable talk was finished, he sat down at one side and said to the Blessed One:

3. "I have had conversations with Master Gotama for a long time. It would be good if Master Gotama would teach me in brief the wholesome and the unwholesome."

"I can teach you the wholesome and the unwholesome in brief, Vaccha, and I can teach you the wholesome and the unwholesome at length. Still I will teach you the wholesome and the unwholesome in brief. Listen and attend closely to what I shall say."

"Yes, sir," he replied. The Blessed One said this:

4. "Vaccha, greed is unwholesome, non-greed is wholesome; hate is unwholesome, non-hate is wholesome; delusion is unwholesome, non-delusion is wholesome. In this way three things are unwholesome and the other three things are wholesome.

5. "Killing living beings is unwholesome, abstention from killing living beings is wholesome; taking what is not given is unwholesome, abstention from taking what is not given is wholesome; misconduct in sensual pleasures is unwholesome, abstention from misconduct in sensual pleasures is wholesome; false speech is unwholesome, abstention from false speech is wholesome; malicious speech [490] is unwholesome, abstention from malicious speech is wholesome; harsh speech is unwholesome, abstention from harsh speech is wholesome; gossip is unwholesome, abstention from gossip is wholesome; covetousness is

unwholesome, uncovetousness is wholesome; ill will is unwholesome, non-ill will is wholesome; wrong view is unwholesome, right view is wholesome. In this way ten things are unwholesome and the other ten things are wholesome.

6. "When a bhikkhu has abandoned craving, cut it off at the root, made it like a palm stump, done away with it so that it is no longer subject to future arising, then that bhikkhu is an arahant with taints destroyed, one who has lived the holy life, done what had to be done, laid down the burden, reached the true goal, destroyed the fetters of being, and is completely liberated through final knowledge."

7. "Apart from Master Gotama, is there any one bhikkhu, Master Gotama's disciple, who by realising for himself with direct knowledge here and now enters upon and abides in the deliverance of mind and deliverance by wisdom that are taintless with the destruction of the taints?"[724]

"There are not only one hundred, Vaccha, or two or three or four or five hundred, but far more bhikkhus, my disciples, who by realising for themselves with direct knowledge here and now enter upon and abide in the deliverance of mind and deliverance by wisdom that are taintless with the destruction of the taints."

8. "Apart from Master Gotama and the bhikkhus, is there any one bhikkhunī, Master Gotama's disciple, who by realising for herself with direct knowledge here and now enters upon and abides in the deliverance of mind and deliverance by wisdom that are taintless with the destruction of the taints?"

"There are not only one hundred...or five hundred, but far more bhikkhunīs, my disciples, who by realising for themselves with direct knowledge here and now enter upon and abide in the deliverance of mind and deliverance by wisdom that are taintless with the destruction of the taints."

9. "Apart from Master Gotama and the bhikkhus and bhikkhunīs, is there any one man lay follower, Master Gotama's disciple, clothed in white leading a life of celibacy who, with the destruction of the five lower fetters, will reappear spontaneously [in the Pure Abodes] and there attain final Nibbāna without ever returning from that world?"[725]

"There are not only one hundred...or five hundred, but far more men lay followers, my disciples, clothed in white leading lives of celibacy who, with the destruction of the five lower fetters, [491] will reappear spontaneously [in the Pure Abodes] and there attain final Nibbāna without ever returning from that world."

10. "Apart from Master Gotama, the bhikkhus and bhikkhunīs, and the men lay followers clothed in white leading lives of celibacy, is there any one man lay follower, Master Gotama's disciple, clothed in white enjoying sensual pleasures, who carries out his instruction, responds to his advice, has gone beyond doubt, become free from perplexity, gained intrepidity, and become independent of others in the Teacher's Dispensation?"[726]

"There are not only one hundred...or five hundred, but far more men lay followers, my disciples, clothed in white enjoying sensual pleasures, who carry out my instruction, respond to my advice, have gone beyond doubt, become free from perplexity, gained intrepidity, and become independent of others in the Teacher's Dispensation."

11. "Apart from Master Gotama, the bhikkhus and bhikkhunīs, and the men lay followers clothed in white, both those leading lives of celibacy and those enjoying sensual pleasures, is there any one woman lay follower, Master Gotama's disciple, clothed in white leading a life of celibacy who, with the destruction of the five lower fetters, will reappear spontaneously [in the Pure Abodes] and there attain final Nibbāna without ever returning from that world?"

"There are not only one hundred...or five hundred, but far more women lay followers, my disciples, clothed in white leading lives of celibacy who, with the destruction of the five lower fetters, will reappear spontaneously [in the Pure Abodes] and there attain final Nibbāna without ever returning from that world."

12. "Apart from Master Gotama, the bhikkhus and bhikkhunīs, and the men lay followers clothed in white, both those leading lives of celibacy and those enjoying sensual pleasures, and the women lay followers clothed in white leading lives of celibacy, is there any one woman lay follower, Master Gotama's disciple, clothed in white enjoying sensual pleasures, who carries out his instruction, responds to his advice, has gone beyond doubt, become free from perplexity, gained intrepidity, and become independent of others in the Teacher's Dispensation?"

"There are not only one hundred...or five hundred, but far more women lay followers, my disciples, clothed in white enjoying sensual pleasures, who carry out my instruction, respond to my advice, have gone beyond doubt, become free of perplexity, gained intrepidity, and become independent of others in the Teacher's Dispensation."

13. "Master Gotama, if only Master Gotama were accomplished in this Dhamma, but no bhikkhus were accomplished, [492] then this holy life would be deficient in that respect; but because Master Gotama and bhikkhus are accomplished in this Dhamma, this holy life is thus complete in that respect. If only Master Gotama and bhikkhus were accomplished in this Dhamma, but no bhikkhunīs were accomplished, then this holy life would be deficient in that respect; but because Master Gotama, bhikkhus, and bhikkhunīs are accomplished in this Dhamma, this holy life is thus complete in that respect. If only Master Gotama, bhikkhus, and bhikkhunīs were accomplished in this Dhamma, but no men lay followers clothed in white leading lives of celibacy were accomplished, then this holy life would be deficient in that respect; but because Master Gotama, bhikkhus and bhikkhunīs, and men lay followers clothed in white leading lives of celibacy are accomplished in this Dhamma, this holy life is thus complete in that respect. If only Master Gotama, bhikkhus and bhikkhunīs, and men lay followers clothed in white leading lives of celibacy were accomplished in this Dhamma, but no men lay followers clothed in white enjoying sensual pleasures were accomplished, then this holy life would be deficient in that respect; but because Master Gotama, bhikkhus and bhikkhunīs, and men lay followers clothed in white, both those leading lives of celibacy and those enjoying sensual pleasures, are accomplished in this Dhamma, this holy life is thus complete in that respect. If only Master Gotama, bhikkhus and bhikkhunīs, and men lay followers clothed in white...were accomplished in this Dhamma, but no women lay followers clothed in white [493] leading lives of celibacy were accomplished, then this holy life would be deficient in that respect; but because Master Gotama, bhikkhus and bhikkhunīs, men lay followers clothed in white...and women lay followers clothed in white leading lives of celibacy are accomplished in this Dhamma, this holy life is thus complete in that respect. If only Master Gotama, bhikkhus and bhikkhunīs, men lay followers clothed in white...and women lay followers clothed in white leading lives of celibacy

were accomplished in this Dhamma, but no women lay followers clothed in white enjoying sensual pleasures were accomplished, then this holy life would be deficient in that respect; but because Master Gotama, bhikkhus and bhikkhunīs, men lay followers clothed in white, both those leading lives of celibacy and those enjoying sensual pleasures, and women lay followers clothed in white, both those leading lives of celibacy and those enjoying sensual pleasures, are accomplished in this Dhamma, this holy life is thus complete in that respect.

14. "Just as the river Ganges inclines towards the sea, slopes towards the sea, flows towards the sea, and merges with the sea, so too Master Gotama's assembly with its homeless ones and its householders inclines towards Nibbāna, slopes towards Nibbāna, flows towards Nibbāna, and merges with Nibbāna.

15. "Magnificent, Master Gotama! Magnificent, Master Gotama! Master Gotama has made the Dhamma clear in many ways, as though he were turning upright what had been overthrown, revealing what was hidden, showing the way to one who was lost, or holding up a lamp in the dark for those with eyesight to see forms. I go to Master Gotama for refuge and to the Dhamma and to the Sangha of bhikkhus. I would receive the going forth under Master Gotama, I would receive the full admission." [494]

16. "Vaccha, one who formerly belonged to another sect and desires the going forth and the full admission in this Dhamma and Discipline lives on probation for four months. At the end of four months, if the bhikkhus are satisfied with him, they give him the going forth and the full admission to the bhikkhus' state. But I recognise individual differences in this matter."

"Venerable sir, if those who formerly belonged to another sect and desire the going forth and the full admission in this Dhamma and Discipline live on probation for four months, and if at the end of the four months the bhikkhus being satisfied with them give them the going forth and the full admission to the bhikkhus' state, then I will live on probation for four years. At the end of the four years if the bhikkhus are satisfied with me, let them give me the going forth and the full admission to the bhikkhus' state."

17. Then the wanderer Vacchagotta received the going forth under the Blessed One, and he received the full admission. Not

long after his full admission, a half-month after his full admission, the venerable Vacchagotta went to the Blessed One, and after paying homage to him, he sat down at one side and told the Blessed One: "Venerable sir, I have attained whatever can be attained by the knowledge of a disciple in higher training, by the true knowledge of a disciple in higher training. Let the Blessed One teach me the Dhamma further."[727]

18. "In that case, Vaccha, develop further two things: serenity and insight. When these two things—serenity and insight—are developed further, they will lead to the penetration of many elements.

19. "To the extent that you may wish: 'May I wield the various kinds of supernormal power: having been one, may I become many; having been many, may I become one; may I appear and vanish; may I go unhindered through a wall, through an enclosure, through a mountain, as though through space; may I dive in and out of the earth as though it were water; may I walk on water without sinking as though it were earth; seated cross-legged, may I travel in space like a bird; with my hand may I touch and stroke the moon and sun so powerful and mighty; may I wield bodily mastery even as far as the Brahma-world'—you will attain the ability to witness any aspect therein, there being a suitable basis.[728]

20. "To the extent that you may wish: 'May I, with the divine ear element, [495] which is purified and surpasses the human, hear both kinds of sounds, the divine and the human, those that are far as well as near'—you will attain the ability to witness any aspect therein, there being a suitable basis.

21. "To the extent that you may wish: 'May I understand the minds of other beings, of other persons, having encompassed them with my own mind. May I understand a mind affected by lust as affected by lust and a mind unaffected by lust as unaffected by lust; may I understand a mind affected by hate as affected by hate and a mind unaffected by hate as unaffected by hate; may I understand a mind affected by delusion as affected by delusion and a mind unaffected by delusion as unaffected by delusion; may I understand a contracted mind as contracted and a distracted mind as distracted; may I understand an exalted mind as exalted and an unexalted mind as unexalted; may I understand a surpassed mind as surpassed and an unsurpassed

mind as unsurpassed; may I understand a concentrated mind as concentrated and an unconcentrated mind as unconcentrated; may I understand a liberated mind as liberated and an unliberated mind as unliberated'—you will attain the ability to witness any aspect therein, there being a suitable basis.

22. "To the extent that you may wish: 'May I recollect my manifold past lives, that is, one birth, two births...(*as Sutta 51, §24*)...Thus with their aspects and particulars may I recollect my manifold past lives'—you will attain the ability to witness any aspect therein, there being a suitable basis. [496]

23. "To the extent that you may wish: 'May I, with the divine eye, which is purified and surpasses the human, see beings passing away and reappearing, inferior and superior, fair and ugly, fortunate and unfortunate...(*as Sutta 51, §25*)...and may I understand how beings pass on according to their actions'—you will attain the ability to witness any aspect therein, there being a suitable basis.

24. "To the extent that you may wish: 'May I, by realising for myself with direct knowledge, here and now enter upon and abide in the deliverance of mind and deliverance by wisdom that are taintless with the destruction of the taints'—you will attain the ability to witness any aspect therein, there being a suitable basis."

25. Then the venerable Vacchagotta, having delighted and rejoiced in the Blessed One's words, rose from his seat, and after paying homage to the Blessed One, keeping him on his right, he departed.

26. Before long, dwelling alone, withdrawn, diligent, ardent, and resolute, the venerable Vacchagotta, by realising for himself with direct knowledge, here and now entered upon and abided in that supreme goal of the holy life for the sake of which clansmen rightly go forth from the home life into homelessness. He directly knew: "Birth is destroyed, the holy life has been lived, what had to be done has been done, there is no more coming to any state of being." And the venerable Vacchagotta became one of the arahants.

27. Now on that occasion a number of bhikkhus were going to see the Blessed One. The venerable Vacchagotta saw them coming in the distance. Seeing them, he went to them and asked them: [497] "Where are the venerable ones going?"

"We are going to see the Blessed One, friend."

"In that case, may the venerable ones pay homage in my name with their heads at the Blessed One's feet, saying: 'Venerable sir, the bhikkhu Vacchagotta pays homage with his head at the Blessed One's feet.' Then say: 'The Blessed One has been worshipped by me, the Sublime One has been worshipped by me.'"[729]

"Yes, friend," those bhikkhus replied. Then they went to the Blessed One, and after paying homage to him, they sat down at one side and told the Blessed One: "Venerable sir, the venerable Vacchagotta pays homage with his head at the Blessed One's feet, and he says: 'The Blessed One has been worshipped by me, the Sublime One has been worshipped by me.'"

28. "Bhikkhus, having encompassed his mind with my own mind, I already knew of the bhikkhu Vacchagotta: 'The bhikkhu Vacchagotta has attained the threefold true knowledge and has great supernormal power and might.' And deities also told me this: 'The bhikkhu Vacchagotta has attained the threefold true knowledge and has great supernormal power and might.'"

That is what the Blessed One said. Those bhikkhus were satisfied and delighted in the Blessed One's words.

74 *Dīghanakha Sutta*
To Dīghanakha

1. THUS HAVE I HEARD. On one occasion the Blessed One was living at Rājagaha in the Boar's Cave on the mountain Vulture Peak.

2. Then the wanderer Dīghanakha went to the Blessed One and exchanged greetings with him.[730] When this courteous and amiable talk was finished, he stood at one side and said to the Blessed One: "Master Gotama, my doctrine and view is this: 'Nothing is acceptable to me.'"[731]

"This view of yours, Aggivessana, 'Nothing is acceptable to me'—is not at least that view acceptable to you?"

"If this view of mine were acceptable to me, Master Gotama, it too would be the same, it too [498] would be the same."[732]

3. "Well, Aggivessana, there are plenty in the world who say: 'It too would be the same, it too would be the same,' yet they do not abandon that view and they take up still some other view. Those are few in the world who say: 'It too would be the same, it too would be the same,' and who abandon that view and do not take up some other view.[733]

4. "Aggivessana, there are some recluses and brahmins whose doctrine and view is this: 'Everything is acceptable to me.' There are some recluses and brahmins whose doctrine and view is this: 'Nothing is acceptable to me.' And there are some recluses and brahmins whose doctrine and view is this: 'Something is acceptable to me, something is not acceptable to me.'[734] Among these, the view of those recluses and brahmins who hold the doctrine and view 'Everything is acceptable to me' is close to lust, close to bondage, close to delighting, close to holding, close to clinging. The view of those recluses and brahmins who hold the doctrine and view 'Nothing is acceptable to me' is close to non-lust, close to non-bondage, close to non-delighting, close to non-holding, close to non-clinging."

5. When this was said, the wanderer Dīghanakha remarked: "Master Gotama commends my point of view, Master Gotama recommends my point of view."

"Aggivessana, as to those recluses and brahmins who hold the doctrine and view 'Something is acceptable to me, something is not acceptable to me'—the view of theirs as to what is acceptable is close to lust, close to bondage, close to delighting, close to holding, close to clinging, while the view of theirs as to what is not acceptable is close to non-lust, close to non-bondage, close to non-delighting, close to non-holding, close to non-clinging.

6. "Now, Aggivessana, a wise man among those recluses and brahmins who hold the doctrine and view 'Everything is acceptable to me' considers thus:[735] 'If I obstinately adhere to my view "Everything is acceptable to me" and declare: "Only this is true, anything else is wrong," then I may clash with the two others: with a recluse or brahmin who holds the doctrine [499] and view "Nothing is acceptable to me" and with a recluse or brahmin who holds the doctrine and view "Something is acceptable to me, something is not acceptable to me." I may clash with these two, and when there is a clash, there are disputes; when there are disputes, there are quarrels; when there are quarrels, there is vexation.' Thus, foreseeing for himself clashes, disputes, quarrels, and vexation, he abandons that view and does not take up some other view. This is how there comes to be the abandoning of these views; this is how there comes to be the relinquishing of these views.

7. "A wise man among those recluses and brahmins who hold the doctrine and view 'Nothing is acceptable to me' considers thus: 'If I obstinately adhere to my view "Nothing is acceptable to me" and declare: "Only this is true, anything else is wrong," then I may clash with the two others: with a recluse or brahmin who holds the doctrine and view "Everything is acceptable to me" and with a recluse or brahmin who holds the doctrine and view "Something is acceptable to me, something is not acceptable to me." I may clash with these two, and when there is a clash, there are disputes; when there are disputes, there are quarrels; when there are quarrels, there is vexation.' Thus, foreseeing for himself clashes, disputes, quarrels, and vexation, he abandons that view and does not take up some other view. This is how there comes to be the abandoning of

these views; this is how there comes to be the relinquishing of these views.

8. "A wise man among those recluses and brahmins who hold the doctrine and view 'Something is acceptable to me, something is not acceptable to me' considers thus: 'If I obstinately adhere to my view "Something is acceptable to me, something is not acceptable to me" and declare: "Only this is true, anything else is wrong," then I may clash with the two others: with a recluse or brahmin who holds the doctrine and view "Everything is acceptable to me" and with a recluse or brahmin who holds the doctrine and view "Nothing is acceptable to me." I may clash with these two, and when there is a clash, there are disputes; when there are disputes, there are quarrels; when there are quarrels, there is vexation.' Thus, foreseeing for himself clashes, disputes, quarrels, and vexation, he abandons that view and does not take up some other view. This is how there comes to be the abandoning of these views; this is how there comes to be the relinquishing of these views. [500]

9. "Now, Aggivessana,[736] this body made of material form, consisting of the four great elements, procreated by a mother and father, and built up out of boiled rice and porridge, is subject to impermanence, to being worn and rubbed away, to dissolution and disintegration. It should be regarded as impermanent, as suffering, as a disease, as a tumour, as a dart, as a calamity, as an affliction, as alien, as disintegrating, as void, as not self. When one regards this body thus, one abandons desire for the body, affection for the body, subservience to the body.

10. "There are, Aggivessana, three kinds of feeling: pleasant feeling, painful feeling, and neither-painful-nor-pleasant feeling. On the occasion when one feels pleasant feeling, one does not feel painful feeling or neither-painful-nor-pleasant feeling; on that occasion one feels only pleasant feeling. On the occasion when one feels painful feeling, one does not feel pleasant feeling or neither-painful-nor-pleasant feeling; on that occasion one feels only painful feeling. On the occasion when one feels neither-painful-nor-pleasant feeling, one does not feel pleasant feeling or painful feeling; on that occasion one feels only neither-painful-nor-pleasant feeling.

11. "Pleasant feeling, Aggivessana, is impermanent, conditioned, dependently arisen, subject to destruction, vanishing,

fading away, and ceasing. Painful feeling too is impermanent, conditioned, dependently arisen, subject to destruction, vanishing, fading away, and ceasing. Neither-painful-nor-pleasant feeling too is impermanent, conditioned, dependently arisen, subject to destruction, vanishing, fading away, and ceasing.

12. "Seeing thus, a well-taught noble disciple becomes disenchanted with pleasant feeling, disenchanted with painful feeling, disenchanted with neither-painful-nor-pleasant feeling. Being disenchanted, he becomes dispassionate. Through dispassion [his mind] is liberated. When it is liberated there comes the knowledge: 'It is liberated.' He understands: 'Birth is destroyed, the holy life has been lived, what had to be done has been done, there is no more coming to any state of being.'

13. "A bhikkhu whose mind is liberated thus, Aggivessana, sides with none and disputes with none; he employs the speech currently used in the world without adhering to it."[737]

14. Now on that occasion the venerable Sāriputta was standing behind the Blessed One, [501] fanning him. Then he thought: "The Blessed One, indeed, speaks to us of the abandoning of these things through direct knowledge; the Sublime One, indeed, speaks to us of the relinquishing of these things through direct knowledge." As the venerable Sāriputta considered this, through not clinging his mind was liberated from the taints.[738]

15. But in the wanderer Dīghanakha the spotless immaculate vision of the Dhamma arose: "All that is subject to arising is subject to cessation." The wanderer Dīghanakha saw the Dhamma, attained the Dhamma, understood the Dhamma, fathomed the Dhamma; he crossed beyond doubt, did away with perplexity, gained intrepidity, and became independent of others in the Teacher's Dispensation.[739]

16. Then he said to the Blessed One: "Magnificent, Master Gotama! Magnificent, Master Gotama! Master Gotama has made the Dhamma clear in many ways, as though he were turning upright what had been overthrown, revealing what was hidden, showing the way to one who was lost, or holding up a lamp in the dark for those with eyesight to see forms. I go to Master Gotama for refuge and to the Dhamma and to the Sangha of bhikkhus. From today let Master Gotama remember me as a lay follower who has gone to him for refuge for life."

75 *Māgandiya Sutta*
To Māgandiya

1. THUS HAVE I HEARD. On one occasion the Blessed One was living in the Kuru country where there was a town of the Kurus named Kammāsadhamma, on a spread of grass in the fire chamber of a brahmin belonging to the Bhāradvāja clan.

2. Then, when it was morning, the Blessed One dressed, and taking his bowl and outer robe, went into Kammāsadhamma for alms. When he had wandered for alms in Kammāsadhamma and had returned from his almsround, after his meal he went to a certain grove for the day's abiding. Having entered the grove, he sat down at the root of a tree for the day's abiding. [502]

3. Then the wanderer Māgandiya, while walking and wandering for exercise, went to the fire chamber of the brahmin belonging to the Bhāradvāja clan. There he saw a spread of grass prepared and asked the brahmin: "For whom has this spread of grass been prepared in Master Bhāradvāja's fire chamber? It seems like it might be a recluse's bed."

4. "Master Māgandiya, there is the recluse Gotama, the son of the Sakyans, who went forth from a Sakyan clan. Now a good report of Master Gotama has been spread to this effect: 'That Blessed One is accomplished, fully enlightened, perfect in true knowledge and conduct, sublime, knower of worlds, incomparable leader of persons to be tamed, teacher of gods and humans, enlightened, blessed.' This bed has been prepared for that Master Gotama."

5. "Indeed, Master Bhāradvāja, it is an ill sight we see when we see the bed of that destroyer of growth,[740] Master Gotama."

"Be careful what you say, Māgandiya, be careful what you say! Many learned nobles, learned brahmins, learned householders, and learned recluses have full confidence in Master

Gotama, and have been disciplined by him in the noble true way, in the Dhamma that is wholesome."

"Master Bhāradvāja, even if we saw that Master Gotama face to face, we would tell him to his face: 'The recluse Gotama is a destroyer of growth.' Why is that? Because that is recorded in our scriptures."

"If Master Māgandiya has no objection, may I tell this to Master Gotama?"

"Let Master Bhāradvāja be at ease. Tell him just what I have said."

6. Meanwhile, with the divine ear, which is purified and surpasses the human, the Blessed One heard this conversation between the brahmin of the Bhāradvāja clan and the wanderer Māgandiya. Then, when it was evening, the Blessed One rose from meditation, went to the brahmin's fire chamber, and sat down on the spread of grass made ready. Then the brahmin of the Bhāradvāja clan went to the Blessed One and exchanged greetings with him. When this courteous and amiable talk was finished, he sat down at one side. The Blessed One asked him: "Bhāradvāja, did you have any conversation with the wanderer Māgandiya [503] about this very same spread of grass?"

When this was said, the brahmin, awestruck and with his hair standing on end, replied: "We wanted to tell Master Gotama about that very thing, but Master Gotama has anticipated us."

7. But this discussion between the Blessed One and the brahmin of the Bhāradvāja clan was left unfinished, for then the wanderer Māgandiya, while walking and wandering for exercise, came to the brahmin's fire chamber and went up to the Blessed One. He exchanged greetings with the Blessed One, and when this courteous and amiable talk was finished, he sat down at one side. The Blessed One said to him:

8. "Māgandiya, the eye delights in forms, takes delight in forms, rejoices in forms; that has been tamed by the Tathāgata, guarded, protected, and restrained, and he teaches the Dhamma for its restraint. Was it with reference to this that you said: 'The recluse Gotama is a destroyer of growth'?"

"It was with reference to this, Master Gotama, that I said: 'The recluse Gotama is a destroyer of growth.' Why is that? Because that is recorded in our scriptures."

"The ear delights in sound...The nose delights in odours...The tongue delights in flavours...The body delights in tangibles...

The mind delights in mind-objects, takes delight in mind-objects, rejoices in mind-objects; that has been tamed by the Tathāgata, guarded, protected, and restrained, and he teaches the Dhamma for its restraint. Was it with reference to this that you said: 'The recluse Gotama is a destroyer of growth'?"

"It was with reference to this, Master Gotama, that I said: 'The recluse Gotama is a destroyer of growth.' Why is that? Because that is recorded in our scriptures."

9. "What do you think, Māgandiya? Here someone [504] may have formerly enjoyed himself with forms cognizable by the eye that are wished for, desired, agreeable, and likeable, connected with sensual desire and provocative of lust. On a later occasion, having understood as they actually are the origin, the disappearance, the gratification, the danger, and the escape in the case of forms, he might abandon craving for forms, remove fever for forms, and abide without thirst, with a mind inwardly at peace. What would you say to him, Māgandiya?"—"Nothing, Master Gotama."

"What do you think, Māgandiya? Here someone may have formerly enjoyed himself with sounds cognizable by the ear...with odours cognizable by the nose...with flavours cognizable by the tongue...with tangibles cognizable by the body that are wished for, desired, agreeable, and likeable, connected with sensual desire and provocative of lust. On a later occasion, having understood as they actually are the origin, the disappearance, the gratification, the danger, and the escape in the case of tangibles, he might abandon craving for tangibles, remove fever for tangibles, and abide without thirst, with a mind inwardly at peace. What would you say to him, Māgandiya?"—"Nothing, Master Gotama."

10. "Māgandiya, formerly when I lived the home life, I enjoyed myself, provided and endowed with the five cords of sensual pleasure: with forms cognizable by the eye...with sounds cognizable by the ear...with odours cognizable by the nose...with flavours cognizable by the tongue...with tangibles cognizable by the body that are wished for, desired, agreeable, and likeable, connected with sensual desire and provocative of lust. I had three palaces, one for the rainy season, one for the winter, and one for the summer. I lived in the rains' palace for the four months of the rainy season, enjoying myself with

musicians, none of whom were men, and I did not go down to the lower palace.[741]

"On a later occasion, having understood as they actually are the origin, the disappearance, the gratification, the danger, and the escape in the case of sensual pleasures, I abandoned craving for sensual pleasures, I removed fever for sensual pleasures, and I abide without thirst, with a mind inwardly at peace. I see other beings who are not free from lust for sensual pleasures being devoured by craving for sensual pleasures, burning with fever for sensual pleasures, indulging in sensual pleasures, and I do not envy them, nor do I delight therein. Why is that? Because there is, Māgandiya, a delight apart from sensual pleasures, apart from unwholesome states, [505] which surpasses even divine bliss.[742] Since I take delight in that, I do not envy what is inferior, nor do I delight therein.

11. "Suppose, Māgandiya, a householder or a householder's son was rich, with great wealth and property, and being provided and endowed with the five cords of sensual pleasure, he might enjoy himself with forms cognizable by the eye...with sounds cognizable by the ear...with odours cognizable by the nose...with flavours cognizable by the tongue...with tangibles cognizable by the body that are wished for, desired, agreeable, and likeable, connected with sensual desire and provocative of lust. Having conducted himself well in body, speech, and mind, on the dissolution of the body, after death, he might reappear in a happy destination, in the heavenly world in the retinue of the gods of the Thirty-three; and there, surrounded by a group of nymphs in the Nandana Grove, he would enjoy himself, provided and endowed with the five cords of divine sensual pleasure. Suppose he saw a householder or a householder's son enjoying himself, provided and endowed with the five cords of [human] sensual pleasure. What do you think, Māgandiya? Would that young god surrounded by the group of nymphs in the Nandana Grove, enjoying himself, provided and endowed with the five cords of divine sensual pleasure, envy the householder or the householder's son for the five cords of human sensual pleasure or would he be enticed by human sensual pleasures?"

"No, Master Gotama. Why not? Because heavenly sensual pleasures are more excellent and sublime than human sensual pleasures."

12. "So too, Māgandiya, formerly when I lived the home life, I enjoyed myself, provided and endowed with the five cords of sensual pleasure: with forms cognizable by the eye...with tangibles cognizable by the body that are wished for, desired, agreeable, and likeable, connected with sensual desire and provocative of lust. On a later occasion, having understood as they actually are the gratification, the danger, and the escape in the case of sensual pleasures, I abandoned craving for sensual pleasures, I removed fever for sensual pleasures, and I abide without thirst, with a mind inwardly at peace. I see other beings who are not free from lust for sensual pleasures being devoured by craving for sensual pleasures, burning with fever for sensual pleasures, [506] indulging in sensual pleasures, and I do not envy them nor do I delight therein. Why is that? Because there is, Māgandiya, a delight apart from sensual pleasures, apart from unwholesome states, which surpasses even divine bliss. Since I take delight in that, I do not envy what is inferior, nor do I delight therein.

13. "Suppose, Māgandiya, there was a leper with sores and blisters on his limbs, being devoured by worms, scratching the scabs off the openings of his wounds with his nails, cauterising his body over a burning charcoal pit. Then his friends and companions, his kinsmen and relatives, would bring a physician to treat him. The physician would make medicine for him, and by means of that medicine the man would be cured of his leprosy and would become well and happy, independent, master of himself, able to go where he likes. Then he might see another leper with sores and blisters on his limbs, being devoured by worms, scratching the scabs off the openings of his wounds with his nails, cauterising his body over a burning charcoal pit. What do you think, Māgandiya? Would that man envy that leper for his burning charcoal pit or his use of medicine?"

"No, Master Gotama. Why is that? Because when there is sickness, there is need for medicine, and when there is no sickness there is no need for medicine."

14. "So too, Māgandiya, formerly when I lived the home life...(*as in §12*)...Since I take delight in that, I do not envy what is inferior, nor do I delight therein. [507]

15. "Suppose, Māgandiya, there was a leper with sores and blisters on his limbs, being devoured by worms, scratching the scabs off the openings of his wounds with his nails, cauterising

his body over a burning charcoal pit. Then his friends and companions, his kinsmen and relatives, brought a physician to treat him. The physician would make medicine for him, and by means of that medicine the man would be cured of his leprosy and would become well and happy, independent, master of himself, able to go where he likes. Then two strong men would seize him by both arms and drag him towards a burning charcoal pit. What do you think, Māgandiya? Would that man twist his body this way and that?"

"Yes, Master Gotama. Why is that? Because that fire is indeed painful to touch, hot, and scorching."

"What do you think, Māgandiya? Is it only now that that fire is painful to touch, hot, and scorching, or previously too was that fire painful to touch, hot, and scorching?"

"Master Gotama, that fire is now painful to touch, hot, and scorching, and previously too that fire was painful to touch, hot, and scorching. For when that man was a leper with sores and blisters on his limbs, being devoured by worms, scratching the scabs off the openings of his wounds with his nails, his faculties were impaired; thus, though the fire was actually painful to touch, he acquired a mistaken perception of it as pleasant."

16. "So too, Māgandiya, in the past sensual pleasures were painful to touch, hot, and scorching; in the future sensual pleasures will be painful to touch, hot, and scorching; and now at present sensual pleasures are painful to touch, hot, and scorching. But these beings who are not free from lust for sensual pleasures, who are devoured by craving for sensual pleasures, who burn with fever for sensual pleasures, have faculties that are impaired; thus, though sensual pleasures are actually painful to touch, they acquire a mistaken perception of them as pleasant.[743]

17. "Suppose, Māgandiya, there was a leper with sores and blisters on his limbs, being devoured by worms, scratching the scabs off the openings of his wounds with his nails, cauterising his body over a burning charcoal pit; the more he scratches the scabs and cauterises his body, [508] the fouler, more evil-smelling and more infected the openings of his wounds would become, yet he would find a certain measure of satisfaction and enjoyment in scratching the openings of his wounds. So too, Māgandiya, beings who are not free from lust for sensual pleasures, who are devoured by craving for sensual pleasures, who

burn with fever for sensual pleasures, still indulge in sensual pleasures; the more such beings indulge in sensual pleasures, the more their craving for sensual pleasures increases and the more they are burned by their fever for sensual pleasures, yet they find a certain measure of satisfaction and enjoyment in dependence on the five cords of sensual pleasure.

18. "What do you think, Māgandiya? Have you ever seen or heard of a king or a king's minister enjoying himself, provided and endowed with the five cords of sensual pleasure who, without abandoning craving for sensual pleasures, without removing fever for sensual pleasures, was able to abide free from thirst, with a mind inwardly at peace, or who is able or who will be able to so abide?"—"No, Master Gotama."

"Good, Māgandiya. I too have never seen or heard of a king or a king's minister enjoying himself, provided and endowed with the five cords of sensual pleasure who, without abandoning craving for sensual pleasures, without removing fever for sensual pleasures, was able to abide free from thirst, with a mind inwardly at peace, or who is able or who will be able to so abide. On the contrary, Māgandiya, those recluses or brahmins who abided or abide or will abide free from thirst, with a mind inwardly at peace, all do so after having understood as they actually are the origin, the disappearance, the gratification, the danger, and the escape in the case of sensual pleasures, and it is after abandoning craving for sensual pleasures and removing fever for sensual pleasures that they abided or abide or will abide free from thirst, with a mind inwardly at peace."

19. Then at that point the Blessed One uttered this exclamation:

"The greatest of all gains is health,
Nibbāna is the greatest bliss,
The eightfold path is the best of paths
For it leads safely to the Deathless."

When this was said, the wanderer Māgandiya said to the Blessed One: "It is wonderful, Master Gotama, it is marvellous how well that has been expressed by Master Gotama: [509]

'The greatest of all gains is health,
Nibbāna is the greatest bliss.'

We too have heard this said by earlier wanderers in the tradition of the teachers, and it agrees, Master Gotama."

"But, Māgandiya, when you heard that said by earlier wanderers in the tradition of the teachers, what is that health, what is that Nibbāna?"

When this was said, the wanderer Māgandiya rubbed his own limbs with his hands and said: "This is that health, Master Gotama, this is that Nibbāna; for I am now healthy and happy and nothing afflicts me."[744]

20. "Māgandiya, suppose there was a man born blind who could not see dark and light forms, who could not see blue, yellow, red, or pink forms, who could not see what was even and uneven, who could not see the stars or the sun and moon. He might hear a man with good eyesight saying: 'Good indeed, sirs, is a white cloth, beautiful, spotless, and clean!' and he would go in search of a white cloth. Then a man would cheat him with a dirty soiled garment thus: 'Good man, here is a white cloth for you, beautiful, spotless, and clean.' And he would accept it and put it on, and being satisfied with it, he would utter words of satisfaction thus: 'Good indeed, sirs, is a white cloth, beautiful, spotless, and clean!' What do you think, Māgandiya? When that man born blind accepted that dirty soiled garment, put it on, and being satisfied with it, uttered words of satisfaction thus: 'Good indeed, sirs, is a white cloth, beautiful, spotless, and clean!'—did he do so knowing and seeing, or out of faith in the man with good eyesight?"

"Venerable sir, he would have done so unknowing and unseeing, [510] out of faith in the man with good eyesight."

21. "So too, Māgandiya, the wanderers of other sects are blind and visionless. They do not know health, they do not see Nibbāna, yet they utter this stanza thus:

> 'The greatest of all gains is health,
> Nibbāna is the greatest bliss.'

This stanza was uttered by the earlier Accomplished Ones, Fully Enlightened Ones, thus:

> 'The greatest of all gains is health,
> Nibbāna is the greatest bliss,

The eightfold path is the best of paths
For it leads safely to the Deathless.'

Now it has gradually become current among ordinary people.[745] And although this body, Māgandiya, is a disease, a tumour, a dart, a calamity, and an affliction, referring to this body you say: 'This is that health, Master Gotama, this is that Nibbāna.' You do not have that noble vision, Māgandiya, by means of which you might know health and see Nibbāna."

22. "I have confidence in Master Gotama thus: 'Master Gotama is capable of teaching me the Dhamma in such a way that I can come to know health and to see Nibbāna.'"

"Māgandiya, suppose there was a man born blind who could not see dark and light forms...or the sun and moon. Then his friends and companions, his kinsmen and relatives, would bring a physician to treat him. The physician would make a medicine for him, yet by means of that medicine the man's vision would not arise or be purified. What do you think, Māgandiya, would that doctor reap weariness and disappointment?"—"Yes, Master Gotama."—"So too, Māgandiya, if I were to teach you the Dhamma thus: 'This is that health, this is that Nibbāna,' you might not know health or see Nibbāna, and that would be wearisome and troublesome for me." [511]

23. "I have confidence in Master Gotama thus: 'Master Gotama is capable of teaching me the Dhamma in such a way that I can come to know health and to see Nibbāna.'"

"Māgandiya, suppose there was a man born blind who could not see dark and light forms...or the sun and moon. He might hear a man with good eyesight saying: 'Good indeed, sirs, is a white cloth, beautiful, spotless, and clean!' and he would go in search of a white cloth. Then a man would cheat him with a dirty soiled garment thus: 'Good man, here is a white cloth for you, beautiful, spotless, and clean.' And he would accept it and put it on. Then his friends and companions, his kinsmen and relatives, would bring a physician to treat him. The physician would make medicine—emetics and purgatives, ointments and counter-ointments and nasal treatment—and by means of that medicine the man's vision would arise and be purified. Together with the arising of his vision, his desire and liking for that dirty soiled garment would be abandoned; then he might burn with indignation and enmity towards that man and might think that he ought to be killed thus: 'Indeed, I have long been tricked, cheated, and defrauded by this man with this dirty soiled garment when he told me: "Good man, here is a white cloth for you, beautiful, spotless, and clean."'

24. "So too, Māgandiya, if I were to teach you the Dhamma thus: 'This is that health, this is that Nibbāna,' you might know health and see Nibbāna. Together with the arising of your vision, your desire and lust for the five aggregates affected by clinging might be abandoned. Then perhaps you might think: 'Indeed, I have long been tricked, cheated, and defrauded by this mind. For when clinging, I have been clinging just to material form, I have been clinging just to feeling, I have been clinging just to perception, I have been clinging just to formations, I have been clinging just to consciousness.[746] With my clinging as condition, being [comes to be]; with being as condition, birth; with birth as condition, ageing and death, sorrow, lamentation, pain, grief, [512] and despair come to be. Such is the origin of this whole mass of suffering.'"

25. "I have confidence in Master Gotama thus: 'Master Gotama is capable of teaching me the Dhamma in such a way that I might rise up from this seat cured of my blindness.'"

"Then, Māgandiya, associate with true men. When you associate with true men, you will hear the true Dhamma. When you hear the true Dhamma, you will practise in accordance with the true Dhamma. When you practise in accordance with the true Dhamma, you will know and see for yourself thus: 'These are diseases, tumours, and darts; but here these diseases, tumours, and darts cease without remainder.[747] With the cessation of my clinging comes cessation of being; with the cessation of being, cessation of birth; with the cessation of birth, ageing and death, sorrow, lamentation, pain, grief, and despair cease. Such is the cessation of this whole mass of suffering.'"

26. When this was said, the wanderer Māgandiya said: "Magnificent, Master Gotama! Magnificent, Master Gotama! Master Gotama has made the Dhamma clear in many ways, as though he were turning upright what had been overthrown, revealing what was hidden, showing the way to one who was lost, or holding up a lamp in the dark for those with eyesight to see forms. I go to Master Gotama for refuge and to the Dhamma

and to the Sangha of bhikkhus. I would receive the going forth under Master Gotama. I would receive the full admission."

27. "Māgandiya, one who formerly belonged to another sect and desires the going forth and the full admission in this Dhamma and Discipline lives on probation for four months. At the end of four months, if the bhikkhus are satisfied with him, they give him the going forth and the full admission to the bhikkhus' state. But I recognise individual differences in this matter."

"Venerable sir, if those who formerly belonged to another sect and desire the going forth and the full admission in this Dhamma and Discipline live on probation for four months, and if at the end of the four months the bhikkhus being satisfied with them give them the going forth and the full admission to the bhikkhus' state, then I will live on probation for four years. At the end of the four years if the bhikkhus are satisfied with me, let them give me the going forth and the full admission to the bhikkhus' state." [513]

28. Then the wanderer Māgandiya received the going forth under the Blessed One, and he received the full admission. And soon, not long after his full admission, dwelling alone, withdrawn, diligent, ardent, and resolute, the venerable Māgandiya, by realising for himself with direct knowledge, here and now entered upon and abided in that supreme goal of the holy life for the sake of which clansmen rightly go forth from the home life into homelessness. He directly knew: "Birth is destroyed, the holy life has been lived, what had to be done has been done, there is no more coming to any state of being." And the venerable Māgandiya became one of the arahants.

76 *Sandaka Sutta*
To Sandaka

1. THUS HAVE I HEARD. On one occasion the Blessed One was living at Kosambī in Ghosita's Park.

2. Now on that occasion the wanderer Sandaka was staying in the Pilakkha-tree Cave with a large assembly of wanderers.

3. Then, when it was evening, the venerable Ānanda rose from meditation and addressed the bhikkhus thus: "Come, friends, let us go to the Devakaṭa Pool to see the cave."—"Yes, friend," those bhikkhus replied. Then the venerable Ānanda went to the Devakaṭa Pool together with a number of bhikkhus.

4. Now on that occasion the wanderer Sandaka was seated with a large assembly of wanderers who were making an uproar, loudly and noisily talking many kinds of pointless talk,[748] such as talk of kings, robbers, ministers, armies, dangers, battles, food, drink, clothing, beds, garlands, perfumes, relatives, vehicles, villages, towns, cities, countries, women, heroes, streets, wells, the dead, trifles, the origin of the world, the origin of the sea, [514] whether things are so or are not so. Then the wanderer Sandaka saw the venerable Ānanda coming in the distance. Seeing him, he quieted his own assembly thus: "Sirs, be quiet; sirs, make no noise. Here comes the recluse Ānanda, a disciple of the recluse Gotama, one of the recluse Gotama's disciples staying in Kosambī. These venerable ones like quiet; they are disciplined in quiet; they commend quiet. Perhaps if he finds our assembly a quiet one, he will think to join us." Then the wanderers became silent.

5. The venerable Ānanda went to the wanderer Sandaka who said to him: "Let Master Ānanda come! Welcome to Master Ānanda! It is long since Master Ānanda found an opportunity to come here. Let Master Ānanda be seated; this seat is ready."

The venerable Ānanda sat down on the seat made ready, and

the wanderer Sandaka took a low seat and sat down at one side. When he had done so, the venerable Ānanda asked him: "For what discussion are you sitting together here now, Sandaka? And what was your discussion that was left unfinished?"

"Master Ānanda, let be the discussion for which we are now sitting together here. Master Ānanda can well hear about it later. It would be good if Master Ānanda would give a talk on his own teacher's Dhamma."

"Then, Sandaka, listen and attend closely to what I shall say."

"Yes, sir," he replied. The venerable Ānanda said this:

6. "Sandaka, these four ways that negate the living of the holy life have been declared by the Blessed One who knows and sees, accomplished and fully enlightened, and also these four kinds of holy life without consolation have been declared, wherein a wise man certainly would not live the holy life, or if he should live it, would not attain the true way, the Dhamma that is wholesome."[749]

"But, Master Ānanda, what are those four ways that negate the living of the holy life that have been declared by the Blessed One who knows and sees, accomplished and fully enlightened, wherein [515] a wise man certainly would not live the holy life, or if he should live it, would not attain the true way, the Dhamma that is wholesome?"

7. "Here, Sandaka, some teacher holds such a doctrine and view as this: 'There is nothing given, nothing offered, nothing sacrificed; no fruit or result of good and bad actions; no this world, no other world; no mother, no father; no beings who are reborn spontaneously; no good and virtuous recluses and brahmins in the world who have themselves realised by direct knowledge and declare this world and the other world. A person consists of the four great elements.[750] When he dies, earth returns and goes back to the body of earth, water returns and goes back to the body of water, fire returns and goes back to the body of fire, air returns and goes back to the body of air; the faculties are transferred to space. [Four] men with the bier as fifth carry away the corpse. The funeral orations last as far as the charnel ground; the bones whiten; burnt offerings end with ashes. Giving is a doctrine of fools. When anyone asserts the doctrine that there is [giving and the like], it is empty, false prattle. Fools and the wise are alike cut off and annihilated with the dissolution of the body; after death they do not exist.'

8. "About this a wise man considers thus: 'This good teacher holds this doctrine and view: "There is nothing given...after death they do not exist." If this good teacher's words are true, then both of us are exactly equal here, we stand on the same level: I who have not practised [this teaching] here and he who has practised it; I who have not lived [the holy life] here and he who has lived it.[751] Yet I do not say that both of us are cut off and annihilated with the dissolution of the body, that after death we shall not exist. But it is superfluous for this good teacher to go about naked, to be shaven, to exert himself in the squatting posture, and to pull out his hair and beard, since I, who live in a house crowded with children, who use Benares sandalwood, who wear garlands, scents, and unguents, and accept gold and silver, shall reap exactly the same destination, the same future course, as this good teacher. What do I know and see that I should lead the holy life under this teacher?' So when he finds that this way negates the living of the holy life, he turns away from it and leaves it.

9. "This is the first way that negates the living of the holy life that has been declared by the Blessed One who knows and sees, accomplished and fully enlightened, wherein a wise man certainly would not live the holy life, [516] or if he should live it, would not attain the true way, the Dhamma that is wholesome.

10. "Again, Sandaka, here some teacher holds such a doctrine and view as this: 'When one acts or makes others act, when one mutilates or makes others mutilate, when one tortures or makes others inflict torture, when one inflicts sorrow or makes others inflict sorrow, when one oppresses or makes others inflict oppression, when one intimidates or makes others inflict intimidation, when one kills living beings, takes what is not given, breaks into houses, plunders wealth, commits burglary, ambushes highways, seduces another's wife, utters falsehood—no evil is done by the doer. If, with a razor-rimmed wheel, one were to make the living beings on this earth into one mass of flesh, into one heap of flesh, because of this there would be no evil and no outcome of evil. If one were to go along the south bank of the Ganges killing and slaughtering, mutilating and making others mutilate, torturing and making others inflict torture, because of this there would be no evil and no outcome of evil. If one were to go along the north bank of

the Ganges giving gifts and making others give gifts, making offerings and making others make offerings, because of this there would be no merit and no outcome of merit. By giving, by taming oneself, by restraint, by speaking truth, there is no merit and no outcome of merit.'

11. "About this a wise man considers thus: 'This good teacher holds this doctrine and view: "When one acts...there is no merit and no outcome of merit." If this good teacher's words are true, then both of us are exactly equal here, we stand on the same level: I who have not practised [this teaching] here and he who has practised it; I who have not lived [the holy life] here and he who has lived it. Yet I do not say that whatever both [of us] do, no evil is done. But it is superfluous for this good teacher...What do I know and see that I should lead the holy life under this teacher?' So when he finds that this way negates the living of the holy life, he turns away from it and leaves it.

12. "This is the second way that negates the living of the holy life that has been declared by the Blessed One who knows and sees, accomplished and fully enlightened...

13. "Again, Sandaka, here some teacher holds such a doctrine and view as this: 'There is no cause or condition for the defilement of beings; beings are defiled without cause or condition. There is no cause or condition for the purification of beings; beings are purified without cause or condition. There is no power, no energy, no manly [517] strength, no manly endurance. All beings, all living things, all creatures, all souls are without mastery, power, and energy; moulded by destiny, circumstance, and nature, they experience pleasure and pain in the six classes.'

14. "About this a wise man considers thus: 'This good teacher holds this doctrine and view: "There is no cause...in the six classes." If this good teacher's words are true, then both of us are exactly equal here, we stand on the same level: I who have not practised [this teaching] here and he who has practised it; I who have not lived [the holy life] here and he who has lived it. Yet I do not say that both [of us] will be purified without cause or condition. But it is superfluous for this good teacher...What do I know and see that I should lead the holy life under this teacher?' So when he finds that this way negates the living of the holy life, he turns away from it and leaves it.

15. "This is the third way that negates the living of the holy life that has been declared by the Blessed One who knows and sees, accomplished and fully enlightened...

16. "Again, Sandaka, here some teacher holds such a doctrine and view as this:[752] 'There are these seven bodies that are unmade, not brought forth, uncreated, without a creator, barren, standing like mountain peaks, standing like pillars. They do not move or change or obstruct each other. None is able [to arouse] pleasure or pain or pleasure-and-pain in another. What are the seven? They are the earth-body, the water-body, the fire-body, the air-body, pleasure, pain, and the soul as the seventh. These seven bodies are unmade...Herein, there is no killer, no slaughterer, no hearer, no speaker, no cognizer, no intimater. Even those who cut off someone's head with a sharp sword do not deprive anyone of life; the sword merely passes through the space between the seven bodies. There are these fourteen hundred thousand principal kinds of generation, and sixty hundred kinds, and six hundred kinds; there are five hundred kinds of action, and five kinds of action, and three kinds of action, and action and half-action; there are sixty-two ways, sixty-two subaeons, six classes, eight planes of man, forty-nine hundred kinds of livelihood, forty-nine kinds of wanderers, forty-nine hundred [518] abodes of serpents, twenty hundred faculties, thirty hundred hells, thirty-six elements of dust, seven percipient breeds, seven non-percipient breeds, seven sheathless breeds, seven kinds of gods, seven kinds of men, seven kinds of demons, seven lakes, seven knots, seven kinds of chasms, seven hundred kinds of chasms, seven kinds of dreams, seven hundred kinds of dreams; and there are eighty-four hundred thousand great aeons wherein, by running and wandering through the round of rebirths, fools and the wise both will make an end of suffering. There is none of this: "By this virtue or observance or asceticism or holy life I shall make unripened action ripen or annihilate ripened action as it comes." Pleasure and pain are meted out. The round of rebirths is limited, there is no shortening or extending it, no increasing or decreasing it. Just as a ball of string when thrown goes as far as the string unwinds, so too, by running and wandering through the round of rebirths, fools and the wise both will make an end of suffering.'

17. "About this a wise man considers thus: 'This good teacher

holds this doctrine and view: "There are these seven bodies… fools and the wise both will make an end of suffering." If this good teacher's words are true, then both of us are exactly equal here, we stand on the same level: I who have not practised [this teaching] here and he who has practised it; I who have not lived [the holy life] here and he who has lived it. Yet I do not say that both of us will make an end of suffering by running and wandering through the round of rebirths. But it is superfluous for this good teacher to go about naked, to be shaven, to exert himself in the squatting position, and to pull out his hair and beard, since I, who live in a house crowded with children, who use Benares sandalwood, who wear garlands, scents, and unguents, and accept gold and silver, shall reap exactly the same destination, the same future course, as this good teacher. What do I know and see that I should lead the holy life under this teacher?' So when he finds that this way negates the living of the holy life, he turns away from it and leaves it.

18. "This is the fourth way that negates the living of the holy life that has been declared by the Blessed One who knows and sees, accomplished and fully enlightened…

19. "These, Sandaka, are the four ways that negate the living of the holy life that have been declared by the Blessed One who knows and sees, accomplished and fully enlightened, [519] wherein a wise man certainly would not live the holy life, or if he should live it, would not attain the true way, the Dhamma that is wholesome."

20. "It is wonderful, Master Ānanda, it is marvellous, how the four ways that negate the living of the holy life have been declared by the Blessed One who knows and sees, accomplished and fully enlightened…But, Master Ānanda, what are those four kinds of holy life without consolation that have been declared by the Blessed One who knows and sees, accomplished and fully enlightened, wherein a wise man certainly would not live the holy life, or if he should live it, would not attain the true way, the Dhamma that is wholesome?"

21. "Here, Sandaka, some teacher claims to be omniscient and all-seeing, to have complete knowledge and vision thus: 'Whether I am walking or standing or sleeping or awake, knowledge and vision are continuously and uninterruptedly present to me.'[753] He enters an empty house, he gets no alms-

food, a dog bites him, he meets with a wild elephant, a wild horse, a wild bull, he asks the name and clan of a woman or a man, he asks the name of a village or a town, and the way to go there. When he is questioned: 'How is this?' he replies: 'I had to enter an empty house, that is why I entered it. I had to get no almsfood, that is why I did not get any. I had to be bitten by a dog, that is why I was bitten. I had to meet with a wild elephant, a wild horse, a wild bull, that is why I met with them. I had to ask the name and clan of a woman or a man, that is why I asked. I had to ask the name of a village or a town and the way to go there, that is why I asked.'

22. "About this a wise man considers thus: 'This good teacher claims to be omniscient and all-seeing, to have complete knowledge and vision...When he is questioned: "How is this?" he replies: "I had to...that is why I asked."' So when he finds that this holy life is without consolation, he turns away from it and leaves it.

23. "This is the first kind of holy life without consolation that has been declared by the Blessed One who knows and sees, accomplished and fully enlightened, [520] wherein a wise man certainly would not live the holy life, or if he should live it, would not attain the true way, the Dhamma that is wholesome.

24. "Again, Sandaka, here some teacher is a traditionalist, one who regards oral tradition as truth; he teaches a Dhamma by oral tradition, by legends handed down, by what has come down in scriptures. But when a teacher is a traditionalist, one who regards oral tradition as truth, some is well transmitted and some badly transmitted,[754] some is true and some is otherwise.

25. "About this a wise man considers thus: 'This good teacher is a traditionalist...some is true and some is otherwise.' So when he finds that this holy life is without consolation, he turns away from it and leaves it.

26. "This is the second kind of holy life without consolation that has been declared by the Blessed One who knows and sees, accomplished and fully enlightened...

27. "Again, Sandaka, here a certain teacher is a reasoner, an inquirer. He teaches a Dhamma hammered out by reasoning, following a line of inquiry as it occurs to him. But when a teacher is a reasoner, an inquirer, some is well reasoned and some is wrongly reasoned, some is true and some is otherwise.

28. "About this a wise man considers thus: 'This good teacher is a reasoner...some is true and some is otherwise.' So when he finds that this holy life is without consolation, he turns away from it and leaves it.

29. "This is the third kind of holy life without consolation that has been declared by the Blessed One who knows and sees, accomplished and fully enlightened...

30. "Again, Sandaka, here a certain teacher is dull and confused. Because he is dull and confused, [521] when he is asked such and such a question, he engages in verbal wriggling, in eel-wriggling: 'I don't say it is like this. And I don't say it is like that. And I don't say it is otherwise. And I don't say it is not so. And I don't say it is not not so.'[755]

31. "About this a wise man considers thus: 'This good teacher is dull and confused...[thus] he engages in verbal wriggling, in eel-wriggling...' So when he finds that this holy life is without consolation, he turns away from it and leaves it.

32. "This is the fourth kind of holy life without consolation that has been declared by the Blessed One who knows and sees, accomplished and fully enlightened...

33. "These, Sandaka, are the four kinds of holy life without consolation that have been declared by the Blessed One who knows and sees, accomplished and fully enlightened, wherein a wise man certainly would not live the holy life, or if he should live it, would not attain the true way, the Dhamma that is wholesome."

34. "It is wonderful, Master Ānanda, it is marvellous, how the four kinds of holy life without consolation have been declared by the Blessed One who knows and sees, accomplished and fully enlightened...But, Master Ānanda, what does that teacher assert, what does he declare, wherein a wise man certainly would live the holy life, and while living it would attain the true way, the Dhamma that is wholesome?'"

35–42. "Here, Sandaka, a Tathāgata appears in the world, accomplished, fully enlightened...(*as Sutta 51, §§12–19*)...he purifies his mind from doubt.

43. "Having thus abandoned these five hindrances, imperfections of the mind that weaken wisdom, quite secluded from sensual pleasures, secluded from unwholesome states, he enters upon and abides in the first jhāna, which is accompanied by applied and sustained thought, with rapture and pleasure born

of seclusion. A wise man certainly would live the holy life with a teacher under whom a disciple attains such a lofty distinction, [522] and while living it he would attain the true way, the Dhamma that is wholesome.

44–46. "Again, with the stilling of applied and sustained thought, he enters upon and abides in the second jhāna...With the fading away as well of rapture...he enters upon and abides in the third jhāna...With the abandoning of pleasure and pain...he enters upon and abides in the fourth jhāna. A wise man certainly would live the holy life with a teacher under whom a disciple attains such a lofty distinction...

47. "When his concentrated mind is thus purified, bright, unblemished, rid of imperfection, malleable, wieldy, steady, and attained to imperturbability, he directs it to knowledge of the recollection of past lives. He recollects his manifold past lives, that is, one birth, two births...(*as Sutta 51, §24*)...Thus with their aspects and particulars he recollects his manifold past lives. A wise man certainly would live the holy life with a teacher under whom a disciple attains such a lofty distinction...

48. "When his concentrated mind is thus purified, bright, unblemished, rid of imperfection, malleable, wieldy, steady, and attained to imperturbability, he directs it to knowledge of the passing away and reappearance of beings...(*as Sutta 51, §25*)...Thus with the divine eye, which is purified and surpasses the human, he sees beings passing away and reappearing, inferior and superior, fair and ugly, fortunate and unfortunate, and he understands how beings pass on according to their actions. A wise man certainly would live the holy life with a teacher under whom a disciple attains such a lofty distinction...

49. "When his concentrated mind is thus purified, bright, unblemished, rid of imperfection, malleable, wieldy, steady, and attained to imperturbability, he directs it to knowledge of the destruction of the taints. He understands as it actually is: 'This is suffering'...(*as Sutta 51, §26*)...He understands as it actually is: 'This is the way leading to the cessation of the taints.'

50. "When he knows and sees thus, his mind is liberated from the taint of sensual desire, from the taint of being, and from the taint of ignorance. When it is liberated there comes the knowledge: 'It is liberated.' He understands: 'Birth is destroyed, the holy life has been lived, what had to be done has been done,

there is no more coming to any state of being.' A wise man certainly would live the holy life with a teacher under whom a disciple attains such a lofty distinction, and while living it he would attain the true way, the Dhamma that is wholesome."

51. "But, Master Ānanda, when a bhikkhu is an arahant with taints destroyed, one who has lived the holy life, done what had to be done, laid down the burden, reached his own goal, destroyed the fetters of being, and is completely liberated through final knowledge, [523] could he enjoy sensual pleasures?"

"Sandaka, when a bhikkhu is an arahant with taints destroyed ...and is completely liberated through final knowledge, he is incapable of transgression in five cases. A bhikkhu whose taints are destroyed is incapable of deliberately depriving a living being of life; he is incapable of taking what is not given, that is, of stealing; he is incapable of indulging in sexual intercourse; he is incapable of knowingly speaking falsehood; he is incapable of enjoying sensual pleasures by storing them up as he did formerly in lay life.[756] When a bhikkhu is an arahant with taints destroyed...he is incapable of transgression in these five cases."[757]

52. "But, Master Ānanda, when a bhikkhu is an arahant with taints destroyed...is his knowledge and vision that his taints are destroyed continuously and uninterruptedly present to him whether he is walking or standing or sleeping or awake?"

"As to that, Sandaka, I shall give you a simile, for some wise men here understand the meaning of a statement by means of a simile. Suppose a man's hands and feet were cut off. Whether he is walking or standing or sleeping or awake, his hands and feet are continuously and uninterruptedly cut off, but he would know this only when he reviews the fact. So too, Sandaka, when a bhikkhu is an arahant with taints destroyed...his knowledge and vision that his taints are destroyed is not continuously and uninterruptedly present to him whether he is walking or standing or sleeping or awake; rather, he knows 'My taints are destroyed' only when he reviews this fact."[758]

53. "How many emancipators[759] are there in this Dhamma and Discipline, Master Ānanda?"

"There are not only one hundred, Sandaka, or two hundred, three hundred, four hundred or five hundred, but far more emancipators than that in this Dhamma and Discipline."

"It is wonderful, Master Ānanda, it is marvellous! There is no lauding of one's own Dhamma and no disparaging of the Dhamma of others; there is the teaching of the Dhamma in its full range, [524] and so many emancipators. But these Ājīvakas, those mothers' dead sons, laud themselves and disparage others, and they recognise only three emancipators, namely, Nanda Vaccha, Kisa Sankicca, and Makkhali Gosāla."[760]

54. Then the wanderer Sandaka addressed his own assembly: "Go, sirs. The holy life is to be lived under the recluse Gotama. It is not easy for us now to give up gain, honour, and renown."

That is how the wanderer Sandaka exhorted his own assembly to live the holy life under the Blessed One.

77 *Mahāsakuludāyi Sutta* The Greater Discourse to Sakuludāyin

[1] 1. THUS HAVE I HEARD. On one occasion the Blessed One was living at Rājagaha in the Bamboo Grove, the Squirrels' Sanctuary.

2. Now on that occasion a number of well-known wanderers were staying at the Peacocks' Sanctuary, the wanderers' park—that is, Annabhāra, Varadhara, and the wanderer Sakuludāyin, as well as other well-known wanderers.

3. Then, when it was morning, the Blessed One dressed, and taking his bowl and outer robe, went into Rājagaha for alms. Then he thought: "It is still too early to wander for alms in Rājagaha. Suppose I went to the wanderer Sakuludāyin in the Peacocks' Sanctuary, the wanderers' park."

4. Then the Blessed One went to the Peacocks' Sanctuary, the wanderers' park. Now on that occasion the wanderer Sakuludāyin was seated with a large assembly of wanderers who were making an uproar, loudly and noisily talking many kinds of pointless talk, such as talk of kings...(*as Sutta 76, §4*) [2]... whether things are so or are not so. Then the wanderer Sakuludāyin saw the Blessed One coming in the distance. Seeing him, he quieted his own assembly thus: "Sirs, be quiet; sirs, make no noise. Here comes the recluse Gotama. This venerable one likes quiet and commends quiet. Perhaps if he finds our assembly a quiet one, he will think to join us." Then the wanderers became silent.

5. The Blessed One went to the wanderer Sakuludāyin, who said to him: "Let the Blessed One come, venerable sir! Welcome to the Blessed One! It is long since the Blessed One found an opportunity to come here. Let the Blessed One be seated; this seat is ready."

The Blessed One sat down on the seat made ready, and the wanderer Sakuludāyin took a low seat and sat down at one side.

When he had done so, the Blessed One asked him: "For what discussion are you sitting together here now, Udāyin? And what was your discussion that was interrupted?"

6. "Venerable sir, let be the discussion for which we are now sitting together here. The Blessed One can well hear about it later. In recent days, venerable sir, when recluses and brahmins of various sects have been gathering together and sitting together in the debating hall, this topic has arisen: 'It is a gain for the people of Anga and Magadha, it is a great gain for the people of Anga and Magadha that these recluses and brahmins, heads of orders, heads of groups, teachers of groups, well-known and famous founders of sects regarded by many as saints, have come to spend the Rains at Rājagaha. There is this Pūraṇa Kassapa, the head of an order, the head of a group, the teacher of a group, the well-known and famous founder of a sect regarded by many as a saint: he has come to spend the Rains at Rājagaha. There is also this Makkhali Gosāla...this Ajita Kesakambalin... this Pakudha Kaccāyana...this Sañjaya Belaṭṭhiputta...this Nigaṇṭha Nātaputta, the head of an order, the head of a group, the teacher of a group, [3] the well-known and famous founder of a sect regarded by many as a saint: he too has come to spend the Rains at Rājagaha. There is also this recluse Gotama, the head of an order, the head of a group, the teacher of a group, the well-known and famous founder of a sect regarded by many as a saint: he too has come to spend the Rains at Rājagaha. Now among these worthy recluses and brahmins, heads of orders...regarded by many as saints, who is honoured, respected, revered, and venerated by his disciples? And how, honouring and respecting him, do they live in dependence on him?'

"Thereupon some said this: 'This Pūraṇa Kassapa is the head of an order...regarded by many as a saint, yet he is not honoured, respected, revered, and venerated by his disciples, nor do his disciples live in dependence on him, honouring and respecting him. Once Pūraṇa Kassapa was teaching his Dhamma to an assembly of several hundred followers. Then a certain disciple of his made a noise thus: "Sirs, do not ask Pūraṇa Kassapa this question. He does not know that. We know that. Ask us that question. We will answer that for you, sirs." It happened that Pūraṇa Kassapa did not get his way, though he waved his arms and wailed: "Be quiet, sirs, make no noise, sirs. They are not asking you, sirs. They are asking us. We will answer them." Indeed, many of his disciples left him after refuting his doctrine thus: "You do not understand this Dhamma and Discipline. I understand this Dhamma and Discipline. How could you understand this Dhamma and Discipline? Your way is wrong. My way is right. I am consistent. You are inconsistent. What should have been said first, you said last. What should have been said last, you said first. What you had so carefully thought up has been turned inside out. Your doctrine is refuted. You are proved wrong. Go and learn better, or disentangle yourself if you can!" Thus Pūraṇa Kassapa is not honoured, respected, revered, and venerated by his disciples, nor do his disciples live in dependence on him, honouring and respecting him. Indeed, he is scorned by the scorn shown to his Dhamma.' [4]

"And some said this: 'This Makkhali Gosāla...this Ajita Kesakambalin...this Pakudha Kaccāyana...this Sañjaya Belaṭṭhiputta...this Nigaṇṭha Nātaputta is the head of an order...[but he] is not honoured, respected, revered, and venerated by his disciples, nor do his disciples live in dependence on him, honouring and respecting him. Indeed, he is scorned by the scorn shown to his Dhamma.'

"And some said this: 'This recluse Gotama is the head of an order, the head of a group, the teacher of a group, the well-known and famous founder of a sect regarded by many as a saint. He is honoured, respected, revered, and venerated by his disciples, and his disciples live in dependence on him, honouring and respecting him. Once the recluse Gotama was teaching his Dhamma to an assembly of several hundred followers and there a certain disciple of his cleared his throat. Thereupon one of his companions in the holy life nudged him with his knee [to indicate]: [5] "Be quiet, venerable sir, make no noise; the Blessed One, the Teacher, is teaching us the Dhamma." When the recluse Gotama is teaching the Dhamma to an assembly of several hundred followers, on that occasion there is no sound of his disciples' coughing or clearing their throats. For then that large assembly is poised in expectancy: "Let us hear the Dhamma the Blessed One is about to teach." Just as though a man were at a crossroads pressing out pure honey and a large group of people were poised in expectancy, so too, when the recluse Gotama is teaching the Dhamma to an assembly of several hundred followers, on that occasion there is no sound of his disciples' coughing or clearing their throats. For then that large assembly is poised in expectancy: "Let us hear the Dhamma the Blessed One is about to teach." And even those disciples of his who fall out with their companions in the holy life and abandon the training to return to the low life—even they praise the Master and the Dhamma and the Sangha; they blame themselves instead of others, saying: "We were unlucky, we have little merit; for though we went forth into homelessness in such a well-proclaimed Dhamma, we were unable to live the perfect and pure holy life for the rest of our lives." Having become monastery attendants or lay followers, they undertake and observe the five precepts. Thus the recluse Gotama is honoured, respected, revered, and venerated by his disciples, and his disciples live in dependence on him, honouring and respecting him.'"

7. "But, Udāyin, how many qualities do you see in me because of which my disciples honour, respect, revere, and venerate me, and live in dependence on me, honouring and respecting me?"

8. "Venerable sir, I see five qualities in the Blessed One because of which his disciples honour, respect, revere, and venerate him, and live in dependence on him, honouring and respecting him. What are the five? First, venerable sir, the Blessed One eats little and commends eating little; this I see as the first quality of the Blessed One because of which his disciples honour, respect, revere, and venerate him, and live in dependence on him, honouring and respecting him. [6] Again, venerable sir, the Blessed One is content with any kind of robe and commends contentment with any kind of robe; this I see as the second quality of the Blessed One...Again, venerable sir, the Blessed One is content with any kind of almsfood and commends contentment with any kind of almsfood; this I see as the third quality of the Blessed One...Again, venerable sir, the Blessed One is content with any kind of resting place and commends contentment with any kind of resting place; this I see as the fourth quality of the Blessed One...Again, venerable sir, the Blessed One is secluded and commends seclusion; this I see as the fifth quality of the Blessed One...Venerable sir, these are the five qualities I see in the Blessed One because of which his disciples honour, respect, revere, and venerate him, and live in dependence on him, honouring and respecting him."

9. "Suppose, Udāyin, my disciples honoured, respected, revered, and venerated me, and lived in dependence on me, honouring and respecting me, with the thought: 'The recluse Gotama eats little and commends eating little.' Now there are disciples of mine who live on a cupful or half a cupful of food, a bilva fruit's or half a bilva fruit's quantity of food, [7] while I sometimes eat the full contents of my almsbowl or even more. So if my disciples honoured me...with the thought: 'The recluse Gotama eats little and commends eating little,' then those disciples of mine who live on a cupful of food...should not honour, respect, revere, and venerate me for this quality, nor should they live in dependence on me, honouring and respecting me.

"Suppose, Udāyin, my disciples honoured, respected, revered, and venerated me, and lived in dependence on me, honouring and respecting me, with the thought: 'The recluse Gotama is content with any kind of robe and commends contentment with any kind of robe.' Now there are disciples of mine who are refuse-rag wearers, wearers of coarse robes; they collect rags from the charnel ground, rubbish heaps, or shops, make them into patched robes, and wear them. But I sometimes wear robes given by householders, robes so fine that pumpkin hair is coarse in comparison. So if my disciples honoured me...with the thought: 'The recluse Gotama is content with any kind of robe and commends contentment with any kind of robe,' then those disciples of mine who are refuse-rag wearers, wearers of coarse robes...should not honour, respect, revere, and venerate me for this quality, nor should they live in dependence on me, honouring and respecting me.

"Suppose, Udāyin, my disciples honoured, respected, revered, and venerated me, and lived in dependence on me, honouring and respecting me, with the thought: 'The recluse Gotama is content with any kind of almsfood and commends contentment with any kind of almsfood.' Now there are disciples of mine who are almsfood eaters, who go on unbroken almsround from house to house, who delight in gathering their food; when they have entered among the houses they will not consent even when invited to sit down. But I sometimes eat on invitation meals of choice rice [8] and many sauces and curries. So if my disciples honoured me...with the thought: 'The recluse Gotama is content with any kind of almsfood and commends contentment with any kind of almsfood,' then those disciples of mine who are almsfood eaters...should not honour, respect, revere, and venerate me for this quality, nor should they live in dependence on me, honouring and respecting me.

"Suppose, Udāyin, my disciples honoured, respected, revered, and venerated me, and lived in dependence on me, honouring and respecting me, with the thought: 'The recluse Gotama is content with any kind of resting place and commends contentment with any kind of resting place.' Now there are disciples of mine who are tree-root dwellers and open-air dwellers, who do not use a roof for eight months [of the year], while I sometimes live in gabled mansions plastered within and without, protected against the wind, secured by door bolts, with shuttered windows. So if my disciples honoured me...with the thought: 'The recluse Gotama is content with any kind of resting place and commends contentment with any kind of resting place,' then those disciples of mine who are tree-root dwellers and open-air dwellers...should not honour, respect, revere, and venerate me for this quality, nor should they live in dependence on me, honouring and respecting me.

"Suppose, Udāyin, my disciples honoured, respected, revered, and venerated me, and lived in dependence on me, honouring and respecting me, with the thought: 'The recluse Gotama is secluded and commends seclusion.' Now there are disciples of mine who are forest dwellers, dwellers in remote resting places, who live withdrawn in remote jungle-thicket resting places and return to the midst of the Sangha once each half-month for the recitation of the Pātimokkha. But I sometimes live surrounded by bhikkhus and bhikkhunīs, by men and women lay followers, by kings and kings' ministers, by other sectarians and their disciples. So if my disciples honoured me...with the thought: 'The recluse Gotama is secluded and commends seclusion,' [9] then those disciples of mine who are forest dwellers...should not honour, respect, revere, and venerate me for this quality, nor should they live in dependence on me, honouring and respecting me. Thus, Udāyin, it is not because of these five qualities that my disciples honour, respect, revere, and venerate me, and live in dependence on me, honouring and respecting me.

10. "However, Udāyin, there are five other qualities because of which my disciples honour, respect, revere, and venerate me, and live in dependence on me, honouring and respecting me. What are the five?

(I. THE HIGHER VIRTUE)

11. "Here, Udāyin, my disciples esteem me for the higher virtue thus: 'The recluse Gotama is virtuous, he possesses the supreme aggregate of virtue.' This is the first quality because of which my disciples honour, respect, revere, and venerate me, and live in dependence on me, honouring and respecting me.

(II. KNOWLEDGE AND VISION)

12. "Again, Udāyin, my disciples esteem me for my excellent knowledge and vision thus: 'When the recluse Gotama says "I know," he truly knows; when he says "I see," he truly sees. The recluse Gotama teaches the Dhamma through direct knowledge, not without direct knowledge; he teaches the Dhamma with a sound basis, not without a sound basis; he teaches the Dhamma in a convincing manner, not in an unconvincing manner.' This is the second quality because of which [10] my disciples honour me...

(III. THE HIGHER WISDOM)

13. "Again, Udāyin, my disciples esteem me for the higher wisdom thus: 'The recluse Gotama is wise; he possesses the supreme aggregate of wisdom. It is impossible that he should not foresee the future courses of doctrine[761] or that he should not be able to confute with reasons the current doctrines of others.' What do you think, Udāyin? Would my disciples, knowing and seeing thus, break in and interrupt me?"—"No, venerable sir."—"I do not expect instruction from my disciples; invariably, it is my disciples who expect instruction from me. This is the third quality because of which my disciples honour me...

(IV. THE FOUR NOBLE TRUTHS)

14. "Again, Udāyin, when my disciples have met with suffering and become victims of suffering, prey to suffering, they come to me and ask me about the noble truth of suffering. Being asked, I explain to them the noble truth of suffering, and I satisfy their minds with my explanation. They ask me about the noble truth of the origin of suffering...about the noble truth of the cessation of suffering...about the noble truth of the way leading to the cessation of suffering. Being asked, I explain to them the noble truth of the way leading to the cessation of suffering, and I satisfy their minds with my explanation. This is the fourth quality [11] because of which my disciples honour me...

(V. THE WAY TO DEVELOP WHOLESOME STATES)

(*1. The Four Foundations of Mindfulness*)

15. "Again, Udāyin, I have proclaimed to my disciples the way to develop the four foundations of mindfulness.[762] Here a bhikkhu abides contemplating the body as a body, ardent, fully aware, and mindful, having put away covetousness and grief for the world. He abides contemplating feelings as feelings...He abides contemplating mind as mind...He abides contemplating mind-objects as mind-objects, ardent, fully aware, and mindful, having put away covetousness and grief for the world. And thereby many disciples of mine abide having reached the consummation and perfection of direct knowledge.[763]

(*2. The Four Right Kinds of Striving*)

16. "Again, Udāyin, I have proclaimed to my disciples the way to develop the four right kinds of striving. Here a bhikkhu awakens zeal for the non-arising of unarisen evil unwholesome states, and he makes effort, arouses energy, exerts his mind, and strives. He awakens zeal for the abandoning of arisen evil unwholesome states...He awakens zeal for the arising of unarisen wholesome states...He awakens zeal for the continuance, non-disappearance, strengthening, increase, and fulfilment by development of arisen wholesome states, and he makes

effort, arouses energy, exerts his mind, and strives. And thereby many disciples of mine abide having reached the consummation and perfection of direct knowledge.

(*3. The Four Bases for Spiritual Power*)

17. "Again, Udāyin, I have proclaimed to my disciples the way to develop the four bases for spiritual power. Here a bhikkhu develops the basis for spiritual power consisting in concentration due to zeal and determined striving. He develops the basis for spiritual power consisting in concentration due to energy and determined striving. He develops the basis for spiritual power consisting in concentration due to [purity of] mind and determined striving. He develops the basis for spiritual power consisting in concentration due to investigation and determined striving. And thereby many disciples of mine abide having reached the consummation and perfection of direct knowledge.

(*4. The Five Faculties*)

18. "Again, Udāyin, I have proclaimed to my disciples the way to develop the five spiritual faculties. Here [12] a bhikkhu develops the faculty of faith, which leads to peace, leads to enlightenment. He develops the faculty of energy...the faculty of mindfulness... the faculty of concentration...the faculty of wisdom, which leads to peace, leads to enlightenment. And thereby many disciples of mine abide having reached the consummation and perfection of direct knowledge.

(*5. The Five Powers*)

19. "Again, Udāyin, I have proclaimed to my disciples the way to develop the five powers. Here a bhikkhu develops the power of faith, which leads to peace, leads to enlightenment. He develops the power of energy...the power of mindfulness...the power of concentration...the power of wisdom, which leads to peace, leads to enlightenment. And thereby many disciples of mine abide having reached the consummation and perfection of direct knowledge.

(*6. The Seven Enlightenment Factors*)

20. "Again, Udāyin, I have proclaimed to my disciples the way to develop the seven enlightenment factors. Here a bhikkhu develops the mindfulness enlightenment factor, which is supported by seclusion, dispassion, and cessation, and results in relinquishment. He develops the investigation-of-states enlightenment factor...the energy enlightenment factor...the rapture enlightenment factor...the tranquillity enlightenment factor...the concentration enlightenment factor...the equanimity enlightenment factor, which is supported by seclusion, dispassion, and cessation, and results in relinquishment. And thereby many disciples of mine abide having reached the consummation and perfection of direct knowledge.

(*7. The Noble Eightfold Path*)

21. "Again, Udāyin, I have proclaimed to my disciples the way to develop the Noble Eightfold Path. Here a bhikkhu develops right view, right intention, right speech, right action, right livelihood, right effort, right mindfulness, and right concentration. And thereby many disciples of mine abide having reached the consummation and perfection of direct knowledge.

(*8. The Eight Liberations*)

22. "Again, Udāyin, I have proclaimed to my disciples the way to develop the eight liberations.[764] Possessed of material form, one sees forms: this is the first liberation. Not perceiving form internally, one sees forms externally: this is the second liberation. One is resolved only upon the beautiful: this is the third liberation. [13] With the complete surmounting of perceptions of form, with the disappearance of perceptions of sensory impact, with non-attention to perceptions of diversity, aware that 'space is infinite,' one enters upon and abides in the base of infinite space: this is the fourth liberation. By completely surmounting the base of infinite space, aware that 'consciousness is infinite,' one enters upon and abides in the base of infinite consciousness: this is the fifth liberation. By completely surmounting the base of infinite consciousness, aware that 'there is nothing,' one enters

upon and abides in the base of nothingness: this is the sixth liberation. By completely surmounting the base of nothingness, one enters upon and abides in the base of neither-perception-nor-non-perception: this is the seventh liberation. By completely surmounting the base of neither-perception-nor-non-perception, one enters upon and abides in the cessation of perception and feeling: this is the eighth liberation. And thereby many disciples of mine abide having reached the consummation and perfection of direct knowledge.

(*9. The Eight Bases for Transcendence*)

23. "Again, Udāyin, I have proclaimed to my disciples the way to develop the eight bases for transcendence.[765] Perceiving form internally, one sees forms externally, limited, fair and ugly; by transcending them, one perceives thus: 'I know, I see.' This is the first base for transcendence.[766] Perceiving form internally, one sees forms externally, immeasurable, fair and ugly; by transcending them, one perceives thus: 'I know, I see.' This is the second base for transcendence. Not perceiving form internally, one sees forms externally, limited, fair and ugly; by transcending them, one perceives thus: 'I know, I see.' This is the third base for transcendence.[767] Not perceiving form internally, one sees forms externally, immeasurable, fair and ugly; by transcending them, one perceives thus: 'I know, I see.' This is the fourth base for transcendence. Not perceiving form internally, one sees forms externally, blue, of blue colour, blue in appearance, with blue luminosity. Just like a flax flower, which is blue, of blue colour, blue in appearance, with blue luminosity, or just like Benares cloth smoothened on both sides, which is blue, of blue colour, blue in appearance, with blue luminosity; so too, not perceiving form internally, one sees forms externally...with blue luminosity; by transcending them, one perceives thus: 'I know, I see.' This is the fifth [14] base for transcendence. Not perceiving form internally, one sees forms externally, yellow, of yellow colour, yellow in appearance, with yellow luminosity. Just like a kaṇṇikāra flower, which is yellow, of yellow colour, yellow in appearance, with yellow luminosity, or just like Benares cloth smoothened on both sides, which is yellow, of yellow colour, yellow in appearance, with yellow luminosity; so too,

not perceiving form internally, one sees forms externally...with yellow luminosity; by transcending them, one perceives thus: 'I know, I see.' This is the sixth base for transcendence. Not perceiving form externally, one sees forms externally, red, of red colour, red in appearance, with red luminosity. Just like a hibiscus flower, which is red, of red colour, red in appearance, with red luminosity, or just like Benares cloth smoothened on both sides, which is red, of red colour, red in appearance, with red luminosity; so too, not perceiving form internally, one sees forms externally...with red luminosity; by transcending them, one perceives thus: 'I know, I see.' This is the seventh base for transcendence. Not perceiving form internally, one sees forms externally, white, of white colour, white in appearance, with white luminosity. Just like the morning star, which is white, of white colour, white in appearance, with white luminosity, or just like Benares cloth smoothened on both sides, which is white, of white colour, white in appearance, with white luminosity; so too, not perceiving form internally, one sees forms externally...with white luminosity; by transcending them, one perceives thus: 'I know, I see.' This is the eighth base for transcendence. And thereby many disciples of mine abide having reached the consummation and perfection of direct knowledge.

(*10. The Ten Kasiṇas*)

24. "Again, Udāyin, I have proclaimed to my disciples the way to develop the ten kasiṇa bases.[768] One contemplates the earth-kasiṇa above, below, and across, undivided and immeasurable. Another contemplates the water-kasiṇa...Another contemplates the fire-kasiṇa...Another contemplates the air-kasiṇa...Another contemplates the blue-kasiṇa...Another contemplates the yellow-kasiṇa...Another contemplates the red-kasiṇa...Another contemplates the white-kasiṇa...Another contemplates the space-kasiṇa...Another contemplates the consciousness-kasiṇa [15] above, below, and across, undivided and immeasurable. And thereby many disciples of mine abide having reached the perfection and consummation of direct knowledge.

(11. The Four Jhānas)

25. "Again, Udāyin, I have proclaimed to my disciples the way to develop the four jhānas. Here, quite secluded from sensual pleasures, secluded from unwholesome states, a bhikkhu enters upon and abides in the first jhāna, which is accompanied by applied and sustained thought, with rapture and pleasure born of seclusion. He makes the rapture and pleasure born of seclusion drench, steep, fill, and pervade this body, so that there is no part of his whole body unpervaded by the rapture and pleasure born of seclusion.[769] Just as a skilled bath man or a bath man's apprentice heaps bath powder in a metal basin and, sprinkling it gradually with water, kneads it till the moisture wets his ball of bath powder, soaks it and pervades it inside and out, yet the ball itself does not ooze; so too, a bhikkhu makes the rapture and pleasure born of seclusion drench, steep, fill, and pervade this body, so that there is no part of his whole body unpervaded by the rapture and pleasure born of seclusion.

26. "Again, with the stilling of applied and sustained thought, a bhikkhu enters upon and abides in the second jhāna, which has self-confidence and singleness of mind without applied and sustained thought, with rapture and pleasure born of concentration. He makes the rapture and pleasure born of concentration drench, steep, fill, and pervade this body, so that there is no part of his whole body unpervaded by the rapture and pleasure born of concentration. Just as though there were a lake whose waters welled up from below and it had no inflow from east, west, north, or south [16] and would not be replenished from time to time by showers of rain, then the cool fount of water welling up in the lake would make the cool water drench, steep, fill, and pervade the lake, so that there would be no part of the whole lake unpervaded by cool water; so too, a bhikkhu makes the rapture and pleasure born of concentration drench, steep, fill, and pervade this body, so that there is no part of his whole body unpervaded by the rapture and pleasure born of concentration.

27. "Again, with the fading away as well of rapture, a bhikkhu abides in equanimity, and mindful and fully aware, still feeling pleasure with the body, he enters upon and abides in the third jhāna, on account of which noble ones announce: 'He has a pleasant abiding who has equanimity and is mindful.' He makes

the pleasure divested of rapture drench, steep, fill, and pervade this body, so that there is no part of his whole body unpervaded by the pleasure divested of rapture. Just as in a pond of blue or red or white lotuses, some lotuses that are born and grow in the water thrive immersed in the water without rising out of it, and cool water drenches, steeps, fills, and pervades them to their tips and their roots, so that there is no part of all those lotuses unpervaded by cool water; so too, a bhikkhu makes the pleasure divested of rapture drench, steep, fill, and pervade this body, so that there is no part of his whole body unpervaded by the pleasure divested of rapture.

28. "Again, with the abandoning of pleasure and pain, and with the previous disappearance of joy and grief, a bhikkhu enters upon and abides in the fourth jhāna, which has neither-pain-nor-pleasure and purity of mindfulness due to equanimity. He sits pervading this body with a pure bright mind, so that there is no part of his whole body unpervaded by the pure bright mind. Just as though a man were sitting covered from the head down with a white cloth, so that there would be no part of his whole body not covered by the white cloth; so too, a bhikkhu sits pervading this body with a pure bright mind, so that there is no part of his whole body [17] unpervaded by the pure bright mind. And thereby many disciples of mine abide having reached the consummation and perfection of direct knowledge.

(*12. Insight Knowledge*)

29. "Again, Udāyin, I have proclaimed to my disciples the way to understand thus:[770] 'This body of mine, made of material form, consisting of the four great elements, procreated by a mother and father, and built up out of boiled rice and porridge, is subject to impermanence, to being worn and rubbed away, to dissolution and disintegration, and this consciousness of mine is supported by it and bound up with it.' Suppose there were a beautiful beryl gem of purest water, eight-faceted, well cut, clear and limpid, possessed of all good qualities, and through it a blue, yellow, red, white, or brown thread would be strung. Then a man with good sight, taking it in his hand, might review it thus: 'This is a beautiful beryl gem of purest water, eight-faceted, well cut, clear and limpid, possessed of all good qualities, and

through it is strung a blue, yellow, red, white, or brown thread.' So too, I have proclaimed to my disciples the way to understand thus: 'This body of mine...is subject to impermanence, to being worn and rubbed away, to dissolution and disintegration, and this consciousness of mine is supported by it and bound up with it.' And thereby many disciples of mine abide having reached the consummation and perfection of direct knowledge.

(*13. The Mind-Made Body*)

30. "Again, Udāyin, I have proclaimed to my disciples the way to create from this body another body having form, mind-made, with all its limbs, lacking no faculty. Just as though a man were to pull out a reed from its sheath and think thus: 'This is the sheath, this is the reed; the sheath is one, the reed is another; it is from the sheath that the reed has been pulled out'; or just as though a man were to pull out a sword from its scabbard and think thus: 'This is the sword, this is the scabbard; the sword is one, the scabbard another; it is from the scabbard that the sword has been pulled out'; [18] or just as though a man were to pull a snake out of its slough and think thus: 'This is the snake, this is the slough; the snake is one, the slough another; it is from the slough that the snake has been pulled out.' So too, I have proclaimed to my disciples the way to create from this body another body having form, mind-made, with all its limbs, lacking no faculty. And thereby many disciples of mine abide having reached the consummation and perfection of direct knowledge.

(*14. The Kinds of Supernormal Power*)

31. "Again, Udāyin, I have proclaimed to my disciples the way to wield the various kinds of supernormal power: having been one, they become many; having been many, they become one; they appear and vanish; they go unhindered through walls, through enclosures, through mountains, as though through space; they dive in and out of the earth as though it were water; they walk on water without sinking as though it were earth; seated cross-legged, they travel in space like birds; with their hands they touch and stroke the moon and sun so powerful and mighty; they wield bodily mastery even as far as the Brahma-world. Just

as a skilled potter or his apprentice might create and fashion out of well-prepared clay any shape of pot he wished; or just as a skilled ivory-worker or his apprentice might create and fashion out of well-prepared ivory any ivory work of art he wished; or just as a skilled goldsmith or his apprentice might create and fashion out of well-prepared gold any gold work of art he wished; so too, I have proclaimed to my disciples the way to wield the various kinds of supernormal power...[19]...they wield bodily mastery even as far as the Brahma-world. And thereby many disciples of mine abide having reached the consummation and perfection of direct knowledge.

(*15. The Divine Ear Element*)

32. "Again, Udāyin, I have proclaimed to my disciples the way whereby with the divine ear element, which is purified and surpasses the human, they hear both kinds of sounds, the divine and the human, those that are far as well as near. Just as a vigorous trumpeter might make himself heard without difficulty in the four quarters; so too, I have proclaimed to my disciples the way whereby with the divine ear element...far as well as near. And thereby many disciples of mine abide having reached the consummation and perfection of direct knowledge.

(*16. Understanding the Minds of Others*)

33. "Again, Udāyin, I have proclaimed to my disciples the way to understand the minds of other beings, of other persons, having encompassed them with their own minds. They understand a mind affected by lust as affected by lust and a mind unaffected by lust as unaffected by lust; they understand a mind affected by hate as affected by hate and a mind unaffected by hate as unaffected by hate; they understand a mind affected by delusion as affected by delusion and a mind unaffected by delusion as unaffected by delusion; they understand a contracted mind as contracted and a distracted mind as distracted; they understand an exalted mind as exalted and an unexalted mind as unexalted; they understand a surpassed mind as surpassed and an unsurpassed mind as unsurpassed; they understand a concentrated mind as concentrated and an unconcentrated mind as unconcentrated; they understand

a liberated mind as liberated and an unliberated mind as unliberated. Just as a man or a woman—young, youthful, and fond of ornaments—on viewing the image of his or her own face in a clean bright mirror or in a bowl of clear water, would know if there were a spot thus: 'There is a spot,' [20] or would know if there were no spot thus: 'There is no spot'; so too, I have proclaimed to my disciples the way to understand...an unliberated mind as unliberated. And thereby many disciples of mine abide having reached the consummation and perfection of direct knowledge.

(17. *The Recollection of Past Lives*)

34. "Again, Udāyin, I have proclaimed to my disciples the way to recollect their manifold past lives, that is, one birth, two births, three births, four births, five births, ten births, twenty births, thirty births, forty births, fifty births, a hundred births, a thousand births, a hundred thousand births, many aeons of world-contraction, many aeons of world-expansion, many aeons of world-contraction and expansion: 'There I was so named, of such a clan, with such an appearance, such was my nutriment, such my experience of pleasure and pain, such my life-term; and passing away from there, I reappeared elsewhere; and there too I was so named...and passing away from there, I reappeared here.' Thus with their aspects and particulars they recollect their manifold past lives. Just as a man might go from his own village to another village and then back again to his own village. He might think: 'I went from my own village to that village, and there I stood in such a way, sat in such a way, spoke in such a way, kept silent in such a way; and from that village I went to that other village and there [21] I stood in such a way...kept silent in such a way; and from that village I came back again to my own village.' So too, I have proclaimed to my disciples the way to recollect their manifold lives...Thus with their aspects and particulars they recollect their manifold past lives. And thereby many disciples of mine abide having reached the consummation and perfection of direct knowledge.

(*18. The Divine Eye*)

35. "Again, Udāyin, I have proclaimed to my disciples the way whereby with the divine eye, which is purified and surpasses the human, they see beings passing away and reappearing, inferior and superior, fair and ugly, fortunate and unfortunate. They understand how beings pass on according to their actions thus: 'These worthy beings who were ill conducted in body, speech, and mind, revilers of noble ones, wrong in their views, giving effect to wrong view in their actions, on the dissolution of the body, after death, have reappeared in a state of deprivation, in a bad destination, in perdition, even in hell; but these worthy beings who were well conducted in body, speech, and mind, not revilers of noble ones, right in their views, giving effect to right view in their actions, on the dissolution of the body, after death, have reappeared in a good destination, even in the heavenly world.' Thus with the divine eye, which is purified and surpasses the human, they see beings passing away and reappearing, inferior and superior, fair and ugly, fortunate and unfortunate, and they understand how beings pass on according to their actions. Just as though there were two houses with doors and a man with good sight standing there between them saw people entering the houses and coming out and passing to and fro. So too, I have proclaimed to my disciples the way whereby with the divine eye...They understand how beings pass on according to their actions. And thereby many disciples of mine abide having reached the consummation and perfection of direct knowledge. [22]

(*19. The Destruction of the Taints*)

36. "Again, Udāyin, I have proclaimed to my disciples the way whereby by realising for themselves with direct knowledge, they here and now enter upon and abide in the deliverance of mind and deliverance by wisdom that are taintless with the destruction of the taints. Just as if there were a lake in a mountain recess, clear, limpid, and undisturbed, so that a man with good sight standing on the bank could see shells, gravel, and pebbles, and also shoals of fish swimming about and resting. He might think: 'There is this lake, clear, limpid, and undisturbed, and there are

these shells, gravel, and pebbles, and also these shoals of fish swimming about and resting.' So too, I have proclaimed to my disciples the way whereby by realising for themselves with direct knowledge, they here and now enter upon and abide in the deliverance of mind and deliverance by wisdom that are taintless with the destruction of the taints. And thereby many disciples of mine abide having reached the consummation and perfection of direct knowledge.

37. "This, Udāyin, is the fifth quality because of which my disciples honour, respect, revere, and venerate me, and live in dependence on me, honouring and respecting me.

38. "These, Udāyin, are the five qualities because of which my disciples honour, respect, revere, and venerate me, and live in dependence on me, honouring and respecting me."

That is what the Blessed One said. The wanderer Udāyin was satisfied and delighted in the Blessed One's words.

78 *Samaṇamaṇḍikā Sutta*
Samaṇamaṇḍikāputta

1. THUS HAVE I HEARD. On one occasion the Blessed One was living at Sāvatthī in Jeta's Grove, Anāthapiṇḍika's Park. Now on that occasion the wanderer Uggāhamāna Samaṇamaṇḍikāputta was staying in Mallikā's Park, the single-halled Tinduka plantation for philosophical debates,[771] [23] together with a large following of wanderers, with as many as three hundred wanderers.

2. The carpenter Pañcakanga went out from Sāvatthī at midday in order to see the Blessed One. Then he thought: "It is not the right time to see the Blessed One; he is still in retreat. And it is not the right time to see bhikkhus worthy of esteem; they are still in retreat. Suppose I went to Mallikā's Park, to the wanderer Uggāhamāna Samaṇamaṇḍikāputta?" And he went to Mallikā's Park.

3. Now on that occasion the wanderer Uggāhamāna was seated with a large assembly of wanderers who were making an uproar, loudly and noisily talking many kinds of pointless talk, such as talk of kings...(*as Sutta 76, §4*)...whether things are so or are not so.

The wanderer Uggāhamāna Samaṇamaṇḍikāputta saw the carpenter Pañcakanga coming in the distance. Seeing him, he quieted his own assembly thus: "Sirs, be quiet; sirs make no noise. Here comes the carpenter Pañcakanga, a disciple of the recluse Gotama, one of the recluse Gotama's white-clothed lay disciples staying at Sāvatthī. These venerable ones like quiet; they are disciplined in quiet; they commend quiet. Perhaps if he finds our assembly a quiet one, he will think to join us." Then the wanderers became silent.

4. The carpenter Pañcakanga went to the wanderer Uggāhamāna and exchanged greetings with him. [24] When this courteous and amiable talk was finished, he sat down at one side. The wanderer Uggāhamāna then said to him:

5. "Carpenter, when a man possesses four qualities, I describe him as accomplished in what is wholesome, perfected in what is wholesome, an ascetic invincible attained to the supreme attainment. What are the four? Here he does no evil bodily actions, he utters no evil speech, he has no evil intentions, and he does not make his living by any evil livelihood. When a man possesses these four qualities, I describe him as accomplished in what is wholesome, perfected in what is wholesome, an ascetic invincible attained to the supreme attainment."

6. Then the carpenter Pañcakanga neither approved nor disapproved of the wanderer Uggāhamāna's words. Without doing either he rose from his seat and went away, thinking: "I shall learn the meaning of this statement in the presence of the Blessed One."

7. Then he went to the Blessed One, and after paying homage to him, he sat down at one side and reported to the Blessed One his entire conversation with the wanderer Uggāhamāna. Thereupon the Blessed One said:

8. "If that were so, carpenter, then a young tender infant lying prone is accomplished in what is wholesome, perfected in what is wholesome, an ascetic invincible attained to the supreme attainment, according to the wanderer Uggāhamāna's statement. For a young tender infant lying prone does not even have the notion 'body,' so how should he do an evil bodily action beyond mere wriggling? A young tender infant lying prone does not even have the notion 'speech,' so how should he utter evil speech beyond mere whining? A young tender infant lying prone does not even have the notion 'intention,' so how should he have evil intentions beyond mere sulking? A young tender infant lying prone does not even have the notion 'livelihood,' so how [25] should he make his living by evil livelihood beyond being suckled at his mother's breast? If that were so, carpenter, then a young tender infant lying prone is accomplished in what is wholesome...according to the wanderer Uggāhamāna's statement.

"When a man possesses four qualities, carpenter, I describe him, not as accomplished in what is wholesome or perfected in what is wholesome or an ascetic invincible attained to the supreme attainment, but as one who stands in the same category as the young tender infant lying prone. What are the four? Here he does no evil bodily actions, he utters no evil speech, he has no evil intentions, and he does not make his living by any evil livelihood. When a man possesses these four qualities, I describe him, not as accomplished...but as one who stands in the same category as the young tender infant lying prone.

9. "When a man possesses ten qualities, carpenter, I describe him as accomplished in what is wholesome, perfected in what is wholesome, an ascetic invincible attained to the supreme attainment. [But first of all] I say, it must be understood thus:[772] 'These are unwholesome habits,' and thus: 'Unwholesome habits originate from this,' and thus: 'Unwholesome habits cease without remainder here,' and thus: 'One practising in this way is practising the way to the cessation of unwholesome habits.' And I say, it must be understood thus: 'These are wholesome habits,' and thus: 'Wholesome habits originate from this,' and thus: 'Wholesome habits cease without remainder here,' and thus: 'One practising in this way is practising the way to the cessation of wholesome habits.' And I say, it must be understood thus: 'These are unwholesome intentions,' and thus: 'Unwholesome intentions originate from this,' [26] and thus: 'Unwholesome intentions cease without remainder here,' and thus: 'One practising in this way is practising the way to the cessation of unwholesome intentions.' And I say, it must be understood thus: 'These are wholesome intentions,' and thus: 'Wholesome intentions originate from this,' and thus: 'Wholesome intentions cease without remainder here,' and thus: 'One practising in this way is practising the way to the cessation of wholesome intentions.'

10. "What are unwholesome habits? They are unwholesome bodily actions, unwholesome verbal actions, and evil livelihood. These are called unwholesome habits.

"And what do these unwholesome habits originate from? Their origin is stated: they should be said to originate from mind. What mind? Though mind is multiple, varied, and of different aspects, there is mind affected by lust, by hate, and by delusion. Unwholesome habits originate from this.

"And where do these unwholesome habits cease without remainder? Their cessation is stated: here a bhikkhu abandons bodily misconduct and develops good bodily conduct; he abandons verbal misconduct and develops good verbal conduct; he abandons mental misconduct and develops good mental conduct;

he abandons wrong livelihood and gains a living by right livelihood.[773] It is here that unwholesome habits cease without remainder.

"And how practising does he practise the way to the cessation of unwholesome habits? Here a bhikkhu awakens zeal for the non-arising of unarisen evil unwholesome states and he makes effort, arouses energy, exerts his mind, and strives. He awakens zeal for the abandoning of arisen evil unwholesome states...He awakens zeal for the arising of unarisen wholesome states...He awakens zeal for the continuance, non-disappearance, strengthening, increase, and fulfilment by development of arisen wholesome states, and he makes effort, arouses energy, exerts his mind, and strives. [27] One so practising practises the way to the cessation of unwholesome habits.[774]

11. "What are wholesome habits? They are wholesome bodily actions, wholesome verbal actions, and purification of livelihood. These are called wholesome habits.

"And what do these wholesome habits originate from? Their origin is stated: they should be said to originate from mind. What mind? Though mind is multiple, varied, and of different aspects, there is mind unaffected by lust, by hate, or by delusion. Wholesome habits originate from this.

"And where do these wholesome habits cease without remainder? Their cessation is stated: here a bhikkhu is virtuous, but he does not identify with his virtue, and he understands as it actually is that deliverance of mind and deliverance by wisdom where these wholesome habits cease without remainder.[775]

"And how practising does he practise the way to the cessation of wholesome habits? Here a bhikkhu awakens zeal for the non-arising of unarisen evil unwholesome states...for the continuance, non-disappearance, strengthening, increase, and fulfilment by development of arisen wholesome states, and he makes effort, arouses energy, exerts his mind, and strives. One so practising practises the way to the cessation of wholesome habits.[776]

12. "What are unwholesome intentions? They are the intention of sensual desire, the intention of ill will, and the intention of cruelty. These are called unwholesome intentions.

"And what do these unwholesome intentions originate from? Their origin is stated: they should be said to originate from perception. What perception? Though perception is multiple, varied, and of different aspects, there is perception of sensual desire, perception of ill will, and perception of cruelty. Unwholesome intentions originate from this.

"And where do these unwholesome intentions cease without remainder? Their cessation is stated: here, quite secluded from sensual pleasures, secluded from [28] unwholesome states, a bhikkhu enters upon and abides in the first jhāna, which is accompanied by applied and sustained thought, with rapture and pleasure born of seclusion. It is here that unwholesome intentions cease without remainder.[777]

"And how practising does he practise the way to the cessation of unwholesome intentions? Here a bhikkhu awakens zeal for the non-arising of unarisen evil unwholesome states...for the continuance, non-disappearance, strengthening, increase, and fulfilment by development of arisen wholesome states, and he makes effort, arouses energy, exerts his mind, and strives. One so practising practises the way to the cessation of unwholesome intentions.[778]

13. "What are wholesome intentions? They are the intention of renunciation, the intention of non-ill will, and the intention of non-cruelty. These are called wholesome intentions.

"And what do these wholesome intentions originate from? Their origin is stated: they should be said to originate from perception. What perception? Though perception is multiple, varied, and of different aspects, there is perception of renunciation, perception of non-ill will, and perception of non-cruelty. Wholesome intentions originate from this.

"And where do these wholesome intentions cease without remainder? Their cessation is stated: here with the stilling of applied and sustained thought, a bhikkhu enters upon and abides in the second jhāna, which has self-confidence and singleness of mind without applied and sustained thought, with rapture and pleasure born of concentration. It is here that these wholesome intentions cease without remainder.[779]

"And how practising does he practise the way to the cessation of wholesome intentions? Here a bhikkhu awakens zeal for the non-arising of unarisen evil unwholesome states...for the continuance, non-disappearance, strengthening, increase, and fulfilment by development of arisen wholesome states, and he makes effort, arouses energy, exerts his mind, and strives. One so practising practises the way to the cessation of wholesome intentions.[780]

14. "Now, carpenter, when a man possesses what ten qualities [29] do I describe him as accomplished in what is wholesome, perfected in what is wholesome, an ascetic invincible attained to the supreme attainment? Here a bhikkhu possesses the right view of one beyond training,[781] the right intention of one beyond training, the right speech of one beyond training, the right action of one beyond training, the right livelihood of one beyond training, the right effort of one beyond training, the right mindfulness of one beyond training, the right concentration of one beyond training, the right knowledge of one beyond training, and the right deliverance of one beyond training. When a man possesses these ten qualities, I describe him as accomplished in what is wholesome, perfected in what is wholesome, an ascetic invincible attained to the supreme attainment."

That is what the Blessed One said. The carpenter Pañcakanga was satisfied and delighted in the Blessed One's words.

79 *Cūḷasakuludāyi Sutta*
The Shorter Discourse to Sakuludāyin

1. THUS HAVE I HEARD. On one occasion the Blessed One was living at Rājagaha in the Bamboo Grove, the Squirrels' Sanctuary. Now on that occasion the wanderer Sakuludāyin was staying in the Peacocks' Sanctuary, the wanderers' park, with a large assembly of wanderers.

2. Then, when it was morning, the Blessed One dressed, and taking his bowl and outer robe, went to Rājagaha for alms. Then he thought: "It is still too early to wander for alms in Rājagaha. Suppose I went to the wanderer Sakuludāyin in the Peacocks' Sanctuary, the wanderers' park."

3–4. Then the Blessed One went to the Peacocks' Sanctuary, the wanderers' park. Now on that occasion the wanderer Sakuludāyin was seated with a large assembly of wanderers who were making an uproar...(*as Sutta 77, §§4–5*) [30]..."For what discussion are you sitting together here now, Udāyin? And what was your discussion that was interrupted?"

5. "Venerable sir, let be the discussion for which we are now sitting together here. The Blessed One can well hear about it later. Venerable sir, when I do not come to this assembly, then it sits talking many kinds of pointless talk. But when I have come to this assembly, then it sits looking up to me, thinking: 'Let us hear the Dhamma that the recluse Udāyin expounds.' However, when [31] the Blessed One comes, then both I and this assembly sit looking up to the Blessed One, thinking: 'Let us hear the Dhamma that the Blessed One expounds.'"

6. "Then, Udāyin, suggest something that I should speak about."

"Venerable sir, in recent days there was one claiming to be omniscient and all-seeing, to have complete knowledge and vision thus: 'Whether I am walking or standing or sleeping or awake, knowledge and vision are continuously and uninterruptedly present to me.' When I asked him a question about the past, he prevaricated, led the talk aside, and showed anger, hate, and bitterness. Then rapture regarding the Blessed One arose in me thus: 'Ah, surely it is the Blessed One, surely it is the Sublime One who is skilled in these things.'"

"But, Udāyin, who was it that claimed to be omniscient and all-seeing...yet when asked a question by you about the past, prevaricated, led the talk aside, and showed anger, hate, and bitterness?"

"It was the Nigaṇṭha Nātaputta, venerable sir."

7. "Udāyin, if someone should recollect his manifold past lives, that is, one birth, two births...thus, with their aspects and particulars, should he recollect his manifold past lives, then either he might ask me a question about the past or I might ask him a question about the past, and he might satisfy my mind with his answer to my question or I might satisfy his mind with my answer to his question. If someone with the divine eye, which is purified and surpasses the human, should see beings passing away and reappearing, inferior and superior, fair and ugly, fortunate and unfortunate...and understand how beings pass on according to their actions, then either he might ask me a question about the future [32] or I might ask him a question about the future, and he might satisfy my mind with his answer to my question or I might satisfy his mind with my answer to his question. But let be the past, Udāyin, let be the future. I shall teach you the Dhamma: When this exists, that comes to be; with the arising of this, that arises. When this does not exist, that does not come to be; with the cessation of this, that ceases."[782]

8. "Venerable sir, I cannot even recollect with their aspects and particulars all that I have experienced within this present existence, so how should I recollect my manifold past lives, that is, one birth, two births...with their aspects and particulars, as the Blessed One does? And I cannot now even see a mud-goblin, so how should I with the divine eye, which is purified and surpasses the human, see beings passing away and reappearing, inferior and superior, fair and ugly, fortunate and unfortunate...and understand how beings pass on according to their actions, as the Blessed One does? But, venerable sir, when the Blessed One told me: 'But let be the past, Udāyin, let be the future. I shall teach you the Dhamma: When this exists, that comes to be; with the arising of this, that arises. When this does not exist, that does not come to be;

with the cessation of this, that ceases'—that is even more unclear to me. Perhaps, venerable sir, I might satisfy the Blessed One's mind by answering a question about our own teachers' doctrine."

9. "Well, Udāyin, what is taught in your own teachers' doctrine?"

"Venerable sir, it is taught that in our own teachers' doctrine: 'This is the perfect splendour, this is the perfect splendour!'"

"But, Udāyin, since it is taught in your own teachers' doctrine: 'This is the perfect splendour, this is the perfect splendour!'—what is that perfect splendour?"

"Venerable sir, that splendour is the perfect splendour which is unsurpassed by any other splendour higher or more sublime."

"But, Udāyin, what is that splendour which is unsurpassed by any other splendour higher or more sublime?" [33]

"Venerable sir, that splendour is the perfect splendour which is unsurpassed by any other splendour higher or more sublime."

10. "Udāyin, you might continue for a long time in this way. You say: 'Venerable sir, that splendour is the perfect splendour which is unsurpassed by any other splendour higher or more sublime,' yet you do not indicate what that splendour is. Suppose a man were to say: 'I am in love with the most beautiful girl in this country.' Then they would ask him: 'Good man, that most beautiful girl in this country with whom you are in love—do you know whether she is from the noble class or the brahmin class or the merchant class or the worker class?' and he would reply: 'No.' Then they would ask him: 'Good man, that most beautiful girl in this country with whom you are in love—do you know her name and clan?...Whether she is tall or short or of middle height?...Whether she is dark or brown or golden-skinned?...What village or town or city she lives in?' and he would reply: 'No.' And then they would ask him: 'Good man, do you then love a girl you have never known or seen?' and he would reply: 'Yes.' What do you think, Udāyin, that being so, would not that man's talk amount to nonsense?"

"Surely, venerable sir, that being so, that man's talk would amount to nonsense."

"But in the same way, Udāyin, you say thus: 'That splendour is the perfect splendour which is unsurpassed by any other splendour higher or more sublime,' yet you do not indicate what that splendour is."

11. "Venerable sir, just as a beautiful beryl gem of purest

water, eight-faceted, well cut, lying on red brocade, glows, radiates, and shines, of such splendour is the self [surviving] unimpaired after death."[783]

12. "What do you think, Udāyin? This beautiful beryl gem of purest water, eight-faceted, well cut, lying on red brocade, [34] which glows, radiates, and shines, or a glowworm in the thick darkness of the night—of these two, which gives off the splendour that is more excellent and sublime?"—"The glowworm in the thick darkness of the night, venerable sir."

13. "What do you think, Udāyin? This glowworm in the thick darkness of the night or an oil-lamp in the thick darkness of the night—of these two, which gives off the splendour that is more excellent and sublime?"—"The oil-lamp, venerable sir."

14. "What do you think, Udāyin? This oil-lamp in the thick darkness of the night or a great bonfire in the thick darkness of the night—of these two, which gives off the splendour that is more excellent and sublime?"—"The great bonfire, venerable sir."

15. "What do you think, Udāyin? This great bonfire in the thick darkness of the night or the morning star towards dawn in a clear cloudless sky—of these two, which gives off the splendour that is more excellent and sublime?"—"The morning star towards dawn in a clear cloudless sky, venerable sir."

16. "What do you think, Udāyin? The morning star towards dawn in a clear cloudless sky or the full moon at midnight in a clear cloudless sky on the Uposatha day of the fifteenth—of these two, which gives off the splendour that is more excellent and sublime?"—"The full moon at midnight in a clear cloudless sky on the Uposatha day of the fifteenth, venerable sir." [35]

17. "What do you think, Udāyin? The full moon at midnight in a clear cloudless sky on the Uposatha day of the fifteenth, or the full disk of the sun at midday in a clear cloudless sky in autumn in the last month of the rainy season—of these two, which gives off the splendour that is more excellent and sublime?"—"The full disk of the sun at midday in a clear cloudless sky in autumn in the last month of the rainy season, venerable sir."

18. "Beyond this, Udāyin, I know of very many gods [whose splendour] the radiance of the sun and moon does not match, yet I do not say that there is no other splendour higher or more sublime than that splendour. But you, Udāyin, say of that splendour

which is lower and meaner than a glowworm's: 'This is the perfect splendour,' yet you do not indicate what that splendour is."

19. "The Blessed One has terminated the discussion; the Sublime One has terminated the discussion."

"But, Udāyin, why do you say that?"

"Venerable sir, it is taught in our own teachers' doctrine: 'This is the perfect splendour, this is the perfect splendour.' But on being pressed and questioned and cross-questioned about our own teachers' doctrine by the Blessed One, we are found empty, hollow, and mistaken."

20. "How is it, Udāyin, is there an exclusively pleasant world? Is there a practical way to realise an exclusively pleasant world?"

"Venerable sir, it is taught in our own teachers' doctrine: 'There is an exclusively pleasant world; there is a practical way to realise an exclusively pleasant world.'"

21. "But, Udāyin, what is that practical way to realise an exclusively pleasant world?"

"Here, venerable sir, abandoning the killing of living beings, someone abstains from killing living beings; abandoning the taking of what is not given, he abstains from taking what is not given; abandoning misconduct in sensual pleasures, he abstains from misconduct in sensual pleasures; [36] abandoning false speech, he abstains from false speech; or else he undertakes and practises some kind of asceticism. This is the practical way to realise an exclusively pleasant world."

22. "What do you think, Udāyin? On an occasion when he abandons the killing of living beings and abstains from killing living beings, does his self then feel only pleasure or both pleasure and pain?"

"Both pleasure and pain, venerable sir."

"What do you think, Udāyin? On an occasion when he abandons the taking of what is not given and abstains from taking what is not given...when he abandons misconduct in sensual pleasures and abstains from misconduct in sensual pleasures... when he abandons false speech and abstains from false speech, does his self then feel only pleasure or both pleasure and pain?"

"Both pleasure and pain, venerable sir."

"What do you think, Udāyin? On an occasion when he undertakes and practises some kind of asceticism, does his self then feel only pleasure or both pleasure and pain?"

"Both pleasure and pain, venerable sir."

"What do you think, Udāyin? Does the realisation of an exclusively pleasant world come about by following a way of mixed pleasure and pain?"

23. "The Blessed One has terminated the discussion; the Sublime One has terminated the discussion."

"But, Udāyin, why do you say that?"

"Venerable sir, it is taught in our own teachers' doctrine: 'There is an exclusively pleasant world; there is a practical way to realise an exclusively pleasant world.' But on being pressed and questioned and cross-questioned about our own teachers' doctrine by the Blessed One, we are found empty, hollow, and mistaken. But how is it, venerable sir, is there an exclusively pleasant world? Is there a practical way to realise an exclusively pleasant world?" [37]

24. "There is an exclusively pleasant world, Udāyin; there is a practical way to realise an exclusively pleasant world."

"Venerable sir, what is that practical way to realise an exclusively pleasant world?"

25. "Here, Udāyin, quite secluded from sensual pleasures, secluded from unwholesome states, a bhikkhu enters upon and abides in the first jhāna...With the stilling of applied and sustained thought, he enters upon and abides in the second jhāna...in the third jhāna...This is the practical way to realise an exclusively pleasant world."

"Venerable sir, that is not the practical way to realise an exclusively pleasant world; at that point an exclusively pleasant world has already been realised."

"Udāyin, at that point an exclusively pleasant world has not yet been realised; that is only the practical way to realise an exclusively pleasant world."

26. When this was said, the wanderer Sakuludāyin's assembly made an uproar, saying very loudly and noisily: "We are lost along with our own teachers' doctrines! We are lost along with our own teachers' doctrines! We know nothing higher than that!"[784]

Then the wanderer Sakuludāyin quieted those wanderers and asked the Blessed One:

27. "Venerable sir, at what point is an exclusively pleasant world realised?"

"Here, Udāyin, with the abandoning of pleasure and pain, and with the previous disappearance of joy and grief, a bhikkhu enters upon and abides in the fourth jhāna, which has neither-pain-nor-pleasure and purity of mindfulness due to equanimity. He dwells with those deities who have arisen in an entirely pleasant world and he talks with them and enters into conversation with them.[785] It is at this point that an exclusively pleasant world has been realised."

28. "Venerable sir, surely it is for the sake of realising that exclusively pleasant world that bhikkhus lead the holy life under the Blessed One."

"It is not for the sake of realising that exclusively pleasant world that bhikkhus lead the holy life under me. There are other states, Udāyin, higher and more sublime [than that] and it is for the sake of realising them that bhikkhus lead the holy life under me." [38]

"What are those higher and more sublime states, venerable sir, for the sake of realising which bhikkhus lead the holy life under the Blessed One?"

29–36. "Here, Udāyin, a Tathāgata appears in the world, accomplished, fully enlightened...(*as Sutta 51, §§12–19*)...he purifies his mind from doubt.

37. "Having thus abandoned these five hindrances, imperfections of the mind that weaken wisdom, quite secluded from sensual pleasures, secluded from unwholesome states, a bhikkhu enters upon and abides in the first jhāna...This, Udāyin, is a higher and more sublime state for the sake of realising which bhikkhus lead the holy life under me.

38–40. "Again, with the stilling of applied and sustained thought, a bhikkhu enters upon and abides in the second jhāna...the third jhāna...the fourth jhāna. This too, Udāyin, is a higher and more sublime state for the sake of realising which bhikkhus lead the holy life under me.

41. "When his concentrated mind is thus purified, bright, unblemished, rid of imperfection, malleable, wieldy, steady, and attained to imperturbability, he directs it to knowledge of the recollection of past lives. He recollects his manifold past lives, that is, one birth, two births...(*as Sutta 51, §24*)...Thus with their aspects and particulars he recollects his manifold past lives. This too, Udāyin, is a higher and more sublime state for the sake of realising which bhikkhus lead the holy life under me.

42. "When his concentrated mind is thus purified, bright, unblemished, rid of imperfection, malleable, wieldy, steady, and attained to imperturbability, he directs it to knowledge of the passing away and reappearance of beings...(*as Sutta 51, §25*)... Thus with the divine eye, which is purified and surpasses the human, he sees beings passing away and reappearing, inferior and superior, fair and ugly, fortunate and unfortunate, and he understands how beings pass on according to their actions. This too, Udāyin, is a higher and more sublime state for the sake of realising which bhikkhus lead the holy life under me.

43. "When his concentrated mind is thus purified, bright, unblemished, rid of imperfection, malleable, wieldy, steady, and attained to imperturbability, he directs it to knowledge of the destruction of the taints. He understands as it actually is: 'This is suffering'...(*as Sutta 51, §26*) [39]...He understands as it actually is: 'This is the way leading to the cessation of the taints.'

44. "When he knows and sees thus, his mind is liberated from the taint of sensual desire, from the taint of being, and from the taint of ignorance. When it is liberated there comes the knowledge: 'It is liberated.' He understands: 'Birth is destroyed, the holy life has been lived, what had to be done has been done, there is no more coming to any state of being.' This too, Udāyin, is a higher and more sublime state for the sake of realising which bhikkhus lead the holy life under me.

"These, Udāyin, are those higher and more sublime states for the sake of realising which bhikkhus lead the holy life under me."

45. When this was said, the wanderer Sakuludāyin said to the Blessed One: "Magnificent, venerable sir! Magnificent, venerable sir! The Blessed One has made the Dhamma clear in many ways, as though he were turning upright what had been overthrown, revealing what was hidden, showing the way to one who was lost, or holding up a lamp in the dark for those with eyesight to see forms. I go to the Blessed One for refuge and to the Dhamma and to the Sangha of bhikkhus. I would receive the going forth under the Blessed One, venerable sir, I would receive the full admission."

46. When this was said, the wanderer Sakuludāyin's assembly addressed him thus: "Do not lead the holy life under the recluse Gotama, Master Udāyin. Having been a teacher, Master Udāyin, do not live as a pupil. For Master Udāyin to do so would be as if

a water jug were to become a pitcher. Do not lead the holy life under the recluse Gotama, Master Udāyin. Having been a teacher, Master Udāyin, do not live as a pupil."

That is how the wanderer Sakuludāyin's assembly obstructed him from leading the holy life under the Blessed One.[786]

80 *Vekhanassa Sutta*
To Vekhanassa

[40] 1. THUS HAVE I HEARD. On one occasion the Blessed One was living at Sāvatthī in Jeta's Grove, Anāthapiṇḍika's Park.

2. Then the wanderer Vekhanassa went to the Blessed One and exchanged greetings with him.[787] When this courteous and amiable talk was finished, he stood at one side and in the Blessed One's presence he uttered this exclamation:

"This is the perfect splendour, this is the perfect splendour!"

"But, Kaccāna, why do you say: 'This is the perfect splendour, this is the perfect splendour!'? What is that perfect splendour?"

"Master Gotama, that splendour is the perfect splendour which is unsurpassed by any other splendour higher or more sublime."

"But, Kaccāna, what is that splendour that is unsurpassed by any other splendour higher or more sublime?"

"Master Gotama, that splendour is the perfect splendour that is unsurpassed by any other splendour higher or more sublime."

3–11. "Kaccāna, you might continue for a long time in this way...(*as Sutta 79, §§10–18*)...[41, 42] yet you do not indicate what that splendour is.

12. "Kaccāna, there are these five cords of sensual pleasure.[788] What five? Forms cognizable by the eye that are wished for, desired, agreeable, and likeable, connected with sensual desire and provocative of lust. Sounds cognizable by the ear...Odours cognizable by the nose...Flavours cognizable by the tongue... Tangibles cognizable by the body [43] that are wished for, desired, agreeable, and likeable, connected with sensual desire and provocative of lust. These are the five cords of sensual pleasure.

13. "Now, Kaccāna, the pleasure and joy that arise dependent on these five cords of sensual pleasure are called sensual

pleasure. Thus sensual pleasure [arises] through sensual pleasures, but beyond sensual pleasure there is a pleasure higher than the sensual, and that is declared to be the highest among them."[789]

14. When this was said, the wanderer Vekhanassa said: "It is wonderful, Master Gotama, it is marvellous, how well that has been expressed by Master Gotama: 'Thus sensual pleasure [arises] through sensual pleasures, but beyond sensual pleasure there is a pleasure higher than the sensual, and that is declared to be the highest among them.'"

"Kaccāna, for you who are of another view, who accept another teaching, who approve of another teaching, who pursue a different training, who follow a different teacher, it is hard to know what sensuality is, or what sensual pleasure is, or what the pleasure higher than the sensual is. But those bhikkhus who are arahants with taints destroyed, who have lived the holy life, done what had to be done, laid down the burden, reached the true goal, destroyed the fetters of being, and are completely liberated through final knowledge—it is they who would know what sensuality is, what sensual pleasure is, and what the pleasure higher than the sensual is."

15. When this was said, the wanderer Vekhanassa was angry and displeased, and he reviled, disparaged, and censured the Blessed One, saying: "The recluse Gotama will be worsted." He then said to the Blessed One: "So then there are some recluses and brahmins here who, without knowing the past and without seeing the future, yet claim: 'Birth is destroyed, the holy life has been lived, what had to be done has been done, there is no more coming to any state of being.' What they say turns out to be ridiculous; it turns out to be mere words, empty and hollow."

16. "If any recluses and brahmins [44], without knowing the past and without seeing the future, yet claim: 'Birth is destroyed, the holy life has been lived, what had to be done has been done, there is no more coming to any state of being,' they can be reasonably confuted. Rather, let the past be, Kaccāna, and let the future be. Let a wise man come, one who is honest and sincere, a man of rectitude. I instruct him, I teach him the Dhamma in such a way that by practising as instructed he will soon know and see for himself: 'Thus, indeed, there rightly comes to be liberation from the bond, that is, from the bond of

ignorance.' Suppose, Kaccāna, there were a young tender infant lying prone, bound by stout bonds [at the four limbs] with the fifth at the neck; and later on, as a result of his growth and the maturing of his faculties, those bonds loosened, then he would know 'I am free' and there would be no more bondage. So too, let a wise man come...'Thus, indeed, there rightly comes to be liberation from the bond, that is, from the bond of ignorance.'"

17. When this was said, the wanderer Vekhanassa said to the Blessed One: "Magnificent, Master Gotama! Magnificent, Master Gotama! Master Gotama has made the Dhamma clear...(*as Sutta 79, §19*)...for those with eyesight to see forms. I go to Master Gotama for refuge and to the Dhamma and to the Sangha of bhikkhus. From today let the Blessed One remember me as a lay follower who has gone to him for refuge for life."

4
The Division on Kings
(*Rājavagga*)

81 *Ghaṭīkāra Sutta*
Ghaṭīkāra the Potter

[45] 1. THUS HAVE I HEARD. On one occasion the Blessed One was wandering among the Kosalans together with a large Sangha of bhikkhus.

2. Then in a certain place beside the main road the Blessed One smiled. It occurred to the venerable Ānanda: "What is the reason, what is the cause, for the Blessed One's smile? Tathāgatas do not smile for no reason." So he arranged his upper robe on one shoulder, and extending his hands in reverential salutation towards the Blessed One, asked him: "Venerable sir, what is the reason, what is the cause, for the Blessed One's smile? Tathāgatas do not smile for no reason."

3. "Once, Ānanda, in this place there was a prosperous and busy market town called Vebhalinga, with many inhabitants and crowded with people. Now the Blessed One Kassapa, accomplished and fully enlightened, lived near the market town Vebhalinga. It was here, in fact, that the Blessed One Kassapa, accomplished and fully enlightened, had his monastery; it was here, in fact, that the Blessed One Kassapa, accomplished and fully enlightened, resided and advised the Sangha of bhikkhus."

4. Then the venerable Ānanda folded his patchwork cloak in four, and spreading it out, said to the Blessed One: "Then, venerable sir, let the Blessed One be seated. Thus this place will have been used by two Accomplished Ones, Fully Enlightened Ones."

The Blessed One sat down on the seat that had been made ready and addressed the venerable Ānanda thus:

5. "Once, Ānanda, in this place there was a prosperous and busy market town called Vebhalinga, with many inhabitants and crowded with people. Now the Blessed One Kassapa, accomplished and fully enlightened, lived near the market town Vebhalinga. It was here, in fact, that the Blessed One Kassapa,

accomplished and fully enlightened, had his monastery; it was here, in fact, that the Blessed One Kassapa, accomplished and fully enlightened, resided [46] and advised the Sangha of bhikkhus.

6. "In Vebhalinga the Blessed One Kassapa, accomplished and fully enlightened, had as a supporter, as his chief supporter, a potter named Ghaṭikāra. Ghaṭikāra the potter had as a friend, as his close friend, a brahmin student named Jotipāla.[790]

"One day the potter Ghaṭikāra addressed the brahmin student Jotipāla thus: 'My dear Jotipāla, let us go and see the Blessed One Kassapa, accomplished and fully enlightened. I hold that it is good to see that Blessed One, accomplished and fully enlightened.' The brahmin student Jotipāla replied: 'Enough, my dear Ghaṭikāra, what is the use of seeing that bald-pated recluse?'

"A second and third time the potter Ghaṭikāra said: 'My dear Jotipāla, let us go and see the Blessed One Kassapa, accomplished and fully enlightened. I hold that it is good to see that Blessed One, accomplished and fully enlightened.' And a second and a third time the brahmin student Jotipāla replied: 'Enough, my dear Ghaṭikāra, what is the use of seeing that bald-pated recluse?'—'Then, my dear Jotipāla, let us take a loofah and bath powder and go to the river to bathe.'—'Very well,' Jotipāla replied.

7. "So the potter Ghaṭikāra and the brahmin student Jotipāla took a loofah and bath powder and went to the river to bathe. Then Ghaṭikāra said to Jotipāla: 'My dear Jotipāla, there is the monastery of the Blessed One Kassapa, accomplished and fully enlightened, quite nearby. Let us go and see the Blessed One Kassapa, accomplished and fully enlightened. I hold that it is good to see that Blessed One, accomplished and fully enlightened.' Jotipāla replied: 'Enough, my dear Ghaṭikāra, what is [47] the use of seeing that bald-pated recluse?'

"A second and a third time Ghaṭikāra said: 'My dear Jotipāla, there is the monastery of the Blessed One Kassapa...' And a second and a third time the brahmin student Jotipāla replied: 'Enough, my dear Ghaṭikāra, what is the use of seeing that bald-pated recluse?'[791]

8. "Then the potter Ghaṭikāra seized the brahmin student Jotipāla by the belt and said: 'My dear Jotipāla, there is the monastery of the Blessed One Kassapa, accomplished and fully enlightened, quite nearby. Let us go and see the Blessed One

Kassapa, accomplished and fully enlightened. I hold that it is good to see that Blessed One, accomplished and fully enlightened.' Then the brahmin student Jotipāla undid his belt and said: 'Enough, my dear Ghaṭikāra, what is the use of seeing that bald-pated recluse?'

9. "Then, when the brahmin student Jotipāla had washed his head, the potter Ghaṭikāra seized him by the hair and said:[792] 'My dear Jotipāla, there is the monastery of the Blessed One Kassapa, accomplished and fully enlightened, quite nearby. Let us go and see the Blessed One Kassapa, accomplished and fully enlightened. I hold that it is good to see that Blessed One, accomplished and fully enlightened.'

"Then the brahmin student Jotipāla thought: 'It is wonderful, it is marvellous that this potter Ghaṭikāra, who is of a different birth, should presume to seize me by the hair when we have washed our heads! Surely this can be no simple matter.' And he said to the potter Ghaṭikāra: 'You go as far as this, my dear Ghaṭikāra?'—'I go as far as this, my dear Jotipāla; for so much [48] do I hold that it is good to see that Blessed One, accomplished and fully enlightened!'—'Then, my dear Ghaṭikāra, let go of me. Let us visit him.'

10. "So Ghaṭikāra the potter and Jotipāla the brahmin student went to the Blessed One Kassapa, accomplished and fully enlightened. Ghaṭikāra, after paying homage to him, sat down at one side, while Jotipāla exchanged greetings with him, and when this courteous and amiable talk was finished, he too sat down at one side. Ghaṭikāra then said to the Blessed One Kassapa, accomplished and fully enlightened: 'Venerable sir, this is the brahmin student Jotipāla, my friend, my close friend. Let the Blessed One teach him the Dhamma.'

"Then the Blessed One Kassapa, accomplished and fully enlightened, instructed, urged, roused, and gladdened Ghaṭikāra the potter and Jotipāla the brahmin student with an exposition of the Dhamma. At the conclusion of the exposition, having delighted and rejoiced in the Blessed One Kassapa's words, they rose from their seats, and after paying homage to the Blessed One Kassapa, accomplished and fully enlightened, keeping him on their right, they departed.

11. "Then Jotipāla asked Ghaṭikāra: 'Now that you have heard this Dhamma, my dear Ghaṭikāra, why don't you go forth from

the home life into homelessness?'—'My dear Jotipāla, don't you know that I support my blind and aged parents?'—'Then, my dear Ghaṭīkāra, I shall go forth from the home life into homelessness.'

12. "So Ghaṭīkāra the potter and Jotipāla the brahmin student went to the Blessed One Kassapa, accomplished and fully enlightened. [49] After paying homage to him, they sat down at one side and Ghaṭīkāra the potter said to the Blessed One Kassapa, accomplished and fully enlightened: 'Venerable sir, this is the brahmin student Jotipāla, my friend, my close friend. Let the Blessed One give him the going forth.' And the brahmin student Jotipāla received the going forth from the Blessed One Kassapa, accomplished and fully enlightened, and he received the full admission.[793]

13. "Then not long after Jotipāla the brahmin student had received the full admission, a half-month after he had received the full admission, the Blessed One Kassapa, accomplished and fully enlightened, having stayed at Vebhalinga as long as he chose, set out to wander towards Benares. Wandering by stages, he eventually arrived at Benares, and there he went to live in the Deer Park at Isipatana.

14. "Now King Kikī of Kāsi heard: 'It seems that the Blessed One Kassapa, accomplished and fully enlightened, has reached Benares and is living in the Deer Park at Isipatana.' So he had a number of state carriages made ready, and mounting a state carriage, drove out from Benares with the full pomp of royalty in order to see the Blessed One Kassapa, accomplished and fully enlightened. He went thus as far as the road was passable for carriages, and then he got down from his carriage and went forward on foot to the Blessed One Kassapa, accomplished and fully enlightened. After paying homage to him, he sat down at one side and the Blessed One Kassapa, accomplished and fully enlightened, instructed, urged, roused, and gladdened King Kikī of Kāsi with an exposition of the Dhamma.

15. "At the conclusion of the exposition, King Kikī of Kāsi said: [50] 'Venerable sir, let the Blessed One together with the Sangha of bhikkhus consent to accept tomorrow's meal from me.' And the Blessed One Kassapa, accomplished and fully enlightened, accepted in silence. Then, knowing that the Blessed One Kassapa, accomplished and fully enlightened, had accepted,

he rose from his seat and after paying homage to him, keeping him on his right, he departed.

16. "Then, when the night had ended, King Kikī of Kāsi had good food of various kinds prepared in his own dwelling—red rice stored in the sheaf with the dark grains picked out, along with many sauces and curries—and he had the time announced to the Blessed One Kassapa, accomplished and fully enlightened, thus: 'It is time, venerable sir, the meal is ready.'

17. "Then, it being morning, the Blessed One Kassapa, accomplished and fully enlightened, dressed, and taking his bowl and outer robe, he went with the Sangha of bhikkhus to the dwelling of King Kikī of Kāsi and sat down on the seat made ready. Then, with his own hands, King Kikī of Kāsi served and satisfied the Sangha of bhikkhus headed by the Buddha with the various kinds of good food. When the Blessed One Kassapa, accomplished and fully enlightened, had eaten and had put his bowl aside, King Kikī of Kāsi took a low seat, sat down at one side and said: 'Venerable sir, let the Blessed One accept from me a residence for the Rains in Benares; that will be helpful for the Sangha.'—'Enough, king, my residence for the Rains has already been provided for.'

"A second and a third time King Kikī of Kāsi said: 'Venerable sir, let the Blessed One accept from me a residence for the Rains in Benares; that will be helpful for the Sangha.'—'Enough, king, my residence for the Rains has already been provided for.'

"The king thought: 'The Blessed One Kassapa, [51] accomplished and fully enlightened, does not accept from me a residence for the Rains in Benares,' and he was very disappointed and sad.

18. "Then he said: 'Venerable sir, have you a better supporter than I am?'—'I have, great king. There is a market town called Vebhalinga where a potter named Ghaṭīkāra lives. He is my supporter, my chief supporter. Now you, great king, thought: "The Blessed One Kassapa, accomplished and fully enlightened, does not accept from me a residence for the Rains in Benares," and you were very disappointed and sad; but the potter Ghaṭīkāra is not and will not be so. The potter Ghaṭīkāra has gone for refuge to the Buddha, the Dhamma, and the Sangha. He abstains from killing living beings, from taking what is not given, from misconduct in sensual pleasures, from false speech,

and from wine, liquor, and intoxicants, which are the basis of negligence. He has perfect confidence in the Buddha, the Dhamma, and the Sangha, and he possesses the virtues loved by noble ones. He is free from doubt about suffering, about the origin of suffering, about the cessation of suffering, and about the way leading to the cessation of suffering. He eats only one meal a day, he observes celibacy, he is virtuous, of good character. He has laid aside gems and gold, he has given up gold and silver. He does not dig the ground for clay using a pick with his own hand; what is left over from embankments or thrown up by rats, he brings home in a carrier; when he has made a pot he says: "Let anyone who likes set down some selected rice or selected beans or selected lentils, and let him take away whatever he likes."⁷⁹⁴ He supports his blind and aged parents. [52] Having destroyed the five lower fetters, he is one who will reappear spontaneously [in the Pure Abodes] and there attain final Nibbāna without ever returning from that world.

19. "'On one occasion when I was living at Vebhalinga, it being morning, I dressed, and taking my bowl and outer robe, I went to the potter Ghaṭīkāra's parents and asked them: "Where has the potter gone, please?"—"Venerable sir, your supporter has gone out; but take rice from the cauldron and sauce from the saucepan and eat."

"'I did so and went away. Then the potter Ghaṭīkāra went to his parents and asked: "Who has taken rice from the cauldron and sauce from the saucepan, eaten and gone away?"—"My dear, the Blessed One Kassapa, accomplished and fully enlightened, did."

"'Then the potter Ghaṭīkāra thought: "It is a gain for me, it is a great gain for me that the Blessed One Kassapa, accomplished and fully enlightened, has so much trust in me!" And rapture and happiness never left him for a half-month or his parents for a week.

20. "'On another occasion when I was living at Vebhalinga, it being morning, I dressed, and taking my bowl and outer robe, I went to the potter Ghaṭīkāra's parents and asked them: "Where has the potter gone, please?"—"Venerable sir, your supporter has gone out; but take some porridge from the vessel and sauce from the saucepan and eat."

"'I did so [53] and went away. Then the potter Ghaṭīkāra went to his parents and asked: "Who has taken porridge from the vessel and sauce from the saucepan, eaten and gone away?"—"My dear, the Blessed One Kassapa, accomplished and fully enlightened, did."

"'Then the potter Ghaṭīkāra thought: "It is a gain for me, it is a great gain for me that the Blessed One Kassapa, accomplished and fully enlightened, has so much trust in me!" And rapture and happiness never left him for a half-month or his parents for a week.

21. "'On another occasion when I was living at Vebhalinga my hut leaked. Then I addressed the bhikkhus thus: "Go, bhikkhus, and find out if there is any grass at the potter Ghaṭīkāra's house."—"Venerable sir, there is no grass at the potter Ghaṭīkāra's house; there is the grass thatch on his roof."—"Go, bhikkhus, and remove the grass from the potter Ghaṭīkāra's house."

"'They did so. Then the potter Ghaṭīkāra's parents asked the bhikkhus: "Who is removing the grass from the house?"—"Sister, the hut of the Blessed One Kassapa, accomplished and fully enlightened, is leaking."—"Take it, venerable sirs, take it, dear ones!"

"'Then the potter Ghaṭīkāra went to his parents and asked: "Who has removed the grass from the roof?"—"The bhikkhus did, my dear; the hut of the Blessed One Kassapa, accomplished and fully enlightened, is leaking."

"'Then the potter Ghaṭīkāra thought: "It is a gain for me, it is a great gain for me that the Blessed One Kassapa, accomplished and fully enlightened, has so much trust in me!" And [54] the rapture and happiness never left him for a half-month or his parents for a week. Then that house remained three whole months with the sky for a roof, and yet no rain came in. Such is the potter Ghaṭīkāra.'

"'It is a gain for the potter Ghaṭīkāra, it is a great gain for him that the Blessed One Kassapa, accomplished and fully enlightened, relies on him thus.'

22. "Then King Kikī of Kāsi dispatched to the potter Ghaṭīkāra five hundred cartloads of red rice stored in the sheaf, and also sauce materials to go with it. Then the king's men went to the potter Ghaṭīkāra and told him: 'Venerable sir, there are five hundred cartloads of red rice stored in the sheaf, and also sauce materials to go with it, dispatched to you by King Kikī of Kāsi;

please accept them.'—'The king is very busy and has much to do. I have enough. Let this be for the king himself.'[795]

23. "Now, Ānanda, you may think thus: 'Certainly, someone else was the brahmin student Jotipāla on that occasion.' But it should not be regarded thus. I was the brahmin student Jotipāla on that occasion."

That is what the Blessed One said. The venerable Ānanda was satisfied and delighted in the Blessed One's words.

82 *Raṭṭhapāla Sutta*
On Raṭṭhapāla

1. THUS HAVE I HEARD. On one occasion the Blessed One was wandering in the Kuru country with a large Sangha of bhikkhus, and eventually he arrived at a Kuru town named Thullakoṭṭhita.

2. The brahmin householders of Thullakoṭṭhita heard: "The recluse Gotama, the son of the Sakyans who went forth from a Sakyan clan, has been wandering in the Kuru country [55] with a large Sangha of bhikkhus and has come to Thullakoṭṭhita. Now a good report of Master Gotama has been spread to this effect: 'That Blessed One is accomplished, fully enlightened, perfect in true knowledge and conduct, sublime, knower of worlds, incomparable leader of persons to be tamed, teacher of gods and humans, enlightened, blessed. He declares this world with its gods, its Māras, and its Brahmās, this generation with its recluses and brahmins, its princes and its people, which he has himself realised with direct knowledge. He teaches the Dhamma good in the beginning, good in the middle, and good in the end, with the right meaning and phrasing, and he reveals a holy life that is utterly perfect and pure.' Now it is good to see such arahants."

3. Then the brahmin householders of Thullakoṭṭhita went to the Blessed One. Some paid homage to the Blessed One and sat down at one side; some exchanged greetings with him, and when this courteous and amiable talk was finished, sat down at one side; some extended their hands in reverential salutation towards the Blessed One and sat down at one side; some pronounced their name and clan in the Blessed One's presence and sat down at one side; some kept silent and sat down at one side. When they were seated, the Blessed One instructed, urged, roused, and gladdened them with talk on the Dhamma.

4. Now at that time a clansman named Raṭṭhapāla, the son of the leading clan in that same Thullakoṭṭhita, was sitting in the assembly.[796] Then it occurred to him: "As I understand the Dhamma taught by the Blessed One, it is not easy while living in a home to lead the holy life, utterly perfect and pure as a polished shell. Suppose I shave off my hair and beard, put on the yellow robe, and go forth from the home life into homelessness."

5. Then the brahmin householders of Thullakoṭṭhita, having been instructed, urged, roused, and gladdened by the Blessed One with talk on the Dhamma, delighted and rejoiced in his words. They then rose from their [56] seats, and after paying homage to him, they departed, keeping him on their right.

6. Soon after they had gone, the clansman Raṭṭhapāla went to the Blessed One, and after paying homage to him, he sat down at one side and said to the Blessed One: "Venerable sir, as I understand the Dhamma taught by the Blessed One, it is not easy while living in a home to lead the holy life, utterly perfect and pure as a polished shell. Venerable sir, I wish to shave off my hair and beard, put on the yellow robe, and go forth from the home life into homelessness. I would receive the going forth under the Blessed One, I would receive the full admission."

"Have you been permitted by your parents, Raṭṭhapāla, to go forth from the home life into homelessness?"

"No, venerable sir, I have not been permitted by my parents."

"Raṭṭhapāla, Tathāgatas do not give the going forth to anyone who does not have his parents' permission."

"Venerable sir, I shall see to it that my parents permit me to go forth from the home life into homelessness."

7. Then the clansman Raṭṭhapāla rose from his seat, and after paying homage to the Blessed One, he departed, keeping him on his right. He went to his parents and told them: "Mother and father, as I understand the Dhamma taught by the Blessed One, it is not easy while living in a home to lead the holy life, utterly perfect and pure as a polished shell. I wish to shave off my hair and beard, put on the yellow robe, and go forth from the home life into homelessness. Give me permission to go forth from the home life into homelessness."

When he had said this, his parents replied: "Dear Raṭṭhapāla, you are our only son, dear and beloved. You have been raised in comfort, brought up in comfort; you know nothing of suffering, dear Raṭṭhapāla.[797] [57] Even in case of your death we would lose you unwillingly, so how could we give you our permission to go forth from the home life into homelessness while you are still living?"

For the second time...For the third time the clansman Raṭṭhapāla said to his parents: "Mother and father...give me permission to go forth from the home life into homelessness."

For the third time his parents replied: "Dear Raṭṭhapāla...how could we give you our permission to go forth from the home life into homelessness while you are still living?"

Then, not receiving his parents' permission to go forth, the clansman Raṭṭhapāla lay down there on the bare floor, saying: "Right here I shall either die or receive the going forth." [58]

8. Then the clansman Raṭṭhapāla's parents said to him: "Dear Raṭṭhapāla, you are our only son, dear and beloved. You have been raised in comfort, brought up in comfort; you know nothing of suffering, dear Raṭṭhapāla. Get up, dear Raṭṭhapāla, eat, drink, and amuse yourself. While eating, drinking, and amusing yourself, you can be happy enjoying sensual pleasures and making merit. We do not permit you to go forth from the home life into homelessness. Even in the case of your death we would lose you unwillingly, so how could we give you our permission to go forth from the home life into homelessness while you are still living?" When this was said, the clansman Raṭṭhapāla was silent.

For the second time...For the third time his parents said to him: "Dear Raṭṭhapāla...how could we give you our permission to go forth from the home life into homelessness while you are still living?" For the third time the clansman Raṭṭhapāla was silent.

9. Then the clansman Raṭṭhapāla's parents went to his friends and said to them: "Dears, the clansman Raṭṭhapāla has lain down on the bare floor, having said: 'Right here I shall either die or receive the going forth.' Come, dears, go to the clansman Raṭṭhapāla and say to him: 'Friend Raṭṭhapāla, you are your parents' only son...Get up, friend Raṭṭhapāla, eat, drink, and amuse yourself...[59] how could your parents give you their permission to go forth from the home life into homelessness while you are still living?'"

10. Then the clansman Raṭṭhapāla's friends went to him and said: "Friend Raṭṭhapāla, you are your parents' only son, dear and beloved. You have been raised in comfort, brought up in

comfort; you know nothing of suffering, friend Raṭṭhapāla. Get up, friend Raṭṭhapāla, eat, drink, and amuse yourself. While eating, drinking, and amusing yourself, you can be happy enjoying sensual pleasures and making merit. Your parents do not permit you to go forth from the home life into homelessness. Even in case of your death they would lose you unwillingly, so how could they give you their permission to go forth from the home life into homelessness while you are still living?" When this was said, the clansman Raṭṭhapāla was silent.

For the second time…For the third time his friends said to him: "Friend Raṭṭhapāla…how could they give you their permission to go forth from the home life into homelessness while you are still living?" For the third time the clansman Raṭṭhapāla was silent.

11. Then the clansman Raṭṭhapāla's friends went to his parents and said to them: "Mother and father, the clansman Raṭṭhapāla is lying down there on the bare floor, having said: 'Right here I shall either die or [60] receive the going forth.' Now if you do not give him your permission to go forth from the home life into homelessness, he will die there. But if you give him your permission, you will see him after he has gone forth. And if he does not enjoy the going forth, what else can he do then but return here? So give him your permission to go forth from the home life into homelessness."

"Then, dears, we give the clansman Raṭṭhapāla permission to go forth from the home life into homelessness. But when he has gone forth, he must visit his parents."

Then the clansman Raṭṭhapāla's friends went to him and told him: "Get up, friend Raṭṭhapāla. Your parents permit you to go forth from the home life into homelessness. But when you have gone forth, you must visit your parents."

12. The clansman Raṭṭhapāla then got up, and when he had regained his strength, he went to the Blessed One, and after paying homage to him, he sat down at one side and told him: "Venerable sir, I have my parents' permission to go forth from the home life into homelessness. Let the Blessed One give me the going forth." Then the clansman Raṭṭhapāla received the going forth under the Blessed One, and he received the full admission.

13. Then not long after the venerable Raṭṭhapāla had received the full admission, a half-month after he had received the full

admission, the Blessed One, having stayed at Thullakoṭṭhita as long as he chose, set out to wander towards Sāvatthī. Wandering by stages, he eventually arrived at Sāvatthī, and there [61] he lived at Sāvatthī in Jeta's Grove, Anāthapiṇḍika's Park.

14. Before long, dwelling alone, withdrawn, diligent, ardent, and resolute, the venerable Raṭṭhapāla, by realising for himself with direct knowledge, here and now entered upon and abided in that supreme goal of the holy life for the sake of which clansmen rightly go forth from the home life into homelessness.[798] He directly knew: "Birth is destroyed, the holy life has been lived, what had to be done has been done, there is no more coming to any state of being." And the venerable Raṭṭhapāla became one of the arahants.

15. Then the venerable Raṭṭhapāla went to the Blessed One, and after paying homage to him, he sat down at one side and told him: "Venerable sir, I wish to visit my parents, if I have the Blessed One's permission."

Then the Blessed One penetrated mentally the thoughts in venerable Raṭṭhapāla's mind. When he knew that the clansman Raṭṭhapāla was incapable of abandoning the training and returning to the low life, he told him: "You may go, Raṭṭhapāla, at your own convenience."

16. Then the venerable Raṭṭhapāla rose from his seat, and after paying homage to the Blessed One, he departed, keeping him on his right. He then set his resting place in order, and taking his bowl and outer robe, set out to wander towards Thullakoṭṭhita. Wandering by stages, he eventually arrived at Thullakoṭṭhita. There he lived in Thullakoṭṭhita in King Koravya's Migācira Garden. Then, when it was morning, he dressed, and taking his bowl and outer robe, went into Thullakoṭṭhita for alms. As he was wandering for alms from house to house in Thullakoṭṭhita, he came to his own father's house.

17. Now on that occasion the venerable Raṭṭhapāla's father was sitting in the hall of the central door having his hair dressed. When he saw the venerable Raṭṭhapāla coming in the distance, he said: "Our only son, dear and beloved, was made to go forth by these bald-pated recluses." [62] Then at his own father's house the venerable Raṭṭhapāla received neither alms nor a polite refusal; instead, he received only abuse.

18. Just then a slavewoman belonging to one of his relatives was about to throw away some old porridge. Seeing this, the

venerable Raṭṭhapāla said to her: "Sister, if that stuff is to be thrown away, then pour it into my bowl here."

While she was doing so, she recognised the characteristic features of his hands, his feet, and his voice. Then she went to his mother and said: "Please know, my lady, that my lord's son Raṭṭhapāla has arrived."

"Gracious! If what you say is true, you are no longer a slave!"

Then the venerable Raṭṭhapāla's mother went to his father and said: "Please know, householder, they say that the clansman Raṭṭhapāla has arrived."

19. Just then the venerable Raṭṭhapāla was eating the old porridge by the wall of a certain shelter. His father went to him and said: "Raṭṭhapāla, my dear, surely there is...and you will be eating old porridge![799] Is there not your own house to go to?"

"How could we have a house, householder, when we have gone forth from the home life into homelessness? We are homeless, householder. We went [63] to your house, but we received neither alms nor a polite refusal there; instead we received only abuse."

"Come, dear Raṭṭhapāla, let us go to the house."

"Enough, householder, my meal for today is finished."

"Then, dear Raṭṭhapāla, consent to accept tomorrow's meal." The venerable Raṭṭhapāla consented in silence.

20. Then, knowing that the venerable Raṭṭhapāla had consented, his father went back to his own house where he had gold coins and bullion made into a large heap and covered it with mats. Then he told the venerable Raṭṭhapāla's former wives: "Come, daughters-in-law, adorn yourselves with ornaments in the way Raṭṭhapāla found you most dear and loveable."

21. When night had ended, the venerable Raṭṭhapāla's father had good food of various kinds prepared in his own house and had the time announced to the venerable Raṭṭhapāla: "It is time, dear Raṭṭhapāla, the meal is ready."

22. Then, it being morning, the venerable Raṭṭhapāla dressed, and taking his bowl and outer robe, he went to his own father's house and sat down on the seat made ready. Then his father had the pile of gold coins and bullion uncovered and said: "Dear Raṭṭhapāla, this is your maternal fortune; your paternal fortune is another and your ancestral fortune is yet another. Dear Raṭṭhapāla, you can enjoy the wealth and make merit. Come

then, dear, [64] abandon the training and return to the low life, enjoy the wealth and make merit."

"Householder, if you would follow my advice, then have this pile of gold coins and bullion loaded on carts and carried away to be dumped midstream in the river Ganges. Why is that? Because, householder, on account of this there will arise for you sorrow, lamentation, pain, grief, and despair."

23. Then the venerable Raṭṭhapāla's former wives clasped his feet and said to him: "What are they like, my lord's son, the nymphs for whose sake you lead the holy life?"

"We do not lead the holy life for the sake of nymphs, sisters."

"Our lord's son Raṭṭhapāla calls us 'sisters,'" they cried and right there they fainted.

24. Then the venerable Raṭṭhapāla told his father: "Householder, if there is a meal to be given, then give it. Do not harass us."

"Eat then, dear Raṭṭhapāla, the meal is ready."

Then, with his own hands, the venerable Raṭṭhapāla's father served and satisfied him with the various kinds of good food. When the venerable Raṭṭhapāla had eaten and had put his bowl aside, he stood up and uttered these stanzas:

25. "Behold a puppet here pranked out,[800]
A body built up out of sores,
Sick, an object for concern,
Where no stability abides.

Behold a figure here pranked out
With jewellery and earrings too,
A skeleton wrapped up in skin,
Made attractive by its clothes.

Its feet adorned with henna dye
And powder smeared upon its face:
It may beguile a fool, but not
A seeker of the further shore. [65]

Its hair is dressed in eightfold plaits
And unguent smeared upon its eyes:
It may beguile a fool, but not
A seeker of the further shore.

A filthy body well adorned
Like a new-painted unguent pot:
It may beguile a fool, but not
A seeker of the further shore.

The deer-hunter set out the snare
But the deer did not spring the trap;
We ate the bait and now depart
Leaving the hunters to lament."

26. After the venerable Raṭṭhapāla had stood up and uttered these stanzas, he went to King Koravya's Migācīra garden and sat down at the root of a tree for the day's abiding.

27. Then King Koravya addressed his gamekeeper thus: "Good gamekeeper, tidy up the Migācīra Garden so that we may go to the pleasure garden to see a pleasing spot."—"Yes, sire," he replied. Now while he was tidying up the Migācīra Garden, the gamekeeper saw the venerable Raṭṭhapāla seated at the root of a tree for the day's abiding. When he saw him, he went to King Koravya and told him: "Sire, the Migācīra Garden has been tidied up. The clansman Raṭṭhapāla is there, the son of the leading clan in this same Thullakoṭṭhita, of whom you have always spoken highly;[801] he is seated at the root of a tree for the day's abiding."

"Then, good gamekeeper, enough of the pleasure garden for today. Now we shall go to pay respects to that Master Raṭṭhapāla."

28. Then, saying: "Give away all the food that has been prepared there," King Koravya had a number of state carriages prepared, and mounting one of them, accompanied by the other carriages, he drove out from Thullakoṭṭhita with the full pomp of royalty to see the venerable Raṭṭhapāla. He drove thus as far as the road was passable for carriages, and then he dismounted from his carriage and went forward on foot with a following of the most eminent officials to where the venerable Raṭṭhapāla was. [66] He exchanged greetings with the venerable Raṭṭhapāla, and when this courteous and amiable talk was finished, he stood at one side and said: "Here is an elephant rug. Let Master Raṭṭhapāla be seated on it."

"There is no need, great king. Sit down. I am sitting on my own mat."

King Koravya sat down on a seat made ready and said:

29. "Master Raṭṭhapāla, there are four kinds of loss. Because they have undergone these four kinds of loss, some people here shave off their hair and beard, put on the yellow robe, and go forth from the home life into homelessness. What are the four? They are loss through ageing, loss through sickness, loss of wealth, and loss of relatives.

30. "And what is loss through ageing? Here, Master Raṭṭhapāla, someone is old, aged, burdened with years, advanced in life, come to the last stage. He considers thus: 'I am old, aged, burdened with years, advanced in life, come to the last stage. It is no longer easy for me to acquire unacquired wealth or to augment wealth already acquired. Suppose I shave off my hair and beard, put on the yellow robe, and go forth from the home life into homelessness.' Because he has undergone that loss through ageing, he shaves off his hair and beard, puts on the yellow robe, and goes forth from the home life into homelessness. This is called loss through ageing. But Master Raṭṭhapāla is now still young, a black-haired young man endowed with the blessing of youth, in the prime of life. Master Raṭṭhapāla has not undergone any loss through ageing. What has he known or seen or heard that he has gone forth from the home life into homelessness?

31. "And what is loss through sickness? Here, Master Raṭṭhapāla, someone is afflicted, suffering, and gravely ill. He considers thus: 'I am afflicted, suffering, and gravely ill. It is no longer easy for me to acquire unacquired wealth...[67]...into homelessness.' Because he has undergone that loss through sickness...he goes forth from the home life into homelessness. This is called loss through sickness. But Master Raṭṭhapāla now is free from illness and affliction; he possesses a good digestion that is neither too cool nor too warm but medium. Master Raṭṭhapāla has not undergone any loss through sickness. What has he known or seen or heard that he has gone forth from the home life into homelessness?

32. "And what is loss of wealth? Here, Master Raṭṭhapāla, someone is rich, of great wealth, of great possessions. Gradually his wealth dwindles away. He considers thus: 'Formerly I was rich, of great wealth, of great possessions. Gradually my wealth has dwindled away. It is no longer easy for me to acquire unacquired wealth...into homelessness.' Because he has

undergone that loss of wealth...he goes forth from the home life into homelessness. This is called loss of wealth. But Master Raṭṭhapāla is the son of the leading clan in this same Thullakoṭṭhita. Master Raṭṭhapāla has not undergone any loss of wealth. What has he known or seen or heard that he has gone forth from the home life into homelessness?

33. "And what is loss of relatives? Here, Master Raṭṭhapāla, someone has many friends and companions, kinsmen and relatives. Gradually those relatives of his dwindle away. He considers thus: 'Formerly I had many friends and companions, kinsmen and relatives. Gradually those relatives of mine have dwindled away. It is no longer easy for me to acquire unacquired wealth...[68]...into homelessness.' Because he has undergone that loss of relatives...he goes forth from the home life into homelessness. This is called loss of relatives. But Master Raṭṭhapāla has many friends and companions, kinsmen and relatives, in this same Thullakoṭṭhita. Master Raṭṭhapāla has not undergone any loss of relatives. What has he known or seen or heard that he has gone forth from the home life into homelessness?

34. "Master Raṭṭhapāla, these are the four kinds of loss. Because they have undergone these four kinds of loss, some people here shave off their hair and beard, put on the yellow robe, and go forth from the home life into homelessness. Master Raṭṭhapāla has not undergone any of these. What has he known or seen or heard that he has gone forth from the home life into homelessness?"

35. "Great king, there are four summaries of the Dhamma that have been taught by the Blessed One who knows and sees, accomplished and fully enlightened. Knowing and seeing and hearing them, I went forth from the home life into homelessness. What are the four?

36. (1) "'[Life in] any world is unstable, it is swept away':[802] this is the first summary of the Dhamma taught by the Blessed One who knows and sees, accomplished and fully enlightened. Knowing and seeing and hearing this, I went forth from the home life into homelessness.

(2) "'[Life in] any world has no shelter and no protector':[803] this is the second summary of the Dhamma taught by the Blessed One who knows and sees...

(3) "'[Life in] any world has nothing of its own; one has to

leave all and pass on':[804] this is the third summary of the Dhamma taught by the Blessed One who knows and sees...

(4) "'[Life in] any world is incomplete, insatiate, the slave of craving':[805] this is the fourth summary of the Dhamma taught by the Blessed One who knows and sees...

37. "Great king, these are the four summaries of the Dhamma that have been taught by the Blessed One who knows and sees, accomplished and fully enlightened. [69] Knowing and seeing and hearing them, I went forth from the home life into homelessness."

38. "Master Raṭṭhapāla said: '[Life in] any world is unstable, it is swept away.' How should the meaning of that statement be understood?"

"What do you think, great king? When you were twenty or twenty-five years old, were you an expert rider of elephants, an expert horseman, an expert charioteer, an expert archer, an expert swordsman, strong in thighs and arms, sturdy, capable in battle?"

"When I was twenty or twenty-five years old, Master Raṭṭhapāla, I was an expert rider of elephants...strong in thighs and arms, sturdy, capable in battle. Sometimes I wonder if I had supernormal power then. I do not see anyone who could equal me in strength."

"What do you think, great king? Are you now as strong in thighs and arms, as sturdy and as capable in battle?"

"No, Master Raṭṭhapāla. Now I am old, aged, burdened with years, advanced in life, come to the last stage; my years have turned eighty. Sometimes I mean to put my foot here and I put my foot somewhere else."

"Great king, it was on account of this that the Blessed One who knows and sees, accomplished and fully enlightened, said: '[Life in] any world is unstable, it is swept away'; and when I knew and saw and heard this, I went forth from the home life into homelessness."

"It is wonderful, Master Raṭṭhapāla, it is marvellous how well that has been expressed by the Blessed One who knows and sees, accomplished and fully enlightened: '[Life in] any world is unstable, it is swept away.' It is indeed so!

39. "Master Raṭṭhapāla, there exist in this court elephant troops and cavalry and chariot troops and infantry, which will serve to subdue any threats to us. [70] Now Master Raṭṭhapāla

said: '[Life in] any world has no shelter and no protector.' How should the meaning of that statement be understood?"

"What do you think, great king? Do you have any chronic ailment?"

"I have a chronic wind ailment, Master Raṭṭhapāla. Sometimes my friends and companions, kinsmen and relatives, stand around me, thinking: 'Now King Koravya is about to die, now King Koravya is about to die!'"

"What do you think, great king? Can you command your friends and companions, your kinsmen and relatives: 'Come, my good friends and companions, my kinsmen and relatives. All of you present share this painful feeling so that I may feel less pain'? Or do you have to feel that pain yourself alone?"

"I cannot command my friends and companions, my kinsmen and relatives thus, Master Raṭṭhapāla. I have to feel that pain alone."

"Great king, it was on account of this that the Blessed One who knows and sees, accomplished and fully enlightened, said: '[Life in] any world has no shelter and no protector'; and when I knew and saw and heard this, I went forth from the home life into homelessness."

"It is wonderful, Master Raṭṭhapāla, it is marvellous how well that has been expressed by the Blessed One who knows and sees, accomplished and fully enlightened: '[Life in] any world has no shelter and no protector.' It is indeed so!

40. "Master Raṭṭhapāla, there exist in this court abundant gold coins and bullion stored away in vaults and depositories. Now Master Raṭṭhapāla said: '[Life in] any world has nothing of its own; one has to leave all and pass on.' How should the meaning of that statement be understood?"

"What do you think, great king? You now [71] enjoy yourself provided and endowed with the five cords of sensual pleasure, but will you be able to have it of the life to come: 'Let me likewise enjoy myself provided and endowed with these same five cords of sensual pleasure'? Or will others take over this property, while you will have to pass on according to your actions?"

"I cannot have it thus of the life to come, Master Raṭṭhapāla. On the contrary, others will take over this property while I shall have to pass on according to my actions."

"Great king, it was on account of this that the Blessed One

who knows and sees, accomplished and fully enlightened, said: '[Life in] any world has nothing of its own; one has to leave all and pass on'; and when I knew and saw and heard this, I went forth from the home life into homelessness."

"It is wonderful, Master Raṭṭhapāla, it is marvellous how well that has been expressed by the Blessed One who knows and sees, accomplished and fully enlightened: '[Life in] any world has nothing of its own; one has to leave all and pass on.' It is indeed so!

41. "Now Master Raṭṭhapāla said: '[Life in] any world is incomplete, insatiate, the slave of craving.' How should the meaning of that statement be understood?"

"What do you think, great king? Do you reign over the rich Kuru country?"

"Yes, Master Raṭṭhapāla, I do."

"What do you think, great king? Suppose a trustworthy and reliable man came to you from the east and said: 'Please know, great king, that I have come from the east, and there I saw a large country, powerful and rich, very populous and crowded with people. There are plenty of elephant troops there, plenty of cavalry, chariot troops and infantry; there is plenty of ivory there, and plenty of gold coins and bullion both unworked and worked, and plenty of women for wives. With your present forces you can conquer it. Conquer it then, great king.' What would you do?" [72]

"We would conquer it and reign over it, Master Raṭṭhapāla."

"What do you think, great king? Suppose a trustworthy and reliable man came to you from the west...from the north...from the south...from across the sea and said: 'Please know, great king, that I have come from across the sea, and there I saw a large country, powerful and rich...Conquer it then, great king.' What would you do?"

"We would conquer it too and reign over it, Master Raṭṭhapāla."

"Great king, it was on account of this that the Blessed One who knows and sees, accomplished and fully enlightened, said: '[Life in] any world is incomplete, insatiate, the slave of craving'; and when I knew and saw and heard this, I went forth from the home life into homelessness."

"It is wonderful, Master Raṭṭhapāla, it is marvellous how well that has been expressed by the Blessed One who knows and sees, accomplished and fully enlightened: '[Life in] any world is incomplete, insatiate, the slave of craving.' It is indeed so!"

42. That is what the venerable Raṭṭhapāla said. And having said that he said further:

"I see men wealthy in the world, who yet
From ignorance give not their gathered wealth.
Greedily they hoard away their riches
Longing still for further sensual pleasures.

A king who has conquered the earth by force
And rules over the land the ocean bounds
Is yet unsated with the sea's near shore
And hungers for its further shore as well. [73]

Most other people too, not just a king,
Encounter death with craving unabated;
[With plans] still incomplete they leave the corpse;
Desires remain unsated in the world.

His relatives lament and rend their hair,
Crying, 'Ah me! Alas! Our love is dead!'
They bear away the body wrapped in shrouds
To place it on a pyre and burn it there.

Clad in a shroud, he leaves his wealth behind,
Prodded with stakes he burns [upon the pyre].
And as he dies, no relatives or friends
Can offer him shelter and refuge here.

While his heirs take over his wealth, this being
Must pass on according to his actions;
And as he dies nothing can follow him;
Not child nor wife nor wealth nor royal estate.

Longevity is not acquired with wealth
Nor can prosperity banish old age;
Short is this life, as all the sages say,
Eternity it knows not, only change.

The rich and poor alike shall feel [Death's] touch,
The fool and sage as well shall feel it too;
But while the fool lies stricken by his folly,
No sage will ever tremble at the touch.

Better is wisdom here than any wealth,
Since by wisdom one gains the final goal.
For people through ignorance do evil deeds
While failing to reach the goal from life to life.

As one goes to the womb and the next world,
Renewing the successive round of births,
Another of little wisdom, trusting him,
Goes also to the womb and the next world. [74]

Just as a robber caught in burglary
Is made to suffer for his evil deed,
So people after death, in the next world,
Are made to suffer for their evil deeds.

Sensual pleasures, varied, sweet, delightful,
In many different ways disturb the mind:
Seeing the danger in these sensual ties
I chose to lead the homeless life, O King.

As fruits fall from the tree, so people too,
Both young and old, fall when this body breaks.
Seeing this too, O King, I have gone forth:
Better is the recluse's life assured."

83 *Makhādeva Sutta*
King Makhādeva

1. THUS HAVE I HEARD.[806] On one occasion, the Blessed One was living at Mithilā in the Makhādeva Mango Grove.[807]

2. Then in a certain place the Blessed One smiled. It occurred to the venerable Ānanda: "What is the reason, what is the cause, for the Blessed One's smile? Tathāgatas do not smile for no reason." So he arranged his upper robe on one shoulder, and extending his hands in reverential salutation towards the Blessed One, he asked him: "Venerable sir, what is the reason, what is the cause, for the Blessed One's smile? Tathāgatas do not smile for no reason."

3. "Once, Ānanda, in this same Mithilā there was a king named Makhādeva. He was a righteous king who ruled by the Dhamma, a great king who was established in the Dhamma.[808] He conducted himself by the Dhamma among brahmins and householders, among town-dwellers and countryfolk, and he observed the Uposatha days [75] on the fourteenth, fifteenth, and eighth of the fortnight.[809]

4. "Now at the end of many years, many hundred years, many thousand years, King Makhādeva addressed his barber thus: 'Good barber, when you see any grey hairs growing on my head, then tell me.'—'Yes, sire,' he replied. And after many years, many hundred years, many thousand years, the barber saw grey hairs growing on King Makhādeva's head.[810] When he saw them, he said to the king: 'The divine messengers have appeared, sire; grey hairs are to be seen growing on your majesty's head.'—'Then, good barber, pull out those grey hairs carefully with tweezers and put them in my palm.'—'Yes, sire,' he replied, and he pulled out those grey hairs carefully with tweezers and put them in the king's palm.

"Then King Makhādeva gave the best township to his barber,

and calling the prince, his eldest son, he said: 'Dear prince, the divine messengers have appeared;[811] grey hairs are seen growing on my head. I have enjoyed human sensual pleasures; now it is time to seek divine sensual pleasures. Come, dear prince, take over the kingship. I shall shave off my hair and beard, put on the yellow robe, and go forth from the home life into homelessness. And now, dear prince, when you too see grey hairs growing on your head, then after giving the best township to your barber, and after carefully instructing the prince, your eldest son, in kingship, shave off your hair and beard, put on the yellow robe, and go forth from the home life into homelessness. Continue this good practice instituted by me and do not be the last man. Dear prince, when there are two men living, he under whom there occurs a breach of this good practice—he is the last man among them. Therefore, dear prince, I say to you: Continue this good practice [76] instituted by me and do not be the last man.'

5. "Then, after giving the best township to his barber and after carefully instructing the prince, his eldest son, in kingship, in the Makhādeva Mango Grove he shaved off his hair and beard, put on the yellow robe, and went forth from the home life into homelessness.

"He abided pervading one quarter with a mind imbued with loving-kindness, likewise the second, likewise the third, likewise the fourth; so above, below, around, and everywhere, and to all as to himself, he abided pervading the all-encompassing world with a mind imbued with loving-kindness, abundant, exalted, immeasurable, without hostility and without ill will.

"He abided pervading one quarter with a mind imbued with compassion...with a mind imbued with altruistic joy...with a mind imbued with equanimity, likewise the second, likewise the third, likewise the fourth; so above, below, around, and everywhere, and to all as to himself, he abided pervading the all-encompassing world with a mind imbued with equanimity, abundant, exalted, immeasurable, without hostility and without ill will.

6. "For eighty-four thousand years King Makhādeva played childish games; for eighty-four thousand years he acted as vice-regent; for eighty-four thousand years he governed the kingdom; for eighty-four thousand years he led the holy life in this Makhādeva Mango Grove after shaving off his hair and beard,

putting on the yellow robe, and going forth from the home life into homelessness. By developing the four divine abodes, on the dissolution of the body, after death, he passed on to the Brahma-world.

7–9. "Now at the end of many years, many hundred years, many thousand years, King Makhādeva's son addressed his barber thus:...(*as above, §§4–6, reading* "King Makhādeva's son" *throughout*)...[77, 78]...By developing the four divine abodes, on the dissolution of the body, after death, he passed on to the Brahma-world.

10. "The descendants of King Makhādeva's son to the number of eighty-four thousand kings in succession, after shaving off their hair and beard and putting on the yellow robe, went forth from the home life into homelessness in this Makhādeva Mango Grove. They abided pervading one quarter with a mind imbued with loving-kindness...with compassion...with altruistic joy...with equanimity...without ill will.

11. "For eighty-four thousand years they played childish games; for eighty-four thousand years they acted as vice-regents; for eighty-four thousand years they governed the kingdom; for eighty-four thousand years they led the holy life in this Makhādeva Mango Grove after shaving off their hair and beard, putting on the yellow robe, and going forth from the home life into homelessness. By developing the four divine abodes, on the dissolution of the body, after death, they passed on to the Brahma-world.

12. "Nimi was the last of those kings. He was a righteous king who ruled by the Dhamma, a great king who was established in the Dhamma. He conducted himself by the Dhamma among brahmins and householders, among town-dwellers and country-folk, and he observed the Uposatha days on the fourteenth, fifteenth, and eighth of the fortnight.

13. "Once, Ānanda, when the gods of the Thirty-three [79] had met together and were seated in the Sudhamma Assembly, this discussion arose among them: 'It is a gain, sirs, for the people of Videha, it is a great gain for the people of Videha that their King Nimi is a righteous king who rules by the Dhamma, a great king who is established in the Dhamma. He conducts himself by the Dhamma among brahmins and householders, among town-dwellers and countryfolk, and he observes the

Uposatha days on the fourteenth, fifteenth, and eighth of the fortnight.'

"Then Sakka, ruler of gods, addressed the gods of the Thirty-three: 'Good sirs, do you want to see King Nimi?'—'Good sir, we want to see King Nimi.'

"Now on that occasion, it being the Uposatha day of the fifteenth, King Nimi had washed his head and ascended to the upper palace chamber, where he was seated for the Uposatha observance. Then, just as quickly as a strong man might extend his flexed arm or flex his extended arm, Sakka, ruler of gods, vanished among the gods of the Thirty-three and appeared in the presence of King Nimi. He said: 'It is a gain for you, great king, it is a great gain for you, great king. When the gods of the Thirty-three had met together and were seated in the Sudhamma Assembly, this discussion arose among them: "It is a gain, sirs, for the people of Videha...eighth of the fortnight." Great king, the gods want to see you. I shall send a chariot harnessed to a thousand thoroughbreds for you, great king. Great king, mount the divine chariot without misgiving.'

"King Nimi consented in silence. Then, just as quickly as a strong man might extend his flexed arm or flex his extended arm, Sakka, ruler of gods, vanished in the presence of King Nimi and appeared among the gods of the Thirty-three.

14. "Then Sakka, ruler of gods, addressed the charioteer Mātali thus: 'Come, good Mātali, prepare a chariot harnessed to a thousand thoroughbreds, and go to King Nimi and say: "Great king, this chariot harnessed to a thousand thoroughbreds has been sent for you by Sakka, ruler of gods. Great king, mount the divine [80] chariot without misgiving."'

"'May your words be held sacred,' the charioteer Mātali replied. And having prepared a chariot harnessed to a thousand thoroughbreds, he went to King Nimi and said: 'Great king, this chariot harnessed to a thousand thoroughbreds has been sent for you by Sakka, ruler of gods. Great king, mount the divine chariot without misgiving. But, great king, by which route shall I drive you: by that on which doers of evil experience the results of evil actions, or by that on which doers of good experience the results of good actions?'—'Drive me by both routes, Mātali.'[812]

15. "Mātali brought King Nimi to the Sudhamma Assembly.

Sakka, ruler of gods, saw King Nimi coming in the distance and said to him: 'Come, great king! Welcome, great king! The gods of the Thirty-three, great king, seated in the Sudhamma Assembly, have expressed themselves thus: "It is a gain, sirs, for the people of Videha...eighth of the fortnight." Great king, the gods of the Thirty-three want to see you. Great king, enjoy divine might among the gods.'

"'Enough, good sir. Let the charioteer drive me back to Mithilā. There I will conduct myself by the Dhamma among brahmins and householders, among town-dwellers and countryfolk; there I will observe the Uposatha days on the fourteenth, fifteenth, and eighth of the fortnight.'

16. "Then Sakka, ruler of gods, told the charioteer Mātali: 'Come, good Mātali, prepare the chariot harnessed to a thousand thoroughbreds and drive King Nimi back to Mithilā.'

"'May your word be held sacred,' the charioteer Mātali replied. And having prepared the chariot harnessed to a thousand thoroughbreds, he drove King Nimi back to Mithilā. And there, indeed, King Nimi conducted himself by the Dhamma among brahmins and householders, among town-dwellers and countryfolk; and there [81] he observed the Uposatha days on the fourteenth, fifteenth, and eighth of the fortnight.

17–19. "Then at the end of many years, many hundred years, many thousand years, King Nimi addressed his barber thus: ...(*as above, §§4–6, reading* "King Nimi" *throughout*)...[82]...By developing the four divine abodes, on the dissolution of the body, after death, he passed on to the Brahma-world.

20. "Now King Nimi had a son named Kaḷārajanaka. He did not go forth from the home life into homelessness. He broke that good practice. He was the last man among them.

21. "Now, Ānanda, it may be that you think thus: 'Certainly, on that occasion someone else was King Makhādeva, who instituted that good practice.' But it should not be regarded thus. I was King Makhādeva on that occasion. I instituted that good practice and later generations continued that good practice instituted by me. But that kind of good practice does not lead to disenchantment, to dispassion, to cessation, to peace, to direct knowledge, to enlightenment, to Nibbāna, but only to reappearance in the Brahma-world. But there is this kind of good practice that has been instituted by me now, which leads to complete

disenchantment, to dispassion, to cessation, to peace, to direct knowledge, to enlightenment, to Nibbāna. And what is that good practice? It is this Noble Eightfold Path; that is, right view, right intention, right speech, right action, right livelihood, [83] right effort, right mindfulness, and right concentration. This is the good practice instituted by me now, which leads to complete disenchantment, to dispassion, to cessation, to peace, to direct knowledge, to enlightenment, to Nibbāna.

"Ānanda, I say to you: continue this good practice instituted by me and do not be the last man. Ānanda, when there are two men living, he under whom there occurs a breach of this good practice—he is the last man among them. Therefore, Ānanda, I say to you: continue this good practice instituted by me and do not be the last man."[813]

That is what the Blessed One said. The venerable Ānanda was satisfied and delighted in the Blessed One's words.

84 *Madhurā Sutta*
At Madhurā

1. THUS HAVE I HEARD. On one occasion the venerable Mahā Kaccāna was living at Madhurā in the Gundā Grove.[814]

2. King Avantiputta of Madhurā heard: "The recluse Kaccāna is living at Madhurā in the Gundā Grove. Now a good report of Master Kaccāna has been spread to this effect: 'He is wise, discerning, sagacious, learned, articulate, and perspicacious; he is aged and he is an arahant. It is good to see such arahants.'"

3. Then King Avantiputta of Madhurā had a number of state carriages made ready, and mounting a state carriage, he drove out from Madhurā with the full pomp of royalty in order to see the venerable Mahā Kaccāna. He went thus as far as the road was passable for carriages, and then he got down from his carriage and went forward on foot to the venerable Mahā Kaccāna. [84] He exchanged greetings with him, and when this courteous and amiable talk was finished, he sat down at one side and said:

4. "Master Kaccāna, the brahmins say thus: 'Brahmins are the highest caste, those of any other caste are inferior; brahmins are the fairest caste, those of any other caste are dark; only brahmins are purified, not non-brahmins; brahmins alone are the sons of Brahmā, the offspring of Brahmā, born of his mouth, born of Brahmā, created by Brahmā, heirs of Brahmā.' What does Master Kaccāna say about that?"

5. "It is just a saying in the world, great king, that 'Brahmins are the highest caste...heirs of Brahmā.' And there is a way whereby it can be understood how that statement of the brahmins is just a saying in the world.

"What do you think, great king? If a noble prospers in wealth, grain, silver, or gold, will there be nobles who rise before him and retire after him, who are eager to serve him, who seek to please him and speak sweetly to him, and will there also be brahmins, merchants, and workers who do likewise?"

"There will be, Master Kaccāna."

"What do you think, great king? If a brahmin prospers in wealth, grain, silver, or gold, will there be brahmins who rise before him and retire after him, who are eager to serve him, who seek to please him and speak sweetly to him, and will there also be merchants, workers, and nobles [85] who do likewise?"

"There will be, Master Kaccāna."

"What do you think, great king? If a merchant prospers in wealth, grain, silver, or gold, will there be merchants who rise before him and retire after him, who are eager to serve him, who seek to please him and speak sweetly to him, and will there also be workers, nobles, and brahmins who do likewise?"

"There will be, Master Kaccāna."

"What do you think, great king? If a worker prospers in wealth, grain, silver, or gold, will there be workers who rise before him and retire after him, who are eager to serve him, who seek to please him and speak sweetly to him, and will there also be nobles, brahmins, and merchants who do likewise?"[815]

"There will be, Master Kaccāna."

"What do you think, great king? If that is so, then are these four castes all the same, or are they not, or how does it appear to you in this case?" [86]

"Surely if that is so, Master Kaccāna, then these four castes are all the same: there is no difference between them at all that I see."

"That is a way, great king, whereby it can be understood how that statement of the brahmins is just a saying in the world.

6. "What do you think, great king? Suppose a noble were to kill living beings, take what is not given, misconduct himself in sensual pleasures, speak falsely, speak maliciously, speak harshly, gossip, be covetous, have a mind of ill will, and hold wrong view. On the dissolution of the body, after death, would he [be likely to] reappear in a state of deprivation, in an unhappy destination, in perdition, even in hell, or not, or how does it appear to you in this case?"

"If a noble were such, Master Kaccāna, he would [be likely to] reappear in a state of deprivation, in an unhappy destination, in perdition, even in hell. That is how it appears to me in this case, and thus I have heard from the arahants."

"Good, good, great king! What you think is good, great king, and what you have heard from the arahants is good. What do you think, great king? Suppose a brahmin...a merchant...a worker were to kill living beings...and hold wrong view. On the dissolution of the body, after death, would he [be likely to] reappear in a state of deprivation, in an unhappy destination, in perdition, even in hell, or not, or how does it appear to you in this case?"

"If a brahmin...a merchant...a worker were such, Master Kaccāna, he would [be likely to] reappear in a state of deprivation, in an unhappy destination, in perdition, even in hell. That is how it appears to me in this case, and thus I have heard from the arahants."

"Good, good, great king! What you think is good, great king, and what you have heard from the arahants is good. What do you think, great king? If that is so, then are these four castes all the same, or are they not, or how does it appear to you in this case?" [87]

"Surely if that is so, Master Kaccāna, then these four castes are all the same: there is no difference between them at all that I see."

"That is also a way, great king, whereby it can be understood how that statement of the brahmins is just a saying in the world.

7. "What do you think, great king? Suppose a noble were to abstain from killing living beings, from taking what is not given, from misconduct in sensual pleasures, from false speech, from malicious speech, from harsh speech, and from gossip, and were to be uncovetous, to have a mind without ill will, and to hold right view. On the dissolution of the body, after death, would he [be likely to] reappear in a happy destination, even in the heavenly world, or not, or how does it appear to you in this case?"

"If a noble were such, Master Kaccāna, he would [be likely to] reappear in a happy destination, even in the heavenly world. That is how it appears to me in this case, and thus I have heard from the arahants."

"Good, good, great king! What you think is good, great king, and what you have heard from the arahants is good. What do you think, great king? Suppose a brahmin...a merchant...a worker were to abstain from killing living beings...and to hold right view. On the dissolution of the body, after death, would he [be likely to] reappear in a happy destination, even in the heavenly world, or not, or how does it appear to you in this case?"

"If a brahmin...a merchant...a worker were such, Master Kaccāna, he would [be likely to] reappear in a happy destination, even in the heavenly world. That is how it appears to me in this case, and thus I have heard from the arahants."

"Good, good, great king! What you think is good, great king, and what you have heard from the arahants is good. What do you think, great king? If that is so, then are these four castes all the same, or are they not, or how does it appear to you in this case?" [88]

"Surely if that is so, Master Kaccāna, then these four castes are all the same: there is no difference between them at all that I see."

"That is also a way, great king, whereby it can be understood how that statement of the brahmins is just a saying in the world.

8. "What do you think, great king? Suppose a noble were to break into houses, plunder wealth, commit burglary, ambush highways, or seduce another's wife, and if your men arrested him and produced him, saying: 'Sire, this is the culprit; command what punishment for him you wish,' how would you treat him?"

"We would have him executed, Master Kaccāna, or we would have him fined, or we would have him exiled, or we would do with him as he deserved. Why is that? Because he has lost his former status of a noble, and is simply reckoned as a robber."

"What do you think, great king? Suppose a brahmin...a merchant...a worker were to break into houses...or seduce another's wife, and if your men arrested him and produced him, saying: 'Sire, this is the culprit; command what punishment for him you wish,' how would you treat him?"

"We would have him executed, Master Kaccāna, or we would have him fined, or we would have him exiled, or we would do with him as he deserved. Why is that? Because he has lost his former status of a brahmin...a merchant...a worker, and is simply reckoned as a robber."

"What do you think, great king? If that is so, then are these four castes all the same, or are they not, or how does it appear to you in this case?"

"Surely if that is so, Master Kaccāna, then these four castes are all the same; there is no difference between them at all that I see."

"That is also a way, great king, whereby it can be understood how that statement of the brahmins is just a saying in the world. [89]

9. "What do you think, great king? Suppose a noble, having shaved off his hair and beard, put on the yellow robe, and gone forth from the home life into homelessness, were to abstain from killing living beings, from taking what is not given, and from false speech. Refraining from eating at night, he would eat only in one part of the day, and would be celibate, virtuous, of good character. How would you treat him?"

"We would pay homage to him, Master Kaccāna, or we would rise up for him, or invite him to be seated; or we would invite him to accept robes, almsfood, resting place, and medicinal requisites; or we would arrange for him lawful guarding, defence, and protection. Why is that? Because he has lost his former status of a noble, and is simply reckoned as a recluse."

"What do you think, great king? Suppose a brahmin...a merchant...a worker, having shaved off his hair and beard...and would be celibate, virtuous, of good character. How would you treat him?"

"We would pay homage to him, Master Kaccāna, or rise up for him, or invite him to be seated; or we would invite him to accept robes, almsfood, resting place, and medicinal requisites; or we would arrange for him lawful guarding, defence, and protection. Why is that? Because he has lost his former status of a brahmin...a merchant...a worker, and is simply reckoned as a recluse."

"What do you think, great king? If that is so, then are these four castes all the same, or are they not, or how does it appear to you in this case?"

"Surely if that is so, Master Kaccāna, then these four castes are all the same; there is no difference between them at all that I see."

"That is also a way, great king, whereby it can be understood how that statement of the brahmins is just a saying in the world." [90]

10. When this was said, King Avantiputta of Madhurā said to the venerable Mahā Kaccāna: "Magnificent, Master Kaccāna! Magnificent, Master Kaccāna! Master Kaccāna has made the Dhamma clear in many ways, as though he were turning upright what had been overthrown, revealing what was hidden,

showing the way to one who is lost, or holding up a lamp in the dark for those with eyesight to see forms. I go to Master Kaccāna for refuge and to the Dhamma and to the Sangha of bhikkhus. From today let Master Kaccāna remember me as a lay follower who has gone to him for refuge for life."

"Do not go to me for refuge, great king. Go for refuge to that same Blessed One to whom I have gone for refuge."

"Where is he living now, Master Kaccāna, that Blessed One, accomplished and fully enlightened?"

"That Blessed One, accomplished and fully enlightened, has attained to final Nibbāna, great king."

11. "If we heard that that Blessed One was within ten leagues, we would go ten leagues in order to see that Blessed One, accomplished and fully enlightened. If we heard that that Blessed One was within twenty leagues...thirty leagues...forty leagues...fifty leagues...a hundred leagues, we would go a hundred leagues in order to see that Blessed One, accomplished and fully enlightened. But since that Blessed One has attained to final Nibbāna, we go to that Blessed One for refuge and to the Dhamma and to the Sangha of bhikkhus. From today let Master Kaccāna remember me as a lay follower who has gone for refuge for life."

85 *Bodhirājakumāra Sutta*
To Prince Bodhi

[91] 1. THUS HAVE I HEARD. On one occasion the Blessed One was living in the Bhagga country at Suṁsumāragira in the Bhesakaḷā Grove, the Deer Park.

2. Now on that occasion a palace named Kokanada had recently been built for Prince Bodhi, and it had not yet been inhabited by any recluse or brahmin or any human being at all.[816]

3. Then Prince Bodhi addressed the brahmin student Sañjikāputta thus: "Come, my dear Sañjikāputta, go to the Blessed One and pay homage in my name with your head at his feet, and ask whether he is free from illness and affliction and is healthy, strong, and abiding in comfort, saying: 'Venerable sir, Prince Bodhi pays homage with his head at the Blessed One's feet, and he asks whether the Blessed One is free from illness...and abiding in comfort.' Then say this: 'Venerable sir, let the Blessed One together with the Sangha of bhikkhus consent to accept tomorrow's meal from Prince Bodhi.'"

"Yes, sir," Sañjikāputta replied, and he went to the Blessed One and exchanged greetings with him. When this courteous and amiable talk was finished, he sat down at one side and said: "Master Gotama, Prince Bodhi pays homage with his head at Master Gotama's feet and asks whether he is free from illness...and abiding in comfort. And he says this: 'Let Master Gotama together with the Sangha of bhikkhus consent to accept tomorrow's meal from Prince Bodhi.'"

4. The Blessed One consented in silence. Then, knowing that the Blessed One had consented, Sañjikāputta rose from his seat, went to Prince Bodhi, and told him what had happened [92], adding: "The recluse Gotama has consented."

5. Then, when the night had ended, Prince Bodhi had good food of various kinds prepared in his own residence, and he had

the Kokanada Palace spread with white cloth down to the last step of the staircase. Then he addressed the brahmin student Sañjikāputta thus: "Come, my dear Sañjikāputta, go to the Blessed One and announce that it is time thus: 'It is time, venerable sir, the meal is ready.'"

"Yes, sir," Sañjikāputta replied, and he went to the Blessed One and announced that it was time thus: "It is time, Master Gotama, the meal is ready."

6. Then, it being morning, the Blessed One dressed, and taking his bowl and outer robe, went to Prince Bodhi's residence.

7. Now on that occasion Prince Bodhi was standing in the outer porch waiting for the Blessed One. When he saw the Blessed One coming in the distance, he went out to meet him and paid homage to him; and then, allowing the Blessed One to precede him, he proceeded to the Kokanada Palace. But the Blessed One stopped at the lowest step of the staircase. Prince Bodhi said to him: "Venerable sir, let the Blessed One step on the cloth, let the Sublime One step on the cloth, that it may lead to my welfare and happiness for a long time." When this was said, the Blessed One was silent.[817]

A second time...A third time Prince Bodhi said to him: "Venerable sir, let the Blessed One step on the cloth, let the Sublime One step on the cloth, that it may lead to my welfare and happiness for a long time."

The Blessed One looked at the venerable Ānanda. [93] The venerable Ānanda said to Prince Bodhi: "Prince, let the cloth be removed. The Blessed One will not step on a strip of cloth; the Tathāgata has regard for future generations."[818]

8. So Prince Bodhi had the cloth removed, and he had seats prepared in the upper apartments of the Kokanada Palace. The Blessed One and the Sangha of bhikkhus ascended the Kokanada Palace and sat down on the seats that had been prepared.

9. Then, with his own hands, Prince Bodhi served and satisfied the Sangha of bhikkhus headed by the Buddha with the various kinds of good food. When the Blessed One had eaten and had put his bowl aside, Prince Bodhi took a low seat, sat down at one side, and said to the Blessed One: "Venerable sir, we have thought thus: 'Pleasure is not to be gained through pleasure; pleasure is to be gained through pain.'"[819]

10. "Prince, before my enlightenment, while I was still only

an unenlightened Bodhisatta, I too thought thus: 'Pleasure is not to be gained through pleasure; pleasure is to be gained through pain.'

11–14. "Later, prince, while still young, a black-haired young man endowed with the blessing of youth, in the prime of life... (*as Sutta 26, §§15–17*)...And I sat down there thinking: 'This will serve for striving.'

15–42. "Now three similes occurred to me spontaneously, never heard before...(*as Sutta 36, §§17–44, but in the present sutta in §§18–23—corresponding to §§20–25 of Sutta 36—the sentence* "But such painful feeling that arose in me did not invade my mind and remain" *does not occur; and in the present sutta in §§37, 39 and 42—corresponding to §§39, 41, and 44 of Sutta 36—the sentence* "But such pleasant feeling that arose in me did not invade my mind and remain" *does not occur*)...as happens in one who abides diligent, ardent, and resolute.

43–53. "I considered: 'This Dhamma that I have attained is profound'...(*as Sutta 26, §§19–29*) [94]...and the six of us lived on what those two bhikkhus brought back from their almsround.

54. "Then the bhikkhus of the group of five, not long after being thus taught and instructed by me, by realising for themselves with direct knowledge, here and now entered upon and abided in that supreme goal of the holy life for the sake of which clansmen rightly go forth from the home life into homelessness."

55. When this was said, Prince Bodhi said to the Blessed One: "Venerable sir, when a bhikkhu finds the Tathāgata to discipline him, how long is it until by realising for himself with direct knowledge, he here and now enters upon and abides in that supreme goal of the holy life for the sake of which clansmen rightly go forth from the home life into homelessness?"

"As to that, prince, I shall ask you a question in return. Answer it as you choose. What do you think, prince? Are you skilled in the art of wielding a goad while riding an elephant?"

"Yes, venerable sir, I am."

56. "What do you think, prince? Suppose a man came here thinking: 'Prince Bodhi knows the art of wielding a goad while riding an elephant; I shall train in that art under him.' If he had no faith, he could not achieve what can be achieved by one who has faith; if he had much illness, he could not achieve what can be achieved by one who is free from illness; if he was fraudulent

and deceitful, he could not achieve what can be achieved by one who is honest and sincere; if he was lazy, he could not achieve what can be achieved by one who is energetic; if he was not wise, he could not achieve what can be achieved by one who is wise. What do you think, prince? Could that man train under you in the art of wielding a goad while riding an elephant?"

"Venerable sir, even if he had one of those deficiencies, he could not train under me, so what of the five?"

57. "What do you think, prince? Suppose a man came here thinking: [95] 'Prince Bodhi knows the art of wielding a goad while riding an elephant; I shall train in that art under him.' If he had faith, he could achieve what can be achieved by one who has faith; if he was free from illness, he could achieve what can be achieved by one who is free from illness; if he was honest and sincere, he could achieve what can be achieved by one who is honest and sincere; if he was energetic, he could achieve what can be achieved by one who is energetic; if he was wise, he could achieve what can be achieved by one who is wise. What do you think, prince? Could that man train under you in the art of wielding a goad while riding an elephant?"

"Venerable sir, even if he had one of those qualities he could train under me, so what of the five?"

58. "So too, prince, there are these five factors of striving. What five? Here a bhikkhu has faith, he places his faith in the Tathāgata's enlightenment thus: 'That Blessed One is accomplished, fully enlightened, perfect in true knowledge and conduct, sublime, knower of worlds, incomparable leader of persons to be tamed, teacher of gods and humans, enlightened, blessed.'

"Then he is free from illness and affliction, possessing a good digestion that is neither too cool nor too warm but medium and able to bear the strain of striving.

"Then he is honest and sincere, and shows himself as he actually is to the Teacher and his companions in the holy life.

"Then he is energetic in abandoning unwholesome states and in undertaking wholesome states, steadfast, launching his effort with firmness and persevering in cultivating wholesome states.

"Then he is wise; he possesses wisdom regarding rise and disappearance that is noble and penetrative and leads to the complete destruction of suffering. These are the five factors of striving.

59. "Prince, when a bhikkhu who possesses these five factors

of striving finds a Tathāgata to discipline him, he might dwell seven years until by realising for himself with direct knowledge, he here and now enters upon and abides in that supreme goal of the holy life for the sake of which clansmen rightly go forth from the home life into homelessness. [96]

"Let alone seven years, prince. When a bhikkhu who possesses these five factors of striving finds a Tathāgata to discipline him, he might dwell six years...five years...four years...three years...two years...one year...Let alone one year, prince,...he might dwell seven months...six months...five months...four months...three months...two months...one month...half a month...Let alone half a month, prince,...he might dwell seven days and nights...six days and nights...five days and nights... four days and nights...three days and nights...two days and nights...one day and night.

"Let alone one day and night, prince. When a bhikkhu who possesses these five factors of striving finds a Tathāgata to discipline him, then being instructed in the evening, he might arrive at distinction in the morning; being instructed in the morning, he might arrive at distinction in the evening."

60. When this was said, Prince Bodhi said to the Blessed One: "Oh the Buddha! Oh the Dhamma! Oh, how well proclaimed is the Dhamma! For one instructed in the evening might arrive at distinction in the morning, and one instructed in the morning might arrive at distinction in the evening."

61. When this was said, the brahmin student Sañjikāputta said to Prince Bodhi: "Master Bodhi says: 'Oh the Buddha! Oh the Dhamma! Oh, how well proclaimed is the Dhamma!' But he does not say: 'I go to Master Gotama for refuge and to the Dhamma and to the Sangha of bhikkhus.'"

"Do not say that, my dear Sañjikāputta, do not say that. I heard and learned this from my mother's lips: [97] There was an occasion when the Blessed One was living at Kosambī in Ghosita's Park. Then my mother, who was pregnant, went to the Blessed One, and after paying homage to him, she sat down at one side and said to him: 'Venerable sir, the prince or princess in my womb, whichever it may be, goes to the Blessed One for refuge and to the Dhamma and to the Sangha of bhikkhus. Let the Blessed One remember [the child] as a lay follower who has gone to him for refuge for life.' There was also an occasion when the Blessed One was living here in the country of the Bhaggas at Suṁsumāragira in the Bhesakaḷā Grove, the Deer Park. Then my nurse, carrying me on her hip, went to the Blessed One, and after paying homage to him, she stood at one side and said to him: 'Venerable sir, this Prince Bodhi goes to the Blessed One for refuge and to the Dhamma and to the Sangha of bhikkhus. Let the Blessed One remember him as a lay follower who has gone to him for refuge for life.' Now, my dear Sañjikāputta, for the third time I go to the Blessed One for refuge and to the Dhamma and to the Sangha of bhikkhus. Let the Blessed One remember me as a lay follower who has gone to him for refuge for life."

86 *Angulimāla Sutta*
On Angulimāla

1. THUS HAVE I HEARD. On one occasion the Blessed One was living at Sāvatthī in Jeta's Grove, Anāthapiṇḍika's Park.

2. Now on that occasion there was a bandit in the realm of King Pasenadi of Kosala named Angulimāla, who was murderous, bloody-handed, given to blows and violence, merciless to living beings. Villages, towns, [98] and districts were laid waste by him. He was constantly murdering people and he wore their fingers as a garland.[820]

3. Then, when it was morning, the Blessed One dressed, and taking his bowl and outer robe, went into Sāvatthī for alms. When he had wandered for alms in Sāvatthī and had returned from his almsround, after his meal he set his resting place in order, and taking his bowl and outer robe, set out on the road leading towards Angulimāla. Cowherds, shepherds, ploughmen, and travellers saw the Blessed One walking along the road leading towards Angulimāla and told him: "Do not take this road, recluse. On this road is the bandit Angulimāla, who is murderous, bloody-handed, given to blows and violence, merciless to living beings. Villages, towns, and districts have been laid waste by him. He is constantly murdering people and he wears their fingers as a garland. Men have come along this road in groups of ten, twenty, thirty, and even forty, but still they have fallen into Angulimāla's hands." When this was said the Blessed One went on in silence.

For the second time...For the third time the cowherds, shepherds, ploughmen, and travellers told this to the Blessed One, but still the Blessed One went on in silence.

4. The bandit Angulimāla saw the Blessed One coming in the distance. When he saw him, he thought: "It is wonderful, it is marvellous! Men have come along this road in groups of ten,

twenty, [99] thirty, and even forty, but still they have fallen into my hands. But now this recluse comes alone, unaccompanied, as if driven by fate. Why shouldn't I take this recluse's life?" Angulimāla then took up his sword and shield, buckled on his bow and quiver, and followed close behind the Blessed One.

5. Then the Blessed One performed such a feat of supernormal power that the bandit Angulimāla, though walking as fast as he could, could not catch up with the Blessed One, who was walking at his normal pace. Then the bandit Angulimāla thought: "It is wonderful, it is marvellous! Formerly I could catch up even with a swift elephant and seize it; I could catch up even with a swift horse and seize it; I could catch up even with a swift chariot and seize it; I could catch up even with a swift deer and seize it; but now, though I am walking as fast as I can, I cannot catch up with this recluse who is walking at his normal pace!" He stopped and called out to the Blessed One: "Stop, recluse! Stop, recluse!"

"I have stopped, Angulimāla, you stop too."

Then the bandit Angulimāla thought: "These recluses, sons of the Sakyans, speak truth, assert truth; but though this recluse is still walking, he says: 'I have stopped, Angulimāla, you stop too.' Suppose I question this recluse."

6. Then the bandit Angulimāla addressed the Blessed One in stanzas thus:

"While you are walking, recluse, you tell me you have stopped;
But now, when I have stopped, you say I have not stopped.
I ask you now, O recluse, about the meaning:
How is it that you have stopped and I have not?"

"Angulimāla, I have stopped forever,
I abstain from violence towards living beings;
But you have no restraint towards things that live:
That is why I have stopped and you have not." [100]

"Oh, at long last this recluse, a venerated sage,
Has come to this great forest for my sake.[821]
Having heard your stanza teaching me the Dhamma,
I will indeed renounce evil forever."

So saying, the bandit took his sword and weapons
And flung them in a gaping chasm's pit;
The bandit worshipped the Sublime One's feet,
And then and there asked for the going forth.

The Enlightened One, the Sage of Great Compassion,
The Teacher of the world with [all] its gods,
Addressed him with these words, "Come, bhikkhu."
And that was how he came to be a bhikkhu.

7. Then the Blessed One set out to wander back to Sāvatthī with Angulimāla as his attendant. Wandering by stages, he eventually arrived at Sāvatthī, and there he lived at Sāvatthī in Jeta's Grove, Anāthapiṇḍika's Park.

8. Now on that occasion great crowds of people were gathering at the gates of King Pasenadi's inner palace, very loud and noisy, crying: "Sire, the bandit Angulimāla is in your realm; he is murderous, bloody-handed, given to blows and violence, merciless to living beings! Villages, towns, and districts have been laid waste by him! He is constantly murdering people and he wears their fingers as a garland! The king must put him down!"

9. Then in the middle of the day King Pasenadi of Kosala drove out of Sāvatthī with a cavalry of five hundred men and set out for the park. He drove thus as far as the road was passable for carriages, and then he dismounted from his carriage and went forward on foot to the Blessed One. [101] After paying homage to the Blessed One, he sat down at one side, and the Blessed One said to him: "What is it, great king? Is King Seniya Bimbisāra of Magadha attacking you, or the Licchavis of Vesālī, or other hostile kings?"

10. "Venerable sir, King Seniya Bimbisāra of Magadha is not attacking me, nor are the Licchavis of Vesālī, nor are other hostile kings. But there is a bandit in my realm named Angulimāla, who is murderous, bloody-handed, given to blows and violence, merciless to living beings. Villages, towns, and districts have been laid waste by him. He is constantly murdering people and he wears their fingers as a garland. I shall never be able to put him down, venerable sir."

11. "Great king, suppose you were to see that Angulimāla had shaved off his hair and beard, put on the yellow robe, and gone

forth from the home life into homelessness; that he was abstaining from killing living beings, from taking what is not given and from false speech; that he was eating only one meal a day, and was celibate, virtuous, of good character. If you were to see him thus, how would you treat him?"

"Venerable sir, we would pay homage to him, or rise up for him, or invite him to be seated; or we would invite him to accept robes, almsfood, a resting place, or medicinal requisites; or we would arrange for him lawful guarding, defence, and protection. But, venerable sir, how could such an immoral man, one of evil character, ever have such virtue and restraint?"

12. Now on that occasion the venerable Angulimāla was sitting not far from the Blessed One. Then the Blessed One extended his right arm and said to King Pasenadi of Kosala: "Great king, this is Angulimāla."

Then King Pasenadi was frightened, alarmed, and terrified. Knowing this, the Blessed One told him: "Do not be afraid, great king, do not be afraid. There is nothing for you to fear from him."

Then the king's fear, [102] alarm, and terror subsided. He went over to the venerable Angulimāla and said: "Venerable sir, is the noble lord really Angulimāla?"

"Yes, great king."

"Venerable sir, of what family is the noble lord's father? Of what family is his mother?"

"My father is a Gagga, great king; my mother is a Mantāṇi."

"Let the noble lord Gagga Mantāṇiputta rest content. I shall provide robes, almsfood, resting place, and medicinal requisites for the noble lord Gagga Mantāṇiputta."

13. Now at that time the venerable Angulimāla was a forest dweller, an almsfood eater, a refuse-rag wearer, and restricted himself to three robes. He replied: "Enough, great king, my triple robe is complete."

King Pasenadi then returned to the Blessed One, and after paying homage to him, he sat down at one side and said: "It is wonderful, venerable sir, it is marvellous how the Blessed One tames the untamed, brings peace to the unpeaceful, and leads to Nibbāna those who have not attained Nibbāna. Venerable sir, we ourselves could not tame him with force and weapons, yet the Blessed One has tamed him without force or weapons. And now, venerable sir, we depart. We are busy and have much to do."

"You may go, great king, at your own convenience."

Then King Pasenadi of Kosala rose from his seat, and after paying homage to the Blessed One, keeping him on his right, he departed.

14. Then, when it was morning, the venerable Angulimāla dressed, and taking his bowl and outer robe, went into Sāvatthī for alms. As he was wandering for alms from house to house in Sāvatthī, he saw a certain woman in difficult labour, in painful labour. [103] When he saw this, he thought: "How beings are afflicted! Indeed, how beings are afflicted!"[822]

When he had wandered for alms in Sāvatthī and had returned from his almsround, after his meal he went to the Blessed One, and after paying homage to him, he sat down at one side and said: "Venerable sir, in the morning I dressed, and taking my bowl and outer robe, went into Sāvatthī for alms. As I was wandering for alms from house to house in Sāvatthī, I saw a certain woman in difficult labour, in painful labour. When I saw that, I thought: 'How beings are afflicted! Indeed, how beings are afflicted!'"

15. "In that case, Angulimāla, go into Sāvatthī and say to that woman: 'Sister, since I was born, I do not recall that I have ever intentionally deprived a living being of life. By this truth, may you be well and may your infant be well!'"

"Venerable sir, wouldn't I be telling a deliberate lie, for I have intentionally deprived many living beings of life?"

"Then, Angulimāla, go into Sāvatthī and say to that woman: 'Sister, since I was born with the noble birth, I do not recall that I have ever intentionally deprived a living being of life. By this truth, may you be well and may your infant be well!'"[823]

"Yes, venerable sir," the venerable Angulimāla replied, and having gone into Sāvatthī, he told that woman: "Sister, since I was born with the noble birth, I do not recall that I have ever intentionally deprived a living being of life. By this truth, may you be well and may your infant be well!" Then the woman and the infant became well.

16. Before long, dwelling alone, withdrawn, diligent, ardent, and resolute, the venerable Angulimāla, by realising for himself with direct knowledge, here and now entered upon and abided in that supreme goal of the holy life for the sake of which clansmen rightly go forth from the home life into homelessness. He

directly knew: "Birth is destroyed, the holy life has been lived, what had to be done has been done, there is no more coming to any state of being." [104] And the venerable Angulimāla became one of the arahants.

17. Then, when it was morning, the venerable Angulimāla dressed, and taking his bowl and outer robe, went into Sāvatthī for alms. Now on that occasion someone threw a clod and hit the venerable Angulimāla's body, someone else threw a stick and hit his body, and someone else threw a potsherd and hit his body. Then, with blood running from his cut head, with his bowl broken, and with his outer robe torn, the venerable Angulimāla went to the Blessed One. The Blessed One saw him coming in the distance and told him: "Bear it, brahmin! Bear it, brahmin! You are experiencing here and now the result of deeds because of which you might have been tortured in hell for many years, for many hundreds of years, for many thousands of years."[824]

18. Then, while the venerable Angulimāla was alone in retreat experiencing the bliss of deliverance, he uttered this exclamation:[825]

> "Who once did live in negligence
> And then is negligent no more,
> He illuminates this world
> Like the moon freed from a cloud.
>
> Who checks the evil deeds he did
> By doing wholesome deeds instead,
> He illuminates this world
> Like the moon freed from a cloud.
>
> The youthful bhikkhu who devotes
> His efforts to the Buddha's teaching,
> He illuminates this world
> Like the moon freed from a cloud.
>
> Let my enemies hear discourse on the Dhamma,
> Let them be devoted to the Buddha's teaching,
> Let my enemies wait on those good people
> Who lead others to accept the Dhamma.

[105] Let my enemies give ear from time to time
And hear the Dhamma of those who preach forbearance,
Of those who speak as well in praise of kindness,
And let them follow up with kind deeds.

For surely then they would not wish to harm me,
Nor would they think of harming other beings,
So those who would protect all, frail or strong,
Let them attain the all-surpassing peace.

Conduit-makers guide the water,
Fletchers straighten out the arrow-shaft,
Carpenters straighten out the timber,
But wise men seek to tame themselves.

There are some that tame with beatings,
Some with goads and some with whips;
But I was tamed by such alone
Who has no rod nor any weapon.

'Harmless' is the name I bear,
Though I was dangerous in the past.[826]
The name I bear today is true:
I hurt no living being at all.

And though I once lived as a bandit
Known to all as 'Finger-garland,'
One whom the great flood swept along,
I went for refuge to the Buddha.

And though I once was bloody-handed
With the name of 'Finger-garland,'
See the refuge I have found:
The bond of being has been cut.

While I did many deeds that lead
To rebirth in the evil realms,
Yet their result has reached me now,
And so I eat free from debt.[827]

They are fools and have no sense
Who give themselves to negligence,
But those of wisdom guard diligence
And treat it as their greatest good.

Do not give way to negligence
Nor seek delight in sensual pleasures,
But meditate with diligence
So as to reach the perfect bliss.

So welcome to that choice of mine
And let it stand, it was not ill made;
Of all the teachings resorted to,
I have come to the very best.

So welcome to that choice of mine
And let it stand, it was not ill made;
I have attained the triple knowledge
And done all that the Buddha teaches."

87 *Piyajātika Sutta*
Born from Those Who Are Dear

[106] 1. THUS HAVE I HEARD. On one occasion the Blessed One was living at Sāvatthī in Jeta's Grove, Anāthapiṇḍika's Park.

2. Now on that occasion a certain householder's dear and beloved only son had died. After his son's death, he had no more desire to work or to eat. He kept going to the charnel ground and crying: "My only son, where are you? My only son, where are you?"

3. Then that householder went to the Blessed One, and after paying homage to him, sat down at one side. The Blessed One said to him: "Householder, your faculties are not those of one in control of his own mind. Your faculties are deranged."

"How could my faculties not be deranged, venerable sir? For my dear and beloved only son has died. Since he died I have no more desire to work or to eat. I keep going to the charnel ground and crying: 'My only son, where are you? My only son, where are you?'"

"So it is, householder, so it is! Sorrow, lamentation, pain, grief, and despair are born from those who are dear, arise from those who are dear."

"Venerable sir, who would ever think that sorrow, lamentation, pain, grief, and despair are born from those who are dear, arise from those who are dear? Venerable sir, happiness and joy are born from those who are dear, arise from those who are dear." Then, displeased with the Blessed One's words, disapproving of them, the householder rose from his seat and left.

4. Now on that occasion some gamblers were playing with dice not far from the Blessed One. Then the householder went to those gamblers and said: "Just now, sirs, [107] I went to the recluse Gotama, and after paying homage to him, I sat down at one side. When I had done so, the recluse Gotama said to me:

'Householder, your faculties are not those of one in control of his own mind.'...(*repeat the entire conversation as above*)...'Venerable sir, happiness and joy are born from those who are dear, arise from those who are dear.' Then, displeased with the recluse Gotama's words, disapproving of them, I rose from my seat and left."

"So it is, householder, so it is! Happiness and joy are born from those who are dear, arise from those who are dear."

Then the householder left thinking: "I agree with the gamblers."

5. Eventually this story reached the king's palace. Then King Pasenadi of Kosala told Queen Mallikā: "This is what has been said by the recluse Gotama, Mallikā: 'Sorrow, lamentation, pain, grief, and despair are born from those who are dear, arise from those who are dear.'"

"If that has been said by the Blessed One, sire, then it is so."

"No matter what the recluse Gotama says, Mallikā applauds it thus: 'If that has been said by the Blessed One, sire, then it is so.' Just as a pupil applauds whatever his teacher says to him, saying: 'So it is, teacher, so it is!'; so too, Mallikā, no matter what the recluse Gotama says, you applaud it thus: 'If that [108] has been said by the Blessed One, sire, then it is so.' Be off, Mallikā, away with you!"

6. Then Queen Mallikā addressed the brahmin Nāḷijangha: "Come, brahmin, go to the Blessed One and pay homage in my name with your head at his feet, and ask whether he is free from illness and affliction and is healthy, strong, and abiding in comfort, saying: 'Venerable sir, Queen Mallikā pays homage with her head at the Blessed One's feet and asks whether the Blessed One is free from illness...and abiding in comfort.' Then say this: 'Venerable sir, have these words been uttered by the Blessed One: "Sorrow, lamentation, pain, grief, and despair are born from those who are dear, arise from those who are dear"?' Learn well what the Blessed One replies and report it to me; for Tathāgatas do not speak untruth."

"Yes, madam," he replied, and he went to the Blessed One and exchanged greetings with him. When this courteous and amiable talk was finished, he sat down at one side and said: "Master Gotama, Queen Mallikā pays homage with her head at Master Gotama's feet and asks whether he is free from illness...and abiding in comfort. And she says this: 'Venerable sir, have these words been spoken by the Blessed One: "Sorrow, lamentation, pain, grief, and despair are born from those who are dear, arise from those who are dear"?'"

7. "So it is, brahmin, so it is! Sorrow, lamentation, pain, grief, and despair are born from those who are dear, arise from those who are dear.

8. "It can be understood from this, brahmin, how sorrow, lamentation, pain, grief, and despair are born from those who are dear, arise from those who are dear. Once in this same Sāvatthī there was a certain woman whose mother died. Owing to her mother's death, she went mad, lost her mind, and wandered from street to street and from crossroad to crossroad, saying: 'Have you seen my mother? Have you seen my mother?' [109]

9–14. "And it can also be understood from this how sorrow, lamentation, pain, grief, and despair are born from those who are dear, arise from those who are dear. Once in this same Sāvatthī there was a certain woman whose father died...whose brother died...whose sister died...whose son died...whose daughter died...whose husband died. Owing to her husband's death, she went mad, lost her mind, and wandered from street to street and from crossroad to crossroad, saying: 'Have you seen my husband? Have you seen my husband?'

15–21. "And it can also be understood from this how sorrow, lamentation, pain, grief, and despair are born from those who are dear, arise from those who are dear. Once in this same Sāvatthī there was a certain man whose mother died...whose father died...whose brother died...whose sister died...whose son died...whose daughter died...whose wife died. Owing to his wife's death, he went mad, lost his mind, and wandered from street to street and from crossroad to crossroad, saying: 'Have you seen my wife? Have you seen my wife?'

22. "And it can also be understood from this how sorrow, lamentation, pain, grief, and despair are born from those who are dear, arise from those who are dear. Once in this same Sāvatthī there was a certain woman who went to live with her relatives' family. Her relatives wanted to divorce her from her husband and give her to another whom she did not want. Then the woman said to her husband: 'Lord, these relatives of mine want to divorce me from you and give me to another whom I

do not want.' Then the man cut the woman in two and [110] committed suicide, thinking: 'We shall be together in the afterlife.' It can also be understood from this how sorrow, lamentation, pain, grief, and despair are born from those who are dear, arise from those who are dear."

23. Then, delighting and rejoicing in the Blessed One's words, the brahmin Nāḷijangha rose from his seat, went to Queen Mallikā, and reported to her his entire conversation with the Blessed One.

24. Then Queen Mallikā went to King Pasenadi of Kosala and asked him: "What do you think, sire? Is Princess Vajīrī dear to you?"

"Yes, Mallikā, Princess Vajīrī is dear to me."

"What do you think, sire? If change and alteration[828] took place in Princess Vajīrī, would sorrow, lamentation, pain, grief, and despair arise in you?"

"Change and alteration in Princess Vajīrī would mean an alteration in my life. How could sorrow, lamentation, pain, grief, and despair not arise in me?"

"It was with reference to this, sire, that the Blessed One who knows and sees, accomplished and fully enlightened, said: 'Sorrow, lamentation, pain, grief, and despair are born from those who are dear, arise from those who are dear.'

25–28. "What do you think, sire? Is the noble Queen Vāsabhā dear to you?...Is General Viḍūḍabha dear to you?...[111]...Am I dear to you?...Are Kāsi and Kosala dear to you?"[829]

"Yes, Mallikā, Kāsi and Kosala are dear to me. We owe it to Kāsi and Kosala that we use Kāsi sandalwood and wear garlands, scents, and unguents."

"What do you think, sire? If change and alteration took place in Kāsi and Kosala, would sorrow, lamentation, pain, grief, and despair arise in you?"

"Change and alteration in Kāsi and Kosala would mean an alteration in my life. How could sorrow, lamentation, pain, grief, and despair not arise in me?"

"It was with reference to this, sire, that the Blessed One who knows and sees, accomplished and fully enlightened, said: 'Sorrow, lamentation, pain, grief, and despair are born from those who are dear, arise from those who are dear.'"

29. "It is wonderful, Mallikā, it is marvellous how far [112] the

Blessed One penetrates with wisdom and sees with wisdom! Come, Mallikā, give me the ablution water."[830]

Then King Pasenadi of Kosala rose from his seat, and arranging his upper robe on one shoulder, he extended his hands in reverential salutation towards the Blessed One and uttered this exclamation three times: "Honour to the Blessed One, accomplished and fully enlightened! Honour to the Blessed One, accomplished and fully enlightened! Honour to the Blessed One, accomplished and fully enlightened!"

88 *Bāhitika Sutta*
The Cloak

1. THUS HAVE I HEARD. On one occasion the Blessed One was living at Sāvatthī in Jeta's Grove, Anāthapiṇḍika's Park.

2. Then, when it was morning, the venerable Ānanda dressed, and taking his bowl and outer robe, went into Sāvatthī for alms. When he had wandered for alms in Sāvatthī and had returned from his almsround, after his meal he went to the Eastern Park, to the Palace of Migāra's Mother, for the day's abiding.

3. Now on that occasion King Pasenadi of Kosala had mounted the elephant Ekapuṇḍarīka and was riding out from Sāvatthī at midday. He saw the venerable Ānanda coming in the distance and asked the minister Sirivaḍḍha: "That is the venerable Ānanda, is it not?"—"Yes, sire, that is the venerable Ānanda."

4. Then King Pasenadi of Kosala told a man: "Come, good man, go to the venerable Ānanda and pay homage in my name with your head at his feet, saying: 'Venerable sir, King Pasenadi of Kosala pays homage with his head at the venerable Ānanda's feet.' Then say this: 'Venerable sir, if the venerable Ānanda has no urgent business, perhaps the venerable Ānanda would wait [113] a moment, out of compassion.'"

5. "Yes, sire," the man replied, and he went to the venerable Ānanda, and after paying homage to him, he stood at one side and said to the venerable Ānanda: "Venerable sir, King Pasenadi of Kosala pays homage with his head at the venerable Ānanda's feet and he says this: 'Venerable sir, if the venerable Ānanda has no urgent business, perhaps the venerable Ānanda would wait a moment, out of compassion.'"

6. The venerable Ānanda consented in silence. Then King Pasenadi went by elephant as far as the elephant could go, and then he dismounted and went to the venerable Ānanda on foot. After paying homage to him, he stood at one side and said to the

venerable Ānanda: "If, venerable sir, the venerable Ānanda has no urgent business, it would be good if he would go to the bank of the river Aciravatī, out of compassion."

7. The venerable Ānanda consented in silence. He went to the bank of the river Aciravatī and sat down at the root of a tree on a seat made ready. Then King Pasenadi went by elephant as far as the elephant could go, and then he dismounted and went to the venerable Ānanda on foot. After paying homage to him, he stood at one side and said to the venerable Ānanda: "Here, venerable sir, is an elephant rug. Let the venerable Ānanda be seated on it."

"There is no need, great king. Sit down. I am sitting on my own mat."

8. King Pasenadi of Kosala sat down on a seat made ready and said: "Venerable Ānanda, would the Blessed One behave with the body in such a way that he could be censured by wise recluses and brahmins?"[831]

"No, great king, the Blessed One would not behave with the body in such a way that he could be censured by wise recluses and brahmins." [114]

"Would the Blessed One, venerable Ānanda, behave with speech...behave with the mind in such a way that he could be censured by wise recluses and brahmins?"

"No, great king, the Blessed One would not behave with speech...behave with the mind in such a way that he could be censured by wise recluses and brahmins."

9. "It is wonderful, venerable sir, it is marvellous! For what we were unable to accomplish with a question has been accomplished by the venerable Ānanda with the answer to the question. We do not recognise anything of value in the praise and blame of others spoken by foolish ignorant persons, who speak without having investigated and evaluated; but we recognise as valuable the praise and blame of others spoken by wise, intelligent, and sagacious persons who speak after having investigated and evaluated.

10. "Now, venerable Ānanda, what kind of bodily behaviour is censured by wise recluses and brahmins?"

"Any bodily behaviour that is unwholesome, great king."

"Now, venerable Ānanda, what kind of bodily behaviour is unwholesome?"

"Any bodily behaviour that is blameworthy, great king."

"Now, venerable Ānanda, what kind of bodily behaviour is blameworthy?"

"Any bodily behaviour that brings affliction, great king."

"Now, venerable Ānanda, what kind of bodily behaviour brings affliction?"

"Any bodily behaviour that has painful results, great king."

"Now, venerable Ānanda, what kind of bodily behaviour has painful results?"

"Any bodily behaviour, great king, that leads to one's own affliction, or to the affliction of others, or to the affliction of both, and on account of which unwholesome states increase and wholesome states diminish. Such bodily behaviour is censured by wise recluses and brahmins, great king."[832]

11. "Now, venerable Ānanda, what kind of verbal behaviour is censured by wise recluses and brahmins?"

"Any verbal behaviour that is unwholesome...(*complete as in §10, substituting* "verbal behaviour" *for* "bodily behaviour")..."

12. "Now, venerable Ānanda, what kind of mental behaviour is censured by wise recluses and brahmins?"

"Any mental behaviour that is unwholesome...(*complete as in §10, substituting* "mental behaviour" *for* "bodily behaviour") [115]..."

13. "Now, venerable Ānanda, does the Blessed One praise only the abandoning of all unwholesome states?"

"The Tathāgata, great king, has abandoned all unwholesome states and he possesses wholesome states."[833]

14. "Now, venerable Ānanda, what kind of bodily behaviour is uncensured by wise recluses and brahmins?"

"Any bodily behaviour that is wholesome, great king."

"Now, venerable Ānanda, what kind of bodily behaviour is wholesome?"

"Any bodily behaviour that is blameless, great king."

"Now, venerable Ānanda, what kind of bodily behaviour is blameless?"

"Any bodily behaviour that does not bring affliction, great king."

"Now, venerable Ānanda, what kind of bodily behaviour does not bring affliction?"

"Any bodily behaviour that has pleasant results, great king."

"Now, venerable Ānanda, what kind of bodily behaviour has pleasant results?"

"Any bodily behaviour, great king, that does not lead to one's own affliction, or to the affliction of others, or to the affliction of both, and on account of which unwholesome states diminish and wholesome states increase. Such bodily behaviour, great king, is uncensured by wise recluses and brahmins."

15. "Now, venerable Ānanda, what kind of verbal behaviour is uncensured by wise recluses and brahmins?"

"Any verbal behaviour that is wholesome...(*complete as in §14, substituting* "verbal behaviour" *for* "bodily behaviour")..."

16. "Now, venerable Ānanda, what kind of mental behaviour is uncensured by wise recluses and brahmins?"

"Any mental behaviour that is wholesome...(*complete as in §14, substituting* "mental behaviour" *for* "bodily behaviour") [116]..."

17. "Now, venerable Ānanda, does the Blessed One praise only the undertaking of all wholesome states?"

"The Tathāgata, great king, has abandoned all unwholesome states and possesses wholesome states."

18. "It is wonderful, venerable sir, it is marvellous how well that has been expressed by the venerable Ānanda! And we are satisfied and pleased by what has been so well expressed by him. Venerable sir, we are so satisfied and pleased with what has been so well expressed by the venerable Ānanda that if the elephant-treasure were allowed to him, we would give it to him; if the horse-treasure were allowed to him, we would give it to him; if the boon of a village were allowed to him, we would give it to him. But we know, venerable sir, that these are not allowable for the venerable Ānanda. But there is this cloak of mine,[834] venerable sir, which was sent to me packed in a royal umbrella case by King Ajātasattu of Magadha, sixteen hands long and eight hands wide. Let the venerable Ānanda accept it out of compassion."

"It is not necessary, great king. My triple robe is complete." [117]

19. "Venerable sir, this river Aciravatī has been seen both by the venerable Ānanda and by ourselves when a great cloud has rained heavily on the mountains; then this river Aciravatī overflows both its banks. So too, venerable sir, the venerable Ānanda can make a triple robe for himself out of this cloak, and he can share out his old triple robe among his companions in the holy life. In this way, our offering will overflow. Venerable sir, let the venerable Ānanda accept the cloak."

20. The venerable Ānanda accepted the cloak. Then King Pasenadi of Kosala said: "And now, venerable sir, we depart. We are busy and have much to do."

"You may go, great king, at your own convenience."

Then King Pasenadi of Kosala, having delighted and rejoiced in the venerable Ānanda's words, rose from his seat, and after paying homage to the venerable Ānanda, keeping him on his right, he departed.

21. Then soon after he had left, the venerable Ānanda went to the Blessed One, and after paying homage to him, he sat down at one side, related to him his entire conversation with King Pasenadi of Kosala, and presented the cloak to the Blessed One.

22. Then the Blessed One addressed the bhikkhus: "It is a gain, bhikkhus, for King Pasenadi of Kosala, it is a great gain for King Pasenadi of Kosala that he has had the opportunity of seeing and paying respect to Ānanda."

That is what the Blessed One said. The bhikkhus were satisfied and delighted in the Blessed One's words.

89 *Dhammacetiya Sutta*
Monuments to the Dhamma

[118] 1. THUS HAVE I HEARD. On one occasion the Blessed One was living in the Sakyan country where there was a town of the Sakyans named Medaḷumpa.

2. Now on that occasion King Pasenadi of Kosala had arrived at Nagaraka for some business or other. Then he addressed Dīgha Kārāyaṇa:[835] "Dear Kārāyaṇa, have the state carriages prepared. Let us go to the pleasure garden to see a pleasing spot."

"Yes, sire," Dīgha Kārāyaṇa replied. When the state carriages were prepared, he informed the king: "Sire, the state carriages are ready for you. You may go at your own convenience."

3. Then King Pasenadi mounted a state carriage, and accompanied by the other carriages, he drove out from Nagaraka with the full pomp of royalty and proceeded towards the park. He went thus as far as the road was passable for carriages and then dismounted from his carriage and entered the park on foot.

4. As he walked and wandered in the park for exercise, King Pasenadi saw roots of trees that were lovely and inspiring, quiet and undisturbed by voices, with an atmosphere of seclusion, remote from people, favourable for retreat. The sight of these reminded him of the Blessed One thus: "These roots of trees are lovely and inspiring, quiet and undisturbed by voices, with an atmosphere of seclusion, remote from people, favourable for retreat, like the places where we used to pay respect to the Blessed One, accomplished and fully enlightened." Then he told Dīgha Kārāyaṇa what he had thought and asked: "Where is he living now, [119] the Blessed One, accomplished and fully enlightened?"

5. "There is, sire, a town of the Sakyans named Medaḷumpa. The Blessed One, accomplished and fully enlightened, is now living there."

"How far is it from Nagaraka to Medaḷumpa?"

"It is not far, sire, three leagues.[836] There is still daylight enough to go there."

"Then, dear Kārāyaṇa, have the state carriages prepared. Let us go and see the Blessed One, accomplished and fully enlightened."

"Yes, sire," he replied. When the state carriages were prepared, he informed the king: "Sire, the state carriages are ready for you. You may go at your own convenience."

6. Then King Pasenadi mounted a state carriage, and accompanied by the other carriages, set out from Nagaraka towards the Sakyan town of Medaḷumpa. He arrived there while it was still daylight and proceeded towards the park. He went thus as far as the road was passable for carriages, and then he dismounted from his carriage and entered the park on foot.

7. Now on that occasion a number of bhikkhus were walking up and down in the open. Then King Pasenadi went to them and asked: "Venerable sirs, where is he living now, the Blessed One, accomplished and fully enlightened? We want to see the Blessed One, accomplished and fully enlightened."

8. "That is his dwelling, great king, with the closed door. Go up to it quietly, without hurrying, enter the porch, clear your throat, and tap on the panel. The Blessed One will open the door for you." King Pasenadi handed over his sword and turban to Dīgha Kārāyaṇa then and there. Then Dīgha Kārāyaṇa thought: "So the king is going into secret session now! And I have to wait here alone now!"[837] Without hurrying, King Pasenadi went quietly up to the dwelling with the closed door, entered the porch, cleared his throat, and tapped on the panel. The Blessed One opened the door.

9. Then King Pasenadi [120] entered the dwelling. Prostrating himself with his head at the Blessed One's feet, he covered the Blessed One's feet with kisses and caressed them with his hands, pronouncing his name: "I am King Pasenadi of Kosala, venerable sir; I am King Pasenadi of Kosala, venerable sir."

"But, great king, what reason do you see for doing such supreme honour to this body and for showing such friendship?"

10. "Venerable sir, I infer according to Dhamma about the Blessed One: 'The Blessed One is fully enlightened, the Dhamma is well proclaimed by the Blessed One, the Sangha of the Blessed One's disciples is practising the good way.' Now, venerable sir, I

see some recluses and brahmins leading a limited holy life for ten years, twenty years, thirty years, or forty years, and then on a later occasion I see them well groomed and well anointed, with trimmed hair and beards, enjoying themselves provided and endowed with the five cords of sensual pleasure. But here I see bhikkhus leading the perfect and pure holy life as long as life and breath last. Indeed, I do not see any other holy life elsewhere as perfect and pure as this. This is why, venerable sir, I infer according to Dhamma about the Blessed One: 'The Blessed One is fully enlightened, the Dhamma is well proclaimed by the Blessed One, the Sangha of the Blessed One's disciples is practising the good way.'

11. "Again, venerable sir, kings quarrel with kings, nobles with nobles, brahmins with brahmins, householders with householders; mother quarrels with son, son with mother, father with son, son with father; brother quarrels with brother, brother with sister, sister with brother, friend with friend.[838] But here I see bhikkhus living in concord, with mutual appreciation, without disputing, blending like milk and water, [121] viewing each other with kindly eyes. I do not see any other assembly elsewhere with such concord. This too, venerable sir, is why I infer according to Dhamma about the Blessed One: 'The Blessed One is fully enlightened, the Dhamma is well proclaimed by the Blessed One, the Sangha of the Blessed One's disciples is practising the good way.'

12. "Again, venerable sir, I have walked and wandered from park to park and from garden to garden. There I have seen some recluses and brahmins who are lean, wretched, unsightly, jaundiced, with veins standing out on their limbs, such that people would not want to look at them again. I have thought: 'Surely these venerable ones are leading the holy life in discontent, or they have done some evil deed and are concealing it, so lean and wretched are they...such that people would not want to look at them again.' I went up to them and asked: 'Why are you venerable ones so lean and wretched...such that people would not want to look at you again?' Their reply was: 'It is our family sickness, great king.' But here I see bhikkhus smiling and cheerful, sincerely joyful, plainly delighting, their faculties fresh, living at ease, unruffled, subsisting on what others give, abiding with mind [as aloof] as a wild deer's. I have thought: 'Surely

these venerable ones perceive successive states of lofty distinction in the Blessed One's Dispensation, since they abide thus smiling and cheerful...with mind [as aloof] as a wild deer's.' This too, venerable sir, is why I infer according to Dhamma about the Blessed One: 'The Blessed One is fully enlightened, the Dhamma is well proclaimed by the Blessed One, the Sangha of the Blessed One's disciples is practising the good way.'

13. "Again, venerable sir, being a head-anointed noble king, [122] I am able to have executed those who should be executed, to fine those who should be fined, to exile those who should be exiled. Yet when I am sitting in council, they break in and interrupt me. Though I say: 'Gentlemen, do not break in and interrupt me when I am sitting in council; wait till the end of my speech,' still they break in and interrupt me. But here I see bhikkhus while the Blessed One is teaching the Dhamma[839] to an assembly of several hundred followers and then there is not even the sound of a disciple of the Blessed One coughing or clearing his throat. Once the Blessed One was teaching the Dhamma to an assembly of several hundred followers and there a disciple of his cleared his throat. Thereupon one of his companions in the holy life nudged him with his knee to indicate: 'Be quiet, venerable sir, make no noise; the Blessed One, the Teacher, is teaching us the Dhamma.' I thought: 'It is wonderful, it is marvellous how an assembly can be so well disciplined without force or weapon!' Indeed, I do not see any other assembly elsewhere so well disciplined. This too, venerable sir, is why I infer according to Dhamma about the Blessed One: 'The Blessed One is fully enlightened, the Dhamma is well proclaimed by the Blessed One, the Sangha of the Blessed One's disciples is practising the good way.'

14. "Again, venerable sir, I have seen here certain learned nobles who were clever, knowledgeable about the doctrines of others, as sharp as hairsplitting marksmen;[840] they wander about, as it were, demolishing the views of others with their sharp wits. When they hear: 'The recluse Gotama will visit such and such a village or town,' they formulate a question thus: 'We will go to the recluse Gotama and ask him this question. If he is asked like this, he will answer like this, and so we will refute his doctrine in this way; and if he is asked like that, he will answer like that, and so we will refute his doctrine in that way.' They

hear: 'The recluse Gotama has come to visit such and such a village or town.' They go to the Blessed One, and the Blessed One instructs, urges, rouses, [123] and gladdens them with a talk on the Dhamma. After they have been instructed, urged, roused, and gladdened by the Blessed One with a talk on the Dhamma, they do not so much as ask him the question, so how should they refute his doctrine? In actual fact, they become his disciples. This too, venerable sir, is why I infer according to Dhamma about the Blessed One: 'The Blessed One is fully enlightened, the Dhamma is well proclaimed by the Blessed One, the Sangha of the Blessed One's disciples is practising the good way.'

15. "Again, venerable sir, I have seen here certain learned brahmins...

16. "Again, venerable sir, I have seen here certain learned householders...

17. "Again, venerable sir, I have seen here certain learned recluses...They do not so much as ask him the question, so how should they refute his doctrine? In actual fact, they ask the Blessed One to allow them to go forth from the home life into homelessness, and he gives them the going forth. Not long after they have thus gone forth, dwelling alone, withdrawn, diligent, ardent, and resolute, by realising for themselves with direct knowledge they here and now enter upon and abide in that supreme goal of the holy life for the sake of which clansmen rightly go forth from the home life into homelessness. They say thus: 'We were very nearly lost, we very nearly perished, for formerly we claimed that we were recluses though we were not really recluses; we claimed that we were brahmins though we were not really brahmins; we claimed that we were arahants though we were not really arahants. But now we are recluses, now we are brahmins, now we are arahants.' This too, venerable sir, is why I infer according to Dhamma about the Blessed One: 'The Blessed One is fully enlightened, the Dhamma is well proclaimed by the Blessed One, the Sangha of the Blessed One's disciples is practising the good way.'

18. "Again, venerable sir, Isidatta and Purāṇa,[841] my two inspectors, eat my food and use my carriages; I provide them with a livelihood and bring them fame. Yet in spite of this, they are less respectful towards me [124] than they are towards the Blessed One. Once when I had gone out leading an army and

was testing these inspectors, Isidatta and Purāṇa, I happened to put up in very cramped quarters. Then these two inspectors, Isidatta and Purāṇa, after spending much of the night in talk on the Dhamma, lay down with their heads in the direction where they had heard that the Blessed One was staying and with their feet towards me. I thought: 'It is wonderful, it is marvellous! These two inspectors, Isidatta and Purāṇa, eat my food and use my carriages; I provide them with a livelihood and bring them fame. Yet in spite of this, they are less respectful towards me than they are towards the Blessed One. Surely these good people perceive successive states of lofty distinction in the Blessed One's Dispensation.' This too, venerable sir, is why I infer according to Dhamma about the Blessed One: 'The Blessed One is fully enlightened, the Dhamma is well proclaimed by the Blessed One, the Sangha of the Blessed One's disciples is practising the good way.'

19. "Again, venerable sir, the Blessed One is a noble and I am a noble; the Blessed One is a Kosalan and I am a Kosalan; the Blessed One is eighty years old and I am eighty years old.[842] Since that is so, I think it proper to do such supreme honour to the Blessed One and to show such friendship.

20. "And now, venerable sir, we depart. We are busy and have much to do."

"You may go, great king, at your own convenience."

Then King Pasenadi of Kosala rose from his seat, and after paying homage to the Blessed One, keeping him on his right, he departed.[843]

21. Then soon after he had left, the Blessed One addressed the bhikkhus thus: "Bhikkhus, before rising from his seat and departing, this King Pasenadi uttered monuments to the Dhamma.[844] Learn the monuments to the Dhamma, bhikkhus; master [125] the monuments to the Dhamma; remember the monuments to the Dhamma. The monuments to the Dhamma are beneficial, bhikkhus, and they belong to the fundamentals of the holy life."

That is what the Blessed One said. The bhikkhus were satisfied and delighted in the Blessed One's words.

90 *Kaṇṇakatthala Sutta*
At Kaṇṇakatthala

1. THUS HAVE I HEARD. On one occasion the Blessed One was living at Ujuññā, in the Kaṇṇakatthala Deer Park.

2. Now on that occasion King Pasenadi of Kosala had arrived at Ujuññā for some business or other. Then he told a man: "Come, good man, go to the Blessed One and pay homage in my name with your head at his feet, and ask whether he is free from illness and affliction, and is healthy, strong, and abiding in comfort, saying: 'Venerable sir, King Pasenadi of Kosala pays homage with his head at the Blessed One's feet, and he asks whether the Blessed One is free from illness...and abiding in comfort.' And say this: 'Venerable sir, today King Pasenadi of Kosala will come to see the Blessed One after he has had his breakfast.'"

"Yes, sire," the man replied, and he went to the Blessed One, and after paying homage to him, he sat down at one side and delivered his message.

3. The sisters Somā and Sakulā[845] heard: "Today [126] King Pasenadi of Kosala will go to see the Blessed One after he has had his breakfast."

Then, while the meal was being served, the two sisters went to the king and said: "Sire, pay homage in our name with your head at the Blessed One's feet, and ask whether he is free from illness...and abiding in comfort, saying: 'Venerable sir, the sisters Somā and Sakulā pay homage with their heads at the Blessed One's feet, and they ask whether he is free from illness...and abiding in comfort.'"

4. Then, when he had finished his breakfast, King Pasenadi of Kosala went to the Blessed One, and after paying homage to him, he sat down at one side and delivered the message of the sisters Somā and Sakulā.

"But, great king, could the sisters Somā and Sakulā find no other messenger?"

"Venerable sir, the sisters Somā and Sakulā heard: 'Today King Pasenadi of Kosala will go to see the Blessed One after he has had his breakfast.' Then, while the meal was being served, the sisters Somā and Sakulā came to me and said: 'Sire, pay homage in our names with your head at the Blessed One's feet, and ask whether he is free from illness...and abiding in comfort.'"

"May the sisters Somā and Sakulā be happy, great king."

5. Then King Pasenadi of Kosala said to the Blessed One: "Venerable sir, I have heard this: 'The recluse Gotama says: "There is no recluse or brahmin who is omniscient and all-seeing, who can claim to have complete knowledge and vision; that is not possible."' Venerable sir, do those who speak thus [127] say what has been said by the Blessed One, and not misrepresent him with what is contrary to fact? Do they explain in accordance with the Dhamma in such a way that nothing that provides a ground for censure can be legitimately deduced from their assertions?"

"Great King, those who speak thus do not say what has been said by me, but misrepresent me with what is untrue and contrary to fact."

6. Then King Pasenadi of Kosala addressed General Viḍūḍabha: "General, who introduced this story into the palace?"

"It was Sañjaya, sire, the brahmin of the Ākāsa clan."

7. Then King Pasenadi of Kosala told a man: "Come, good man, in my name tell Sañjaya, the brahmin of the Ākāsa clan: 'Venerable sir, King Pasenadi of Kosala calls you.'"

"Yes, sire," the man replied. He went to Sañjaya, the brahmin of the Ākāsa clan, and told him: "Venerable sir, King Pasenadi of Kosala calls you."

8. Meanwhile King Pasenadi of Kosala said to the Blessed One: "Venerable sir, could something else have been said by the Blessed One referring to that, and the person understood it wrongly? In what way does the Blessed One recall making that utterance?"

"I recall having actually made the utterance in this way, great king: 'There is no recluse or brahmin who knows all, who sees all, simultaneously; that is not possible.'"[846]

"What the Blessed One has said appears reasonable, what the Blessed One has said appears to be supported by reason: 'There is no recluse or brahmin [128] who knows all, who sees all, simultaneously; that is not possible.'"

9. "There are these four castes, venerable sir: the nobles, the brahmins, the merchants, and the workers. Is there any distinction or difference among them?"

"There are these four castes, great king: the nobles, the brahmins, the merchants, and the workers. Two of them, that is, the nobles and the brahmins, are held to be superior since men pay homage to them, rise up for them, and accord them reverential salutation and polite services."

10. "Venerable sir, I was not asking about this present life; I was asking about the life to come.[847] There are these four castes, venerable sir: the nobles, the brahmins, the merchants, and the workers. Is there any distinction or difference among them?"

"Great king, there are these five factors of striving.[848] What five? Here a bhikkhu has faith, he places his faith in the Tathāgata's enlightenment thus: 'The Blessed One is accomplished, fully enlightened, perfect in true knowledge and conduct, sublime, knower of worlds, incomparable leader of persons to be tamed, teacher of gods and humans, enlightened, blessed.' Then he is free from illness and affliction, possessing a good digestion that is neither too cool nor too warm but medium and able to bear the strain of striving. Then he is honest and sincere, and shows himself as he actually is to his teacher and his companions in the holy life. Then he is energetic in abandoning unwholesome states and in undertaking wholesome states, steadfast, launching his effort with firmness and persevering in cultivating wholesome states. Then he is wise; he possesses wisdom regarding rise and disappearance that is noble and penetrative and leads to the complete destruction of suffering. These are the five factors of striving.

"There are these four castes, great king: the nobles, the brahmins, the merchants, and the workers. Now if they possessed these five factors of striving, it would lead to their welfare and happiness for a long time."

11. "Venerable sir, there are these four castes: the nobles, the brahmins, the merchants, [129] and the workers. Now if they possessed these five factors of striving, would there be any difference among them here in that respect?"

"Here, great king, I say that the difference among them would lie in the diversity of their striving. Suppose there were two tamable elephants or tamable horses or tamable oxen that were well tamed and well disciplined, and two tamable elephants or tamable horses or tamable oxen that were untamed and undisciplined. What do you think, great king? Would the two tamable elephants or tamable horses or tamable oxen that were well tamed and well disciplined, being tamed, acquire the behaviour of the tamed, would they arrive at the grade of the tamed?"

"Yes, venerable sir."

"And would the two tamable elephants or tamable horses or tamable oxen that were untamed and undisciplined, being untamed, acquire the behaviour of the tamed, would they arrive at the grade of the tamed, like the two elephants or horses or oxen that were well tamed and well disciplined?"

"No, venerable sir."

"So too, great king, it is not possible that what can be achieved by one who has faith, who is free from illness, who is honest and sincere, who is energetic, and who is wise, can be achieved by one who has no faith, who has much illness, who is fraudulent and deceitful, who is lazy, and who is not wise."

12. "What the Blessed One has said appears reasonable, what the Blessed One has said appears to be supported by reason.

"There are these four castes, venerable sir: the nobles, the brahmins, the merchants, and the workers. Now if they possessed these five factors of striving, and if their striving was right, would there be any difference among them in that respect?"

"Here, great king, in this respect I say that among them there is no difference, that is, between the deliverance of one and the deliverance of the others. Suppose a man took dry sāka wood, lit a fire, and produced heat; and then another man took dry sāla wood, lit a fire, and produced heat; [130] and then another man took dry mango wood, lit a fire, and produced heat; and then another man took dry fig wood, lit a fire, and produced heat. What do you think, great king? Would there be any difference among these fires lit with different kinds of wood, that is, between the flame of one and the flames of the others, or between the colour of one and the colours of the others, or between the radiance of one and the radiances of the others?"

"No, venerable sir."

"So too, great king, when a fire is kindled by energy, lit by striving, there is, I say, no difference, that is, between the deliverance of one and the deliverance of the others."

13. "What the Blessed One has said appears reasonable, what the Blessed One has said appears to be supported by reason. But, venerable sir, how is it: are there gods?"

"Why do you ask that, great king?"

"Venerable sir, I was asking whether those gods come back to this [human] state or whether they do not."

"Great king, those gods who are still subject to affliction come back to this [human] state, those gods who are no longer subject to affliction do not come back to this [human] state."[849]

14. When this was said, General Viḍūḍabha asked the Blessed One: "Venerable sir, can those gods who are still subject to affliction and who come back to this [human] state topple or banish from that place those gods who are no longer subject to affliction and who do not come back to this [human] state?"

Then the venerable Ānanda thought: "This General Viḍūḍabha is the son of King Pasenadi of Kosala, and I am the son of the Blessed One. This is the time for one son to talk with the other." He said to General Viḍūḍabha: "General, I shall ask you a question in return. Answer it as you choose. General, what do you think? There is the whole extent of King Pasenadi of Kosala's realm, where [131] he exercises lordship and sovereignty; now can King Pasenadi of Kosala topple or banish from that place any recluse or brahmin, irrespective of whether that recluse or brahmin has merit or not and whether he leads the holy life or not?"

"He can do so, sir."

"What do you think, general? There is the whole extent that is not King Pasenadi of Kosala's realm, where he does not exercise lordship and sovereignty; now can King Pasenadi of Kosala topple or banish from that place any recluse or brahmin, irrespective of whether that recluse or brahmin has merit or not and whether he leads the holy life or not?"

"He cannot do so, sir."

"General, what do you think? Have you heard of the gods of the Thirty-three?"

"Yes, sir, I have heard of them. And King Pasenadi of Kosala has heard of them too."

"General, what do you think? Can King Pasenadi of Kosala topple the gods of the Thirty-three or banish them from that place?"

"Sir, King Pasenadi of Kosala cannot even see the gods of the Thirty-three, so how could he topple them or banish them from that place?"

"So too, general, those gods who are still subject to affliction and who come back to this [human] state cannot even see those gods who are no longer subject to affliction and who do not come back to this [human] state; so how could they topple them or banish them from that place?"

15. Then King Pasenadi of Kosala asked the Blessed One: "Venerable sir, what is this bhikkhu's name?"

"His name is Ānanda, great king."

"Ānanda [joy] he is indeed, venerable sir, and Ānanda he appears. What [132] the venerable Ānanda has said appears reasonable, what he has said appears to be supported by reason. But, venerable sir, how is it: are there Brahmās?"

"Why do you ask that, great king?"

"Venerable sir, I was asking whether those Brahmās come back to this [human] state or whether they do not."

"Great king, any Brahmā who is still subject to affliction comes back to this [human] state, any Brahmā who is no longer subject to affliction does not come back to this [human] state."

16. Then a man announced to King Pasenadi of Kosala: "Great king, Sañjaya, the brahmin of the Ākāsa clan, has come."

King Pasenadi of Kosala asked Sañjaya, the brahmin of the Ākāsa clan: "Brahmin, who introduced this story to the palace?"

"Sire, it was General Viḍūḍabha."

General Viḍūḍabha said: "Sire, it was Sañjaya, the brahmin of the Ākāsa clan."

17. Then a man announced to King Pasenadi of Kosala: "Sire, it is time to depart."

King Pasenadi of Kosala said to the Blessed One: "Venerable sir, we have asked the Blessed One about omniscience, and the Blessed One has answered about omniscience; we approve of and accept that answer, and so we are satisfied. We have asked the Blessed One about purification in the four castes, and the Blessed One has answered about purification in the four castes; we approve of and accept that answer, and so we are satisfied. We have asked the Blessed One about the gods, and the Blessed

One has answered about the gods; we approve of and accept that answer, and so we are satisfied. We have asked the Blessed One about the Brahmās, and the Blessed One has answered about the Brahmās; we approve of and accept that answer, and so we are satisfied. Whatever we asked the Blessed One, that the Blessed One has answered; we approve of and accept those answers, and so we are satisfied. [133] And now, venerable sir, we depart. We are busy and have much to do."

"You may go, great king, at your own convenience."

18. Then King Pasenadi of Kosala, having delighted and rejoiced in the Blessed One's words, rose from his seat, and after paying homage to the Blessed One, keeping him on his right, he departed.

5

The Division on Brahmins

(*Brāhmaṇavagga*)

91 *Brahmāyu Sutta*
Brahmāyu

1. THUS HAVE I HEARD. On one occasion the Blessed One was wandering in the country of the Videhans with a large Sangha of bhikkhus, with five hundred bhikkhus.

2. Now on that occasion the brahmin Brahmāyu was living at Mithilā. He was old, aged, burdened with years, advanced in life, and come to the last stage; he was in his hundred and twentieth year. He was a master of the Three Vedas with their vocabularies, liturgy, phonology, and etymology, and the histories as a fifth; skilled in philology and grammar, he was fully versed in natural philosophy and in the marks of a Great Man.[850]

3. The brahmin Brahmāyu heard: "The recluse Gotama, the son of the Sakyans who went forth from a Sakyan clan, has been wandering in the country of the Videhans with a large Sangha of bhikkhus, with five hundred bhikkhus. Now a good report of Master Gotama has been spread to this effect: 'The Blessed One is accomplished, fully enlightened, perfect in true knowledge and conduct, sublime, knower of worlds, incomparable leader of persons to be tamed, teacher of gods and humans, enlightened, blessed. He declares this world with its gods, its Māras, and its Brahmās, this generation with its recluses and brahmins, with its princes and its people, which he has himself realised with direct knowledge. He teaches the Dhamma that is good in the beginning, good in the middle, and good in the end, with the right meaning and phrasing, and he reveals a holy life that is utterly perfect and pure.' Now it is good to see such arahants." [134]

4. Now at that time the brahmin Brahmāyu had a young brahmin student named Uttara who was a master of the Three Vedas...fully versed in natural philosophy and in the marks of a Great Man. He told his student: "My dear Uttara, the recluse Gotama, the son of the Sakyans who went forth from a Sakyan

clan, has been wandering in the country of the Videhans with a large Sangha of bhikkhus, with five hundred bhikkhus...Now it is good to see such arahants. Come, my dear Uttara, go to the recluse Gotama and find out whether the report spread about him is true or not, and whether Master Gotama is one such as this or not. Thus we shall know about Master Gotama through you."

5. "But how shall I find out, sir, whether the report spread about Master Gotama is true or not, and whether Master Gotama is one such as this or not?"

"My dear Uttara, the thirty-two marks of a Great Man have been handed down in our hymns, and the Great Man who is endowed with them has only two possible destinies, no other.[851] If he lives the home life, he becomes a Wheel-turning Monarch, a righteous king who rules by the Dhamma, master of the four quarters, all-victorious, who has stabilised his country and possesses the seven treasures. He has these seven treasures: the wheel-treasure, the elephant-treasure, the horse-treasure, the jewel-treasure, the woman-treasure, the steward-treasure, and the counsellor-treasure as the seventh.[852] His children, who exceed a thousand, are brave and heroic, and crush the armies of others; over this earth bounded by the ocean, he rules without a rod, without a weapon, by means of the Dhamma. But if he goes forth from the home life into homelessness, he becomes an Accomplished One, a Fully Enlightened One, who draws aside the veil in the world.[853] But I, my dear Uttara, am the giver of the hymns; you are the receiver of them."

6. "Yes, sir," he replied. He rose from his seat, and after paying homage to the brahmin Brahmāyu, keeping him on his right, he left for the country of the Videhans, where the Blessed One was wandering. [135] Travelling by stages, he came to the Blessed One and exchanged greetings with him. When this courteous and amiable talk was finished, he sat down at one side and looked for the thirty-two marks of a Great Man on the Blessed One's body. He saw, more or less, the thirty-two marks of a Great Man on the Blessed One's body, except two; he was doubtful and uncertain about two of the marks, and he could not decide and make up his mind about them: about the male organ being enclosed in a sheath and about the largeness of the tongue.

Then it occurred to the Blessed One: "This brahmin student Uttara sees, more or less, the thirty-two marks of a Great Man on me, except two; he is doubtful and uncertain about two of the marks, and he cannot decide and make up his mind about them: about the male organ being enclosed in a sheath and about the largeness of the tongue."

7. Then the Blessed One worked such a feat of supernormal power that the brahmin student Uttara saw that the Blessed One's male organ was enclosed in a sheath.[854] Next the Blessed One extruded his tongue, and he repeatedly touched both ear holes and both nostrils, and he covered the whole of his forehead with his tongue.

8. Then the brahmin student Uttara thought: "The recluse Gotama is endowed with the thirty-two marks of a Great Man. Suppose I were to follow the recluse Gotama and observe his behaviour?"

Then he followed the Blessed One for seven months like a shadow, never leaving him. At the end of the seven months in the country of the Videhans, he set out to journey to Mithilā where the brahmin Brahmāyu was. When he arrived, he paid homage to him and sat down at one side. Thereupon, the brahmin Brahmāyu asked him: "Well, my dear Uttara, is the report that has been spread about Master Gotama [136] true or not? And is Master Gotama one such as this or not?"

9. "The report that has been spread about Master Gotama is true, sir, and not otherwise; and Master Gotama is one such as this and not otherwise. He possesses the thirty-two marks of a Great Man.

Master Gotama sets his foot down squarely—this is a mark of a Great Man in Master Gotama.

On the soles of his feet there are wheels with a thousand spokes and ribs and hubs all complete...

He has projecting heels...

He has long fingers and toes...

His hands and feet are soft and tender...

He has netted hands and feet...

His feet are arched...

He has legs like an antelope's...

When he stands without stooping, the palms of both his hands touch and rub against his knees...

His male organ is enclosed in a sheath...

He is the colour of gold, his skin has a golden sheen...

He is fine-skinned, and because of the fineness of his skin, dust and dirt do not stick on his body…

His body-hairs grow singly, each body-hair growing alone in a hair socket…

The tips of his body-hairs turn up; the up-turned body-hairs are blue-black, the colour of collyrium, curled and turned to the right…

He has the straight limbs of a Brahmā…

He has seven convexities…[855]

He has the torso of a lion…

The furrow between his shoulders is filled in…

He has the spread of a banyan tree; the span of his arms equals the height of his body, and the height of his body equals the span of his arms…

His neck and his shoulders are even…

His taste is supremely acute…[856]

He is lion-jawed…[137]

He has forty teeth…

His teeth are even…

His teeth are without gaps…

His teeth are quite white…

He has a large tongue…

He has a divine voice, like the call of the Karavīka bird…

His eyes are deep blue…

He has the eyelashes of an ox…

He has hair growing in the space between his eyebrows, which is white with the sheen of soft cotton…

His head is shaped like a turban—this is a mark of a Great Man in Master Gotama.[857]

Master Gotama is endowed with these thirty-two marks of a Great Man.

10. "When he walks, he steps out with the right foot first. He does not extend his foot too far or put it down too near. He walks neither too quickly nor too slowly. He walks without his knees knocking together. He walks without his ankles knocking together. He walks without raising or lowering his thighs, or bringing them together or keeping them apart. When he walks, only the lower part of his body oscillates, and he does not walk with bodily effort. When he turns to look, he does so with his whole body. He does not look straight up; he does not look

straight down. He does not walk looking about. He looks a plough-yoke's length before him; beyond that he has unhindered knowledge and vision.

11. "When he goes indoors, he does not raise or lower his body, or bend it forward or back. [138] He turns round neither too far from the seat nor too near it. He does not lean on the seat with his hand. He does not throw his body onto the seat.

12. "When seated indoors, he does not fidget with his hands. He does not fidget with his feet. He does not sit with his knees crossed. He does not sit with his ankles crossed. He does not sit with his hand holding his chin. When seated indoors he is not afraid, he does not shiver and tremble, he is not nervous. Being unafraid, not shivering or trembling or nervous, his hair does not stand up and he is intent on seclusion.

13. "When he receives the water for the bowl, he does not raise or lower the bowl or tip it forwards or backwards. He receives neither too little nor too much water for the bowl. He washes the bowl without making a splashing noise. He washes the bowl without turning it round. He does not put the bowl on the floor to wash his hands: when his hands are washed, the bowl is washed; and when the bowl is washed, his hands are washed. He pours the water for the bowl neither too far nor too near and he does not pour it about.

14. "When he receives rice, he does not raise or lower the bowl or tip it forwards or backwards. He receives neither too little rice nor too much rice. He adds sauces in the right proportion; he does not exceed the right amount of sauce in the mouthful. He turns the mouthful over two or three times in his mouth and then swallows it, and no rice kernel enters his body unchewed, and no rice kernel remains in his mouth; then he takes another mouthful. He takes his food experiencing the taste, though not experiencing greed for the taste. The food he takes has eight factors: it is neither for amusement nor for intoxication nor for the sake of physical beauty and attractiveness, but only for the endurance and continuance of his body, for the ending of discomfort, and for assisting the holy life; [139] he considers: 'Thus I shall terminate old feelings without arousing new feelings and I shall be healthy and blameless and shall live in comfort.'[858]

15. "When he has eaten and receives water for the bowl, he does not raise or lower the bowl or tip it forwards or backwards.

He receives neither too little nor too much water for the bowl. He washes the bowl without making a splashing noise. He washes the bowl without turning it round. He does not put the bowl on the floor to wash his hands: when his hands are washed, the bowl is washed; and when the bowl is washed, his hands are washed. He pours the water for the bowl neither too far nor too near and he does not pour it about.

16. "When he has eaten, he puts the bowl on the floor neither too far nor too near; and he is neither careless of the bowl nor over-solicitous about it.

17. "When he has eaten, he sits in silence for a while, but he does not let the time for the blessing go by.[859] When he has eaten and gives the blessing, he does not do so criticising the meal or expecting another meal; he instructs, urges, rouses, and gladdens that audience with talk purely on the Dhamma. When he has done so, he rises from his seat and departs.

18. "He walks neither too fast nor too slow, and he does not go as one who wants to get away.

19. "His robe is worn neither too high nor too low on his body, nor too tight against his body, nor too loose on his body, nor does the wind blow his robe away from his body. Dust and dirt do not soil his body.

20. "When he has gone to the monastery, he sits down on a seat made ready. Having sat down, he washes his feet, though he does not concern himself with grooming his feet. Having washed his feet, he seats himself cross-legged, sets his body erect, and establishes mindfulness in front of him. He does not occupy his mind with self-affliction, or the affliction of others, or the affliction of both; he sits with his mind set on his own welfare, on the welfare of others, and on the welfare of both, even on the welfare of the whole world. [140]

21. "When he has gone to the monastery, he teaches the Dhamma to an audience. He neither flatters nor berates that audience; he instructs, urges, rouses, and encourages it with talk purely on the Dhamma. The speech that issues from his mouth has eight qualities: it is distinct, intelligible, melodious, audible, ringing, euphonious, deep, and sonorous. But while his voice is intelligible as far as the audience extends, his speech does not issue out beyond the audience. When the people have been instructed, urged, roused, and gladdened by him, they rise from

their seats and depart looking only at him and concerned with nothing else.

22. "We have seen Master Gotama walking, sir, we have seen him standing, we have seen him entering indoors, we have seen him indoors seated in silence, we have seen him eating indoors, we have seen him seated in silence after eating, we have seen him giving the blessing after eating, we have seen him going to the monastery, we have seen him in the monastery seated in silence, we have seen him in the monastery teaching the Dhamma to an audience. Such is the Master Gotama; such he is, and more than that."[860]

23. When this was said, the brahmin Brahmāyu rose from his seat, and after arranging his upper robe on one shoulder, he extended his hands in reverential salutation towards the Blessed One and uttered this exclamation three times: "Honour to the Blessed One, accomplished and fully enlightened! Honour to the Blessed One, accomplished and fully enlightened! Honour to the Blessed One, accomplished and fully enlightened! Perhaps sometime or other we might meet Master Gotama, perhaps we might have some conversation with him."

24. Then, in the course of his wandering, the Blessed One eventually arrived at Mithilā. There the Blessed One lived in Makhādeva's Mango Grove. The brahmin householders of Mithilā heard: [141] "The recluse Gotama, the son of the Sakyans who went forth from a Sakyan clan, has been wandering in the country of the Videhans with a large Sangha of bhikkhus, with five hundred bhikkhus, and he has now come to Mithilā and is living in Makhādeva's Mango Grove. Now a good report of Master Gotama has been spread to this effect...(*as in §3 above*)...Now it is good to see such arahants."

25. Then the brahmin householders of Mithilā went to the Blessed One. Some paid homage to the Blessed One and sat down at one side; some exchanged greetings with him, and when this courteous and amiable talk was finished, sat down at one side; some extended their hands in reverential salutation towards him and sat down at one side; some pronounced their name and clan in the Blessed One's presence and sat down at one side; some kept silent and sat down at one side.

26. The brahmin Brahmāyu heard: "The recluse Gotama, the son of the Sakyans who went forth from the Sakyan clan, has

arrived in Mithilā and is living in Makhādeva's Mango Grove in Mithilā."

Then the brahmin Brahmāyu went to Makhādeva's Mango Grove with a number of brahmin students. When he came to the Mango Grove, he thought: "It is not proper that I should go to the recluse Gotama without first being announced." Then he addressed a certain brahmin student: "Come, brahmin student, go to the recluse Gotama and ask in my name whether the recluse Gotama is free from illness and affliction, and is healthy, strong, and abiding in comfort, saying: 'Master Gotama, the brahmin Brahmāyu asks whether Master Gotama is free from illness...abiding in comfort,' and say this: 'The brahmin Brahmāyu, Master Gotama, is old, aged, burdened with years, advanced in life, and come to the last stage; he is in his hundred and twentieth year. He is a master of the Three Vedas with their vocabularies, liturgy, phonology, and etymology, and the histories as a fifth; skilled in philology and grammar, he is fully versed in natural philosophy and in the marks of a Great Man. Of all the brahmin householders who live in Mithilā, the brahmin Brahmāyu is pronounced the foremost of them in wealth, in knowledge of the hymns, [142] and in age and fame. He wants to see Master Gotama.'"

"Yes, sir," the brahmin student replied. He went to the Blessed One and exchanged greetings with him, and when this courteous and amiable talk was finished, he stood at one side and delivered his message. [The Blessed One said:]

"Student, let the brahmin Brahmāyu come at his own convenience."

27. Then the brahmin student went to the brahmin Brahmāyu and said: "Permission has been granted by the recluse Gotama. You may come, sir, at your own convenience."

So the brahmin Brahmāyu went to the Blessed One. The assembly saw him coming in the distance, and they at once made way for him as for one who was well known and famous. Then the brahmin Brahmāyu said to the assembly: "Enough, sirs, let each sit down in his own seat. I shall sit here next to the recluse Gotama."

28. Then he went to the Blessed One and exchanged greetings with him, and when this courteous and amiable talk was finished, he sat down at one side and looked for the thirty-two

marks of a Great Man on the Blessed One's body. [143] He saw, more or less, the thirty-two marks of a Great Man on the Blessed One's body, except two; he was doubtful about two of the marks, and he could not decide and make up his mind about them: about the male organ being enclosed in a sheath and about the largeness of the tongue.

29. Then the brahmin Brahmāyu addressed the Blessed One in stanzas:

> "The two-and-thirty marks I learned
> That are the signs of a Great Man—
> I still do not see two of these
> Upon your body, Gotama.
> Is what should be concealed by cloth
> Hid in a sheath, greatest of men?
> Though called by a word of feminine gender,[861]
> Perhaps your tongue is a manly one?
> Perhaps your tongue is large as well,
> According to what we have been taught?
> Please put it out a little bit
> And so, O Seer, cure our doubt
> For welfare in this very life
> And happiness in lives to come.
> And now we crave for leave to ask
> Something that we aspire to know."

30. Then it occurred to the Blessed One: "This brahmin Brahmāyu sees, more or less, the thirty-two marks of a Great Man on me, except two; he is doubtful and uncertain about two of the marks, and he cannot decide and make up his mind about them: about the male organ being enclosed in a sheath and about the largeness of the tongue."

Then the Blessed One worked such a feat of supernormal power that the brahmin Brahmāyu saw that the Blessed One's male organ was enclosed in a sheath. Next the Blessed One extruded his tongue, and he repeatedly touched both ear holes and both nostrils, and he covered the whole of his forehead with his tongue.

31. Then the Blessed One spoke these stanzas in reply to the brahmin Brahmāyu:

"The two-and-thirty marks you learned
That are the signs of a Great Man—
All on my body can be found:
So, brahmin, doubt no more on that.

What must be known is directly known,
What must be developed has been developed,
What must be abandoned has been abandoned,
Therefore, brahmin, I am a Buddha.[862] [144]

For welfare in this very life
And happiness in lives to come,
Since leave is given you, please ask
Whatever you aspire to know."

32. Then the brahmin Brahmāyu thought: "Permission has been granted me by the recluse Gotama. Which should I ask him about: good in this life or good in the lives to come?" Then he thought: "I am skilled in the good of this life, and others too ask me about good in this life. Why shouldn't I ask him only about good in the lives to come?" Then he addressed the Blessed One in stanzas:

"How does one become a brahmin?
And how does one attain to knowledge?[863]
How has one the triple knowledge?
And how is one called a holy scholar?
How does one become an arahant?
And how does one attain completeness?
How is one a silent sage?
And how is one called a Buddha?"[864]

33. Then the Blessed One spoke these stanzas in reply:

"Who knows about his former lives,
Sees heaven and states of deprivation,
And has arrived at birth's destruction—
A sage who knows by direct knowledge,
Who knows his mind is purified,
Entirely freed from every lust,

Who has abandoned birth and death,
Who is complete in the holy life,
Who has transcended everything—
One such as this is called a Buddha."[865]

34. When this was said, the brahmin Brahmāyu rose from his seat, and after arranging his upper robe on one shoulder, he prostrated himself with his head at the Blessed One's feet, and he covered the Blessed One's feet with kisses and caressed them with his hands, pronouncing his name: "I am the brahmin Brahmāyu, Master Gotama; I am the brahmin Brahmāyu, Master Gotama."

35. Those in the assembly wondered and marvelled, and they said: "It is wonderful, sirs, it is marvellous, what great power and great might the recluse Gotama has, for the well-known and famous brahmin Brahmāyu to make such a display of humility!"

Then the Blessed One said to the brahmin Brahmāyu: [145] "Enough, brahmin, arise; sit down in your own seat since your mind has confidence in me."

The brahmin Brahmāyu then rose and sat down in his own seat.

36. The Blessed One then gave him progressive instruction,[866] that is, talk on giving, talk on virtue, talk on the heavens; he explained the danger, degradation, and defilement in sensual pleasures and the blessing of renunciation. When he knew that the brahmin Brahmāyu's mind was ready, receptive, free from hindrances, elated, and confident, he expounded to him the teaching special to the Buddhas: suffering, its origin, its cessation, and the path. Just as a clean cloth with all marks removed would take dye evenly, so too, while the brahmin Brahmāyu sat there, the spotless immaculate vision of the Dhamma arose in him: "All that is subject to arising is subject to cessation." Then the brahmin Brahmāyu saw the Dhamma, attained the Dhamma, understood the Dhamma, fathomed the Dhamma; he crossed beyond doubt, did away with perplexity, gained intrepidity, and became independent of others in the Teacher's Dispensation.

37. Then he said to the Blessed One: "Magnificent, Master Gotama! Magnificent, Master Gotama! Master Gotama has made the Dhamma clear in many ways, as though he were turning upright what had been overthrown, revealing what was hidden,

showing the way to one who was lost, or holding up a lamp in the dark for those with eyesight to see forms. I go to Master Gotama for refuge and to the Dhamma and to the Sangha of bhikkhus. From today let Master Gotama remember me as a lay follower who has gone to him for refuge for life. Let the Blessed One, together with the Sangha of bhikkhus, consent to accept tomorrow's meal from me."

The Blessed One consented in silence. Then, knowing that the Blessed One had consented, the brahmin Brahmāyu rose from his seat, and after paying homage to the Blessed One, keeping him on his right, he departed.

38. Then, when the night had ended, the brahmin Brahmāyu had good food of various kinds prepared in his residence, and he had the time announced to the Blessed One: "It is time, Master Gotama, the meal is ready." [146]

Then, it being morning, the Blessed One dressed, and taking his bowl and outer robe, he went with the Sangha of bhikkhus to the brahmin Brahmāyu's residence and sat down on the seat made ready. Then, for a week, with his own hands, the brahmin Brahmāyu served and satisfied the Sangha of bhikkhus headed by the Buddha with various kinds of good food.

39. At the end of that week, the Blessed One set out to wander in the country of the Videhans. Soon after he had gone, the brahmin Brahmāyu died. Then a number of bhikkhus went to the Blessed One, and after paying homage to him, they sat down at one side and said: "Venerable sir, the brahmin Brahmāyu has died. What is his destination? What is his future course?"

"Bhikkhus, the brahmin Brahmāyu was wise, he entered into the way of the Dhamma, and he did not trouble me in the interpretation of the Dhamma. With the destruction of the five lower fetters, he has reappeared spontaneously [in the Pure Abodes] and will there attain final Nibbāna, without ever returning from that world."

That is what the Blessed One said. The bhikkhus were satisfied and delighted in the Blessed One's words.

92 *Sela Sutta*
To Sela

1. THUS HAVE I HEARD.[867] On one occasion the Blessed One was wandering in the country of the Anguttarāpans with a large Sangha of bhikkhus, [102] with twelve hundred and fifty bhikkhus, and eventually he arrived at a town of the Anguttarāpans named Āpaṇa.

2. The matted-hair ascetic Keṇiya heard: "The recluse Gotama, the son of the Sakyans who went forth from a Sakyan clan, has been wandering in the country of the Anguttarāpans with a large Sangha of bhikkhus, with twelve hundred and fifty [103] bhikkhus, and he has come to Āpaṇa. Now a good report of Master Gotama has been spread to this effect...(*as Sutta 91, §3*)...Now it is good to see such arahants."

3. Then the matted-hair ascetic Keṇiya went to the Blessed One and exchanged greetings with him, and when this courteous and amiable talk was finished, he sat down at one side. The Blessed One instructed, urged, roused, and gladdened him with a talk on the Dhamma. Then, having been instructed, urged, roused, and gladdened by the Blessed One with a talk on the Dhamma, the matted-hair ascetic Keṇiya said to the Blessed One: "Let Master Gotama together with the Sangha of bhikkhus consent to accept tomorrow's meal from me."

When this was said, the Blessed One told him: "The Sangha of bhikkhus is large, Keṇiya, [104] consisting of twelve hundred and fifty bhikkhus, and you place full confidence in the brahmins."

A second time the matted-hair ascetic Keṇiya said to the Blessed One: "Although the Sangha of bhikkhus is large, Master Gotama, consisting of twelve hundred and fifty bhikkhus, and although I place full confidence in the brahmins, still let Master Gotama, together with the Sangha of bhikkhus, consent to accept tomorrow's meal from me." A second time the Blessed One told him: "The Sangha of bhikkhus is large, Keṇiya..."

A third time the matted-hair ascetic Keṇiya said to the Blessed One: "Although the Sangha is large, Master Gotama...still let Master Gotama together with the Sangha of bhikkhus consent to accept tomorrow's meal from me." The Blessed One consented in silence.

4. Then, knowing that the Blessed One had consented, the matted-hair ascetic Keṇiya rose from his seat and went to his own hermitage where he addressed his friends and companions, his kinsmen and relatives thus: "Hear me, sirs, my friends and companions, my kinsmen and relatives. The recluse Gotama has been invited by me for tomorrow's meal together with the Sangha of bhikkhus. Make the necessary purchases and preparations for me."

"Yes, sir," they replied, and some dug out ovens, some chopped wood, some washed dishes, some set out water jugs, some prepared seats, while the matted-hair ascetic Keṇiya himself set up a pavilion.

5. Now on that occasion the brahmin Sela was staying at Āpaṇa. [105] He was a master of the Three Vedas with their vocabularies, liturgy, phonology, and etymology, and the histories as a fifth; skilled in philology and grammar, he was fully versed in natural philosophy and in the marks of a Great Man, and was teaching the recitation of the hymns to three hundred brahmin students.

6. At the time the matted-hair ascetic Keṇiya had placed full confidence in the brahmin Sela. Then the brahmin Sela, while walking and wandering for exercise attended by his three hundred brahmin students, came to the matted-hair ascetic Keṇiya's hermitage. There he saw some men digging out ovens, some chopping wood, some washing dishes, some setting out water jugs, some preparing seats, while the matted-hair ascetic Keṇiya himself was setting up a pavilion.

7. When he saw this, he asked the matted-hair ascetic Keṇiya: "What, is Master Keṇiya to hold a marriage or a giving in marriage? Or is there some great sacrifice? Or has King Seniya Bimbisāra of Magadha been invited with a large retinue for tomorrow's meal?"

8. "I will not be holding a marriage or a giving in marriage,

Master Sela, nor has King Seniya Bimbisāra of Magadha been invited with a large retinue for tomorrow's meal, but I am planning a great sacrifice. The recluse Gotama, the son of the Sakyans who went forth from a Sakyan clan, has been wandering in the country of the Anguttarāpans with a large Sangha of bhikkhus, with twelve hundred and fifty bhikkhus, and has come to Āpaṇa. [106] Now a good report of Master Gotama has been spread to this effect: 'That Blessed One is accomplished, fully enlightened, perfect in true knowledge and conduct, sublime, knower of worlds, incomparable leader of persons to be tamed, teacher of gods and humans, enlightened [*buddha*], blessed.' He has been invited by me for tomorrow's meal together with the Sangha of bhikkhus."

9. "Did you say 'Buddha,' Keṇiya?"

"I said 'Buddha,' Sela."

"Did you say 'Buddha,' Keṇiya?"

"I said 'Buddha,' Sela."

10. Then it occurred to the brahmin Sela: "Even this sound 'Buddha' is hard to come across in this world. Now the thirty-two marks of a Great Man have been handed down in our hymns, and the Great Man who is endowed with them has only two possible destinies, no other. If he lives the home life he becomes a Wheel-turning Monarch, a righteous king who rules by the Dhamma, master of the four quarters, all-victorious, who has stabilised his country and possesses the seven treasures. He has these seven treasures: the wheel-treasure, the elephant-treasure, the horse-treasure, the jewel-treasure, the woman-treasure, the steward-treasure, and the counsellor-treasure as the seventh. His children, who exceed a thousand, are brave and heroic and crush the armies of others; over this earth bounded by the ocean he rules without a rod, without a weapon, by means of the Dhamma. But if he goes forth from the home life into homelessness, he becomes an Accomplished One, a Fully Enlightened One, who draws aside the veil in the world."

11. [He said]: "My good Keṇiya, where is Master Gotama, the Accomplished One, the Fully Enlightened One, now living?"

When this was said, the matted-hair ascetic Keṇiya extended his right arm and said: [107] "There, where that green line of the grove is, Master Sela."

12. Then the brahmin Sela went with the three hundred brahmin

students to the Blessed One. He addressed the brahmin students: "Come quietly, sirs, tread carefully; for these Blessed Ones are difficult to approach, they wander alone like lions. When I am speaking with the recluse Gotama, do not break in and interrupt me, but wait until our talk is finished."

13. Then the brahmin Sela went to the Blessed One and exchanged greetings with him. When this courteous and amiable talk was finished, he sat down at one side and looked for the thirty-two marks of a Great Man on the Blessed One's body. He saw, more or less, the thirty-two marks of a Great Man on the Blessed One's body, except two; he was doubtful and uncertain about two of the marks, and he could not decide and make up his mind about them: about the male organ being enclosed in a sheath and about the largeness of the tongue.

Then it occurred to the Blessed One: "This brahmin Sela sees the thirty-two marks of a Great Man on me, except two; he is doubtful and uncertain about two of the marks, and he cannot decide and make up his mind about them: about the male organ being enclosed in a sheath and about the largeness of the tongue."

14. Then the Blessed One worked such a feat of supernormal power that the brahmin Sela saw that the Blessed One's male organ was enclosed in a sheath. [108] Next the Blessed One extruded his tongue, and he repeatedly touched both ear holes and both nostrils, and he covered the whole of his forehead with his tongue.

15. Then the brahmin Sela thought: "The recluse Gotama is endowed with the thirty-two marks of a Great Man; they are complete, not incomplete. But I do not know whether he is a Buddha or not. However, I have heard from elder aged brahmins who speak according to the lineage of teachers that those who are the Accomplished Ones, Fully Enlightened Ones, reveal themselves as such when their praise is spoken. Suppose I extol the recluse Gotama to his face with fitting stanzas."

Then he extolled the Blessed One to his face with fitting stanzas:

16. *Sela*

"O perfect in body, well favoured,
Well fashioned and lovely to behold;
O Blessed One, golden is your colour,
And white your teeth; you are strong.
The features are seen one and all

That distinguish a man as well born;
They are all to be found on your body,
These marks that reveal a Great Man.
With eyes clear, with countenance bright,
Majestic, erect as a flame,
In the midst of this body of recluses
You shine like the blazing sun.
A bhikkhu so lovely to look on
With skin of so golden a sheen—
With beauty so rare why should you
Be content with the life of a recluse?
You are fit to be a king, a lord of chariots,
A monarch who makes the wheel turn,
A victor in all the four quarters
And lord of the Jambu-tree Grove.[868] [109]
With warriors and great princes
All devoted to your service,
O Gotama, you should reign
As ruler of men, king above all kings."

17. *Buddha*
"I am already a king, O Sela,"
the Blessed One replied.
"I am supreme king of the Dhamma,
I make the Wheel of Dhamma revolve,
The wheel that none can stop."

18. *Sela*
"You claim full enlightenment," the brahmin Sela said,
"You tell me, O Gotama,
'I am supreme king of the Dhamma,
I make the Wheel of Dhamma revolve.'

Who is your general, that disciple
Who follows in the Master's own way?
Who is it who helps you to turn
The wheel set in motion by you?"

19. *Buddha*
"The wheel set in motion by me,"

The Blessed One replied,
"That same supreme Wheel of Dhamma,
Sāriputta the Tathāgata's son
Helps me in turning this wheel.

What must be known is directly known,
What must be developed has been developed,
What must be abandoned has been abandoned,
Therefore, brahmin, I am a Buddha.

So let your doubts about me cease
And let resolution take their place,
For it is always hard to gain
Sight of the Enlightened Ones. [110]

I am the one whose presence in the world
Is very rarely come upon,
I am the Fully Enlightened One,
I, O brahmin, am the supreme physician.

I am the holy one beyond compare
Who has crushed all Māra's teeming hordes;
Having defeated all my enemies,
I rejoice free from fear."

20. *Sela*
"O sirs, hear this, hear what he says,
The man of vision, the physician,
The mighty hero who roars
Like a lion in the forest.

Who, even though of outcast birth,
Would not believe him when he saw
That he is the holy one beyond compare
Who has crushed all Māra's teeming hordes?

Now let him follow me who wants
And who wants not, let him depart.
For I will go forth under him,
This man of lofty wisdom."

21. *Pupils*
"If, O sir, you now approve
This teaching of the Enlightened One,
We too will go forth under him,
This man of lofty wisdom."

22. *Sela*
"There are three hundred brahmins here
Who with uplifted hands implore:
'O may we live the holy life
Under you, O Blessed One.'"

23. *Buddha*
"The holy life is well proclaimed,
O Sela," said the Blessed One,
"To be seen here and not delayed;
One who trains with diligence
Will find a fruitful going forth."

24. Then the brahmin Sela and his assembly received the going forth under the Blessed One, and they received the full admission.

25. Then, when the night had ended, the matted-hair ascetic Keṇiya had good food of various kinds prepared in his own hermitage [111] and had the time announced to the Blessed One: "It is time, Master Gotama, the meal is ready." Then, it being morning, the Blessed One dressed, and taking his bowl and outer robe, he went with the Sangha of bhikkhus to the hermitage of the matted-hair ascetic Keṇiya and sat down on the seat made ready. Then, with his own hands, the matted-hair ascetic Keṇiya served and satisfied the Sangha of bhikkhus headed by the Buddha with various kinds of good food. When the Blessed One had eaten and had put his bowl aside, the matted-hair ascetic Keṇiya took a low seat and sat down on one side. Thereupon the Blessed One gave him his blessing with these stanzas:

26. "Burnt offerings are the glory of fires,
Sāvitrī the glory of Vedic hymns,
Glory of human beings, a king,
Glory of flowing rivers, the sea;

The moon is the glory of the stars,
The sun is the glory of all that shine;
Merit is the glory of all who aspire;
The Sangha, glory of those who give."

When the Blessed One had given his blessing with these stanzas, he rose from his seat and departed.

27. Then, not long after their full admission, dwelling alone, withdrawn, diligent, ardent, and resolute, the venerable Sela and his assembly, [112] by realising for themselves with direct knowledge, here and now entered upon and abided in that supreme goal of the holy life for the sake of which clansmen rightly go forth from the home life into homelessness. They directly knew: "Birth is destroyed, the holy life has been lived, what had to be done has been done, there is no more coming to any state of being." And the venerable Sela together with his assembly became arahants.

28. Then the venerable Sela together with his assembly went to the Blessed One. Having arranged his upper robe on one shoulder, extending his hands in reverential greeting towards the Blessed One, he addressed him with these stanzas:

"Eight days have passed, All-Seeing One,
Since we went to you for refuge.
In these seven nights, O Blessed One,
We have been tamed in your teaching.

You are the Buddha, you are the Teacher,
You are the Sage, the conqueror of Māra.
Having cut off all evil tendencies,
You have crossed and guide humanity across.

You have surmounted all acquisitions,
You have removed all the taints.
You are a lion free from clinging,
You have abandoned fear and dread.

Here these three hundred bhikkhus stand
With hands held out in adoration.
O Hero, extend your feet,
And let these great beings worship the Teacher."

93 *Assalāyana Sutta*
To Assalāyana

[147] 1. THUS HAVE I HEARD. On one occasion the Blessed One was living at Sāvatthī in Jeta's Grove, Anāthapiṇḍika's Park.

2. Now at that time five hundred brahmins from diverse provinces were staying at Sāvatthī for some business or other. Then those brahmins thought: "This recluse Gotama describes purification for all the four castes.[869] Who is there able to dispute with him about this assertion?"

3. Now on that occasion a brahmin student named Assalāyana was staying at Sāvatthī. Young, shaven-headed, sixteen years old, he was a master of the Three Vedas with their vocabularies, liturgy, phonology, and etymology, and the histories as a fifth; skilled in philology and grammar, he was fully versed in natural philosophy and in the marks of a Great Man. Then the brahmins thought: "There is this young brahmin student named Assalāyana staying at Sāvatthī. Young...fully versed in natural philosophy and in the marks of a Great Man. He will be able to dispute with the recluse Gotama about this assertion."

4. So the brahmins went to the brahmin student Assalāyana and said to him: "Master Assalāyana, this recluse Gotama describes purification for all the four castes. Let Master Assalāyana come and dispute with the recluse Gotama about this assertion."

When this was said, the brahmin student Assalāyana replied: "Sirs, the recluse Gotama is one who speaks the Dhamma. Now those who speak the Dhamma are difficult to dispute with. I am not able to dispute with the recluse Gotama about this assertion."

A second time the brahmins said to him: "Master Assalāyana, this recluse Gotama describes purification for all the four castes. Let Master Assalāyana come [148] and dispute with the recluse Gotama about this assertion. For the training of a wanderer has been completed by Master Assalāyana."[870]

For the second time the brahmin student Assalāyana replied: "Sirs, the recluse Gotama is one who speaks the Dhamma. Now those who speak the Dhamma are difficult to dispute with. I am not able to dispute with the recluse Gotama about this assertion."

A third time the brahmins said to him: "Master Assalāyana, this recluse Gotama describes purification for all the four castes. Let Master Assalāyana come and dispute with the recluse Gotama about this assertion. For the training of a wanderer has been completed by Master Assalāyana. Let not the Master Assalāyana be defeated without having even fought the battle."

When this was said, the brahmin student Assalāyana replied: "Surely, Sirs, I am not getting through to you when I say: 'The recluse Gotama is one who speaks the Dhamma.' Now those who speak the Dhamma are difficult to dispute with. I am not able to dispute with the recluse Gotama about this assertion. Still, sirs, at your bidding I will go."

5. Then the brahmin student Assalāyana went with a large number of brahmins to the Blessed One and exchanged greetings with him. When this courteous and amiable talk was finished, he sat down at one side and said to the Blessed One: "Master Gotama, the brahmins say thus: 'Brahmins are the highest caste, those of any other caste are inferior; brahmins are the fairest caste, those of any other caste are dark; only brahmins are purified, not non-brahmins; brahmins alone are the sons of Brahmā, the offspring of Brahmā, born of his mouth, born of Brahmā, created by Brahmā, heirs of Brahmā.' What does Master Gotama say about that?"

"Now, Assalāyana, the brahmin women are seen having their periods, becoming pregnant, giving birth, and giving suck.[871] And yet those brahmins, though born from the womb, say thus: 'Brahmins are the highest caste...brahmins alone are the sons of Brahmā, the offspring of Brahmā, born of his mouth, born of Brahmā, created by Brahmā, heirs of Brahmā.'" [149]

6. "Although Master Gotama says this, still the brahmins think thus: 'Brahmins are the highest caste...heirs of Brahmā.'"

"What do you think, Assalāyana? Have you heard that in Yona and Kamboja[872] and in other outland countries there are only two castes, masters and slaves, and that masters become slaves and slaves masters?"

"So I have heard, sir."

"Then on the strength of what [argument] or with the support of what [authority] do the brahmins in this case say thus: 'Brahmins are the highest caste...heirs of Brahmā'?"

7. "Although Master Gotama says this, still the brahmins think thus: 'Brahmins are the highest caste...heirs of Brahmā.'"

"What do you think, Assalāyana?[873] Suppose a noble were to kill living beings, take what is not given, misconduct himself in sensual pleasures, speak falsely, speak maliciously, speak harshly, gossip, be covetous, have a mind of ill will, and hold wrong view. On the dissolution of the body, after death, would only he [be likely to] reappear in a state of deprivation, in an unhappy destination, in perdition, even in hell—and not a brahmin? Suppose a merchant...a worker were to kill living beings...and hold wrong view. On the dissolution of the body after death, would only he [be likely to] reappear in a state of deprivation, in an unhappy destination, in perdition, even in hell—and not a brahmin?"

"No, Master Gotama. Whether it be a noble, or a brahmin, or a merchant, or a worker—those of all four castes who kill living beings [150]...and hold wrong view, on the dissolution of the body, after death, [are likely to] reappear in a state of deprivation, in an unhappy destination, in perdition, even in hell."

"Then on the strength of what [argument] or with the support of what [authority] do the brahmins in this case say thus: 'Brahmins are the highest caste...heirs of Brahmā'?"

8. "Although Master Gotama says this, still the brahmins think thus: 'Brahmins are the highest caste...heirs of Brahmā.'"

"What do you think, Assalāyana? Suppose a brahmin were to abstain from killing living beings, from taking what is not given, from misconduct in sensual pleasures, from false speech, from malicious speech, from harsh speech, and from gossip, and were to be uncovetous, to have a mind without ill will, and to hold right view. On the dissolution of the body, after death, would only he [be likely to] reappear in a happy destination, even in the heavenly world—and not a noble, or a merchant, or a worker?"

"No, Master Gotama. Whether it be a noble, or a brahmin, or a merchant, or a worker—those of all four castes who abstain from killing living beings...and hold right view, on the dissolution of the body, after death, [are likely to] reappear in a happy destination, even in the heavenly world."

"Then on the strength of what [argument] or with the support of what [authority] do the brahmins in this case say thus: 'Brahmins are the highest caste...heirs of Brahmā'?"

9. "Although Master Gotama says this, [151] still the brahmins think thus: 'Brahmins are the highest caste...heirs of Brahmā.'"

"What do you think, Assalāyana? Is only a brahmin capable of developing a mind of loving-kindness towards a certain region, without hostility and without ill will, and not a noble, or a merchant, or a worker?"

"No, Master Gotama. Whether it be a noble, or a brahmin, or a merchant, or a worker—those of all four castes are capable of developing a mind of loving-kindness towards a certain region, without hostility and without ill will."

"Then on the strength of what [argument] or with the support of what [authority] do the brahmins in this case say thus: 'Brahmins are the highest caste...heirs of Brahmā'?"

10. "Although Master Gotama says this, still the brahmins think thus: 'Brahmins are the highest caste...heirs of Brahmā.'"

"What do you think, Assalāyana? Is only a brahmin capable of taking a loofah and bath powder, going to the river, and washing off dust and dirt, and not a noble, or a merchant, or a worker?"

"No, Master Gotama. Whether it be a noble, or a brahmin, or a merchant, or a worker—those of all four castes are capable of taking a loofah and bath powder, going to the river, and washing off dust and dirt."

"Then on the strength of what [argument] or with the support of what [authority] do the brahmins in this case say thus: 'Brahmins are the highest caste...heirs of Brahmā'?"

11. "Although Master Gotama says this, still the brahmins think thus: 'Brahmins are the highest caste...heirs of Brahmā.'"

"What do you think, Assalāyana? [152] Suppose a head-anointed noble king were to assemble here a hundred men of different birth and say to them: 'Come, sirs, let any here who have been born into a noble clan or a brahmin clan or a royal clan take an upper fire-stick of sāla wood, salala wood, sandalwood, or padumaka wood and light a fire and produce heat. And also let any who have been born into an outcast clan, a trapper clan, a wicker workers' clan, a cartwrights' clan, or a scavengers' clan take an upper fire-stick made from a dog's drinking trough, from a pig's trough, from a dustbin, or from castor-oil wood and light a fire and produce heat.'

"What do you think, Assalāyana? When a fire is lit and heat is produced by someone in the first group, would that fire have a flame, a colour, and a radiance, and would it be possible to use it for the purposes of fire, while when a fire is lit and heat is produced by someone of the second group, that fire would have no flame, no colour, and no radiance, and it would not be possible to use it for the purposes of fire?"

"No, Master Gotama. When a fire is lit and heat is produced by someone in the first group, that fire would have a flame, a colour, and a radiance, and it would be possible to use it for the purposes of fire. And when a fire is lit and heat is produced by someone of the second group, that fire too would have a flame, a colour, and a radiance, and it would be possible to use it for the purposes of fire. For all fire has a flame, [153] a colour, and a radiance, and it is possible to use all fire for the purposes of fire."

"Then on the strength of what [argument] or with the support of what [authority] do the brahmins in this case say thus: 'Brahmins are the highest caste...heirs of Brahmā'?"

12. "Although Master Gotama says this, still the brahmins think thus: 'Brahmins are the highest caste...heirs of Brahmā.'"

"What do you think, Assalāyana? Suppose a noble youth were to cohabit with a brahmin girl, and a son was born from their cohabitation. Should a son born from a noble youth and a brahmin girl be called a noble after the father or a brahmin after the mother?"

"He could be called both, Master Gotama."

13. "What do you think, Assalāyana? Suppose a brahmin youth here were to cohabit with a noble girl, and a son were to be born from their cohabitation. Should the son born from a brahmin youth and a noble girl be called a noble after the mother or a brahmin after the father?"

"He could be called both, Master Gotama."

14. "What do you think, Assalāyana? Suppose a mare were to be mated with a male donkey, and a foal were to be born as the result. Should the foal be called a horse after the mother or a donkey after the father?"

"It is a mule, Master Gotama, since it does not belong to either kind. [154] I see the difference in this last case, but I see no difference in either of the former cases."

15. "What do you think, Assalāyana? Suppose there were two

brahmin students who were brothers, born of the same mother, one studious and acute, and one neither studious nor acute. Which of them would brahmins feed first at a funeral feast, or at a ceremonial milk-rice offering, or at a sacrificial feast, or at a feast for guests?"

"On such occasions, brahmins would feed first the one who was studious and acute, Master Gotama; for how could what is given to one who is neither studious nor acute bring great fruit?"

16. "What do you think, Assalāyana? Suppose there were two brahmin students who were brothers, born of the same mother, one studious and acute, but immoral and of bad character, and one neither studious nor acute, but virtuous and of good character. Which of them would brahmins feed first at a funeral feast, or at a ceremonial milk-rice offering, or at a sacrificial feast, or at a feast for guests?"

"On such occasions, brahmins would feed first the one who was neither studious nor acute, but virtuous and of good character, Master Gotama; for how could what is given to one who is immoral and of bad character bring great fruit?"

17. "First, Assalāyana, you took your stand on birth, and after that you took your stand on scriptural learning, and after that you have come to take your stand on the very ground that purification is for all four castes, as I describe it."

When this was said, the brahmin student Assalāyana sat silent and dismayed, with shoulders drooping and head down, glum, and without response. Knowing this, the Blessed One said to him:

18. "Once, Assalāyana, when seven brahmin seers were dwelling in leaf huts in the forest, this pernicious view arose in them: 'Brahmins are the highest caste…[155]…heirs of Brahmā.' Now the seer Devala the Dark heard this.[874] Then he arranged his hair and beard, dressed in ochre-coloured garments, put on stout sandals, and taking a staff made of gold, he appeared in the courtyard of the seven brahmin seers. Then, while walking up and down the courtyard of the seven brahmin seers, the seer Devala the Dark spoke thus: 'Where have those worthy brahmin seers gone? Where have those worthy brahmin seers gone?' Then the seven brahmin seers thought: 'Who is walking up and down in the courtyard of the seven brahmin seers like a village lout speaking thus: "Where have those worthy brahmin seers

gone? Where have those worthy brahmin seers gone?" Let us curse him!' Then the seven brahmin seers cursed the seer Devala the Dark thus: 'Be ashes, vile one! Be ashes, vile one!' But the more the seven brahmin seers cursed him, the more comely, beautiful, and handsome the seer Devala the Dark became. Then the seven brahmin seers thought: 'Our asceticism is in vain, our holy life is fruitless; for formerly when we cursed anyone thus: "Be ashes, vile one! Be ashes, vile one!" he always became ashes; but the more we curse this one, the more comely, beautiful, and handsome he becomes.'

"'Your asceticism is not in vain, sirs, your holy life is not fruitless. But, sirs, put away your hatred towards me.' [156]

"'We have put away our hatred towards you, sir. Who are you?'

"'Have you heard of the seer Devala the Dark, sirs?'—'Yes, sir.'—'I am he, sirs.'

"Then the seven brahmin seers went to the seer Devala the Dark and paid homage to him. Then he said to them: 'Sirs, I heard that while the seven brahmin seers were dwelling in leaf huts in the forest, this pernicious view arose in them: "Brahmins are the highest caste...heirs of Brahmā."'—'That is so, sir.'

"'But, sirs, do you know if the mother who bore you went only with a brahmin and never with a non-brahmin?'—'No, sir.'

"'But, sirs, do you know if your mother's mothers back to the seventh generation went only with brahmins and never with non-brahmins?'—'No, sir.'

"'But, sirs, do you know if the father who begot you went only with a brahmin woman and never with a non-brahmin woman?'—'No, sir.'

"'But, sirs, do you know if your father's fathers back to the seventh generation went only with brahmin women and never with non-brahmin women?'—'No, sir.'

"'But, sirs, do you know how the descent of an embryo comes about?'

"'Sir, we know how the descent of an embryo comes about. [157] Here, there is the union of the mother and father, and the mother is in season, and the *gandhabba* is present. Thus the descent of an embryo comes about through the union of these three things.'[875]

"'Then, sirs, do you know for sure whether that *gandhabba* is a noble, or a brahmin, or a merchant, or a worker?'

"'Sir, we do not know for sure whether that *gandhabba* is a noble, or a brahmin, or a merchant, or a worker.'

"'That being so, sirs, then what are you?'

"'That being so, sir, we do not know what we are.'

"Now, Assalāyana, even those seven brahmin seers, on being pressed and questioned and cross-questioned by the seer Devala the Dark on their own assertion about birth, were unable to support it. But how shall you, on being pressed and questioned and cross-questioned by me now on your assertion about birth, be able to support it? You, who rely on the teachers' doctrines, are not [even fit to be] their spoon-holder Puṇṇa."[876]

19. When this was said, the brahmin student Assalāyana said to the Blessed One: "Magnificent, Master Gotama! Magnificent, Master Gotama!...(*as Sutta 91, §37*)...From today let Master Gotama remember me as a lay follower who has gone to him for refuge for life."

94 *Ghoṭamukha Sutta*
To Ghoṭamukha

1. THUS HAVE I HEARD. On one occasion the venerable Udena was living at Benares in the Khemiya Mango Grove.

2. Now on that occasion the brahmin Ghoṭamukha had arrived in Benares for some business or other. As he was [158] walking and wandering for exercise, he came to the Khemiya Mango Grove. At the time the venerable Udena was walking up and down in the open. Then the brahmin Ghoṭamukha went up to the venerable Udena and exchanged greetings with him. When this courteous and amiable talk was finished, still walking up and down with the venerable Udena, he said this: "Worthy recluse, there is no wanderers' life that accords with the Dhamma: so it seems to me here, and that may be because I have not seen such venerable ones as yourself or [because I have not seen] the Dhamma here."

3. When this was said, the venerable Udena stepped down from the walk and went into his dwelling, where he sat down on a seat made ready.[877] And Ghoṭamukha too stepped down from the walk and went into the dwelling, where he stood at one side. Then the venerable Udena said to him: "There are seats, brahmin, sit down if you wish."

"We did not sit down because we were waiting for Master Udena [to speak]. For how could one like myself presume to sit down on a seat without first being invited to do so?"

4. Then the brahmin Ghoṭamukha took a low seat, sat down at one side, and said to the venerable Udena: "Worthy recluse, there is no wanderers' life that accords with the Dhamma: so it seems to me here, and that may be because I have not seen such venerable ones as yourself or [because I have not seen] the Dhamma here."

"Brahmin, if you think any statement of mine is to be agreed with, then agree with it; if you think any statement of mine is to be argued against, then argue against it; and if you do not understand the meaning of any statement of mine, ask me to clarify it thus: 'How is this, Master Udena? What is the meaning of this?' In this way we can discuss this matter."

"Master Udena, if I think any statement of Master Udena's is to be agreed with, I shall agree with it; if I think any statement of his is to be argued against, I shall argue against it; and if I [159] do not understand the meaning of any statement of Master Udena's, then I shall ask Master Udena to clarify it thus: 'How is this Master Udena? What is the meaning of this?' In this way let us discuss this matter."

5–6. "Brahmin, there are four kinds of persons to be found existing in the world. What four?"...(*as Sutta 51, §§5–6*) [160]...

"But, Master Udena, the kind of person who does not torment himself or pursue the practice of torturing himself and who does not torment others or pursue the practice of torturing others; who, since he torments neither himself nor others, is here and now hungerless, extinguished, and cooled, and abides experiencing bliss, having himself become holy—he does not torment and torture either himself or others, both of whom desire pleasure and recoil from pain. That is why this kind of person satisfies my mind."

7. "Brahmin, there are two kinds of assembly. What two? Here a certain assembly lusts after jewels and earrings and seeks wives and children, men and women slaves, fields and land, gold and silver. But here a certain assembly does not lust after jewels and earrings, but having abandoned wives and children, men and women slaves, fields and land, gold and silver, has gone forth from the home life into homelessness. Now there is this kind of person who does not torment himself or pursue the practice of torturing himself and who does not torment others or pursue the practice of torturing others; who, since he torments neither himself nor others, is here and now hungerless, extinguished, and cooled, and abides experiencing bliss, having himself become holy. In which of the two kinds of assembly do you usually see this person, brahmin—in the assembly that lusts after jewels and earrings and seeks wives and children, men and women slaves, fields and land, gold and silver; or in the assembly that does not lust after jewels and earrings, but having abandoned wives and children...has gone forth from the home life into homelessness?"

[161] "I usually see this kind of person, Master Udena, in the assembly that does not lust after jewels and earrings, but having abandoned wives and children...has gone forth from the home life into homelessness."

8. "But only just now, brahmin, we understood you to say: 'Worthy recluse, there is no wanderers' life that accords with the Dhamma: so it seems to me here, and that may be because I have not seen such venerable ones as yourself or [because I have not seen] the Dhamma here.'"

"Certainly, Master Udena, it was in order to learn that I spoke those words. There is a wanderers' life that accords with the Dhamma; so it seems to me here, and may Master Udena remember me [to have spoken] thus. It would be good if, out of compassion, Master Udena would expound to me in detail those four kinds of persons he mentioned in brief."

9. "Then, brahmin, listen and attend closely to what I shall say."—"Yes, sir," the brahmin Ghoṭamukha replied. The venerable Udena said this:

10–30. "Brahmin, what kind of person torments himself and pursues the practice of torturing himself? Here a certain person goes naked...(*as Sutta 51, §§8–28*) [162]...and abides experiencing bliss, having himself become holy."

31. When this was said, the brahmin Ghoṭamukha said to the venerable Udena: "Magnificent, Master Udena! Magnificent, Master Udena! Master Udena has made the Dhamma clear in many ways, as though he were turning upright what had been overthrown, revealing what was hidden, showing the way to one who was lost, or holding up a lamp in the dark for those with eyesight to see forms. I go to Master Udena for refuge and to the Dhamma and to the Sangha of bhikkhus. From today let Master Udena remember me as a lay follower who has gone to him for refuge for life."

32. "Do not go to me for refuge, brahmin. Go for refuge to that same Blessed One to whom I have gone for refuge."

"Where is he living now, that Master Gotama, accomplished and fully enlightened, Master Udena?"

"That Blessed One, accomplished and fully enlightened, has attained final Nibbāna, brahmin."

"If we heard that Master Gotama was within ten leagues, we would go ten leagues in order to see that Master Gotama, accomplished and fully enlightened. If we heard that Master Gotama was within twenty leagues...thirty leagues...forty leagues...fifty leagues...a hundred leagues, [163] we would go a hundred leagues in order to see that Master Gotama, accomplished and fully enlightened. But since that Master Gotama has attained to final Nibbāna, we go to that Master Gotama for refuge and to the Dhamma and to the Sangha of bhikkhus. From today let Master Udena remember me as a lay follower who has gone for refuge for life.

33. "Now, Master Udena, the king of Anga gives me a daily donation. Let me give Master Udena one regular donation from that."

"What kind of regular daily donation does the king of Anga give you, brahmin?"

"Five hundred *kahāpaṇas*, Master Udena."[878]

"It is not allowable for us to accept gold and silver, brahmin."

"If it is not allowable for Master Udena, I will have a monastery built for Master Udena."

"If you desire to have a monastery built for me, brahmin, have an assembly hall built for the Sangha at Pāṭaliputta."[879]

"I am still more satisfied and pleased that Master Udena suggests that I give a gift to the Sangha. So with this regular donation and another regular donation, I shall have an assembly hall built for the Sangha at Pāṭaliputta."

Then with that regular donation [which he offered to Master Udena] and another regular donation [added to it], the brahmin Ghoṭamukha had an assembly hall built for the Sangha at Pāṭaliputta. And that is now known as the Ghoṭamukhī.

95 *Cankī Sutta*
With Cankī

[164] 1. THUS HAVE I HEARD.[880] On one occasion the Blessed One was wandering in the Kosalan country with a large Sangha of bhikkhus, and eventually he arrived at a Kosalan brahmin village named Opasāda. There the Blessed One stayed in the Gods' Grove,[881] the Sāla-tree Grove to the north of Opasāda.

2. Now on that occasion the brahmin Cankī was ruling over Opasāda, a crown property abounding in living beings, rich in grasslands, woodlands, waterways, and grain, a royal endowment, a sacred grant given to him by King Pasenadi of Kosala.

3. The brahmin householders of Opasāda heard: "The recluse Gotama...(*as Sutta 91, §3*)...Now it is good see such arahants."

4. Then the brahmin householders of Opasāda set forth from Opasāda in groups and bands and headed northwards to the Gods' Grove, the Sāla-tree Grove.

5. Now on that occasion the brahmin Cankī had retired to the upper storey of his palace for his midday rest. Then he saw the brahmin householders of Opasāda setting forth from Opasāda in groups and bands and heading northwards to the Gods' Grove, the Sāla-tree Grove. When he saw them, he asked his minister: "Good minister, why are the brahmin householders of Opasāda setting forth from Opasāda in groups and bands and heading northwards to the Gods' Grove, the Sāla-tree Grove?"

6. "Sir, there is the recluse Gotama, the son of the Sakyans who went forth from a Sakyan clan, who has been wandering in the Kosalan country...(*as Sutta 91, §3*)...They are going to see that Master Gotama."

"Then, good minister, go to the brahmin householders of Opasāda and tell them: 'Sirs, the brahmin Cankī says this: "Please wait, sirs. The brahmin Cankī will also go to see the recluse Gotama."'"

"Yes, sir," the minister replied, [165] and he went to the brahmin householders of Opasāda and gave them the message.

7. Now on that occasion five hundred brahmins from various states were staying at Opasāda for some business or other. They heard: "The brahmin Cankī, it is said, is going to see the recluse Gotama." Then they went to the brahmin Cankī and asked him: "Sir, is it true that you are going to see the recluse Gotama?"

"So it is, sirs. I am going to see the recluse Gotama."

8. "Sir, do not go to see the recluse Gotama. It is not proper, Master Cankī, for you to go to see the recluse Gotama; rather, it is proper for the recluse Gotama to come to see you. For you, sir, are well born on both sides, of pure maternal and paternal descent seven generations back, unassailable and impeccable in respect of birth. Since that is so, Master Cankī, it is not proper for you to go to see the recluse Gotama; rather, it is proper for the recluse Gotama to come to see you. You, sir, are rich, with great wealth and great possessions. You, sir, are a master of the Three Vedas with their vocabularies, liturgy, phonology, and etymology, and the histories as a fifth; skilled in philology and grammar, you are fully versed in natural philosophy and in the marks of a Great Man. You, sir, are handsome, comely, and graceful, possessing supreme beauty of complexion, with sublime beauty and sublime presence, remarkable to behold. You, sir, are virtuous, mature in virtue, possessing mature virtue. You, sir, are a good speaker with a good delivery; [166] you speak words that are courteous, distinct, flawless, and communicate the meaning. You, sir, teach the teachers of many, and you teach the recitation of the hymns to three hundred brahmin students. You, sir, are honoured, respected, revered, venerated, and esteemed by King Pasenadi of Kosala. You, sir, are honoured, respected, revered, venerated, and esteemed by the brahmin Pokkharasāti.[882] You, sir, rule over Opasāda, a crown property abounding in living beings...a sacred grant given to you by King Pasenadi of Kosala. Since this is so, Master Cankī, it is not proper for you to go to see the recluse Gotama; rather, it is proper for the recluse Gotama to come to see you."

9. When this was said, the brahmin Cankī told those brahmins: "Now, sirs, hear from me why it is proper for me to go to see Master Gotama, and why it is not proper for Master Gotama to come to see me. Sirs, the recluse Gotama is well born on both

sides, of pure maternal and paternal descent seven generations back, unassailable and impeccable in respect of birth. Since this is so, sirs, it is not proper for Master Gotama to come to see me; rather, it is proper for me to go to see Master Gotama. Sirs, the recluse Gotama went forth abandoning much gold and bullion stored away in vaults and depositories. Sirs, the recluse Gotama went forth from the home life into homelessness while still young, a black-haired young man endowed with the blessing of youth, in the prime of life. Sirs, the recluse Gotama shaved off his hair and beard, put on the yellow robe, and went forth from the home life into homelessness though his mother and father wished otherwise and wept with tearful faces. Sirs, the recluse Gotama is handsome, comely, and graceful, possessing supreme beauty of complexion, [167] with sublime beauty and sublime presence, remarkable to behold. Sirs, the recluse Gotama is virtuous, with noble virtue, with wholesome virtue, possessing wholesome virtue. Sirs, the recluse Gotama is a good speaker with a good delivery; he speaks words that are courteous, distinct, flawless, and communicate the meaning. Sirs, the recluse Gotama is a teacher of the teachers of many. Sirs, the recluse Gotama is free from sensual lust and without personal vanity. Sirs, the recluse Gotama holds the doctrine of the moral efficacy of action, the doctrine of the moral efficacy of deeds; he does not seek any harm for the line of brahmins. Sirs, the recluse Gotama went forth from an aristocratic family, from one of the original noble families. Sirs, the recluse Gotama went forth from a rich family, from a family of great wealth and great possessions. Sirs, people come from remote kingdoms and remote districts to question the recluse Gotama. Sirs, many thousands of deities have gone for refuge for life to the recluse Gotama. Sirs, a good report of the recluse Gotama has been spread to this effect: 'That Blessed One is accomplished, fully enlightened, perfect in true knowledge and conduct, sublime, knower of worlds, incomparable leader of persons to be tamed, teacher of gods and humans, enlightened, blessed.' Sirs, the recluse Gotama possesses the thirty-two marks of a Great Man. Sirs, King Seniya Bimbisāra of Magadha and his wife and children have gone for refuge for life to the recluse Gotama. Sirs, King Pasenadi of Kosala and his wife and children have gone for refuge for life to the recluse Gotama. Sirs, the brahmin Pokkharasāti and his wife and children have gone for refuge for life to the recluse Gotama. Sirs, the recluse Gotama has arrived at Opasāda and is living at Opasāda in the Gods' Grove, the Sāla-tree Grove to the north of Opasāda. Now any recluses or brahmins that come to our town are our guests, and guests should be honoured, respected, revered, and venerated by us. Since the recluse Gotama has arrived at Opasāda, he is our guest, and as our guest should be honoured, respected, revered, and venerated by us. [168] Since this is so, sirs, it is not proper for Master Gotama to come to see me; rather, it is proper for me to go to see Master Gotama.

"Sirs, this much is the praise of Master Gotama that I have learned, but the praise of Master Gotama is not limited to that, for the praise of Master Gotama is immeasurable. Since Master Gotama possesses each one of these factors, it is not proper for him to come to see me; rather, it is proper for me to go to see Master Gotama. Therefore, sirs, let all of us go to see the recluse Gotama."

10. Then the brahmin Cankī, together with a large company of brahmins, went to the Blessed One and exchanged greetings with him. When this courteous and amiable talk was finished, he sat down at one side.

11. Now on that occasion the Blessed One was seated finishing some amiable talk with some very senior brahmins. At the time, sitting in the assembly, was a brahmin student named Kāpaṭhika. Young, shaven-headed, sixteen years old, he was a master of the Three Vedas with their vocabularies, liturgy, phonology, and etymology, and the histories as a fifth; skilled in philology and grammar, he was fully versed in natural philosophy and in the marks of a Great Man. While the very senior brahmins were conversing with the Blessed One, he often broke in and interrupted their talk. Then the Blessed One rebuked the brahmin student Kāpaṭhika thus: "Let not the venerable Bhāradvāja break in and interrupt the talk of the very senior brahmins while they are conversing. Let the venerable Bhāradvāja wait until the talk is finished."

When this was said, the brahmin Cankī said to the Blessed One: "Let not Master Gotama rebuke the brahmin student Kāpaṭhika. The brahmin student Kāpaṭhika is a clansman, he is very learned, he has a good delivery, he is wise; he is capable of taking part in this discussion with Master Gotama."

12. Then the Blessed One thought: "Surely, [169] since the brahmins honour him thus, the brahmin student Kāpaṭhika must be accomplished in the scriptures of the Three Vedas."

Then the brahmin student Kāpaṭhika thought: "When the recluse Gotama catches my eye, I shall ask him a question."

Then, knowing with his own mind the thought in the brahmin student Kāpaṭhika's mind, the Blessed One turned his eye towards him. Then the brahmin student Kāpaṭhika thought: "The recluse Gotama has turned towards me. Suppose I ask him a question." Then he said to the Blessed One: "Master Gotama, in regard to the ancient brahmanic hymns that have come down through oral transmission and in the scriptural collections, the brahmins come to the definite conclusion: 'Only this is true, anything else is wrong.' What does Master Gotama say about this?"

13. "How then, Bhāradvāja, among the brahmins is there even a single brahmin who says thus: 'I know this, I see this: only this is true, anything else is wrong'?"—"No, Master Gotama."

"How then, Bhāradvāja, among the brahmins is there even a single teacher or a single teacher's teacher back to the seventh generation of teachers who says thus: 'I know this, I see this: only this is true, anything else is wrong'?"—"No, Master Gotama."

"How then, Bhāradvāja, the ancient brahmin seers, the creators of the hymns, the composers of the hymns, whose ancient hymns that were formerly chanted, uttered, and compiled, the brahmins nowadays still chant and repeat, repeating what was spoken and reciting what was recited—that is, Aṭṭhaka, Vāmaka, Vāmadeva, Vessāmitta, Yamataggi, Angirasa, Bhāradvāja, Vāseṭṭha, Kassapa, and Bhagu[883]—did even these ancient brahmin seers say thus: 'We know this, we see this: only this is true, anything else is wrong'?"—[170] "No, Master Gotama."

"So, Bhāradvāja, it seems that among the brahmins there is not even a single brahmin who says thus: 'I know this, I see this: only this is true, anything else is wrong.' And among the brahmins there is not even a single teacher or a single teacher's teacher back to the seventh generation of teachers, who says thus: 'I know this, I see this: only this is true, anything else is wrong.' And the ancient brahmin seers, the creators of the hymns, the composers of the hymns...even these ancient brahmin seers did not say thus: 'We know this, we see this: only this is true, anything else is wrong.' Suppose there were a file of blind men each in touch with the next: the first one does not see, the middle one does not see, and the last one does not see. So too, Bhāradvāja, in regard to their statement the brahmins seem to be like a file of blind men: the first one does not see, the middle one does not see, and the last one does not see. What do you think, Bhāradvāja, that being so, does not the faith of the brahmins turn out to be groundless?"

14. "The brahmins honour this not only out of faith, Master Gotama. They also honour it as oral tradition."

"Bhāradvāja, first you took your stand on faith, now you speak of oral tradition. There are five things, Bhāradvāja, that may turn out in two different ways here and now. What five? Faith, approval, oral tradition, reasoned cogitation, and reflective acceptance of a view.[884] These five things may turn out in two different ways here and now. Now something may be fully accepted out of faith, yet it may be empty, hollow, and false; but something else may not be fully accepted out of faith, yet it may be factual, true, and unmistaken. Again, [171] something may be fully approved of...well transmitted...well cogitated...well reflected upon, yet it may be empty, hollow, and false; but something else may not be well reflected upon, yet it may be factual, true, and unmistaken. [Under these conditions] it is not proper for a wise man who preserves truth to come to the definite conclusion: 'Only this is true, anything else is wrong.'"[885]

15. "But, Master Gotama, in what way is there the preservation of truth?[886] How does one preserve truth? We ask Master Gotama about the preservation of truth."

"If a person has faith, Bhāradvāja, he preserves truth when he says: 'My faith is thus'; but he does not yet come to the definite conclusion: 'Only this is true, anything else is wrong.' In this way, Bhāradvāja, there is the preservation of truth; in this way he preserves truth; in this way we describe the preservation of truth. But as yet there is no discovery of truth.[887]

"If a person approves of something...if he receives an oral tradition...if he [reaches a conclusion based on] reasoned cogitation...if he gains a reflective acceptance of a view, he preserves truth when he says: 'My reflective acceptance of a view is thus'; but he does not yet come to the definite conclusion: 'Only this is true, anything else is wrong.' In this way too, Bhāradvāja, there is the preservation of truth; in this way he preserves truth; in this way we describe the preservation of truth. But as yet there is no discovery of truth."

16. "In that way, Master Gotama, there is the preservation of truth; in that way one preserves truth; in that way we recognise the preservation of truth. But in what way, Master Gotama, is there the discovery of truth? In what way does one discover truth? We ask Master Gotama about the discovery of truth."

17. "Here, Bhāradvāja, a bhikkhu may be living in dependence on some village or town.[888] Then a householder or a householder's son goes to him and investigates him in regard to three kinds of states: [172] in regard to states based on greed, in regard to states based on hate, and in regard to states based on delusion: 'Are there in this venerable one any states based on greed such that, with his mind obsessed by those states, while not knowing he might say, "I know," or while not seeing he might say, "I see," or he might urge others to act in a way that would lead to their harm and suffering for a long time?' As he investigates him he comes to know: 'There are no such states based on greed in this venerable one. The bodily behaviour and the verbal behaviour of this venerable one are not those of one affected by greed. And the Dhamma that this venerable one teaches is profound, hard to see and hard to understand, peaceful and sublime, unattainable by mere reasoning, subtle, to be experienced by the wise. This Dhamma cannot easily be taught by one affected by greed.'

18. "When he has investigated him and has seen that he is purified from states based on greed, he next investigates him in regard to states based on hate: 'Are there in this venerable one any states based on hate such that, with his mind obsessed by those states...he might urge others to act in a way that would lead to their harm and suffering for a long time?' As he investigates him, he comes to know: 'There are no such states based on hate in this venerable one. The bodily behaviour and the verbal behaviour of this venerable one are not those of one affected by hate. And the Dhamma that this venerable one teaches is profound...to be experienced by the wise. This Dhamma cannot easily be taught by one affected by hate.'

19. "When he has investigated him and has seen that he is purified from states based on hate, [173] he next investigates him in regard to states based on delusion: 'Are there in this venerable

one any states based on delusion such that, with his mind obsessed by those states...he might urge others to act in a way that would lead to their harm and suffering for a long time?' As he investigates him, he comes to know: 'There are no such states based on delusion in this venerable one. The bodily behaviour and the verbal behaviour of this venerable one are not those of one affected by delusion. And the Dhamma that this venerable one teaches is profound...to be experienced by the wise. This Dhamma cannot easily be taught by one affected by delusion.'

20. "When he has investigated him and has seen that he is purified from states based on delusion, then he places faith in him; filled with faith he visits him and pays respect to him; having paid respect to him, he gives ear; when he gives ear, he hears the Dhamma; having heard the Dhamma, he memorises it and examines the meaning of the teachings he has memorised; when he examines their meaning, he gains a reflective acceptance of those teachings; when he has gained a reflective acceptance of those teachings, zeal springs up; when zeal has sprung up, he applies his will; having applied his will, he scrutinises;[889] having scrutinised, he strives;[890] resolutely striving, he realises with the body the supreme truth and sees it by penetrating it with wisdom.[891] In this way, Bhāradvāja, there is the discovery of truth; in this way one discovers truth; in this way we describe the discovery of truth. But as yet there is no final arrival at truth."[892]

21. "In that way, Master Gotama, there is the discovery of truth; in that way one discovers truth; in that way we recognise the discovery of truth. But in what way, Master Gotama, is there the final arrival at truth? In what way does one finally arrive at truth? We ask Master Gotama about the final arrival at truth." [174]

"The final arrival at truth, Bhāradvāja, lies in the repetition, development, and cultivation of those same things. In this way, Bhāradvāja, there is the final arrival at truth; in this way one finally arrives at truth; in this way we describe the final arrival at truth."

22. "In that way, Master Gotama, there is the final arrival at truth; in that way one finally arrives at truth; in that way we recognise the final arrival at truth. But what, Master Gotama, is most helpful for the final arrival at truth? We ask Master Gotama about the thing most helpful for the final arrival at truth."

"Striving is most helpful for the final arrival at truth, Bhāradvāja. If one does not strive, one will not finally arrive at truth; but because one strives, one does finally arrive at truth. That is why striving is most helpful for the final arrival at truth."

23. "But what, Master Gotama, is most helpful for striving? We ask Master Gotama about the thing most helpful for striving."

"Scrutiny is most helpful for striving, Bhāradvāja. If one does not scrutinise, one will not strive; but because one scrutinises, one strives. That is why scrutiny is most helpful for striving."

24. "But what, Master Gotama, is most helpful for scrutiny? We ask Master Gotama about the thing most helpful for scrutiny."

"Application of the will is most helpful for scrutiny, Bhāradvāja. If one does not apply one's will, one will not scrutinise; but because one applies one's will, one scrutinises. That is why application of the will is most helpful for scrutiny."

25. "But what, Master Gotama, is most helpful for application of the will? We ask the Master Gotama about the thing most helpful for application of the will."

"Zeal is most helpful for application of the will, Bhāradvāja. If one does not arouse zeal, one will not apply one's will; but because one arouses zeal, one applies one's will. That is why zeal is most helpful for application of the will."

26. "But what, Master Gotama, is most helpful for zeal? [175] We ask Master Gotama about the thing most helpful for zeal."

"A reflective acceptance of the teachings is most helpful for zeal, Bhāradvāja. If one does not gain a reflective acceptance of the teachings, zeal will not spring up; but because one gains a reflective acceptance of the teachings, zeal springs up. That is why a reflective acceptance of the teachings is most helpful for zeal."

27. "But what, Master Gotama, is most helpful for a reflective acceptance of the teachings? We ask Master Gotama about the thing most helpful for a reflective acceptance of the teachings."

"Examination of the meaning is most helpful for a reflective acceptance of the teachings, Bhāradvāja. If one does not examine their meaning, one will not gain a reflective acceptance of the teachings; but because one examines their meaning, one gains a reflective acceptance of the teachings. That is why examination of the meaning is most helpful for a reflective acceptance of the teachings."

28. "But what, Master Gotama, is most helpful for examination of the meaning? We ask Master Gotama about the thing most helpful for examination of meaning."

"Memorising the teachings is most helpful for examining the meaning, Bhāradvāja. If one does not memorise a teaching, one will not examine its meaning; but because one memorises a teaching, one examines its meaning."

29. "But what, Master Gotama, is most helpful for memorising the teachings? We ask Master Gotama about the thing most helpful for memorising the teachings."

"Hearing the Dhamma is most helpful for memorising the teachings, Bhāradvāja. If one does not hear the Dhamma, one will not memorise the teachings; but because one hears the Dhamma, one memorises the teachings. That is why hearing the Dhamma is most helpful for memorising the teachings."

30. "But what, Master Gotama, is most helpful for hearing the Dhamma? We ask Master Gotama about the thing most helpful for hearing the Dhamma."

"Giving ear is most helpful for hearing the Dhamma, Bhāradvāja. [176] If one does not give ear, one will not hear the Dhamma; but because one gives ear, one hears the Dhamma. That is why giving ear is most helpful for hearing the Dhamma."

31. "But what, Master Gotama, is most helpful for giving ear? We ask Master Gotama about the thing most helpful for giving ear."

"Paying respect is most helpful for giving ear, Bhāradvāja. If one does not pay respect, one will not give ear; but because one pays respect, one gives ear. That is why paying respect is most helpful for giving ear."

32. "But what, Master Gotama, is most helpful for paying respect? We ask Master Gotama about the thing most helpful for paying respect."

"Visiting is most helpful for paying respect, Bhāradvāja. If one does not visit [a teacher], one will not pay respect to him; but because one visits [a teacher], one pays respect to him. That is why visiting is most helpful for paying respect."

33. "But what, Master Gotama, is most helpful for visiting? We ask Master Gotama about the thing most helpful for visiting."

"Faith is most helpful for visiting, Bhāradvāja. If faith [in a teacher] does not arise, one will not visit him; but because faith [in a teacher] arises, one visits him. That is why faith is most helpful for visiting."

34. "We asked Master Gotama about the preservation of truth, and Master Gotama answered about the preservation of truth; we approve of and accept that answer, and so we are satisfied. We asked Master Gotama about the discovery of truth, and Master Gotama answered about the discovery of truth; we approve of and accept that answer, and so we are satisfied. We asked Master Gotama about the final arrival at truth, and Master Gotama answered about the final arrival at truth; we approve of and accept that answer, and so we are satisfied. [177] We asked Master Gotama about the thing most helpful for the final arrival at truth, and Master Gotama answered about the thing most helpful for the final arrival at truth; we approve of and accept that answer, and so we are satisfied. Whatever we asked Master Gotama about, that he has answered us; we approve of and accept that answer, and so we are satisfied. Formerly, Master Gotama, we used to think: 'Who are these bald-pated recluses, these swarthy menial offspring of the Kinsman's feet, that they would understand the Dhamma?'[893] But Master Gotama has indeed inspired in me love for recluses, confidence in recluses, reverence for recluses.

35. "Magnificent, Master Gotama! Magnificent, Master Gotama!...(*as Sutta 91, §37*)...From today let Master Gotama remember me as a lay follower who has gone to him for refuge for life."

96 *Esukārī Sutta*

To Esukārī

1. THUS HAVE I HEARD. On one occasion the Blessed One was living at Sāvatthī in Jeta's Grove, Anāthapiṇḍika's Park.

2. Then the brahmin Esukārī went to the Blessed One and exchanged greetings with him. When this courteous and amiable talk was finished, he sat down at one side and said:

3. "Master Gotama, the brahmins prescribe four levels of service. They prescribe the level of service towards a brahmin, the level of service towards a noble, the level of service towards a merchant, and the level of service towards a worker. Therein, Master Gotama, the brahmins prescribe this as the level of service towards a brahmin: a brahmin may serve a brahmin, a noble may serve a brahmin, a merchant may serve a brahmin, and a worker may serve a brahmin. That is the level of service towards a brahmin [178] that the brahmins prescribe. Master Gotama, the brahmins prescribe this as the level of service towards a noble: a noble may serve a noble, a merchant may serve a noble, and a worker may serve a noble. That is the level of service towards a noble that the brahmins prescribe. Master Gotama, the brahmins prescribe this as the level of service towards a merchant: a merchant may serve a merchant and a worker may serve a merchant. That is the level of service towards a merchant that the brahmins prescribe. Master Gotama, the brahmins prescribe this as the level of service towards a worker: only a worker may serve a worker; for who else could serve a worker? That is the level of service towards a worker that the brahmins prescribe. What does Master Gotama say about this?"

4. "Well, brahmin, has all the world authorised the brahmins to prescribe these four levels of service?"—"No, Master Gotama."—"Suppose, brahmin, they were to force a cut of meat

upon a poor, penniless, destitute man and tell him: 'Good man, you must eat this meat and pay for it'; so too, without the consent of those [other] recluses and brahmins, the brahmins nevertheless prescribe those four levels of service.

5. "I do not say, brahmin, that all are to be served, nor do I say that none are to be served. For if, when serving someone, one becomes worse and not better because of that service, then I say that he should not be served. And if, when serving someone, one becomes better and not worse because of that service, then I say that he should be served.

6. "If they were to ask a noble thus: 'Which of these should you serve—one in whose service you become worse and not better when serving him, or one in whose service you become better and not worse when serving him: [179] answering rightly, a noble would answer thus: 'I should not serve the one in whose service I become worse and not better when serving him; I should serve the one in whose service I become better and not worse when serving him.'

"If they were to ask a brahmin...to ask a merchant...to ask a worker...answering rightly, a worker would answer thus: 'I should not serve the one in whose service I become worse and not better when serving him; I should serve the one in whose service I become better and not worse when serving him.'

7. "I do not say, brahmin, that one is better because one is from an aristocratic family, nor do I say that one is worse because one is from an aristocratic family. I do not say that one is better because one is of great beauty, nor do I say that one is worse because one is of great beauty. I do not say that one is better because one is of great wealth, nor do I say that one is worse because one is of great wealth.

8. "For here, brahmin, one from an aristocratic family may kill living beings, take what is not given, misconduct himself in sensual pleasures, speak falsely, speak maliciously, speak harshly, gossip, be covetous, have a mind of ill will, and hold wrong view. Therefore I do not say that one is better because one is from an aristocratic family. But also, brahmin, one from an aristocratic family may abstain from killing living beings, from taking what is not given, from misconduct in sensual pleasures, from false speech, from malicious speech, from harsh speech, and from gossip, and he may be uncovetous, have a

mind without ill will, and hold right view. Therefore I do not say that one is worse because one is from an aristocratic family.

"Here, brahmin, one of great beauty...one of great wealth may kill living beings...and hold wrong view. Therefore I do not say that one is better because one is of great beauty...of great wealth. But also, brahmin, one of great beauty...of great wealth may abstain from killing living beings...and hold right view. Therefore [180] I do not say that one is worse because one is of great beauty...of great wealth.

9. "I do not say, brahmin, that all are to be served, nor do I say that none are to be served. For if, when serving someone, one's faith, virtue, learning, generosity, and wisdom increase in his service, then I say that he should be served."

10. When this was said, the brahmin Esukārī said to the Blessed One: "Master Gotama, the brahmins prescribe four types of wealth. They prescribe the wealth of a brahmin, the wealth of a noble, the wealth of a merchant, and the wealth of a worker.

"Therein, Master Gotama, the brahmins prescribe this as the wealth of a brahmin—wandering for alms;[894] a brahmin who spurns his own wealth, wandering for alms, abuses his duty like a guard who takes what has not been given. That is the wealth of a brahmin which the brahmins prescribe. Master Gotama, the brahmins prescribe this as the wealth of a noble—the bow and quiver; a noble who spurns his own wealth, the bow and quiver, abuses his duty like a guard who takes what has not been given. That is the wealth of a noble which the brahmins prescribe. Master Gotama, the brahmins prescribe this as the wealth of a merchant—farming and cattle-breeding;[895] a merchant who spurns his own wealth, farming and cattle-breeding, abuses his duty like a guard who takes what has not been given. That is the wealth of a merchant which the brahmins prescribe. Master Gotama, the brahmins prescribe this as the wealth of a worker—the sickle and carrying-pole; a worker who spurns his own wealth, the sickle and carrying-pole, abuses his duty like a guard who takes what has not been given. That is the wealth of a worker which the brahmins prescribe. What does Master Gotama say about this?"

11. "Well, brahmin, has all the world authorised the brahmins to prescribe these four types of wealth?"—[181] "No, Master Gotama."—"Suppose, brahmin, they were to force a cut of meat

upon a poor, penniless, destitute man and tell him: 'Good man, you must eat this meat and pay for it'; so too, without the consent of those [other] recluses and brahmins, the brahmins nevertheless prescribe these four types of wealth.

12. "I, brahmin, declare the noble supramundane Dhamma as a person's own wealth.[896] But recollecting his ancient maternal and paternal family lineage, he is reckoned according to wherever he is reborn.[897] If he is reborn in a clan of nobles, he is reckoned as a noble; if he is reborn in a clan of brahmins, he is reckoned as a brahmin; if he is reborn in a clan of merchants, he is reckoned as a merchant; if he is reborn in a clan of workers, he is reckoned as a worker. Just as fire is reckoned by the particular condition dependent on which it burns—when fire burns dependent on logs, it is reckoned as a log fire; when fire burns dependent on faggots, it is reckoned as a faggot fire; when fire burns dependent on grass, it is reckoned as a grass fire; when fire burns dependent on cowdung, it is reckoned as a cowdung fire—so too, brahmin, I declare the noble supramundane Dhamma as a person's own wealth. But recollecting his ancient maternal and paternal lineage, he is reckoned according to wherever he is reborn. If he is reborn...in a clan of workers, he is reckoned as a worker.

13. "If, brahmin, anyone from a clan of nobles goes forth from the home life into homelessness, and after encountering the Dhamma and Discipline proclaimed by the Tathāgata, he abstains from killing living beings, from taking what is not given, from incelibacy, from false speech, from malicious speech, from harsh speech, and from gossip, and is uncovetous, has a mind without ill will, and holds right view, he is one who is accomplishing the true way, the Dhamma that is wholesome. [182]

"If, brahmin, anyone from a clan of brahmins goes forth...If anyone from a clan of merchants goes forth...If anyone from a clan of workers goes forth from the home life into homelessness, and after encountering the Dhamma and Discipline proclaimed by the Tathāgata, he abstains from killing living beings...and holds right view, he is one who is accomplishing the true way, the Dhamma that is wholesome.

14. "What do you think, brahmin? Is only a brahmin capable of developing a mind of loving-kindness towards a certain region, without hostility and without ill will, and not a noble, or a merchant, or a worker?"

"No, Master Gotama. Whether it be a noble, or a brahmin, or a merchant, or a worker—those of all four castes are capable of developing a mind of loving-kindness towards a certain region, without hostility and without ill will."

"So too, brahmin, if anyone from a clan of nobles goes forth...(*repeat §13*)...he is one who is accomplishing the true way, the Dhamma that is wholesome.

15. "What do you think, brahmin? Is only a brahmin capable of taking a loofah and bath powder, going to the river, and washing off dust and dirt, and not a noble, or a merchant, or a worker?"

"No, Master Gotama. Whether it be a noble, or a brahmin, or a merchant, [183] or a worker—those of all four castes are capable of taking a loofah and bath powder, going to the river, and washing off dust and dirt."

"So too, brahmin, if anyone from a clan of nobles goes forth...(*repeat §13*)...he is one who is accomplishing the true way, the Dhamma that is wholesome.

16. "What do you think, brahmin? Suppose a head-anointed noble king were to assemble here a hundred men of different birth"...(*as Sutta 93, §13*) [184]..."For all fire has a flame, a colour, and a radiance, and it is possible to use all fire for the purposes of fire."

"So too, brahmin, if anyone from a clan of nobles goes forth...(*repeat §13*)...he is one who is accomplishing the true way, the Dhamma that is wholesome."

17. When this was said, the brahmin Esukārī said to the Blessed One: "Magnificent, Master Gotama! Magnificent, Master Gotama!...From today let Master Gotama remember me as a lay follower who has gone to him for refuge for life."

97 *Dhānañjāni Sutta*
To Dhānañjāni

1. THUS HAVE I HEARD. On one occasion the Blessed One was living at Rājagaha in the Bamboo Grove, the Squirrels' Sanctuary.

2. Now on that occasion the venerable Sāriputta was wandering in the Southern Hills with a large Sangha of bhikkhus. Then a certain [185] bhikkhu who had spent the Rains at Rājagaha went to the venerable Sāriputta in the Southern Hills and exchanged greetings with him. When this courteous and amiable talk was finished, he sat down at one side and the venerable Sāriputta asked him: "Is the Blessed One well and strong, friend?"

"The Blessed One is well and strong, friend."

"Is the Sangha of bhikkhus well and strong, friend?"

"The Sangha of bhikkhus too is well and strong, friend."

"Friend, there is a brahmin named Dhānañjāni living at the Taṇḍulapāla Gate. Is that brahmin Dhānañjāni well and strong?"

"That brahmin Dhānañjāni too is well and strong, friend."

"Is he diligent, friend?"

"How could he be diligent, friend? He plunders brahmin householders in the name of the king, and he plunders the king in the name of the brahmin householders. His wife, who had faith and came from a clan with faith, has died and he has taken another wife, a woman without faith who comes from a clan without faith."

"This is bad news that we hear, friend. It is bad news indeed to hear that the brahmin Dhānañjāni has become negligent. Perhaps sometime or other we might meet the brahmin Dhānañjāni and have some conversation with him."

3. Then, having stayed in the Southern Hills as long as he chose, the venerable Sāriputta set out to wander towards Rājagaha. Wandering by stages he eventually arrived at Rājagaha, and there he lived in the Bamboo Grove, the Squirrels' Sanctuary.

4. Then, when it was morning, the venerable Sāriputta dressed, and taking his bowl and outer robe, went into Rājagaha for alms. [186] Now at that time the brahmin Dhānañjāni was having his cows milked in a cowshed outside the city. So when the venerable Sāriputta had wandered for alms in Rājagaha and had returned from his almsround, after his meal he went to the brahmin Dhānañjāni. The brahmin Dhānañjāni saw the venerable Sāriputta coming in the distance, and he went to him and said: "Drink some of this fresh milk, Master Sāriputta, until it is time for the meal."

"Enough, brahmin, I have finished my meal for today. I shall be at the root of that tree for the day's abiding. You may come there."

"Yes, sir," he replied.

5. And then, after he had eaten his morning meal, the brahmin Dhānañjāni went to the venerable Sāriputta and exchanged greetings with him. When this courteous and amiable talk was finished, he sat down at one side and the venerable Sāriputta asked him: "Are you diligent, Dhānañjāni?"

"How can we be diligent, Master Sāriputta, when we have to support our parents, our wife and children, and our slaves, servants, and workers; when we have to do our duty towards our friends and companions, towards our kinsmen and relatives, towards our guests, towards our departed ancestors, towards the deities, and towards the king; and when this body must also be refreshed and nourished?"

6. "What do you think, Dhānañjāni? Suppose someone here were to behave contrary to the Dhamma, to behave unrighteously for the sake of his parents, and then because of such behaviour the wardens of hell were to drag him off to hell. Would he be able [to free himself by pleading thus]: 'It was for the sake of my parents that I behaved contrary to the Dhamma, that I behaved unrighteously, so let not the wardens of hell [drag me off] to hell'? [187] Or would his parents be able [to free him by pleading thus]: 'It was for our sake that he behaved contrary to the Dhamma, that he behaved unrighteously, so let not the wardens of hell [drag him off] to hell'?"

"No, Master Sāriputta. Even while he was crying out, the wardens of hell would fling him into hell."

7–15. "What do you think, Dhānañjāni? Suppose someone here were to behave contrary to the Dhamma, to behave unrighteously for the sake of his wife and children...for the sake of his slaves, servants, and workers...for the sake of his friends and companions...for the sake of his kinsmen and relatives...for the sake of his guests...[188] for the sake of his departed ancestors...for the sake of the deities...for the sake of the king...for the sake of refreshing and nourishing this body, and because of such behaviour the wardens of hell were to drag him off to hell. Would he be able [to free himself by pleading thus]: 'It was for the sake of refreshing and nourishing this body that I behaved contrary to the Dhamma, that I behaved unrighteously, so let not the wardens of hell [drag me off] to hell'? Or would others be able [to free him by pleading thus]: 'It was for the sake of refreshing and nourishing this body that he behaved contrary to the Dhamma, that he behaved unrighteously, so let not the wardens of hell [drag him off] to hell'?"

"No, Master Sāriputta. Even while he was crying out, the wardens of hell would fling him into hell."

16. "What do you think, Dhānañjāni? Who is the better, one who for the sake of his parents behaves contrary to the Dhamma, behaves unrighteously, or one who for the sake of his parents behaves according to the Dhamma, behaves righteously?"

"Master Sāriputta, the one who for the sake of his parents behaves contrary to the Dhamma, behaves unrighteously, is not the better; the one who for the sake of his parents behaves according to the Dhamma, behaves righteously, is the better."

"Dhānañjāni, there are other kinds of work, profitable and in accordance with the Dhamma, by means of which one can support one's parents and at the same time both avoid doing evil and practise merit.

17–25. "What do you think, Dhānañjāni? Who is the better, one who for the sake of his wife and children...[189]...for the sake of his slaves, servants, and workers...for the sake of his friends and companions...[190]...for the sake of his kinsmen and relatives...for the sake of his guests...for the sake of his departed ancestors...for the sake of the deities...[191]...for the sake of the king...for the sake of refreshing and nourishing this body behaves contrary to the Dhamma, behaves unrighteously, or one who for the sake of refreshing and nourishing this body behaves according to the Dhamma, behaves righteously?"

"Master Sāriputta, the one who for the sake of refreshing and nourishing this body behaves contrary to the Dhamma, behaves unrighteously, is not the better; the one who for the sake of refreshing and nourishing this body behaves according to the Dhamma, behaves righteously, is the better."

"Dhānañjāni, there are other kinds of work, profitable and in accordance with the Dhamma, by means of which one can refresh and nourish this body and at the same time both avoid doing evil and practise merit."

26. Then the brahmin Dhānañjāni, having delighted and rejoiced in the venerable Sāriputta's words, rose from his seat and departed.

27. On a later occasion the brahmin Dhānañjāni became afflicted, suffering, and gravely ill. Then he told a man: "Come, good man, [192] go to the Blessed One, pay homage in my name with your head at his feet, and say: 'Venerable sir, the brahmin Dhānañjāni is afflicted, suffering, and gravely ill; he pays homage with his head at the Blessed One's feet.' Then go to the venerable Sāriputta, pay homage in my name with your head at his feet, and say: 'Venerable sir, the brahmin Dhānañjāni is afflicted, suffering, and gravely ill; he pays homage with his head at the venerable Sāriputta's feet.' Then say thus: 'It would be good, venerable sir, if the venerable Sāriputta would come to the house of the brahmin Dhānañjāni, out of compassion.'"

"Yes, venerable sir," the man replied, and he went to the Blessed One, and after paying homage to the Blessed One, he sat down at one side and delivered his message. Then he went to the venerable Sāriputta and after paying homage to the venerable Sāriputta, he delivered his message, saying: "It would be good, venerable sir, if the venerable Sāriputta would come to the residence of the brahmin Dhānañjāni, out of compassion." The venerable Sāriputta consented in silence.

28. Then the venerable Sāriputta dressed, and taking his bowl and outer robe, he went to the residence of the brahmin Dhānañjāni, sat down on a seat made ready, and said to the brahmin Dhānañjāni: "I hope you are getting well, brahmin, I hope you are comfortable. I hope your painful feelings are subsiding and not increasing, and that their subsiding, not their increase, is apparent."

29. "Master Sāriputta, I am not getting well, I am not comfortable. My painful feelings are increasing, not subsiding; their

increase and not their subsiding is apparent. Just as if [193] a strong man were splitting my head open with a sharp sword, so too, violent winds cut through my head. I am not getting well...Just as if a strong man were tightening a tough leather strap around my head as a headband, so too, there are violent pains in my head. I am not getting well...Just as if a skilled butcher or his apprentice were to carve up an ox's belly with a sharp butcher's knife, so too, violent winds are carving up my belly. I am not getting well...Just as if two strong men were to seize a weaker man by both arms and roast him over a pit of hot coals, so too, there is a violent burning in my body. I am not getting well, I am not comfortable. My painful feelings are increasing, not subsiding; their increase and not their subsiding is apparent."

30. "What do you think, Dhānañjāni? Which is better—hell or the animal realm?"—"The animal realm, Master Sāriputta."—"Which is better—the animal realm or the realm of ghosts?"—"The realm of ghosts, Master Sāriputta."—"Which is better—the realm of ghosts or the realm of human beings?"—"Human beings, Master Sāriputta." [194] "Which is better—human beings or the gods of the heaven of the Four Great Kings?"—"The gods of the heaven of the Four Great Kings, Master Sāriputta."—"Which is better—the gods of the heaven of the Four Great Kings or the gods of the heaven of the Thirty-three?"—"The gods of the heaven of the Thirty-three, Master Sāriputta."—"Which is better—the gods of the heaven of the Thirty-three or the Yāma gods?"—"The Yāma gods, Master Sāriputta."—"Which is better—the Yāma gods or the gods of the Tusita heaven?"—"The gods of the Tusita heaven, Master Sāriputta."—"Which is better—the gods of the Tusita heaven or the gods who delight in creating?"—"The gods who delight in creating, Master Sāriputta."—"Which is better—the gods who delight in creating or the gods who wield power over others' creations?"—"The gods who wield power over others' creations, Master Sāriputta."

31. "What do you think, Dhānañjāni? Which is better—the gods who wield power over others' creations or the Brahma-world?"—"Master Sāriputta said 'the Brahma-world.' Master Sāriputta said 'the Brahma-world.'"

Then the venerable Sāriputta thought: "These brahmins are

devoted to the Brahma-world. Suppose I teach the brahmin Dhānañjāni the path to the company of Brahmā?" [And he said:] "Dhānañjāni, I shall teach you the path to the company of Brahmā. Listen and attend closely to what I shall say."—"Yes, sir," he replied. [195] The venerable Sāriputta said this:

32. "What is the path to the company of Brahmā? Here, Dhānañjāni, a bhikkhu abides pervading one quarter with a mind imbued with loving-kindness, likewise the second, likewise the third, likewise the fourth; so above, below, around, and everywhere, and to all as to himself, he abides pervading the all-encompassing world with a mind imbued with loving-kindness, abundant, exalted, immeasurable, without hostility and without ill will. This is the path to the company of Brahmā.

33–35. "Again, Dhānañjāni, a bhikkhu abides pervading one quarter with a mind imbued with compassion...with a mind imbued with altruistic joy...with a mind imbued with equanimity, likewise the second, likewise the third, likewise the fourth; so above, below, around, and everywhere, and to all as to himself, he abides pervading the all-encompassing world with a mind imbued with equanimity, abundant, exalted, immeasurable, without hostility and without ill will. This too is the path to the company of Brahmā."

36. "Then, Master Sāriputta, pay homage in my name with your head at the Blessed One's feet, and say: 'Venerable sir, the brahmin Dhānañjāni is afflicted, suffering, and gravely ill; he pays homage with his head at the Blessed One's feet.'"

Then the venerable Sāriputta, having established the brahmin Dhānañjāni in the inferior Brahma-world, rose from his seat and departed while there was still more to be done.[898] Soon after the venerable Sāriputta had left, the brahmin Dhānañjāni died and reappeared in the Brahma-world.

37. Then the Blessed One addressed the bhikkhus thus: "Bhikkhus, Sāriputta, having established the brahmin Dhānañjāni in the inferior Brahma-world, rose from his seat and departed while there was still more to be done."

38. Then the venerable Sāriputta went to the Blessed One, and after paying homage to him, he sat down at one side and said: "Venerable sir, the brahmin Dhānañjāni is afflicted, suffering, and gravely ill; he pays homage with his head at the Blessed One's feet."

"Sāriputta, having established the brahmin Dhānañjāni [196] in the inferior Brahma-world, why did you rise from your seat and leave while there was still more to be done?"

"Venerable sir, I thought thus: 'These brahmins are devoted to the Brahma-world. Suppose I teach the brahmin Dhānañjāni the path to the company of Brahmā.'"

"Sāriputta, the brahmin Dhānañjāni has died and has reappeared in the Brahma-world."[899]

98 *Vāseṭṭha Sutta*
To Vāseṭṭha

[115] 1. THUS HAVE I HEARD.[900] On one occasion the Blessed One was living at Icchānangala, in the wood near Icchānangala.

2. Now on that occasion a number of well-known, well-to-do brahmins were staying at Icchānangala, that is, the brahmin Cankī, the brahmin Tārukkha, the brahmin Pokkharasāti, the brahmin Jāṇussoṇi, the brahmin Todeyya, and other well-known, well-to-do brahmins.

3. Then, while the brahmin students Vāseṭṭha and Bhāradvāja were walking and wandering for exercise, this discussion arose between them: "How is one a brahmin?" The brahmin student Bhāradvāja said: "When one is well born on both sides, of pure maternal and paternal descent seven generations back, unassailable and impeccable in respect of birth, then one is a brahmin." The brahmin student Vāseṭṭha said: "When one is virtuous and fulfils the observances, then one is a brahmin."

4. But the brahmin student Bhāradvāja could not [116] convince the brahmin student Vāseṭṭha, nor could the brahmin student Vāseṭṭha convince the brahmin student Bhāradvāja.

5. Then the brahmin student Vāseṭṭha addressed the brahmin student Bhāradvāja: "Sir, the recluse Gotama, the son of the Sakyans who went forth from a Sakyan clan, is living at Icchānangala, in the wood near Icchānangala. Now a good report of Master Gotama has been spread to this effect: 'That Blessed One is accomplished, fully enlightened, perfect in true knowledge and conduct, sublime, knower of worlds, incomparable leader of persons to be tamed, teacher of gods and humans, enlightened, blessed.' Come, Bhāradvāja, let us go to the recluse Gotama and ask him about this matter. As he answers, so we will remember it."—"Yes, sir," the brahmin student Bhāradvāja replied.

6. Then the two brahmin students, Vāseṭṭha and Bhāradvāja, went to the Blessed One and exchanged greetings with him. When this courteous and amiable talk was finished, they sat down at one side and the brahmin student Vāseṭṭha addressed the Blessed One in stanzas thus:

7. *Vāseṭṭha*

1. "We are both acknowledged to possess
The knowledge we claim of the Triple Veda,
For I am Pokkharasāti's pupil
And he a pupil of Tārukkha.

2. We have attained full mastery
Over all that the Vedic experts teach;
Skilled in philology and grammar
We match our teachers in discussion. [117]

3. A dispute has arisen between us, Gotama,
Concerning the question of birth and class:
Bhāradvāja says one is a brahmin by birth,
While I hold one is a brahmin by action.[901]
Know this, O Seer, as our debate.

4. Since neither of us could convince the other,
Or make him see his point of view,
We have come to ask you, sir,
Widely famed to be a Buddha.

5. As people turn with palms upraised
Towards the moon when it reaches fullness,
So in the world do they venerate you
And pay homage to you, Gotama.

6. So now we ask of you, Gotama,
The eye uprisen in the world:
Is one a brahmin by birth or action?
Explain to us who do not know
How we should recognise a brahmin."

8. *Buddha*

7. "I will explain to you as they really are,
Vāseṭṭha," said the Blessed One,
"The generic divisions of living beings;
For many are the kinds of birth.

8. Know first the grass and trees:
Though they lack self-awareness,
Their birth is their distinctive mark;
For many are the kinds of birth. [118]

9. Next come the moths and butterflies
And so on through as far as ants:
Their birth is their distinctive mark;
For many are the kinds of birth.

10. Then know the kinds of quadrupeds
[Of varied sorts] both small and large:
Their birth is their distinctive mark;
For many are the kinds of birth.

11. Know those whose bellies are their feet,
To wit, the long-backed class of snakes:
Their birth is their distinctive mark;
For many are the kinds of birth.

12. Know too the water-dwelling fish
That pasture in the liquid world:
Their birth is their distinctive mark;
For many are the kinds of birth.

13. Next know the birds that wing their way
As they range in open skies:
Their birth is their distinctive mark;
For many are the kinds of birth.

9.

14. "While in these births the differences
Of birth make their distinctive mark,
With humans no differences of birth

Make a distinctive mark in them.

15. Nor in the hairs nor in the head
Nor in the ears nor in the eyes
Nor in the mouth nor in the nose
Nor in the lips nor in the brows;

16. Nor in the shoulders or the neck
Nor in the belly or the back
Nor in the buttocks or the breast
Nor in the anus or genitals;

17. Nor in the hands nor in the feet
Nor in the fingers or the nails
Nor in the knees nor in the thighs
Nor in their colour or in voice:
Here birth makes no distinctive mark
As with the other kinds of birth. [119]

18. In human bodies in themselves
Nothing distinctive can be found.
Distinction among human beings
Is purely verbal designation.[902]

10.
19. "Who makes his living among men[903]
By agriculture, you should know
Is called a farmer, Vāseṭṭha;
He is not a brahmin.

20. Who makes his living among men
By varied crafts, you should know
Is called a craftsman, Vāseṭṭha;
He is not a brahmin.

21. Who makes his living among men
By merchandise, you should know
Is called a merchant, Vāseṭṭha;
He is not a brahmin.

22. Who makes his living among men
By serving others, you should know
Is called a servant, Vāseṭṭha;
He is not a brahmin.

23. Who makes his living among men
By stealing, you should know
Is called a robber, Vāseṭṭha;
He is not a brahmin.

24. Who makes his living among men
By archery, you should know
Is called a soldier, Vāseṭṭha;
He is not a brahmin.

25. Who makes his living among men
By priestly craft, you should know
Is called a chaplain, Vāseṭṭha;
He is not a brahmin.

26. Whoever governs among men
The town and realm, you should know
Is called a ruler, Vāseṭṭha;
He is not a brahmin.

11.
27. "I call him not a brahmin
Because of his origin and lineage.
If impediments still lurk in him,
He is just one who says 'Sir.'[904]
Who is unimpeded and clings no more:
He is the one I call a brahmin.

28. Who has cut off all fetters
And is no more by anguish shaken,
Who has overcome all ties, detached:
He is the one I call a brahmin. [120]

29. Who has cut each strap and thong,
The reins and bridle-band as well,

Whose shaft is lifted, the awakened one:
He is the one I call a brahmin.

30. Who endures without a trace of hate
Abuse, violence, and bondage too,
With strength of patience well arrayed:
He is the one I call a brahmin.

31. Who does not flare up with anger,
Dutiful, virtuous, and humble,
Subdued, bearing his final body:
He is the one I call a brahmin.

32. Who, like the rain on lotus leaves,
Or mustard seed on the point of an awl,
Clings not at all to sensual pleasures:
He is the one I call a brahmin.

33. Who knows right here within himself
The destruction of all suffering,
With burden lowered, and detached:
He is the one I call a brahmin.

34. Who with deep understanding, wise,
Can tell the path from the not-path
And has attained the goal supreme:
He is the one I call a brahmin.

35. Aloof alike from householders
And those gone into homelessness,
Who wanders without home or wish:
He is the one I call a brahmin.

36. Who has laid aside the rod
Against all beings frail or bold,
Who does not kill or have them killed:
He is the one I call a brahmin.

37. Who is unopposed among opponents,
Peaceful among those given to violence,

Who does not cling among those who cling:
He is the one I call a brahmin.

38. Who has dropped all lust and hate,
Dropped conceit and contempt,
Like mustard seed on the point of an awl:
He is the one I call a brahmin. [121]

39. Who utters speech free from harshness,
Full of meaning, ever truthful,
Which does not damage anyone:
He is the one I call a brahmin.

40. Who in the world will never take
What is not given, long or short,
Small or big or fair or foul:
He is the one I call a brahmin.

41. Who has no more inner yearnings
Regarding this world and the next,
Who lives unyearning and detached:
He is the one I call a brahmin.

42. Who has no more indulgences
No more perplexity since he knows
Through having reached the Deathless Sphere:
He is the one I call a brahmin.

43. Who, by transcending all ties here
About both merit and evil deeds,
Is sorrowless, stainless, and pure:
He is the one I call a brahmin.

44. Who, pure as the spotless moon,
Is clear and limpid, and in whom
Delight and being have been destroyed:
He is the one I call a brahmin.

45. Who has passed beyond the swamp,
The mire, saṁsāra, all delusion,

Who has crossed to the further shore
And meditates within the jhānas,
Is unperturbed and unperplexed,
Attained Nibbāna through no clinging:
He is the one I call a brahmin.

46. Who has abandoned sensual pleasures
And wanders here in homelessness
With sense desires and being destroyed:
He is the one I call a brahmin.

47. Who has abandoned craving too,
And wanders here in homelessness,
With craving and being both destroyed:
He is the one I call a brahmin.

48. Who leaves behind all human bonds
And has cast off the bonds of heaven,
Detached from all bonds everywhere:
He is the one I call a brahmin.

49. Who leaves behind delight and discontent,
Who is cool and acquisitionless,
The hero who has transcended the whole world:
He is the one I call a brahmin. [122]

50. Who knows how beings pass away
To reappear in many a mode,
Unclutching he, sublime, awake:
He is the one I call a brahmin.

51. Whose destination is unknown
To gods, to spirits, and to men,
An arahant with taints destroyed:
He is the one I call a brahmin.

52. Who has no impediments at all,
Before, behind, or in the middle,
Who is unimpeded and clings no more:
He is the one I call a brahmin.

53. The herd's leader, perfected hero,
The great seer whose victory is won,
Unperturbed, cleansed, awakened:
He is the one I call a brahmin.

54. Who knows his manifold past lives
And sees the heavens and states of woe,
Who has reached the destruction of birth:
He is the one I call a brahmin.

12.
55. "For name and clan are assigned
As mere designations in the world;
Originating in conventions,
They are assigned here and there.

56. For those who do not know this fact,
Wrong views have long underlain their hearts;
Not knowing, they declare to us:
'One is a brahmin by birth.'

57. One is not a brahmin by birth,
Nor by birth a non-brahmin.
By action is one a brahmin,
By action is one a non-brahmin.

58. For men are farmers by their acts,[905]
And by their acts are craftsmen too;
And men are merchants by their acts,
And by their acts are servants too.

59. And men are robbers by their acts,
And by their acts are soldiers too;
And men are chaplains by their acts,
And by their acts are rulers too. [123]

13.
60. "So that is how the truly wise
See action as it really is,

Seers of dependent origination,
Skilled in action and its results.[906]

61. Action makes the world go round,
Action makes this generation turn.
Living beings are bound by action
Like the chariot wheel by the pin.

62. Asceticism, the holy life,
Self-control and inner training—
By this one becomes a brahmin,
In this supreme brahminhood lies.[907]

63. One possessing the triple knowledge,
Peaceful, with being all destroyed:
Know him thus, O Vāseṭṭha,
As Brahmā and Sakka for those who understand."

14. When this was said, the brahmin students Vāseṭṭha and Bhāradvāja said to the Blessed One: "Magnificent, Master Gotama! Magnificent, Master Gotama!...From today let Master Gotama remember us as lay followers who have gone to him for refuge for life."

99 *Subha Sutta*
To Subha

1. THUS HAVE I HEARD. On one occasion the Blessed One was living at Sāvatthī in Jeta's Grove, Anāthapiṇḍika's Park.

2. Now on that occasion the brahmin student Subha, Todeyya's son, was staying at the residence of a certain householder in Sāvatthī for some business or other.[908] Then the brahmin student Subha, Todeyya's son, asked the householder in whose residence he was staying: "Householder, I have heard that Sāvatthī is not devoid of arahants. What recluse or brahmin may we go to today to pay our respects?"

"Venerable sir, this Blessed One is living at Sāvatthī in Jeta's Grove, Anāthapiṇḍika's Park. You may go to pay your respects to that Blessed One, venerable sir." [197]

3. Then, having assented to the householder, the brahmin student Subha, Todeyya's son, went to the Blessed One and exchanged greetings with him. When this courteous and amiable talk was finished, he sat down at one side and asked the Blessed One:

4. "Master Gotama, the brahmins say this: 'The householder is accomplishing the true way, the Dhamma that is wholesome. The one gone forth [into homelessness] is not accomplishing the true way, the Dhamma that is wholesome.' What does Master Gotama say about this?"

"Here, student, I am one who speaks after making an analysis;[909] I do not speak one-sidedly. I do not praise the wrong way of practice on the part either of a householder or one gone forth; for whether it be a householder or one gone forth, one who has entered on the wrong way of practice, by reason of his wrong way of practice, is not accomplishing the true way, the Dhamma that is wholesome. I praise the right way of practice on the part either of a householder or one gone forth; for whether it be a householder or one gone forth, one who has entered on the right way of practice, by reason of his right way of practice, is accomplishing the true way, the Dhamma that is wholesome."

5. "Master Gotama, the brahmins say this: 'Since the work of the household life involves a great deal of activity, great functions, great engagements, and great undertakings, it is of great fruit. Since the work of those gone forth involves a small amount of activity, small functions, small engagements, and small undertakings, it is of small fruit.' What does Master Gotama say about this?"

"Here too, student, I am one who speaks after making an analysis; I do not speak one-sidedly. There is work involving a great deal of activity, great functions, great engagements, and great undertakings, which, when it fails, is of small fruit. There is work involving a great deal of activity, great functions, great engagements, and great undertakings, which, when it succeeds, is of great fruit. There is work involving a small amount of activity, small functions, small engagements, and small undertakings, which, when it fails, is of small fruit. There is work involving a small amount of activity, small functions, small engagements, and small undertakings, which, when it succeeds, is of great fruit.

6. "What, [198] student, is that work involving a great deal of activity...which, when it fails, is of small fruit? Agriculture is that work involving a great deal of activity...which, when it fails, is of small fruit. And what, student, is that work involving a great deal of activity...which, when it succeeds, is of great fruit? Agriculture again is that work involving a great deal of activity...which, when it succeeds, is of great fruit. And what, student, is that work involving a small amount of activity... which, when it fails, is of small fruit? Trade is that work involving a small amount of activity...which, when it fails, is of small fruit.[910] And what, student, is that work involving a small amount of activity...which, when it succeeds, is of great fruit? Trade again is that work involving a small amount of activity...which, when it succeeds, is of great fruit.

7. "Just as agriculture, student, is work that involves a great deal of activity...but is of small fruit when it fails, so the work of the household life involves a great deal of activity, great functions, great engagements, and great undertakings, but is of small

fruit when it fails. Just as agriculture is work that involves a great deal of activity...and is of great fruit when it succeeds, so the work of the household life involves a great deal of activity, great functions, great engagements, and great undertakings, and is of great fruit when it succeeds. Just as trade is work that involves a small amount of activity...and is of small fruit when it fails, so the work of those gone forth involves a small amount of activity, small functions, small engagements, and small undertakings, and is of small fruit when it fails. Just as trade is work that involves a small amount of activity...but is of great fruit when it succeeds, so [199] the work of those gone forth involves a small amount of activity, small functions, small engagements, and small undertakings, but is of great fruit when it succeeds."

8. "Master Gotama, the brahmins prescribe five things for the performance of merit, for accomplishing the wholesome."

"If it is not troublesome for you, student, please state to this assembly the five things that the brahmins prescribe for the performance of merit, for accomplishing the wholesome."

"It is not troublesome for me, Master Gotama, when such venerable ones as yourself and others are sitting [in the assembly]."

"Then state them, student."

9. "Master Gotama, truth is the first thing that the brahmins prescribe for the performance of merit, for accomplishing the wholesome. Asceticism is the second thing...Celibacy is the third thing...Study is the fourth thing...Generosity is the fifth thing that the brahmins prescribe for the performance of merit, for accomplishing the wholesome. These are the five things that the brahmins prescribe for the performance of merit, for accomplishing the wholesome. What does Master Gotama say about this?"

"How then, student,[911] among the brahmins is there even a single brahmin who says thus: 'I declare the result of these five things having realised it myself with direct knowledge'?"—"No, Master Gotama."

"How then, student, among the brahmins is there even a single teacher or teacher's teacher back to the seventh generation of teachers who says thus: 'I declare the result of these five things having realised it myself with direct knowledge'?"—"No, Master Gotama." [200]

"How then, student, the ancient brahmin seers, the creators of the hymns, the composers of the hymns, whose ancient hymns that were formerly chanted, uttered, and compiled the brahmins nowadays still chant and repeat, repeating what was spoken, reciting what was recited—that is, Aṭṭhaka, Vāmaka, Vāmadeva, Vessāmitta, Yamataggi, Angirasa, Bhāradvāja, Vāseṭṭha, Kassapa, and Bhagu—did even these ancient brahmin seers say thus: 'We declare the result of these five things having realised it ourselves with direct knowledge'?"—"No, Master Gotama."

"So, student, it seems that among the brahmins there is not even a single brahmin who says thus: 'I declare the result of these five things having realised it myself with direct knowledge.' And among the brahmins there is not even a single teacher or a single teacher's teacher back to the seventh generation of teachers, who says thus: 'I declare the result of these five things having realised it myself with direct knowledge.' And the ancient brahmin seers, the creators of the hymns, the composers of the hymns...even these ancient brahmin seers did not say thus: 'We declare the result of these five things having realised it ourselves with direct knowledge.' Suppose there were a file of blind men each in touch with the next: the first one does not see, the middle one does not see, and the last one does not see. So too, student, in regard to their statement the brahmins seem to be like a file of blind men: the first one does not see, the middle one does not see, and the last one does not see."

10. When this was said, the brahmin student Subha, Todeyya's son, was angry and displeased with the simile of the file of blind men, and he reviled, disparaged, and censured the Blessed One, saying: "The recluse Gotama will be worsted." Then he said to the Blessed One: "Master Gotama, the brahmin Pokkharasāti of the Upamañña clan, lord of the Subhaga Grove, says thus:[912] 'Some recluses and brahmins here claim superhuman states, distinctions in knowledge and vision worthy of the noble ones. But what they say [201] turns out to be ridiculous; it turns out to be mere words, empty and hollow. For how could a human being know or see or realise a superhuman state, a distinction in knowledge and vision worthy of the noble ones? That is impossible.'"

11. "How then, student, does the brahmin Pokkharasāti understand the minds of all recluses and brahmins, having encompassed them with his own mind?"

"Master Gotama, the brahmin Pokkharasāti does not even

understand the mind of his slavewoman Puṇṇikā, having encompassed it with his own mind, so how could he understand thus the minds of all recluses and brahmins?"

12. "Student, suppose there were a man born blind who could not see dark and light forms, who could not see blue, yellow, red, or pink forms, who could not see what was even and uneven, who could not see the stars or the sun and moon. He might say thus: 'There are no dark and light forms, and no one who sees dark and light forms; there are no blue, yellow, red, or pink forms, and no one who sees blue, yellow, red, or pink forms; there is nothing even and uneven, and no one who sees anything even and uneven; there are no stars and no sun and moon, and no one who sees stars and the sun and moon. I do not know these, I do not see these, therefore these do not exist.' Speaking thus, student, would he be speaking rightly?"

"No, Master Gotama. There are dark and light forms, and those who see dark and light forms...there are the stars and the sun and moon, and those who see the stars and the sun and moon. [202] Saying, 'I do not know these, I do not see these, therefore these do not exist,' he would not be speaking rightly."

13. "So too, student, the brahmin Pokkharasāti is blind and visionless. That he could know or see or realise a superhuman state, a distinction in knowledge and vision worthy of the noble ones—this is impossible. What do you think, student? What is better for those well-to-do brahmins of Kosala such as the brahmin Cankī, the brahmin Tārukkha, the brahmin Pokkharasāti, the brahmin Jāṇussoṇi, or your father, the brahmin Todeyya—that the statements they make accord with worldly convention or flaunt worldly convention?"—"That they accord with worldly convention, Master Gotama."

"What is better for them, that the statements they make be thoughtful or thoughtless?"—"Thoughtful, Master Gotama."—"What is better for them, that they make their statements after reflecting or without reflecting?"—"After reflecting, Master Gotama."—"What is better for them, that the statements they make be beneficial or unbeneficial?"—"Beneficial, Master Gotama."

14. "What do you think, student? If that is so, did the statement made by the brahmin Pokkharasāti accord with worldly convention or flaunt worldly convention?"—"It flaunted

worldly convention, Master Gotama."—"Was the statement made thoughtful or thoughtless?"—"Thoughtless, Master Gotama."—"Was the statement made after reflecting or without reflecting?"—"Without reflecting, Master Gotama."—"Was the statement made beneficial or unbeneficial?"—"Unbeneficial, Master Gotama." [203]

15. "Now there are these five hindrances, student. What are the five? The hindrance of sensual desire, the hindrance of ill will, the hindrance of sloth and torpor, the hindrance of restlessness and remorse, and the hindrance of doubt. These are the five hindrances. The brahmin Pokkharasāti is obstructed, hindered, blocked, and enveloped by these five hindrances. That he could know or see or realise a superhuman state, a distinction in knowledge and vision worthy of the noble ones—this is impossible.

16. "Now there are these five cords of sensual pleasure, student. What are the five? Forms cognizable by the eye that are wished for, desired, agreeable, and likeable, connected with sensual desire and provocative of lust. Sounds cognizable by the ear...Odours cognizable by the nose...Flavours cognizable by the tongue...Tangibles cognizable by the body that are wished for, desired, agreeable, and likeable, connected with sensual desire and provocative of lust. These are the five cords of sensual pleasure. The brahmin Pokkharasāti is tied to these five cords of sensual pleasure, infatuated with them and utterly committed to them; he enjoys them without seeing the danger in them or understanding the escape from them. That he could know or see or realise a superhuman state, a distinction in knowledge and vision worthy of the noble ones—this is impossible.

17. "What do you think, student? Which of these two fires would have a [better] flame, colour, and radiance—a fire that might burn in dependence on fuel, such as grass and wood, or a fire that might burn independent of fuel, such as grass and wood?"

"If it were possible, Master Gotama, for a fire to burn independent of fuel such as grass and wood, that fire would have a [better] flame, colour, and radiance."

"It is impossible, student, it cannot happen that a fire could burn independent of fuel such as grass or wood except through [the exercise of] supernormal power. Like the fire that burns dependent on fuel such as grass and wood, I say, is the rapture

[204] that is dependent on the five cords of sensual pleasure. Like the fire that burns independent of fuel such as grass and wood, I say, is the rapture that is apart from sensual pleasures, apart from unwholesome states. And what, student, is the rapture that is apart from sensual pleasures, apart from unwholesome states? Here, quite secluded from sensual pleasures, secluded from unwholesome states, a bhikkhu enters upon and abides in the first jhāna, which is accompanied by applied and sustained thought, with rapture and pleasure born of seclusion. This is a rapture apart from sensual pleasures, apart from unwholesome states. Again, with the stilling of applied and sustained thought, a bhikkhu enters upon and abides in the second jhāna, which has self-confidence and singleness of mind without applied and sustained thought, with rapture and pleasure born of concentration. This too is a rapture apart from sensual pleasures, apart from unwholesome states.

18. "Of those five things, student, that the brahmins prescribe for the performance of merit, for accomplishing the wholesome, which of the five do they prescribe as the most fruitful for the performance of merit, for accomplishing the wholesome?"

"Of those five things, Master Gotama, that the brahmins prescribe for the performance of merit, for accomplishing the wholesome, they prescribe generosity as the most fruitful for the performance of merit, for accomplishing the wholesome."

19. "What do you think, student? Here a brahmin might be holding a great sacrifice, and two other brahmins would go there thinking to take part in that great sacrifice. One brahmin among them would think: 'Oh, that only I might get the best seat, the best water, the best almsfood in the refectory; that no other brahmin might get the best seat, the best water, the best almsfood in the refectory!' And it is possible that the other brahmin, not that brahmin, gets the best seat, the best water, the best almsfood in the refectory. Thinking about this, [205] the first brahmin might become angry and displeased. What kind of result do the brahmins describe for this?"

"Master Gotama, brahmins do not give gifts in such a way, thinking: 'Let the others become angry and displeased because of this.' Rather, brahmins give gifts motivated by compassion."

"That being so, student, isn't this the brahmins' sixth basis for the performance of merit, that is, the motive of compassion?"[913]

"That being so, Master Gotama, this is the brahmins' sixth basis for the performance of merit, that is, the motive of compassion."

20. "Those five things, student, that the brahmins prescribe for the performance of merit, for accomplishing the wholesome—where do you often see those five things, among householders or among those gone forth?"

"Those five things, Master Gotama, that the brahmins prescribe for the performance of merit, for accomplishing the wholesome, I often see among those gone forth, seldom among householders. For the householder has a great deal of activity, great functions, great engagements, and great undertakings: he does not constantly and invariably speak the truth, practise asceticism, observe celibacy, engage in study, or engage in generosity. But one gone forth has a small amount of activity, small functions, small engagements, and small undertakings: he constantly and invariably speaks the truth, practises asceticism, observes celibacy, engages in study, and engages in generosity. Thus those five things that the brahmins prescribe for the performance of merit, for accomplishing the wholesome, I often see among those gone forth, seldom among householders."

21. "Those five things, student, that the brahmins prescribe for the performance of merit, for accomplishing the wholesome, [206] I call equipment of the mind, that is, for developing a mind that is without hostility and without ill will. Here, student, a bhikkhu is a speaker of truth. Thinking, 'I am a speaker of truth,' he gains inspiration in the meaning, gains inspiration in the Dhamma, gains gladness connected with the Dhamma. It is that gladness connected with the wholesome that I call an equipment of the mind. Here, student, a bhikkhu is an ascetic...one who is celibate...one who engages in study...one who engages in generosity. Thinking, 'I am one who engages in generosity,' he gains inspiration in the meaning, gains inspiration in the Dhamma, gains gladness connected with the Dhamma. It is that gladness connected with the wholesome that I call an equipment of the mind. Thus those five things that the brahmins prescribe for the performance of merit, for accomplishing the wholesome, I call equipment of the mind, that is, for developing a mind that is without hostility and without ill will."

22. When this was said, the brahmin student Subha, Todeyya's

son, said to the Blessed One: "Master Gotama, I have heard that the recluse Gotama knows the path to the company of Brahmā."

"What do you think, student? Is the village of Naḷakāra near here, not far from here?"

"Yes, sir, the village of Naḷakāra is near here, not far from here."

"What do you think, student? Suppose there was a man born and raised in the village of Naḷakāra, and as soon as he had left Naḷakāra they asked him about the path to the village. Would that man be slow or hesitant in answering?"

"No, Master Gotama. Why is that? Because that man has been born and raised in Naḷakāra, and is well acquainted with all the paths to the village."

"Still, a man born and raised in the village of Naḷakāra [207] might be slow or hesitant in answering when asked about the path to the village, but a Tathāgata, when asked about the Brahma-world or the way leading to the Brahma-world, would never be slow or hesitant in answering. I understand Brahmā, student, and I understand the Brahma-world, and I understand the way leading to the Brahma-world, and I understand how one should practise to reappear in the Brahma-world."[914]

23. "Master Gotama, I have heard that the recluse Gotama teaches the path to the company of Brahmā. It would be good if Master Gotama would teach me the path to the company of Brahmā."

"Then, student, listen and attend closely to what I shall say."

"Yes, sir," he replied. The Blessed One said this:

24. "What, student, is the path to the company of Brahmā? Here a bhikkhu abides pervading one quarter with a mind imbued with loving-kindness, likewise the second, likewise the third, likewise the fourth; so above, below, around, and everywhere, and to all as to himself, he abides pervading the all-encompassing world with a mind imbued with loving-kindness, abundant, exalted, immeasurable, without hostility, and without ill will. When the deliverance of mind by loving-kindness is developed in this way, no limiting action remains there, none persists there. Just as a vigorous trumpeter could make himself heard without difficulty in the four quarters, so too, when the deliverance of mind by loving-kindness is developed in this way, no limiting action remains there, none persists there.[915] This is the path to the company of Brahmā.

25–27. "Again, a bhikkhu abides pervading one quarter with a mind imbued with compassion...with a mind imbued with altruistic joy...with a mind imbued with equanimity, likewise the second, likewise the third, likewise the fourth; so above, below, around, and everywhere, and to all as to himself, he abides pervading the all-encompassing world with a mind imbued with equanimity, abundant, exalted, [208] immeasurable, without hostility, and without ill will. When the deliverance of mind by equanimity is developed in this way, no limiting action remains there, none persists there. Just as a vigorous trumpeter could make himself heard without difficulty in the four quarters, so too, when the deliverance of mind by equanimity is developed in this way, no limiting action remains there, none persists there. This too is the path to the company of Brahmā."

28. When this was said, the brahmin student Subha, Todeyya's son, said to the Blessed One: "Magnificent, Master Gotama! Magnificent, Master Gotama! Master Gotama has made the Dhamma clear in many ways, as though he were turning upright what had been overturned, revealing what was hidden, showing the way to one who was lost, or holding up a lamp in the dark for those with eyesight to see forms. I go to Master Gotama for refuge and to the Dhamma and to the Sangha of bhikkhus. Let Master Gotama remember me as a lay follower who has gone to him for refuge for life.

29. "And now, Master Gotama, we depart. We are busy and have much to do."

"You may go, student, at your own convenience."

Then the brahmin student Subha, Todeyya's son, having delighted and rejoiced in the Blessed One's words, rose from his seat, and after paying homage to the Blessed One, keeping him on his right, he departed.

30. Now on that occasion the brahmin Jāṇussoṇi was driving out of Sāvatthī in the middle of the day in an all-white chariot drawn by white mares.[916] He saw the brahmin student Subha, Todeyya's son, coming in the distance and asked him: "Now where is Master Bhāradvāja coming from in the middle of the day?"

"Sir, I am coming from the presence of the recluse Gotama."

"What does Master Bhāradvāja think of the recluse Gotama's lucidity of wisdom? He is wise, is he not?" [209]

"Sir, who am I to know the recluse Gotama's lucidity of wisdom? One would surely have to be his equal to know the recluse Gotama's lucidity of wisdom."

"Master Bhāradvāja praises the recluse Gotama with high praise indeed."

"Sir, who am I to praise the recluse Gotama? The recluse Gotama is praised by the praised as best among gods and humans. Sir, those five things that the brahmins prescribe for the performance of merit, for accomplishing the wholesome, the recluse Gotama calls equipment of the mind, that is, for developing a mind that is without hostility and without ill will."

31. When this was said, the brahmin Jāṇussoṇi got down from his all-white chariot drawn by white mares, and after arranging his upper robe on one shoulder, he extended his hands in reverential salutation towards the Blessed One and uttered this exclamation: "It is a gain for King Pasenadi of Kosala, it is a great gain for King Pasenadi of Kosala that the Tathāgata, accomplished and fully enlightened, lives in his realm."

100 *Sangārava Sutta*
To Sangārava

1. THUS HAVE I HEARD. On one occasion the Blessed One was wandering in the Kosalan country with a large Sangha of bhikkhus.

2. Now on that occasion a brahmin woman named Dhānañjānī was staying at Caṇḍalakappa, having full confidence in the Buddha, the Dhamma, and the Sangha.[917] One time she stumbled, and [on recovering her balance] exclaimed three times: "Honour to the Blessed One, accomplished and fully enlightened! Honour to the Blessed One, accomplished and fully enlightened! Honour to the Blessed One, accomplished [210] and fully enlightened!"

3. At the time there was a brahmin student named Sangārava staying at Caṇḍalakappa. He was a master of the Three Vedas, with their vocabularies, liturgy, phonology, and etymology, and the histories as the fifth; skilled in philology and grammar, he was fully versed in natural philosophy and in the marks of a Great Man. Having heard the brahmin woman Dhānañjānī utter those words, he said to her: "This brahmin woman Dhānañjānī must be disgraced and degraded, since when there are brahmins around she praises that bald-pated recluse."

[She replied:] "My dear sir, you do not know the virtue and wisdom of the Blessed One. If you knew that Blessed One's virtue and wisdom, my dear sir, you would never think of abusing and reviling him."

"Then, madam, inform me when the recluse Gotama comes to Caṇḍalakappa."

"Yes, dear sir," the brahmin woman Dhānañjāni replied.

4. Then, after wandering by stages in the Kosalan country, the Blessed One eventually arrived at Caṇḍalakappa. There in Caṇḍalakappa the Blessed One lived in the Mango Grove belonging to the brahmins of the Todeyya clan.

5. The brahmin woman Dhānañjānī heard that the Blessed One had arrived, so she went to the brahmin student Saṅgārava and told him: "My dear sir, the Blessed One has arrived in Caṇḍalakappa and he is living here in Caṇḍalakappa in the Mango Grove belonging to the brahmins of the Todeyya clan. Now, dear Sir, you may go at your own convenience."

"Yes, madam," he replied. Then he went to the Blessed One and exchanged greetings with him. When this courteous [211] and amiable talk was finished, he sat down at one side and said:

6. "Master Gotama, there are some recluses and brahmins who claim [to teach] the fundamentals of the holy life after having reached the consummation and perfection of direct knowledge here and now.[918] Where among these recluses and brahmins does Master Gotama stand?"

7. "Bhāradvāja, I say that there is a diversity among those recluses and brahmins who claim [to teach] the fundamentals of the holy life after having reached the consummation and perfection of direct knowledge here and now. There are some recluses and brahmins who are traditionalists, who on the basis of oral tradition claim [to teach] the fundamentals of the holy life after having reached the consummation and perfection of direct knowledge here and now; such are the brahmins of the Three Vedas. There are some recluses and brahmins who, entirely on the basis of mere faith, claim [to teach] the fundamentals of the holy life after having reached the consummation and perfection of direct knowledge here and now; such are the reasoners and investigators.[919] There are some recluses and brahmins who, having directly known the Dhamma for themselves[920] among things not heard before, claim [to teach] the fundamentals of the holy life after having reached the consummation and perfection of direct knowledge here and now.

8. "I, Bhāradvāja, am one of those recluses and brahmins who, having directly known the Dhamma for themselves among things not heard before, claim [to teach] the fundamentals of the holy life after having reached the consummation and perfection of direct knowledge here and now. As to how I am one of those recluses and brahmins, that may be understood in the following way.

9. "Here, Bhāradvāja, before my enlightenment, while I was still only an unenlightened Bodhisatta, I considered thus:

'Household life is crowded and dusty; life gone forth is wide open. It is not easy while living in a home to lead the holy life utterly perfect and pure as a polished shell. Suppose I shave off my hair and beard, put on the yellow robe, and go forth from the home life into homelessness.'

10–13. "Later, Bhāradvāja, [212] while still young...(*as Sutta 26, §§14–17*)...And I sat down thinking: 'This will serve for striving.'

14–30. "Now these three similes occurred to me spontaneously never heard before...(*as Sutta 36, §§17–33; but in the present sutta in §§17–22—corresponding to §§20–25 of Sutta 36—the sentence* "But such painful feeling that arose in me did not invade my mind and remain" *does not occur*)...the five bhikkhus were disgusted and left me, thinking: 'The recluse Gotama now lives luxuriously; he has given up his striving and reverted to luxury.'

31–41. "Now when I had eaten solid food and regained my strength, then quite secluded from sensual pleasures, secluded from unwholesome states...(*as Sutta 36, §§34–44; but in the present sutta in §§36, 38, and 41—corresponding to §§39, 41, and 44 of Sutta 36—the sentence* "But such pleasant feeling that arose in me did not invade my mind and remain" *does not occur*)...as happens in one who abides diligent, ardent, and resolute."

42. When this was said, the brahmin student Sangārava said to the Blessed One: "Master Gotama's striving was unfaltering, Master Gotama's striving was that of a true man, as it should be for an Accomplished One, a Fully Enlightened One. But how is it, Master Gotama, are there gods?"

"It is known to me to be the case, Bhāradvāja, that there are gods."

"But how is this, Master Gotama, that when you are asked, 'Are there gods?' you say: 'It is known to me to be the case, Bhāradvāja, that there are gods'? If that is so, isn't what you say empty and false?"[921]

"Bhāradvāja, when one is asked, 'Are there gods?' [213] whether one answers, 'There are gods,' or 'It is known to me to be the case [that there are gods],' a wise man can draw the definite conclusion that there are gods."

"But why didn't Master Gotama answer me in the first way?"

"It is widely accepted in the world, Bhāradvāja, that there are gods."

43. When this was said, the brahmin student Sangārava said to

the Blessed One: "Magnificent, Master Gotama! Magnificent, Master Gotama! Master Gotama has made the Dhamma clear in many ways, as though he were turning upright what had been overturned, revealing what was hidden, showing the way to one who was lost, or holding up a lamp in the dark for those with eyesight to see forms. I go to Master Gotama for refuge and to the Dhamma and to the Sangha of bhikkhus. Let Master Gotama remember me as a lay follower who has gone to him for refuge for life."

Part Three
The Final Fifty Discourses
(*Uparipaṇṇāsapāḷi*)

1

The Division at Devadaha

(*Devadahavagga*)

101 *Devadaha Sutta*
At Devadaha

[214] 1. THUS HAVE I HEARD. On one occasion the Blessed One was living in the Sakyan country where there was a town of the Sakyans named Devadaha. There the Blessed One addressed the bhikkhus thus: "Bhikkhus."—"Venerable sir," they replied. The Blessed One said this:

2. "Bhikkhus, there are some recluses and brahmins who hold such a doctrine and view as this: 'Whatever this person feels, whether pleasure or pain or neither-pain-nor-pleasure, all that is caused by what was done in the past.[922] So by annihilating with asceticism past actions[923] and by doing no fresh actions, there will be no consequence in the future. With no consequence in the future, there is the destruction of action. With the destruction of action, there is the destruction of suffering. With the destruction of suffering, there is the destruction of feeling. With the destruction of feeling, all suffering will be exhausted.' So speak the Nigaṇṭhas, bhikkhus.

3. "I go to the Nigaṇṭhas who speak thus and I say: 'Friend Nigaṇṭhas, is it true that you hold such a doctrine and view as this: "Whatever this person feels…all suffering will be exhausted"?' If, when they are asked thus, the Nigaṇṭhas admit this and say 'Yes,' I say to them:

4. "'But, friends, do you know that you existed in the past, and that it is not the case that you did not exist?'—'No, friend.'—'But, friends, do you know that you did evil actions in the past and did not abstain from them?'—'No, friend.'—'But, friends, do you know that you did such and such evil actions?'—'No, friend.'—'But, friends, do you know that so much suffering has already been exhausted, or that so much suffering has still to be exhausted, or that when so much suffering has been exhausted all suffering will have been exhausted?'—[215] 'No, friend.'—'But, friends, do you

know what the abandoning of unwholesome states is and what the cultivation of wholesome states is here and now?'—'No, friend.'

5. "'So, friends, it seems that you do not know that you existed in the past and that it is not the case that you did not exist; or that you did evil actions in the past and did not abstain from them; or that you did such and such evil actions; or that so much suffering has already been exhausted, or that so much suffering has still to be exhausted, or that when so much suffering has been exhausted all suffering will have been exhausted; or what the abandoning of unwholesome states is and what the cultivation of wholesome states is here and now. That being so, it is not fitting for the venerable Nigaṇṭhas to declare: "Whatever this person feels, whether pleasure or pain or neither-pain-nor-pleasure, all that is caused by what was done in the past. So by annihilating with asceticism past actions and by doing no fresh actions, there will be no consequence in the future. With no consequence in the future...all suffering will be exhausted."

6. "'If, friend Nigaṇṭhas, you knew that you existed in the past and that it is not the case that you did not exist; or that you did evil actions in the past and did not abstain from them; or that you did such and such evil actions; or that so much suffering has already been exhausted, or that so much suffering has still to be exhausted, or that when so much suffering has been exhausted all suffering will have been exhausted; or what the abandoning of unwholesome states is and what the cultivation of wholesome states is here and now; that being so, it would be fitting for the venerable Nigaṇṭhas to declare: "Whatever this person feels...[216]...all suffering will be exhausted."

7. "'Friend Nigaṇṭhas, suppose a man were wounded by an arrow thickly smeared with poison, and because of this he felt painful, racking, piercing feelings. Then his friends and companions, kinsmen and relatives, brought a surgeon. The surgeon would cut around the opening of the wound with a knife, probe for the arrow with a probe, pull out the arrow, and apply a medicinal cauteriser to the opening of the wound, and at each step the man would feel painful, racking, piercing feelings. Then on a later occasion, when the wound was healed and covered with skin, the man would be well and happy, independent, master of himself, able to go where he likes. He might think: "Formerly I was pierced by an arrow thickly smeared with poison, and

because of this I felt painful, racking, piercing feelings. Then my friends and companions, kinsmen and relatives, brought a surgeon. The surgeon cut around the opening of the wound with a knife, probed for the arrow with a probe, pulled out the arrow, and applied a medicinal cauteriser to the opening of the wound, and at each step I felt painful, racking, piercing feelings. [217] But now that the wound is healed and covered with skin, I am well and happy, independent, my own master, able to go where I like."

8. "'So too, friend Nigaṇṭhas, if you knew that you existed in the past and that it is not the case that you did not exist...or what the abandoning of unwholesome states is and what the cultivation of wholesome states is here and now; that being so, it would be fitting for the venerable Nigaṇṭhas to declare: "Whatever this person feels...all suffering will be exhausted."

9. "'But since, friend Nigaṇṭhas, you do not know that you existed in the past and that it is not the case that you did not exist...or what the abandoning of unwholesome states is and what the cultivation of wholesome states is here and now, it is not fitting for the venerable Nigaṇṭhas to declare: "Whatever this person feels...all suffering will be exhausted."'

10. "When this was said, the Nigaṇṭhas told me: [218] 'Friend, the Nigaṇṭha Nātaputta is omniscient and all-seeing and claims to have complete knowledge and vision thus: "Whether I am walking or standing or asleep or awake, knowledge and vision are continuously and uninterruptedly present to me." He says thus: "Nigaṇṭhas, you have done evil actions in the past; exhaust them with the performance of piercing austerities. And when you are here and now restrained in body, speech, and mind, that is doing no evil actions for the future. So by annihilating with asceticism past actions and by doing no fresh actions, there will be no consequence in the future. With no consequence in the future...all suffering will be exhausted." We approve of and accept this, and so we are satisfied.'

11. "When this was said, I told the Nigaṇṭhas:[924] 'There are five things, friend Nigaṇṭhas, that may turn out in two different ways here and now. What five? They are: faith, approval, oral tradition, reasoned cogitation, and reflective acceptance of a view. These five things may turn out in two different ways here and now. Herein, what kind of faith do the venerable Nigaṇṭhas

have in a teacher who speaks about the past? What kind of approval, what kind of oral tradition, what kind of reasoned cogitation, what kind of reflective acceptance of a view?' Speaking thus, bhikkhus, I did not see any legitimate defence of their position by the Nigaṇṭhas.

12. "Again, bhikkhus, I said to the Nigaṇṭhas: 'What do you think, friend Nigaṇṭhas? When there is intense exertion, intense striving, do you then feel painful, racking, piercing feelings due to intense exertion? But when there is no intense exertion, no intense striving, do you then not feel any painful, racking, piercing feelings due to intense exertion?'—'When there is intense exertion, friend Gotama, intense striving, then we feel painful, racking, piercing feelings due to intense exertion; [219] but when there is no intense exertion, no intense striving, then we do not feel any painful, racking, piercing feelings due to intense exertion.'

13. "'So it seems, friend Nigaṇṭhas, that when there is intense exertion...you feel painful, racking, piercing feelings due to intense exertion; but when there is no intense exertion...you do not feel any painful, racking, piercing feelings due to intense exertion. That being so, it is not fitting for the venerable Nigaṇṭhas to declare:[925] "Whatever this person feels, whether pleasure or pain or neither-pain-nor-pleasure, all that is caused by what was done in the past. So by annihilating with asceticism past actions and by doing no fresh actions, there will be no consequence in the future. With no consequence...all suffering will be exhausted."

14. "'If, friend Nigaṇṭhas, when there was intense exertion, intense striving, then painful, racking, piercing feelings due to intense exertion were present, and when there was no intense exertion, no intense striving, then painful, racking, piercing feelings due to intense exertion were still present; that being so, it would be fitting for the venerable Nigaṇṭhas to declare: "Whatever this person feels...all suffering will be exhausted."

15. "'But since, friend Nigaṇṭhas, when there is intense exertion, intense striving, then you feel painful, racking, piercing feelings due to intense exertion, but when there is no intense exertion, no intense striving, then you do not feel painful, racking, piercing feelings due to intense exertion, you are therefore feeling only the painful, racking, piercing feelings of your self-

imposed exertion, and it is through ignorance, unknowing, and delusion [220] that you mistakenly hold: "Whatever this person feels...all suffering will be exhausted."' Speaking thus, bhikkhus, I did not see any legitimate defence of their position by the Nigaṇṭhas.

16. "Again, bhikkhus, I said to the Nigaṇṭhas: 'What do you think, friend Nigaṇṭhas? Is it possible that an action [whose result] is to be experienced here and now[926] can, through exertion and striving, become one [whose result] is to be experienced in the next life?'—'No, friend.'—'But is it possible that an action [whose result] is to be experienced in the next life can, through exertion and striving, become one [whose result] is to be experienced here and now?'—'No, friend.'

17. "'What do you think, friend Nigaṇṭhas? Is it possible that an action [whose result] is to be experienced as pleasant can, through exertion and striving, become one [whose result] is to be experienced as painful?'—'No, friend.'—'But is it possible that an action [whose result] is to be experienced as painful can, through exertion and striving, become one [whose result] is to be experienced as pleasant?'—'No, friend.'

18. "'What do you think, friend Nigaṇṭhas? Is it possible that an action [whose result] is to be experienced in a matured [personality] can, by exertion and striving, become one [whose result] is to be experienced in an unmatured [personality]?'[927]—'No, friend.'—'But is it possible that an action [whose result] is to be experienced in an unmatured [personality] can, by exertion and striving, become one [whose result] is to be experienced in a matured personality?'—'No, friend.'

19. "'What do you think, friend Nigaṇṭhas? [221] Is it possible that an action [whose result] is to be much experienced can, through exertion and striving, become one [whose result] is to be little experienced?'—'No, friend.'—'But is it possible that an action [whose result] is to be little experienced can, through exertion and striving, become one [whose result] is to be much experienced?'—'No, friend.'

20. "'What do you think, friend Nigaṇṭhas? Is it possible that an action [whose result] is to be experienced can, through exertion and striving, become one [whose result] is not to be experienced?'[928]—'No, friend.'—'But is it possible that an action [whose result] is not to be experienced can, through exertion

and striving, become one [whose result] is to be experienced?'—'No, friend.'

21. "'So it seems, friend Niganṭhas, that it is impossible that an action [whose result] is to be experienced here and now can, through exertion and striving, become one [whose result] is to be experienced in the next life, and impossible that an action [whose result] is to be experienced in the next life can, through exertion and striving, become one [whose result] is to be experienced here and now; impossible that an action [whose result] is to be experienced as pleasant can, through exertion and striving, become one [whose result] is to be experienced as painful, and impossible that an action [whose result] is to be experienced as painful can, through exertion and striving, become one [whose result] is to be experienced as pleasant; impossible that an action [whose result] is to be experienced in a matured [personality] can, by exertion and striving, become one [whose result] is to be experienced in an unmatured [personality], and impossible that an action [whose result] is to be experienced in an unmatured [personality] can, through exertion and striving, become one [whose result] is to be experienced in a matured [personality]; impossible that an action [whose result] is to be much experienced can, through exertion and striving, become one [whose result] is to be little experienced, and impossible that an action [whose result] is to be little experienced can, through exertion and striving, become one [whose result] is to be much experienced; impossible that an action [whose result] is to be experienced can, through exertion and striving, become one [whose result] is not to be experienced, and impossible that an action [whose result] is not to be experienced can, through exertion and striving, become one [whose result] is to be experienced. That being so, the venerable Niganṭhas' exertion is fruitless, [222] their striving is fruitless.'

22. "So speak the Niganṭhas, bhikkhus. And because the Niganṭhas speak thus, there are ten legitimate deductions from their assertions that provide ground for censuring them:

(1) "If the pleasure and pain that beings feel are caused by what was done in the past, then the Niganṭhas surely must have done bad deeds in the past, since they now feel such painful, racking, piercing feelings.

(2) "If the pleasure and pain that beings feel are caused by the

creative act of a Supreme God,[929] then the Nigaṇṭhas surely must have been created by an evil Supreme God, since they now feel such painful, racking, piercing feelings.

(3) "If the pleasure and pain that beings feel are caused by circumstance and nature,[930] then the Nigaṇṭhas surely must have bad luck, since they now feel such painful, racking, piercing feelings.

(4) "If the pleasure and pain that beings feel are caused by class [among the six classes of birth],[931] then the Nigaṇṭhas surely must belong to a bad class, since they now feel such painful, racking, piercing feelings.

(5) "If the pleasure and pain that beings feel are caused by exertion here and now, then the Nigaṇṭhas surely must strive badly here and now, since they now feel such painful, racking, piercing feelings.

(6) "If the pleasure and pain that beings feel are caused by what was done in the past, then the Nigaṇṭhas are to be censured; if not, then the Nigaṇṭhas are still to be censured.

(7) "If the pleasure and pain that beings feel are caused by the creative act of a Supreme God, then the Nigaṇṭhas are to be censured; if not, they are still to be censured.

(8) "If the pleasure and pain that beings feel are caused by chance, then the Nigaṇṭhas are to be censured; if not, they are still to be censured.

(9) "If the pleasure and pain that beings feel are caused by class, then the Nigaṇṭhas are to be censured; if not, they are still to be censured.

(10) "If the pleasure and pain that beings feel are caused by exertion here and now, [223] then the Nigaṇṭhas are to be censured; if not, they are still to be censured.

"So speak the Nigaṇṭhas, bhikkhus. And because the Nigaṇṭhas speak thus, these ten legitimate deductions from their assertions provide grounds for censuring them. Thus their exertion is fruitless, their striving is fruitless.

23. "And how is exertion fruitful, bhikkhus, how is striving fruitful? Here, bhikkhus, a bhikkhu is not overwhelmed by suffering and does not overwhelm himself with suffering; and he does not give up the pleasure that accords with Dhamma, yet he is not infatuated with that pleasure.[932] He knows thus: 'When I strive with determination, this particular source of suffering

fades away in me because of that determined striving; and when I look on with equanimity, this particular source of suffering fades away in me while I develop equanimity.'[933] He strives with determination in regard to that particular source of suffering which fades away in him because of that determined striving; and he develops equanimity in regard to that particular source of suffering which fades away in him while he is developing equanimity. When he strives with determination, such and such a source of suffering fades away in him because of that determined striving; thus that suffering is exhausted in him. When he looks on with equanimity, such and such a source of suffering fades away in him while he develops equanimity; thus that suffering is exhausted in him.

24. "Suppose, bhikkhus, a man loved a woman with his mind bound to her by intense desire and passion. He might see that woman standing with another man, chatting, joking, and laughing. What do you think, bhikkhus? Would not sorrow, lamentation, pain, grief, and despair arise in that man when he sees that woman standing with another man, chatting, joking, and laughing?"

"Yes, venerable sir. Why is that? Because that man loves that woman with his mind bound to her by intense desire and passion; [224] that is why sorrow, lamentation, pain, grief, and despair would arise in him when he sees her standing with another man, chatting, joking, and laughing."

25. "Then, bhikkhus, the man might think: 'I love this woman with my mind bound to her by intense desire and passion; thus sorrow, lamentation, pain, grief, and despair arise in me when I see her standing with another man, chatting, joking, and laughing. What if I were to abandon my desire and lust for that woman?' He would abandon his desire and lust for that woman. On a later occasion he might see that woman standing with another man, chatting, joking, and laughing. What do you think, bhikkhus? Would sorrow, lamentation, pain, grief, and despair arise in that man when he sees that woman standing with another man...?"

"No, venerable sir. Why is that? Because that man no longer loves that woman; that is why sorrow, lamentation, pain, grief, and despair do not arise in him when he sees that woman standing with another man..."

26. "So too, bhikkhus, when a bhikkhu is not overwhelmed by suffering and does not overwhelm himself with suffering...(*as in §23 above*) [225]...thus that suffering is exhausted in him. Thus, bhikkhus, the exertion is fruitful, the striving is fruitful.

27. "Again, bhikkhus, a bhikkhu considers thus: 'While I live according to my pleasure, unwholesome states increase in me and wholesome states diminish; but when I exert myself in what is painful, unwholesome states diminish in me and wholesome states increase. What if I exert myself in what is painful?' He exerts himself in what is painful. When he does so, unwholesome states diminish in him and wholesome states increase.[934] At a later time he does not exert himself in what is painful. Why is that? The purpose for which that bhikkhu exerted himself in what is painful has been achieved; that is why at a later time he does not exert himself in what is painful.

28. "Suppose, bhikkhus, an arrowsmith were warming and heating an arrow shaft between two flames, making it straight and workable. When the arrow shaft had been warmed and heated between the two flames and had been made straight and workable, then at a later time he would not again warm and heat the arrow shaft and make it straight and workable. Why is that? The purpose for which that arrowsmith had warmed and heated the arrow and made it straight and workable has been achieved; that is why at a later time he would not again warm and heat the arrow shaft and make it straight and workable.

29. "So too, a bhikkhu considers thus...(*as in §27 above*) [226]...that is why at a later time he does not exert himself in what is painful. Thus too, bhikkhus, the exertion is fruitful, the striving is fruitful.

30–37. "Again, bhikkhus, here a Tathāgata appears in the world, accomplished, fully enlightened...(*as Sutta 51, §§12–19*)... he purifies his mind from doubt.

38. "Having thus abandoned these five hindrances, imperfections of the mind that weaken wisdom, quite secluded from sensual pleasures, secluded from unwholesome states, he enters upon and abides in the first jhāna, which is accompanied by applied and sustained thought, with rapture and pleasure born of seclusion. Thus too, bhikkhus, the exertion is fruitful, the striving is fruitful.

39. "Again, bhikkhus, with the stilling of applied and sustained thought, a bhikkhu enters upon and abides in the second jhāna, which has self-confidence and singleness of mind without applied and sustained thought, with rapture and pleasure born of concentration. Thus too, bhikkhus, the exertion is fruitful, the striving is fruitful.

40. "Again, bhikkhus, with the fading away as well of rapture, a bhikkhu abides in equanimity, and mindful and fully aware, still feeling pleasure with the body, he enters upon and abides in the third jhāna, on account of which noble ones announce: 'He has a pleasant abiding who has equanimity and is mindful.' Thus too, bhikkhus, the exertion is fruitful, the striving is fruitful.

41. "Again, bhikkhus, with the abandoning of pleasure and pain, and with the previous disappearance of joy and grief, a bhikkhu enters upon and abides in the fourth jhāna, which has neither-pain-nor-pleasure and purity of mindfulness due to equanimity. Thus too, bhikkhus, the exertion is fruitful, the striving is fruitful.

42. "When his concentrated mind is thus purified, bright, unblemished, rid of imperfection, malleable, wieldy, steady, and attained to imperturbability, he directs it to knowledge of the recollection of past lives. He recollects his manifold past lives, that is, one birth, two births...(*as Sutta 51, §24*)...Thus with their aspects and particulars he recollects his manifold past lives. Thus too, bhikkhus, the exertion is fruitful, the striving is fruitful.

43. "When his concentrated mind is thus purified, bright, unblemished, rid of imperfection, malleable, wieldy, steady, and attained to imperturbability, he directs it to knowledge of the passing away and reappearance of beings...(*as Sutta 51, §25*)... Thus with the divine eye, which is purified and surpasses the human, he sees beings passing away and reappearing, inferior and superior, fair and ugly, fortunate and unfortunate, and he understands how beings pass on according to their actions. Thus too, bhikkhus, the exertion is fruitful, the striving is fruitful. [227]

44. "When his concentrated mind is thus purified, bright, unblemished, rid of imperfection, malleable, wieldy, steady, and attained to imperturbability, he directs it to knowledge of the destruction of the taints. He understands as it actually is: 'This is suffering';...'This is the origin of suffering';...'This is the cessation of suffering';...'This is the way leading to the cessation of

suffering';...'These are the taints';...'This is the origin of the taints';...'This is the cessation of the taints';...'This is the way leading to the cessation of the taints.'

45. "When he knows and sees thus, his mind is liberated from the taint of sensual desire, from the taint of being, and from the taint of ignorance. When it is liberated there comes the knowledge: 'It is liberated.' He understands: 'Birth is destroyed, the holy life has been lived, what had to be done has been done, there is no more coming to any state of being.' Thus too, bhikkhus, the exertion is fruitful, the striving is fruitful.

46. "So the Tathāgata speaks, bhikkhus. And because the Tathāgata speaks thus, there are ten legitimate grounds for praising him:

(1) "If the pleasure and pain that beings feel are caused by what was done in the past, then the Tathāgata surely must have done good deeds in the past, since he now feels such taintless pleasant feelings.

(2) "If the pleasure and pain that beings feel are caused by the creative act of a Supreme God, then the Tathāgata surely must have been created by a good Supreme God, since he now feels such taintless pleasant feelings.

(3) "If the pleasure and pain that beings feel are caused by circumstance and nature, then the Tathāgata surely must have good luck, since he now feels such taintless pleasant feelings.

(4) "If the pleasure and pain that beings feel are caused by class [among the six classes of birth], then the Tathāgata surely must belong to a good class, since he now feels such taintless pleasant feelings.

(5) "If the pleasure and pain that beings feel are caused by exertion here and now, then the Tathāgata surely must strive well here and now, since he now feels such taintless pleasant feelings.

(6) "If the pleasure and pain that beings feel are caused by what was done in the past, then the Tathāgata is to be praised; if not, then the Tathāgata is still to be praised.

(7) "If the pleasure and pain that beings feel are caused by the creative act of a Supreme God, then the Tathāgata is to be praised; if not, then the Tathāgata is still to be praised.

(8) "If the pleasure and pain that beings feel are caused by chance, then the Tathāgata is to be praised; if not, then the Tathāgata is still to be praised.

(9) "If the pleasure and pain that beings feel are caused by class, then the Tathāgata is to be praised; if not, then the Tathāgata is still to be praised.

(10) "If the pleasure and pain that beings feel are caused by exertion here and now, then the Tathāgata is to be praised; if not, [228] then the Tathāgata is still to be praised.

"So the Tathāgata speaks, bhikkhus. And because the Tathāgata speaks thus, there are these ten legitimate grounds for praising him."

That is what the Blessed One said. The bhikkhus were satisfied and delighted in the Blessed One's words.

102 *Pañcattaya Sutta*
The Five and Three

1. THUS HAVE I HEARD.[935] On one occasion the Blessed One was living at Sāvatthī in Jeta's Grove, Anāthapiṇḍika's Park. There he addressed the bhikkhus thus: "Bhikkhus."—"Venerable sir," they replied. The Blessed One said this:

(SPECULATIONS ABOUT THE FUTURE)

2. "Bhikkhus, there are some recluses and brahmins who speculate about the future and hold views about the future, who assert various doctrinal propositions concerning the future.

(I) Some assert thus: 'The self is percipient and unimpaired after death.'

(II) Some assert thus: 'The self is non-percipient and unimpaired after death.'

(III) Some assert thus: 'The self is neither percipient nor non-percipient and unimpaired after death.'

(IV) Or they describe the annihilation, destruction, and extermination of an existing being [at death].

(V) Or some assert Nibbāna here and now.[936]

"Thus (a) they either describe an existing self that is unimpaired after death; (b) or they describe the annihilation, destruction, and extermination of an existing being [at death]; (c) or they assert Nibbāna here and now. Thus these [views] being five become three, and being three become five. This is the summary of the 'five and three.'

3. (I) "Therein, bhikkhus, those recluses and brahmins [229] who describe the self as percipient and unimpaired after death describe such a self, percipient and unimpaired after death, to be either:

material;
or immaterial;
or both material and immaterial;
or neither material nor immaterial;
or percipient of unity;
or percipient of diversity;
or percipient of the limited;
or percipient of the immeasurable.[937]

Or else, among those few who go beyond this, some make assertions about the consciousness-kasiṇa, immeasurable and imperturbable.[938]

4. "The Tathāgata, bhikkhus, understands this thus: 'Those good recluses and brahmins who describe the self as percipient and unimpaired after death describe such a self to be either material... or they describe it to be percipient of the immeasurable. Or else, [230] some make assertions about the base of nothingness, immeasurable and imperturbable; [for them] "there is nothing" is declared to be the purest, supreme, best, and unsurpassed of those perceptions—whether perceptions of form or of the formless, of unity or diversity.[939] That is conditioned and gross, but there is cessation of formations.' Having known 'There is this,' seeing the escape from that, the Tathāgata has gone beyond that.[940]

5. (II) "Therein, bhikkhus, those recluses and brahmins who describe the self as non-percipient and unimpaired after death describe such a self, non-percipient and unimpaired after death, to be either:

material;
or immaterial;
or both material and immaterial;
or neither material nor immaterial.[941]

6. "Therein, bhikkhus, these criticise those recluses and brahmins who describe the self as percipient and unimpaired after death. Why is that? Because they say: 'Perception is a disease, perception is a tumour, perception is a dart; this is peaceful, this is sublime, that is, non-perception.'

7. "The Tathāgata, bhikkhus, understands this thus: 'Those good recluses and brahmins who describe the self as non-percipient and unimpaired after death describe such a self, non-percipient and unimpaired after death, to be either material...or neither material nor immaterial. That any recluse or brahmin

could say: "Apart from material form, apart from feeling, apart from perception, apart from formations, I shall describe the coming and going of consciousness, its passing away and re-appearance, its growth, increase, and maturation"—that is impossible.[942] That is conditioned and gross, but there is [231] cessation of formations.' Having known 'There is this,' seeing the escape from that, the Tathāgata has gone beyond that.

8. (III) "Therein, bhikkhus, those recluses and brahmins who describe the self as neither percipient nor non-percipient and unimpaired after death describe such a self, neither percipient nor non-percipient and unimpaired after death, to be either:

material;
or immaterial;
or both material and immaterial;
or neither material nor immaterial.[943]

9. "Therein, bhikkhus, these criticise those good recluses and brahmins who describe the self as percipient and unimpaired after death, and they criticise those good recluses and brahmins who describe the self as non-percipient and unimpaired after death. Why is that? Because they say: 'Perception is a disease, perception is a tumour, perception is a dart, and non-perception is stupefaction;[944] this is peaceful, this is sublime, that is, neither-perception-nor-non-perception.'

10. "The Tathāgata, bhikkhus, understands this thus: 'Those good recluses and brahmins who describe the self as neither percipient nor non-percipient and unimpaired after death describe such a self, neither percipient nor non-percipient and unimpaired after death, to be either material...or neither material nor immaterial. If any recluses or brahmins describe the entering upon this base to come about through a measure of formations regarding what is seen, heard, sensed, and cognized, that is declared to be a disaster for entering upon this base.[945] [232] For this base, it is declared, is not to be attained as an attainment with formations; this base, it is declared, is to be attained as an attainment with a residue of formations.[946] That is conditioned and gross, but there is cessation of formations.' Having known 'There is this,' seeing the escape from that, the Tathāgata has gone beyond that.

11. (IV) "Therein, bhikkhus, those recluses and brahmins who describe the annihilation, destruction, and extermination of an existing being [at death][947] criticise those good recluses and

brahmins who describe the self as percipient and unimpaired after death, and they criticise those good recluses and brahmins who describe the self as non-percipient and unimpaired after death, and they criticise those good recluses and brahmins who describe the self as neither percipient nor non-percipient and unimpaired after death. Why is that? All these good recluses and brahmins, rushing onwards, assert their attachment thus: 'We shall be thus after death, we shall be thus after death.' Just as a merchant going to market thinks: 'Through this, that will be mine; with this, I will get that'; so too, these good recluses and brahmins seem like merchants when they declare: 'We shall be thus after death, we shall be thus after death.'

12. "The Tathāgata, bhikkhus, understands this thus: 'Those good recluses and brahmins who describe the annihilation, destruction, and extermination of an existing being [at death], through fear of identity and disgust with identity, keep running and circling around that same identity.[948] Just as a dog bound by a leash tied to a firm post or pillar [233] keeps on running and circling around that same post or pillar; so too, these good recluses and brahmins, through fear of identity and disgust with identity, keep running and circling around that same identity. That is conditioned and gross, but there is cessation of formations.' Having known 'There is this,' seeing the escape from that, the Tathāgata has gone beyond that.

13. "Bhikkhus, any recluses or brahmins who speculate about the future and hold views about the future, who assert various doctrinal propositions concerning the future, all assert these five bases or a certain one among them.[949]

(SPECULATIONS ABOUT THE PAST)

14. "Bhikkhus, there are some recluses and brahmins who speculate about the past and hold views about the past, who assert various doctrinal propositions concerning the past.

(1) Some assert thus: 'The self and the world are eternal: only this is true, anything else is wrong.'[950]

(2) Some assert thus: 'The self and the world are not eternal: only this is true, anything else is wrong.'[951]

(3) Some assert thus: 'The self and the world are both eternal and not eternal: only this is true, anything else is wrong.'[952]

(4) Some assert thus: 'The self and the world are neither eternal nor not eternal: only this is true, anything else is wrong.'[953]

(5) Some assert thus: 'The self and the world are finite: only this is true, anything else is wrong.'[954]

(6) Some assert thus: 'The self and the world are infinite: only this is true, anything else is wrong.'

(7) Some assert thus: 'The self and the world are both finite and infinite: only this is true, anything else is wrong.'

(8) Some assert thus: 'The self and the world are neither finite nor infinite: only this is true, anything else is wrong.'

(9) Some assert thus: 'The self and the world are percipient of unity: only this is true, anything else is wrong.'[955]

(10) Some assert thus: 'The self and the world are percipient of diversity: only this is true, anything else is wrong.'

(11) Some assert thus: 'The self and the world are percipient of the limited: only this is true, anything else is wrong.'

(12) Some assert thus: 'The self and the world are percipient of the immeasurable: only this is true, anything else is wrong.'

(13) Some assert thus: 'The self and the world [experience] exclusively pleasure: only this is true, anything else is wrong.'

(14) Some assert thus: 'The self and the world [experience] exclusively pain: only this is true, anything else is wrong.' [234]

(15) Some assert thus: 'The self and the world [experience] both pleasure and pain: only this is true, anything else is wrong.'

(16) Some assert thus: 'The self and the world [experience] neither pleasure nor pain: only this is true, anything else is wrong.'

15. (1) "Therein, bhikkhus, as to those recluses and brahmins who hold such a doctrine and view as this: 'The self and the world are eternal: only this is true, anything else is wrong,' that apart from faith, apart from approval, apart from oral tradition, apart from reasoned cogitation, apart from reflective acceptance of a view, they will have any pure and clear personal knowledge of this—that is impossible.[956] Since they have no pure and clear personal knowledge, even the mere fragmentary knowledge that those good recluses and brahmins clarify [about their view] is declared to be clinging on their part.[957] That is conditioned and gross, but there is cessation of formations. Having known'There is this,' seeing the escape from that, the Tathāgata has gone beyond that.

16. (2–16) "Therein, bhikkhus, as to those recluses and brahmins

who hold such a doctrine and view as this: 'The self and the world are not eternal...both eternal and not eternal...neither eternal nor not eternal...finite...infinite...both finite and infinite...neither finite nor infinite...percipient of unity...percipient of diversity...percipient of the limited...percipient of the immeasurable...[experience] exclusively pleasure...[experience] exclusively pain...[experience] both pleasure and pain...[experience] neither pleasure nor pain: only this is true, anything else is wrong,' that apart from faith, apart from approval, apart from oral tradition, apart from reasoned cogitation, apart from reflective acceptance of a view, they will have any pure and clear personal knowledge of this—that is impossible. [235] Since they have no pure and clear personal knowledge, even the mere fragmentary knowledge that those good recluses and brahmins clarify [about their view] is declared to be clinging on their part. That is conditioned and gross, but there is cessation of formations. Having known 'There is this,' seeing the escape from that, the Tathāgata has gone beyond that.[958]

(NIBBĀNA HERE AND NOW)[959]

17. (V) "Here, bhikkhus,[960] some recluse or brahmin, with the relinquishing of views about the past and the future and through complete lack of resolve upon the fetters of sensual pleasure, enters upon and abides in the rapture of seclusion.[961] He thinks: 'This is the peaceful, this is the sublime, that I enter upon and abide in the rapture of seclusion.' That rapture of seclusion ceases in him. With the cessation of the rapture of seclusion, grief arises, and with the cessation of grief, the rapture of seclusion arises.[962] Just as the sunlight pervades the area that the shadow leaves, and the shadow pervades the area that the sunlight leaves, so too, with the cessation of the rapture of seclusion, grief arises, and with the cessation of grief, the rapture of seclusion arises.

18. "The Tathāgata, bhikkhus, understands this thus: 'This good recluse or brahmin, with the relinquishing of views about the past and the future...and with the cessation of grief, the rapture of seclusion arises. That is conditioned and gross, but there is cessation of formations.' Having known 'There is this,' seeing the escape from that, the Tathāgata has gone beyond that.

19. "Here, bhikkhus, some recluse or brahmin, with the relinquishing of views about the past and the future, through complete lack of resolve upon the fetters of sensual pleasure, and with the surmounting of the rapture of seclusion, enters upon and abides in unworldly pleasure.[963] He thinks: 'This is the peaceful, this is the sublime, that I enter upon and abide in unworldly pleasure.' That unworldly pleasure ceases in him. With the cessation of unworldly pleasure, the rapture of seclusion arises, and with the cessation of the rapture of seclusion, unworldly pleasure arises. [236] Just as the sunlight pervades the area that the shadow leaves, and the shadow pervades the area that the sunlight leaves, so too, with the cessation of unworldly pleasure, the rapture of seclusion arises and with the cessation of the rapture of seclusion, unworldly pleasure arises.

20. "The Tathāgata, bhikkhus, understands this thus: 'This good recluse or brahmin, with the relinquishing of views about the past and the future...and with the cessation of the rapture of seclusion, unworldly pleasure arises. That is conditioned and gross, but there is cessation of formations.' Having known 'There is this,' seeing the escape from that, the Tathāgata has gone beyond that.

21. "Here, bhikkhus, some recluse or brahmin, with the relinquishing of views about the past and the future, through complete lack of resolve upon the fetters of sensual pleasure, and with the surmounting of the rapture of seclusion and unworldly pleasure, enters upon and abides in neither-painful-nor-pleasant feeling.[964] He thinks: 'This is the peaceful, this is the sublime, that I enter upon and abide in neither-painful-nor-pleasant feeling.' That neither-painful-nor-pleasant feeling ceases in him. With the cessation of neither-painful-nor-pleasant feeling, unworldly pleasure arises, and with the cessation of unworldly pleasure, neither-painful-nor-pleasant feeling arises. Just as the sunlight pervades the area that the shadow leaves, and the shadow pervades the area that the sunlight leaves, so too, with the cessation of neither-painful-nor-pleasant feeling, unworldly pleasure arises, and with the cessation of unworldly pleasure, neither-painful-nor-pleasant feeling arises.

22. "The Tathāgata, bhikkhus, understands this thus: 'This good recluse or brahmin, with the relinquishing of views about the past and the future...[237]...and with the cessation of

unworldly pleasure, neither-painful-nor-pleasant feeling arises. That is conditioned and gross, but there is cessation of formations.' Having known 'There is this,' seeing the escape from that, the Tathāgata has gone beyond that.

23. "Here, bhikkhus, some recluse or brahmin, with the relinquishing of views about the past and the future, through complete lack of resolve upon the fetters of sensual pleasure, and with the surmounting of the rapture of seclusion, unworldly pleasure, and neither-painful-nor-pleasant feeling, regards himself thus: '*I* am at peace, *I* have attained Nibbāna, *I* am without clinging.'[965]

24. "The Tathāgata, bhikkhus, understands this thus: 'This good recluse or brahmin, with the relinquishing of views about the past and the future...regards himself thus: "*I* am at peace, *I* have attained Nibbāna, *I* am without clinging." Certainly this venerable one asserts the way directed to Nibbāna. Yet this good recluse or brahmin still clings, clinging either to a view about the past or to a view about the future or to a fetter of sensual pleasure or to the rapture of seclusion or to unworldly pleasure or to neither-painful-nor-pleasant feeling. And when this venerable one regards himself thus: "*I* am at peace, *I* have attained Nibbāna, *I* am without clinging," that too is declared to be clinging on the part of this good recluse or brahmin.[966] That is conditioned and gross, but there is cessation of formations.' Having understood 'There is this,' seeing the escape from that, the Tathāgata has gone beyond that.

25. "Bhikkhus, this supreme state of sublime peace has been discovered by the Tathāgata, that is, liberation through not clinging,[967] by understanding as they actually are the origination, the disappearance, the gratification, the danger, and the escape in the case of the six bases of contact. Bhikkhus, that is the supreme state of sublime peace discovered by the Tathāgata, [238], that is, liberation through not clinging, by understanding as they actually are the origination, the disappearance, the gratification, the danger, and the escape in the case of the six bases of contact."[968]

That is what the Blessed One said. The bhikkhus were satisfied and delighted in the Blessed One's words.

103 *Kinti Sutta*
What Do You Think About Me?

1. THUS HAVE I HEARD. On one occasion the Blessed One was living at Kusinārā, in the Grove of Offerings. There he addressed the bhikkhus thus: "Bhikkhus."—"Venerable sir," they replied. The Blessed One said this:

2. "What do you think about me, bhikkhus? That the recluse Gotama teaches the Dhamma for the sake of robes? Or that the recluse Gotama teaches the Dhamma for the sake of almsfood? Or that the recluse Gotama teaches the Dhamma for the sake of a resting place? Or that the recluse Gotama teaches the Dhamma for the sake of some better state of being?"[969]

"We do not think thus about the Blessed One: 'The recluse Gotama teaches the Dhamma for the sake of robes, or for the sake of almsfood, or for the sake of a resting place, or for the sake of some better state of being.'"

"So, bhikkhus, you do not think thus about me: 'The recluse Gotama teaches the Dhamma for the sake of robes...or for the sake of some better state of being.' Then what do you think about me?"

"Venerable sir, we think thus about the Blessed One: 'The Blessed One is compassionate and seeks our welfare; he teaches the Dhamma out of compassion.'"

"So, bhikkhus, you think thus about me: 'The Blessed One is compassionate and seeks our welfare; he teaches the Dhamma out of compassion.'

3. "So, bhikkhus, these things that I have taught you after directly knowing them—that is, the four foundations of mindfulness, the four right kinds of striving, the four bases for spiritual power, the five faculties, the five powers, the seven [239] enlightenment factors, the Noble Eightfold Path—in these things you should all train in concord, with mutual appreciation, without disputing.

4. "While you are training in concord, with mutual appreciation, without disputing, two bhikkhus might make different assertions about the higher Dhamma.[970]

5. "Now if you should think thus: 'These venerable ones differ about both the meaning and the phrasing,'[971] then whichever bhikkhu you think is the more reasonable should be approached and addressed thus: 'The venerable ones differ about both the meaning and the phrasing. The venerable ones should know that it is for this reason that there is difference about the meaning and difference about the phrasing; let them not fall into a dispute.' Then whichever bhikkhu you think is the most reasonable of those who side together on the opposite part should be approached and addressed thus: 'The venerable ones differ about the meaning and the phrasing. The venerable ones should know that it is for this reason that there is difference about the meaning and difference about the phrasing; let them not fall into a dispute.' So what has been wrongly grasped should be borne in mind as wrongly grasped. Bearing in mind what has been wrongly grasped as wrongly grasped, what is Dhamma and what is Discipline should be expounded.

6. "Now if you should think thus: 'These venerable ones differ about the meaning but agree about the phrasing,' then whichever bhikkhu you think is the more reasonable should be approached and addressed thus: 'The venerable ones differ about the meaning but agree about the phrasing. The venerable ones should know that it is for this reason that there is difference about the meaning but agreement about the phrasing; let them not fall into a dispute.' Then whichever bhikkhu you think is the most reasonable of those who side together on the opposite part should be approached and addressed thus: 'The venerable ones differ about the meaning but agree about the phrasing. The venerable ones should know that it is for this reason that there is difference about the meaning but agreement about the phrasing; let them not fall into a dispute.' [240] So what has been wrongly grasped should be borne in mind as wrongly grasped and what has been rightly grasped should be borne in mind as rightly grasped. Bearing in mind what has been wrongly grasped as wrongly grasped, and bearing in mind what has been rightly grasped as rightly grasped, what is Dhamma and what is Discipline should be expounded.

7. "Now if you think thus: 'These venerable ones agree about the meaning but differ about the phrasing,' then whichever bhikkhu you think is the more reasonable should be approached and addressed thus: 'The venerable ones agree about the meaning but differ about the phrasing. The venerable ones should know that it is for this reason that there is agreement about the meaning but difference about the phrasing. But the phrasing is a mere trifle. Let the venerable ones not fall into a dispute over a mere trifle.'[972] Then whichever bhikkhu you think is the most reasonable of those who side together on the opposite part should be approached and addressed thus: 'The venerable ones agree about the meaning but differ about the phrasing. The venerable ones should know that it is for this reason that there is agreement about the meaning but difference about the phrasing. But the phrasing is a mere trifle. Let the venerable ones not fall into a dispute over a mere trifle.' So what has been rightly grasped should be borne in mind as rightly grasped and what has been wrongly grasped should be borne in mind as wrongly grasped. Bearing in mind what has been rightly grasped as rightly grasped, and bearing in mind what has been wrongly grasped as wrongly grasped, what is Dhamma and what is Discipline should be expounded.

8. "Now if you should think thus: 'These venerable ones agree about both the meaning and the phrasing,' then whichever bhikkhu you think is the more reasonable should be approached and addressed thus: 'The venerable ones agree about both the meaning and the phrasing. The venerable ones should know that it is for this reason that there is agreement about both the meaning and the phrasing; let the venerable ones not fall into a dispute.' Then whichever bhikkhu you think is the most reasonable of those who side together on the opposite part should be approached and addressed thus: 'The venerable ones agree about both the meaning and the phrasing. The venerable ones should know that it is for this reason that there is agreement about both the meaning and the phrasing; let the venerable ones not [241] fall into a dispute.' So what has been rightly grasped should be borne in mind as rightly grasped. Bearing in mind what has been rightly grasped as rightly grasped, what is Dhamma and what is Discipline should be expounded.

9. "While you are training in concord, with mutual appreciation, without disputing, some bhikkhu might commit an offence or a transgression.[973]

10. "Now, bhikkhus, you should not hurry to reprove him; rather, the person should be examined thus: 'I shall not be troubled and the other person will not be hurt; for the other person is not given to anger and resentment, he is not firmly attached to his view and he relinquishes easily, and I can make that person emerge from the unwholesome and establish him in the wholesome.' If such occurs to you, bhikkhus, it is proper to speak.

11. "Then it may occur to you, bhikkhus: 'I shall not be troubled, but the other person will be hurt, for the other person is given to anger and resentment. However, he is not firmly attached to his view and he relinquishes easily, and I can make that person emerge from the unwholesome and establish him in the wholesome. It is a mere trifle that the other person will be hurt, but it is a much greater thing that I can make that person emerge from the unwholesome and establish him in the wholesome.' If such occurs to you, bhikkhus, it is proper to speak.

12. "Then it may occur to you, bhikkhus: 'I shall be troubled, but the other person will not be hurt; for the other person is not given to anger and resentment, though he is firmly attached to his view and he relinquishes with difficulty; yet I can make that person emerge from the unwholesome and establish him in the wholesome. It is a mere trifle that I shall be troubled, but it is a much greater thing that I can make that person emerge from the unwholesome and establish him in the wholesome.' If such occurs to you, bhikkhus, it is proper to speak.

13. "Then it may occur to you, bhikkhus: 'I shall be troubled and the other person will be hurt; [242] for the other person is given to anger and resentment, and he is firmly attached to his view and he relinquishes with difficulty; yet I can make that person emerge from the unwholesome and establish him in the wholesome. It is a mere trifle that I shall be troubled and the other person hurt, but it is a much greater thing that I can make that person emerge from the unwholesome and establish him in the wholesome.' If such occurs to you, bhikkhus, it is proper to speak.

14. "Then it may occur to you, bhikkhus: 'I shall be troubled and the other person will be hurt; for the other person is given to anger and resentment, and he is firmly attached to his view

and he relinquishes with difficulty; and I cannot make that person emerge from the unwholesome and establish him in the wholesome.' One should not underrate equanimity towards such a person.

15. "While you are training in concord, with mutual appreciation, without disputing, there might arise mutual verbal friction, insolence in views, mental annoyance, bitterness, and dejection. Then whichever bhikkhu you think is the most reasonable of those who side together on the one part should be approached and addressed thus: 'While we were training in concord, friend, with mutual appreciation, without disputing, there arose mutual verbal friction, insolence in views, mental annoyance, bitterness, and dejection. If the Recluse knew, would he censure that?'[974] Answering rightly, the bhikkhu would answer thus: 'While we were training...If the Recluse knew, he would censure that.'

"'But, friend, without abandoning that thing, can one realise Nibbāna?' Answering rightly, the bhikkhu would answer thus: 'Friend, without abandoning that thing, one cannot realise Nibbāna.'[975]

16. "Then whichever bhikkhu you think is the most reasonable of those who side together on the opposite part should be approached and addressed thus: 'While we were training in concord, friend, with mutual appreciation, without disputing, there arose mutual verbal friction, insolence in views, mental annoyance, bitterness, and dejection. If the Recluse knew, would he censure that?' Answering rightly, the bhikkhu would answer thus: 'While we were training...If the Recluse knew, he would censure that.'

"'But, friend, without abandoning that thing, can one realise Nibbāna?' Answering rightly, the bhikkhu would answer thus: [243] 'Friend, without abandoning that thing, one cannot realise Nibbāna.'

17. "If others should ask that bhikkhu thus: 'Was it the venerable one who made those bhikkhus emerge from the unwholesome and established them in the wholesome?' answering rightly, the bhikkhu would answer thus: 'Here, friends, I went to the Blessed One. The Blessed One taught me the Dhamma. Having heard that Dhamma, I spoke to those bhikkhus. The bhikkhus heard that Dhamma, and they emerged from the unwholesome and became established in the wholesome.' Answering thus, the

bhikkhu neither exalts himself nor disparages others; he answers in accordance with the Dhamma in such a way that nothing which provides a ground for censure can be legitimately deduced from his assertion."

That is what the Blessed One said. The bhikkhus were satisfied and delighted in the Blessed One's words.

104 *Sāmagāma Sutta*
At Sāmagāma

1. THUS HAVE I HEARD. On one occasion the Blessed One was living in the Sakyan country at Sāmagāma.

2. Now on that occasion the Nigaṇṭha Nātaputta had just died at Pāvā.[976] On his death the Nigaṇṭhas divided, split into two; and they had taken to quarrelling and brawling and were deep in disputes, stabbing each other with verbal daggers: "You do not understand this Dhamma and Discipline. I understand this Dhamma and Discipline. How could you understand this Dhamma and Discipline? Your way is wrong. My way is right. I am consistent. You are inconsistent. What should have been said first [244] you said last. What should have been said last you said first. What you had so carefully thought up has been turned inside out. Your assertion has been shown up. You are refuted. Go and learn better, or disentangle yourself if you can!" It seemed as if there were nothing but slaughter among the Nigaṇṭha Nātaputta's pupils. And his white-clothed lay disciples were disgusted, dismayed, and disappointed with the Nigaṇṭha Nātaputta's pupils, as they were with his badly proclaimed and badly expounded Dhamma and Discipline, which was unemancipating, unconducive to peace, expounded by one not fully enlightened, and was now with its shrine broken, left without a refuge.[977]

3. Then the novice Cunda,[978] who had spent the Rains at Pāvā, went to the venerable Ānanda, and after paying homage to him, he sat down at one side and told him what was taking place.

The venerable Ānanda then said to the novice Cunda: "Friend Cunda, this is news that should be told to the Blessed One. Come, let us approach the Blessed One and tell him this."

"Yes, venerable sir," the novice Cunda replied.

4. Then the venerable Ānanda and the novice Cunda went

together to the Blessed One. After paying homage to him, they sat down at one side, and [245] the venerable Ānanda said to the Blessed One: "This novice Cunda, venerable sir, says thus: 'Venerable sir, the Nigaṇṭha Nātaputta has just died. On his death the Nigaṇṭhas divided, split into two...and is now with its shrine broken, left without a refuge.' I thought, venerable sir: 'Let no dispute arise in the Sangha when the Blessed One has gone. For such a dispute would be for the harm and unhappiness of many, for the loss, harm, and suffering of gods and humans.'"

5. "What do you think, Ānanda? These things that I have taught you after directly knowing them—that is, the four foundations of mindfulness, the four right kinds of striving, the four bases for spiritual power, the five faculties, the five powers, the seven enlightenment factors, the Noble Eightfold Path—do you see, Ānanda, even two bhikkhus who make differing assertions about these things?"

"No, venerable sir, I do not see even two bhikkhus who make differing assertions about these things. But, venerable sir, there are people who live deferential towards the Blessed One who might, when he has gone, create a dispute in the Sangha about livelihood and about the Pātimokkha.[979] Such a dispute would be for the harm and unhappiness of many, for the loss, harm, and suffering of gods and humans."

"A dispute about livelihood or about the Pātimokkha would be trifling, Ānanda. But should a dispute arise in the Sangha about the path or the way,[980] such a dispute would be for the harm and unhappiness of many, for the loss, harm, and suffering of gods and humans.

6. "There are, Ānanda, these six roots of disputes.[981] What six? Here, Ānanda, a bhikkhu is angry and resentful. Such a bhikkhu dwells disrespectful and undeferential towards the Teacher, towards the Dhamma, and towards the Sangha, and he does not fulfil the training. A bhikkhu who dwells disrespectful and undeferential towards the Teacher, towards the Dhamma, and towards the Sangha, [246] and who does not fulfil the training, creates a dispute in the Sangha, which would be for the harm and unhappiness of many, for the loss, harm, and suffering of gods and humans. Now if you see any such root of dispute either in yourselves or externally, you should strive to abandon that same evil root of dispute. And if you do not see any such root of

dispute either in yourselves or externally, you should practise in such a way that that same evil root of dispute does not erupt in the future. Thus there is the abandoning of that evil root of dispute; thus there is the non-eruption of that evil root of dispute in the future.

7–11. "Again, a bhikkhu is contemptuous and insolent...envious and avaricious...deceitful and fraudulent...has evil wishes and wrong view...adheres to his own views, holds on to them tenaciously, and relinquishes them with difficulty. Such a bhikkhu dwells disrespectful and undeferential towards the Teacher, towards the Dhamma, and towards the Sangha, and he does not fulfil the training. A bhikkhu who dwells disrespectful and undeferential towards the Teacher, towards the Dhamma, and towards the Sangha, and who does not fulfil the training, creates a dispute in the Sangha, which would be for the harm and unhappiness of many, for the loss, harm, and suffering of gods and humans. Now if you see any such root of dispute either in yourselves or externally, you should strive to abandon that same evil root of dispute. And if you do not see any such root of dispute either in yourselves or externally, you should practise in such a way that that same evil root of dispute does not erupt in the future. [247] Thus there is the abandoning of that evil root of dispute; thus there is the non-eruption of that evil root of dispute in the future. These are the six roots of dispute.

12. "Ānanda, there are these four kinds of litigation. What four? Litigation because of a dispute, litigation because of an accusation, litigation because of an offence, and litigation concerning proceedings. These are the four kinds of litigation.[982]

13. "Ānanda, there are these seven kinds of settlement of litigation.[983] For the settlement and pacification of litigations whenever they arise: removal of litigation by confrontation may be provided, removal of litigation on account of memory may be provided, removal of litigation on account of past insanity may be provided, the effecting of acknowledgement of an offence, the opinion of the majority, the pronouncement of bad character against someone, and covering over with grass.

14. "And how is there removal of litigation by confrontation?[984] Here bhikkhus are disputing: 'It is Dhamma,' or 'It is not Dhamma,' or 'It is Discipline,' or 'It is not Discipline.' Those bhikkhus should all meet together in concord. Then, having met

together, the guideline of the Dhamma should be drawn out.[985] Once the guideline of the Dhamma has been drawn out, that litigation should be settled in a way that accords with it. Such is the removal of litigation by confrontation. And so there comes to be the settlement of some litigations here by removal of litigation by confrontation.

15. "And how is there the opinion of a majority? If those bhikkhus cannot settle that litigation in that dwelling place, they should go to a dwelling place where there is a greater number of bhikkhus. There they should all meet together in concord. Then, having met together, the guideline of the Dhamma should be drawn out. Once the guideline of the Dhamma has been drawn out, that litigation should be settled in a way that accords with it. Such is the opinion of a majority. And so there comes to be the settlement of some litigations here by the opinion of a majority.

16. "And how is there removal of litigation on account of memory?[986] Here one bhikkhu reproves another bhikkhu for such and such a grave offence, one involving defeat or bordering on defeat:[987] 'Does the venerable one remember having committed such and such a grave offence, one involving defeat or bordering on defeat?' He says: 'I do not, friends, remember having committed such and such a grave offence, one involving defeat or bordering on defeat.' [248] In his case removal of litigation on account of memory should be pronounced. Such is the removal of litigation on account of memory. And so there comes to be the settlement of some litigations here by removal of litigation on account of memory.

17. "And how is there removal of litigation on account of past insanity?[988] Here one bhikkhu reproves another bhikkhu for such and such a grave offence, one involving defeat or bordering on defeat: 'Does the venerable one remember having committed such and such a grave offence, one involving defeat or bordering on defeat?' He says: 'I do not, friends, remember having committed such and such a grave offence, one involving defeat or bordering on defeat.' Despite the denial, the former presses the latter further: 'Surely the venerable one must know quite well if he remembers having committed such and such a grave offence, one involving defeat or bordering on defeat?' He says: 'I had gone mad, friend, I was out of my mind, and when I was mad I said and did many things improper for a recluse. I do not

remember, I was mad when I did that.' In his case removal of litigation on account of past insanity should be pronounced. Such is the removal of litigation on account of past insanity. And so there comes to be the settlement of some litigations here by removal of litigation on account of past insanity.

18. "And how is there the effecting of acknowledgement of an offence? Here a bhikkhu, whether reproved or unreproved, remembers an offence, reveals it, and discloses it. He should go to a senior bhikkhu, and after arranging his robe on one shoulder, he should pay homage at his feet. Then, sitting on his heels, he should raise his hands palms together and say: 'Venerable sir, I have committed such and such an offence; I confess it.' The other says: 'Do you see?'—'Yes, I see.'—'Will you practise restraint in the future?'—'I will practise restraint in the future.' Such is the effecting of acknowledgement of an offence.[989] And so there comes to be the settlement of some litigations here by the effecting of acknowledgement of an offence. [249]

19. "And how is there the pronouncement of bad character against someone?[990] Here one bhikkhu reproves another for such and such a grave offence, one involving defeat or bordering on defeat: 'Does the venerable one remember having committed such and such a grave offence, one involving defeat or bordering on defeat?' He says: 'I do not, friends, remember having committed such and such a grave offence, one involving defeat or bordering on defeat.' Despite the denial, the former presses the latter further: 'Surely the venerable one must know quite well if he remembers having committed such and such a grave offence, one involving defeat or bordering on defeat?' He says: 'I do not, friends, remember having committed such and such a grave offence, one involving defeat or bordering on defeat. But, friends, I remember having committed such and such a minor offence.' Despite the denial, the former presses the latter further: 'Surely the venerable one must know quite well if he remembers having committed such and such a grave offence, one involving defeat or bordering on defeat?' He says: 'Friends, when not asked I acknowledge having committed this minor offence; so when asked, why shouldn't I acknowledge having committed such and such a grave offence, one involving defeat or bordering on defeat?' The other says: 'Friend, if you had not been asked, you would not have acknowledged committing this

minor offence; so why, when asked, would you acknowledge having committed such and such a grave offence, one involving defeat or bordering on defeat? Surely the venerable one must know quite well if he remembers having committed such and such a grave offence, one involving defeat or bordering on defeat?' He says: 'I remember, friends, having committed such and such a grave offence, one involving defeat or bordering on defeat. I was joking, I was raving, when I said that I did not remember having committed such and such a grave offence, one involving defeat or bordering on defeat.' Such is the pronouncement of bad character against someone. And so there comes to be the settlement of some litigations here by the pronouncement of bad character against someone. [250]

20. "And how is there covering over with grass?[991] Here when bhikkhus have taken to quarreling and brawling and are deep in disputes, they may have said and done many things improper for a recluse. Those bhikkhus should all meet together in concord. When they have met together, a wise bhikkhu among the bhikkhus who side together on the one part should rise from his seat, and after arranging his robe on one shoulder, he should raise his hands, palms together, and call for an enactment of the Sangha thus: 'Let the venerable Sangha hear me. When we took to quarreling and brawling and were deep in disputes, we said and did many things improper for a recluse. If it is approved by the Sangha, then for the good of these venerable ones and for my own good, in the midst of the Sangha I shall confess, by the method of covering over with grass, any offences of these venerable ones and any offences of my own, except for those which call for serious censure and those connected with the laity.'[992]

"Then a wise bhikkhu among the bhikkhus who side together on the other part should rise from his seat, and after arranging his robe on one shoulder, he should raise his hands, palms together, and call for an enactment of the Sangha thus: 'Let the venerable Sangha hear me. When we took to quarreling and brawling and were deep in disputes, we said and did many things improper for a recluse. If it is approved by the Sangha, then for the good of these venerable ones and for my own good, in the midst of the Sangha I shall confess, by the method of covering over with grass, any offences of these venerable ones and any offences of my own, except for those which call for serious censure and those connected with the laity.' Such is the covering over with grass. And so there comes to be the settlement of some litigations here by the covering over with grass.

21. "Ānanda, there are these six principles of cordiality that create love and respect, and conduce to cohesion, to non-dispute, to concord, and to unity.[993] What are the six?

"Here a bhikkhu maintains bodily acts of loving-kindness both in public and in private towards his companions in the holy life. This is a principle of cordiality that creates love and respect, and conduces to cohesion, to non-dispute, to concord, and to unity.

"Again, a bhikkhu maintains verbal acts of loving-kindness both in public and in private towards his companions in the holy life. This too is a principle of cordiality that creates love and respect, and conduces to...unity.

"Again, a bhikkhu maintains mental acts of loving-kindness both in public and in private towards his companions in the holy life. This too is a principle of cordiality that creates love [251] and respect, and conduces to...unity.

"Again, a bhikkhu enjoys things in common with his virtuous companions in the holy life; without making reservations, he shares with them any gain of a kind that accords with the Dhamma and has been obtained in a way that accords with the Dhamma, including even what is in his bowl. This too is a principle of cordiality that creates love and respect, and conduces to...unity.

"Again, a bhikkhu dwells both in public and in private possessing in common with his companions in the holy life those virtues that are unbroken, untorn, unblotched, unmottled, liberating, commended by the wise, not misapprehended, and conducive to concentration. This too is a principle of cordiality that creates love and respect and conduces to...unity.

"Again, a bhikkhu dwells both in public and in private possessing in common with his companions in the holy life that view that is noble and emancipating, and leads the one who practises in accordance with it to the complete destruction of suffering. This too is a principle of cordiality that creates love and respect, and conduces to cohesion, to non-dispute, to concord, and to unity.

"These are the six principles of cordiality that create love and respect, and conduce to cohesion, to non-dispute, to concord, and to unity.

22. "If, Ānanda, you undertake and maintain these six principles of cordiality, do you see any course of speech, trivial or gross, that you could not endure?"[994]—"No, venerable sir."—"Therefore, Ānanda, undertake and maintain these six principles of cordiality. That will lead to your welfare and happiness for a long time."

That is what the Blessed One said. The venerable Ānanda was satisfied and delighted in the Blessed One's words.

105 *Sunakkhatta Sutta*
To Sunakkhatta

[252] 1. THUS HAVE I HEARD. On one occasion the Blessed One was living at Vesālī in the Great Wood in the Hall with the Peaked Roof.

2. Now on that occasion a number of bhikkhus had declared final knowledge in the presence of the Blessed One thus: "We understand: Birth is destroyed, the holy life has been lived, what had to be done has been done, there is no more coming to any state of being."

3. Sunakkhatta, son of the Licchavis,[995] heard: "A number of bhikkhus, it seems, have declared final knowledge in the presence of the Blessed One thus: 'We understand: Birth is destroyed ...there is no more coming to any state of being.'" Then Sunakkhatta, son of the Licchavis, went to the Blessed One, and after paying homage to him, he sat down at one side and said to the Blessed One:

4. "I have heard, venerable sir, that a number of bhikkhus have declared final knowledge in the presence of the Blessed One. Did they do so rightly or are there some bhikkhus here who declare final knowledge because they overestimate themselves?"

5. "When those bhikkhus, Sunakkhatta, declared final knowledge in my presence, there were some bhikkhus who declared final knowledge rightly and there were some who declared final knowledge because they overestimated themselves.[996] Therein, when bhikkhus declare final knowledge rightly, their declaration is true. But when bhikkhus declare final knowledge because they overestimate themselves, the Tathāgata thinks: 'I should teach them the Dhamma.'[997] Thus it is in this case, Sunakkhatta, that the Tathāgata thinks: 'I should teach them the Dhamma.' But some misguided men here formulate a question, come to the Tathāgata, and ask it. In that case, Sunakkhatta, [253] though the

Tathāgata has thought: 'I should teach them the Dhamma,' he changes his mind."[998]

6. "This is the time, Blessed One, this is the time, Sublime One, for the Blessed One to teach the Dhamma. Having heard it from the Blessed One, the bhikkhus will remember it."

"Then listen, Sunakkhatta, and attend closely to what I shall say."

"Yes, venerable sir," Sunakkhatta, son of the Licchavis, replied to the Blessed One. The Blessed One said this:

7. "There are, Sunakkhatta, these five cords of sensual pleasure. What are the five? Forms cognizable by the eye that are wished for, desired, agreeable, and likeable, connected with sensual desire and provocative of lust. Sounds cognizable by the ear...Odours cognizable by the nose...Flavours cognizable by the tongue...Tangibles cognizable by the body that are wished for, desired, agreeable, and likeable, connected with sensual desire and provocative of lust. These are the five cords of sensual pleasure.

8. "It is possible, Sunakkhatta, that some person here may be intent on worldly material things.[999] When a person is intent on worldly material things, only talk concerning that interests him, and his thinking and pondering are in line with that, and he associates with that kind of person, and he finds satisfaction in that. But when talk about the imperturbable is going on, he will not listen to it or give it ear or exert his mind to understand it. He does not associate with that kind of person, and he does not find satisfaction in that.

9. "Suppose, Sunakkhatta, a man had left his own village or town a long time ago, and he were to see another man who had only recently left that village or town. He would ask that man whether the people of that village or town were safe, prosperous, and healthy, and that man would tell him whether the people of that village or town were safe, prosperous, [254] and healthy. What do you think, Sunakkhatta? Would that first man listen to him, give him ear, and exert his mind to understand?"—"Yes, venerable sir."—"So too, Sunakkhatta, it is possible that some person here may be intent on worldly material things. When a person is intent on worldly material things...and he does not find satisfaction in that. He should be understood as a person who is intent on worldly material things.

10. "It is possible, Sunakkhatta, that some person here may be intent on the imperturbable.[1000] When a person is intent on the imperturbable, only talk concerning that interests him, and his thinking and pondering are in line with that, and he associates with that kind of person, and he finds satisfaction in that. But when talk about worldly material things is going on, he will not listen to it or give it ear or exert his mind to understand it. He does not associate with that kind of person, and he does not find satisfaction in that.

11. "Just as a yellow leaf that has fallen from its stalk is incapable of becoming green again, so too, Sunakkhatta, when a person is intent on the imperturbable he has shed the fetter of worldly material things. He should be understood as a person detached from the fetter of worldly material things who is intent on the imperturbable.

12. "It is possible, Sunakkhatta, that some person here may be intent on the base of nothingness. When a person is intent on the base of nothingness, only talk concerning that interests him, and his thinking and pondering are in line with that, and he associates with that kind of person, and he finds satisfaction in that. [255] But when talk about the imperturbable is going on, he will not listen to it or give it ear or exert his mind to understand it. He does not associate with that kind of person, and he does not find satisfaction in that.

13. "Just as a thick stone that has split in two cannot be joined together again, so too, Sunakkhatta, when a person is intent on the base of nothingness his fetter of the imperturbable has been split. He should be understood as a person detached from the fetter of the imperturbable who is intent on the base of nothingness.

14. "It is possible, Sunakkhatta, that some person here may be intent on the base of neither-perception-nor-non-perception. When a person is intent on the base of neither-perception-nor-non-perception, only talk concerning that interests him, and his thinking and pondering are in line with that, and he associates with that kind of person, and he finds satisfaction in that. But when talk about the base of nothingness is going on, he will not listen to it or give it ear or exert his mind to understand it. He does not associate with that kind of person, and he does not find satisfaction in that.

15. "Suppose a person has eaten some delicious food and thrown it up. What do you think, Sunakkhatta? Could that man have any desire to eat that food again?"

"No, venerable sir. Why is that? Because that food is considered repulsive."

"So too, Sunakkhatta, when a person is intent on the base of neither-perception-nor-non-perception, his fetter of the base of nothingness has been rejected. He should be understood as a person detached from the fetter of the base of nothingness who is intent on the base of neither-perception-nor-non-perception.

16. "It is possible, Sunakkhatta, that some person here may be completely intent on Nibbāna. When a person is completely intent on Nibbāna, only talk concerning that interests him, and his thinking and pondering are in line with that, and he associates with that kind of person, and he finds satisfaction in that. But when talk about the base of neither-perception-nor-non-perception is going on, [256] he will not listen to it or give it ear or exert his mind to understand it. He does not associate with that kind of person, and he does not find satisfaction in that.

17. "Just as a palm tree with its top cut off is incapable of growing again, so too, Sunakkhatta, when a person is completely intent on Nibbāna, his fetter of the base of neither-perception-nor-non-perception has been cut off—cut off at the root, made like a palm stump, done away with so that it is no longer subject to future arising. He should be understood as a person detached from the fetter of the base of neither-perception-nor-non-perception who is completely intent on Nibbāna.

18. "It is possible, Sunakkhatta, that some bhikkhu here might think thus: 'Craving has been called an arrow by the Recluse;[1001] the poisonous humour of ignorance is spread about by desire, lust, and ill will. That arrow of craving has been removed from me; the poisonous humour of ignorance has been expelled. I am one who is completely intent on Nibbāna.' Since he conceives himself thus, though it is contrary to fact,[1002] he might pursue those things that are unsuitable for one completely intent on Nibbāna. He might pursue the sight of unsuitable forms with the eye, he might pursue unsuitable sounds with the ear, unsuitable odours with the nose, unsuitable flavours with the tongue, unsuitable tangibles with the body, or unsuitable mind-objects with the mind. When he pursues the sight of unsuitable forms

with the eye...unsuitable mind-objects with the mind, lust invades his mind. With his mind invaded by lust, he would incur death or deadly suffering.

19. "Suppose, Sunakkhatta, a man were wounded by an arrow thickly smeared with poison, and his friends and companions, his kinsmen and relatives, brought a surgeon. The surgeon would cut around the opening of the wound with a knife, then he would probe for the arrow with a probe, [257] then he would pull out the arrow and would expel the poisonous humour, leaving a trace of it behind. Thinking that no trace was left behind,[1003] he would say: 'Good man, the arrow has been pulled out from you; the poisonous humour has been expelled with no trace left behind, and it is incapable of harming you. Eat only suitable food; do not eat unsuitable food or else the wound may suppurate. From time to time wash the wound and from time to time anoint its opening, so that pus and blood do not cover the opening of the wound. Do not walk around in the wind and sun or else dust and dirt may infect the opening of the wound. Take care of your wound, good man, and see to it that the wound heals.'

20. "The man would think: 'The arrow has been pulled out from me; the poisonous humour has been expelled with no trace left behind, and it is incapable of harming me.' He would eat unsuitable food, and the wound would suppurate. He would not wash the wound from time to time nor would he anoint its opening from time to time, and pus and blood would cover the opening of the wound. He would walk around in the wind and sun, and dust and dirt would infect the opening of the wound. He would not take care of his wound, nor would he see to it that the wound heals. Then, both because he does what is unsuitable and because a trace was left behind when the foul poisonous humour was expelled, the wound would swell, and with its swelling he would incur death or deadly suffering.

21. "So too, Sunakkhatta, it is possible that some bhikkhu here might think thus: 'Craving has been called an arrow by the Recluse; the poisonous humour of ignorance is spread about by desire, lust, and ill will. That arrow of craving has been removed from me; [258] the poisonous humour of ignorance has been expelled. I am one who is completely intent upon Nibbāna.' Because he conceives himself thus, though it is contrary to fact,

he might pursue those things that are unsuitable for one completely intent on Nibbāna...(*as above*)...With his mind invaded by lust, he would incur death or deadly suffering.

22. "For it is death in the Discipline of the Noble One, Sunakkhatta, when one abandons the training and reverts to the low life; and it is deadly suffering when one commits some defiled offence.[1004]

23. "It is possible, Sunakkhatta, that some bhikkhu here might think thus: 'Craving has been called an arrow by the Recluse; the poisonous humour of ignorance is spread about by desire, lust, and ill will. That arrow of craving has been removed from me; the poisonous humour of ignorance has been expelled. I am one who is completely intent on Nibbāna.' Being one who really is completely intent on Nibbāna, he would not pursue those things that are unsuitable for one completely intent on Nibbāna. He would not pursue the sight of unsuitable forms with the eye, he would not pursue unsuitable sounds with the ear, unsuitable odours with the nose, unsuitable flavours with the tongue, unsuitable tangibles with the body, or unsuitable mind-objects with the mind. Because he does not pursue the sight of unsuitable forms with the eye...unsuitable mind-objects with the mind, lust does not invade his mind. [259] Because his mind is not invaded by lust, he would not incur death or deadly suffering.

24. "Suppose, Sunakkhatta, a man were wounded by an arrow thickly smeared with poison, and his friends and companions, his kinsmen and relatives, brought a surgeon. The surgeon would cut around the opening of the wound with a knife, then he would probe for the arrow with a probe, then he would pull out the arrow and would expel the poisonous humour without leaving a trace of it behind. Knowing that no trace was left behind, he would say: 'Good man, the arrow has been pulled out from you; the poisonous humour has been expelled with no trace left behind, and it is incapable of harming you. Eat only suitable food; do not eat unsuitable food or else the wound may suppurate. From time to time wash the wound and from time to time anoint its opening, so that pus and blood do not cover the opening of the wound. Do not walk around in the wind and sun or else dust and dirt may infect the opening of the wound. Take care of your wound, good man, and see to it that the wound heals.'

25. "The man would think: 'The arrow has been pulled out from me; the poisonous humour has been expelled with no trace left behind, and it is incapable of harming me.' He would eat only suitable food, and the wound would not suppurate. From time to time he would wash the wound and from time to time he would anoint its opening, and pus and blood would not cover the opening of the wound. He would not walk around in the wind and sun, and dust and dirt would not infect the opening of the wound. He would take care of his wound and would see to it that the wound heals. Then, both because he does what is suitable and because no trace was left behind when the foul poisonous humour was expelled, the wound would heal, and because it had healed and was covered with skin, he would not incur death or deadly suffering.

26. "So too, Sunakkhatta, it is possible that some bhikkhus here might think thus: 'Craving has been called an arrow by the Recluse; [260] the poisonous humour of ignorance is spread about by desire, lust, and ill will. That arrow of craving has been pulled out from me; the poisonous humour of ignorance has been expelled. I am one who is completely intent on Nibbāna.' Being one who really is completely intent on Nibbāna, he would not pursue those things unsuitable for one completely intent on Nibbāna...(*as above*)...Because his mind is not invaded by lust, he would not incur death or deadly suffering.

27. "Sunakkhatta, I have given this simile in order to convey a meaning. This is the meaning here: 'Wound' is a term for the six internal bases. 'Poisonous humour' is a term for ignorance. 'Arrow' is a term for craving. 'Probe' is a term for mindfulness. 'Knife' is a term for noble wisdom. 'Surgeon' is a term for the Tathāgata, the Accomplished One, the Fully Enlightened One.

28. "That bhikkhu, Sunakkhatta, is one who practises restraint in the six bases of contact. Having understood that acquisition is the root of suffering,[1005] being acquisitionless, liberated in the destruction of the acquisitions, it is not possible that he would direct his body or arouse his mind towards any acquisition.

29. "Suppose, Sunakkhatta, there were a bronze cup of beverage possessing a good colour, smell, and taste, but it was mixed with poison, and a man came who wanted to live, not to die, who wanted pleasure and recoiled from pain.[1006] What do you think, Sunakkhatta, would that man drink that cup of beverage,

knowing: 'If I drink this I will incur death or deadly suffering'?"—"No, venerable sir." [261]—"So too, that bhikkhu is one who practises restraint in the six bases of contact. Having understood that acquisition is the root of suffering, being acquisitionless, liberated in the destruction of acquisitions, it is not possible that he would direct his body or arouse his mind towards any acquisition.

30. "Suppose, Sunakkhatta, there were a deadly poisonous snake, and a man came who wanted to live, not to die, who wanted pleasure and recoiled from pain. What do you think, Sunakkhatta, would that man give that deadly poisonous snake his hand or his thumb, knowing: 'If I am bitten by him I will incur death or deadly suffering'?"—"No, venerable sir."—"So too, when a bhikkhu practises restraint in the six bases of contact, and having understood that attachment is the root of suffering, is without attachment, liberated by the destruction of attachment, it is not possible that he would direct his body or arouse his mind towards any object of attachment."

That is what the Blessed One said. Sunakkhatta, son of the Licchavis, was satisfied and delighted in the Blessed One's words.

106 *Āneñjasappāya Sutta*
The Way to the Imperturbable

1. THUS HAVE I HEARD.[1007] On one occasion the Blessed One was living in the Kuru country where there was a town of the Kurus named Kammāsadhamma. There the Blessed One addressed the bhikkhus thus: "Bhikkhus."—"Venerable sir," they replied. The Blessed One said this:

2. "Bhikkhus, sensual pleasures[1008] are impermanent, hollow, false, deceptive; they are illusory, the prattle of fools. Sensual pleasures here and now and sensual pleasures in lives to come, [262] sensual perceptions here and now and sensual perceptions in lives to come—both alike are Māra's realm, Māra's domain, Māra's bait, Māra's hunting ground. On account of them, these evil unwholesome mental states such as covetousness, ill will, and presumption arise, and they constitute an obstruction to a noble disciple in training here.

(THE IMPERTURBABLE)

3. "Therein, bhikkhus, a noble disciple considers thus: 'Sensual pleasures here and now and sensual pleasures in lives to come...constitute an obstruction to a noble disciple in training here. Suppose I were to abide with a mind abundant and exalted, having transcended the world and made a firm determination with the mind.[1009] When I do so, there will be no more evil unwholesome mental states such as covetousness, ill will, and presumption in me, and with the abandoning of them my mind will be unlimited, immeasurable, and well developed.' When he practises in this way and frequently abides thus, his mind acquires confidence in this base.[1010] Once there is full confidence, he either attains to the imperturbable now or else he resolves [upon it] with wisdom. On the dissolution of the body,

after death, it is possible that the evolving consciousness may pass on [to rebirth] in the imperturbable.[1011] This, bhikkhus, is declared to be the first way directed to the imperturbable.

4. "Again, bhikkhus, a noble disciple considers thus:[1012] '[There are] sensual pleasures here and now and sensual pleasures in lives to come, sensual perceptions here and now and sensual perceptions in lives to come; whatever material form [there is], all material form is the four great elements and the material form derived from the four great elements.' When he practises in this way and frequently abides thus, his mind acquires confidence in this base. Once there is full confidence, he either attains to the imperturbable now or else he resolves [upon it] with wisdom. On the dissolution of the body, after death, it is possible that the evolving consciousness may pass on [to rebirth] in the imperturbable. This, bhikkhus, is declared to be the second way directed to the imperturbable. [263]

5. "Again, bhikkhus, a noble disciple considers thus:[1013] 'Sensual pleasures here and now and sensual pleasures in lives to come, sensual perceptions here and now and sensual perceptions in lives to come, material forms here and now and material forms in lives to come, perceptions of forms here and now and perceptions of forms in lives to come—both alike are impermanent. What is impermanent is not worth delighting in, not worth welcoming, not worth holding to.' When he practises in this way and frequently abides thus, his mind acquires confidence in this base. Once there is full confidence, he either attains to the imperturbable now or else he resolves [upon it] with wisdom. On the dissolution of the body, after death, it is possible that the evolving consciousness may pass on [to rebirth] in the imperturbable. This, bhikkhus, is declared to be the third way directed to the imperturbable.

(THE BASE OF NOTHINGNESS)

6. "Again, bhikkhus, a noble disciple considers thus:[1014] 'Sensual pleasures here and now and sensual pleasures in lives to come, sensual perceptions here and now and sensual perceptions in lives to come, material forms here and now and material forms in lives to come, perceptions of forms here and now and perceptions of forms in lives to come, and perceptions of the

imperturbable—all are perceptions. Where these perceptions cease without remainder, that is the peaceful, that is the sublime, namely, the base of nothingness.' When he practises in this way and frequently abides thus, his mind acquires confidence in this base. Once there is full confidence, he either attains to the base of nothingness now or else he resolves [upon it] with wisdom. On the dissolution of the body, after death, it is possible that the evolving consciousness may pass on [to rebirth] in the base of nothingness. This, bhikkhus, is declared to be the first way directed to the base of nothingness.

7. "Again, bhikkhus, a noble disciple, gone to the forest or to the root of a tree or to an empty hut, considers thus: 'This is void of a self or of what belongs to a self.'[1015] When he practises in this way and frequently abides thus, his mind acquires confidence in this base. Once there is full confidence, he either attains to the base of nothingness now or else he resolves [upon it] with wisdom. On the dissolution of the body, after death, it is possible that the evolving consciousness may pass on [to rebirth] in the base of nothingness. This, bhikkhus, is declared to be the second way directed to the base of nothingness.

8. "Again, bhikkhus, a noble disciple considers thus: 'I am not anything belonging to anyone anywhere, [264] nor is there anything belonging to me in anyone anywhere.'[1016] When he practises in this way and frequently abides thus, his mind acquires confidence in this base. Once there is full confidence, he either attains to the base of nothingness now or else he resolves [upon it] with wisdom. On the dissolution of the body, after death, it is possible that the evolving consciousness may pass on [to rebirth] in the base of nothingness. This, bhikkhus, is declared to be the third way directed to the base of nothingness.

(THE BASE OF NEITHER-PERCEPTION-NOR-NON-PERCEPTION)

9. "Again, bhikkhus, a noble disciple considers thus: 'Sensual pleasures here and now and sensual pleasures in lives to come, sensual perceptions here and now and sensual perceptions in lives to come, material forms here and now and material forms in lives to come, perceptions of forms here and now and perceptions of forms in lives to come, perceptions of the imperturbable,

and perceptions of the base of nothingness—all are perceptions. Where these perceptions cease without remainder, that is the peaceful, that is the sublime, namely, the base of neither-perception-nor-non-perception.' When he practises in this way and frequently abides thus, his mind acquires confidence in this base. Once there is full confidence, he either attains to the base of neither-perception-nor-non-perception now or else he resolves [upon it] with wisdom. On the dissolution of the body, after death, it is possible that the evolving consciousness may pass on [to rebirth] in the base of neither-perception-nor-non-perception. This, bhikkhus, is declared to be the way directed to the base of neither-perception-nor-non-perception."

(NIBBĀNA)

10. When this was said, the venerable Ānanda said to the Blessed One: "Venerable sir, here a bhikkhu is practising thus: 'It might not be, and it might not be mine; it will not be, and it will not be mine. What exists, what has come to be, that I am abandoning.' Thus he obtains equanimity.[1017] Venerable sir, does such a bhikkhu attain Nibbāna?"

"One bhikkhu here, Ānanda, might attain Nibbāna, another bhikkhu here might not attain Nibbāna."

"What is the cause and reason, venerable sir, why one bhikkhu here might attain Nibbāna, while another bhikkhu here might not attain Nibbāna?"

"Here, Ānanda, a bhikkhu is practising thus: 'It might not be, and it might not be mine; it will not be, and it will not be mine. What exists, [265] what has come to be, that I am abandoning.' Thus he obtains equanimity. He delights in that equanimity, welcomes it, and remains holding to it. As he does so, his consciousness becomes dependent on it and clings to it. A bhikkhu with clinging, Ānanda, does not attain Nibbāna."[1018]

11. "But, venerable sir, when that bhikkhu clings, what does he cling to?"

"To the base of neither-perception-nor-non-perception, Ānanda."

"When that bhikkhu clings, venerable sir, it seems he clings to the best [object of] clinging."

"When that bhikkhu clings, Ānanda, he clings to the best

[object of] clinging; for this is the best [object of] clinging, namely, the base of neither-perception-nor-non-perception.[1019]

12. "Here, Ānanda, a bhikkhu is practising thus: 'It might not be, and it might not be mine; it will not be, and it will not be mine. What exists, what has come to be, that I am abandoning.' Thus he obtains equanimity. He does not delight in that equanimity, welcome it, or remain holding to it. Since he does not do so, his consciousness does not become dependent on it and does not cling to it. A bhikkhu without clinging, Ānanda, attains Nibbāna."

13. "It is wonderful, venerable sir, it is marvellous! The Blessed One, indeed, has explained to us the crossing of the flood in dependence upon one support or another.[1020] But, venerable sir, what is noble liberation?"[1021]

"Here, Ānanda, a noble disciple considers thus: 'Sensual pleasures here and now and sensual pleasures in lives to come, sensual perceptions here and now and sensual perceptions in lives to come, material forms here and now and material forms in lives to come, perceptions of forms here and now and perceptions of forms in lives to come, perceptions of the imperturbable, perceptions of the base of nothingness, and perceptions of the base of neither-perception-nor-non-perception—this is identity as far as identity extends.[1022] This is the Deathless, namely, the liberation of the mind through not clinging.'[1023]

14. "Thus, Ānanda, I have taught the way directed to the imperturbable, I have taught the way directed to the base of nothingness, I have taught the way directed to the base of neither-perception-nor-non-perception, I have taught the crossing of the flood in dependence upon one support or another, I have taught noble liberation.

15. "What should be done for his disciples out of compassion by a teacher who seeks their welfare and has compassion for them, [266] that I have done for you, Ānanda. There are these roots of trees, these empty huts. Meditate, Ānanda, do not delay, or else you will regret it later. This is our instruction to you."

That is what the Blessed One said. The venerable Ānanda was satisfied and delighted in the Blessed One's words.

107 *Gaṇakamoggallāna Sutta*
To Gaṇaka Moggallāna

[1] 1. THUS HAVE I HEARD. On one occasion the Blessed One was living at Sāvatthī in the Eastern Park, in the Palace of Migāra's Mother. Then the brahmin Gaṇaka Moggallāna went to the Blessed One and exchanged greetings with him. When this courteous and amiable talk was finished, he sat down at one side and said to the Blessed One:

2. "Master Gotama, in this Palace of Migāra's Mother there can be seen gradual training, gradual practice, and gradual progress, that is, down to the last step of the staircase.[1024] Among these brahmins too, there can be seen gradual training, gradual practice, and gradual progress, that is, in study. Among archers too, there can be seen gradual training...that is, in archery. And also among accountants[1025] like us, who earn our living by accountancy, there can be seen gradual training...that is, in computation. For when we get an apprentice first we make him count: one one, two twos, three threes, four fours, five fives, six sixes, seven sevens, eight eights, nine nines, ten tens; and we make him count a hundred too. Now is it also possible, Master Gotama, to describe gradual training, gradual practice, and gradual progress in this Dhamma and Discipline?" [2]

3. "It is possible, brahmin, to describe gradual training, gradual practice, and gradual progress in this Dhamma and Discipline. Just as, brahmin, when a clever horse-trainer obtains a fine thoroughbred colt, he first makes him get used to wearing the bit, and afterwards trains him further,[1026] so when the Tathāgata obtains a person to be tamed he first disciplines him thus: 'Come, bhikkhu, be virtuous, restrained with the restraint of the Pātimokkha, be perfect in conduct and resort, and seeing fear in the slightest fault, train by undertaking the training precepts.'

4. "When, brahmin, the bhikkhu is virtuous...and seeing fear in the slightest fault, trains by undertaking the training precepts, then the Tathāgata disciplines him further: 'Come, bhikkhu, guard the doors of your sense faculties. On seeing a form with the eye, do not grasp at its signs and features. Since, if you were to leave the eye faculty unguarded, evil unwholesome states of covetousness and grief might invade you, practise the way of its restraint, guard the eye faculty, undertake the restraint of the eye faculty. On hearing a sound with the ear...On smelling an odour with the nose...On tasting a flavour with the tongue...On touching a tangible with the body...On cognizing a mind-object with the mind, do not grasp at its signs and features. Since, if you were to leave the mind faculty unguarded, evil unwholesome states might invade you, practise the way of its restraint, guard the mind faculty, undertake the restraint of the mind faculty.'

5. "When, brahmin, the bhikkhu guards the doors of his sense faculties, then the Tathāgata disciplines him further: 'Come, bhikkhu, be moderate in eating. Reflecting wisely, you should take food neither for amusement nor for intoxication nor for the sake of physical beauty and attractiveness, but only for the endurance and continuance of this body, for ending discomfort, and for assisting the holy life, considering: "Thus I shall terminate old feelings without arousing new feelings and I shall be healthy and blameless and shall live in comfort."'

6. "When, [3] brahmin, the bhikkhu is moderate in eating, then the Tathāgata disciplines him further: 'Come, bhikkhu, be devoted to wakefulness. During the day, while walking back and forth and sitting, purify your mind of obstructive states. In the first watch of the night, while walking back and forth and sitting, purify your mind of obstructive states. In the middle watch of the night you should lie down on the right side in the lion's pose with one foot overlapping the other, mindful and fully aware, after noting in your mind the time for rising. After rising, in the third watch of the night, while walking back and forth and sitting, purify your mind of obstructive states.'

7. "When, brahmin, the bhikkhu is devoted to wakefulness, then the Tathāgata disciplines him further: 'Come, bhikkhu, be possessed of mindfulness and full awareness. Act in full awareness when going forward and returning; act in full awareness when looking ahead and looking away; act in full awareness

when flexing and extending your limbs; act in full awareness when wearing your robes and carrying your outer robe and bowl; act in full awareness when eating, drinking, consuming food, and tasting; act in full awareness when defecating and urinating; act in full awareness when walking, standing, sitting, falling asleep, waking up, talking, and keeping silent.'

8. "When, brahmin, the bhikkhu possesses mindfulness and full awareness, then the Tathāgata disciplines him further: 'Come, bhikkhu, resort to a secluded resting place: the forest, the root of a tree, a mountain, a ravine, a hillside cave, a charnel ground, a jungle thicket, an open space, a heap of straw.'

9. "He resorts to a secluded resting place: the forest...a heap of straw. On returning from his almsround, after his meal he sits down, folding his legs crosswise, setting his body erect, and establishing mindfulness before him. Abandoning covetousness for the world, he abides with a mind free from covetousness; he purifies his mind from covetousness. Abandoning ill will and hatred, he abides with a mind free from ill will, compassionate for the welfare of all living beings; he purifies his mind from ill will and hatred. Abandoning sloth and torpor, he abides free from sloth and torpor, percipient of light, mindful and fully aware; he purifies his mind from sloth and torpor. Abandoning restlessness and remorse, he abides unagitated with a mind inwardly peaceful; he purifies his mind from restlessness and remorse. Abandoning doubt, he abides having gone beyond doubt, unperplexed about wholesome states; he purifies his mind from doubt. [4]

10. "Having thus abandoned these five hindrances, imperfections of the mind that weaken wisdom, quite secluded from sensual pleasures, secluded from unwholesome states, he enters upon and abides in the first jhāna, which is accompanied by applied and sustained thought, with rapture and pleasure born of seclusion. With the stilling of applied and sustained thought, he enters upon and abides in the second jhāna, which has self-confidence and singleness of mind without applied and sustained thought, with rapture and pleasure born of concentration. With the fading away as well of rapture, he abides in equanimity, and mindful and fully aware, still feeling pleasure with the body, he enters upon and abides in the third jhāna, on account of which noble ones announce: 'He has a pleasant

abiding who has equanimity and is mindful.' With the abandoning of pleasure and pain, and with the previous disappearance of joy and grief, he enters upon and abides in the fourth jhāna, which has neither-pain-nor-pleasure and purity of mindfulness due to equanimity.

11. "This is my instruction, brahmin, to those bhikkhus who are in the higher training, whose minds have not yet attained the goal, who abide aspiring to the supreme security from bondage. But these things conduce both to a pleasant abiding here and now and to mindfulness and full awareness for those bhikkhus who are arahants with taints destroyed, who have lived the holy life, done what had to be done, laid down the burden, reached their own goal, destroyed the fetters of being, and are completely liberated through final knowledge."[1027]

12. When this was said, the brahmin Gaṇaka Moggallāna asked the Blessed One: "When Master Gotama's disciples are thus advised and instructed by him, do they all attain Nibbāna, the ultimate goal, or do some not attain it?"

"When, brahmin, they are thus advised and instructed by me, some of my disciples attain Nibbāna, the ultimate goal, and some do not attain it."

13. "Master Gotama, since Nibbāna exists and the path leading to Nibbāna exists and Master Gotama is present as the guide, what is the cause and reason why, when Master Gotama's disciples are thus advised and instructed by him, some of them attain Nibbāna, the ultimate goal, and some do not attain it?"

14. "As to that, brahmin, I will ask you a question in return. Answer it as you choose. [5] What do you think, brahmin? Are you familiar with the road leading to Rājagaha?"

"Yes, Master Gotama, I am familiar with the road leading to Rājagaha."

"What do you think, brahmin? Suppose a man came who wanted to go to Rājagaha, and he approached you and said: 'Venerable sir, I want to go to Rājagaha. Show me the road to Rājagaha.' Then you told him: 'Now, good man, this road goes to Rājagaha. Follow it for awhile and you will see a certain village, go a little further and you will see a certain town, go a little further and you will see Rājagaha with its lovely parks, groves, meadows, and ponds.' Then, having been thus advised and instructed by you, he would take a wrong road and would go to the west. Then a second man came who wanted to go to Rājagaha, and he approached you and said: 'Venerable sir, I want to go to Rājagaha. Show me the road to Rājagaha.' Then you told him: 'Now, good man, this road goes to Rājagaha. Follow it for a while...and you will see Rājagaha with its lovely parks, groves, meadows, and ponds.' Then, having been thus advised and instructed by you, he would arrive safely in Rājagaha. Now, brahmin, since Rājagaha exists and the path leading to Rājagaha exists and you are present as the guide, what is the cause and reason why, when those men have been thus advised and instructed by you, one man takes a wrong road and goes to the west and one arrives safely in Rājagaha?" [6]

"What can I do about that, Master Gotama? I am one who shows the way."

"So too, brahmin, Nibbāna exists and the path leading to Nibbāna exists and I am present as the guide. Yet when my disciples have been thus advised and instructed by me, some of them attain Nibbāna, the ultimate goal, and some do not attain it. What can I do about that, brahmin? The Tathāgata is one who shows the way."[1028]

15. When this was said, the brahmin Gaṇaka Moggallāna said to the Blessed One:[1029] "There are persons who are faithless and have gone forth from the home life into homelessness not out of faith but seeking a livelihood, who are fraudulent, deceitful, treacherous, haughty, hollow, personally vain, rough-tongued, loose-spoken, unguarded in their sense faculties, immoderate in eating, undevoted to wakefulness, unconcerned with recluseship, not greatly respectful of training, luxurious, careless, leaders in backsliding, neglectful of seclusion, lazy, wanting in energy, unmindful, not fully aware, unconcentrated, with straying minds, devoid of wisdom, drivellers. Master Gotama does not dwell together with these.

"But there are clansmen who have gone forth out of faith from the home life into homelessness, who are not fraudulent, deceitful, treacherous, haughty, hollow, personally vain, rough-tongued, and loose-spoken; who are guarded in their sense faculties, moderate in eating, devoted to wakefulness, concerned with recluseship, greatly respectful of training, not luxurious or careless, who are keen to avoid backsliding, leaders in seclusion, energetic, resolute, established in mindfulness, fully aware, concentrated, with unified minds, possessing wisdom, not drivellers. Master Gotama dwells together with these.

16 "Just as black orris root is reckoned as the best of root perfumes and red sandalwood is reckoned as the best of wood perfumes and jasmine is reckoned as the best of flower perfumes, [7] so too, Master Gotama's advice is supreme among the teachings of today.[1030]

17. "Magnificent, Master Gotama! Magnificent, Master Gotama! Master Gotama has made the Dhamma clear in many ways, as though he were turning upright what had been overturned, revealing what was hidden, showing the way to one who was lost, or holding up a lamp in the dark for those with eyesight to see forms. I go to Master Gotama for refuge and to the Dhamma and to the Sangha of bhikkhus. Let Master Gotama remember me as a lay follower who has gone to him for refuge for life."

108 *Gopakamoggallāna Sutta*
With Gopaka Moggallāna

1. THUS HAVE I HEARD. On one occasion the venerable Ānanda was living at Rājagaha in the Bamboo Grove, the Squirrels' Sanctuary, not long after the Blessed One had attained to final Nibbāna.[1031]

2. Now on that occasion King Ajātasattu Vedehiputta of Magadha, being suspicious of King Pajjota, was having Rājagaha fortified.[1032]

3. Then, when it was morning, the venerable Ānanda dressed, and taking his bowl and outer robe, went into Rājagaha for alms. Then the venerable Ānanda thought: "It is still too early to wander for alms in Rājagaha. Suppose I went to the brahmin Gopaka Moggallāna at his workplace."

4. So the venerable Ānanda went to the brahmin Gopaka Moggallāna at his workplace. The brahmin Gopaka Moggallāna saw the venerable Ānanda coming in the distance and said to him: "Let Master Ānanda come! Welcome to Master Ānanda! It is long since Master Ānanda found an opportunity to come here. Let Master Ānanda be seated; this seat is ready." The venerable Ānanda sat down on the seat made ready. [8] The brahmin Gopaka Moggallāna took a low seat, sat down at one side, and asked the venerable Ānanda:

5. "Master Ānanda, is there any single bhikkhu who possesses in each and every way all those qualities that were possessed by Master Gotama, accomplished and fully enlightened?"

"There is no single bhikkhu, brahmin, who possesses in each and every way all those qualities that were possessed by the Blessed One, accomplished and fully enlightened. For the Blessed One was the arouser of the unarisen path, the producer of the unproduced path, the declarer of the undeclared path; he was the knower of the path, the finder of the path, the one skilled in the path. But his disciples now abide following that path and become possessed of it afterwards."

6. But this discussion between the venerable Ānanda and the brahmin Gopaka Moggallāna was interrupted; for then the brahmin Vassakāra, the chief minister of Magadha,[1033] while supervising the work at Rājagaha, went to the venerable Ānanda at the workplace of the brahmin Gopaka Moggallāna. He exchanged greetings with the venerable Ānanda, and when this courteous and amiable talk was finished, he sat down at one side and asked the venerable Ānanda: "For what discussion are you sitting together here now, Master Ānanda? And what was your discussion that was interrupted?"

"Brahmin, the brahmin Gopaka Moggallāna asked me: 'Master Ānanda, is there any single bhikkhu who possesses in each and every way all those qualities that were possessed by Master Gotama, accomplished and fully enlightened?' I replied to the brahmin Gopaka Moggallāna: 'There is no single bhikkhu, brahmin, who possesses in each and every way all those qualities that were possessed by the Blessed One, accomplished and fully enlightened. For the Blessed One was the arouser of the unarisen path [9]...But his disciples now abide following that path and become possessed of it afterwards.' This was our discussion that was interrupted when you arrived."

7. "Is there, Master Ānanda, any single bhikkhu who was appointed by Master Gotama thus: 'He will be your refuge when I am gone,' and whom you now have recourse to?"

"There is no single bhikkhu, brahmin, who was appointed by the Blessed One who knows and sees, accomplished and fully enlightened, thus: 'He will be your refuge when I am gone,' and whom we now have recourse to."

8. "But is there, Master Ānanda, any single bhikkhu who has been chosen by the Sangha and appointed by a number of elder bhikkhus thus: 'He will be our refuge after the Blessed One has gone,' and whom you now have recourse to?"

"There is no single bhikkhu, brahmin, who has been chosen by the Sangha and appointed by a number of elder bhikkhus thus: 'He will be our refuge after the Blessed One has gone,' and whom we now have recourse to."

9. "But if you have no refuge, Master Ānanda, what is the cause for your concord?"

"We are not without a refuge, brahmin. We have a refuge; we have the Dhamma as our refuge."

10. "But when you were asked: 'Is there, Master Ānanda, any single bhikkhu who was appointed by Master Gotama thus: "He will be your refuge when I am gone," and whom you now have recourse to?' you answered: 'There is no such single bhikkhu... whom we now have recourse to.' When you were asked: 'Is there, Master Ānanda, any single bhikkhu who has been chosen by the Sangha and appointed by a number of elder bhikkhus thus: "He will be our refuge after the Blessed One has gone," and whom you now have recourse to?' you answered: 'There is no such single bhikkhu...[10]...whom we now have recourse to.' When you were asked: 'But if you have no refuge, Master Ānanda, what is the cause for your concord?' you answered: 'We are not without a refuge, brahmin. We have a refuge; we have the Dhamma as our refuge.' Now how should the meaning of these statements be regarded, Master Ānanda?"

"Brahmin, the Blessed One who knows and sees, accomplished and fully enlightened, has prescribed the course of training for bhikkhus and he has laid down the Pātimokkha. On the Uposatha day as many of us as live in dependence upon a single village district meet together in unison, and when we meet we ask one who knows the Pātimokkha to recite it. If a bhikkhu remembers an offence or a transgression while the Pātimokkha is being recited, we deal with him according to the Dhamma in the way we have been instructed. It is not the worthy ones who deal with us; it is the Dhamma that deals with us."[1034]

11. "Is there, Master Ānanda, any single bhikkhu whom you now honour, respect, revere, and venerate, and on whom you live in dependence honouring and respecting him?"

"There is a single bhikkhu, brahmin, whom we now honour, respect, revere, and venerate, and on whom we live in dependence honouring and respecting him."

12. "But when you were asked: 'Is there, Master Ānanda, any single bhikkhu who was appointed by Master Gotama...?' you answered 'There is no such single bhikkhu...' When you were asked: 'Is there, Master Ānanda, any single bhikkhu who has been chosen by the Sangha...?' [11] you answered: 'There is no such single bhikkhu...' When you were asked: 'Is there, Master Ānanda, any single bhikkhu whom you honour, respect, revere,

and venerate, and on whom you live in dependence honouring and respecting him?' you answered: 'There is such a single bhikkhu whom we now honour...and on whom we live in dependence honouring and respecting him.' Now how should the meaning of these statements be regarded, Master Ānanda?"

13. "There are, brahmin, ten qualities inspiring confidence that have been declared by the Blessed One who knows and sees, accomplished and fully enlightened. When these qualities are found in anyone among us, we honour, respect, revere, and venerate him, and live in dependence on him honouring and respecting him. What are the ten?

14. (1) "Here, brahmin, a bhikkhu is virtuous, he dwells restrained with the restraint of the Pātimokkha, he is perfect in conduct and resort, and seeing fear in the slightest faults, he trains himself by undertaking the training precepts.

15. (2) "He has learned much, remembers what he has learned, and consolidates what he has learned. Such teachings as are good in the beginning, good in the middle, and good in the end, with the right meaning and phrasing, and which affirm a holy life that is utterly perfect and pure—such teachings as these he has learned much of, remembered, mastered verbally, investigated with the mind, and penetrated well by view.

16. (3) "He is content with his robes, almsfood, resting place, and medicinal requisites.

17. (4) "He obtains at will, without trouble or difficulty, the four jhānas that constitute the higher mind and provide a pleasant abiding here and now.

18. (5) "He wields the various kinds of supernormal power: having been one, he becomes many; having been many, he becomes one; he appears and vanishes; he goes unhindered through a wall, through an enclosure, through a mountain as though through space; he dives in and out of the earth as though it were water; he walks on water without sinking as though it were earth; [12] seated cross-legged, he travels in space like a bird; with his hand he touches and strokes the moon and sun so powerful and mighty; he wields bodily mastery even as far as the Brahma-world.

19. (6) "With the divine ear element, which is purified and surpasses the human, he hears both kinds of sounds, the divine and the human, those that are far as well as near.

20. (7) "He understands the minds of other beings, of other persons, having encompassed them with his own mind. He understands a mind affected by lust as affected by lust and a mind unaffected by lust as unaffected by lust; he understands a mind affected by hate as affected by hate and a mind unaffected by hate as unaffected by hate; he understands a mind affected by delusion as affected by delusion and a mind unaffected by delusion as unaffected by delusion; he understands a contracted mind as contracted and a distracted mind as distracted; he understands an exalted mind as exalted and an unexalted mind as unexalted; he understands a surpassed mind as surpassed and an unsurpassed mind as unsurpassed; he understands a concentrated mind as concentrated and an unconcentrated mind as unconcentrated; he understands a liberated mind as liberated and an unliberated mind as unliberated.

21. (8) "He recollects his manifold past lives, that is, one birth, two births...(*as Sutta 51, §24*)...Thus with their aspects and particulars he recollects his manifold past lives.

22. (9) "With the divine eye, which is purified and surpasses the human, he sees beings passing away and reappearing, inferior and superior, fair and ugly, fortunate and unfortunate, and he understands how beings pass on according to their actions.

23. (10) "By realising for himself with direct knowledge, he here and now enters upon and abides in the deliverance of mind and deliverance by wisdom that are taintless with the destruction of the taints.

"These, brahmin, are the ten qualities inspiring confidence that have been declared by the Blessed One who knows and sees, accomplished and fully enlightened. When these qualities are found in anyone among us, we honour, respect, revere, and venerate him, and live in dependence on him honouring and respecting him." [13]

24. When this was said, the brahmin Vassakāra, the minister of Magadha, said to General Upananda: "What do you think, general? When these worthy ones honour one who should be honoured, respect one who should be respected, revere one who should be revered, and venerate one who should be venerated, surely they honour one who should be honoured...and venerate one who should be venerated. For if these worthy ones did not honour, respect, revere, and venerate such a person, then whom

could they honour, respect, revere, and venerate, and on whom could they live in dependence honouring and respecting?"

25. Then the brahmin Vassakāra, the minister of Magadha, said to the venerable Ānanda: "Where is Master Ānanda living now?"

"Now I am living in the Bamboo Grove, brahmin."

"I hope, Master Ānanda, that the Bamboo Grove is pleasant, quiet and undisturbed by voices, with an atmosphere of seclusion, remote from people, favourable for retreat."

"Indeed, brahmin, that the Bamboo Grove is pleasant... favourable for retreat is because of such guardian protectors as yourself."

"Indeed, Master Ānanda, that the Bamboo Grove is pleasant...favourable for retreat is because of the worthy ones who are meditators and cultivate meditation. The worthy ones are meditators and cultivate meditation. On one occasion, Master Ānanda, Master Gotama was living at Vesālī in the Hall with the Peaked Roof in the Great Wood. Then I went there and approached Master Gotama, and in many ways he gave a talk about meditation. Master Gotama was a meditator and cultivated meditation, and he praised every type of meditation."

26. "The Blessed One, brahmin, did not praise every type of meditation, nor did he condemn every type of meditation. What kind [14] of meditation did the Blessed One not praise? Here, brahmin, someone abides with his mind obsessed by sensual lust, a prey to sensual lust, and he does not understand as it actually is the escape from arisen sensual lust. While he harbours sensual lust within, he meditates, premeditates, out-meditates, and mismeditates.[1035] He abides with his mind obsessed by ill will, a prey to ill will...with his mind obsessed by sloth and torpor, a prey to sloth and torpor...with his mind obsessed by restlessness and remorse, a prey to restlessness and remorse...with his mind obsessed by doubt, a prey to doubt, and he does not understand as it actually is the escape from arisen doubt. While he harbours doubt within, he meditates, premeditates, out-meditates, and mismeditates. The Blessed One did not praise that kind of meditation.

27. "And what kind of meditation did the Blessed One praise? Here, brahmin, quite secluded from sensual pleasures, secluded from unwholesome states, a bhikkhu enters upon and abides in the first jhāna...With the stilling of applied and sustained

thought, he enters upon and abides in the second jhāna...With the fading away as well of rapture...he enters upon and abides in the third jhāna...With the abandoning of pleasure and pain...he enters upon and abides in the fourth jhāna...The Blessed One praised that kind of meditation."

28. "It seems, Master Ānanda, that Master Gotama censured that kind of meditation that should be censured and praised that kind of meditation that should be praised. And now, Master Ānanda, we depart. We are busy and have much to do."

"You may go, brahmin, at your own convenience." [15]

Then the brahmin Vassakāra, the minister of Magadha, having delighted and rejoiced in the venerable Ānanda's words, rose from his seat and departed.

29. Then, soon after he had left, the brahmin Gopaka Moggallāna said to the venerable Ānanda: "Master Ānanda has not yet answered what we asked him."

"Did we not tell you, brahmin: 'There is no single bhikkhu, brahmin, who possesses in each and every way all those qualities that were possessed by the Blessed One, accomplished and fully enlightened. For the Blessed One was the arouser of the unarisen path, the producer of the unproduced path, the declarer of the undeclared path; he was the knower of the path, the finder of the path, the one skilled in the path. But his disciples now abide following that path and become possessed of it afterwards'?"

109 *Mahāpuṇṇama Sutta* The Greater Discourse on the Full-Moon Night

1. THUS HAVE I HEARD. On one occasion the Blessed One was living at Sāvatthī in the Eastern Park, in the Palace of Migāra's Mother.

2. On that occasion—on the Uposatha day of the fifteenth,[1036] on the full-moon night—the Blessed One was seated in the open surrounded by the Sangha of bhikkhus.

3. Then a certain bhikkhu rose from his seat,[1037] arranged his upper robe on one shoulder, and extending his hands in reverential salutation towards the Blessed One, said to him: "Venerable sir, I would ask the Blessed One about a certain point, if the Blessed One would grant me an answer to my question."—"Sit on your own seat, bhikkhu, and ask what you like." So the bhikkhu sat on his own seat and said to the Blessed One:

4. "Are these not, venerable sir, the five aggregates affected by clinging; [16] that is, the material form aggregate affected by clinging, the feeling aggregate affected by clinging, the perception aggregate affected by clinging, the formations aggregate affected by clinging, and the consciousness aggregate affected by clinging?"

"These, bhikkhus, are the five aggregates affected by clinging; that is, the material form aggregate affected by clinging...and the consciousness aggregate affected by clinging."

Saying, "Good, venerable sir," the bhikkhu delighted and rejoiced in the Blessed One's words. Then he asked him a further question:

5. "But, venerable sir, in what are these five aggregates affected by clinging rooted?"

"These five aggregates affected by clinging are rooted in desire,[1038] bhikkhu."

6. "Venerable sir, is that clinging the same as these five aggregates affected by clinging, or is the clinging something apart from the five aggregates affected by clinging?"[1039]

"Bhikkhu, that clinging is neither the same as these five aggregates affected by clinging, nor is the clinging something apart from the five aggregates affected by clinging. It is the desire and lust in regard to the five aggregates affected by clinging that is the clinging there."

7. "But, venerable sir, can there be diversity in the desire and lust regarding these five aggregates affected by clinging?"

"There can be, bhikkhu," the Blessed One said. "Here, bhikkhu, someone thinks thus: 'May my material form be thus in the future; may my feeling be thus in the future; may my perception be thus in the future; may my formations be thus in the future; may my consciousness be thus in the future.' Thus there is diversity in the desire and lust regarding these five aggregates affected by clinging."

8. "But, venerable sir, in what way does the term 'aggregates' apply to the aggregates?"

"Bhikkhu, any kind of material form whatever, whether past, future, or present, internal or external, gross or subtle, inferior or superior, far or near—this is the material form aggregate. [17] Any kind of feeling whatever...far or near—this is the feeling aggregate. Any kind of perception whatever...far or near—this is the perception aggregate. Any kind of formations whatever... far or near—this is the formations aggregate. Any kind of consciousness whatever...far or near—this is the consciousness aggregate. It is in this way, bhikkhu, that the term 'aggregate' applies to the aggregates."

9. "What is the cause and condition, venerable sir, for the manifestation of the material form aggregate? What is the cause and condition for the manifestation of the feeling aggregate... the perception aggregate...the formations aggregate...the consciousness aggregate?"

"The four great elements, bhikkhu, are the cause and condition for the manifestation of the material form aggregate. Contact is the cause and condition for the manifestation of the feeling aggregate. Contact is the cause and the condition for the manifestation of the perception aggregate. Contact is the cause and condition for the manifestation of the formations aggregate. Mentality-materiality is the cause and condition for the manifestation of the consciousness aggregate."[1040]

10. "Venerable sir, how does identity view come to be?"[1041]

"Here, bhikkhu, an untaught ordinary person, who has no regard for noble ones and is unskilled and undisciplined in their Dhamma, who has no regard for true men and is unskilled and undisciplined in their Dhamma, regards material form as self, or self as possessed of material form, or material form as in self, or self as in material form. He regards feeling as self...perception as self...formations as self...consciousness as self, or self as possessed of consciousness, [18] or consciousness as in self, or self as in consciousness. That is how identity view comes to be."

11. "But, venerable sir, how does identity view not come to be?"

"Here, bhikkhu, a well-taught noble disciple, who has regard for noble ones and is skilled and disciplined in their Dhamma, who has regard for true men and is skilled and disciplined in their Dhamma, does not regard material form as self, or self as possessed of material form, or material form as in self, or self as in material form. He does not regard feeling as self...perception as self...formations as self...consciousness as self, or self as possessed of consciousness, or consciousness as in self, or self as in consciousness. That is how identity view does not come to be."

12. "What, venerable sir, is the gratification, what is the danger, and what is the escape in the case of material form? What is the gratification, what is the danger, and what is the escape in the case of feeling...in the case of perception...in the case of formations...in the case of consciousness?"

"The pleasure and joy, bhikkhu, that arise in dependence on material form—this is the gratification in the case of material form. Material form is impermanent, suffering, and subject to change—this is the danger in the case of material form. The removal of desire and lust, the abandonment of desire and lust for material form—this is the escape in the case of material form.

"The pleasure and joy that arise in dependence on feeling...in dependence on perception...in dependence on formations...in dependence on consciousness—this is the gratification in the case of consciousness. Consciousness is impermanent, suffering, and subject to change—this is the danger in the case of consciousness. The removal of desire and lust, the abandonment of desire and lust for consciousness—this is the escape in the case of consciousness."

13. "Venerable sir, how does one know, how does one see, so

that in regard to this body with its consciousness and all external signs, there is no I-making, mine-making, and underlying tendency to conceit?"

"Bhikkhu, any kind of material form whatever, whether past or present, internal or external, gross or subtle, inferior [19] or superior, far or near—one sees all material form as it actually is with proper wisdom thus: 'This is not mine, this I am not, this is not my self.' Any kind of feeling whatever...Any kind of perception whatever...Any kind of formations whatever...Any kind of consciousness whatever...one sees all consciousness as it actually is with proper wisdom thus: 'This is not mine, this I am not, this is not my self.' It is when one knows and sees thus that in regard to this body with its consciousness and all external signs there is no I-making, mine-making, or underlying tendency to conceit."

14. Then, in the mind of a certain bhikkhu this thought arose: "So, it seems, material form is not self, feeling is not self, perception is not self, formations are not self, consciousness is not self. What self, then, will actions done by the not-self affect?"[1042]

Then the Blessed One, knowing in his mind the thought in the mind of that bhikkhu, addressed the bhikkhus thus: "It is possible, bhikkhus, that some misguided man here, obtuse and ignorant, with his mind dominated by craving, might think that he can outstrip the Teacher's Dispensation thus: 'So, it seems, material form is not self...consciousness is not self. What self, then, will actions done by the not-self affect?' Now, bhikkhus, you have been trained by me through interrogation on various occasions in regard to various things.[1043]

15. "Bhikkhus, what do you think? Is material form permanent or impermanent?"—"Impermanent, venerable sir."—"Is what is impermanent suffering or happiness?"—"Suffering, venerable sir."—"Is what is impermanent, suffering, and subject to change fit to be regarded thus: 'This is mine, this I am, this is my self'?"—"No, venerable sir."

"Bhikkhus, what do you think: Is feeling...perception...formations...consciousness permanent or impermanent?"—"Impermanent, venerable sir."—[20] "Is what is impermanent suffering or happiness?"—"Suffering, venerable sir."—"Is what is impermanent, suffering, and subject to change fit to be regarded thus: 'This is mine, this I am, this is my self'?"—"No, venerable sir."

16. "Therefore, bhikkhus, any kind of material form whatever, whether past, future, or present...all material form should be seen as it actually is with proper wisdom thus: 'This is not mine, this I am not, this is not my self.' Any kind of feeling whatever... Any kind of perception whatever...Any kind of formations whatever...Any kind of consciousness whatever...all consciousness should be seen as it actually is with proper wisdom thus: 'This is not mine, this I am not, this is not my self.'

17. "Seeing thus, a well-taught noble disciple becomes disenchanted with material form, disenchanted with feeling, disenchanted with perception, disenchanted with formations, disenchanted with consciousness.

18. "Being disenchanted, he becomes dispassionate. Through dispassion [his mind] is liberated. When it is liberated there comes the knowledge: 'It is liberated.' He understands: 'Birth is destroyed, the holy life has been lived, what had to be done has been done, there is no more coming to any state of being.'"

That is what the Blessed One said. The bhikkhus were satisfied and delighted in the Blessed One's words. Now while this discourse was being spoken, through not clinging the minds of sixty bhikkhus were liberated from the taints.[1044]

110 *Cūḷapuṇṇama Sutta* The Shorter Discourse on the Full-Moon Night

1. THUS HAVE I HEARD. On one occasion the Blessed One was living at Sāvatthī in the Eastern Park, in the Palace of Migāra's Mother.

2. On that occasion—the Uposatha day of the fifteenth, on the full-moon night—[21] the Blessed One was seated in the open surrounded by the Sangha of bhikkhus. Then, surveying the silent Sangha of bhikkhus, he addressed them thus:

3. "Bhikkhus, would an untrue man[1045] know of an untrue man: 'This person is an untrue man'?"—"No, venerable sir."—"Good, bhikkhus. It is impossible, it cannot be, that an untrue man should know of an untrue man: 'This person is an untrue man.' But would an untrue man know of a true man: 'This person is a true man'?"—"No, venerable sir."—"Good, bhikkhus. It is impossible, it cannot be, that an untrue man should know of a true man: 'This person is a true man.'

4. "Bhikkhus, an untrue man is possessed of bad qualities; he associates as an untrue man, he wills as an untrue man, he counsels as an untrue man, he speaks as an untrue man, he acts as an untrue man, he holds views as an untrue man, and he gives gifts as an untrue man.

5. "And how is an untrue man possessed of bad qualities? Here an untrue man has no faith, no shame, no fear of wrongdoing; he is unlearned, lazy, forgetful, and unwise. That is how an untrue man is possessed of bad qualities.

6. "And how does an untrue man associate as an untrue man? Here an untrue man has for friends and companions those recluses and brahmins who have no faith, no shame, no fear of wrongdoing; who are unlearned, lazy, forgetful, and unwise. That is how an untrue man associates as an untrue man.

7. "And how does an untrue man will as an untrue man? Here an untrue man wills for his own affliction, for the affliction of

others, and for the affliction of both. That is how an untrue man wills as an untrue man.

8. "And how does an untrue man counsel as an untrue man? Here an untrue man counsels for his own affliction, for the affliction of others, and for the affliction of both. [22] That is how an untrue man counsels as an untrue man.

9. "And how does an untrue man speak as an untrue man? Here an untrue man speaks false speech, malicious speech, harsh speech, and gossip. That is how an untrue man speaks as an untrue man.

10. "And how does an untrue man act as an untrue man? Here an untrue man kills living beings, takes what is not given, and misconducts himself in sensual pleasures. That is how an untrue man acts as an untrue man.

11. "And how does an untrue man hold views as an untrue man? Here an untrue man holds such a view as this: 'There is nothing given, nothing offered, nothing sacrificed; no fruit or result of good and bad actions; no this world, no other world; no mother, no father; no beings who are reborn spontaneously; no good and virtuous recluses and brahmins in the world who have realised for themselves by direct knowledge and declare this world and the other world.' That is how an untrue man holds views as an untrue man.

12. "And how does an untrue man give gifts as an untrue man? Here an untrue man gives a gift carelessly, gives it not with his own hand, gives it without showing respect, gives what is to be discarded, gives it with the view that nothing will come of it. That is how an untrue man gives gifts as an untrue man.

13. "That untrue man—thus possessed of bad qualities, who thus associates as an untrue man, wills as an untrue man, counsels as an untrue man, speaks as an untrue man, acts as an untrue man, holds views as an untrue man, and gives gifts as an untrue man—on the dissolution of the body, after death, reappears in the destination of untrue men. And what is the destination of untrue men? It is hell or the animal world.

14. "Bhikkhus, would a true man know of a true man: 'This person is a true man'?" [23]—"Yes, venerable sir."—"Good, bhikkhus. It is possible that a true man would know of a true man: 'This person is a true man.' But would a true man know of an untrue man: 'This person is an untrue man'?"—"Yes, venerable

sir."—"Good, bhikkhus. It is possible that a true man would know of an untrue man: 'This person is an untrue man.'

15. "Bhikkhus, a true man is possessed of good qualities; he associates as a true man, he wills as a true man, he counsels as a true man, he speaks as a true man, he acts as a true man, he holds views as a true man, and he gives gifts as a true man.

16. "And how is a true man possessed of good qualities? Here a true man has faith, shame, and fear of wrongdoing; he is learned, energetic, mindful, and wise. That is how a true man is possessed of good qualities.

17. "And how does a true man associate as a true man? Here a true man has for his friends and companions those recluses and brahmins who have faith, shame, and fear of wrongdoing; who are learned, energetic, mindful, and wise. That is how a true man associates as a true man.

18. "And how does a true man will as a true man? Here a true man does not will for his own affliction, for the affliction of others, or for the affliction of both. That is how a true man wills as a true man.

19. "And how does a true man counsel as a true man? Here a true man does not counsel for his own affliction, for the affliction of others, or for the affliction of both. That is how a true man counsels as a true man.

20. "And how does a true man speak as a true man? Here a true man abstains from false speech, from malicious speech, from harsh speech, and from gossip. That is how a true man speaks as a true man.

21. "And how does a true man act as a true man? Here a true man abstains from killing living beings, from taking what is not given, [24] and from misconduct in sensual pleasures. That is how a true man acts as a true man.

22. "And how does a true man hold views as a true man? Here a true man holds such a view as this: 'There is what is given and what is offered and what is sacrificed; there is fruit and result of good and bad actions; there is this world and the other world; there is mother and father; there are beings who are reborn spontaneously; there are good and virtuous recluses and brahmins in the world who have realised for themselves by direct knowledge and declare this world and the other world.' That is how a true man holds views as a true man.

23. "And how does a true man give gifts as a true man? Here a true man gives a gift carefully, gives it with his own hand, gives it showing respect, gives a valuable gift, gives it with the view that something will come of it. That is how a true man gives gifts as a true man.

24. "That true man—thus possessed of good qualities, who thus associates as a true man, wills as a true man, counsels as a true man, speaks as a true man, acts as a true man, holds views as a true man, and gives gifts as a true man—on the dissolution of the body, after death, reappears in the destination of true men. And what is the destination of true men? It is greatness among the gods or greatness among human beings."

That is what the Blessed One said. The bhikkhus were satisfied and delighted in the Blessed One's words.

2

The Division of One by One

(*Anupadavagga*)

111 *Anupada Sutta*
One by One As They Occurred

[25] 1. THUS HAVE I HEARD. On one occasion the Blessed One was living at Sāvatthī in Jeta's Grove, Anāthapiṇḍika's Park. There he addressed the bhikkhus thus: "Bhikkhus."—"Venerable, sir," they replied. The Blessed One said this:

2. "Bhikkhus, Sāriputta is wise; Sāriputta has great wisdom; Sāriputta has wide wisdom; Sāriputta has joyous wisdom; Sāriputta has quick wisdom; Sāriputta has keen wisdom; Sāriputta has penetrative wisdom. During half a month, bhikkhus, Sāriputta gained insight into states one by one as they occurred.[1046] Now Sāriputta's insight into states one by one as they occurred was this:

3. "Here, bhikkhus, quite secluded from sensual pleasures, secluded from unwholesome states, Sāriputta entered upon and abided in the first jhāna, which is accompanied by applied and sustained thought, with rapture and pleasure born of seclusion.

4. "And the states in the first jhāna—the applied thought, the sustained thought, the rapture, the pleasure, and the unification of mind; the contact, feeling, perception, volition, and mind; the zeal, decision, energy, mindfulness, equanimity, and attention—these states were defined by him one by one as they occurred;[1047] known to him those states arose, known they were present, known they disappeared. He understood thus: 'So indeed, these states, not having been, come into being; having been, they vanish.' Regarding those states, he abided unattracted, unrepelled, independent, detached, free, dissociated, with a mind rid of barriers.[1048] He understood: 'There is an escape beyond,' and with the cultivation of that [attainment], he confirmed that there is.[1049]

5. "Again, bhikkhus, with the stilling of applied and sustained thought, Sāriputta entered and abided in [26] the second jhāna,

which has self-confidence and singleness of mind without applied and sustained thought, with rapture and pleasure born of concentration.

6. "And the states in the second jhāna—the self-confidence, the rapture, the pleasure, and the unification of mind; the contact, feeling, perception, volition, and mind; the zeal, decision, energy, mindfulness, equanimity, and attention—these states were defined by him one by one as they occurred; known to him those states arose, known they were present, known they disappeared. He understood thus:...and with the cultivation of that [attainment], he confirmed that there is.

7. "Again, bhikkhus, with the fading away as well of rapture, Sāriputta abided in equanimity, and mindful and fully aware, still feeling pleasure with the body, he entered upon and abided in the third jhāna, on account of which noble ones announce: 'He has a pleasant abiding who has equanimity and is mindful.'

8. "And the states in the third jhāna—the equanimity, the pleasure, the mindfulness, the full awareness, and the unification of mind; the contact, feeling, perception, volition, and mind; the zeal, decision, energy, mindfulness, equanimity, and attention—these states were defined by him one by one as they occurred; known to him those states arose, known they were present, known they disappeared. He understood thus:...and with the cultivation of that [attainment], he confirmed that there is.

9. "Again, bhikkhus, with the abandoning of pleasure and pain, and with the previous disappearance of joy and grief, Sāriputta entered upon and abided in the fourth jhāna, which has neither-pain-nor-pleasure and purity of mindfulness due to equanimity.

10. "And the states in the fourth jhāna—the equanimity, the neither-painful-nor-pleasant feeling, the mental unconcern due to tranquillity,[1050] the purity of mindfulness, and the unification of mind; the contact, feeling, perception, volition, and mind; the zeal, decision, energy, mindfulness, equanimity, and attention—these states were defined by him one by one as they occurred; known to him those states arose, known they were present, [27] known they disappeared. He understood thus:...and with the cultivation of that [attainment], he confirmed that there is.

11. "Again, bhikkhus, with the complete surmounting of perceptions of form, with the disappearance of perceptions of

sensory impact, with non-attention to perceptions of diversity, aware that 'space is infinite,' Sāriputta entered upon and abided in the base of infinite space.

12. "And the states in the base of infinite space—the perception of the base of infinite space and the unification of mind; the contact, feeling, perception, volition, and mind; the zeal, decision, energy, mindfulness, equanimity, and attention—these states were defined by him one by one as they occurred; known to him those states arose, known they were present, known they disappeared. He understood thus:...and with the cultivation of that [attainment], he confirmed that there is.

13. "Again, bhikkhus, by completely surmounting the base of infinite space, aware that 'consciousness is infinite,' Sāriputta entered upon and abided in the base of infinite consciousness.

14. "And the states in the base of infinite consciousness—the perception of the base of infinite consciousness and the unification of mind; the contact, feeling, perception, volition, and mind; the zeal, decision, energy, mindfulness, equanimity, and attention—these states were defined by him one by one as they occurred; known to him those states arose, known they were present, known they disappeared. He understood thus:...and with the cultivation of that [attainment], he confirmed that there is. [28]

15. "Again, bhikkhus, by completely surmounting the base of infinite consciousness, aware that 'there is nothing,' Sāriputta entered upon and abided in the base of nothingness.

16. "And the states in the base of nothingness—the perception of the base of nothingness and the unification of mind; the contact, feeling, perception, volition, and mind; the zeal, decision, energy, mindfulness, equanimity, and attention—these states were defined by him one by one as they occurred; known to him those states arose, known they were present, known they disappeared. He understood thus:...and with the cultivation of that [attainment], he confirmed that there is.

17. "Again, bhikkhus, by completely surmounting the base of nothingness, Sāriputta entered upon and abided in the base of neither-perception-nor-non-perception.

18. "He emerged mindful from that attainment. Having done so, he contemplated the states that had passed, ceased, and changed, thus: 'So indeed, these states, not having been, come into being; having been, they vanish.'[1051] Regarding those states,

he abided unattracted, unrepelled, independent, detached, free, dissociated, with a mind rid of barriers. He understood: 'There is an escape beyond,' and with the cultivation of that [attainment], he confirmed that there is.

19. "Again, bhikkhus, by completely surmounting the base of neither-perception-nor-non-perception, Sāriputta entered upon and abided in the cessation of perception and feeling. And his taints were destroyed by his seeing with wisdom.[1052]

20. "He emerged mindful from that attainment. Having done so, he recalled the states that had passed, ceased, and changed, thus: 'So indeed, these states, not having been, come into being; having been, they vanish.'[1053] Regarding those states, he abided unattracted, unrepelled, independent, detached, free, dissociated, with a mind rid of barriers. He understood: 'There is no escape beyond,' and with the cultivation of that [attainment], he confirmed that there is not.[1054]

21. "Bhikkhus, rightly speaking, were it to be said of anyone: 'He has attained mastery and perfection[1055] in noble virtue, [29] attained mastery and perfection in noble concentration, attained mastery and perfection in noble wisdom, attained mastery and perfection in noble deliverance,' it is of Sāriputta indeed that rightly speaking this should be said.

22. "Bhikkhus, rightly speaking, were it to be said of anyone: 'He is the son of the Blessed One, born of his breast, born of his mouth, born of the Dhamma, created by the Dhamma, an heir in the Dhamma, not an heir in material things,' it is of Sāriputta indeed that rightly speaking this should be said.

23. "Bhikkhus, the matchless Wheel of the Dhamma set rolling by the Tathāgata is kept rolling rightly by Sāriputta."

That is what the Blessed One said. The bhikkhus were satisfied and delighted in the Blessed One's words.

112 *Chabbisodhana Sutta*
The Sixfold Purity

1. THUS HAVE I HEARD. On one occasion the Blessed One was living at Sāvatthī in Jeta's Grove, Anāthapiṇḍika's Park. There he addressed the bhikkhus thus: "Bhikkhus."—"Venerable sir," they replied. The Blessed One said this:

2. "Here, bhikkhus, a bhikkhu makes a declaration of final knowledge thus: 'I understand: Birth is destroyed, the holy life has been lived, what had to be done has been done, there is no more coming to any state of being.'

3. "That bhikkhu's words should neither be approved nor disapproved. Without approving or disapproving, a question should be put thus: 'Friend, there are four kinds of expression rightly proclaimed by the Blessed One who knows and sees, accomplished and fully enlightened. What four? Telling the seen as it is seen; telling the heard as it is heard; telling the sensed as it is sensed; telling the cognized as it is cognized.[1056] [30] These, friend, are the four kinds of expression rightly proclaimed by the Blessed One who knows and sees, accomplished and fully enlightened. How does the venerable one know, how does he see, regarding these four kinds of expression, so that through not clinging his mind is liberated from the taints?'

4. "Bhikkhus, when a bhikkhu is one with taints destroyed, who has lived the holy life, done what had to be done, laid down the burden, reached the true goal, destroyed the fetters of being, and is completely liberated through final knowledge, this is the nature of his answer:

"'Friends, regarding the seen I abide unattracted, unrepelled, independent, detached, free, dissociated, with a mind rid of barriers.[1057] Regarding the heard...Regarding the sensed...Regarding the cognized I abide unattracted, unrepelled, independent, detached, free, dissociated, with a mind rid of barriers. It is by knowing thus, seeing thus, regarding these four kinds of expression, that through not clinging my mind is liberated from the taints.'

5. "Saying 'good,' one may delight and rejoice in that bhikkhu's words. Having done so, a further question may be put thus:

"'Friend, there are these five aggregates affected by clinging, rightly proclaimed by the Blessed One who knows and sees, accomplished and fully enlightened. What five? They are the material form aggregate affected by clinging, the feeling aggregate affected by clinging, the perception aggregate affected by clinging, the formations aggregate affected by clinging, and the consciousness aggregate affected by clinging. These, friend, are the five aggregates affected by clinging, rightly proclaimed by the Blessed One who knows and sees, accomplished and fully enlightened. How does the venerable one know, how does he see, regarding these five aggregates affected by clinging, so that through not clinging his mind is liberated from the taints?'

6. "Bhikkhus, when a bhikkhu is one with taints destroyed... and is completely liberated through final knowledge, this is the nature of his answer:

"'Friends, having known material form to be feeble, fading away, and comfortless, [31] with the destruction, fading away, cessation, giving up, and relinquishing of attraction and clinging regarding material form, of mental standpoints, adherences, and underlying tendencies regarding material form,[1058] I have understood that my mind is liberated.

"'Friends, having known feeling...Having known perception...Having known formations...Having known consciousness to be feeble, fading away, and comfortless, with the destruction, fading away, cessation, giving up, and relinquishing of attraction and clinging regarding consciousness, of mental standpoints, adherences, and underlying tendencies regarding consciousness, I have understood that my mind is liberated.

"'It is by knowing thus, seeing thus, regarding these five aggregates affected by clinging, that through not clinging my mind is liberated from the taints.'

7. "Saying 'good,' one may delight and rejoice in that bhikkhu's words. Having done so, a further question may be put thus:

"'Friend, there are these six elements rightly proclaimed by the Blessed One who knows and sees, accomplished and fully enlightened. What six? They are the earth element, the water element, the fire element, the air element, the space element, and the consciousness element. These, friend, are the six elements rightly proclaimed by the Blessed One who knows and sees, accomplished and fully enlightened. How does the venerable one know, how does he see, regarding these six elements, so that through not clinging his mind is liberated from the taints?'

8. "Bhikkhus, when a bhikkhu is one with taints destroyed... and is completely liberated through final knowledge, this is the nature of his answer:

"'Friends, I have treated the earth element as not self, with no self based on the earth element.[1059] And with the destruction, fading away, cessation, giving up, and relinquishing of attraction and clinging based on the earth element, of mental standpoints, adherences, and underlying tendencies based on the earth element, I have understood that my mind is liberated.

"'Friends, I have treated the water element...the fire element...the air element...the space element...the consciousness element as not self, with no self based on the consciousness element. And with the destruction, fading away, cessation, giving up, and relinquishing of attraction and clinging based on the consciousness element, of mental standpoints, adherences, and underlying tendencies based on the consciousness element, I have understood that my mind is liberated.

"'It is by knowing thus, seeing thus, regarding these six elements, that through not clinging my mind is liberated from the taints.'

9. "Saying 'good,' [32] one may delight and rejoice in that bhikkhu's words. Having done so, a further question may be put thus:

"'But, friend, there are these six internal and external bases rightly proclaimed by the Blessed One who knows and sees, accomplished and fully enlightened. What six? They are the eye and forms, the ear and sounds, the nose and odours, the tongue and flavours, the body and tangibles, the mind and mind-objects. These, friend, are the six internal and external bases rightly proclaimed by the Blessed One who knows and sees, accomplished and fully enlightened. How does the venerable one know, how does he see, regarding these six internal and external bases, so that through not clinging his mind is liberated from the taints?'

10. "Bhikkhus, when a bhikkhu is one with taints destroyed... and is completely liberated through final knowledge, this is the nature of his answer:

"'Friends, with the destruction, fading away, cessation, giving up, and relinquishing of desire, lust, delight, craving, attraction, and clinging, and of mental standpoints, adherences, and underlying tendencies regarding the eye, forms, eye-consciousness, and things cognizable [by the mind] through eye-consciousness, I have understood that my mind is liberated.[1060]

"'With the destruction, fading away, cessation, giving up, and relinquishing of desire, lust, delight, craving, attraction, and clinging, and of mental standpoints, adherences, and underlying tendencies regarding the ear, sounds, ear-consciousness, and things cognizable [by the mind] through ear-consciousness... regarding the nose, odours, nose-consciousness, and things cognizable [by the mind] through nose-consciousness...regarding the tongue, flavours, tongue-consciousness, and things cognizable [by the mind] through tongue consciousness...regarding the body, tangibles, body-consciousness, and things cognizable [by the mind] through body-consciousness...regarding the mind, mind-objects, mind-consciousness, and things cognizable [by the mind] through mind-consciousness, I have understood that my mind is liberated.

"'It is by knowing thus, seeing thus, regarding these six internal and external bases, that through not clinging my mind is liberated from the taints.'

11. "Saying 'good,' one may delight and rejoice in that bhikkhu's words. Having done so, a further question may be put thus:

"'But, friend, how does the venerable one know, how does he see, so that in regard to this body with its consciousness and all external signs, I-making, mine-making, and the underlying tendency to conceit have been eradicated in him?'[1061] [33]

12. "Bhikkhus, when a bhikkhu is one with taints destroyed... and is completely liberated through final knowledge, this is the nature of his answer:

"'Friends, formerly when I lived the home life I was ignorant. Then the Tathāgata or his disciple taught me the Dhamma. On hearing the Dhamma I acquired faith in the Tathāgata. Possessing that faith, I considered thus: "Household life is crowded and dusty; life gone forth is wide open. It is not easy while living in a home to lead the holy life utterly perfect and pure as a polished shell. Suppose I shave off my hair and beard, put on the yellow robe, and go forth from the home life into homelessness." On a later occasion, abandoning a small or a large fortune, abandoning a small or a large circle of relations, I shaved off my hair and beard, put on the yellow robe, and went forth from the home life into homelessness.

13–17. "'Having thus gone forth and possessing the bhikkhus' training and way of life...(*as Sutta 51, §§14–19*) [34, 35]...I purified my mind from doubt. [36]

18. "'Having thus abandoned these five hindrances, imperfections of the mind that weaken wisdom, quite secluded from sensual pleasures, secluded from unwholesome states, I entered upon and abided in the first jhāna, which is accompanied by applied and sustained thought, with rapture and pleasure born of seclusion. With the stilling of applied and sustained thought, I entered upon and abided in the second jhāna...With the fading away as well of rapture...I entered upon and abided in the third jhāna...With the abandoning of pleasure and pain...I entered upon and abided in the fourth jhāna, which has neither-pain-nor-pleasure and purity of mindfulness due to equanimity.

19. "'When my concentrated mind was thus purified, bright, unblemished, rid of imperfections, malleable, wieldy, steady, and attained to imperturbability, I directed it to knowledge of the destruction of the taints.[1062] I directly knew as it actually is: "This is suffering"..."This is the origin of suffering"..."This is the cessation of suffering"..."This is the way leading to the cessation of suffering." I directly knew as it actually is: "These are the taints"..."This is the origin of the taints"..."This is the cessation of the taints"..."This is the way leading to the cessation of the taints."

20. "'When I knew and saw thus, my mind was liberated from the taint of sensual desire, from the taint of being, and from the taint of ignorance. When it was liberated there came the knowledge: "It is liberated." I directly knew: "Birth is destroyed, the holy life has been lived, what had to be done has been done, there is no more coming to any state of being."

"'It is by knowing thus, seeing thus, friends, that in regard to this body with its consciousness and all external signs, I-making, mine-making, and the underlying tendency to conceit have been eradicated in me.'

21. "Saying 'good,' bhikkhus, one may delight and rejoice in that bhikkhu's words. Having done so, one should say to him: 'It is a gain for us, friend, [37] it is a great gain for us, friend, that we see such a companion in the holy life as the venerable one.'"[1063]

That is what the Blessed One said. The bhikkhus were satisfied and delighted in the Blessed One's words.

113 *Sappurisa Sutta*
The True Man

1. THUS HAVE I HEARD. On one occasion the Blessed One was living at Sāvatthī in Jeta's Grove, Anāthapiṇḍika's Park. There he addressed the bhikkhus thus: "Bhikkhus."—"Venerable sir," they replied. The Blessed One said this:

2. "Bhikkhus, I shall teach you the character of a true man and the character of an untrue man.[1064] Listen and attend closely to what I shall say."—"Yes, venerable sir," the bhikkhus replied. The Blessed One said this:

3. "Bhikkhus, what is the character of an untrue man? Here an untrue man who has gone forth from an aristocratic family considers thus: 'I have gone forth from an aristocratic family; but these other bhikkhus have not gone forth from aristocratic families.' So he lauds himself and disparages others because of his aristocratic family. This is the character of an untrue man.

"But a true man considers thus: 'It is not because of one's aristocratic family that states of greed, hatred, or delusion are destroyed. Even though someone may not have gone forth from an aristocratic family, yet if he has entered upon the way that accords with the Dhamma, entered upon the proper way, [38] and conducts himself according to the Dhamma, he should be honoured for that, he should be praised for that.' So, putting the practice of the way first, he neither lauds himself nor disparages others because of his aristocratic family. This is the character of a true man.

4–6. "Moreover, an untrue man who has gone forth from a great family...from a wealthy family...from an influential family considers thus: 'I have gone forth from an influential family; but these other bhikkhus have not gone forth from influential families.' So he lauds himself and disparages others because of his influential family. This too is the character of an untrue man.

"But a true man considers thus: 'It is not because of one's influential family that states of greed, hatred, or delusion are destroyed. Even though someone may not have gone forth from an influential family, yet if he has entered upon the way that accords with the Dhamma, entered upon the proper way, and conducts himself according to the Dhamma, he should be honoured for that, he should be praised for that.' So, putting the practice of the way first, he neither lauds himself nor disparages others because of his influential family. This too is the character of a true man.

7. "Moreover, an untrue man who is well known and famous considers thus: 'I am well known and famous; but these other bhikkhus are unknown and of no account.' So he lauds himself and disparages others because of his renown. This too is the character of an untrue man.

"But a true man considers thus: 'It is not because of one's renown that states of greed, hatred, or delusion are destroyed. Even though someone may not be well known and famous, yet if he has entered upon the way that accords with the Dhamma, entered upon the proper way, and conducts himself according to the Dhamma, he should be honoured for that, he should be praised for that.' So, putting the practice of the way first, he neither lauds himself nor disparages others because of his renown. This too is the character of a true man. [39]

8. "Moreover, an untrue man who gains robes, almsfood, resting places, and requisites of medicine considers thus: 'I gain robes, almsfood, resting places, and requisites of medicine; but these other bhikkhus do not gain these things.' So he lauds himself and disparages others because of gain. This too is the character of an untrue man.

"But a true man considers thus: 'It is not because of gain that states of greed, hatred, or delusion are destroyed. Even though someone has no gain, yet if he has entered upon the way that accords with the Dhamma, entered upon the proper way, and conducts himself according to the Dhamma, he should be honoured for that, he should be praised for that.' So, putting the practice of the way first, he neither lauds himself nor disparages others because of gain. This too is the character of a true man.

9–20. "Moreover, an untrue man who is learned...who is expert in the Discipline...[40]...who is a preacher of the Dhamma...who is a forest dweller...who is a refuse-rag wearer...[41]...an almsfood eater...a tree-root dweller...[42]...a charnel-ground dweller...an open-air dweller...a continual sitter...an any-bed user...a one-session eater considers thus: 'I am a one-session eater; but these other bhikkhus are not one-session eaters.'[1065] So he lauds himself and disparages others because of his being a one-session eater. This too is the character of an untrue man.

"But a true man considers thus: 'It is not because of being a one-session eater that states of greed, hatred, or delusion are destroyed. Even though someone may not be a one-session eater, yet if he has entered upon the way that accords with the Dhamma, entered upon the proper way, and conducts himself according to the Dhamma, he should be honoured for that, he should be praised for that.' So, putting the practice of the way first, he neither lauds himself nor disparages others because of his being a one-session eater. This too is the character of a true man.

21. "Moreover, quite secluded from sensual pleasures, secluded from unwholesome states, an untrue man enters upon and abides in the first jhāna, which is accompanied by applied and sustained thought, with rapture and pleasure born of seclusion. He considers thus: 'I have gained the attainment of the first jhāna; but these other bhikkhus have not gained the attainment of the first jhāna.' So he lauds himself and disparages others because of his attainment of the first jhāna. This too is the character of an untrue man.

"But a true man considers thus: 'Non-identification even with the attainment of the first jhāna has been declared by the Blessed One; for in whatever way they conceive, the fact is ever other than that.'[1066] [43] So, putting non-identification first, he neither lauds himself nor disparages others because of his attainment of the first jhāna. This too is the character of a true man.

22–24. "Moreover, with the stilling of applied and sustained thought, an untrue man enters upon and abides in the second jhāna...With the fading away as well of rapture...he enters upon and abides in the third jhāna...With the abandoning of pleasure and pain...he enters upon and abides in the fourth jhāna...

25. "Moreover, with the complete surmounting of perceptions of form, with the disappearance of perceptions of sensory impact, with non-attention to perceptions of diversity, aware

that 'space is infinite,' an untrue man enters upon and abides in the base of infinite space...

26. "Moreover, by completely surmounting the base of infinite space, aware that 'consciousness is infinite,' an untrue man enters upon and abides in the base of infinite consciousness...[44]...

27. "Moreover, by completely surmounting the base of infinite consciousness, aware that 'there is nothing,' an untrue man enters upon and abides in the base of nothingness...

28. "Moreover, by completely surmounting the base of nothingness, an untrue man enters upon and abides in the base of neither-perception-nor-non-perception. He considers thus: 'I have gained the attainment of the base of neither-perception-nor-non-perception; but these other bhikkhus have not gained the attainment of the base of neither-perception-nor-non-perception.' So he lauds himself and disparages others because of his attainment of the base of neither-perception-nor-non-perception. This too is the character of an untrue man.

"But a true man considers thus: 'Non-identification even with the attainment of the base of neither-perception-nor-non-perception has been declared by the Blessed One; for in whatever way they conceive, the fact is ever other than that.' So, putting non-identification first, he neither lauds himself nor disparages others because of his attainment of the base of neither-perception-nor-non-perception. This too is the character of a true man. [45]

29. "Moreover, by completely surmounting the base of neither-perception-nor-non-perception, a true man enters upon and abides in the cessation of perception and feeling.[1067] And his taints are destroyed by his seeing with wisdom. This bhikkhu does not conceive anything, he does not conceive in regard to anything, he does not conceive in any way."[1068]

That is what the Blessed One said. The bhikkhus were satisfied and delighted in the Blessed One's words.

114 *Sevitabbāsevitabba Sutta*
To Be Cultivated and Not to Be Cultivated

1. THUS HAVE I HEARD. On one occasion the Blessed One was living at Sāvatthī in Jeta's Grove, Anāthapiṇḍika's Park. There he addressed the bhikkhus thus: "Bhikkhus."—"Venerable sir," they replied. The Blessed One said this:

2. "Bhikkhus, I shall teach you a discourse on what should be cultivated and what should not be cultivated. Listen and attend closely to what I shall say."—"Yes, venerable sir," the bhikkhus replied. The Blessed One said this:

(FIRST EXPOSITION)

3. "Bhikkhus,[1069] bodily conduct is of two kinds, I say: to be cultivated and not to be cultivated. And bodily conduct is either the one or the other.[1070] Verbal conduct is of two kinds, I say: to be cultivated and not to be cultivated. And verbal conduct is either the one or the other. Mental conduct is of two kinds, I say: to be cultivated and not to be cultivated. And mental conduct is either the one or the other. Inclination of mind is of two kinds, I say: to be cultivated and not to be cultivated. And inclination of mind is either the one or the other. [46] The acquisition of perception is of two kinds, I say: to be cultivated and not to be cultivated. And the acquisition of perception is either the one or the other. The acquisition of view is of two kinds, I say: to be cultivated and not to be cultivated. And the acquisition of view is either the one or the other. The acquisition of individuality is of two kinds, I say: to be cultivated and not to be cultivated. And the acquisition of individuality is either the one or the other."

(FIRST ELABORATION)

4. When this was said, the venerable Sāriputta said to the Blessed One: "Venerable sir, I understand the detailed meaning of the Blessed One's utterance, which he has spoken in brief without expounding the detailed meaning, to be thus:

5. "'Bhikkhus, bodily conduct is of two kinds, I say: to be cultivated and not to be cultivated. And bodily conduct is either the one or the other.' So it was said by the Blessed One. And with reference to what was this said?

"Venerable sir, such bodily conduct as causes unwholesome states to increase and wholesome states to diminish in one who cultivates it should not be cultivated. But such bodily conduct as causes unwholesome states to diminish and wholesome states to increase in one who cultivates it should be cultivated.

"And what kind of bodily conduct causes unwholesome states to increase and wholesome states to diminish in one who cultivates it? Here someone kills living beings; he is murderous, bloody-handed, given to blows and violence, merciless to living beings. He takes what is not given; he takes by way of theft the wealth and property of others in the village or in the forest. He misconducts himself in sensual pleasures; he has intercourse with such women as are protected by their mother, father, mother and father, brother, sister, or relatives, who have a husband, who are protected by law, and even with those who are garlanded in token of betrothal. Such bodily conduct [47] causes unwholesome states to increase and wholesome states to diminish in one who cultivates it.

"And what kind of bodily conduct causes unwholesome states to diminish and wholesome states to increase in one who cultivates it? Here someone, abandoning the killing of living beings, abstains from killing living beings; with rod and weapon laid aside, gently and kindly, he abides compassionate to all living beings. Abandoning the taking of what is not given, he abstains from taking what is not given; he does not take by way of theft the wealth and property of others in the village or in the forest. Abandoning misconduct in sensual pleasures, he abstains from misconduct in sensual pleasures; he does not have intercourse with such women as are protected by their mother, father, mother and father, brother, sister, or relatives, who have a husband, who are protected by law, or with those who are garlanded in token of betrothal. Such bodily conduct causes unwholesome states to diminish and wholesome states to increase in one who cultivates it.

"So it was with reference to this that it was said by the Blessed One: 'Bhikkhus, bodily conduct is of two kinds, I say: to be cultivated and not to be cultivated. And bodily conduct is either the one or the other.'

6. "'Bhikkhus, verbal conduct is of two kinds, I say: to be cultivated and not to be cultivated. And verbal conduct is either the one or the other.' So it was said by the Blessed One. And with reference to what was this said?

"Venerable sir, such verbal conduct as causes unwholesome states to increase and wholesome states to diminish in one who cultivates it should not be cultivated. But such verbal conduct as causes unwholesome states to diminish and wholesome states to increase in one who cultivates it should be cultivated.

"And what kind of verbal conduct causes unwholesome states to increase and wholesome states to diminish in one who cultivates it? Here someone speaks falsehood; when summoned to a court, or to a meeting, [48] or to his relatives' presence, or to his guild, or to the royal family's presence, and questioned as a witness thus: 'So, good man, tell what you know,' not knowing, he says, 'I know,' or knowing, he says, 'I do not know'; not seeing, he says, 'I see,' or seeing, he says, 'I do not see'; in full awareness he speaks falsehood for his own ends, or for another's ends, or for some trifling worldly end. He speaks maliciously; he repeats elsewhere what he has heard here in order to divide [those people] from these, or he repeats to these people what he has heard elsewhere in order to divide [these people] from those; thus he is one who divides those who are united, a creator of divisions, who enjoys discord, rejoices in discord, delights in discord, a speaker of words that create discord. He speaks harshly; he utters such words as are rough, hard, hurtful to others, offensive to others, bordering on anger, unconducive to concentration. He is a gossip; he speaks at the wrong time, speaks what is not fact, speaks what is useless, speaks contrary to the Dhamma and the Discipline; at the wrong time he speaks such words as are worthless, unreasonable, immoderate, and unbeneficial. Such verbal conduct causes unwholesome states to increase and wholesome states to diminish in one who cultivates it.

"And what kind of verbal conduct causes unwholesome states to diminish and wholesome states to increase in one who cultivates it? Here someone, abandoning false speech, abstains from false speech; when summoned to a court, or to a meeting, or to his relatives' presence, or to his guild, or to the royal family's presence, and questioned as a witness thus: 'So, good man, tell what you know,' not knowing, he says, 'I do not know,' or knowing, he says, 'I know'; not seeing, he says, 'I do not see,' or seeing, he says, 'I see'; [49] he does not in full awareness speak falsehood for his own ends, or for another's ends, or for some trifling worldly end. Abandoning malicious speech, he abstains from malicious speech; he does not repeat elsewhere what he has heard here in order to divide [those people] from these, nor does he repeat to these people what he has heard elsewhere in order to divide [these people] from those; thus he is one who reunites those who are divided, a promoter of friendships, who enjoys concord, rejoices in concord, delights in concord, a speaker of words that promote concord. Abandoning harsh speech, he abstains from harsh speech; he speaks such words as are gentle, pleasing to the ear, and loveable, as go to the heart, are courteous, desired by many, and agreeable to many. Abandoning gossip, he abstains from gossip; he speaks at the right time, speaks what is fact, speaks on what is good, speaks on the Dhamma and the Discipline; at the right time he speaks such words as are worth recording, reasonable, moderate, and beneficial. Such verbal conduct causes unwholesome states to diminish and wholesome states to increase in one who cultivates it.

"So it was with reference to this that it was said by the Blessed One: 'Bhikkhus, verbal conduct is of two kinds, I say: to be cultivated and not to be cultivated. And verbal conduct is either the one or the other.'

7. "'Mental conduct is of two kinds, I say: to be cultivated and not to be cultivated. And mental conduct is either the one or the other.' So it was said by the Blessed One. And with reference to what was this said?

"Venerable sir, such mental conduct as causes unwholesome states to increase and wholesome states to diminish in one who cultivates it should not be cultivated. But such mental conduct as causes unwholesome states to diminish and wholesome states to increase in one who cultivates it should be cultivated.

"And what kind of mental conduct causes unwholesome states to increase and wholesome states to diminish in one who cultivates it? Here someone is covetous; he covets the wealth and property of others thus: 'Oh, may what belongs to another be mine!' Or he has a mind of ill will and intentions of hate [50] thus: 'May these beings be slain and slaughtered, may they be cut off, perish, or be annihilated!' Such mental conduct causes unwholesome states to increase and wholesome states to diminish in one who cultivates it.

"And what kind of mental conduct causes unwholesome states to diminish and wholesome states to increase in one who cultivates it? Here someone is not covetous; he does not covet the wealth and property of others thus: 'Oh, may what belongs to another be mine!' His mind is without ill will and he has intentions free from hate thus: 'May these beings be free from enmity, affliction, and anxiety! May they live happily!' Such mental conduct causes unwholesome states to diminish and wholesome states to increase in one who cultivates it.

"So it was with reference to this that it was said by the Blessed One: 'Bhikkhus, mental conduct is of two kinds, I say: to be cultivated and not to be cultivated. And mental conduct is either the one or the other.'[1071]

8. "'Inclination of mind is of two kinds, I say: to be cultivated and not to be cultivated. And inclination of mind is either the one or the other.' So it was said by the Blessed One. And with reference to what was this said?

"Venerable sir, such inclination of mind as causes unwholesome states to increase and wholesome states to diminish in one who cultivates it should not be cultivated. But such inclination of mind as causes unwholesome states to diminish and wholesome states to increase in one who cultivates it should be cultivated.

"And what kind of inclination of mind causes unwholesome states to increase and wholesome states to diminish in one who cultivates it? Here someone is covetous and abides with his mind imbued with covetousness; he has ill will and abides with his mind imbued with ill will; he is cruel and abides with his mind imbued with cruelty.[1072] Such inclination of mind causes unwholesome states to increase and wholesome states to diminish in one who cultivates it.

"And what kind of inclination of mind causes unwholesome states to diminish and wholesome states to increase [51] in one who cultivates it? Here someone is uncovetous and abides with his mind detached from covetousness; he is without ill will and abides with his mind detached from ill will; he is uncruel and abides with his mind detached from cruelty. Such inclination of mind causes unwholesome states to diminish and wholesome states to increase in one who cultivates it.

"So it was with reference to this that it was said by the Blessed One: 'Bhikkhus, inclination of mind is of two kinds, I say: to be cultivated and not to be cultivated. And inclination of mind is either the one or the other.'

9. "'The acquisition of perception is of two kinds, I say: to be cultivated and not to be cultivated. And the acquisition of perception is either the one or the other.' So it was said by the Blessed One. And with reference to what was this said?

"Venerable sir, such acquisition of perception as causes unwholesome states to increase and wholesome states to diminish in one who cultivates it should not be cultivated. But such acquisition of perception as causes unwholesome states to diminish and wholesome states to increase in one who cultivates it should be cultivated.

"And what kind of acquisition of perception causes unwholesome states to increase and wholesome states to diminish in one who cultivates it? Here someone is covetous and abides with his perception imbued with covetousness; he has ill will and abides with his perception imbued with ill will; he is cruel and abides with his perception imbued with cruelty. Such acquisition of perception causes unwholesome states to increase and wholesome states to diminish in one who cultivates it.

"And what kind of acquisition of perception causes unwholesome states to diminish and wholesome states to increase in one who cultivates it? Here someone is uncovetous and abides with his perception detached from covetousness; he is without ill will and abides with his perception detached from ill will; he is uncruel and abides with his perception detached from cruelty. Such acquisition of perception causes unwholesome states to diminish and wholesome states to increase in one who cultivates it.

"So it was with reference to this that it was said by the Blessed One: 'Bhikkhus, the acquisition of perception is of two kinds, I say: to be cultivated and not to be cultivated. And the acquisition of perception is either the one or the other.' [52]

10. "'The acquisition of view is of two kinds, I say: to be cultivated and not to be cultivated. And the acquisition of view is either the one or the other.' So it was said by the Blessed One. And with reference to what was this said?

"Venerable sir, such acquisition of view as causes unwholesome states to increase and wholesome states to diminish in one who cultivates it should not be cultivated. But such acquisition of view as causes unwholesome states to diminish and wholesome states to increase in one who cultivates it should be cultivated.

"And what kind of acquisition of view causes unwholesome states to increase and wholesome states to diminish in one who cultivates it? Here someone holds such a view as this: 'There is nothing given, nothing offered, nothing sacrificed; no fruit or result of good and bad actions; no this world, no other world; no mother, no father; no beings who are reborn spontaneously; no good and virtuous recluses and brahmins in the world who have realised for themselves by direct knowledge and declare this world and the other world.' Such acquisition of view causes unwholesome states to increase and wholesome states to diminish in one who cultivates it.

"And what kind of acquisition of view causes unwholesome states to diminish and wholesome states to increase in one who cultivates it? Here someone holds such a view as this: 'There is what is given and what is offered and what is sacrificed; there is fruit and result of good and bad actions; there is this world and the other world; there is mother and father; there are beings who are reborn spontaneously; there are good and virtuous recluses and brahmins in the world who have realised for themselves by direct knowledge and declare this world and the other world.' Such acquisition of view causes unwholesome states to diminish and wholesome states to increase in one who cultivates it.

"So it was with reference to this that it was said by the Blessed One: 'Bhikkhus, the acquisition of view is of two kinds, I say: to be cultivated and not to be cultivated. And the acquisition of view is either the one or the other.'

11. "'The acquisition of individuality is of two kinds, I say:[1073] to be cultivated and not to be cultivated. And the acquisition of individuality is either the one or the other.' So it was said by the Blessed One. And with reference to what was this said?

"Venerable sir, [53] such acquisition of individuality as causes unwholesome states to increase and wholesome states to diminish in one who cultivates it should not be cultivated. But such acquisition of individuality as causes unwholesome states to diminish and wholesome states to increase in one who cultivates it should be cultivated.

"And what kind of acquisition of individuality causes unwholesome states to increase and wholesome states to diminish in one who cultivates it? When a person generates an acquisition of individuality that is subject to affliction, unwholesome states increase and wholesome states diminish in him, preventing him from reaching the consummation.[1074]

"And what kind of acquisition of individuality causes unwholesome states to diminish and wholesome states to increase in one who cultivates it? When a person generates an acquisition of individuality that is free from affliction, unwholesome states diminish and wholesome states increase in him, enabling him to reach the consummation.

"So it was with reference to this that it was said by the Blessed One: 'Bhikkhus, the acquisition of individuality is of two kinds, I say: to be cultivated and not to be cultivated. And the acquisition of individuality is either the one or the other.'

12. "Venerable sir, I understand the detailed meaning of the Blessed One's utterance, which he has spoken in brief without expounding the detailed meaning, to be thus."

(FIRST APPROVAL AND RECAPITULATION)

13. "Good, good, Sāriputta! It is good that you understand the detailed meaning of my utterance, which I spoke in brief without expounding the detailed meaning, to be thus.

14–20. [54, 55] (*In these paragraphs the Buddha repeats verbatim §§5–11, with the substitution of* "Sāriputta" *for* "venerable sir" *and of* "by me" *for* "by the Blessed One.")

21. "Sāriputta, the detailed meaning of my utterance, which I spoke in brief, should be regarded thus.

(SECOND EXPOSITION)

22. "Sāriputta, forms cognizable by the eye are of two kinds, I say: [56] to be cultivated and not to be cultivated.[1075] Sounds cognizable by the ear are of two kinds, I say: to be cultivated and not to be cultivated. Odours cognizable by the nose are of two kinds, I say: to be cultivated and not to be cultivated. Flavours cognizable by the tongue are of two kinds, I say: to be cultivated and not to be cultivated. Tangibles cognizable by the body are of two kinds, I say: to be cultivated and not to be cultivated. Mind-objects cognizable by the mind are of two kinds, I say: to be cultivated and not to be cultivated."

(SECOND ELABORATION)

23. When this was said, the venerable Sāriputta said to the Blessed One: "Venerable sir, I understand the detailed meaning of the Blessed One's utterance, which he has spoken in brief without expounding the detailed meaning, to be thus:

24. "'Sāriputta, forms cognizable by the eye are of two kinds, I say: [56] to be cultivated and not to be cultivated.' So it was said by the Blessed One. And with reference to what was this said?

"Venerable sir, such forms cognizable by the eye as cause unwholesome states to increase and wholesome states to diminish in one who cultivates them should not be cultivated. But such forms cognizable by the eye as cause unwholesome states to diminish and wholesome states to increase in one who cultivates them should be cultivated.

"So it was with reference to this that it was said by the Blessed One: 'Sāriputta, forms cognizable by the eye are of two kinds, I say: to be cultivated and not to be cultivated.'

25. "'Sounds cognizable by the ear are of two kinds, I say'...

26. "'Odours cognizable by the nose are of two kinds, I say'...[57]

27. "'Flavours cognizable by the tongue are of two kinds, I say'...

28. "'Tangibles cognizable by the body are of two kinds, I say'...

29. "'Mind-objects cognizable by the mind are of two kinds, I say: to be cultivated and not to be cultivated.' So it was said by the Blessed One. And with reference to what was this said?

"Venerable sir, such mind-objects cognizable by the mind as

cause unwholesome states to increase and wholesome states to diminish in one who cultivates them should not be cultivated. [58] But such mind-objects cognizable by the mind as cause unwholesome states to diminish and wholesome states to increase in one who cultivates them should be cultivated.

"So it was with reference to this that it was said by the Blessed One: 'Mind-objects cognizable by the mind are of two kinds, I say: to be cultivated and not to be cultivated.'

30. "Venerable sir, I understand the detailed meaning of the Blessed One's utterance, which he has spoken in brief without expounding the detailed meaning, to be thus."

(SECOND APPROVAL AND RECAPITULATION)

31. "Good, good, Sāriputta! It is good that you understand the detailed meaning of my utterance, which I spoke in brief without expounding the detailed meaning, to be thus.

32–37. (*In these paragraphs the Buddha repeats verbatim §§24–29, with the necessary substitutions.*)

38. "Sāriputta, the detailed meaning of my utterance, which I spoke in brief, should be regarded thus.

(THIRD EXPOSITION)

39. "Sāriputta, robes are of two kinds, I say: to be cultivated and not to be cultivated. Almsfood is of two kinds, I say: to be cultivated and not to be cultivated. Resting places are of two kinds, I say: to be cultivated and not to be cultivated. Villages are of two kinds, I say: to be cultivated and not to be cultivated. Towns are of two kinds, I say: to be cultivated and not to be cultivated. Cities are of two kinds, I say: to be cultivated and not to be cultivated. Districts are of two kinds, I say: to be cultivated and not to be cultivated. Persons are of two kinds, I say: to be cultivated and not to be cultivated." [59]

40. When this was said, the venerable Sāriputta said to the Blessed One: "Venerable sir, I understand the detailed meaning of the Blessed One's utterance, which he has spoken in brief without expounding the detailed meaning, to be thus:

41. "'Sāriputta, robes are of two kinds, I say: to be cultivated

and not to be cultivated.' So it was said by the Blessed One. And with reference to what was this said?

"Venerable sir, such robes as cause unwholesome states to increase and wholesome states to diminish in one who cultivates them should not be cultivated. But such robes as cause unwholesome states to diminish and wholesome states to increase in one who cultivates them should be cultivated.

"So it was with reference to this that it was said by the Blessed One: 'Sāriputta, robes are of two kinds, I say: to be cultivated and not to be cultivated.'

42. "'Almsfood is of two kinds, I say'...

43. "'Resting places are of two kinds, I say'...

44. "'Villages are of two kinds, I say'...

45. "'Towns are of two kinds, I say'...

46. "'Cities are of two kinds, I say'...

47. "'Districts are of two kinds, I say'...

48. "'Persons are of two kinds, I say: to be cultivated and not to be cultivated.' So it was said by the Blessed One. And with reference to what was this said?

"Venerable sir, [association with] such persons as causes unwholesome states to increase and wholesome states to diminish in one who cultivates it should not be cultivated. But [association with] such persons as causes unwholesome states to diminish and wholesome states to increase in one who cultivates it should be cultivated.

"So it was with reference to this that it was said by the Blessed One: 'Persons are of two kinds, I say: to be cultivated and not to be cultivated.'

49. "Venerable sir, I understand the detailed meaning of the Blessed One's utterance, which he has spoken in brief without expounding the detailed meaning, to be thus."

(THIRD APPROVAL AND RECAPITULATION)

50. "Good, good, Sāriputta! It is good that you understand the detailed meaning of my utterance, which I spoke in brief without expounding the detailed meaning, to be thus.

51–58. (*In these paragraphs the Buddha repeats verbatim §§41–48 with the necessary substitutions.*) [60]

59. "Sāriputta, the detailed meaning of my utterance, which I spoke in brief, should be regarded thus.

(CONCLUSION)

60. "Sāriputta, if all nobles understood thus the detailed meaning of my utterance, which I spoke in brief, it would lead to their welfare and happiness for a long time.[1076] If all brahmins...all merchants...all workers understood thus the meaning of my utterance, which I spoke in brief, it would lead to their welfare and happiness for a long time. If the world with its gods, its Māras, and its Brahmās, this generation with its recluses and brahmins, its princes and its people, understood thus the detailed meaning of my utterance, which I spoke in brief, it would lead to the welfare and happiness of the world for a long time." [61]

That is what the Blessed One said. The venerable Sāriputta was satisfied and delighted in the Blessed One's words.

115 *Bahudhātuka Sutta*
The Many Kinds of Elements

1. THUS HAVE I HEARD. On one occasion the Blessed One was living at Sāvatthī in Jeta's Grove, Anāthapiṇḍika's Park. There he addressed the bhikkhus thus: "Bhikkhus."—"Venerable sir," they replied. The Blessed One said this:

2. "Bhikkhus, whatever fears arise, all arise because of the fool, not because of the wise man; whatever troubles arise, all arise because of the fool, not because of the wise man; whatever calamities arise, all arise because of the fool, not because of the wise man. Just as a fire that starts in a shed made of rushes or grass burns down even a house with a peaked roof, with walls plastered inside and outside, shut off, secured by bars, with shuttered windows; so too, bhikkhus, whatever fears arise...all arise because of the fool, not because of the wise man. Thus the fool brings fear, the wise man brings no fear; the fool brings trouble, the wise man brings no trouble; the fool brings calamity, the wise man brings no calamity. No fear comes from the wise man, no trouble comes from the wise man, no calamity comes from the wise man. Therefore, bhikkhus, you should train thus: 'We shall be wise men, we shall be inquirers.'" [62]

3. When this was said, the venerable Ānanda asked the Blessed One: "In what way, venerable sir, can a bhikkhu be called a wise man and an inquirer?"

"When, Ānanda, a bhikkhu is skilled in the elements, skilled in the bases, skilled in dependent origination, skilled in what is possible and what is impossible, in that way he can be called a wise man and an inquirer."

(THE ELEMENTS)

4. "But, venerable sir, in what way can a bhikkhu be called skilled in the elements?"

"There are, Ānanda, these eighteen elements: the eye element, the form element, the eye-consciousness element; the ear element, the sound element, the ear-consciousness element; the nose element, the odour element, the nose-consciousness element; the tongue element, the flavour element, the tongue-consciousness element; the body element, the tangible element, the body-consciousness element; the mind element, the mind-object element, the mind-consciousness element. When he knows and sees these eighteen elements, a bhikkhu can be called skilled in the elements."[1077]

5. "But, venerable sir, might there be another way in which a bhikkhu can be called skilled in the elements?"

"There might be, Ānanda. There are, Ānanda, these six elements: the earth element, the water element, the fire element, the air element, the space element, and the consciousness element. When he knows and sees these six elements, a bhikkhu can be called skilled in the elements."

6. "But, venerable sir, might there be another way in which a bhikkhu can be called skilled in the elements?"

"There might be, Ānanda. There are, Ānanda, these six elements: the pleasure element, the pain element, the joy element, the grief element, the equanimity element, and the ignorance element. When he knows and sees these six elements, a bhikkhu can be called skilled in the elements."[1078]

7. "But, venerable sir, might there be another way in which a bhikkhu can be called skilled in the elements?"

"There might be, Ānanda. There are, Ānanda, these six elements: the sensual desire element, the renunciation element, the ill will element, the non-ill will element, [63] the cruelty element, and the non-cruelty element. When he knows and sees these six elements, a bhikkhu can be called skilled in the elements."[1079]

8. "But, venerable sir, might there be another way in which a bhikkhu can be called skilled in the elements?"

"There might be, Ānanda. There are, Ānanda, these three elements: the sense-sphere element, the fine-material element, and the immaterial element. When he knows and sees these three elements, a bhikkhu can be called skilled in the elements."[1080]

9. "But, venerable sir, might there be another way in which a bhikkhu can be called skilled in the elements?"

"There might be, Ānanda. There are, Ānanda, these two elements: the conditioned element and the unconditioned element. When he knows and sees these two elements, a bhikkhu can be called skilled in the elements."[1081]

(THE BASES)

10. "But, venerable sir, in what way can a bhikkhu be called skilled in the bases?"

"There are, Ānanda, these six internal and external bases: the eye and forms, the ear and sounds, the nose and odours, the tongue and flavours, the body and tangibles, the mind and mind-objects.[1082] When he knows and sees these six internal and external bases, a bhikkhu can be called skilled in the bases."

(DEPENDENT ORIGINATION)

11. "But, venerable sir, in what way can a bhikkhu be called skilled in dependent origination?"[1083]

"Here, Ānanda, a bhikkhu knows thus: 'When this exists, that comes to be; with the arising of this, that arises. When this does not exist, that does not come to be; with the cessation of this, that ceases. That is, with ignorance as condition, formations [come to be]; with formations as condition, consciousness; with consciousness as condition, mentality-materiality; with mentality-materiality as condition, the sixfold base; with the sixfold base as condition, contact; with contact as condition, feeling; with feeling as condition, craving; with craving as condition, clinging; with clinging as condition, [64] being; with being as condition, birth; with birth as condition, ageing and death, sorrow, lamentation, pain, grief, and despair come to be. Such is the origin of this whole mass of suffering.

"'But with the remainderless fading away and cessation of ignorance comes cessation of formations; with the cessation of formations, cessation of consciousness; with the cessation of consciousness, cessation of mentality-materiality; with the cessation of mentality-materiality, cessation of the sixfold base; with the cessation of the sixfold base, cessation of contact; with the cessation of contact, cessation of feeling; with the cessation of feeling, cessation of craving; with the cessation of craving, cessation of clinging; with the cessation of clinging, cessation of being; with the cessation of being, cessation of birth; with the cessation of birth, ageing and death, sorrow, lamentation, pain, grief, and despair cease. Such is the cessation of this whole mass of suffering.' In this way, Ānanda, a bhikkhu can be called skilled in dependent origination."

(THE POSSIBLE AND THE IMPOSSIBLE)

12. "But, venerable sir, in what way can a bhikkhu be called skilled in what is possible and what is impossible?"

"Here, Ānanda, a bhikkhu understands: 'It is impossible, it cannot happen that a person possessing right view could treat any formation as permanent—there is no such possibility.'[1084] And he understands: 'It is possible that an ordinary person might treat some formation as permanent—there is such a possibility.' He understands: 'It is impossible, it cannot happen that a person possessing right view could treat any formation as pleasurable—there is no such possibility.'[1085] And he understands: 'It is possible that an ordinary person might treat some formation as pleasurable—there is such a possibility.' He understands: 'It is impossible, it cannot happen that a person possessing right view could treat anything as self—there is no such possibility.' And he understands: 'It is possible that an ordinary person might treat something as self—there is such a possibility.'[1086]

13. "He understands: 'It is impossible, it cannot happen that a person possessing right view could deprive his mother of life—there is no such possibility.'[1087] And he understands: 'It is possible that an ordinary person might deprive his mother of life—there is such a possibility.' He understands: 'It is impossible, it cannot happen that [65] a person possessing right view could deprive his father of life...could deprive an arahant of life—there is no such possibility.' And he understands: 'It is possible that an ordinary person might deprive his father of life...might deprive an arahant of life—there is such a possibility.' He understands: 'It is impossible, it cannot happen that a person possessing right view could, with a mind of hate, shed a Tathāgata's blood—there is no such possibility.' And he understands: 'It is possible that an ordinary person might, with a mind of hate, shed a Tathāgata's blood—there is such a possibility.' He understands: 'It is impossible, it

cannot happen that a person possessing right view could cause a schism in the Sangha...could acknowledge another teacher[1088]—there is no such possibility.' And he understands: 'It is possible that an ordinary person might cause a schism in the Sangha...might acknowledge another teacher—there is such a possibility.'

14. "He understands: 'It is impossible, it cannot happen that two Accomplished Ones, Fully Enlightened Ones, could arise contemporaneously in one world-system—there is no such possibility.'[1089] And he understands: 'It is possible that one Accomplished One, a Fully Enlightened One, might arise in one world-system—there is such a possibility.' He understands: 'It is impossible, it cannot happen that two Wheel-turning Monarchs could arise contemporaneously in one world-system...It is possible that one Wheel-turning Monarch might arise in one world-system—there is such a possibility.'

15. "He understands: 'It is impossible, it cannot happen that a woman could be an Accomplished One, a Fully Enlightened One—there is no such possibility.'[1090] And he understands: 'It is possible that a man might be an Accomplished One, a Fully Enlightened One—there is such a possibility.' He understands: 'It is impossible, it cannot happen that a woman could be a Wheel-turning Monarch...that a woman could occupy the position of Sakka [66]...that a woman could occupy the position of Māra...that a woman could occupy the position of Brahmā—there is no such possibility.' And he understands: 'It is possible that a man might be a Wheel-turning Monarch...that a man might occupy the position of Sakka...that a man might occupy the position of Māra...that a man might occupy the position of Brahmā—there is such a possibility.'

16. "He understands: 'It is impossible, it cannot happen that a wished for, desired, agreeable result could be produced from bodily misconduct...from verbal misconduct...from mental misconduct—there is no such possibility.' And he understands: 'It is possible that an unwished for, undesired, disagreeable result might be produced from bodily misconduct...from verbal misconduct...from mental misconduct—there is such a possibility.'

17. "He understands: 'It is impossible, it cannot happen that an unwished for, undesired, disagreeable result could be produced from good bodily conduct...from good verbal conduct...from good mental conduct—there is no such possibility.' And he understands:

'It is possible that a wished for, desired, agreeable result might be produced from good bodily conduct...from good verbal conduct...from good mental conduct—there is such a possibility.'

18. "He understands: 'It is impossible, it cannot happen that a person engaging in bodily misconduct [67]...engaging in verbal misconduct...engaging in mental misconduct could on that account, for that reason, on the dissolution of the body, after death, reappear in a happy destination, even in the heavenly world—there is no such possibility.'[1091] And he understands: 'It is possible that a person engaging in bodily misconduct...engaging in verbal misconduct...engaging in mental misconduct might on that account, for that reason, on the dissolution of the body, after death, reappear in a state of deprivation, in an unhappy destination, in perdition, even in hell—there is such a possibility.'

19. "He understands: 'It is impossible, it cannot happen that a person engaging in good bodily conduct...engaging in good verbal conduct...engaging in good mental conduct could on that account, for that reason, on the dissolution of the body, after death, reappear in a state of deprivation, in an unhappy destination, in perdition, even in hell—there is no such possibility.' And he understands: 'It is possible that a person engaging in good bodily conduct...engaging in good verbal conduct... engaging in good mental conduct might on that account, for that reason, on the dissolution of the body, after death, reappear in a happy destination, even in the heavenly world.'

"In this way, Ānanda, a bhikkhu can be called skilled in what is possible and what is impossible."

(CONCLUSION)

20. When this was said, the venerable Ānanda said to the Blessed One: "It is wonderful, venerable sir, it is marvellous! What is the name of this discourse on the Dhamma?"

"You may remember this discourse on the Dhamma, Ānanda, as 'The Many Kinds of Elements' and as 'The Four Cycles'[1092] and as 'The Mirror of the Dhamma' and as 'The Drum of the Deathless' and as 'The Supreme Victory in Battle.'"

That is what the Blessed One said. The venerable Ānanda was satisfied and delighted in the Blessed One's words.

116 *Isigili Sutta*
Isigili: The Gullet of the Seers

[68] 1. THUS HAVE I HEARD.[1093] On one occasion the Blessed One was living at Rājagaha, at Isigili—the Gullet of the Seers. There he addressed the bhikkhus thus: "Bhikkhus."—"Venerable sir," they replied. The Blessed One said this:

2. "You see, bhikkhus, do you not, that mountain Vebhāra?"[1094]—"Yes, venerable sir."

"There used to be another name, another designation, for that mountain Vebhāra. You see, bhikkhus, do you not, that mountain Paṇḍava?"—"Yes, venerable sir."

"There used to be another name, another designation, for that mountain Paṇḍava. You see, bhikkhus, do you not, that mountain Vepulla?"—"Yes, venerable sir."

"There used to be another name, another designation, for that mountain Vepulla. You see, bhikkhus, do you not, that mountain Gijjhakuṭa—the Vulture Peak?"—"Yes, venerable sir."

"There used to be another name, another designation, for that mountain Gijjhakuṭa—the Vulture Peak. You see, bhikkhus, do you not, that mountain Isigili—the Gullet of the Seers?"—"Yes, venerable sir."

3. "There used to be this same name, this same designation, for this mountain Isigili—the Gullet of the Seers. For in former times five hundred paccekabuddhas[1095] dwelt long on this mountain, the Gullet of the Seers. They were seen entering into this hill; once gone in, they were no longer seen. People who saw this said: 'This mountain swallows up these seers.'[1096] And so it was that this came to be named 'The Gullet of the Seers.' I shall tell you, bhikkhus, the names of the paccekabuddhas, I shall relate to you the names of the paccekabuddhas, I shall teach you [69] the names of the paccekabuddhas. Listen and

attend closely to what I shall say."—"Yes, venerable sir," the bhikkhus replied. The Blessed One said this:

4. "Bhikkhus, the paccekabuddha Ariṭṭha dwelt long on this mountain Isigili. The paccekabuddha Upariṭṭha dwelt long on this mountain Isigili. The paccekabuddha Tagarasikhin[1097]... Yasassin...Sudassana...Piyadassin...Gandhāra...Piṇḍola... Upāsabha...Nītha...Tatha...Sutavā...Bhāvitatta dwelt long on this mountain Isigili.

5. "These saintly beings, desireless, rid of suffering,
Who each achieved awakening by himself—
Hear me relate the names of these, the greatest
Of men, who have plucked out the dart [of pain].

Ariṭṭha, Upariṭṭha, Tagarasikhin, Yasassin,
Sudassana, and Piyadassin the enlightened,
Gandhāra, Piṇḍola, Upāsabha as well,
Nītha, Tatha, Sutavā, Bhāvitatta. [70]

6. "Sumbha, Subha, Methula, and Aṭṭhama,[1098]
Then Assumegha, Anīgha, Sudāṭha—
And Hingū, and Hinga, the greatly powerful,
Paccekabuddhas no more led to being.

Two sages named Jāli, and Aṭṭhaka,
Then Kosala the enlightened, then Subāhu,
Upanemi, and Nemi, and Santacitta
Right and true, immaculate and wise.

Kāḷa, Upakāḷa, Vijita, and Jita;
Anga, and Panga, and Gutijjita too;
Passin conquered acquisition, the root of suffering;
Aparājita conquered Māra's power.

Satthar, Pavattar, Sarabhanga, Lomahaṁsa,
Uccangamāya, Asita, Anāsava,
Manomaya, and Bandhumant the free from pride,
Tadādhimutta stainless and resplendent;

Ketumbarāga, Mātanga, and Ariya,
Then Accuta, Accutagāma, Byāmaka,
Sumangala, Dabbila, Supatiṭṭhita,
Asayha, Khemābhirata, and Sorata,

Durannaya, Sangha, and then Ujjaya;
Another sage, Sayha, of noble endeavour.
And twelve between—Ānandas, Nandas, and Upanandas—
And Bhāradvāja bearing his last body;

Then Bodhi, Mahānāma the supreme,
Bhāradvāja with fair-crested mane;
Tissa and Upatissa not bound to being;
Upasīdarin, and Sīdarin, free from craving.

Enlightened was Mangala, free from lust;
Usabha cut the net, the root of suffering.
Upanīta attained the state of peace,
Purified, excellent, truly named.

Jeta, Jayanta, Paduma, and Uppala,
Padumuttara, Rakkhita, and Pabbata, [71]
Mānatthaddha glorious, Vītarāga
And Kaṇha enlightened with mind released.

7. "These and also other great and mighty
Paccekabuddhas no more led to being—
Honour these sages who, transcending craving,
Have attained final Nibbāna, past all measure."

117 *Mahācattārīsaka Sutta*
The Great Forty

1. THUS HAVE I HEARD. On one occasion the Blessed One was living at Sāvatthī in Jeta's Grove, Anāthapiṇḍika's Park. There he addressed the bhikkhus thus: "Bhikkhus."—"Venerable sir," they replied. The Blessed One said this:

2. "Bhikkhus, I shall teach you noble right concentration with its supports and its requisites.[1099] Listen and attend closely to what I shall say."—"Yes, venerable sir," the bhikkhus replied. The Blessed One said this:

3. "What, bhikkhus, is noble right concentration with its supports and its requisites, that is, right view, right intention, right speech, right action, right livelihood, right effort, and right mindfulness? Unification of mind equipped with these seven factors is called noble right concentration with its supports and its requisites.

(VIEW)

4. "Therein, bhikkhus, right view comes first.[1100] And how does right view come first? One understands wrong view as wrong view and right view as right view: this is one's right view.[1101]

5. "And what, bhikkhus, is wrong view? 'There is nothing given, nothing offered, nothing sacrificed; no fruit or result of good and bad actions; no this world, no other world; no mother, no father; no beings who are reborn spontaneously; no [72] good and virtuous recluses and brahmins in the world who have realised for themselves by direct knowledge and declare this world and the other world.' This is wrong view.

6. "And what, bhikkhus, is right view? Right view, I say, is twofold: there is right view that is affected by taints, partaking of merit, ripening in the acquisitions;[1102] and there is right view that is noble, taintless, supramundane, a factor of the path.

7. "And what, bhikkhus, is right view that is affected by the taints, partaking of merit, ripening in the acquisitions? 'There is what is given and what is offered and what is sacrificed; there is fruit and result of good and bad actions; there is this world and the other world; there is mother and father; there are beings who are reborn spontaneously; there are in the world good and virtuous recluses and brahmins who have realised for themselves by direct knowledge and declare this world and the other world.' This is right view affected by taints, partaking of merit, ripening in the acquisitions.

8. "And what, bhikkhus, is right view that is noble, taintless, supramundane, a factor of the path? The wisdom, the faculty of wisdom, the power of wisdom, the investigation-of-states enlightenment factor, the path factor of right view in one whose mind is noble, whose mind is taintless, who possesses the noble path and is developing the noble path:[1103] this is right view that is noble, taintless, supramundane, a factor of the path.

9. "One makes an effort to abandon wrong view and to enter upon right view: this is one's right effort. Mindfully one abandons wrong view, mindfully one enters upon and abides in right view: this is one's right mindfulness. Thus these three states run and circle around right view, that is, right view, right effort, and right mindfulness.[1104]

(INTENTION)

10. "Therein, bhikkhus, right view comes first. And how does right view come first? One understands wrong intention as wrong intention and right intention as right intention: this is one's [73] right view.[1105]

11. "And what, bhikkhus, is wrong intention? The intention of sensual desire, the intention of ill will, and the intention of cruelty: this is wrong intention.

12. "And what, bhikkhus, is right intention? Right intention, I say, is twofold: there is right intention that is affected by taints, partaking of merit, ripening in the acquisitions, and there is right intention that is noble, taintless, supramundane, a factor of the path.

13. "And what, bhikkhus, is right intention that is affected by taints, partaking of merit, ripening in the acquisitions? The

intention of renunciation, the intention of non-ill will, and the intention of non-cruelty:[1106] this is right intention that is affected by taints…ripening in the acquisitions.

14. "And what, bhikkhus, is right intention that is noble, taintless, supramundane, a factor of the path? The thinking, thought, intention, mental absorption, mental fixity, directing of mind, verbal formation in one whose mind is noble, whose mind is taintless, who possesses the noble path and is developing the noble path:[1107] this is right intention that is noble…a factor of the path.

15. "One makes an effort to abandon wrong intention and to enter upon right intention: this is one's right effort. Mindfully one abandons wrong intention, mindfully one enters upon and abides in right intention: this is one's right mindfulness. Thus these three states run and circle around right intention, that is, right view, right effort, and right mindfulness.[1108]

(SPEECH)

16. "Therein, bhikkhus, right view comes first. And how does right view come first? One understands wrong speech as wrong speech and right speech as right speech: this is one's right view.

17. "And what, bhikkhus, is wrong speech? False speech, malicious speech, harsh speech, and gossip: this is wrong speech.

18. "And what, bhikkhus, is right speech? Right speech, I say, is twofold: there is right speech that is affected by taints, partaking of merit, ripening in the acquisitions; and there is [74] right speech that is noble, taintless, supramundane, a factor of the path.

19. "And what, bhikkhus, is right speech that is affected by taints, partaking of merit, ripening in the acquisitions? Abstinence from false speech, abstinence from malicious speech, abstinence from harsh speech, abstinence from gossip: this is right speech that is affected by taints…ripening in the acquisitions.

20. "And what, bhikkhus, is right speech that is noble, taintless, supramundane, a factor of the path? The desisting from the four kinds of verbal misconduct, the abstaining, refraining, abstinence from them in one whose mind is noble, whose mind is taintless, who possesses the noble path and is developing the noble path:[1109] this is right speech that is noble…a factor of the path.

21. "One makes an effort to abandon wrong speech and to enter upon right speech: this is one's right effort. Mindfully one abandons wrong speech, mindfully one enters upon and abides in right speech: this is one's right mindfulness. Thus these three states run and circle around right speech, that is, right view, right effort, and right mindfulness.

(ACTION)

22. "Therein, bhikkhus, right view comes first. And how does right view come first? One understands wrong action as wrong action and right action as right action: this is one's right view.

23. "And what, bhikkhus, is wrong action? Killing living beings, taking what is not given, and misconduct in sensual pleasures: this is wrong action.

24. "And what, bhikkhus, is right action? Right action, I say, is twofold: there is right action that is affected by taints, partaking of merit, ripening in the acquisitions; and there is right action that is noble, taintless, supramundane, a factor of the path.

25. "And what, bhikkhus, is right action that is affected by taints, partaking of merit, ripening in the acquisitions? Abstinence from killing living beings, abstinence from taking what is not given, abstinence from misconduct in sensual pleasures: this is right action that is affected by taints...ripening in the acquisitions.

26. "And what, bhikkhus, is right action that is noble, taintless, supramundane, a factor of the path? The desisting from the three kinds of bodily misconduct, the abstaining, refraining, abstinence from them in one whose mind is noble, whose mind is taintless, who possesses the noble path and is developing the noble path: this is right action [75] that is noble...a factor of the path.

27. "One makes an effort to abandon wrong action and to enter upon right action: this is one's right effort. Mindfully one abandons wrong action, mindfully one enters upon and dwells in right action: this is one's right mindfulness. Thus these three states run and circle around right action, that is, right view, right effort, and right mindfulness.

(LIVELIHOOD)

28. "Therein, bhikkhus, right view comes first. And how does right view come first? One understands wrong livelihood as wrong livelihood and right livelihood as right livelihood: this is one's right view.

29. "And what, bhikkhus, is wrong livelihood? Scheming, talking, hinting, belittling, pursuing gain with gain: this is wrong livelihood.[1110]

30. "And what, bhikkhus, is right livelihood? Right livelihood, I say, is twofold: there is right livelihood that is affected by taints, partaking of merit, ripening in the acquisitions; and there is right livelihood that is noble, taintless, supramundane, a factor of the path.

31. "And what, bhikkhus, is right livelihood that is affected by taints, partaking of merit, ripening in the acquisitions? Here, bhikkhus, a noble disciple abandons wrong livelihood and gains his living by right livelihood: this is right livelihood that is affected by taints...ripening in the acquisitions.

32. "And what, bhikkhus, is right livelihood that is noble, taintless, supramundane, a factor of the path? The desisting from wrong livelihood, the abstaining, refraining, abstinence from it in one whose mind is noble, whose mind is taintless, who possesses the noble path and is developing the noble path: this is right livelihood that is noble...a factor of the path.

33. "One makes an effort to abandon wrong livelihood and to enter upon right livelihood: this is one's right effort. Mindfully one abandons wrong livelihood, mindfully one enters upon and dwells in right livelihood: this is one's right mindfulness. Thus these three states run and circle around right livelihood, that is, right view, right effort, and right mindfulness.

(THE GREAT FORTY)

34. "Therein, bhikkhus, right view comes first. And how does right view come first? [76] In one of right view, right intention comes into being;[1111] in one of right intention, right speech comes into being; in one of right speech, right action comes into being; in one of right action, right livelihood comes into being; in one of right livelihood, right effort comes into being; in one of

right effort, right mindfulness comes into being; in one of right mindfulness, right concentration comes into being; in one of right concentration, right knowledge comes into being; in one of right knowledge, right deliverance comes into being. Thus, bhikkhus, the path of the disciple in higher training possesses eight factors, the arahant possesses ten factors.[1112]

35. "Therein, bhikkhus, right view comes first. And how does right view come first? In one of right view, wrong view is abolished, and the many evil unwholesome states that originate with wrong view as condition are also abolished, and the many wholesome states that originate with right view as condition come to fulfilment by development.

"In one of right intention, wrong intention is abolished, and the many evil unwholesome states that originate with wrong intention as condition are also abolished, and the many wholesome states that originate with right intention as condition come to fulfilment by development.

"In one of right speech, wrong speech is abolished...In one of right action, wrong action is abolished...In one of right livelihood, wrong livelihood is abolished [77]...In one of right effort, wrong effort is abolished...In one of right mindfulness, wrong mindfulness is abolished...In one of right concentration, wrong concentration is abolished...In one of right knowledge, wrong knowledge is abolished...In one of right deliverance, wrong deliverance is abolished, and the many evil unwholesome states that originate with wrong deliverance as condition are also abolished, and the many wholesome states that originate with right deliverance as condition come to fulfilment by development.

36. "Thus, bhikkhus, there are twenty factors on the side of the wholesome, and twenty factors on the side of the unwholesome.[1113] This Dhamma discourse on the Great Forty has been set rolling and cannot be stopped by any recluse or brahmin or god or Māra or Brahmā or anyone in the world.

37. "Bhikkhus, if any recluse or brahmin thinks that this Dhamma discourse on the Great Forty should be censured and rejected, then there are ten legitimate deductions from his assertions that would provide grounds for censuring him here and now. If that worthy one censures right view, then he would honour and praise those recluses and brahmins who are of wrong view. If that worthy one censures right intention, [78] then he

would honour and praise those recluses and brahmins who are of wrong intention. If that worthy one censures right speech... right action...right livelihood...right effort...right mindfulness...right concentration...right knowledge...right deliverance, then he would honour and praise those recluses and brahmins who are of wrong deliverance. If any recluse or brahmin thinks that this Dhamma discourse on the Great Forty should be censured and rejected, then these are ten legitimate deductions from his assertions that would provide grounds for censuring him here and now.

38. "Bhikkhus, even those teachers from Okkala, Vassa and Bhañña,[1114] who held the doctrine of non-causality, the doctrine of non-doing, and the doctrine of nihilism, would not think that this Dhamma discourse on the Great Forty should be censured and rejected. Why is that? For fear of blame, attack, and confutation."

That is what the Blessed One said. The bhikkhus were satisfied and delighted in the Blessed One's words.

118 *Ānāpānasati Sutta*
Mindfulness of Breathing

(INTRODUCTORY SECTION)

1. THUS HAVE I HEARD. On one occasion the Blessed One was living at Sāvatthī in the Eastern Park, in the Palace of Migāra's Mother, together with many very well known elder disciples—the venerable Sāriputta, the venerable Mahā Moggallāna, the venerable Mahā Kassapa, the venerable Mahā Kaccāna, the venerable Mahā Koṭṭhita, the venerable Mahā Kappina, the venerable Mahā Cunda, [79] the venerable Anuruddha, the venerable Revata, the venerable Ānanda, and other very well known elder disciples.

2. Now on that occasion elder bhikkhus had been teaching and instructing new bhikkhus; some elder bhikkhus had been teaching and instructing ten bhikkhus, some elder bhikkhus had been teaching and instructing twenty...thirty...forty bhikkhus. And the new bhikkhus, taught and instructed by the elder bhikkhus, had achieved successive stages of high distinction.

3. On that occasion—the Uposatha day of the fifteenth, on the full-moon night of the Pavāraṇā ceremony[1115]—the Blessed One was seated in the open surrounded by the Sangha of bhikkhus. Then, surveying the silent Sangha of bhikkhus, he addressed them thus:

4. "Bhikkhus, I am content with this progress. My mind is content with this progress. So arouse still more energy to attain the unattained, to achieve the unachieved, to realise the unrealised. I shall wait here at Sāvatthī for the Komudī full moon of the fourth month."[1116]

5. The bhikkhus of the countryside heard: "The Blessed One will wait there at Sāvatthī for the Komudī full moon of the fourth month." And the bhikkhus of the countryside left in due course for Sāvatthī to see the Blessed One.

6. And elder bhikkhus still more intensively taught and instructed new bhikkhus; some elder bhikkhus taught and instructed ten bhikkhus, some elder bhikkhus taught and instructed twenty...thirty...forty bhikkhus. And the new bhikkhus, taught and instructed by the elder bhikkhus, [80] achieved successive stages of high distinction.

7. On that occasion—the Uposatha day of the fifteenth, the full-moon night of the Komudī full moon of the fourth month—the Blessed One was seated in the open surrounded by the Sangha of bhikkhus. Then, surveying the silent Sangha of bhikkhus, he addressed them thus:

8. "Bhikkhus, this assembly is free from prattle, this assembly is free from chatter. It consists purely of heartwood. Such is this Sangha of bhikkhus, such is this assembly. Such an assembly as is worthy of gifts, worthy of hospitality, worthy of offerings, worthy of reverential salutation, an incomparable field of merit for the world—such is this Sangha of bhikkhus, such is this assembly. Such an assembly that a small gift given to it becomes great and a great gift greater—such is this Sangha of bhikkhus, such is this assembly. Such an assembly as is rare for the world to see—such is this Sangha of bhikkhus, such is this assembly. Such an assembly as would be worth journeying many leagues with a travel-bag to see—such is this Sangha of bhikkhus, such is this assembly.

9. "In this Sangha of bhikkhus there are bhikkhus who are arahants with taints destroyed, who have lived the holy life, done what had to be done, laid down the burden, reached their own goal, destroyed the fetters of being, and are completely liberated through final knowledge—such bhikkhus are there in this Sangha of bhikkhus.

10. "In this Sangha of bhikkhus there are bhikkhus who, with the destruction of the five lower fetters, are due to reappear spontaneously [in the Pure Abodes] and there attain final Nibbāna, without ever returning from that world—such bhikkhus are there in this Sangha of bhikkhus.

11. "In this Sangha of bhikkhus there are bhikkhus who, with the destruction of three fetters and with the attenuation of lust, hate, and delusion, are once-returners, returning once to this world [81] to make an end of suffering—such bhikkhus are there in this Sangha of bhikkhus.

12. "In this Sangha of bhikkhus there are bhikkhus who, with the destruction of the three fetters, are stream-enterers, no longer subject to perdition, bound [for deliverance], headed for enlightenment—such bhikkhus are there in this Sangha of bhikkhus.

13. "In this Sangha of bhikkhus there are bhikkhus who abide devoted to the development of the four foundations of mindfulness—such bhikkhus are there in this Sangha of bhikkhus. In this Sangha of bhikkhus there are bhikkhus who abide devoted to the development of the four right kinds of striving...of the four bases for spiritual power...of the five faculties...of the five powers...of the seven enlightenment factors...of the Noble Eightfold Path—such bhikkhus are there in this Sangha of bhikkhus.

14. "In this Sangha of bhikkhus there are bhikkhus who abide devoted to the development of loving-kindness [82]...of compassion...of altruistic joy...of equanimity...of the meditation on foulness...of the perception of impermanence—such bhikkhus are there in this Sangha of bhikkhus. In this Sangha of bhikkhus there are bhikkhus who abide devoted to the development of mindfulness of breathing.

(MINDFULNESS OF BREATHING)

15. "Bhikkhus, when mindfulness of breathing is developed and cultivated, it is of great fruit and great benefit. When mindfulness of breathing is developed and cultivated, it fulfils the four foundations of mindfulness. When the four foundations of mindfulness are developed and cultivated, they fulfil the seven enlightenment factors. When the seven enlightenment factors are developed and cultivated, they fulfil true knowledge and deliverance.

16. "And how, bhikkhus, is mindfulness of breathing developed and cultivated, so that it is of great fruit and great benefit?

17. "Here a bhikkhu, gone to the forest or to the root of a tree or to an empty hut, sits down; having folded his legs crosswise, set his body erect, and established mindfulness in front of him, ever mindful he breathes in, mindful he breathes out.

18. "Breathing in long, he understands:[1117] 'I breathe in long'; or breathing out long, he understands: 'I breathe out long.' Breathing in short, he understands: 'I breathe in short'; or breathing out short, he understands: 'I breathe out short.' He

trains thus: 'I shall breathe in experiencing the whole body [of breath]'; he trains thus: 'I shall breathe out experiencing the whole body [of breath].' He trains thus: 'I shall breathe in tranquillising the bodily formation'; he trains thus: 'I shall breathe out tranquillising the bodily formation.'

19. "He trains thus: 'I shall breathe in experiencing rapture'; he trains thus: 'I shall breathe out experiencing rapture.'[1118] He trains thus: 'I shall breathe in experiencing pleasure'; [83] he trains thus: 'I shall breathe out experiencing pleasure.' He trains thus: 'I shall breathe in experiencing the mental formation'; he trains thus: 'I shall breathe out experiencing the mental formation.' He train thus: 'I shall breathe in tranquillising the mental formation'; he trains thus: 'I shall breathe out tranquillising the mental formation.'[1119]

20. "He trains thus: 'I shall breathe in experiencing the mind'; he trains thus: 'I shall breathe out experiencing the mind.' He trains thus: 'I shall breathe in gladdening the mind'; he trains thus: 'I shall breathe out gladdening the mind.' He trains thus: 'I shall breathe in concentrating the mind'; he trains thus: 'I shall breathe out concentrating the mind.' He trains thus: 'I shall breathe in liberating the mind'; he trains thus: 'I shall breathe out liberating the mind.'[1120]

21. "He trains thus: 'I shall breathe in contemplating impermanence'; he trains thus: 'I shall breathe out contemplating impermanence.' He trains thus: 'I shall breathe in contemplating fading away'; he trains thus: 'I shall breathe out contemplating fading away.' He trains thus: 'I shall breathe in contemplating cessation'; he trains thus: 'I shall breathe out contemplating cessation.' He trains thus: 'I shall breathe in contemplating relinquishment'; he trains thus: 'I shall breathe out contemplating relinquishment.'[1121]

22. "Bhikkhus, that is how mindfulness of breathing is developed and cultivated, so that it is of great fruit and great benefit.

(FULFILMENT OF THE FOUR FOUNDATIONS OF MINDFULNESS)

23. "And how, bhikkhus, does mindfulness of breathing, developed and cultivated, fulfil the four foundations of mindfulness?

24. "Bhikkhus, on whatever occasion a bhikkhu, breathing in long, understands: 'I breathe in long,' or breathing out long,

understands: 'I breathe out long'; breathing in short, understands: 'I breathe in short,' or breathing out short, understands: 'I breathe out short'; trains thus: 'I shall breathe in experiencing the whole body [of breath]'; trains thus: 'I shall breathe out experiencing the whole body [of breath]'; trains thus: 'I shall breathe in tranquillising the bodily formation'; trains thus: 'I shall breathe out tranquillising the bodily formation'—on that occasion a bhikkhu abides contemplating the body as a body, ardent, fully aware, and mindful, having put away covetousness and grief for the world. I say that this is a certain body among the bodies, namely, in-breathing and out-breathing.[1122] That is why on that occasion a bhikkhu abides contemplating the body as a body, ardent, fully aware, and mindful, having put away covetousness and grief for the world.

25. "Bhikkhus, on whatever occasion [84] a bhikkhu trains thus: 'I shall breathe in experiencing rapture'; trains thus: 'I shall breathe out experiencing rapture'; trains thus: 'I shall breathe in experiencing pleasure'; trains thus: 'I shall breathe out experiencing pleasure'; trains thus: 'I shall breathe in experiencing the mental formation'; trains thus: 'I shall breathe out experiencing the mental formation'; trains thus: 'I shall breathe in tranquillising the mental formation'; trains thus: 'I shall breathe out tranquillising the mental formation'—on that occasion a bhikkhu abides contemplating feelings as feelings, ardent, fully aware, and mindful, having put away covetousness and grief for the world. I say that this is a certain feeling among the feelings, namely, giving close attention to in-breathing and out-breathing.[1123] That is why on that occasion a bhikkhu abides contemplating feelings as feelings, ardent, fully aware, and mindful, having put away covetousness and grief for the world.

26. "Bhikkhus, on whatever occasion a bhikkhu trains thus: 'I shall breathe in experiencing the mind'; trains thus: 'I shall breathe out experiencing the mind'; trains thus: 'I shall breathe in gladdening the mind'; trains thus: 'I shall breathe out gladdening the mind'; train thus: 'I shall breathe in concentrating the mind'; trains thus: 'I shall breathe out concentrating the mind'; trains thus: 'I shall breathe in liberating the mind'; trains thus: 'I shall breathe out liberating the mind'—on that occasion a bhikkhu abides contemplating mind as mind, ardent, fully aware, and mindful, having put away covetousness and grief for

the world. I do not say that there is the development of mindfulness of breathing for one who is forgetful, who is not fully aware. That is why on that occasion a bhikkhu abides contemplating mind as mind, ardent, fully aware, and mindful, having put away covetousness and grief for the world.[1124]

27. "Bhikkhus, on whatever occasion a bhikkhu trains thus: 'I shall breathe in contemplating impermanence'; trains thus: 'I shall breathe out contemplating impermanence'; trains thus: 'I shall breathe in contemplating fading away'; trains thus: 'I shall breathe out contemplating fading away'; trains thus: 'I shall breathe in contemplating cessation'; trains thus: 'I shall breathe out contemplating cessation'; trains thus: 'I shall breathe in contemplating relinquishment'; trains thus: 'I shall breathe out contemplating relinquishment'—on that occasion a bhikkhu abides contemplating mind-objects as mind-objects, ardent, fully aware, and mindful, having put away covetousness and grief for the world. Having seen with wisdom the abandoning of covetousness and grief, [85] he closely looks on with equanimity.[1125] That is why on that occasion a bhikkhu abides contemplating mind-objects as mind-objects, ardent, fully aware, and mindful, having put away covetousness and grief for the world.

28. "Bhikkhus, that is how mindfulness of breathing, developed and cultivated, fulfils the four foundations of mindfulness.

(FULFILMENT OF THE SEVEN ENLIGHTENMENT FACTORS)

29. "And how, bhikkhus, do the four foundations of mindfulness, developed and cultivated, fulfil the seven enlightenment factors?

30. "Bhikkhus, on whatever occasion a bhikkhu abides contemplating the body as a body, ardent, fully aware, and mindful, having put away covetousness and grief for the world—on that occasion unremitting mindfulness is established in him. On whatever occasion unremitting mindfulness is established in a bhikkhu—on that occasion the mindfulness enlightenment factor is aroused in him, and he develops it, and by development, it comes to fulfilment in him.

31. "Abiding thus mindful, he investigates and examines that state with wisdom and embarks upon a full inquiry into it. On whatever occasion, abiding thus mindful, a bhikkhu investigates and examines that state with wisdom and embarks upon a full

inquiry into it—on that occasion the investigation-of-states enlightenment factor is aroused in him, and he develops it, and by development it comes to fulfilment in him.

32. "In one who investigates and examines that state with wisdom and embarks upon a full inquiry into it, tireless energy is aroused. On whatever occasion tireless energy is aroused in a bhikkhu who investigates and examines that state with wisdom and embarks upon a full inquiry into it—on that occasion the energy enlightenment factor is aroused in him, and he develops it, and by development it comes to fulfilment in him.

33. "In one who has aroused energy, unworldly rapture arises. On whatever occasion unworldly rapture arises in a bhikkhu who has aroused energy—[86] on that occasion the rapture enlightenment factor is aroused in him, and he develops it, and by development it comes to fulfilment in him.

34. "In one who is rapturous, the body and the mind become tranquil. On whatever occasion the body and the mind become tranquil in a bhikkhu who is rapturous—on that occasion the tranquillity enlightenment factor is aroused in him, and he develops it, and by development it comes to fulfilment in him.

35. "In one whose body is tranquil and who feels pleasure, the mind becomes concentrated. On whatever occasion the mind becomes concentrated in a bhikkhu whose body is tranquil and who feels pleasure—on that occasion the concentration enlightenment factor is aroused in him, and he develops it, and by development it comes to fulfilment in him.

36. "He closely looks on with equanimity at the mind thus concentrated. On whatever occasion a bhikkhu closely looks on with equanimity at the mind thus concentrated—on that occasion the equanimity enlightenment factor is aroused in him, and he develops it, and by development it comes to fulfilment in him.

37. "Bhikkhus, on whatever occasion a bhikkhu abides contemplating feelings as feelings, ardent, fully aware, and mindful, having put away covetousness and grief for the world...(*repeat as at §§30–36*)...the equanimity enlightenment factor is aroused in him, and he develops it, and by development it comes to fulfilment in him.

38. "Bhikkhus, on whatever occasion a bhikkhu abides contemplating mind as mind, ardent, fully aware, and mindful,

having put away covetousness and grief for the world...(*repeat as at §§30–36*)...the equanimity enlightenment factor is aroused in him, and he develops it, and by development it comes to fulfilment in him.

39. "Bhikkhus, on whatever occasion a bhikkhu abides contemplating mind-object as mind-objects, ardent, fully aware, and mindful, having put away covetousness and grief for the world...(*repeat as at §§30–36*)...[87]...the equanimity enlightenment factor is aroused in him, and he develops it, and by development it comes to fulfilment in him.

40. "Bhikkhus, that is how the four foundations of mindfulness, developed and cultivated, fulfil the seven enlightenment factors.[1126] [88]

(FULFILMENT OF TRUE KNOWLEDGE AND DELIVERANCE)

41. "And how, bhikkhus, do the seven enlightenment factors, developed and cultivated, fulfil true knowledge and deliverance?

42. "Here, bhikkhus, a bhikkhu develops the mindfulness enlightenment factor, which is supported by seclusion, dispassion, and cessation, and ripens in relinquishment.[1127] He develops the investigation-of-states enlightenment factor...the energy enlightenment factor...the rapture enlightenment factor...the tranquillity enlightenment factor...the concentration enlightenment factor...the equanimity enlightenment factor, which is supported by seclusion, dispassion, and cessation, and ripens in relinquishment.

43. "Bhikkhus, that is how the seven enlightenment factors, developed and cultivated, fulfil true knowledge and deliverance."[1128]

That is what the Blessed One said. The bhikkhus were satisfied and delighted in the Blessed One's words.

119 *Kāyagatāsati Sutta*
Mindfulness of the Body

1. THUS HAVE I HEARD. On one occasion the Blessed One was living at Sāvatthī in Jeta's Grove, Anāthapiṇḍika's Park.

2. Now a number of bhikkhus were sitting in the assembly hall, where they had met together on returning from their almsround, after their meal, when this discussion arose among them: "It is wonderful, friends, it is marvellous, how it has been said by the Blessed One who knows and sees, accomplished and fully enlightened, that mindfulness of the body, when developed and cultivated, is of great fruit and great benefit."

However, their discussion was interrupted; for the Blessed One rose from meditation when it was evening, went to the assembly hall, and sat down on a seat made ready. Then he addressed the bhikkhus thus: "Bhikkhus, for what discussion are you sitting together here now? And what was your discussion that was interrupted?" [89]

"Here, venerable sir, we were sitting in the assembly hall, where we had met together on returning from our almsround, after our meal, when this discussion arose among us: 'It is wonderful, friends, it is marvellous, how it has been said by the Blessed One who knows and sees, accomplished and fully enlightened, that mindfulness of the body, when developed and cultivated, is of great fruit and great benefit.' This was our discussion, venerable sir, that was interrupted when the Blessed One arrived."

3. "And how, bhikkhus, is mindfulness of the body developed and cultivated so that it is of great fruit and great benefit?

(MINDFULNESS OF BREATHING)

4. "Here a bhikkhu,[1129] gone to the forest or to the root of a tree or to an empty hut, sits down; having folded his legs crosswise,

set his body erect, and established mindfulness in front of him, ever mindful he breathes in, mindful he breathes out. Breathing in long, he understands: 'I breathe in long'; or breathing out long, he understands: 'I breathe out long.' Breathing in short, he understands: 'I breathe in short'; or breathing out short, he understands: 'I breathe out short.' He trains thus: 'I shall breathe in experiencing the whole body'; he trains thus: 'I shall breathe out experiencing the whole body.' He trains thus: 'I shall breathe in tranquillising the bodily formation'; he trains thus: 'I shall breathe out tranquillising the bodily formation.' As he abides thus diligent, ardent, and resolute, his memories and intentions based on the household life are abandoned; with their abandoning his mind becomes steadied internally, quieted, brought to singleness, and concentrated. That is how a bhikkhu develops mindfulness of the body.

(THE FOUR POSTURES)

5. "Again, bhikkhus, when walking, a bhikkhu understands: 'I am walking'; when standing, he understands: 'I am standing'; when sitting, he understands: 'I am sitting'; when lying down, he understands: 'I am lying down'; or he understands accordingly however his body is disposed. As he abides thus diligent, ardent, and resolute, his memories and intentions based on the household life are abandoned...That too is how a bhikkhu develops mindfulness of the body. [90]

(FULL AWARENESS)

6. "Again, bhikkhus, a bhikkhu is one who acts in full awareness when going forward and returning; who acts in full awareness when looking ahead and looking away; who acts in full awareness when flexing and extending his limbs; who acts in full awareness when wearing his robes and carrying his outer robe and bowl; who acts in full awareness when eating, drinking, consuming food, and tasting; who acts in full awareness when defecating or urinating; who acts in full awareness when walking, standing, sitting, falling asleep, waking up, talking, and keeping silent. As he abides thus diligent, ardent, and resolute, his memories and intentions based on the household life are

abandoned...That too is how a bhikkhu develops mindfulness of the body.

(FOULNESS—THE BODILY PARTS)

7. "Again, bhikkhus, a bhikkhu reviews this same body up from the soles of the feet and down from the top of the hair, bounded by skin, as full of many kinds of impurity thus: 'In this body there are head-hairs, body-hairs, nails, teeth, skin, flesh, sinews, bones, bone-marrow, kidneys, heart, liver, diaphragm, spleen, lungs, intestines, mesentery, contents of the stomach, feces, bile, phlegm, pus, blood, sweat, fat, tears, grease, spittle, snot, oil of the joints, and urine.' Just as though there were a bag with an opening at both ends full of many sorts of grain, such as hill rice, red rice, beans, peas, millet, and white rice, and a man with good eyes were to open it and review it thus: 'This is hill rice, this is red rice, these are beans, these are peas, this is millet, this is white rice'; so too, a bhikkhu reviews this same body as full of many kinds of impurity thus: 'In this body there are head-hairs...and urine.' As he abides thus diligent, ardent, and resolute, his memories and intentions based on the household life are abandoned...That too is how a bhikkhu develops mindfulness of the body. [91]

(ELEMENTS)

8. "Again, bhikkhus, a bhikkhu reviews this same body, however it is placed, however disposed, as consisting of elements thus: 'In this body there are the earth element, the water element, the fire element, and the air element.' Just as though a skilled butcher or his apprentice had killed a cow and were seated at the crossroads with it cut up into pieces; so too, a bhikkhu reviews this same body however it is placed, however disposed, as consisting of elements thus: 'In this body there are the earth element, the water element, the fire element, and the air element.' As he abides thus diligent, ardent, and resolute, his memories and intentions connected with the household life are abandoned...That too is how a bhikkhu develops mindfulness of the body.

(THE NINE CHARNEL GROUND CONTEMPLATIONS)

9. "Again, bhikkhus, as though he were to see a corpse thrown aside in a charnel ground, one, two, or three days dead, bloated, livid, and oozing matter, a bhikkhu compares this same body with it thus: 'This body too is of the same nature, it will be like that, it is not exempt from that fate.' As he abides thus diligent... That too is how a bhikkhu develops mindfulness of the body.

10. "Again, as though he were to see a corpse thrown aside in a charnel ground, being devoured by crows, hawks, vultures, dogs, jackals, or various kinds of worms, a bhikkhu compares this same body with it thus: 'This body too is of the same nature, it will be like that, it is not exempt from that fate.' As he abides thus diligent...That too is how a bhikkhu develops mindfulness of the body. [92]

11–14. "Again, as though he were to see a corpse thrown aside in a charnel ground, a skeleton with flesh and blood, held together with sinews...a fleshless skeleton smeared with blood, held together with sinews...a skeleton without flesh and blood, held together with sinews...disconnected bones scattered in all directions—here a hand-bone, there a foot-bone, here a shin-bone, there a thigh-bone, here a hip-bone, there a back-bone, here a rib-bone, there a breast-bone, here an arm-bone, there a shoulder-bone, here a neck-bone, there a jaw-bone, here a tooth, there the skull—a bhikkhu compares this same body with it thus: 'This body too is of the same nature, it will be like that, it is not exempt from that fate.' As he abides thus diligent...That too is how a bhikkhu develops mindfulness of the body.

15–17. "Again, as though he were to see a corpse thrown aside in a charnel ground, bones bleached white, the colour of shells...bones heaped up, more than a year old...bones rotted and crumbled to dust, a bhikkhu compares this same body with it thus: 'This body too is of the same nature, it will be like that, it is not exempt from that fate.' As he abides thus diligent...That too is how a bhikkhu develops mindfulness of the body.

(THE JHĀNAS)

18. "Again, bhikkhus, quite secluded from sensual pleasures, secluded from unwholesome states, a bhikkhu enters upon and

abides in the first jhāna, which is accompanied by applied and sustained thought, with rapture and pleasure born of seclusion. He makes the rapture and pleasure born of seclusion drench, steep, fill, and pervade this body, so that there is no part of his whole body unpervaded by the rapture and pleasure born of seclusion. Just as a skilled bath man or a bath man's apprentice[1130] heaps bath powder in a metal basin and, sprinkling it gradually with water, kneads it till the moisture wets his ball of bath powder, soaks it and pervades it inside and out, yet the ball itself does not ooze; so too, a bhikkhu makes the rapture and pleasure born of seclusion [93] drench, steep, fill, and pervade this body, so that there is no part of his whole body unpervaded by the rapture and pleasure born of seclusion. As he abides thus diligent...That too is how a bhikkhu develops mindfulness of the body.

19. "Again, bhikkhus, with the stilling of applied and sustained thought, a bhikkhu enters upon and abides in the second jhāna, which has self-confidence and singleness of mind without applied and sustained thought, with rapture and pleasure born of concentration. He makes the rapture and pleasure born of concentration drench, steep, fill, and pervade this body, so that there is no part of his whole body unpervaded by the rapture and pleasure born of concentration. Just as though there were a lake whose waters welled up from below and it had no inflow from east, west, north, or south, and would not be replenished from time to time by showers of rain, then the cool fount of water welling up in the lake would make the cool water drench, steep, fill, and pervade the lake, so that there would be no part of the whole lake unpervaded by cool water; so too, a bhikkhu makes the rapture and pleasure born of concentration drench, steep, fill, and pervade this body, so that there is no part of his whole body unpervaded by the rapture and pleasure born of concentration. As he abides thus diligent...That too is how a bhikkhu develops mindfulness of the body.

20. "Again, bhikkhus, with the fading away as well of rapture, a bhikkhu abides in equanimity, and mindful and fully aware, still feeling pleasure with the body, he enters upon and abides in the third jhāna, on account of which noble ones announce: 'He has a pleasant abiding who has equanimity and is mindful.' He

makes the pleasure divested of rapture drench, steep, fill, and pervade this body, so that there is no part of his whole body unpervaded by the pleasure divested of rapture. Just as in a pond of blue or white or red lotuses, some lotuses that are born and grow in the water thrive immersed in the water without rising out of it, [94] and cool water drenches, steeps, fills, and pervades them to their tips and their roots, so that there is no part of all those lotuses unpervaded by cool water; so too, a bhikkhu makes the pleasure divested of rapture drench, steep, fill, and pervade this body, so that there is no part of his whole body unpervaded by the pleasure divested of rapture. As he abides thus diligent...That too is how a bhikkhu develops mindfulness of the body.

21. "Again, bhikkhus, with the abandoning of pleasure and pain, and with the previous disappearance of joy and grief, a bhikkhu enters upon and abides in the fourth jhāna, which has neither-pain-nor-pleasure and purity of mindfulness due to equanimity. He sits pervading this body with a pure bright mind, so that there is no part of his whole body unpervaded by the pure bright mind. Just as though a man were sitting covered from head down with a white cloth, so that there would be no part of his whole body not covered by the white cloth; so too, a bhikkhu sits pervading this body with a pure bright mind, so that there is no part of his body unpervaded by the pure bright mind. As he abides thus diligent, ardent, and resolute, his memories and intentions based on the household life are abandoned; with their abandoning his mind becomes steadied internally, quieted, brought to singleness, and concentrated. That too is how a bhikkhu develops mindfulness of the body.

(PROGRESS THROUGH MINDFULNESS OF THE BODY)

22. "Bhikkhus, anyone who has developed and cultivated mindfulness of the body has included within himself whatever wholesome states there are that partake of true knowledge.[1131] Just as anyone who has extended his mind over the great ocean has included within it whatever streams there are that flow into the ocean; so too, anyone who has developed and cultivated mindfulness of the body has included within himself whatever wholesome states there are that partake of true knowledge.

23. "Bhikkhus, when anyone has not developed and cultivated mindfulness of the body, Māra finds an opportunity and a support in him. Suppose a man were to throw a heavy stone ball upon a mound of wet clay. What do you think, bhikkhus? Would that heavy ball find entry into that mound of wet clay?"—"Yes, venerable sir."—[95] "So too, bhikkhus, when anyone has not developed and cultivated mindfulness of the body, Māra finds an opportunity and a support in him.

24. "Suppose there were a dry sapless piece of wood, and a man came with an upper fire-stick, thinking: 'I shall light a fire, I shall produce heat.' What do you think, bhikkhus? Could the man light a fire and produce heat by rubbing the dry sapless piece of wood with an upper fire-stick?"—"Yes, venerable sir."—"So too, bhikkhus, when anyone has not developed and cultivated mindfulness of the body, Māra finds an opportunity and a support in him.

25. "Suppose there were a hollow empty water jug set out on a stand, and a man came with a supply of water. What do you think, bhikkhus? Could the man pour the water into the jug?"—"Yes, venerable sir."—"So too, bhikkhus, when anyone has not developed and cultivated mindfulness of the body, Māra finds an opportunity and a support in him.

26. "Bhikkhus, when anyone has developed and cultivated mindfulness of the body, Māra cannot find an opportunity or a support in him. Suppose a man were to throw a light ball of string at a door-panel made entirely of heartwood. What do you think, bhikkhus? Would that light ball of string find entry through that door-panel made entirely of heartwood?"—"No, venerable sir."—"So too, bhikkhus, when anyone has developed and cultivated mindfulness of the body, Māra cannot find an opportunity or a support in him.

27. "Suppose there were a wet sappy piece of wood, and a man came with an upper fire-stick, thinking: 'I shall light a fire, I shall produce heat.' [96] What do you think, bhikkhus? Could the man light a fire and produce heat by taking the upper fire-stick and rubbing it against the wet sappy piece of wood?"—"No, venerable sir."—"So too, bhikkhus, when anyone has developed and cultivated mindfulness of the body, Māra cannot find an opportunity or a support in him.

28. "Suppose, set out on a stand, there were a water jug full of

water right up to the brim so that crows could drink from it, and a man came with a supply of water. What do you think, bhikkhus? Could the man pour the water into the jug?"—"No, venerable sir."—"So too, bhikkhus, when anyone has developed and cultivated mindfulness of the body, Māra cannot find an opportunity or a support in him.

29. "Bhikkhus, when anyone has developed and cultivated mindfulness of the body, then when he inclines his mind towards realising any state that may be realised by direct knowledge, he attains the ability to witness any aspect therein, there being a suitable basis. Suppose, set out on a stand, there were a water jug full of water right up to the brim so that crows could drink from it. Whenever a strong man tips it, would water come out?"—"Yes, venerable sir."—"So too, bhikkhus, when anyone has developed and cultivated mindfulness of the body, then when he inclines his mind towards realising any state that may be realised by direct knowledge, he attains the ability to witness any aspect therein, there being a suitable basis.

30. "Suppose there were a square pond on level ground, surrounded by an embankment, full of water right up to the brim so that crows could drink from it. Whenever a strong man loosens the embankment, would water come out?"—[97] "Yes, venerable sir."—"So too, bhikkhus, when anyone has developed and cultivated mindfulness of the body...he attains the ability to witness any aspect therein, there being a suitable basis.

31. "Suppose there were a chariot on even ground at the crossroads, harnessed to thoroughbreds, waiting with goad lying ready, so that a skilled trainer, a charioteer of horses to be tamed, might mount it, and taking the reins in his left hand and the goad in his right hand, might drive out and back by any road whenever he likes. So too, bhikkhus, when anyone has developed and cultivated mindfulness of the body...he attains the ability to witness any aspect therein, there being a suitable basis.

(BENEFITS OF MINDFULNESS OF THE BODY)

32. "Bhikkhus, when mindfulness of the body has been repeatedly practised, developed, cultivated, used as a vehicle, used as a basis, established, consolidated, and well undertaken, these ten benefits may be expected. What ten?

33. (i) "One becomes a conqueror of discontent and delight, and discontent does not conquer oneself; one abides overcoming discontent whenever it arises.

34. (ii) "One becomes a conqueror of fear and dread, and fear and dread do not conquer oneself; one abides overcoming fear and dread whenever they arise.

35. (iii) "One bears cold and heat, hunger and thirst, and contact with gadflies, mosquitoes, wind, the sun, and creeping things; one endures ill-spoken, unwelcome words and arisen bodily feelings that are painful, racking, sharp, piercing, disagreeable, distressing, and menacing to life.

36. (iv) "One obtains at will, without trouble or difficulty, the four jhānas that constitute the higher mind and [98] provide a pleasant abiding here and now.

37. (v) "One wields the various kinds of supernormal power... (*as Sutta 108, §18*)...one wields bodily mastery even as far as the Brahma-world.

38. (vi) "With the divine ear element, which is purified and surpasses the human, one hears both kinds of sounds, the divine and the human, those that are far as well as near.

39. (vii) "One understands the minds of other beings, of other persons, having encompassed them with one's own mind. One understands a mind affected by lust as affected by lust...(*as Sutta 108, §20*)...an unliberated mind as unliberated.

40. (viii) "One recollects one's manifold past lives, that is, [99] one birth, two births...(*as Sutta 51, §24*)...Thus with their aspects and particulars one recollects one's manifold past lives.

41. (ix) "With the divine eye, which is purified and surpasses the human, one sees beings passing away and reappearing, inferior and superior, fair and ugly, fortunate and unfortunate, and one understands how beings pass on according to their actions.

42. (x) "By realising for oneself with direct knowledge, one here and now enters upon and abides in the deliverance of mind and deliverance by wisdom that are taintless with the destruction of the taints.

43. "Bhikkhus, when mindfulness of the body has been repeatedly practised, developed, cultivated, used as a vehicle, used as a basis, established, consolidated, and well undertaken, these ten benefits may be expected."

That is what the Blessed One said. The bhikkhus were satisfied and delighted in the Blessed One's words.

120 *Sankhārupapatti Sutta*
Reappearance by Aspiration

1. THUS HAVE I HEARD. On one occasion the Blessed One was living at Sāvatthī in Jeta's Grove, Anāthapiṇḍika's Park. There he addressed the bhikkhus thus: "Bhikkhus."—"Venerable sir," they replied. The Blessed One said this:

2. "Bhikkhus, I shall teach you reappearance in accordance with one's aspiration.[1132] Listen and attend closely to what I shall say."—"Yes, venerable sir," the bhikkhus replied. The Blessed One said this:

3. "Here, bhikkhus, a bhikkhu possesses faith, virtue, learning, generosity, and wisdom. He thinks: 'Oh, that on the dissolution of the body, after death, I might reappear in the company of well-to-do nobles!' He fixes his mind on that, resolves upon it, develops it. [100] These aspirations and this abiding of his, thus developed and cultivated, lead to his reappearance there. This, bhikkhus, is the path, the way that leads to reappearance there.[1133]

4–5. "Again, a bhikkhu possesses faith...and wisdom. He thinks: 'Oh, that on the dissolution of the body, after death, I might reappear in the company of well-to-do brahmins!...in the company of well-to-do householders!' He fixes his mind on that...This, bhikkhus, is the path, the way that leads to reappearance there.

6. "Again, a bhikkhu possesses faith...and wisdom. He hears that the gods of the heaven of the Four Great Kings are long-lived, beautiful, and enjoy great happiness. He thinks: 'Oh, that on the dissolution of the body, after death, I might reappear in the company of the gods of the heaven of the Four Great Kings!' He fixes his mind on that...This, bhikkhus, is the path, the way that leads to reappearance there.

7–11. "Again, a bhikkhu possesses faith...and wisdom. He

hears that the gods of the heaven of the Thirty-three...the Yāma gods...the gods of the Tusita heaven...the gods who delight in creating...the gods who wield power over others' creations are long-lived, beautiful, and enjoy great happiness. He thinks: 'Oh, that on the dissolution of the body, after death, I might reappear in the company of the gods who wield power over others' creations!' He fixes his mind on that...This, bhikkhus, is the path, the way that leads to reappearance there.

12. "Again, a bhikkhu possesses faith [101]...and wisdom. He hears that the Brahmā of a Thousand is long-lived, beautiful, and enjoys great happiness. Now the Brahmā of a Thousand abides resolved on pervading a world-system of a thousand worlds, and he abides resolved on pervading the beings that have reappeared there.[1134] Just as a man with good sight might take a gallnut in his hand and review it, so the Brahmā of a Thousand abides resolved on pervading a world-system of a thousand [worlds], and he abides resolved on pervading the beings that have reappeared there. The bhikkhu thinks: 'Oh, that on the dissolution of the body, after death, I might reappear in the company of the Brahmā of a Thousand!' He fixes his mind on that...This, bhikkhus, is the path, the way that leads to reappearance there.

13–16. "Again, a bhikkhu possesses faith...and wisdom. He hears that the Brahmā of Two Thousand...the Brahmā of Three Thousand...the Brahmā of Four Thousand...the Brahmā of Five Thousand is long-lived, beautiful, and enjoys great happiness. Now the Brahmā of Five Thousand abides resolved on pervading a world-system of five thousand worlds, and he abides resolved on pervading the beings that have reappeared there. Just as a man with good sight might take five gallnuts in his hand and review them, so the Brahmā of Five Thousand abides resolved on pervading a world-system of five thousand worlds, and he abides resolved on pervading the beings that have reappeared there. The bhikkhu thinks: 'Oh, that on the dissolution of the body, after death, I might reappear in the company of the Brahmā of Five Thousand!' He fixes his mind on that...This, bhikkhus, is the path, the way that leads to reappearance there.

17. "Again, a bhikkhu possesses faith...and wisdom. He hears that the Brahmā of Ten Thousand is long-lived, beautiful, and enjoys great happiness. Now the Brahmā of Ten Thousand abides resolved on pervading [102] a world-system of ten thousand

worlds, and he abides resolved on pervading the beings that have reappeared there. Just as a fine beryl gem of purest water, eight-faceted, well cut, lying on red brocade, glows, radiates, and shines, so the Brahmā of Ten Thousand abides resolved on pervading a world-system of ten thousand worlds, and he abides resolved on pervading the beings that have reappeared there. The bhikkhu thinks: 'Oh, that on the dissolution of the body, after death, I might reappear in the company of the Brahmā of Ten Thousand!' He fixes his mind on that...This, bhikkhus, is the path, the way that leads to reappearance there.

18. "Again, a bhikkhu possesses faith...and wisdom. He hears that the Brahmā of a Hundred Thousand is long-lived, beautiful, and enjoys great happiness. Now the Brahmā of a Hundred Thousand abides resolved on pervading a world-system of a hundred thousand worlds, and he abides resolved on pervading the beings that have reappeared there. Just as an ornament of finest gold, very skilfully wrought in the furnace by a clever goldsmith, lying on red brocade, glows, radiates, and shines, so the Brahmā of a Hundred Thousand abides resolved on pervading a world-system of a hundred thousand worlds, and he abides resolved on pervading the beings that have reappeared there. The bhikkhu thinks: 'Oh, that on the dissolution of the body, after death, I might reappear in the company of the Brahmā of a Hundred Thousand!' He fixes his mind on that...This, bhikkhus, is the path, the way that leads to reappearance there.

19–32. "Again, a bhikkhu possesses faith...and wisdom. He hears that the gods of Radiance[1135]...the gods of Limited Radiance...the gods of Immeasurable Radiance...the gods of Streaming Radiance...the gods of Glory...the gods of Limited Glory...the gods of Immeasurable Glory...the gods of Refulgent Glory...[103]...the gods of Great Fruit...the Aviha gods...the Atappa gods...the Sudassa gods...the Sudassī gods...the Akaniṭṭha gods are long-lived, beautiful, and enjoy great happiness. He thinks: 'Oh, that on the dissolution of the body, after death, I might reappear in the company of the Akaniṭṭha gods!' He fixes his mind on that...This, bhikkhus, is the path, the way that leads to reappearance there.

33–36. "Again, a bhikkhu possesses faith...and wisdom. He hears that the gods of the base of infinite space...the gods of the base of infinite consciousness...the gods of the base of nothingness...the gods of the base of neither-perception-nor-non-perception are long-lived, long-enduring, and enjoy great happiness. He thinks: 'Oh, that on the dissolution of the body, after death, I might reappear in the company of the gods of the base of neither-perception-nor-non-perception!' He fixes his mind on that, resolves on it, develops it. These aspirations and this abiding of his, thus developed and cultivated, lead to his reappearance there. This, bhikkhus, is the path, the way that leads to reappearance there.

37. "Again, a bhikkhu possesses faith, virtue, learning, generosity, and wisdom. He thinks: 'Oh, that by realising for myself with direct knowledge, I might here and now enter upon and abide in the deliverance of mind and deliverance by wisdom that are taintless with the destruction of the taints!' And by realising for himself with direct knowledge, he here and now enters upon and abides in the deliverance of mind and deliverance by wisdom that are taintless with the destruction of the taints. Bhikkhus, this bhikkhu does not reappear anywhere at all."[1136]

That is what the Blessed One said. The bhikkhus were satisfied and delighted in the Blessed One's words.

3

The Division on Voidness

(*Suññatavagga*)

121 *Cūḷasuññata Sutta*
The Shorter Discourse on Voidness

[104] 1. THUS HAVE I HEARD. On one occasion the Blessed One was living at Sāvatthī in the Eastern Park, in the Palace of Migāra's Mother.

2. Then, when it was evening, the venerable Ānanda rose from meditation, went to the Blessed One, and after paying homage to him, he sat down at one side and said to the Blessed One:

3. "Venerable sir, on one occasion the Blessed One was living in the Sakyan country where there is a town of the Sakyans named Nagaraka. There, venerable sir, I heard and learned this from the Blessed One's own lips: 'Now, Ānanda, I often abide in voidness.'[1137] Did I hear that correctly, venerable sir, did I learn that correctly, attend to that correctly, remember that correctly?"

"Certainly, Ānanda, you heard that correctly, learned that correctly, attended to that correctly, remembered that correctly. As formerly, Ānanda, so now too I often abide in voidness.

4. "Ānanda, just as this Palace of Migāra's Mother is void of elephants, cattle, horses, and mares, void of gold and silver, void of the assembly of men and women, and there is present only this non-voidness, namely, the singleness dependent on the Sangha of bhikkhus; so too, a bhikkhu—not attending to the perception of village, not attending to the perception of people—attends to the singleness dependent on the perception of forest.[1138] His mind enters into that perception of forest and acquires confidence, steadiness, and resolution. He understands thus: 'Whatever disturbances there might be dependent on the perception of village, those are not present here; whatever disturbances there might be dependent on the perception of people, those are not present here. There is present only this amount of disturbance, namely, the singleness dependent on the perception of forest.'[1139] He understands: 'This field of perception is

void of the perception of village; this field of perception is void of the perception of people. There is present only this non-voidness, namely, the singleness dependent on the perception of forest.' Thus he regards it as void of what is not there, but as to what [105] remains there he understands that which is present thus: 'This is present.' Thus, Ānanda, this is his genuine, undistorted, pure descent into voidness.

5. "Again, Ānanda, a bhikkhu—not attending to the perception of people, not attending to the perception of forest—attends to the singleness dependent on the perception of earth.[1140] His mind enters into that perception of earth and acquires confidence, steadiness, and resolution. Just as a bull's hide becomes free from folds when fully stretched with a hundred pegs; so too, a bhikkhu—not attending to any of the ridges and hollows of this earth, to the rivers and ravines, the tracts of stumps and thorns, the mountains and uneven places—attends to the singleness dependent on the perception of earth. His mind enters into that perception of earth and acquires confidence, steadiness, and resolution. He understands thus: 'Whatever disturbances there might be dependent on the perception of people, those are not present here; whatever disturbances there might be dependent on the perception of forest, those are not present here. There is present only this amount of disturbance, namely, the singleness dependent on the perception of earth.' He understands: 'This field of perception is void of the perception of people; this field of perception is void of the perception of forest. There is present only this non-voidness, namely, the singleness dependent on the perception of earth.' Thus he regards it as void of what is not there, but as to what remains there he understands that which is present thus: 'This is present.' Thus, Ānanda, this too is his genuine, undistorted, pure descent into voidness.

6. "Again, Ānanda, a bhikkhu—not attending to the perception of forest, not attending to the perception of earth—attends to the singleness dependent on the perception of the base of infinite space.[1141] His mind enters into that perception of the base of infinite space and acquires confidence, steadiness, and resolution. He understands thus: 'Whatever disturbances there might be dependent on the perception of forest, those are not present here; whatever disturbances there might be [106] dependent on the perception of earth, those are not present here. There is

present only this amount of disturbance, namely, the singleness dependent on the perception of the base of infinite space.' He understands: 'This field of perception is void of the perception of forest; this field of perception is void of the perception of earth. There is present only this non-voidness, namely, the singleness dependent on the perception of the base of infinite space.' Thus he regards it as void of what is not there, but as to what remains there he understands that which is present thus: 'This is present.' Thus, Ānanda, this too is his genuine, undistorted, pure descent into voidness.

7. "Again, Ānanda, a bhikkhu—not attending to the perception of earth, not attending to the perception of the base of infinite space—attends to the singleness dependent on the perception of the base of infinite consciousness. His mind enters into that perception of the base of infinite consciousness and acquires confidence, steadiness, and resolution. He understands thus: 'Whatever disturbances there might be dependent on the perception of earth, those are not present here; whatever disturbances there might be dependent on the perception of the base of infinite space, those are not present here. There is present only this amount of disturbance, namely, the singleness dependent on the perception of the base of infinite consciousness.' He understands: 'This field of perception is void of the perception of earth; this field of perception is void of the perception of the base of infinite space. There is present only this non-voidness, namely, the singleness dependent on the perception of the base of infinite consciousness.' Thus he regards it as void of what is not there, but as to what remains there he understands that which is present thus: 'This is present.' Thus, Ānanda, this too is his genuine, undistorted, pure descent into voidness.

8. "Again, Ānanda, a bhikkhu—not attending to the perception of the base of infinite space, not attending to the perception of the base of infinite consciousness—attends to the singleness dependent on the perception of the base of nothingness. His mind enters into that perception of the base of nothingness and acquires confidence, steadiness, and resolution. He understands thus: 'Whatever disturbances there might be dependent on the perception of the base of infinite space, those are not present here; whatever disturbances there might be dependent on the perception of the base of infinite consciousness, those are not

present here. There is present only this amount of disturbance, namely, the singleness dependent on the perception of the base of nothingness.' He understands: 'This field of perception is void of the perception of the base of infinite space; [107] this field of perception is void of the perception of the base of infinite consciousness. There is present only this non-voidness, namely, the singleness dependent on the perception of the base of nothingness.' Thus he regards it as void of what is not there, but as to what remains there he understands that which is present thus: 'This is present.' Thus, Ānanda, this too is his genuine, undistorted, pure descent into voidness.

9. "Again, Ānanda, a bhikkhu—not attending to the perception of the base of infinite consciousness, not attending to the perception of the base of nothingness—attends to the singleness dependent on the perception of the base of neither-perception-nor-non-perception. His mind enters into that perception of the base of neither-perception-nor-non-perception and acquires confidence, steadiness, and resolution. He understands thus: 'Whatever disturbances there might be dependent on the perception of the base of infinite consciousness, those are not present here; whatever disturbances there might be dependent on the perception of the base of nothingness, those are not present here. There is present only this amount of disturbance, namely, the singleness dependent on the perception of the base of neither-perception-nor-non-perception.' He understands: 'This field of perception is void of the perception of the base of infinite consciousness; this field of perception is void of the perception of the base of nothingness. There is present only this non-voidness, namely, the singleness dependent on the perception of the base of neither-perception-nor-non-perception.' Thus he regards it as void of what is not there, but as to what remains there he understands that which is present thus: 'This is present.' Thus, Ānanda, this too is his genuine, undistorted, pure descent into voidness.

10. "Again, Ānanda, a bhikkhu—not attending to the perception of the base of nothingness, not attending to the perception of the base of neither-perception-nor-non-perception—attends to the singleness dependent on the signless concentration of mind.[1142] His mind enters into that signless concentration of mind and acquires confidence, steadiness, and resolution. He understand thus: 'Whatever disturbances there might be

dependent on the perception of the base of nothingness, those are not present here; whatever disturbances there might be dependent on the perception of the base of neither-perception-nor-non-perception, those are not present here. There is present only this amount of disturbance, namely, that connected with the six bases that are dependent on this body and [108] conditioned by life.' He understands: 'This field of perception is void of the perception of the base of nothingness; this field of perception is void of the perception of the base of neither-perception-nor-non-perception. There is present only this non-voidness, namely, that connected with the six bases that are dependent on this body and conditioned by life.' Thus he regards it as void of what is not there, but as to what remains there he understands that which is present thus: 'This is present.' Thus, Ānanda, this too is his genuine, undistorted, pure descent into voidness.

11. "Again, Ānanda, a bhikkhu—not attending to the perception of the base of nothingness, not attending to the perception of the base of neither-perception-nor-non-perception—attends to the singleness dependent on the signless concentration of mind. His mind enters into that signless concentration of mind and acquires confidence, steadiness, and resolution. He understands thus: 'This signless concentration of mind is conditioned and volitionally produced. But whatever is conditioned and volitionally produced is impermanent, subject to cessation.'[1143] When he knows and sees thus, his mind is liberated from the taint of sensual desire, from the taint of being, and from the taint of ignorance. When it is liberated there comes the knowledge: 'It is liberated.' He understands: 'Birth is destroyed, the holy life has been lived, what had to be done has been done, there is no more coming to any state of being.'

12. "He understands thus: 'Whatever disturbances there might be dependent on the taint of sensual desire, those are not present here; whatever disturbances there might be dependent on the taint of being, those are not present here; whatever disturbances there might be dependent on the taint of ignorance, those are not present here. There is present only this amount of disturbance, namely, that connected with the six bases that are dependent on this body and conditioned by life.' He understands: 'This field of perception is void of the taint of sensual desire; this field of perception is void of the taint of being; this

field of perception is void of the taint of ignorance. There is present only this non-voidness, namely, that connected with the six bases that are dependent on this body and conditioned by life.' Thus he regards it as void of what is not there, but as to what remains there he understands that which is present thus: 'This is present.' Thus, Ānanda, this is his genuine, [109] undistorted, pure descent into voidness, supreme and unsurpassed.[1144]

13. "Ānanda, whatever recluses and brahmins in the past entered upon and abided in pure, supreme, unsurpassed voidness, all entered upon and abided in this same pure, supreme, unsurpassed voidness. Whatever recluses and brahmins in the future will enter upon and abide in pure, supreme, unsurpassed voidness, all will enter upon and abide in this same pure, supreme, unsurpassed voidness. Whatever recluses and brahmins in the present enter upon and abide in pure, supreme, unsurpassed voidness, all enter upon and abide in this same pure, supreme, unsurpassed voidness. Therefore, Ānanda, you should train thus: 'We will enter upon and abide in pure, supreme, unsurpassed voidness.'"

That is what the Blessed One said. The venerable Ānanda was satisfied and delighted in the Blessed One's words.

122 *Mahāsuññata Sutta*
The Greater Discourse on Voidness

1. THUS HAVE I HEARD.[1145] On one occasion the Blessed One was living in the Sakyan country at Kapilavatthu in Nigrodha's Park.

2. Then, when it was morning, the Blessed One dressed, and taking his bowl and outer robe, went into Kapilavatthu for alms. When he had wandered for alms in Kapilavatthu and had returned from his almsround, after his meal he went for his daytime abiding to the dwelling of Kāḷakhemaka the Sakyan. Now on that occasion there were many resting places prepared in Kāḷakhemaka the Sakyan's dwelling.[1146] When the Blessed One saw this, [110] he thought: "There are many resting places prepared in Kāḷakhemaka the Sakyan's dwelling. Do many bhikkhus live there?"

Now on that occasion the venerable Ānanda, along with many bhikkhus, was busy making robes at Ghāṭā the Sakyan's dwelling. Then, when it was evening, the Blessed One rose from retreat and went to Ghāṭā the Sakyan's dwelling. There he sat down on a seat made ready and asked the venerable Ānanda:

"Ānanda, there are many resting places prepared in Kāḷakhemaka the Sakyan's dwelling. Do many bhikkhus live there?"[1147]

"Venerable sir, many resting places have been prepared in Kāḷakhemaka the Sakyan's dwelling. Many bhikkhus are living there. This is our time for making robes, venerable sir."[1148]

3. "Ānanda, a bhikkhu does not shine by delighting in company, by taking delight in company, by devoting himself to delight in company; by delighting in society, by taking delight in society, by rejoicing in society. Indeed, Ānanda, it is not possible that a bhikkhu who delights in company, takes delight in company, and devotes himself to delight in company, who delights in society, takes delight in society, and rejoices in society, will ever obtain at will, without trouble or difficulty, the bliss of

renunciation, the bliss of seclusion, the bliss of peace, the bliss of enlightenment.[1149] But it can be expected that when a bhikkhu lives alone, withdrawn from society, he will obtain at will, without trouble or difficulty, the bliss of renunciation, the bliss of seclusion, the bliss of peace, the bliss of enlightenment.

4. "Indeed, Ānanda, it is not possible that a bhikkhu who delights in company, takes delight in company, and devotes himself to delight in company, who delights in society, takes delight in society, and rejoices in society, will ever enter upon and abide in either the deliverance of mind that is temporary and delectable or in [the deliverance of mind] that is perpetual and unshakeable.[1150] But it can be expected that when a bhikkhu lives alone, withdrawn from society, he will enter upon and abide in the deliverance of mind that is temporary and delectable or in [the deliverance of mind] that is perpetual and unshakeable. [111]

5. "I do not see even a single kind of form, Ānanda, from the change and alteration of which there would not arise sorrow, lamentation, pain, grief, and despair in one who lusts for it and takes delight in it.

6. "However, Ānanda, there is this abiding discovered by the Tathāgata: to enter and abide in voidness internally by giving no attention to all signs.[1151] If, while the Tathāgata is abiding thus, he is visited by bhikkhus or bhikkhunīs, by men or women lay followers, by kings or kings' ministers, by other sectarians or their disciples, then with a mind leaning to seclusion, tending and inclining to seclusion, withdrawn, delighting in renunciation, and altogether done away with things that are the basis for taints, he invariably talks to them in a way concerned with dismissing them.

7. "Therefore, Ānanda, if a bhikkhu should wish: 'May I enter upon and abide in voidness internally,' he should steady his mind internally, quiet it, bring it to singleness, and concentrate it. And how does he steady his mind internally, quiet it, bring it to singleness, and concentrate it?

8. "Here, Ānanda, quite secluded from sensual pleasures, secluded from unwholesome states, a bhikkhu enters upon and abides in the first jhāna...the second jhāna...the third jhāna...the fourth jhāna, which has neither-pain-nor-pleasure and purity of mindfulness due to equanimity. That is how a bhikkhu steadies

his mind internally, quiets it, brings it to singleness, and concentrates it. [112]

9. "Then he gives attention to voidness internally.[1152] While he is giving attention to voidness internally, his mind does not enter into voidness internally or acquire confidence, steadiness, and decision. When that is so, he understands thus: 'While I am giving attention to voidness internally, my mind does not enter into voidness internally or acquire confidence, steadiness, and decision.' In this way he has full awareness of that.

"He gives attention to voidness externally...He gives attention to voidness internally and externally...He gives attention to imperturbability.[1153] While he is giving attention to imperturbability, his mind does not enter into imperturbability or acquire confidence, steadiness, and decision. When that is so, he understands thus: 'While I am giving attention to imperturbability, my mind does not enter into imperturbability or acquire confidence, steadiness, and decision.' In this way he has full awareness of that.

10. "Then that bhikkhu should steady his mind internally, quiet it, bring it to singleness, and concentrate it on that same sign of concentration as before.[1154] Then he gives attention to voidness internally. While he is giving attention to voidness internally, his mind enters into voidness internally and acquires confidence, steadiness, and decision. When that is so, he understands thus: 'While I am giving attention to voidness internally, my mind enters into voidness internally and acquires confidence, steadiness, and decision.' In this way he has full awareness of that.

"He gives attention to voidness externally...He gives attention to voidness internally and externally...He gives attention to imperturbability. While he is giving attention to imperturbability, his mind enters into imperturbability and acquires confidence, steadiness, and decision. When that is so, he understands thus: 'While I am giving attention to imperturbability, my mind enters into imperturbability and acquires confidence, steadiness, and decision.' In this way he has full awareness of that.

11. "When a bhikkhu abides thus, if his mind inclines to walking, he walks, thinking: 'While I am walking thus, no evil unwholesome states of covetousness and grief will beset me.' [113] In this way he has full awareness of that. And when a bhikkhu abides thus, if his mind inclines to standing, he

stands...If his mind inclines to sitting, he sits...If his mind inclines to lying down, he lies down, thinking: 'While I am lying down thus, no evil unwholesome states will beset me.' In this way he has full awareness of that.

12. "When a bhikkhu abides thus, if his mind inclines to talking, he resolves: 'Such talk as is low, vulgar, coarse, ignoble, unbeneficial, and which does not lead to disenchantment, dispassion, cessation, peace, direct knowledge, enlightenment, and Nibbāna, that is, talk of kings, robbers, ministers, armies, dangers, battles, food, drink, clothing, beds, garlands, perfumes, relatives, vehicles, villages, towns, cities, countries, women, heroes, streets, wells, the dead, trivialities, the origin of the world, the origin of the sea, whether things are so or are not so: such talk I shall not utter.' In this way he has full awareness of that.

"But he resolves: 'Such talk as deals with effacement, as favours the mind's release, and which leads to complete disenchantment, dispassion, cessation, peace, direct knowledge, enlightenment, and Nibbāna, that is, talk on wanting little, on contentment, seclusion, aloofness from society, arousing energy, virtue, concentration, wisdom, deliverance, knowledge and vision of deliverance: such talk I shall utter.' In this way he has full awareness of that.

13. "When a bhikkhu abides thus, [114] if his mind inclines to thinking, he resolves: 'Such thoughts as are low, vulgar, coarse, ignoble, unbeneficial, and which do not lead to disenchantment, dispassion, cessation, peace, direct knowledge, enlightenment, and Nibbāna, that is, thoughts of sensual desire, thoughts of ill will, and thoughts of cruelty: such thoughts I shall not think.' In this way he has full awareness of that.

"But he resolves: 'Such thoughts as are noble and emancipating, and lead the one who practises in accordance with them to the complete destruction of suffering, that is, thoughts of renunciation, thoughts of non-ill will, and thoughts of non-cruelty: such thoughts I shall think.' In this way he has full awareness of that.

14. "Ānanda, there are these five cords of sensual pleasure.[1155] What five? Forms cognizable by the eye that are wished for, desired, agreeable, and likeable, connected with sensual desire and provocative of lust. Sounds cognizable by the ear...Odours cognizable by the nose...Flavours cognizable by the tongue...

Tangibles cognizable by the body that are wished for, desired, agreeable, and likeable, connected with sensual desire and provocative of lust. These are the five cords of sensual pleasure.

15. "Herein a bhikkhu should constantly review his own mind thus: 'Does any mental excitement concerning any base among these five cords of sensual pleasure ever arise in me?' If, on reviewing his mind, the bhikkhu understands: 'Mental excitement concerning a certain base among these five cords of sensual pleasure does arise in me,' then he understands: 'Desire and lust for the five cords of sensual pleasure are unabandoned in me.' In this way he has full awareness of that. But if, on reviewing his mind, the bhikkhu understands: 'No mental excitement concerning any base among these five cords of sensual pleasure arises in me,' then he understands: 'Desire and lust for the five cords of sensual pleasure are abandoned in me.' In this way he has full awareness of that.

16. "Ānanda, there are these five aggregates affected by clinging,[1156] in regard to which a bhikkhu should abide contemplating rise and fall thus: 'Such is material form, such its arising, such its disappearance; such is feeling, such [115] its arising, such its disappearance; such is perception, such its arising, such its disappearance; such are formations, such their arising, such their disappearance; such is consciousness, such its arising, such its disappearance.'

17. "When he abides contemplating rise and fall in these five aggregates affected by clinging, the conceit 'I am' based on these five aggregates affected by clinging is abandoned in him. When that is so, that bhikkhu understands: 'The conceit "I am" based on these five aggregates affected by clinging is abandoned in me.' In that way he has full awareness of that.

18. "These states have an entirely wholesome basis; they are noble, supramundane, and inaccessible to the Evil One.

19. "What do you think, Ānanda? What good does a disciple see that he should seek the Teacher's company even if he is told to go away?"

"Venerable sir, our teachings are rooted in the Blessed One, guided by the Blessed One, have the Blessed One as their resort. It would be good if the Blessed One would explain the meaning of these words. Having heard it from the Blessed One, the bhikkhus will remember it."

20. "Ānanda, a disciple should not seek the Teacher's company for the sake of discourses, stanzas, and expositions. Why is that? For a long time, Ānanda, you have learned the teachings, remembered them, recited them verbally, examined them with the mind, and penetrated them well by view. But such talk as deals with effacement, as favours the mind's release, and which leads to complete disenchantment, dispassion, cessation, peace, direct knowledge, enlightenment, and Nibbāna, that is, talk on wanting little, on contentment, seclusion, aloofness from society, arousing energy, virtue, concentration, wisdom, deliverance, knowledge and vision of deliverance: for the sake of such talk a disciple should seek the Teacher's company even if he is told to go away.

21. "Since this is so, Ānanda, a teacher's undoing may come about, a pupil's undoing may come about, and the undoing of one who lives the holy life may come about.[1157]

22. "And how does a teacher's undoing come about? Here some teacher resorts to a secluded resting place: the forest, the root of a tree, a mountain, a ravine, a hillside cave, a charnel ground, [116] a jungle thicket, an open space, a heap of straw. While he lives thus withdrawn, brahmins and householders from town and country visit him, and as a result he goes astray, becomes filled with desire, succumbs to craving, and reverts to luxury. This teacher is said to be undone by the teacher's undoing. He has been struck down by evil unwholesome states that defile, bring renewal of being, give trouble, ripen in suffering, and lead to future birth, ageing, and death. This is how the teacher's undoing comes about.

23. "And how does a pupil's undoing come about? A pupil of that teacher, emulating the teacher's seclusion, resorts to a secluded resting place: the forest...a heap of straw. While he lives thus withdrawn, brahmins and householders from town and country visit him, and as a result he goes astray, becomes filled with desire, succumbs to craving, and reverts to luxury. This pupil is said to be undone by the pupil's undoing. He has been struck down by evil unwholesome states that defile, bring renewal of being, give trouble, ripen in suffering, and lead to future birth, ageing, and death. This is how the pupil's undoing comes about.

24. "And how does the undoing of one who lives the holy life

come about? Here a Tathāgata appears in the world, accomplished and fully enlightened, perfect in true knowledge and conduct, sublime, knower of worlds, incomparable leader of persons to be tamed, teacher of gods and humans, enlightened, blessed. He resorts to a secluded resting place: the forest...a heap of straw. While he lives thus withdrawn, brahmins and householders from town and country visit him, yet he does not go astray, or become filled with desire, succumb to craving, and revert to luxury. [117] But a disciple of this teacher, emulating his teacher's seclusion, resorts to a secluded resting place: the forest...a heap of straw. While he lives thus withdrawn, brahmins and householders from town and country visit him, and as a result he goes astray, becomes filled with desire, succumbs to craving, and reverts to luxury. This one who lives the holy life is said to be undone by the undoing of one who lives the holy life. He has been struck down by evil unwholesome states that defile, bring renewal of being, give trouble, ripen in suffering, and lead to future birth, ageing, and death. Thus there comes to be the undoing of one who leads the holy life. And herein, Ānanda, the undoing of one who leads the holy life has a more painful result, a more bitter result, than the teacher's undoing or the pupil's undoing, and it even leads to perdition.[1158]

25. "Therefore, Ānanda, behave towards me with friendliness, not with hostility. That will lead to your welfare and happiness for a long time. And how do disciples behave towards the Teacher with hostility, not with friendliness? Here, Ānanda, compassionate and seeking their welfare, the Teacher teaches the Dhamma to the disciples out of compassion: 'This is for your welfare, this is for your happiness.' His disciples do not want to hear or give ear or exert their minds to understand; they err and turn aside from the Teacher's Dispensation. Thus do disciples behave towards the Teacher with hostility, not with friendliness.

26. "And how do disciples behave towards the Teacher with friendliness, not with hostility? Here, Ānanda, compassionate and seeking their welfare, the Teacher teaches the Dhamma to the disciples out of compassion: 'This is for your welfare, this is for your happiness.' His disciples want to hear and give ear and exert their minds to understand; they do not err and turn aside from the Teacher's Dispensation. Thus do disciples behave towards the Teacher with friendliness, not with hostility. [118]

Therefore, Ānanda, behave towards me with friendliness, not with hostility. That will lead to your welfare and happiness for a long time.

27. "I shall not treat you as the potter treats the raw damp clay. Repeatedly restraining you, I shall speak to you, Ānanda. Repeatedly admonishing you, I shall speak to you, Ānanda. The sound core will stand [the test]."[1159]

That is what the Blessed One said. The venerable Ānanda was satisfied and delighted in the Blessed One's words.

123 *Acchariya-abbhūta Sutta*
Wonderful and Marvellous

1. THUS HAVE I HEARD. On one occasion the Blessed One was living at Sāvatthī in Jeta's Grove, Anāthapiṇḍika's Park.

2. Now a number of bhikkhus were sitting in the assembly hall, where they had met together on returning from their almsround, after their meal, when this discussion arose among them: "It is wonderful, friends, it is marvellous, how mighty and powerful is the Tathāgata! For he is able to know about the Buddhas of the past—who attained to final Nibbāna, cut [the tangle of] proliferation, broke the cycle, ended the round, and surmounted all suffering—that for those Blessed Ones their birth was thus, their names were thus, their clans were thus, their virtue was thus, their state [of concentration] was thus, their wisdom was thus, their abiding [in attainments] was thus, their deliverance was thus."[1160]

When this was said, the venerable Ānanda told the bhikkhus: "Friends, Tathāgatas are wonderful and have wonderful qualities. Tathāgatas are marvellous and have marvellous qualities." [119]

However, their discussion was interrupted; for the Blessed One rose from meditation when it was evening, went to the assembly hall, and sat down on a seat made ready. Then he addressed the bhikkhus thus: "Bhikkhus, for what discussion are you sitting together here now? And what was your discussion that was interrupted?"

"Here, venerable sir, we were sitting in the assembly hall, where we had met together on returning from our almsround, after our meal, when this discussion arose among us: 'It is wonderful, friends, it is marvellous...their deliverance was thus.' When this was said, venerable sir, the venerable Ānanda said to us: 'Friends, Tathāgatas are wonderful and have wonderful qualities. Tathāgatas are marvellous and have marvellous qualities.'

This was our discussion, venerable sir, that was interrupted when the Blessed One arrived."

Then the Blessed One addressed the venerable Ānanda: "That being so, Ānanda, explain more fully the Tathāgata's wonderful and marvellous qualities."

3. "I heard and learned this, venerable sir, from the Blessed One's own lips: 'Mindful and fully aware, Ānanda, the Bodhisatta appeared in the Tusita heaven.'[1161] That [120] mindful and fully aware the Bodhisatta appeared in the Tusita heaven—this I remember as a wonderful and marvellous quality of the Blessed One.

4. "I heard and learned this from the Blessed One's own lips: 'Mindful and fully aware the Bodhisatta remained in the Tusita heaven.' This too I remember as a wonderful and marvellous quality of the Blessed One.

5. "I heard and learned this from the Blessed One's own lips: 'For the whole of his life-span the Bodhisatta remained in the Tusita heaven.' This too I remember as a wonderful and marvellous quality of the Blessed One.

6. "I heard and learned this from the Blessed One's own lips: 'Mindful and fully aware the Bodhisatta passed away from the Tusita heaven and descended into his mother's womb.' This too I remember as a wonderful and marvellous quality of the Blessed One.

7. "I heard and learned this from the Blessed One's own lips: 'When the Bodhisatta passed away from the Tusita heaven and descended into his mother's womb, then a great immeasurable light surpassing the splendour of the gods appeared in the world with its gods, its Māras, and its Brahmās, in this generation with its recluses and brahmins, with its princes and its people. And even in those abysmal world interspaces of vacancy, gloom, and utter darkness, where the moon and the sun, mighty and powerful as they are, cannot make their light prevail—there too a great immeasurable light surpassing the splendour of the gods appeared.[1162] And the beings born there perceived each other by that light: "So other beings, indeed, have appeared here." And this ten-thousandfold world system shook and quaked and trembled, and there too a great immeasurable light surpassing the splendour of the gods appeared.' This too I remember as a wonderful and marvellous quality of the Blessed One.

8. "I heard and learned this from the Blessed One's own lips: 'When the Bodhisatta had descended into his mother's womb, four young deities came to guard him at the four quarters so that no humans or non-humans or anyone at all could harm the Bodhisatta or his mother.'[1163] This too I remember as a wonderful and marvellous quality of the Blessed One.

9. "I heard and learned this from the Blessed One's own lips: 'When the Bodhisatta had descended into his mother's womb, she became intrinsically virtuous, refraining from killing living beings, from taking what is not given, from misconduct in sensual pleasures, from false speech, and from wines, liquors, and intoxicants, which are the basis of negligence.' This too I remember as a wonderful and marvellous quality of the Blessed One. [121]

10. "I heard and learned this from the Blessed One's own lips: 'When the Bodhisatta had descended into his mother's womb, no sensual thought arose in her concerning men, and she was inaccessible to any man having a lustful mind.' This too I remember as a wonderful and marvellous quality of the Blessed One.

11. "I heard and learned this from the Blessed One's own lips: 'When the Bodhisatta had descended into his mother's womb, she obtained the five cords of sensual pleasure, and furnished and endowed with them, she enjoyed herself with them.' This too I remember as a wonderful and marvellous quality of the Blessed One.

12. "I heard and learned this from the Blessed One's own lips: 'When the Bodhisatta had descended into his mother's womb, no kind of affliction arose in her; she was blissful and free from bodily fatigue. She saw the Bodhisatta within her womb with all his limbs, lacking no faculty. Suppose a blue, yellow, red, white, or brown thread were strung through a fine beryl gem of purest water, eight-faceted, well cut, and a man with good sight were to take it in his hand and review it thus: "This is a fine beryl gem of purest water, eight-faceted, well cut, and through it is strung a blue, yellow, red, white, or brown thread"; so too when the Bodhisatta had descended into his mother's womb...she saw the Bodhisatta within her womb with all his limbs, lacking no faculty.' This too I remember as a wonderful and marvellous quality of the Blessed One. [122]

13. "I heard and learned this from the Blessed One's own lips:

'Seven days after the birth of the Bodhisatta, his mother died and reappeared in the Tusita heaven.'[1164] This too I remember as a wonderful and marvellous quality of the Blessed One.

14. "I heard and learned this from the Blessed One's own lips: 'Other women give birth after carrying the child in the womb for nine or ten months, but not so the Bodhisatta's mother. The Bodhisatta's mother gave birth to him after carrying him in her womb for exactly ten months.' This too I remember as a wonderful and marvellous quality of the Blessed One.

15. "I heard and learned this from the Blessed One's own lips: 'Other women give birth seated or lying down, but not so the Bodhisatta's mother. The Bodhisatta's mother gave birth to him standing up.' This too I remember as a wonderful and marvellous quality of the Blessed One.

16. "I heard and learned this from the Blessed One's own lips: 'When the Bodhisatta came forth from his mother's womb, first gods received him, then human beings.' This too I remember as a wonderful and marvellous quality of the Blessed One.

17. "I heard and learned this from the Blessed One's own lips: 'When the Bodhisatta came forth from his mother's womb, he did not touch the earth. The four young gods received him and set him before his mother saying: "Rejoice, O queen, a son of great power has been born to you."' This too I remember as a wonderful and marvellous quality of the Blessed One.

18. "I heard and learned this from the Blessed One's own lips: 'When the Bodhisatta came forth from his mother's womb, he came forth unsullied, unsmeared [123] by water or humours or blood or any kind of impurity, clean, and unsullied. Suppose there were a gem placed on Kāsi cloth, then the gem would not smear the cloth or the cloth the gem. Why is that? Because of the purity of both. So too when the Bodhisatta came forth...clean and unsullied.' This too I remember as a wonderful and marvellous quality of the Blessed One.

19. "I heard and learned this from the Blessed One's own lips: 'When the Bodhisatta came forth from his mother's womb, two jets of water appeared to pour from the sky, one cool and one warm, for bathing the Bodhisatta and his mother.' This too I remember as a wonderful and marvellous quality of the Blessed One.

20. "I heard and learned this from the Blessed One's own lips:

'As soon as the Bodhisatta was born, he stood firmly with his feet on the ground; then he took seven steps facing north, and with a white parasol held over him, he surveyed each quarter and uttered the words of the Leader of the Herd: "I am the highest in the world; I am the best in the world; I am the foremost in the world. This is my last birth; now there is no renewal of being for me."'[1165] This too I remember as a wonderful and marvellous quality of the Blessed One.

21. "I heard and learned this from the Blessed One's own lips: 'When the Bodhisatta came forth from his mother's womb, then a great immeasurable light surpassing the splendour of the gods appeared in the world with its gods, its Māras, and its Brahmās, in this generation with its recluses and brahmins, with its princes and its people. And even in those abysmal world interspaces of vacancy, gloom, and utter darkness, where the moon and the sun, mighty and powerful as they are, cannot make their light prevail—[124] there too a great immeasurable light surpassing the splendour of the gods appeared. And the beings born there perceived each other by that light: "So other beings, indeed, have appeared here." And this ten-thousandfold world system shook and quaked and trembled, and there too a great immeasurable light surpassing the splendour of the gods appeared.' That when the Bodhisatta came forth from his mother's womb, then a great immeasurable light surpassing the splendour of the gods appeared...this too I remember as a wonderful and marvellous quality of the Blessed One."

22. "That being so, Ānanda, remember this too as a wonderful and marvellous quality of the Tathāgata: Here, Ānanda, for the Tathāgata feelings are known as they arise, as they are present, as they disappear; perceptions are known as they arise, as they are present, as they disappear; thoughts are known as they arise, as they are present, as they disappear.[1166] Remember this too, Ānanda, as a wonderful and marvellous quality of the Tathāgata."

23. "Venerable sir, since for the Blessed One feelings are known as they arise, as they are present, as they disappear; perceptions are known as they arise, as they are present, as they disappear; thoughts are known as they arise, as they are present, as they disappear—this too I remember as a wonderful and marvellous quality of the Blessed One."

That is what the venerable Ānanda said. The Teacher approved. The bhikkhus were satisfied and delighted in the venerable Ānanda's words.

124 *Bakkula Sutta*
Bakkula

1. THUS HAVE I HEARD. On one occasion the venerable Bakkula was living at Rājagaha in the Bamboo Grove, the Squirrels' Sanctuary.[1167]

2. Then Acela Kassapa, a former companion of the venerable Bakkula in his lay life, [125] went to the venerable Bakkula and exchanged greetings with him. When this courteous and amiable talk was finished, he sat down at one side and asked the venerable Bakkula:

3. "Friend Bakkula, how long is it since you went forth?"

"It is eighty years since I went forth, friend."

"Friend Bakkula, in these eighty years how many times have you engaged in sexual intercourse?"

"Friend Kassapa, you should not ask me such a question as that. You should ask me such a question as this: 'Friend Bakkula, in these eighty years how many times have perceptions of sensual desire arisen in you?'"

"Friend Bakkula, in these eighty years how many times have perceptions of sensual desire arisen in you?"

"Friend Kassapa, in the eighty years since I went forth I do not recall any perception of sensual desire to have ever arisen in me."

> [That in the eighty years since he went forth the venerable Bakkula did not recall any perception of sensual desire to have ever arisen in him—this we remember as a wonderful and marvellous quality of the venerable Bakkula.][1168]

4–5. "Friend, in the eighty years since I went forth I do not recall any perception of ill will...any perception of cruelty to have ever arisen in me."

> [That in the eighty years since he went forth the venerable Bakkula did not recall any perception of ill will... any perception of cruelty to have ever arisen in him—

this we remember as a wonderful and marvellous quality of the venerable Bakkula.]

6. "Friend, in the eighty years since I went forth I do not recall any thought of sensual desire to have ever arisen in me."

[...this too we remember as a wonderful and marvellous quality of the venerable Bakkula.]

7–8. "Friend, in the eighty years since I went forth I do not recall any thought of ill will...any thought of cruelty to have ever arisen in me."

[...this too we remember as a wonderful and marvellous quality of the venerable Bakkula.] [126]

9–15. "Friend, in the eighty years since I went forth I do not recall ever having accepted a robe from a householder[1169]...ever having worn a robe given by a householder...ever having cut a robe with a cutter...ever having sewn a robe with a needle... ever having coloured a robe with dye...ever having sewn a robe at the *kaṭhina* time...ever having worked on making robes for my companions in the holy life."

[...this too we remember as a wonderful and marvellous quality of the venerable Bakkula.]

16–19. "Friend, in the eighty years since I went forth I do not recall ever having accepted an invitation to a meal...ever having given rise to the thought: 'Oh, may someone invite me to a meal!'...ever having sat down inside a house...ever having eaten inside a house."

[...this too we remember as a wonderful and marvellous quality of the venerable Bakkula.]

20–25. "Friend, in the eighty years since I went forth I do not recall ever having grasped at the signs and features of a woman...ever having taught the Dhamma to a woman, even as much as a four-line stanza...ever having gone to the bhikkhunīs' quarters...ever having taught the Dhamma to a bhikkhunī... ever having taught the Dhamma to a female probationer...ever having taught the Dhamma to a female novice."

[...this too we remember as a wonderful and marvellous quality of the venerable Bakkula.]

26–29. "Friend, in the eighty years since I went forth I do not recall ever having given the going forth...ever having given the full admission...ever having given dependence...ever having had a novice wait on me."

[...this too we remember as a wonderful and marvellous quality of the venerable Bakkula.]

30–37. "Friend, in the eighty years since I went forth I do not recall ever having bathed in a bath house...ever having bathed with bath powder...ever having undertaking the work of massaging the limbs of my companions in the holy life [127]...ever having had an affliction arise in me even for as long as it takes to milk a cow...ever having taken medicine, even as much as a piece of gallnut...ever having used a bolster...ever having made up a bed...ever having entered upon residence for the Rains in a resting place inside a village."

[...this too we remember as a wonderful and marvellous quality of the venerable Bakkula.]

38. "Friend, for seven days after going forth I ate the country's almsfood as a debtor; on the eighth day final knowledge arose."[1170]

[That for seven days the venerable Bakkula ate the country's almsfood as a debtor, and on the eighth day final knowledge arose—this too we remember as a wonderful and marvellous quality of the venerable Bakkula.]

39. [Then Acela Kassapa said:] "I would receive the going forth in this Dhamma and Discipline, I would receive the full admission." And Acela Kassapa received the going forth in this Dhamma and Discipline, he received the full admission.[1171] And soon, not long after his full admission, dwelling alone, withdrawn, diligent, ardent, and resolute, the venerable Kassapa, by realising for himself with direct knowledge, here and now entered upon and abided in that supreme goal of the holy life for the sake of which clansmen rightly go forth from the home life into homelessness. He knew directly: "Birth is destroyed, the holy life has been lived, what had to be done has been done, there is no more coming to any state of being." And the venerable Kassapa became one of the arahants.

40. Then, on a later occasion, the venerable Bakkula took a key and went from cell to cell, saying: "Come forth, venerable sirs; come forth, venerable sirs. Today I shall attain final Nibbāna."

[That the venerable Bakkula took a key and went from cell to cell saying: "Come forth, venerable sirs; come forth, venerable sirs. Today I shall attain final Nibbāna"—this too we remember as a wonderful and marvellous quality of the venerable Bakkula.] [128]

41. Then, seated in the midst of the Sangha of bhikkhus, the venerable Bakkula attained final Nibbāna.[1172]

[That seated in the midst of the Sangha of bhikkhus, the venerable Bakkula attained final Nibbāna—this too we remember as a wonderful and marvellous quality of the venerable Bakkula.][1173]

125 *Dantabhūmi Sutta*
The Grade of the Tamed

1. THUS HAVE I HEARD. On one occasion the Blessed One was living at Rājagaha in the Bamboo Grove, the Squirrels' Sanctuary.

2. Now on that occasion the novice Aciravata was living in a forest hut. Then Prince Jayasena, while wandering and walking for exercise, went to the novice Aciravata and exchanged greetings with him.[1174] When this courteous and amiable talk was finished, he sat down at one side and said to the novice Aciravata: "Master Aggivessana, I have heard that a bhikkhu who abides here diligent, ardent, and resolute can achieve unification of mind."

"That is so, prince, that is so. A bhikkhu who abides here diligent, ardent, and resolute can achieve unification of mind."

3. "It would be good if Master Aggivessana would teach me the Dhamma as he has heard it and mastered it."

"I cannot teach you the Dhamma, prince, as I have heard it and mastered it. For if I were to teach you the Dhamma as I have heard it and mastered it, you would not understand the meaning of my words, and that would be wearying and troublesome for me." [129]

4. "Let Master Aggivessana teach me the Dhamma as he has heard it and mastered it. Perhaps I can understand the meaning of his words."

"I shall teach you the Dhamma, prince, as I have heard it and mastered it. If you can understand the meaning of my words, that will be good. But if you cannot understand the meaning, then leave it at that and do not question me about it further."

"Let Master Aggivessana teach me the Dhamma as he has heard it and mastered it. If I can understand the meaning of his words, that will be good. If I cannot understand the meaning, then I will leave it at that and I will not question him about it further."

5. Then the novice Aciravata taught Prince Jayasena the Dhamma as he had heard it and mastered it. After he had spoken, Prince Jayasena remarked: "It is impossible, Master Aggivessana, it cannot happen that a bhikkhu who abides diligent, ardent, and resolute can achieve unification of mind." Then, having declared to the novice Aciravata that this was impossible and could not happen, Prince Jayasena rose from his seat and departed.

6. Soon after Prince Jayasena had left, the novice Aciravata went to the Blessed One. After paying homage to the Blessed One, he sat down at one side and reported to the Blessed One his entire conversation with Prince Jayasena. When he had finished, the Blessed One said to him:

7. "Aggivessana, how is it possible that Prince Jayasena, living in the midst of sensual pleasures, enjoying sensual pleasures, being devoured by thoughts of sensual pleasures, being consumed by the fever of sensual pleasures, bent on the search for sensual pleasures, [130] could know, see, or realise that which must be known through renunciation, seen through renunciation, attained through renunciation, realised through renunciation? That is impossible.

8. "Suppose,[1175] Aggivessana, there were two tamable elephants, horses, or oxen that were well tamed and well disciplined, and two tamable elephants, horses, or oxen that were untamed and undisciplined. What do you think, Aggivessana? Would the two tamable elephants, horses, or oxen that were well tamed and well disciplined, being tamed, acquire the behaviour of the tamed, would they arrive at the grade of the tamed?"—"Yes, venerable sir."—"But would the two tamable elephants, horses, or oxen that were untamed and undisciplined, being untamed, acquire the behaviour of the tamed, would they arrive at the grade of the tamed, like the two tamable elephants, horses, or oxen that were well tamed and well disciplined?"—"No, venerable sir."—"So too, Aggivessana, it is impossible that Prince Jayasena, living in the midst of sensual pleasures,...could know, see, or realise that which must be known through renunciation, seen through renunciation, attained through renunciation, realised through renunciation.

9. "Suppose, Aggivessana, there were a high mountain not far from a village or town, and two friends would leave the village

or town and approach the mountain hand in hand. Having reached it, one friend would remain below at the foot of the mountain while the other would climb to the top. Then the friend who remained below at the foot of the mountain would say to the friend who stood on the top: 'Well, friend, what do you see, standing on top of the mountain?' And the other replied: 'Standing on top of the mountain, friend, I see lovely parks, lovely groves, lovely meadows, and lovely ponds.' Then the first friend would say: 'It is impossible, [131] friend, it cannot happen that while standing on top of the mountain you should see lovely parks, lovely groves, lovely meadows, and lovely ponds.'

"Then the other friend would come down to the foot of the mountain, take his friend by the arm, and make him climb to the top of the mountain. After giving him a few moments to catch his breath, he would ask: 'Well, friend, standing on top of the mountain, what do you see?' And his friend would reply: 'Standing on top of the mountain, friend, I see lovely parks, lovely groves, lovely meadows, and lovely ponds.' Then the other would say: 'Friend, just a little earlier we heard you say: "It is impossible, friend, it cannot happen that while standing on top of the mountain you should see lovely parks...lovely ponds." But just now we heard you say: "Standing on top of the mountain, friend, I see lovely parks...lovely ponds."' Then the first friend would reply: 'Because I was obstructed by this high mountain, friend, I did not see what was there to be seen.'

10. "So too, Aggivessana, Prince Jayasena is obstructed, hindered, blocked, and enveloped by a still greater mass than this—the mass of ignorance. Thus it is impossible that Prince Jayasena, living in the midst of sensual pleasures,...could know, see, or realise that which must be known through renunciation, seen through renunciation, attained through renunciation, realised through renunciation.

11. "Aggivessana, if these two similes had occurred to you [with reference] to Prince Jayasena, he would have spontaneously acquired confidence in you, and being confident, would have shown his confidence to you."

"Venerable sir, how could these two similes have occurred to me [with reference] to Prince Jayasena as they occur to the Blessed One, since they are spontaneous and have never been heard before?"

[132] 12. "Suppose, Aggivessana, a head-anointed noble king addresses his elephant woodsman thus: 'Good elephant woodsman, mount the king's elephant, enter the elephant wood, and when you see a forest elephant, bind him by the neck to the king's elephant.' Having replied 'Yes, sire,' the elephant woodsman mounts the king's elephant, enters the elephant wood, and when he sees a forest elephant, binds him by the neck to the king's elephant. The king's elephant leads him out into the open. It is in this way that a forest elephant comes out into the open; for the forest elephant clings to the elephant wood.

"Then the elephant woodsman informs the head-anointed noble king: 'Sire, the forest elephant has come out into the open.' The king addresses his elephant tamer thus: 'Come, good elephant tamer, tame the forest elephant. Subdue his forest habits, subdue his forest memories and intentions, subdue his distress, fatigue, and fever over leaving the forest. Get him to take delight in the town, inculcate in him habits congenial to human beings.' Having replied 'Yes, sire,' the elephant tamer plants a large post in the earth and binds the forest elephant to it by the neck in order to subdue his forest habits...and to inculcate in him habits congenial to human beings.

"Then the elephant tamer addresses the elephant with words that are gentle, pleasing to the ear, and loveable, as go to the heart, are courteous, desired by many, and agreeable to many. When the forest elephant [133] is addressed by such words, he listens, gives ear, and exerts his mind to understand. The elephant tamer next rewards him with grass-fodder and water. When the forest elephant accepts the grass-fodder and water from him, the elephant tamer knows: 'Now the king's elephant will live!'

"Then the elephant tamer trains him further thus: 'Take up, put down!' When the king's elephant obeys his tamer's orders to take up and put down and carries out his instructions, the elephant tamer trains him further thus: 'Go forward, go back!' When the king's elephant obeys his tamer's orders to go forward and go back and carries out his instructions, the elephant tamer trains him further thus: 'Get up, sit down!' When the king's elephant obeys his tamer's orders to get up and sit down and carries out his instructions, the elephant tamer trains him further in the task called imperturbability. He ties a giant plank to his trunk; a man with a lance in his hand sits on his neck; men with lances in their hands surround him on all sides; and the elephant tamer himself stands in front of him holding a long lance pole. When the elephant is being trained in the task of imperturbability, he does not move his forelegs or his hindlegs; he does not move his forequarters or his hindquarters; he does not move his head, ears, tusks, tail, or trunk. The king's elephant is able to endure blows from spears, blows from swords, blows from arrows, blows from other beings, and the thundering sounds of drums, kettledrums, trumpets, and tomtoms. Being rid of all faults and defects, purged of flaws, he is worthy of the king, in the king's service, considered one of the factors of a king. [134]

13–14. "So too, Aggivessana, a Tathāgata appears in the world, accomplished, fully enlightened...(*as Sutta 51, §§12–13*)...he shaves off his hair and beard, puts on the yellow robe, and goes forth from the home life into homelessness. It is in this way that a noble disciple comes out into the open; for gods and humans cling to the five cords of sensual pleasure.

15. "Then the Tathāgata disciplines him further: 'Come, bhikkhu, be virtuous, restrained with the restraint of the Pātimokkha, be perfect in conduct and resort, and seeing fear in the slightest fault, train by undertaking the training precepts.'

16. "When, Aggivessana, the noble disciple is virtuous...and seeing fear in the slightest fault, trains by undertaking the training precepts, then the Tathāgata disciplines him further: 'Come, bhikkhu, guard the doors of your sense faculties. On seeing a form with the eye, do not grasp at its signs and features. Since, if you were to leave the eye faculty unguarded, evil unwholesome states of covetousness and grief might invade you, practise the way of its restraint, guard the eye faculty, undertake the restraint of the eye faculty. On hearing a sound with the ear...On smelling an odour with the nose...On tasting a flavour with the tongue...On touching a tangible with the body...On cognizing a mind-object with the mind, do not grasp at its signs and features. Since, if you were to leave the mind faculty unguarded, evil unwholesome states of covetousness and grief might invade you, practise the way of its restraint, guard the mind faculty, undertake the restraint of the mind faculty.'

17. "When, Aggivessana, the noble disciple guards the doors of his sense faculties, then the Tathāgata disciplines him further:

'Come, bhikkhu, be moderate in eating. Reflecting wisely, you should take food neither for amusement nor for intoxication nor for the sake of physical beauty and attractiveness, but only for the endurance and continuance of this body, for ending discomfort, and for assisting the holy life, considering: "Thus I shall terminate old feelings without arousing new feelings and I shall be healthy and blameless and shall live in comfort."'

18. "When, [135] Aggivessana, the noble disciple is moderate in eating, then the Tathāgata disciplines him further: 'Come, bhikkhu, be devoted to wakefulness. During the day, while walking back and forth and sitting, purify your mind of obstructive states. In the first watch of the night, while walking back and forth and sitting, purify your mind of obstructive states. In the middle watch of the night you should lie down on the right side in the lion's pose with one foot overlapping the other, mindful and fully aware, after noting in your mind the time for rising. After rising, in the last watch of the night, while walking back and forth and sitting, purify your mind of obstructive states.'

19. "When, Aggivessana, the noble disciple is devoted to wakefulness, then the Tathāgata disciplines him further: 'Come, bhikkhu, be possessed of mindfulness and full awareness. Act in full awareness when going forward and returning...when looking ahead and looking away...when flexing and extending your limbs...when wearing your robes and carrying your outer robe and bowl...when eating, drinking, consuming food, and tasting...when defecating and urinating...when walking, standing, sitting, falling asleep, waking up, talking, and keeping silent.'

20. "When, Aggivessana, the noble disciple possesses mindfulness and full awareness, then the Tathāgata disciplines him further: 'Come, bhikkhu, resort to a secluded resting place: the forest, the root of a tree, a mountain, a ravine, a hillside cave, a charnel ground, a jungle thicket, an open space, a heap of straw.'

21. "He resorts to a secluded resting place: the forest...a heap of straw. On returning from his almsround, after his meal he sits down, folding his legs crosswise, setting his body erect, and establishing mindfulness before him. Abandoning covetousness for the world, he abides with a mind free from covetousness; he purifies his mind from covetousness. Abandoning ill will and hatred, he abides with a mind free from ill will, compassionate for the welfare of all living beings; he purifies his mind from ill

will and hatred. Abandoning sloth and torpor, he abides free from sloth and torpor, percipient of light, mindful, and fully aware; he purifies his mind from sloth and torpor. Abandoning restlessness and remorse, he abides unagitated with a mind inwardly peaceful; he purifies his mind from restlessness and remorse. [136] Abandoning doubt, he abides having gone beyond doubt, unperplexed about wholesome states; he purifies his mind from doubt.

22. "Having thus abandoned these five hindrances, imperfections of the mind that weaken wisdom, he abides contemplating the body as a body, ardent, fully aware, and mindful, having put away covetousness and grief for the world. He abides contemplating feelings as feelings...mind as mind...mind-objects as mind-objects, ardent, fully aware, and mindful, having put away covetousness and grief for the world.[1176]

23. "Just as, Aggivessana, the elephant tamer plants a large post in the earth and binds the forest elephant to it by the neck in order to subdue his forest habits...and to inculcate in him habits congenial to human beings, so these four foundations of mindfulness are the bindings for the mind of the noble disciple in order to subdue his habits based on the household life, to subdue his memories and intentions based on the household life, to subdue his distress, fatigue, and fever based on the household life, and in order that he may attain the true way and realise Nibbāna.

24. "Then the Tathāgata disciplines him further: 'Come, bhikkhu, abide contemplating the body as a body, but do not think thoughts of sensual desire. Abide contemplating feelings as feelings...mind as mind...mind-objects as mind-objects, but do not think thoughts of sensual desire.'[1177]

25. "With the stilling of applied and sustained thought, he enters upon and abides in the second jhāna...the third jhāna...the fourth jhāna.

26–29. "When his concentrated mind is thus purified...(*as Sutta 51, §§24–27*)...He understands: 'Birth is destroyed, the holy life has been lived, what had to be done has been done, there is no more coming to any state of being.'

30. "That bhikkhu is able to endure cold and heat, hunger and thirst, and contact with gadflies, mosquitoes, wind, the sun, and creeping things; he is able to endure ill-spoken, unwelcome words

and arisen bodily [137] feelings that are painful, racking, sharp, piercing, disagreeable, distressing, and menacing to life. Being rid of all lust, hate, and delusion, purged of flaws, he is worthy of gifts, worthy of hospitality, worthy of offerings, worthy of reverential salutations, an unsurpassed field of merit for the world.

31. "If, Aggivessana, the king's elephant dies in old age untamed and undisciplined, then he is considered an old elephant that has died an untamed death. If the king's elephant dies when middle-aged untamed and undisciplined, then he is considered a middle-aged elephant that has died an untamed death. If the king's elephant dies when young untamed and undisciplined, then he is considered a young elephant that has died an untamed death. So too, Aggivessana, if an elder bhikkhu dies with his taints undestroyed, then he is considered an elder bhikkhu who has died an untamed death. If a bhikkhu of middle status dies with his taints undestroyed, then he is considered a bhikkhu of middle status who has died an untamed death. If a newly ordained bhikkhu dies with his taints undestroyed, then he is considered a newly ordained bhikkhu who has died an untamed death.

32. "If, Aggivessana, the king's elephant dies in old age well tamed and well disciplined, then he is considered an old elephant that has died a tamed death. If the king's elephant dies when middle-aged well tamed and well disciplined, then he is considered a middle-aged elephant that has died a tamed death. If the king's elephant dies when young well tamed and well disciplined, then he is considered a young elephant that has died a tamed death. So too, Aggivessana, if an elder bhikkhu dies with his taints destroyed, then he is considered an elder bhikkhu who has died a tamed death. If a bhikkhu of middle status dies with his taints destroyed, then he is considered a bhikkhu of middle status who has died a tamed death. If a newly ordained bhikkhu dies with his taints destroyed, then he is considered a newly ordained bhikkhu who has died a tamed death."

That is what the Blessed One said. The novice Aciravata was satisfied and delighted in the Blessed One's words.

126 *Bhūmija Sutta*
Bhūmija

[138] 1. THUS HAVE I HEARD. On one occasion the Blessed One was living at Rājagaha in the Bamboo Grove, the Squirrels' Sanctuary.

2. Then, when it was morning, the venerable Bhūmija dressed, and taking his bowl and outer robe, went to the house of Prince Jayasena and sat down on a seat made ready.[1178]

3. Then Prince Jayasena went to the venerable Bhūmija and exchanged greetings with him. When this courteous and amiable talk was finished, he sat down at one side and said to the venerable Bhūmija: "Master Bhūmija, there are some recluses and brahmins who make such assertions and hold such views as this: 'If one makes an aspiration[1179] and one leads the holy life, one is unable to procure any fruit; if one makes no aspiration and one leads the holy life, one is still unable to procure any fruit; if one both makes an aspiration and makes no aspiration and one leads the holy life, one is still unable to procure any fruit; if one neither makes an aspiration nor makes no aspiration and one leads the holy life, one is still unable to procure any fruit.' What does the venerable Bhūmija's teacher say here, what does he declare?"

4. "I have not heard and learned that from the Blessed One's own lips, prince. But it is possible that the Blessed One might say this: 'If one makes an aspiration and one leads the holy life unwisely, one is unable to procure any fruit; if one makes no aspiration and one leads the holy life unwisely, one is still unable to procure any fruit; if one both makes an aspiration and makes no aspiration and one leads the holy life unwisely, one is still unable to procure any fruit; if one neither makes an aspiration nor makes no aspiration and one leads the holy life unwisely, one is still unable to procure any fruit. However, if one makes

an aspiration and one leads the holy life wisely, one is able to procure fruit; [139] if one makes no aspiration and one leads the holy life wisely, one is still able to procure fruit; if one both makes an aspiration and makes no aspiration and one leads the holy life wisely, one is still able to procure fruit; if one neither makes an aspiration nor makes no aspiration and one leads the holy life wisely, one is still able to procure fruit.' I have not heard and learned this from the Blessed One's own lips, prince, but it is possible that the Blessed One would answer as I have stated."

5. "If Master Bhūmija's teacher speaks thus, if he declares thus, then it certainly seems that the venerable Bhūmija's teacher stands ahead of all the ordinary recluses and brahmins."

6. Then Prince Jayasena served the venerable Bhūmija from his own dish of milk rice.

7. Then, when the venerable Bhūmija had returned from his almsround after his meal, he went to the Blessed One. After paying homage to him, he sat down at one side and told the Blessed One what had occurred, adding: "Venerable sir, I hope that when I was asked such a question and answered thus, I said what has been said by the Blessed One and did not misrepresent him with what is contrary to fact. I hope I explained in accordance with the Dhamma in such a way that nothing which provides a ground for censure can be legitimately deduced from my assertion." [140]

8. "Surely, Bhūmija, when you were asked such a question and answered thus, you said what has been said by me and did not misrepresent me with what is contrary to fact. You explained in accordance with the Dhamma in such a way that nothing which provides a ground for censure can be legitimately deduced from your assertion.

9. "Whatever recluses and brahmins have wrong view, wrong intention, wrong speech, wrong action, wrong livelihood, wrong effort, wrong mindfulness, and wrong concentration, if they make an aspiration and they lead the holy life, they are unable to procure any fruit; if they make no aspiration and they lead the holy life, they are still unable to procure any fruit; if they both make an aspiration and make no aspiration and they lead the holy life, they are still unable to procure any fruit; if they neither make an aspiration nor make no aspiration and they lead the holy life, they are still unable to procure any fruit. Why

is that? Because that [wrong path] is not a proper method for procuring fruit.

10. "Suppose a man needing oil, seeking oil, wandering in search of oil, were to heap up gravel in a tub, sprinkle it all over with water, and press it. Then, if he made an aspiration and acted thus, he would be unable to procure any oil; if he made no aspiration and acted thus, he would still be unable to procure any oil; if he both made an aspiration and made no aspiration and acted thus, he would still be unable to procure any oil; if he neither made an aspiration nor made no aspiration and acted thus, he would still be unable to procure any oil. Why is that? Because that [way of acting] is not a proper method for procuring oil. So too, whatever recluses and brahmins have wrong view...they are still unable to procure any fruit. [141] Why is that? Because that [wrong path] is not a proper method for procuring fruit.

11. "Suppose a man needing milk, seeking milk, wandering in search of milk, were to pull a recently-calved cow by her horn. Then, if he made an aspiration...if he made no aspiration...if he both made an aspiration and made no aspiration...if he neither made an aspiration nor made no aspiration and acted thus, he would still be unable to procure any milk. Why is that? Because that [way of acting] is not a proper method for procuring milk. So too, whatever recluses and brahmins have wrong view...they are still unable to procure any fruit. Why is that? Because that [wrong path] is not a proper method for procuring fruit.

12. "Suppose a man needing butter, seeking butter, wandering in search of butter, were to pour water into a churn and churn it with a churning-stick. Then, if he made an aspiration...if he made no aspiration...if he both made an aspiration and made no aspiration...if he neither made an aspiration nor made no aspiration and acted thus, he would still be unable to procure any butter. Why is that? Because that [way of acting] is not a proper method for procuring butter. So too, whatever recluses and brahmins have wrong view...they are still unable to procure any fruit. Why is that? Because that [wrong path] is not a proper method for procuring fruit.

13. "Suppose a man needing fire, seeking fire, wandering in search of fire, were to take an [142] upper fire-stick and rub a wet sappy piece of wood with it. Then, if he made an aspiration...if

he made no aspiration...if he both made an aspiration and made no aspiration...if he neither made an aspiration nor made no aspiration and acted thus, he would still be unable to procure any fire. Why is that? Because that [way of acting] is not a proper method for procuring fire. So too, whatever recluses and brahmins have wrong view...they are still unable to procure any fruit. Why is that? Because that [wrong path] is not a proper method for procuring fruit.

14. "Whatever recluses and brahmins have right view, right intention, right speech, right action, right livelihood, right effort, right mindfulness, and right concentration, if they make an aspiration and they lead the holy life, they are able to procure fruit; if they make no aspiration and they lead the holy life, they are still able to procure fruit; if they both make an aspiration and make no aspiration and they lead the holy life, they are still able to procure fruit; if they neither make an aspiration nor make no aspiration and they lead the holy life, they are still able to procure fruit. Why is that? Because that [right path] is a proper method for procuring fruit.

15. "Suppose a man needing oil, seeking oil, wandering in search of oil, were to heap up sesamum flour in a tub, sprinkle it all over with water, and press it. Then, if he made an aspiration and acted thus, he would be able to procure oil; if he made no aspiration and acted thus, he would still be able to procure oil; if he both made an aspiration and made no aspiration and acted thus, he would still be able to procure oil; if he neither made an aspiration nor made no aspiration and acted thus, he would still be able to procure oil. Why is that? Because that [way of acting] is a proper method for procuring oil. So too, whatever recluses and brahmins have right view [143]...they are still able to procure fruit. Why is that? Because that [right path] is a proper method for procuring fruit.

16. "Suppose a man needing milk, seeking milk, wandering in search of milk, were to pull a recently-calved cow by her udder. Then, if he made an aspiration...if he made no aspiration...if he both made an aspiration and made no aspiration...if he neither made an aspiration nor made no aspiration and acted thus, he would still be able to procure milk. Why is that? Because that [way of acting] is a proper method for procuring milk. So too, whatever recluses and brahmins have right view...they are still

able to procure fruit. Why is that? Because that [right path] is a proper method for procuring fruit.

17. "Suppose a man needing butter, seeking butter, wandering in search of butter, were to pour curd into a churn and churn it with a churning-stick. Then, if he made an aspiration...if he made no aspiration...if he both made an aspiration and made no aspiration...if he neither made an aspiration nor made no aspiration and acted thus, he would still be able to procure butter. Why is that? Because that [way of acting] is a proper method for procuring butter. So too, whatever recluses and brahmins have right view...they are still able to procure fruit. Why is that? Because that [right path] is a proper method for procuring fruit.

18. "Suppose a man needing fire, seeking fire, wandering in search of fire, were to take an upper fire-stick and rub a dry sapless piece of wood with it. Then, if he made an aspiration...[144] if he made no aspiration...if he both made an aspiration and made no aspiration...if he neither made an aspiration nor made no aspiration and acted thus, he would still be able to procure fire. Why is that? Because that [way of acting] is a proper method for procuring fire. So too, whatever recluses and brahmins have right view...they are still able to procure fruit. Why is that? Because that [right path] is a proper method for procuring fruit.

19. "Bhūmija, if these four similes had occurred to you [with reference] to Prince Jayasena, he would have spontaneously acquired confidence in you, and being confident, would have shown his confidence to you."

"Venerable sir, how could these four similes have occurred to me [with reference] to Prince Jayasena as they occur to the Blessed One, since they are spontaneous and have never been heard before?"

That is what the Blessed One said. The venerable Bhūmija was satisfied and delighted in the Blessed One's words.

127 *Anuruddha Sutta*
Anuruddha

1. THUS HAVE I HEARD. On one occasion the Blessed One was living at Sāvatthī in Jeta's Grove, Anāthapiṇḍika's Park.

2. Then the carpenter Pañcakanga addressed a certain man thus: "Come, good man, go to the venerable Anuruddha, [145] pay homage in my name with your head at his feet, and say: 'Venerable sir, the carpenter Pañcakanga pays homage with his head at the venerable Anuruddha's feet and says: "Venerable sir, let the venerable Anuruddha with three others consent to accept tomorrow's meal from the carpenter Pañcakanga; and let the venerable Anuruddha arrive punctually as the carpenter Pañcakanga is very busy and has much work to do for the king."'"

"Yes, sir," that man replied, and he went to the venerable Anuruddha. After paying homage to the venerable Anuruddha, he sat down at one side and delivered his message. The venerable Anuruddha consented in silence.

3. Then, when the night had ended, it being morning, the venerable Anuruddha dressed, and taking his bowl and outer robe, he went to the carpenter Pañcakanga's house and sat down on a seat made ready. Then, with his own hands, the carpenter Pañcakanga served and satisfied the venerable Anuruddha with the various kinds of good food. Then, when the venerable Anuruddha had eaten and had put his bowl aside, the carpenter Pañcakanga took a low seat, sat down at one side, and said to the venerable Anuruddha:

4. "Here, venerable sir, elder bhikkhus have come to me and said: 'Householder, develop the immeasurable deliverance of mind'; and some elders have said: 'Householder, develop the exalted deliverance of mind.' Venerable sir, the immeasurable deliverance of mind and the exalted deliverance of mind[1180]—

are these states different in meaning and [146] different in name, or are they one in meaning and different only in name?"

5. "Explain it as you see it, householder. Afterwards it will be cleared up for you."

"Venerable sir, I think thus: the immeasurable deliverance of mind and the exalted deliverance of mind—these states are one in meaning and different only in name."

6. "Householder, the immeasurable deliverance of mind and the exalted deliverance of mind—these states are different in meaning and different in name. And it should be understood as follows how these states are different in meaning and different in name.

7. "What, householder, is the immeasurable deliverance of mind? Here a bhikkhu abides pervading one quarter with a mind imbued with loving-kindness, likewise the second, likewise the third, likewise the fourth; so above, below, around, and everywhere, and to all as to himself, he abides pervading the all-encompassing world with a mind imbued with loving-kindness, abundant, exalted, immeasurable, without hostility and without ill will. He abides pervading one quarter with a mind imbued with compassion...He abides pervading one quarter with a mind imbued with altruistic joy...He abides pervading one quarter with a mind imbued with equanimity...abundant, exalted, immeasurable, without hostility and without ill will. This is called the immeasurable deliverance of mind.

8. "And what, householder, is the exalted deliverance of mind? Here a bhikkhu abides resolved upon an area the size of the root of one tree, pervading it as exalted: this is called the exalted deliverance of mind.[1181] Here a bhikkhu abides resolved upon an area the size of the roots of two or three trees, pervading it as exalted: this too is called the exalted deliverance of mind. Here a bhikkhu abides resolved upon an area the size of one village, pervading it as exalted...[147]...an area the size of two or three villages...an area the size of one major kingdom... an area the size of two or three major kingdoms...an area the size of the earth bounded by the ocean, pervading it as exalted: this too is called the exalted deliverance of mind. It is in this way, householder, that it can be understood how these states are different in meaning and different in name.

9. "There are, householder, these four kinds of reappearance [in a future state of] being.[1182] What four? Here someone abides

resolved upon and pervading 'limited radiance'; on the dissolution of the body, after death, he reappears in the company of the gods of Limited Radiance. Here someone abides resolved upon and pervading 'immeasurable radiance'; on the dissolution of the body, after death, he reappears in the company of the gods of Immeasurable Radiance. Here someone abides resolved upon and pervading 'defiled radiance'; on the dissolution of the body, after death, he reappears in the company of the gods of Defiled Radiance. Here someone abides resolved upon and pervading 'pure radiance'; on the dissolution of the body, after death, he reappears in the company of the gods of Pure Radiance. These are the four kinds of reappearance [in a future state of] being.[1183]

10. "There is an occasion, householder, when those deities assemble in one place. When they have assembled in one place, a difference in their colour can be discerned but no difference in their radiance. Just as, if a man were to bring several oil-lamps into a house, a difference in the flames of the lamps might be discerned but no difference in their radiance; so too, there is an occasion when those deities assemble in one place [148]...but no difference in their radiance.

11. "There is an occasion, householder, when those deities disperse from there. When they have dispersed, a difference in their colours can be discerned and also a difference in their radiance. Just as, if the man were to remove those several oil-lamps from that house, a difference might be discerned in the flames of the lamps and also a difference in their radiance; so too, there is an occasion when those deities disperse from there...and also a difference in their radiance.

12. "It does not occur to those deities: 'This [life] of ours is permanent, everlasting, and eternal,' yet wherever those deities settle down, there they find delight. Just as, when flies are being carried along on a carrying-pole or on a basket, it does not occur to them: 'This [life] of ours is permanent, everlasting, or eternal,' yet wherever those flies settle down, there they find delight; so too, it does not occur to those deities...yet wherever they settle down, there they find delight."

13. When this was said, the venerable Abhiya Kaccāna said to the venerable Anuruddha: "Good, venerable Anuruddha, yet I have something further to ask: Are all those radiant ones deities

of Limited Radiance, or are some of them deities of Immeasurable Radiance?"

"By reason of the factor [responsible for rebirth], friend Kaccāna, some are deities of Limited Radiance, some deities of Immeasurable Radiance."

14. "Venerable Anuruddha, what is the cause and reason why among those deities that have reappeared in a single order of gods, [149] some are deities of Limited Radiance, some deities of Immeasurable Radiance?"

"As to that, friend Kaccāna, I shall ask you a question in return. Answer it as you choose. What do you think, friend Kaccāna? When one bhikkhu abides resolved upon an area the size of the root of one tree, pervading it as exalted, and another bhikkhu abides resolved upon the area the size of the roots of two or three trees, pervading it as exalted—which of these types of mental development is more exalted?"—"The second, venerable sir."

"What do you think, friend Kaccāna? When one bhikkhu abides resolved upon an area the size of the roots of two or three trees, pervading it as exalted, and another bhikkhu abides resolved upon an area the size of one village, pervading it as exalted...an area the size of one village and an area the size of two or three villages...an area the size of two or three villages [150] and an area the size of one major kingdom...an area the size of one major kingdom and an area the size of two or three major kingdoms...an area the size of two or three major kingdoms and an area the size of the earth bounded by the ocean, pervading it as exalted—which of these two types of mental development is more exalted?"—"The second, venerable sir."

"This is the cause and reason, friend Kaccāna, why among those deities that have reappeared in a single order of gods, some are deities of Limited Radiance, some deities of Immeasurable Radiance."

15. "Good, venerable Anuruddha, yet I have something further to ask: Are all those radiant ones deities of Defiled Radiance, or are some of them deities of Pure Radiance?" [151]

"By reason of the factor [responsible for rebirth], friend Kaccāna, some are deities of Defiled Radiance, some deities of Pure Radiance."

16. "Venerable Anuruddha, what is the cause and reason why

among those deities that have reappeared in a single order of gods, some are deities of Defiled Radiance, some deities of Pure Radiance?"

"As to that, friend Kaccāna, I shall give a simile, for some wise men here understand the meaning of a statement by means of a simile. Suppose an oil-lamp is burning with impure oil and an impure wick; because of the impurity of its oil and its wick it burns dimly. So too, here a bhikkhu abides resolved upon and pervading [an area with] a defiled radiance. His bodily inertia has not fully subsided, his sloth and torpor have not been fully eliminated, his restlessness and remorse have not been fully removed; because of this he meditates, as it were, dimly.[1184] On the dissolution of the body, after death, he reappears in the company of the gods of Defiled Radiance.

"Suppose an oil-lamp is burning with pure oil and a pure wick; because of the purity of its oil and its wick it does not burn dimly. So too, here a bhikkhu abides resolved upon and pervading [an area with] a pure radiance. His bodily inertia has fully subsided, his sloth and torpor have been fully eliminated, his restlessness and remorse have been fully removed; because of this he meditates, as it were, brightly. On the dissolution of the body, after death, he reappears in the company of the gods of Pure Radiance. [152]

"This is the cause and reason, friend Kaccāna, why among those deities that have reappeared in the same order of gods, some are deities of Defiled Radiance, some deities of Pure Radiance."

17. When this was said, the venerable Abhiya Kaccāna said to the venerable Anuruddha: "Good, venerable Anuruddha. The venerable Anuruddha does not say: 'Thus have I heard' or 'It should be thus.' Rather, the venerable Anuruddha says: 'These gods are thus and those gods are such.' It occurs to me, venerable sir, that the venerable Anuruddha certainly has previously associated with those deities and talked with them and held conversations with them."

"Certainly, friend Kaccāna, your words are offensive and discourteous, but still I will answer you. Over a long time I have previously associated with those deities and talked with them and held conversations with them."[1185]

18. When this was said, the venerable Abhiya Kaccāna said to

the carpenter Pañcakanga: "It is a gain for you, householder, it is a great gain for you that you have abandoned your state of doubt and have had the opportunity to hear this discourse on the Dhamma."

128 *Upakkilesa Sutta*
Imperfections

1. THUS HAVE I HEARD. On one occasion the Blessed One was living at Kosambī in Ghosita's Park.

2. Now on that occasion the bhikkhus at Kosambī had taken to quarrelling and brawling and were deep in disputes, stabbing each other with verbal daggers.[1186]

3. Then a certain bhikkhu went to the Blessed One, [153] and after paying homage to him, he stood at one side and said: "Venerable sir, the bhikkhus here at Kosambī have taken to quarrelling and brawling and are deep in disputes, stabbing each other with verbal daggers. It would be good, venerable sir, if the Blessed One would go to those bhikkhus out of compassion." The Blessed One consented in silence.

4. Then the Blessed One went to those bhikkhus and said to them: "Enough, bhikkhus, let there be no quarrelling, brawling, wrangling, or dispute." When this was said, a certain bhikkhu said to the Blessed One: "Wait, venerable sir! Let the Blessed One, the Lord of the Dhamma, live at ease devoted to a pleasant abiding here and now. We are the ones who will be responsible for this quarrelling, brawling, wrangling, and dispute."

For a second time...For a third time the Blessed One said: "Enough, bhikkhus, let there be no quarrelling, brawling, wrangling, or dispute." For a third time that bhikkhu said to the Blessed One: "Wait, venerable sir!...We are the ones who will be responsible for this quarrelling, brawling, wrangling, and dispute."

5. Then, when it was morning, the Blessed One dressed, and taking his bowl and outer robe, entered Kosambī for alms. When he had wandered for alms in Kosambī and had returned from his almsround, after his meal he set his resting place in order, took his bowl and outer robe, and while still standing uttered these stanzas: [154]

6. "When many voices shout at once
None considers himself a fool;
Though the Sangha is being split
None thinks himself to be at fault.

They have forgotten thoughtful speech,
They talk obsessed by words alone.
Uncurbed their mouths, they bawl at will;
None knows what leads him so to act.

'He abused me, he struck me,[1187]
He defeated me, he robbed me'—
In those who harbour thoughts like these
Hatred will never be allayed.

For in this world hatred is never
Allayed by further acts of hate.
It is allayed by non-hatred:
That is the fixed and ageless law.

Those others do not recognise
That here we should restrain ourselves.
But those wise ones who realise this
At once end all their enmity.

Breakers of bones and murderers,
Those who steal cattle, horses, wealth,
Those who pillage the entire realm—
When even these can act together
Why can you not do so too?

If one can find a worthy friend,
A virtuous, steadfast companion,
Then overcome all threats of danger
And walk with him content and mindful.

But if one finds no worthy friend,
No virtuous, steadfast companion,
Then as a king leaves his conquered realm,
Walk like a tusker in the woods alone.

Better it is to walk alone,
There is no companionship with fools.
Walk alone and do no evil,
At ease like a tusker in the woods."

7. Then, having uttered these stanzas while standing, the Blessed One went to the village of Bālakaloṇakāra. On that occasion [155] the venerable Bhagu was living at the village of Bālakaloṇakāra. When the venerable Bhagu saw the Blessed One coming in the distance, he prepared a seat and set out water for washing the feet. The Blessed One sat down on the seat made ready and washed his feet. The venerable Bhagu paid homage to the Blessed One and sat down at one side, and the Blessed One said to him: "I hope you are keeping well, bhikkhu, I hope you are comfortable, I hope you are not having any trouble getting almsfood."

"I am keeping well, Blessed One, I am comfortable, and I am not having any trouble getting almsfood."

Then the Blessed One instructed, urged, roused, and gladdened the venerable Bhagu with talk on the Dhamma, after which he rose from his seat and went to the Eastern Bamboo Park.

8. Now on that occasion the venerable Anuruddha, the venerable Nandiya and the venerable Kimbila were living at the Eastern Bamboo Park.[1188] The park keeper saw the Blessed One coming in the distance and told him: "Do not enter this park, recluse. There are three clansmen here seeking their own good. Do not disturb them."

9. The venerable Anuruddha heard the park keeper speaking to the Blessed One and told him: "Friend park keeper, do not keep the Blessed One out. It is our Teacher, the Blessed One, who has come." Then the venerable Anuruddha went to the venerable Nandiya and the venerable Kimbila and said: "Come out, venerable sirs, come out! Our Teacher, the Blessed One, has come."

10. Then all three went to meet the Blessed One. One took his bowl and outer robe, one prepared a seat, and one set out water for washing the feet. The Blessed One sat down on the seat made ready and washed his feet. Then those three venerable ones paid homage to the Blessed One and sat down at one side, and the Blessed One said to them: "I hope you are all keeping

well, Anuruddha, I hope you are comfortable, I hope you are not having any trouble getting almsfood." [156]

"We are keeping well, Blessed One, we are comfortable, and we are not having any trouble getting almsfood."

11. "I hope, Anuruddha, that you are all living in concord, with mutual appreciation, without disputing, blending like milk and water, viewing each other with kindly eyes."

"Surely, venerable sir, we are living in concord, with mutual appreciation, without disputing, blending like milk and water, viewing each other with kindly eyes."

"But, Anuruddha, how do you live thus?"

12. "Venerable sir, as to that, I think thus: 'It is a gain for me, it is a great gain for me that I am living with such companions in the holy life.' I maintain bodily acts of loving-kindness towards these venerable ones both openly and privately; I maintain verbal acts of loving-kindness towards them both openly and privately; I maintain mental acts of loving-kindness towards them both openly and privately. I consider: 'Why should I not set aside what I wish to do and do what these venerable ones wish to do?' Then I set aside what I wish to do and do what these venerable ones wish to do. We are different in body, venerable sir, but one in mind."

The venerable Nandiya and the venerable Kimbila each spoke likewise, adding: "That is how, venerable sir, we are living in concord, with mutual appreciation, without disputing, blending like milk and water, viewing each other with kindly eyes."

13. "Good, good, Anuruddha. I hope that you all abide diligent, ardent, and resolute." [157]

"Surely, venerable sir, we abide diligent, ardent, and resolute."

"But, Anuruddha, how do you abide thus?"

14. "Venerable sir, as to that, whichever of us returns first from the village with almsfood prepares the seats, sets out the water for drinking and for washing, and puts the refuse bucket in its place. Whichever of us returns last eats any food left over, if he wishes; otherwise he throws it away where there is no greenery or drops it into water where there is no life. He puts away the seats and the water for drinking and for washing. He puts away the refuse bucket after washing it, and he sweeps out the refectory. Whoever notices that the pots of water for drinking, washing, or the latrine are low or empty takes care of them.

If they are too heavy for him, he calls someone else by a signal of the hand and they move it by joining hands, but because of this we do not break out into speech. But every five days we sit together all night discussing the Dhamma. That is how we abide diligent, ardent, and resolute."

15. "Good, good, Anuruddha. But while you abide thus diligent, ardent, and resolute, have you attained any superhuman states, a distinction in knowledge and vision worthy of the noble ones, a comfortable abiding?"

"Venerable sir, as we abide here diligent, ardent, and resolute, we perceive both light and a vision of forms.[1189] Soon afterwards the light and the vision of forms disappear, but we have not discovered the cause for that."

16. "You should discover the cause for that,[1190] Anuruddha. Before my enlightenment, while I was still only an unenlightened Bodhisatta, I too perceived both light and a vision of forms. Soon afterwards the light [158] and the vision of forms disappeared. I thought: 'What is the cause and condition why the light and the vision of forms have disappeared?' Then I considered thus: 'Doubt arose in me, and because of the doubt my concentration fell away; when my concentration fell away, the light and the vision of forms disappeared. I shall so act that doubt will not arise in me again.'

17. "As, Anuruddha, I was abiding diligent, ardent, and resolute, I perceived both light and a vision of forms. Soon afterward the light and the vision of forms disappeared. I thought: 'What is the cause and condition why the light and the vision of forms have disappeared?' Then I considered thus: 'Inattention arose in me, and because of inattention my concentration fell away; when my concentration fell away, the light and the vision of forms disappeared. I shall so act that neither doubt nor inattention will arise in me again.'

18. "As, Anuruddha, I was abiding diligent...I considered thus: 'Sloth and torpor arose in me, and because of sloth and torpor my concentration fell away; when my concentration fell away, the light and the vision of forms disappeared. I shall so act that neither doubt nor inattention nor sloth and torpor will arise in me again.'

19. "As, Anuruddha, I was abiding diligent...I considered thus: 'Fear arose in me, and because of fear my concentration fell

away; when my concentration fell away, the light and the vision of forms disappeared.' Suppose a man set out on a journey and murderers leaped out on both sides of him; then fear would arise in him because of that. So too, fear arose in me...the light and the vision of forms disappeared. [I considered thus:] 'I shall so act [159] that neither doubt nor inattention nor sloth and torpor nor fear will arise in me again.'

20. "As, Anuruddha, I was abiding diligent...I considered thus: 'Elation arose in me, and because of elation my concentration fell away; when my concentration fell away, the light and the vision of forms disappeared.' Suppose a man seeking one entrance to a hidden treasure came all at once upon five entrances to a hidden treasure;[1191] then elation would arise in him because of that. So too, elation arose in me...the light and the vision of forms disappeared. [I considered thus:] 'I shall so act that neither doubt nor inattention...nor fear nor elation will arise in me again.'

21. "As, Anuruddha, I was abiding diligent...I considered thus: 'Inertia arose in me, and because of inertia my concentration fell away; when my concentration fell away, the light and the vision of forms disappeared. I shall so act that neither doubt nor inattention...nor elation nor inertia will arise in me again.'

22. "As, Anuruddha, I was abiding diligent...I considered thus: 'Excess of energy arose in me, and because of excess of energy my concentration fell away; when my concentration fell away, the light and the vision of forms disappeared.' Suppose a man were to grip a quail tightly with both hands; it would die then and there. So too, an excess of energy arose in me...the light and the vision of forms disappeared. [I considered thus:] 'I shall so act that neither doubt nor inattention...nor inertia nor excess of energy will arise in me again.'

23. "As, Anuruddha, I was abiding diligent...I considered thus: 'Deficiency of energy arose in me, [160] and because of deficiency of energy my concentration fell away; when my concentration fell away, the light and the vision of forms disappeared.' Suppose a man were to grip a quail loosely; it would fly out of his hands. So too, a deficiency of energy arose in me...the light and the vision of forms disappeared. [I considered thus:] 'I shall so act that neither doubt nor inattention...nor excess of energy nor deficiency of energy will arise in me again.'

24. "As, Anuruddha, I was abiding diligent...I considered thus: 'Longing arose in me, and because of that longing my concentration fell away; when my concentration fell away, the light and the vision of forms disappeared. I shall so act that neither doubt nor inattention...nor deficiency of energy nor longing will arise in me again.'

25. "As, Anuruddha, I was abiding diligent...I considered thus: 'Perception of diversity arose in me,[1192] and because of perception of diversity my concentration fell away; when my concentration fell away, the light and the vision of forms disappeared. I shall so act that neither doubt nor inattention...nor longing nor perception of diversity will arise in me again.'

26. "As, Anuruddha, I was abiding diligent...I considered thus: 'Excessive meditation upon forms arose in me,[1193] and because of excessive meditation upon forms my concentration fell away; when my concentration fell away, the light and the vision of forms disappeared. I shall so act that neither doubt nor inattention...nor perception of diversity nor excessive meditation upon forms will arise in me again.'

27. "When, Anuruddha, I understood that doubt is an imperfection of the mind,[1194] I abandoned doubt, an imperfection of the mind. When I understood that inattention...sloth and torpor...fear...elation...inertia...excess of energy...deficiency of energy...longing...perception of diversity...excessive meditation upon forms [161] is an imperfection of the mind, I abandoned excessive meditation upon forms, an imperfection of the mind.

28. "As, Anuruddha, I was abiding diligent, ardent, and resolute, I perceived light but I did not see forms; I saw forms but I did not perceive light, even for a whole night or a whole day or a whole day and night. I thought: 'What is the cause and condition for this?' Then I considered thus: 'On the occasion when I do not attend to the sign of forms but attend to the sign of light, I then perceive light but do not see forms. On the occasion when I do not attend to the sign of light but attend to the sign of forms, I then see forms but do not perceive light, even for a whole night or a whole day or a whole day and night.'

29. "As, Anuruddha, I was abiding diligent, ardent, and resolute, I perceived limited light and saw limited forms; I perceived immeasurable light and saw immeasurable forms, even for a whole night or a whole day or a whole day and night. I

thought: 'What is the cause and condition for this?' Then I considered thus: 'On the occasion when concentration is limited, my vision is limited, and with limited vision I perceive limited light and limited forms. But on the occasion when concentration is immeasurable, my vision is immeasurable, and with immeasurable vision I perceive immeasurable light and see immeasurable forms, even for a whole night or a whole day or a whole day and night.'

30. "When, [162] Anuruddha, I understood that doubt is an imperfection of the mind and had abandoned doubt, an imperfection of the mind; when I understood that inattention is an imperfection of the mind and had abandoned inattention... abandoned sloth and torpor...abandoned fear...abandoned elation...abandoned inertia...abandoned excess of energy...abandoned deficiency of energy...abandoned longing...abandoned perception of diversity...abandoned excessive meditation upon forms, an imperfection of the mind; then I thought: 'I have abandoned those imperfections of the mind. Let me now develop concentration in three ways.'[1195]

31. "Thereupon, Anuruddha, I developed concentration with applied thought and sustained thought; I developed concentration without applied thought but with sustained thought only; I developed concentration without applied thought and without sustained thought; I developed concentration with rapture; I developed concentration without rapture; I developed concentration accompanied by enjoyment; I developed concentration accompanied by equanimity.[1196]

32. "When, Anuruddha, I had developed concentration with applied thought and sustained thought...when I had developed concentration accompanied by equanimity, the knowledge and vision arose in me: 'My deliverance is unshakeable; this is my last birth; now there is no renewal of being.'"[1197]

That is what the Blessed One said. The venerable Anuruddha was satisfied and delighted in the Blessed One's words.

129 *Bālapaṇḍita Sutta*
Fools and Wise Men

[163] 1. THUS HAVE I HEARD. On one occasion the Blessed One was living at Sāvatthī in Jeta's Grove, Anāthapiṇḍika's Park. There he addressed the bhikkhus thus: "Bhikkhus."—"Venerable sir," they replied. The Blessed One said this:

(THE FOOL)

2. "Bhikkhus, there are these three characteristics of a fool, signs of a fool, attributes of a fool. What three? Here a fool is one who thinks bad thoughts, speaks bad words, and does bad deeds. If a fool were not so, how would the wise know him thus: 'This person is a fool, an untrue man'? But because a fool is one who thinks bad thoughts, speaks bad words, and does bad deeds, the wise know him thus: 'This person is a fool, an untrue man.'

3. "A fool feels pain and grief here and now in three ways. If a fool is seated in an assembly or along a street or in a square and people there are discussing certain pertinent and relevant matters, then, if the fool is one who kills living beings, takes what is not given, misconducts himself in sensual pleasures, speaks falsehood, and indulges in wine, liquor, and intoxicants, which are the basis of negligence, he thinks: 'These people are discussing certain pertinent and relevant matters; these things are found in me, and I am seen engaging in those things.' This is the first kind of pain and grief that a fool feels here and now.

4. "Again, when a robber culprit is caught, a fool sees kings having many kinds of torture inflicted on him:[1198] [164] having him flogged with whips, beaten with canes, beaten with clubs; having his hands cut off, his feet cut off, his hands and feet cut off; his ears cut off, his nose cut off, his ears and nose cut off;

having him subjected to the 'porridge pot,' to the 'polished-shell shave,' to the 'Rāhu's mouth,' to the 'fiery wreath,' to the 'flaming hand,' to the 'blades of grass,' to the 'bark dress,' to the 'antelope,' to the 'meat hooks,' to the 'coins,' to the 'lye pickling,' to the 'pivoting pin,' to the 'rolled-up palliasse'; and having him splashed with boiling oil, and having him thrown to be devoured by dogs, and having him impaled alive on stakes, and having his head cut off with a sword. Then the fool thinks thus: 'Because of such evil actions as those, when a robber culprit is caught, kings have many kinds of tortures inflicted on him: they have him flogged with whips...and have his head cut off with a sword. Those things are found in me, and I am seen engaging in those things.' This is the second kind of pain and grief that a fool feels here and now.

5. "Again, when a fool is on his chair or on his bed or resting on the ground, then the evil actions that he did in the past—his bodily, verbal, and mental misconduct—cover him, overspread him, and envelop him. Just as the shadow of a great mountain peak in the evening covers, overspreads, and envelops the earth, so too, when a fool is on his chair or on his bed or resting on the ground, [165] then the evil actions that he did in the past—his bodily, verbal, and mental misconduct—cover him, overspread him, and envelop him. Then the fool thinks: 'I have not done what is good, I have not done what is wholesome, I have not made myself a shelter from anguish. I have done what is evil, I have done what is cruel, I have done what is wicked. When I pass away, I shall go to the destination of those who have not done what is good...who have done what is wicked.' He sorrows, grieves, and laments, he weeps beating his breast and becomes distraught. This is the third kind of pain and grief that a fool feels here and now.

6. "A fool who has given himself over to misconduct of body, speech, and mind, on the dissolution of the body, after death, reappears in a state of deprivation, in an unhappy destination, even in hell.

(HELL)

7. "Were it rightly speaking to be said of anything: 'That is utterly unwished for, utterly undesired, utterly disagreeable,' it is of

hell that, rightly speaking, this should be said, so much so that it is hard to find a simile for the suffering in hell."

When this was said, a bhikkhu asked the Blessed One: "But, venerable sir, can a simile be given?"

8. "It can, bhikkhu," the Blessed One said.[1199] "Bhikkhus, suppose men caught a robber culprit and presented him to the king, saying: 'Sire, here is a robber culprit. Order what punishment you will for him.' Then the king said: 'Go and strike this man in the morning with a hundred spears.' And they struck him in the morning with a hundred spears. Then at noon the king asked: 'How is that man?'—'Sire, he is still alive.' Then the king said: 'Go and strike that man at noon with a hundred spears.' And they struck him at noon with a hundred spears. Then in the evening the king asked: 'How is that man?'—'Sire, he is still alive.' Then the king said: 'Go and strike that man in the evening with a hundred spears.' And they struck him in the evening with a hundred spears. [166] What do you think, bhikkhus? Would that man experience pain and grief because of being struck with the three hundred spears?"

"Venerable sir, that man would experience pain and grief because of being struck with even one spear, let alone three hundred."

9. Then, taking a small stone the size of his hand, the Blessed One addressed the bhikkhus thus: "What do you think, bhikkhus? Which is the greater, this small stone that I have taken, the size of my hand, or Himalaya, the king of mountains?"

"Venerable sir, the small stone that the Blessed One has taken, the size of his hand, does not count beside Himalaya, the king of mountains; it is not even a fraction, there is no comparison."

"So too, bhikkhus, the pain and grief that the man would experience because of being struck with the three hundred spears does not count beside the suffering of hell; it is not even a fraction, there is no comparison.

10. "Now the wardens of hell torture him with the fivefold transfixing. They drive a red-hot iron stake through one hand, they drive a red-hot iron stake through the other hand, they drive a red-hot iron stake through one foot, they drive a red-hot iron stake through the other foot, they drive a red-hot iron stake through his belly. There he feels painful, racking, piercing

feelings. Yet he does not die so long as that evil action has not exhausted its result.

11. "Next the wardens of hell throw him down and pare him with axes. There he feels painful, racking, piercing feelings. Yet he does not die so long as that evil action has not exhausted its result.

12. "Next the wardens of hell set him with his feet up and his head down and pare him with adzes. There he feels painful, racking, piercing feelings. Yet he does not die so long as that evil action has not exhausted its result.

13. "Next the wardens of hell harness him to a chariot and drive him back and forth across ground that is burning, blazing, and glowing. [167] There he feels painful, racking, piercing feelings. Yet he does not die so long as that evil action has not exhausted its result.

14. "Next the wardens of hell make him climb up and down a great mound of coals that are burning, blazing, and glowing. There he feels painful, racking, piercing feelings. Yet he does not die so long as that evil action has not exhausted its result.

15. "Next the wardens of hell take him feet up and head down and plunge him into a red-hot metal cauldron that is burning, blazing, and glowing. He is cooked there in a swirl of froth. And as he is being cooked there in a swirl of froth, he is swept now up, now down, and now across. There he feels painful, racking, piercing feelings. Yet he does not die so long as that evil action has not exhausted its result.

16. "Next the wardens of hell throw him into the Great Hell. Now as to that Great Hell, bhikkhus:

> It has four corners and is built
> With four doors, one set in each side,
> Walled up with iron and all around
> And shut in with an iron roof.
> Its floor as well is made of iron
> And heated till it glows with fire.
> The range is a full hundred leagues
> Which it covers all-pervasively.

17. "Bhikkhus, I could tell you in many ways about hell.[1200] So much so that it is hard to finish describing the suffering in hell.

(THE ANIMAL KINGDOM)

18. "Bhikkhus, there are animals that feed on grass. They eat by cropping fresh or dried grass with their teeth. And what animals feed on grass? Horses, cattle, donkeys, goats, and deer, and any other such animals. A fool who formerly delighted in tastes here and did evil actions here, on the dissolution of the body, after death, reappears in the company of animals that feed on grass.

19. "There are animals that feed on dung. They smell dung from a distance and run to it, thinking: 'We can eat, we can eat!' Just as brahmins run to the smell of a sacrifice, thinking: 'We can eat here, we can eat here!' so too these animals that feed on dung [168] smell dung from a distance and run to it, thinking: 'We can eat here, we can eat here!' And what animals feed on dung? Fowls, pigs, dogs, and jackals, and any other such animals. A fool who formerly delighted in tastes here and did evil actions here, on the dissolution of the body, after death, reappears in the company of animals that feed on dung.

20. "There are animals that are born, age, and die in darkness. And what animals are born, age, and die in darkness? Moths, maggots, and earthworms, and any other such animals. A fool who formerly delighted in tastes here and did evil actions here, on the dissolution of the body, after death, reappears in the company of animals that are born, age, and die in darkness.

21. "There are animals that are born, age, and die in water. And what animals are born, age, and die in water? Fish, turtles, and crocodiles, and any other such animals. A fool who formerly delighted in tastes here and did evil actions here, on the dissolution of the body, after death, reappears in the company of animals that are born, age, and die in water.

22. "There are animals that are born, age, and die in filth. And what animals are born, age, and die in filth? Those animals that are born, age, and die in a rotten fish or in a rotten corpse or in rotten porridge or in a cesspit or in a sewer. [169] A fool who formerly delighted in tastes here and did evil actions here, on the dissolution of the body, after death, reappears in the company of animals that are born, age, and die in filth.

23. "Bhikkhus, I could tell you in many ways about the animal

kingdom, so much so that it is hard to finish describing the suffering in the animal kingdom.

24. "Suppose a man threw into the sea a yoke with one hole in it, and the east wind carried it to the west, and the west wind carried it to the east, and the north wind carried it to the south, and the south wind carried it to the north. Suppose there were a blind turtle that came up once at the end of each century. What do you think, bhikkhus? Would that blind turtle put his neck into that yoke with one hole in it?"

"He might, venerable sir, sometime or other at the end of a long period."

"Bhikkhus, the blind turtle would sooner put his neck into that yoke with a single hole in it than a fool, once gone to perdition, would take to regain the human state, I say. Why is that? Because there is no practising of the Dhamma there, no practising of what is righteous, no doing of what is wholesome, no performance of merit. There mutual devouring prevails, and the slaughter of the weak.

25. "If, sometime or other, at the end of a long period, that fool comes back to the human state, it is into a low family that he is reborn—into a family of outcasts or hunters or bamboo-workers or cartwrights or scavengers—one that is poor with little to eat and drink, surviving with difficulty, where he scarcely finds food and clothing; and he is ugly, unsightly, and misshapen, sickly, blind, cripple-handed, lame, or paralysed; he gets no food, drink, clothes, [170] vehicles, garlands, scents and unguents, bed, lodging, and light; he misconducts himself in body, speech, and mind, and having done that, on the dissolution of the body, after death, he reappears in a state of deprivation, in an unhappy destination, in perdition, even in hell.

26. "Bhikkhus, suppose a gambler at the very first unlucky throw loses his child and his wife and all his property and furthermore goes into bondage himself, yet an unlucky throw such as that is negligible; it is a far more unlucky throw when a fool who misconducts himself in body, speech, and mind, on the dissolution of the body, after death, reappears in a state of deprivation, in an unhappy destination, in perdition, even in hell. This is the complete perfection of the fool's grade.[1201]

(THE WISE MAN)

27. "Bhikkhus, there are these three characteristics of a wise man, signs of a wise man, attributes of a wise man. What three? Here a wise man is one who thinks good thoughts, speaks good words, and does good deeds. If a wise man were not so, how would the wise know him thus: 'This person is a wise man, a true man'? But because a wise man is one who thinks good thoughts, speaks good words, and does good deeds, the wise know him thus: 'This person is a wise man, a true man.'

28. "A wise man feels pleasure and joy here and now in three ways. If a wise man is seated in an assembly or along a street or in a square and people there are discussing certain pertinent and relevant matters, then, if the wise man is one who abstains from killing living beings, from taking what is not given, from misconduct in sensual pleasures, [171] from false speech, from wine, liquor, and intoxicants, which are the basis of negligence, he thinks: 'These people are discussing certain pertinent and relevant matters; those things are not found in me, and I am not seen engaging in them.'[1202] This is the first kind of pleasure and joy that a wise man feels here and now.

29. "Again, when a robber culprit is caught, a wise man sees kings having many kinds of torture inflicted on him...(*as in §4*)...Then the wise man thinks thus: 'Because of such evil actions as those, when a robber culprit is caught, kings have many kinds of tortures inflicted on him. Those things are not found in me, and I am not seen engaging in those things.' This is the second kind of pleasure and joy that a wise man feels here and now.

30. "Again, when a wise man is on his chair or on his bed or resting on the ground, then the good actions that he did in the past—his good bodily, verbal, and mental conduct—cover him, overspread him, and envelop him. Just as the shadow of a great mountain peak in the evening covers, overspreads, and envelops the earth, so too, when a wise man is on his chair or on his bed or resting on the ground, then the good actions that he did in the past—his good bodily, verbal, and mental conduct—cover him, overspread him, and envelop him. Then the wise man thinks: 'I have not done what is evil, I have not done what is cruel, I have not done what is wicked. I have done what is good, I have done what is wholesome, I have made myself a

shelter from anguish. When I pass away, I shall go to the destination of those who have not done what is evil...who have made themselves a shelter from anguish.' He does not sorrow, grieve, and lament, he does not weep beating his breast and become distraught. This is the third kind of pleasure and joy that a wise man feels here and now.

31. "A wise man who has given himself over to good conduct of body, speech, and mind, [172] on the dissolution of the body, after death, reappears in a happy destination, even in heaven.

(HEAVEN)

32. "Were it rightly speaking to be said of anything: 'That is utterly wished for, utterly desired, utterly agreeable,' it is of heaven that, rightly speaking, this should be said, so much so that it is hard to finish describing the happiness of heaven."

When this was said, a bhikkhu asked the Blessed One: "But, venerable sir, can a simile be given?"

33. "It can, bhikkhu," the Blessed One said. "Bhikkhus, suppose that a Wheel-turning Monarch[1203] possessed the seven treasures and the four kinds of success, and because of that experienced pleasure and joy.

34. "What are the seven treasures? Here, when a head-anointed noble king has bathed his head on the Uposatha day of the fifteenth[1204] and has ascended to the upper palace chamber for the Uposatha, there appears to him the divine wheel-treasure with its thousand spokes, its tire, and its nave, complete in every aspect. On seeing it, the head-anointed noble king thinks thus: 'Now it has been heard by me that when a head-anointed noble king has bathed his head on the Uposatha day of the fifteenth and has ascended to the upper palace chamber for the Uposatha, and there appears to him the divine wheel-treasure with its thousand spokes, its tire, and its nave, complete in every aspect, then that king becomes a Wheel-turning Monarch. Am I then a Wheel-turning Monarch?'

35. "Then the head-anointed noble king rises from his seat, and taking a water vessel in his left hand, he sprinkles the wheel-treasure with his right hand, saying: 'Turn forward, good wheel-treasure; triumph, good wheel-treasure!' Then the wheel-treasure turns forward rolling in the eastern direction and the

Wheel-turning Monarch follows it with his four-constituent army. Now in whatever region the wheel-treasure pauses, there the Wheel-turning Monarch takes up his abode with his four-constituent army. And [173] opposing kings in the eastern direction come to the Wheel-turning Monarch and speak thus: 'Come, great king; welcome, great king; command, great king; advise, great king.' The Wheel-turning Monarch speaks thus: 'You should not kill living beings; you should not take what has not been given; you should not misconduct yourselves in sensual pleasures; you should not speak falsehood; you should not drink intoxicants; you should eat what you are accustomed to eat.' And the opposing kings in the eastern direction submit to the Wheel-turning Monarch.

"Then the wheel-treasure plunges into the eastern ocean and emerges again. And then it turns forward rolling in the southern direction…And the opposing kings in the southern direction submit to the Wheel-turning Monarch. Then the wheel-treasure plunges into the southern ocean and emerges again. And then it turns forward rolling in the western direction…And the opposing kings in the western direction submit to the Wheel-turning Monarch. Then the wheel-treasure plunges into the western ocean and emerges again. And then it turns forward rolling in the northern direction…And the opposing kings in the northern direction submit to the Wheel-turning Monarch.

"Now when the wheel-treasure has triumphed over the earth to the ocean's edge, it returns to the royal capital and remains as if fixed on its axle at the gate of the Wheel-turning Monarch's inner palace, as an adornment to the gate of his inner palace. Such is the wheel-treasure that appears to a Wheel-turning Monarch.

36. "Again, the elephant-treasure appears to the Wheel-turning Monarch, all white, with sevenfold stance, with supernormal power, flying through the air, the king of elephants named 'Uposatha.' On seeing him, the Wheel-turning Monarch's mind has confidence in him thus: 'It would be wonderful to ride the elephant, if he would undergo taming!' Then the elephant-treasure [174] undergoes taming just like a fine thoroughbred elephant well tamed for a long time. And it so happens that the Wheel-turning Monarch, when testing the elephant-treasure, mounts him in the morning, and after traversing the whole earth to the edge of the ocean, he returns to the royal capital to take his

morning meal. Such is the elephant-treasure that appears to a Wheel-turning Monarch.

37. "Again, the horse-treasure appears to the Wheel-turning Monarch, all white, with raven-black head, with mane like muñja grass, with supernormal power, flying through the air, the king of horses named 'Valāhaka' ['Thundercloud']. On seeing him, the Wheel-turning Monarch's mind has confidence in him thus: 'It would be wonderful to ride the horse, if he would undergo taming!' Then the horse-treasure undergoes taming just like a fine thoroughbred horse well tamed for a long time. And it so happens that the Wheel-turning Monarch, when testing the horse-treasure, mounts him in the morning, and after traversing the whole earth to the edge of the ocean, he returns to the royal capital to take his morning meal. Such is the horse-treasure that appears to a Wheel-turning Monarch.

38. "Again, the jewel-treasure appears to the Wheel-turning Monarch. The jewel is fine beryl of purest water, eight-faceted, and well cut. Now the radiance of the jewel-treasure spreads around for a whole league. And it so happens that when the Wheel-turning Monarch is testing the jewel-treasure, he draws up his four-constituent army in array, and mounting the jewel on top of his banner, he sets forth in the darkness and gloom of the night. Then all the [inhabitants of the] villages nearby begin their work by its light, thinking that it is day. Such is the jewel-treasure that appears to a Wheel-turning Monarch.

39. "Again, the woman-treasure appears to the Wheel-turning Monarch, beautiful, comely and graceful, possessing the supreme beauty of complexion, neither too tall nor too short, [175] neither too slim nor too stout, neither too dark nor too fair, surpassing human beauty without reaching divine beauty. The touch of the woman-treasure is such that it is like a tuft of kapok or a tuft of cotton-wool. When it is cool, her limbs are warm; when it is warm, her limbs are cool. From her body the scent of sandalwood comes forth, and from her mouth the scent of lotuses. She rises before the Wheel-turning Monarch and retires after him. She is eager to serve, agreeable in conduct, and sweet in speech. Since she is never unfaithful to the Wheel-turning Monarch even in thought, how could she be so in body? Such is the woman-treasure that appears to a Wheel-turning Monarch.

40. "Again, the steward-treasure appears to the Wheel-turning

Monarch. The divine eye born of past action is manifested in him whereby he sees hidden stores of treasure both with owners and ownerless. He approaches the Wheel-turning Monarch and says: 'Sire, you remain at ease. I shall take care of your monetary affairs.' And it so happens that when the Wheel-turning Monarch is testing the steward-treasure, he boards a boat, and putting out into the river Ganges, in midstream he tells the steward-treasure: 'I need gold and bullion, steward.'—'Then, sire, let the boat be steered towards one bank.'—'Steward, it is actually here that I need gold and bullion.' Then the steward-treasure plunges both hands into the water and draws up a pot full of gold and bullion, and he tells the Wheel-turning Monarch: 'Is this enough, sire? Is enough done, enough offered?'—'This is enough, steward, enough is done, enough offered.' Such is the steward-treasure that appears to a Wheel-turning Monarch.

41. "Again, the counsellor-treasure appears [176] to the Wheel-turning Monarch, wise, shrewd, and sagacious, capable of getting the Wheel-turning Monarch to promote that which is worthy of being promoted, to dismiss that which should be dismissed, and to establish that which should be established. He approaches the Wheel-turning Monarch and says: 'Sire, you remain at ease. I shall govern.' Such is the counsellor-treasure that appears to a Wheel-turning Monarch.

"These are the seven treasures that a Wheel-turning Monarch possesses.

42. "What are the four kinds of success? Here a Wheel-turning Monarch is handsome, comely, and graceful, possessing the supreme beauty of complexion, and he surpasses other human beings in that respect. This is the first kind of success that a Wheel-turning Monarch possesses.

43. "Again, a Wheel-turning Monarch lives long and endures long, and he surpasses other human beings in that respect. This is the second kind of success that a Wheel-turning Monarch possesses.

44. "Again, a Wheel-turning Monarch is free from illness and affliction, possessing a good digestion that is neither too cool nor too warm, and he surpasses other human beings in that respect. This is the third kind of success that a Wheel-turning Monarch possesses.

45. "Again, a Wheel-turning Monarch is dear and agreeable to

brahmins and householders. Just as a father is dear and agreeable to his children, so too a Wheel-turning Monarch is dear and agreeable to brahmins and householders. Brahmins and householders, too, are dear and agreeable to a Wheel-turning Monarch. Just as children are dear and agreeable to a father, so too brahmins and householders are dear and agreeable to a Wheel-turning Monarch. Once a Wheel-turning Monarch was driving in a pleasure park with his four-constituent army. Then brahmins and householders went to him and spoke thus: 'Sire, drive slowly that we may see you longer.' And so he told his charioteer: [177] 'Charioteer, drive slowly that I may see the brahmins and householders longer.' This is the fourth kind of success that a Wheel-turning Monarch possesses.

"These are the four kinds of success that a Wheel-turning Monarch possesses.

46. "What do you think, bhikkhus? Would a Wheel-turning Monarch experience pleasure and joy because of possessing these seven treasures and these four kinds of success?"

"Venerable sir, a Wheel-turning Monarch would experience pleasure and joy because of possessing even one treasure, let alone seven treasures and four kinds of success."

47. Then, taking a small stone the size of his hand, the Blessed One addressed the bhikkhus thus: "What do you think, bhikkhus? Which is the greater, this small stone that I have taken, the size of my hand, or Himalaya, the king of mountains?"

"Venerable sir, the small stone that the Blessed One has taken, the size of his hand, does not count beside Himalaya, the king of mountains; it is not even a fraction, there is no comparison."

"So too, bhikkhus, the pleasure and joy that a Wheel-turning Monarch would experience because of possessing the seven treasures and the four kinds of success does not count beside the happiness of heaven; it is not even a fraction, there is no comparison.

48. "If, some time or other, at the end of a long period, the wise man comes back to the human state, it is into a high family that he is reborn—into a family of well-to-do nobles, or well-to-do brahmins, or well-to-do householders—one that is rich, of great wealth, of great possessions, with abundant gold and silver, with abundant assets and means, and with abundant money and grain. He is handsome, comely and graceful, possessing the

supreme beauty of complexion. He obtains food and drink, clothes, vehicles, garlands, scents and unguents, bed, lodging, and light. He conducts himself well in body, speech, and mind, [178] and having done so, on the dissolution of the body, after death, he reappears in a happy destination, even in the heavenly world.

49. "Bhikkhus, suppose a gambler at the very first lucky throw won a great fortune, yet a lucky throw such as that is negligible; it is a far more lucky throw when a wise man who conducts himself well in body, speech, and mind, on the dissolution of the body, after death, reappears in a happy destination, even in the heavenly world.[1205] This is the complete perfection of the wise man's grade."

That is what the Blessed One said. The bhikkhus were satisfied and delighted in the Blessed One's words.

130 *Devadūta Sutta*
The Divine Messengers

1. THUS HAVE I HEARD. On one occasion the Blessed One was living at Sāvatthī in Jeta's Grove, Anāthapiṇḍika's Park. There he addressed the bhikkhus thus: "Bhikkhus."—"Venerable sir," they replied. The Blessed One said this:

2. "Bhikkhus, suppose there were two houses with doors and a man with good sight standing there between them saw people going in and coming out and passing to and fro. So too, with the divine eye, which is purified and surpasses the human, I see beings passing away and reappearing, inferior and superior, fair and ugly, fortunate and unfortunate. I understand how beings pass on according to their actions thus: 'These worthy beings who were well conducted in body, speech, and mind, not revilers of noble ones, right in their views, giving effect to right views in their actions, on the dissolution of the body, after death, have reappeared in a happy destination, even in the heavenly world. Or these worthy beings who were well conducted in body, speech, and mind, not [179] revilers of noble ones, right in their views, giving effect to right views in their actions, on the dissolution of the body, after death, have reappeared among human beings. But these worthy beings who were ill conducted in body, speech, and mind, revilers of noble ones, wrong in their views, giving effect to wrong views in their actions, on the dissolution of the body, after death, have reappeared in the realm of ghosts. Or these worthy beings who were ill conducted...on the dissolution of the body, after death, have reappeared in the animal world. Or these worthy beings who were ill conducted ...on the dissolution of the body, after death, have reappeared in a state of deprivation, in an unhappy destination, in perdition, even in hell.'

3. "Now the wardens of hell seize such a being by the arms

and present him to King Yama,[1206] saying: 'Sire, this man has ill-treated his mother, ill-treated his father, ill-treated recluses, ill-treated brahmins; he has had no respect for the elders of his clan. Let the king order his punishment.'

4. "Then King Yama presses and questions and cross-questions him about the first divine messenger: 'Good man, did you not see the first divine messenger to appear in the world?'[1207] He says: 'I did not, venerable sir.' Then King Yama says: 'Good man, have you never seen in the world a young tender infant lying prone, fouled in his own excrement and urine?' He says: 'I have, venerable sir.'

"Then King Yama says: 'Good man, did it never occur to you—an intelligent and mature man—"I too am subject to birth, I am not exempt from birth: surely I had better do good by body, speech, and mind"?' He says: 'I was unable, venerable sir, I was negligent.' Then King Yama says: 'Good man, through negligence you have failed to do good by body, speech, and mind. Certainly they will deal with you according to your negligence. But this evil action of yours was not done by your mother or your father, [180] or by your brother or your sister, or by your friends and companions, or by your kinsmen and relatives, or by recluses and brahmins, or by gods: this evil action was done by you yourself, and you yourself will experience its result.'

5. "Then, after pressing and questioning and cross-questioning him about the first divine messenger, King Yama presses and questions and cross-questions him about the second divine messenger: 'Good man, did you not see the second divine messenger to appear in the world?' He says: 'I did not, venerable sir.' Then King Yama says: 'Good man, have you never seen in the world a man—or a woman—at eighty, ninety, or a hundred years, aged, as crooked as a roof bracket, doubled up, supported by a walking stick, tottering, frail, youth gone, teeth broken, grey-haired, scanty-haired, bald, wrinkled, with limbs all blotchy?' He says: 'I have, venerable sir.'

"Then King Yama says: 'Good man, did it never occur to you—an intelligent and mature man—"I too am subject to ageing, I am not exempt from ageing: surely I had better do good by body, speech, and mind"?' He says: 'I was unable, venerable sir, I was negligent.' Then King Yama says: 'Good man, through negligence you have failed to do good by body, speech, and mind.

Certainly they will deal with you according to your negligence. But this evil action of yours was not done by your mother...or by gods: this evil action was done by you yourself, and you yourself will experience its result.'

6. "Then, after pressing and questioning and cross-questioning him about the second divine messenger, King Yama presses and questions and cross-questions him about the third divine messenger: [181] 'Good man, did you not see the third divine messenger to appear in the world?' He says: 'I did not, venerable sir.' Then King Yama says: 'Good man, have you never seen in the world a man—or a woman—afflicted, suffering, and gravely ill, lying fouled in his own excrement and urine, lifted up by some and set down by others?' He says: 'I have, venerable sir.'

"Then King Yama says: 'Good man, did it never occur to you—an intelligent and mature man—"I too am subject to sickness, I am not exempt from sickness: surely I had better do good by body, speech, and mind"?' He says: 'I was unable, venerable sir, I was negligent.' Then King Yama says: 'Good man, through negligence you have failed to do good by body, speech, and mind. Certainly they will deal with you according to your negligence. But this evil action of yours was not done by your mother...or by gods: this evil action was done by you yourself, and you yourself will experience its result.'

7. "Then, after pressing and questioning and cross-questioning him about the third divine messenger, King Yama presses and questions and cross-questions him about the fourth divine messenger: 'Good man, did you not see the fourth divine messenger to appear in the world?' He says: 'I did not, venerable sir.' Then King Yama says: 'Good man, have you never seen in the world, when a robber culprit is caught, kings having many kinds of tortures inflicted on him: having him flogged with whips...(*as Sutta 129, §4*)...and having his head cut off with a sword?' He says: 'I have, venerable sir.'

"Then King Yama says: 'Good man, did it never occur to you—an intelligent and mature man—"Those who do evil actions have such tortures of various kinds inflicted on them here and now; [182] so what in the hereafter? Surely I had better do good by body, speech, and mind"?' He says: 'I was unable, venerable sir, I was negligent.' Then King Yama says: 'Good man, through negligence you have failed to do good by body, speech, and mind. Certainly they will deal with you according to your negligence. But this evil action of yours was not done by your mother...or by gods: this evil action was done by you yourself, and you yourself will experience its result.'

8. "Then, after pressing and questioning and cross-questioning him about the fourth divine messenger, King Yama presses and questions and cross-questions him about the fifth divine messenger: 'Good man, did you not see the fifth divine messenger to appear in the world?' He says: 'I did not, venerable sir.' Then King Yama says: 'Good man, have you never seen in the world a man—or a woman—one-day dead, two-days dead, three-days dead, bloated, livid, and oozing with matter?' He says: 'I have, venerable sir.'

"Then King Yama says: 'Good man, did it never occur to you—an intelligent and mature man—"I too am subject to death, I am not exempt from death: surely I had better do good by body, speech, and mind"?' He says: 'I was unable, venerable sir, I was negligent.' Then King Yama says: 'Good man, through negligence you have failed to do good by body, speech, and mind. Certainly they will deal with you according to your negligence. But this evil action of yours was not done by your mother...or by gods: this evil action was done by you yourself, and you yourself will experience its result.'

9. "Then, after pressing and questioning and cross-questioning him about the fifth divine messenger, King Yama is silent.

10. "Now the wardens of hell [183] torture him with the fivefold transfixing.[1208] They drive a red-hot iron stake through one hand, they drive a red-hot iron stake through the other hand, they drive a red-hot iron stake through one foot, they drive a red-hot iron stake through the other foot, they drive a red-hot iron stake through his belly. There he feels painful, racking, piercing feelings. Yet he does not die so long as that evil action has not exhausted its result.

11. "Next the wardens of hell throw him down and pare him with axes. There he feels painful, racking, piercing feelings. Yet he does not die so long as that evil action has not exhausted its result.

12. "Next the wardens of hell set him with his feet up and his head down and pare him with adzes. There he feels painful, racking, piercing feelings. Yet he does not die so long as that evil action has not exhausted its result.

13. "Next the wardens of hell harness him to a chariot and drive him back and forth across ground that is burning, blazing, and glowing. There he feels painful, racking, piercing feelings. Yet he does not die so long as that evil action has not exhausted its result.

14. "Next the wardens of hell make him climb up and down a great mound of coals that are burning, blazing, and glowing. There he feels painful, racking, piercing feelings. Yet he does not die so long as that evil action has not exhausted its result.

15. "Next the wardens of hell take him feet up and head down and plunge him into a red-hot metal cauldron that is burning, blazing, and glowing. He is cooked there in a swirl of froth. And as he is being cooked there in a swirl of froth, he is swept now up, now down, and now across. There he feels painful, racking, piercing feelings. Yet he does not die so long as that evil action has not exhausted its result.

16. "Next the wardens of hell throw him into the Great Hell. Now as to that Great Hell, bhikkhus:

> It has four corners and is built
> With four doors, one set in each side,
> Walled up with iron all around
> And shut in with an iron roof.
> Its floor as well is made of iron
> And heated till it glows with fire.
> The range is a full hundred leagues
> Which it covers all-pervasively.

17. "Now the flames that surge out from the Great Hell's eastern wall dash against its western wall. The flames that surge out from its western wall dash against [184] its eastern wall. The flames that surge out from its northern wall dash against its southern wall. The flames that surge out from its southern wall dash against its northern wall. The flames that dash out from the bottom dash against the top. And the flames that surge out from the top dash against the bottom. There he feels painful, racking, piercing feelings. Yet he does not die so long as that evil action has not exhausted its result.

18. "Some time or other, bhikkhus, at the end of a long period, there comes an occasion when the Great Hell's eastern door is

opened. He runs towards it, treading quickly. As he does so, his outer skin burns, his inner skin burns, his flesh burns, his sinews burn, his bones turn to smoke; and it is the same when his foot is uplifted. When at long last he reaches the door, then it is shut. There he feels painful, racking, piercing feelings. Yet he does not die so long as that evil action has not exhausted its result.

"Some time or other, at the end of a long period, there comes an occasion when the Great Hell's western door is opened... when its northern door is opened...when its southern door is opened. He runs towards it, treading quickly...When at long last he reaches the door, then it is shut. There he feels painful, racking, piercing feelings. Yet he does not die so long as that evil action has not exhausted its result.

19. "Some time or other, bhikkhus, at the end of a long period, there comes an occasion when the Great Hell's eastern door is opened. He runs towards it, treading quickly. As he does so, his outer skin burns, his inner skin burns, his flesh burns, his sinews burn, his bones turn to smoke; and it is the same when his foot is uplifted. He comes out by that door.

20. "Immediately next to the Great Hell [185] is the vast Hell of Excrement. He falls into that. In that Hell of Excrement needle-mouthed creatures bore through his outer skin and bore through his inner skin and bore through his flesh and bore through his sinews and bore through his bones and devour his marrow. There he feels painful, racking, piercing feelings. Yet he does not die so long as that evil action has not exhausted its result.

21. "Immediately next to the Hell of Excrement is the vast Hell of Hot Embers. He falls into that. There he feels painful, racking, piercing feelings. Yet he does not die so long as that evil action has not exhausted its result.

22. "Immediately next to the Hell of Hot Embers is the vast Wood of Simbali Trees, a league high, bristling with thorns sixteen finger-breadths long, burning, blazing, and glowing. They make him climb up and down those trees. There he feels painful, racking, piercing feelings. Yet he does not die so long as that evil action has not exhausted its result.

23. "Immediately next to the Wood of Simbali Trees is a vast Wood of Sword-leaf Trees. He goes into that. The leaves, stirred by the wind, cut his hands and cut his feet and cut his hands and feet; they cut his ears and cut his nose and cut his ears and nose.

There he feels painful, racking, piercing feelings. Yet he does not die so long as that evil action has not exhausted its result.

24. "Immediately next to the Wood of Sword-leaf Trees is a great river of caustic water. He falls into that. There he is swept along the stream and against the stream and both along and against the stream. There he feels painful, racking, piercing feelings. Yet he does not die so long as that evil action has not exhausted its result.

25. "Next the wardens of hell pull him out with a hook, [186] and setting him on the ground, they ask him: 'Good man, what do you want?' He says: 'I am hungry, venerable sirs.' Then the wardens of hell prise open his mouth with red-hot iron tongs, burning, blazing, and glowing, and they throw into his mouth a red-hot metal ball, burning, blazing, and glowing. It burns his lips, it burns his mouth, it burns his throat, it burns his stomach, and it passes out below carrying with it his intestines and mesentery. There he feels painful, racking, piercing feelings. Yet he does not die so long as that evil action has not exhausted its result.

26. "Next the wardens of hell ask him: 'Good man, what do you want?' He says: 'I am thirsty, venerable sirs.' Then the wardens of hell prise open his mouth with red-hot iron tongs, burning, blazing, and glowing, and they pour into his mouth molten copper, burning, blazing, and glowing. It burns his lips, it burns his mouth, it burns his throat, it burns his stomach, and it passes out below carrying with it his intestines and mesentery. There he feels painful, racking, piercing feelings. Yet he does not die so long as that evil action has not exhausted its result.

27. "Then the wardens of hell throw him back again into the Great Hell.

28. "It has happened that King Yama thought: 'Those in the world who do evil unwholesome actions indeed have all these many kinds of tortures inflicted on them. Oh, that I might attain the human state, that a Tathāgata, accomplished and fully enlightened, might appear in the world, that I might wait on that Blessed One, that the Blessed One might teach me the Dhamma, and that I might come to understand that Blessed One's Dhamma!'

29. "Bhikkhus, I tell you this not as something I heard from another recluse or brahmin. I tell you this as something that I have actually known, seen, and discovered by myself." [187]

30. That is what the Blessed One said. When the Sublime One had said that, the Teacher said further:

"Though warned by the divine messengers,
Full many are the negligent,
And people may sorrow long indeed
Once gone down to the lower world.
But when by the divine messengers
Good people here in this life are warned,
They do not dwell in negligence
But practise well the noble Dhamma.
Clinging they look upon with fear
For it produces birth and death;
And by not clinging they are freed
In the destruction of birth and death.
They dwell in bliss for they are safe
And reach Nibbāna here and now.
They are beyond all fear and hate;
They have escaped all suffering."

4

The Division of Expositions

(*Vibhangavagga*)

131 *Bhaddekaratta Sutta*
A Single Excellent Night

1. THUS HAVE I HEARD.[1209] On one occasion the Blessed One was living at Sāvatthī in Jeta's Grove, Anāthapiṇḍika's Park. There he addressed the bhikkhus thus: "Bhikkhus."—"Venerable sir," they replied. The Blessed One said this:

2. "Bhikkhus, I shall teach you the summary and exposition of 'One Who Has Had a Single Excellent Night.'[1210] Listen and attend closely to what I shall say."—"Yes, venerable sir," the bhikkhus replied. The Blessed One said this:

3. "Let not a person revive the past
Or on the future build his hopes;[1211]
For the past has been left behind
And the future has not been reached.
Instead with insight let him see
Each presently arisen state;[1212]
Let him know that and be sure of it,
Invincibly, unshakeably.[1213]
Today the effort must be made;
Tomorrow Death may come, who knows?
No bargain with Mortality
Can keep him and his hordes away,
But one who dwells thus ardently,
Relentlessly, by day, by night—
It is he, the Peaceful Sage has said,[1214]
Who has had a single excellent night. [188]

4. "How, bhikkhus, does one revive the past? One finds delight there thinking, 'I had such material form in the past.'[1215] One finds delight there thinking, 'I had such feeling in the past,'...'I had such perception in the past,'...'I had such formations

in the past,'...'I had such consciousness in the past.' That is how one revives the past.

5. "And how, bhikkhus, does one not revive the past? One does not find delight there thinking, 'I had such material form in the past.'[1216] One does not find delight there thinking, 'I had such feeling in the past,'...'I had such perception in the past,'...'I had such formations in the past,'...'I had such consciousness in the past.' That is how one does not revive the past.

6. "And how, bhikkhus, does one build up hope upon the future? One finds delight there thinking, 'May I have such material form in the future!'[1217] One finds delight there thinking, 'May I have such feeling in the future!'...'May I have such perception in the future!'...'May I have such formations in the future!'...'May I have such consciousness in the future!' That is how one builds up hope upon the future.

7. "And how, bhikkhus, does one not build up hope upon the future? One does not find delight there thinking, 'May I have such material form in the future!' One does not find delight there thinking, 'May I have such feeling in the future!'...'May I have such perception in the future!'...'May I have such formations in the future!'...'May I have such consciousness in the future!' That is how one does not build up hope upon the future.

8. "And how, bhikkhus, is one vanquished in regard to presently arisen states?[1218] Here, bhikkhus, an untaught ordinary person, who has no regard for noble ones and is unskilled and undisciplined in their Dhamma, who has no regard for true men and is unskilled and undisciplined in their Dhamma, regards material form as self, or self as possessed of material form, or material form as in self, or self as in material form. He regards feeling as self...perception as self...formations as self [189]...consciousness as self, or self as possessed of consciousness, or consciousness as in self, or self as in consciousness. That is how one is vanquished in regard to presently arisen states.

9. "And how, bhikkhus, is one invincible in regard to presently arisen states? Here, bhikkhus, a well-taught noble disciple, who has regard for noble ones and is skilled and disciplined in their Dhamma, who has regard for true men and is skilled and disciplined in their Dhamma, does not regard material form as self, or self as possessed of material form, or material form as in self, or self as in material form. He does not regard feeling as

self...perception as self...formations as self...consciousness as self, or self as possessed of consciousness, or consciousness as in self, or self as in consciousness. That is how one is invincible in regard to presently arisen states.

10. "Let not a person revive the past...
Who has had a single excellent night.

11. "So it was with reference to this that it was said: 'Bhikkhus, I shall teach you the summary and exposition of "One Who Has Had a Single Excellent Night."'"

That is what the Blessed One said. The bhikkhus were satisfied and delighted in the Blessed One's words.

132 *Ānandabhaddekaratta Sutta*
Ānanda and A Single Excellent Night

1. THUS HAVE I HEARD. On one occasion the Blessed One was living at Sāvatthī in Jeta's Grove, Anāthapiṇḍika's Park.

2. Now on that occasion the venerable Ānanda was instructing, urging, rousing, and gladdening [190] the bhikkhus with talk on the Dhamma in the assembly hall. He was reciting the summary and exposition of "One Who Has Had a Single Excellent Night."

Then, in the evening, the Blessed One rose from meditation and went to the assembly hall. He sat down on a seat made ready and asked the bhikkhus: "Bhikkhus, who has been instructing, urging, rousing, and gladdening the bhikkhus with talk on the Dhamma in the assembly hall? Who has been reciting the summary and exposition of 'One Who Has Had a Single Excellent Night'?"

"It was the venerable Ānanda, venerable sir."

Then the Blessed One asked the venerable Ānanda: "Ānanda, how were you instructing, urging, rousing, and gladdening the bhikkhus with talk on the Dhamma, and reciting the summary and exposition of 'One Who Has Had a Single Excellent Night'?"

3–10. "I was doing so thus, venerable sir: [191]

> 'Let not a person revive the past…
> (*Repeat the whole of the last sutta, §§3–10 up to:*)
> Who has had a single excellent night.'

11. "I was instructing, urging, rousing, and gladdening the bhikkhus with talk on the Dhamma thus, and reciting the summary and exposition of 'One Who Has Had a Single Excellent Night' thus."

"Good, good, Ānanda! It is good that you were instructing, urging, rousing, and gladdening the bhikkhus with talk on the

Dhamma thus, and reciting the summary and exposition of 'One Who Has Had a Single Excellent Night' thus:

> 12–19. "Let not a person revive the past…
> (*Repeat the whole of the last sutta, §§3–10 up to:*)
> Who has had a single excellent night."

That is what the Blessed One said. The venerable Ānanda was satisfied and delighted in the Blessed One's words.

133 *Mahākaccānabhaddekaratta Sutta*
Mahā Kaccāna and A Single Excellent Night

[192] 1. THUS HAVE I HEARD. On one occasion the Blessed One was living at Rājagaha in the Park of the Hot Springs. Then, when it was near dawn, the venerable Samiddhi went to the hot springs to bathe his limbs. After bathing he came up out of the water and stood dressed in one robe, drying his limbs. Then, when the night was well advanced, a certain deity of beautiful appearance who illuminated the whole of the Hot Springs, approached the venerable Samiddhi. Standing at one side, the deity said to him:

2. "Bhikkhu, do you remember the summary and exposition of 'One Who Has Had a Single Excellent Night'?"

"Friend, I do not remember the summary and exposition of 'One Who Has Had a Single Excellent Night.' But, friend, do you remember the summary and exposition of 'One Who Has Had a Single Excellent Night'?"

"Bhikkhu, I too do not remember the summary and exposition of 'One Who Has Had a Single Excellent Night.' But, bhikkhu, do you remember the stanzas of 'One Who Has Had a Single Excellent Night'?"

"Friend, I do not remember the stanzas of 'One Who Has Had a Single Excellent Night.' But, friend, do you remember the stanzas of 'One Who Has Had a Single Excellent Night'?"

"Bhikkhu, I too do not remember the stanzas of 'One Who Has Had a Single Excellent Night.' But, bhikkhu, learn the summary and exposition of 'One Who Has Had a Single Excellent Night.' Bhikkhu, master the summary and exposition of 'One Who Has Had a Single Excellent Night.' Bhikkhu, remember the summary and exposition of 'One Who Has Had a Single

Excellent Night.' Bhikkhu, the summary and exposition of 'One Who Has Had a Single Excellent Night' is beneficial, it belongs to the fundamentals of the holy life."

That is what was said by the deity, who thereupon vanished at once.

3. Then, when the night was over, the venerable Samiddhi went to the Blessed One. After paying homage to him, he sat down at one side, [193] told the Blessed One all that had occurred, and said: "It would be good, venerable sir, if the Blessed One would teach me the summary and exposition of 'One Who Has Had a Single Excellent Night.'"

4. "Then, bhikkhu, listen and attend closely to what I shall say."—"Yes, venerable sir," the venerable Samiddhi replied. The Blessed One said:

5. "Let not a person revive the past
Or on the future build his hopes;
For the past has been left behind
And the future has not been reached.
Instead with insight let him see
Each presently arisen state;
Let him know that and be sure of it,
Invincibly, unshakeably.
Today the effort must be made;
Tomorrow Death may come, who knows?
No bargain with Mortality
Can keep him and his hordes away.
But one who dwells thus ardently,
Relentlessly, by day, by night—
It is he, the Peaceful Sage has said,
Who has had a single excellent night."

6. That is what the Blessed One said. Having said this, the Sublime One rose from his seat and went into his dwelling.

7. Then, soon after the Blessed One had gone, the bhikkhus considered:[1219] "Now, friends, the Blessed One has risen from his seat and gone into his dwelling after giving a summary in brief without expounding the detailed meaning. Now who will expound this in detail?" [194] Then they considered: "The venerable Mahā Kaccāna is praised by the Teacher and

esteemed by his wise companions in the holy life. He is capable of expounding the detailed meaning. Suppose we went to him and asked him the meaning of this."

8. Then the bhikkhus went to the venerable Mahā Kaccāna and exchanged greetings with him. When this courteous and amiable talk was finished, they sat down to one side and they told him what had taken place, adding: "Let the venerable Mahā Kaccāna expound it to us."

9. [The venerable Mahā Kaccāna replied:] "Friends, it is as though a man needing heartwood, seeking heartwood, wandering in search of heartwood, [195] thought that heartwood should be sought for among the branches and leaves of a great tree standing possessed of heartwood, after he had passed over the root and the trunk. And so it is with you, venerable sirs, that you think that I should be asked about the meaning of this, after you passed the Blessed One by when you were face to face with the Teacher. For knowing, the Blessed One knows; seeing, he sees; he is vision, he is knowledge, he is the Dhamma, he is the holy one; he is the sayer, the proclaimer, the elucidator of meaning, the giver of the Deathless, the lord of the Dhamma, the Tathāgata. That was the time when you should have asked the Blessed One the meaning. As he told you, so you should have remembered it."

10. "Surely, friend Kaccāna, knowing, the Blessed One knows; seeing, he sees; he is vision...the Tathāgata. That was the time when we should have asked the Blessed One the meaning. As he told us, so we should have remembered it. Yet the venerable Mahā Kaccāna is praised by the Teacher and esteemed by his wise companions in the holy life. The venerable Mahā Kaccāna is capable of expounding the detailed meaning of this summary given in brief by the Blessed One without expounding the detailed meaning. Let the venerable Mahā Kaccāna expound it without finding it troublesome."

11. "Then listen, friends, and attend closely to what I shall say."—"Yes, friend," the bhikkhus replied. The venerable Mahā Kaccāna said this:

12. "Friends, when the Blessed One rose from his seat and went into his dwelling after giving a summary in brief without expounding the detailed meaning, that is:

'Let not a person revive the past...
Who has had a single excellent night,'

I understand the detailed meaning of it to be as follows.

13. "How, friends, does one revive the past? [196] One's consciousness becomes bound up with desire and lust there thinking, 'My eye was thus in the past and forms were thus.'[1220] Because one's consciousness is bound up with desire and lust, one delights in that. When one delights in that, one revives the past.

"One's consciousness becomes bound up with desire and lust there thinking, 'My ear was thus in the past and sounds were thus...My nose and odours...My tongue and flavours...My body and tangibles...My mind was thus in the past and mind-objects were thus.' Because one's consciousness is bound up with desire and lust, one delights in that. When one delights in that, one revives the past. That is how one revives the past.

14. "How does one not revive the past? One's consciousness does not become bound up with desire and lust there thinking, 'My eye was thus in the past and forms were thus.' Because one's consciousness is not bound up with desire and lust, one does not delight in that. When one does not delight in that, one does not revive the past.

"One's consciousness does not become bound up with desire and lust there thinking, 'My ear was thus in the past and sounds were thus...My nose and odours...My tongue and flavours...My body and tangibles...My mind was thus in the past and mind-objects were thus.' Because one's consciousness is not bound up with desire and lust, one does not delight in that. When one does not delight in that, one does not revive the past. That is how one does not revive the past.

15. "How, friends, does one build up hope upon the future? One sets one's heart on obtaining what has not yet been obtained, thinking, 'May my eye be thus in the future and forms be thus!' Because one sets one's heart thus, one delights in that. When one delights in that, one builds up hope upon the future.

"One sets one's heart on obtaining what has not yet been obtained, thinking, 'May my ear be thus in the future and sounds be thus!...May my nose and odours...May my tongue and flavours...May my body and tangibles...May my mind be thus in the future and [197] mind-objects be thus!' Because one sets one's heart thus, one delights in that. When one delights in that, one builds up hope upon the future. That is how one builds up hope upon the future.

16. "How, friends, does one not build up hope upon the future? One does not set one's heart on obtaining what has not yet been obtained, thinking, 'May my eye be thus in the future and forms be thus!' Because one does not set one's heart thus, one does not delight in that. When one does not delight in that, one does not build up hope upon the future.

"One does not set one's heart on obtaining what has not yet been obtained, thinking, 'May my ear be thus in the future and sounds be thus!...May my nose and odours...May my tongue and flavours...May my body and tangibles...May my mind be thus in the future and mind-objects be thus!' Because one does not set one's heart thus, one does not delight in that. When one does not delight in that, one does not build up hope upon the future. That is how one does not build up hope upon the future.

17. "How is one vanquished in regard to presently arisen states? In regard to the eye and forms that are presently arisen, one's consciousness is bound up with desire and lust for that which is presently arisen. Because one's consciousness is bound up with desire and lust, one delights in that. When one delights in that, one is vanquished in regard to presently arisen states.

"In regard to the ear and sounds that are presently arisen...the nose and odours...the tongue and flavours...the body and tangibles...the mind and mind-objects that are presently arisen, one's consciousness is bound up with desire and lust for that which is presently arisen. Because one's consciousness is bound up with desire and lust, one delights in that. When one delights in that, one is vanquished in regard to presently arisen states. That is how one is vanquished in regard to presently arisen states.

18. "How is one invincible in regard to presently arisen states? In regard to the eye and forms that are presently arisen, one's consciousness is not bound up with desire and lust for that which is presently arisen. Because one's consciousness is not bound up with desire and lust, one does not delight in that. When one does not delight in that, one is invincible in regard to presently arisen states.

"In regard to the ear and sounds that are presently arisen... the nose and odours...the tongue and flavours...the body and tangibles...the mind and mind-objects that are presently arisen, [198] one's consciousness is not bound up with desire and lust for that which is presently arisen. Because one's consciousness is not bound up with desire and lust, one does not delight in that. When one does not delight in that, one is invincible in regard to presently arisen states. That is how one is invincible in regard to presently arisen states.

19. "Friends, when the Blessed One rose from his seat and went into his dwelling after giving a summary in brief without expounding the detailed meaning, that is:

> 'Let not a person revive the past...
> Who has had a single excellent night,'

I understand the detailed meaning of this summary to be thus. Now, friends, if you wish, go to the Blessed One and ask him about the meaning of this. As the Blessed One explains it to you, so you should remember it."

20. Then the bhikkhus, having delighted and rejoiced in the venerable Mahā Kaccāna's words, rose from their seats and went to the Blessed One. After paying homage to him, they sat down at one side and told the Blessed One all that had taken place after he had left, adding: [199] "Then, venerable sir, we went to the venerable Mahā Kaccāna and asked him about the meaning. The venerable Mahā Kaccāna expounded the meaning to us with these terms, statements, and phrases."

21. "Mahā Kaccāna is wise, bhikkhus, Mahā Kaccāna has great wisdom. If you had asked me the meaning of this, I would have explained it to you in the same way that Mahā Kaccāna has explained it. Such is its meaning, and so you should remember it."

That is what the Blessed One said. The bhikkhus were satisfied and delighted in the Blessed One's words.

134 *Lomasakangiyabhaddekaratta Sutta*
Lomasakangiya and A Single Excellent Night

1. THUS HAVE I HEARD. On one occasion the Blessed One was living at Sāvatthī in Jeta's Grove, Anāthapiṇḍika's Park. Now on that occasion the venerable Lomasakangiya was living in the Sakyan country at Kapilavatthu in Nigrodha's Park.[1221]

2. Then, when the night was well advanced, Candana, a young deity of beautiful appearance who illuminated the whole of Nigrodha's Park, approached the venerable Lomasakangiya. Standing at one side, Candana the young deity said to him:

"Bhikkhu, do you remember the summary and exposition of 'One Who Has Had a Single Excellent Night'?" [200]

"Friend, I do not remember the summary and exposition of 'One Who Has Had a Single Excellent Night.' But, friend, do you remember the summary and exposition of 'One Who Has Had a Single Excellent Night'?"

"Bhikkhu, I too do not remember the summary and exposition of 'One Who Has Had a Single Excellent Night.' But, bhikkhu, do you remember the stanza of 'One Who Has Had a Single Excellent Night'?"

"Friend, I do not remember the stanza of 'One Who Has Had a Single Excellent Night.' But, friend, do you remember the stanza of 'One Who Has Had a Single Excellent Night'?"

"Bhikkhu, I remember the stanza of 'One Who Has Had a Single Excellent Night.'"

"But, friend, in what way do you remember the stanza of 'One Who Has Had a Single Excellent Night'?"

"Bhikkhu, once the Blessed One was living among the gods of the heaven of the Thirty-three, on the Red Marble Stone at the root of the Pāricchattaka tree.[1222] There the Blessed One recited the summary and exposition of 'One Who Has Had a Single Excellent Night' to the gods of the heaven of the Thirty-three:

3. 'Let not a person revive the past
Or on the future build his hopes;
For the past has been left behind
And the future has not been reached.
Instead with insight let him see
Each presently arisen state;
Let him know that and be sure of it,
Invincibly, unshakeably.
Today the effort must be made;
Tomorrow Death may come, who knows?
No bargain with Mortality
Can keep him and his hordes away.
But one who dwells thus ardently,
Relentlessly, by day, by night—
It is he, the Peaceful Sage has said,
Who has had a single excellent night.'

4. "Bhikkhu, I remember the stanza of 'One Who Has Had a Single Excellent Night' thus. Bhikkhu, learn the summary and exposition of 'One Who Has Had a Single Excellent Night.' Bhikkhu, master the summary and exposition of 'One Who Has Had A Single Excellent Night.' Bhikkhu, remember the summary and exposition of 'One Who Has Had a Single Excellent Night.' Bhikkhu, the summary and exposition of 'One Who Has Had a Single Excellent Night' is beneficial, it belongs to the fundamentals of the holy life."

That is what was said by Candana the young deity, who thereupon vanished at once.

5. Then, when the night was over, the venerable Lomasakangiya set his resting place in order, and taking his bowl and outer robe, set out to wander by stages to Sāvatthī. He [201] at length arrived at Sāvatthī, and went to the Blessed One in Jeta's Grove, Anāthapiṇḍika's Park. After paying homage to him, he sat down at one side, told the Blessed One all that had occurred, and said: "It would be good, venerable sir, if the Blessed One would teach me the summary and exposition of 'One Who Has Had a Single Excellent Night.'"

6. "Bhikkhu, do you know that young deity?"

"No, venerable sir."

"Bhikkhu, that young deity is named Candana. He heeds the

Dhamma, gives it attention, engages it with all his mind, hears it with eager ears. So, bhikkhu, listen and attend closely to what I shall say."

"Yes, venerable sir," the venerable Lomasakangiya replied to the Blessed One. The Blessed One said this:

7–14. "Let not a person revive the past…
(*Repeat the whole of Sutta 131, §§3–10 up to:*) [202]
Who has had a single excellent night."

That is what the Blessed One said. The Venerable Lomasakangiya was satisfied and delighted in the Blessed One's words.

135 *Cūḷakammavibhaṅga Sutta*
The Shorter Exposition of Action

1. THUS HAVE I HEARD. On one occasion the Blessed One was living at Sāvatthī in Jeta's Grove, Anāthapiṇḍika's Park.

2. Then the brahmin student Subha, Todeyya's son, went to the Blessed One and exchanged greetings with him.[1223] When this courteous and amiable talk was finished, he sat down at one side and asked the Blessed One:

3. "Master Gotama, what is the cause and condition why human beings are seen to be inferior and superior? For people are seen to be short-lived and long-lived, sickly and healthy, ugly and beautiful, uninfluential and influential, poor and wealthy, low-born and high-born, stupid and [203] wise. What is the cause and condition, Master Gotama, why human beings are seen to be inferior and superior?"

4. "Student, beings are owners of their actions, heirs of their actions; they originate from their actions, are bound to their actions, have their actions as their refuge. It is action that distinguishes beings as inferior and superior."

"I do not understand in detail the meaning of Master Gotama's statement, which he spoke in brief without expounding the meaning in detail. It would be good if Master Gotama would teach me the Dhamma so that I might understand in detail the meaning of Master Gotama's statement."

"Then, student, listen and attend closely to what I shall say."

"Yes, sir," the brahmin student Subha replied. The Blessed One said this:

5. "Here, student, some man or woman kills living beings and is murderous, bloody-handed, given to blows and violence, merciless to living beings. Because of performing and undertaking such action, on the dissolution of the body, after death, he reappears in a state of deprivation, in an unhappy destination, in

perdition, even in hell. But if on the dissolution of the body, after death, he does not reappear in a state of deprivation, in an unhappy destination, in perdition, in hell, but instead comes back to the human state, then wherever he is reborn he is short-lived.[1224] This is the way, student, that leads to short life, namely, one kills living being and is murderous, bloody-handed, given to blows and violence, merciless to living beings.

6. "But here, student, some man or woman, abandoning the killing of living beings, abstains from killing living beings; with rod and weapon laid aside, gentle and kindly, he abides compassionate to all living beings. Because of performing and undertaking such action, on the dissolution of the body, after death, he reappears in a happy destination, even in the heavenly world. But if on the dissolution of the body, after death, he does not reappear in a happy destination, in the heavenly world, but instead comes back to the human state, then wherever he is reborn he is long-lived.[1225] This is the way, student, that leads to long life, namely, abandoning the killing of living beings, [204] one abstains from killing living beings; with rod and weapon laid aside, gentle and kindly, one abides compassionate to all living beings.

7. "Here, student, some man or woman is given to injuring beings with the hand, with a clod, with a stick, or with a knife. Because of performing and undertaking such action, on the dissolution of the body, after death, he reappears in a state of deprivation...But if instead he comes back to the human state, then wherever he is reborn he is sickly. This is the way, student, that leads to sickliness, namely, one is given to injuring beings with the hand, with a clod, with a stick, or with a knife.

8. "But here, student, some man or woman is not given to injuring beings with the hand, with a clod, with a stick, or with a knife. Because of performing and undertaking such action, on the dissolution of the body, after death, he reappears in a happy destination...But if instead he comes back to the human state, then wherever he is reborn he is healthy. This is the way, student, that leads to health, namely, one is not given to injuring beings with the hand, with a clod, with a stick, or with a knife.

9. "Here, student, some man or woman is of an angry and irritable character; even when criticised a little, he is offended, becomes angry, hostile, and resentful, and displays anger, hate,

and bitterness. Because of performing and undertaking such action...he reappears in a state of deprivation...But if instead he comes back to the human state, then wherever he is reborn he is ugly. This is the way, student, that leads to ugliness, namely, one is of an angry and irritable character...and displays anger, hate, and bitterness.

10. "But here, student, some man or woman is not of an angry and irritable character; even when criticised a little, he is not offended, does not become angry, hostile, and resentful, and does not display anger, hate, and bitterness. Because of performing and undertaking such action...he reappears in a happy destination...But if instead he comes back to the human state, then wherever he is reborn he is beautiful. This is the way, student, that leads to being beautiful, namely, one is not of an angry and irritable character...and does not display anger, hate, and bitterness.

11. "Here, student, some man or woman is envious, one who envies, resents, and begrudges the gains, honour, respect, reverence, salutations, and veneration received by others. Because of performing and undertaking such action...he reappears in a state of deprivation...But if instead he comes back to the human state, then wherever he is reborn he is uninfluential. This is the way, student, that leads to being uninfluential, namely, one is envious...towards the gains, honour, respect, reverence, salutations, and veneration received by others. [205]

12. "But here, student, some man or woman is not envious, one who does not envy, resent, and begrudge the gains, honour, respect, reverence, salutations, and veneration received by others. Because of performing and undertaking such action...he reappears in a happy destination...But if instead he comes back to the human state, then wherever he is reborn he is influential. This is the way, student, that leads to being influential, namely, one is not envious...towards the gains, honour, respect, reverence, salutations, and veneration received by others.

13. "Here, student, some man or woman does not give food, drink, clothing, carriages, garlands, scents, unguents, beds, dwelling, and lamps to recluses or brahmins. Because of performing and undertaking such action...he reappears in a state of deprivation...But if instead he comes back to the human state, then wherever he is reborn he is poor. This is the way, student,

that leads to poverty, namely, one does not give food...and lamps to recluses or brahmins.

14. "But here, student, some man or woman gives food...and lamps to recluses or brahmins. Because of performing and undertaking such action...he reappears in a happy destination...But if instead he comes back to the human state, then wherever he is reborn he is wealthy. This is the way, student, that leads to wealth, namely, one gives food...and lamps to recluses or brahmins.

15. "Here, student, some man or woman is obstinate and arrogant; he does not pay homage to one who should receive homage, does not rise up for one in whose presence he should rise up, does not offer a seat to one who deserves a seat, does not make way for one for whom he should make way, and does not honour, respect, revere, and venerate one who should be honoured, respected, revered, and venerated. Because of performing and undertaking such action...he reappears in a state of deprivation...But if instead he comes back to the human state, then wherever he is reborn he is low-born. This is the way, student, that leads to low birth, namely, one is obstinate and arrogant...and does not honour, respect, revere, and venerate one who should be honoured, respected, revered, and venerated.

16. "But here, student, some man or woman is not obstinate and arrogant; he pays homage to one who should receive homage, rises up for one in whose presence he should rise up, offers a seat to one who deserves a seat, makes way for one for whom he should make way, and honours, respects, reveres, and venerates one who should be honoured, respected, revered, and venerated. Because of performing and undertaking such action...he reappears in a happy destination...But if instead he comes back to the human state, then wherever he is reborn he is high-born. This is the way, student, that leads to high birth, namely, one is not obstinate and arrogant...and honours, respects, reveres, and venerates one who should be honoured, respected, revered, and venerated.

17. "Here, student, some man or woman does not visit a recluse or a brahmin and ask: 'Venerable sir, what is wholesome? What is unwholesome? What is blameable? What is blameless? What should be cultivated? What should not be cultivated? What kind of action will lead to my harm and suffering for a long time? What kind of action will lead to my welfare and happiness for a long

time?' Because of performing and undertaking such action...he reappears in a state of deprivation...But if instead he comes back to the human state, then wherever he is reborn he is stupid. This is the way, student, that leads to stupidity, namely, one does not visit a recluse or brahmin and ask such questions. [206]

18. "But here, student, some man or woman visits a recluse or a brahmin and asks: 'Venerable sir, what is wholesome?...What kind of action will lead to my welfare and happiness for a long time?' Because of performing and undertaking such action...he reappears in a happy destination...But if instead he comes back to the human state, then wherever he is reborn he is wise. This is the way, student, that leads to wisdom, namely, one visits a recluse or brahmin and asks such questions.

19. "Thus, student, the way that leads to short life makes people short-lived, the way that leads to long life makes people long-lived; the way that leads to sickliness makes people sickly, the way that leads to health makes people healthy; the way that leads to ugliness makes people ugly, the way that leads to beauty makes people beautiful; the way that leads to being uninfluential makes people uninfluential, the way that leads to being influential makes people influential; the way that leads to poverty makes people poor, the way that leads to wealth makes people wealthy; the way that leads to low birth makes people low-born, the way that leads to high birth makes people high-born; the way that leads to stupidity makes people stupid, the way that leads to wisdom makes people wise.

20. "Beings are owners of their actions, student, heirs of their actions; they originate from their actions, are bound to their actions, have their actions as their refuge. It is action that distinguishes beings as inferior and superior."

21. When this was said, the brahmin student Subha, Todeyya's son, said to the Blessed One: "Magnificent, Master Gotama! Magnificent, Master Gotama! Master Gotama has made the Dhamma clear in many ways, as though he were turning upright what had been overturned, revealing what was hidden, showing the way to one who was lost, or holding up a lamp in the dark for those with eyesight to see forms. I go to Master Gotama for refuge and to the Dhamma and to the Sangha of bhikkhus. Let Master Gotama remember me as a lay follower who has gone to him for refuge for life."

136 *Mahākammavibhanga Sutta*
The Greater Exposition of Action

[207] 1. THUS HAVE I HEARD. On one occasion the Blessed One was living at Rājagaha, in the Bamboo Grove, the Squirrels' Sanctuary.

2. Now on that occasion the venerable Samiddhi was living in a forest hut. Then the wanderer Potaliputta, while wandering and walking for exercise, went to the venerable Samiddhi and exchanged greetings with him. When this courteous and amiable talk was finished, he sat down at one side and said to the venerable Samiddhi:

"Friend Samiddhi, I heard and learned this from the recluse Gotama's own lips: 'Bodily action is vain, verbal action is vain, only mental action is real.' And: 'There is that attainment on entering which one does not feel anything at all.'"[1226]

"Do not say so, friend Potaliputta, do not say so. Do not misrepresent the Blessed One; it is not good to misrepresent the Blessed One. The Blessed One would not speak thus: 'Bodily action is vain, verbal action is vain, only mental action is real.' But, friend, there is that attainment on entering which one does not feel anything at all."

"How long is it since you went forth, friend Samiddhi?"

"Not long, friend: three years."

"There now, what shall we say to the elder bhikkhus when a young bhikkhu thinks the Teacher is to be defended thus? Friend Samiddhi, having done an intentional action by way of body, speech, or mind, what does one feel?"

"Having done an intentional action by way of body, speech, or mind, one feels suffering, friend Potaliputta."

Then, neither approving nor disapproving of the venerable Samiddhi's words, the wanderer Potaliputta rose from his seat and departed.

3. Soon after the wanderer Potaliputta had left, the venerable Samiddhi went to the venerable Ānanda [208] and exchanged greetings with him. When this courteous and amiable talk was finished, he sat down at one side and reported to the venerable Ānanda his entire conversation with the wanderer Potaliputta. After he had spoken, the venerable Ānanda told him: "Friend Samiddhi, this conversation should be told to the Blessed One. Come, let us approach the Blessed One and tell him this. As the Blessed One explains to us, so we shall bear it in mind."—"Yes, friend," the venerable Samiddhi replied.

4. Then the venerable Ānanda and the venerable Samiddhi went together to the Blessed One, and after paying homage to him, they sat down at one side. The venerable Ānanda reported to the Blessed One the entire conversation between the venerable Samiddhi and the wanderer Potaliputta.

5. When he had finished, the Blessed One told the venerable Ānanda: "Ānanda, I do not even recall ever having seen the wanderer Potaliputta, so how could there have been this conversation? Though the wanderer Potaliputta's question should have been analysed before being answered, this misguided man Samiddhi answered it one-sidedly."

6. When this was said, the venerable Udāyin said to the Blessed One: "Venerable sir, perhaps the venerable Samiddhi spoke thus referring to [the principle]: 'Whatever is felt is included in suffering.'"[1227]

Then the Blessed One addressed the venerable Ānanda: "See, Ānanda, how this misguided man Udāyin interferes. I knew, Ānanda, that this misguided man Udāyin would unduly interfere right now. From the start the wanderer Potaliputta had asked about the three kinds of feeling. This misguided man Samiddhi [209] would have answered the wanderer Potaliputta rightly if, when asked thus, he would have explained: 'Friend Potaliputta, having done an intentional action by way of body, speech, or mind [whose result is] to be felt as pleasant, one feels pleasure. Having done an intentional action by way of body, speech, or mind [whose result is] to be felt as painful, one feels pain. Having done an intentional action by way of body, speech, or mind [whose result is] to be felt as neither-pain-nor-pleasure, one feels neither-pain-nor-pleasure.' But who are these foolish, thoughtless wanderers of other sects, that they could understand the Tathāgata's great exposition of action? You should listen, Ānanda, to the Tathāgata as he expounds the great exposition of action."

7. "This is the time, Blessed One, this is the time, Sublime One, for the Blessed One to expound the great exposition of action. Having heard it from the Blessed One, the bhikkhus will remember it."

"Then listen, Ānanda, and attend closely to what I shall say."

"Yes, venerable sir," the venerable Ānanda replied. The Blessed One said this:

8. "Ānanda,[1228] there are four kinds of persons to be found existing in the world. What four? Here some person kills living beings, takes what is not given, misconducts himself in sensual pleasures, speaks falsehood, speaks maliciously, speaks harshly, gossips; he is covetous, has a mind of ill will, and holds wrong view. On the dissolution of the body, after death, he reappears in a state of deprivation, in an unhappy destination, in perdition, even in hell.

"But here some person kills living beings...and holds wrong view. On the dissolution of the body, after death, he reappears in a happy destination, even in the heavenly world.

"Here some person abstains from killing living beings, from taking what is not given, from misconduct in sensual pleasures, from false speech, from malicious speech, [210] from harsh speech, from gossip; he is not covetous, his mind is without ill will, and he holds right view. On the dissolution of the body, after death, he reappears in a happy destination, even in the heavenly world.

"But here some person abstains from killing living beings... and he holds right view. On the dissolution of the body, after death, he reappears in a state of deprivation, in an unhappy destination, in perdition, even in hell.

9. "Here, Ānanda, by means of ardour, endeavour, devotion, diligence, and right attention, some recluse or brahmin attains such concentration of mind that, when his mind is concentrated, with the divine eye, which is purified and surpasses the human, he sees that person here who kills living beings...and holds wrong view, and he sees that on the dissolution of the body, after death, he has reappeared in a state of deprivation, in an unhappy destination, in perdition, even in hell. He says thus:

'Indeed, there are evil actions, there is result of misconduct; for I saw a person here who killed living beings...and held wrong view, and I see that on the dissolution of the body, after death, he has reappeared in a state of deprivation...even in hell.' He says thus: 'On the dissolution of the body, after death, everyone who kills living beings...and holds wrong view reappears in a state of deprivation...even in hell. Those who know thus know rightly; those who think otherwise are mistaken.' Thus he obstinately adheres to what he himself has known, seen, and discovered, insisting: 'Only this is true, anything else is wrong.'

10. "But here, Ānanda, [211] by means of ardour...some recluse or brahmin attains such a concentration of mind that, when his mind is concentrated, with the divine eye, which is purified and surpasses the human, he sees that person here who kills living beings...and holds wrong view, and he sees that on the dissolution of the body, after death, he has reappeared in a happy destination, even in the heavenly world. He says thus: 'Indeed, there are no evil actions, there is no result of misconduct; for I saw a person here who killed living beings...and held wrong view, and I see that on the dissolution of the body, after death, he has reappeared in a happy destination, even in the heavenly world.' He says thus: 'On the dissolution of the body, after death, everyone who kills living beings...and holds wrong view reappears in a happy destination, even in the heavenly world. Those who know thus know rightly; those who think otherwise are mistaken.' Thus he obstinately adheres to what he himself has known, seen, and discovered, insisting: 'Only this is true, anything else is wrong.'

11. "Here, Ānanda, by means of ardour...some recluse or brahmin attains such a concentration of mind that, when his mind is concentrated, with the divine eye, which is purified and surpasses the human, he sees that person here who abstains from killing living beings...and holds right view, and he sees that on the dissolution of the body, after death, he has reappeared in a happy destination, even in the heavenly world. He says thus: 'Indeed, there are good actions, there is result of good conduct; for I saw a person here who abstained from killing living beings...and held right view, and I see that on the dissolution of the body, after death, he has reappeared in a happy destination, even in the heavenly world.' He says thus: 'On the dissolution of

the body, after death, everyone who abstains from killing living beings...and holds right view reappears in a happy destination, even in the heavenly world. Those who know thus know rightly; those who think otherwise are mistaken.' Thus he obstinately adheres to what he himself has known, seen, and discovered, insisting: 'Only this is true, anything else is wrong.'

12. "But here, Ānanda, [212] by means of ardour...some recluse or brahmin attains such a concentration of mind that, when his mind is concentrated, with the divine eye, which is purified and surpasses the human, he sees that person here who abstains from killing living beings...and holds right view, and he sees that on the dissolution of the body, after death, he reappears in a state of deprivation, in an unhappy destination, in perdition, even in hell. He says thus: 'Indeed, there are no good actions, there is no result of good conduct; for I saw a person here who abstained from killing living beings...and held right view, and I see that on the dissolution of the body, after death, he has reappeared in a state of deprivation...even in hell.' He says thus: 'On the dissolution of the body, after death, everyone who abstains from killing living beings...and holds right view reappears in a state of deprivation...even in hell. Those who know thus know rightly; those who think otherwise are mistaken.' Thus he obstinately adheres to what he himself has known, seen, and discovered, insisting: 'Only this is true, anything else is wrong.'

13. "Therein, Ānanda,[1229] when a recluse or brahmin says: 'Indeed, there are evil actions, there is result of misconduct,' I grant him this. When he says: 'I saw a person here who killed living beings...and held wrong view, and I see that on the dissolution of the body, after death, he has reappeared in a state of deprivation...even in hell,' I also grant him this. But when he says: 'On the dissolution of the body, after death, everyone who kills living beings...and holds wrong view reappears in a state of deprivation...even in hell,' I do not grant him this. And when he says: 'Those who know thus know rightly; those who think otherwise are mistaken,' I also do not grant him this. And when he obstinately adheres to what he himself has known, seen, and discovered, insisting: 'Only this is true, anything else is wrong,' I also do not grant him this. Why is that? Because, Ānanda, the Tathāgata's knowledge of the great exposition of action is otherwise.

14. "Therein, Ānanda, when a recluse or brahmin says: 'Indeed, there are no evil actions, there is no result of misconduct,' I do not grant him this. When he says: 'I saw a person here who killed living beings...and held wrong view, and I see that on the dissolution of the body, after death, he has reappeared in a happy destination, even in the heavenly world,' I grant him this. But when he says: "On the dissolution of the body, after death, everyone who kills living beings...and holds wrong view reappears in a happy destination, even in the heavenly world,' [213] I do not grant him this. And when he says: 'Those who know thus know rightly; those who think otherwise are mistaken,' I also do not grant him this. And when he obstinately adheres to what he himself has known, seen, and discovered, insisting: 'Only this is true, anything else is wrong,' I also do not grant him this. Why is that? Because, Ānanda, the Tathāgata's knowledge of the great exposition of action is otherwise.

15. "Therein, Ānanda, when a recluse or brahmin says: 'Indeed, there are good actions, there is result of good conduct,' I grant him this. And when he says: 'I saw a person here who abstained from killing living beings...and held right view, and I see that on the dissolution of the body, after death, he has reappeared in a happy destination, even in the heavenly world,' I also grant him this. But when he says: 'On the dissolution of the body, after death, everyone who abstains from killing living beings...and holds right view reappears in a happy destination, even in the heavenly world,' I do not grant him this. And when he says: 'Those who know thus know rightly; those who think otherwise are mistaken,' I also do not grant him this. And when he obstinately adheres to what he himself has known, seen, and discovered, insisting: 'Only this is true, anything else is wrong,' I also do not grant him this. Why is that? Because, Ānanda, the Tathāgata's knowledge of the great exposition of action is otherwise.

16. "Therein, Ānanda, when a recluse or brahmin says: 'Indeed, there are no good actions, there is no result of good conduct,' I do not grant him this. When he says: 'I saw a person here who abstained from killing living beings...and held right view, and I see that on the dissolution of the body, after death, he has reappeared in a state of deprivation...even in hell,' I grant him

this. But when he says: 'On the dissolution of the body, after death, everyone who abstains from killing living beings...and holds right view reappears in a state of deprivation...even in hell,' I do not grant him this. And when he says: [214] 'Those who know thus know rightly; those who think otherwise are mistaken,' I also do not grant him this. And when he obstinately adheres to what he himself has known, seen, and discovered, insisting: 'Only this is true, anything else is wrong,' I also do not grant him this. Why is that? Because, Ānanda, the Tathāgata's knowledge of the great exposition of action is otherwise.

17. "Therein, Ānanda,[1230] as to the person here who kills living beings...and holds wrong view, and on the dissolution of the body, after death, reappears in a state of deprivation...even in hell: either earlier he did an evil action to be felt as painful, or later he did an evil action to be felt as painful, or at the time of death he acquired and undertook wrong view.[1231] Because of that, on the dissolution of the body, after death, he has reappeared in a state of deprivation...even in hell. And since he has here killed living beings...and held wrong view, he will experience the result of that either here and now, or in his next rebirth, or in some subsequent existence.[1232]

18. "Therein, Ānanda, as to the person here who kills living beings...and holds wrong view, and on the dissolution of the body, after death, reappears in a happy destination, even in the heavenly world: either earlier he did a good action to be felt as pleasant, or later he did a good action to be felt as pleasant, or at the time of death he acquired and undertook right view.[1233] Because of that, on the dissolution of the body, after death, he has reappeared in a happy destination, even in the heavenly world. But since he has here killed living beings...and held wrong view, he will experience the result of that either here and now, or in his next rebirth, or in some subsequent existence.

19. "Therein, Ānanda, as to the person here who abstains from killing living beings...and holds right view, and on the dissolution of the body, after death, reappears in a happy destination, even in the heavenly world: either earlier he did a good action to be felt as pleasant, or later he did a good action to be felt as pleasant, or at the time of death he acquired and undertook right view. Because of that, on the dissolution of the body, after death, he has reappeared in a happy destination, even in the

heavenly world. And since he has here abstained from killing living beings [215]...and held right view, he will experience the result of that either here and now, or in his next rebirth, or in some subsequent existence.

20. "Therein, Ānanda, as to the person here who abstains from killing living beings...and holds right view, and on the dissolution of the body, after death, reappears in a state of deprivation...even in hell: either earlier he did an evil action to be felt as painful, or later he did an evil action to be felt as painful, or at the time of death he acquired and undertook wrong view. Because of that, on the dissolution of the body, after death, he has reappeared in a state of deprivation...even in hell. But since he has here abstained from killing living beings...and held right view, he will experience the result of that either here and now, or in his next rebirth, or in some subsequent existence.

21. "Thus, Ānanda, there is action that is incapable and appears incapable; there is action that is incapable and appears capable; there is action that is capable and appears capable; and there is action that is capable and appears incapable."[1234]

That is what the Blessed One said. The venerable Ānanda was satisfied and delighted in the Blessed One's words.

137 *Saḷāyatanavibhanga Sutta*
The Exposition of the Sixfold Base

1. THUS HAVE I HEARD. On one occasion the Blessed One was living at Sāvatthī in Jeta's Grove, Anāthapiṇḍika's Park. There he addressed the bhikkhus thus: "Bhikkhus."—"Venerable sir," they replied. The Blessed One said this:

2. "Bhikkhus, I shall teach you an exposition of the sixfold base. Listen and attend closely to what I shall say."—"Yes, venerable sir," the bhikkhus replied. The Blessed One said this: [216]

3. "The six internal bases should be understood. The six external bases should be understood. The six classes of consciousness should be understood. The six classes of contact should be understood. The eighteen kinds of mental exploration should be understood. The thirty-six positions of beings should be understood. Therein, by depending on this, abandon that. There are three foundations of mindfulness that the Noble One cultivates, cultivating which the Noble One is a teacher fit to instruct a group. Among the teachers of training it is he that is called the incomparable leader of persons to be tamed. This is the summary of the exposition of the sixfold base.

4. "'The six internal bases should be understood.' So it was said. And with reference to what was this said? There are the eye-base, the ear-base, the nose-base, the tongue-base, the body-base, and the mind-base. So it was with reference to this that it was said: 'The six internal bases should be understood.'

5. "'The six external bases should be understood.' So it was said. And with reference to what was this said? There are the form-base, the sound-base, the odour-base, the flavour-base, the tangible-base, and the mind-object-base. So it was with reference to this that it was said: 'The six external bases should be understood.'

6. "'The six classes of consciousness should be understood.' So

it was said. And with reference to what was this said? There are eye-consciousness, ear-consciousness, nose-consciousness, tongue-consciousness, body-consciousness, and mind-consciousness. So it was with reference to this that it was said: 'The six classes of consciousness should be understood.'

7. "'The six classes of contact should be understood.' So it was said. And with reference to what was this said? There are eye-contact, ear-contact, nose-contact, tongue-contact, body-contact, and mind-contact. So it was with reference to this that it was said: 'The six classes of contact should be understood.'

8. "'The eighteen kinds of mental exploration should be understood.'[1235] So it was said. And with reference to what was this said?

"On seeing a form with the eye, one explores a form productive of joy, one explores a form productive of grief, one explores a form productive of equanimity.[1236] On hearing a sound with the ear...On smelling an odour with the nose...On tasting a flavour with the tongue...[217] On touching a tangible with the body... On cognizing a mind-object with the mind, one explores a mind-object productive of joy, one explores a mind-object productive of grief, one explores a mind-object productive of equanimity. Thus there are six kinds of exploration with joy, six kinds of exploration with grief, and six kinds of exploration with equanimity. So it was with reference to this that it was said: 'The eighteen kinds of mental exploration should be understood.'

9. "'The thirty-six positions of beings should be understood.'[1237] So it was said. And with reference to what was this said? There are six kinds of joy based on the household life and six kinds of joy based on renunciation.[1238] There are six kinds of grief based on the household life and six kinds of grief based on renunciation. There are six kinds of equanimity based on the household life and six kinds of equanimity based on renunciation.

10. "Herein, what are the six kinds of joy based on the household life? When one regards as a gain the gain of forms cognizable by the eye that are wished for, desired, agreeable, gratifying, and associated with worldliness—or when one recalls what was formerly obtained that has passed, ceased, and changed—joy arises. Such joy as this is called joy based on the household life.

"When one regards as a gain the gain of sounds cognizable by the ear...the gain of odours cognizable by the nose...the gain of flavours cognizable by the tongue...the gain of tangibles cognizable by the body...the gain of mind-objects cognizable by the mind that are wished for, desired, agreeable, gratifying, and associated with worldliness—or when one recalls what was formerly obtained that has passed, ceased, and changed—joy arises. Such joy as this is called joy based on the household life. These are the six kinds of joy based on the household life.

11. "Herein, what are the six kinds of joy based on renunciation? When, by knowing the impermanence, change, fading away, and cessation of forms, one sees as it actually is with proper wisdom that forms both formerly and now are all impermanent, suffering, and subject to change, joy arises. Such joy as this is called joy based on renunciation.[1239]

"When, by knowing the impermanence, change, fading away, and cessation of sounds...of odours...of flavours...of tangibles...[218] of mind-objects, one sees as it actually is with proper wisdom that mind-objects both formerly and now are all impermanent, suffering, and subject to change, joy arises. Such joy as this is called joy based on renunciation. These are the six kinds of joy based on renunciation.

12. "Herein, what are the six kinds of grief based on the household life? When one regards as a non-gain the non-gain of forms cognizable by the eye that are wished for, desired, agreeable, gratifying, and associated with worldliness—or when one recalls what was formerly not obtained that has passed, ceased, and changed—grief arises. Such grief as this is called grief based on the household life.

"When one regards as a non-gain the non-gain of sounds cognizable by the ear...the non-gain of odours cognizable by the nose...the non-gain of flavours cognizable by the tongue...the non-gain of tangibles cognizable by the body...the non-gain of mind-objects cognizable by the mind that are wished for, desired, agreeable, gratifying, and associated with worldliness—or when one recalls what was formerly not obtained that has passed, ceased, and changed—grief arises. Such grief as this is called grief based on the household life. These are the six kinds of grief based on the household life.

13. "Herein, what are the six kinds of grief based on renunciation? When, by knowing the impermanence, change, fading away, and cessation of forms, one sees as it actually is with proper wisdom that forms both formerly and now are all impermanent, suffering, and subject to change, one generates a longing for the supreme liberations thus: 'When shall I enter upon and abide in that base that the noble ones now enter upon and abide in?'[1240] In one who generates thus a longing for the supreme liberations, grief arises with that longing as condition. Such grief as this is called grief based on renunciation.

"When, by knowing the impermanence, change, fading away, and cessation of sounds...of odours...of flavours...of tangibles ...of mind-objects, one sees as it actually is with proper wisdom that mind-objects both formerly and now are all impermanent, suffering, and subject to change, [219] one generates a longing for the supreme liberations thus: 'When shall I enter upon and abide in that base that the noble ones now enter upon and abide in?' In one who thus generates a longing for the supreme liberations, grief arises with that longing as condition. Such grief as this is called grief based on renunciation. These are the six kinds of grief based on renunciation.

14. "Herein, what are the six kinds of equanimity based on the household life? On seeing a form with the eye, equanimity arises in a foolish infatuated ordinary person, in an untaught ordinary person who has not conquered his limitations or conquered the results [of action] and who is blind to danger. Such equanimity as this does not transcend the form; that is why it is called equanimity based on the household life.[1241]

"On hearing a sound with the ear...On smelling an odour with the nose...On tasting a flavour with the tongue...On touching a tangible with the body...On cognizing a mind-object with the mind, equanimity arises in a foolish infatuated ordinary person, in an untaught ordinary person who has not conquered his limitations or conquered the results [of action] and who is blind to danger. Such equanimity as this does not transcend the mind-object; that is why it is called equanimity based on the household life. These are the six kinds of equanimity based on the household life.

15. "Herein, what are the six kinds of equanimity based on renunciation? When, by knowing the impermanence, change,

fading away, and cessation of forms, one sees as it actually is with proper wisdom that forms both formerly and now are all impermanent, suffering, and subject to change, equanimity arises. Such equanimity as this transcends the form; that is why it is called equanimity based on renunciation.[1242]

"When, by knowing the impermanence, change, fading away, and cessation of sounds...of odours...of flavours...of tangibles... of mind-objects, one sees as it actually is with proper wisdom that mind-objects both formerly and now are all impermanent, suffering, and subject to change, equanimity arises. Such equanimity as this transcends the mind-object; that is why it is called equanimity based on renunciation. These are the six kinds of equanimity based on renunciation.

"So it was with reference to this that it was said: 'The thirty-six positions of beings should be understood.' [220]

16. "'Therein, by depending on this, abandon that.' So it was said. And with reference to what was this said?

"Here, bhikkhus, by depending and relying on the six kinds of joy based on renunciation, abandon and surmount the six kinds of joy based on the household life. It is thus they are abandoned; it is thus they are surmounted. By depending and relying on the six kinds of grief based on renunciation, abandon and surmount the six kinds of grief based on the household life. It is thus they are abandoned; it is thus they are surmounted. By depending and relying on the six kinds of equanimity based on renunciation, abandon and surmount the six kinds of equanimity based on the household life. It is thus they are abandoned; it is thus they are surmounted.

"By depending and relying on the six kinds of joy based on renunciation, abandon and surmount the six kinds of grief based on renunciation. It is thus they are abandoned; it is thus they are surmounted. By depending and relying on the six kinds of equanimity based on renunciation, abandon and surmount the six kinds of joy based on renunciation. It is thus they are abandoned; it is thus they are surmounted.

17. "There is, bhikkhus, equanimity that is diversified, based on diversity; and there is equanimity that is unified, based on unity.[1243]

18. "And what, bhikkhus, is equanimity that is diversified, based on diversity? There is equanimity regarding forms,

sounds, odours, flavours, and tangibles. This, bhikkhus, is equanimity that is diversified, based on diversity.

19. "And what, bhikkhus, is equanimity that is unified, based on unity? There is equanimity regarding the base of infinite space, the base of infinite consciousness, the base of nothingness, and the base of neither-perception-nor-non-perception. This, bhikkhus, is equanimity that is unified, based on unity.

20. "Here, bhikkhus, by depending and relying on equanimity that is unified, based on unity, abandon and surmount equanimity that is diversified, based on diversity. It is thus this is abandoned; it is thus this is surmounted.[1244]

"Bhikkhus, by depending and relying on non-identification,[1245] abandon and surmount equanimity that is unified, based on unity. It is thus this is abandoned; it is thus this is surmounted. [221]

"So it was in reference to this that it was said: 'Therein, by depending on this, abandon that.'

21. "'There are three foundations of mindfulness that the Noble One cultivates, cultivating which the Noble One is a teacher fit to instruct a group.'[1246] So it was said. And with reference to what was this said?

22. "Here, bhikkhus, compassionate and seeking their welfare, the Teacher teaches the Dhamma to the disciples out of compassion: 'This is for your welfare; this is for your happiness.' His disciples do not want to hear or give ear or exert their minds to understand; they err and turn aside from the Teacher's Dispensation. With that the Tathāgata is not satisfied and feels no satisfaction; yet he dwells unmoved, mindful, and fully aware. This, bhikkhus, is called the first foundation of mindfulness that the Noble One cultivates, cultivating which the Noble One is a teacher fit to instruct a group.

23. "Furthermore, bhikkhus, compassionate and seeking their welfare, the Teacher teaches the Dhamma to the disciples out of compassion: 'This is for your welfare; this is for your happiness.' Some of his disciples will not hear or give ear or exert their minds to understand; they err and turn aside from the Teacher's Dispensation. Some of his disciples will hear and give ear and exert their minds to understand; they do not err and turn aside from the Teacher's Dispensation. With that the Tathāgata is not satisfied and feels no satisfaction, and he is not dissatisfied and

feels no dissatisfaction; remaining free from both satisfaction and dissatisfaction, he dwells in equanimity, mindful, and fully aware. This, bhikkhus, is called the second foundation of mindfulness that the Noble One cultivates, cultivating which the Noble One is a teacher fit to instruct a group.

24. "Furthermore, bhikkhus, compassionate and seeking their welfare, the Teacher teaches the Dhamma to the disciples out of compassion: 'This is for your welfare; this is for your happiness.' His disciples will hear and give ear and exert their minds to understand; they do not err and turn aside from the Teacher's Dispensation. With that the Tathāgata is satisfied and feels satisfaction; yet he dwells unmoved, mindful, and fully aware. This, bhikkhus, is called the third foundation of mindfulness that the Noble One cultivates, cultivating which the Noble One is a teacher fit to instruct a group. [222]

"So it was with reference to this that it was said: 'There are three foundations of mindfulness that the Noble One cultivates, cultivating which the Noble One is a teacher fit to instruct a group.'

25. "'Among the teachers of training it is he that is called the incomparable leader of persons to be tamed.'[1247] So it was said. And with reference to what was this said?

"Guided by the elephant tamer, bhikkhus, the elephant to be tamed goes in one direction—east, west, north, or south. Guided by the horse tamer, bhikkhus, the horse to be tamed goes in one direction—east, west, north, or south. Guided by the ox tamer, bhikkhus, the ox to be tamed goes in one direction—east, west, north, or south.

26. "Bhikkhus, guided by the Tathāgata, accomplished and fully enlightened, the person to be tamed goes in eight directions.[1248]

"Possessed of material form, he sees forms: this is the first direction. Not perceiving forms internally, he sees forms externally: this is the second direction. He is resolved only upon the beautiful: this is the third direction. With the complete surmounting of perceptions of form, with the disappearance of perceptions of sensory impact, with non-attention to perceptions of diversity, aware that 'space is infinite,' he enters upon and abides in the base of infinite space: this is the fourth direction. By completely surmounting the base of infinite space, aware that 'consciousness is infinite,' he enters upon and abides in the base of infinite consciousness: this is the fifth direction. By completely surmounting the base of infinite consciousness, aware that 'there is nothing,' he enters upon and abides in the base of nothingness: this is the sixth direction. By completely surmounting the base of nothingness, he enters upon and abides in the base of neither-perception-nor-non-perception: this is the seventh direction. By completely surmounting the base of neither-perception-nor-non-perception, he enters upon and abides in the cessation of perception and feeling: this is the eighth direction.

"Bhikkhus, guided by the Tathāgata, accomplished and fully enlightened, the person to be tamed goes in these eight directions.

28. "So it was with reference to this that it was said: 'Among the teachers of training it is he that is called the incomparable leader of persons to be tamed.'"

That is what the Blessed One said. The bhikkhus were satisfied and delighted in the Blessed One's words.

138 *Uddesavibhaṅga Sutta*
The Exposition of a Summary

[223] 1. THUS HAVE I HEARD. On one occasion the Blessed One was living at Sāvatthī in Jeta's Grove, Anāthapiṇḍika's Park. There the Blessed One addressed the bhikkhus thus: "Bhikkhus."—"Venerable sir," they replied. The Blessed One said this:

2. "Bhikkhus, I shall teach you a summary and an exposition. Listen and attend closely to what I shall say."—"Yes, venerable sir," the bhikkhus replied. The Blessed One said this:

3. "Bhikkhus, a bhikkhu should examine things in such a way that while he is examining them, his consciousness is not distracted and scattered externally nor stuck internally, and by not clinging he does not become agitated. If his consciousness is not distracted and scattered externally nor stuck internally, and if by not clinging he does not become agitated, then for him there is no origination of suffering—of birth, ageing, and death in the future."

4. That is what the Blessed One said. Having said this, the Sublime One rose from his seat and went into his dwelling.[1249]

5. Then, soon after the Blessed One had gone, the bhikkhus considered: "Now, friends, the Blessed One has risen from his seat and gone into his dwelling after giving a summary in brief without expounding the detailed meaning. Now who will expound this in detail?" Then they considered: "The venerable Mahā Kaccāna is praised by the Teacher and esteemed by his wise companions in the holy life. He is capable of expounding the detailed meaning. Suppose we went to him and asked him the meaning of this."

6–8. [224, 225] (*As at Sutta 133, §§8–10.*)

9. "Then listen, friends, and attend closely to what I shall say."

"Yes, friend," the bhikkhus replied. The venerable Mahā Kaccāna said this:

10. "How, friends, is consciousness called 'distracted and scattered externally'?[1250] Here, when a bhikkhu has seen a form with the eye, if his consciousness follows after the sign of form, is tied and shackled by gratification in the sign of form,[1251] is fettered by the fetter of gratification in the sign of form, then his consciousness is called 'distracted and scattered externally.'

"When he has heard a sound with the ear...smelt an odour with the nose...tasted a flavour with the tongue...touched a tangible with the body...cognized a mind-object with the mind, if his consciousness follows after the sign of the mind-object, is tied and shackled by gratification in the sign of the mind-object, is fettered by the fetter of gratification in the sign of the mind-object, then his consciousness is called 'distracted and scattered externally.'

11. "And how, friends, is consciousness called 'not distracted and scattered externally'? Here, when a bhikkhu has seen a form with the eye, if his consciousness does not follow after the sign of form, is not tied and shackled by gratification in the sign of form, is not fettered by the fetter of gratification in the sign of form, then his consciousness is called 'not distracted and scattered externally.' [226]

"When he has heard a sound with the ear...smelt an odour with the nose...tasted a flavour with the tongue...touched a tangible with the body...cognized a mind-object with the mind, if his consciousness does not follow after the sign of the mind-object, is not tied and shackled by gratification in the sign of the mind-object, is not fettered by the fetter of gratification in the sign of the mind-object, then his consciousness is called 'not distracted and scattered externally.'

12. "And how, friends, is the mind called 'stuck internally'?[1252] Here, quite secluded from sensual pleasures, secluded from unwholesome states, a bhikkhu enters upon and abides in the first jhāna, which is accompanied by applied and sustained thought, with rapture and pleasure born of seclusion. If his consciousness follows after the rapture and pleasure born of seclusion, is tied and shackled by gratification in the rapture and pleasure born of seclusion, then his mind is called 'stuck internally.'

13. "Again, with the stilling of applied and sustained thought, a bhikkhu enters upon and abides in the second jhāna, which

has self-confidence and singleness of mind without applied and sustained thought, with rapture and pleasure born of concentration. If his consciousness follows after the rapture and pleasure born of concentration...then his mind is called 'stuck internally.'

14. "Again, with the fading away as well of rapture, a bhikkhu abides in equanimity, and mindful and fully aware, still feeling pleasure with the body, he enters upon and abides in the third jhāna, on account of which noble ones announce: 'He has a pleasant abiding who has equanimity and is mindful.' If his consciousness follows after the equanimity...then his mind is called 'stuck internally.'

15. "Again, with the abandoning of pleasure and pain, and with the previous disappearance of joy and grief, a bhikkhu enters upon and abides in the fourth jhāna, which has neither-pain-nor-pleasure and purity of mindfulness due to equanimity. If his consciousness follows after the neither-pain-nor-pleasure, is tied and shackled by gratification in the neither-pain-nor-pleasure, is fettered by the fetter of gratification in the neither-pain-nor-pleasure, then his mind is called 'stuck internally.' That is how the mind is called 'stuck internally.' [227]

16. "And how, friends, is the mind called 'not stuck internally'? Here, quite secluded from sensual pleasures, secluded from unwholesome states, a bhikkhu enters upon and abides in the first jhāna...If his consciousness does not follow after the rapture and pleasure born of seclusion, is not tied and shackled by gratification in the rapture and pleasure born of seclusion, is not fettered by the fetter of gratification in the rapture and pleasure born of seclusion, then his mind is called 'not stuck internally.'

17. "Again, with the stilling of applied and sustained thought, a bhikkhu enters upon and abides in the second jhāna...If his consciousness does not follow after the rapture and pleasure born of concentration...then his mind is called 'not stuck internally.'

18. "Again, with the fading away as well of rapture, a bhikkhu... enters upon and abides in the third jhāna...If his consciousness does not follow after the equanimity...then his mind is called 'not stuck internally.'

19. "Again, with the abandoning of pleasure and pain...a bhikkhu enters upon and abides in the fourth jhāna...If his consciousness does not follow after the neither-pain-nor-pleasure,

is not tied and shackled by gratification in the neither-pain-nor-pleasure, is not fettered by the fetter of gratification in the neither-pain-nor-pleasure, then his mind is called 'not stuck internally.' That is how the mind is called 'not stuck internally.'

20. "How, friends, is there agitation due to clinging?[1253] Here an untaught ordinary person who has no regard for noble ones and is unskilled and undisciplined in their Dhamma, who has no regard for true men and is unskilled and undisciplined in their Dhamma, regards material form as self, or self as possessed of material form, or material form as in self, or self as in material form. That material form of his changes and becomes otherwise. With the change and becoming otherwise of that material form, his consciousness is preoccupied with the change of material form. Agitated mental states born of preoccupation with the change of material form arise together[1254] and remain obsessing his mind. Because his mind is obsessed, he is anxious, distressed, and concerned, and due to clinging he becomes agitated.[1255] [228]

"He regards feeling as self...He regards perception as self...He regards formations as self...He regards consciousness as self, or self as possessed of consciousness, or consciousness as in self, or self as in consciousness. That consciousness of his changes and becomes otherwise. With the change and becoming otherwise of that consciousness, his consciousness is preoccupied with the change of consciousness. Agitated states of mind born of preoccupation with the change of consciousness arise together and remain obsessing his mind. Because his mind is obsessed, he is anxious, distressed, and concerned, and due to clinging he becomes agitated. That is how there is agitation due to clinging.

21. "And how, friends, is there non-agitation due to non-clinging?[1256] Here a well-taught noble disciple who has regard for noble ones and is skilled and disciplined in their Dhamma, who has regard for true men and is skilled and disciplined in their Dhamma, does not regard material form as self, or self as possessed of material form, or material form as in self, or self as in material form. That material form of his changes and becomes otherwise. With the change and becoming otherwise of that material form, his consciousness is not preoccupied with the change of material form. Agitated mental states born of preoccupation with the change of material form do not arise together

and remain obsessing his mind. Because his mind is not obsessed, he is not anxious, distressed, and concerned, and due to non-clinging he does not become agitated.

"He does not regard feeling as self...He does not regard perception as self...He does not regard formations as self...He does not regard consciousness as self, or self as possessed of consciousness, or consciousness as in self, or self as in consciousness. That consciousness of his changes and becomes otherwise. With the change and becoming otherwise of that consciousness, his consciousness is not preoccupied with the change of consciousness. Agitated mental states born of preoccupation with the change of consciousness do not arise together and remain obsessing his mind. Because his mind is not obsessed, he is not anxious, distressed, and concerned, and due to non-clinging he does not become agitated. That is how there is non-agitation due to non-clinging.

22. "Friends, when the Blessed One rose from his seat and went into his dwelling after giving a summary in brief without expounding the detailed meaning, that is: 'Bhikkhus, a bhikkhu should examine things in such a way that while he is examining them, his consciousness is not distracted and scattered externally nor stuck internally, and by not clinging he does not become agitated. If his consciousness is not distracted and scattered externally nor stuck internally, and if by not clinging he does not become agitated, then for him there is no origination of suffering—of birth, ageing, and death in the future,' I understand the detailed meaning of this summary to be thus. [229] Now, friends, if you wish, go to the Blessed One and ask him about the meaning of this. As the Blessed One explains it to you, so you should remember it."

23. Then the bhikkhus, having delighted and rejoiced in the venerable Mahā Kaccāna's words, rose from their seats and went to the Blessed One. After paying homage to him, they sat down at one side and told the Blessed One all that had taken place after he had left, adding: "Then, venerable sir, we went to the venerable Mahā Kaccāna and asked him about the meaning. The venerable Mahā Kaccāna expounded the meaning to us with these terms, statements, and phrases."

24. "Mahā Kaccāna is wise, bhikkhus, Mahā Kaccāna has great wisdom. If you had asked me the meaning of this, I would have

explained it to you in the same way that Mahā Kaccāna has explained it. Such is its meaning, and so you should remember it."

That is what the Blessed One said. The bhikkhus were satisfied and delighted in the Blessed One's words.

139 *Araṇavibhanga Sutta*
The Exposition of Non-Conflict

[230] 1. THUS HAVE I HEARD. On one occasion the Blessed One was living at Sāvatthī in Jeta's Grove, Anāthapiṇḍika's Park. There the Blessed One addressed the bhikkhus thus: "Bhikkhus."—"Venerable sir," they replied. The Blessed One said this:

2. "Bhikkhus, I shall teach you an exposition of non-conflict. Listen and attend closely to what I shall say."—"Yes, venerable sir," the bhikkhus replied. The Blessed One said this:

3. "One should not pursue sensual pleasure, which is low, vulgar, coarse, ignoble, and unbeneficial; and one should not pursue self-mortification, which is painful, ignoble, and unbeneficial. The Middle Way discovered by the Tathāgata avoids both extremes; giving vision, giving knowledge, it leads to peace, to direct knowledge, to enlightenment, to Nibbāna.[1257] One should know what it is to extol and what it is to disparage, and knowing both, one should neither extol nor disparage but should teach only the Dhamma. One should know how to define pleasure, and knowing that, one should pursue pleasure within oneself. One should not utter covert speech, and one should not utter overt sharp speech. One should speak unhurriedly, not hurriedly. One should not insist on local language, and one should not override normal usage. This is the summary of the exposition of non-conflict.

4. "'One should not pursue sensual pleasure, which is low, vulgar, coarse, ignoble, and unbeneficial; and one should not pursue self-mortification, which is painful, ignoble, and unbeneficial.' So it was said. And with reference to what was this said?

"The pursuit of the enjoyment of one whose pleasure is linked to sensual desires[1258]—low, vulgar, coarse, ignoble, and unbeneficial—is a state beset by suffering, vexation, despair, and fever, and it is the wrong way.[1259] [231] Disengagement from the pursuit of the enjoyment of one whose pleasure is linked to sensual desires—low, vulgar, coarse, ignoble, and unbeneficial—is a state without suffering, vexation, despair, and fever, and it is the right way.

"The pursuit of self-mortification—painful, ignoble, and unbeneficial—is a state beset by suffering, vexation, despair, and fever, and it is the wrong way. Disengagement from the pursuit of self-mortification—painful, ignoble, and unbeneficial—is a state without suffering, vexation, despair, and fever, and it is the right way.

"So it was with reference to this that it was said: 'One should not pursue sensual pleasure, which is low, vulgar, coarse, ignoble, and unbeneficial; and one should not pursue self-mortification, which is painful, ignoble, and unbeneficial.'

5. "'The Middle Way discovered by the Tathāgata avoids both these extremes; giving vision, giving knowledge, it leads to peace, to direct knowledge, to enlightenment, to Nibbāna.' So it was said. And with reference to what was this said? It is just this Noble Eightfold Path; that is, right view, right intention, right speech, right action, right livelihood, right effort, right mindfulness, and right concentration. So it was with reference to this that it was said: 'The Middle Way discovered by the Tathāgata avoids both these extremes...to Nibbāna.'

6. "'One should know what it is to extol and what it is to disparage, and knowing both, one should neither extol nor disparage but should teach only the Dhamma.' So it was said. And with reference to what was this said?

7. "How, bhikkhus, does there come to be extolling and disparaging and failure to teach only the Dhamma? When one says: 'All those engaged in the pursuit of the enjoyment of one whose pleasure is linked to sensual desires—low...and unbeneficial—are beset by suffering, vexation, despair, and fever, and they have entered upon the wrong way,' one thus disparages some. When one says: 'All those disengaged from the pursuit of the enjoyment of one whose pleasure is linked to sensual desires—low...and unbeneficial—are without suffering, vexation, despair, and fever, and they have entered upon the right way,' one thus extols some.

"When one says: 'All those engaged in the pursuit of self-mortification—painful, ignoble, and unbeneficial—[232] are beset by suffering, vexation, despair, and fever, and they have entered upon the wrong way,' one thus disparages some. When one says: 'All those disengaged from the pursuit of self-mortification—painful, ignoble, and unbeneficial—are without suffering, vexation, despair, and fever, and they have entered upon the right way,' one thus extols some.

"When one says: 'All those who have not abandoned the fetter of being[1260] are beset by suffering, vexation, despair, and fever, and they have entered upon the wrong way,' one thus disparages some. When one says: 'All those who have abandoned the fetter of being are without suffering, vexation, despair, and fever, and they have entered upon the right way,' one thus extols some. This is how there comes to be extolling and disparaging and failure to teach only the Dhamma.

8. "And how, bhikkhus, does there come to be neither extolling nor disparaging but teaching only the Dhamma? When one does not say: 'All those engaged in the pursuit of the enjoyment of one whose pleasure is linked to sensual desires...have entered upon the wrong way,' but says instead: 'The pursuit is a state beset by suffering, vexation, despair, and fever, and it is the wrong way,' then one teaches only the Dhamma.[1261] When one does not say: 'All those disengaged from the pursuit of the enjoyment of one whose pleasure is linked to sensual desires...have entered upon the right way,' but says instead: 'The disengagement is a state without suffering, vexation, despair, and fever, and it is the right way,' then one teaches only the Dhamma.

"When one does not say: 'All those engaged in the pursuit of self-mortification...have entered upon the wrong way,' but says instead: 'The pursuit is a state beset by suffering, vexation, despair, and fever, and it is the wrong way,' then one teaches only the Dhamma. When one does not say: 'All those disengaged from the pursuit of self-mortification...have entered upon the right way,' but says instead: 'The disengagement is a state without suffering, vexation, despair, and fever, and it is the right way,' then one teaches only the Dhamma.

"When one does not say: 'All those who have not abandoned the fetter of being...have entered upon the wrong way,' [233] but says instead: 'As long as the fetter of being is unabandoned, being too is unabandoned,' then one teaches only the Dhamma.

When one does not say: 'All those who have abandoned the fetter of being...have entered upon the right way,' but says instead: 'When the fetter of being is abandoned, being also is abandoned,' then one teaches only the Dhamma.

"So it was with reference to this that it was said: 'One should know what it is to extol and what it is to disparage, and knowing both, one should neither extol nor disparage but should teach only the Dhamma.'

9. "'One should know how to define pleasure, and knowing that, one should pursue pleasure within oneself.' So it was said. And with reference to what was this said?

"Bhikkhus, there are these five cords of sensual pleasure. What five? Forms cognizable by the eye...sounds cognizable by the ear...odours cognizable by the nose...flavours cognizable by the tongue...tangibles cognizable by the body that are wished for, desired, agreeable, and likeable, connected with sensual desire and provocative of lust. These are the five cords of sensual pleasure. Now the pleasure and joy that arise dependent on these five cords of sensual pleasure are called sensual pleasure—a filthy pleasure, a coarse pleasure, an ignoble pleasure. I say of this kind of pleasure that it should not be pursued, that it should not be developed, that it should not be cultivated, and that it should be feared.

"Here, bhikkhus, quite secluded from sensual pleasures, secluded from unwholesome states, a bhikkhu enters upon and abides in the first jhāna...the second jhāna...the third jhāna... the fourth jhāna. This is called the bliss of renunciation, the bliss of seclusion, the bliss of peace, the bliss of enlightenment. I say of this kind of pleasure that it should be pursued, that it should be developed, that it should be cultivated, and that it should not be feared. [234]

"So it was with reference to this that it was said: 'One should know how to define pleasure, and knowing that, one should pursue pleasure within oneself.'

10. "'One should not utter covert speech, and one should not utter overt sharp speech.' So it was said. And with reference to what was this said?

"Here, bhikkhus, when one knows covert speech to be untrue, incorrect, and unbeneficial, one should on no account utter it. When one knows covert speech to be true, correct, and unbeneficial, one should try not to utter it. But when one knows covert speech to be true, correct, and beneficial, one may utter it, knowing the time to do so.

"Here, bhikkhus, when one knows overt sharp speech to be untrue, incorrect, and unbeneficial, one should on no account utter it. When one knows overt sharp speech to be true, correct, and unbeneficial, one should try not to utter it. But when one knows overt sharp speech to be true, correct, and beneficial, one may utter it, knowing the time to do so.

"So it was with reference to this that it was said: 'One should not utter covert speech, and one should not utter overt sharp speech.'

11. "'One should speak unhurriedly, not hurriedly.' So it was said. And with reference to what was this said?

"Here, bhikkhus, when one speaks hurriedly, one's body grows tired and one's mind becomes excited, one's voice is strained and one's throat becomes hoarse, and the speech of one who speaks hurriedly is indistinct and hard to understand.

"Here, bhikkhus, when one speaks unhurriedly, one's body does not grow tired nor does one's mind become excited, one's voice is not strained nor does one's throat become hoarse, and the speech of one who speaks unhurriedly is distinct and easy to understand.

"So it was with reference to this that it was said: 'One should speak unhurriedly, not hurriedly.'

12. "'One should not insist on local language, and one should not override normal usage.' So it was said. And with reference to what was this said?

"How, bhikkhus, does there come to be insistence on local language and overriding of normal usage? Here, bhikkhus, in different localities they call the same thing a 'dish' [*pāti*], [235] a 'bowl' [*patta*], a 'vessel' [*vittha*], a 'saucer' [*serāva*], a 'pan' [*dhāropa*], a 'pot' [*poṇa*], or a 'basin' [*pisīla*]. So whatever they call it in such and such a locality, one speaks accordingly, firmly adhering [to that expression] and insisting: 'Only this is correct; anything else is wrong.' This is how there comes to be insistence on local language and overriding normal usage.[1262]

"And how, bhikkhus, does there come to be non-insistence on local language and non-overriding of normal usage? Here, bhikkhus, in different localities they call the same thing a 'dish'...or a 'basin.' So whatever they call it in such and such a locality, without adhering [to that expression] one speaks accordingly, thinking: 'These venerable ones, it seems, are speaking with reference to this.' This is how there comes to be non-insistence on local language and non-overriding of normal usage.

"So it was with reference to this that it was said: 'One should not insist on local language, and one should not override normal usage.'

13. "Here, bhikkhus, the pursuit of the enjoyment of one whose pleasure is linked to sensual desires—low...and unbeneficial—is a state beset by suffering, vexation, despair, and fever, and it is the wrong way. Therefore this is a state with conflict.

"Here, bhikkhus, disengagement from the pursuit of the enjoyment of one whose pleasure is linked to sensual desires—low...and unbeneficial—is a state without suffering, vexation, despair, and fever, and it is the right way. Therefore this is a state without conflict.

"Here, bhikkhus, the pursuit of self-mortification—painful, ignoble, and unbeneficial—is a state beset by suffering, vexation, despair, and fever, and it is the wrong way. Therefore this is a state with conflict.

"Here, bhikkhus, disengagement from the pursuit of self-mortification—painful, ignoble, and unbeneficial—is a state without suffering, vexation, despair, and fever, and it is the right way. [236] Therefore this is a state without conflict.

"Here, bhikkhus, the Middle Way discovered by the Tathāgata avoids both these extremes; giving vision, giving knowledge, it leads to peace, to direct knowledge, to enlightenment, to Nibbāna. It is a state without suffering...and it is the right way. Therefore this is a state without conflict.

"Here, bhikkhus, extolling and disparaging and failure to teach only the Dhamma is a state beset by suffering...and it is the wrong way. Therefore this is a state with conflict.

"Here, bhikkhus, not extolling and not disparaging and teaching only the Dhamma is a state without suffering...and it is the right way. Therefore this is a state without conflict.

"Here, bhikkhus, sensual pleasure—a filthy pleasure, a coarse pleasure, an ignoble pleasure—is a state beset by suffering...and it is the wrong way. Therefore this is a state with conflict.

"Here, bhikkhus, the bliss of renunciation, the bliss of seclusion, the bliss of peace, the bliss of enlightenment, is a state without suffering...and it is the right way. Therefore this is a state without conflict.

"Here, bhikkhus, covert speech that is untrue, incorrect, and unbeneficial is a state beset by suffering...Therefore this is a state with conflict.

"Here, bhikkhus, covert speech that is true, correct, and unbeneficial is a state beset by suffering...Therefore this is a state with conflict.

"Here, bhikkhus, covert speech that is true, correct, and beneficial is a state without suffering...Therefore this is a state without conflict.

"Here, bhikkhus, overt sharp speech that is untrue, incorrect, and unbeneficial is a state beset by suffering...Therefore this is a state with conflict.

"Here, bhikkhus, overt sharp speech that is true, correct, and unbeneficial is a state beset by suffering...Therefore this is a state with conflict.

"Here, bhikkhus, overt sharp speech [237] that is true, correct, and beneficial is a state without suffering...Therefore this is a state without conflict.

"Here, bhikkhus, the speech of one who speaks hurriedly is a state beset by suffering, vexation, despair, and fever, and it is the wrong way. Therefore this is a state with conflict.

"Here, bhikkhus, the speech of one who speaks unhurriedly is a state without suffering...Therefore this is a state without conflict.

"Here, bhikkhus, insistence on local language and overriding of normal usage is a state beset by suffering...Therefore this is a state with conflict.

"Here, bhikkhus, non-insistence on local language and non-overriding of normal usage is a state without suffering, vexation, despair, and fever, and it is the right way. Therefore this is a state without conflict.

14. "Therefore, bhikkhus, you should train yourselves thus: 'We shall know the state with conflict and we shall know the state without conflict, and knowing these, we shall enter upon the way without conflict.' Now, bhikkhus, Subhūti is a clansman who has entered upon the way without conflict."[1263]

That is what the Blessed One said. The bhikkhus were satisfied and delighted in the Blessed One's words.

140 *Dhātuvibhanga Sutta*
The Exposition of the Elements

1. THUS HAVE I HEARD. On one occasion the Blessed One was wandering in the Magadhan country and eventually arrived at Rājagaha. There he went to the potter Bhaggava and said to him:

2. "If it is not inconvenient for you, Bhaggava, I will stay one night in your workshop."

"It is not inconvenient for me, venerable sir, but there is a homeless one already staying there. If he agrees, then stay as long as you like, venerable sir." [238]

3. Now there was a clansman named Pukkusāti who had gone forth from the home life into homelessness out of faith in the Blessed One, and on that occasion he was already staying in the potter's workshop.[1264] Then the Blessed One went to the venerable Pukkusāti and said to him: "If it is not inconvenient for you, bhikkhu, I will stay one night in the workshop."

"The potter's workshop is large enough, friend.[1265] Let the venerable one stay as long as he likes."

4. Then the Blessed One entered the potter's workshop, prepared a spread of grass at one end, and sat down, folding his legs crosswise, setting his body erect, and establishing mindfulness in front of him. Then the Blessed One spent most of the night seated [in meditation], and the venerable Pukkusāti also spent most of the night seated [in meditation]. Then the Blessed One thought: "This clansman conducts himself in a way that inspires confidence. Suppose I were to question him." So he asked the venerable Pukkusāti:

5. "Under whom have you gone forth, bhikkhu? Who is your teacher? Whose Dhamma do you profess?"[1266]

"Friend, there is the recluse Gotama, the son of the Sakyans who went forth from a Sakyan clan. Now a good report of that Blessed Gotama has been spread to this effect: 'That Blessed One is accomplished, fully enlightened, perfect in true knowledge and conduct, sublime, knower of worlds, incomparable leader of persons to be tamed, teacher of gods and humans, enlightened, blessed.' I have gone forth under that Blessed One; that Blessed One is my teacher; I profess the Dhamma of that Blessed One."

"But, bhikkhu, where is that Blessed One, accomplished and fully enlightened, now living?"

"There is, friend, a city in the northern country named Sāvatthī. The Blessed One, accomplished and fully enlightened, is now living there."

"But, bhikkhu, have you ever seen that Blessed One before? Would you recognise him if you saw him?" [239]

"No, friend, I have never seen that Blessed One before, nor would I recognise him if I saw him."

6. Then the Blessed One thought: "This clansman has gone forth from the home life into homelessness under me. Suppose I were to teach him the Dhamma." So the Blessed One addressed the venerable Pukkusāti thus: "Bhikkhu, I will teach you the Dhamma. Listen and attend closely to what I shall say."—"Yes, friend," the venerable Pukkusāti replied. The Blessed One said this:

7. "Bhikkhu, this person consists of six elements, six bases of contact, and eighteen kinds of mental exploration, and he has four foundations.[1267] The tides of conceiving do not sweep over one who stands upon these [foundations], and when the tides of conceiving no longer sweep over him he is called a sage at peace. One should not neglect wisdom, should preserve truth, should cultivate relinquishment, and should train for peace. This is the summary of the exposition of the six elements.

8. "'Bhikkhu, this person consists of six elements.'[1268] So it was said. And with reference to what was this said? There are the earth element, the water element, the fire element, the air element, the space element, and the consciousness element. So it was with reference to this that it was said: 'Bhikkhu, this person consists of six elements.'

9. "'Bhikkhu, this person consists of six bases of contact.' So it was said. And with reference to what was this said? There are the base of eye-contact, the base of ear-contact, the base of nose-contact, the base of tongue-contact, the base of body-contact, and the base of mind-contact. So it was with reference to this that it was said: 'Bhikkhu, this person consists of six bases of contact.'

10. "'Bhikkhu, this person consists of eighteen kinds of mental exploration.'[1269] So it was said. And with reference to what was this said? On seeing a form with the eye, one explores a form productive of joy, one explores a form productive of grief, one explores a form productive of equanimity. On hearing a sound with the ear...[240] On smelling an odour with the nose...On tasting a flavour with the tongue...On touching a tangible with the body...On cognizing a mind-object with the mind, one explores a mind-object productive of joy, one explores a mind-object productive of grief, one explores a mind-object productive of equanimity. So it was with reference to this that it was said: 'Bhikkhu, this person consists of eighteen kinds of mental exploration.'

11. "'Bhikkhu, this person has four foundations.' So it was said. And with reference to what was this said? There are the foundation of wisdom, the foundation of truth, the foundation of relinquishment, and the foundation of peace.[1270] So it was with reference to this that it was said: 'Bhikkhu, this person has four foundations.'

12. "'One should not neglect wisdom, should preserve truth, should cultivate relinquishment, and should train for peace.'[1271] So it was said. And with reference to what was this said?

13. "How, bhikkhu, does one not neglect wisdom?[1272] There are these six elements: the earth element, the water element, the fire element, the air element, the space element, and the consciousness element.

14. "What, bhikkhu, is the earth element? The earth element may be either internal or external. What is the internal earth element? Whatever internally, belonging to oneself, is solid, solidified, and clung-to, that is, head-hairs, body-hairs, nails, teeth, skin, flesh, sinews, bones, bone-marrow, kidneys, heart, liver, diaphragm, spleen, lungs, intestines, mesentery, contents of the stomach, feces, or whatever else internally, belonging to oneself, is solid, solidified, and clung-to: this is called the internal earth element. Now both the internal earth element and the external earth element are simply earth element. And that should be seen as it actually is with proper wisdom thus: 'This is not mine, this I am not, this is not my self.' When one sees it thus as it actually is with proper wisdom, one becomes disenchanted with the earth element and makes the mind dispassionate towards the earth element.

15. "What, bhikkhu, is the water element? The water element may be either [241] internal or external. What is the internal water element? Whatever internally, belonging to oneself, is water, watery, and clung-to, that is, bile, phlegm, pus, blood, sweat, fat, tears, grease, spittle, snot, oil-of-the-joints, urine, or whatever else internally, belonging to oneself, is water, watery, and clung-to: this is called the internal water element. Now both the internal water element and the external water element are simply water element. And that should be seen as it actually is with proper wisdom thus: 'This is not mine, this I am not, this is not my self.' When one sees it thus as it actually is with proper wisdom, one becomes disenchanted with the water element and makes the mind dispassionate towards the water element.

16. "What, bhikkhu, is the fire element? The fire element may be either internal or external. What is the internal fire element? Whatever internally, belonging to oneself, is fire, fiery, and clung-to, that is, that by which one is warmed, ages, and is consumed, and that by which what is eaten, drunk, consumed, and tasted gets completely digested, or whatever else internally, belonging to oneself, is fire, fiery, and clung-to: this is called the internal fire element. Now both the internal fire element and the external fire element are simply fire element. And that should be seen as it actually is with proper wisdom thus: 'This is not mine, this I am not, this is not my self.' When one sees it thus as it actually is with proper wisdom, one becomes disenchanted with the fire element and makes the mind dispassionate towards the fire element.

17. "What, bhikkhu, is the air element? The air element may be either internal or external. What is the internal air element? Whatever internally, belonging to oneself, is air, airy, and clung-to, that is, up-going winds, down-going winds, winds in the belly, winds in the bowels, winds that course through the limbs, in-breath and out-breath, or whatever else internally, belonging to oneself, is air, airy, and clung-to: this is called the internal air element. Now both the internal air element and the external air element are simply air element. And that should be seen as it actually is with proper wisdom thus: 'This is not mine, this I am not, this is not my self.' When one sees it thus as it actually is with proper wisdom, one becomes disenchanted with the air element and makes the mind dispassionate towards the air element.

18. "What, bhikkhu, is the space element? The space element may be either internal or external. What is the internal [242] space element? Whatever internally, belonging to oneself, is space, spatial, and clung-to, that is, the holes of the ears, the nostrils, the door of the mouth, and that [aperture] whereby what is eaten, drunk, consumed, and tasted gets swallowed, and where it collects, and whereby it is excreted from below, or whatever else internally, belonging to oneself, is space, spatial, and clung-to: this is called the internal space element. Now both the internal space element and the external space element are simply space element. And that should be seen as it actually is with proper wisdom thus: 'This is not mine, this I am not, this is not my self.' When one sees it thus as it actually is with proper wisdom, one becomes disenchanted with the space element and makes the mind dispassionate towards the space element.

19. "Then there remains only consciousness, purified and bright.[1273] What does one cognize with that consciousness? One cognizes: '[This is] pleasant'; one cognizes: '[This is] painful'; one cognizes: '[This is] neither-painful-nor-pleasant.' In dependence on a contact to be felt as pleasant there arises a pleasant feeling.[1274] When one feels a pleasant feeling, one understands: 'I feel a pleasant feeling.' One understands: 'With the cessation of that same contact to be felt as pleasant, its corresponding feeling—the pleasant feeling that arose in dependence on that contact to be felt as pleasant—ceases and subsides.' In dependence on a contact to be felt as painful there arises a painful feeling. When one feels a painful feeling, one understands: 'I feel a painful feeling.' One understands: 'With the cessation of that same contact to be felt as painful, its corresponding feeling—the painful feeling that arose in dependence on that contact to be felt as painful—ceases and subsides.' In dependence on a contact to be felt as neither-painful-nor-pleasant there arises a neither-painful-nor-pleasant feeling. When one feels a neither-painful-nor-pleasant feeling, one understands: 'I feel a neither-painful-nor-pleasant feeling.' One understands: 'With the cessation of that same contact to be felt as neither-painful-nor-pleasant, its corresponding feeling—the neither-painful-nor-pleasant feeling that arose in dependence on that contact to be felt as neither-painful-nor-pleasant—ceases and subsides.' Bhikkhu, just as from the contact and friction of two fire-sticks heat is generated

and fire is produced, and with the separation and disjunction of these two fire-sticks the corresponding heat ceases and subsides; so too, [243] in dependence on a contact to be felt as pleasant...to be felt as painful...to be felt as neither-painful-nor-pleasant there arises a neither-painful-nor-pleasant feeling... One understands: 'With the cessation of that same contact to be felt as neither-painful-nor-pleasant, its corresponding feeling...ceases and subsides.'

20. "Then there remains only equanimity, purified and bright, malleable, wieldy, and radiant.[1275] Suppose, bhikkhu, a skilled goldsmith or his apprentice were to prepare a furnace, heat up the crucible, take some gold with tongs, and put it into the crucible. From time to time he would blow on it, from time to time he would sprinkle water over it, and from time to time he would just look on. That gold would become refined, well refined, completely refined, faultless, rid of dross, malleable, wieldy, and radiant. Then whatever kind of ornament he wished to make from it, whether a golden chain or earrings or a necklace or a golden garland, it would serve his purpose. So too, bhikkhu, then there remains only equanimity, purified and bright, malleable, wieldy, and radiant.

21. "He understands thus: 'If I were to direct this equanimity, so purified and bright, to the base of infinite space and to develop my mind accordingly, then this equanimity of mine, supported by that base, clinging to it, would remain for a very long time.[1276] If I were to direct this equanimity, so purified and bright, to the base of infinite consciousness...[244]...to the base of nothingness...to the base of neither-perception-nor-non-perception and to develop my mind accordingly, then this equanimity of mine, supported by that base, clinging to it, would remain for a very long time.'

22. "He understands thus: 'If I were to direct this equanimity, so purified and bright, to the base of infinite space and to develop my mind accordingly, this would be conditioned.[1277] If I were to direct this equanimity, so purified and bright, to the base of infinite consciousness...to the base of nothingness...to the base of neither-perception-nor-non-perception and to develop my mind accordingly, this would be conditioned.' He does not form any condition or generate any volition tending towards either being or non-being.[1278] Since he does not form any condition or generate

any volition tending towards either being or non-being, he does not cling to anything in this world. When he does not cling, he is not agitated. When he is not agitated, he personally attains Nibbāna. He understands thus: 'Birth is destroyed, the holy life has been lived, what had to be done has been done, there is no more coming to any state of being.'[1279]

23. "If he feels a pleasant feeling,[1280] he understands: 'It is impermanent; there is no holding to it; there is no delight in it.' If he feels a painful feeling, he understands: 'It is impermanent; there is no holding to it; there is no delight in it.' If he feels a neither-painful-nor-pleasant feeling, he understands: 'It is impermanent; there is no holding to it; there is no delight in it.'

24. "If he feels a pleasant feeling, he feels it detached; if he feels a painful feeling, he feels it detached; if he feels a neither-painful-nor-pleasant feeling, he feels it detached. When he feels a feeling terminating with the body, he understands: 'I feel a feeling terminating with the body.' [245] When he feels a feeling terminating with life, he understands: 'I feel a feeling terminating with life.'[1281] He understands: 'On the dissolution of the body, with the ending of life, all that is felt, not being delighted in, will become cool right here.'[1282] Bhikkhu, just as an oil-lamp burns in dependence on oil and a wick, and when the oil and wick are used up, if it does not get any more fuel, it is extinguished from lack of fuel; so too when he feels a feeling terminating with the body...a feeling terminating with life, he understands: 'I feel a feeling terminating with life.' He understands: 'On the dissolution of the body, with the ending of life, all that is felt, not being delighted in, will become cool right here.'

25. "Therefore a bhikkhu possessing [this wisdom] possesses the supreme foundation of wisdom. For this, bhikkhu, is the supreme noble wisdom, namely, the knowledge of the destruction of all suffering.[1283]

26. "His deliverance, being founded upon truth, is unshakeable. For that is false, bhikkhu, which has a deceptive nature, and that is true which has an undeceptive nature—Nibbāna. Therefore a bhikkhu possessing [this truth] possesses the supreme foundation of truth. For this, bhikkhu, is the supreme noble truth, namely, Nibbāna, which has an undeceptive nature.

27. "Formerly, when he was ignorant, he undertook and accepted acquisitions;[1284] now he has abandoned them, cut them off at the

root, made them like a palm stump, done away with them so that they are no longer subject to future arising. Therefore a bhikkhu possessing [this relinquishment] possesses the supreme foundation of relinquishment. For this, bhikkhu, is the supreme noble relinquishment, namely, the relinquishing of all acquisitions.

28. "Formerly, when he was ignorant, he experienced covetousness, desire, and lust; now he has abandoned them, cut them off at the root, made them like a palm stump, done away with them so that they are no longer subject to future arising. Formerly, when he was ignorant, he experienced anger, ill will, and hate; now he has abandoned them, cut them off at the root, made them like a palm stump, done away with them so that they are no longer subject to future arising. Formerly, when he was ignorant, he experienced ignorance and delusion; now he has abandoned them, cut them off [246] at the root, made them like a palm stump, done away with them so that they are no longer subject to future arising. Therefore a bhikkhu possessing [this peace] possesses the supreme foundation of peace. For this, bhikkhu, is the supreme noble peace, namely, the pacification of lust, hate, and delusion.

29. "So it was with reference to this that it was said: 'One should not neglect wisdom, should preserve truth, should cultivate relinquishment, and should train for peace.'

30. "'The tides of conceiving do not sweep over one who stands upon these [foundations], and when the tides of conceiving no longer sweep over him he is called a sage at peace.'[1285] So it was said. And with reference to what was this said?

31. "Bhikkhu, 'I am' is a conceiving; 'I am this' is a conceiving; 'I shall be' is a conceiving; 'I shall not be' is a conceiving; 'I shall be possessed of form' is a conceiving; 'I shall be formless' is a conceiving; 'I shall be percipient' is a conceiving; 'I shall be non-percipient' is a conceiving; 'I shall be neither-percipient-nor-non-percipient' is a conceiving. Conceiving is a disease, conceiving is a tumour, conceiving is a dart. By overcoming all conceivings, bhikkhu, one is called a sage at peace. And the sage at peace is not born, does not age, does not die; he is not shaken and is not agitated. For there is nothing present in him by which he might be born.[1286] Not being born, how could he age? Not ageing, how could he die? Not dying, how could he be shaken? Not being shaken, why should he be agitated?

32. "So it was with reference to this that it was said: 'The tides of conceiving do not sweep over one who stands upon these [foundations], and when the tides of conceiving no longer sweep over him he is called a sage at peace.' Bhikkhu, bear in mind this brief exposition of the six elements."

33. Thereupon the venerable Pukkusāti thought: "Indeed, the Teacher has come to me! The Sublime One has come to me! The Fully Enlightened One has come to me!" Then he rose from his seat, arranged his upper robe over one shoulder, and prostrating himself with his head at the Blessed One's feet, he said: "Venerable sir, a transgression overcame me, in that like a fool, confused [247] and blundering, I presumed to address the Blessed One as 'friend.' Venerable sir, may the Blessed One forgive my transgression seen as such for the sake of restraint in the future."

"Surely, bhikkhu, a transgression overcame you, in that like a fool, confused and blundering, you presumed to address me as 'friend.' But since you see your transgression as such and make amends in accordance with the Dhamma, we forgive you. For it is growth in the Noble One's Discipline when one sees one's transgression as such, makes amends in accordance with the Dhamma, and undertakes restraint in the future."

34. "Venerable sir, I would receive the full admission under the Blessed One."

"But are your bowl and robes complete, bhikkhu?"

"Venerable sir, my bowl and robes are not complete."

"Bhikkhu, Tathāgatas do not give the full admission to anyone whose bowl and robes are not complete."

35. Then the venerable Pukkusāti, having delighted and rejoiced in the Blessed One's words, rose from his seat, and after paying homage to the Blessed One, keeping him on his right, he departed in order to search for a bowl and robes. Then, while the venerable Pukkusāti was searching for a bowl and robes, a stray cow killed him.

36. Then a number of bhikkhus went to the Blessed One, and after paying homage to him, they sat down at one side and told him: "Venerable sir, the clansman Pukkusāti, who was given brief instruction by the Blessed One, has died. What is his destination? What is his future course?"

"Bhikkhus, the clansman Pukkusāti was wise. He practised in accordance with the Dhamma and did not trouble me in the interpretation of the Dhamma. With the destruction of the five lower fetters, the clansman Pukkusāti has reappeared spontaneously [in the Pure Abodes] and will attain final Nibbāna there without ever returning from that world."[1287]

That is what the Blessed One said. The bhikkhus were satisfied and delighted in the Blessed One's words.

141 *Saccavibhanga Sutta*
The Exposition of the Truths

[248] 1. THUS HAVE I HEARD. On one occasion the Blessed One was living at Benares in the Deer Park at Isipatana. There he addressed the bhikkhus thus: "Bhikkhus."—"Venerable sir," they replied. The Blessed One said this:

2. "At Benares, bhikkhus, in the Deer Park at Isipatana the Tathāgata, accomplished and fully enlightened, set rolling the matchless Wheel of the Dhamma,[1288] which cannot be stopped by any recluse or brahmin or god or Māra or Brahmā or anyone in the world—that is, the announcing, teaching, describing, establishing, revealing, expounding, and exhibiting of the Four Noble Truths. Of what four?

3. "The announcing, teaching, describing, establishing, revealing, expounding, and exhibiting of the noble truth of suffering. The announcing, teaching, describing, establishing, revealing, expounding, and exhibiting of the noble truth of the origin of suffering...of the noble truth of the cessation of suffering...of the noble truth of the way leading to the cessation of suffering.

4. "At Benares, bhikkhus, in the Deer Park at Isipatana the Tathāgata, accomplished and fully enlightened, set rolling the matchless Wheel of the Dhamma, which cannot be stopped by any recluse or brahmin or god or Māra or Brahmā or anyone in the world—that is, the announcing, teaching, describing, establishing, revealing, expounding, and exhibiting of these Four Noble Truths.

5. "Cultivate the friendship of Sāriputta and Moggallāna, bhikkhus; associate with Sāriputta and Moggallāna. They are wise and helpful to their companions in the holy life. Sāriputta is like a mother; Moggallāna is like a nurse. Sāriputta trains others for the fruit of stream-entry, Moggallāna for the supreme goal.[1289] Sāriputta, bhikkhus, is able to announce, teach, describe, establish, reveal, expound, and exhibit the Four Noble Truths."

6. So the Blessed One said. Having said this, the Sublime One rose from his seat and went into his dwelling. [249]

7. Then, soon after the Blessed One had gone, the venerable Sāriputta addressed the bhikkhus thus: "Friends, bhikkhus."—"Friend," the bhikkhus replied to the venerable Sāriputta. The venerable Sāriputta said this:

8. "At Benares, friends, in the Deer Park at Isipatana the Tathāgata, accomplished and fully enlightened, set rolling the matchless Wheel of the Dhamma...and exhibiting of the Four Noble Truths. Of what four?

9. "The announcing...and exhibiting of the noble truth of suffering...of the noble truth of the origin of suffering...of the noble truth of the cessation of suffering...of the noble truth of the way leading to the cessation of suffering.

10. "And what, friends, is the noble truth of suffering? Birth is suffering; ageing is suffering; death is suffering; sorrow, lamentation, pain, grief, and despair are suffering; not to obtain what one wants is suffering; in short, the five aggregates affected by clinging are suffering.

11. "And what, friends, is birth?[1290] The birth of beings into the various orders of beings, their coming to birth, precipitation [in a womb], generation, the manifestation of the aggregates, obtaining the bases for contact—this is called birth.

12. "And what, friends, is ageing? The ageing of beings in the various orders of beings, their old age, brokenness of teeth, greyness of hair, wrinkling of skin, decline of life, weakness of faculties—this is called ageing.

13. "And what, friends, is death? The passing of beings out of the various orders of beings, their passing away, dissolution, disappearance, dying, completion of time, dissolution of aggregates, laying down of the body—this is called death.

14. "And what, friends, is sorrow? The sorrow, sorrowing, sorrowfulness, inner sorrow, inner sorriness, of one who has encountered some misfortune or is affected by some painful state—this is called sorrow.

15. "And what, friends, is lamentation? The wail and lament, wailing and lamenting, [250] bewailing and lamentation, of one who has encountered some misfortune or is affected by some painful state—this is called lamentation.

16. "And what, friends, is pain? Bodily pain, bodily discomfort,

painful, uncomfortable feeling born of bodily contact—this is called pain.

17. "And what, friends, is grief? Mental pain, mental discomfort, painful, uncomfortable feeling born of mental contact—this is called grief.

18. "And what, friends, is despair? The trouble and despair, the tribulation and desperation, of one who has encountered some misfortune or is affected by some painful state—this is called despair.

19. "And what, friends, is 'not to obtain what one wants is suffering'? To beings subject to birth there comes the wish: 'Oh, that we were not subject to birth! That birth would not come to us!' But this is not to be obtained by wishing, and not to obtain what one wants is suffering. To beings subject to ageing...subject to sickness...subject to death...subject to sorrow, lamentation, pain, grief, and despair, there comes the wish: 'Oh, that we were not subject to sorrow, lamentation, pain, grief, and despair! That sorrow, lamentation, pain, grief, and despair would not come to us!' But this is not to be obtained by wishing, and not to obtain what one wants is suffering.

20. "And what, friends, are the five aggregates affected by clinging that, in short, are suffering? They are: the material form aggregate affected by clinging, the feeling aggregate affected by clinging, the perception aggregate affected by clinging, the formations aggregate affected by clinging, and the consciousness aggregate affected by clinging. These are the five aggregates affected by clinging that, in short, are suffering. This is called the noble truth of suffering.

21. "And what, friends, is the noble truth of the origin of suffering? It is craving, which brings renewal of being, is accompanied by delight and lust, and delights in this and that; that is, craving for sensual pleasures, craving for being, [251] and craving for non-being. This is called the noble truth of the origin of suffering.

22. "And what, friends, is the noble truth of the cessation of suffering? It is the remainderless fading away and ceasing, the giving up, relinquishing, letting go, and rejecting of that same craving. This is called the noble truth of the cessation of suffering.

23. "And what, friends, is the noble truth of the way leading to the cessation of suffering? It is just this Noble Eightfold

Path; that is, right view, right intention, right speech, right action, right livelihood, right effort, right mindfulness, and right concentration.

24. "And what, friends, is right view? Knowledge of suffering, knowledge of the origin of suffering, knowledge of the cessation of suffering, and knowledge of the way leading to the cessation of suffering—this is called right view.

25. "And what, friends, is right intention? Intention of renunciation, intention of non-ill will, and intention of non-cruelty—this is called right intention.

26. "And what, friends, is right speech? Abstaining from false speech, abstaining from malicious speech, abstaining from harsh speech, and abstaining from idle chatter—this is called right speech.

27. "And what, friends, is right action? Abstaining from killing living beings, abstaining from taking what is not given, and abstaining from misconduct in sensual pleasures—this is called right action.

28. "And what, friends, is right livelihood? Here a noble disciple, having abandoned wrong livelihood, earns his living by right livelihood—this is called right livelihood.

29. "And what, friends, is right effort? Here a bhikkhu awakens zeal for the non-arising of unarisen evil unwholesome states, and he makes effort, arouses energy, exerts his mind, and strives. He awakens zeal for the abandoning of arisen evil unwholesome states, and he makes effort, arouses energy, exerts his mind, and strives. He awakens zeal for the arising of unarisen wholesome states, [252] and he makes effort, arouses energy, exerts his mind, and strives. He awakens zeal for the continuance, non-disappearance, strengthening, increase, and fulfilment by development of arisen wholesome states, and he makes effort, arouses energy, exerts his mind, and strives. This is called right effort.

30. "And what, friends, is right mindfulness? Here a bhikkhu abides contemplating the body as a body, ardent, fully aware, and mindful, having put away covetousness and grief for the world. He abides contemplating feelings as feelings, ardent, fully aware, and mindful, having put away covetousness and grief for the world. He abides contemplating mind as mind, ardent, fully aware, and mindful, having put away covetousness

and grief for the world. He abides contemplating mind-objects as mind-objects, ardent, fully aware, and mindful, having put away covetousness and grief for the world. This is called right mindfulness.

31. "And what, friends, is right concentration? Here, quite secluded from sensual pleasures, secluded from unwholesome states, a bhikkhu enters upon and abides in the first jhāna, which is accompanied by applied and sustained thought, with rapture and pleasure born of seclusion. With the stilling of applied and sustained thought, he enters upon and abides in the second jhāna, which has self-confidence and singleness of mind without applied and sustained thought, with rapture and pleasure born of concentration. With the fading away as well of rapture, he abides in equanimity, and mindful and fully aware, still feeling pleasure with the body, he enters upon and abides in the third jhāna, on account of which noble ones announce: 'He has a pleasant abiding who has equanimity and is mindful.' With the abandoning of pleasure and pain, and with the previous disappearance of joy and grief, he enters upon and abides in the fourth jhāna, which has neither-pain-nor-pleasure and purity of mindfulness due to equanimity. This is called right concentration.

"This is called the noble truth of the way leading to the cessation of suffering.

32. "At Benares, friends, in the Deer Park at Isipatana the Tathāgata, accomplished and fully enlightened, set rolling the matchless Wheel of the Dhamma, which cannot be stopped by any recluse or brahmin or god or Māra or Brahmā or anyone in the world—that is, the announcing, teaching, describing, establishing, revealing, expounding, and exhibiting of these Four Noble Truths."

That is what the venerable Sāriputta said. The bhikkhus were satisfied and delighted in the venerable Sāriputta's words.

142 *Dakkhiṇāvibhanga Sutta*
The Exposition of Offerings

[253] 1. THUS HAVE I HEARD. On one occasion the Blessed One was living in the Sakyan country at Kapilavatthu in Nigrodha's Park.

2. Then Mahāpajāpatī Gotamī took a new pair of cloths and went to the Blessed One.[1291] After paying homage to him, she sat down at one side and said to the Blessed One: "Venerable sir, this new pair of cloths has been spun by me, woven by me, especially for the Blessed One. Venerable sir, let the Blessed One accept it from me out of compassion."

When this was said, the Blessed One told her: "Give it to the Sangha, Gotamī. When you give it to the Sangha, both I and the Sangha will be honoured."[1292]

A second time and a third time she said to the Blessed One: "Venerable sir,...accept it from me out of compassion."

A second time and a third time the Blessed One told her: "Give it to the Sangha, Gotamī. When you give it to the Sangha, both I and the Sangha will be honoured."

3. Then the venerable Ānanda said to the Blessed One: "Venerable sir, let the Blessed One accept the new pair of cloths from Mahāpajāpatī Gotamī. Mahāpajāpatī Gotamī has been very helpful to the Blessed One, venerable sir. As his mother's sister, she was his nurse, his foster mother, the one who gave him milk. She suckled the Blessed One when his own mother died. The Blessed One too has been very helpful to Mahāpajāpatī Gotamī, venerable sir. It is owing to the Blessed One that Mahāpajāpatī Gotamī has gone for refuge to the Buddha, the Dhamma, and the Sangha. It is owing to the Blessed One that Mahāpajāpatī Gotamī abstains from killing living beings, from taking what is not given, from misconduct in sensual pleasures, from false speech, and from wine, liquor, and intoxicants, which are the basis of negligence. It is owing to the Blessed One that Mahāpajāpatī Gotamī

possesses perfect confidence in the Buddha, the Dhamma, and the Sangha, and that she possesses [254] the virtues loved by noble ones.[1293] It is owing to the Blessed One that Mahāpajāpatī Gotamī is free from doubt about suffering, about the origin of suffering, about the cessation of suffering, and about the way leading to the cessation of suffering. The Blessed One has been very helpful to Mahāpajāpatī Gotamī."

4. "That is so, Ānanda, that is so! When one person, owing to another, has gone for refuge to the Buddha, the Dhamma, and the Sangha, I say that it is not easy for the former to repay the latter by paying homage to him, rising up for him, according him reverential salutation and polite services, and by providing robes, almsfood, resting places, and medicinal requisites.

"When one person, owing to another, has come to abstain from killing living beings, from taking what is not given, from misconduct in sensual pleasures, from false speech, and from wine, liquor, and intoxicants, which are the basis of negligence, I say that it is not easy for the former to repay the latter by paying homage to him...and medicinal requisites.

"When one person, owing to another, has come to possess perfect confidence in the Buddha, the Dhamma, and the Sangha, and to possess the virtues loved by noble ones, I say that it is not easy for the former to repay the latter by paying homage to him...and medicinal requisites.

"When one person, owing to another, has become free from doubt about suffering, about the origin of suffering, about the cessation of suffering, and about the way leading to the cessation of suffering, I say that it is not easy for the former to repay the latter by paying homage to him...and medicinal requisites.

5. "There are fourteen kinds of personal offerings, Ānanda.[1294] One gives a gift to the Tathāgata, accomplished and fully enlightened; this is the first kind of personal offering. One gives a gift to a paccekabuddha; this is the second kind of personal offering. One gives a gift to an arahant disciple of the Tathāgata; this is the third kind of personal offering. One gives a gift to one who has entered upon the way to the realisation of the fruit of arahantship; this is the fourth kind of personal offering. One gives a gift to a non-returner; this is the fifth kind of personal offering. [255] One gives a gift to one who has entered upon the way to the realisation of the fruit of non-return; this is the sixth

kind of personal offering. One gives a gift to a once-returner; this is the seventh kind of personal offering. One gives a gift to one who has entered upon the way to the realisation of the fruit of once-return; this is the eighth kind of personal offering. One gives a gift to a stream-enterer; this is the ninth kind of personal offering. One gives a gift to one who has entered upon the way to the realisation of the fruit of stream-entry;[1295] this is the tenth kind of personal offering. One gives a gift to one outside [the Dispensation] who is free from lust for sensual pleasures;[1296] this is the eleventh kind of personal offering. One gives a gift to a virtuous ordinary person; this is the twelfth kind of personal offering. One gives a gift to an immoral ordinary person; this is the thirteenth kind of personal offering. One gives a gift to an animal; this is the fourteenth kind of personal offering.

6. "Herein, Ānanda, by giving a gift to an animal, the offering may be expected to repay a hundredfold.[1297] By giving a gift to an immoral ordinary person, the offering may be expected to repay a thousandfold. By giving a gift to a virtuous ordinary person, the offering may be expected to repay a hundred-thousandfold. By giving a gift to one outside [the Dispensation] who is free from lust for sensual pleasures, the offering may be expected to repay a hundred-thousand times a hundred-thousandfold.

"By giving a gift to one who has entered upon the way to the realisation of the fruit of stream-entry, the offering may be expected to repay incalculably, immeasurably. What, then, should be said about giving a gift to a stream-enterer? What should be said about giving a gift to one who has entered upon the way to the realisation of the fruit of once-return…to a once-returner…to one who has entered upon the way to the realisation of the fruit of non-return…to a non-returner…to one who has entered upon the way to the realisation of the fruit of arahantship…to an arahant…to a paccekabuddha? What should be said about giving a gift to a Tathāgata, accomplished and fully enlightened?[1298]

7. "There are seven kinds of offerings made to the Sangha, Ānanda. One gives a gift to a Sangha of both [bhikkhus and bhikkhunīs] headed by the Buddha; this is the first kind of offering made to the Sangha.[1299] One gives a gift to a Sangha of both [bhikkhus and bhikkhunīs] after the Tathāgata has attained final Nibbāna; this is the second kind of offering made to the Sangha.

One gives a gift to a Sangha of bhikkhus; this is the third kind of offering made to the Sangha. One gives a gift to a Sangha of bhikkhunīs; this is the fourth kind of offering made to the Sangha. One gives a gift, saying: 'Appoint so many bhikkhus and bhikkhunīs for me from the Sangha'; [256] this is the fifth kind of offering made to the Sangha. One gives a gift, saying: 'Appoint so many bhikkhus for me from the Sangha'; this is the sixth kind of offering made to the Sangha. One gives a gift, saying: 'Appoint so many bhikkhunīs for me from the Sangha'; this is the seventh kind of offering made to the Sangha.

8. "In future times, Ānanda, there will be members of the clan who are 'yellow-necks,' immoral, of evil character.[1300] People will give gifts to those immoral persons for the sake of the Sangha. Even then, I say, an offering made to the Sangha is incalculable, immeasurable.[1301] And I say that in no way is a gift to a person individually ever more fruitful than an offering made to the Sangha.[1302]

9. "There are, Ānanda, four kinds of purification of offering. What four? There is the offering that is purified by the giver, not by the receiver.[1303] There is the offering that is purified by the receiver, not by the giver. There is the offering that is purified neither by the giver nor by the receiver. There is the offering that is purified both by the giver and by the receiver.

10. "And how is the offering purified by the giver, not by the receiver? Here the giver is virtuous, of good character, and the receiver is immoral, of evil character. Thus the offering is purified by the giver, not by the receiver.

11. "And how is the offering purified by the receiver, not by the giver? Here the giver is immoral, of evil character, and the receiver is virtuous, of good character. Thus the offering is purified by the receiver, not by the giver.

12. "And how is the offering purified neither by the giver nor by the receiver? Here the giver is immoral, of evil character, and the receiver is immoral, of evil character. Thus the offering is purified neither by the giver nor by the receiver.

13. "And how is the offering purified both by the giver and by the receiver? Here the giver is virtuous, of good character, and the receiver is virtuous, of good character. [257] Thus the offering is purified both by the giver and by the receiver. These are the four kinds of purification of offering."

14. That is what the Blessed One said. When the Sublime One had said that, the Teacher said further:

"When a virtuous person to an immoral person gives
With trusting heart a gift righteously obtained,
Placing faith that the fruit of action is great,
The giver's virtue purifies the offering.

When an immoral person to a virtuous person gives
With untrusting heart a gift unrighteously obtained,
Nor places faith that the fruit of action is great,
The receiver's virtue purifies the offering.

When an immoral person to an immoral person gives
With untrusting heart a gift unrighteously obtained,
Nor places faith that the fruit of action is great,
Neither's virtue purifies the offering.

When a virtuous person to a virtuous person gives
With trusting heart a gift righteously obtained,
Placing faith that the fruit of action is great,
That gift, I say, will come to full fruition.

When a passionless person to a passionless person gives
With trusting heart a gift righteously obtained,
Placing faith that the fruit of action is great,
That gift, I say, is the best of worldly gifts."[1304]

5

The Division of the Sixfold Base

(*Saḷāyatanavagga*)

143 *Anāthapiṇḍikovāda Sutta*
Advice to Anāthapiṇḍika

[258] 1. THUS HAVE I HEARD. On one occasion the Blessed One was living at Sāvatthī in Jeta's Grove, Anāthapiṇḍika's Park.

2. Now on that occasion the householder Anāthapiṇḍika was afflicted, suffering, and gravely ill. Then he addressed a certain man thus: "Come, good man, go to the Blessed One, pay homage in my name with your head at his feet, and say: 'Venerable sir, the householder Anāthapiṇḍika is afflicted, suffering, and gravely ill; he pays homage with his head at the Blessed One's feet.' Then go to the venerable Sāriputta, pay homage in my name with your head at his feet, and say: 'Venerable sir, the householder Anāthapiṇḍika is afflicted, suffering, and gravely ill; he pays homage with his head at the venerable Sāriputta's feet.' Then say: 'It would be good, venerable sir, if the venerable Sāriputta would come to the residence of the householder Anāthapiṇḍika, out of compassion.'"

"Yes, sir," the man replied, and he went to the Blessed One, and after paying homage to the Blessed One, he sat down at one side and delivered his message. Then he went to the venerable Sāriputta, and after paying homage to the venerable Sāriputta, he delivered his message, saying: "It would be good, venerable sir, if the venerable Sāriputta would come to the residence of the householder Anāthapiṇḍika, out of compassion." The venerable Sāriputta consented in silence.

3. Then the venerable Sāriputta dressed, and taking his bowl and outer robe, went to the residence of the householder Anāthapiṇḍika with the venerable Ānanda as his attendant. Having gone there, [259] he sat down on a seat made ready and said to the householder Anāthapiṇḍika: "I hope you are getting well, householder, I hope you are comfortable. I hope your

painful feelings are subsiding and not increasing, and that their subsiding, not their increase, is apparent."

4. "Venerable Sāriputta, I am not getting well, I am not comfortable. My painful feelings are increasing, not subsiding; their increase and not their subsiding is apparent. Just as if a strong man were splitting my head open with a sharp sword, so too, violent winds cut through my head. I am not getting well...Just as if a strong man were tightening a tough leather strap around my head as a headband, so too, there are violent pains in my head. I am not getting well...Just as if a skilled butcher or his apprentice were to carve up an ox's belly with a sharp butcher's knife, so too, violent winds are carving up my belly. I am not getting well...Just as if two strong men were to seize a weaker man by both arms and roast him over a pit of hot coals, so too, there is a violent burning in my body. I am not getting well, I am not comfortable. My painful feelings are increasing, not subsiding; their increase and not their subsiding is apparent."

5. "Then, householder, you should train thus: 'I will not cling to the eye, and my consciousness will not be dependent on the eye.'[1305] Thus you should train. You should train thus: 'I will not cling to the ear...I will not cling to the nose...I will not cling to the tongue...I will not cling to the body...I will not cling to the mind, and my consciousness will not be dependent on the mind.' Thus you should train.

6. "Householder, you should train thus: 'I will not cling to forms...I will not cling to sounds...I will not cling to odours...I will not cling to flavours...I will not cling to tangibles...I will not cling to mind-objects, and my consciousness will not be dependent on mind-objects.' Thus you should train.

7. "Householder, you should train thus: 'I will not cling to eye-consciousness...I will not cling to ear-consciousness...I will not cling to nose-consciousness...I will not cling to tongue-consciousness...I will not cling to body-consciousness...I will not cling to mind-consciousness, and my consciousness will not be dependent on mind-consciousness.' Thus you should train.

8. "Householder, you should train thus: 'I will not cling to eye-contact...[260]...I will not cling to ear-contact...I will not cling to nose-contact...I will not cling to tongue-contact...I will not cling to body-contact...I will not cling to mind-contact, and

my consciousness will not be dependent on mind-contact.' Thus you should train.

9. "Householder, you should train thus: 'I will not cling to feeling born of eye-contact...I will not cling to feeling born of ear-contact...I will not cling to feeling born of nose-contact...I will not cling to feeling born of tongue-contact...I will not cling to feeling born of body-contact...I will not cling to feeling born of mind-contact, and my consciousness will not be dependent on feeling born of mind-contact.' Thus you should train.

10. "Householder, you should train thus: 'I will not cling to the earth element...I will not cling to the water element...I will not cling to the fire element...I will not cling to the air element...I will not cling to the space element...I will not cling to the consciousness element, and my consciousness will not be dependent on the consciousness element.' Thus you should train.

11. "Householder, you should train thus: 'I will not cling to material form...I will not cling to feeling...I will not cling to perception...I will not cling to formations...I will not cling to consciousness, and my consciousness will not be dependent on consciousness.' Thus you should train.

12. "Householder, you should train thus: 'I will not cling to the base of infinite space...I will not cling to the base of infinite consciousness...I will not cling to the base of nothingness [261]...I will not cling to the base of neither-perception-nor-non-perception, and my consciousness will not be dependent on the base of neither-perception-nor-non-perception.' Thus you should train.

13. "Householder, you should train thus: 'I will not cling to this world, and my consciousness will not be dependent on this world. I will not cling to the world beyond, and my consciousness will not be dependent on the world beyond.' Thus you should train.

14. "Householder, you should train thus: 'I will not cling to what is seen, heard, sensed, cognized, encountered, sought after, and examined by the mind, and my consciousness will not be dependent on that.' Thus you should train."

15. When this was said, the householder Anāthapiṇḍika wept and shed tears. Then the venerable Ānanda asked him: "Are you foundering, householder, are you sinking?"

"I am not foundering, venerable Ānanda, I am not sinking. But although I have long waited upon the Teacher and bhikkhus worthy of esteem, never before have I heard such a talk on the Dhamma."

"Such talk on the Dhamma, householder, is not given to lay people clothed in white. Such talk on the Dhamma is given to those who have gone forth."[1306]

"Well then, venerable Sāriputta, let such talk on the Dhamma be given to lay people clothed in white. There are clansmen with little dust in their eyes who are wasting away through not hearing [such talk on] the Dhamma. There will be those who will understand the Dhamma."

16. Then, after giving the householder Anāthapiṇḍika this advice, the venerable Sāriputta and the venerable Ānanda rose from their seats and departed. Soon after they had left, [262] the householder Anāthapiṇḍika died and reappeared in the Tusita heaven.

17. Then, when the night was well advanced, Anāthapiṇḍika, now a young god of beautiful appearance, went to the Blessed One, illuminating the whole of Jeta's Grove. After paying homage to the Blessed One, he stood at one side and addressed the Blessed One in stanzas:

"Oh blessed is this Jeta's Grove,
Dwelt in by the sagely Sangha,
Wherein resides the King of Dhamma,
The fount of all my happiness.

By action, knowledge and Dhamma,
By virtue and noble way of life—
By these are mortals purified,
Not by lineage or wealth.

Therefore a wise person who sees
What truly leads to his own good,
Should investigate the Dhamma
And purify himself with it.

Sāriputta has reached the peak
In virtue, peace, and wisdom's ways;

Any bhikkhu who has gone beyond
At best can only equal him."

18. That is what the young god Anāthapiṇḍika said, and the Teacher approved. Then the young god Anāthapiṇḍika, thinking: "The Teacher has approved of me," paid homage to the Blessed One, and keeping him on his right, he vanished at once.

19. When the night had ended, the Blessed One addressed the bhikkhus thus: "Bhikkhus, last night when the night was well advanced, there came to me a certain young god of beautiful appearance who illuminated the whole of Jeta's Grove. After paying homage to me, he stood at one side and addressed me in stanzas thus:

'Oh blessed is this Jeta's Grove...
At best can only equal him.' [263]

That is what the young god said. Then the young god, thinking: 'The Teacher has approved of me,' paid homage to me, and keeping me on his right, he vanished at once."

20. When this was said, the venerable Ānanda said to the Blessed One: "Surely, venerable sir, that young god must have been Anāthapiṇḍika. For the householder Anāthapiṇḍika had perfect confidence in the venerable Sāriputta."

"Good, good, Ānanda! As far as reasoning goes you have drawn the right conclusion. That young god was Anāthapiṇḍika, no one else."

That is what the Blessed One said. The venerable Ānanda was satisfied and delighted in the Blessed One's words.

144 *Channovāda Sutta*
Advice to Channa

1. THUS HAVE I HEARD. On one occasion the Blessed One was living at Rājagaha in the Bamboo Grove, the Squirrels' Sanctuary.

2. Now on that occasion the venerable Sāriputta, the venerable Mahā Cunda, and the venerable Channa were living on the mountain Vulture Peak.

3. On that occasion the venerable Channa was afflicted, suffering, and gravely ill. Then, when it was evening, the venerable Sāriputta rose from meditation, went to the venerable Mahā Cunda, and said to him: "Friend Cunda, let us go to the venerable Channa and ask about his illness."—"Yes, friend," the venerable Mahā Cunda replied.

4. Then the venerable Sāriputta and the venerable Mahā Cunda went to the venerable Channa and exchanged greetings with him. When [264] this courteous and amiable talk was finished, they sat down at one side and the venerable Sāriputta said to the venerable Channa: "I hope you are getting well, friend Channa, I hope you are comfortable. I hope your painful feelings are subsiding and not increasing, and that their subsiding, not their increase, is apparent."

5. "Friend Sāriputta, I am not getting well, I am not comfortable. My painful feelings are increasing, not subsiding;...(*as Sutta 143, §4*)...their increase and not their subsiding is apparent. I shall use the knife,[1307] friend Sāriputta; I have no desire to live."

6. "Let the venerable Channa not use the knife. Let the venerable Channa live. We want the venerable Channa to live. If he lacks suitable food, I will go in search of suitable food for him. If he lacks suitable medicine, I will go in search of suitable medicine for him. If he lacks a proper attendant, I will attend on him. Let the venerable Channa not use the knife. Let the venerable Channa live. We want the venerable Channa to live."

7. "Friend Sāriputta, it is not that I have no suitable food and medicine or no proper attendant. But rather, friend Sāriputta, the Teacher has long been worshipped by me with love, not without love; for it is proper for the disciple to worship the Teacher with love, not without love. Friend Sāriputta, remember this: the bhikkhu Channa will use the knife blamelessly."[1308]

8. "We would ask the venerable Channa certain questions, if the venerable Channa finds it opportune to reply."

"Ask, friend Sāriputta. When I have heard, I shall know."

9. "Friend Channa, do you regard the eye, eye-consciousness, and things cognizable [by the mind] through eye-consciousness thus: 'This is mine, this I am, [265] this is my self'? Do you regard the ear...the nose...the tongue...the body...the mind, mind-consciousness, and things cognizable [by the mind] through mind-consciousness thus: 'This is mine, this I am, this is my self'?"

"Friend Sāriputta, I regard the eye, eye-consciousness, and things cognizable [by the mind] through eye-consciousness thus: 'This is not mine, this I am not, this is not my self.' I regard the ear...the nose...the tongue...the body...the mind, mind-consciousness, and things cognizable [by the mind] through mind-consciousness thus: 'This is not mine, this I am not, this is not my self.'"

10. "Friend Channa, what have you seen and directly known in the eye, in eye-consciousness, and in things cognizable [by the mind] through eye-consciousness, that you regard them thus: 'This is not mine, this I am not, this is not my self'? What have you seen and directly known in the ear...in the nose...in the tongue...in the body...in the mind, in mind-consciousness, and in things cognizable [by the mind] through mind-consciousness, that you regard them thus: 'This is not mine, this I am not, this is not my self'?"

"Friend Sāriputta, it is through seeing and directly knowing cessation in the eye, in eye-consciousness, and in things cognizable [by the mind] through eye-consciousness, that I regard them thus: 'This is not mine, this I am not, this is not my self.' It is through seeing and directly knowing cessation in the ear...in the nose...in the tongue...in the body...in the mind, in mind-consciousness, and in things cognizable [by the mind] through mind-consciousness, [266] that I regard them thus: 'This is not mine, this I am not, this is not my self.'"

11. When this was said, the venerable Mahā Cunda said to the venerable Channa:[1309] "Therefore, friend Channa, this instruction of the Blessed One's is to be constantly given attention: 'There is wavering in one who is dependent, there is no wavering in one who is independent; when there is no wavering, there is tranquillity; when there is tranquillity, there is no bias; when there is no bias, there is no coming and going; when there is no coming and going, there is no passing away and reappearing; when there is no passing away and reappearing, there is no here nor beyond nor in between. This is the end of suffering.'"[1310]

12. Then when the venerable Sāriputta and the venerable Mahā Cunda had advised the venerable Channa thus, they rose from their seats and went away. Then, soon after they had gone, the venerable Channa used the knife.[1311]

13. Then the venerable Sāriputta went to the Blessed One, and after paying homage to him, he sat down at one side and said to the Blessed One: "Venerable sir, the venerable Channa has used the knife. What is his destination, what is his future course?"

"Sāriputta, didn't the bhikkhu Channa declare to you his blamelessness?"[1312]

"Venerable sir, there is a Vajjian village called Pubbajira. There the venerable Channa had friendly families, intimate families, approachable families [as his supporters]."[1313]

"Indeed, Sāriputta, the bhikkhu Channa had friendly families, intimate families, approachable families [as his supporters]; but I do not say that to this extent he was blameworthy. Sāriputta, when one lays down this body and takes up a new body, then I say one is blameworthy. This did not happen in the case of the bhikkhu Channa; the bhikkhu Channa used the knife blamelessly."[1314]

That is what the Blessed One said. The venerable Sāriputta was satisfied and delighted in the Blessed One's words.

145 *Puṇṇovāda Sutta*
Advice to Puṇṇa

[267] 1. THUS HAVE I HEARD. On one occasion the Blessed One was living at Sāvatthī in Jeta's Grove, Anāthapiṇḍika's Park. Then, when it was evening, the venerable Puṇṇa rose from meditation and went to the Blessed One.[1315] After paying homage to the Blessed One, he sat down at one side and said to him:

2. "Venerable sir, it would be good if the Blessed One would give me brief advice. Having heard the Dhamma from the Blessed One, I will abide alone, withdrawn, diligent, ardent, and resolute."

"Well then, Puṇṇa, listen and attend carefully to what I shall say."

"Yes, venerable sir," the venerable Puṇṇa replied. The Blessed One said this:

3. "Puṇṇa, there are forms cognizable by the eye that are wished for, desired, agreeable, and likeable, connected with sensual desire and provocative of lust. If a bhikkhu delights in them, welcomes them, and remains holding to them, delight arises in him. With the arising of delight, Puṇṇa, there is the arising of suffering, I say.[1316] There are, Puṇṇa, sounds cognizable by the ear...odours cognizable by the nose...flavours cognizable by the tongue...tangibles cognizable by the body...mind-objects cognizable by the mind that are wished for, desired, agreeable, and likeable, connected with sensual desire [268] and provocative of lust. If a bhikkhu delights in them, welcomes them, and remains holding to them, delight arises in him. With the arising of delight, Puṇṇa, there is the arising of suffering, I say.

4. "Puṇṇa, there are forms cognizable by the eye...sounds cognizable by the ear...odours cognizable by the nose...flavours cognizable by the tongue...tangibles cognizable by the body...

mind-objects cognizable by the mind that are wished for, desired, agreeable, and likeable, connected with sensual desire and provocative of lust. If a bhikkhu does not delight in them, welcome them, and remain holding to them, delight ceases in him. With the cessation of delight, Puṇṇa, there is the cessation of suffering, I say.

5. "Now that I have given you this brief advice, Puṇṇa, in which country will you dwell?"

"Venerable sir, now that the Blessed One has given me this brief advice, I am going to dwell in the Sunāparanta country."

"Puṇṇa, the people of Sunāparanta are fierce and rough. If they abuse and threaten you, what will you think then?"

"Venerable sir, if the people of Sunāparanta abuse and threaten me, then I shall think: 'These people of Sunāparanta are kind, truly kind, in that they did not give me a blow with the fist.' Then I shall think thus, Blessed One; then I shall think thus, Sublime One."

"But, Puṇṇa, if the people of Sunāparanta do give you a blow with the fist, what will you think then?"

"Venerable sir, if the people of Sunāparanta do give me a blow with the fist, then I shall think: 'These people of Sunāparanta are kind, truly kind, in that they did not give me a blow with a clod.' Then I shall think thus, Blessed One; then I shall think thus, Sublime One."

"But, Puṇṇa, if the people of Sunāparanta do give you a blow with a clod, what will you think then?"

"Venerable sir, if the people of Sunāparanta do give me a blow with a clod, then I shall think: 'These people of Sunāparanta are kind, truly kind, in that they did not give me a blow with a stick.' Then I shall think thus, Blessed One; then I shall think thus, Sublime One." [269]

"But, Puṇṇa, if the people of Sunāparanta do give you a blow with a stick, what will you think then?"

"Venerable sir, if the people of Sunāparanta do give me a blow with a stick, then I shall think: 'These people of Sunāparanta are kind, truly kind, in that they did not give me a blow with a knife.' Then I shall think thus, Blessed One; then I shall think thus, Sublime One."

"But, Puṇṇa, if the people of Sunāparanta do give you a blow with a knife, what will you think then?"

"Venerable sir, if the people of Sunāparanta do give me a blow with a knife, then I shall think: 'These people of Sunāparanta are kind, truly kind, in that they have not taken my life with a sharp knife.' Then I shall think thus, Blessed One; then I shall think thus, Sublime One."

"But, Puṇṇa, if the people of Sunāparanta do take your life with a sharp knife, what will you think then?"

"Venerable sir, if the people of Sunāparanta do take my life with a sharp knife, then I shall think thus: 'There have been disciples of the Blessed One who, being humiliated and disgusted by the body and by life, sought to have their lives deprived by the knife. But I have had my life deprived by the knife without seeking for it.' Then I shall think thus, Blessed One; then I shall think thus, Sublime One."

6. "Good, good, Puṇṇa! Possessing such self-control and peacefulness, you will be able to dwell in the Sunāparanta country. Now, Puṇṇa, it is time to do as you think fit."

7. Then, having delighted and rejoiced in the Blessed One's words, the venerable Puṇṇa rose from his seat, and after paying homage to the Blessed One, departed keeping him on his right. He then set his resting place in order, took his bowl and outer robe, and set out to wander towards the Sunāparanta country. Wandering by stages, he eventually arrived in the Sunāparanta country, and there he lived. Then, during that Rains, the venerable Puṇṇa established five hundred men lay followers and five hundred women lay followers in the practice, and he himself realised the three true knowledges. On a later occasion, the venerable Puṇṇa attained final Nibbāna.[1317]

8. Then a number of bhikkhus went to the Blessed One, and after paying homage to him, they sat down at one side and told him: "Venerable sir, the clansman Puṇṇa, who [270] was given brief advice by the Blessed One, has died. What is his destination? What is his future course?"

"Bhikkhus, the clansman Puṇṇa was wise. He practised in accordance with the Dhamma and did not trouble me in the interpretation of the Dhamma. The clansman Puṇṇa has attained final Nibbāna."

That is what the Blessed One said. The bhikkhus were satisfied and delighted in the Blessed One's words.

146 *Nandakovāda Sutta*
Advice from Nandaka

1. THUS HAVE I HEARD. On one occasion the Blessed One was living at Sāvatthī in Jeta's Grove, Anāthapiṇḍika's Park.

2. Then Mahāpajāpatī Gotamī together with five hundred bhikkhunīs went to the Blessed One. After paying homage to the Blessed One, she stood at one side and said to him: "Venerable sir, let the Blessed One advise the bhikkhunīs, let the Blessed One instruct the bhikkhunīs, let the Blessed One give the bhikkhunīs a talk on the Dhamma."

3. Now on that occasion the elder bhikkhus were taking turns in advising the bhikkhunīs, but the venerable Nandaka did not want to advise them when his turn came.[1318] Then the Blessed One addressed the venerable Ānanda: "Ānanda, whose turn is it today to advise the bhikkhunīs?"

"Venerable sir, it is the venerable Nandaka's turn to advise the bhikkhunīs, but he does not want to advise them even though it is his turn."

4. Then the Blessed One addressed the venerable Nandaka: "Advise the bhikkhunīs, Nandaka. Instruct the bhikkhunīs, Nandaka. Give the bhikkhunīs a talk on the Dhamma, brahmin."

"Yes, venerable sir," [271] the venerable Nandaka replied. Then, in the morning, the venerable Nandaka dressed, and taking his bowl and outer robe, went into Sāvatthī for alms. When he had wandered for alms in Sāvatthī and had returned from his almsround, after his meal he went with a companion to the Rājaka Park. The bhikkhunīs saw the venerable Nandaka coming in the distance and prepared a seat and set out water for the feet. The venerable Nandaka sat down on the seat made ready and washed his feet. The bhikkhunīs paid homage to him and sat down at one side. When they were seated, the venerable Nandaka told the bhikkhunīs:

5. "Sisters, this talk will be in the form of questions. When you understand you should say: 'We understand'; when you do not understand you should say: 'We do not understand'; when you are doubtful or perplexed you should ask me: 'How is this, venerable sir? What is the meaning of this?'"

"Venerable sir, we are satisfied and pleased with the master Nandaka for inviting us in this way."

6. "Sisters, what do you think? Is the eye permanent or impermanent?"—"Impermanent, venerable sir."—"Is what is impermanent suffering or happiness?"—"Suffering, venerable sir."—"Is what is impermanent, suffering, and subject to change fit to be regarded thus: 'This is mine, this I am, this is my self'?"—"No, venerable sir."

"Sisters, what do you think? Is the ear...the nose...the tongue...the body...the mind permanent or impermanent?"—"Impermanent, venerable sir."—"Is what is impermanent suffering or happiness?"—"Suffering, venerable sir."—"Is what is impermanent, suffering, [272] and subject to change fit to be regarded thus: 'This is mine, this I am, this is my self'?"—"No, venerable sir. Why is that? Because, venerable sir, we have already seen this well as it actually is with proper wisdom thus: 'These six internal bases are impermanent.'"[1319]

"Good, good, sisters! So it is with a noble disciple who sees this as it actually is with proper wisdom.

7. "Sisters, what do you think? Are forms...sounds...odours...flavours...tangibles...mind-objects permanent or impermanent?"—"Impermanent, venerable sir."—"Is what is impermanent suffering or happiness?"—"Suffering, venerable sir."—"Is what is impermanent, suffering, and subject to change fit to be regarded thus: 'This is mine, this I am, this is my self'?"—"No, venerable sir. Why is that? Because, venerable sir, we have already seen this well as it actually is with proper wisdom thus: 'These six external bases are impermanent.'"

"Good, good, sisters! So it is with a noble disciple who sees this as it actually is with proper wisdom.

8. "Sisters, what do you think? Is eye-consciousness... [273]...ear-consciousness...nose-consciousness...tongue-consciousness...body-consciousness...mind-consciousness permanent or impermanent?"—"Impermanent, venerable sir."—"Is what is impermanent suffering or happiness?"—"Suffering, venerable sir."—

"Is what is impermanent, suffering, and subject to change fit to be regarded thus: 'This is mine, this I am, this is my self'?"—"No, venerable sir. Why is that? Because, venerable sir, we have already seen this well as it actually is with proper wisdom thus: 'These six classes of consciousness are impermanent.'"

"Good, good, sisters! So it is with a noble disciple who sees this as it actually is with proper wisdom.

9. "Sisters, suppose an oil-lamp is burning: its oil is impermanent and subject to change, its wick is impermanent and subject to change, its flame is impermanent and subject to change, and its radiance is impermanent and subject to change. Now would anyone be speaking rightly who spoke thus: 'While this oil-lamp is burning, its oil, wick, and flame are impermanent and subject to change, but its radiance is permanent, everlasting, eternal, not subject to change'?"

"No, venerable sir. Why is that? Because, venerable sir, while that oil-lamp is burning, its oil, wick, and flame are impermanent and subject to change, so its radiance must be impermanent and subject to change."

"So too, sisters, would anyone be speaking rightly who spoke thus: 'These six internal bases are impermanent and subject to change, but the pleasant, painful, or neither-painful-nor-pleasant feeling that one experiences in dependence upon the six internal bases is permanent, everlasting, eternal, not subject to change'?"

"No, venerable sir. Why is that? Because each feeling arises in dependence upon its corresponding condition,[1320] [274] and with the cessation of its corresponding condition, the feeling ceases."

"Good, good, sisters! So it is with a noble disciple who sees this as it actually is with proper wisdom.

10. "Sisters, suppose a great tree is standing possessed of heartwood: its root is impermanent and subject to change, its trunk is impermanent and subject to change, its branches and foliage are impermanent and subject to change, and its shadow is impermanent and subject to change. Now would anyone be speaking rightly who spoke thus: 'The root, trunk, branches, and foliage of this great tree standing possessed of heartwood are impermanent and subject to change, but its shadow is permanent, everlasting, eternal, not subject to change'?"

"No, venerable sir. Why is that? Because, venerable sir, the root, trunk, branches, and foliage of this great tree standing possessed of heartwood are impermanent and subject to change, so its shadow must be impermanent and subject to change."

"So too, sisters, would anyone be speaking rightly who spoke thus: 'These six external bases are impermanent and subject to change, but the pleasant, painful, or neither-painful-nor-pleasant feeling that one experiences in dependence upon the six external bases is permanent, everlasting, eternal, not subject to change'?"

"No, venerable sir. Why is that? Because each feeling arises in dependence upon its corresponding condition, and with the cessation of its corresponding condition, the feeling ceases."

"Good, good, sisters! So it is with a noble disciple who sees this as it actually is with proper wisdom.

11. "Sisters, suppose a skilled butcher or his apprentice were to kill a cow and carve it up with a sharp butcher's knife. Without damaging the inner mass of flesh and without damaging the outer hide, he would cut, sever, and carve away the inner tendons, sinews, and ligaments with the sharp butcher's knife. [275] Then having cut, severed, and carved all this away, he would remove the outer hide and cover the cow again with that same hide. Would he be speaking rightly if he were to say: 'This cow is joined to this hide just as it was before'?"

"No, venerable sir. Why is that? Because if that skilled butcher or his apprentice were to kill a cow...and cut, sever, and carve all that away, even though he covers the cow again with that same hide and says: 'This cow is joined to this hide just as it was before,' that cow would still be disjoined from that hide."

12. "Sisters, I have given this simile in order to convey a meaning. This is the meaning: 'The inner mass of flesh' is a term for the six internal bases. 'The outer hide' is a term for the six external bases. 'The inner tendons, sinews, and ligaments' is a term for delight and lust. 'The sharp butcher's knife' is a term for noble wisdom—the noble wisdom that cuts, severs, and carves away the inner defilements, fetters, and bonds.

13. "Sisters, there are these seven enlightenment factors[1321] through the development and cultivation of which a bhikkhu, by realising for himself with direct knowledge, here and now enters upon and abides in the deliverance of mind and deliverance by wisdom that are taintless with the destruction of the taints. What are the seven? Here, sisters, a bhikkhu develops the mindfulness enlightenment factor, which is supported by

seclusion, dispassion, and cessation, and ripens in relinquishment. He develops the investigation-of-states enlightenment factor... the energy enlightenment factor...the rapture enlightenment factor...the tranquillity enlightenment factor...the concentration enlightenment factor...the equanimity enlightenment factor, which is supported by seclusion, dispassion, and cessation, and ripens in relinquishment. These are the seven enlightenment factors through the development and cultivation of which a bhikkhu, by realising for himself with direct knowledge, here and now enters upon and abides in the deliverance of mind and deliverance by wisdom that are taintless with the destruction of the taints." [276]

14. When the venerable Nandaka had advised the bhikkhunīs thus, he dismissed them, saying: "Go, sisters, it is time." Then the bhikkhunīs, having delighted and rejoiced in the venerable Nandaka's words, rose from their seats, and after paying homage to the venerable Nandaka, departed keeping him on their right. They went to the Blessed One, and after paying homage to him, stood at one side. The Blessed One told them: "Go, sisters, it is time." Then the bhikkhunīs paid homage to the Blessed One and departed keeping him on their right.

15. Soon after they had left, the Blessed One addressed the bhikkhus: "Bhikkhus, just as on the Uposatha day of the fourteenth people are not doubtful or perplexed as to whether the moon is incomplete or full, since then the moon is clearly incomplete, so too, those bhikkhunīs are satisfied with Nandaka's teaching of the Dhamma, but their intention has not yet been fulfilled."

16–26. Then the Blessed One addressed the venerable Nandaka: "Well then, Nandaka, tomorrow too you should advise those bhikkhunīs in exactly the same way."

"Yes, venerable sir," the venerable Nandaka replied. Then, the next morning, the venerable Nandaka dressed...(*repeat verbatim §§4–14 above, as far as*) [277]...Then the bhikkhunīs paid homage to the Blessed One and departed keeping him on their right.

27. Soon after they had left, the Blessed One addressed the bhikkhus: "Bhikkhus, just as on the Uposatha day of the fifteenth people are not doubtful or perplexed as to whether the moon is incomplete or full, since then the moon is clearly full, so too, those bhikkhunīs are satisfied with Nandaka's teaching of the Dhamma and their intention has been fulfilled. Bhikkhus,

even the least advanced of those five hundred bhikkhunīs is a stream-enterer, no longer subject to perdition, bound [for deliverance], headed for enlightenment."[1322]

That is what the Blessed One said. The bhikkhus were satisfied and delighted in the Blessed One's words.

147 *Cūḷarāhulovāda Sutta*
The Shorter Discourse of Advice to Rāhula

1. THUS HAVE I HEARD. On one occasion the Blessed One was living at Sāvatthī in Jeta's Grove, Anāthapiṇḍika's Park.[1323]

2. Then, while the Blessed One was alone in meditation, a thought arose in his mind thus: "The states that ripen in deliverance have ripened in Rāhula.[1324] Suppose I were to lead him on further to the destruction of the taints."

Then, when it was morning, the Blessed One dressed, and taking his bowl and outer robe, went into Sāvatthī for alms. When he had walked for alms in Sāvatthī and had returned from his almsround, after his meal he addressed the venerable Rāhula thus:

"Take your sitting cloth with you, Rāhula; let us go to the Blind Men's Grove [278] to pass the day."

"Yes, venerable sir," the venerable Rāhula replied, and taking his sitting cloth with him, he followed close behind the Blessed One.

Now on that occasion many thousands of deities followed the Blessed One, thinking: "Today the Blessed One will lead the venerable Rāhula further to the destruction of the taints."[1325] Then the Blessed One went into the Blind Men's Grove and sat down at the root of a certain tree on a seat made ready. And the venerable Rāhula paid homage to the Blessed One and sat down at one side. The Blessed One then said to the venerable Rāhula:

3. "Rāhula, what do you think? Is the eye permanent or impermanent?"—"Impermanent, venerable sir."—"Is what is impermanent suffering or happiness?"—"Suffering, venerable sir."—"Is what is impermanent, suffering, and subject to change fit to be regarded thus: 'This is mine, this I am, this is my self'?"—"No, venerable sir."

"Rāhula, what do you think? Are forms...Is eye-consciousness ...[279]...Is eye-contact...Is anything comprised within the feeling, perception, formations, and consciousness that arise with eye-contact as condition permanent or impermanent?"[1326]—"Impermanent, venerable sir."—"Is what is impermanent suffering or happiness?"—"Suffering, venerable sir."—"Is what is impermanent, suffering, and subject to change fit to be regarded thus: 'This is mine, this I am, this is my self'?"—"No, venerable sir."

4–8. "Rāhula, what do you think? Is the ear permanent or impermanent?...Is the nose permanent or impermanent?...Is the tongue permanent or impermanent?...Is the body permanent or impermanent?...Is the mind permanent or impermanent?...Are mind-objects...Is mind-consciousness...Is mind-contact...Is anything comprised within the feeling, perception, formations, and consciousness that arise with mind-contact as condition permanent or impermanent?"—"Impermanent, venerable sir."—"Is what is impermanent suffering or happiness?"—"Suffering, venerable sir."—"Is what is impermanent, suffering, and subject to change fit to be regarded thus: 'This is mine, this I am, this is my self'?"—"No, venerable sir."

9. "Seeing thus, Rāhula, a well-taught noble disciple becomes disenchanted with the eye, disenchanted with forms, disenchanted with eye-consciousness, disenchanted with eye-contact, and disenchanted with anything comprised within the feeling, perception, formations, and consciousness that arise with eye-contact as condition.

"He becomes disenchanted with the ear...He becomes disenchanted with the nose...He becomes disenchanted with the tongue...He becomes disenchanted with the body...He becomes disenchanted with the mind, disenchanted with mind-objects, disenchanted with mind-consciousness, disenchanted with mind-contact, [280] and disenchanted with anything comprised within the feeling, perception, formations, and consciousness that arise with mind-contact as condition.

That is what the Blessed One said. The venerable Rāhula was satisfied and delighted in the Blessed One's words. Now while this discourse was being spoken, through not clinging the venerable Rāhula's mind was liberated from the taints.

And in those many thousands of deities there arose the spotless immaculate vision of the Dhamma: "All that is subject to arising is subject to cessation."[1327]

148 *Chachakka Sutta*
The Six Sets of Six

1. THUS HAVE I HEARD. On one occasion the Blessed One was living at Sāvatthī in Jeta's Grove, Anāthapiṇḍika's Park. There he addressed the bhikkhus thus: "Bhikkhus."—"Venerable sir," they replied. The Blessed One said this:

2. "Bhikkhus, I shall teach you the Dhamma that is good in the beginning, good in the middle, and good in the end, with the right meaning and phrasing; I shall reveal a holy life that is utterly perfect and pure,[1328] that is, the six sets of six. Listen and attend closely to what I shall say."—"Yes, venerable sir," the bhikkhus replied. The Blessed One said this:

(SYNOPSIS)

3. "The six internal bases should be understood. The six external bases should be understood. The six classes of consciousness should be understood. The six classes of contact should be understood. The six classes of feeling should be understood. The six classes of craving should be understood.

(ENUMERATION)

4. (i) "'The six internal bases should be understood.' So it was said. And with reference to what was this said? There are the eye-base, the ear-base, the nose-base, the tongue-base, the body-base, and the mind-base. So it was with reference to this that it was said: 'The six internal bases should be understood.' This is the first set of six. [281]

5. (ii) "'The six external bases should be understood.' So it was said. And with reference to what was this said? There are the form-base, the sound-base, the odour-base, the flavour-base, the

tangible-base, and the mind-object-base. So it was with reference to this that it was said: 'The six external bases should be understood.' This is the second set of six.

6. (iii) "'The six classes of consciousness should be understood.' So it was said. And with reference to what was this said? Dependent on the eye and forms, eye-consciousness arises; dependent on the ear and sounds, ear-consciousness arises; dependent on the nose and odours, nose-consciousness arises; dependent on the tongue and flavours, tongue-consciousness arises; dependent on the body and tangibles, body-consciousness arises; dependent on the mind and mind-objects, mind-consciousness arises. So it was with reference to this that it was said: 'The six classes of consciousness should be understood.' This is the third set of six.

7. (iv) "'The six classes of contact should be understood.' So it was said. And with reference to what was this said? Dependent on the eye and forms, eye-consciousness arises; the meeting of the three is contact. Dependent on the ear and sounds, ear-consciousness arises; the meeting of the three is contact. Dependent on the nose and odours, nose-consciousness arises; the meeting of the three is contact. Dependent on the tongue and flavours, tongue-consciousness arises; the meeting of the three is contact. Dependent on the body and tangibles, body-consciousness arises; the meeting of the three is contact. Dependent on the mind and mind-objects, mind-consciousness arises; the meeting of the three is contact. So it was with reference to this that it was said: 'The six classes of contact should be understood.' This is the fourth set of six.

8. (v) "'The six classes of feeling should be understood.' So it was said. And with reference to what was this said? Dependent on the eye and forms, eye-consciousness arises; the meeting of the three is contact; with contact as condition there is feeling. Dependent on the ear and sounds, ear-consciousness arises; the meeting of the three is contact; with contact as condition there is feeling. Dependent on the nose and odours, nose-consciousness arises; the meeting of the three is contact; with contact as condition there is feeling. Dependent on the tongue and flavours, tongue-consciousness arises; the meeting of the three is contact; with contact as condition there is feeling. Dependent on the body and tangibles, body-consciousness arises; the

meeting of the three is contact; with contact as condition there is feeling. Dependent on the mind and mind-objects, mind-consciousness arises; the meeting of the three is contact; with contact as condition there is feeling. So it was with reference to this that it was said: 'The six classes of feeling should be understood.' [282] This is the fifth set of six.

9. (vi) "'The six classes of craving should be understood.' So it was said. And with reference to what was this said? Dependent on the eye and forms, eye-consciousness arises; the meeting of the three is contact; with contact as condition there is feeling; with feeling as condition there is craving.[1329] Dependent on the ear and sounds, ear-consciousness arises...with feeling as condition there is craving. Dependent on the nose and odours, nose-consciousness arises...with feeling as condition there is craving. Dependent on the tongue and flavours, tongue-consciousness arises...with feeling as condition there is craving. Dependent on the body and tangibles, body-consciousness arises...with feeling as condition there is craving. Dependent on the mind and mind-objects, mind-consciousness arises; the meeting of the three is contact; with contact as condition there is feeling; with feeling as condition there is craving. So it was with reference to this that it was said: 'The six classes of craving should be understood.' This is the sixth set of six.

(DEMONSTRATION OF NOT SELF)

10. (i) "If anyone says, 'The eye is self,' that is not tenable.[1330] The rise and fall of the eye are discerned, and since its rise and fall are discerned, it would follow: 'My self rises and falls.' That is why it is not tenable for anyone to say, 'The eye is self.' Thus the eye is not self.[1331]

"If anyone says, 'Forms are self'[1332]...That is why it is not tenable for anyone to say, 'Forms are self.' Thus the eye is not self, forms are not self.

"If anyone says, 'Eye-consciousness is self'...That is why it is not tenable for anyone to say, 'Eye-consciousness is self.' Thus the eye is not self, forms are not self, eye-consciousness is not self.

"If anyone says, 'Eye-contact is self'...That is why it is not tenable for anyone to say, 'Eye-contact is self.' Thus the eye is not self, forms are not self, eye-consciousness is not self, eye-contact is not self.

"If anyone says, 'Feeling is self' [283]...That is why it is not tenable for anyone to say, 'Feeling is self.' Thus the eye is not self, forms are not self, eye-consciousness is not self, eye-contact is not self, feeling is not self.

"If anyone says, 'Craving is self'...That is why it is not tenable for anyone to say, 'Craving is self.' Thus the eye is not self, forms are not self, eye-consciousness is not self, eye-contact is not self, feeling is not self, craving is not self.

11. (ii) "If anyone says, 'The ear is self,' that is not tenable. The rise and fall of the ear are discerned, and since its rise and fall are discerned, it would follow: 'My self rises and falls.' That is why it is not tenable for anyone to say, 'The ear is self.' Thus the ear is not self.

"If anyone says, 'Sounds are self,'...'Ear-consciousness is self,'...'Ear-contact is self,'...'Feeling is self,'...'Craving is self'... That is why it is not tenable for anyone to say, 'Craving is self.' Thus the ear is not self, sounds are not self, ear-consciousness is not self, ear-contact is not self, feeling is not self, craving is not self.

12. (iii) "If anyone says, 'The nose is self,' that is not tenable. The rise and fall of the nose are discerned, and since its rise and fall are discerned, it would follow: 'My self rises and falls.' That is why it is not tenable for anyone to say, 'The nose is self.' Thus the nose is not self.

"If anyone says, 'Odours are self,'...'Nose-consciousness is self,' ...'Nose-contact is self,'...'Feeling is self,'...'Craving is self'...That is why it is not tenable for anyone to say, 'Craving is self.' Thus the nose is not self, odours are not self, nose-consciousness is not self, nose-contact is not self, feeling is not self, craving is not self.

13. (iv) "If anyone says, 'The tongue is self,' that is not tenable. The rise and fall of the tongue are discerned, and since its rise and fall are discerned, it would follow: 'My self rises and falls.' That is why it is not tenable for anyone to say, 'The tongue is self.' Thus the tongue is not self.

"If anyone says, 'Flavours are self,'...'Tongue-consciousness is self,'...'Tongue-contact is self,'...'Feeling is self,'...'Craving is self'...That is why it is not tenable for anyone to say, 'Craving is self.' Thus the tongue is not self, flavours are not self, tongue-consciousness is not self, tongue-contact is not self, feeling is not self, craving is not self.

14. (v) "If anyone says, 'The body is self,' that is not tenable. The rise and fall of the body are discerned, and since its rise and fall are discerned, it would follow: 'My self rises and falls.' That is why it is not tenable for anyone to say, 'The body is self.' Thus the body is not self.

"If anyone says, 'Tangibles are self,'...'Body-consciousness is self,'...'Body-contact is self,'...'Feeling is self,'...'Craving is self'...That is why it is not tenable for anyone to say, 'Craving is self.' Thus the body is not self, tangibles are not self, body-consciousness is not self, body-contact is not self, feeling is not self, craving is not self.

15. (vi) "If anyone says, 'The mind is self,' that is not tenable. The rise and fall of the mind are discerned, and since its rise and fall are discerned, it would follow: 'My self rises and falls.' That is why it is not tenable for anyone to say, 'The mind is self.' Thus the mind is not self.

"If anyone says, 'Mind-objects are self,'...'Mind-consciousness is self,'...'Mind-contact is self,'...'Feeling is self,'...[284]...'Craving is self'...That is why it is not tenable for anyone to say, 'Craving is self.' Thus the mind is not self, mind-objects are not self, mind-consciousness is not self, mind-contact is not self, feeling is not self, craving is not self.

(THE ORIGINATION OF IDENTITY)

16. "Now, bhikkhus, this is the way leading to the origination of identity.[1333] (i) One regards the eye thus: 'This is mine, this I am, this is my self.' One regards forms thus...One regards eye-consciousness thus...One regards eye-contact thus...One regards feeling thus...One regards craving thus: 'This is mine, this I am, this is my self.'

17–21. (ii–vi) "One regards the ear thus: 'This is mine, this I am, this is my self.'...One regards the nose thus: 'This is mine, this I am, this is my self.'...One regards the tongue thus: 'This is mine, this I am, this is my self.'...One regards the body thus: 'This is mine, this I am, this is my self.'...One regards the mind thus: 'This is mine, this I am, this is my self.' One regards mind-objects thus...One regards mind-consciousness thus...One regards mind-contact thus...One regards feeling thus...One regards craving thus: 'This is mine, this I am, this is my self.'

(THE CESSATION OF IDENTITY)

22. "Now, bhikkhus, this is the way leading to the cessation of identity.[1334] (i) One regards the eye thus: 'This is not mine, this I am not, this is not my self.' One regards forms thus...One regards eye-consciousness thus...One regards eye-contact thus...One regards feeling thus...One regards craving thus: 'This is not mine, this I am not, this is not my self.'

23–27. (ii–vi) "One regards the ear thus: 'This is not mine, this I am not, this is not my self.'...One regards the nose thus: 'This is not mine, this I am not, this is not my self.'...One regards the tongue thus: 'This is not mine, this I am not, this is not my self.'...One regards the body thus: 'This is not mine, this I am not, this is not my self.'...One regards the mind thus: 'This is not mine, this I am not, this is not my self.' One regards mind-objects thus...One regards mind-consciousness thus...One regards mind-contact thus...One regards feeling [285] thus...One regards craving thus: 'This is not mine, this I am not, this is not my self.'

(THE UNDERLYING TENDENCIES)

28. (i) "Bhikkhus, dependent on the eye and forms,[1335] eye-consciousness arises; the meeting of the three is contact; with contact as condition there arises [a feeling] felt as pleasant or painful or neither-painful-nor-pleasant. When one is touched by a pleasant feeling, if one delights in it, welcomes it, and remains holding to it, then the underlying tendency to lust lies within one. When one is touched by a painful feeling, if one sorrows, grieves and laments, weeps beating one's breast and becomes distraught, then the underlying tendency to aversion lies within one. When one is touched by a neither-painful-nor-pleasant feeling, if one does not understand as it actually is the origination, the disappearance, the gratification, the danger, and the escape in regard to that feeling, then the underlying tendency to ignorance lies within one. Bhikkhus, that one shall here and now make an end of suffering without abandoning the underlying

tendency to lust for pleasant feeling, without abolishing the underlying tendency to aversion towards painful feeling, without extirpating the underlying tendency to ignorance in regard to neither-painful-nor-pleasant feeling, without abandoning ignorance and arousing true knowledge[1336]—this is impossible.

29–33. (ii–vi) "Bhikkhus, dependent on the ear and sounds, ear-consciousness arises...Dependent on the mind and mind-objects, mind-consciousness arises; the meeting of the three is contact; with contact as condition there arises [a feeling] felt as pleasant or painful or neither-painful-nor-pleasant...Bhikkhus, that one should here and now make an end of suffering without abandoning the underlying tendency to lust for pleasant feeling...without abandoning ignorance and arousing true knowledge—this is impossible. [286]

(THE ABANDONMENT OF THE UNDERLYING TENDENCIES)

34. (i) "Bhikkhus, dependent on the eye and forms, eye-consciousness arises; the meeting of the three is contact; with contact as condition there arises [a feeling] felt as pleasant or painful or neither-painful-nor-pleasant. When one is touched by a pleasant feeling, if one does not delight in it, welcome it, and remain holding to it, then the underlying tendency to lust does not lie within one. When one is touched by a painful feeling, if one does not sorrow, grieve and lament, does not weep beating one's breast and become distraught, then the underlying tendency to aversion does not lie within one. When one is touched by a neither-painful-nor-pleasant feeling, if one understands as it actually is the origination, the disappearance, the gratification, the danger, and the escape in regard to that feeling, then the underlying tendency to ignorance does not lie within one. Bhikkhus, that one shall here and now make an end of suffering by abandoning the underlying tendency to lust for pleasant feeling, by abolishing the underlying tendency to aversion towards painful feeling, by extirpating the underlying tendency to ignorance in regard to neither-painful-nor-pleasant feeling, by abandoning ignorance and arousing true knowledge—this is possible.

35–39. (ii–vi) "Bhikkhus, dependent on the ear and sounds, ear-consciousness arises...Dependent on the mind and mind-objects, mind-consciousness arises; the meeting of the three is contact; with contact as condition there arises [a feeling] felt as pleasant or painful or neither-painful-nor-pleasant...Bhikkhus, that one shall here and now make an end of suffering by abandoning the underlying tendency to lust for pleasant feeling...by abandoning ignorance and arousing true knowledge—this is possible.

(LIBERATION)

40. "Seeing thus, bhikkhus, a well-taught noble disciple becomes disenchanted with the eye, disenchanted with forms, disenchanted with eye-consciousness, disenchanted with eye-contact, disenchanted with feeling, disenchanted with craving.

"He becomes disenchanted with the ear...He becomes disenchanted with the nose...He becomes disenchanted with the tongue...He becomes disenchanted with the body...He becomes disenchanted with the mind, disenchanted with mind-objects, disenchanted with mind-consciousness, disenchanted with mind-contact, disenchanted with feeling, disenchanted with craving.

41. "Being disenchanted, [287] he becomes dispassionate. Through dispassion [his mind] is liberated. When it is liberated, there comes the knowledge: 'It is liberated.' He understands: 'Birth is destroyed, the holy life has been lived, what had to be done has been done, there is no more coming to any state of being.'"

That is what the Blessed One said. The bhikkhus were satisfied and delighted in the Blessed One's words. Now while this discourse was being spoken, through not clinging the minds of sixty bhikkhus were liberated from the taints.[1337]

149 *Mahāsaḷāyatanika Sutta*
The Great Sixfold Base

1. THUS HAVE I HEARD. On one occasion the Blessed One was living at Sāvatthī in Jeta's Grove, Anāthapiṇḍika's Park. There he addressed the bhikkhus thus: "Bhikkhus."—"Venerable sir," they replied. The Blessed One said this:

2. "Bhikkhus, I shall teach you a discourse on the great sixfold base. Listen and attend closely to what I shall say."—"Yes, venerable sir," the bhikkhus replied. The Blessed One said this:

3. "Bhikkhus, when one does not know and see the eye as it actually is,[1338] when one does not know and see forms as they actually are, when one does not know and see eye-consciousness as it actually is, when one does not know and see eye-contact as it actually is, when one does not know and see as it actually is [the feeling] felt as pleasant or painful or neither-painful-nor-pleasant that arises with eye-contact as condition, then one is inflamed by lust for the eye, for forms, for eye-consciousness, for eye-contact, for [the feeling] felt as pleasant or painful or neither-painful-nor-pleasant that arises with eye-contact as condition.

"When one abides inflamed by lust, fettered, infatuated, contemplating gratification, then the five aggregates affected by clinging are built up for oneself in the future;[1339] and one's craving—which brings renewal of being, is accompanied by delight and lust, and delights in this and that—increases. One's bodily and [288] mental troubles increase, one's bodily and mental torments increase, one's bodily and mental fevers increase, and one experiences bodily and mental suffering.

4–8. "When one does not know and see the ear as it actually is...When one does not know and see the nose as it actually is...When one does not know and see the tongue as it actually is...When one does not know and see the body as it actually is...

When one does not know and see the mind as it actually is...one experiences bodily and mental suffering.

9. "Bhikkhus, when one knows and sees the eye as it actually is,[1340] when one knows and sees forms as they actually are, when one knows and sees eye-consciousness as it actually is, when one knows and sees eye-contact as it actually is, when one knows and sees as it actually is [the feeling] felt as pleasant or painful or neither-painful-nor-pleasant that arises with eye-contact as condition, then one is not inflamed by lust for the eye, for forms, for eye-consciousness, for eye-contact, for [the feeling] felt as pleasant or painful or neither-painful-nor-pleasant that arises with eye-contact as condition.

"When one abides uninflamed by lust, unfettered, uninfatuated, contemplating danger, then the five aggregates affected by clinging are diminished for oneself in the future; and one's craving—which brings renewal of being, is accompanied by delight and lust, and delights in this or that—is abandoned. One's bodily and mental troubles are abandoned, one's bodily and mental torments are abandoned, one's bodily and mental fevers are abandoned, [289] and one experiences bodily and mental pleasure.

10. "The view of a person such as this is right view. His intention is right intention, his effort is right effort, his mindfulness is right mindfulness, his concentration is right concentration. But his bodily action, his verbal action, and his livelihood have already been well purified earlier.[1341] Thus this Noble Eightfold Path comes to fulfilment in him by development. When he develops this Noble Eightfold Path, the four foundations of mindfulness also come to fulfilment in him by development; the four right kinds of striving also come to fulfilment in him by development; the four bases for spiritual power also come to fulfilment in him by development; the five faculties also come to fulfilment in him by development; the five powers also come to fulfilment in him by development; the seven enlightenment factors also come to fulfilment in him by development. These two things—serenity and insight—occur in him yoked evenly together.[1342] He fully understands by direct knowledge those things that should be fully understood by direct knowledge. He abandons by direct knowledge those things that should be abandoned by direct knowledge. He develops by direct knowledge

those things that should be developed by direct knowledge. He realises by direct knowledge those things that should be realised by direct knowledge.[1343]

11. "And what things should be fully understood by direct knowledge? The answer to that is: the five aggregates affected by clinging, that is, the material form aggregate affected by clinging, the feeling aggregate affected by clinging, the perception aggregate affected by clinging, the formations aggregate affected by clinging, the consciousness aggregate affected by clinging. These are the things that should be fully understood by direct knowledge.

"And what things should be abandoned by direct knowledge? Ignorance and craving for being. These are the things that should be abandoned by direct knowledge.

"And what things should be developed by direct knowledge? Serenity and insight.[1344] These are the things that should be developed by direct knowledge. [290]

"And what things should be realised by direct knowledge? True knowledge and deliverance.[1345] These are the things that should be realised by direct knowledge.

12–14. "When one knows and sees the ear as it actually is... These are the things that should be realised by direct knowledge.[1346]

15–17. "When one knows and sees the nose as it actually is... These are the things that should be realised by direct knowledge.

18–20. "When one knows and sees the tongue as it actually is...These are the things that should be realised by direct knowledge.

21–23. "When one knows and sees the body as it actually is... These are the things that should be realised by direct knowledge.

24–26. "When one knows and sees the mind as it actually is... These are the things that should be realised by direct knowledge."

That is what the Blessed One said. The bhikkhus were satisfied and delighted in the Blessed One's words.

150 *Nagaravindeyya Sutta*
To the Nagaravindans

1. THUS HAVE I HEARD. On one occasion the Blessed One was wandering in the Kosalan country with a large Sangha of bhikkhus, and eventually arrived at a Kosalan village named Nagaravinda.

2. The brahmin householders of Nagaravinda heard: "The recluse Gotama, the son of the Sakyans who went forth from a Sakyan clan, has been wandering in the Kosalan country with a large Sangha of bhikkhus [291] and has come to Nagaravinda. Now a good report of Master Gotama has been spread to this effect: 'That Blessed One is accomplished, fully enlightened...(*as Sutta 41, §2*)...he reveals a holy life that is utterly perfect and pure.' Now it is good to see such arahants."

3. Then the brahmin householders of Nagaravinda went to the Blessed One. Some paid homage to the Blessed One and sat down at one side; some exchanged greetings with him, and when this courteous and amiable talk was finished, sat down at one side; some extended their hands in reverential salutation towards the Blessed One and sat down at one side; some pronounced their name and clan in the Blessed One's presence and sat down at one side; some kept silent and sat down at one side. When they were seated, the Blessed One said to them:

4. "Householders, if wanderers of other sects ask you thus: 'Householders, what kind of recluses and brahmins should not be honoured, respected, revered, and venerated?' you should answer them thus: 'Those recluses and brahmins who are not rid of lust, hate, and delusion regarding forms cognizable by the eye, whose minds are not inwardly peaceful, and who conduct themselves now righteously, now unrighteously in body, speech, and mind—such recluses and brahmins should not be honoured, respected, revered, and venerated. Why is that?

Because we ourselves are not rid of lust, hate, and delusion regarding forms cognizable by the eye, our minds are not inwardly peaceful, and we conduct ourselves now righteously, now unrighteously in body, speech, and mind. Since we do not see any higher righteous conduct on the part of those good recluses and brahmins, they should not be honoured, respected, revered, and venerated.

"'Those recluses and brahmins who are not rid of lust, hate, and delusion regarding sounds cognizable by the ear...regarding odours cognizable by the nose...regarding flavours cognizable by the tongue...regarding tangibles cognizable by the body...regarding mind-objects cognizable by the mind, whose minds are not inwardly peaceful, and who conduct themselves now righteously, now unrighteously in body, speech, and mind...should not be honoured...[292]...Since we do not see any higher righteous conduct on the part of those good recluses and brahmins, they should not be honoured, respected, revered, and venerated.' Being thus asked, householders, you should answer those wanderers of other sects in this way.

5. "But, householders, if wanderers of other sects ask you thus: 'Householders, what kind of recluses and brahmins should be honoured, respected, revered, and venerated?' you should answer them thus: 'Those recluses and brahmins who are rid of lust, hate, and delusion regarding forms cognizable by the eye, whose minds are inwardly peaceful, and who conduct themselves righteously in body, speech, and mind—such recluses and brahmins should be honoured, respected, revered, and venerated. Why is that? Because we ourselves are not rid of lust, hate, and delusion regarding forms cognizable by the eye, our minds are not inwardly peaceful, and we conduct ourselves now righteously, now unrighteously, in body, speech, and mind. Since we see higher righteous conduct on the part of those good recluses and brahmins, they should be honoured, respected, revered, and venerated.

"'Those recluses and brahmins who are rid of lust, hate, and delusion regarding sounds cognizable by the ear...regarding odours cognizable by the nose...regarding flavours cognizable by the tongue...regarding tangibles cognizable by the body...regarding mind-objects cognizable by the mind, whose minds are inwardly peaceful, and who conduct themselves righteously in body, speech, and mind…should be honoured… Since we see higher righteous conduct on the part of those good recluses and brahmins, they should be honoured, respected, revered, and venerated.' Being thus asked, householders, you should answer those wanderers of other sects in this way.

6. "Householders, if wanderers of other sects ask you thus: 'But what are your reasons and what is your evidence regarding those venerable ones whereby you say about them: "Surely these venerable ones [293] are either rid of lust or are practising for the removal of lust; they are either rid of hate or are practising for the removal of hate; they are either rid of delusion or are practising for the removal of delusion"?'—being asked thus, you should answer those wanderers of other sects thus: 'It is because those venerable ones resort to remote jungle-thicket resting places in the forest. For there are no forms cognizable by the eye there of a kind that they could look at and delight in. There are no sounds cognizable by the ear there of a kind that they could listen to and delight in. There are no odours cognizable by the nose there of a kind that they could smell and delight in. There are no flavours cognizable by the tongue there of a kind that they could taste and delight in. There are no tangibles cognizable by the body there of a kind that they could touch and delight in. These are our reasons, friends, this is our evidence whereby we say about those venerable ones: "Surely these venerable ones are either rid of lust, hate, and delusion, or are practising for their removal."' Being thus asked, householders, you should answer those wanderers of other sects in this way."

7. When this was said, the brahmin householders of Nagaravinda said to the Blessed One: "Magnificent, Master Gotama! Magnificent, Master Gotama! Master Gotama has made the Dhamma clear in many ways, as though he were turning upright what had been overthrown, revealing what was hidden, showing the way to one who was lost, or holding up a lamp in the darkness for those with eyesight to see forms. We go to Master Gotama for refuge and to the Dhamma and to the Sangha of bhikkhus. From today let Master Gotama accept us as lay followers who have gone to him for refuge for life."

151 *Piṇḍapātapārisuddhi Sutta*
The Purification of Almsfood

1. THUS HAVE I HEARD. On one occasion the Blessed One was living at Rājagaha in the Bamboo Grove, the Squirrels' Sanctuary. Then, when it was evening, the venerable Sāriputta rose from meditation and went to the Blessed One. After paying homage to him, he sat down at one side. The Blessed One then said to him: [294]

2. "Sāriputta, your faculties are clear. The colour of your skin is pure and bright. What abiding do you often abide in now, Sāriputta?"

"Now, venerable sir, I often abide in voidness."[1347]

"Good, good, Sāriputta! Now, indeed, you often abide in the abiding of a great man. For this is the abiding of a great man, namely, voidness.[1348]

3. "So, Sāriputta, if a bhikkhu should wish: 'May I now often abide in voidness,' he should consider thus: 'On the path by which I went to the village for alms, or in the place where I wandered for alms, or on the path by which I returned from the almsround, was there any desire, lust, hate, delusion, or aversion in my mind regarding forms cognizable by the eye?'[1349] If, by so reviewing, he knows thus: 'On the path by which I went to the village for alms, or in the place where I wandered for alms, or on the path by which I returned from the almsround, there was desire, lust, hate, delusion, or aversion in my mind regarding forms cognizable by the eye,' then he should make an effort to abandon those evil unwholesome states. But if, by reviewing, he knows thus: 'On the path by which I went to the village for alms, and in the place where I wandered for alms, and on the path by which I returned from the almsround, there was no desire, lust, hate, delusion, or aversion in my mind regarding forms cognizable by the eye,'

then he can abide happy and glad, training day and night in wholesome states.

4–8. "Again, Sāriputta, a bhikkhu should consider thus: 'On the path by which I went to the village for alms, or in the place where I wandered for alms, or on the path by which I returned from the almsround, was there any desire, lust, hate, delusion, or aversion in my mind regarding sounds cognizable by the ear?...regarding odours cognizable by the nose?...regarding flavours cognizable by the tongue?...regarding tangibles cognizable by the body?...regarding mind-objects cognizable by the mind?' [295] If, by reviewing, he knows thus: 'On the path by which I went to the village for alms...there was desire, lust, hate, delusion, or aversion in my mind regarding mind-objects cognizable by the mind,' then he should make an effort to abandon those evil unwholesome states. But if, by reviewing, he knows thus: 'On the path by which I went to the village for alms...there was no desire, lust, hate, delusion, or aversion in my mind regarding mind-objects cognizable by the mind,' then he can abide happy and glad, training day and night in wholesome states.

9. "Again, Sāriputta, a bhikkhu should consider thus: 'Are the five cords of sensual pleasure abandoned in me?'[1350] If, by reviewing, he knows thus: 'The five cords of sensual pleasure are not abandoned in me,' then he should make an effort to abandon those five cords of sensual pleasure. But if, by reviewing, he knows thus: 'The five cords of sensual pleasure are abandoned in me,' then he can abide happy and glad, training day and night in wholesome states.

10. "Again, Sāriputta, a bhikkhu should consider thus: 'Are the five hindrances abandoned in me?' If, by reviewing, he knows thus: 'The five hindrances are not abandoned in me,' then he should make an effort to abandon those five hindrances. But if, by reviewing, he knows thus: 'The five hindrances are abandoned in me,' then he can abide happy and glad, training day and night in wholesome states.

11. "Again, Sāriputta, a bhikkhu should consider thus: 'Are the five aggregates affected by clinging fully understood by me?' If, by reviewing, he knows thus: 'The five aggregates affected by clinging are not fully understood by me,' then he should make an effort to fully understand those five aggregates

affected by clinging. But if, by reviewing, [296] he knows thus: 'The five aggregates affected by clinging are fully understood by me,' then he can abide happy and glad, training day and night in wholesome states.

12. "Again, Sāriputta, a bhikkhu should consider thus: 'Are the four foundations of mindfulness developed in me?' If, by reviewing, he knows thus: 'The four foundations of mindfulness are not developed in me,' then he should make an effort to develop those four foundations of mindfulness. But if, by reviewing, he knows thus: 'The four foundations of mindfulness are developed in me,' then he can abide happy and glad, training day and night in wholesome states.

13–19. "Again, Sāriputta, a bhikkhu should consider thus: 'Are the four right kinds of striving developed in me?...Are the four bases for spiritual power developed in me?...Are the five faculties developed in me?...Are the five powers developed in me?...Are the seven enlightenment factors developed in me?...Is the Noble Eightfold Path developed in me? [297]...Are serenity and insight developed in me?' If, by reviewing, he knows thus: 'Serenity and insight are not developed in me,' then he should make an effort to develop them. But if, by reviewing, he knows thus: 'Serenity and insight are developed in me,' then he can abide happy and glad, training day and night in wholesome states.

20. "Again, Sāriputta, a bhikkhu should consider thus: 'Are true knowledge and deliverance realised by me?' If, by reviewing, he knows thus: 'True knowledge and deliverance are not realised by me,' then he should make an effort to realise true knowledge and deliverance. But if, by reviewing, he knows thus: 'True knowledge and deliverance are realised by me,' then he can abide happy and glad, training day and night in wholesome states.[1351]

21. "Sāriputta, whatever recluses and brahmins in the past have purified their almsfood have all done so by repeatedly reviewing thus. Whatever recluses and brahmins in the future will purify their almsfood will all do so by repeatedly reviewing thus. Whatever recluses and brahmins in the present are purifying their almsfood are all doing so by repeatedly reviewing thus. Therefore, Sāriputta, you should train thus: 'We will purify our almsfood by repeatedly reviewing thus.'"

That is what the Blessed One said. The venerable Sāriputta was satisfied and delighted in the Blessed One's words.

152 *Indriyabhāvanā Sutta*
The Development of the Faculties

[298] 1. THUS HAVE I HEARD. On one occasion the Blessed One was living at Kajangalā in a grove of mukhelu trees.

2. Then the brahmin student Uttara, a pupil of the brahmin Pārāsariya, went to the Blessed One and exchanged greetings with him. When this courteous and amiable talk was finished, he sat down at one side. The Blessed One then asked him: "Uttara, does the brahmin Pārāsariya teach his disciples the development of the faculties?"

"He does, Master Gotama."

"But, Uttara, how does he teach his disciples the development of the faculties?"

"Here, Master Gotama, one does not see forms with the eye, one does not hear sounds with the ear. That is how the brahmin Pārāsariya teaches his disciples the development of the faculties."

"If that is so, Uttara, then a blind man and a deaf man will have developed faculties, according to what the brahmin Pārāsariya says. For a blind man does not see forms with the eye, and a deaf man does not hear sounds with the ear."

When this was said, the brahmin student Uttara, Pārāsariya's pupil, sat silent, dismayed, with shoulders drooping and head down, glum, and without response.

3. Then, knowing this, the Blessed One addressed the venerable Ānanda: "Ānanda, the brahmin Pārāsariya teaches his disciples the development of the faculties in one way, but in the Noble One's Discipline the supreme development of the faculties is otherwise."[1352]

"Now is the time, Blessed One, now is the time, Sublime One, for the Blessed One [299] to teach the supreme development of the faculties in the Noble One's Discipline. Having heard it from the Blessed One, the bhikkhus will remember it."

"Then listen, Ānanda, and attend closely to what I shall say."

"Yes, venerable sir," he replied. The Blessed One said this:

4. "Now, Ānanda, how is there the supreme development of the faculties in the Noble One's Discipline? Here, Ānanda, when a bhikkhu sees a form with the eye, there arises in him what is agreeable, there arises what is disagreeable, there arises what is both agreeable and disagreeable.[1353] He understands thus: 'There has arisen in me what is agreeable, there has arisen what is disagreeable, there has arisen what is both agreeable and disagreeable. But that is conditioned, gross, dependently arisen; this is peaceful, this is sublime, that is, equanimity.' The agreeable that arose, the disagreeable that arose, and the both agreeable and disagreeable that arose cease in him and equanimity is established.[1354] Just as a man with good sight, having opened his eyes might shut them or having shut his eyes might open them, so too concerning anything at all, the agreeable that arose, the disagreeable that arose, and the both agreeable and disagreeable that arose cease just as quickly, just as rapidly, just as easily, and equanimity is established. This is called in the Noble One's Discipline the supreme development of the faculties regarding forms cognizable by the eye.[1355]

5. "Again, Ānanda, when a bhikkhu hears a sound with the ear, there arises in him what is agreeable, there arises what is disagreeable, there arises what is both agreeable and disagreeable. He understands thus:...and equanimity is established. Just as a strong man might easily snap his fingers, so too concerning anything at all, the agreeable that arose, the disagreeable that arose, and the both agreeable and disagreeable that arose cease just as quickly, just as rapidly, just as easily, and equanimity is established. This is called in the Noble One's Discipline the supreme development of the faculties regarding sounds cognizable by the ear.

6. "Again, Ānanda, when a bhikkhu smells an odour with the nose, there arises in him what is agreeable, there arises what is disagreeable, there arises what is both agreeable and disagreeable. He understands thus:...and equanimity is established. Just as [300] raindrops on a slightly sloping lotus leaf roll off and do not remain there, so too concerning anything at all, the agreeable that arose, the disagreeable that arose, and the both agreeable and disagreeable that arose cease just as quickly, just as

rapidly, just as easily, and equanimity is established. This is called in the Noble One's Discipline the supreme development of the faculties regarding odours cognizable by the nose.

7. "Again, Ānanda, when a bhikkhu tastes a flavour with the tongue, there arises in him what is agreeable, there arises what is disagreeable, there arises what is both agreeable and disagreeable. He understands thus:...and equanimity is established. Just as a strong man might easily spit out a ball of spittle collected on the tip of his tongue, so too concerning anything at all, the agreeable that arose, the disagreeable that arose, and the both agreeable and disagreeable that arose cease just as quickly, just as rapidly, just as easily, and equanimity is established. This is called in the Noble One's Discipline the supreme development of the faculties regarding flavours cognizable by the tongue.

8. "Again, Ānanda, when a bhikkhu touches a tangible with the body, there arises in him what is agreeable, there arises what is disagreeable, there arises what is both agreeable and disagreeable. He understands thus:...and equanimity is established. Just as a strong man might extend his flexed arm or flex his extended arm, so too concerning anything at all, the agreeable that arose, the disagreeable that arose, and the both agreeable and disagreeable that arose cease just as quickly, just as rapidly, just as easily, and equanimity is established. This is called in the Noble One's Discipline the supreme development of the faculties regarding tangibles cognizable by the body.

9. "Again, Ānanda, when a bhikkhu cognizes a mind-object with the mind, there arises in him what is agreeable, there arises what is disagreeable, there arises what is both agreeable and disagreeable. He understands thus:...and equanimity is established. Just as if a man were to let two or three drops of water fall onto an iron plate heated for a whole day, the falling of the drops might be slow but they would quickly vaporise and vanish,[1356] so too concerning anything at all, the agreeable that arose, the disagreeable that arose, and the both agreeable and disagreeable that arose cease just as quickly, just as rapidly, just as easily, and equanimity is established. This is called in the Noble One's Discipline the supreme development of the faculties regarding ideas cognizable by the mind.

"That is how there is the supreme development of the faculties in the Noble One's Discipline.

10. "And how, Ānanda, is one a disciple in higher training, one who has entered upon the way? Here, Ānanda, when a bhikkhu sees a form with the eye...[301] hears a sound with the ear...smells an odour with the nose...tastes a flavour with the tongue...touches a tangible with the body...cognizes a mind-object with the mind, there arises in him what is agreeable, there arises what is disagreeable, there arises what is both agreeable and disagreeable; he is ashamed, humiliated and disgusted by the agreeable that arose, by the disagreeable that arose, and by the both agreeable and disagreeable that arose.[1357] That is how one is a disciple in higher training, one who has entered upon the way.

11–16. "And how, Ānanda, is one a noble one with developed faculties?[1358] Here, Ānanda, when a bhikkhu sees a form with the eye...hears a sound with the ear...smells an odour with the nose...tastes a flavour with the tongue...touches a tangible with the body...cognizes a mind-object with the mind, there arises in him what is agreeable, there arises what is disagreeable, there arises what is both agreeable and disagreeable.[1359] If he should wish: 'May I abide perceiving the unrepulsive in the repulsive,' he abides perceiving the unrepulsive in the repulsive. If he should wish: 'May I abide perceiving the repulsive in the unrepulsive,' he abides perceiving the repulsive in the unrepulsive. If he should wish: 'May I abide perceiving the unrepulsive in the repulsive and the unrepulsive,' he abides perceiving the unrepulsive in that. If he should wish: 'May I abide perceiving the repulsive in the unrepulsive and the repulsive,' he abides perceiving the repulsive in that. If he should wish: 'May I, avoiding both the repulsive and unrepulsive, [302] abide in equanimity, mindful and fully aware,' he abides in equanimity towards that, mindful and fully aware.[1360] That is how one is a noble one with developed faculties.

17. "So, Ānanda, the supreme development of the faculties in the Noble One's Discipline has been taught by me, the disciple in higher training who has entered upon the way has been taught by me, and the noble one with developed faculties has been taught by me.

18. "What should be done for his disciples out of compassion by a Teacher who seeks their welfare and has compassion for them, that I have done for you, Ānanda. There are these roots of

trees, these empty huts. Meditate, Ānanda, do not delay, or else you will regret it later. This is our instruction to you."

That is what the Blessed One said. The venerable Ānanda was satisfied and delighted in the Blessed One's words.

Bibliography

List of Abbreviations

Notes

Pali-English Glossary

Indexes

Bibliography

A. PALI TEXTS

The Majjhima Nikāya. 3 vols. Vol. 1 edited by V. Trenckner; Vols. 2 and 3 edited by Robert Chalmers. First published 1888–99. Reprint. London: Pali Text Society, 1977–79. Roman-script edition.

The Majjhima Nikāya. 3 vols. Rangoon: Buddhasāsana Samiti, 1954. Burmese-script edition published in connection with the Sixth Buddhist Council held in Burma, 1954–56.

The Majjhima Nikāya. 3 vols. Sri Lanka: Lanka Buddha Mandalaya, 1964–74. Sinhala-script edition published in the Buddha Jayanti Tripitaka Series; Sinhala translation on facing pages.

Majjhima Nikāya Aṭṭhakathā (Papañcasūdanī). 4 vols. Rangoon: Buddhasāsana Samiti, 1957. Burmese-script edition of Ācariya Buddhaghosa's commentary to the Majjhima Nikāya.

Majjhima Nikāya Ṭīkā. 3 vols. Rangoon: Buddhasāsana Samiti, 1961. Burmese-script edition of Ācariya Dhammapāla's subcommentary to the Majjhima Nikāya.

B. TRANSLATIONS AND STUDIES

Basham, A.L. *History and Doctrines of the Ājīvikas*. 1951. Reprint. Delhi: Motilal Banarsidass, 1981. Study of a philosophical school to which several of the Buddha's contemporary rivals belonged.

Bodhi, Bhikkhu, trans. *The Discourse on the All-Embracing Net of Views: The Brahmajāla Sutta and Its Commentaries*. BPS, 1978. Translation of the first sutta in the Dīgha Nikāya, a parallel to MN 102.

———, trans. *The Discourse on the Fruits of Recluseship: The Sāmaññaphala Sutta and Its Commentaries.* BPS, 1989. Translation of the second sutta in the Dīgha Nikāya; clarifies views of the six heterodox teachers often mentioned in the Majjhima Nikāya.

———, trans. *The Discourse on the Root of Existence: The Mūlapariyāya Sutta and Its Commentaries.* Translation of MN 1, commentary, portions of subcommentary.

Horner, I.B., trans. *The Book of the Discipline.* 6 vols. London: PTS, 1949–66. Translation of the complete Vinaya Piṭaka.

———, trans. *The Collection of the Middle Length Sayings.* 3 vols. London: PTS, 1954–59. Long-standing translation of the complete Majjhima Nikāya.

———. *Early Buddhism and the Taking of Life.* BPS Wheel No. 104, 1967.

Kloppenborg, Ria. *The Paccekabuddha: A Buddhist Ascetic.* BPS Wheel No. 305/307, 1983. Study of the figure extolled in MN 116.

Ñāṇamoli, Bhikkhu, trans. *The Greater Discourse on Voidness.* BPS Wheel No. 87, 1965. Translation of MN 122 and commentary.

———. *The Life of the Buddha According to the Pali Canon.* BPS, 1972. Biography of the Buddha constructed from canonical texts.

———, trans. *Mindfulness of Breathing.* 2nd ed. BPS, 1964. Includes translation of MN 118 and related texts.

———, trans. *The Minor Readings and The Illustrator of Ultimate Meaning.* London: PTS, 1960. Appendix contains discussion of translator's understanding of Pali technical terms.

———, trans. *The Path of Purification (Visuddhimagga),* 4th ed. BPS, 1980. Encyclopaedic work on Buddhist doctrine and meditation, by Ācariya Buddhaghosa. "Cornerstone" of the commentaries.

———, trans. *A Treasury of the Buddha's Words.* Bangkok: Mahāmakutarājavidyālaya, 1980. Ninety Majjhima suttas, selected and edited by Bhikkhu Khantipālo.

Ñāṇananda, Bhikkhu. *Concept and Reality in Early Buddhism.* BPS, 1971. Includes exposition of MN 18.

———, trans. *Ideal Solitude.* BPS Wheel No. 188, 1973. Translation of MN 131 with introduction and notes.

Norman, K.R. *Elders' Verses I: Theragātha*. London: PTS, 1969.

———. *The Group of Discourses II*. Oxford: PTS, 1992.

Nyanaponika Thera, trans. *The Discourse on the Snake Simile*. BPS Wheel No. 48/49, 1962. Translation of MN 22 with introduction and notes.

———. *The Five Mental Hindrances*. BPS Wheel No. 26, 1961. Includes translation of commentary on similes in MN 39.

———. *The Four Nutriments of Life*. BPS Wheel No. 105/106, 1967. Explicates the nutriments mentioned in MN 9 and MN 38.

———, trans. *The Greater Discourse on the Elephant-Footprint Simile*. BPS Wheel No. 101, 1966. Translation of MN 28 with introduction and notes.

———. *The Heart of Buddhist Meditation*. London: Rider and Co., 1962; BPS, 1992. Includes translation of MN 10 with modern commentary.

———. *The Roots of Good and Evil*. BPS Wheel No. 251/253, 1978. Canonical study of the unwholesome roots and their antidotes.

———, trans. *The Simile of the Cloth and The Discourse on Effacement*. BPS Wheel No. 61/62, 1964. Translation of MN 7 and MN 8 with introduction and notes.

———. *The Threefold Refuge*. BPS Wheel No. 76, 1965. Includes commentary on refuge formula often met with in the Majjhima Nikāya.

Piyadassi Thera. *The Seven Factors of Enlightenment*. BPS Wheel No. 1, 1957.

Skilling, Peter. *Mahāsūtras II, Parts 1 and 2*. Oxford: PTS, 1997.

Soma Thera, trans. *The Removal of Distracting Thoughts*. BPS Wheel No. 21, 1960. Translation of MN 20 with commentary and subcommentary.

———, trans. *The Way of Mindfulness*, 5th ed. BPS, 1981. Translation of MN 10 and its commentary and subcommentary.

Thittila, Sayadaw U, trans. *The Book of Analysis (Vibhanga)*. London: PTS, 1969. Includes explanation of Tathāgata's powers (MN 12), elements and bases (MN 115).

Walshe, Maurice, trans. *Thus Have I Heard: Long Discourses of the Buddha*. London: Wisdom Publications, 1987. Recent translation of the complete Dīgha Nikāya.

Watanabe, Fumimaro. *Philosophy and its Development in the Nikāyas and Abhidhamma*. Delhi: Motilal Banarsidass, 1983.

Chapters on Abhidhamma elements in the Nikāyas and on the Codes (*mātikā*).

Wijesekera, O.H. de A. *Buddhist and Vedic Studies*. Delhi: Motilal Banarsidass, 1994.

List of Abbreviations

AN	Anguttara Nikāya
BBS	Burmese-script Buddhasāsana Samiti edition of the Majjhima Nikāya
BPS	Buddhist Publication Society of Kandy, Sri Lanka
CPD	Critical Pāli Dictionary
Cv	Cūḷavagga (Vinaya Piṭaka)
Dhp	Dhammapada
DN	Dīgha Nikāya
Jāt	Jātaka
Kh	Khandhaka (Vinaya Piṭaka)
MA	Majjhima Nikāya Aṭṭhakathā
Miln	Milindapañha
MLS	Middle Length Sayings (see Bibliography, Horner)
MN	Majjhima Nikāya
Ms	Ven. Ñāṇamoli's manuscript translation of the Majjhima Nikāya
MṬ	Majjhima Nikāya Ṭīkā
Mv	Mahāvagga (Vinaya Piṭaka)
Ñm	Bhikkhu Ñāṇamoli
Pāc	Pācittiya
Pār	Pārājika
PED	Pali-English Dictionary (Pali Text Society)
PTS	Pali Text Society
Pṭs	Paṭisambhidāmagga
Pug	Puggalapaññatti
SBJ	Sinhala-script Buddha Jayanti Tripitaka Series edition of the Majjhima Nikāya
SN	Saṁyutta Nikāya
Sn	Sutta Nipāta

Thag	Theragāthā
Ud	Udāna
Vbh	Vibhanga
Vin	Vinaya Piṭaka
Vsm	Visuddhimagga

In the case of references containing two figures separated by a slash, the figure to the right of the slash is the volume and page number of the PTS edition of the Pali text. Of the figures to the left of the slash, references to the Saṁyutta Nikāya and the Udāna indicate chapter and sutta number; those to the Anguttara Nikāya indicate division and sutta number; those to the Dīgha Nikāya indicate the sutta, section, and verse number assigned in Maurice Walshe's translation, *Thus Have I Heard* (see Bibliography). References to the *Visuddhimagga* are to chapter and section number of Bhikkhu Ñāṇamoli's translation, *The Path of Purification*. All references to the Majjhima Nikāya are to the sutta and section number of the present work.

Notes

SUTTA 1

1 For a fuller treatment of this important and difficult sutta, see Bhikkhu Bodhi, *Discourse on the Root of Existence.* This work contains, besides a translation of the sutta, a lengthy analytical study of its philosophical significance and copious extracts from the very helpful commentarial literature that has accumulated around it. Ñm's rendering of this sutta in Ms was highly conjectural; thus, while I have retained most of his terminology, I have substituted my own rendering of the syntax to bring out the meaning that accords with the traditional interpretation and that seems warranted by the original Pali text as well. The key passages as Ñm rendered them will be given in the Notes.

2 MA explains that the Buddha delivered this sutta to dispel the conceit that had arisen in five hundred bhikkhus on account of their erudition and intellectual mastery of the Buddha's teachings. These bhikkhus were formerly brahmins learned in the Vedic literature, and the Buddha's cryptic utterances may well have been intended to challenge the brahmanic views to which they may still have adhered.

3 *Sabbadhammamūlapariyāya*. MṬ explains that the word "all" (*sabba*) is being used here in the restricted sense of the "all of personal identity" (*sakkāyasabba*), that is, with reference to all states or phenomena (*dhammā*) comprised within the five aggregates affected by clinging (see MN 28.4). Supramundane states—the paths, fruits, and

Nibbāna—are excluded. The "root of all things"—that is, the special condition that maintains the continuity of the process of repeated existence—MṬ explains to be craving, conceit, and views (which are the underlying springs of "conceiving"), and these in turn are underlaid by ignorance, suggested in the sutta by the phrase "he has not fully understood it."

4 The "untaught ordinary person" (*assutavā puthujjana*) is the common worldling, who possesses neither learning nor spiritual accomplishment in the Dhamma of the noble ones, and allows himself to be dominated by the multitude of defilements and wrong views. See Bodhi, *Discourse on the Root of Existence*, pp. 40–46.

5 *Paṭhaviṁ paṭhavito sañjānāti.* Although perceiving "earth as earth" seems to suggest seeing the object as it really is, the aim of Buddhist insight meditation, the context makes it clear that the ordinary person's perception of "earth as earth" already introduces a slight distortion of the object, a distortion that will be blown up into full-fledged misinterpretation when the cognitive process enters the phase of "conceiving." MA explains that the ordinary person seizes upon the conventional expression "it is earth," and applying this to the object, perceives it through a "perversion of perception" (*saññāvipallāsa*). The latter is a technical expression explained as perceiving the impermanent as permanent, the painful as pleasurable, what is not self as self, and what is foul as beautiful (AN 4:49/ii.52). Ñm reads the ablative suffix *-to* of the Pali as signifying derivation and translates the phrase: "From earth he has a percept of earth."

6 The Pali verb "conceives" (*maññati*), from the root *man*, "to think," is often used in the Pali suttas to mean distortional thinking—thought that ascribes to its object characteristics and a significance derived not from the object itself, but from one's own subjective imaginings. The cognitive distortion introduced by conceiving consists, in brief, in the intrusion of the egocentric perspective into the experience already slightly distorted by spontaneous perception. According to the commentaries, the activity of conceiving is governed by three defile-

ments, which account for the different ways it comes to manifestation—craving (*taṇhā*), conceit (*māna*), and views (*diṭṭhi*).

MA paraphrases this text thus: "Having perceived earth with a perverted perception, the ordinary person afterwards conceives it—construes or discriminates it—through the gross proliferating tendencies (*papañca*) of craving, conceit, and views, which are here called 'conceivings.'...He apprehends it in diverse ways contrary [to reality]."

The four ways of conceiving (*maññanā*): The Buddha shows that the conceiving of any object may occur in any of four ways, expressed by the text as a fourfold linguistic pattern: accusative, locative, ablative, and appropriative. The primary significance of this modal pattern—enigmatic in the Pali as well—seems to be ontological. I take the pattern to represent the diverse ways in which the ordinary person attempts to give positive being to his imagined sense of egohood by positing, below the threshold of reflection, a relationship between himself as the subject of cognition and the perceived phenomenon as its object. According to the fourfold pattern given, this relationship may be one either of direct identification ("he conceives X"), or of inherence ("he conceives in X"), or of contrast or derivation ("he conceives from X"), or of simple appropriation ("he conceives X to be 'mine'").

But care is needed in interpreting these phrases. The Pali does not supply any direct object for the second and third modes, and this suggests that the process at work in conceiving proceeds from a deeper and more general level than that involved in the forming of an explicit view of self, as described for example at MN 2.8 or MN 44.7. The activity of conceiving thus seems to comprise the entire range of subjectively tinged cognition, from the impulses and thoughts in which the sense of personal identity is still inchoate to elaborate intellectual structures in which it has been fully explicated.

Ñm, however, understands the implicit object of conceiving to be the percept itself, and accordingly translates: "having had from earth a percept of earth, he conceives [that to be] earth, he conceives [that to be] in earth, he conceives [that to be apart] from earth," etc.

The fifth phrase, "he delights in X," explicitly connects conceiving with craving, which is elsewhere said to "delight here and there." This, moreover, hints at the danger in the worldling's thought processes, since craving is pointed to by the Buddha as the origin of suffering.

MA gives prolific examples illustrating all the different modes of conceiving, and these clearly establish that the intended object of conceiving is the misplaced sense of egoity.

7 MA states that one who fully understands earth does so by the three types of full understanding: the full understanding of the known (*ñātapariññā*)—the definition of the earth element by way of its unique characteristic, function, manifestation, and proximate cause; the full understanding by scrutinization (*tīraṇapariññā*)—the contemplation of the earth element by way of the three general characteristics of impermanence, suffering, and non-self; and the full understanding of abandonment (*pahānapariññā*)—the abandoning of desire and lust for the earth element through the supreme path (of arahantship).

8 *Bhūtā.* MA says that "beings" here signifies only living beings below the heaven of the Four Great Kings, the lowest of the sense-sphere heavens; the higher grades of living beings are covered by the terms to follow. MA exemplifies the application of the three types of conceiving to this situation as follows: When a person becomes attached to beings as a result of sight, hearing, etc., or desires rebirth in a certain class of beings, this is conceiving due to craving. When he ranks himself as superior, equal, or inferior to others, this is conceiving due to conceit. And when he thinks, "Beings are permanent, stable, eternal," etc., this is conceiving due to views.

9 MA: The gods of the six sense-sphere heavenly worlds are meant, except for Māra and his retinue in the heaven of the gods who wield power over others' creations. See the account of Buddhist cosmology in the Introduction, pp. 45–48.

10 Prajāpati, "lord of creation," is a name given by the

Vedas to Indra, Agni, etc., as the highest of the Vedic divinities. But according to MA, *Pajāpati* here is a name for Māra because he is the ruler of this "generation" (*pajā*) made up of living beings.

11 *Brahmā* here is Mahābrahmā, the first deity to be born at the beginning of a new cosmic cycle and whose lifespan lasts for the entire cycle. The Ministers of Brahmā and the Assembly of Brahmā—the other deities whose position is determined by attainment of the first jhāna—are also included.

12 MA: By mentioning these, all beings occupying the plane of the second jhāna—the gods of Limited Radiance and the gods of Immeasurable Radiance—should be included, for all these occupy a single level.

13 MA: By mentioning these, all beings occupying the plane of the third jhāna—the gods of Limited Glory and the gods of Immeasurable Glory—should be included.

14 These are divinities on the plane of the fourth jhāna.

15 *Abhibhū*. MA says this term is a designation for the non-percipient realm, called thus because it vanquishes (*abhibhavati*) the four immaterial aggregates. The identification sounds contrived, especially because the word "*abhibhū*" is a masculine singular noun. Elsewhere (MN 49.5) the word appears as part of Baka the Brahmā's claim to theocratic hegemony, yet MA rejects identifying the Abhibhū with Brahmā here as a redundancy.

16 This and the next three sections deal with conceiving in relation to the four immaterial planes of existence—the cosmological counterparts of the four immaterial meditative attainments. With §18 the division of conceiving by way of planes of existence is completed.

17 In these four sections the phenomena comprising personal identity are considered as objects of perception classified into the four categories of the seen, heard, sensed, and cognized. Here, *sensed* (*muta*) signifies the data of smell, taste, and touch, *cognized* (*viññāta*) the data of introspection, abstract thought, and imagination. The objects of perception are "conceived" when they are cognized in terms of "mine," "I," and "self," or in ways that generate craving, conceit, and views.

18 In this section and the next, the phenomena comprising personal identity are treated as twofold—by way of unity and diversity. The emphasis on *unity* (*ekatta*), MA informs us, is characteristic of one who attains the jhānas, in which the mind occurs in a single mode on a single object. The emphasis on *diversity* (*nānatta*) prevails in the case of the non-attainer who lacks the overwhelming unitive experience of jhānas. Conceivings stressing diversity come to expression in philosophies of pluralism, those stressing unity in philosophies of the monistic type.

19 In this section, all phenomena of personal identity are collected together and shown as singlefold. This idea of totality can form the basis for philosophies of the pantheistic or monistic type, depending on the relation posited between the self and the all.

20 MA understands "Nibbāna" here to refer to the five kinds of "supreme Nibbāna here and now" included among the sixty-two wrong views of the Brahmajāla Sutta (DN 1.3.19–25/i.36–38), that is, Nibbāna identified with the full enjoyment of sense pleasures or with the four jhānas. Enjoying this state, or yearning for it, he conceives it with craving. Priding himself on attaining it, he conceives it with conceit. Holding this imaginary Nibbāna to be permanent, etc., he conceives it with views.

21 The *sekha,* the disciple in higher training, is one who has reached any of the three lower planes of sanctity—stream-entry, once-returning, or non-returning—but must still train further in order to reach the goal, arahantship, the supreme security from bondage. MN 53 is devoted to expounding the training he must undertake. The arahant is sometimes described as *asekha*, one beyond training, in the sense that he has completed the training in the Noble Eightfold Path. Ñm rendered *sekha* as "initiate" and *asekha* as "adept," which have been changed here to avoid their "esoteric" connotations.

22 It should be noted that, whereas the ordinary man is said to *perceive* each of the bases, the one in higher training is said to *directly know* them (*abhijānāti*). MA explains that he knows them with distinguished knowledge, knows them in accordance with their real nature as

impermanent, suffering, and non-self. Ñm rendered: "From earth he has direct knowledge of earth."

23 The disciple in higher training is urged by the Buddha to refrain from conceiving and delight because the dispositions to these mental processes still remain within him. With his attainment of stream-entry he eradicated the fetter of identity view and thus can no longer conceive in terms of wrong views. But the defilements of craving and conceit are only uprooted by the path of arahantship, and thus the *sekha* remains vulnerable to the conceivings to which they are capable of giving rise. Whereas direct knowledge (*abhiññā*) is the province of both the *sekha* and the arahant, full understanding (*pariññā*) is the province exclusively of the arahant, as it involves the full abandoning of all defilements.

24 This is the stock description of the arahant, repeated in many suttas.

25 When ignorance has been abolished by the attainment of full understanding, the subtlest dispositions to craving and conceit are also eradicated. Thus the arahant can no longer engage in conceiving and delight.

26 This section and the following two are stated to show that the arahant does not conceive, not only because he has fully understood the object, but because he has eradicated the three unwholesome roots—lust (or greed), hate, and delusion. The phrase "free from lust through the destruction of lust" is used to stress that the arahant is not merely temporarily without lust, but has destroyed it at the most fundamental level. Similarly with hate and delusion.

27 On this word, the epithet the Buddha uses most often when referring to himself, see the Introduction, p. 24. The commentaries give a long detailed etymology, into which they try to compress virtually the entire Dhamma. The passage has been translated in Bhikkhu Bodhi, *Discourse on the All-Embracing Net of Views*, pp. 331–44.

28 *Pariññātantaṁ tathāgatassa.* So BBS and SBJ and MA, though PTS reads simply *pariññātaṁ.* MA glosses: "fully understood to the conclusion, fully understood to the limit, fully understood without remainder." It explains that while Buddhas and disciple-arahants are alike in

abandoning all defilements, there is a distinction in their range of full understanding: whereas disciples can attain Nibbāna after comprehending with insight only a limited number of formations, Buddhas fully understand all formations without exception.

29 This sentence gives a highly compressed statement of the formula of dependent origination (*paṭicca samuppāda*), usually expounded in twelve factors (as in MN 38). As interpreted by MA, "delight" is the craving of the previous life that brought into being the "suffering" of the five aggregates in the present life, "being" the kammically determinative aspect of the present life that causes future birth, followed by future ageing and death. This passage shows the cause for the Buddha's elimination of conceiving to be his penetration of dependent origination on the night of his enlightenment. The mention of "delight" (*nandī*) as the root of suffering links up with the sutta's title; moreover, by referring to the earlier statement that the ordinary person delights in earth, etc., it shows suffering to be the ultimate consequence of delight.

30 MA explains the sequence of ideas thus: The Tathāgata does not conceive earth and does not delight in earth because he has understood that delight is the root of suffering. Further, by understanding dependent origination, he has completely abandoned the craving here called "delight" and has awakened to supreme full enlightenment. As a result he does not conceive earth or delight in earth.

31 The bhikkhus did *not* delight in the Buddha's words, apparently because the discourse probed too deeply into the tender regions of their own conceit, and perhaps their residual brahmanic views. At a later time, MA tells us, when their pride had been humbled, the Buddha expounded to these same bhikkhus the *Gotamaka Sutta* (AN 3:123/i.276), in the course of which they all attained arahantship.

SUTTA 2

32 The taints (*āsava*), a category of defilements existing at

the deepest and most fundamental level, are discussed in the Introduction, p. 38. MA explains that restraint (*saṁvara*) is fivefold: through virtue, mindfulness, knowledge, energy, and patience. In the present sutta, restraint through virtue is illustrated by avoiding unsuitable seats and resorts (§19); restraint through mindfulness, by restraining the sense faculties (§12); restraint through knowledge, by the repeated phrase "reflecting wisely"; restraint through energy, by the removing of unwholesome thoughts (§20); and restraint through patience, by the passage on enduring (§18).

33 Wise attention (*yoniso manasikāra*) is glossed as attention that is the right means (*upāya*), on the right track (*patha*). It is explained as mental advertence, consideration, or preoccupation that accords with the truth, namely, attention to the impermanent as impermanent, etc. Unwise attention (*ayoniso manasikāra*) is attention that is the wrong means, on the wrong track (*uppatha*), contrary to the truth, namely, attention to the impermanent as permanent, the painful as pleasurable, what is not self as self, and what is foul as beautiful. Unwise attention, MA informs us, is at the root of the round of existence, for it causes ignorance and craving to increase; wise attention is at the root of liberation from the round, since it leads to the development of the Noble Eightfold Path. MA sums up the point of this passage thus: the destruction of the taints is for one who *knows* how to arouse wise attention and who *sees* to it that unwise attention does not arise.

34 Six of these—omitting the taints to be abandoned by seeing—are mentioned in the catechism on the taints in AN 6:58/iii.387–90.

35 The word "seeing" (*dassana*) here refers to the first of the four supramundane paths—the path of stream-entry (*sotāpattimagga*)—so designated because it offers the first glimpse of Nibbāna. The higher three paths are called the paths of development (*bhāvanā*) because they develop the vision of Nibbāna to the point at which all defilements are eradicated.

36 MA makes the important point that there is no fixed determination in things themselves as to whether they

are fit or unfit for attention. The distinction consists, rather, in the mode of attention. That mode of attention that is a causal basis for unwholesome states of mind should be avoided, while that mode of attention that is a causal basis for wholesome states should be developed. This same principle applies to §9.

37 MA illustrates the growth of the taints through unwise attention as follows: When he attends to gratification in the five cords of sensual pleasure, the taint of sensual desire arises and increases; when he attends to gratification in the exalted states (the jhānas), the taint of being arises and increases; and when he attends to any mundane things through the four "perversions" (of permanence, etc.—see n.5), the taint of ignorance arises and increases.

38 According to MA, this passage is undertaken to show the taint of views (*diṭṭhāsava*, not expressly mentioned in the discourse) under the heading of doubt. However, it might be more correct to say that the taint of views, disclosed by §8, emerges out of unwise attention in the form of doubt. The various types of doubt are already pregnant with the wrong views that will come to explicit expression in the next section.

39 Of these six views, the first two represent the simple antinomy of eternalism and annihilationism; the view that "no self exists for me" is *not* the non-self doctrine of the Buddha, but the materialist view that identifies the individual with the body and thus holds that there is no personal continuity beyond death. The next three views may be understood to arise out of the philosophically more sophisticated observation that experience has a built-in reflexive structure that allows for self-consciousness, the capacity of the mind to become cognizant of itself, its contents, and the body with which it is inter-connected. Engaged in a search for his "true nature," the untaught ordinary person will identify self either with both aspects of the experience (view 3), or with the observer alone (view 4), or with the observed alone (view 5). The last view is a full-blown version of eternalism in which all reservations have been discarded.

40 The self as speaker represents the conception of the self

as the agent of action; the self as feeler, the conception of the self as the passive subject. "Here and there" suggests the self as the transmigrating entity that retains its identity through a succession of different incarnations. The same view is maintained by the bhikkhu Sāti at MN 38.2.

41 This is, of course, the formula for the Four Noble Truths, treated as a subject of contemplation and insight. MA says that up to the attainment of the path of stream-entry, attention denotes insight (*vipassanā*), but at the moment of the path it denotes path-knowledge. Insight directly apprehends the first two truths, since its objective range is the mental and material phenomena comprised under *dukkha* and its origin; it can know the latter two truths only inferentially. Path-knowledge makes the truth of cessation its object, apprehending it by penetration as object (*ārammaṇa*). Path-knowledge performs four functions regarding the four truths: it fully understands the truth of suffering, abandons the origin of suffering, realises the cessation of suffering, and develops the way to the cessation of suffering.

42 The path of stream-entry has the function of cutting off the first three fetters binding to saṁsāra. MA says that identity view and adherence to rules and observances, being included in the taint of views, are taints as well as fetters, while doubt is (ordinarily) classified as only a fetter, not a taint; but because it is included here among the "taints to be abandoned by seeing," it may be spoken of as a taint.

43 If abandonment of the taints is understood in the strict sense as their ultimate destruction, then only two of the seven methods mentioned in the sutta effect their abandonment—seeing and development—which between them comprise the four supramundane paths. The other five methods cannot directly accomplish the destruction of the taints, but they can keep them under control during the preparatory stages of practice and thereby facilitate their eventual eradication by the supramundane paths.

44 The primary factor responsible for exercising this restraint over the sense faculties is mindfulness. A fuller formula for sense restraint is given in many other

suttas—e.g., MN 27.15—and analysed in detail at Vsm I, 53–59. MA explains "fever" (*pariḷāha*) in the above passage as the fever of defilements and of their (kammic) results.

45 The passages that follow here have become the standard formulas that bhikkhus use in their daily reflections upon the four requisites of the holy life. They are explained in detail at Vsm I, 85–97.

46 Unsuitable seats are the two kinds mentioned in the Pātimokkha—sitting with a woman on a screened seat convenient for sexual intercourse, and sitting alone with a woman in a private place. Various kinds of unsuitable resort are mentioned at Vsm I, 45.

47 The first three types of unwholesome thought—of sensual desire, ill will, and cruelty—constitute wrong thought or wrong intention, the opposite of the second factor of the Noble Eightfold Path. The three types of wrong thought and their opposites are dealt with more fully in MN 19.

48 These are the seven enlightenment factors (*satta bojjhangā*) included among the thirty-seven requisites of enlightenment, and treated more extensively below at MN 10.42 and MN 118.29–40. The present section explains the seven enlightenment factors specifically as aids for developing the three higher supramundane paths, by which the taints that escaped eradication by the first path will be eradicated. The terms "seclusion" (*viveka*), "dispassion" (*virāga*), and "cessation" (*nirodha*) may all be understood as referring to Nibbāna. Their use in this context signifies that the development of the enlightenment factors is directed to Nibbāna as its goal during the preparatory stages of the path, and as its object with the attainment of the supramundane paths. MA explains that the word *vossagga*, rendered as "relinquishment," has the two meanings of "giving up" (*pariccāga*), i.e., the abandonment of defilements, and "entering into" (*pakkhandana*), i.e., culminating in Nibbāna.

49 The taint of sensual desire is eradicated by the path of non-returning, the taints of being and of ignorance only by the final path, that of arahantship.

50 The ten fetters that must be destroyed to gain full deliver-

ance have been enumerated in the Introduction, pp. 42–43. Conceit, at the most subtle level, is the conceit "I am," which lingers in the mental continuum until the attainment of arahantship. The "penetration of conceit" (*mānābhisamaya*) means seeing *through* conceit and abandoning it, which are both accomplished simultaneously by the path of arahantship. The bhikkhu has "made an end of suffering" in the sense that he has put an end to the suffering of the round of saṁsāra (*vaṭṭadukkha*).

SUTTA 3

51 MA: The Buddha delivered this sutta because many bhikkhus were becoming elated over the gains and honour accruing to the Sangha, to the neglect of their spiritual training. The Buddha obviously could not lay down a training rule prohibiting the use of the requisites, but he wanted to show the practice of the heirs in Dhamma to those bhikkhus who were earnestly desirous of training.

52 MA explains that these five qualities gradually fulfil all the stages of the practice culminating in arahantship.

53 Elder bhikkhus (*thera*) are those with more than ten rainy seasons since ordination (*upasampadā*); middle bhikkhus have between five and nine rains; new bhikkhus less than five rains.

54 The evil qualities mentioned here, and in the sections that follow, are introduced to show the states referred to above (§6) by the statement: "They do not abandon what the Teacher tells them to abandon." They are also the factors that induce a bhikkhu to become an heir of material things rather than an heir of Dhamma. In MN 7.3 the same sixteen qualities, with "ill will" substituted for "hate," are referred to as "the imperfections that defile the mind" (*cittass' upakkilesā*). See n. 87 below.

55 The Noble Eightfold Path is introduced here to show the practice that makes one an "heir in Dhamma." The antithesis between the defilements and the path restates, from a new angle, the contrast between "heirs in material things" and "heirs in Dhamma" with which the Buddha had opened the sutta.

SUTTA 4

56 MA says that Jāṇussoṇi was not a given name but an honorific title meaning "royal chaplain" (*purohita*) bestowed on him by the king. MN 27 is also addressed to the brahmin Jāṇussoṇi.

57 *Bhoto Gotamassa sā janatā diṭṭhānugatiṁ āpajjati.* Ñm renders: "Do these people follow the implications of Master Gotama's view?" And Horner: "These people emulate the views of the honoured Gotama" (MLS 1:22). MA, too, glosses: "These people have the same view, opinion, outlook as Master Gotama." However, it makes much better sense in this context to read *diṭṭha* not as a *sandhi* form of *diṭṭhi*, but as the past participle, and to take this phrase as meaning "following what they have seen of him," i.e., his example. This meaning is clearly required by the phrase in its appearances at SN ii.203, AN i.126, AN iii.108, 251, 422.

58 Ñm originally had rendered this phrase as "perfect in understanding," and the corresponding phrase in the preceding section as "perfect in concentration." However, since it seems inappropriate to ascribe perfection in *samādhi* and *paññā* to the Bodhisatta prior to his enlightenment, I have chosen to render the suffix *sampanna* throughout as "possessed of." MA explains that this is neither the wisdom of insight nor of the path, but the wisdom that defines the nature of its object (*ārammaṇavavatthānapaññā*).

59 The Indian year, according to the ancient system inherited by Buddhism, is divided into three seasons—the cold season, the hot season, and the rainy season—each lasting for four months. The four months are subdivided into eight fortnights (*pakkha*), the third and the seventh containing fourteen days and the others fifteen days. Within each fortnight, the nights of the full moon and the new moon (either the fourteenth or fifteenth) and the night of the half-moon (the eighth) are regarded as especially auspicious. Within Buddhism these days become the Uposatha, the days of religious observance. On the full moon and new moon days the bhikkhus recite their

code of precepts and lay people visit the monasteries to listen to sermons and to practise meditation.

60 The four postures (*iriyāpatha*) often mentioned in the Buddhist texts are walking, standing, sitting, and lying down.

61 Beginning with this section, the Buddha shows the course of practice that led him to the peak of non-delusion.

62 MA says that the Bodhisatta developed the four jhānas using mindfulness of breathing as his meditation subject.

63 Explained in detail at Vsm XIII, 13–71.

64 Explained in detail at Vsm XIII, 72–101.

65 MA: Having shown the Four Noble Truths in their own nature (that is, in terms of suffering), the passage on the taints is stated to show them indirectly by way of the defilements.

66 According to MA, the phrase "When I knew and saw thus" refers to insight and the path, which reaches its climax in the path of arahantship; the phrase "my mind was liberated" shows the moment of the fruit; and the phrase "there came the knowledge: 'It is liberated'" shows reviewing knowledge (see Vsm XXII, 20–21), as does the next sentence beginning "I directly knew."

67 This is the stock canonical announcement of final knowledge or arahantship. MA explains that the statement "Birth is destroyed" means that any type of birth that might have arisen if the path had not been developed has been rendered incapable of arising by the development of the path. The "holy life" that has been lived is the holy life of the path (*maggabrahmacariya*). The phrase "what had to be done has been done" (*kataṁ karaṇīyaṁ*) indicates that the four tasks of the noble path—fully understanding suffering, abandoning its origin, realising its cessation, and developing the path—have now all been completed for each of the four supramundane paths. The fourth phrase, *nāparaṁ itthattāya*, is glossed by MA thus: "Now there is no need for me to develop the path again for 'such a state,' i.e., for the sixteenfold function (of the path) or for the destruction of the defilements. Or alternatively: after 'such a state,' i.e., the continuum of aggregates now occurring, there is no further continuum of aggregates for me. These five aggregates, having been

fully understood, stand like trees that are cut at the root. With the cessation of the last consciousness, they will be extinguished like a fire without fuel." I have opted for the second of these interpretations, but take *itthattāya* as a dative. The word, which literally means "the state of this" or "the state of thus," implies manifestation in a concrete state of existence. Ñm had rendered: "There is no more of this beyond."

68 MA: He has "compassion for future generations" insofar as later generations of monks, seeing that the Buddha resorted to forest dwellings, will follow his example and thus hasten their progress towards making an end of suffering.

SUTTA 5

69 MA, picking up on the venerable Sāriputta's use of the word "person" (*puggala*), explains that the Buddha has a twofold teaching—a conventional teaching (*sammutidesanā*) expressed in terms of persons, beings, women, and men, etc.; and an ultimate teaching (*paramatthadesanā*) expressed solely in terms that possess ultimate ontological validity, such as aggregates, elements, sense bases, impermanent, suffering, not self, etc. The Buddha expounds his teaching through whichever approach is best suited to enable the hearer to penetrate the meaning, dispel delusion, and achieve distinction. The use of the word "person," therefore, does not imply a misconception of the person as a self.

70 *Subhanimitta*: an attractive object that is the basis for lust. The Buddha says that unwise attention to the sign of the beautiful is the nutriment (*āhāra*) for the arising of unarisen sensual desire and for the growth and increase of arisen sensual desire (SN 46:2/v.64).

71 These are strict ascetic practices. The forest dweller, almsfood eater, house-to-house seeker and refuse-rag wearer are explained in Vsm II.

72 These are "softer" practices than those referred to in §29, generally regarded as signs of a less earnest commitment to exertion for the sake of the goal.

73 The Ājīvakas, or Ājīvikas, were a rival sect whose teaching

emphasised severe austerities based on a philosophy bordering on fatalism. See Basham, *History and Doctrines of the Ājīvikas*.

74 The possessive pronouns qualifying heart are not in the Pali, but the sense of the phrase has to be understood by consideration of the simile. Just as Samīti planed the faults out of the felloe as if he knew Paṇḍuputta's heart with his own heart, so does Sāriputta plane out the faults of the bhikkhus as if he knew Moggallāna's wish to have them removed. MLS (1:40) misses the point by translating: "because he knows their hearts with his heart," taking the first reference to be to the monks rather than to Ven. Moggallāna.

75 *Mahānāga*. The *nāgas* are a class of dragonlike beings in Indian mythology believed to inhabit the nether regions of the earth and to be the guardians of hidden treasures. The word comes to represent any gigantic or powerful creature, such as a tusker elephant or a cobra and, by extension, an arahant bhikkhu. See Dhp, ch. 23, Nāgavagga.

SUTTA 6

76 MA says that the expression *sampannasīlā*, translated here as "possessed of virtue," can mean either "perfect in virtue" (*paripuṇṇasīlā*) or "endowed with virtue" (*sīlasamangino*). The Pātimokkha is the code of monastic discipline, which in its Pali version consists of 227 rules. "Resort" (*gocara*) implies a proper resort for alms, though it may also signify the proper deportment of a monk, his serene and self-possessed bearing. The key terms in this passage are analysed at Vsm I, 43–52.

77 MA: The passage beginning with "let him fulfil the precepts," repeated for each of the following sections until the end of the sutta, comprises the entire threefold training. The phrase about fulfilling the precepts signifies the training in higher virtue (*adhisīlasikkhā*); the phrase "be devoted to internal serenity of mind, not neglect meditation" indicates the training in concentration or the higher mind (*adhicittasikkhā*); and the phrase "be possessed of insight" points to the training in the

higher wisdom (*adhipaññāsikkhā*). The phrase "dwell in empty huts" combines the latter two trainings, since one resorts to an empty hut to develop serenity and insight.

78 That is, if the relatives who have been reborn in the realm of ghosts or in some lower deva realm recollect virtuous bhikkhus with confidence, that confidence will become a source of merit for them, protecting them from bad rebirths and becoming a positive condition for the attainment of Nibbāna.

79 These are the four immaterial attainments for which the full formulas are to be found below at MN 8.8–11, MN 25.16–19, etc. MA glosses "body" as "mental body" (*nāmakāya*).

80 The three fetters destroyed by the stream-enterer are identity view, doubt, and adherence to rules and observances, as mentioned at MN 2.11.

81 In addition to the first three fetters, the non-returner destroys the other two "lower fetters" of sensual desire and ill will. The non-returner is reborn in a special region of the Brahma-world called the Pure Abodes, and there makes an end of suffering.

82 §§14–19 present the six kinds of direct knowledge (*abhiññā*). See Introduction, p. 37; for details, see Vsm XII and XIII.

83 MA: In this passage "mind" and "wisdom" signify, respectively, the concentration and wisdom associated with the fruit of arahantship. Concentration is called "deliverance of mind" (*cetovimutti*) because it is liberated from lust; wisdom is called "deliverance by wisdom" (*paññāvimutti*) because it is liberated from ignorance. The former is normally the result of serenity, the latter the result of insight. But when they are coupled and described as taintless (*anāsava*), they jointly result from the destruction of the taints by the supramundane path of arahantship.

SUTTA 7

84 For a more thorough treatment of this sutta and the following one, with helpful introductions and lengthy

explanatory notes, see Nyanaponika Thera, *The Simile of the Cloth and The Discourse on Effacement*.

85 An unhappy destination (*duggati*) is rebirth in the three states of deprivation—hell, the animal kingdom, and the realm of ghosts. A happy destination (*sugati*), mentioned just below, is rebirth in a superior state among humans and in the heavenly worlds.

86 *Cittassa upakkilesā*. The word *upakkilesā* is sometimes used in the sense of blemishes or imperfections of meditative concentration, as at MN 128.27, 30; sometimes in the sense of blemishes or imperfections of insight, as at Vsm XX, 105; and sometimes to signify the minor defilements that arise from the three unwholesome roots—greed, hate, and delusion—either as their modes or their offshoots. Here it is used in this third sense, but to maintain the connection with its first two usages, it has been translated by the phrase "imperfections that defile the mind."

87 MA offers several tentative distinctions between covetousness (*abhijjhā*) and unrighteous greed (*visamalobha*), but then it points out that since, from the standpoint of the higher training, all greed is unrighteous, the two terms can be understood as merely different names for the same mental factor, greed or lust. Here I paraphrase MA's explanations of some of the other mental corruptions: Resentment (*upanāha*) sets in after anger has repeatedly enveloped the mind. *Contempt (makkha)* is the devaluation of benefits conferred on one by others. *Insolence (paḷāsa)* is presumption (*yugaggāha*) arising when one puts oneself at the same level as others who have superior qualities. *Envy (issā)* is resentment over the honours, etc., shown to others; *avarice (macchariya)* is unwillingness to share one's own possessions with others. *Obstinacy (thambha)* is inflexibility, stiffness, rigidity, like a bellows full of air. *Rivalry (sārambha)* is attempting to outdo others, the drive to surpass their achievements. Several of these corruptions are also defined at Vbh §§845–46, 891–94.

88 MA says that the abandoning spoken of here should be understood as "abandonment by eradication" (*samucchedappahāna*), that is, complete uprooting by the supramundane

path. The sixteen defilements are abandoned by the noble paths in the following order:

1. The *path of stream-entry* abandons: contempt, insolence, envy, avarice, deceit, fraud.
2. The *path of non-returning* abandons: ill will, anger, resentment, negligence.
3. The *path of arahantship* abandons: covetousness and unrighteous greed, obstinacy, rivalry, conceit, arrogance, vanity.

MA maintains, by reference to an ancient exegetical source, that in this passage the path of the non-returner is being described. Therefore we must understand that those defilements to be fully abandoned by the path of arahantship have at this point only been abandoned in part, by way of their coarser manifestations.

89 Perfect confidence (*aveccappasāda*) in the Buddha, the Dhamma, and the Sangha is an attribute of a noble disciple at the minimal level of a stream-enterer, whose confidence is perfect because he has seen the truth of the Dhamma for himself. The formulas for recollection of the Buddha, Dhamma, and Sangha given here are explained at length in Vsm VII.

90 This translation follows the reading *yatodhi* and MA's explanation of this as the partial abandoning of defilements by the first three paths, contrasted with the total (*anodhi*) abandoning of defilements by the fourth and final path. Ñm, following the reading *yathodhi*, translates: "And whatever [from among those imperfections] has, according to the limitation [set by whichever of the first three paths he has attained], been given up, has been [forever] dropped, let go, abandoned, relinquished." The two variations seem to be ancient as they are both recognized by MA.

91 *Labhati atthavedaṁ labhati dhammavedaṁ.* Ven. Nyanaponika renders: "He gains enthusiasm for the goal, gains enthusiasm for the Dhamma." MA explains *veda* as meaning joy and the knowledge connected with that joy, and says: "*Atthaveda* is the inspiration arisen in one who reviews his perfect confidence; *dhammaveda* is the inspiration arisen in one who reviews the abandonment of the defilements in part, the cause of that perfect confidence."

92 The Pali equivalents, in noun form, for the terms in this series are: *pāmojja*, gladness; *pīti*, rapture; *passaddhi*, tranquillity; *sukha*, pleasure; *samādhi*, concentration. Tranquillity, by removing the subtle bodily and mental disturbances connected with gladness and rapture, brings the serene pleasure that prepares the mind for deepened concentration.

93 The Pali terms are: *evaṁsīlo evaṁdhammo evaṁpañño*. The middle term, in this context, obviously must refer to the second stage of the threefold training, concentration, though it is puzzling why *samādhi* itself is not used. The commentary to MN 123.2 glosses a parallel expression by *samādhi-pakkha-dhammā*, "states belonging to concentration."

94 This statement underscores his attainment of the stage of non-returner. Since the non-returner has eradicated sensual desire, delicious food cannot impede him in his quest for the final path and fruit.

95 §§13–16 present the standard sutta formulas for the four "divine abodes" (*brahmavihāra*). Briefly, loving-kindness (*mettā*) is the wish for the welfare and happiness of others; compassion (*karuṇā*), the empathy with them in their suffering; altruistic joy (*muditā*), rejoicing in their virtues and success; and equanimity (*upekkhā*), the attitude of detached impartiality towards beings (*not* apathy or indifference). For a fuller treatment, see Vsm IX.

96 MA: The present section shows the non-returner's practice of insight meditation aimed at arahantship and the following section his attainment of arahantship. The phrase "there is this" signifies the truth of suffering; "there is the inferior," the origin of suffering; "the superior," the truth of the path; and "the escape from this whole field of perception" is Nibbāna, the cessation of suffering.

97 MA: The Buddha used this phrase to arouse the attention of the brahmin Sundarika Bhāradvāja, who was in the assembly and believed in purification by ritual bathing. The Buddha foresaw that the brahmin would be inspired to take ordination under him and would attain arahantship.

98 These are rivers and fords that were popularly believed to give purification.

99 The Pali has *phaggu*, a day of brahmanical purification in the month of *Phagguna* (February–March), and *uposatha*, the religious observance days regulated by the lunar calendar. See n.59.

100 The going forth (*pabbajjā*) is the formal ordination of entering the homeless life as a novice (*sāmaṇera*); the full admission (*upasampadā*) confers the status of a bhikkhu, a full member of the Sangha.

SUTTA 8

101 See n.84.

102 Views associated with doctrines of a self (*attavādapaṭisaṁyuttā*), according to MA, are the twenty types of identity view enumerated at MN 44.7, though they may also be understood to include the more elaborate doctrines about a self discussed in MN 102. Views associated with doctrines about the world (*lokavādapaṭisaṁyuttā*) are the eight views: the world is eternal, non-eternal, both, or neither; the world is infinite, finite, both, or neither. See MN 63 and MN 72 for the Buddha's rejection of these views.

103 MA: This question refers to one who has only reached the initial stages of insight meditation without attaining stream-entry. The type of abandonment under discussion is abandoning by eradication, which is effected only by the path of stream-entry. Ven. Mahā Cunda posed this question because some meditators were overestimating their achievement, thinking they had abandoned such views while they had not really eradicated them.

104 MA explains that the word "arise" (*uppajjanti*) refers here to the arising of views that have not arisen before; "underlie" (*anusenti*) to their gathering strength through continued adherence to them; and being "exercised" (*samudācaranti*) to their gaining bodily or verbal expression. The "object" upon which they are based is the five aggregates (*khandha*) that constitute a person or living being—material form, feeling, perception, mental formations, and consciousness.

105 By this statement the Buddha shows the means by which these views are eradicated: contemplation of the five aggregates as "not mine," etc., with the wisdom of insight culminating in the path of stream-entry.

106 MA explains that the Buddha, having answered the Elder's question, now speaks of another type of overestimator—those who attain the eight meditative attainments and believe that they are practising true effacement (*sallekha*). The word *sallekha*, originally meaning austerity or ascetic practice, is used by the Buddha to signify the radical effacing or removal of defilements. Though the eight attainments are elsewhere placed securely within the Buddhist training (see MN 25.12–19, MN 26.34–41), it is here said that they should not be called effacement because the bhikkhu who attains them does not use them as a basis for insight—as described for example in MN 52 and MN 64—but only as a means of enjoying bliss and peace.

107 The forty-four "modes of effacement" to be expounded fall, by and large, into several fixed sets of doctrinal categories as follows. Those not mentioned here do not fit into any fixed set.

(2)–(11) are the ten courses of unwholesome and wholesome action (*kammapatha*)—see MN 9.4, 9.6;

(12)–(18) are the last seven factors of the eightfold path—wrong and right—the first factor being identical with (11);

(19)–(20) are sometimes added to the two eightfold paths—see MN 117.34–36;

(21)–(23) are the last three of the five hindrances—see MN 10.36—the first two being identical with (9) and (10);

(24)–(33) are ten of the sixteen imperfections that defile the mind, mentioned in MN 7.3;

(37)–(43) are the seven bad qualities and the seven good qualities (*saddhammā*) mentioned in MN 53.11–17.

108 MṬ: Non-cruelty (*avihiṁsā*), which is a synonym for compassion, is mentioned at the beginning because it is the root of all virtues, especially the root-cause of morality.

109 MA: This is a description of those who hold firmly to a

view that has occurred to them, believing "This alone is the truth"; they do not relinquish it even if spoken to by the Buddha with reasoned arguments.

110 MA: The inclination of mind is of great benefit because it entails exclusively welfare and happiness, and because it is the cause of the subsequent actions that conform to it.

111 The Pali term rendered by "extinguished" is *parinibbuto,* which can also mean "attained to Nibbāna"; and the Pali term rendered by "help extinguish" is *parinibbāpessati,* which can also mean "help attain Nibbāna" or "bring to Nibbāna." The Pali original for the expression to follow, "by which to extinguish it," *parinibbānaya,* might have been rendered "for attaining Nibbāna." Though in all three cases the alternative rendering would be too strong to insist on literally, its implications contribute to the suggestiveness of the original in a way that cannot be captured in translation.

112 MA points out that this statement can be understood in two ways: (1) one who is himself free from cruelty can use his non-cruelty to help extinguish the cruelty of another person; and (2) one who is himself cruel can develop non-cruelty to extinguish his own cruel disposition. All the following cases should be similarly understood in this twofold way.

113 MA: The compassionate teacher's task is the correct teaching of the Dhamma; beyond that is the practice, which is the work of the disciples.

SUTTA 9

114 MA: Right view is twofold: mundane and supramundane. Mundane right view is again twofold: the view that kamma produces its fruits, which may be held both by Buddhists and outsiders, and the view that accords with the Four Noble Truths, which is exclusive to the Buddha's Dispensation. Supramundane right view is the understanding of the Four Noble Truths attained by penetrating to the four paths and fruits of sanctity. The question posed by the Ven. Sāriputta concerns the *sekha,* the disciple in higher training, who possesses supramundane

right view leading irreversibly to emancipation. This is implied by the phrase "perfect confidence" and "arrived at this true Dhamma."

115 Here the unwholesome (*akusala*) is explained by the ten unwholesome courses of action. The first three of these pertain to bodily action, the middle four to verbal action, the last three to mental action. The ten are explained at greater length at MN 41.8–10.

116 These three are called the roots of the unwholesome because they motivate all unwholesome actions. For a thorough and informative textual study of these factors and their opposites, see Nyanaponika Thera, *The Roots of Good and Evil.*

117 These ten wholesome courses of action are elaborated upon in MN 41.12–14.

118 MA explains the disciple's understanding of these four terms by way of the Four Noble Truths thus: all the courses of action are the truth of suffering; the wholesome and unwholesome roots are the truth of the origin; the non-occurrence of both actions and their roots is the truth of cessation; and the noble path that realises cessation is the truth of the path. To this extent a noble disciple at one of the first three stages has been described—one who has arrived at supramundane right view but has not yet eliminated all defilements.

119 The passage from "he entirely abandons the underlying tendency to lust" until "he makes an end of suffering" shows the work accomplished by the paths of the non-returner and of arahantship—the elimination of the most subtle and obstinate defilements and the achievement of final knowledge. Here, the underlying tendencies to sensual lust and aversion are eliminated by the path of the non-returner, the underlying tendency to the view and conceit "I am" and ignorance by the path of arahantship. MA explains that the expression "underlying tendency to the view and conceit 'I am'" (*asmī ti diṭṭhimānānusaya*) should be interpreted to mean the underlying tendency to conceit that is *similar to* a view because, like the view of self, it occurs apprehending the notion "I am."

120 Here I take *sambhavesīnam* to be an instance of the (rare) future active participle in *-esin*. (See Norman, *Elders' Verses I : Theragāthā*, n.527, and Gelger, *A Pāli Grammar*, 193A.) The commentators, whom I have followed in the first edition of this work, take *-esin* as an adjectival formation from *esati*, to seek, and thus explain the phrase as meaning "those who are seeking a new existence." See too n. 514 below. Nutriment (*āhāra*) is to be understood here in a broad sense as a prominent condition for the individual life-continuity. Physical food (*kabalinkāra āhāra*) is an important condition for the physical body, contact for feeling, mental volition for consciousness, and consciousness for mentality-materiality, the psychophysical organism in its totality. Craving is called the origin of nutriment in that the craving of the previous existence is the source of the present individuality with its dependence upon and continual consumption of the four nutriments in this existence. For an annotated compilation of the canonical and commentarial texts on the nutriments, see Nyanaponika Thera, *The Four Nutriments of Life*.

121 The next twelve sections present, in reverse order, a factor-by-factor examination of dependent origination. The principal terms of the formula are explained briefly in the Introduction, pp. 30–31. The detailed exegesis is in Vsm XVII. Here each factor is patterned after the Four Noble Truths.

122 This refers to the five aggregates. See MN 10.38 and MN 44.2.

123 The six bases for contact are enumerated at §50 below.

124 The three kinds of being are explained in the Introduction, pp. 46–48, in the discussion of Buddhist cosmology. Here, by "being" should be understood both the actual planes of rebirth and the types of kamma that generate rebirth into those planes.

125 Clinging to rules and observances is the adherence to the view that purification can be achieved by adopting certain external rules or following certain observances, particularly of ascetic self-discipline; clinging to a doctrine of self is synonymous with identity view in one or another of its twenty forms (see MN 44.7); clinging to views is the

clinging to all other types of views except the two mentioned separately. Clinging in any of its varieties represents a strengthening of craving, its condition.

126 Craving for mind-objects (*dhammataṇhā*) is the craving for all objects of consciousness except the objects of the five kinds of sense consciousness. Examples would be the craving for fantasies and mental imagery, for abstract ideas and intellectual systems, for feelings and emotional states, etc.

127 Contact (*phassa*) is explained at MN 18.16 as the meeting of sense faculty, its object, and consciousness.

128 Mind-base (*manāyatana*) is a collective term for all classes of consciousness. One part of this base—the "life continuum" (*bhavanga*) or subliminal consciousness—is the "door" for the arising of mind-consciousness. See n.130.

129 Mentality-materiality (*nāmarūpa*) is an umbrella term for the psychophysical organism exclusive of consciousness. The five mental factors mentioned under *nāma* are indispensable to consciousness and thus pertain to all conscious experience. The four great elements concretely represent matter's essential properties of solidity, cohesion, heat, and distension. The material form derived from the elements includes, according to the Abhidhamma analysis, the sensitive substance of the five sense faculties; four sense objects—colour, sound, smell, and taste (tangibles being the three elements of earth, fire, and air); the physical life faculty, nutritive essence, sex determination, and other types of material phenomena. See also the Introduction, p. 56.

130 Mind-consciousness (*manoviññāṇa*) comprises all consciousness except the five types of sense consciousness just mentioned. It includes consciousness of mental images, abstract ideas, and internal states of mind, as well as the consciousness in reflection upon sense objects.

131 In the context of the doctrine of dependent origination, formations (*sankhārā*) are wholesome and unwholesome volitions, or, in short, kamma. The bodily formation is volition that is expressed through the body, the verbal formation volition that is expressed by speech, and the mental formation volition that remains internal without coming to bodily or verbal expression.

132 It should be noted that while ignorance is a condition for the taints, the taints—which include the taint of ignorance—are in turn a condition for ignorance. MA says that this conditioning of ignorance by ignorance should be understood to mean that the ignorance in any one existence is conditioned by the ignorance in the preceding existence. Since this is so, the conclusion follows that no first point can be discovered for ignorance, and thus that saṁsāra is without discernible beginning.

SUTTA 10

133 This is one of the most important suttas in the Pali Canon, containing the most comprehensive statement of the most direct way to the attainment of the Buddhist goal. Virtually the identical sutta is found as well at DN 22, though with an expanded analysis of the Four Noble Truths attached, which accounts for its greater length. The sutta, its commentary, and copious extracts from its difficult but illuminating subcommentary have been presented together in translation by Soma Thera in *The Way of Mindfulness*. A very readable translation of the sutta, with a modern commentary excelling in clarity and depth, will be found in Nyanaponika Thera, *The Heart of Buddhist Meditation*.

134 This town is said by some scholars to have been in the vicinity of modern Delhi.

135 The Pali reads *ekāyano ayaṁ bhikkhave maggo*, and virtually all translators understand this as a statement upholding *satipaṭṭhāna* as an exclusive path. Thus Ven. Soma renders it: "This is the only way, O bhikkhus," and Ven. Nyanaponika: "This is the sole way, monks." Ñm, however, points out that *ekāyana magga* at MN 12.37–42 has the unambiguous contextual meaning of "a path that goes in one way only," and so he rendered the phrase in this passage, too. The expression used here, "the direct path," is an attempt to preserve this meaning in a more streamlined phrasing. MA explains *ekāyana magga* as a single path, not a divided path; as a way that has to be walked by oneself alone, without a companion; and as a

way that goes to one goal, Nibbāna. Though there is neither canonical nor commentarial basis for this view, it might be maintained that *satipaṭṭhāna* is called *ekāyana magga*, the direct path, to distinguish it from the approach to meditative attainment that proceeds through the jhānas or *brahmavihāras*. While the latter can lead to Nibbāna, they do not do so necessarily but can lead to sidetracks, whereas *satipaṭṭhāna* leads invariably to the final goal.

136 The word *satipaṭṭhāna* is a compound term. The first part, *sati*, originally meant "memory," but in Pali Buddhist usage it far more frequently bears the meaning of attentiveness directed to the present—hence the makeshift rendering "mindfulness." The second part is explained in two ways: either as a shortened form of *upaṭṭhāna*, meaning "setting up" or "establishing"—here, of mindfulness; or as *paṭṭhāna*, meaning "domain" or "foundation"—again, of mindfulness. Thus the four *satipaṭṭhānas* may be understood as either the four ways of setting up mindfulness or as the four objective domains of mindfulness, to be amplified in the rest of the sutta. The former seems to be the etymologically correct derivation (confirmed by the Sanskrit *smṛtyupasthāna*), but the Pali commentators, while admitting both explanations, have a predilection for the latter.

137 MA says that in this context, "bhikkhu" is a term indicating a person who earnestly endeavours to accomplish the practice of the teaching: "Whoever undertakes that practice...is here comprised under the term 'bhikkhu.'"

138 The repetition in the phrase "contemplating the body as a body" (*kāye kāyānupassī*), according to MA, has the purpose of precisely determining the object of contemplation and of isolating that object from others with which it might be confused. Thus, in this practice, the body should be contemplated as such, and not one's feelings, ideas, and emotions concerning it. The phrase also means that the body should be contemplated simply as a body and not as a man, a woman, a self, or a living being. Similar considerations apply to the repetitions in the case of each of the other three foundations of mindfulness. "Covetousness and grief," MA says, stands for sensual

desire and ill will, the principal hindrances that must be overcome for the practice to succeed, enumerated separately below in §36.

139 The structure of this sutta is fairly simple. Following the preamble, the body of the discourse falls into four parts by way of the four foundations of mindfulness:

I. *Contemplation of the body*, which comprises fourteen exercises: mindfulness of breathing; contemplation of the four postures; full awareness; attention to foulness; attention to the elements; and nine "charnel ground contemplations"—reflection on corpses in different stages of decomposition.

II. *Contemplation of feeling*, considered one exercise.

III. *Contemplation of mind*, also one exercise.

IV. *Contemplation of mind-objects*, which has five subdivisions—the five hindrances; the five aggregates; the six sense bases; the seven enlightenment factors; and the Four Noble Truths.

Thus the sutta expounds altogether twenty-one exercises in contemplation. Each exercise in turn has two aspects: the basic exercise, explained first, and a supplementary section on insight (essentially the same for all the exercises), which indicates how the contemplation is to be developed to deepen understanding of the phenomenon under investigation.

Finally the sutta concludes with a statement of assurance in which the Buddha personally vouches for the effectiveness of the method by declaring the fruits of continuous practice to be either arahantship or non-returning.

140 The practice of mindfulness of breathing (*ānāpānasati*) involves no deliberate attempt to regulate the breath, as in hatha yoga, but a sustained effort to fix awareness on the breath as it moves in and out in its natural rhythm. Mindfulness is set up at the nostrils or the upper lip, wherever the impact of the breath is felt most distinctly; the length of the breath is noted but not consciously controlled. The complete development of this meditation method is expounded in MN 118. For a collection of texts on this subject, see Bhikkhu Ñāṇamoli, *Mindfulness of Breathing*. See too Vsm VIII, 145–244.

141 MA explains "experiencing the whole body" (*sabbakāya-paṭisaṁvedī*) as signifying that the meditator becomes aware of each in-breath and out-breath through its three phases of beginning, middle, and end. In the first edition I followed this explanation and added in brackets "of breath" after "the whole body." In retrospect, however, this interpretation seems forced, and I now prefer to take the phrase quite literally. It is also difficult to see how *paṭisaṁvedī* could mean "is aware of," as it is based on a verb meaning "to experience."

142 The "bodily formation" (*kāyasankhāra*) is defined at MN 44.13 as in-and-out breathing itself. Thus, as MA explains, with the successful development of the practice, the meditator's breathing becomes increasingly quiet, tranquil, and peaceful.

143 MA: "Internally": contemplating the breathing in his own body. "Externally": contemplating the breathing occurring in the body of another. "Internally and externally": contemplating the breathing in his own body and in the body of another alternately, with uninterrupted attention. A similar explanation applies to the refrain that follows each of the other sections, except that under the contemplation of feeling, mind, and mind-objects, the contemplation externally, apart from those possessing telepathic powers, must be inferential.

144 The expression *samudayadhammānupassī kāyasmiṁ viharati* is usually translated "he abides contemplating in the body its arising factors" (as was done in the first edition), on the assumption that the compound contains a plural, *samudayadhammā*. A plural sense, however, is not mandatory, and it is more consistent with the use of the suffix *-dhamma* elsewhere to take it to mean "subject to" or "having the nature of" here as well. The commentarial explanation of the conditioning factors for each of the four foundations does not imply that the commentary understands *-dhamma* to mean the actual conditioning factors.

MA explains that the arising nature (*samudayadhamma*) of the body can be observed in its conditioned origination through ignorance, craving, kamma, and food, as well as in the moment-by-moment origination of material phenomena in the body. In the case of mindfulness of breathing, an additional condition is the physiological apparatus of respiration. The "vanishing nature" (*vaya-dhamma*) of the body is seen in the cessation of bodily phenomena through the cessation of their conditions as well as in the momentary dissolution of bodily phenomena.

145 MA: For the sake of a wider and wider and higher and higher measure of knowledge and mindfulness.

146 The understanding of the bodily postures referred to in this exercise is not our ordinary natural knowledge of our bodily activity, but a close, constant, and careful awareness of the body in every position, coupled with an analytical examination intended to dispel the delusion of a self as the agent of bodily movement.

147 *Sampajañña*, also translated as "clear comprehension" (Soma, Nyanaponika), is analysed in the commentaries into four types: full awareness of the purpose of one's action; full awareness of the suitability of one's means; full awareness of the domain, that is, not abandoning the subject of meditation during one's daily routine; and full awareness of reality, the knowledge that behind one's activities there is no abiding self. See *The Way of Mindfulness*, pp. 60–100; *The Heart of Buddhist Meditation*, pp. 46–55.

148 In later Pali works the brain is added to the above list to form thirty-two parts. The details of this meditation practice are explained at Vsm VIII, 42–144.

149 These four elements are explained by Buddhist tradition as the primary attributes of matter—solidity, cohesion, heat, and distension. The detailed explanation is found at Vsm XI, 27–117.

150 The phrase "as though" (*seyyathāpi*) suggests that this meditation, and those to follow, need not be based upon an actual encounter with a corpse in the state of decay described, but can be performed as an imaginative exercise. "This same body" is, of course, the meditator's own body.

151 Each of the four types of corpse mentioned here, and the three types below, may be taken as a separate and self-sufficient subject of meditation; or the entire set may be used as a progressive series for impressing on the mind

the idea of the body's transience and insubstantiality. The progression continues in §§26–30.

152 Feeling (*vedanā*) signifies the affective quality of experience, bodily and mental, either pleasant, painful, or neither, i.e., neutral feeling. Examples of the "worldly" and "unworldly" forms of these feelings are given at MN 137.9–15 under the rubric of the six kinds of joy, grief, and equanimity based respectively on the household life and renunciation.

153 The conditions for the arising and vanishing of feeling are the same as those for the body (see n.144) except that food is replaced by contact, since contact is the condition for feeling (see MN 9.42).

154 Mind (*citta*) as an object of contemplation refers to the general state and level of consciousness. Since consciousness itself, in its own nature, is the bare knowing or cognizing of an object, the quality of any state of mind is determined by its associated mental factors, such as lust, hate, and delusion or their opposites, as mentioned by the sutta.

155 The paired examples of *citta* given in this passage contrast states of mind of wholesome and unwholesome, or developed and undeveloped character. An exception, however, is the pair "contracted" and "distracted," which are both unwholesome, the former due to sloth and torpor, the latter due to restlessness and remorse. MA explains "exalted mind" and "unsurpassed mind" as the mind pertaining to the level of the jhānas and immaterial meditative attainments, and "unexalted mind" and "surpassed mind" as the mind pertaining to the level of sense-sphere consciousness. "Liberated mind" must be understood as a mind temporarily and partly freed from defilements through insight or the jhānas. Since the practice of *satipaṭṭhāna* pertains to the preliminary phase of the path aimed at the supramundane paths of deliverance, this last category should not be understood as a mind liberated through attainment of the supramundane paths.

156 The conditions for the arising and vanishing of mind are the same as those for the body except that food is replaced by mentality-materiality, since the latter is the condition for consciousness (see DN 15.22/ii.63).

157 The word rendered here as "mind-objects" is the polymorphous *dhammā*. In this context *dhammā* can be understood as comprising all phenomena classified by way of the categories of the Dhamma, the Buddha's teaching of actuality. This contemplation reaches its climax in the penetration of the teaching at the heart of the Dhamma—the Four Noble Truths.

158 The five hindrances (*pañcanīvaraṇā*) are the main inner impediments to the development of concentration and insight. Sensual desire arises through attending unwisely to a sensually attractive object and is abandoned by meditation on a foul object (as in §10 and §§14–30); ill will arises through attending unwisely to a repugnant object and is abandoned by developing loving-kindness; sloth and torpor arise by submitting to boredom and laziness and are abandoned by arousing energy; restlessness and remorse arise through unwisely reflecting on disturbing thoughts and are abandoned by wisely reflecting on tranquillity; doubt arises through unwisely reflecting on dubious matters and is abandoned by study, investigation, and inquiry. The hindrances are fully eradicated only by the supramundane paths. For a fuller treatment, see *The Way of Mindfulness*, pp. 119–130; Nyanaponika Thera, *The Five Mental Hindrances*; and also below, MN 27.18 and MN 39.13–14.

159 The five aggregates affected by clinging (*pañc'upādānakkhandhā*) are the five groups of factors comprising the individual personality. The aggregates are discussed in the Introduction, pp. 26–27, and are analysed and explained in terms of their origin and disappearance at MN 109.9.

160 The internal bases are, as shown, the six sense faculties; the external bases, their respective objects. The fetter that arises dependent upon the pairs may be understood by way of the ten fetters explained in the Introduction, pp. 42–43, or more simply as attraction (greed), aversion (hatred), and the underlying delusion.

161 How the seven enlightenment factors unfold in progressive sequence is explained at MN 118.29–40. For a more detailed discussion, see Piyadassi Thera, *The Seven Factors of Enlightenment*.

162 "Investigation of states" (*dhammavicaya*) means the scrutiny of the mental and physical phenomena presented to the meditator's mind by mindfulness.

163 The commentaries explain in detail the conditions that conduce to the maturation of the enlightenment factors. See *The Way of Mindfulness*, pp. 134–149.

164 With this section, the contemplation of *dhammā* culminates in the understanding of *the* Dhamma in its core formulation as the Four Noble Truths. The longer *Mahāsatipaṭṭhāna Sutta* of the Dīgha Nikāya gives extended definitions and elaborations of each of the truths.

165 Final knowledge, *aññā*, is the arahant's knowledge of final deliverance. Non-return (*anāgāmitā*) is, of course, the state of a non-returner, who is reborn in a higher world where he attains final Nibbāna without ever returning to the human world.

SUTTA 11

166 The phrase "only here" means only in the Buddha's Dispensation. The four recluses (*samaṇa*) referred to are the four grades of noble disciples—the stream-enterer, once-returner, non-returner, and arahant. A "lion's roar" (*sīhanāda*), according to MA, is a roar of supremacy and fearlessness, a roar that cannot be confuted. In connection with the Buddha's proclamation, see also his discussion with Subhadda in the *Mahāparinibbāna Sutta* (DN 16:5.27/ii.151–52).

167 MA: Even though the adherents of other sects all declare arahantship—understood in a general way as spiritual perfection—to be the goal, they point out other attainments as the goal in accordance with their views. Thus the brahmins declare the Brahma-world to be the goal, the ascetics declare the gods of Streaming Radiance, the wanderers the gods of Refulgent Glory, and the Ājīvakas the non-percipient state, which they imagine to be "infinite mind."

168 "Favouring and opposing" (*anurodhapaṭivirodha*) means reacting with attraction through lust and with aversion through hate.

169 Proliferation (*papañca*), according to MA, is here mental activity governed by craving and views. For more on this important term, see n.229.

170 The view of being (*bhavadiṭṭhi*) is eternalism, the belief in an eternal self; the view of non-being (*vibhavadiṭṭhi*) is annihilationism, the denial of any principle of continuity as a basis for rebirth and kammic retribution. The adoption of one view entailing opposition to the other ties up with the earlier statement that the goal is for one who does not favour and oppose.

171 As the origin (*samudaya*) of these views, MA mentions eight conditions: the five aggregates, ignorance, contact, perception, thought, unwise attention, bad friends, and the voice of another. Their disappearance (*atthangama*) is the path of stream-entry, which eradicates all wrong views. Their gratification (*assāda*) may be understood as the satisfaction of psychological need that they provide; their danger (*ādīnava*) is the continual bondage that they entail; the escape (*nissaraṇa*) from them is Nibbāna.

172 MA glosses full understanding (*pariññā*) here as overcoming, transcending (*samatikkama*), with reference to the commentarial notion of *pahānapariññā*, "full understanding as abandonment." See n.7.

173 This passage clearly states that the critical factor differentiating the Buddha's teaching from all other religious and philosophical creeds is its "full understanding of clinging to a doctrine of self." This means, in effect, that the Buddha alone is able to show how to overcome all views of self by developing penetration of the truth of non-self. Since the other spiritual teachers lack this understanding of non-self, their claims to fully understand the three other kinds of clinging are also suspect.

174 MA: That is, the Buddha teaches how clinging to sense pleasures (understood as comprising all forms of greed, MṬ) is abandoned by the path of arahantship, the other three clingings by the path of stream-entry.

175 This passage is stated to show how clinging is to be abandoned. Clinging is traced back to its root-cause in ignorance, and then the destruction of ignorance is shown to be the means to eradicate clinging.

176 The Pali idiom, *n'eva kāmupādānaṁ upādiyati*, would have to be rendered literally as "he does not cling to the clinging to sense pleasures," which may obscure the sense rather than convey it. *Upādāna* in Pali is the object of its own verb form, while "clinging" in English is not. At one stage in his translation Ñm tried to circumvent this problem by borrowing the word *upādāna*'s other meaning of "fuel" and translating: "he no longer clings to sensual desires [as fuel for] clinging." This, however, also borders on obscurity, and I have therefore attempted to cut through the difficulty by translating directly in accordance with the sense rather than in conformity with the Pali idiom.

SUTTA 12

177 The *Sunakkhatta Sutta* (MN 105) had been expounded to him by the Buddha, apparently before he joined the Sangha; the account of his defection is given in the *Pāṭika Sutta* (DN 24). He became dissatisfied and left the Order because the Buddha would not perform any miracles for him or explain to him the beginning of things.

178 Superhuman states (*uttari manussadhammā*) are states, virtues, or attainments higher than the ordinary human virtues comprised in the ten wholesome courses of action (see MN 9.6); they include the jhānas, the kinds of direct knowledge, and the paths and fruits. "Distinction in knowledge and vision worthy of the noble ones" (*alamariyañāṇadassanavisesa*), a frequently occurring expression in the suttas, signifies all higher degrees of meditative knowledge characteristic of the noble individual. Here, according to MA, it means specifically the supramundane path, which Sunakkhatta is denying of the Buddha.

179 The gist of his criticism is that the Buddha teaches a doctrine that he has merely worked out in thought rather than one he has realised through transcendental wisdom. Apparently he believes that being led to the complete destruction of suffering is, as a goal, inferior to the acquisition of miraculous powers.

180 All the sections to follow are intended as a rebuttal of Sunakkhatta's criticism of the Buddha. §§6–8 cover the

first three of the six direct knowledges (*abhiññā*), the last three appearing as the last of the ten powers of the Tathāgata. The latter, according to MA, are to be understood as powers of knowledge (*ñāṇabala*) that are attained by all Buddhas as the fruit of their accumulation of merit. The Vibhanga (§§809–31/440–51) of the Abhidhamma Piṭaka provides an elaborate analysis of them.

181 On the Buddha's sounding of his lion's roar, see SN 22:78/iii.84–86. The Wheel of Brahmā is the supreme, best, most excellent wheel, the Wheel of the Dhamma (*dhammacakka*) in its twofold meaning: the knowledge penetrating the truth and the knowledge of how to expound the teaching (MA).

182 Vbh §809 explicates this knowledge by quoting at length MN 115.12–17. MA, however, explains it differently as the knowledge of the correlations between causes and their results.

183 This knowledge can be exemplified by the Buddha's analysis of kamma in MN 57, MN 135, and MN 136. MA explains the possibility (*ṭhāna*) as the realm, circumstances, time, and effort—factors that can either impede or reinforce the result; the cause (*hetu*) is the kamma itself.

184 This knowledge will be elucidated in §§35–42 below.

185 The Tathāgata's understanding of the many elements constituting the world will be found in MN 115.4–9.

186 Vbh §813 explains that the Tathāgata understands that beings are of inferior inclinations and superior inclinations, and that they gravitate towards those who share their own inclinations.

187 Vbh §§814–27 gives a detailed analysis. MA states the meaning more concisely as the Tathāgata's knowledge of the superiority and inferiority of beings' faculties of faith, energy, mindfulness, concentration, and wisdom.

188 Vbh §828: The "defilement" (*sankilesa*) is a state causing deterioration, "cleansing" (*vodāna*) a state causing excellence, "emergence" (*vuṭṭhāna*) is both cleansing and the rising out of an attainment. The eight liberations (*vimokkhā*) are enumerated in MN 77.22 and MN 137.26; the nine attainments (*samāpatti*) are the four jhānas, four

immaterial attainments, and the cessation of perception and feeling as in MN 25.12–20.

189 The idiom *yathābhataṁ nikkhitto evaṁ niraye* is knotty; the rendering here follows the commentary: "He will be put in hell as if carried off and put there by the wardens of hell."

190 In later Buddhist tradition the *asuras*, titans or "anti-gods," are added as a separate realm to make six destinations.

191 MA: Even though the description is the same as that of the bliss of the heavenly world, the meaning is different. For the bliss of the heavenly world is not really extremely pleasant because the fevers of lust, etc., are still present there. But the bliss of Nibbāna is extremely pleasant in every way through the subsiding of all fevers.

192 At this juncture, MA informs us, the Buddha related this account of his past ascetic practices because Sunakkhatta was a great admirer of extreme asceticism (as the *Pāṭika Sutta* shows) and the Buddha wanted to make it known that there was no one who could equal him in the practice of austerities. The passages to follow should be collated with MN 4.20 and MN 36.20–30 for a fuller picture of the Bodhisatta's experiment with the extreme of self-mortification.

193 The idea seems to be that his pity was directed, not towards the microbes in a drop of water (as the rendering in the first edition implied), but towards the creatures that might be hurt or killed by carelessly discarded water.

194 The "eight-days interval of frost" refers to a regular cold spell that occurs in northern India in late December or early January.

195 That is, they hold the view that beings are purified by reducing their intake of food.

196 Rebirth into the Pure Abodes (*suddhāvāsa*) is possible only for non-returners.

197 The Pali for the four terms is: *sati, gati, dhiti, paññāveyyattiya*. MA explains *sati* as the ability to grasp in mind a hundred or a thousand phrases as they are being spoken; *gati* as the ability to bind them and retain them in the mind; *dhiti* as the ability to recite back what has been

grasped and retained; and *paññāveyyattiya* as the ability to discern the meaning and logic of those phrases.

198 Ven. Nāgasamāla had been a personal attendant of the Buddha during the first twenty years of his ministry.

199 *Lomahaṁsanapariyāya*. The sutta is referred to by that name at Miln 398 and in the commentary to the Dīgha Nikāya.

SUTTA 13

200 MA: "Full understanding" (*pariññā*) here means overcoming (*samatikkama*) or abandoning (*pahāna*). The wanderers of other sects identify the full understanding of sensual pleasures with the first jhāna, the full understanding of material form with the immaterial planes of being, and the full understanding of feelings with the impercipient plane of being. The Buddha, in contrast, describes the full understanding of sensual pleasures as the path of the non-returner, and the full understanding of both material form and feelings as the path of arahantship.

201 MA gives a graphic description of each of these forms of torture.

202 It should be noted that while the previous dangers in sensual pleasures were called "a mass of suffering visible here and now" (*sandiṭṭhiko dukkhakkhandho*), this one is called "a mass of suffering in the life to come" (*samparāyiko dukkhakkhandho*).

203 MA says that Nibbāna is the removal and abandonment of desire and lust for sensual pleasures, for in dependence on Nibbāna, desire and lust are removed and abandoned. It might also be taken to include the path of the non-returner, which accomplishes the abandoning of desire and lust for sensual pleasures.

204 To expose the danger in feelings, the Buddha chooses the most refined and exalted type of mundane pleasure, the bliss and peacefulness of the jhānas, and shows that even those states are impermanent and therefore unsatisfactory.

SUTTA 14

205 Mahānāma the Sakyan was a cousin of the Buddha and the brother of the monks Anuruddha and Ānanda. He chose to remain a householder and let Anuruddha become a monk. The story is told in Ñāṇamoli, *The Life of the Buddha*, pp. 80–81.

206 According to MA, Mahānāma had long ago attained the fruit of the once-returner, which only weakens greed, hate, and delusion but does not eradicate them. MA says that he had the mistaken notion that greed, hate, and delusion are eradicated by the path of the once-returner. Thus, when he saw that they still arose in his mind, he realised that they were not abandoned and inquired from the Buddha the cause for their arising. Noble disciples can be mistaken about which defilements are abandoned by which path.

207 From the ensuing discussion on the danger in sensual pleasures, it seems that the "state" (*dhamma*) unabandoned by Mahānāma was sensual desire, which kept him tied to the home life and the enjoyment of sensual pleasures.

208 The "rapture and pleasure that are apart from sensual pleasures" are the rapture and pleasure pertaining to the first and second jhānas; the states "more peaceful than that" are the higher jhānas. From this passage it seems that a disciple may attain even to the second path and fruit without possessing mundane jhāna.

209 The Nigaṇṭhas or Jains, followers of the teacher Nigaṇṭha Nātaputta (also known as Mahāvīra), stressed the practice of austerities to wear off the accumulations of past evil kamma. The purpose of this passage, according to MA, is to show the *escape*, which was not shown earlier along with the gratification and the danger in sensual pleasures. The Buddha brings in the Jain practice of asceticism to demonstrate that his own teaching is a "middle way" free from the two extremes of sensual indulgence and self-mortification.

210 The Jains held the view that whatever a person experiences is caused by past kamma. If that were so, the Buddha argues, the severe pains to which they subjected

themselves as part of their ascetic discipline would have to be rooted in grave actions of their previous lives.

211 MA: This refers to his own experience of the pleasure of fruition attainment, i.e., the attainment of the fruit of arahantship (*arahattaphalasamāpatti*).

SUTTA 15

212 *Vadantu*, meaning literally "let them speak to me," has the implied sense: "Let them speak to me by way of instruction and exhortation" (MA).

213 See MN 5.10–29.

214 See MN 8.44 and n.109.

215 It is from this passage that the sutta acquires its name.

216 MA: The ancients called this sutta the "Bhikkhupātimokkha." A bhikkhu should review himself three times daily in the way described in the sutta. If he cannot do so three times, then he should do so twice, or, at the minimum, once.

SUTTA 16

217 MA explains *cetokhila*, translated "wilderness in the heart," as rigidity, rubbish, or a stump in the mind. It explains *cetaso vinibandha* as something that binds the mind, clenching it like a fist; hence "shackle in the heart." The former, as will be seen, consists of four cases of doubt, one of hate; the latter of five varieties of greed.

218 MA explains "Dhamma" here as the scriptural teaching and penetration to the paths, fruits, and Nibbāna. The Dhamma as practice is mentioned separately just below as the training (*sikkhā*)—that is, the threefold training in virtue, concentration, and wisdom.

219 "Body" here is his own body, while "form" just below is outer forms, the bodies of others.

220 The four bases for spiritual power (*iddhipāda*) are included among the thirty-seven aids to enlightenment; they are the special foundation for the five mundane kinds of direct knowledge (*abhiññā*). According to MA, enthusiasm (*ussoḷhi*) is energy, which is to be applied everywhere.

221 The fifteen factors are the abandoning of the five wildernesses of the heart, the abandoning of the five shackles, and the five just mentioned. "Supreme security from bondage" (*anuttara yogakkhema*) is arahantship, as at MN 1.27.

222 This simile appears again at MN 53.19–22 in connection with the disciple's breaking out to the three types of true knowledge (*tevijjā*).

SUTTA 17

223 The pattern on which §§3–6 are constructed may be stated simply as follows:
no progress and requisites are scarce = depart;
no progress and requisites are plentiful = depart;
progress and requisites are scarce = stay;
progress and requisites are plentiful = stay.

224 The same pattern is applied in §§7–22 to village, town, city, and country.

225 PTS, in reading here *anāpucchā,* "without taking leave," seems to be mistaken. BBS and SBJ read *āpucchā,* "after taking leave," which seems more fitting. As the person on whom the bhikkhu relied—presumably a teacher or a lay supporter—provided the requisites in adequate measure, courtesy requires that the bhikkhu take leave of him before departing.

SUTTA 18

226 Daṇḍapāni, whose name means "stick-in-hand," was so called because he used to walk around ostentatiously with a golden walking stick, even though he was still young and healthy. According to MA, he sided with Devadatta, the Buddha's arch foe, when the latter attempted to create a schism in the Buddha's following. His manner of asking the question is arrogant and deliberately provocative.

227 The first part of the Buddha's reply directly counters Daṇḍapāni's aggressive attitude. MA quotes in this connection SN 22:94/iii.138: "Bhikkhus, I do not dispute

with the world, it is the world that disputes with me. A speaker of Dhamma does not dispute with anyone in the world." The second part may be taken to mean that, for the arahant (spoken of here as "that brahmin" with reference to the Buddha himself), perceptions no longer awaken the dormant underlying tendencies to defilements, to be enumerated in §8.

228 This response seems to be an expression of frustration and bewilderment.

229 The interpretation of this cryptic passage hinges on the word *papañca* and the compound *papañca-saññā-sankhā.* Ñm had translated the former as "diversification" and the latter as "calculations about perceptions of diversification." It seems, however, that the primary problem to which the term *papañca* points is not "diversification," which may be quite in place when the sensory field itself displays diversity, but the propensity of the worldling's imagination to erupt in an effusion of mental commentary that obscures the bare data of cognition. In a penetrative study, *Concept and Reality in Early Buddhism,* Bhikkhu Ñāṇananda explains *papañca* as "conceptual proliferation," and I follow him in substituting "proliferation" for Ñm's "diversification." The commentaries identify the springs of this proliferation as the three factors—craving, conceit, and views—on account of which the mind "embellishes" experience by interpreting it in terms of "mine," "I" and "my self." *Papañca* is thus closely akin to *maññanā,* "conceiving," in MN 1—see n.6.

The compound *papañca-saññā-sankhā* is more problematic. Ven. Ñāṇananda interprets it to mean "concepts characterised by the mind's prolific tendency," but this explanation still leaves the word *saññā* out of account. MA glosses *sankhā* by *koṭṭhāsa,* "portion," and says that *saññā* is either perception associated with *papañca* or *papañca* itself. I go along with Ñāṇananda in taking *sankhā* to mean concept or notion (Ñm's "calculation" is too literal) rather than portion. My decision to treat *saññā-sankhā* as a *dvanda* compound, "perceptions and notions," may be questioned, but as the expression *papañca-saññā-sankhā* occurs but rarely in the Canon and is never verbally analysed, no rendering is utterly beyond doubt. On alternative interpretations of its components, the expression might have been rendered "notions [arisen from] the proliferation of perceptions" or "perceptual notions [arisen from] proliferation."

The sequel will make it clear that the process of cognition is itself "the source through which perceptions and notions [born of] mental proliferation beset a man." If nothing in the process of cognition is found to delight in, to welcome, or to hold to, the underlying tendencies of the defilements will come to an end.

230 Ven. Mahā Kaccāna was declared by the Buddha to be the most eminent disciple in expounding the detailed meaning of a brief saying. MN 133 and MN 138 were also spoken by him under similar circumstances.

231 *Cakkhubhūto ñāṇabhūto dhammabhūto brahmabhūto.* MA: He is vision in the sense that he is the leader in vision; he is knowledge in the sense that he makes things known; he is the Dhamma in the sense that he consists of the Dhamma that he utters verbally after considering it in his heart; he is Brahmā, the holy one, in the sense of the best.

232 This passage shows how *papañca*, emerging from the process of cognition, gives rise to perceptions and notions that overwhelm and victimise their hapless creator. Ms contains a note by Ñm: "The meeting of eye, form, and eye-consciousness is called contact. Contact, according to dependent origination, is the principal condition of feeling. Feeling and perception are inseparable (MN 43.9). What is perceived as 'this' is thought about in its differences and is thus diversified from 'that' and from 'me.' This diversification—involving craving for form, wrong view about permanence of form, etc., and the conceit 'I am'—leads to preoccupation with calculating the desirability of past and present forms with a view to obtaining desirable forms in the future." Perhaps the key to the interpretation of this passage is Ven. Mahā Kaccāna's explanation of the Bhaddekaratta verses in MN 133. There too delight in the elements of cognition plays a prominent role in causing bondage, and the elaboration of the verses in terms of the three

periods of time links up with the reference to the three times in this sutta.

233 The Pali idiom *phassapaññattiṁ paññāpessati,* in which the verb takes an object derived from itself, is difficult. Ñm originally rendered "that one will describe a description of contact." "To point out a manifestation" is less literal, but it should do justice to the meaning without jeopardising intelligibility. MA says that this passage is intended to show the entire round of existence (*vaṭṭa*) by way of the twelve sense bases; §18 shows the cessation of the round (*vivaṭṭa*) by the negation of the twelve sense bases.

234 A large sweet cake or a ball made from flour, ghee, molasses, honey, sugar, etc. See also AN 5:194/iii.237.

SUTTA 19

235 The Bodhisatta's twofold division of thought occurred during his six-year struggle for enlightenment.

236 Thoughts of non-ill will and thoughts of non-cruelty may also be explained positively as thoughts of loving-kindness (*mettā*) and thoughts of compassion (*karuṇā*).

237 MA: Excessive thinking and pondering leads to agitation. To tame and soften the mind, the Bodhisatta would enter a meditative attainment, then he would emerge from it and develop insight.

SUTTA 20

238 This sutta together with its commentary is available in a translation by Soma Thera, *The Removal of Distracting Thoughts*.

239 MA: The higher mind (*adhicitta*) is the mind of the eight meditative attainments used as a basis for insight; it is called "higher mind" because it is higher than the ordinary (wholesome) mind of the ten wholesome courses of action. The five "signs" (*nimitta*) may be understood as practical methods of removing the distracting thoughts. They should be resorted to only when the distractions become persistent or obtrusive; at other times the meditator should remain with his primary subject of meditation.

240 MA: When thoughts of sensual desire arise directed towards living beings, the "other sign" is the meditation on foulness (see MN 10.10); when the thoughts are directed to inanimate things, the "other sign" is attention to impermanence. When thoughts of hate arise directed towards living beings, the "other sign" is the meditation on loving-kindness; when they are directed to inanimate things, the "other sign" is attention to the elements (see MN 10.12). The remedy for thoughts connected with delusion is living under a teacher, studying the Dhamma, inquiring into its meaning, listening to the Dhamma, and inquiring into causes.

241 This method can be illustrated by the reflections of the Bodhisatta in MN 19.3–5. Calling to mind the unworthiness of the evil thoughts produces a sense of shame (*hiri*); calling to mind their dangerous consequences produces fear of wrongdoing (*ottappa*).

242 *Vitakka-sankhāra-saṇṭhānaṁ*. MA understands *sankhāra* here as condition, cause, or root, and takes the compound to mean "stopping the cause of the thought." This is accomplished by inquiring, when an unwholesome thought has arisen: "What is its cause? What is the cause of its cause?" etc. Such an inquiry, according to MA, brings about a slackening, and eventually the cessation, of the flow of unwholesome thought.

243 MA: He should crush the unwholesome state of mind with a wholesome state of mind.

244 This shows the attainment of arahantship. See n.50.

SUTTA 21

245 At SN 12:12/ii.13 Moliya Phagguna puts a series of questions to the Buddha, which the Buddha rejects as wrongly formulated. Later it is reported that he reverted to lay life (SN 12:32/ii.50).

246 According to MA, the Buddha said this because Phagguna still did not wish to comply with his advice but continued to resist him, and this induced the Buddha to speak praise of the compliant bhikkhus during an earlier part of his ministry. For the passage on eating at a single session, see MN 65.2 and MN 70.2.

247 *Tadārammaṇaṁ,* lit. "with him as the object." MA: First one develops loving-kindness towards the person who addresses one with one or another of the five courses of speech, then one directs that mind of loving-kindness towards all beings, making the entire world the object.

SUTTA 22

248 This sutta with a fine introduction and detailed notes is available in a translation by Nyanaponika Thera, *The Discourse on the Snake Simile.*

249 In making this assertion he directly contradicts the third of the four intrepidities of the Tathāgata—see MN 12.25. According to MA, while reflecting in seclusion he came to the conclusion that there would be no harm if bhikkhus were to engage in sexual relations with women and he maintained that this should not be prohibited by the monastic rules. Though his statement does not expressly mention the sexual issue, the similes about sensual pleasures brought forth by the bhikkhus lend credence to the commentary.

250 The first seven similes for sense pleasures are expanded upon at MN 54.15–21.

251 This first part of the Ariṭṭha episode occurs twice in the Vinaya Piṭaka. At Vin ii.25 it leads to the Sangha announcing an act of suspension (*ukkhepaniyakamma*) against Ariṭṭha for refusing to give up his wrong view. At Vin iv.133–34 his refusal to give up his wrong view after repeated admonitions is defined as a monastic offence of the Pācittiya class.

252 Though the Pali uses the one word *kāma* in all four cases, from the context the first phrase must be understood to refer to objective sensual pleasures, i.e., sensually enjoyable objects, the other phrases to refer to subjective defilements connected with sensuality, i.e., sensual desire. MA glosses "that one can engage in sensual pleasures" with "that one can indulge in sexual intercourse." MṬ says that other physical acts expressive of sexual desire such as hugging and stroking should be included.

253 MA explains that this passage is stated in order to show

the fault in wrongly motivated acquisition of intellectual knowledge of the Dhamma—apparently the pitfall into which Ariṭṭha fell. The "good (*attha*) for the sake of which they learned the Dhamma" is the paths and fruits.

254 This famous "simile of the raft" continues the same argument against misuse of learning introduced by the simile of the snake. One who is preoccupied with using the Dhamma to stir up controversy and win debates carries the Dhamma around on his head instead of using it to cross the flood.

255 *Dhammā pi vo pahātabbā pageva adhammā.* The word *dhammā* is ambiguous here. MA interprets it as meaning good states, which it identifies with serenity and insight (*samatha-vipassanā*) thus in its paraphrase of the text: "I teach, bhikkhus, even the abandoning of desire and attachment to such peaceful and sublime states as serenity and insight, how much more so to that low, vulgar, contemptible, coarse, and impure thing that this foolish Ariṭṭha sees as harmless when he says that there is no obstruction in desire and lust for the five cords of sensual pleasure." The commentator cites MN 66.26–33 as an example of the Buddha teaching the abandonment of attachment to serenity, MN 38.14 as an example of his teaching the abandonment of attachment to insight. Note that in each case it is the *attachment* to the good states that should be abandoned, not the good states themselves.

Despite MA, it seems to me that *dhammā* here signifies, not good states themselves, but the teachings, the correct attitude to which was delineated just above in the simile of the snake. The simile of the raft thus intimates that even the teachings that are to be rightly grasped must finally be relinquished. This, however, is not an invitation to moral nihilism, but a warning that even attachment to the noble teachings is an obstacle to progress. What is contrary to the teachings, *adhammā,* would include the moral laxity that the bhikkhu Ariṭṭha advocated.

256 This section evidently has the purpose of forestalling another type of misconception and misrepresentation of the Dhamma, i.e., the introduction of a view of self into the teaching. According to MA, standpoints for views

(*diṭṭhiṭṭhāna*) are wrong views themselves as grounds for other more elaborate wrong views; the objects of views, i.e., the five aggregates; and the conditions for views, i.e., such factors as ignorance, perverted perception, and false thoughts, etc.

257 MA states that the notion "this is mine" is induced by craving, the notion "this I am" by conceit, and the notion "this is my self" by wrong views. These three—craving, conceit, and views—are called the three obsessions (*gāha*). They are also the mainsprings behind conceiving (MN 1) and mental proliferation (MN 18).

258 This series of terms shows the aggregate of consciousness indirectly, by way of its object. The "seen" points to eye-consciousness, the "heard" to ear-consciousness, the "sensed" to the other three kinds of sense consciousness, and the remaining terms to mind-consciousness.

259 This is a full-fledged eternalist view arisen on the basis of one of the earlier, more rudimentary types of personality view; here it becomes itself an object of craving, conceit, and the false view of self. Ven. Nyanaponika contends that this view expresses the identity of the self with the universe, though this interpretation is purely hypothetical as the Pali is ambiguous and could just as well be pointing to a fundamental dualism of self and world along the lines of Sānkhya philosophy with its distinction between changeable Nature (*prakṛti*) and changeless Spirit (*puruṣa*)

260 *Asati na paritassati.* The noun form *paritassanā*, according to MA, has the twofold connotation of fear and craving, thus "agitation" was chosen as comprehending both. Agitation about what is non-existent externally (§18) refers to the worldling's despair over the loss or non-acquisition of possessions; agitation about what is non-existent internally (§20) to the eternalist's despair when he misinterprets the Buddha's teaching on Nibbāna as a doctrine of annihilation.

261 *Pariggahaṁ pariganheyyātha*, lit. "you may possess that possession." This links up with §18 on agitation about external possessions.

262 *Attavādupādānaṁ upādiyetha*, lit. "you may cling to that

clinging to a doctrine of self." On the problem this idiom involves for translation, see n.176. This passage links up with §20 on agitation arising from a view of self.

263 The support of views (*diṭṭhinissaya*), according to MA, is the sixty-two views mentioned in the Brahmajāla Sutta (DN 1), which emerge from personality view or "doctrine of a self." It might also include the pernicious view adopted by Ariṭṭha at the beginning of the sutta.

264 The notion "what belongs to self" or "self's property" (*attaniya*) is ascribed to whichever among the five aggregates are not identified as self, as well as to all the individual's external possessions. This passage shows the mutual dependence, and thus the equal untenability, of the twin notions "I" and "mine."

265 According to the commentaries, disenchantment (*nibbidā*, also rendered "revulsion" or "disgust") signifies the culminating stages of insight, dispassion (*virāga*) the attainment of the supramundane path, and liberation (*vimutti*) the fruit. The arahant's reviewing knowledge (*paccavekkhaṇañāṇa*) is shown by the phrase "there comes the knowledge" and "he understands: 'Birth is destroyed...'."

266 "Thus gone" is, in Pali, *tathāgata*, the usual epithet of the Buddha, but here applied more broadly to the arahant. MA interprets this passage in two alternative ways thus: (1) The arahant even while alive is here and now untraceable as a being or individual (in the sense of an abiding self) because in the ultimate sense there is no being (as self). (2) The arahant is untraceable here and now because it is impossible for the gods, etc., to find the support for his insight-mind, path-mind, or fruition-mind (*vipassanācitta, maggacitta, phalacitta*); that is, the object being Nibbāna, his mind cannot be known by the worldling.

267 This refers back to §20, where the eternalist misunderstands the Buddha's teaching on Nibbāna, the cessation of being, to involve the annihilation of an existing being considered as self.

268 The import of this statement is deeper than appears on the surface. In the context of the false accusations of §37, the Buddha is stating that he teaches that a living being is not

a self but a mere conglomeration of factors, material and mental events, linked together in a process that is inherently *dukkha,* and that Nibbāna, the cessation of suffering, is not the annihilation of a being but the termination of that same unsatisfactory process. This statement should be read in conjunction with SN 12:15/ii.17, where the Buddha says that one with right view, who has discarded all doctrines of a self, sees that whatever arises is only *dukkha* arising, and whatever ceases is only *dukkha* ceasing.

269 "What earlier was fully understood" (*pubbe pariññātaṁ*) are the five aggregates. Since it is only these to which honour and abuse are shown, not an "I" or self, there is no reason for elation or dejection.

270 MA points out that it is the attachment to the five aggregates that should be abandoned; the aggregates themselves cannot be torn apart or pulled out.

271 MA: "*Chinna-pilotika*: *pilotikā* is a torn and worn-out rag stitched and knotted here and there; there is nothing (in the Dhamma) like this—torn, worn-out, stitched and knotted by way of hypocrisy and other deceptions."

272 That is, as the arahants have achieved deliverance from the entire round of existence, it is impossible to point to any plane within the round where they might be reborn.

273 These are two classes of individuals standing on the path of stream-entry. "Dhamma-followers" (*dhammānusārin*) are disciples in whom the faculty of wisdom (*paññindriya*) is predominant and who develop the noble path with wisdom in the lead; when they attain the fruit they are called "attained-to-view" (*diṭṭhipatta*). "Faith-followers" (*saddhānusārin*) are disciples in whom the faculty of faith (*saddhindriya*) is predominant and who develop the noble path with faith in the lead; when they attain the fruit they are called "liberated-by-faith" (*saddhāvimutta*). See MN 70.20, 21; also Pug 1:35–36/15 and Vsm XXI, 75.

274 MA says that this refers to persons devoted to the practice of insight meditation who have not reached any supramundane attainment. Note that they are headed only for heaven, not for enlightenment, though if their practice matures they can attain the path of stream-entry and thus gain assurance of enlightenment. The expression

saddhāmattaṁ pemamattaṁ might be rendered "simply faith, simply love" or "mere faith, mere love" (as it sometimes is), but this could not explain the guarantee of rebirth in heaven. It therefore seems obligatory to take the suffix *matta* here as implying a requisite amount of faith and love, not simple possession of these qualities.

SUTTA 23

275 Ven. Kumāra Kassapa was an adopted son of King Pasenadi of Kosala, born of a woman who, not knowing she was pregnant, had gone forth as a bhikkhunī after having conceived him. At the time this sutta was delivered he was still a *sekha*; he attained arahantship using this sutta as his subject of meditation.

276 According to MA, this deity was a non-returner living in the Pure Abodes. He and Kumāra Kassapa had been members of a group of five fellow monks who, in the Dispensation of the previous Buddha Kassapa, had practised meditation together on a mountain-top. It was this same deity who spurred Bāhiya Dāruciriya, another former member of the group, to visit the Buddha (see Ud 1:10/7).

277 The meaning of the deity's imagery will be explained later on in the sutta itself.

278 *Kummāsa*: The Vinaya and commentaries explain it as something made of *yava*, barley. Ñm had translated the word as bread, but from MN 82.18 it is clear that *kummāsa* is viscous and spoils overnight. PED defines it as junket; Horner translates it as "sour milk."

279 MA: Just as a bar across the entrance to a city prevents people from entering it, so ignorance prevents people from attaining Nibbāna.

280 *Dvedhāpatha* might also have been rendered "a forked path," an obvious symbol for doubt.

281 MA states that the four feet and head of a tortoise are similar to the five aggregates.

282 MA: Beings desiring sensual enjoyments are chopped up by the butcher's knife of sensual desires upon the block of sense objects.

283 The symbolism is explicated at MN 54.16.

284 This is an arahant. For the symbolism, see n.75.

SUTTA 24

285 The parenthetical specification is supplied from MA. The Buddha's native land is Kapilavatthu, at the foot of the Himalayas.

286 The last five items form a set called the five aggregates of Dhamma (*dhammakkhandhā*). "Deliverance" is identified with the noble fruits, "the knowledge and vision of deliverance" with reviewing knowledge.

287 Ven. Puṇṇa Mantāṇiputta belonged to a brahmin family and was ordained by Ven. Aññā Kondañña at Kapilavatthu, where he continued to reside until he decided to visit the Buddha at Sāvatthī. He was later declared by the Buddha the most eminent bhikkhu among the preachers of the Dhamma.

288 Although these seven purifications (*satta visuddhi*) are mentioned elsewhere in the Pali Canon (at DN iii.288, with two added: purification by wisdom and purification by deliverance), it is curious that they are not analysed as a set anywhere in the Nikāyas; and this becomes even more puzzling when both these great disciples seem to recognise them as a fixed group of doctrinal categories. The sevenfold scheme forms, however, the scaffolding for the entire *Visuddhimagga*, which defines the different stages by means of the fully developed commentarial traditions on concentration and insight meditation.

In brief, "purification of virtue" (*sīlavisuddhi*) is the unbroken adherence to the moral precepts one has undertaken, explained by Vsm with reference to the moral training of a bhikkhu as the "fourfold purification of virtue." "Purification of mind" (*cittavisuddhi*) is the overcoming of the five hindrances through the attainment of access concentration and the jhānas. "Purification of view" (*diṭṭhivisuddhi*) is the understanding that defines the nature of the five aggregates constituting a living being. "Purification by overcoming doubt" (*kankhāvitaraṇavisuddhi*) is the understanding of conditionality.

"Purification by knowledge and vision of what is the path and what is not the path" (*maggāmaggañāṇadassana-visuddhi*) is the correct discrimination between the false path of the ecstatic, exhilarating experiences and the true path of insight into impermanence, suffering, and not self. "Purification by knowledge and vision of the way" (*paṭipadāñāṇadassanavisuddhi*) comprises the ascending series of insight knowledges up to the supramundane paths. And "purification by knowledge and vision" (*ñāṇadassanavisuddhi*) is the supramundane paths.

289 MA glosses *anupādā parinibbāna* as *appaccayaparinibbāna*, "final Nibbāna that has no condition," explaining that *upādāna* has two meanings: grasping (*gahaṇa*), as in the usual passage on the four types of clinging; and condition (*paccaya*), as illustrated by this passage. The commentators explain "final Nibbāna without clinging" either as the fruit of arahantship, because it cannot be grasped by any of the four types of clinging; or as Nibbāna the unconditioned, because it has not arisen through any condition.

290 MA explains that the first six stages are "accompanied by clinging" in the sense both of being conditioned and of existing in one who still has grasping; the seventh stage, being supramundane, only in the sense of being conditioned.

291 MA says that Sāriputta asked this only as a way of greeting Puṇṇa Mantāṇiputta since he already knew his name. Puṇṇa, however, had never seen Sāriputta before and so must have been genuinely surprised to meet the great disciple.

292 *Satthukappa.* MA says that this is the highest praise that can be spoken of a disciple.

SUTTA 25

293 *Cetovimutti*: MA explains that they simply abandoned their resolution to live in the wilds, though it could well be that these ascetics had attained—and lost—the eight meditative attainments that are usually implied by the term *cetovimutti*.

294 These are the ten speculative views debated by the ascetic philosophers of the Buddha's age. All were rejected by the Buddha as being unconnected with the fundamentals of the holy life and unconducive to liberation from suffering. See MN 63, MN 72.

295 The eight meditative attainments here must be understood, as MA explains, as bases for insight. When a bhikkhu has entered such a jhāna, Māra cannot see how his mind is proceeding. This immunity from Māra's influence, however, is as yet only temporary.

296 This last bhikkhu, by destroying the taints, has become not only temporarily invisible to Māra but permanently inaccessible to him. On the cessation of perception and feeling, see Introduction, p. 41.

SUTTA 26

297 This title follows the PTS and SBJ eds. of MN. The BBS ed. of MN, and both the PTS and BBS eds. of MA, refer to this discourse as the *Pāsarāsi Sutta,* The Heap of Snares, with reference to the simile in §§32–33.

298 MA points out that the second jhāna and one's basic meditation subject are both called "noble silence" (*ariyo tuṇhībhāvo*). Those who cannot attain the second jhāna are advised to maintain noble silence by attending to their basic meditation subject.

299 *Upadhi*: The root meaning is foundation, basis, ground (PED). In the commentaries various kinds of *upadhi* are enumerated, among them the five aggregates, objects of sensual pleasure, defilements, and kamma. Ñm renders the term consistently throughout as "essentials of existence," which often obscures its clear contextual meaning. I have tried to capture the several connotations of the word by rendering it "acquisitions" where its objective meaning is prominent (as it is here) and as "acquisition" where its subjective meaning is prominent. At MN 26.19 Nibbāna is called "the relinquishing of all acquisitions" (*sabb'ūpadhipaṭinissagga*), with both meanings intended.

300 Gold and silver are excluded from the things subject to sickness, death, and sorrow, but they are subject to

defilement, according to MA, because they can be alloyed with metals of lesser worth.

301 MA: He taught him the seven attainments (of serenity meditation) ending in the base of nothingness, the third of the four immaterial attainments. Though these attainments are spiritually exalted, they are still mundane and not in themselves directly conducive to Nibbāna.

302 That is, it leads to rebirth in the plane of existence called the base of nothingness, the objective counterpart of the seventh meditative attainment. Here the lifespan is supposed to be 60,000 aeons, but when that has elapsed one must pass away and return to a lower world. Thus one who attains this is still not free from birth and death but is caught in the trap of Māra (MA). Horner misses the point that rebirth is the issue by translating "only as far as reaching the plane of no-thing" (MLS 1:209).

303 Both Horner in MLS and Ñm in Ms err in their translations of the account of the Bodhisatta's meeting with Uddaka Rāmaputta by assuming that Uddaka is identical with Rāma. However, as his name indicates, Uddaka was the son (*putta*) of Rāma, who must have already passed away before the Bodhisatta arrived on the scene. It should be noted that all references to Rāma are in the past tense and the third person, and that Uddaka in the end places the Bodhisatta in the position of teacher. Though the text does not allow for definite conclusions, this suggests that he himself had not yet reached the fourth immaterial attainment.

304 MN 36, which includes the account of the Bodhisatta's meetings with Āḷāra Kālāma and Uddaka Rāmaputta, continues from this point with the story of the extreme ascetic practices that brought him to the verge of death and his subsequent discovery of the middle way that led to enlightenment.

305 MA identifies "this Dhamma" with the Four Noble Truths. The two truths or states (*ṭhāna*) spoken of just below—dependent origination and Nibbāna—are the truths of the origin of suffering and the cessation of suffering, which respectively imply the truths of suffering and the path.

306 *Ālaya*. It is difficult to find for this word a suitable English equivalent that has not already been assigned to a more frequently occurring Pali term. Horner renders it as "sensual pleasure," which appropriates the usual rendering of *kāma* and may be too narrow. In Ms and in other published works Ñm translates it as "something to rely on," which may draw upon a connotation of the word that is not the one intended here. MA explains *ālaya* as comprising both objective sense pleasures and the thoughts of craving concerned with them; thus "worldliness" has been chosen as sharing this twofold meaning of the original.

307 MA raises the question why, when the Bodhisatta had long ago made an aspiration to reach Buddhahood in order to liberate others, his mind now inclined towards inaction. The reason, the commentator says, is that only now, after reaching enlightenment, did he become fully cognizant of the strength of the defilements in people's minds and of the profundity of the Dhamma. Also, he wanted Brahmā to entreat him to teach so that beings who venerated Brahmā would recognise the precious value of the Dhamma and desire to listen to it.

308 These five monks attended on the Bodhisatta during his period of self-mortification, convinced that he would attain enlightenment and teach them the Dhamma. However, when he abandoned his austerities and resumed taking solid food, they lost faith in him, accused him of reverting to luxury, and deserted him. See MN 36.33.

309 *Anantajina*: perhaps this was an Ājīvakan epithet for the spiritually perfected individual.

310 According to MA, Upaka thereafter fell in love with a hunter's daughter and married her. When his marriage turned out to be an unhappy one, he returned to the Buddha, entered the Sangha, and became a non-returner. He was reborn in the Avīha heaven, where he attained arahantship.

311 *Āvuso*: a familiar term of address used among equals.

312 See n.178.

313 The change in address from "friend" to "venerable sir" (*bhante*) indicates that they have now accepted the

Buddha's claim and are prepared to regard him as their superior.

314 At this point the Buddha preached to them his first sermon, the *Dhammacakkappavattana Sutta,* The Setting in Motion of the Wheel of Dhamma, on the Four Noble Truths. Several days later, after they had all become stream-enterers, he taught them the *Anattalakkhaṇa Sutta,* The Characteristic of Non-self, upon hearing which they all attained arahantship. The complete narrative, found in the Mahāvagga (Vin i.7–14), is included in Ñāṇamoli, *The Life of the Buddha,* pp. 42–47.

315 This section reverts to the theme of the noble and ignoble quests with which the Buddha's discourse opened. It is intended to show that the adoption of the monastic life is no guarantee that one has embarked on the noble quest, for the ignoble quest makes inroads upon the monastic life as well.

316 This refers to the use of the four requisites with reflection upon their proper purpose in the life of renunciation. See MN 2.13–16.

317 See n.295.

318 See n.296.

SUTTA 27

319 According to the chronicles of Sri Lanka, this was the first sutta preached by Mahinda Thera following his arrival in Sri Lanka.

320 Vacchāyana is Pilotika's clan name.

321 Ñm had translated *ekabhattika* as "eating only in one part of the day," following the commentary. According to the Vinaya the proper time for bhikkhus to eat is between dawn and noon. From noon until the next dawn only liquids are allowed.

322 This formula is analysed at Vsm I, 53–59. Briefly, the signs (*nimitta*) are the most distinctive qualities of the object which, when grasped at unmindfully, can kindle defiled thoughts; the features (*anubyañjana*) are the details that may subsequently catch the attention when the first perceptual contact has not been followed up by

restraint. "States of covetousness and grief" signifies the alternative reactions of desire and aversion, attraction and repulsion, towards sense objects.

323 Covetousness (*abhijjhā*) here is synonymous with sensual desire (*kāmacchanda*), the first of the five hindrances.

324 MA: He does not come to this conclusion about the Triple Gem because the jhānas and the (mundane) direct knowledges are held in common with those outside the Buddha's Dispensation.

325 This, according to MA, shows the moment of the path, and since at this point the noble disciple has still not completed his task, he has not yet come to a conclusion (*na tveva niṭṭhaṁ gato hoti*) about the Triple Gem; rather, he is in the process of coming to a conclusion (*niṭṭhaṁ gacchati*). The sutta employs a pun on the meaning of the expression "coming to a conclusion" that is as viable in English as in Pali.

326 This shows the occasion when the disciple has attained the fruit of arahantship, and having completed all his tasks in every way, has come to the conclusion about the Triple Gem.

SUTTA 28

327 This discourse has been published separately with introduction and notes by Nyanaponika Thera, *The Greater Discourse on the Elephant-Footprint Simile.*

328 The structure of this discourse may be outlined as follows: Ven. Sāriputta first enumerates the Four Noble Truths (§2). He then takes up the truth of suffering for analysis into its various aspects (§3). From among these, he selects the last and enumerates the five aggregates affected by clinging (§4). He next selects the first aggregate, that of material form (§5). Taking up each of the great elements in turn, he shows it to have two aspects—internal and external—the former being selected for detailed analysis, the latter only briefly mentioned for the sake of completeness and comparison (e.g., §§6–7). Each of the elements is expounded as a basis for insight meditation as well as for developing patience, faith, and

equanimity (e.g., §§8–10). Having finished examining the elements, Ven. Sāriputta next takes up the aspects of the Four Noble Truths he earlier had put aside. He introduces derivative material form by way of the sense faculties and their objects (§27, etc.), which he then relates to the other four aggregates of the first noble truth. Finally he sets this whole complex of ideas in relation to the other three noble truths (§28, etc.).

329 *Upādinna*, "clung-to," is used in the Abhidhamma as a technical term applicable to bodily phenomena that are produced by kamma. Here, however, it is used in a more general sense as applicable to the entire body insofar as it is grasped as "mine" and misapprehended as a self. The phrase "whatever else" is intended to include the earth element comprised in those parts of the body not included in the above enumeration. According to the Abhidhamma analysis of matter, the four primary elements are inseparable, and thus each element is also included, though in a subordinate role, in the bodily phenomena listed under the other three elements.

330 MA: This statement is made to underscore the insentient nature (*acetanābhāva*) of the internal earth element by yoking it to the external earth element, the insentient nature of which is much more easily discerned.

331 According to ancient Indian cosmology the cyclical destruction of the world may be due to either water, fire, or wind. See Vsm XIII, 30–65.

332 The notions "I," "mine," and "I am," represent the three obsessions of identity view, craving, and conceit, respectively.

333 MA explains that this passage, referring to a bhikkhu who practises meditation on the elements, is intended to show his strength of mind in applying his comprehension of things to undesirable objects arisen at the "door" of the ear. By contemplating the experience by way of conditionality and impermanence, he transforms the potentially provocative situation of being subjected to abuse into an opportunity for insight.

334 *Tassa dhātārammaṇam eva cittaṁ pakkhandati.* This sentence can be construed in two alternative ways, depending on

how the compound *dhātārammaṇam* is understood. Ven. Nyanaponika takes it as the object of the verb *pakkhandati,* and he understands *dhātu* here as "an impersonal element in general" capable of including sound, contact, feeling, etc. Thus he translates: "And his mind enters into that very object [taking it just as an impersonal] element." Ñm reads the compound as an adjunct qualifying *citta,* and supplies the object of the verb in parenthesis. MA seems to support the former reading; MṬ explicitly identifies *dhātu* as the earth element, thus supporting the latter reading. MA explains the phrase "acquires resolution" to mean that the meditator contemplates the situation by way of elements and thus has neither attachment nor aversion concerning it.

335 MA: This passage is intended to show the strength of the meditating bhikkhu on an occasion when he is subjected to affliction by way of the body.

336 See MN 21.20.

337 MA: The recollection of the Buddha is undertaken here by recalling that the Blessed One spoke this simile of the saw, the recollection of the Dhamma by recalling the advice given in the simile of the saw, and the recollection of the Sangha by recalling the virtues of the bhikkhu who can endure such abuse without giving rise to a mind of hate. "Equanimity supported by the wholesome" (*upekkhā kusalanissitā*) is the equanimity of insight, the sixfold equanimity of neither attraction nor aversion towards agreeable and disagreeable objects that appear at the six sense doors. Strictly speaking, the sixfold equanimity pertains only to the arahant, but it is here ascribed to the monk in training because his insight approximates to the perfect equanimity of the arahant.

338 This is said to stress once again the egoless nature of the body. MṬ: He shows that the four elements are only mere elements not belonging to a self; they are without a being, without a soul.

339 This section is set forth, according to MA, to introduce the material form derived from the four great elements. Derived material form, according to the Abhidhamma analysis of matter, includes the five sense faculties

(*pasādarūpa*) and the first four kinds of sense object, the tangible object being identified with the primary elements themselves. "Corresponding (conscious) engagement" (*tajjo samannāhāro*) is explained by MA as attention (*manasikāra*) arising in dependence on the eye and forms; it is identified with the "five-door adverting consciousness" (*pañcadvārāvajjanacitta*), which breaks off the flow of the life continuum (*bhavanga*) to initiate a process of cognition. Even when forms come into range of the eye, if attention is not engaged by the form because one is occupied with something else, there is still no manifestation of the "corresponding class of consciousness," i.e., eye-consciousness.

340 This section is set forth to show the Four Noble Truths by way of the sense doors. "What has thus come to be" (*tathābhūta*) is the entire complex of factors arisen by way of eye-consciousness. By analysing this complex into the five aggregates, Ven. Sāriputta shows that any occasion of sense experience is comprised within the truth of suffering.

341 This statement has not been traced directly to the Buddha in any of the existing suttas in the Pali Canon. MA glosses, perhaps with too little sensitivity to the statement's profounder implications: "One who sees dependent origination sees dependently arisen states (*paṭicca samuppanne dhamme*); one who sees dependently arisen states sees dependent origination."

342 The four terms—*chanda, ālaya, anunaya, ajjhosāna*—are synonyms for craving (*taṇhā*).

343 Though only three of the Four Noble Truths are explicitly shown in the text, the fourth truth is implied. According to MA, it is the penetration of these three truths by the development of the eight factors of the path.

344 MA identifies "mind" (*mano*) in this passage with the life-continuum consciousness (*bhavangacitta*).

345 MA illustrates this case by the mind's preoccupation with a familiar object when it does not notice the familiar details of that object. The "corresponding class of consciousness" here is mind-consciousness (*manoviññāṇa*), which takes non-sensuous objects as its sphere of cognition.

SUTTA 29

346 After Devadatta had unsuccessfully attempted to kill the Buddha and usurp control of the Sangha, he broke away from the Buddha and tried to establish his own sect with himself at the head. See Ñāṇamoli, *The Life of the Buddha,* pp. 266–69.

347 "Knowledge and vision" (*ñāṇadassana*) here refers to the divine eye (MA), the ability to see subtle forms invisible to normal vision.

348 This translation follows BBS and SBJ, which read *asamaya-vimokkhaṁ* in the preceding sentence and *asamayavimut-tiyā* in this sentence. The PTS ed., on which both Horner and Ñm based their translations, is evidently mistaken in reading *samaya* in the two compounds and *ṭhānaṁ* instead of *aṭṭhānaṁ*. MA cites the *Paṭisambhidāmagga* (ii.40) for a definition of *asamayavimokkha* (lit., non-temporary or "perpetual" liberation) as the four paths, four fruits, and Nibbāna, and of *samayavimokkha* (tempo-rary liberation) as the four jhānas and four formless attainments. See also MN 122.4.

349 "Unshakeable deliverance of mind" is the fruit of ara-hantship (MA). Thus "perpetual liberation"—as including all four paths and fruits—has a wider range of meaning than "unshakeable deliverance of mind," which alone is declared to be the goal of the holy life.

SUTTA 30

350 These six teachers, the Buddha's senior contemporaries, all stood outside the fold of orthodox Brahmanism, and their doctrines are indicative of the speculative audacity of the Buddha's age. The six are often mentioned together in the Canon. Their teachings, as understood by the Buddhist community, are stated at DN 2.17–32/ii.52–59.

351 Precisely the same question is posed to the Buddha on the eve of his Parinibbāna by the wanderer Subhadda at DN 16.5.26–27/ii.150–52.

352 It is this sentence, used in place of the sentence beginning "He becomes intoxicated...," that distinguishes these

passages of this sutta from the corresponding passages of the preceding sutta.

353 Although the jhānas may also have been included in the attainment of concentration set forth in §10, and knowledge and vision was described as higher than the attainment of concentration, the jhānas now become higher than knowledge and vision because they are being treated as the basis for the attainment of cessation and the destruction of the taints (in §21).

SUTTA 31

354 Ven. Anuruddha was the Buddha's cousin; Vens. Nandiya and Kimbila were Anuruddha's friends and constant companions.

355 These are three of the "six principles of cordiality" explained at MN 48.6.

356 MA identifies this *yakkha* as a celestial king (*devarāja*) included among the twenty-eight commanders of the *yakkhas* mentioned at DN 32.10/iii.205.

SUTTA 32

357 The four assemblies are those of bhikkhus, bhikkhunīs, men lay followers, and women lay followers. The seven underlying tendencies are enumerated at MN 18.8. Ven. Ānanda was declared by the Buddha to be the pre-eminent disciple among those who had learned much, and his discourses are said to have delighted the four assemblies (DN 16.5.16/ii.145).

358 *Yathā sakaṁ paṭibhānaṁ.* This phrase might also be rendered "according to his own intuition" or "according to his own ideal." Ñm renders "as it occurs to him"; Horner, "according to his own capacity."

359 Ven. Revata was declared the pre-eminent disciple among those who are meditators.

360 Ven. Anuruddha was the pre-eminent disciple among those who possessed the divine eye.

361 Mahā Kassapa was the pre-eminent disciple among those who observed the ascetic practices.

362 *Abhidhamma.* Though the word cannot refer here to the Piṭaka of that name—obviously the product of a phase of Buddhist thought later than the Nikāyas—it may well indicate a systematic and analytical approach to the doctrine that served as the original nucleus of the Abhidhamma Piṭaka. In a careful study of the contexts in which the word "Abhidhamma" occurs in the Sutta Piṭakas of several early recensions, the Japanese Pali scholar Fumimaro Watanabe concludes that the Buddha's own disciples formed the conception of Abhidhamma as an elementary philosophical study that attempted to define, analyse, and classify *dhammas* and to explore their mutual relations. See his *Philosophy and its Development in the Nikāyas and Abhidhamma*, pp. 34–36.

363 While the replies of the disciples hold up as the ideal a bhikkhu who has already achieved proficiency in a particular sphere of the renunciant life, the Buddha's reply, by focusing on a bhikkhu still striving for the goal, underscores the ultimate purpose of the holy life itself.

SUTTA 33

364 See MN 129.2, 27.

365 The Codes (*mātikā*) are probably the rules of the Pātimokkha abstracted from their explanatory matrix, as well as lists of the primary doctrinal categories used for expounding the Dhamma. For more on the *mātikās* see Watanabe, *Philosophy and its Development in the Nikāyas and Abhidhamma*, pp. 42–45.

366 See n.89.

367 At SN 47:6/v.148 the four foundations of mindfulness are called the proper pasture (*gocara*) of a bhikkhu, in the sense of being the proper sphere of his activity.

SUTTA 34

368 See n.273.

SUTTA 35

369 According to MA, Saccaka was the son of Nigaṇṭha (Jain) parents who were both skilled in philosophical debate. He had learned a thousand doctrines from his parents and many more philosophical systems from others. In the discussion below he is referred to by his clan name, Aggivessana.

370 Ven. Assaji was one of the first five disciples of the Buddha.

371 This summary of the doctrine omits the second of the three characteristics, *dukkha* or suffering. MA explains that Assaji omitted this in order to avoid giving Saccaka the opportunity to attempt a refutation of the Buddha's doctrine.

372 MA explains that men play this game when preparing hemp cloth. They bind up handfuls of rough hemp, immerse them in the water, and beat them on planks to the left, right, and middle. A royal elephant saw this game, and plunging into the water, he took up water in his trunk and sprayed it on his belly, his body, both sides, and his groin.

373 In asserting the five aggregates to be self he is, of course, directly contradicting the Buddha's teaching of *anattā*. He ascribes this view to the "great multitude" with the thought that "the majority cannot be wrong."

374 The Buddha is here suggesting that the aggregates are not self because they lack one of the essential characteristics of selfhood—being susceptible to the exercise of mastery. What cannot come under my mastery or perfect control cannot be identified as "my self."

375 MA identifies this spirit (*yakkha*) as Sakka, ruler of the gods.

376 The text between the asterisks is absent from the PTS ed. but is supplied from BBS and SBJ. The five aggregates are here called suffering because they are impermanent and not susceptible to the exercise of mastery.

377 These are the characteristics of a *sekha*. The arahant, in contrast, not only possesses the right view of non-self, but has used it to eradicate all clinging, as the Buddha will explain in §25.

378 MA gives several alternative explanations of these three terms. They are mundane and supramundane wisdom, practice, and deliverance. Or they are entirely supramundane: the first is the right view of the path of arahantship, the second the remaining seven path factors, the third the supreme fruit (of arahantship). Or the first is the vision of Nibbāna, the second the path factors, the third the supreme fruit.

379 Though Saccaka admitted defeat in debate, he must have still considered himself a saint, and thus did not feel impelled to go for refuge to the Triple Gem. Also, because he continued to regard himself as a saint, he must have felt that it was not proper for him to dedicate the merit of the alms offering to himself, and thus he wished to dedicate the merit to the Licchavis. But the Buddha replies that the Licchavis will gain the merit of providing Saccaka with food to offer to the Buddha, while Saccaka himself will gain the merit of offering the food to the Buddha. The merit of giving alms differs in quality according to the purity of the recipient, as explained at MN 142.6.

SUTTA 36

380 MA: Saccaka approached with the intention of refuting the Buddha's doctrine, which he failed to do in his earlier encounter with the Buddha (in MN 35). But this time he came alone, thinking that if he were to suffer defeat no one would know about it. He intended to refute the Buddha with his question about sleeping during the day, which he does not ask until close to the end of the sutta (§45).

381 MA: Ānanda says this out of compassion for Saccaka, thinking that if he gets to see the Buddha and to hear the Dhamma, it will lead to his welfare and happiness for a long time.

382 It will become clear from §5 that Saccaka identifies "development of body" (*kāyabhāvanā*) with the practice of self-mortification. Because he does not see the Buddhist bhikkhus engaged in self-mortification, he maintains that they do not pursue development of the body. But the

Buddha (according to MA) understands "development of body" as insight meditation, "development of mind" (*citta-bhāvanā*) as serenity meditation.

383 These are the three mentors of the Ājīvakas; the last was a contemporary of the Buddha, the former two are near legendary figures whose identities remain obscure. The Bodhisatta had adopted their practices during his period of asceticism—see MN 12.45—but subsequently rejected them as unconducive to enlightenment.

384 MA explains that "development of body" here is insight, and "development of mind" concentration. When the noble disciple experiences pleasant feeling, he does not become overwhelmed by it because, through his development of insight, he understands the feeling to be impermanent, unsatisfactory, and not self; and when he experiences painful feeling, he does not become overwhelmed by it because, through his development of concentration, he is able to escape from it by entering into one of the meditative absorptions.

385 Now the Buddha will answer Saccaka's questions by showing first the extremely painful feelings he experienced during his course of ascetic practices, and thereafter the extremely pleasant feelings he experienced during his meditative attainments preceding his enlightenment.

386 PTS is certainly mistaken in reading here *avūpakaṭṭho*, "not withdrawn." In the first edition I translated this passage on the basis of BBS, which has *kāyena c'eva cittena ca*. But PTS and SBJ omit *cittena*, and it seems difficult to understand how these ascetics can be described as "mentally withdrawn" from sensual pleasures when they have not stilled sensual desire within themselves. I therefore follow PTS and SBJ.

387 It is puzzling that in the following paragraphs the Bodhisatta is shown engaging in self-mortification *after* he had here come to the conclusion that such practices are useless for the attainment of enlightenment. This dissonant juxtaposition of ideas raises a suspicion that the narrative sequence of the sutta has become jumbled. The appropriate place for the simile of the fire-sticks, it seems, would be at the end of the Bodhisatta's period of ascetic

experimentation, when he has acquired a sound basis for rejecting self-mortification. Nevertheless, MA accepts the sequence as given and raises the question why the Bodhisatta undertook the practice of austerities if he could have attained Buddhahood without doing so. It answers: He did so, first, in order to show his own exertion to the world, because the quality of invincible energy gave him joy; and second, out of compassion for later generations, by inspiring them to strive with the same determination that he applied to the attainment of enlightenment.

388 This sentence, repeated at the end of each of the following sections as well, answers the second of the two questions posed by Saccaka in §11.

389 MA: During the Bodhisatta's boyhood as a prince, on one occasion his father led a ceremonial ploughing at a traditional festival of the Sakyans. The prince was brought to the festival and a place was prepared for him under a rose-apple tree. When his attendants left him to watch the ploughing ceremony, the prince, finding himself all alone, spontaneously sat up in the meditation posture and attained the first jhāna through mindfulness of breathing. When the attendants returned and found the boy seated in meditation, they reported this to the king, who came and bowed down in veneration to his son.

390 This passage marks a change in the Bodhisatta's evaluation of pleasure; now it is no longer regarded as something to be feared and banished by the practice of austerities, but, when born of seclusion and detachment, is seen as a valuable accompaniment of the higher stages along the path to enlightenment. See MN 139.9 on the twofold division of pleasure.

391 This sentence answers the first of the two questions posed by Saccaka in §11.

392 MA explains the "sign of concentration" (*samādhinimitta*) here as the fruition attainment of emptiness (*suññata-phalasamāpatti*). See also MN 122.6.

393 This was the question that Saccaka originally intended to ask the Buddha. MA explains that though arahants have eliminated all sloth and torpor, they still need to sleep in order to dispel the physical tiredness intrinsic to the body.

394 MA explains that even though Saccaka did not reach any attainment or even become established in the Three Refuges, the Buddha taught him two long suttas in order to deposit in him a mental impression (*vāsanā*) that would come to maturity in the future. For he foresaw that at a later time, after the Dispensation became established in Sri Lanka, Saccaka would be reborn there and would attain arahantship as the great arahant, Kāḷa Buddharakkhita Thera.

SUTTA 37

395 MA expands: "Briefly, to what extent is he said to be liberated in the destruction of craving, that is, in Nibbāna, the destruction of craving through the liberatedness of his mind [which occurs] by taking it [Nibbāna] as object. Teach me briefly the preliminary practice of the arahant bhikkhu by means of which he is liberated in the destruction of craving."

396 MA explains this passage as follows: "Everything" (*sabbe dhammā*) is the five aggregates, the twelve bases, the eighteen elements. These are "not worth adhering to" by way of craving and views because they turn out in actuality to be different from the way they are grasped: grasped as permanent, pleasurable, and self, they turn out to be impermanent, suffering, and not self. He "directly knows" them as impermanent, suffering, and not self, and "fully understands" them by scrutinising them in the same way. "Contemplating impermanence," etc., is accomplished by the insight knowledges of rise and fall and of destruction and disappearance. "He does not cling" to any formation by way of craving and views, does not become agitated because of craving, and personally attains Nibbāna by the extinguishing of all defilements.

397 A personal name of Sakka, meaning "the owl."

398 The gods and titans (*asura*) are depicted in the Pali Canon as being perpetually in a state of war with each other. See especially the Sakkasaṁyutta (SN i.216–28).

399 One of the Four Great Kings, the ruler of the *yakkhas*, his kingdom being in the north.

400 MA: He did this by entering into meditation on the water-kasiṇa and then resolving: "Let the foundation of the palace be like water."

401 Sakka can refer to Ven. Mahā Moggallāna as a "companion in the holy life" because he himself had earlier attained to stream-entry (DN 21.2.10/ii.289) and was thus a noble disciple bound for the same deliverance that Mahā Moggallāna had already achieved.

SUTTA 38

402 According to MA, through faulty reasoning based on the fact of rebirth, Sāti came to the conclusion that a persisting consciousness transmigrating from one existence to another is necessary to explain rebirth. The first part of the sutta (down to §8) replicates the opening of MN 22, the only difference being in the view espoused.

403 This is the last of the six views described at MN 2.8. See n.40.

404 MA: The purpose of the simile is to show that there is no transmigration of consciousness across the sense doors. Just as a log fire burns in dependence on logs and ceases when its fuel is finished, without transmigrating to faggots and becoming reckoned as a faggot fire, so too, consciousness arisen in the eye door dependent on the eye and forms ceases when its conditions are removed, without transmigrating to the ear, etc., and becoming reckoned as ear-consciousness, etc. Thus the Buddha says in effect: "In the occurrence of consciousness there is not even the mere transmigration from door to door, so how can this misguided Sāti speak of transmigration from existence to existence?"

405 *Bhūtam idan ti.* MA: "This" refers to the five aggregates. Having shown the conditionality of consciousness, the Buddha states this passage to show the conditionality of all the five aggregates, which come into being through conditions, their "nutriment," and pass out of being with the ceasing of those conditions. In the following *tadāhārasambhavaṁ,* MA takes the *tad* as a nominative representing the subject (= *taṁ khandhapañcakaṁ*), but it

seems more likely that it qualifies *āhāra* and that both should be taken as ablatives, the subject *idaṁ* being understood. This interpretation seems confirmed by the third statement, *tadāhāranirodhā yaṁ bhūtaṁ taṁ nirodha-dhammaṁ*. Horner's "This is the origination of nutriment" is clearly wrong.

406 This is said to show the bhikkhus that they should not cling even to the right view of insight meditation. The simile of the raft refers to MN 22.13.

407 On the four nutriments, see n.120. MA: The Buddha states this passage and the following one linking up the nutriments with dependent origination in order to show that he knows not merely the five aggregates but the entire chain of conditions responsible for their being.

408 This is a statement of the abstract principle of dependent origination exemplified by the twelvefold formula. The abstract principle on cessation is stated at §22. Ñm had rendered the principle of arising thus: "That is when this is; that arises with the arising of this." And the principle of cessation: "That is not when this is not; that ceases with the cessation of this."

409 The best reading is SBJ: *samaṇavacanena ca mayaṁ*. Ñm apparently translated from PTS *samaṇā ca na ca mayaṁ* and thus rendered it, "and so do [other] monks, but we do not speak thus." "The Recluse" is the Buddha.

410 The following portion of the discourse may be understood as a concrete application of dependent origination—so far expressed only as a doctrinal formula—to the course of individual existence. The passage §§26–29 may be taken to show the factors from consciousness through feeling that result from past ignorance and formations, §40 the causal factors of craving and clinging as they build up a continuation of the saṁsāric round. The following section (§§31–40), connecting dependent origination to the appearance of the Buddha and his teaching of the Dhamma, shows the practice of the Dhamma to be the means of bringing the round to an end.

411 MA: The *gandhabba* is the being arriving there. It is not someone (i.e., a disembodied spirit) standing nearby watching the future parents having intercourse, but a

being driven on by the mechanism of kamma, due to be reborn on that occasion.

The exact import of the word *gandhabba* in relation to the rebirth process is not explained in the Nikāyas, and the word in this sense occurs only here and at 93.18. DN 15/ii.63 speaks of consciousness as "descending into the mother's womb," this being a condition for rebirth to take place. Thus we might identify the *gandhabba* here as the stream of consciousness, conceived more animistically as coming over from the previous existence and bringing along its total accumulation of kammic tendencies and personality traits. The fullest study of the concept of the *gandhabba* is Wijesekera, "Vedic Gandharva and Pali Gandhabba," in *Buddhist and Vedic Studies*, pp. 191–202.

412 MA explains that he delights in the painful feeling by clinging to it with thoughts of "I" and "mine." In confirmation of the statement that a worldling may delight in painful feelings, one thinks not only of full-fledged masochism but also of the common tendency of people to put themselves into distressing situations in order to reinforce their sense of ego.

413 MA: An immeasurable mind (*appamāṇacetaso*) is a supramundane mind; this means that he possesses the path.

414 This statement reveals that the chain of dependent origination is broken at the link between feeling and craving. Feeling arises necessarily because the body acquired through past craving is subject to the maturation of past kamma. However, if one does not delight in feeling, craving will not have the opportunity to arise and set off reactions of like and dislike that provide further fuel for the round, and thus the round will come to an end.

SUTTA 39

415 "Brahmin" should be understood in the sense explained below, §24.

416 Shame (*hiri*) and fear of wrongdoing (*ottappa*) are two complementary qualities designated by the Buddha "the guardians of the world" (AN i.51) because they serve as the foundation for morality. *Shame* has the characteristic

of disgust with evil, is dominated by a sense of self-respect, and manifests itself as conscience. *Fear of wrong-doing* has the characteristic of dread of evil, is dominated by a concern for the opinions of others, and manifests itself as fear of doing evil. See Vsm XIV, 142.

417 MA quotes SN 45:35–36/v.25: "What, bhikkhus, is recluseship (*sāmañña*)? The Noble Eightfold Path...—this is called recluseship. And what, bhikkhus, is the goal of recluseship (*sāmaññattho*)? The destruction of greed, hate, and delusion—this is called the goal of recluseship."

418 MA gives a detailed elaboration of each of the five similes. An English translation can be found in Nyanaponika Thera, *The Five Mental Hindrances*, pp. 27–34.

419 Each of the explanations to follow involves a word play that cannot be reproduced in English, e.g., a bhikkhu is a recluse (*samaṇa*) because he has quieted down (*samita*) evil states, a brahmin because he has expelled (*bāhita*) evil states, etc.

420 The term "washed" (*nhātaka*) refers to a brahmin who, at the end of his discipleship under his teacher, has taken a ceremonial bath marking the end of his training. See Sn 521.

421 The Pali word *sotthiya* (Skt, *śrotriya*) means a brahmin well versed in the Vedas, one conversant with sacred knowledge.

SUTTA 40

422 Where the previous sutta used the phrase "things that make one a recluse" (*dhammā samaṇakaraṇā*), the present sutta speaks of "the way proper to the recluse" (*samaṇa-samīcipaṭipadā*).

423 The first ten of these twelve "stains for a recluse" are included among the sixteen "imperfections that defile the mind" at MN 7.3.

424 MA: Because he has quieted down (*samita*) all defilements, he is a recluse in the highest sense (*paramattha-samaṇa*).

SUTTA 41

425 This is a morally nihilistic materialist view that denies an afterlife and kammic retribution. "There is nothing given" means that there is no fruit of giving; "no this world, no other world" that there is no rebirth into either this world or a world beyond; "no mother, no father" that there is no fruit of good conduct and bad conduct towards mother and father. The statement about recluses and brahmins denies the existence of Buddhas and arahants.

426 MA explains that "the gods of Radiance" is not a separate class of gods but a collective name for the three classes that follow; the same applies to "the gods of Glory." This celestial hierarchy is explained in the Introduction, pp. 46–48.

427 It should be noted that while "conduct in accordance with the Dhamma" as described in the sutta is a necessary condition for rebirth in the higher heavenly worlds and for the destruction of the taints, it is by no means a sufficient condition. Rebirth into the realms beginning with the gods of Brahmā's retinue requires the attainment of jhāna, rebirth into the Pure Abodes (the five beginning with the Avihā gods) the attainment of the stage of non-returner, rebirth into the immaterial planes the corresponding immaterial attainments, and the destruction of the taints requires the full practice of the Noble Eightfold Path up to the path of arahantship.

SUTTA 43

428 Ven. Mahā Koṭṭhita was declared by the Buddha the foremost disciple of those who have attained the analytical knowledges (*paṭisambhidā*).

429 According to MA, the understanding of the Four Noble Truths being discussed here is penetration by the supramundane path. Thus the lowest type of person to be described as "one who is wise" (*paññavā*) is the person on the path of stream-entry. The rendering of *paññā* as "wisdom" (which I substituted for Ñm's "understanding") has the disadvantage of severing the tie, evident in the

Pali, with the verb *pajānāti*. To preserve the connection, here and in the preceding paragraph, the verb has been rendered "wisely understand."

430 The Pali phrase defining consciousness uses only the verb, *vijānāti vijānāti*, and this could as well be understood to mean "One cognizes, one cognizes." Although Ñm had translated this phrase without any pronoun, the pronoun has been inserted for greater intelligibility. The renderings of the verb definitions of feeling and perception at §7 and §8 have been similarly augmented by the addition of the pronoun.

431 MA: The question concerns the consciousness with which the person described as "one who is wise" examines formations; that is, the consciousness of insight by which that person arrived (at his attainment), the mind which does the work of meditation. Ven. Sāriputta answers by explaining the meditation subject of feeling, in the way it has come down in the Discourse on the Foundations of Mindfulness (MN 10.32). The Pali construction, *sukhan ti pi vijānāti*, indicates that the feeling is being treated as a direct object of consciousness rather than as an affective tone of the experience; to show this the words "this is" have been supplied in brackets and the entire phrase set in quotation marks.

432 MA: This statement refers to the wisdom and consciousness on the occasions of both insight and the supramundane path. The two are conjoined in that they arise and cease simultaneously and share a single sense base and object. However, the two are not inseparably conjoined since, while wisdom always requires consciousness, consciousness can occur without wisdom.

433 Wisdom, being the path factor of right view, is to be developed as a factor of the path. Consciousness, being included among the five aggregates that pertain to the noble truth of suffering, is to be fully understood—as impermanent, suffering, and not self.

434 MA says that the question and reply refer to mundane feelings that are the objective range of insight. The Pali construction here, *sukham pi vedeti*, etc., shows feeling as simultaneously a quality of the object and an affective

tone of the experience by which it is apprehended. MA points out that feeling itself feels; there is no other (separate) feeler.

435 MA: The question and reply refer to mundane perceptions that are the objective range of insight.

436 MA: Wisdom has been excluded from this exchange because the intention is to show only the states that are conjoined on every occasion of consciousness.

437 MA: Purified mind-consciousness (*parisuddha manoviññāṇa*) is the consciousness of the fourth jhāna. It can know the immaterial attainments insofar as one established in the fourth jhāna is capable of reaching them. The base of neither-perception-nor-non-perception is excluded here because, owing to its subtlety, it does not come into the direct range of contemplation for the attainment of insight.

438 MA: The eye of wisdom (*paññācakkhu*) is wisdom itself, called an eye in the sense that it is an organ of spiritual vision.

439 For the distinction between direct knowledge (*abhiññā*) and full understanding (*pariññā*), see n.23.

440 MA: "The voice of another" (*parato ghosa*) is the teaching of beneficial Dhamma. These two conditions are necessary for disciples to arrive at the right view of insight and the right view of the supramundane path. But paccekabuddhas arrive at their enlightenment and fully enlightened Buddhas at omniscience solely in dependence on wise attention without "the voice of another."

441 MA: Right view here is the right view pertaining to the path of arahantship. "Deliverance of mind" and "deliverance by wisdom" both refer to the fruit of arahantship; see n.83. When one fulfils these five factors, the path of arahantship arises and yields its fruit.

442 "Renewal of being in the future" (*āyatiṁ punabbhavābhinibbatti*) is rebirth, the continuation of the round. This question and the next may be regarded as synoptic approaches to the entire twelvefold formula of dependent origination laid out in MN 38.17 and 20.

443 The five outer sense faculties each have their own unique object—forms for the eye, sounds for the ear, etc.—but

the mind faculty is able to experience the objects of all five sense faculties as well as the mental objects exclusive to itself. Hence the other five faculties have mind as their resort (*manopaṭisaraṇaṁ*).

444 MA identifies vitality (*āyu*) with the life faculty (*jīvit-indriya*), which has the function of maintaining and vitalising the other material phenomena of the living body.

445 Heat (*usmā*) is the kamma-born heat intrinsic to the living body.

446 "Vital formations" (*āyusankhārā*), according to MA, denotes vitality itself. They cannot be states of feeling because they are required to keep the body of a bhikkhu alive when he has attained to the cessation of perception and feeling. This special meditative attainment, in which all mental activity ceases, is accessible only to non-returners and arahants who also have mastery over the eight attainments on the side of serenity. For a brief discussion see the Introduction, p. 41, and for the full scholastic account, Vsm XXIII, 16–52. The cessation of perception and feeling will be taken up again in MN 44.

447 That is, dead. The departure of consciousness from the body is not sufficient to constitute death; vitality and the vital heat must also perish.

448 The bodily formations are in-and-out breathing, the verbal formations are applied thought and sustained thought, the mental formations are perception and feeling—see MN 44.14–15. MA says that the faculties during the ordinary course of life, being impinged upon by sense objects, are afflicted and soiled like a mirror set up at a crossroads; but the faculties of one in cessation become exceptionally clear like a mirror placed in a case and deposited in a box.

449 MA: The "signless deliverance of mind" (*animittā cetovimutti*) is the attainment of fruition; the "signs" are objects such as forms, etc.; the "signless element" is Nibbāna, in which all signs of conditioned things are absent.

450 MA identifies this *suññatā cetovimutti* with insight into the voidness of selfhood in persons and things.

451 As above, the signless deliverance of mind is identified

by MA with the attainment of fruition. Of the four deliverances of mind mentioned in §30, this one alone is supramundane. The first three—the *brahmavihāras*, the third immaterial attainment, and insight into the voidness of formations—all pertain to the mundane level.

452 Lust, hate, and delusion may be understood as "makers of measurement" (*pamāṇakaraṇa*) in that they impose limitations upon the range and depths of the mind; MA, however, explains this phrase to mean that the defilements enable one to measure a person as a worldling, a stream-enterer, a once-returner, or a non-returner.

453 MA: There are twelve immeasurable deliverances of mind: the four *brahmavihāras*, the four paths, and the four fruits. The unshakeable deliverance of mind is the fruit of arahantship. The statement that this unshakeable deliverance is void of lust, hate, and delusion—repeated at the end of §36 and §37 as well—also identifies it as the supramundane deliverance of mind through voidness.

454 The word *kiñcana* is explained by MA as meaning "impediment" or "obstacle." Ñm rendered it as "owning." I have gone back to the original meaning "something" to maintain coherence with the statement that its abandonment issues in deliverance of mind through nothingness.

455 MA: There are nine deliverances of mind through nothingness: the base of nothingness and the four paths and fruits.

456 MA interprets the phrase "maker of signs" (*nimittakaraṇa*) to mean that lust, hate, and delusion brand a person as a worldling or a noble one, as lustful, hating, or deluded. But it may also mean that these defilements cause the mind to ascribe a false significance to things as being permanent, pleasurable, self, or beautiful.

457 MA: There are thirteen signless deliverances of mind: insight, because it removes the signs of permanence, pleasure, and self; the four immaterial attainments, because they lack the sign of material form; and the four paths and fruits, because of the absence of the sign of defilements.

458 All the four deliverances of mind are one in meaning in that they all refer to the fruition attainment of arahantship.

MA also points out that the four deliverances are one in meaning because the terms—the immeasurable, nothingness, voidness, and the signless—are all names for Nibbāna, which is the object of the fruition attainment of arahantship.

SUTTA 44

459 Visākha was a wealthy merchant of Rājagaha and a non-returner. Dhammadinnā, his former wife in lay life, had attained arahantship soon after her ordination as a bhikkhunī. She was declared by the Buddha the foremost bhikkhunī disciple in expounding the Dhamma.

460 MA explains the compound *pañc'upādānakkhandhā* as the five aggregates that become the condition for clinging (MṬ: as its objects). Since these five aggregates are, in brief, the entire noble truth of suffering (MN 9.15; 28.3), it will be seen that the first four questions pose an inquiry into the Four Noble Truths expressed in terms of personal identity rather than suffering.

461 MA: Because clinging is only one part of the aggregate of formations (as defined here, greed), it is not the same as the five aggregates; and because clinging cannot be altogether disconnected from the aggregates, there is no clinging apart from the aggregates.

462 These are the twenty kinds of identity view. MA quotes Pṭs i.144–45 to illustrate the four basic modes of identity view in regard to material form. One may regard material form as self, in the way the flame of a burning oil-lamp is identical with the colour (of the flame). Or one may regard self as possessing material form, as a tree possesses a shadow; or one may regard material form as in self, as the scent is in the flower; or one may regard self as in material form, as a jewel is in a casket.

463 The word *khandha* here has a different meaning than in the more common context of the five aggregates affected by clinging. It here refers to a body of training principles, the three divisions of the Noble Eightfold Path into virtue (*sīla*), concentration (*samādhi*), and wisdom (*paññā*).

464 The four foundations of mindfulness are the basis of

concentration (*samādhinimitta*) in the sense of being its condition (MA). Here it would seem incorrect to translate *nimitta* as "sign," in the sense of either distinctive mark or object. The four right kinds of striving are explained at MN 77.16.

465 MA: Dhammadinnā anticipated Visākha's intention to ask about the formations that cease when one enters the attainment of cessation. Thus she explained the three formations in this way rather than as wholesome and unwholesome volitions of body, speech, and mind, the meaning relevant within the context of dependent origination.

466 MA explains further that the bodily formation and the mental formation are said to be formations "bound up" with the body and the mind in the sense that they *are formed by* the body and *by* the mind, while the verbal formation is a formation in the sense that it *forms* speech. The verb form *vitakketvā vicāretvā* has been rendered in a way that maintains consistency with the rendering of the nouns *vitakka* and *vicāra* as "applied thought" and "sustained thought."

467 Cessation can be attained only by a non-returner or an arahant with mastery over the eight jhānic attainments. The meditator enters each attainment in turn, emerges from it, and contemplates it with insight as impermanent, suffering, and not self. After completing this procedure through the base of nothingness, he attends to certain preliminary duties, and then determines to be without mind for a particular length of time. He then briefly enters the base of neither-perception-nor-non-perception, after which mind and mental functions utterly cease. Thus his determination, backed by his previous accomplishments and preparations, leads him into the attainment of cessation. See Vsm XXIII, 32–43.

468 Applied and sustained thought cease first in the second jhāna; in-and-out breathing cease next in the fourth jhāna; and perception and feeling cease last in the attainment of cessation itself.

469 When the time decided upon by the determination for the attainment has lapsed, by reason of that prior determination

the meditator spontaneously emerges from the attainment of cessation and the mind-process resumes.

470 MA: When one emerges from cessation, the consciousness of fruition attainment arises first, and the perception and feeling associated with that are the mental formation that arises first. Then, with the subsequent descent into the life continuum, the bodily formation, i.e., breathing, recommences. And subsequently, when the meditator resumes his ordinary activity, the verbal formation arises.

471 The first state of consciousness to arise on emerging from cessation is that of fruition attainment, which is called voidness, the signless, and the desireless because of its own inherent quality and because of its object, Nibbāna. Here these three names for fruition are assigned to the contact associated with fruition.

472 MṬ: Nibbāna, the object of the fruition consciousness that arises on emerging from cessation, is called seclusion (*viveka*) because it is secluded from all conditioned things.

473 MṬ: The three defilements are called *anusaya*, underlying tendencies, in the sense that they have not been abandoned in the mental continuum to which they belong and because they are capable of arising when a suitable cause presents itself.

474 MA explains that the bhikkhu suppresses the tendency to lust and attains the first jhāna. Having made the tendency to lust well suppressed by the jhāna, he develops insight and eradicates the tendency to lust by the path of the non-returner. But because it has been suppressed by the jhāna, it is said "the underlying tendency to lust does not underlie that."

475 MA identifies "that base" (*tadāyatana*), as well as "the supreme liberations," with arahantship. The grief that arises because of that longing is elsewhere called "the grief based on renunciation" (MN 137.13). MA explains that one does not actually abandon the tendency to aversion by means of that grief; rather, spurred on by the longing for the supreme liberations, one takes up the practice with firm determination and eradicates the tendency to aversion by attaining the path of the non-returner.

476 MA: The bhikkhu suppresses the tendency to ignorance with the fourth jhāna, makes it well suppressed, and then eradicates the tendency to ignorance by attaining the path of arahantship.

477 The word "counterpart" (*paṭibhāga*) is used to express the relationships of both opposition and supplementation.

478 Ignorance is its counterpart because neither-painful-nor-pleasant feeling is subtle and difficult to recognise.

479 MṬ: Nibbāna does have an opposite counterpart, namely, conditioned states. But in the strict sense it has no supplementary counterpart, for how can there be anything to supplement Nibbāna, the unconditioned?

480 MA: By saying this, the Buddha makes this sutta Word of the Conqueror, stamped as it were with the seal of the Conqueror.

SUTTA 46

481 A full analysis of the things that should and should not be followed is presented in MN 114.

SUTTA 47

482 *Parassa cetopariyāyaṁ ajānantena,* reading the last word with BBS and SBJ rather than with PTS as *ājānantena,* which gives the positive sense "knowing." In the context the negative is clearly required, since the bhikkhu who cannot know by direct cognition of the Buddha's mind that he is fully enlightened must arrive at this conclusion by inference from his bodily and verbal behaviour and the other evidence adduced by the sutta.

483 Bodily actions are "states cognizable through the eye." Words are "states cognizable through the ear." MA: Just as one infers the presence of fish from the rippling and bubbling of water, so from a defiled action or utterance one infers that the mind originating it is defiled.

484 MṬ: "Mixed states" (*vītimissā dhammā*) refers to the conduct of one who is engaged in purifying his conduct but is unable to keep to it consistently. Sometimes his conduct is pure or bright, sometimes impure or dark.

485 MA: The dangers are conceit, arrogance, etc. For some bhikkhus, as long as they have not become well known or acquired a following, these dangers are not found, and they are very calm and quiet; but when they have become famous and have acquired a following, they go about behaving improperly, attacking other bhikkhus like a leopard pouncing on a herd of deer.

486 MA: The opposite of those who teach a group—those who dwell detached from a group—though not mentioned, should be understood.

487 MA: This passage shows the Buddha's impartiality (*tādibhāva*) towards beings: he does not extol some and disparage others.

488 *No ca tena tammayo.* MA glosses: "I do not identify with that purified virtue, I am without craving for it."

489 *So tasmiṁ dhamme abhiññāya idh'ekaccaṁ dhammaṁ dhammesu niṭṭhaṁ gacchati.* In order to convey the intended meaning I have rendered the second occurrence of *dhamma* here as "teaching," i.e., the particular doctrine taught to him, the plural *dhammesu* as "teachings," and *tasmiṁ dhamme* as "that Dhamma," in the sense of the total teaching. MA and MṬ together explicate the meaning thus: When the Dhamma has been taught by the Teacher, by directly knowing the Dhamma through penetration of the path, fruit, and Nibbāna, the bhikkhu comes to a conclusion about the preliminary teaching of the Dhamma on the aids to enlightenment (*bodhipakkhiyā dhammā*).

490 *Ākāravatī saddhā dassanamūlikā daḷhā.* This phrase refers to the faith of a stream-enterer who has seen the Dhamma through the supramundane path and can never point to any other teacher than the Buddha.

SUTTA 48

491 The background to this sutta is the quarrel at Kosambī, which is related at Vin Mv Kh 10 (Vin i.337 ff.) and in Ñāṇamoli, *The Life of the Buddha*, pp. 109–19. The quarrel, which began with a casual misunderstanding of a minor disciplinary rule, quickly flared up and divided a large

part of the Sangha and laity resident at Kosambī into two hostile factions.

492 *Cha dhammā sārāṇiyā.* Ñm had rendered this expression "six memorable qualities," which was adopted in the first edition. In this he follows the commentaries, which gloss the phrase, "fit to be remembered; not to be forgotten even with the passage of time" (*saritabbayuttā addhāne atikkante pi na pamusitabbā*). The correct derivation, however, as PED notes, is from Skt *saṁrañjanīya*, "causing delight."

493 MA: This is the right view belonging to the noble path.

494 The Four Noble Truths.

495 *Dhammatā.*

496 This is a breach of the code of monastic discipline from which a bhikkhu can be rehabilitated either by a formal act of the Sangha or by confession to another bhikkhu. Even though a noble disciple may commit such an offence unintentionally or through lack of knowledge, he makes no attempt to conceal it but immediately discloses it and seeks the means of rehabilitation.

497 See n.91.

498 MA calls those seven factors the "great reviewing knowledges" (*mahāpaccavekkhaṇañāṇa*) of a stream-enterer. On the reviewing knowledges see Vsm XXII, 19–21.

SUTTA 49

499 The *Mūlapariyāya Sutta* (MN 1) was also delivered by the Buddha while he was living in the Subhaga Grove at Ukkaṭṭhā, and the similarity in formulation and theme between these two suttas—perhaps the only two recorded as originating at Ukkaṭṭhā—is striking. It is even possible to see the present sutta as a dramatic representation of the same ideas set forth by the *Mūlapariyāya* in abstract philosophical terms. Thus Baka the Brahmā may be taken to represent *being* (*bhava*) or personality (*sakkāya*) in its most eminent form, blindly engaged in the activity of *conceiving (maññanā)*, sustaining itself with its delusions of permanence, pleasure, and selfhood. Underlying being is *craving*, symbolised by Māra—seemingly inconspicuous

in the assembly, yet the real author of all the outpourings of conceiving, the one who holds the entire universe in his grip. The alliance of Brahmā and Māra, God and Satan, an incomprehensible union from the perspective of Western theism, points to the thirst for continued being as the hidden root of all world affirmation, whether theistic or non-theistic. In the sutta the superficial theoretical contest between Baka and the Buddha soon gives way to a gripping deep-level confrontation between Māra and the Buddha—Māra as craving demanding the affirmation of being, the Enlightened One pointing to the cessation of being through the uprooting of delight.

500 A similar encounter between the Buddha and Baka is recorded at SN 6:4/i.142–44, though without the dramatic trappings of this meeting and with an extended exchange in verse. According to MA and MṬ, he held this eternalist view with regard to both his own individual personality and the world over which he presided. His denial of an "escape beyond" is a rejection of the higher jhāna planes, the paths and fruits, and Nibbāna, none of which he even knows exist.

501 MA: When Māra discovered that the Buddha had gone to the Brahma-world, he became anxious that the Brahmās might be won over to the Dhamma and escape from his control; thus he went there to discourage the Buddha from teaching the Dhamma.

502 MA: Because they considered it to be impermanent, suffering, and not self.

503 MA: In the four states of deprivation. Here, and at §10 and §29, the word "body" (*kāya*) is used to mean plane of existence.

504 MA: They lauded it by speaking praise of it as permanent, everlasting, eternal, etc., and delighted in it by way of craving and views.

505 MA: In the Brahma-world.

506 MA: Māra's intention is to show: "If you do as Brahmā says without overstepping his word, you too will shine with the same splendour and glory as that with which the Brahmā's Assembly shines."

507 MA says that by the first two terms he tries to cajole the Buddha, by the remaining two terms he threatens him. To "hold to earth" is to grasp it by way of craving, conceit, and views. The list of categories here, though condensed, is reminiscent of MN 1.

508 MA: Baka Brahmā was a Brahmā exercising sovereignty over a thousand world-systems, but above him there are Brahmās exercising sovereignty over two, three, four, five, ten thousand, and a hundred thousand world-systems.

509 The body of Streaming Radiance is a realm of rebirth pertaining to the second jhāna, while Baka Brahmā's realm pertains only to the first jhāna. The body of Refulgent Glory and the body of Great Fruit in the next paragraph pertain to the third and fourth jhānas.

510 In the *Brahmajāla Sutta* (DN 1.2.2–6/ii.17–19) the Buddha shows how Mahā Brahmā gives rise to the delusion that he is the supreme creator God. When the world begins to form again after a period of dissolution, a being of great merit is the first to be reborn in the newly formed Brahma-world. Subsequently, other beings take rebirth in the Brahma-world and this causes Mahā Brahmā to imagine that he is their creator and master. See Bodhi, *The Discourse on the All-Embracing Net of Views*, pp. 69–70, 159–166.

511 This passage, parallel in structure to the corresponding passage of MN 1, is a difficult one. The negative verb differs among the three editions I consulted. PTS has *nāhosi,* BBS *nāpahosiṁ,* SBJ *nāhosiṁ.* Ñm preferred *nāpahosiṁ,* which he took to be an aorist of *pabhavati,* meaning "to produce, to give being to." It is much more likely, however, that *nāpahosiṁ* should be resolved simply as *na + api + ahosiṁ.* Thus the meaning does not differ significantly between BBS and SBJ. MA glosses: "I did not grasp earth through the obsessions of craving, conceit, and views." Ñm had rendered *ananubhūtaṁ* as "not co-essential with." This has been replaced by "not partaken of by," following MA's gloss, "not reached by earth" and MṬ: "Its nature is not shared with earth." MA says that what is "not partaken of by the earthness of earth" is Nibbāna, which is detached from all that is conditioned.

512 PTS is surely mistaken in omitting here the *ti* ending a direct quotation; this misleads Horner into ascribing the following passage to Baka rather than to the Buddha (MLS 1:392). BBS and SBJ supply *ti*. Baka seems to be suggesting that since the object of the Buddha's knowledge "is not partaken of by the allness of all," it might be merely an empty concept.

513 In the first edition, I retained Ñm's own translation of these lines, which read:

> The consciousness that makes no showing,
> Nor has to do with finiteness,
> Not claiming being with respect to all.

In retrospect, I find this rendering far from satisfactory and thus here offer my own. These lines (which also appear as part of a full verse at DN 11.85/i.223) have been a perennial challenge to Buddhist scholarship, and even Ācariya Buddhaghosa seems to founder over them. MA takes the subject of the sentence to be Nibbāna, called "consciousness" (*viññāṇaṁ*) in the sense that "it can be cognized" (*vijānitabbaṁ*). This derivation is hardly credible, since nowhere in the Nikāyas is Nibbāna described as consciousness, nor is it possible to derive an active noun from the gerundive. MA explains *anidassanaṁ* as meaning invisible, "because it (Nibbāna) does not come within range of eye-consciousness," but again this is a trite explanation. The word *anidassana* occurs at MN 21.14 in the description of empty space as an unsuitable medium for painting pictures; thus the idea seems to be that of not making manifest.

MA offers three explanations of *sabbato pabhaṁ*: (1) completely possessed of luminosity (*pabhā*); (2) possessing being (*pabhūtaṁ*) everywhere; and (3) a ford (*pabhaṁ*) accessible from all sides, i.e., through any of the thirty-eight meditation objects. Only the first of these seems to have any linguistic legitimacy. Ñm, in Ms, explains that he takes *pabhaṁ* to be a negative present participle of *pabhavati*—*apabhaṁ*—the negative-prefix a dropping off in conjunction with *sabbato*: "The sense can be paraphrased freely by 'not predicating being in relation to "all,"' or 'not assuming of "all" that it is or is not in an absolute sense.'" But if we take *pabhaṁ* as "luminous," which seems better justified, the verse links up with the idea of the mind as intrinsically luminous (*pabhassaram idaṁ cittaṁ*, AN i.10) and also suggests the light of wisdom (*paññāpabhā*), called the best of lights (AN ii.139). I understand this consciousness to be, not Nibbāna itself, but the arahant's consciousness during the meditative experience of Nibbāna. See in this connection AN v.7–10, 318–26. Note that this meditative experience does not make manifest any conditioned phenomena of the world, and thus may be truly described as "non-manifesting."

514 The Buddha's disappearance seems to be a "visible" demonstration of his verse. Having extirpated delight in being, he is able to vanish from the sight of Baka, the supreme representative of being and world affirmation. But Baka, bound to being by clinging, cannot transcend the range of the Buddha's knowledge, which encompasses both being and non-being at the same time that it transcends them.

515 This is the same inclination that arose in the Buddha's mind in the period immediately after his enlightenment—see MN 26.19. Compare also DN 16.3.34/ii.112 where Māra attempts to persuade the newly enlightened Buddha to pass away peacefully at once.

516 *Tādiso*: that is, whether he teaches or not he remains the Tathāgata.

SUTTA 50

517 The name means "the Corrupter" or "the Corrupted One." In the Buddhist conception of the universe the position of Māra, like that of Mahā Brahmā, is a fixed one that is assumed by different individuals in accordance with their kamma.

518 Kakusandha was the first Buddha to arise in this present cosmological cycle called the "Auspicious Age." He was followed by the Buddhas Konāgamaṇa and Kassapa, after whom the present Buddha Gotama arose.

519 The name means "the Unrivalled."

520 One who has attained to cessation, it seems, is not subject to injury or death within the attainment itself. At Vsm XXIII, 37 it is said that the attainment protects even his belongings such as his robes and seat from destruction.

521 The name means "the Survivor."

522 That is, by causing defilements to arise in their minds, he will prevent them from escaping from saṁsāra.

523 MA takes pains to point out that Māra did not exercise control over their actions, in which case he alone would have been responsible and the brahmins could not have generated bad kamma by their deeds. Rather, Māra caused the brahmins to imagine scenes of the bhikkhus engaged in improper conduct, and this aroused their antagonism and induced them to harass the bhikkhus. Māra's intent in doing so was to make the bhikkhus give rise to anger and dejection.

524 "The Kinsman" (*bandhu*) is Brahmā, who was called thus by the brahmins because they regarded him as their primal ancestor. MA explains that it was a belief among the brahmins that they themselves were the offspring of Brahmā's mouth, the *khattiyas* of his breast, the *vessas* of his belly, the *suddas* of his legs, and *samaṇas* of the soles of his feet.

525 *Jhāyanti pajjhāyanti nijjhāyanti apajjhāyanti.* Though the verbs individually do not have an established pejorative sense, the string is obviously intended as a denigration. At MN 108.26 the four verbs are used to describe the meditation of one whose mind is obsessed by the five hindrances.

526 The four *brahmavihāras* are the appropriate antidote for the hostility of others, as well as for the tendencies to anger and dejection in one's own mind.

527 This time Māra's intent was to cause the bhikkhus to fall victim to pride, complacency, and negligence.

528 MA quotes a sutta (AN 7:46/iv.46–53) stating that these four meditations are the antidotes, respectively, for sexual desire, craving for tastes, attraction to the world, and infatuation with gain, honour, and praise.

529 MA: The elephant look (*nāgapalokita*) means that without twisting his neck, he turns his whole body in order to look. The Māra Dūsī did not die *because* of the Buddha's

elephant look, but because the evil kamma he generated in wronging a great disciple cut off his life right on the spot.

530 The Great Hell, also called Avīci, is described in greater detail in MN 130.16–19.

531 MA: This feeling, experienced in the auxiliary (*ussada*) of the Great Hell, is said to be more painful than the feelings experienced in the Great Hell itself.

532 The Buddha Kakusandha is called a brahmin in the sense of MN 39.24.

533 The reference is to SN 51:14/v.269–70.

534 See MN 37.11.

535 See MN 37.12.

536 The reference is to SN 6:5/i.145.

537 This verse refers to Ven. Moggallāna's mastery over the supernormal power of travelling in space like a bird.

SUTTA 51

538 From this difference in their manner of greeting the Buddha it is evident that Pessa is a follower of the Buddha, whereas Kandaraka—despite his respect and admiration—belongs to a different religious community.

539 MA: Out of respect for the Buddha and because of their training, the bhikkhus did not converse with one another, nor did they even clear their throats. Unmoving in body, undistracted in mind, they sat surrounding the Blessed One like ruddy clouds surrounding the peak of Mount Sineru. Kandaraka must have been privately comparing this assembly of the bhikkhus with the assemblies of wanderers as described in MN 76.4.

540 MA explains that Kandaraka did not have direct knowledge of the Buddhas of the past and future. He made this statement as a way of expressing his admiration for the well-trained, disciplined, and calm Sangha of bhikkhus. The Buddha, however, confirms this on the basis of direct knowledge.

541 MA: The four foundations of mindfulness are brought in to show the *cause* for the calm and tranquil deportment of the Sangha. On the foundations of mindfulness, see MN 10.

542 MA glosses: "We too, when we get an opportunity, from time to time attend to this; we are also practitioners; we do not completely neglect meditation."

543 The point of this statement is that an animal's guile and trickery is very limited, while that of human beings is inexhaustible.

544 MA explains that this passage is introduced as a sequel to Pessa's statement that the Blessed One knows the welfare and harm of beings; for the Buddha shows that the first three kinds of persons are practising in harmful ways, while the fourth is practising in a beneficial way. The passage can also be connected with Kandaraka's praise of the Sangha; for the Buddha will show three ways in which he does not train the Sangha and the one way in which all the Buddhas of the past, present, and future train their Sanghas.

545 *Sukhapaṭisaṁvedī brahmabhūtena attanā*. MA: He experiences the bliss of the jhānas, paths, fruits, and Nibbāna. "Brahma" here should be understood in the sense of holy or excellent (*seṭṭha*). There may be an allusion here to the main theme of the Upanishads, the identity of the *ātman* with *brahman*.

546 MA: Pessa would have attained the fruit of stream-entry, but he rose from his seat and left before the Buddha had completed his discourse. The benefits he did receive are two: he gained greater confidence in the Sangha, and he gave rise to a new method for comprehending the foundations of mindfulness.

547 This passage details the austerities undertaken by many of the Buddha's ascetic contemporaries, as well as by the Bodhisatta himself during his period of striving for enlightenment. See MN 12.45.

548 This passage shows the practice of one who torments himself in the hope of gaining merit and then offers sacrifices that involve the slaughter of many animals and the oppression of his workers.

549 This is the arahant. To show clearly that he torments neither himself nor others, the Buddha next undertakes to describe the path of practice by which he arrived at arahantship.

SUTTA 52

550 All these expressions are descriptive of arahantship.

551 *Abhisankhataṁ abhisañcetayitaṁ.* The two terms are frequently used in conjunction to indicate a conditioned state in which volition (*cetanā*) is the most prominent conditioning factor.

552 This passage explains a method for developing "insight preceded by serenity" (*samathapubbangamā vipassanā*; see AN 4:170/ ii.157). Having first attained a jhāna, the meditator emerges from it and contemplates that state as brought into being by conditions, particularly volition. On the basis of this, he ascertains its impermanence, and then contemplates the jhāna with insight into the three marks of impermanence, suffering, and non-self. See also MN 64.9–15 for a somewhat different approach to developing insight on the basis of the jhānas.

553 *Dhammarāgena dhammanandiyā.* MA: These two terms signify desire and attachment (*chandarāga*) with respect to serenity and insight. If one is able to discard all desire and attachment concerning serenity and insight, one becomes an arahant; if one cannot discard them, one becomes a non-returner and is reborn in the Pure Abodes.

554 The base of neither-perception-nor-non-perception is not mentioned because it is too subtle a state for its constituent factors to be used as objects of insight contemplation.

555 The eleven "doors to the Deathless" are the four jhānas, the four *brahmavihāras*, and the first three immaterial attainments used as bases for the development of insight and attainment of arahantship.

556 This would be five hundred *kahāpaṇas,* the latter being the standard monetary unit of the time.

SUTTA 53

557 It was believed to be a source of merit for those who construct a new dwelling to invite an eminent religious personage to dwell in it even for a single night before they inhabit it themselves. This belief still continues in

Buddhist lands today, and people who have built a new house for themselves will often invite bhikkhus to hold an all-night recitation of *paritta* (protective) suttas in their new home before they move in.

558 *Sekho pāṭipado*. On the *sekha*, see n.21.

559 On the distinction between shame (*hiri*) and fear of wrongdoing (*ottappa*), see n.416.

560 Here the text explains *sati*, mindfulness, by reference to its original meaning of memory. The relationship between the two senses of *sati*—memory and attentiveness—may be formulated thus: keen attentiveness to the present forms the basis for an accurate memory of the past. MA takes the mention of *sati* here to imply all seven factors of enlightenment, among which it is the first.

561 MA: This is the wisdom of insight and of the path, capable of penetrating the rise and fall of the five aggregates. Path wisdom is called "penetrative" (*nibbedhikā*) because it pierces through and eradicates the mass of greed, hate, and delusion; insight wisdom is called penetrative because it pierces through them temporarily and because it leads to penetration by the path.

562 As at MN 16.26.

563 This refers to the fourth jhāna, which is the foundation for the three knowledges to follow.

564 At this point he ceases to be a *sekha* and becomes an arahant.

565 These constitute the traditional list of fifteen factors making up conduct (*caraṇa*), which are often conjoined with the three following types of knowledge in the complete course of training. The two together enter into the common epithet of the Buddha and the arahants, *vijjācaraṇasampanna*, "perfect in true knowledge and conduct." See Vsm VII, 30–31.

566 The verse was approved by the Buddha at DN 3.1.28/i.99. The Brahmā Sanankumāra, "Forever Young," according to MA was a youth who attained jhāna, passed away, and was reborn in the Brahma-world, retaining the same handsome form he possessed in his existence in the human world. See DN 18.17–29/ii.210–218.

SUTTA 54

567 Translated literally the Pali reads simply "no rapacious greed." Since, in the English idiom, it is difficult to see how the mere absence of an evil can serve as a support, I have added the phrase "refraining from" here and in the next two cases, which are also expressed as simple negatives in the Pali.

568 MA: Although the killing of living beings is not included among the ten fetters and five hindrances, it may be called a fetter in the sense of binding one to the round of rebirths and a hindrance in the sense of obstructing one's true welfare.

569 MA: Killing and taking what is not given are to be abandoned by bodily virtue; false speech and malicious speech, by verbal virtue; rapacious greed, angry despair, and arrogance, by mental virtue. Spiteful scolding (which can include violent reprisals) is to be abandoned by both bodily and verbal virtue.

570 These similes for the dangers in sensual pleasures are alluded to at MN 22.3, though this sutta does not elaborate on the last three similes mentioned there.

571 According to MA, the "equanimity that is based on diversity" is equanimity (i.e., apathy, indifference) related to the five cords of sensual pleasure; the "equanimity that is based on unity" is the equanimity of the fourth jhāna.

572 In Ms, Ñm had followed the gloss of MA in rendering *ājānīya* as "those who know" (taking the word as derived from *ājānāti*); it seems far preferable, however, to understand the word here as "thoroughbred." See MN 65.32 for *assājānīya*, "thoroughbred colt," and for *purisājānīya*, "thoroughbred man" (i.e., an arahant), see AN 9:10/v, 324.

SUTTA 55

573 Jīvaka was the abandoned child of a courtesan. Discovered and raised by Prince Abhaya, he studied medicine at Takkasilā and was later appointed the personal

physician of the Buddha. He became a stream-enterer after hearing the Buddha teach the Dhamma.

574 This passage states clearly and explicitly the regulations on meat-eating laid down by the Buddha for the Sangha. It will be noted that the Buddha does not require the bhikkhus to observe a vegetarian diet, but permits them to consume meat when they are confident that the animal has not been slaughtered especially to provide them with food. Such meat is called *tikoṭiparisuddha,* "pure in three aspects," because it is not seen, heard, or suspected to come from an animal killed specifically for the bhikkhu. The lay Buddhist's precept of abstaining from the taking of life would prohibit him from killing for his food, but does not proscribe purchasing meat prepared from animals already dead. For more on this issue see Vin Mv Kh 6/i.237–38, and I.B. Horner, *Early Buddhism and the Taking of Life,* pp. 20–26.

575 Here the Buddha shows that he does not merely abide in loving-kindness by suppressing his ill will with jhāna based on loving-kindness, as the divinity Brahmā does, but has eradicated the roots of ill will through his attainment of arahantship.

576 Cruelty, discontent, and aversion (*vihesā, arati, paṭigha*) are the opposites of compassion, altruistic joy, and equanimity respectively.

577 It is puzzling that Jīvaka here declares himself a lay follower as if for the first time when he had already been established in stream-entry. Perhaps this formula was used as a means of reaffirming one's dedication to the Triple Gem and was not restricted to an initial profession of going for refuge.

SUTTA 56

578 This means "Tall Ascetic," a name given to him because of his height.

579 *Daṇḍa,* originally a stick or staff, acquires the meaning of rod as an instrument of punishment, and subsequently comes to mean punishment or infliction itself, even without reference to an instrument. Its use here suggests that

the Jains regarded bodily, verbal, and mental activity as instruments by which the individual torments himself by prolonging his bondage in saṁsāra and torments others by causing them harm.

580 MA: The Nigaṇṭhas held that the first two "rods" create kamma independently of the involvement of the mind (*acittaka*) just as, when the wind blows, the branches sway and the leaves rustle without any initiative of mind.

581 The Buddha may have said this because in his teaching volition (*cetanā*), a mental factor, is the essential ingredient of kamma, and in its absence—that is, in the case of unintentional bodily or verbal activity—no kamma is created. MA, however, maintains that the Buddha said this referring to wrong view with fixed consequences (*niyatā micchā diṭṭhi*), and it quotes in support AN 1:18.3/i.33: "Bhikkhus, I see nothing so blameworthy as wrong view. Wrong view is the most blameworthy of all things." These types of wrong view are described at MN 60.5, 13 and 21.

582 As at MN 35.5.

583 The parenthetical additions in the previous paragraph, inserted by Ñm, are supplied from MA. Ñm, in Ms, sums up the argument thus: The Nigaṇṭhas are not allowed to use cold water (because they regard it as containing living beings). By his bodily and verbal refusal of cold water he has kept his bodily and verbal conduct pure, but if he longs in his mind for cold water his mental conduct is impure, and thus he is reborn among the "mind-bound gods" (*manosattā devā*).

584 At §15 Upāli admits that at this point he had already acquired confidence in the Buddha. However, he continued to oppose him because he wished to hear the Buddha's varied solutions to the problem.

585 This statement, at DN 2.29/i.57, is ascribed to the Nigaṇṭha Nātaputta himself as a formulation of the Jain doctrine. Ñm points out in Ms that it may involve a pun on the word *vāri*, which can mean both "water" and "curb" (from *vāreti*, to ward off). In my translation of the *Sāmaññaphala Sutta, The Discourse on the Fruits of Recluseship*, p. 24, I render it based on the Dīgha commentary as

follows: "A Nigaṇṭha is restrained with regard to all water; he is endowed with the avoidance of all evil; he is cleansed by the avoidance of all evil; he is suffused with the avoidance of all evil." Though the statement conveys a concern for moral purity, the tone is decidedly different from that of the Buddha's teachings.

586 The Buddha points to a contradiction between the Jain thesis that, even in the absence of volition, the "bodily rod" is the most reprehensible of all, and their assertion that the presence of volition significantly alters the moral character of an action.

587 See Jāt iii.463, v.133ff., 267; v.144; vi.389, v.267; v.114, 267; Miln 130.

588 MA: Vision of the Dhamma (*dhammacakkhu*) is the path of stream-entry. The phrase "All that is subject to arising is subject to cessation" shows the mode in which the path arises. The path takes cessation (Nibbāna) as its object, but its function is to penetrate all conditioned states as subject to arising and cessation.

589 The "Dhamma" referred to here is the Four Noble Truths. Having seen these truths for himself, he has cut off the fetter of doubt and now possesses the "view that is noble and emancipating and (which) leads the one who practises in accordance with it to the complete destruction of suffering" (MN 48.7).

590 MA: Upāli says this referring to the path of stream-entry he had penetrated earlier.

591 See MN 16.3–7.

592 PTS and SBJ read *vessantarassa*; the BBS ed. of text and MA read *vesamantarassa*; MṬ supports the former reading. MA explains: "He has transcended the unrighteous state (*visama*) of lust, etc."

593 *Monapattassa*. The "silence" is wisdom, related to *muni*, silent sage.

594 The "banner" is the conceit "I am." See MN 22.35.

595 *Nippapañcassa*. See n.229.

596 *Isisattamassa*. MA interprets this to mean "the seventh seer"—in line with the brahmanic conception of the seven rishis—and takes it as referring to Gotama's status as the seventh Buddha since Vipassī (see DN 14.1.4/ii.2).

It is more probable, however, that *sattama* here is the superlative of *sad*, and thus that the compound means "the best of seers." The expression *isisattama* occurs at Sn 356, and the commentary to that verse allows both interpretations, offering *uttama* as a gloss on *sattama*.

597 This refers to the absence of attachment and repulsion.

598 Ñm translates from a Siamese v.l. *appabhītassa*, pointing out that PTS's *appahīnassa* does not make good sense here.

599 MA: A heavy sorrow arose in him because of the loss of his lay supporter, and this produced a bodily disorder that resulted in his vomiting hot blood. After vomiting hot blood, few beings can survive. Thus they brought him to Pāvā on a litter, and shortly thereafter he passed away.

SUTTA 57

600 MA: Puṇṇa wore horns on his head, tied a tail to his backside, and went about eating grass together with the cows. Seniya performed all the actions typical of a dog.

601 It should be noted that a wrong ascetic practice has less severe consequences when it is undertaken without wrong view than when it is accompanied by wrong view. Although few nowadays will take up the dog-duty practice, many other deviant lifestyles have become widespread, and to the extent that these are justified by a wrong view, their consequences become that much more harmful.

602 *Sabyābajjhaṁ kāyasankhāraṁ* (*vacīsankhāraṁ, manosankhāraṁ*) *abhisankharoti*. Here an "afflictive bodily formation" may be understood as the volition responsible for the three courses of unwholesome bodily action; an "afflictive verbal formation" as the volition responsible for the four courses of unwholesome verbal action; and an "afflictive mental formation" as the volition responsible for the three courses of unwholesome mental action. See MN 9.4.

603 He is reborn in one of the states of deprivation—hell, the animal kingdom, or the realm of ghosts.

604 *Bhūtā bhūtassa upapatti hoti*. MA: Beings are reborn through the actions they perform and in ways conforming to

those actions. The implications of this thesis are explored more fully in MN 135 and MN 136.

605 Here the volitions responsible for the ten courses of wholesome action, together with the volitions of the jhānas, are intended.

606 He is reborn in a heavenly world.

607 Strictly speaking, no volitional action can be simultaneously both wholesome and unwholesome, for the volition responsible for the action must be either one or the other. Thus here we should understand that the being engages in a medley of wholesome and unwholesome actions, none of which is particularly dominant.

608 MA: This is the volition of the four supramundane paths culminating in arahantship. Although the arahant performs deeds, his deeds no longer have any kammic potency to generate new existence or to bring forth results even in the present existence.

609 MA explains that *pabbajjā*, the going forth, is mentioned here only in a loose figure of speech. In actual fact, he receives the going forth before the probationary period and then lives on probation for four months before being entitled to receive *upasampadā*, full admission to the Sangha.

610 MA: The Buddha can decide: "This person must live on probation, this one need not live on probation."

SUTTA 58

611 Prince Abhaya was a son of King Bimbisāra of Magadha, though not the heir to the throne.

612 Both horns of the dilemma devised by the Nigaṇṭha Nātaputta presupposed that the Buddha would give a one-sided answer. Now that a one-sided answer has been rejected, the dilemma becomes inapplicable.

613 The Buddha does not hesitate to rebuke and admonish his disciples when he sees that such speech will promote their welfare.

614 MA says that *dhammadhātu* ("element of things") refers to the Buddha's knowledge of omniscience. *Dhammadhātu* here should not be confused with the same term

used to signify the element of mind-objects among the eighteen elements, nor does it bear the meaning of an all-embracing cosmic principle that the term acquires in Mahāyāna Buddhism.

SUTTA 59

615 Pañcakanga, the carpenter for King Pasenadi of Kosala, was a devoted follower of the Buddha. He reappears in MN 78 and MN 127.

616 The *two kinds* of feeling are bodily and mental feeling, or (less commonly) the two mentioned by Pañcakanga in §3. The *three kinds* are the three mentioned by Udāyin in §3. The *five kinds* are the faculties of (bodily) pleasure, (mental) joy, (bodily) pain, (mental) grief, and equanimity. The *six kinds* are the feelings born of contact through the six sense faculties. The *eighteen kinds* are the eighteen kinds of mental exploration—exploring the six sense objects that are productive of joy, productive of grief, and productive of equanimity (see MN 137.8). The *thirty-six kinds* are the thirty-six positions of beings—the six kinds of joy, grief, and equanimity each based either on the household life or on renunciation (see MN 137.9–15). The *hundred and eight kinds* are the previous thirty-six considered as referring to the past, present, and future.

617 MA points out that by speaking of the neither-painful-nor-pleasant feeling of the fourth jhāna as a kind of pleasure, the Buddha is implicitly endorsing the view put forth by Pañcakanga.

618 MA: Both felt pleasure and unfelt pleasure are found (the latter being the pleasure pertaining to the attainment of cessation). The Tathāgata describes both as pleasure in the sense that they are without suffering (*niddukkhabhāva*).

SUTTA 60

619 MA: The Buddha began by asking this question because the village of Sālā was situated at the entrance to a forest, and many recluses and brahmins of diverse creeds would stay there overnight, expounding their own views

and tearing down the views of their opponents. This left the villagers perplexed, unable to commit themselves to a particular teaching.

620 *Apaṇṇakadhamma.* MA explains this as a teaching that is uncontradictable, free from ambiguity, definitely acceptable (*aviraddho advejjhagāmī ekaṁsagāhiko*). The term also occurs at AN 3:16/i.113 and AN 4:71/ii.76.

621 The three views discussed in §§5, 13 and 21 are called wrong views with fixed evil result (*niyatā micchā diṭṭhi*). To adhere to them with firm conviction closes off the prospect of a heavenly rebirth and the attainment of liberation. For a fuller discussion see Bodhi, *Discourse on the Fruits of Recluseship*, pp. 79–83.

The examination of these views unfolds according to the following pattern: The Buddha discloses the wrong view A and its antithesis B. Taking up A for examination first, in A.i he shows the pernicious effect of this view on bodily, verbal, and mental conduct. In A.ii he proceeds from the judgement that the view is actually wrong and elicits additional negative consequences of its adoption. Then in A.iii he shows how a wise person comes to the conclusion that whether or not the view is true, it serves his best interest to reject it.

Next, position B is considered. In B.i the Buddha describes the wholesome influence of this view on conduct. In B.ii he elicits additional positive consequences of adopting such a view. And in B.iii he shows how a wise person comes to the conclusion that, irrespective of its actual veracity, it serves his best interest to conduct his affairs as though the view is true.

622 See n.425 for clarification of several expressions used in the formulation of this view.

623 The Pali terms are *susīlya* and *dusīlya*. Since "corrupt virtue" sounds self-contradictory, "conduct" has been used in my rendering of the latter expression. Ñm had used "unvirtuousness."

624 He has made himself safe (*sotthi*) in the sense that he will not be subject to suffering in a future existence. However, he is still liable to the types of suffering to be encountered in this existence, which the Buddha is about to mention.

625 *Natthikavāda*, lit. "the doctrine of non-existence," is so called because it denies the existence of an afterlife and of kammic retribution.

626 His undertaking of the incontrovertible teaching "extends only to one side" in the sense that he makes himself safe with regard to the next life only on the presupposition that there is no afterlife, while if there is an afterlife he loses on both counts.

627 *Atthikavāda*: the affirmation of the existence of an afterlife and of kammic retribution.

628 His undertaking "extends to both sides" since he reaps the benefits of his view affirming the afterlife whether or not an afterlife actually exists.

629 This doctrine of non-doing (*akiriyavāda*), in the *Sāmaññaphala Sutta* (DN 2.17/i.52–53), is attributed to Pūraṇa Kassapa. Although on first encounter the view seems to rest on materialist premises, as the previous nihilistic view does, there is canonical evidence that Pūraṇa Kassapa subscribed to a fatalistic doctrine. Thus his moral antinomianism probably follows from the view that all action is predestined in ways that abrogate the ascription of moral responsibility to its agent. See Basham, *History and Doctrines of the Ājīvikas*, p. 84.

630 This is the doctrine of non-causality (*ahetukavāda*) maintained by the Ājīvaka leader Makkhali Gosāla, called in the *Sāmaññaphala Sutta* the doctrine of purification by saṁsāra (*saṁsārasuddhi*, DN 2.21/i.54). The philosophy of Makkhali Gosāla has been examined in detail by Basham, *History and Doctrines of the Ājīvikas*, Chapters 12 and 13. A translation of the Dīgha commentary on this doctrine will be found in Bodhi, *Discourse on the Fruits of Recluseship*, pp. 70–77.

631 *Niyati*, destiny or fate, is the primary explanatory principle in Makkhali's philosophy, "circumstance and nature" (*sangatibhāva*) seem to be its modes of operation in external events and in the constitution of the individual, respectively. The six classes (*abhijāti*) are six gradations of human beings according to their level of spiritual development, the highest being reserved for the three mentors of the Ājīvakas mentioned at MN 36.5. On the

six classes, see Bodhi, *Discourse on the Fruits of Recluseship*, pp. 73–75. Also, AN 6:57/iii.383–84.

632 This is a denial of the four immaterial planes of existence, the objective counterparts of the four immaterial meditative attainments.

633 These are the gods of the planes corresponding to the four jhānas. They possess bodies of subtle matter, unlike the gods of the immaterial planes who consist entirely of mind without any admixture of matter.

634 MA: Even though the wise man discussed here has doubts about the existence of the immaterial planes, he attains the fourth jhāna, and on the basis of that he attempts to attain the immaterial absorptions. If he fails he is certain of rebirth in the fine-material planes, but if he succeeds he will be reborn in the immaterial planes. Thus for him this wager is an "incontrovertible teaching."

635 MA: Cessation of being (*bhavanirodha*) here is Nibbāna.

636 MA: Even though this person has doubts about the existence of Nibbāna, he attains the eight meditative attainments, and then, using one of those attainments as a basis, he develops insight, thinking: "If there is cessation, then I will reach arahantship and attain Nibbāna." If he fails he is certain of rebirth in the immaterial planes, but if he succeeds he reaches arahantship and attains Nibbāna.

SUTTA 61

637 Rāhula was the only son of the Buddha, born on the day his father left the palace to seek enlightenment. At the age of seven he was ordained as a novice by Ven. Sāriputta on the occasion of the Buddha's first return visit to Kapilavatthu after his enlightenment. The Buddha declared him the foremost disciple among those desirous of training. According to MA, this discourse was taught to Rāhula when he was seven years old, thus very shortly after his ordination. At MN 147 he attains arahantship after listening to a discourse by the Buddha on the development of insight.

638 To acknowledge a wrong deed as such, confess it, and

undertake restraint for the future leads to growth in the discipline of the Noble One. See MN 65.13.

639 In this section, however, the phrase "then you should confess such a bodily action...and laid it open" is replaced by the following: "Then you should be repelled, humiliated, and disgusted by that mental action. Having become repelled, humiliated, and disgusted by that mental action..." This substitution is made because unwholesome thoughts, unlike bodily and verbal transgressions, do not require confession as a means of exoneration. Both Horner in MLS and Ñm in Ms missed this variation.

SUTTA 62

640 According to MA, this discourse was taught to Rāhula when he was eighteen years old, for the purpose of dispelling desire connected with the household life. The Shorter Discourse of Advice to Rāhula is MN 147.

641 MA: While Rāhula was following the Buddha, he noted with admiration the physical perfection of the Master and reflected that he himself was of similar appearance, thinking: "I too am handsome like my father the Blessed One. The Buddha's form is beautiful and so too is mine." The Buddha read Rāhula's thought and decided to admonish him at once, before such vain thoughts led him into greater difficulties. Hence the Buddha framed his advice in terms of contemplating the body as neither a self nor the possession of a self.

642 MA: Ven. Sāriputta, Rāhula's teacher, gave Rāhula this advice unaware that he had already been given different meditation instructions by the Buddha. He was misled by Rāhula's cross-legged posture into thinking that he was practising mindfulness of breathing.

643 MA: The Buddha here explains the meditation on the four great elements rather than mindfulness of breathing in order to dispel Rāhula's attachment to the body, which had not yet been removed by the brief instruction on the egolessness of material form. See n.329 for explanation of terms requiring comment.

644 Space (*ākāsa*) is not a primary material element but is classified under derivative material form (*upādā rūpa*).

645 MA: This passage (§13–17) is taught to show the quality of impartiality (*tādibhāva*).

646 For explanations of unclear terms in this first tetrad on mindfulness of breathing (§26), see nn.140–142. Terms needing clarification in the following three tetrads will be explained in the notes to MN 118, the *Ānāpānasati Sutta*.

647 That is, the meditator dies calmly, with mindfulness and awareness.

SUTTA 63

648 Those who have always wondered about the fate of the monk who almost left the Buddha to satisfy his metaphysical curiosity will be gladdened to know that in his old age Mālunkyāputta received a brief discourse on the six sense bases from the Buddha, went off into solitary meditation, and attained arahantship. See SN 35:95/ iv.72–76. His verses are at Thag 399–404 and 794–817.

SUTTA 64

649 The five lower fetters (*orambhāgiyāni saṁyojanāni*) are so called because they lead to rebirth in the sense-sphere planes. They are eradicated in their entirety only by the non-returner.

650 MA: The question may be raised: "When the Buddha had asked about the fetters and the Elder replied in terms of the fetters, why does the Buddha criticise his reply?" The reason is that Mālunkyāputta held the view that a person is fettered by the defilements only at times when they assail him, while at other times he is not fettered by them. The Buddha spoke as he did to show the error in this view.

651 *Anuseti tvev'assa sakkāyadiṭṭhānusayo.* On the *anusayas* or underlying tendencies, see n.473. In the commentaries the defilements are distinguished as occurring at three levels: the *anusaya* level, where they remain as mere latent dispositions in the mind; the *pariyuṭṭhāna* level,

where they rise up to obsess and enslave the mind (referred to in §5 of this discourse); and the *vītikkama* level, where they motivate unwholesome bodily and verbal action. The point of the Buddha's criticism is that the fetters, even when they do not come to active manifestation, continue to exist at the *anusaya* level so long as they have not been eradicated by the supramundane path.

652 *Dhammā*. This could also have been rendered "things."

653 MA: The fetter and the underlying tendency are in principle not distinct things; rather, it is the same defilement that is called a fetter in the sense of binding, and an underlying tendency in the sense of being unabandoned.

654 *Upadhivivekā*. MA glosses *upadhi* here as the five cords of sensual pleasure. Though the first three clauses of this statement seem to express the same ideas as the two more usual clauses that follow, MṬ indicates that they are intended to show the *means* for becoming "quite secluded from sensual pleasures, secluded from unwholesome states."

655 This passage shows the development of insight (*vipassanā*) upon a basis of serenity (*samatha*), using the jhāna on which the practice of insight is based as the object of insight contemplation. See MN 52.4 and n.552. Here two terms—impermanent and disintegrating—show the characteristic of impermanence; three terms—alien, void, and not self—show the characteristic of non-self; the remaining six terms show the characteristic of suffering.

656 MA: He "turns his mind away" from the five aggregates included within the jhāna, which he has seen to be stamped with the three characteristics. The "deathless element" (*amatā dhātu*) is Nibbāna. First "he directs his mind to it" with the insight consciousness, having heard it praised and described as "the peaceful and sublime," etc. Then, with the supramundane path, "he directs his mind to it" by making it an object and penetrating it as the peaceful and sublime, etc.

657 See n.553.

658 It should be noted that, when the immaterial attainments are made the basis for insight contemplation, the aggregate of material form is not included among the objects

of insight. Thus only the four immaterial aggregates are mentioned here.

659 MA: Among those who proceed by way of serenity, one bhikkhu emphasises unification of mind—he is said to gain deliverance of mind; another emphasises wisdom—he is said to gain deliverance by wisdom. Among those who proceed by way of insight, one emphasises wisdom—he is said to gain deliverance by wisdom; another emphasises unification of mind—he is said to gain deliverance of mind. The two chief disciples attained arahantship by emphasising both serenity and insight, but Ven. Sāriputta became one who gained deliverance by wisdom and Ven. Mahā Moggallāna became one who gained deliverance of mind. Thus the reason (for the different designations) is the difference in their faculties, i.e., between the predominance of the concentration faculty and of the wisdom faculty.

SUTTA 65

660 This refers to the Buddha's practice of eating a single meal in the forenoon only. According to the Pātimokkha, the bhikkhus are prohibited from eating from noon until the following dawn, though the single-session practice is only recommended but not required.

661 MA: He would be worried and anxious whether he could live the holy life for his entire life.

662 His anxiety persisted because he would still have to finish his meal of the remains by noon.

663 This is the rule prohibiting eating outside the proper time limits. See Vin Pāc 37/iv.35.

664 The seven terms used in this section represent a sevenfold classification of noble individuals. They are explicated at MN 70.14–21.

665 Both Ñm and Horner take *sankameyya* here to mean that the bhikkhu makes himself a plank, i.e., lies down across the mud. This, however, is contradicted by Bhaddāli's negative answer. Thus it would seem more correct to take this verb to mean that he crosses over himself (as the verb literally does mean), in disregard of the Buddha's

injunction. MA points out that the Buddha would never give such a command to his disciples, but only says this to emphasise the recalcitrant behaviour of Bhaddāli.

666 MA: He maintains himself by a measure of worldly faith and worldly love towards his preceptor and teacher. Because the other bhikkhus help him, he remains in the homeless life and may eventually become a great monk who has attained to the direct knowledges.

667 This passage refers to the fixed principle that the Buddha does not lay down a training rule until a case arises that requires the promulgation of an appropriate training rule. See Vin Pār 1/iii.9–10.

668 *Tasmiṁ ṭhāne parinibbāyati.* The verb used here is the verbal form of *parinibbāna,* and could be literally, though erroneously, translated, "He attains final Nibbāna in that action."

669 "One beyond training" (*asekha*) is an arahant. MA explains these ten factors as constituents of the fruit of arahantship.

670 Right knowledge (*sammā ñāṇa*) is the knowledge pertaining to the fruit of arahantship, right deliverance (*sammā vimutti*) the arahant's liberation from all defilements.

SUTTA 66

671 From this passage and that to follow, it appears that the Buddha restricted the allowable time for bhikkhus' meals in two successive stages, first prohibiting only the afternoon meal and allowing a night meal. However, in the Vinaya account of the origin of Pāc 37 (Vin iv.85) no mention is made of this successive prohibition. To the contrary, the text seems to assume it to be an item of common knowledge that monks should not consume food past noon, and it shows the Buddha laying down the rule against untimely eating with one categorical pronouncement valid for all meals past noon.

672 The utterance is in what appears to be very colloquial Pali. MA explains: If one's mother and father were alive, they would give their son various kinds of food and offer him a place to sleep, and thus he would not have to wander about for food at night.

673 MA: The Buddha undertakes this teaching in order to

analyse the person who abandons what he is told to abandon (§9) into four distinct types of individuals.

674 *Upadhi.* MA glosses: For the abandoning of four kinds of *upadhi*—the aggregates, defilements, volitional formations, and cords of sensual pleasure (*khandh'upadhi kiles'upadhi abhisankhār'upadhi kāmaguṇ'upadhi*).

675 MA: The ordinary man, the stream-enterer, the once-returner, and the non-returner can all be included under the first category (§14), the non-returner because the craving for being still exists in him and thus at times he can delight in thoughts of worldly enjoyment. The same four can be included in the second category (§15), the ordinary man because he may suppress arisen defilements, arouse energy, develop insight, and eradicate defilements by attaining the supramundane path.

676 This type is distinguished from the previous type only by his sluggishness in arousing mindfulness to abandon arisen defilements.

677 This is the arahant, who alone has eradicated all the fetters.

678 Here I have departed from Ñm in rendering *sukha* as "bliss" rather than "pleasure" in order to avoid the awkward-sounding phrases that would result from strict consistency. MA explains the jhānas as *nekkhammasukha* because they yield the bliss of renouncing sensual pleasures; as *pavivekasukha* because they yield the bliss of being secluded from the crowd and from defilements; as *upasamasukha* because their bliss is for the purpose of quieting down the defilements; and as *sambodhasukha* because their bliss is for the purpose of attaining enlightenment. The jhānas themselves, of course, are not states of enlightenment.

679 All states of mind below the fourth jhāna are classified as "the perturbable" (*iñjita*). The fourth jhāna and all higher states are called "the imperturbable" (*aniñjita*). See n.1000.

680 MA: It is not fitting to become attached to it with craving, and one should not come to a standstill at this point.

681 The cessation of perception and feeling is not simply one more higher attainment along the scale of concentration, but here implies the full development of insight brought to its climax in arahantship.

SUTTA 67

682 *Kevaṭṭā maññe macchavilope.* MA gives two explanations: one favours this rendering, the other suggests "fisherman hauling in fish."

683 It was the Brahmā Sahampati who entreated the newly enlightened Buddha to teach the Dhamma to the world. See MN 26.20.

684 MA: In this case Ven. Sāriputta erred in not recognising his responsibility, for the Sangha is the responsibility of the two great elders. Thus the Buddha rebuked him but commended Ven. Moggallāna, who recognised his responsibility.

685 MA: The Buddha undertook this teaching to show that there are four fears (or dangers, *bhaya*) in his Dispensation. Those who can overcome these four fears will become established in the Dispensation, the others will not become established.

686 Pali uses two distinct words signifying different types of food: *khādaniya*, "food to be consumed," includes all varieties of vegetables, nuts, fruits, yams, etc.; *bhojanīya*, "food to be eaten," includes food made of grain, meat, and fish. Things to be tasted (*sāyitabba*) would include light refreshments.

687 The proper time is from dawn to noon, beyond which only liquids may be drunk.

SUTTA 68

688 The "rapture and pleasure secluded from sensual pleasures" signifies the first and second jhānas, "something more peaceful than that" the higher jhānas and the four paths.

689 See MN 2.4. These are practices undertaken by one in training to prevent the arising of latent taints that have not yet been abandoned.

690 This refers to the Buddha's ability to discover by clairvoyance the states in which his disciples have taken rebirth.

691 *Aññā*: the knowledge attained by the arahant. It should

be noted that whereas the declarations of attainment made by monks and nuns begin with arahantship, those for men and women lay followers begin with non-returning (in §18, §21). Though early Buddhism recognises the possibility of lay persons attaining arahantship, in all such cases attested to in the Nikāyas, they do so either when on the verge of death or just before requesting admission into the Sangha.

SUTTA 69

692 This is prohibited by Pāc 46 (Vin iv.98–101). A bhikkhu may visit families at these times only if he has informed another bhikkhu in the monastery of his intentions, except during the season for making and giving robes.

693 *Abhidhamma abhivinaya.* MA says that he should apply himself to learning the text and commentary to the Abhidhamma Piṭaka and the Vinaya Piṭaka. This is clearly anachronistic. On Abhidhamma in the context of the suttas, see n.362. Although there is no corresponding body of literature called "Abhivinaya," it seems probable the word refers to a systematic and analytical approach to the study of the Vinaya, perhaps that embedded in the Suttavibhanga of the Vinaya Piṭaka.

694 MA: This refers to the eight meditative attainments. As a minimum he should become proficient in the preliminary work of one meditation subject, such as a kasiṇa.

695 MA: This refers to all the supramundane states. As a minimum he should become proficient in one approach to developing insight up to arahantship.

SUTTA 70

696 See n.671. In agreement with MN 66.6, MA explains that the Buddha had first prohibited the afternoon meal and then at a later time prohibited the night meal. He did this out of concern for the delicate bhikkhus in the Order, since they might have become fatigued too quickly if both late meals were prohibited simultaneously.

697 In the Vinaya Piṭaka, Assaji and Punabbasuka are

described as "unscrupulous and depraved" monks and are shown indulging in various kinds of bad conduct that corrupt the laity. At Kiṭāgiri an act of banishment was pronounced against them, and their refusal to obey led to the promulgation of Sanghādisesa 13 (Vin iii.179–84).

698 MA: This statement is made with pointed reference to pleasure experienced in eating a night meal, which does not conduce to the practice of a monk's duties.

699 MA: The former type of pleasant feeling is the joy based on the household life, the latter the joy based on renunciation. Similarly, the next two sentences refer to the grief and equanimity based, respectively, on the household life and on renunciation. See MN 137.9–15.

700 §§8–10 serve to provide, by appeal to the Buddha's perfect understanding, the grounds for his injunction to abandon all feelings based on the household life and to develop the feelings based on renunciation.

701 Here follows a sevenfold classification of noble individuals which categorises them not merely on the basis of their path and fruit attainment—as the more familiar eightfold scheme does—but according to their dominant faculty. Alternative definitions of these seven are offered by Pug 1:30–36/14–15.

702 *Ubhatobhāgavimutta*. MA: He is "liberated-in-both-ways" because he is liberated from the physical body by the immaterial attainments and from the mental body by the path (of arahantship). The Pug definition reads: "He contacts with the body and abides in the eight liberations, and his taints are destroyed by his seeing with wisdom." MA says that the *ubhatobhāgavimutta* includes those who attain arahantship after emerging from one or another of the four immaterial attainments and the one who attains it after emerging from the attainment of cessation.

703 *Paññāvimutta*. MA: This includes those who attain arahantship either as dry-insight meditators (*sukkha-vipassaka*) or after emerging from one or another of the four jhānas. The Pug definition merely substitutes the eight liberations for "those liberations…transcending forms."

704 *Kāyasakkhin*. MA: This type includes the six individuals—

from the one established in the fruit of stream-entry up to the one on the path of arahantship—who first contact the (immaterial) jhānas and subsequently realise Nibbāna. MṬ stresses that one or another of the immaterial attainments including cessation is needed to qualify as *kāyasakkhin*. The Pug definition merely substitutes the eight liberations.

705 *Diṭṭhipatta*. MA says that this type includes the same six individuals included under *kayasakkhin*—from the stream-enterer to the one on the path of arahantship—but without possession of the immaterial attainments. Pug defines him as one who has understood the Four Noble Truths and who has reviewed and examined with wisdom the teachings proclaimed by the Tathāgata.

706 *Saddhāvimutta*. MA says that this type too includes the same six. Pug defines him in the same way as it defines the *diṭṭhipatta*, but adds that he has not reviewed and examined the teachings with wisdom to the same extent that the *diṭṭhipatta* has.

707 MA says that this type, the *dhammānusārin*, and the next, the *saddhānusārin*, are individuals on the path of stream-entry, the former with predominance of wisdom, the latter with predominance of faith. For more on these two types, see n.273.

708 MA: With the mental body he realises Nibbāna, the ultimate truth, and he penetrates it with the wisdom pertaining to the supramundane path.

709 That is, these bhikkhus have not had the faith required to undertake the training laid down for them by the Buddha.

710 MA says that the "four-phrased statement" (*catuppadaṁ veyyākaraṇaṁ*) is the teaching of the Four Noble Truths. However, no mention is made here of the four truths. Possibly, the four-phrased statement is the resolution on effort just below, with each clause counting as a phrase (the conditional clause being taken as two phrases).

711 MA: By this the Buddha shows that the ideal disciple practises by arousing his energy and resolving: "I shall not rise up so long as I have not attained arahantship."

SUTTA 71

712 This sutta and the following two seem to present a chronological account of Vacchagotta's spiritual evolution. The Saṁyutta Nikāya contains a whole section of short discussions between the Buddha and Vacchagotta, SN 33/iii.257–62. See also SN 44:7–11/iv.391–402.

713 This is the type of omniscience that the Jain teacher the Nigaṇṭha Nātaputta claims at MN 14.17.

714 MA explains that even though part of the statement is valid, the Buddha rejects the entire statement because of the portion that is invalid. The part of the statement that is valid is the assertion that the Buddha is omniscient and all-seeing; the part that is excessive is the assertion that knowledge and vision are continuously present to him. According to the Theravāda exegetical tradition the Buddha is omniscient in the sense that all knowable things are potentially accessible to him. He cannot, however, know everything simultaneously and must advert to whatever he wishes to know. At MN 90.8 the Buddha says that it is possible to know and see all, though not simultaneously, and at AN 4:24/ii.24 he claims to know all that can be seen, heard, sensed, and cognized. This is understood by the Theravāda commentators as an assertion of omniscience in the qualified sense. See too in this connection Miln 102–7.

715 MA explains "the fetter of householdership" (*gihisaṁyojana*) as attachment to the requisites of a householder, which MṬ details as land, ornaments, wealth, grain, etc. MA says that even though the texts mention some individuals who attained arahantship as laymen, by the path of arahantship they destroyed all attachment to worldly things and thus either went forth as monks or passed away immediately after their attainment. The question of lay arahants is discussed at Miln 264.

716 On the Ājīvakas see MN 5.5.

717 Since this Ājīvaka believed in the moral efficacy of action, he could not have subscribed to the orthodox philosophical fatalism of the Ājīvakas, which denied the effective role of kamma and volitional deeds in modifying human

destiny. MA identifies this Ājīvaka with the Bodhisatta in a previous birth.

SUTTA 72

718 The view that the soul (*jīva*) and the body are the same is materialism, which reduces the soul to the body. The following view that the soul and the body are different is an eternalist view, which regards the soul as a persisting spiritual principle that can exist independently of the body.

719 The view that a Tathāgata exists after death is a form of eternalism that regards the Tathāgata, or spiritually perfect individual, as possessing a self that attains eternal deliverance after the death of the body. The view that a Tathāgata does not exist after death also identifies the Tathāgata as self, but holds that this self is annihilated upon the death of the body. The third view attempts a synthesis of these two, which the Buddha rejects because both components involve a wrong view. The fourth view seems to be a sceptical attempt to reject both alternatives or to avoid taking a definite stand.

720 In the Pali a word play is involved between *diṭṭhigata*, "speculative view," which the Tathāgata has put away, and *diṭṭha*, what has been "seen" by the Tathāgata with direct vision, namely, the rise and fall of the five aggregates.

721 MA says that "does not reappear" actually does apply, in the sense that the arahant does not undergo a new existence. But if Vacchagotta were to hear this he would misapprehend it as annihilationism, and thus the Buddha denies that it applies in the sense that annihilation is not a tenable position.

722 MA says this is the material form by which one would describe the Tathāgata as a being (or self) possessing material form. MṬ adds that the material form has been abandoned by the abandonment of the fetters connected with it, and it has thus become incapable of arising again in the future.

723 This passage should be connected with the simile of the extinguished fire. Just as the extinguished fire cannot be described as having gone to any direction, so the

Tathāgata who has attained to final Nibbāna cannot be described in terms of the four alternatives. The simile concerns solely the legitimacy of conceptual and linguistic usage and is not intended to suggest, as some scholars have held, that the Tathāgata attains to some mystical absorption in the Absolute. The words "profound, immeasurable, hard to fathom" point to the transcendental dimension of the liberation attained by the Accomplished One, its inaccessibility to discursive thought.

It seems that at this point in the dialogue, the Buddha resorts to imagery to suggest what concepts cannot convey. The two images—of the extinguished fire and the deep ocean—establish between themselves a dialectical tension, and thus both must be taken into account to avoid falling into one-sided views. The image of the extinguished fire, taken alone, veers in the direction of total extinction, and thus must be balanced by the image of the ocean; the image of the ocean, taken alone, suggests some eternal mode of being, and thus must be balanced by the image of the extinguished fire. Again, the truth lies in the middle that transcends untenable extremes.

SUTTA 73

724 This question and the next refer to arahantship, which (according to MA) Vacchagotta thought may have been an exclusive prerogative of the Buddha.

725 This question refers to the non-returner. Even though a non-returner may remain in the lay life, he necessarily observes celibacy because he has cut off the fetter of sensual desire.

726 This question refers to the stream-enterer and the once-returner, who may still indulge in sensual pleasures if they remain in the lay life.

727 MA: He had attained the fruit of the non-returner and came to ask the Buddha about the practice of insight for attaining the path of arahantship. However, the Buddha saw that he had the supporting conditions for the six

direct knowledges. Thus he taught him serenity for producing the five mundane direct knowledges and insight for reaching arahantship.

728 The suitable basis (*āyatana*) is the fourth jhāna for the five direct knowledges and insight for arahantship.

729 *Paricinṇo me Bhagavā, paricinṇo me Sugato.* This is an indirect way of informing the Buddha of his attainment of arahantship. The bhikkhus did not understand this, and therefore the Buddha interprets its significance for them.

SUTTA 74

730 Dīghanakha was Ven. Sāriputta's nephew. At the time he approached the Buddha, Sāriputta had been a bhikkhu for only two weeks and was still a stream-enterer.

731 MA holds that Dīghanakha is an annihilationist (*ucchedavādin*) and explains this assertion to mean: "No [mode of] rebirth is acceptable to me." However, the text itself does not give any concrete evidence supporting this interpretation. It seems much more likely that Dīghanakha's statement, "Nothing is acceptable to me" (*sabbaṁ me na khamati*), is intended to apply specifically to other philosophical views, and thus shows Dīghanakha to be a radical sceptic of the class satirically characterised at MN 76.30 as "eel-wrigglers". His assertion would then be tantamount to a wholesale repudiation of all philosophical views.

732 This exchange, as interpreted by MA and MṬ, should be understood as follows: The Buddha suggests, by his question, that Dīghanakha's assertion involves an inherent contradiction. For he cannot reject everything without also rejecting his own view, and this would entail the opposite position, namely, that something is acceptable to him. However, though Dīghanakha recognises the implication of the Buddha's question, he continues to insist on his view that nothing is acceptable to him.

733 MA says that the first sentence refers to those who first take up a basic eternalist or annihilationist view and then subsequently adopt secondary variations on that view; the second sentence refers to those who abandon their basic view without adopting an alternative. But if, as

seems plausible, Dīghanakha was a radical sceptic, then the Buddha's statement might be understood to point to an unsatisfactoriness inherent in the sceptic's position: it is psychologically uncomfortable to insist on remaining in the dark. Thus most sceptics, while professing a rejection of all views, surreptitiously adopt some definite view, while a few abandon their scepticism to seek a path to personal knowledge.

734 MA identifies the three views here as eternalism, annihilationism, and partial eternalism. The eternalist view is close to lust (*sārāgāya santike*), etc., because it affirms and delights in existence in however sublimated a form; annihilationism is close to non-lust, etc., because, though involving a wrong conception of self, it leads to disenchantment with existence. If the second view is understood as radical scepticism, it could also be seen as close to non-lust in that it expresses disillusionment with the attempt to buttress the attachment to existence with a theoretical foundation and thus represents a tentative, though mistaken, step in the direction of dispassion.

735 MA: This teaching is undertaken to show Dīghanakha the danger in his view and thereby encourage him to discard it.

736 MA: At this point Dīghanakha has discarded his annihilationist view. Thus the Buddha now undertakes to teach him insight meditation, first by way of the impermanence of the body and then by way of the impermanence of the mental factors under the heading of feeling.

737 MA quotes a verse that says that an arahant may use the words "I" and "mine" without giving rise to conceit or misconceiving them as referring to a self or ego (SN 1:5/i.14). See too DN 9.53/i.202, where the Buddha says of expressions employing the word "self": "These are merely names, expressions, turns of speech, designations in common use in the world, which the Tathāgata uses without misapprehending them."

738 MA: Having reflected on the discourse spoken to his nephew, Ven. Sāriputta developed insight and attained arahantship. Dīghanakha attained the fruit of stream-entry.

739 See nn.588–89.

SUTTA 75

740 *Bhūnahuno*. In Ms, Ñm had rendered this cryptic expression "a wrecker of being." I follow Horner in translating after the commentarial gloss *hatavaḍḍhino mariyādakārakassa*. MA explains that he held the view that "growth" should be accomplished in the six senses by experiencing whatever sense objects one has never experienced before without clinging to those that are already familiar. His view thus seems close to the contemporary attitude that intensity and variety of experience is the ultimate good and should be pursued without inhibitions or restrictions. The reason for his disapproval of the Buddha will become clear in §8.

741 MA glosses the term *nippurisa*, lit. "non-men," as meaning that they were all women. Not only the musicians, but all posts in the palace, including the door-keepers, were filled by women. His father, the king, had provided him with three palaces and the entourage of women in hopes of keeping him confined to the lay life and distracting him from thoughts of renunciation.

742 MA: This is said referring to the attainment of the fruit of arahantship based on the fourth jhāna.

743 The expression *viparītasaññā* alludes to the "perverted perception" (*saññāvipallāsa*) of perceiving pleasure in what is really painful. MṬ says that sensual pleasures are painful because they arouse the painful defilements and because they yield painful fruits in the future. Horner misses the point by translating the line "(they may) receive a change of sensation and think it pleasant" (MLS 2:187).

744 Māgandiya evidently understands the verse in line with the fifty-eighth wrong view of the *Brahmajāla Sutta*: "When this self, furnished and supplied with the five strands of sense pleasures, revels in them—at this point the self attains supreme Nibbāna here and now" (DN 1.3.20/i.36).

745 MA: The full verse had been recited by the previous Buddhas seated in the midst of their fourfold assemblies. The multitude learned it as "a verse concerned with the

good." After the last Buddha passed away, it spread among the wanderers, who were able to preserve only the first two lines in their books.

746 The emphatic *yeva*, "just," implies that he was clinging to material form, feeling, etc., misconceived to be "I," "mine," and "my self." With the arising of vision—a metaphorical expression for the path of stream-entry—identity view is eradicated and he understands the aggregates to be mere empty phenomena devoid of the selfhood that he had earlier imputed to them.

747 "These" refers to the five aggregates.

SUTTA 76

748 *Tiracchānakathā*. Many translators render this expression as "animal talk." However, *tiracchāna* means literally "going horizontally," and though this term is used as a designation for animals, MA explains that in the present context it means talk that goes "horizontally" or "perpendicularly" to the path leading to heaven and liberation.

749 The "four ways that negate the living of the holy life" (*abrahmacariyavāsā*, lit. "ways that are not living the holy life") are teachings that in principle nullify the prospect of attaining the ultimate fruits of spiritual discipline. As the sutta will show, their proponents—inconsistently with their own principles—did observe celibacy and practise austerities. The "four kinds of holy life without consolation" (*anassāsikāni brahmacariyāni*) do not undermine the principles of the holy life, but they fail to offer the prospect of attaining the ultimate fruits of spiritual discipline.

750 The following passage makes explicit the materialist premises of the nihilistic view already set forth at MN 60.7. The *Sāmaññaphala Sutta* ascribes this view to Ajita Kesakambalin (DN 2.23/i.55).

751 The point seems to be that even if one does not live the holy life, one ultimately reaps the same rewards as one who does, as the rest of the passage will make clear.

752 In the *Sāmaññaphala Sutta* the view that follows, as far as "the space between the seven bodies," is ascribed to

Pakudha Kaccāyana (DN 2.26/i.56). However, in that sutta the following passage on the elaborate system of classifications, down to "fools and the wise both will make an end of suffering," is connected with the view of non-causality and follows immediately upon the statement of the doctrine of non-causality set forth in this sutta at §13. The entire view is there assigned to Makkhali Gosāla. Since there are evident connections between the non-causality doctrine and items in the system of classifications (e.g., the reference to the "six classes"), and since both are known to have been typical of the Ājīvaka movement headed by Makkhali Gosāla, it seems that the inclusion of this system of classifications here under the doctrine of the seven bodies came about through an error of oral transmission. The correct version would thus be the one preserved by the Dīgha Nikāya. For the commentary on the system of classification, see Bodhi, *The Discourse on the Fruits of Recluseship*, pp. 72–77.

753 This is the claim made by the Jain teacher the Nigaṇṭha Nātaputta at MN 14.17, and both the latter and Pūraṇa Kassapa at AN 9:38/iv.428–29. The fact that he makes bad judgements and must ask questions belies his claim to omniscience.

754 With BBS and SBJ we should read *sussutaṁ* and *dussutaṁ*. PTS *sussataṁ* and *dussataṁ* are clearly mistaken.

755 MA: This position is called eel-wriggling (*amarāvikkhepa*) because the doctrine roams about here and there, like an eel diving in and out of the water, and thus it is impossible to catch hold of it. In the *Sāmaññaphala Sutta* this position is ascribed to Sañjaya Belaṭṭhiputta (DN 2.32/1.58–59). It is quite possible that the "eel-wrigglers" were a class of radical sceptics who questioned the entire prospect of apodictic knowledge about ultimate issues.

756 MA: He is incapable of storing up food provisions and other pleasurable goods and subsequently enjoying them.

757 At DN 29.26/iii.133 four other things that the arahant cannot do are mentioned: he cannot take a wrong course of action because of desire, hatred, fear, or delusion.

758 The translation of this passage follows SBJ and PTS. The BBS version is more elaborate.

759 *Niyyātāro*: Ñm had rendered this as "guides," Horner as "great leaders." Evidently both followed PED, which takes *niyyātar* to be an agent noun related to *niyyāma(ka)*, pilot or helmsman. But *niyyātar* must be an agent noun of the verb *niyyāti*, "to go out (to final emancipation)," and thus it has been rendered here as "emancipator." This may be the only place in the Nikāyas where this word occurs.

760 On these three mentors of the Ājīvakas, see MN 36.5 and n.383. MA explains the phrase *puttamatāya puttā*, "mother's dead sons," thus: The idea occurred to him, "The Ājīvakas are dead; their mother had dead sons."

SUTTA 77

761 *Anāgataṁ vādapathaṁ*. Ñm had translated: "a future logical consequence of an assertion." The meaning seems to be that the Buddha understands all the unexpressed implications of his own doctrine as well as of his opponents' doctrines. The phrase may also imply that, in such suttas as the *Brahmajāla Sutta*, the Buddha has laid down a critique applicable to any doctrine that might arise in the future course of religio-philosophical thought.

762 Explained in full in MN 10. The first seven groups of "wholesome states" (§§15–21) constitute the thirty-seven aids to enlightenment (*bodhipakkhiyā dhammā*).

763 *Abhiññāvosānapāramippatta*. MA explains as the attainment of arahantship. This may be the only sense that the word *pāramī* bears in the four Nikāyas. In the later Theravāda literature, beginning perhaps with such works as the Buddhavaṁsa, this word comes to signify the perfect virtues that a bodhisatta must fulfil over many lives in order to attain Buddhahood. In that context it corresponds to the *pāramitā* of the Mahāyāna literature, though the numerical lists of virtues overlap only in part.

764 MA explains liberation (*vimokkha*) here as meaning the mind's full (but temporary) release from the opposing states and its full (but temporary) release by delighting in the object. The first liberation is the attainment of the four jhānas using a kasiṇa (see §24 and n.768) derived from a

coloured object in one's own body; the second is the attainment of the jhānas using a kasiṇa derived from an external object; the third can be understood as the attainment of the jhānas through either a very pure and beautiful coloured kasiṇa or the four *brahmavihāras*. The remaining liberations are the immaterial attainments and the attainment of cessation.

765 MA explains that these are called bases of transcendence (*abhibhāyatana*) because they transcend (*abhibhavati*, overcome) the opposing states and the objects, the former through the application of the appropriate antidote, the latter through the arising of knowledge.

766 MA: The meditator does the preliminary work on an internal form—e.g., the blue of the eyes for a blue-kasiṇa, the skin for a yellow kasiṇa, the blood for a red-kasiṇa, the teeth for a white-kasiṇa—but the sign of concentration (*nimitta*) arises externally. The "transcending" of the forms is the attainment of absorption together with the arising of the sign. The perception "I know, I see" is the advertence (*ābhoga*) that occurs after he emerges from the attainment, not within the attainment. The second base of transcendence differs from the first only by the extension of the sign from limited to unlimited dimensions.

767 MA: The third and fourth bases involve preliminary work done on an external form and the arising of the sign externally. The fifth through eighth bases differ from the third and fourth in the superior purity and luminosity of their colours.

768 The *kasiṇa* is a meditation object derived from a physical device that provides a support for acquiring the inwardly visualised sign. Thus, for example, a disk made of clay can be used as the preliminary object for practising the earth-kasiṇa, a bowl of water for practising the water-kasiṇa. The kasiṇas are explained in detail in Vsm IV and V. There, however, the space-kasiṇa is restricted to limited space, and the consciousness-kasiṇa is replaced by the light-kasiṇa.

769 The similes for the jhānas also appear in MN 39, as do the similes for the last three types of knowledge at §§34–36.

770 §§29–36 describe eight varieties of higher knowledge

which, in the *Sāmaññaphala Sutta*, are designated superior fruits of recluseship.

SUTTA 78

771 MA: The park had been built by Queen Mallikā, the wife of King Pasenadi of Kosala, and beautified with flower trees and fruit trees. At first only one hall was built, which accounts for its name, but afterwards many halls were built. Various companies of brahmins and wanderers would assemble here to expound and discuss their doctrines.

772 MA: First the Buddha shows the plane of the arahant, the one beyond training (i.e., by mentioning the ten qualities), then he sets up an outline applicable to the *sekha*, the disciple in higher training. The word rendered as "habits" is *sīla*, which in some contexts can assume a wider range of meaning than "virtue."

773 MA explains that this refers to the fruit of stream-entry, for it is at that point that the virtue of restraint by the Pātimokkha is fulfilled (and, for a lay Buddhist, the observance of the Five Precepts). MA will also explain the subsequent passages by reference to the other supramundane paths and fruits. Although the text of the sutta does not expressly mention these attainments, the commentarial interpretation seems to be justified by the expression "cease without remainder" (*aparisesā nirujjhanti*), for it is only with the attainment of the respective paths and fruits that a total cessation of the particular defilement occurs. The commentary's view is further supported by the culmination of the entire discourse in the figure of the arahant.

774 MA: As far as the path of stream-entry he is said to be practising for their cessation; when he has attained the fruit of stream-entry they are said to have ceased.

775 This passage shows the arahant, who maintains virtuous conduct but no longer identifies with his virtue by conceiving it as "I" and "mine." Since his virtuous habits no longer generate kamma, they are not describable as "wholesome."

776 MA: As far as the path of arahantship he is said to be

practising for their cessation; when he has attained the fruit of arahantship they are said to have ceased.

777 MA: This refers to the first jhāna pertaining to the fruit of non-returning. The path of non-returning eradicates sensual desire and ill will, and thus prevents any future arising of the three unwholesome intentions—those of sensual desire, ill will, and cruelty.

778 MA: As far as the path of non-returning he is said to be practising for their cessation; when he has attained the fruit of non-returning they are said to have ceased.

779 MA: This refers to the second jhāna pertaining to the fruit of arahantship.

780 MA: As far as the path of arahantship he is said to be practising for their cessation; when he has obtained the fruit of arahantship they are said to have ceased. The virtuous intentions of the arahant are not described as "wholesome."

781 See MN 65.34.

SUTTA 79

782 See n.408.

783 *Evaṁvaṇṇo attā hoti arogo paraṁ maraṇā.* The word *arogo,* normally meaning healthy, here should be understood to mean permanent. MA says that he speaks with reference to rebirth in the heavenly world of Refulgent Glory, the objective counterpart of the third jhāna, of which he has heard without actually attaining it. His view would seem to fall into the class described at MN 102.3.

784 Previous translators seem to have been perplexed by the verb *anassāma.* Thus Ñm in Ms renders the line: "We don't renounce our teachers' doctrines for this reason." And Horner: "We have heard to here from our own teachers." But *anassāma* is a first-person plural aorist of *nassati,* "to perish, to be lost." The same form occurs at MN 27.7. MA explains that they knew that in the past meditators would do the preparatory work on the kasiṇa, attain the third jhāna, and be reborn in the world of Refulgent Glory. But as time went on, the preparatory work on the kasiṇa was no longer understood and

meditators were not able to attain the third jhāna. The wanderers only learned that "an entirely pleasant world" exists and that the five qualities mentioned at §21 were the "practical way" to it. They knew of no entirely pleasant world higher than the third jhāna, and of no practical way higher than the five qualities.

785 MA: Having attained the fourth jhāna, by supernormal power he goes to the world of Refulgent Glory and converses with the deities there.

786 MA explains that in a previous life, as a monk during the time of the Buddha Kassapa, he had persuaded another monk to return to lay life in order to gain his robes and bowl, and this obstructive kamma prevented him from going forth under the Buddha in this life. But the Buddha taught him two long suttas to provide him with a condition for future attainment. During the reign of King Asoka he attained arahantship as the Elder Assagutta, who excelled in the practice of loving-kindness.

SUTTA 80

787 MA identifies Vekhanassa as Sakuludāyin's teacher.

788 MA: Even though he was a wanderer, he was keenly intent on sensual pleasures. The Buddha undertook this teaching in order to make him recognise his strong concern with sensual pleasures, and thus the discourse would be beneficial to him.

789 In the Pali this sentence takes the form of a riddle, and the translation here is conjectural. MA explains that the "pleasure higher than the sensual" (or "the highest sensual pleasure," *kāmaggasukhaṁ*) is Nibbāna.

SUTTA 81

790 At the end of this sutta the Buddha will state that at that time he himself was Jotipāla. At SN 1:50/i,35–36 the deity Ghaṭikāra visits the Buddha Gotama and recalls their ancient friendship.

791 This seems to have been a common pejorative expression used by the brahmin householders with reference to

those who led a full-time renunciate life, contrary to their own ideal of maintaining the family lineage.

792 In the East it is considered, under normal circumstances, a serious breach of etiquette for one of lower birth to touch one of superior birth on the head. MA explains that Ghaṭikāra was prepared to risk that breach in order to persuade Jotipāla to meet the Buddha.

793 MA states that bodhisattas go forth under the Buddhas, purify their virtue, learn the Buddha's teachings, practise the meditative life, and develop insight up to conformity knowledge (*anulomañāṇa*). But they do not make effort to attain the paths and fruits (which would terminate their bodhisatta career).

794 His conduct approximates as closely to that of a monk as is possible for one still leading the household life. MA explains that he does not trade in the pottery he makes but merely engages in a free exchange of services with his neighbours.

795 MA explains that he refused because of his fewness of wishes (*appicchatā*). He realised that the king had sent the foodstuffs because he had heard the Buddha's report about his own virtues, but he thought: "I have no need of this. With what I acquire through my work I can support my parents and make offerings to the Buddha."

SUTTA 82

796 Because of his readiness to risk death in order to obtain his parents' permission to go forth, he was later declared by the Buddha the foremost of those gone forth in faith. His verses are at Thag 769–93.

797 I omit here the lines beginning *ehi tvaṁ Raṭṭhapāla*, found in SBJ but given in brackets in PTS and in a note by BBS. The lines seem to fit better into §8 below, with the verb *uṭṭhehi* in place of *ehi*.

798 Although the stock phrase "before long" is used here, MA says that it took Raṭṭhapāla twelve years of striving to attain arahantship. This statement seems correct in view of the fact that on his return journey to his parents' home his father did not immediately recognise him.

799 MA explains that his father meant to say: "Raṭṭhapāla, my dear, there is our wealth—we cannot be called poor—yet you sit in such a place eating old porridge!" However, the householder was afflicted with such sorrow that he was unable to complete his utterance.

800 The verses obviously refer to his former wives, adorned in order to entice him back to the lay life. Strangely, no mention is made of the wives in the portion of the sutta conceived in his pre-ordination days.

801 MA: Recalling the Elder, the king would speak praise of him in the midst of his army or his harem: "That young man has done a difficult thing—having abandoned great wealth, he went forth without turning back or looking aside."

802 *Upanīyati loko addhuvo.* MA: It is swept away towards ageing and death.

803 *Attāṇo loko anabhissaro.* MA: There is no one able to offer it shelter or to console it with a refuge. This statement, of course, does not deny a refuge *from* the world, which is just what the Dhamma offers.

804 *Assako loko sabbaṁ pahāya gamanīyaṁ.*

805 *Ūno loko atitto taṇhādāso.*

SUTTA 83

806 See *Makhādeva Jātaka* (No. 9) and *Nimi Jātaka* (No. 54). King Makhādeva and King Nimi were earlier births of the Buddha Gotama.

807 The grove was originally planted by Makhādeva and thus was still named after him.

808 MA: He was established in the ten wholesome courses of action.

809 The Uposatha is the religious observance day of ancient India, also absorbed as such into Buddhism. See n.59.

810 According to Buddhist cosmology, the lifespan of human beings oscillates between a minimum of ten years and a maximum of many thousands of years. Makhādeva lived at a time when the lifespan was at the long end of the spectrum.

811 On the "divine messengers"—the foretokens of old age, illness, and death—see MN 130.

812 MA: Mātali led him first through the hells, then he turned back and led him through the heavenly world.

813 MA: The good practice is being broken by a virtuous bhikkhu when he thinks, "I cannot obtain arahantship" and does not exert energy. It has been broken by a corrupt bhikkhu. It is being continued by the seven *sekhas*. It has been continued by the arahant.

SUTTA 84

814 See n.230.

815 From this passage it seems that despite a tendency to rigidification, the Indian class system was at the time considerably more elastic than the later caste system that evolved from it.

SUTTA 85

816 Prince Bodhi was the son of King Udena of Kosambī; his mother was the daughter of King Caṇḍappajjota of Avantī. The portion of the sutta from §2 through §8 is also found at Vin Cv Kh 5/ii.127–29, where it leads to the formulation of the rule mentioned in the following note.

817 MA explains that Prince Bodhi was childless and desired a son. He had heard that people can fulfil their wishes by making special offerings to the Buddha, so he spread the white cloth with the idea: "If I am to have a son, the Buddha will step on the cloth; if I am not to have a son, he will not step on the cloth." The Buddha knew that by reason of past evil kamma, he and his wife were destined to remain childless. Hence he did not step on the cloth. Later he laid down a disciplinary rule prohibiting the bhikkhus from stepping on a white cloth, but subsequently modified the rule to allow bhikkhus to step on a cloth as a blessing for householders.

818 *Pacchimaṁ janataṁ Tathāgato apaloketi.* The Vin version here reads *anukampati*, "has compassion," which is preferable. MA explains that Ven. Ānanda said this with the thought in mind: "In later times people will come to regard honour to the bhikkhus as a way of ensuring the

fulfilment of their mundane wishes and will lose faith in the Sangha if their displays of honour do not bring the success they desire."

819 This is the basic tenet of the Jains, as at MN 14.20.

SUTTA 86

820 The name "Angulimāla" is an epithet meaning "garland (*mālā*) of fingers (*anguli*)." He was the son of the brahmin Bhaggava, a chaplain to King Pasenadi of Kosala. His given name was Ahiṁsaka, meaning "harmless one." He studied at Takkasilā, where he became his teacher's favourite. His fellow students, jealous of him, told the teacher that Ahiṁsaka had committed adultery with his wife. The teacher, intent on bringing Ahiṁsaka to ruin, commanded him to bring him a thousand human right-hand fingers as an honorarium. Ahiṁsaka lived in the Jālinī forest, attacking travellers, cutting off a finger of each, and wearing them as a garland around his neck. At the time the sutta opens he was one short of a thousand and had made a determination to kill the next person to come along. The Buddha saw that Angulimāla's mother was on her way to visit him, and aware that Angulimāla had the supporting conditions for arahantship, he intercepted him shortly before his mother was due to arrive.

821 MA explains that Angulimāla had just realised that the monk before him was the Buddha himself and that he had come to the forest for the express purpose of transforming him.

822 MṬ explains the expression *mūḷhagabbha* to mean that the fetus had turned over only partly in the womb and was being expelled horizontally, so that its exit was blocked. MA says that although Angulimāla had killed almost a thousand people, he had never given rise to a thought of compassion. But now, through the power of his ordination, compassion arose in him as soon as he saw the woman in painful labour.

823 Even today this utterance is often recited by Buddhist monks as a protective charm (*paritta*) for pregnant women close to their time of delivery.

824 MA explains that any volitional action (*kamma*) is capable of yielding three kinds of result: a result to be experienced here and now, i.e., in the same life in which the deed is committed; a result to be experienced in the next existence; and a result to be experienced in any life subsequent to the next, as long as one's sojourn in saṁsāra continues. Because he had attained arahantship, Angulimāla had escaped the latter two types of result but not the first, since even arahants are susceptible to experiencing the present-life results of actions they performed before attaining arahantship.

825 Several of the verses to follow also appear in the Dhammapada. Angulimāla's verses are found in full at Thag 866–91.

826 Although MA says that Ahiṁsaka, "Harmless," was Angulimāla's given name, the commentary to the Theragāthā says his original name was Hiṁsaka, meaning "dangerous."

827 Whereas virtuous bhikkhus short of arahants are said to eat the country's almsfood as an inheritance from the Buddha, the arahant eats "free from debt" because he has made himself fully worthy of receiving alms. See Vsm I, 125–27.

SUTTA 87

828 The expression is often used to mean serious illness and death.

829 Viḍūḍabha was the king's son, who eventually overthrew him. Kāsi and Kosala are lands over which the king ruled.

830 MA: He used this to wash his hands and feet and clean his mouth before saluting the Buddha.

SUTTA 88

831 MA explains that the king asked this question with reference to the case involving the female wanderer Sundarī, which was pending investigation at the time. Wishing to discredit the Buddha, some wandering ascetics persuaded

Sundarī to visit Jeta's Grove at night and then let herself be seen returning at dawn, so people would become suspicious. After some time they had her murdered and buried near Jeta's Grove, and when her body was discovered there, they pointed an accusing finger at the Buddha. After a week the false report was exposed when the king's spies found out the real story behind the murder. See Ud 4:8/42–45.

832 Briefly, this passage offers five criteria of evil actions: *unwholesomeness* underscores the psychological quality of the action, its unhealthy effect upon the mind; its being *blameworthy* underscores its morally detrimental nature; its capacity to produce *painful results* calls attention to its undesirable kammic potential; and the last statement calls attention to both its evil *motivation* and the harmful long-range *consequences* such action entails for both oneself and others. The opposite explanation applies to good action, discussed in §14.

833 MA: Ven. Ānanda's answer goes beyond the question, for he shows not only that the Buddha praises the abandoning of all unwholesome states, but that he acts in accordance with his word by having abandoned all unwholesome states as well.

834 MA explains the word *bāhitikā*, after which the sutta is named, as a cloak produced in a foreign country.

SUTTA 89

835 Dīgha Kārāyaṇa was the commander-in-chief of King Pasenadi's forces. He was the nephew of Bandhula, chief of the Mallas and a former friend of King Pasenadi, whom the king had killed together with his thirty-two sons through the treacherous contrivance of his corrupt ministers. Kārāyaṇa was in secret collusion with Prince Viḍūḍabha, Pasenadi's son, to help the latter usurp his father's throne.

836 Three leagues (*yojana*) would be approximately twenty miles.

837 MA says that he thought: "Previously, after conferring in private with the recluse Gotama, the king arrested my

uncle and his thirty-two sons. Perhaps this time he will arrest me." The royal insignia entrusted to Dīgha Kārāyaṇa also included the fan, parasol, and sandals. Dīgha Kārāyaṇa hurried back to the capital with the royal insignia and crowned Viḍūḍabha king.

838 At MN 13.11 these quarrels are said to arise because of sensual pleasures.

839 As at MN 77.6.

840 As at MN 27.4–7.

841 At the time of their deaths both were declared by the Buddha to be once-returners. See AN 6:44/iii.348.

842 This statement indicates that this sutta can be assigned to the last year of the Buddha's life.

843 When King Pasenadi returned to the place where he had left Dīgha Kārāyaṇa, he found only a servant woman who reported the news to him. He then hurried on to Rājagaha to enlist the aid of his nephew, King Ajātasattu. But since he arrived late, he found the city gates closed. Exhausted by the journey, he lay down in a hall outside the city and died during the night.

844 MA: "Monuments to the Dhamma" means words expressing reverence to the Dhamma. Whenever reverence is shown towards any of the Three Jewels, it is also shown to the others.

SUTTA 90

845 MA: These two sisters are the king's wives (not his sisters!).

846 MA: There is no one who can know and see all—past, present, and future—with one act of mental adverting, with one act of consciousness; thus this problem is discussed in terms of a single act of consciousness (*ekacitta*). On the question of the kind of omniscience the Theravāda tradition attributes to the Buddha, see n.714.

847 That is, he is not inquiring about their social status but about their prospects for spiritual progress and attainment.

848 As at MN 85.58.

849 MA's explanation of this reply suggests that the former class of gods are non-returners, while the latter class are gods who have not attained the status of non-returners.

The same would apply to the question on Brahmās in §15. The two key terms that here distinguish the two types of gods appear in the PTS ed. as *savyāpajjhā* and *abyāpajjhā*, which would be rendered as "subject to ill will" and "free from ill will," respectively. The BBS reading accepted here, *sabyābajjhā* and *abyābajjhā*, has the support of MA, which glosses the former as "who have not abandoned mental suffering by eradicating it," and the latter as "who have eradicated suffering." As either reading would be applicable to non-returners, no significant difference is entailed. Note that the word *itthatta*, which in the stock declaration of arahantship signifies any state of manifest existence, is here glossed by MA as *manussaloka*, the human world.

SUTTA 91

850 This is a stock description of a learned brahmin. According to MA, the Three Vedas are the Iru, Yaju, and Sāma (= Rig, Yajur, and Sāman). The fourth Veda, the Atharva, is not mentioned, but MA says its existence is implied when the histories (Itihāsa) are called "the fifth," i.e., of the works regarded as authoritative by the brahmins. It is more likely, however, that the histories are called "the fifth" in connection with the four branches of study auxiliary to the Vedas that precede them in the description. The translation of technical terms here follows MA, with the help of Monier-William's *Sanskrit-English Dictionary* (Oxford, 1899). On the marks of a Great Man, MA says that this was a science based on 12,000 works explaining the characteristics of great men, such as Buddhas, paccekabuddhas, chief disciples, great disciples, Wheel-turning Monarchs, etc. These works included 16,000 verses called "The Buddha Mantra."

851 The thirty-two marks, enumerated in §9 below, are the subject of an entire sutta in the Dīgha Nikāya, DN 30, *Lakkhaṇa Sutta*. There each of the marks is explained as the kammic consequence of a particular virtue perfected by the Buddha during his earlier existences as a bodhisatta.

852 The seven treasures are discussed in MN 129.34–41. The

acquisition of the wheel-treasure explains why he is called a "Wheel-turning Monarch."

853 *Loke vivattacchaddo*. For hypotheses about the original form and meaning of this expression, see Norman, *Group of Discourses II*, n. to 372, pp. 217–18. MA: The world, enveloped in the darkness of the defilements, is covered by seven veils: lust, hate, delusion, conceit, views, ignorance, and immoral conduct. Having removed these veils, the Buddha abides generating light all around. Thus he is one who draws aside the veil in the world. Or else *vivattacchado* can be resolved into *vivatto* and *vicchaddo*; that is, he is devoid of the round (*vaṭṭarahito*) and devoid of veils (*chadanarahito*). By the absence of the round (i.e., *saṁsāra*) he is an arahant; by the absence of veils, a Fully Enlightened One.

854 MA explains that the Buddha worked this feat after first ascertaining that Uttara's teacher, Brahmāyu, had the potential for achieving the fruit of non-returning, and that his attainment of this fruit depended upon the dispelling of Uttara's doubts.

855 The seven are the backs of the four limbs, the two shoulders, and the trunk.

856 *Rasaggasaggī*. The *Lakkhaṇa Sutta* expands (DN 30.2.7/iii.166): "Whatever he touches with the tip of his tongue he tastes in his throat, and the taste is dispersed everywhere." It is difficult, however, to understand either how this quality could be considered a physical characteristic or how it could be perceived by others.

857 This mark, the *uṇhīsa*, accounts for the protuberance commonly seen on the top of the head of Buddha images.

858 This is the standard reflection on the proper use of almsfood, as at MN 2.14.

859 The blessing (*anumodanā*) is a short talk following the meal, instructing the donors in some aspect of the Dhamma and expressing the wish that their meritorious kamma will bring them abundant fruit.

860 I here follow BBS, which is fuller than SBJ and PTS. MA: This is the intention: "The excellent qualities I have not described are far more numerous than those I have

described. The excellent qualities of Master Gotama are like the great earth and the great ocean; expounded in detail they are infinite and immeasurable, like space."

861 The Pali word for the tongue, *jivhā*, is of the feminine gender.

862 What must be directly known (*abhiññeyya*) are the Four Noble Truths, what must be developed (*bhāvetabba*) is the Noble Eightfold Path, and what must be abandoned (*pahātabba*) are the defilements headed by craving. Here the context requires that the word "Buddha" be understood in the specific sense of a Fully Enlightened One (*sammāsambuddha*).

863 *Vedagū*. This term and the following two—*tevijja* and *sotthiya*—seem to have represented ideal types among the brahmins; see too MN 39.24, 26, and 27. The sixth and seventh terms—*kevalī* and *muni*—were probably ideal types among the non-Vedic ascetic orders. By his reply, the Buddha endows these terms with new meanings derived from his own spiritual system.

864 Here and in the reply the word "Buddha" may signify simply one who is enlightened or awakened, in a sense applicable to any arahant, though Brahmāyu's response also suggests it may be intended in the narrower sense of a Fully Enlightened One.

865 MA offers an involved explanation of how the Buddha's reply answers all eight of Brahmāyu's questions.

866 As at MN 56.18.

SUTTA 92

867 The text of this sutta has not been included in the PTS ed. of the Majjhima Nikāya, as it is identical with the sutta of the same name in the Sutta Nipāta, published in two different versions by the PTS. The bracketed page numbers here therefore refer to the more recent PTS ed. of Sn, edited by Dines Anderson and Helmer Smith.

868 That is, Jambudīpa, the Indian subcontinent.

SUTTA 93

869 The argument in favour of this thesis is set forth at MN 90.10–12.

870 MA: They speak thus intending to say: "Having studied the Three Vedas, you have trained in the mantras by which those who go forth undertake their going forth and the mantras they maintain after they have gone forth. You have practised their mode of conduct. Therefore, you will not be defeated. Victory will be yours."

871 This statement is intended to show that brahmins are born of women, just like other human beings, and there is thus no substance to their claim that they are born of Brahmā's mouth.

872 Yona is probably the Pali equivalent of Ionia, the reference being to the Bactrian Greeks. Kamboja is a district in India to the north of the Middle Country.

873 The argument of §§7–8 here is substantially identical with that of MN 84.

874 MA identifies Devala the Dark, Asita Devala, with the Buddha in an earlier life. The Buddha undertakes this teaching to show: "In the past, when you were of a superior birth and I was of an inferior birth, you could not answer a question I asked you about an assertion concerning birth. So how can you do so now, when you are inferior and I have become a Buddha?"

875 As in MN 38.26. See n. 411. Note that the dialogue just below establishes the meaning of *gandhabba* as the deceased being about to be reborn.

876 MA: Puṇṇa was the name of a servant of the seven seers; he would take a spoon, cook leaves, and serve them.

SUTTA 94

877 MA: He did this after recognising that a lengthy discussion would be required.

878 The *kahāpaṇa* was the principal monetary unit of the time.

879 During the Buddha's last days, this city was still a small town known as Pāṭaligāma. At DN 16.1.28/iii.87, the Buddha predicts its future greatness. It eventually became

the capital of Magadha. Its present-day descendent is the city of Patna, capital of the state of Bihar.

SUTTA 95

880 The opening passage of this sutta, down to §10, is virtually identical with the opening of the *Soṇadaṇḍa Sutta* (DN 4).

881 MA: It was called thus because offerings were made there to the gods.

882 Another wealthy brahmin who resided in Ukkaṭṭhā, a crown property given to him by King Pasenadi. At DN 2.21/i.110 he hears a discourse from the Buddha, attains stream-entry, and goes for refuge along with his family and retinue.

883 These are the ancient rishis whom the brahmins regarded as the divinely inspired authors of the Vedic hymns.

884 In Pali: *saddhā, ruci, anussava, ākāraparivitakka, diṭṭhi-nijjhānakkhanti*. Of these five grounds for arriving at a conviction, the first two seem to be primarily emotive, the third to be a blind acceptance of tradition, and the last two primarily rational or cognitive. The "two different ways" each may turn out are true and false.

885 It is not proper for him to come to this conclusion because he has not personally ascertained the truth of his conviction but only accepts it on a ground that is not capable of yielding certainty.

886 *Saccānurakkhana*: or, the safeguarding of truth, the protection of truth.

887 *Saccānubodha*: or, the awakening to truth.

888 The procedure for the discovery of truth recommended in this sutta appears to be an elaboration of the approach described in MN 47.

889 *Tūleti*. MA: He investigates things in terms of impermanence, and so forth. This stage thus seems to be that of insight contemplation.

890 Although applying the will (*ussahati*) appears similar to striving (*padahati*), the former may be understood as the exertion undertaken prior to insight contemplation, the latter as the exertion that brings insight up to the level of the supramundane path.

891 MA: He realises Nibbāna with the mental body (of the path of stream-entry), and having penetrated the defilements, he sees Nibbāna with wisdom, making it clear and evident.

892 While the discovery of truth in this context appears to signify the attainment of stream-entry, the final arrival at truth (*saccānuppatti*) seems to mean the full attainment of arahantship.

893 See n.524.

SUTTA 96

894 MA: It had been an ancient practice among the brahmins to wander for alms even when they possessed great wealth.

895 Although agriculture may seem a strange occupation for one described as a merchant, it should be understood that the *vessas* not only ran the urban business enterprises, but also owned and supervised agrarian undertakings.

896 *Ariyaṁ kho ahaṁ brāhmaṇa lokuttaraṁ dhammaṁ purisassa sandhanaṁ paññāpemi.*

897 *Attabhāvassa abhinibbatti*: literally, "wherever the reconception of his individuality takes place."

SUTTA 97

898 *Sati uttarakaraṇīye.* Ven. Sāriputta had left without giving him a teaching that would have enabled him to arrive at the supramundane path and become fixed in destination for enlightenment. Compared to this even rebirth in the Brahma-world is described as "inferior" (*hīna*).

899 This remark has the force of a gentle reproach. The Buddha must have seen that Dhānañjāni had the potential to attain the supramundane path, since elsewhere (e.g., MN 99.24–27) he himself teaches only the way to the Brahma-world when that potential is lacking in his listener.

SUTTA 98

900 The text of this sutta has not been included in the PTS ed. of the Majjhima Nikāya, for the same reason given

in n.867. The bracketed page numbers refer to the Anderson-Smith ed. of Sn.

901 Here the word "kamma" has to be understood as present action or deed, and not past action producing its present consequences.

902 *Sāmaññā*. MA: Among animals the diversity in the shape of their bodily parts is determined by their species (*yoni*), but that (species differentiation) is not found in the individual bodies of brahmins and other classes of humans. Such being the case, the distinction between brahmins, *khattiyas*, etc., is purely a verbal designation; it is spoken of as mere conventional expression.

903 MA: Up to this point the Buddha has criticised the assertion of Bhāradvāja that birth makes one a brahmin. Now he will uphold the assertion of Vāseṭṭha that action makes one a brahmin. For the ancient brahmins and other wise ones in the world would not recognise the brahminhood of one defective in livelihood, virtue, and conduct.

904 *Bhovādi*. *Bho*, "sir," was a mode of address used among the brahmins. From this point on the Buddha will identify the true brahmin with the arahant. Verses 27–54 here are identical with Dhp 396–423, except for an additional couplet in Dhp 423.

905 MA: By the present volitional action which accomplishes the work of farming, etc.

906 With this verse the word "kamma" undergoes a shift in meaning signalled by the term "dependent origination." "Kamma" here no longer means simply present action determining one's social status, but action in the special sense of a force binding beings to the round of existence. This same line of thought becomes even clearer in the next verse.

907 This verse and the following one again refer to the arahant. Here, however, the contrast is not between the arahant as the one made holy by his actions and the born brahmin unworthy of his designation, but between the arahant as the one liberated from the bondage of action and result and all other beings who remain tied by their actions to the wheel of birth and death.

SUTTA 99

908 Todeyya was a wealthy brahmin, the overlord of Tudigāma, a village near Sāvatthī. MN 135 was also spoken to this same Subha.

909 *Vibhajjavādo kho aham ettha*. Such statements account for the later designation of Buddhism as *vibhajjavāda*, "the doctrine of analysis." As the context makes clear, the Buddha calls himself a *vibhajjavādin*, not because he analyses things into their constituents (as is popularly believed), but because he distinguishes the different implications of a question without answering one-sidedly.

910 Obviously at the time trade was still in an early stage of development. The same statement could hardly be made today!

911 As at MN 95.13.

912 This statement must have been made before Pokkharasāti became a follower of the Buddha, as is mentioned at MN 95.9.

913 *Anukampājātika*.

914 This knowledge pertains to the third of the Tathāgata's powers, knowing the ways to all destinations. See MN 12.12.

915 MA explains limiting action (*pamāṇakataṁ kammaṁ*) as kamma pertaining to the sense sphere (*kāmāvacara*). It is contrasted with a limitless or immeasurable action, namely, the jhānas pertaining to the fine-material sphere or the immaterial sphere. In this case the *brahmavihāras* developed to the jhānic level are intended. When a jhāna pertaining to the fine-material sphere or the immaterial sphere is attained and mastered, a kamma pertaining to the sense sphere cannot overpower it and gain the opportunity to yield its own result. Rather, the kamma pertaining to the fine-material sphere or the immaterial sphere overpowers the sense-sphere kammas and produces its results. Obstructing the result of the sense-sphere kammas, the *brahmavihāra* that has been mastered leads to rebirth in the company of Brahmā.

916 As at MN 27.2.

SUTTA 100

917 Dhānañjānī was a stream-enterer. MA says that Sangārava was her husband's younger brother.

918 *Diṭṭhadhammābhiññāvosānapāramippattā ādibrahmacariyaṁ paṭijānanti.* MA glosses: They claim to be the originators, creators, producers of a holy life, saying: "Having directly known here and now in this present existence and having reached the consummation, we have attained Nibbāna, called 'perfection' because it is the transcendence of everything."

919 It is puzzling that the reasoners and investigators (*takkī, vīmaṁsī*) are here said to rely on the basis of mere faith (*saddhāmattakena*). Elsewhere faith and reasoning are contrasted as two different grounds of conviction (MN 95.14), and "mere faith" seems more closely allied with reliance on oral tradition than with reasoning and investigation.

920 *Sāmaṁ yeva dhammaṁ abhiññāya.* This phrase emphasises direct personal realisation as the foundation for promulgating a holy life.

921 MA says that Sangārava had the idea that the Buddha spoke thus without actual knowledge, and he therefore accuses the Buddha of false speech. The sequence of ideas in this passage is difficult to follow and it is likely that the text is corrupt.

SUTTA 101

922 This doctrine, which is here ascribed to the Jains, is also taken up for criticism by the Buddha at SN 36:21/iv.230–31 and AN 3:61/i.173–74. The Buddha's teaching recognises the existence of feeling that is not the result of past action but a concomitant of present action, and also admits feeling that is neither kammically active nor kammic result.

923 From here until §5, "That being so…," also at MN 14.17–19. The statement of the Nigaṇṭha Nātaputta, which at MN 14.17 introduces the Nigaṇṭhas' position, here comes afterwards, at §10, as the Nigaṇṭhas' justification for their assertion.

924 As at MN 95.14.

925 It is not fitting for them to make that declaration because their "intense exertion," i.e., their ascetic practice, is the cause for their painful feelings, as the Buddha states in §15.

926 This is a technical expression for an action that is to ripen in this present life.

927 MA: "An action [whose result] is to be experienced in a matured [personality]" is a synonym for an action [whose result] is to be experienced here and now. "An action [whose result] is to be experienced in an unmatured personality" is a synonym for action [whose result] is to be experienced in the next life. But a specification is made as follows: any action that yields its result in the same life is one to be experienced here and now, but only an action that produces its result *within seven days* is called one to be experienced in a matured personality.

928 This is an action that does not gain the opportunity to yield its result and thereby becomes defunct.

929 *Issaranimmānahetu*. This doctrine of the theists is criticised by the Buddha at AN 3:61/i.174.

930 *Sangatibhāvahetu*. This alludes to the doctrine of Makkhali Gosāla, criticised at length at MN 60.21 and AN 3:61/ i.175.

931 *Abhijātihetu*. This also refers to a tenet of Makkhali Gosāla.

932 This is a formulation of the Buddha's Middle Way, which avoids the extreme of self-mortification without falling into the other extreme of infatuation with sensual pleasure.

933 MA explains the source of suffering to be craving, so called because it is the root of the suffering comprised in the five aggregates. The passage shows two alternative approaches toward overcoming craving—one employing energetic striving, the other detached equanimity. The "fading away" of the source is identified by MA with the supramundane path. The passage is said to illustrate the practice of one who progresses on a pleasant path with quick direct knowledge (*sukhapaṭipadā khippābhiññā*).

934 This passage is brought forth to show the Buddha's reason for permitting his monks to undertake the ascetic practices (*dhutanga*): the moderate use of austerities is conducive to overcoming the defilements; but they are not undertaken to wear away old kamma and to purify the soul, as the Jains and other ascetic sects believed. MA

says that this passage illustrates the practice of one who progresses on a difficult path with sluggish direct knowledge (*dukkhapaṭipadā dandhābhiññā*).

SUTTA 102

935 This sutta is a "middle length" counterpart of the longer *Brahmajāla Sutta,* included in the Dīgha Nikāya and published in translation with its commentaries in Bodhi, *Discourse on the All-Embracing Net of Views.* Detailed explanations for almost all the views mentioned in this sutta will be found in the Introduction and Part Two of that work. There exists a Tibetan translation of the *Pañcatraya Sūtra,* the counterpart of this text belonging to the Mūlasarvāstivāda school, whose collections were preserved in Skt. This text is discussed by Peter Skilling at *Mahāsūtras II,* pp. 469–511. Skilling highlights the interesting contrasts between this version of the text and the Pali version.

936 Skilling points out that in the Tibetan *Pañcatraya,* assertions of Nirvāṇa here and now are not comprised under views about the future but constitute a separate category. The *Brahmajāla Sutta* places assertions of supreme Nibbāna here and now among views about the future, but the arrangement in the Tibetan counterpart seems to be more logical.

937 In the *Brahmajāla Sutta* sixteen varieties of this view are mentioned, the eight given here and two other tetrads: the self as finite, infinite, both, and neither; and the self as experiencing exclusively pleasure, exclusively pain, a mixture of both, and neither. In the present sutta these two tetrads are incorporated under speculations about the past in §14, but at SN 24:37-44/iii.219-20 they describe the self *after death.*

938 Evidently, in the above list the views of the self as immaterial, percipient of unity, and percipient of the immeasurable are based on attainment of the base of infinite space. MṬ explains the consciousness-kasiṇa as the base of infinite consciousness, stating that these theorists declare that base to be the self.

939 The perception within the third immaterial meditation—the base of nothingness—is the subtlest and most refined of all mundane perceptions. Although there is still a kind of perception in the fourth immaterial attainment, it is so subtle that it is no longer appropriate to designate it perception.

940 MA paraphrases thus: "All those types of perceptions together with the views are conditioned, and because they are conditioned, they are gross. But there is Nibbāna, called the cessation of formations, that is, of the conditioned. Having known 'There is this,' that there is Nibbāna, seeing the escape from the conditioned, the Tathāgata has gone beyond the conditioned."

941 The second tetrad of §3 is dropped here since the self is conceived as non-percipient. In the *Brahmajāla Sutta* eight varieties of this view are mentioned, these four plus the finite-infinite tetrad.

942 MA points out that this statement is made with reference to those planes of existence where all five aggregates exist. In the immaterial planes consciousness occurs without the aggregate of material form, and in the non-percipient plane there is material form without consciousness. But consciousness never occurs without the three other mental aggregates.

943 The *Brahmajāla Sutta* mentions eight varieties of this view, these four plus the finite-infinite tetrad.

944 *Sammoha*, here obviously having a different meaning than the usual "confusion" or "delusion."

945 MA explains the compound *diṭṭhasutamutaviññātabba* as meaning "what is to be cognized as the seen, heard, and sensed" and takes it to refer to sense-door cognitions. However, it can also comprise all grosser mind-door cognitions as well. To enter the fourth immaterial attainment, all the ordinary "mental formations" involved in other cognitive processes must be overcome, for their persistence is an obstacle to entering this attainment. Hence it is called "not percipient" (*n'eva saññī*).

946 *Sasankhārāvasesasamāpatti*. Within the fourth immaterial attainment a residue of extremely subtle mental formations remains. Hence it is called "not non-percipient" (*nāsaññī*).

947 The *Brahmajāla* explains seven types of annihilationism, here all collected together as one.

948 The "fear and disgust with identity" is an aspect of *vibhavataṇhā*, the craving for non-existence. The annihilationist view to which it gives rise still involves an identification with self—a self that is annihilated at death—and thus, despite his denial, it binds the theorist to the round of existence.

949 So far only four of the original five classes of speculations about the future have been analysed, yet the Buddha speaks as if they were all explicated. MA tries to resolve the problem by explaining that assertions of "Nibbāna here and now" were comprised by the terms "percipient of unity" and "percipient of diversity" in §3. This explanation, however, is not convincing. Ñm, in Ms, had added the heading "Nibbāna Here and Now" over §17, and §§17–21 do seem to correspond with the last four of the five doctrines of Nibbāna here and now in the *Brahmajāla*. However, this interpretation seems contradicted by §13 and by the phrase used in §17, §19, and §21, "with the relinquishing of views about the past and the future," which would exclude the doctrines of Nibbāna here and now from views about the future (though it is placed among such views in the preamble). The problem seems insoluble, and raises the suspicion that the text was to some degree corrupted in the course of its oral transmission. The insertion of the views about the past just below is also problematic. Not only are such views not mentioned in the preamble, but the placing of the past after the future inverts the normal time sequence. Skilling suggests this passage may have been part of an oral commentary on the sutta which, at some point, was absorbed into the text.

950 This view includes all four of the eternalists who speculate about the past mentioned in the *Brahmajāla*.

951 Since this is a view referring to the past, it may be taken to imply that at some point in the past the self and the world arose spontaneously out of nothing. Thus it would comprise the two doctrines of fortuitous origination of the *Brahmajāla*, as MA maintains.

952 This includes the four types of partial eternalism.
953 This may include the four types of endless equivocation or "eel-wriggling" of the *Brahmajāla*.
954 Views 5–8 correspond exactly to the four extensionists of the *Brahmajāla*.
955 The eight views (9–16) are, in the *Brahmajāla*, included among the doctrines of percipient immortality comprised under speculations about the future.
956 That is, they must accept their doctrine on some ground other than knowledge, one involving belief or reasoning. At MN 95.14, it is said that these five grounds of conviction yield conclusions that can turn out to be either true or false.
957 MA: That is not really knowledge but wrong understanding; thus it is declared to be clinging to views.
958 MA says that at this point all sixty-two of the views set forth in the *Brahmajāla Sutta* have been incorporated, yet this sutta has an even wider range since it includes an exposition of identity view (most notably implied by §24).
959 This section title, and the following Roman numeral "V", were inserted by Ñm on the supposition that this passage presents the doctrines of Nibbāna here and now, mentioned but not explicated earlier.
960 MA: This section is intended to show how all sixty-two speculative views arise predominated over by identity view.
961 *Pavivekaṁ pītiṁ.* This refers to the first two jhānas, which include *pīti.*
962 MA explains that this is the grief caused by the loss of the jhāna. The grief does not arise immediately upon the cessation of the jhāna, but only after reflection upon its disappearance.
963 *Nirāmisaṁ sukhaṁ.* This is the pleasure of the third jhāna.
964 The fourth jhāna.
965 *Santo'ham asmi, nibbuto'ham asmi, anupādāno'ham asmi.* In the Pali the expression *aham asmi,* "I am," reveals that he is still involved with clinging, as the Buddha will point out.
966 MA takes this to be an allusion to identity view. Thus he is still clinging to a view.
967 MA states that elsewhere the expression "liberation

through not clinging" (*anupādā vimokkha*) signifies Nibbāna, but here it means the attainment of the fruit of arahantship.

968 The *Brahmajāla Sutta* too points to the understanding of the origination, etc., of the six bases of contact as the way to transcend all views.

SUTTA 103

969 *Bhavābhavahetu*. MA: "Do you think that he teaches the Dhamma as a means of gaining merit so that he can experience happiness in this or that [higher] state of being?"

970 *Abhidhamma*. MA says that this refers to the thirty-seven aids to enlightenment mentioned in the previous paragraph. See n.362.

971 Meaning (*attha*) and phrasing (*byañjana*) are the two aspects of the Dhamma taught by the Buddha. The following passage, §§5–8, should be compared with DN 29.18–21/iii.128–29, which also expresses a concern for the preservation of the correct meaning and phrasing of the Dhamma.

972 This statement is made because slight deviations from the correct phrasing are not necessarily an obstacle to a proper understanding of the meaning. But elsewhere (e.g., AN 2:20/i.59) the Buddha points out that the wrong expression of the letter and the wrong interpretation of the meaning are two factors responsible for the distortion and disappearance of the true Dhamma.

973 The general principle underlying §§10–14 is this: If the offending bhikkhu can be rehabilitated, then despite the hurt to him and the trouble to oneself, one should try to correct him. But if he is not susceptible to being rehabilitated, one should just maintain one's own equanimity.

974 "The Recluse" (*samaṇa*) is glossed by MA with *satthā*, the Teacher, referring to the Buddha. A similar use of the term is found at MN 105.18, 21.

975 The "thing" (*dhamma*) intended, MA says, is quarrelling.

SUTTA 104

976 The opening of this sutta is the same as that of DN 29, which is also concerned with preserving harmony in the Sangha after the Buddha's demise.

977 MA: The "shrine" and "refuge" are the Nigaṇṭha Nātaputta, who is now dead.

978 The novice Cunda was the younger brother of Ven. Sāriputta.

979 Even while the Buddha was still alive such a dispute had already broken out among the bhikkhus at Kosambī, referred to at MN 48.2.

980 This would be a dispute about the Noble Eightfold Path or the other aids to enlightenment.

981 The first four pairs are included among the "imperfections that defile the mind" at MN 7.3.

982 *Adhikaraṇa*. Horner translates "legal questions." They are dealt with at length at Vin Cv Kh 4/Vin ii.88–93; see Horner, *Book of the Discipline*, 5:117–25. Briefly, litigation because of a dispute (*vivādādhikaraṇa*) arises when bhikkhus dispute about the Dhamma and the Discipline; litigation because of an accusation (*anuvādādhikaraṇa*) when bhikkhus accuse a bhikkhu of committing a transgression of the monastic rules; litigation because of an offence (*āpattādhikaraṇa*) when a bhikkhu who has committed a transgression seeks to exonerate himself from it; and litigation concerning procedures (*kiccādhikaraṇa*) deals with the enactment of the formal functions of the Sangha.

983 *Adhikaraṇasamatha*. They are dealt with in detail in Vin Cv Kh 4. How the seven means of settlement are to be applied for the resolution of the four kinds of litigation is discussed at Vin ii.93–104; see Horner, *Book of the Discipline*, 5:125–40.

984 *Sammukhāvinaya*. Horner translates "verdict in the presence of." At Vin ii.93, this is explained as confrontation with (or presence of) the Sangha, the Dhamma, the Discipline, and the individuals who are parties to the dispute. This kind of settlement applies to all four kinds of litigation, with minor differences in formulation.

985 *Dhammanetti samanumajjitabbā*. MA gives as an example

of *dhammanetti* the ten courses of wholesome and unwholesome conduct, but says that here the Dhamma and Discipline themselves are meant.

986 *Sativinaya*. Horner renders "verdict of innocence". At Vin ii.80, it is said that this is given when a bhikkhu is pure and without offences and he is reproached with an offence; he must ask the Sangha to give him such a verdict by appeal to his full and accurate recollection of his behaviour.

987 An offence involving defeat, a *pārājika* offence, requires expulsion from the Sangha. An offence bordering on defeat is either a *saṅghādisesa* offence, which requires a formal meeting of the Sangha and a period of temporary penalisation, or the preliminary steps leading to a *pārājika* offence. I follow BBS and SBJ, which have one bhikkhu as accuser, rather than PTS, which uses a plural form. So too below.

988 *Amūḷhavinaya*. A verdict of past insanity is given when a bhikkhu commits offences during a period of madness. The criterion for determining insanity is that he must have no recollection of his behaviour during the period for which the verdict is requested.

989 The procedure described is the established method by which a bhikkhu obtains exoneration for his transgression when he has fallen into any offence that can be cleared by confession.

990 *Pāpiyyāsikā*. Horner renders "decision for specific depravity." This verdict is pronounced against a bhikkhu who is a maker of strife and quarrels in the Sangha, who is ignorant and full of offences, or who lives in unbecoming association with householders.

991 *Tiṇavatthāraka*. This means of settlement is resorted to when the Sangha has been involved in a dispute in the course of which the bhikkhus committed many minor offences. Since to pursue charges for these offences might prolong the conflict, the offences are cleared by the means described in the sutta. MA explains that this method is like throwing grass over excrement to remove the bad smell, hence the name "covering over with grass."

992 Offences calling for serious censure are those of the *pārājika* and *saṅghādisesa* classes. Those connected with the laity are cases where a bhikkhu reviles and disparages householders.

993 As at MN 48.6.

994 At MN 21.21, this is said with reference to the simile of the saw.

SUTTA 105

995 See MN 12 and n.177.

996 *Adhimānena.* MA: They declare this out of conceit, considering themselves to have attained what they have not attained.

997 MA: To make clear to them their level of attainment.

998 MA: Because they are motivated by desire, the Tathāgata's thought of teaching the Dhamma, which arises towards true practitioners, changes (i.e., fades away).

999 *Lokāmisa.* These are the five cords of sensual pleasure.

1000 *Āneñja* (BBS); *āṇañja* (PTS). This is a technical term for the meditative attainments from the fourth jhāna through the four immaterial attainments. But since the highest two immaterial attainments are dealt with separately, it seems that in this sutta only the fourth jhāna and the lower two immaterial attainments are intended as "the imperturbable."

1001 The Buddha.

1002 Reading with BBS, *evaṁmāni assa atathaṁ samānaṁ.* CPD suggests *atathaṁ samānaṁ* may be an accusative absolute. This passage refers back to the problem of self-overestimation with which the discourse began.

1003 I follow PTS here, whose reading seems supported by all versions prior to BBS. Because the surgeon is later compared to the Tathāgata, and the text cannot ascribe an error in judgement to the Buddha, BBS insists on a strict application of the simile and has thus "corrected" the text to read *sa-upādiseso ti jānamāno.* I followed this reading in the first edition, but now believe it was a mistake on the part of BBS to alter the received text; strict parallelism in the application of the simile need not be expected. SBJ follows BBS in reading *sa-upādiseso,* but retains *maññamāno,* which verges on incoherence. All eds. have *janamāno* as the participle in the contrasting version of the simile found below. Where PTS has *alañ* just below, we should read *analañ* with BBS and SBJ, also supported by the gloss in MA.

1004 Any offence of the two classes, *pārājika* and *sanghādisesa;* see n.987. The analogy is difficult to apply with complete precision, since if craving and ignorance had truly been removed from him with only a trace left behind, the bhikkhu would be a *sekha;* yet it is inconceivable that a *sekha* would abandon the training or commit a defiled offence. It seems that in this case the analogy must be applied loosely, and the bhikkhu should be understood as one who falsely imagines that craving and ignorance have been removed from him.

1005 See MN 66.17. MA: The arahant, liberated in Nibbāna, the destruction of craving [by taking it] as object, would never divert his body or arouse his mind to indulge in the five cords of sensual pleasure.

1006 As at MN 46.19. I follow BBS and SBJ, which include *rasasampanno,* missing in PTS.

SUTTA 106

1007 See n.1000. Here, too, the term "imperturbable" seems to comprise only the fourth jhāna and the two lower immaterial attainments.

1008 MA says both objective sensual pleasures and sensual defilements are intended.

1009 MA glosses: "having transcended the sense-sphere world and having determined with a mind that has jhāna as its objective."

1010 MA explains the phrase "his mind acquires confidence in this base" to mean that he attains either insight aimed at reaching arahantship or the access to the fourth jhāna. If he gains access to the fourth jhāna, this becomes his basis for attaining "the imperturbable," i.e., the fourth jhāna itself. But if he gains insight, then "he resolves [upon it] with wisdom" by deepening his insight in order to reach arahantship. The expression "resolution with wisdom" may explain why so many of the following sections of this sutta, though culminating in attainments along the scale of concentration, are expressed in phrasing appropriate to the development of insight.

1011 MA explains that this passage describes the rebirth process of one who could not realise arahantship after reaching the fourth jhāna. The "evolving consciousness" (*saṁvattanikaṁ viññāṇaṁ*) is the resultant consciousness by which this person is reborn, and this has the same imperturbable nature as the kammically formative consciousness that attained to the fourth jhāna. Since it is the fourth-jhāna consciousness that determines rebirth, this person will be reborn in one of the exalted realms corresponding to the fourth jhāna.

1012 MA says that this is the reflection of one who has attained the fourth jhāna. Since he includes material form among the things to be transcended, if he attains to the imperturbable he reaches the base of infinite space, and if he does not attain arahantship he is reborn in the plane of infinite space.

1013 MA says that this is the reflection of one who has attained the base of infinite space. If he attains to the imperturbable, he reaches the base of infinite consciousness and is reborn in that plane if he does not reach arahantship.

1014 This is the reflection of one who has attained the base of infinite consciousness and aims at attaining the base of nothingness.

1015 MA calls this two-pointed voidness—the absence of "I" and "mine"—and says that this teaching of the base of nothingness is expounded by way of insight rather than concentration, the approach taken in the previous section. At MN 43.33, this contemplation is said to lead to the deliverance of mind through voidness.

1016 MA calls this four-pointed voidness and explains thus: (i) he does not see his self anywhere; (ii) he does not see a self of his own that can be treated as something belonging to another, e.g., as a brother, friend, assistant, etc.; (iii) he does not see the self of another; (iv) he does not see the self of another that can be treated as something belonging to him. Ms has a note by Ñm: "These expressions [in this paragraph and the next] seem to have been stereotyped slogans or descriptions of the attainments of nothingness and neither-perception-nor-non-perception, primarily non-Buddhist, and sometimes used as a basis for the existing-body [=identity] view." See Ñm's note 19 to Vsm XXI, 53 for further discussion and other references.

1017 MA glosses: "If the round of kamma had not been accumulated by me, now there would not be for me the round of results; if the round of kamma is not accumulated by me now, in the future there will not be the round of results." "What exists, what has come to be" are the five aggregates. The first part of the formula again seems to be a condensed formulation of a view held by non-Buddhists. Several suttas identify it as an expression for the annihilationist view, adapted by the Buddha with new meanings assigned to it. For other occurrences of this formula, see SN iii.55–56, 99, 183, 206; AN iv.69–72, v.63.

MA says that he obtains the equanimity of insight, but from §11 it seems that the equanimity of the base of neither-perception-nor-non-perception is also intended.

1018 There is word play here that cannot be successfully reproduced in translation. The verb *parinibbāyati*, rendered "to attain Nibbāna," is also applied to the going out of a fire. The attainment of Nibbāna is thus the "going out" of the fires of lust, hatred, and delusion. *Upādāna*, "clinging," also designates the fuel which a fire consumes. Thus consciousness continues on in the round of rebirths so long as it is sustained by the fuel of clinging. When the defilements are extinguished, there is no more fuel for consciousness to burn, and thus the bhikkhu without clinging "goes out" by the attainment of Nibbāna. The subtlest object of clinging, thus the subtlest fuel (as the following exchange will show), is the base of neither-perception-nor-non-perception.

1019 MA: This is said with reference to the rebirth of one who attains the base of neither-perception-nor-non-perception. The meaning is that he takes rebirth in the best, the highest, plane of existence.

1020 *Nissāya nissāya oghassa nittharaṇā*. MA: The Buddha has explained the crossing of the flood for a bhikkhu who uses as the basis (for reaching arahantship) any of the attainments from the third jhāna up to the fourth immaterial attainment.

1021 MA: Ānanda's question is intended to elicit from the Buddha an account of the practice of the dry-insight meditator (*sukkhavipassaka*), who attains arahantship without depending on a jhānic attainment.

1022 *Esa sakkāyo yāvatā sakkāyo*. MA: This is the personal identity in its entirety—the round of the three realms of existence; there is no personal identity outside of this.

1023 MA says that the arahantship of the dry-insight meditator is intended. MṬ adds that arahantship is called "the Deathless" because it has the flavour of the Deathless, being attained on the basis of Nibbāna the Deathless.

SUTTA 107

1024 MA: It is not possible to construct a seven-storied mansion in a single day. Once the site is cleared, from the time the foundation is laid until the paint job is finished there is gradual progress.

1025 *Gaṇaka*. His name means "Moggallāna the Accountant."

1026 See MN 65.33.

1027 While the preceding steps of practice are necessary measures for bhikkhus in training to attain arahantship, they are also beneficial to arahants in that they conduce to "a pleasant abiding here and now." MA identifies this "abiding" with the attainment of the fruit of arahantship, and explains that some arahants can enter fruition easily at any time while others must apply themselves diligently to the steps of practice to enter fruition.

1028 *Maggakkhāyī Tathāgato*. Compare Dhp 276: "You yourselves must strive; the Tathāgatas only point the way."

1029 The following as at MN 5.32.

1030 *Paramajjadhammesu*. MA: The doctrine of Gotama is supreme, the highest, among contemporary teachings—the teachings of the six outside teachers.

SUTTA 108

1031 MA says that after the Buddha's relics had been distributed, Ven. Ānanda had come to Rājagaha for the recitation of the Dhamma (at the first Great Council).

1032 King Pajjota was a friend of King Bimbisāra of Magadha, who had been killed by his son Ajātasattu. According to MA, Ajātasattu thought King Pajjota might seek to avenge his friend's murder.

1033 See DN 16.1.2–5/iii.72–76.

1034 The import of this statement is that the Sangha is not governed by the personal judgements of its members but by the Dhamma and disciplinary code laid down for it by the Buddha. In this the bhikkhus follow the Buddha's final injunction: "What I have taught and explained to you as Dhamma and Discipline will, at my passing, be your teacher" (DN 16.6.1/ii.154).

1035 See n.525.

SUTTA 109

1036 The fifteenth day of the fortnight. See n.59 and n.809.

1037 MA explains that this bhikkhu was himself an arahant and the teacher of sixty other bhikkhus who lived with him in the forest, striving in meditation. With their teacher's guidance they had developed various insight knowledges but could not attain the paths and fruits. Therefore their teacher brought them to see the Buddha in the hope that he could guide them to the supramundane attainments. The teacher asks the questions, not because he has doubts, but in order to dispel the doubts of his disciples.

1038 *Chandamūlakā.* MA glosses *chanda* by *taṇhā,* craving, which is the origin of the suffering comprised by the five aggregates.

1039 As at MN 44.6.

1040 In the material form aggregate each of the four great elements is a condition for the other three and for derived material form. Contact is a condition for each of the three middle aggregates, as it is said: "Contacted one feels, bhikkhus; contacted one perceives; contacted one wills" (SN 35:93/iv.68). MA explains that at the moment of conception, the material phenomena and the three mental aggregates that arise are the mentality-materiality that is a condition for the rebirth consciousness. During the course of life the physical sense faculties and the sense objects together with the three mental aggregates are the mentality-materiality that is a condition for sense consciousness.

1041 As at MN 44.7–8.

1042 It seems that this bhikkhu had difficulty in understanding how kamma can produce results without a self to receive them.

1043 The readings of this sentence are highly divergent in different editions. The same sutta appears at SN 22:82/iii.104, and the reading there (*paṭipucchā vinītā*) seems preferable to the reading here (in PTS, *paṭicca vinītā*; in BBS, *paṭivinītā*). The translation here follows the Saṁyutta text. Ñm's translation, based on the PTS Majjhima text, reads: "Now, bhikkhus, you have been trained by me in dependent [conditionality] in various instances." Neither version is idiomatic Pali, and the commentaries to both Nikāyas are silent.

1044 MA: The sixty bhikkhus discarded their original meditation subjects and investigated a new subject (based on the Buddha's discourse, MṬ). Without breaking their posture, right in their seats they attained arahantship.

SUTTA 110

1045 *Asappurisa.* MA glosses by *pāpapurisa,* an evil man.

SUTTA 111

1046 *Anupadadhammavipassanā.* MA explains that he developed insight into states in successive order by way of the meditative attainments and the jhāna factors, as will be described. The two-week period referred to fell from the time of Ven. Sāriputta's ordination under the Buddha to his attainment of arahantship while listening to the

Buddha explain the comprehension of feeling to Dīghanakha (see MN 74.14).

1047 The first five states in the list are the jhāna factors proper of the first jhāna; the following states are additional components each performing their individual functions within the jhāna. This minute analysis of mental states into their components anticipates the methodology of the Abhidhamma, and it is thus no coincidence that the name of Sāriputta is so closely linked with the emergence of the Abhidhamma literature.

1048 All these terms signify the temporary suppression of the defilements by the power of the jhāna, not the full liberation from defilements through their eradication by the highest path, which Ven. Sāriputta had yet to attain.

1049 The "escape beyond" (*uttariṁ nissaraṇaṁ*) here is the next higher attainment, the second jhāna.

1050 Reading with the BBS ed. *passaddhattā cetaso anābhogo.* MA explains that the mental concern with pleasure, which persists in the third jhāna, is now considered to be gross, and when it subsides there is "mental unconcern due to tranquillity." The PTS ed. reading, *passi vedanā,* is unintelligible and clearly an error.

1051 This indirect introspective method must be used to contemplate the fourth immaterial attainment because this attainment, being extremely subtle, does not enter into the direct range of investigation for disciples. Only fully enlightened Buddhas are able to contemplate it directly.

1052 MA offers this explanation of the passage, transmitted by "the elders of India": "The Elder Sāriputta cultivated serenity and insight in paired conjunction and realised the fruit of non-returning. Then he entered the attainment of cessation, and after emerging from it he attained arahantship."

1053 Since there are no mental factors in the attainment of cessation, MA says that "these states" here must refer either to the states of material form that were occurring while he attained cessation, or to the mental factors of the preceding fourth immaterial attainment.

1054 Note the realisation that there is "*no* escape beyond" the attainment of arahantship.

1055 *Vasippatto pāramipatto.* See n.763.

SUTTA 112

1056 See n.17.

1057 As at MN 111.4, but here these terms are intended to express the complete eradication of defilements by the path of arahantship.

1058 MA: All these terms signify craving and views.

1059 MA: The first phrase negates the consideration of the earth element as self, the second negates the consideration of the material and mental factors other than the earth element as self. The same method applies to the other elements.

1060 The text appears redundant in mentioning both forms (*rūpā*) and things cognizable (by the mind) through eye-consciousness (*cakkhuviññāṇa-viññātabbā dhammā*). MA mentions two opinions proposed to resolve this problem. One holds that "forms" refers to visible things that actually enter into cognition, "things cognizable..." to visible things that cease without being cognized. The second holds that the former term signifies all form without distinction, the latter term the three mental aggregates that function in association with eye-consciousness.

1061 MA explains "I-making" (*ahankāra*) as conceit and "mine-making" (*mamankāra*) as craving. "All external signs" (*nimitta*) are external objects.

1062 MA: The recollection of past lives and the knowledge of the passing away and reappearance of beings (usually included in this type of exposition) are here omitted because the original question at §11 concerned the attainment of arahantship, not mundane attainments.

1063 MA says that this sutta is also called the *Ekavissajjita Sutta* (The Single Answer Discourse). MA finds it difficult to account for the "sixfold" mentioned in the original title, since only five questions and answers have come down in the discourse. It suggests dividing the last item into two—one's own body with its consciousness and the conscious bodies of others—and also mentions another opinion that the four nutriments should be brought in as the sixth. Neither of these suggestions, however, appears cogent, and it seems likely that a part of the text has been lost.

SUTTA 113

1064 *Sappurisadhamma; asappurisadhamma.*

1065 These are nine of the thirteen ascetic practices discussed in Vsm II.

1066 MA explains "non-identification" (*atammayatā*, lit. "not consisting of that") as the absence of craving. However, the context suggests that the absence of conceit may be the meaning. The statement "for in whatever way they conceive, the fact is ever other than that" (*yena yena hi maññanti tato taṁ hoti aññathā*) is a philosophical riddle appearing also at Sn 588, Sn 757, and Ud 3:10. Though MA is silent, the Udāna commentary (to Ud 3:10) explains it to mean that in whatever way worldly people conceive any of the five aggregates—as self or self's belonging, etc.—the thing conceived turns out to be other than the aspect ascribed to it: it is not self or self's belonging, not "I" or "mine."

1067 It should be noted that there is no passage on the untrue man entering the cessation of perception and feeling. Unlike the jhānas and immaterial attainments, which can be attained by worldlings, cessation is the domain exclusively of non-returners and arahants.

1068 *Na kiñci maññati, na kuhiñci maññati, na kenaci maññati.* This is a brief statement of the same situation described in full at MN 1.51–146. On "conceiving" see n.6

SUTTA 114

1069 This first paragraph offers merely a "table of contents," to be elaborated in the body of the sutta.

1070 *Aññamaññaṁ.* MA: The two are mutually exclusive, and there is no way by which the one can be regarded as the other.

1071 Although wrong view and right view are usually included under mental conduct, in this sutta they are shown separately in §10 as "the acquisition of view."

1072 Whereas the covetousness and ill will described in §7 possess the strength of a full course of action (*kammapatha*), in this section on inclination of mind (*cittuppāda*) they are shown in their nascent stage as mere dispositions that have not yet erupted into obsessive volitions.

1073 "Acquisition of individuality" (*attabhāvapaṭilābha*) here refers to mode of rebirth.

1074 *Apariniṭṭhitabhāvāya*. The expression may be unique to this sutta. MA glosses it with *bhavānaṁ apariniṭṭhitabhāvāya* and explains: There are four modes of individual existence "subject to affliction" (*sabyābajjhattabhāvā*). The first is the worldling who is unable to reach the consummation of existence in that particular life; for him, from the time of rebirth on, unwholesome states increase and wholesome states diminish, and he generates an individuality accompanied by suffering. So too the stream-enterer, once-returner, and non-returner. Even non-returners still have not abandoned craving for being, and thus have not reached consummation. The individuals [mentioned just below in the text] who acquire individual existence "free from affliction" (*abyābajjhattabhāvā*) are the same four when they enter the final existence in which they are to attain arahantship. Even the worldling in his last existence is able to consummate existence, like the serial killer Angulimāla. Their existence is said to be free from affliction, and they are said to reach consummation.

1075 MA points out that the clause "Forms are either the one or the other" is not used here because the distinction does not lie in the object but in the approach to it. For one person lust and other defilements arise towards a particular form, but another person develops dispassion and detachment in regard to the same form.

1076 MA says that those who study the text and commentary to this sutta without practising in accordance with it cannot be said to "understand the detailed meaning." Only those who practise accordingly can be so described.

SUTTA 115

1077 The eighteen elements are defined at Vbh §§183–84/87–90 and are explained in detail at Vsm XV, 17–43. Briefly, the mind element (*manodhātu*), according to the Abhidhamma, includes the consciousness that adverts to the five sense objects impinging on the five sense faculties (*pañcadvārāvajjana-citta*) and the consciousness that receives the object after it has been cognized through the senses (*sampaṭicchana-citta*). The mind-consciousness element (*manoviññāṇadhātu*) includes all types of consciousness except the five sense consciousnesses and the mind-element. The mind-object element (*dhammadhātu*) includes the types of subtle material phenomena not involved in sense cognition, the three mental aggregates of feeling, perception, and formations, and Nibbāna. It does not include concepts, abstract ideas, judgements, etc. Though these latter are included in the notion of mind-object (*dhammārammaṇa*), the mind-object *element* includes only things that exist by their own nature, not things constructed by the mind.

1078 These are defined at Vbh §180/85–86. The pleasure and pain elements are bodily pleasant and painful feeling; the joy and grief elements are mental pleasant and painful feeling; the equanimity element is neither-painful-nor-pleasant feeling. MA says that ignorance is brought in because of its apparent similarity to the equanimity element.

1079 Vbh §183/86–87 defines these as the six corresponding types of applied thought (*vitakka*); see MN 19.2.

1080 MA explains the sense-sphere element as the five aggregates pertaining to the sense-sphere (*kāmāvacara*), the fine-material element as the five aggregates pertaining to the fine-material sphere (*rūpāvacara*), and the immaterial element as the four aggregates pertaining to the immaterial sphere (*arūpāvacara*).

1081 MA: the conditioned element includes everything produced by conditions and is a designation for the five aggregates. The unconditioned element is Nibbāna.

1082 The twelve bases are defined at Vbh §§155–167/70–73 and explained at Vsm XV, 1–16. The mind base includes all types of consciousness, and thus comprises all seven elements that exercise the function of consciousness. The mind-object base is identical with the mind-object element.

1083 On the terms in the formula of dependent origination, see Introduction, pp. 30–31.

1084 MA: A person possessing right view (*diṭṭhisampanno*) is one possessing the view of the path, a noble disciple at the minimal level of a stream-enterer. "Formation" here is to be understood as a conditioned formation (*sankhata-sankhāra*), i.e., anything conditioned.

1085 MA points out that a noble disciple below the level of arahantship can still apprehend formations as pleasurable with a mind dissociated from wrong view, but he cannot adopt the view that any formation is pleasurable. Although perceptions and thoughts of formations as pleasurable arise in him, he knows reflectively that such notions are mistaken.

1086 In the passage on self, *sankhāra*, "formation," is replaced by *dhamma*, "thing." MA explains that this substitution is made to include concepts, such as a kasiṇa sign, etc., which the ordinary person is also prone to identify as self. However, in view of the fact that Nibbāna is described as imperishable (*accuta*) and as bliss (*sukha*), and is also liable to be misconceived as self (see MN 1.26), the word *sankhāra* may be taken to include only the conditioned, while *dhamma* includes both the conditioned and the unconditioned. This interpretation, however, is not endorsed by the commentaries of Ācariya Buddhaghosa.

1087 This section distinguishes the ordinary person and noble disciple in terms of the five heinous crimes. MA points out that a noble disciple is in fact incapable of intentionally depriving any living being of life, but the contrast is made here by way of matricide and patricide to stress the dangerous side of the ordinary person's condition and the strength of the noble disciple.

1088 That is, could acknowledge anyone other than the Buddha as the supreme spiritual teacher.

1089 MA: The arising of another Buddha is impossible from the time a bodhisatta takes his final conception in his mother's womb until his Dispensation has completely disappeared. The problem is discussed at Miln 236–39.

1090 This statement asserts only that a Fully Enlightened Buddha always has the male sex, but does not deny that a person who is now a woman may become a Fully Enlightened Buddha in the future. To do so, however, at an earlier point she will have had to be reborn as a man.

1091 In this passage the phrase "on that account, for that reason" (*tannidānā tappaccayā*) is of prime importance. As the Buddha will show in MN 136, a person who engages in evil conduct may be reborn in a heavenly world and a person who engages in good conduct may be reborn in a lower world. But in those cases the rebirth will be caused by some kamma different from the kamma in which the person habitually engages. Strict lawfulness applies only to the relation between kamma and its result.

1092 The "four cycles" are the elements, the bases, dependent origination, and the possible and the impossible.

SUTTA 116

1093 In Sri Lanka this sutta is regularly recited as a protective discourse and is included in the medieval compilation, *Mahā Pirit Pota*, "The Great Book of Protection."

1094 This and the following are mountains surrounding Rājagaha.

1095 A paccekabuddha is one who attains enlightenment and liberation on his own, without relying on the Dhamma taught by the Buddha, but is not capable of teaching the Dhamma to others and establishing the Dispensation. Paccekabuddhas arise only at a time when no Dispensation of a Buddha exists in the world. For a fuller study of the subject see Ria Kloppenborg, *The Paccekabuddha: A Buddhist Ascetic*.

1096 *Ayaṁ pabbato ime isī gilati*: a word play is involved here. The *gili* in Isigili is certainly a dialectical variant of *giri*, hill, but the text connects it to the verb *gilati*, to swallow, and to *gala*, throat, gullet.

1097 Tagarasikhin is referred to at Ud 5:4/50 and SN 3:20/i.92.

1098 Ñm remarks in Ms that without the aid of the commentary it is extremely difficult to distinguish the proper names of the paccekabuddhas from their descriptive epithets.

SUTTA 117

1099 *Ariyaṁ sammā samādhiṁ sa-upanisaṁ saparikkhāraṁ.* MA explains "noble" here as supramundane, and says that this is the concentration pertaining to the supramundane path. Its "supports and requisites," as will be shown, are the other seven path factors.

1100 *Pubbangamā,* lit. "the forerunner." MA says that two kinds of right view are forerunners: the right view of insight, which investigates formations as impermanent, suffering, and non-self; and the right view of the path, which arises as a consequence of insight and effects the radical destruction of defilements. The right view of insight as the forerunner seems to be shown in §§4, 10, 16, 22 and 28; the right view of the path as forerunner in §§34 and 35.

1101 This statement suggests that in order to acquire right view about the nature of reality, one must first be able to distinguish between wrong and right teachings on the nature of reality. MA says that this is the right view of insight which understands wrong view as an object by penetrating its characteristics of impermanence, etc., and which understands right view by exercising the function of comprehension and by clearing away confusion.

1102 This is mundane right view, a meritorious factor that conduces to a favourable rebirth but does not by itself transcend conditioned existence. The expression *upadhivepakka* is glossed by MA to mean that it gives results consisting in the acquisitions [MṬ: = the continuity of the five aggregates].

1103 This definition defines supramundane right view as the wisdom (*paññā*) found among the aids to enlightenment as a faculty, power, enlightenment factor, and path factor. The definition is formulated by way of the cognitive function rather than the objective content of right view. Elsewhere (MN 141.24) the right view of the path is defined as knowledge of the Four Noble Truths. We may understand that the conceptual comprehension of the four truths falls under mundane right view, while the direct penetration of the truths by realising Nibbāna with the path constitutes supramundane right view.

1104 MA: They accompany right view as its co-existents and precursors. Right effort and right mindfulness are co-existent with supramundane right view; the right view of insight is the precursor of supramundane right view.

1105 MA explains this as the right view of insight which understands right intention by way of its function and by clearing away confusion. It seems, though, that a more elementary discrimination of the two kinds of intention is the issue.

1106 This is the standard definition of right intention as a factor of the Noble Eightfold Path; see MN 141.25.

1107 In this definition, the factor of intention (*sankappa*) is identified with applied thought (*vitakka*), which is further specified as the factor responsible for absorption by fixing and directing the mind upon its object. For applied thought as "verbal formation," see MN 44.15.

1108 MA: This statement refers exclusively to the co-existent factors accompanying supramundane right intention. In the preliminary phase of the practice, the three mundane right intentions arise separately, but at the moment of the supramundane path, a single right intention arises cutting off the threefold wrong intention. Thus the supramundane right intention may also be described as the intention of renunciation, non-ill will, and non-cruelty. The same method applies to right speech, etc.

1109 Whereas mundane right speech is exercised in four different modes according to the type of wrong speech from which there is abstinence, on the occasion of the supramundane path, the single factor of right speech exercises the fourfold function of cutting off the tendencies towards the four kinds of wrong speech. The same principle applies to right action.

1110 These are wrong means for bhikkhus to acquire their requisites; they are explained at Vsm I, 61–65. MA says that those mentioned in the sutta are not the only kinds of wrong livelihood, which include any mode of earning one's living that involves transgression of the precepts.

At AN 5:177/iii.208, the Buddha mentions five kinds of wrong livelihood for lay people: dealing in arms, beings, meat, intoxicants, and poisons.

1111 MA explains that for one having the right view of the path, the right intention of the path comes into being; similarly, for one having the right view of the fruit, the right intention of the fruit comes into being. Similarly, the following factors except the last two also refer to the supramundane path.

1112 The additional two factors possessed by the arahant are right knowledge, which can be identified with his reviewing knowledge that he has destroyed all the defilements, and right deliverance, which can be identified with his experience of liberation from all defilements.

1113 The twenty factors on the wholesome side are the ten right factors and the wholesome states that originate from each; the twenty factors on the unwholesome side are the ten wrong factors and the unwholesome states that originate from each. Hence the name "The Great Forty."

1114 MA says only that these two were individuals who lived in the country of Okkala. Otherwise their identity is unknown.

SUTTA 118

1115 The Pavāraṇā is the ceremony that concludes the rains residence, at which each bhikkhu invites all the others to admonish him for his transgressions.

1116 Komudī is the full-moon day of the month of Kattika, the fourth month of the rainy season; it is called by this name because the white water-lily (*kumuda*) is said to bloom at that time.

1117 Explanatory notes for the first tetrad will be found at nn.140–142. MN 10.4 differs from this passage only by the addition of the simile. Since Ācariya Buddhaghosa has commented on the four tetrads on mindfulness of breathing in the *Visuddhimagga,* in MA he merely refers the reader to the latter work for explanation. Notes 1118–21 are drawn from Vsm VIII, 226–37, also included by Ñm in his *Mindfulness of Breathing*.

1118 One experiences rapture in two ways: by attaining one of the lower two jhānas in which rapture is present, one experiences rapture in the mode of serenity; by emerging from that jhāna and contemplating that rapture as subject to destruction, one experiences rapture in the mode of insight.

1119 The same method of explanation as in n.1118 applies to the second and third clauses, except that the second comprises the three lower jhānas and the third all four jhānas. The mental formation is perception and feeling (see MN 44.14), which is tranquillised by the development of successively higher levels of serenity and insight.

1120 "Experiencing the mind" is to be understood by way of the four jhānas. "Gladdening the mind" is explained either as the attainment of the two jhānas containing rapture or as the penetration of those jhānas with insight as subject to destruction, etc. "Concentrating the mind" refers either to the concentration pertaining to the jhāna or to the momentary concentration that arises along with insight. "Liberating the mind" means liberating it from hindrances and grosser jhānic factors by successively higher levels of concentration, and from the cognitive distortions by way of insight knowledge.

1121 This tetrad deals entirely with insight, unlike the previous three, which deal with both serenity and insight. "Contemplating fading away" and "contemplating cessation" can be understood both as the insight into the impermanence of formations and as the supramundane path realising Nibbāna, called the fading away of lust (i.e., dispassion, *virāga*) and the cessation of suffering. "Contemplating relinquishment" is the giving up of defilements through insight and the entering into Nibbāna by attainment of the path.

1122 MA: In-and-out breathing is to be counted as the air element among the four elements making up the body. It should also be included in the base of tangibles among bodily phenomena (since the object of attention is the touch sensation of the breath entering and leaving the nostrils).

1123 MA explains that close attention (*sādhuka manasikāra*) is not itself actually feeling, but is spoken of as such only figuratively. In the second tetrad the actual feeling is the pleasure mentioned in the second clause and also the feeling comprised by the expression "mental formation" in the third and fourth clauses.

1124 MA: Although the meditating bhikkhu takes as his object the sign of in-and-out breathing, he is said to be "contemplating mind as mind" because he maintains his mind on the object by arousing mindfulness and full awareness, two factors of mind.

1125 MA: Covetousness and grief signify the first two hindrances, sensual desire and ill will, and thus represent the contemplation of mind-objects, which begins with the five hindrances. The bhikkhu sees the abandoning of the hindrances effected by the contemplations of impermanence, fading away, cessation, and relinquishment, and thus comes to look upon the object with equanimity.

1126 MA says that the above passage shows the enlightenment factors existing together in each mind-moment in the practice of insight meditation.

1127 See n.48.

1128 MA: The mindfulness that comprehends breathing is mundane; the mundane mindfulness of breathing perfects the mundane foundations of mindfulness; the mundane foundations of mindfulness perfect the supramundane enlightenment factors; and the supramundane enlightenment factors perfect (or fulfil) true knowledge and deliverance, i.e., the fruit and Nibbāna.

SUTTA 119

1129 §§4–17 of this sutta is identical with MN 10.4–30, except that here the refrain on insight has been replaced by the refrain that begins "As he abides thus diligent." This change indicates a shift in emphasis from insight in MN 10 to concentration in the present sutta. This shift reappears in the passage on the jhānas at §§18–21 and the passage on the direct knowledges at §§37–41, both of which distinguish this sutta from MN 10.

1130 The similes for the jhānas are also found at MN 39.15–18 and MN 77.25–28.

1131 *Vijjābhāgiyā dhammā*. MA explains these states as the eight types of knowledge expounded at MN 77.29–36.

SUTTA 120

1132 Although I have attempted to render *sankhārā* consistently throughout as "formations," here it seemed that the content required a different rendering to bring the intended meaning to light. Ñm had used "determinations," his own consistent choice for *sankhārā*. MA initially explains *sankhārupapatti* as meaning either reappearance (i.e., rebirth) *of mere formations*, not of a being or person, or reappearance of the aggregates in a new existence *through a meritorious kamma-formation*. However, in subsequent passages, MA glosses *sankhārā* with *patthanā*, a word unambiguously meaning aspiration.

1133 MA: "The way" is the five qualities beginning with faith, together with the aspiration. One who has either the five qualities without the aspiration, or the aspiration without the qualities, does not have a fixed destination. The destination can only be fixed when both factors are present.

1134 MA explains that there are five kinds of pervasion: pervasion of mind, i.e., knowing the thoughts of the beings throughout a thousand worlds; pervasion of the kasiṇa, i.e., extending the kasiṇa image to a thousand worlds; pervasion of the divine eye, i.e., seeing a thousand worlds with the divine eye; pervasion of light, which is the same as the previous pervasion; and pervasion of body, i.e., extending one's bodily aura to a thousand worlds.

1135 See n.426.

1136 MA: The five qualities mentioned are sufficient for rebirth into the sense-sphere realm, but for the higher modes of rebirth and the destruction of the taints, more is required. Basing oneself on the five qualities, if one attains the jhānas, one is reborn in the Brahma-world; if one attains the immaterial attainments, one is reborn in the immaterial world; if one develops insight and attains the fruit of non-returning, one is reborn in the Pure Abodes; and if one reaches the path of arahantship, one attains the destruction of the taints.

SUTTA 121

1137 *Suññatāvihāra*. The discourse will gradually make it clear that this refers to the fruition attainment of voidness (*suññataphala-samāpatti*), the fruition attainment of arahantship that is entered by focusing upon the void aspect of Nibbāna. See n.458.

1138 MA: He attends to the perception of forest dependent on the single forest itself, thinking: "This is a forest, this is a tree, this is a mountain, this a grove." In the next sentence I read with BBS and SBJ *adhimuccati*, as against PTS *vimuccati*.

1139 MA and MṬ explain the sense of this passage thus: The disturbance of defilements—attraction and repulsion—that arise through perception of people are not present here. But there is still the disturbance caused by the occurrence of gross states due to lack of the necessary tranquillity.

1140 MA: He abandons the perception of forest and attends to the perception of earth because one cannot achieve any distinction in meditation through the perception of forest, neither access concentration nor full absorption. But earth can be used as the preliminary object for kasiṇa, on the basis of which one produces jhāna, develops insight, and attains arahantship.

1141 Having used the perception of earth to attain the four jhānas, he extends the earth-kasiṇa and then removes the kasiṇa sign to attain the base of infinite space. See Vsm X, 6–7.

1142 *Animitta cetosamādhi*. MA: This is the concentration of the mind in insight; it is called "signless" because it is devoid of the signs of permanence, etc.

1143 See MN 52.4. MA calls this "counter-insight" (*paṭivipassanā*), i.e., the application of the principles of insight to the act of consciousness that exercises the function of insight. On the basis of this he attains arahantship.

1144 Here the words "supreme and unsurpassed" (*paramānuttarā*) have been added. MA says that this is the arahant's fruition attainment of voidness.

SUTTA 122

1145 This sutta together with its full commentary has been published in translation by Ñm as *The Greater Discourse on Voidness.*

1146 MA: This was a dwelling built in Nigrodha's Park by Kāḷakhemaka the Sakyan. Beds, chairs, mattresses, and mats were prepared, and they were so close together that the dwelling looked like the residence of a society of bhikkhus.

1147 MA explains that this was merely a rhetorical question, since the Buddhas can know by direct knowledge whatever they wish to know. The Buddha asked this with the thought in mind: "As soon as these bhikkhus form into a society and delight in society, they will act in improper ways. I shall expound the Great Practice of Voidness which will be like a training rule [prohibiting delight in society]."

1148 MA: Ven. Ānanda intended to say: "These bhikkhus are living this way not just because they delight in being busy, but on account of making robes."

1149 See MN 66.20 and n.678.

1150 The former is deliverance through the jhānas and the immaterial attainments, the latter deliverance through the supramundane paths and fruits. See also MN 29.6 and n.348.

1151 MA: The Buddha begins the present passage in order to ward off the criticism that while he enjoins his disciples to live in solitude, he himself is often surrounded by a large retinue. "Voidness" here is the fruition attainment of voidness; see n.1137.

1152 MA explains voidness internally as that connected with one's own five aggregates, voidness externally as that connected with the aggregates of others. The voidness spoken of here thus must be the temporary deliverance of mind reached through the insight contemplation of non-self, as explained at MN 43.33. When the insight into non-self is brought to the level of the path, it issues in the fruition experiencing Nibbāna by way of its aspect of voidness.

1153 MA: He gives attention to an imperturbable immaterial meditative attainment.

1154 MA: This refers to the jhāna that was used as the basis for insight. If, after emerging from the basic jhāna, his mind does not enter into voidness through insight contemplation on his own aggregates or those of others, and he also cannot attain the imperturbable immaterial attainment, he should return to the same basic jhāna that he originally developed and attend to it again and again.

1155 According to MA, up to this point the Buddha has shown the training for the attainment of the first two paths, those of stream-entry and once-returning. He now speaks the present passage (§§14–15) to point out the insight needed to attain the path of non-returning, which culminates in the abandoning of sensual desire.

1156 This passage (§§16–17) points out the insight needed to attain the path of arahantship, which culminates in the abandoning of the conceit "I am."

1157 *Ācariyūpaddava, antevāsūpaddava, brahmacariyūpaddava. Upaddava* may also be rendered as disaster, calamity. MA explains that the Buddha speaks the present passage to show the danger in solitude when one does not fulfil the proper purpose of solitary living. The "teacher" is a teacher outside the Buddha's Dispensation.

1158 MA: The going forth into homelessness outside the Dispensation brings small gain, so one who falls away from that falls away only from mundane attainment; he meets with no great suffering, as one who falls from the back of a donkey merely becomes covered with dust. But the going forth in the Buddha's Dispensation brings great gain—the paths, fruits, and Nibbāna. Thus one who falls away from this meets great suffering, like one who falls from the back of an elephant.

1159 The contrast in this simile is between the way the potter treats the raw damp clay and the way he treats the baked pots produced from the clay. MA paraphrases: "After advising once I shall not be silent; I shall advise and instruct by repeatedly admonishing you. Just as the potter tests the baked pots, puts aside those that are cracked, split, or faulty, and keeps only those that pass the test, so I shall advise and instruct by repeatedly testing you. Those among you who are sound, having reached the paths and fruits, will stand the test." MA adds that the mundane virtuous qualities are also intended as a criterion of soundness.

SUTTA 123

1160 This ability is exemplified by DN 14, which provides detailed information about the six Buddhas preceding Gotama.

1161 This refers to the Bodhisatta's rebirth in the Tusita heaven, which followed his preceding human existence as Vessantara and preceded his birth in the human world as Siddhattha Gotama.

1162 MA: Between every three world systems there is an interspace measuring 8,000 yojanas; it is like the space between three cartwheels or almsbowls touching one another. The beings who live there have taken rebirth there because of committing some heavy, terrible offence against their parents or righteous recluses and brahmins, or because of some habitual evil deed like killing animals, etc.

1163 MA: The four deities were the Four Great Kings (the presiding deities of the heaven of the Four Great Kings).

1164 MA: This happened, not through a defect in the birth, but through the expiration of her lifespan; for the place (in the womb) occupied by the Bodhisatta, like the inner chamber of a cetiya, is not to be used by others.

1165 MA explains each aspect of this event as a foretoken of the Buddha's later attainments. Thus, his standing with his feet (*pāda*) firmly on the ground was a foretoken of his attaining the four bases for spiritual power (*iddhipāda*); his facing the north, of his going above and beyond the multitude; his seven steps, of his acquiring the seven enlightenment factors; the white parasol, of his acquiring the parasol of deliverance; his surveying the quarters, of his acquiring the unobstructed knowledge of omniscience; his uttering the words of the Leader of the Herd, of his setting in motion the irreversible Wheel of the Dhamma; his statement "This is my last birth," of his passing away into the Nibbāna element with no residue remaining (of the factors of existence).

1166 This statement seems to be the Buddha's way of calling attention to the quality he regarded as the true wonder and marvel.

SUTTA 124

1167 According to MA, Ven. Bakkula became a monk in his eightieth year, which would make him 160 at the time this sutta takes place. He was declared by the Buddha to be the foremost disciple with respect to good health.

1168 MA says that the passages here enclosed in brackets were added by the elders who compiled the Dhamma.

1169 This passage and those to follow show Ven. Bakkula as an observer of the ascetic practices. The *kaṭhina* time is the period following the three-month rains residence when bhikkhus make new robes from the cloth they have received.

1170 MA says that after he went forth, he was an ordinary man for seven days, but on the eighth day he attained arahantship together with the analytical knowledges (*paṭisambhidā*).

1171 MA: Ven. Bakkula himself did not give the ordination (which would have been a violation of his mode of practice) but arranged for other bhikkhus to give it.

1172 MA: Ven. Bakkula had considered that all his life he had never made himself a burden to the other bhikkhus, and he did not want his body to be a burden after his death. Thus he entered into meditation on the heat element and attained final Nibbāna by causing his entire body to be consumed by the blaze. Only the relics remained.

1173 MA says that this sutta was recited at the second compilation of the Dhamma, held about a hundred years after the Buddha's passing away.

SUTTA 125

1174 MA identifies Prince Jayasena as a son of King Bimbisāra.

1175 The simile as at MN 90.11.

1176 Note that here the four foundations of mindfulness are expounded in the place usually reserved for the four jhānas.

1177 I translate on the basis of BBS and SBJ (supported by a 1937 Sinhala edition) rather than PTS. Both BBS and SBJ abridge the passage; where PTS reads *kāyūpasaṁhitaṁ* and *dhammūpasaṁhitaṁ*, these two eds. read *kāmūpasaṁhitaṁ* in both places, a significant difference. I am told that the Chinese translation of the Madhyama Āgama (the Skt counterpart of MN) has a reading that corresponds to that of BBS and SBJ. The Chinese version mentions all four jhānas.

SUTTA 126

1178 MA says that Ven. Bhūmija was the uncle of Prince Jayasena.

1179 *Āsaṁ karitvā*: if one makes a wish, if one raises a hope or expectation. The recluses and brahmins who held this view must have been the sceptics or the annihilationists.

SUTTA 127

1180 *Appamāṇā cetovimutti, mahaggatā cetovimutti.* At MN 43.31, as here, the immeasurable deliverance of mind is explained as the four *brahmavihāras*. Since the formula for each *brahmavihāra* includes the word "exalted," Pañcakanga was apparently misled into supposing that the two deliverances were the same in meaning.

1181 MA: He covers an area the size of one tree root with his kasiṇa sign, and he abides resolved upon that kasiṇa sign, pervading it with the exalted jhāna. The same method of explanation applies to the following cases.

1182 MA: This teaching is undertaken to show the kinds of rebirth that result from the attainment of the exalted deliverance.

1183 MA explains that there are no separate realms of gods called those of "Defiled Radiance" and those of "Pure Radiance." Both are subdivisions within the two realms—the gods of Limited Radiance and the gods of

Immeasurable Radiance. Rebirth among the gods of Limited Radiance is determined by the attainment of the (second) jhāna with a limited kasiṇa sign, rebirth among the gods of Immeasurable Radiance by the attainment of the same jhāna with an extended kasiṇa sign. Rebirth with defiled radiance is for those who have not mastered the jhāna and purified it of obstructive states; rebirth with pure radiance is for those who have acquired this mastery and purification.

1184 A pun is involved here. In Pali the verb *jhāyati* means both to burn and to meditate, though the two meanings are derived from different Sanskrit verbs: *kshāyati* is to burn, *dhyāyati* to meditate.

1185 Abhiya's words, it seems, are discourteous because they inquire very bluntly into the personal experience of Ven. Anuruddha. MA says that while fulfilling the perfections (*pāramīs*) in past lives, Anuruddha had gone forth as a recluse, reached the meditative attainments, and passed three hundred existences without interruption in the Brahma-world. Hence his reply.

SUTTA 128

1186 The opening of this sutta is the same as that of MN 48.

1187 This verse and the next two appear at Dhp 3, 5–6. The last three verses are at Dhp 328–30.

1188 The passage at §§8–15 is nearly identical with MN 31.3–10. From the sequel, however, it is clear that the present sutta is set at an earlier time, for in MN 31 all three bhikkhus have reached arahantship while here they are still striving for the goal.

1189 It is here that the present sutta continues differently from MN 31. MA explains light (*obhāsa*) as the preliminary light, which MṬ glosses as the light produced by the access to jhāna. MṬ adds that one who gains the fourth jhāna develops the light-kasiṇa as the preliminary to arousing the divine eye. The "vision of forms" (*dassanaṁ rūpānaṁ*) is the seeing of forms with the divine eye. Ven. Anuruddha was later declared by the Buddha to be the foremost disciple in the exercise of the divine eye.

1190 *Nimittaṁ paṭivijjhitabbaṁ.* Lit. "You should penetrate that sign."

1191 See MN 52.15.

1192 MA paraphrases: "While I was attending to a single type of form, longing arose. Thinking 'I will attend to different kinds of forms,' sometimes I directed my attention towards the heavenly world, sometimes towards the human world. As I attended to different kinds of forms, perception of diversity arose in me."

1193 *Atinijjhāyitattaṁ rūpānaṁ.* MA: "When perception of diversity arose, I thought I would attend to one type of form, whether agreeable or disagreeable. As I did so, excessive meditation upon forms arose in me."

1194 *Cittassa upakkileso.* The same term is used at MN 7.3, though here it means imperfections in the development of concentration. Hence the expression has been rendered slightly differently in the two cases.

1195 The "three ways" seem to be the first three types of concentration mentioned in the next paragraph, also spoken of as a triad at DN 33.1.10/iii.219. Of these, the first is the first jhāna and the third covers the three higher jhānas of the usual fourfold scheme. The second type of concentration has no place in the fourfold scheme, but appears as the second jhāna in a fivefold division of jhānas expounded in the Abhidhamma Piṭaka. This second jhāna of the fivefold scheme is attained by those who cannot overcome applied thought and sustained thought simultaneously but must eliminate them successively.

1196 MA: The concentration with rapture is the two lower jhānas; without rapture, the two higher jhānas; accompanied by enjoyment (*sāta*), the three lower jhānas; accompanied by equanimity, the fourth jhāna. PTS omits *sātasahagato pi samādhi bhāvito ahosi*, found in the other eds.

1197 MA says that the Buddha developed these concentrations in the last watch of the night on the night of his enlightenment while sitting at the foot of the Bodhi tree.

SUTTA 129

1198 As at MN 13.14.

1199 The following simile is employed at SN 12:63/ii.100 to illustrate the nutriment of consciousness (*viññāṇāhāra*).

1200 And he will—at MN 130.17–27.

1201 MA: That is, the fool engages in the three types of misconduct, because of which he is reborn in hell. By the residue of that kamma, when he comes back to the human state he is reborn in a low family. Having again engaged in the three types of misconduct, he is again reborn in hell.

1202 Although the Pali does not contain the negative particle *na*, it seems to be required here to yield the intended meaning, and it does appear in the parallel clauses of the following paragraph.

1203 See MN 91.5. The legend of the Wheel-turning Monarch is treated more extensively in DN 17 and DN 26.

1204 See n.809.

1205 MA: That is, the wise man engages in the three types of good conduct, because of which he is reborn in heaven. Returning to the human world, he is reborn in a good family with wealth and beauty. He engages in the three types of good conduct and is again reborn in heaven. It should be noted that the "complete perfection of the wise man's grade" is entirely mundane and takes no account of the more excellent stages along the path to liberation.

SUTTA 130

1206 Yama is the god of death. MA says that he is a king of spirits possessing a celestial mansion. Sometimes he lives in his celestial mansion enjoying celestial pleasures, sometimes he experiences the result of kamma; he is a righteous king. MA adds that there are in fact four Yamas, one at each of four gates (of hell?).

1207 According to Buddhist legend, three of the divine messengers—the old man, the sick man, and the dead man—appeared to the Bodhisatta while he was living in the palace, destroying his enchantment with the worldly life and awakening in him a desire to seek the way to deliverance. See AN 3:38/i.145–46 for the psychological nucleus out of which the legend must have developed.

1208 The following description of hell, down to §16, is also found at MN 129.10–16.

SUTTA 131

1209 This discourse with a lengthy introduction and notes is available separately in a translation by Bhikkhu Ñāṇananda under the title *Ideal Solitude*.

1210 In the first edition I followed Ñm in rendering *bhaddekaratta* as "one fortunate attachment." At the suggestion of Ven. Thānissaro Bhikkhu, however, I have changed it to "a single excellent night," which seems more likely to be correct. *Ratta* and *ratti* could be taken to represent respectively either Skt *rātra* and *rātri* (= night) or Skt *rakta* and *rakti* (= attachment). Ñm had taken the words in the latter sense, but the fact that neither MA nor MṬ glosses *ratta* implies that "night" is intended; for if the word were used to mean attachment, an unwholesome state in typical Buddhist discourse, some commentarial clarification would surely have been offered. The Central Asian Skt version, the Skt title at the head of the Tibetan version, and the Tibetan translation itself all use *bhadrakarātri*. This confirms the identification of *ratta* with "night"; the change from *-e-* to *-a-* can be understood as an attempt to convert a difficult reading into a more familiar one. (I am indebted to Peter Skilling for this information.) The Chinese Madhyama Āgama has merely transliterated the title of the Skt version and thus offers no help.

Apart from this series of suttas, the expression *bhaddekaratta* does not occcur elsewhere in the Pali Canon. MA merely says: "'A single-excellent-nighter' is one with a single night who is excellent because of possessing application to insight" (*bhaddekarattassā ti vipassanāyogasamannāgatattā bhaddekassa ekarattassa*). MṬ simply gives word resolutions (*ekā ratti ekaratto; bhaddo ekaratto etassā ti bhaddekarattaṁ*) and says this refers to a person cultivating insight. As the verse emphasises the urgent need to conquer death by developing insight, the title probably describes a meditator who has had a single excellent night (and day) devoted to practising insight meditation "invincibly, unshakeably." Ñm says in Ms: "It might be supposed that the expression *'bhaddekaratta'* was a popular phrase taken over by the Buddha and given a special sense by him, as was not infrequently done, but there seems to be no reason to do so and there is no evidence for it in this case. It is more likely to be a term coined by the Buddha himself to describe a certain aspect of development."

1211 More literally the first two lines would be translated: "Let not a person run back to the past or live in expectation of the future." The meaning will be elucidated in the expository passage of the sutta.

1212 MA: He should contemplate each presently arisen state, just where it has arisen, by way of the seven contemplations of insight (insight into impermanence, suffering, non-self, disenchantment, dispassion, cessation, relinquishment).

1213 *Asaṁhīraṁ asankuppaṁ.* MA explains that this is said for the purpose of showing insight and counter-insight (see n.1143); for insight is "invincible, unshakeable" because it is not vanquished or shaken by lust and other defilements. Elsewhere the expression "the invincible, the unshakeable" is used as a description of Nibbāna (e.g., Sn v.1149) or of the liberated mind (e.g., Thag v.649), but here it seems to refer to a stage in the development of insight. The recurrence of the verb form *saṁhīrati* in §8 and §9 suggests that the intended meaning is contemplation of the present moment without being misled into the adoption of a view of self.

1214 The "Peaceful Sage" (*santo muni*) is the Buddha.

1215 MA: One "finds delight" by bringing to bear upon the past either craving or a view associated with craving. It should be noted that it is not the mere recollection of the past through memory that causes bondage, but the reliving of past experiences with thoughts of craving. In this respect the Buddha's teaching differs significantly from that of Krishnamurti, who seems to regard memory itself as the villain behind the scene.

1216 The syntax of the Pali allows this sentence to be interpreted in two ways, as stating either that one thinks, "I had such form in the past," yet does not find delight in that thought; or that one does not find delight in the past by thinking such a thought. Horner, Ñāṇananda (in *Ideal Solitude*), and Ñm (in Ms) construe the sentence in the former way; I had preserved Ñm's rendering in the first edition. On reconsideration, I now believe that the second interpretation is more true to the intention of the text. This also ties in better with the stanzas themselves, which enjoin the disciple not to dwell in the past and the future but to contemplate "each presently arisen state" just as it presents itself.

1217 In the first edition, this sentence was rendered: "Thinking, 'I may have such material form in the future,' one finds delight in that." In retrospect, it now seems to me more likely that the sentence expresses an exclamatory wish for the future.

1218 The verb here and in the next paragraph, *saṁhīrati*, refers back to the line in the verse, "invincibly, unshakeably." MA glosses: "One is dragged along by craving and views because of the lack of insight."

SUTTA 133

1219 Down to §12, as at MN 18.10–15.

1220 MA: In the two previous suttas and in the one to follow the Buddha set up the outline and analysis by way of the five aggregates, but here he set it up so that it could be analysed by way of the twelve sense bases. Understanding the Buddha's intention, Ven. Mahā Kaccāna spoke as he did, and because of his skill in grasping the method even when it was not explicitly shown, the Buddha appointed him the foremost disciple in explaining in detail a teaching stated in brief.

SUTTA 134

1221 According to the commentary to Thag, Ven. Lomasakangiya had been a bhikkhu in the time of the Buddha Kassapa. After the Buddha Kassapa had taught the *Bhaddekaratta Sutta*, a certain bhikkhu spoke about it to Lomasakangiya. Unable to understand it, he exclaimed: "In the future, may I be able to teach you this sutta!" The other answered: "May I ask you about it!" In the present age Lomasakangiya was born into a Sakyan family at Kapilavatthu, while the other bhikkhu became the god Candana.

1222 MA explains that this occurred in the seventh year after the Buddha's enlightenment, at the time when he spent the three months of the rainy season in the heaven of the Thirty-three teaching the Abhidhamma to the gods who had assembled from ten thousand world-systems.

SUTTA 135

1223 See MN 99. According to MA, his father, the brahmin Todeyya, was reborn as a dog in his own house because of his extreme stinginess. The Buddha identified him to Subha by getting the dog to dig up some hidden treasure Subha's father had buried before his death. This inspired Subha's confidence in the Buddha and moved him to approach and inquire about the workings of kamma.

1224 If the kamma of killing directly determines the mode of rebirth, it will produce rebirth in one of the states of deprivation. But if a wholesome kamma brings about a human rebirth—and rebirth as a human being is always the result of wholesome kamma—the kamma of killing will operate in a manner contrary to that of the rebirth-generative kamma by causing various adversities that may eventuate in a premature death. The same principle holds for the subsequent cases in which unwholesome kamma comes to maturity in a human existence: in each case the unwholesome kamma counteracts the wholesome kamma responsible for the human rebirth by engendering a specific type of misfortune corresponding to its own distinctive quality.

1225 In this case the wholesome kamma of abstaining from killing may be directly responsible for either the heavenly rebirth or the longevity in a human existence. The same principle applies in all the passages on the maturation of wholesome kamma.

SUTTA 136

1226 MA says that Potaliputta did not actually hear this personally from the Buddha, but had heard a report that these statements were made by the Buddha. The former is a distorted version of the Buddha's declaration at MN 56.5 that mental action is the most reprehensible of the three types of deeds for the performance of evil action. The latter derives from the Buddha's discussion of the cessation of perception in the *Poṭṭhapāda Sutta* (DN 9). MA glosses the word "vain" by "fruitless."

1227 This statement is made by the Buddha at SN 36:11/ iv.216, with reference to the suffering inherent in all formations by reason of their impermanence. Though the statement itself is true, Samiddhi seems to have misinterpreted it to mean that all feeling is felt as suffering, which is patently false.

1228 MA: This section is not the expounding of the Tathāgata's knowledge of the great exposition of action, but the setting up of the outline for the purpose of presenting that exposition.

1229 MA: This too is not the expounding of the knowledge of the great exposition of action, but is still the setting up of the outline. The purpose here is to show what can be accepted and what should be rejected in the claims of the outside recluses and brahmins. Briefly put, the propositions that report their direct observations can be accepted, but the generalisations they derive from those observations must be rejected.

1230 Here begins the expounding of the knowledge of the great exposition of action.

1231 MA: The person who was seen with the divine eye

killing living beings, etc., is reborn in hell because of another evil deed he had done earlier than the deed of killing, etc., or because of an evil deed he did afterwards, or because of a wrong view he accepted at the time of death. Although the Pali seems to be saying that he was necessarily reborn in hell on account of some action other than the one he was seen performing, this should not be understood as an apodictic pronouncement but only as a statement of possibility. That is, while it may be true that he was reborn in hell because of the evil action he was seen performing, it is also possible that he was reborn there because of some other evil action he did earlier or later or because of wrong view.

1232 This statement shows that even if his evil kamma does not generate the mode of rebirth, it will still mature for him in some other way either in this life, in the next life, or in some more distant future life.

1233 In this case the heavenly rebirth must be due to some action other than the one he was seen performing, since an evil action cannot produce a fortunate mode of rebirth.

1234 MA explains *abhabba*, incapable, as the unwholesome (*akusala*), called "incapable" because it is devoid of the capacity for growth; and *bhabba*, capable, as the wholesome, called "capable" because it has the capacity for growth. This explanation sounds suspect; *bhabba* (Skt *bhavya*) may simply mean "potent, capable of producing results," without implying any particular moral valuation. MA gives two explanations of the tetrad. The first devolves on taking the suffix *-ābhāsa* to mean "outshine" or "overcome," and thus the four terms exemplify the way a kamma of one quality can "outshine" another in generating its result. The second explanation, which seems more cogent, takes *-ābhāsa* to mean "appears," which I follow in the translation. On this explanation, the first type is illustrated by the person who kills living beings and is reborn in hell: his action is incapable (of good result) because it is unwholesome, and it appears incapable because, since he is reborn in hell, it seems to be the cause for his rebirth there. The second is illustrated by the person who kills living beings and is reborn in heaven: his action is incapable (of good result) because it is unwholesome, yet it appears capable because he is reborn in heaven; thus to the outside recluses and brahmins it seems to be the cause for his rebirth in heaven. The remaining two terms should be understood along the same lines, with appropriate changes.

SUTTA 137

1235 MA: Mental exploration (*manopavicāra*) is applied thought and sustained thought. One explores (or examines, *upavicarati*) the object by the occurrence of sustained thought (*vicāra*), and applied thought is associated with the latter.

1236 MA: Having seen a form with eye-consciousness, one explores a form which, as an object, is a cause of joy (grief, equanimity).

1237 MA: These are positions (*pada*) for beings who are intent on the round of existence and for those intent on the cessation of the round.

1238 MA: "Based on the household life" means connected with the cords of sensual pleasure; "based on renunciation" means connected with insight.

1239 MA: This is the joy that arises when one has set up insight and is sitting watching the breakup of formations with a current of sharp and bright insight knowledge focused on formations.

1240 MA explains "the supreme liberations" and "that base" as arahantship. See MN 44.28.

1241 MA: This is the equanimity of unknowing that arises in one who has not conquered the limitations imposed by the defilements or the future results (of action). It "does not transcend the form" because it is stuck, fastened to the object like flies to a ball of sugar.

1242 MA: This is the equanimity associated with insight knowledge. It does not become lustful towards desirable objects that come into range of the senses, nor does it become angry because of undesirable objects.

1243 MA says that previously worldly equanimity was discussed, but here the contrast is between the equanimity in differentiated sense experience and the equanimity of the meditative attainments.

1244 MA paraphrases: "By the equanimity of the immaterial attainments, abandon the equanimity of the fine-material attainments; by insight into the immaterial sphere, abandon insight into the fine-material sphere."

1245 MA says that non-identification (*atammayatā*—see n.1066) here refers to "insight leading to emergence," i.e., the insight immediately preceding the arising of the supramundane path; for this effects the abandonment of the equanimity of the immaterial attainments and the equanimity of insight.

1246 *Satipaṭṭhāna* here obviously has a different meaning than usual, as the sequel will make clear. The "Noble One" is the Buddha.

1247 This is one of the nine epithets of the Buddha in the usual enumeration of the Buddha's qualities.

1248 These "eight directions" are the eight liberations, on which see n.764.

SUTTA 138

1249 It is strange that the Buddha, having announced that he will teach a summary and an exposition, should recite only the summary and leave without giving the exposition. Although elsewhere the Buddha departs suddenly after making an enigmatic statement (e.g., in MN 18), on those occasions he had not previously declared his intention to give an exposition. MA offers no explanation.

1250 MA: Consciousness is "distracted and scattered externally," i.e., among external objects, when it occurs by way of attachment towards an external object.

1251 MṬ: The form itself is called the sign of form (*rūpanimitta*) in that it is the cause for the arising of defilements. One "follows after it" by way of lust.

1252 MA: The mind is "stuck internally" by way of attachment to an internal object. The text of the sutta itself makes the shift from *viññāṇa* in the Buddha's summary to *citta* in Mahā Kaccāna's exposition.

1253 All known editions of the Pali text of MN 138 read here *anupādā paritassanā,* literally "agitation due to non-clinging," which obviously contradicts what the Buddha consistently teaches: that agitation arises from clinging, and ceases with the removal of clinging. However, this reading apparently predates the commentaries, for MA accepts *anupādā* as correct and offers the following explanation: "In what sense is there agitation due to non-clinging? Through the non-existence of anything to cling to. For if there existed any formation that were permanent, stable, a self, or the belonging of a self, it would be possible to cling to it. Then this agitation would be agitation due to clinging (something to cling to). But because there is no formation that can be clung to thus, then even though material form, etc., are clung to with the idea 'material form is self,' etc., they are not clung to (in the way they are conceived). Thus, what is here called 'agitation due to non-clinging' is in meaning agitation due to clinging by way of views." Ñm had followed this reading, and on the basis of MA's explanation, had rendered the phrase "anguish [agitation] due to not finding anything to cling to." He did not discuss the problem in his notes.

A sutta in the Saṁyutta Nikāya (SN 22:7/iii, 16) is virtually identical with this passage of MN 138, except that here it reads, as we should expect, *upādā paritassanā,* "agitation due to clinging." From the Saṁyutta text we may safely infer that the Majjhima reading is an ancient error that should be discounted. My rendering here is based on the reading of SN 22:7. Horner too follows the latter text in MLS.

1254 MA explains the unusual phrase *paritassanā dhammasamuppādā* as "the agitation of craving and the arising of (other) unwholesome states."

1255 The agitation thus results from the lack of any permanent essence in things that could provide a refuge from the suffering precipitated by their change and instability.

1256 This phrase is identical in both the Majjhima and Saṁyutta versions.

SUTTA 139

1257 This is substantially identical with the proclamation with which the newly enlightened Buddha opened his first discourse to the five bhikkhus, before teaching them the Four Noble Truths.

1258 This is a more complicated expression for the pursuit of sensual pleasure.

1259 MA: It is "beset by suffering, vexation," etc., through the suffering and vexation, etc., of its results and the suffering and vexation, etc., of its attendant defilements.

1260 This is craving for being. Just below we should read again *bhavasaṁyojanaṁ* (with BBS and SBJ) as against PTS *vibhavasaṁyojanaṁ*.

1261 That is, extolling and disparaging come about when one frames one's statements in terms of persons, some of whom are praised and others blamed. One teaches "only the Dhamma" when one frames one's statements in terms of the state (*dhamma*)—the mode of practice—without explicit references to persons.

1262 This problem of "insistence on local language" must have been particularly acute in the Sangha, when the bhikkhus lived a life of constant wandering and had to pass through many localities each with their distinct dialects.

1263 Ven. Subhūti was the younger brother of Anāthapiṇḍika and became a bhikkhu on the day Jeta's Grove was offered to the Sangha. The Buddha appointed him the foremost disciple in two categories—those who live without conflict and those who are worthy of gifts.

SUTTA 140

1264 According to MA, Pukkusāti had been the king of Takkasilā and had entered into a friendship with King Bimbisāra of Magadha through merchants who travelled between the two countries for purposes of trade. In an exchange of gifts Bimbisāra sent Pukkusāti a golden plate on which he had inscribed descriptions of the Three Jewels and various aspects of the Dhamma. When Pukkusāti read the inscription, he was filled with joy and decided to renounce the world. Without taking formal ordination, he shaved his head, put on yellow robes, and left the palace. He went to Rājagaha intending to meet the Buddha, who was then in Sāvatthī, about 300 miles away. The Buddha saw Pukkusāti with his clairvoyant knowledge, and recognising his capacity to attain the paths and fruits, he journeyed alone on foot to Rājagaha to meet him. To avoid being recognised, by an act of will the Buddha caused his special physical attributes such as the marks of a Great Man to be concealed, and he appeared just like an ordinary wandering monk. He arrived at the potter's shed shortly after Pukkusāti had arrived there intending to leave for Sāvatthī the next day in order to meet the Buddha.

1265 Pukkusāti, unaware that the new arrival is the Buddha, addresses him by the familiar appellation *"āvuso."*

1266 MA: The Buddha asked these questions merely as a way to start a conversation, as he already knew that Pukkusāti had gone forth on account of himself.

1267 MA: Since Pukkusāti had already purified the preliminary practice of the path and was able to attain the fourth jhāna through mindfulness of breathing, the Buddha began directly with a talk on insight meditation, expounding the ultimate voidness that is the foundation for arahantship.

1268 MA: Here the Buddha expounds the non-truly existent by way of the truly existent; for the elements are truly existent but the person is not truly existent. This is meant: "That which you perceive as a person consists of six elements. Ultimately there is no person here. 'Person' is a mere concept."

1269 As at MN 137.8.

1270 *Paññādhiṭṭhāna, saccādhiṭṭhāna, cāgādhiṭṭhāna, upasamādhiṭṭhāna.* Ñm, in Ms, had first rendered *adhiṭṭhāna* as "resolve," and then replaced it with "mode of expression," neither of which seems suitable for this context. MA glosses the word with *patiṭṭhā,* which clearly means foundation, and explains the sense of the statement thus: "This person who consists of the six elements, the six bases of contact, and the eighteen kinds of mental approach—when he turns away from these and attains arahantship, the supreme accomplishment, he does so established upon these four bases." The four foundations will be individually elucidated by the sequel, §§12–29.

1271 MA: From the start one should not neglect the wisdom born of concentration and insight in order to penetrate through to the wisdom of the fruit of arahantship. One should preserve truthful speech in order to realise Nibbāna, the ultimate truth. One should cultivate the relinquishment of defilements in order to relinquish all defilements by the path of arahantship. From the start one should train in the pacification of defilements in order to pacify all defilements by the path of arahantship. Thus the wisdom, etc., born of serenity and insight are spoken of as the preliminary foundations for achieving the foundations of wisdom, etc. (distinctive of arahantship).

1272 MA: The non-neglecting of wisdom is explained by way of the meditation on the elements. The analysis of the elements here is identical with that of MN 28.6, 11, 16, 21 and MN 62.8–12.

1273 MA: This is the sixth element, which "remains" in that it has yet to be expounded by the Buddha and penetrated by Pukkusāti. Here it is explained as the consciousness that accomplishes the work of insight contemplation on the elements. Under the heading of consciousness, the contemplation of feeling is also introduced.

1274 This passage shows the conditionality of feeling and its impermanence through the cessation of its condition.

1275 MA identifies this as the equanimity of the fourth jhāna. According to MA, Pukkusāti had already achieved the fourth jhāna and had a strong attachment to it. The Buddha first praises this equanimity to inspire Pukkusāti's confidence, then he gradually leads him to the immaterial jhānas and the attainment of the paths and fruits.

1276 The sense is: If he attains the base of infinite space and should pass away while still attached to it, he would be reborn in the plane of infinite space and would live there for the full lifespan of 20,000 aeons specified for that plane. In the higher three immaterial planes the lifespan is respectively 40,000 aeons, 60,000 aeons, and 84,000 aeons.

1277 MA: This is said in order to show the danger in the

immaterial jhānas. By the one phrase, "This would be conditioned," he shows: "Even though the lifespan there is 20,000 aeons, that is conditioned, fashioned, built up. It is thus impermanent, unstable, not lasting, transient. It is subject to perishing, breaking up, and dissolution; it is involved with birth, ageing, and death, grounded upon suffering. It is not a shelter, a place of safety, a refuge. Having passed away there as a worldling, one can still be reborn in the four states of deprivation."

1278 *So n'eva abhisankharoti nābhisañcetayati bhavāya vā vibhavāya.* The two verbs suggest the notion of volition as a constructive power that builds up the continuation of conditioned existence. Ceasing to will for either being or non-being shows the extinction of craving for eternal existence and annihilation, culminating in the attainment of arahantship.

1279 MA says that at this point Pukkusāti penetrated three paths and fruits, becoming a non-returner. He realised that his teacher was the Buddha himself, but he could not express his realisation since the Buddha still continued with his discourse.

1280 This passage shows the arahant's abiding in the Nibbāna element with a residue remaining (of the factors of conditioned existence, *sa-upādisesa nibbānadhātu*). Though he continues to experience feelings, he is free from lust towards pleasant feeling, from aversion towards painful feeling, and from ignorance about neutral feeling.

1281 That is, he continues to experience feeling only as long as the body with its life faculty continues, but not beyond that.

1282 This refers to his attainment of the Nibbāna-element with no residue remaining (*anupādisesa nibbānadhātu*)—the cessation of all conditioned existence with his final passing away.

1283 This completes the exposition of the first foundation, which began at §13. MA says that the knowledge of the destruction of all suffering is the wisdom pertaining to the fruit of arahantship.

1284 MA mentions four kinds of acquisitions (*upadhi*) here: see n.674.

1285 The "tides of conceiving" (*maññussavā*), as the following paragraph will show, are thoughts and notions originating from the three roots of conceiving—craving, conceit, and views. For a fuller explanation, see n.6. The "sage at peace" (*muni santo*) is the arahant.

1286 That which is not present in him is craving for being, which leads those who have not eradicated it back to a new birth following death.

1287 MA says that he was reborn in the Pure Abode called Avihā and attained arahantship as soon as he took rebirth there. It quotes a verse from the Saṁyutta Nikāya (SN 1:50/i.35) mentioning Pukkusāti as one of seven bhikkhus who were reborn in Avihā and attained deliverance by transcending the celestial bonds.

SUTTA 141

1288 This refers to the Buddha's first sermon, delivered to the five bhikkhus in the Deer Park at Isipatana.

1289 MA: Ven. Sāriputta trains them until he knows they have attained the fruit of stream-entry, then he lets them develop the higher paths on their own and he takes on a new batch of pupils. But Ven. Moggallāna continues to train his pupils until they have attained arahantship.

1290 The definitions of birth, ageing, and death are also found at MN 9.22, 26. This entire detailed analysis of the Four Noble Truths is included in the *Mahāsatipaṭṭhāna Sutta*, with an even more elaborate exposition of the second and third truths. See DN 22.18–21/ii.305–13.

SUTTA 142

1291 Mahāpajāpatī Gotamī was the younger sister of Queen Mahāmāyā, the Buddha's mother, and was also the wife of King Suddhodana. After Mahāmāyā's death, she became the Buddha's foster mother. The present sutta takes place at an early point in the Buddha's ministry, on one of his return visits to his native city. After King Suddhodana's death, Mahāpajāpatī pleaded with the Buddha to admit women into the Sangha, and her acceptance marked the beginning of the Bhikkhunī Sangha, the Order of Nuns. The story is found at Vin Cv Kh 10/ii.253–56 (see Ñāṇamoli, *The Life of the Buddha*, pp. 104–7).

An interesting anachronism in this sutta was brought to my notice by Ven. Ajahn Sucitto of Cittaviveka Monastery. The sutta depicts Mahāpajāpatī Gotamī as a devout lay Buddhist and refers to the Bhikkhunī Sangha as if it were an existing reality, yet the canonical account of the founding of the Bhikkhunī Sangha shows Mahāpajāpatī to have been the first historical bhikkhunī. Thus the Bhikkhunī Sangha could not have existed at the time the sutta was spoken if Mahāpajāpatī was still a lay woman. We might resolve the discrepancy (unnoticed by the commentator) by supposing that the original discourse was later modified after the founding of the Bhikkhunī Sangha to bring the latter into the scheme of offerings to the Sangha.

1292 MA: The Buddha asked her to give the gift to the Sangha because he wanted her volition of generosity to be directed both to the Sangha and to himself, as the combined volition would yield merit conducive to her welfare and happiness for a long time to come. He also said this so that later generations would be inspired to show respect towards the Sangha, and by supporting the Sangha with the four physical requisites would contribute towards the longevity of the Dispensation.

1293 These are the four factors of stream-entry. Thus it is clear that at the time this sutta takes place, Mahāpajāpatī Gotamī was already a stream-enterer.

1294 MA: The Buddha undertakes this teaching because the sutta began with a personal gift presented to him, and he wishes to make clear the comparative value of personal gifts and gifts offered to the Sangha.

1295 MA and MṬ explain that this term can be loosely extended to include even a lay follower who has gone for refuge to the Triple Gem, as well as lay people and monks intent on fulfilling the moral training and the practice of concentration and insight. In the strict technical sense it refers only to those possessing the supramundane path of stream-entry.

1296 This is a non-Buddhist contemplative who attains the jhānas and the mundane kinds of direct knowledge.

1297 MA: In a hundred existences it gives long life, beauty, happiness, strength, and intelligence, and it makes one free of agitation. The following attainments should be understood accordingly.

1298 MA says that although the results of giving in each of these cases is incalculable, there is still an ascending gradation in their incalculability, similar to the ascending incalculability of the waters in a great river, etc., up to that of the waters in the ocean. Perhaps the "incalculable, immeasurable" value of these gifts consists in their becoming a supporting condition for attainment of the paths, fruits, and Nibbāna.

1299 MA: There is no gift equal in measure to this gift. This is the kind of gift Mahāpajāpatī would be giving by offering the pair of cloths to the Sangha.

1300 MA: "Members of the clan" (*gotrabhuno*) are those who are monks merely in name. They will go about with a piece of yellow cloth tied around their necks or arms, and will support their wives and children by engaging in trade and farming, etc.

1301 The gift is incalculable and immeasurable in value because it is offered, by way of the intention of the donor, not to the "yellow-necks" as individuals but to the Sangha as a corporate whole. Thus the recipient body includes all the virtuous bhikkhus of the past, even those who have long passed away.

1302 MA states that a gift offered to an immoral bhikkhu taken to represent the entire Sangha is more fruitful than a gift offered on a personal basis to an arahant. But for the gift to be properly presented to the Sangha, the donor must take no account of the personal qualities of the recipient but must see him solely as representing the Sangha as a whole.

1303 MA: Here the word "purified" has the meaning "made fruitful."

1304 MA: This last verse refers to the gift one arahant gives to another arahant. Although the arahant believes in the fruit of kamma, because he is without desire and lust for existence his own act of giving is not productive of any fruits. It is a mere functional action (*kiriya*) that leaves no traces behind.

SUTTA 143

1305 MA says that clinging to the eye takes place by way of desire and lust; consciousness is dependent on the eye by way of craving and views. However, since Anāthapiṇḍika was already a stream-enterer, dependence for him would have involved only craving, views having been eradicated by the path of stream-entry.

1306 This statement does not imply that there is any inherent exclusiveness or arbitrary discrimination in the Buddha's way of presenting his teaching. But as those who remain in lay life must look after their families, possessions, and occupations, such talk leading to complete detachment would not have been appropriate for them.

SUTTA 144

1307 This is an elliptical expression for committing suicide.

1308 By making this statement he is implicitly claiming arahantship, as will be made clear at §13. Whether his claim at this point was valid or not is uncertain, the commentary regarding it as a case of self-overestimation.

1309 MA says that Ven. Mahā Cunda gave him this instruction thinking that he must still be an ordinary person, since he could not endure the deadly pains and wanted to commit suicide.

1310 The sense of this instruction might be explained with the help of MA thus: One is dependent because of craving and views and becomes independent by abandoning them with the attainment of arahantship. Bias (*nati*, lit. bending) comes about through craving, and its absence means there is no inclination or desire for existence. There is no coming and going by the ending of rebirth and death, no here nor beyond nor in between by the transcendence of this world, the world beyond, and the passage between one and the other. This is the end of the suffering of defilements and the suffering of the round.

1311 MA: He cut his throat, and just at that moment the fear of death descended on him and the sign of future rebirth appeared. Recognising that he was still an ordinary person, he was aroused and developed insight. Comprehending the formations, he attained arahantship just before he expired.

1312 MA: Although this declaration (of blamelessness) was made while Channa was still a worldling, as his attainment of final Nibbāna followed immediately, the Buddha answered by referring to that very declaration.

It should be noted that this commentarial interpretation is imposed on the text from the outside, as it were. If one sticks to the actual wording of the text it seems that Channa was already an arahant when he made his declaration, the dramatic punch being delivered by the failure of his two brother-monks to recognise this. The implication, of course, is that excruciating pain might motivate even an arahant to take his own life—not from aversion but simply from a wish to be free from unbearable pain.

1313 The terms used to describe the lay families which supported the Venerable Channa—*mittakulāni suhajjakulāni upavajjakulāni*—are obviously synonymous. The third term gives the opportunity for a word play. MA glosses it *upasankamitabbakulāni*, "families to be approached" (that is, for his requisites). According to CPD, *upavajja* here represents Skt *upavrajya*; the word in this sense is not in PED, though this may be the only instance where it bears such a meaning. The word is homonymous with another word meaning "blameworthy," representing Skt *upavadya*, thus linking up with Channa's earlier avowal that he would kill himself blamelessly (*anupavajja*). See the following note.

1314 This statement seems to imply that Channa was an arahant at the time he committed suicide, though the commentary explains otherwise.

When the Buddha speaks about the conditions under which one is blameworthy (*sa-upavajja*), *upavajja* represents *upavadya*. Though earlier MA explained the correct sense of *upavajjakulāni,* here the commentator seems oblivious to the pun and comments as if Channa had actually been at fault for associating too closely with lay people: "The Elder Sāriputta, showing the fault of intimacy with families (*kulasaṁsaggadosa*) in the preliminary stage of practice, asks: 'When that bhikkhu had such supporters, could he have attained final Nibbāna?' The Blessed One answers showing that he was not intimate with families."

SUTTA 145

1315 This Puṇṇa is a different person from Puṇṇa Mantāṇiputta of MN 24. He was from a family of merchants residing in the port city of Suppāraka in the Sunāparanta country (present-day Maharashtra). On a business trip to Sāvatthī he heard the Buddha give a discourse and renounced the home life to become a bhikkhu.

1316 MA explains this instruction as a short teaching on the Four Noble Truths. Delight (*nandī*) is an aspect of craving. Through the arising of delight in regard to the eye and forms there arises the suffering of the five aggregates. Thus in this first part of the instruction the Buddha teaches the round of existence by way of the first two truths—suffering and its origin—as they occur through the six senses. In the second part (§4) he teaches the ending of the round by way of the second two truths—cessation and the path—expressed as the abandoning of delight in the six senses and their objects.

1317 That is, he expired. Since the Buddha still refers to Puṇṇa as a clansman (*kulaputta*), he must have died within a short time after returning to the Sunāparanta country. The texts leave no record of how he died. The version of this sutta at SN 35:88 (iv.60–63) says that he expired during his first rains retreat there.

SUTTA 146

1318 One of the eight important rules laid down by the Buddha when he established the Bhikkhunī Sangha stipulated that every fortnight the bhikkhunī should request the bhikkhus to send a bhikkhu for the purpose of giving them an exhortation. According to MA, in a previous life Ven. Nandaka had been a king and those bhikkhunīs had been his concubines. He wanted to avoid his turn in advising the bhikkhunīs because he thought that another bhikkhu possessing the knowledge of past lives, seeing him giving an exhortation surrounded by the bhikkhunīs, would think that he still could not separate himself from his former concubines. But the Buddha saw that Nandaka's discourse to the bhikkhunīs would benefit them and thus he requested him to instruct them.

1319 MA: They have seen this with the wisdom of insight.

1320 *Tajjaṁ tajjaṁ paccayaṁ paṭicca tajjā tajjā vedanā uppajjanti.* The coming together of the eye, forms, and eye-consciousness is eye-contact, and this is the primary condition for the arising of feeling born of eye-contact. With the cessation of the eye, one of the factors responsible for eye-contact is removed. Thus eye-contact ceases, and with its cessation the feeling born of eye-contact also ceases.

1321 MA: He undertakes this teaching on the enlightenment factors because wisdom is not able to cut away the defilements by itself, but only when accompanied by the other six enlightenment factors (wisdom being equivalent to the investigation-of-states enlightenment factor).

1322 MA: She who was last in regard to good qualities had become a stream-enterer, but those whose intentions were to become once-returners, non-returners, and arahants each achieved the fulfilment of their intentions. Because of these results, the Buddha named Ven. Nandaka the foremost bhikkhu in instructing the bhikkhunīs.

SUTTA 147

1323 MA says that this discourse was spoken to Rāhula shortly after his higher ordination, presumably at the age of twenty.

1324 *Vimuttiparipācanīyā dhammā.* MA interprets these as the fifteen qualities that purify the five faculties (faith, energy, mindfulness, concentration, and wisdom), namely, in regard to each faculty: avoiding people who lack the faculty, associating with those endowed with it, and reflecting on suttas that inspire its maturation. MA brings in another set of fifteen qualities: the five faculties again; the five perceptions partaking of penetration, namely, perception of impermanence, suffering, non-self, abandoning, and dispassion; and the five qualities taught to Meghiya, namely, noble friendship, the virtue of the monastic rules, suitable conversation, energy, and wisdom (see AN 9:3/iv.356; Ud 4:1/36).

1325 MA says that these deities, who came from various celestial realms, had been companions of Rāhula's during the previous life in which he first made the aspiration to attain arahantship as the son of a Buddha.

1326 It should be noted that the last four items mentioned are the four mental aggregates. Thus this discourse covers not only the sense bases but also the five aggregates, the aggregate of material form being implied by the physical sense faculties and their objects.

1327 According to MA, stream-entry was the minimal attainment of those deities, but some attained the higher paths and fruits up to arahantship.

SUTTA 148

1328 This string of epithets, usually descriptions of the Dhamma as a whole, here serves to emphasise the importance of the discourse the Buddha is about to deliver.

1329 The last two clauses in this sequence are also found in the standard formulation of dependent origination, which is thus implicitly incorporated into this discourse on the six sets of six.

1330 The verb *upapajjati* (the PTS ed. reading, *uppajjati*, is an error), normally means "reappears" or "is reborn," but it also has a special usage in logic to mean "to be tenable, to be acceptable," as it does here.

1331 The argument derives the principle of non-self from the verifiable premise of impermanence. The structure of the argument may be briefly set out thus: Whatever is self must be permanent; X is directly perceived to be impermanent, i.e., marked by rise and fall; therefore X is not self.

1332 The full argument of the previous paragraph is repeated for each of the remaining five terms in each set of six.

1333 MA explains that this passage is stated to show two noble truths—suffering and its origin—by way of the three obsessions (*gāha*). The truth of suffering is shown by the term "identity," elsewhere explicated as the five aggregates affected by clinging (MN 44.2). The three obsessions are craving, conceit, and views, which respectively give rise to the notions "mine," "I am" and "my self." The two truths together constitute the round of existence.

1334 MA: This passage is stated to show the other two noble truths—cessation and the path—by the repudiation of the three obsessions. These two truths constitute the ending of the round.

1335 MA: This passage shows the round of existence once again, this time by way of the underlying tendencies. On the underlying tendencies and their correlation with the three types of feeling, see MN 44.25–28.

1336 MA: The first-mentioned ignorance is only the lack of understanding of the origination, etc., of neither-painful-nor-pleasant feeling. The second-mentioned is the ignorance that is at the root of the round.

1337 MA: There is nothing wonderful in the fact that sixty bhikkhus attained arahantship when the Buddha first taught this sutta. But each time Sāriputta, Moggallāna, and the eighty great disciples taught it, sixty bhikkhus attained arahantship. In Sri Lanka the Elder Maliyadeva taught this sutta in sixty places, and each time sixty bhikkhus attained arahantship. But when the Elder Tipiṭaka Cūḷanāga taught this sutta to a vast assembly of humans and gods, at the end of the discourse a thousand bhikkhus attained arahantship, and among the gods only one remained a worldling.

SUTTA 149

1338 MA: When one does not know and see the eye by way of insight knowledge and path knowledge.

1339 That is, the craving that arises and settles on the eye and forms, etc., holds to them with clinging, and this produces kamma that can generate a new set of five aggregates in the next existence.

1340 When one knows and sees the eye by insight and the path.

1341 The eight factors of the path mentioned here seem to pertain to the preliminary or mundane portion of the path. MṬ identifies them with the factors possessed by a person at the highest level of insight development, immediately prior to the emergence of the supramundane path. In this stage only the former five path factors are actively operative, the three factors of the morality group having been purified prior to the undertaking of insight meditation. But when the supramundane path arises, all eight factors occur simultaneously, the three factors of the morality group exercising the function of eradicating the defilements responsible for moral transgression in speech, action, and livelihood.

1342 MA says that this refers to the simultaneous arising of serenity and insight in the supramundane path. The former is present under the heading of right concentration, the latter under the heading of right view.

1343 These are the four functions exercised by the supramundane path: fully understanding the truth of suffering, abandoning the cause of suffering, realising the cessation of suffering, and developing the path leading to the end of suffering.

1344 Here serenity and insight represent the entire Noble Eightfold Path.

1345 MA identifies "true knowledge" with the knowledge of the path of arahantship, "deliverance" with the fruit of arahantship. Here these take the place usually reserved for Nibbāna, the true cessation of suffering.

1346 This passage and each of the following passages repeat the entire text of §§9–11, the only change being in the sense faculty and object.

SUTTA 151

1347 MA: The arahant's fruition attainment of voidness. See n.458 and n.1144.

1348 MA: This is the abiding of such great men (*mahāpurisa*) as

Buddhas, paccekabuddhas, and the great disciples of the Tathāgatas.

1349 Among the five terms, desire and lust are synonymous as are hate and aversion.

1350 Beginning with this section a sequence of development may be discerned. The abandoning of the five cords of sensual pleasure is the preliminary step for developing the jhānas, and the abandoning of the five hindrances (§10) the immediate antecedent to the attainment of the first jhāna. The full understanding of the five aggregates (§11) indicates the insight wisdom necessary to attain the path of stream-entry, and the sections on the thirty-seven aids to enlightenment (§§12–18) the cultivation of the factors needed to arrive at the intermediate stages of sanctity. The section on serenity and insight (§19), though applicable to all stages, can be seen as fully actualised by the non-returner striving for arahantship. Finally, the section on true knowledge and deliverance signifies the attainment of the path and fruit of arahantship.

1351 Although the arahant, who has fully realised true knowledge and deliverance, has no need for further training, he continues to cultivate serenity and insight in order to enter into the bliss of the jhānas, the fruition attainment of arahantship, and the cessation of perception and feeling.

SUTTA 152

1352 The expression "the development of the faculties" (*indriyabhāvanā*) properly signifies the development *of the mind* in responding to the objects experienced through the sense faculties. The more rudimentary aspect of this practice, the restraint of the sense faculties (*indriyasaṁvara*), involves controlling the mind in such a way that one does not grasp at the "signs and features" of things, their distinctive attractive and repulsive attributes. The development of the faculties carries this process of control through to the point where, by an act of will, one can immediately set up insight even in the course of sense perception. At the highest level one acquires the ability to radically transform the subjective significance of perceptual objects themselves, making them appear in a mode that is the very opposite of the way they are normally apprehended.

1353 MA explains that when a desirable form comes into range of the eye, an agreeable state (*manāpa*) arises; when an undesirable form appears, a disagreeable state (*amanāpa*) arises; and when an indifferent form appears, a state that is both agreeable and disagreeable arises. It should be noted that though these three terms are ordinarily used to qualify the sense objects, here they also seem to signify subtle states of liking, aversion, and dull indifference that arise due to the influence of the underlying tendencies. MṬ identifies "the agreeable" with wholesome and unwholesome states of mind associated with joy, "the disagreeable" with unwholesome states of mind associated with grief (displeasure), and "the agreeable and disagreeable" with states of mind associated with equanimous feeling.

1354 MA: This equanimity is the equanimity of insight (*vipassan'upekkhā*). The bhikkhu does not allow his mind to be overcome by lust, hate, or delusion, but comprehends the object and sets up insight in the neutral state. MṬ explains this to mean that he enters into equanimity regarding formations (*sankhār'upekkhā*), a particular stage of insight knowledge (see Vsm XXI, 61–66).

1355 MṬ: The noble development of the faculties is the suppression of lust, etc., arisen through the eye, and the establishment of the equanimity of insight.

1356 The same simile appears at MN 66.16.

1357 Although the *sekha* has already entered upon the way to final deliverance, he is still prone to subtle states of liking, aversion, and dull indifference in regard to sense objects. He experiences these, however, as impediments to his progress, and thus becomes repelled, humiliated, and disgusted by them.

1358 *Ariya bhāvitindriya*: the arahant is meant.

1359 Since the arahant has eradicated all the defilements along with their underlying tendencies, in this passage the three terms—the agreeable, etc.—must be understood simply as the feelings that arise through contact with sense objects, and not as the subtle traces of liking, aversion, and indifference relevant to the preceding passage.

1360 The Paṭisambhidāmagga calls this practice "the noble supernormal power" (*ariya iddhi*) and explains it thus (ii.212): To abide perceiving the unrepulsive in the repulsive, one pervades a repulsive being with loving-kindness, or one attends to a repulsive object (either animate or inanimate) as a mere assemblage of impersonal elements. To abide perceiving the repulsive in the unrepulsive, one pervades a (sensually) attractive person with the idea of the foulness of the body, or one attends to an attractive object (either animate or inanimate) as impermanent. The third and fourth methods involve the application of the first and second contemplations to both repulsive and unrepulsive objects, without discrimination. The fifth method involves the avoidance of joy and sorrow in response to the six sense objects, thus enabling one to abide in equanimity, mindful and fully aware.

Although this fivefold contemplation is ascribed to the arahant as a power perfectly under his control, elsewhere the Buddha teaches it to bhikkhus still in training as a way to overcome the three unwholesome roots. See AN 5:144/iii.169–70; and for a thoughtful commentary on that sutta, see Nyanaponika Thera, *The Roots of Good and Evil*, pp. 73–78.

Pali-English Glossary

THIS GLOSSARY INCLUDES only (a) important doctrinal terms, and (b) words and meanings not found in the PTS's *Pali-English Dictionary*. The latter, compiled by Ven. Ñāṇamoli in a section of his manuscript, are here marked by an asterisk and are followed by references to the Majjhima passage where they occur. All terms are defined only by way of the meanings they bear in the Majjhima Nikāya, and no account is taken of meanings they may have in other Buddhist texts. The Pali words are listed here in Indian alphabetical order.

PALI	ENGLISH
akālika	immediately effective
akiriyavāda	doctrine of non-doing
akuppa	unshakeable
akusala	unwholesome
**akkhāyati*	to be plain (evident) (11.13)
anga	factor
angaṇa	blemish
**accādāya*	overlapping (39.10; 53.10; 107.6; 125.18)
**accokkaṭṭha*	too low (91.19)
ajjhatta	internal(ly)
ajjhosāna	holding
aññā	final knowledge
aṭṭhāna	impossibility
**atammayatā*	non-identification (113.21; 137.20)
**atināmeti*	to exceed (the right amount) (91.14)
**atinijjhāyitatta*	excessive meditation (128.26)
**atipāteti*	to shoot across (12.62)
atimāna	arrogance
attakilamatha	self-mortification
attabhāva	individuality

PALI	ENGLISH
attā	self
attha	(1) meaning; (2) purpose; (3) good
atthangama	disappearance
adukkhamasukha	neither-painful-nor-pleasant
adosa	non-hate
**adduva*	knee (91.10)
adhikaraṇa	litigation
adhicitta	higher mind
adhiṭṭhāna	(1) decision; (2) foundation
adhimāna	overestimation
adhimuccati	to resolve upon
adhivāsanā	endurance
**adhisallekhata*	too exacting (66.7)
anagāriya	homelessness
anattā	not self
**anapāya*	unrepelled (111.4; 112.4)
anāgamin	non-returner
anicca	impermanent
animitta	signless
anissita	independent
anukampā	compassion
anupassanā	contemplation
**anupāya*	unattracted (111.4; 112.4)
anubyañjana	feature
anusaya	underlying tendency
anussati	recollection
anussava	oral tradition
**anvākāri*	flung (86.6)
**anvāgameti*	to follow after (131.3)
**apakaṭṭha*	too loose (91.19)
apadāna	attribute (129.2)
apāya	state of deprivation
**appaṭivibhattabhogin*	one who shares without reservation (48.6; 104.21)
appaṇihita	desireless
**appabaddha*	coherent (32.4)
appamāṇa	immeasurable
appamāda	diligence
**abbyāyeyya*	would pull out (105.19)
abyāpāda	non-ill will
abhijjhā	covetousness
abhiññā	direct knowledge
abhinandati	to delight in
**abhinipphajjati*	to come to, to be achieved (13.9)

PALI	ENGLISH
**abhinipphanna*	achieved, produced (101.28)
abhinivesa	adherence
abhibhāyatana	base for transcendence
abhibhū	overlord
abhivadati	to welcome, to affirm
abhisankhata	conditioned
abhisankharoti	to generate, to perform
abhisañcetayita	volitionally produced
abhisamaya	penetration
amata	deathless
amanasikāra	inattention
amarāvikkhepa	eel-wriggling
amoha	non-delusion
ayoniso	unwise
arati	discontent
**arahati*	to be proper (95.8)
arahant	untranslated: (1) a liberated person; (2) accomplished, Accomplished One
ariya	noble, noble one
ariyasacca	noble truth
ariyasāvaka	noble disciple
arūpa	immaterial
alobha	non-greed
avacara	sphere
**avadhāna*	giving (ear) (95.30)
**avaloketi*	to turn to look (91.10)
avijjā	ignorance
**avisārin*	euphonious (91.21)
avihiṁsā	non-cruelty
aveccappasāda	perfect confidence
asankhata	unconditioned
asappurisa	untrue man
asamaya	perpetual
asāmāyika	perpetual
asita	sickle (96.10)
asubha	foulness
asura	titan
asekha	one beyond training
asmimāna	the conceit "I am"
assāda	gratification
ahankāra	I-making
ākāsa	space
ākāsānañcāyatana	base of infinite space

PALI	ENGLISH
ākiñcañña	nothingness
ākiñcaññāyatana	base of nothingness
**ācariyaka*	teacher's doctrine (26.15; 79.8)
ājīva	livelihood
ādīnava	danger
ānāpānasati	mindfulness of breathing
āneñja	imperturbable
āpatti	offence
**āpādetar*	nurse (141.5)
āpo	water
ābhicetasika	pertaining to the higher mind
**āmaṇḍa*	gallnut (120.12)
āmisa	material thing, worldly
āyatana	base
**āyatika*	having as a basis (122.18)
āyu	life, life-term, vitality
āruppa	immaterial, immaterial realm
ālaya	adhesion
āsava	taint
**āhañcaṁ*	I will beat (26.25)
**āhattar*	one who brings (89.18)
āhāra	nutriment
**icchati*	to stir (28.22)
iñjita	perturbable
iddhābhisankhāra	feat of supernormal power
iddhi	(1) supernormal power; (2) spiritual power; (3) success
iddhipāda	basis for spiritual power
indriya	faculty
iriyāpatha	posture
issā	envy
uccheda	annihilation
**uttarāraṇi*	upper fire-stick (36.17; 93.11; 126.13)
uttarimanussadhamma	superhuman state
udayabbaya	rise and fall
uddhacca	restlessness
**upakāri*	bastion (13.13)
upakkilesa	imperfection
**upadussati*	to resent (135.11)
**upadhā*	cushion (12.45)
upadhi	acquisition(s)
upanāha	resentment
**upapajjati*	also: to be tenable (148.10)

PALI	ENGLISH
upapatti	reappearance (by way of rebirth)
**upavicarati*	to explore (137.8)
upavicāra	mental exploration
**upasankamitar*	one who approaches, visitor (12.30)
upasama	peace
upasampadā	full admission (to Sangha)
upādāna	clinging
upādinna	clung-to
upāyāsa	despair
upāsaka	man lay follower
upāsikā	woman lay follower
upekkhā	equanimity
ubbilla	elation
usmā	heat
**ussaṭa*	eminent (not as in PED) (82.28)
ussoḷhi	enthusiasm
**ūruṇḍa*	large enough (140.3)
ekaggatā	unification (of mind)
ekatta	unity
ekāyana	direct, going in one direction
ekodibhāva	singleness (of mind)
**etaparama*	at most (12.52)
**okkappaniya*	believable (36.45)
ottappa	fear of wrongdoing
**odhasta*	lying ready (21.7; 119.31)
**opakkama*	due to exertion (101.14)
**opārambha*	censurable (88.8)
obhāsa	light
kathā	talk
kappa	aeon
kamma	action
kammanta	action
karuṇā	compassion
**kalabhāga*	fraction (129.9)
kalyāṇa	good
kasiṇa	untranslated: meditation device
**kasimāna*	emaciation (12.52; 25.9)
**kākātidayin*	open to crows (66.11)
kāma	(1) sensual pleasure; (2) sensual desire; (3) sense-sphere (being)
kāmaguṇa	cord of sensual pleasure

PALI	ENGLISH
kāmacchanda	sensual desire
kāya	body
kāyasakkhin	body-witness
**kisora*	foal (93.14)
**kukkuka*	fruit-bud core (of plantain tree) (35.22)
kukkucca	remorse
kusala	wholesome
**ko*	also: where (81.20; 93.18)
kodha	anger
kopa	anger
khattiya	noble (caste)
khanti	(1) forbearance; *(2) acceptance (of a view) (22.11; 70.23; 95.14)
khandha	aggregate, mass
khaya	destruction
**kharigata*	solidified (28.6; 62.8; 140.14)
**khīṇa*	also: sharp (139.10)
**khurakā*	prancing (65.33)
khurappa	hoof-tipped (kind of arrowhead) (63.5)
**khulukhulukāraka*	making a splashing noise (91.15)
gaṇa	group, company
gati	(1) destination; (2) retentiveness
**gāmaṇḍala*	village lout (93.18)
gocara	resort
**cangarava*	sieve (23.2)
caraṇa	conduct
**carasā*	prowling (66.6)
cāga	(1) generosity; (2) relinquishment
citta	mind
cittuppāda	inclination of mind
**cilīma*	tendon (146.11)
cīvara	robe
cuti	passing away
cetanā	volition
ceto	mind, heart
cetokhila	wilderness in heart
cetovimutti	deliverance of mind
chanda	(1) desire; (2) zeal
chambhitatta	fear

PALI	ENGLISH
jarā	ageing
jāgariya	wakefulness
jāti	birth
**jātibhūmi*	native land (24.2)
**jāpeti*	to fine (caus. of jahati) (35.12; 89.13)
jīva	soul
jīvita	life
jhāna	(1) untranslated: meditative absorption; (2) meditation
**ñatta*	renown (47.8)
ñāṇa	knowledge
ñāya	true way
ṭhāna	(1) state; (2) possibility
takka	reasoning
**tacchati*	to pare, to plane (5.31; 130.12)
taṇhā	craving
tathāgata	untranslated: Thus Come One, Thus Gone One
tiracchānakathā	pointless talk
tiracchānayoni	animal realm
tulanā	scrutiny
**tūlinī*	silky (21.18)
tejo	fire
**telamasikata*	dirty, oily (75.23)
thambha	obstinacy
thīna	sloth
daratha	disturbance
dassana	seeing, vision
dāna	giving, gift
diṭṭha	seen
diṭṭhi	view
diṭṭhiṭṭhāna	standpoint for views
diṭṭhippatta	one attained-to-view
dibbacakkhu	divine eye
dibbasota	divine ear
**dukkarakārikā*	performance of austerities (12.56; 26.27)
dukkha	suffering, pain, painful

Pali	English
duggati	bad destination
duccarita	misconduct
**duṭṭhulla*	inertia (64.9; 127.16; 128.21)
**dubbaca*	difficult to admonish (15.2)
deva	god
devatā	deity
devadūta	divine messenger
domanassa	grief
dosa	hate
dhamma	(1) untranslated: the Buddha's teaching; (2) things, states, factors; (3) mind-objects; (4) qualities; (5) teachings; (6) (as suffix) subject to
dhammavicaya	investigation-of-states
dhammānusārin	Dhamma-follower
dhātu	element
**dhutta*	(brewer's) mixer (35.5; 56.7)
dhuva	everlasting
natthikavāda	nihilism
nandī	delight
**narassika*	manly (91.29)
nānatta	diversity
nāma	mentality
nāmarūpa	mentality-materiality
nicca	permanent
**niccakappaṁ*	constantly (144.11)
niṭṭhā	(1) goal; (2) conclusion
nibbāna	untranslated: final deliverance from suffering
nibbidā	disenchantment
nimitta	(1) sign; (2) basis
**nimmathita*	kindled (90.12)
niraya	hell
nirāmisa	unworldly
nirodha	cessation
**nisevita*	scraping (27.10)
nissaraṇa	escape
nissita	dependent
**nihaniṁ*	instituted (aor.) (83.21)
nīvaraṇa	hindrance
**nīhata*	faultless (140.20)
nekkhamma	renunciation

PALI	ENGLISH
nevasaññānāsaññāyatana	base of neither-perception-nor-non-perception
paccanubhoti	to experience
paccaya	condition
paccavekkhaṇa	reviewing, reflection
paccekabuddha	untranslated: a solitary enlightened one
pajā	generation
paññā	wisdom
paññāvimutta	one liberated-by-wisdom
paññāvimutti	deliverance by wisdom
**paṭikaroti*	to carry out (instructions), to obey (125.12)
paṭikkūla	repulsive
paṭigha	(1) sensory impact; (2) aversion
paṭicca samuppāda	dependent origination
paṭinissagga	relinquishment
paṭipadā	(1) way, practice; (2) progress
**paṭivānarūpa*	disappointed (104.2)
**paṭiveti*	to disappear (111.4)
paṭisallāna	meditation
**paṭṭhita*	gone out (12.49)
paṭhavī	earth
paṇīta	sublime
**paṇopanavidhā*	haggling, bargaining (70.26)
paṇḍita	wise, wise man
**paṇḍumutika*	(rice) stored in a sheaf (81.16)
**padumaka*	(kind of wood) (93.11)
padhāna	striving
papañca	proliferation
**papatati*	to flee (12.48)
pabbajjā	going forth (into homelessness)
pabhava	production
**pabhāvika*	arising from (87.3)
**pabhivatta*	selected (81.18)
pamāda	negligence
parāmāsa	adherence
**parikkamana*	avoidance (8.14)
parikkhāra	requisite
**parikkhepeti*	to utterly destroy (35.21)
pariggaha	possession
pariññā	full understanding
paritassanā	agitation
parideva	lamentation

PALI	ENGLISH
parinibbāna	(1) final Nibbāna; (2) extinguishing
paribbājaka	wanderer
pariyuṭṭhāna	obsession
pariyesanā	search
paḷāsa	insolence
**pavaṭṭikā*	ornamental chain (140.20)
**pavana*	wilds (of forest) (19.25; 26.34)
paviveka	seclusion
pasāda	confidence
passaddhi	tranquillity
pahāna	abandonment
pahitatta	resolute
**pāṭipuggalika*	personal, for a particular person (142.5)
pāṇa	living being
pāṇātipāta	killing living beings
**pāṇupeta*	for life (until the end of one's life) (4.35)
**pātavyatā*	gulping down (45.3)
pātimokkha	untranslated: code of monastic rules
pāpa	evil
pāpicchā	evil desire
pāmojja	gladness
pāramī	perfection
pāripūri	fulfilment
pārisuddhi	purification
**pāsādanīya*	inspiring, pleasing (89.4)
piṇḍapāta	almsfood
pisuṇā vācā	malicious speech
pīti	rapture
puggala	person
puñña	merit
puthujjana	ordinary person
punabbhava	renewal of being
pubbenivāsa	past life
**purindada*	first of givers (56.29)
peta	ghost
pharati	to pervade
pharusā vācā	harsh speech
phala	fruit, fruition
phassa	contact
**baddha*	imprisoned (39.14)
**bandha*	imprisonment (19.7)
**bandhana*	imprisonment (39.14)

PALI	ENGLISH
bala	power
bahiddhā	external(ly)
bahulīkata	cultivated
bahussuta	learned
bāla	fool
**bāhulika*	luxurious (26.26)
buddha	(1) untranslated; (2) enlightened, Enlightened One
bojjhanga	enlightenment factor
bodhisatta	untranslated: a future Buddha
byañjana	phrasing
byāpāda	ill will
**byābangī*	carrying-pole (96.10)
brahmacariya	holy life, celibacy
brahmavihāra	divine abode
brahmā	untranslated: (1) supreme God (for brahmins); (2) class of deities (for Buddhists)
brāhmaṇa	brahmin (caste)
bhagavā	blessed, Blessed One
bhaya	fear
bhava	being
**bhavyatā*	ability (119.29)
bhāvanā	development
bhāvita	developed
bhikkhu	untranslated: Buddhist monk
bhikkhunī	untranslated: Buddhist nun
bhūta	(1) a being; (2) what has come to be
makkha	contempt
magga	path
macchariya	avarice
maññati	to conceive
maññita	conceiving
**maññussava*	tide of conceiving (140.30)
**mattaṭṭhaka*	lasting for a moment (28.7)
**mattha*	churning-stick (126.17)
mada	vanity
manasikāra	attention
manussa	human
mano	mind, mental
mamankāra	mine-making
maraṇa	death

PALI	ENGLISH
mahaggata	exalted
**mahacca*	pomp (82.28)
mahāpurisa	great man
mahābhūta	great element
**mahī*	greatness (35.30)
mahesakkha	influential
mātikā	codes (summaries of teachings)
māna	conceit
māyā	deceit
micchā	wrong
micchācāra	misconduct
middha	torpor
muta	sensed
muditā	altruistic joy
muni	sage
musāvāda	false speech
mūla	root
mettā	loving-kindness
moha	delusion
yathābhūta	as it actually is
**yāvetadohi*	as far as this (81.9)
yogakkhema	security from bondage
yoni	(mode of) generation
yoniso	wise, thorough
raṇa	conflict
rati	delight
rāga	lust
ruci	approval
rūpa	(1) form (visible object); (2) material form, materiality; (3) fine-material (being)
lābha	gain
loka	world
lokuttara	supramundane
lobha	greed
vacī	speech, verbal
vaṭṭa	round (of existence)
vata	observance
vaya	vanishing
vācā	speech

PALI	ENGLISH
vāyāma	effort
vāyo	air
**vāla*	strainer (35.5; 56.7)
vicaya	investigation
vicāra	sustained thought
vicikicchā	doubt
vijjā	true knowledge
viññāṇa	consciousness
viññāṇañcāyatana	base of infinite consciousness
viññāta	cognized
**viṭabhi*	canopy (45.4)
vitakka	thought, applied thought
vinaya	(1) discipline; (2) removal
vinipāta	perdition
vinibandha	shackle
**vipakkamati*	to disperse (127.11)
vipariṇāma	change
**vipariyāsa*	(mental) derangement (104.17)
vipassanā	insight
vipāka	result
**vipekkhati*	to look about (91.10)
vibhava	non-being, extermination
vimutta	liberated
vimutti	deliverance
vimokkha	liberation
virāga	(1) dispassion; (2) fading away (as impermanence)
viriya	energy
vivaṭṭa	world-expansion
vivāda	dispute
viveka	seclusion
visama	unrighteous
visuddhi	purification
vihiṁsā	cruelty
vīmaṁsā	investigation
**vuddhasīla*	mature virtue (95.9)
**vekurañjā*	not of either kind (?) (93.14)
veda	(1) untranslated: ancient Indian scripture; (2) inspiration
vedanā	feeling
vedayita	what is felt, feeling
veramaṇī	abstinence
vessa	merchant (caste)
vossagga	relinquishment

PALI	ENGLISH
vohāra	expression
**vyāpajjitar*	one who undertakes (work) (124.32)
saṁyojana	fetter
saṁvaṭṭa	world-contraction
saṁvara	restraint
saṁvega	sense of urgency
saṁsāra	round of births
sakadāgāmin	once-returner
sakkāya	identity
sakkāyadiṭṭhi	identity view
sakkāra	honour
sagga	heaven
sankappa	intention
sankilesa	defilement
sankhata	conditioned
sankhāra	formation
sanganika	society
sangha	untranslated: (1) the Buddhist monastic order; (2) the community of noble disciples
sacca	truth
**saññūḷha*	concocted (56.30)
sati	mindfulness
satipaṭṭhāna	foundation of mindfulness
satta	being
sattapada	position of beings
saddhamma	(1) true Dhamma; (2) good quality
saddhā	faith
saddhānusārin	faith-follower
santa	peaceful
santi	peace
santosa	contentment
sandiṭṭhika	visible here and now
sappurisa	true man
sabba	all
sabbaññū	omniscient
sama	righteous
samaṇa	recluse
samatha	(1) serenity; (2) stilling (of formations); (3) settlement (of litigation)
**samanvāneti*	to find (131.4)
samācāra	conduct, behaviour
samādhi	concentration

Pali	English
samāpatti	attainment (in meditation)
samudaya	origin, arising
sampajañña	full awareness
samphappalāpa	gossip
sambojjhanga	enlightenment factor
sambodhi	enlightenment
sammā	(1) fully, completely; (2) right(ly)
saraṇa	refuge
sallekha	effacement
saḷāyatana	sixfold base
sassata	eternal
sāṭheyya	fraud
sāmaggī	concord
sārambha	rivalry
sāsana	Dispensation (of Buddha)
sikkhā	training
sikkhāpada	training precept
siloka	praise
sīla	(1) virtue; (2) habit; (3) rule
sīlabbata	rules and observances
sukha	pleasure, pleasant, bliss
sugata	sublime, Sublime One
sugati	good destination
suññatā	voidness
suta	(1) heard; (2) learning
sudda	worker (caste)
suddhāvāsa	Pure Abodes
subha	beauty, beautiful
**suvaca*	easy to admonish (15.4)
**suvihata*	fully stretched out (121.5)
**susamanniṭṭha*	well investigated (pp. *su* + *samannesati*) (47.16)
sekha	disciple in higher training
senāsana	resting place
soka	sorrow
sotāpanna	stream-enterer
somanassa	joy
**hassaka*	ridiculous (80.15; 99.10)
hita	welfare
hiri	shame
hetu	cause

Index of Subjects

THIS INDEX LISTS SIGNIFICANT REFERENCES only. Italicised numbers refer to the page numbers of the Introduction; references to sutta passages give sutta number followed by section number. The abbreviation "ff." is here used to indicate that the term of entry pertains to a continuing or repetitive sequence of sections and does not necessarily mean that the term occurs in every section of the sequence. References may be listed under an entry even when the term itself does not appear in the text, as long as the passage is pertinent to the term of entry.

When a stock formulation is applied to each term in a set of categories, the reference is usually given only under the name of the set, not under the individual items belonging to that set. For example, the passage on the enlightenment factors at 2.21 is registered under Enlightenment factors, but not under the names of the individual factors. Cross-references ensure that essential references are not overlooked.

Pali equivalents are provided for all key doctrinal terms, though not for terms of lesser importance or for entries without an exact Pali counterpart. With few exceptions, the Pali term is given in the singular, even though the English entry may be plural. When two Pali words with a different denotation are rendered by a single English word, the two are listed as separate entries—e.g., Mind is listed twice, corresponding to *citta* and to *mano*. When a single English word represents two Pali words with overlapping meanings but different contextual usage, the two sets of references are classified within the same entry separated by a slash—e.g., Compassion as a rendering for both *karuṇā* and *anukampā*.

106.3ff.; manifestation of, 28.27; mind-c., n.130, 43.10, n.437; not self, 35.19, 146.8, 147.3ff., 148.10ff.; stuck internally, 138.12ff. *See also* Aggregates

Contact (*phassa*), 9.45ff., 18.16, 28.8, 38.17ff., 44.20, 57.8ff., 62.13ff., 109.9, n.1040, 137.7, 140.19, 143.9, 147.3ff., 148.7; not self, 148.10ff.

Contempt (*makkha*), 3.10, 7.3ff., 15.3ff., 40.3, 40.7, 104.7

Contentment (*santosa*), 24.2, 27.14, 32.7, 51.15, 77.8f., 108.16

Converting magic, 56.8, 56.25f.

Cordiality, principles of (*sārāṇīyā dhammā*), 48.6, 104.21f.

Counsellor-treasure, 129.41

Covering with grass, 104.20

Covetousness (*abhijjhā*), 7.3ff., 10.2ff., 40.3, 41.10, 114.7, 114.8, 114.9, 140.28; abandoning of, 27.18, 39.13, 40.7, 41.14, 51.19, 114.7ff., 140.28. *See also* Greed; Lust; Sensual desire

Craving (*taṇhā*), *29*, n.6, 9.11, 9.37ff., n.126, 11.5, 16.8ff., 38.17ff., 82.41, 148.9, 149.3f.; abandoned, 1.171, 2.22, 20.8, 22.33, 73.6, 149.9f.; as arrow, 105.18, 105.23; deliverance from, 37.3, 38.41; not self, 148.10ff.; origin of personality, 44.3; origin of suffering, 9.16, 141.21. *See also* Four Noble Truths; Taints

Cruelty (*vihiṁsā*), 2.20, 19.5, 33.6, 33.19, 51.9f., 62.19, 114.8f., 135.7. *See also* Killing

Death (*maraṇa*), 9.22, 26.9, 130.8, 141.13; in Noble One's Discipline, 105.22; realm of, 33.3, 33.5

Deathless (*amata*), 26.12, 26.18, 26.20f., 52.15, 64.9ff., 106.13, n.1023. *See also* Nibbāna

Deceit (*māyā*), 3.12, 7.3ff., 15.3ff., 40.3, 40.7, 104.9

Defiled Radiance, gods of (*sankiliṭṭhābhā devatā*), 127.9ff.

Defilement (*sankilesa*), 26.11

Delight (*nandī*), 1.3ff., 1.171, n.29, 18.8, 38.30, 43.15, 49.5, 49.27f., 131.4ff., 133.13ff., 145.3f., n.1316, 148.28ff.; and lust, 19.26, 23.4, 146.12; in Dhamma, 52.4ff., 64.9ff. / (*rati*), 6.7, 75.10, 119.33

Delight in creating, gods who (*nimmānaratī devā*), 31.21, 41.22, 97.30 120.10

Deliverance (*vimutti*), 22.29, 24.2, 32.7, 37.8, 38.41, 44.29, 74.12, 90.12, 109.18, 118.41ff., 147.10, 148.41, 149.11, 151.20; by wisdom (*paññāvimutti*), 6.19, n.83, 12.36, 12.42, 38.40, 40.14, 41.43, 43.14, 53.22, 54.24, 71.9, 73.24, 77.36, 78.11, 108.23, 119.42, 120.37, 146.13; of mind (*cetovimutti*), 6.19, n.83, 12.36, 12.42,

Steward-treasure, 129.40
Stream-enterer (*sotāpanna*), *42*, n.35, 6.11, n.80, n.88, 22.45, 34.9, 48.15, 68.13ff., 118.12, 142.5f., 146.27. *See also* Disciple in higher training; Noble disciple
Streaming Radiance, gods of (*ābhassarā devā*), 1.11, n.12, 49.10, 49.19
Striving (*padhāna*), 16.26, 70.23, 77.17, 95.22, 101.23ff.; five factors of, 85.58f., 90.10ff.; right, 44.12, 77.16, 78.10ff., 103.3, 104.5, 118.13, 149.10, 151.13
Stupidity, 135.17
Success (*iddhi*), 129.42ff.
Suffering (*dukkha*), *25ff.*, n.29, 2.8, 10.2, 11.7f., 13.8ff., 22.38, 29.2ff., 30.8ff., 35.21, 67.17ff., 68.5, 77.14, 87.3ff., 101.23, 136.2, 136.6, 138.3, 139.4, 139.13, 145.3f., 149.3; as noble truth, 2.11, 9.15, 10.44, 28.3, 141.10ff.; end of, 2.22, 12.2, 12.26, 14.17, 20.8, 48.6ff., 144.11, 148.28ff. *See also* Four Noble Truths; Impermanence: suffering, not self
Suicide, 144.5ff.
Superhuman states (*uttarimanussadhamma*), 12.2, n.178, 26.27, 31.10ff., 65.14f., 69.19, 99.10ff., 128.15
Supernormal power (*iddhi*), 6.14, 11.6, 37.11, 56.13, 73.19, 77.31, 108.13, 119.37, n.1360. *See also* Buddha: supernormal powers
Sustained thought (*vicāra*), 43.19f., 44.15. *See also* Jhāna

Taints (*āsava*), *38*, 2.2ff., n.32, n.37, 9.69ff., 36.47, 49.30, 68.7, 121.12; bases for, 65.30f.; liberation from, 2.3, n.33, n.49, 6.19, 7.18. 12.24, 12.36. 12.42, 25.20, 26.42, 30.21, 31.18, 32.17, 40.14, 41.43, 52.3ff., 53.22, 54.24, 64.9ff., 71.9, 73.24, 74.14, 77.36, 108.23, 112.3ff., 119.42, 121.11, 146.13, 147.10. *See also* Deliverance: by wisdom; Knowledge of destruction of taints
Taking what is not given (*adinnādāna*), 41.8, 54.4, 54.7, 114.5; abstention from, 27.13, 41.12, 51.14, 114.5
Talk (*kathā*): pointless, 76.4, 77.4, 78.3, 79.5, 122.12; suitable, 26.4, 43.14, 122.12, 122.20
Tathāgata, *24f.*, 1.147ff., 11.14, 19.26, 47.16, 55.7ff., 58.8, 58.11, 72.15, 72.20, n.723, 88.13, 88.17, 101.46, 102.4, 105.27, 107.3, 107.14, 142.5f.; abiding in voidness, 121.2, 122.6; after death, 25.10, 63.2ff., 72.9ff., 72.20, n.719; appears in world, 27.11, 51.12; footprints of, 27.19ff.; free from taints, 36.47, 49.30, 68.7; intrepidities, 12.22ff.; investigation of, 47.4ff.; powers of, 12.9ff.; wonderful qualities of, 123.2ff., 123.22. *See also* Buddha

Index of Proper Names

Index of Similes

Air, meditation like, 62.16
Archer, 12.62
Arrowsmith, 101.28

Bag of grain, 10.10, 119.7
Ball of string, 119.26
Bath powder, 39.15, 77.25, 119.18
Beryl gem on thread, 77.29, 123.12
Bhikkhu, 12.21
Blind turtle, 129.24
Borrowed goods, 22.3, 54.20
Bronze dish, 5.4ff.
Butcher carving ox, 36.24, 97.29, 143.4
Butter from curd, 126.17
Butter from water, 126.12

Calf, 67.7
Carcass on neck, 20.4
Cat awaiting mouse, 50.13
Catching snake, 22.10ff.
Catskin bag, 21.18
Cesspit, 12.38
Changing postures, 20.6
Charcoal pit, 12.37, 22.3, 54.18
Chariot, 21.7, 119.31
Chest of garments, 32.9
Cloth, 7.2, 7.12
Cowherd, 19.7, 19.12, 33.2, 33.15, 34.2, 34.4
Cow with calf, 48.12
Crab, 35.24
Creating artworks, 77.31
Crossing desert, 39.14
Cut-up cow, 10.12, 119.8

Daughter-in-law, 28.10, 37.9
Delicious food, 105.15
Dog circling post, 102.12
Donkey, 50.13
Drawing in space, 21.14
Dream, 22.3, 54.19
Drink of curd, 46.21
Drops on hot plate, 66.16, 152.9

Earth, meditation like, 62.13
Elephant at play, 35.5, 56.7
Elephant's footprint, 27.3ff., 28.2
Extending arm, 26.20, 37.6, 37.13, 49.3, 67.8, 152.8

File of blind men, 95.13, 99.9
Filling a jug, 119.25, 119.28
Fire extinguished, 72.19
Fire from woods, 90.12, 93.11
Fire in grass-shed, 115.2
Fire, meditation like, 62.15

Index of Pali Terms Discussed in Introduction and Notes

THE PALI WORDS are listed here in Indian alphabetical order.

About the Translators

BHIKKHU ÑĀṆAMOLI was born in England in 1905 and entered the Buddhist monastic order in Sri Lanka in 1949. During his eleven years in the Sangha he translated the Pali into lucid English some of the most difficult texts of the Theravada Buddhism, including the *Visuddhimagga*. He passed away in 1960 due to heart failure.

BHIKKHU BODHI is an American monk born in New York City in 1944. He was ordained as a monk in Sri Lanka in 1972 and is currently the president and editor of the Buddhist Publication Society in Kandy. His previous publications include four major Pali suttas along with their commentaries.

The Barre Center for Buddhist Studies

THE BARRE CENTER FOR BUDDHIST STUDIES represents a new vision of the study and practice of Buddha's teachings in America, dedicated to bringing together teachers, students, scholars, and practitioners who are committed to exploring Buddhist thought and practice as a living tradition that is faithful to its origins and lineage yet adaptable and alive in each new time and place. The Study Center, offers a variety of study and research opportunities, lectures, classes, seminars, workshops, conferences, retreats, independent study, and, in the future, a scholars-in-residence program. Its vision calls for dialogue between different schools of Buddhism, and discussions with other religious and scientific traditions.

The Study Center has recently started Dhamma Dana Publications, which endeavors to bring a long-standing tradition to America by making high-quality books on Buddhist teachings available for free distribution. Anyone wishing to sponsor the publication and free distribution of a manuscript may contact the director of the Barre Center for Buddhist Studies.

The Study Center is located on ninety acres of wooded land in rural, central Massachusetts, one-half mile from the Insight Meditation Society. Founded in 1989, the complex has residential facilities for staff and course participants, a library, offices, and a dining hall. Visitors are welcome at all times.

Barre Center for Buddhist Studies
149 Lockwood Road
Barre MA 01005 USA
Telephone: (978) 355-2347
www.dharma.org/bcbs.htm

Wisdom Publications

Wisdom Publications, a not-for-profit publisher, is dedicated to making available authentic Buddhist works for the benefit of all. We publish translations of the sutras and tantras, commentaries and teachings of past and contemporary Buddhist masters, and original works by the world's leading Buddhist scholars. We publish our titles with the appreciation of Buddhism as a living philosophy and with the special commitment to preserve and transmit important works from all the major Buddhist traditions.

If you would like to learn more about Wisdom, or to browse our books online, visit our website at www.wisdompubs.org. If you would like to receive a copy of our mail-order catalog, please write to:

Wisdom Publications
199 Elm Street, Somerville MA 02144
Telephone: (617) 776-7416 • Fax: (617) 776-7841
Email: info@wisdompubs.org • www.wisdompubs.org

The Wisdom Trust

As a non-profit publisher, Wisdom is dedicated to the publication of fine Dharma books for the benefit of all sentient beings. We depend upon sponsors in order to publish books like the one you are holding in your hand.

If you would like to make a donation to the Wisdom Trust Fund to help us continue our Dharma work or to receive information about opportunities for planned giving, please write to our Boston office. Thank you so much.

Wisdom Publications is a non-profit, charitable 501(c)(3) organization affiliated with the Foundation for the Preservation of the Mahayana Tradition (FPMT).